THE OXFORD HANDBOOK

POLITICAL
METHODOLOGY

THE
OXFORD
HANDBOOKS
OF
POLITICAL
SCIENCE

GENERAL EDITOR: ROBERT E. GOODIN

The *Oxford Handbooks of Political Science* is a ten-volume set of reference books offering authoritative and engaging critical overviews of all the main branches of political science.

The series as a whole is under the General Editorship of Robert E. Goodin, with each volume being edited by a distinguished international group of specialists in their respective fields:

POLITICAL THEORY
John S. Dryzek, Bonnie Honig & Anne Phillips

POLITICAL INSTITUTIONS
R. A. W. Rhodes, Sarah A. Binder & Bert A. Rockman

POLITICAL BEHAVIOR
Russell J. Dalton & Hans-Dieter Klingemann

COMPARATIVE POLITICS
Carles Boix & Susan C. Stokes

LAW & POLITICS
Keith E. Whittington, R. Daniel Kelemen & Gregory A. Caldeira

PUBLIC POLICY
Michael Moran, Martin Rein & Robert E. Goodin

POLITICAL ECONOMY
Barry R. Weingast & Donald A. Wittman

INTERNATIONAL RELATIONS
Christian Reus-Smit & Duncan Snidal

CONTEXTUAL POLITICAL ANALYSIS
Robert E. Goodin & Charles Tilly

POLITICAL METHODOLOGY
Janet M. Box-Steffensmeier, Henry E. Brady & David Collier

This series aspires to shape the discipline, not just to report on it. Like the Goodin–Klingemann *New Handbook of Political Science* upon which the series builds, each of these volumes will combine critical commentaries on where the field has been together with positive suggestions as to where it ought to be heading.

THE OXFORD HANDBOOK OF

POLITICAL METHODOLOGY

Edited by

JANET M. BOX-STEFFENSMEIER
HENRY E. BRADY

and

DAVID COLLIER

OXFORD
UNIVERSITY PRESS

OXFORD
UNIVERSITY PRESS

Great Clarendon Street, Oxford OX2 6DP

Oxford University Press is a department of the University of Oxford.
It furthers the University's objective of excellence in research, scholarship,
and education by publishing worldwide in

Oxford New York

Auckland Cape Town Dar es Salaam Hong Kong Karachi
Kuala Lumpur Madrid Melbourne Mexico City Nairobi
New Delhi Shanghai Taipei Toronto

With offices in

Argentina Austria Brazil Chile Czech Republic France Greece
Guatemala Hungary Italy Japan Poland Portugal Singapore
South Korea Switzerland Thailand Turkey Ukraine Vietnam

Oxford is a registered trade mark of Oxford University Press
in the UK and in certain other countries

Published in the United States
by Oxford University Press Inc., New York

British Library Cataloguing in Publication Data
Data available

Library of Congress Cataloging in Publication Data
The Oxford handbook of political methodlogy / edited by Janet M.
Box-Steffensmeier, Henry E. Brady and David Collier.
p.   cm.
ISBN 978–0–19–928654–6
1. Political science–Methodology–Handbooks, manuals, etc.
I. Box-Steffensmeier, Janet M., 1965   II. Brady, Henry E.
III. Collier, David, 1942
JA71.O948   2008
320.01–dc22   2008024395

Typeset by SPI Publisher Services, Pondicherry, India
Printed in Great Britain
on acid-free paper by
CPI Group (UK) Ltd, Croydon, CR0 4YY

ISBN 978–0–19–928654–6 (hbk.)
ISBN 978–0–19–958556–4 (pbk.)

7 9 10 8

For those who instilled in us a passion for methods,
and the confidence to strive for excellence
in pursuing rigor and high standards

James Lindsay, Peter McCormick,
Tse-Min Lin, and Herbert Weisberg

–JBS

Christopher Achen, Walter Dean Burnham,
Douglas Hibbs, and Daniel McFadden

–HEB

Giovanni Sartori, Alexander George,
Christopher Achen, and David Freedman

–DC

ACKNOWLEDGMENTS

We thank all the authors for their excellent contributions, and their responsiveness to our requests. Robert Goodin, General Editor of the *Oxford Handbooks of Political Science*, provided steadfast and insightful guidance on substance and editorial duties. To Dominic Byatt, Chief Editor at Oxford University Press, our gratitude for his patience and assistance through to the end. Elizabeth Suffling, Assistant Commissioning Editor, deserves our thanks for her quick and always helpful responses. We also thank Quintin Beazer, Kyle Kopko, Corwin Smidt, and David Zelenka for research assistance.

CONTENTS

PART IV CAUSALITY AND EXPLANATION IN SOCIAL RESEARCH

PART V EXPERIMENTS, QUASI-EXPERIMENTS AND NATURAL EXPERIMENTS

PART VI QUANTITATIVE TOOLS FOR DESCRIPTIVE AND CAUSAL INFERENCE: GENERAL METHODS

PART VII QUANTITATIVE TOOLS FOR DESCRIPTIVE AND CAUSAL INFERENCE: SPECIAL TOPICS

PART VIII QUALITATIVE TOOLS FOR DESCRIPTIVE AND CAUSAL INFERENCE

PART IX ORGANIZATIONS, INSTITUTIONS, AND MOVEMENTS IN THE FIELD OF METHODOLOGY

About the Contributors

John H. Aldrich is Pfizer-Pratt University Professor of Political Science, Duke University.

James E. Alt is Frank G. Thomson Professor of Government, Harvard University.

R. Michael Alvarez is Professor of Political Science in the Division of the Humanities and Social Sciences, California Institute of Technology.

Nathaniel Beck is Professor and Chair of the Wilf Family Department of Political Science, New York University.

Andrew Bennett is Professor of Government, Georgetown University.

Mark Bevir is Professor in the Charles and Louise Travers Department of Political Science, University of California, Berkeley.

Kenneth A. Bollen is Henry Rudolph Immerwahr Distinguished Professor of Sociology and Director of Odum Institute for Research in Social Sciences, University of North Carolina, Chapel Hill.

Janet M. Box-Steffensmeier is Vernal Riffe Professor of Political Science and Sociology, Director of the Program in Statistics Methodology, Ohio State University.

Henry E. Brady is Class of 1941 Monroe Deutsch Professor in the Charles and Louise Travers Department of Political Science and the Goldman School of Public Policy, and Director of the Survey Research Center, UC DATA, and California Census Research Data Center, University of California, Berkeley.

Jason D. Brozek is Stephen E. Scarff Assistant Professor of International Affairs in the Government Department, Lawrence University.

Wendy K. Tam Cho is Associate Professor of Political Science and Statistics and Senior Research Scientist at the National Center for Supercomputing Applications, University of Illinois at Urbana-Champaign.

David Collier is Robson Professor in the Charles and Louise Travers Department of Political Science, University of California, Berkeley.

Scott de Marchi is Associate Professor of Political Science, Duke University.

Colin Elman is Associate Professor of Political Science, The Maxwell School, Syracuse University.

James D. Fearon is Theodore and Frances Geballe Professor of Political Science, Stanford University.

Charles H. Franklin is Professor of Political Science, University of Wisconsin, Madison.

Robert J. Franzese, Jr. is Associate Professor of Political Science and Research Associate Professor in the Center for Political Studies, University of Michigan, Ann Arbor.

David A. Freedman is Professor of Statistics and Mathematics, University of California, Berkeley.

Alan S. Gerber is Professor of Political Science and Director of the Center for the Study of American Politics, Yale University.

John Gerring is Professor of Political Science, Boston University.

Garrett Glasgow is Associate Professor of Political Science, University of California, Santa Barbara.

Gary Goertz is Professor of Political Science, University of Arizona.

Jonathan Golub is Lecturer in Politics and International Relations, University of Reading.

Donald P. Green is A. Whitney Griswold Professor of Political Science and Director of the Institution for Social and Policy Studies, Yale University.

Russell Hardin is Professor in the Wilf Family Department of Political Science, New York University.

Jude C. Hays is Assistant Professor of Political Science, University of Illinois at Urbana-Champaign.

Peter Hedström is Professor of Sociology, Nuffield College, University of Oxford.

Simon Jackman is Professor of Political Science, Stanford University.

John E. Jackson is M. Kent Jennings Collegiate Professor of Political Science, University of Michigan, Ann Arbor.

Bradford S. Jones is Associate Professor of Political Science, University of California at Davis.

Richard Johnston is Professor of Political Science, Research Director of the National Annenberg Election Study, University of Pennsylvania.

David D. Laitin is James T. Watkins IV and Elise V. Watkins Professor of Political Science, Stanford University.

Jody LaPorte is a Doctoral Candidate in the Charles and Louise Travers Department of Political Science, University of California, Berkeley.

Jack S. Levy is Board of Governors' Professor of Political Science, Rutgers University.

Michael S. Lewis-Beck is F. Wendell Miller Distinguished Professor of Political Science, University of Iowa.

Arthur Lupia is Hal R. Varian Collegiate Professor of Political Science, University of Michigan.

James Mahoney is Professor of Political Science and Sociology, Northwestern University.

Charles F. Manski is Board of Trustees Professor and Chair of Economics, Northwestern University.

Andrew D. Martin is Professor and Chair of Political Science, and Professor of Law, Washington University, St Louis.

Rebecca B. Morton is Professor in the Wilf Family Department of Political Science, New York University.

Scott E. Page is Professor of Political Science, Research Professor in Center for Political Studies, and Associate Director of Center for the Study of Complex Systems, University of Michigan, Ann Arbor.

Jon C. Pevehouse is Associate Professor at the Irving B. Harris School of Public Policy, University of Chicago.

Keith T. Poole is Professor of Political Science, University of California, San Diego.

Sophia Rabe-Hesketh is Professor of Educational Statistics and Professor of Biostatistics at the University of California, Berkeley, and Chair of Social Statistics at the Institute of Education, University of London.

Charles C. Ragin is Professor of Political Science and Sociology, University of Arizona, Tucson.

Brian C. Rathbun is Assistant Professor of Political Science, University of Southern California.

Benoît Rihoux is Professor of Political Science, Université catholique de Louvain.

Jason Seawright is Assistant Professor of Political Science, Northwestern University.

Jasjeet S. Sekhon is Associate Professor in the Charles and Louise Travers Department of Political Science, University of California, Berkeley.

Anders Skrondal is Director of the Methodology Institute and Professor of Statistics at the London School of Economics.

P. Larkin Terrie is a Doctoral Candidate in Political Science, Northwestern University.

Kenneth C. Williams is Professor of Political Science, Michigan State University.

PART I

INTRODUCTION

CHAPTER 1

....

POLITICAL SCIENCE METHODOLOGY

....

JANET M. BOX-STEFFENSMEIER
HENRY E. BRADY
DAVID COLLIER

"You say you want a revolution
Well, you know,
We all want to change the world."
The Beatles

PEOPLE of the 1960s generation did not argue much with the Beatles—we listened to them with rapt attention. But are they right? What do they mean by a revolution? Do we all want to change the world? What would change the world? Would the result be good or bad?

Political methodology provides the practicing political scientist with tools for attacking all these questions, although it leaves to normative political theory the question of what is ultimately good or bad. Methodology provides techniques for clarifying the theoretical meaning of concepts such as revolution and for developing definitions of revolutions. It offers descriptive indicators for comparing the scope of revolutionary change, and sample surveys for gauging the support for revolutions. And it offers an array of methods for making causal inferences that provide insights into the causes and consequences of revolutions. All these tasks are important and strongly

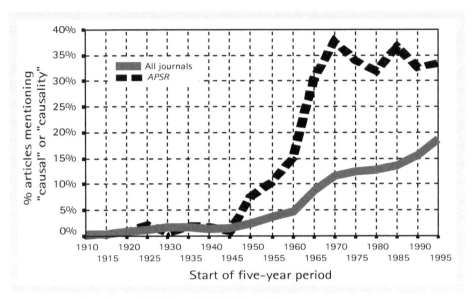

Fig. 1.1. Growth of "causal thinking" in JSTOR articles from 1910 to 1999

interconnected. While causal inference is fundamental in political science, making good inferences depends entirely on adequate conceptualization and measurement of the phenomena under study—tasks that receive substantial attention in this volume. Yet time and again our authors return to the question of what might constitute a valid causal inference using qualitative or quantitative data, small-N or large-n data, in-depth interviews or sample surveys, historical narratives or experimental data.

Although not all of modern political science is about causal inference, between 1995 and 1999 about 33 percent of the articles in the *American Political Science Review* (*APSR*) mentioned these words and 19 percent of all the journal articles in JSTOR for this period mentioned them. The proportions rise to 60 percent for all journals and 67 percent for the *APSR* if we add the words "cause" or "causes," but these words do not have the same technical meaning as "causal" or "causality" so we will stick with the narrower measure of our concept, even though it might be an underestimate of the scope of causal thinking.[1] As shown in Figure 1.1, the concern with causality is increasing, and the mentions of these terms grew rapidly from less than 2 percent of JSTOR articles from 1910 to 1950 to an increasing proportion from 1950 onwards, with the *APSR* apparently leading the way.

What is behind this dramatic increase in mentions of "causal" or "causality?" Does it tell us something meaningful about political science in the twentieth century? Have we measured a useful concept (i.e. "causal thinking in political science")

---

[1] If we just search for the words "cause" or "causes" alone in all political science articles, we find that the proportion of these words is 55 percent in 1995–9 which is not a very dramatic increase since 1910–19 when it was 50 percent. This suggests that the words "cause" or "causes" measure something different from "causality" and "causal." As we shall see, political methodology often grapples with questions like this about construct validity.

with our JSTOR search? Have we described accurately the rise of causal thinking in the twentieth century? Can we explain this rise? The methods contained in this handbook are expressly designed to answer social science questions of this sort. Our discussion of causality may be just a "toy example," but it does have the virtue that it is familiar to and perhaps interesting to political scientists. And it has the additional virtue that explaining the increasing concern with a new perspective such as "causal thinking" within political science is a miniature and simpler version of explaining the rise of "revolutionary" perspectives in politics—the emergence of eighteenth-century liberalism, nineteenth-century socialism, early to mid-twentieth-century New Deal liberalism, late twentieth-century neoliberalism, and the modern environmental movement. If we can understand the difficulties of *explaining* the rise of causal thinking within political science, indeed the difficulties of merely *describing* whether or not causal thinking actually increased during the twentieth century, we will not only provide an overview of this handbook, but we will also learn a lot about what methodologists can contribute to doing political science research. If along the way the reader grimaces over some of our methodological approaches, we hope this reaction has the effect of raising questions about what can and cannot be done with these methods. Perhaps it will also help us all develop some modesty about what our craft can accomplish.

1 Social Theory and Approaches to Social Science Methodology

How do we think about explaining the rise of causal thinking in political science? One place to start is with social theory which asks questions about the ontology and epistemology of our enterprise. Ontology deals with the things that we think exist in the world, and epistemology with how we come to know about those things. Hardin (Chapter 2) suggests that we should start social science inquiry with individuals, their motivations, and the kinds of transactions they undertake with one another. He starts with self-interest (although he quickly suggests that there are other motivations as well), and this provides a useful starting place for understanding the increasing focus on causality in political science. Self-interest suggests that people publish in order to advance their careers and that they will do what is necessary to achieve that end, but it begs the question of why causal thinking is a common goal of the political science profession.

Hardin describes four basic schools of social theory: conflict, shared-values, exchange, and coordination theories. Several of these might help to explain why political scientists have adopted causal thinking as a goal for their enterprise. Political scientists might be adhering to shared "scientific" values about understanding the world through the exploration of causal relationships. And this scientific value might have become important to science in the twentieth century because it allowed humans to manipulate their world and to shape it in their self-interest. According to this explanation, the social sciences simply adopted this value because, well, it was valuable. Alternatively, political scientists might be exchanging their causal knowledge for resources garnered from the larger society. Or they might be coordinating on the topic of causality in order to have a common standard for evaluating research, although this leaves open why they chose this solution to the coordination problem. One answer might be that a focal point was created through the invention of some convenient tool that promised to help political scientists with their research. Two obvious methodological tools of the early twentieth century are correlation analysis (Pearson 1909) and regression analysis (Pearson 1896; Yule 1907), although as we shall see, only regression analysis provided at least rhetorical support for causal inference.

Bevir (Chapter 3) provides some explanations for the rise of causal thinking as the "behavioral revolution's" reaction to the nineteenth century's teleological narratives about history ("developmental historicism") and early twentieth-century emphasis on classifications, correlations, and systems ("modernist empiricism"). The behavioral revolution took a somewhat different direction and emphasized general theories and the testing of causal hypotheses. Bevir's chapter suggests that the rise of causal thinking might have been a corollary of this development. But Bevir warns that there are new currents in philosophy which have moved beyond behavioralism.

De Marchi and Page (Chapter 4) explore one kind of mathematical modeling, agent-based modeling, that has become increasingly common in political science. We might have included chapters on other theoretical perspectives (rational choice, social network modeling, historical narratives, etc.) but this one was especially apt for a methodology handbook since agent-based modeling is not only an approach to modeling; it is also a way of simulating models to generate testable hypotheses and even of generating data that can then be analyzed. Agent-based models suggest that we should think of political scientists as agents with goals who interact according to some rules—including rule-changing rules. These "rule-changing rules" might include changes in what is valued or in how people coordinate—such as a change towards emphasizing causal thinking over other kinds of inquiry.

Three possible causes of the increased emphasis on causality follow from this discussion. Two of them look to the development of a new tool, either regression or correlation, that made it easier to determine causality so that more scholars focused upon that problem. The third suggests value change with the rise of behavioralism. There may be other plausible explanations, but these provide us with a trio of possibilities for developing our example. Indeed, these categories of explanation—new inventions and new values—crop up again and again in social science. The rise of capitalism, for example, has been explained as the result of inventions such as markets, corporations, and industrial processes that made individual accumulation possible, and it has been explained as the result of an emphasis on particular values such as a protestant ethic that valued accumulation and accomplishment.

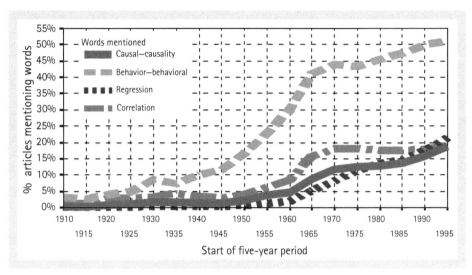

Fig. 1.2. Growth of mentions of words related to causal thinking in political science in JSTOR articles from 1910 to 1999

2 CONCEPTS AND MEASUREMENT

To proceed with our investigation of the rise in causal thinking, we must clarify our concepts and develop measures. Our concepts are "the study of causality in political science," the use of the tools of "regression analysis" or "correlation," and changes in values due to the "behavioral revolution." Continuing with what we have already done, we measure them using word searches in JSTOR. For regression and correlation, we look for "regression" or "correlation."[2] We risk, of course, the possibility that these terms are being used in nonstatistical ways ("regression to his childhood" or "the correlation of forces"), but we assume for the moment that these uses stay relatively constant over time.

In order to determine the utility of this approach, we focus on the definition of "behavioral revolution," but if we had more space we could have added similar discussions about measuring "the study of causality in political science" or "correlation" or "regression." To measure the extent of the behavioral revolution, we look for the words "behavior" or "behavioral." When we count these various terms over the ninety years we get the results in Figure 1.2.

Goertz (Chapter 5) provides guidance on how to think about our concepts. Not surprisingly, he tells us that we must start by thinking about the theory embedded in the concept, and we must think about the plausible method for aggregating indicators

---

[2] We might also search for the term "least squares" but almost whenever it appears (88 percent of the time), the term "regression" also appears, so not much is gained by searching for it as well.

of the concept. For measuring the extent of the "the behavioral revolution" we want to measure those habits and perspectives of inquiry that distinguished those researchers who were concerned with general theories of behavior from those who went before them. Simply counting words may seem like a poor way to do this—at first blush it would seem that we should use a more sophisticated method that codes articles based on whether or not they proposed general hypotheses, collected data to test them, and carried out some tests to do just that. At the very least, we might look for the word "behavioralism" or "behaviorism" to make sure that the authors subscribed to the movement. But from 1910 to 1999, "behavioralism" is only mentioned in 338 articles— out of a total of 78,046 (about 0.4 percent). And "behaviorism" is mentioned in even fewer articles, which is not too surprising since political scientists (although not psychologists) tended to prefer the term "behavioralism."

The words "behavioral" and "behavior" turn out to be better measures as judged by tests of criterion and convergent validity (Jackman, Chapter 6). The word behavioral is mentioned in 8.9 percent of the articles and the word "behavior" in 31.3 percent. These two words (behavior and behavioral) are almost always mentioned when the criterion words of behavioralism or behaviorism are mentioned (about 95 percent of the time). Moreover, in a test of convergent validity, the articles of those people known to be leaders of the behavioral movement used these terms more frequently than the authors of the average article. Between 1930 and 1990, we find that the average article mentioned one or more of the four terms 33 percent of the time, but the articles by the known behavioralists mentioned one or more of the four terms 66 percent of the time.[3] Hence, these words appear to be closely related to the behavioral movement, and we will often refer to mentions of them as indicators of "behavioralism." Similarly, we will often refer to mentions of "causal" and "causality" as indicators of "causal thinking."

In our running example, we used JSTOR categories to describe scientific disciplines (political science, sociology, etc.) and to classify journals and items (as articles or book reviews or editorials) according to these categories. Collier, LaPorte, and Seawright (Chapter 7) and Ragin (Chapter 8) remind us that these are important decisions with significant implications for conceptualization and calibration.

Collier, LaPorte, and Seawright (Chapter 7) discuss categories and typologies as an optic for looking at concept formation and measurement. Working with typologies is crucial not only to the creation and refinement of concepts, but it also contributes to constructing categorical variables involving nominal, partially ordered, and ordinal scales. Although typologies might be seen as part of the qualitative tradition of research, in fact they are also employed by quantitative analysts, and this chapter

---

[3] Using a list of presidents of the American Political Science Association, we coded those people known to be "behavioralists" from 1950 to 1980—we coded sixteen of the 31 presidents in this way (Odegard, Herring, Lasswell, Schattschneider, Key, Truman, Almond, Dahl, Easton, Deutsch, Lane, Eulau, Leiserson, Ranney, Wahlke, and Miller). Using different time periods yields similar results. (For example, the 1950–80 period yields 35 percent for a general article and 78 percent for those by the famous behavioralists.)

therefore provides one of the many bridges between these two approaches that are crucial to the approach of this handbook.

Ragin (Chapter 8) distinguishes between "measurement" and "calibration," arguing that with calibration the researcher achieves a tighter integration of measurement and theory. For example, a political science theory about "developed countries" will probably not be the same as a theory about "developing countries," so that careful thought must be given to how the corresponding categories are conceptualized, and how countries are assigned to them. In our running example, articles in political science will probably be different from those in other disciplines, so care must be taken in defining the scope of the discipline. Yet we have rather cavalierly allowed JSTOR to define this membership, even though by JSTOR's categorization, political science thereby includes the journals *Social Science History*, the *Journal of Comparative Law*, and *Asian Studies*. We have also allowed JSTOR to treat articles as examples of "causal thinking" when they have at least one mention of "causal" or "causality" even though there might be a substantial difference between articles that mention these terms only once versus those that mention them many times. Alternative calibration decisions are certainly possible. Perhaps only journals with political, politics, or some similar word in their titles should be considered political science journals. Perhaps we should require a threshold number of mentions of "causal" or "causality" before considering an article as an example of "causal thinking." Perhaps we should revisit the question of whether "cause" and "causes" should be used as measures of "causal thinking." Ragin provides a "fuzzy-set" framework for thinking about these decisions, and thereby offers both direct and indirect methods for calibration.

Jackman (Chapter 6) also focuses on measurement, starting from the classic test theory model in which an indicator is equal to a latent variable plus some error. He reminds us that good measures must be both valid and reliable, and defines these standards carefully. He demonstrates the dangers of unreliability, and discusses the estimation of various measurement models using Bayesian methods. Jackman's argument reminds us to consider the degree to which our counts of articles that mention specific words represent the underlying concepts, and he presents a picture of measurement in which multiple indicators are combined—typically additively—to get better measures of underlying concepts. Goertz's chapter suggests that there is an alternative approach in which indicators are combined according to some logical formula. Our approach to measuring behavioralism at the article level has more in common with Goertz's approach because it requires that either "behavior" or "behavioral" be present in the article, but it has more in common with Jackman's approach when we assume that our time series of proportions of articles mentioning these terms is a valid and relatively reliable measure of the degree to which behavioralism has infused the discipline.

Poole (Chapter 9), Jackman (Chapter 6), and Bollen et al. (Chapter 18) consider whether concepts are multidimensional. Any measurement effort should consider this possibility, but political scientists must be especially careful because the dimensionality of politics matters a great deal for understanding political contestation. To take just one example, multidimensional voting spaces typically lead to voting cycles

Table 1.1. Two dimensions of political
science discourse, 1970–1999

	Component	
	Causal	Interpretive
Narrative	.018	.759
Interpretive	.103	.738
Causal/causality	.700	.105
Hypothesis	.750	−.073
Explanation	.701	.131

Extraction method: principal component analysis.
Rotation method: oblimin with Kaiser normalization.

(Arrow 1963) and "chaos" theorems (McKelvey 1979; Schofield 1983; Saari 1999) for voting systems. Poole reviews how the measurement of political issue spaces has developed in the past eighty years through borrowings from psychometrics (scaling, factor analysis, and unfolding), additions from political science theories (the spatial theory of voting and ideal points), and confronting the special problems of political survey, roll-call, and interest-group ratings data. Bollen et al. show how factor analysis methods for determining dimensionality can be combined with structural equation modeling (SEM).

There does not seem to be any obvious need to consider dimensions for our data, but suppose we broaden our inquiry by asking whether there are different dimensions of political science discourse. Based upon our relatively detailed qualitative knowledge of "political science in America," we chose to search for all articles from 1970 to 1999 on five words that we suspected might have a two-dimensional structure: the words "narrative," "interpretive," "causal or causality," "hypothesis," and "explanation." After obtaining their correlations across articles,[4] we used principal components and an oblimin rotation as described in Jackman (Chapter 6). We found two eigenvalues with values larger than one which suggested a two dimensional principal components solution reported in Table 1.1. There is a "causal dimension" which applies to roughly one-third of the articles and an "interpretive" dimension which applies to about 6 percent of the articles.[5] Although we expected this two-dimensional structure, we were somewhat surprised to find that the word "explanation" was almost entirely connected with "causal or cauality" and with "hypothesis." And we were surprised that the two dimensions were completely distinctive, since they are essentially uncorrelated at .077. Moreover, in a separate analysis, we found

[4] We constructed variables for each word with a zero value if the word was not present in an article and a one if it was mentioned at least once. Then we obtained the ten correlations between pairs of the five variables with articles as the unit of analysis.

[5] Each word appears in a different number of articles, but one or the other or both of the words "narrative" or "interpretive" appear in about 5.9 percent of the articles and the words "hypothesis" or "causal" or "causality" appear in almost one-third (31.3 percent). "Explanation" alone appears in 35.4 percent of the articles.

that whereas the increase in "causal thinking" occurred around 1960 or maybe even 1950 in political science (see Figure 1.1), the rise in the use of the terms "narrative" and "interpretive" came in 1980.[6]

This result reminds us that "causal thinking" is not the only approach to political science discourse. Our volume recognizes this by including chapters that consider historical narrative (Mahoney and Terrie, Chapter 32) and intensive interviewing (Rathbun, Chapter 28), but there is also a rich set of chapters in a companion volume, the *Oxford Handbook of Contextual Political Analysis*, which the interested reader might want to consult.

This discussion leads us to think a bit more about our measure of "causal thinking." The chapters on "Concepts and Measurement" suggest that we have been a bit cavalier in our definition of concepts. Perhaps we should be thinking about measuring "scientific thinking" instead of just "causal thinking." How can we do that? In fact, like many researchers, we started with an interesting empirical fact (i.e. the mentions of "causal" and "causality" in political science articles), and worked from there. At this point, some hard thinking and research (which will be mostly qualitative) about our concepts would be useful. Philosophical works about the nature of science and social science should be consulted. Some well-known exemplars of good social science research should be reviewed. And something like the following can be done.

Based upon our reflections about the nature of scientific thinking (and the factor analysis above), we believe that the words "hypothesis" and "explanation" as well as "causal or causality" might be thought of as indicators of a "scientific" frame of mind.[7] Consider the frequency of these words in all articles in JSTOR in various disciplines from 1990 to 1999. Table 1.2 sorts the results in terms of the discipline with the highest use of any of the words at the top of the table. Note that by these measures, ecology and evolutionary biology, sociology, and economics are most "scientific" while "history," "film studies," and "performing arts" are least "scientific." Also note that the highest figures in each row (excluding the final column) are in bold. Note that we put "scientific" in quotations because we want to emphasize our special and limited definition of the term.

Ecology and evolutionary biology and economics refer to "hypothesis" to a greater degree than other disciplines which mention "explanation" more. But also note that political science (17.2 percent) and sociology (25.2 percent) tend to be high in mentions of "causal" or "causality." In contrast, "performing arts" has a 3.6 percent rate of mention of "causal" or "causality" and "film studies" has a 5.8 percent rate.

As researchers, we might at this point rethink our dependent variable, but we are going to stay with mentions of "causal or causality" for two reasons. First, these words

---

[6] In 1980–4, the words "narrative" or "interpretive" were mentioned only 4.1 percent of the time in political science journals; in the succeeding five-year periods, the words increased in use to 6.1 percent, 8.1 percent, and finally 10.1 percent for 1995–9.

[7] At least two other words might be relevant: "law" and "theory." The first gets at the notion of the need for "law-like" statements, but searching for it on JSTOR obviously leads to many false positives—mentions of public laws, the rule of law, the study of law, and the exercise of law. Similarly, "theory" gets at the notion of "theories" lying behind hypotheses, but the subfield of "political theory" uses theory in a much different sense.

Table 1.2. Mentions of "scientific" terms in various disciplines, 1990–9 (%)

	Causal/causality	Hypothesis	Explanation	Any of these words
Ecology & evolutionary biology	7.9	50.0	31.7	62.3
Sociology	25.1	37.3	40.6	61.7
Economics	10.0	44.6	36.1	61.2
Political science	17.2	27.3	38.0	52.2
Anthropology	12.5	22.8	39.1	52.0
History	8.1	14.3	36.4	44.6
Film studies	5.8	5.3	19.3	25.4
Performing arts	3.6	4.8	18.5	23.8

Source: Searches of JSTOR archive by authors.

come closest to measuring the concerns of many authors in our book. Second, the narrowness of this definition (in terms of the numbers of articles mentioning the terms) may make it easier to explain. But the foregoing analysis (including our discussion of narrative and interpretive methods) serves as a warning that we have a narrow definition of what political science is doing.

3 CAUSALITY AND EXPLANATION IN SOCIAL RESEARCH

Brady (Chapter 10) presents an overview of causal thinking by characterizing four approaches to causal inference. The Humean regularity approach focuses on "lawlike" constant conjunction and temporal antecedence, and many statistical methods—preeminently regression analysis—are designed to provide just the kind of information to satisfy the requirements of the Humean model. Regression analysis can be used to determine whether a dependent variable is still correlated ("constantly conjoined") with an independent variable when other plausible causes of the dependent variable are held constant by being included in the regression; and time-series regressions can look for temporal antecedence by regressing a dependent variable on lagged independent variables.

In our running example, if the invention of regression analysis actually led to the emphasis upon causality in political science, then we would expect to find two things. First in a regression of "causal thinking" (that is, mentions of "causal or causality") on mentions of "regression," mentions of "correlation," and mentions of "behavioralism," we expect to find a significant regression coefficient on the "regression" variable. Second, we would expect that the invention of the method of regression and its introduction into political science would pre-date the onset of "causal thinking" in political science. In addition, in a time-series regression of mentions of "causal thinking" on lagged values of mentions of "regression," "correlation," and "behavioralism" we would expect a significant coefficient on lagged "regression." We shall discuss this approach in detail later on.

The counterfactual approach to causation asks what would have happened had a putative cause not occurred in the most similar possible world without the cause. It requires either finding a similar situation in which the cause is not present or imagining what such a situation would be like. In our running example, if we want to determine whether or not the introduction of regression analysis led to an efflorescence of causal thinking in political science, we must imagine what would have happened if regression analysis had not been invented by Pearson and Yule. In this imagined world, we would not expect causal thinking to develop to such a great extent as in our present world. Or alternatively, we must find a "similar" world (such as the study of politics in some European country such as France) where regression was not introduced until much later than in the United States. In this most similar world, we would not expect to see mentions of "causal thinking" in the political science literature until much later as well.

The manipulation approach asks what happens when we actively manipulate the cause: Does it lead to the putative effect? In our running example, we might consider what happened when the teaching of regression was introduced into some scholarly venue. When graduate programs introduced regression analysis, do we find that their new Ph.Ds focused on causal issues in their dissertations? Does the manipulation of the curriculum by teaching regression analysis lead to "causal thinking?"

Finally, as we shall see below, the mechanism and capacities approach asks what detailed steps lead from the cause to the effect. In our running example, it asks about the exact steps that could lead from the introduction of regression analysis in a discipline to a concern with causality.

Brady also discusses the INUS model which considers the complexity of causal factors. This model gets beyond simple necessary or sufficient conditions for an effect by arguing that often there are different sufficient pathways (but no pathway is strictly necessary) to causation—each pathway consisting of an *insufficient* but *nonredundant* part of an *unnecessary* but *sufficient* (INUS) condition for the effect.

Sekhon (Chapter 11) provides a detailed discussion of the Neyman–Rubin model of causal inference that combines counterfactual thinking with the requirement for manipulation in the design of experiments. This model also makes the basic test of a causal relationship a probabilistic one: whether or not the probability of the effect goes up when the cause is present.[8] Sekhon shows how with relatively weak assumptions (but see below) this approach can lead to valid causal inferences. He

---

[8] Thus if C is cause and E is effect, a necessary condition for causality is that $\text{Prob}(E|C) > \text{Prob}(E|\text{not } C)$. Of course, this also means that the expectation goes up $E(E|C) > E(E|\text{not } C)$.

also discusses under what conditions "matching" approaches can lead to valid inferences, and what kinds of compromises sometimes have to be made with respect to generalizability (external validity) to ensure valid causal inferences (internal validity).

Freedman (Chapter 12) argues that "substantial progress also derives from informal reasoning and qualitative insights." Although he has written extensively on the Neyman–Rubin framework and believes that it should be employed whenever possible because it sets the gold standard for causal inferences, Freedman knows that in the real world, we must sometimes fall back on observational data. What do we do then? The analysis of large "observational" data-sets is one approach, but he suggests that another strategy relying upon "causal process observations" (CPOs) might be useful as a complement to them. CPOs rely on detailed observations of situations to look for hints and signs that one or another causal process might be at work. These case studies sometimes manipulate the putative cause, as in Jenner's vaccinations. Or they rule out alternative explanations, as in Semmelweis's rejection of "atmospheric, cosmic, telluric changes" as the causes for puerperal fever. They take advantage of case studies such as the death of Semmelweis's colleague by "cadaveric particles," Fleming's observation of an anomaly in a bacterial culture in his laboratory that led to the discovery of penicillin, or the death of a poor soul in London who next occupied the same room as a newly arrived and cholera infected seaman. Or a lady's death by cholera from what Snow considered the infected water from the "Broad Street Pump" even though she lived far from the pump but, it turned out, liked the taste of the water from the pump.

Hedström (Chapter 13) suggests that explanation requires understanding mechanisms which are the underlying "cogs and wheels" which connect the cause and the effect. The mechanism, for example, which explains how vaccinations work to provide immunity from an illness is the interaction between a weakened form of a virus and the body's immune system which confers long-term immunity. In social science, the rise in a candidate's popularity after an advertisement might be explained by a psychological process that works on a cognitive or emotional level to process messages in the advertisement. Hedström inventories various definitions of "mechanism." He provides examples of how they might work, and he presents a framework for thinking about the mechanisms underlying individual actions.

In our running example, it would be useful to find out how regression might have become a tool for supposedly discovering causality. Some of the mechanisms include the following. Regression is inherently asymmetrical leading to an identification of the "dependent" variable with the effect and the "independent" variables with possible causes. The interpretation of regression coefficients to mean that a unit change in the independent variable would lead to a change in the dependent variable equal to the regression coefficient (everything else equal) strongly suggests that regression coefficients can be treated as causal effects, and it provides a simple and powerful way to describe and quantify the causal effect for someone. The names for regression techniques may have played a role from about 1966 onwards when there was a steady growth for the next twenty-five years in articles that described regression analyses as "causal models" or "causal modeling"[9] even though some authors would argue that the names were often seriously misleading—even amounting to a "con job" (Leamer 1983; Freedman 2005). And the relative ease with which regression could be taught and used (due to the advent of computers) might also explain why it was adopted by political scientists.

4 EXPERIMENTS, QUASI-EXPERIMENTS, AND NATURAL EXPERIMENTS

Experiments are the gold standard for establishing causality. Combining R. A. Fisher's notion of randomized experiment (1925) with the Neyman–Rubin model (Neyman 1923; Rubin 1974; 1978; Holland 1986) provides a recipe for valid causal inference as long as several assumptions are met. At least one of these, the Stable Unit Treatment Value Assumption (SUTVA), is not trivial,[10] but some of the others are relatively innocuous so that when an experiment can be done, the burden of good inference is to properly implement the experiment. Morton and Williams (Chapter 14) note that the number of experiments has increased dramatically in political science in the last thirty-five years because of their power for making causal inferences.[11] At the same time, they directly confront the Achilles heel of experiments—their external validity. They argue that external validity can be achieved if a result can be replicated across a variety of data-sets and situations. In some cases this means trying experiments in the field, in surveys, or on the internet; but they also argue that the control possible in laboratory experimentation can make it possible to induce a wider range of variation than in the field—thus increasing external validity. They link formal models with experimentation by showing how experiments can be designed to test them.

For Gerber and Green (Chapter 15) field experiments and natural experiments are a way to overcome the external validity limitations of laboratory experiments. They show that despite early skepticism about what could be done with experiments, social scientists are increasingly finding ways to experiment in areas such as criminal justice, the provision of social welfare, schooling, and even politics. But they

---

[9] Not until the 1960s are there any articles that use the term "regression" and either "causal model" or "causal modeling." Then the number grows from 25 in the 1960s, to 124 in the 1970s, to 129 in the 1980s. It drops to 103 in the 1990s.

[10] SUTVA means that a subject's response depends only on that subject's assignment, not the assignment of other subjects. SUTVA will be violated if the number of units getting the treatment versus the control status affects the outcome (as in a general equilibrium situation where many people getting the treatment of more education affects the overall value of education more than when just a few people get education), or if there is more communication of treatment to controls depending on the way assignment is done.

[11] The observant reader will note that these authors make a causal claim about the power of an invention (in this case experimental methods) to further causal discourse.

admit that "there remain important domains of political science that lie beyond the reach of randomized experimentation." Gerber and Green review the Neyman–Rubin framework, discuss SUTVA, and contrast experimental and observational inference. They also discuss the problems of "noncompliance" and "attrition" in experiments. Noncompliance occurs when medical subjects do not take the medicines they are assigned or citizens do not get the phone calls that were supposed to to encourage their participation in politics. Attrition is a problem for experiments when people are more likely to be "lost" in one condition (typically, but not always, the control condition) than another. They end with a discussion of natural experiments where some naturally occurring process such as a lottery for the draft produces a randomized or nearly randomized treatment.

With the advice of these articles in hand, we can return to our running example. We are encouraged to think hard about how we might do an experiment to find out about the impact of new techniques (regression or correlation) or changes in values (the behavioral revolution) on causal thinking. We could, for example, randomly assign students to either a 1970s-style curriculum in which they learned about "causal modeling" methods such as regression analysis or a 1930s-style curriculum in which they did not. We could then observe what kinds of dissertations they produced. It would also be interesting to see which group got more jobs, although we suspect that human subjects committees (not to mention graduate students) would look askance at these scientific endeavors. Moreover, there is the great likelihood that SUTVA would be violated as the amount of communication across the two groups might depend on their assignment. All in all, it is hard to think of experiments that can be done in this area. This example reminds us that for some crucial research questions, experiments may be impossible or severely limited in their usefulness.

5 QUANTITATIVE TOOLS FOR CAUSAL AND DESCRIPTIVE INFERENCE: GENERAL METHODS

Our discussion of the rise of causal thinking in political science makes use of the JSTOR database. Political science is increasingly using databases that are available on the internet. But scientific surveys provided political scientists with the first opportunities to collect micro-data on people's attitudes, beliefs, and behaviors, and surveys continue to be an immensely important method of data collection. Other handbooks provide information on some of these other methods of data collection, but the discussion of survey methods provides a template for thinking about data collection issues. Johnston (Chapter 16) considers three dimensions for data collection: mode, space, and time. For sample surveys, the modes include mail, telephone, in-person, and internet. Space and time involve the methods of data collection (clustered samples versus completely random samples) and the design of the survey (cross-sectional or panels). Beyond mode, space, and time, Johnston goes on to consider the problems of adequately representing persons by ensuring high response rates and measuring opinions validly and reliably through the design of high-quality questions.

In our running example, our data come from a computerized database of articles, but we could imagine getting very useful data from other modes such as surveys, in-depth interviews, or old college catalogs and reading lists for courses. Our JSTOR data provide a fairly wide cross-section of extant journals at different locations at any moment in time, and they provide over-time data extending back to when many journals began publishing. We can think of the data as a series of repeated cross-sections, or if we wish to consider a number of journals, as a panel with repeated observations on each journal. As for the quality of the data, we can ask, as does Johnston in the survey context about the veracity of question responses, whether our articles and coding methods faithfully represent people's beliefs and attitudes.

The rest of this section and all of the next section of the handbook discuss regression-like statistical methods and their extensions. These methods can be used for two quite different purposes that are sometimes seriously conflated and unfortunately confused. They can be used for *descriptive inferences* about phenomena, or they can be used to make *causal inferences* about them (King, Keohane, and Verba 1994). Establishing the Humean conditions of constant conjunction and temporal precedence with regression-like methods often takes pride of place when people use these methods, but they can also be thought of as ways to describe complex data-sets by estimating parameters that tell us important things about the data. For example, Autoregressive Integrated Moving Average (ARIMA) models can quickly tell us a lot about a time series through the standard "p,d,q" parameters which are the order of the autoregression (p), the level of differencing (d) required for stationarity, and the order of the moving average component (q). And a graph of a hazard rate over time derived from an events history model reveals at a glance important facts about the ending of wars or the dissolution of coalition governments. Descriptive inference is often underrated in the social sciences (although survey methodologists proudly focus on this problem), but more worrisome is the tendency for social scientists to mistake description using a statistical technique for valid causal inferences. For example, most regression analyses in the social sciences are probably useful descriptions of the relationships among various variables, but they often cannot properly be used for causal inferences because they omit variables, fail to deal with selection bias and endogeneity, and lack theoretical grounding.

Let us illustrate this with our running example. The classic regression approach to causality suggests estimating a simple regression equation such as the following for cross-sectional data on all political science articles in JSTOR between 1970 and 1979. For each article we score a mention of either "causality or causal" as a one and no mention of these terms as a zero. We then regress these zero–one values of the "dependent variable" on zero–one values for "independent variables" measuring

Table 1.3. Results of regressing whether "causal thinking" was mentioned among potential explanatory factors for 1970–1979—all political science journal articles in JSTOR

Independent variables	Regression coefficient (standard error)	
	One	Two
Behavior	.122 (.006)***	.110 (.006)***
Regression	.169 (.010)***	.061 (.021)**
Correlation	.157 (.008)***	.150 (.015)***
Behavior × regression		.135 (.022)***
Behavior × correlation		.004 (.017)
Regression × correlation		.027 (.021)
Constant	.022 (.008)***	.028 (.004)***
R^2/N	.149/ 12,305	.152/ 12,305

***Significant at .001 level; **Significant at .01 level; *Significant at .05 level.

whether or not the article mentioned "regression," "correlation," or "behavioralism." When we do this, we get the results in column one in Table 1.3.

If we use the causal interpretation of regression analysis to interpret these results, we might conclude that all three factors led to the emphasis on "causal thinking" in political science because each coefficient is substantively large and statistically highly significant. But this interpretation ignores a multitude of problems.

Given the INUS model of causation which emphasizes the complexity of necessary and sufficient conditions, we might suspect that there is some interaction among these variables so we should include interactions between each pair of variables. These interactions require that both concepts be present in the article so that a "regression × correlation" interaction requires that both regression and correlation are mentioned. The results from estimating this model are in column two of the table. Interestingly, only the "behavior × regression" interaction is significant, suggesting that it is the combination of the behavioral revolution and the development of regression analysis that "explains" the prevalence of causal thinking in political science. (The three-way interaction is not reported and is insignificant.) Descriptively this result is certainly correct—it appears that a mention of behavioralism alone increases the probability of "causal thinking" in an article by about 11 percent, the mention of regression increases the probability by about 6 percent, the mention of correlation increases the probability by about 15 percent, and the mention of both behavioralism and regression together further increases the probability of causal thinking by about 13.5 percent.

But are these causal effects? This analysis is immediately open to the standard criticisms of the regression approach when it is used to infer causation: Maybe some other factor (or factors) causes these measures (especially "behavioral," "regression," and "causality") to cohere during this period. Maybe these are all spurious relationships which appear to be significant because the true cause is omitted from the equation.

Or maybe causality goes both ways and all these variables are endogenous. Perhaps "causal thinking" causes mentions of the words "behavioral or behavior" and "regression" and "correlation."

Although the problem of spurious relationships challenged the regression approach from the very beginning (see Yule 1907), many people (including Yule) thought that it could be overcome by simply adding enough variables to cover all potential causes. The endogeneity problem posed a greater challenge which only became apparent to political scientists in the 1970s. If all variables are endogenous, then there is a serious identification problem with cross-sectional data that cannot be overcome no matter how much data are collected. For example, in the bivariate case where "causal thinking" may influence "behavioralism" as well as "behavioralism" influencing "causal thinking," the researcher only observes a single correlation which cannot produce the two distinctive coefficients representing the impact of "behavioralism" on "causal thinking" and the impact of "causal thinking" on "behavioralism."

The technical solution to this problem is the use of "instrumental variables" known to be exogenous and known to be correlated with the included endogenous variables, but the search for instruments proved elusive in many situations. Jackson (Chapter 17) summarizes the current situation with respect to "endogeneity and structural equation estimation" through his analysis of a simultaneous model of electoral support and congressional voting records. Jackson's chapter covers a fundamental problem with grace and lucidity, and he is especially strong in discussing "Instrumental Variables in Practice" and tests for endogeneity. Jackson's observations on these matters are especially appropriate because he was a member of the group that contributed to the 1973 Goldberger and Duncan volume on *Structural Equation Models in the Social Sciences* which set the stage for several decades of work using these methods to explore causal relationships.

The most impressive accomplishment of this effort was the synthesis of factor analysis and causal modeling to produce what became known as LISREL, covariance structure, path analysis, or structural equation models. Bollen, Rabe-Hesketh, and Skrondal (Chapter 18) summarize the results of these efforts which typically used factor analysis types of models to develop measures of latent concepts which were then combined with causal models of the underlying latent concepts. These techniques have been important on two levels. At one level they simply provide a way to estimate more complicated statistical models that take into account both causal and measurement issues. At another level, partly through the vivid process of preparing "path diagrams," they provide a metaphor for understanding the relationships between concepts and their measurements, latent variables and causation, and the process of going from theory to empirical estimation. Unfortunately, the models have also sometimes led to baroque modeling adventures and a reliance on linearity and additivity that at once complicates and simplifies things too much. Perhaps the biggest problem is the reliance upon "identification" conditions that often require heroic assumptions about instruments.

One way out of the instrumental variables problem is to use time-series data. At the very least, time series give us a chance to see whether a putative cause "jumps" before a supposed effect. We can also consider values of variables that occur earlier in time to be "predetermined"—not quite exogenous but not endogenous either. Pevehouse and Brozek (Chapter 19) describe time-series methods such as simple time-series regressions, ARIMA models, vector autoregression (VAR) models, and unit root and error correction models (ECM). There are two tricky problems in this literature. One is the complex but tractable difficulty of autocorrelation, which typically means that time series have less information in them per observation than cross-sectional data and which suggest that some variables have been omitted from the specification (Beck and Katz 1996; Beck 2003). The second is the more pernicious problem of unit roots and commonly trending (co-integrated) data which can lead to nonsense correlations. In effect, in time-series data, time is almost always an "omitted" variable that can lead to spurious relationships which cannot be easily (or sensibly) disentangled by simply adding time to the regression. And thus, the special adaptation of methods designed for these data.

For our running example, we estimate a time-series autoregressive model for eighteen five-year periods from 1910 to 1999. The model regresses the proportion of articles mentioning "causal thinking" on the lagged proportions mentioning the words "behavioral or behavior," "regression," or "correlation." Table 1.4 shows that mentions of "correlation" do not seem to matter (the coefficient is negative and the standard error is bigger than the coefficient), but mentions of "regression" or "behavioralism" are substantively large and statistically significant. (Also note that the autoregressive parameter is insignificant.) These results provide further evidence that it might have been the combination of behavioralism and regression that led to an increase in causal thinking in political science.

A time series often throws away lots of cross-sectional data that might be useful in making inferences. Time-series cross-sectional (TSCS) methods try to remedy this problem by using both sorts of information together. Beck (Chapter 20) summarizes this literature nicely. Not surprisingly, TSCS methods encounter all the

Table 1.4. Mentions of "causal thinking" for five-year periods regressed on mentions of "behavioral or behavior," "regression," and "correlation" for five-year periods for 1910–1999

Independent variables lagged	Regression coefficients (standard errors)
Behavior	.283 (.065)***
Regression	.372 (.098)**
Correlation	−.159 (.174)
AR (1)	.276 (.342)
Constant	−.002 (.005)
N	17 (one dropped for lags)

Significant: .05 (*), .01 (**), .001 (***).

problems that beset both cross-sectional and time-series data. Beck starts by considering the time-series properties including issues of nonstationarity. He then moves to cross-sectional issues including heteroskedasticity and spatial autocorrelation. He pays special attention to the ways that TSCS methods deal with heterogeneous units through fixed effects and random coefficient models. He ends with a discussion of binary variables and their relationship to event history models which are discussed in more detail in Golub (Chapter 23).

Martin (Chapter 21) surveys modern Bayesian methods of estimating statistical models. Before the 1990s, many researchers could write down a plausible model and the likelihood function for what they were studying, but the model presented insuperable estimation problems. Bayesian estimation was often even more daunting because it required not only the evaluation of likelihoods, but the evaluation of posterior distributions that combined likelihoods and prior distributions. In the 1990s, the combination of Bayesian statistics, Markov Chain Monte Carlo (MCMC) methods, and powerful computers provided a technology for overcoming these problems. These methods make it possible to simulate even very complex distributions and to obtain estimates of previously intractable models.

Using the methods in this chapter, we could certainly estimate a complex time-series cross-sectional model with latent variable indicators for the rise of causal thinking in the social sciences. We might, for example, gather yearly data from 1940 onwards on our various indicators for six different political science journals that have existed since then.[12] We could collect yearly indicators for each latent variable that represents a concept (e.g. "causal" or "causality" for "causal thinking" and "behavior" or "behavioral" for "behavioralism"). We could postulate some time-series cross-sectional model for the data which includes fixed effects for each journal and lagged effects of the explanatory variables. We might want to constrain the coefficients on the explanatory variables to be similar across journals or allow them to vary in some way. But we will leave this task to others.

6 QUANTITATIVE TOOLS FOR CAUSAL AND DESCRIPTIVE INFERENCE: SPECIAL TOPICS

Often our research requires that we use more specially defined methods to answer our research questions. In our running example, we have so far ignored the fact that our dependent variable is sometimes a dichotomous variable (as in Table 1.3 above), but there are good reasons to believe that we should take this into account. Discrete

---

[12] *American Political Science Review* (1906), *Annals of the American Academy of Political and Social Science* (1890), *Journal of Politics* (1939), *Political Science Quarterly* (1886), *Public Opinion Quarterly* (1937), and *Review of Politics* (1939).

choice modeling (Chapter 22) by Glasgow and Alvarez presents methods for dealing with dichotomous variables and with ordered and unordered choices. These methods are probably especially important for our example because each journal article that we code represents a set of choices by the authors which should be explicitly modeled. Alvarez and Glasgow take readers to the forefront of this methodological research area by discussing how to incorporate heterogeneity into these models.

Golub's discussion of survival analysis (Chapter 23) presents another way to in-corporate temporal information into our analysis in ways that provide advantages similar to those from using time series. In our running example, we could consider when various journals began to publish significant numbers of articles mentioning "causality" or "causal" to see how these events are related to the characteristics of the journals (perhaps their editorial boards or editors) and to characteristics of papers (such as the use of regression or behavioral language). As well as being a useful way to model the onset of events, survival analysis, also known as event history analysis, reveals the close ties and interaction that can occur between quantitative and qualitative research. For example, Elliott (2005) brings together narrative and event history analysis in her work on methodology.

A statistical problem that has commanded the attention of scholars for over a hundred years is addressed by Cho and Manski (Chapter 24). Scholars face this problem of "cross-level inference" whenever they are interested in the behavior of individuals but the data are aggregated at the precinct or census tract level. Cho and Manskid's chapter lays out the main methodological approaches to this problem; they do so by first building up intuitions about the problem. The chapter wraps up by placing the ecological inference problem within the context of the literature on partial identification and by describing recent work generalizing the use of logical bounds to produce solutions that are "regions" instead of point estimates for parameters.

The chapters on spatial analysis (Chapter 25) by Franzese and Hays and hierarchical modeling (Chapter 26) by Jones point to ways we can better capture the spatial and logical structure of data. In our running example, the smallest data unit was the use of words such as "causality" within the article, but these articles were then nested within journals and within years (and even in some of our analysis, within different disci-plines). A complete understanding of the development of "causal thinking" within the sciences would certainly require capturing the separate effects of years, journals, and disciplines. It would also require understanding the interdependencies across years, journals, and disciplines.

Franzese and Hayes consider the role of "spatial interdependence" between units of analysis by employing a symmetric weighting matrix for the units of observation whose elements reflect the relative connectivity between unit i and unit j. By includ-ing this matrix in estimation in much the same way that we include lagged values of the dependent variable in time series, we can discover the impact of different forms of interdependence. In our example, if we had separate time series for journals, we could consider the impact of the "closeness" of editorial boards within disciplines based upon overlapping membership or overlapping places of training. These in-terdependencies could be represented by a "spatial" weighting matrix whose entries represent the degree of connection between the journals. The inclusion of this matrix in analyses poses a number of difficult estimation problems, but Franzese and Hayes provide an excellent overview of the problems and their solutions.

Jones considers multilevel models in which units are nested within one another. The classic use of multilevel models is in educational research, where students are in classrooms which are in schools which are in school districts that are in states. Data can be collected at each level: test scores for the students, educational attainment and training for the teachers, student composition for the schools, taxing and spending for the school districts, and so forth. Multilevel methods provide a way of combining these data to determine their separate impacts on outcome variables.

At the moment, spatial and multilevel information cannot be easily incorporated in all types of statistical models. But these two chapters suggest that progress is being made, and that further innovations are on the way.

7 QUALITATIVE TOOLS FOR CAUSAL INFERENCE

Throughout this chapter, we have been using our qualitative knowledge of American political science to make decisions regarding our quantitative analysis. We have used this knowledge to choose the time period of our analysis, to choose specific journals for analysis, to name our concepts and to select the words by which we have measured them by searching in JSTOR, to think about our model specifications, and to interpret our results. Now we use qualitative thinking more directly to further dissect our research problem.

Levy (Chapter 27) suggests that counterfactuals can be used along with case studies to make inferences, although strong theories are needed to do this. He argues that game theory is one (but not the only) approach that provides this kind of theory because a game explicitly models all of the actors' options including those possibilities that are not chosen. Game theory assumes that rational actors will choose an equilibrium path through the extensive form of the game, and all other routes are considered "off the equilibrium path"—counterfactual roads not taken. Levy argues that any counterfactual argument requires a detailed and explicit description of the alternative antecedent (i.e. the cause which did not occur in the counterfactual world) which is plausible and involves a minimal rewrite of history, and he suggests that one of the strengths of game theory is its explicitness about alternatives. Levy also argues that any counterfactual argument requires some evidence that the alternative antecedent would have actually led to a world in which the outcome is different from what we observe with the actual antecedent.

Short of developing game theory models to understand the history of political science, Levy tells us that we must at least try to specify some counterfactuals clearly to see what they might entail. One of our explanations for the rise of "causal thinking" is the invention of regression. Hence, one counterfactual is that regression analysis is not invented and therefore not brought into political science. Would there be less emphasis on causality in this case? It seems likely. As noted earlier, regression analysis, much more than correlation analysis, provides a seductive technology for exploring causality. Its asymmetry with a dependent variable that depends on a number of independent variables lends itself to discussions of causes (independent variables) and effects (dependent variables), whereas correlation (even partial correlation) analysis is essentially symmetric. Indeed, path analysis uses diagrams which look just like causal arrows between variables. Econometricians and statisticians provide theorems which show that if the regression model satisfies certain conditions, then the regression coefficients will be an unbiased estimate of the impact of the independent variables on the dependent variables. Regression analysis also provides the capacity to predict that if there is a one-unit change in some independent variable, then there will be a change in the dependent variable equal to the value of the independent variable's regression coefficient. In short, regression analysis delivers a great deal whereas correlation analysis delivers much less.

Yet, it is hard to believe that regression analysis would have fared so well unless the discipline valued the discussion of causal effects—and this valuation depended on the rise of behavioralism in political science to begin with. It seems likely that behavioralism and regression analysis complemented one another. In fact, if we engage in a counterfactual thought experiment in which behavioralism does not arise, we speculate that regression alone would not have led to an emphasis on causal thinking. After reflection, it seems most likely that behavioralism produced fertile ground for thinking about causality. Regression analysis then took advantage of this fertile soil to push forward a "causal modeling" research agenda.[13]

It would be useful to have some additional corroboration of this story. With so many journal articles to hand in JSTOR, it seems foolhardy not to read some of them, but how do we choose cases? We cannot read all 78,046 articles from 1910 to 1999. Gerring (Chapter 28) provides some guidance by cataloging nine different techniques for case selection: typical, diverse, extreme, deviant, influential, crucial, pathway, most similar, and most different. Our judgment is that we should look for influential, crucial, or pathway cases. Influential cases are those with an influential configuration of the independent variables. Gerring suggests that if the researcher

---

[13] The time-series analysis provides some support for this idea. If we regress the proportion of articles mentioning behavioralism on its lagged value and the lagged values of the proportion of articles mentioning regression, correlation, and causality, only behavioralism lagged has a significant coefficient and causality and correlation have the wrong signs. Behavioralism, it seems, is only predicted by its lagged value. If we do the same analysis by regressing causality on its lagged value and the lagged values of regression, correlation, and behavioralism, we find that only behavioralism is significant and correlation has the wrong sign. If we eliminate correlation, then causality has the wrong sign. If we then eliminate it, we are left with significant coefficients for behavioralism and regression suggesting that mentions of causality come from both sources.

is starting from a quantitative database, then methods for finding influential out-liers can be used. Crucial cases are those most or least likely to exhibit a given outcome. Pathway cases help to illuminate the mechanisms that connect causes and effects.

To investigate the role of behavioralism, we chose a set of four cases (sorted by JSTOR's relevance algorithm) that had "behavioralism" or "behavioral" in their titles or abstracts and that were written between 1950 and 1969. We chose them on the grounds that they might be pathway cases for behavioralism. The first article, by John P. East (1968), is a criticism of behavioralism, but in its criticism it notes that the behavioralist's "plea for empirical or causal theory over value theory is well known" (601) and that behavioralism "employs primarily empirical, quantitative, mathematical, and statistical methods" (597). The second article by Norman Luttbeg and Melvin Kahn (1968) reports on a survey of Ph.D. training in political science. The data are cross-tabulated by "behavioral" versus "traditional" departments with the former being much more likely to offer "behavioral" courses on "Use and Limits of Scientific Method" (60 percent to 20 percent), "Empirically Oriented Political Theory (60 percent to 24 percent), or "Empirical Research Methods" (84 percent to 48 percent) and being much more likely to require "Statistical Competence" (43 percent to 4 percent). The third article ("The Role for Behavioral Science in a University Medical Center") is irrelevant to our topic, but the fourth is "A Network of Data Archives for the Behavioral Sciences" by Philip Converse (1964). Converse mentions regression analysis in passing, but the main line of his argument is that with the grow-ing abundance of survey and other forms of data and with the increasing power of computers, it makes sense to have a centralized data repository. The effort described in this article led to the ICPSR whose fortunes are reviewed in a later chapter in this handbook. After reading these four cases, it seems even more likely to us that behavioralism came first, and regression later. More reading might be useful in other areas such as "causal modeling" or "regression analysis" during the 1970s.

Rathbun (Chapter 29) offers still another method for understanding phenomena. He recommends intensive, in-depth interviews which can help to establish moti-vations and preferences, even though they must deal with the perils of "strategic reconstruction." Certainly it seems likely that interviews with those who lived through the crucial period of the 1950s to the 1970s would shed light on the rise of causal thinking in political science. Lacking the time to undertake these interviews, two of us who are old enough to remember at least part of this period offer our own perspectives. We both remember the force with which statistical regression meth-ods pervaded the discipline in the 1970s. There was a palpable sense that statistical methods could uncover important causal truths and that they provided political scientists with real power to understand phenomena. One of us remembers thinking that causal modeling could surely unlock causal mechanisms and explain political phenomena.

Andrew Bennett (Chapter 30) offers an overview of process tracing, understood as an analytic procedure through which scholars make fine-grained observations to test ideas about causal mechanisms and causal sequences. He argues that the logic of process tracing has important features in common with Bayesian analysis: It requires clear prior expectations linked to the theory under investigation, examines highly detailed evidence relevant to those expectations, and then considers appropriate revisions to the theory in light of observed evidence. With process tracing, the movement from theoretical expectations to evidence takes diverse forms, and Bennett reviews these alternatives and illustrates them with numerous examples.

Benoît Rihoux (Chapter 31) analyzes the tradition of case-oriented configurational research, focusing specifically on qualitative comparative analysis (QCA) as a tool for causal inference. This methodology employs both conventional set theory and fuzzy-set analysis, thereby seeking to capture in a systematic framework the more intuitive procedures followed by many scholars as they seek to "make sense of their cases." Rihoux explores the contrasts between QCA procedures and correlation-based methods, reviews the diverse forms of QCA, and among these diverse forms presents a valuable discussion of what he sees as the "best practices."

Much of what we have been doing in our running example in this chapter is to try to fathom the course of history—albeit a rather small political science piece of it. Comparative historical analysis provides an obvious approach to understanding complicated, drawn-out events. Mahoney and Terrie (Chapter 32) suggest that comparative historical analysis is complementary to statistical analysis because it deals with "causes of effects" rather than "effects of causes." Whereas statistical analysis starts from some treatment or putative cause and asks whether it has an effect, comparative historical analysis tends to start with a revolution, a war, or a discipline concerned with causal analysis, and asks what caused these outcomes, just as a doctor asks what caused someone's illness. In some cases, these are singular events which pose especially difficult problems—for doctors, patients, and political science researchers.

After providing a diagnosis of the distinctive features of historical research, Mahoney and Terrie go on to provide some ideas about how we can tackle the problems posed by engaging in comparative historical inquiry. In our case, it seems likely that some comparative histories of American and European political science might yield some insights about the role of behavioralism and regression analysis. Another comparative approach would be to compare articles in journals with different kinds of editorial boards. Figure 1.3 suggests that there are substantial differences in the growth of mentions of "causal thinking" in the *American Political Science Review* (APSR), *Journal of Politics* (JOP), and *Review of Politics* (ROP) between 1940 and 1999. It would be useful to compare the histories of these journals.

Fearon and Laitin (Chapter 33) discuss how qualitative and quantitative tools can be used jointly to strengthen causal inference. Large-n correlational analysis offers a valuable point of entry for examining empirical relationships, but if it is not used in conjunction with fully specified statistical models and insight into mechanisms, it makes only a weak contribution to causal inference. While case studies do not play a key role in ascertaining whether these overall empirical relations exist, they are valuable for establishing if the empirical relationships can be interpreted causally. Fearon and Laitin argue that this use of case studies will be far more valuable if the cases

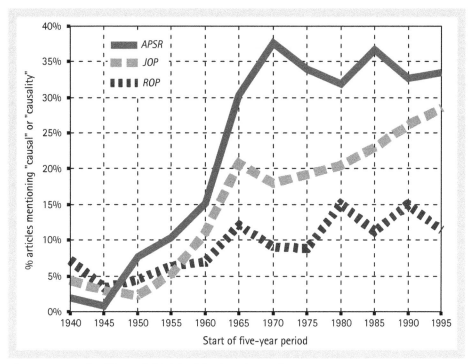

Fig. 1.3. Growth of "causal thinking" in three journals 1940–1999

are chosen randomly. In our running example, this suggests that we should choose a number of articles in JSTOR at random and read them carefully. We might even stratify our sample so that we get more coverage for some kinds of articles than others.

8 ORGANIZATIONS, INSTITUTIONS, AND MOVEMENTS IN THE FIELD OF METHODOLOGY

If nothing else, the preceding pages should convince most people that organizations, institutions, and movements matter in political science. They certainly mattered for the behavioralists, and they have mattered for political methodologists. The final chapters review some of these movements—several of which involved the present authors at first hand.[14]

---

[14] Brady was a founding member and early president of the Political Methodology Society. He was a co-principal investigator (with PI Paul Sniderman and Phil Tetlock) of the Multi-Investigator Study which championed the use of experiments in surveys and which provided the base for the TESS program. And he was present at the meeting convened by Jim Granato at NSF which conceived of the EITM idea, and he is a co-PI of one of the two EITM summer programs. Janet Box-Steffensmeier was an

A clear trajectory in our discipline is that more and more attention is being devoted to methodology writ large. There is ample evidence for this assertion. The two methodology sections of the American Political Science Association are two of the largest of thirty-eight sections. There is an increasing demand for training in methodology. The discipline has expanded its ability to train its own graduate students (instead of sending them to economics or some other discipline), and there is an increasing capacity to better train our undergraduates in methodology as well. Training is now available at the venerable Inter-University Consortium for Political and Social Research (ICPSR) Summer Training Program in methods, the Empirical Implications of Theoretical Models (EITM) summer programs that link formal models and empirical testing, and the winter Consortium on Qualitative Research Methods (CQRM) training program on qualitative methods. Methodology is taught more and more by political scientists to political scientists. Political methodology is also finding more and more connections with theory. Beck (2000) draws the contrast between statisticians and political methodologists in that "statisticians work hard to get the data to speak, whereas political scientists are more interested in testing theory." The focus on theory draws both quantitative and qualitative political scientists to the substance of politics, and it helps unite political methodologists to the political science community.

The rapid development of institutions for the study of qualitative methods in the past decade is discussed by Collier and Elman (Chapter 34). The discipline's welcoming response to these institutions reflects the pent-up need for them and the pluralistic culture of political science which facilitated the development of both the CQRM and the American Political Science Association's organized section on Qualitative Methods, recently renamed the Qualitative and Multi-Method Research Section.

Franklin (Chapter 35) traces the history of the quantitative methodology institutions, ICPSR, and the American Political Science Association's Political Methodology Section. ICPSR has the longest history, having been established in the 1960s in response to the needs of a newly quantitative field that lacked a tradition of training in statistical techniques. It was not until 1984 that the Political Methodology Section was formed to respond to the intellectual concerns driving the field.

Lewis-Beck (Chapter 36) discusses the forty-year history of publications in quantitative political methodology. He shows that the range and scope of outlets now available stands in dramatic contrast to what existed forty years ago.

Finally, Aldrich, Alt, and Lupia (Chapter 37) discuss the National Science Foundation's initiative to close the gap between theory and methods. The original goal of the Empirical Implications of Theoretical Models (EITM) initiative was to create a new generation of scholars who knew enough formal theory and enough about methods to build theories that could be tested, and methods that could test theories. Aldrich, Alt, and Lupia talk about the EITM as currently understood as a way of thinking

early graduate student member of the Political Methodology Society and a recent President. David Collier was the founding President of the APSA qualitative methods section, and the Chair of CQRM's Academic Council.

about causal inference in service to causal reasoning. The empirical tool kit is seen as encompassing statistical approaches, experiments, and qualitative methods.

As Franklin rightly points out, academic institutions develop and are sustained because there are intellectual and professional needs that they serve. And these institutions matter. We know this as political scientists and see it in the development of our methodology field. Based on the vibrancy of our institutions, the future of political methodology looks bright indeed.

9 What Have We Learned?

The field of political methodology has changed dramatically in the past thirty years. Not only have new methods and techniques been developed, but the Political Methodology Society and the Qualitative and Multi-Method Research Section of the American Political Science Association have engaged in ongoing research and training programs that have advanced both quantitative and qualitative methodology. The *Oxford Handbook of Political Methodology* is designed to reflect these developments. Like other handbooks, it provides overviews of specific methodologies, but it also emphasizes three things.

- *Utility for understanding politics*—Techniques should be the servants of improved data collection, measurement, and conceptualization and of better understanding of meanings and enhanced identification of causal relationships. The handbook describes techniques with the aim of showing how they contribute to these tasks, and the emphasis is on developing good research designs. The need for strong research designs unites both quantitative and qualitative research and provides the basis upon which to carry out high-quality research. Solid research design "... ensures that the results have internal, external, and ecological validity" (Educational Psychology).
- *Pluralism of approaches*—There are many different ways that these tasks can be undertaken in the social sciences through description and modeling, case-study and large-n designs, and quantitative and qualitative research.
- *Cutting across boundaries*—Techniques can and should cut across boundaries and should be useful for many different kinds of researchers. For example, in this handbook, those describing large-n statistical techniques provide examples of how their methods inform, or may even be adopted by, those doing case studies or interpretive work. Similarly, authors explaining how to do comparative historical work or process tracing reach out to explain how it could inform those doing time-series studies.

Despite its length and heft, our volume does not encompass all of methodology. As we indicated earlier, there is a rich set of chapters contained in a companion volume, the *Oxford Handbook of Contextual Political Analysis*. This volume discusses inter-pretive and constructivist methods, along with broader issues of situating alternative analytic tools in relation to an understanding of culture. The chapter by Mark Bevir insightfully addresses questions of meta-methodology, a topic explored more widely in the other volume in discussions of epistemology, ontology, logical positivism, and postmodernism. Another important focus in the other volume is narrative analysis, as both a descriptive and an explanatory tool. Finally, in the traditions of research represented in our volume, the issues of context that arise in achieving measurement validity and establishing causal homogeneity are of great importance. But, corre-sponding to its title—i.e. *contextual political analysis*—the companion volume offers considerably more discussion of context and contextualized comparison which can be seen as complementary to our volume.

We hope that our running example on American political science has shown that at least some research problems (and perhaps all of them) can benefit from the use of both quantitative and qualitative methods. We find that quantitative methods provide some important insights about the size and scope of phenomena and about the linkages among variables, but quantitative methods are often maddeningly opaque with respect to the exact causal mechanisms that link our variables. Qualitative methods fill in some of these dark corners, but they sometimes lead to worries about the possibility that we have simply stumbled across an idiosyncratic causal path. We find ourselves oscillating back and forth between the methods, trying to see if insights from one approach can be verified and explicated by the other. But both are certainly helpful.

With respect to our running example, we conclude, with some trepidation given the incompleteness of our analysis, that values and inventions both help explain the rise of "causal thinking" in political science. The behavioral movement furthered "scientific values" like causal thinking, and regression provided an invention that seemingly provided political scientists with estimates of causal effects with minimal fuss and bother. As this handbook shows, however, regression is not the philoso-pher's stone that can turn base observational studies into gold-standard experimental studies. And even experimental studies have their limits, so that we are forced to develop an armamentarium of methods, displayed in this handbook, for dragging causal effects out of nature and for explaining political phenomena.

References

ARROW, K. J. 1963. *Social Choice and Individual Values*, 2nd edn. New Haven, Cann.: Yale University Press.

BECK, N. 2000. Political methodology: a welcoming discipline. *Journal of the American Statis-tical Association*, 95: 651–4.

—— 2003. Time-series cross-section data: what have we learned in the past few years? *Annual Review of Political Science*, 4: 271–93.

—— and KATZ, J. N. 1996. Nuisance vs. substance: specifying and estimating time-series cross-section models. *Political Analysis*, 89: 634–47.

CONVERSE, P. 1964. A network of data archives for the behavioral sciences. *Public Opinion Quarterly*, 28: 273–86.

EAST, J. P. 1968. Pragmatism and behavioralism. *Western Political Science Quarterly*, 21: 597–605.

ELLIOTT, J. 2005. *Using Narrative in Social Research: Qualitative and Quantitative Approaches.* London: Sage.

FISHER, R. A. 1925. *Statistical Methods for Research Workers.* Edinburgh: Oliver and Boyd.

FREEDMAN, D. A. 2005. *Statistical Models: Theory and Practice.* Cambridge: Cambridge University Press.

GOLDBERGER, A., and DUNCAN, O. D. 1973. *Structural Equation Models in the Social Sciences.* New York: Seminar Press.

HOLLAND, P. W. 1986. Statistics and causal inference. *Journal of the American Statistical Association*, 81: 945–60.

KING, G., KEOHANE, R. O., and VERBA, S. 1994. *Designing Social Inquiry: Scientific Inference in Qualitative Research.* Princeton, NJ: Princeton University Press.

LEAMER, E. E. 1983. Let's take the con out of econometrics. *American Economic Review*, 73: 31–43.

LUTTBEG, N. R., and KAHN, M. A. 1968. Ph.D. training in political science. *Midwest Journal of Political Science*, 12: 303–29.

MCKELVEY, R. D. 1979. General conditions for global intransitivities in formal voting models. *Econometrica*, 47: 1085–112.

NEYMAN, J. 1923. On the application of probability theory to agricultural experiments: essay on principles, section 9; trans. 1990. *Statistical Science*, 5: 465–80.

PEARSON, K. 1896. Mathematical contributions to the theory of evolution: III. regression, heredity, and panmixia. *Philosophical Transactions of the Royal Society of London*, 187: 253–318.

—— 1909. Determination of the coefficient of correlation. *Science*, 30: 23–5.

RUBIN, D. B. 1974. Estimating causal effects of treatments in randomized and nonrandomized studies. *Journal of Educational Psychology*, 66: 688–701.

—— 1978. Bayesian inference for causal effects: the role of randomization. *Annals of Statistics*, 6: 34–58.

SAARI, D. G. 1999. Chaos, but in voting and apportionments? *Proceedings of the National Academy of Sciences of the United States of America*, 96: 10568–71.

SCHOFIELD, N. J. 1983. Generic instability of majority rule. *Review of Economic Studies*, 50: 695–705.

YULE, G. U. 1907. On the theory of correlation for any number of variables, treated by a new system of notation. *Proceedings of the Royal Society of London*, 79: 182–93.

PART II

APPROACHES TO SOCIAL SCIENCE METHODOLOGY

CHAPTER 2

....

NORMATIVE METHODOLOGY

....

RUSSELL HARDIN

MODERN political philosophy begins with Thomas Hobbes, David Hume, and others who train their focus on the individual and on interactions between individuals. The purpose of politics in their view is to regulate the behavior of individuals to enable them to be peaceful and productive. They treat of behavior and virtually ignore beliefs. They are interested in social order and its maintenance, not in the salvation of the soul, the creation of a heavenly city, or the ideal society. Hobbes's (1642; 1651) great works of political theory, *De Cive* and *Leviathan*, were published in the first and last years, respectively, of the English Civil Wars, one of the most devastating periods of English history. Against this background, his view of the role of political theory is the explanation and therefore the enablement of social order, a focus that continued through Locke and Hume, although they are increasingly concerned with the working of government and the nature of politics. If any of these three theorists were concerned with "the good society," they would have meant a society that is good for individuals. In an important sense, they are normatively behaviorist. That is to say, they attempt to explain rather than to justify political institutions and behavior. They are also forerunners of the modern self-interest and rational-choice schools of social thought. They are normative theorists only in the very limited sense of *explaining* what would get us to better states of affairs, in the sense of those states' being de facto in our interest or better for us by our own lights. From this vision, the main contemporary approaches to explanation derive. In contemporary normative social theory, there are three main schools—conflict, shared-value, and exchange theories—based, respectively, on interests, shared values, and agreement (as in contractarian theories of both explanation and justification).

The first move in much of normative social science, especially in normative political theory, is to establish a background of self-interested motivation and behavior.
Indeed, the transformation of political theory by Hume in his *Treatise of Human
Nature* is based on an account of normative issues that is not specifically a theory
of those issues and how we should deal with them but is rather an account of how
we see them and why we see them that way (Hume 2000 [1739–40], book 3; Hardin
2007, ch. 5). His account is essentially psychological. The way we see normative issues
is to fit them to our interests. In keeping with their program to explain, not to
justify, Hobbes and Hume are naturalists. Their explanations are grounded in the
assumption that people are essentially self-interested and that their actions can be
explained from this fact. From their time forward, the development of normative
social science has depended heavily on the assumption that individuals are relatively
self-interested.

1 SELF-INTEREST

One need not suppose that people are wholly self-interested, but a preponderance
or a strong element of self-interest makes behavior explicable in fairly consistent
terms. Consistency of individual motivations is central to the task of general explanation of behavior. Many normative or moral theories might yield explanations of
behavior but only idiosyncratically, so that we can explain much of your behavior
and commitments but not those of your neighbor. No standard moral theory comes
close to the general applicability of self-interest as a motivation for large numbers of
people.

Hobbes and Hume are not alone in this view. Bernard Mandeville,[1] Adam Smith,
and Alexis de Tocqueville, among many others, conclude that self-seeking behavior in
certain very important and pervasive contexts promotes the good of society in the—
to them—only meaningful sense, which is promoting the good of individuals. Consider Tocqueville (1966 [1835 and 1840], ii, ch. 8) who, with his characteristic clarity,
justifies the interest-based normative program in a forceful chapter on "Individualism
and the doctrine of self-interest properly understood." He says that the doctrine of
self-interest properly understood is *the best moral theory for our time*. He comes from
a background in which French Catholic virtue theory was the dominant strain of
moral judgment. He notes that in the United States, where he famously toured as de
facto an ethnographer, there was no talk of virtue. Clearly he approves of this fact.
In virtue theory, he says, one does good without self-interest. The American trick
combines interest and charity because it is in the interest of each to work for the

---

[1] Mandeville's subtitle is "Private Vices, Publick Virtues."

good of all, although they need not know or intend this. This is Smith's argument from the invisible hand and it leads us to a resolution of the logic of collective action in the provision of large-scale public benefits. I seek my own good, you seek yours, and all together we promote the good of all. The happiness of all comes from the selfishness of each (ii. 376). Recall one of Smith's most quoted aphorisms, that it is "not from the benevolence of the butcher, the brewer, or the baker, that we expect our dinner, but from their regard to their own interest" (Smith 1976 [1776], 1.2.2, 26–7). Arguably, Tocqueville's central thesis is that, if you give democratic peoples education and freedom and leave them alone, they will extract from the world all the good things it has to offer (Tocqueville 1966 [1835 and 1840], ii. 543). This is, of course, a collective achievement based on individually motivated actions.

This view is not strictly only a modern vision. Aristotle states a partial version of it, in passing, in his praise of farmers as especially good citizens for democracy: "For the many strive for profit more than honor" (*Politics*, 1318b16–17). Aristotle says this with approval. If his claim were not true, he supposes that society would not cohere, because it is founded on the generality and stability of the motivations of farmers, whose productivity is fundamentally important for the good of all in the society. The scale of the contributions of farmers to the good of society remained relatively constant from the time of Aristotle until roughly two or three centuries ago in Europe when industrial production began to displace it as the main locus of employment. Today 2 or 3 percent of the workforce in the advanced economies suffices for agricultural production. It is an extraordinary fact that all of our main strands of political theory originate in the earlier era, when social structure was radically different.

A slight variant of the Aristotle–Hobbes–Hume view of the role of interest in the ordering of society is an assumption at the foundation of John Rawls's theory of justice. Rawls (1999, 112 [1971, 128]; see also Hardin 2003, 3–8) supposes that citizens are *mutually disinterested*. By this he means that my assessment of *my own benefits* from the social order established under his theory of justice does not depend on *your benefits* from that order. For example, I do not envy you and you do not envy me. Our social order has been established as just and there is no alternative that is similarly just and that would better serve my interests.[2] If we are mutually disinterested, then we have no direct concern with the aggregate outcome, but only with our own part or share in that outcome. This is a fundamentally important assumption in Rawls's theory, without which the theory would not go, but it is not often addressed in the massive literature on that theory. But even that theory, put forward in a nonagricultural world, builds on earlier visions of society.

---

[2] There could be two equally qualified just orderings, in one of which I am better off than I am in the other. It does not follow that a society of people who are committed to justice would rank the one of these equally qualified orderings in which I am better off above the other, because someone else will be worse off in that ordering. Hence, there would be no mutual advantage move that would make both of us better off.

2 THREE SCHOOLS OF SOCIAL THEORY

One can do normative political analysis without starting from rational choice principles and, indeed, such analysis is often done as an alternative to rational choice theories. But one cannot do very systematic, coherent political analysis without a clear delineation of basic principles on which the analyses are to be built. So for example, there are three grand theories—or schools of theory—on social order, each of which is based on a systematic set of theoretical assumptions. First are *conflict*, as represented by Thrasymachus (in Plato's *Republic*), Karl Marx, and Ralf Dahrendorf (1968; also see Wrong 1994). Hobbes is also commonly considered strictly a conflict theorist, but I think that this is wrong; that, as noted below, he is largely a coordination theorist. Conflict theories commonly turn to coercion or the threat of coercion to resolve issues. Hence, they almost inherently lead us into normative discussions of the justification of coercion in varied political contexts (Hardin 1990). They can also lead to debates about the nature of power and compliance as in Machiavelli, Marx, Gramsci, Nietzsche, or Foucault.

Second are *shared-value theories*, as represented by John Locke, Ibn Khaldun, and Talcott Parsons (1968 [1937], 89–94). Religious visions of social order are usually shared-value theories and, as Tocqueville notes, interest is the chief means used by religions to guide people. Religious and theological theories and justifications once held sway but are now of little import in Western social science. Now religious commitments and beliefs are merely social facts to be explained. Many contemporary shared-value theorists in the social sciences in the West are followers of Parsons. These followers are mostly sociologists and anthropologists—there are virtually no economists and there are now few political scientists in the Parsons camp. There was a grand Parsonian movement in political science from the 1950s through some time in the 1970s. The most notable and creative example of this movement is the civic culture of Gabriel Almond and Sidney Verba (1963) and others. Although there is not much of a grand-synthesis view of norms that remains in political science or even in much of sociology, there are still ad hoc theories of norms. For example, political scientists often explain the voting that occurs as public spirited, altruistic, or duty driven. And there is today a rising chorus of political scientists who take a more or less ad hoc stand on the importance of a value consensus, as represented by those concerned with the supposed declines in trust, family values, and community (e.g. Putnam 2000).

Contractarians in social theory are typically shared-value theorists. This may sound odd, because legal contracts typically govern exchanges. But social contract theory requires a motivation for fulfilling one's side of a contractual arrangement and a social contract is not analogous to a legal contract in this respect. Because there is no enforcer of it, a social contract is commonly therefore seen to require a normative commitment—essentially the same normative commitment from everyone (see Hardin 1999, ch. 3). For example, in the view of Thomas Scanlon (1982, 115 n.; 1999; see further Barry 1995 and Hardin 1998) the motivation to keep to a social contract is the desire to achieve reasonable agreement on cooperative arrangements. This appears to entail a straightforward factual issue about the existence of this desire. Is this desire prevalent? Because of the difficulty of defining reasonable agreement, it seems unlikely. The methodological task of demonstrating the prevalence of such a desire seems simple enough, but the reasonable agreement theorists have not bothered to test their assumption. It seems very unlikely that there is such a desire, so that Scanlon's contractualism cannot undergird social cooperation or, therefore, social theory. Contracts for ordinary exchanges are backed by various incentives to perform, especially by the threat of legal enforcement, by the interest the parties have in maintaining the relationship for future exchanges, or in maintaining their reputations. Social contracts have none of these to back them.

And, third, there are *exchange*, which are relatively more recent than the other two schools, with Bernard Mandeville and Adam Smith among the first major figures, and, in our time, George Homans and many social choice theorists and economists.[3] At the core of an exchange theory is individualism. Tocqueville (1966 [1835 and 1840], vol. ii. 506–08), writing in the 1830s, says "individualism" is a new term. It turns on the calm feeling that disposes each to isolate himself from the mass and to live among family and friends. It tends to isolate us from our past and our contemporaries. The rigorous, uncompromising focus on individuals is a distinctive contribution of Hobbes, the contribution that puts us on the track to modern political philosophy and that makes Hobbes at least partially an exchange theorist. For him, the assumption of individualism is de facto a method for focusing on what is central to social order. It is also, of course, a descriptive fact of the social world that he analyzes. It becomes Tocqueville's assumption in analyzing American society two centuries later, when it is also the basis for criticizing his own French society. He says that, at the head of any undertaking, where in France we would find government and in England some territorial magnate, in the United States we are sure to find an association (513). These associations are made up of individuals who voluntarily take on their roles; they are not appointed to these roles, which are not part of any official hierarchy. Tocqueville has a forceful method: go to the core of any activity to explain the form of its successes and failures. And when we do that for America in the 1830s, we find individuals motivated by their own interests. When we do it for France, we find government agents and regulations. Anyone who has lived in both France and the United States might reasonably conclude that the two societies have moved toward one another in this respect, but that they still differ in the way Tocqueville finds nearly two centuries ago.

Note that these three sets of assumptions—individualism, self-interest, and the collective benefits of self-seeking behavior—are the assumptions of both positive and normative theories. This should not be a surprise because the world we wish to judge normatively is the same world we wish to explain positively. Moreover, all of the normative theories we might address are likely to have positive elements that

---

[3] There are also many theories and assumptions, such as structural theories as represented by Marx and articulated by many structuralist sociologists in our time, that are much less broadly applicable, both positively and normatively.

we could analyze from the perspective of relevant positive theories. For example, to argue persuasively for shared-value theories we must be able to show that there are shared values. This is often not done very well or even at all, but is merely assumed as though it were obvious. A fully adequate normative theory must therefore fit both positive and normative assumptions and must depend on both positive and normative methodologies. Often this must mean that the methodological demands of normative claims are more stringent than the methodological demands of any parallel positive claims. Normative claims must pass muster on both positive and normative methodological standards.

Given the pervasiveness of shared-value theories in contemporary social and political theory, we should consider whether there are shared values of the relevant kind and force. This is, again, a positive issue and it should not be hard to handle. Once we establish that there are or are not relevant shared values, we can go on to discuss how they are constructed and what implications they might have for social theory, actual institutions, and political behavior.

3 Shared Values

Suppose it is established that we do share some important set of political values, X, Y, and Z. What follows? Our shared values do not directly entail any particular actions because acting on those values might conflict with our interests in other things, and acting on our shared values might cost you heavily enough to block you from acting in our common interest. Superficially it might seem that interest, for example in the form of resources, is merely another value, or rather a proxy for values that could compare to X, Y, and Z. But this will commonly be wrong. For an important political example, suppose we are all or almost all patriotic. Your patriotism benefits me if it motivates you to act in certain ways, but acting in those ways likely has costs for you, so that although we share the value of patriotism we may not have incentives to act in ways that benefit each other. Given that we share the value of patriotism to a particular nation, we might want to ask on what that value commitment is founded. It could be founded on interests, identity, or bald commitment to our nation, right or wrong. It might not be easy to establish which, if any, of these plays a role. Tocqueville supposes that patriotism founded on interests must be fragile, because interests can change (Tocqueville 1966 [1835 and 1840], i. 373). We might also suppose that our interests in patriotism here could be compromised in favor of other interests.

Perhaps our commitment turns on our ethnic identity, as is commonly claimed for nationalist commitments. There can typically be no compromise on ethnicity and the costs of defending one's ethnicity may be discounted heavily for that reason. You cannot trade half of your ethnic commitments for half of mine. Of course, the next generation might do exactly that. They might marry across our ethnic divide, engage in joint corporate activities, and have friendship groups that straddle ethnic lines. Sadly, such actions and even merely their possibility might be sources of deep conflict between our groups. On economic issues, there commonly is some possibility of compromise that lets the parties split differences to allow all to gain from staying involved with each other, even cooperating together and coordinating on many fundamentally important activities. This is, for Smith and many other political economists, a major unintended benefit of the market for exchange.

Contract or agreement theories suggest a need or at least an urge to explain why we agree, and the answer often must be that it is in our interest to agree on some particular social arrangement or that we share the values on which we are to contract. Hence, agreement theories threaten to reduce to simple interest or to shared-value theories or explanations. But even then they have a strength that shared-value theories often lack. Once your interests, pro and con, are established, there is likely no further need to explain why you act in relevant ways. Motivations and interests tend to collapse into each other if they are fully defined. Unless someone's commitment to some value translates in standard terms into their interests (hence, the odd locution "can be cashed out" as), we still face the task of determining how that value commitment will motivate action, if at all. In sum, interest is both a value and a motivation. Shared-value theories must first establish what values are shared and then give an account of how commitment to them motivates action. Both steps here may be very difficult. Indeed, each of these steps might challenge some of our standard methodologies for establishing social and psychological facts.

An important subcategory of shared-value theory is the body of norms that regulate our behavior in social interaction. The category of norms is much broader than that for social order, but it is these that matter for political theory. We may parse the category of norms in many ways. The most common move is simply to list many norms and to apply them to particular problems, as with the putative norms on voting. In a far more systematic approach, Edna Ullmann-Margalit (1977) lays out several categories as based on the game-theoretic structure of the underlying problems that the norms help to resolve or at least address. Her deep insight is that norms must handle the strategic structure of the incentives people face if the norms are to get them to behave cooperatively. Her modal strategic categories are prisoner's dilemma, coordination and unequal coordination, and conflict. Some of Ullmann-Margalit's norms help us, respectively, to coordinate, to cooperate, or to manage conflict in these contexts.

It is striking that Ullmann-Margalit's book from only four decades ago is among the first serious efforts to bring strategic analysis systematically to bear on normative theory and problems. Indeed, we might well speak of the strategic turn in social theory, a turn that has been heavily influenced and even guided by game theory, which was invented roughly during the Second World War (Neumann and Morgenstern 1953 [1944]). That turn has influenced both positive and normative theory. There are standard norms that address all of Ullmann-Margalit's strategic categories and those norms have vernacular standing in ordinary life contexts. But Ullmann-Margalit shows that many norms are strategically related and thereby shows how they are grounded in incentives. In political theory, the norms that most interest us are those that regulate social order (Hardin 1995, chs. 4 and 5).

4 A FOURTH THEORY: COORDINATION

Because there generally is conflict in any moderately large society, coercion is a sine qua non for social order. But it is only one sine qua non. Two others are exchange and coordination. All are needed because the strategic structures of our potential interactions are quite varied, and we need devices for handling all of these reasonably well if we are to have desirable order and prosperity. In a subsistence agricultural society, coercion might be very nearly the only point of government. But in a complex society, coercion seems to be a minor element in the actual lives of most people, although the threat of it might stand behind more of our actions than we suppose. In such a society, exchange and coordination loom very large, radically larger than in the subsistence economy.

The three grand, broadly established schools of political thought—conflict, shared values, and agreement or exchange—are right about particular aspects of social order. But they miss the central mode of social order in a complex modern society, which is coordination (Lindblom 1977; Schelling 1960). We do not necessarily share values but we can coordinate to allow each of us to pursue our own values without destructive interaction or exchange. To grossly simplify much of the problem of social order in a complex society, consider the relatively trivial problem of maintaining order in traffic on roads. There are two main coordinations at stake. The first is the obvious one of merely getting all drivers to drive on the same side of the road—either all on their left or all on their right—in order to prevent constant accidents and difficult problems of negotiating who gets to go first. The second is the problem of controlling the flow of traffic at intersections, for which traffic signals and signs are used when the traffic is heavy enough. Two striking things about the collection of drivers are that *they are not genuinely in conflict* and that *they do not typically have to share any general social values* in order for these coordinations to work well. Furthermore, *there is no exchange* that they can make to solve the problems arising from their interactions. I have my purposes, you have yours, and we want merely to avoid getting in each other's way while going about our own affairs. The seeming miracle is that often we can do all of this spontaneously. For example, some coordinations can be managed by relying on focal points (Schelling 1960) that make a particular solution obvious or on institutions, which can define a resolution. Getting everyone to drive right is an instance of the first of these devices; managing traffic flow at intersections is an instance of the second.

As are conflict theories, coordination is an interest theory. Hobbes is perhaps the first major coordination theorist.[4] But David Hume (2000 [1739–40], book 3), Adam Smith (1976 [1776]), and C. E. Lindblom (1977) see much of social order as a matter of coordinating the disparate interests of many people. A shared-value theory could be essentially a coordination theory if the values motivate coordinated actions, but *coordination does not require broadly shared values*. This is the chief reason why coordination is fundamentally important in modern social and political theory. Shared-value theories typically make adherence to relevant values a matter of overriding one's interests and, when put into political power, overriding the interests of many citizens. For example, I help to defend my community despite the risks that such effort entails, I submerge my identity in the collective identity (whatever that might mean), or I vote despite the burden to me of doing so and despite the virtual irrelevance of the effect of my vote on my interests. But against the strenuous and implausible view of Parsons, a collection of quite diverse pluralists can coordinate on an order for the society in which they seek their diverse values. In sum, coordination interactions are especially important for politics and political theory and probably for sociology, although exchange relations might be most of economics, or at least of classical economics. In a sense, the residual Parsonians are right to claim that conflict relations are not the whole of political order, although not for reasons that they might recognize. They are right, again, because the core or modal character of social order is coordination.

While at a commonsense level the problem of coordination is typically not difficult to grasp, its general significance and its compelling nature have not been central understandings in the social sciences or in political philosophy. Hobbes had a nascent coordination theory in his vision of our coordinating on a single sovereign (Hardin 1991). Had he been more supple in his views, he might have recognized that the dreadful problem of civil war in his England was a matter of *multiple coordinations* of various groups in mortal conflict with each other. There was no war of all against all but only war between alternative factions for rule, each of which was well enough coordinated to wreak havoc on the others and on nonparticipant bystanders. Hume made the outstanding philosophical contribution to understanding coordination problems, but his insights were largely ignored for two centuries or more after he wrote and they are still commonly misread.[5] Thomas Schelling (1960, 54–8) gave the first insightful game-theoretic account of coordination problems and their strategic and incentive structures. But their pervasive importance in social life is still not a standard part of social scientific and philosophical understanding.

In social life, coordination occurs in two very different forms: spontaneously and institutionally. We can coordinate and we can be coordinated as in the two-part coordination of traffic. In Philadelphia in 1787 a small number of people coordinated spontaneously to create the framework to organize the new US nation institutionally.

---

[4] Not all Hobbes scholars would agree with this assessment. For an argument for understanding him as a coordination theorist, see Hardin (1991).

[5] Hume's arguments may have been overlooked because they are chiefly in a series of long footnotes in Hume (2000 [1739–40], 3.2.3.4 n–11 n).

Once they had drafted their constitution, its adoption was beneficial to enough of the politically significant groups in the thirteen states that, for them, it was mutually advantageous (Hardin 1999). Therefore, they were able to *coordinate spontaneously on that constitution* to subject themselves to being *coordinated institutionally by it* thereafter. This is the story of very many institutional structures that govern our social lives, and the more often this story plays out in varied realms, the more pervasively we can expect to see it carried over to other realms and to organize our institutions, practices, and even, finally, our preferences, tastes, and values. As it does so, it might be expected then to drive out or to dominate alternative ways to create and justify our social organization.

5 CONCLUDING REMARKS

In the era of Hobbes, writing during the English Civil War, the first focus of political theory was social order in which individuals might survive and prosper. Success in managing order has pushed worry about social order out of its formerly central place, even virtually out of concern altogether for many political theorists. The meaning of justice has changed to match this development. Through Hume's writings, justice is commonly conceived as "justice as order," as in Henry Sidgwick's (1907, 440) somewhat derisive term. This is more or less the justice that legal authorities and courts achieve in the management of criminal law and of the civil law of contracts and property relations. By Sidgwick's time, it begins to be conceived as, or at least to include, distributive justice, as in the theory of John Rawls (1999 [1971]). Hume and John Stuart Mill (1977 [1861]) also shift the focus toward the institutions of government, which in large modern societies entails representative government. This move brings back classical and Renaissance political thought. It also makes great demands on causal understandings and therefore on positive theory and methodology, again tying the normative and the positive tightly together in a single account. Rawls's theory also requires massive positive understandings when he says that now the task is to design institutions capable of delivering distributive justice, a task that he leaves to others, who have so far generally failed to take it up. Rawls's and Hobbes's theories are relatively holistic and general; Hume's and Mill's are relatively piecemeal and specific. Perhaps no methodology gives us serious entrée to handling holistic social and political theory at the level and scale required by Hobbes and Rawls. Eventually, therefore, we must want to break down the institutional moves entailed by Rawls's theory to make them piecemeal and manageable.

It is an interesting fact that normative methodologies have changed substantially over the past several decades. Methodologies in many fields of social theory and explanation have been refined extensively during that period, especially under the influence of rational choice and game theory but few if any of them have been dropped or developed *de novo*. Today's three leading normative methods have come into their own during that period, so much so that it is hard to imagine what normative theories would be like today without those methods driving their articulation and refinement. Developments have not been equally dramatic in all three methods. Two of the methods, shared-value and contractarian arguments, threaten to be narrowed down to use by academic moral theorists with little resonance beyond that narrow community. Any method that becomes as esoteric as much of contemporary moral theory has become is apt to be ignored and even dismissed by the overwhelming majority of social theorists as irrelevant. That would be a profoundly sad separation of normative from positive theory, the worst such separation in the history of social theory, worse than the separation of economic from utilitarian value theory wrought by G. E. Moore (1903, 84) a century ago, when he literally took utility into the vacuousness of outer space.

The theorists who work in the normative vineyard often seem to strive more for novelty than for comprehensiveness or even comprehension. Great novelty cannot generally be a worthy goal for us in social theory. The occasional major novel invention, such as Hobbes's all-powerful sovereign as a form of institutionally enforced coordination, Hume's convention as a form of spontaneously enforced coordination, Smith's classical economics, Vilfredo Pareto's (1971 [1927]) value theory, John von Neumann and Oskar Morgenstern's (1953 [1944]) game theory, or Schelling's (1960) coordination theory takes a long time to be incorporated into the main stream of theory and explanation of social institutions and practices. A flood of supposedly novel contributions is apt to be ignored or openly dismissed. Creativity in social theory is not likely to depend on such major innovations except on relatively rare occasions. *Most of the creativity we see is in the application of well-established innovations across many realms.*

Over the past four or five decades, rational-choice normative theory, the third major branch of contemporary normative methodology, has become a vast program that increasingly leaves the other two branches behind in its scope and sheer quantity of work. This development is made more readily possible by the clarity and systematic structure of game theory and game-theoretic rational choice. Game theory and rational choice methodology are very well laid out and easily put to use. Perhaps at least partially because of that fact, rational choice methods are taking over normative theorizing and theories. Early steps along the way in this seeming conquest include Richard Braithwaite's (1955) use of game theory in moral reasoning, David Lewis's (1969) analysis of convention in the spirit of Hume, Ullmann-Margalit's (1977) theory of norms, and a flood of other works from the 1980s on.

In this program, method and theory tend to merge. One might wonder whether this is a typical tendency for relatively developed theories and the methods successfully associated with them. Shared-value theory is perhaps becoming the most commonly asserted alternative to rational choice in our time as contractarian reasoning recedes from center stage in the face of challenges to the story of contracting that lies behind it and the difficulty of believing people actually think they have consciously agreed to their political order, as long ago noted by Hume (1985 [1748]). But it faces a harder task than rational-choice normative theory because it has barely begun at the basic level of establishing a set of demonstrably shared values other than own welfare. Own welfare is, of course, the shared value that shared-value theorists most want to reject, although one wonders how many of the most ardent opponents of that value as a general guiding principle in social theory would actually reject that value in their own lives.

References

ALMOND, G., and VERBA, S. 1963. *The Civic Culture: Political Attitudes and Democracy in Five Nations*. Boston: Little, Brown.

ARISTOTLE 1958 [4th century BC]. *Politics*, trans. E. Barker. New York: Oxford University Press.

BARRY, B. 1995. *Justice as Impartiality*. Oxford: Oxford University Press.

BRAITHWAITE, R. 1955. *Theory of Games as a Tool for the Moral Philosopher*. Oxford: Oxford University Press.

DAHRENDORF, R. 1968. In praise of Thrasymachus. Pp. 129–50 in Dahrendorf, *Essays in the Theory of Society*. Stanford, Calif.: Stanford University Press.

HARDIN, R. 1990. Rationally justifying political coercion. *Journal of Philosophical Research*, 15: 79–91.

—— 1991. Hobbesian political order. *Political Theory*, 19: 156–80.

—— 1995. *One for All: The Logic of Group Conflict*. Princeton, NJ: Princeton University Press.

—— 1998. Reasonable agreement: political not normative. Pp. 137–53 in *Impartiality, Neutrality and Justice: Re-Reading Brian Barry's* Justice as Impartiality, ed. P. J. Kelly. Edinburgh: Edinburgh University Press.

—— 1999. *Liberalism, Constitutionalism, and Democracy*. Oxford: Oxford University Press.

—— 2003. *Indeterminacy and Society*. Princeton, NJ: Princeton, University Press.

—— 2007. *David Hume: Moral and Political Theorist*. Oxford: Oxford University Press.

HOBBES, T. 1983 [1642]. *De Cive*, ed. H. Warrender, trans. from the Latin. Oxford: Oxford University Press.

—— 1994 [1651]. *Leviathan*, ed. E. Curley. Indianapolis: Hackett.

HUME, D. 2000 [1739–40]. *A Treatise of Human Nature*, ed. D. F. Norton and M. J. Norton. Oxford: Oxford University Press.

—— 1985 [1748]. Of the original contract. Pp. 465–87 in *David Hume: Essays Moral, Political, and Literary*, ed. E. F. Miller. Indianapolis: Liberty Classics.

LEWIS, D. K. 1969. *Convention*. Cambridge, Mass.: Harvard University Press.

LINDBLOM, C. E. 1977. *Politics and Markets: The World's Political-Economic Systems*. New York: Basic Books.

MILL, J. S. 1977 [1861]. *Considerations on Representative Government*. Pp. 376–613 in Mill, *Essays on Politics and Society*, vol. xix of *Collected Works of John Stuart Mill*, ed. J. M. Robson. Toronto: University of Toronto Press.

MOORE, G. E. 1903. *Principia Ethica*. Cambridge: Cambridge University Press.

NEUMANN, J. VON, and MORGENSTERN, O. 1953 [1944]. *Theory of Games and Economic Behavior*, 3rd edn. Princeton, NJ: Princeton University Press.

PARETO, V. 1971 [1927]. *Manual of Political Economy*, trans. from French edition. New York: Kelley.

PARSONS, T. 1968 [1937]. *The Structure of Social Action*. New York: Free Press.

PUTNAM, R. D. 2000. *Bowling Alone: The Collapse and Revival of American Community*. New York: Simon and Schuster.

RAWLS, J. 1999 [1971]. *A Theory of Justice*. Cambridge, Mass.: Harvard University Press.

SCANLON, T. M. 1982. Contractualism and utilitarianism. Pp. 103–28 in *Utilitarianism and Beyond*, ed. A. Sen and B. Williams. Cambridge: Cambridge University Press.

——1999. *What We Owe to Each Other*. Cambridge, Mass.: Harvard University Press.

SCHELLING, T. C. 1960. *The Strategy of Conflict*. Cambridge, Mass.: Harvard University Press.

SIDGWICK, H. 1907. *The Methods of Ethics*, 7th edn. London: Macmillan.

SMITH, A. 1976 [1776]. *An Inquiry into the Nature and Causes of the Wealth of Nations*. Oxford: Oxford University Press.

TOCQUEVILLE, A. DE 1966 [1835 and 1840]. *Democracy in America*, trans. G. Lawrence. New York: Harper and Row.

ULLMANN-MARGALIT, E. 1977. *The Emergence of Norms*. Oxford: Oxford University Press.

WRONG, D. 1994. *The Problem of Order: What Unites and Divides Society*. New York: Free Press.

....

CHAPTER 3

META-METHODOLOGY: CLEARING THE UNDERBRUSH

....

MARK BEVIR

META-METHODOLOGY is in many ways just another word for philosophy. The meta-methodology of political science is the philosophy of social science. More particularly, meta-methodology is the deliberate attempt to reflect theoretically about what methods are appropriate to the study of what aspects of politics and on what occasions. It is the attempt to clarify what kind of knowledge and what kind of explanations fit the kinds of objects that are the concern of political science.

The importance of meta-methodology should now be clear. Only when we know what kinds of knowledge and explanation are apt for political science can we intelligently decide what methods are best suited to producing them. Whether any method is apt in any given instance always depends on underlying philosophical issues. We should not let the importance of methodological rigor obscure what are prior philosophical issues about the adequacy of the commitments entailed by any claim that a particular method is an appropriate means of generating knowledge about a given type of object.

In this chapter, I explore the philosophical issues that are indispensable to any discussion of the role of a given methodology. At times I press the claims of certain positions, notably holism, constructivism, and historicism. But my main point is simply that political methodologists are dangerously out of touch. Philosophical thinking has altered dramatically in ways that render highly problematic the meta-methodological assumptions of many political scientists. Discussion of methods and their utility are profoundly impoverished by a lack of thought about their epistemological, ontological, and explanatory assumptions.

1 META-METHODOLOGICAL CONCEPTS

The concepts of concern here generally refer to traditions, subfields, or doctrines. A grasp of the differences between these three types of concepts will help us appreciate the structure of this chapter. Some meta-methodological concepts refer to traditions. Examples include behavioralism, rational choice, and institutionalism. While traditions are often recognizable by political scientists, there can be something misleading about couching meta-methodological debate in such terms. For debates to be couched in terms of traditions, the traditions would have to contain coherent and stable philosophical ideas. But traditions generally include philosophical ideas that need not logically go together, and, moreover, the content of a tradition can change dramatically over time. Hence meta-methodology often involves clearing the underbrush of confusion that arises when people reflect on methods in terms set by familiar traditions. It unpacks traditions of political science so as to relate them to specific philosophical doctrines. In this chapter, the next section on "Traditions of Political Science" discusses the philosophical doctrines that are associated with modernist empiricism, behavioralism, institutionalism, and rational choice.

Other meta-methodological concepts refer to philosophical subfields. Prominent examples include epistemology, which is the theory of knowledge, and ontology, which is the theory of what kinds of objects exist. Any political methodology, any application of any method, and indeed any study of anything entails philosophical commitments. Yet political scientists often leave their commitments implicit and fail to reflect on them. In contrast, meta-methodology is the attempt to think explicitly about philosophical issues and their implications for political science. Typically there are numerous positions that someone might adopt on the relevant philosophical issues. No doubt most of us will believe, moreover, that political science should be a pluralistic space in which different people might adopt different epistemological and ontological positions. But it is one thing to believe one's colleagues should be allowed their own views, and it is quite another to believe that any individual political scientist can hold incompatible philosophical ideas. If a particular individual adopts one philosophical stance toward one problem and another toward some other problem, they are showing themselves to be not generously pluralistic but rather intellectually confused. Hence meta-methodology is also the attempt to promote particular philosophical ideas. Any meta-methodology tries to develop clear, defensible, and consistent ideas across the relevant philosophical subfields. In this chapter, each section after that on traditions of political science concerns a particular subfield of philosophy—epistemology, ontology, and explanation.

Still other meta-methodological concepts refer to particular doctrines. The particular theories that we hold, whether implicitly or explicitly, constitute our meta-methodology. Substantive meta-methodological debates are about the adequacy of various doctrines and what they do or do not imply about the adequacy of approaches and methods in political science. This chapter explores the main doctrines in each subfield. The section on epistemology studies theories such as falsificationism and Bayesianism. The section on ontology considers theories such as realism and constructivism. The section on explanation considers theories such as the covering-law one and historicism.

It is important to add, finally, that disparate meta-methodological doctrines are sometimes clumped together under collective labels that are used to refer to philosophical traditions. A good example is positivism. If we were to define positivism, we would surely have to appeal to theories perhaps including verificationism and naturalism (that is, belief in the unity of science). These bundled philosophical concepts can be useful: They help intellectual historians who want to examine the history of meta-methodological and philosophical ideas; they help philosophers who want to debate the merits of various types of philosophy; and they can have a role in political science provided we clearly stipulate the ideas we associate with them. Nonetheless, we should remember that these bundled philosophical concepts are like the traditions of political science mentioned above: Their content might change dramatically over time, and they often combine positions that need not logically go together. Certainly logical positivism in the twentieth century had little in common with the evolutionary positivism of the late nineteenth century, let alone Auguste Comte's religious and ethical ideas. In this chapter, I generally use these bundled philosophical concepts to refer to broad intellectual movements. Indeed, one aim of the next section is to relate familiar approaches to political science, such as institutionalism and behavioralism, to broader intellectual movements, such as modernist empiricism and positivism.

2 TRADITIONS OF POLITICAL SCIENCE

Political scientists often make much of the distinctions between various traditions in their discipline—behavioralism, rational choice, and institutionalism. One aim of this section is to flatten these distinctions. Of course there are philosophical differences between behavioralism and rational choice, and some of these differences will concern us. Nonetheless, with the partial exception of rational choice, the leading approaches to political science rely on an empiricist epistemology, realist ontology, and formal modes of explanation. To understand the dominance of these philosophical ideas, we may briefly look back at the emergence of modern political science.[1]

---

[1] The broad historical sweep of what follows draws on Adcock, Bevir, and Stimson (2007).

2.1 Modernist Empiricism

The emergence of modernist empiricism in political science must be set against the backdrop of developmental historicism. Nineteenth-century political scientists relied on historical narratives to make sense of the world. They were committed to empiricism and induction: They believed that valid narratives depended on the systematic and impartial collection and sifting of facts. Yet they made sense of the facts by locating them in a teleological narrative about the gradual development of principles such as nationality and liberty along fairly fixed paths. In their view, nation states were organic units defined by ethical and cultural ties, and political scientists made sense of the facts by showing how they fitted within an account of a state as a developing historical expression of just such an organic nation. Political science was, to echo E. A. Freeman's famous remark, "present history."

During the early twentieth century, this developmental historicism gave way to modernist empiricism. The First World War more or less decisively undermined the idea of developmental progress. Political scientists increasingly replaced historical narratives with modernist modes of knowing. They remained committed to induction: knowledge arose from accumulating facts. But they increasingly made sense of facts by locating them not in historical narratives but in ahistorical classifications, correlations, or systems.

Modernist empiricism has been the dominant orientation of political science since the early twentieth century. Modernist empiricism is atomistic and analytic. It broke up the continuities and gradual changes of elder narratives, dividing the world into discrete, discontinuous units. Modernist empiricism then makes sense of these discrete units by means of formal, ahistorical explanations such as calculations, typologies, and appeals to function. Consider one notable example: In 1921 Herman Finer included in a study of comparative government an analytical index of topics to enable the reader to compare similar institutions across countries; in 1932 his new study of modern government moved from analytical topic to analytical topic, treating an institution in relation to ones in other states that he classified alongside it rather than in the specific history of its own state (Finer 1921; 1932). More generally, the shift from historicist to formal modes of explanation brought appeals to new theories and objects. Behavior was explained by reference to increasingly formal psychological theories. Processes were explained in terms of structures and systems.

The meta-methodological orientation of modernist empiricism continues to dominate much political science. Consider each of the philosophical subfields that are explored later in this chapter. In epistemology (the theory of knowledge), modernist empiricists justified their claims to knowledge inductively by reference to accumulated facts based on experience. In ontology (the theory of what exists), modernist empiricists ascribed a real existence and causal properties to formal objects such as structures and systems. Finally, in terms of explanation, modernist empiricists rejected historicism in favor of formal approaches such as classifications and correlations; they treated history as a source of data, not a way of explaining data.

2.2 Behavioralism

As modernist empiricism spread, so some political scientists began to worry about "hyperfactualism" (e.g. Easton 1953, 66–78). This hyperfactualism arose precisely because political scientists had given up on the narratives by which developmental historicists controlled and managed facts. Ironically, it was the rejection of developmental historicism that thus created the space in which behavioralists were soon to promote their general theories.

By the 1950s, the behavioralists were drawing on a relatively new positivist concept of science. Modernist empiricists equated science with the rigorous collection and sifting of facts: theories emerged from accumulated facts. In contrast, twentieth-century positivists often emphasized the role of general theories as a source of hypotheses that were then confirmed or refuted by factual investigations.

It is worth emphasizing that this new concept of science was all that was really new about the so-called "behavioral revolution". Neither the techniques nor the topics associated with behavioralism were particularly novel: Modernist empiricists had long used a range of statistical techniques to study topics such as policy networks, parties, and voting behavior. What behavioralists challenged was the modernist empiricist view of science. David Easton argued that political science was falsely wedded to "a view of science as the objective collection and classification of facts and the relating of them into singular generalizations" (Easton 1953, 65–6). What behavioralists promoted was a view of science that privileged general theories as a source of verifiable hypotheses. As Easton again argued (p. 25), "the purpose of scientific rules of procedure is to make possible the discovery of highly generalized theory."

While the behavioralists promoted general theory, they rarely strayed too far from modernist empiricism. Their epistemology remained empiricist, albeit that it shifted slightly from an inductive empiricism to what we might call a more experimentalist orientation. In their view, general theories can only generate hypotheses, not establish knowledge. All theories are ultimately confirmed or refuted by the way they stand up to experiments and other factual experiences. Similarly, the behavioralists' ontology remained realist. If some of them toyed with the idea of referring only to observable phenomena, most were happy to treat data as evidence of real if unobservable attitudes, and most were happy to appeal in their general theories to structures and systems as if these too were real objects with causal properties. Finally, the behavioralists favored formal, ahistorical explanations. The whole point of theories such as structural-functionalism and systems analysis was that they were to apply across time and space.

2.3 Institutionalism

The rise of behaviouralism led some modernist empiricists to define themselves in terms almost diametrically opposed to those with which their predecessors broke with developmental historicism. Historical institutionalism emerged as modernist empiricists defined their approach as comparative and historical in contrast to the general theories of the behavioralists. Ironically the historical institutionalists thereby forget their own debt to the modernist empiricist rejection of developmental historicism in favor of formal correlations and classifications.

Historical institutionalists are skeptical of general theories as a source of hypotheses, and some of them even appear to be hostile to large-N statistical analyses. Nonetheless, they do not return to historicism, but only restate modernist empiricism. Historical institutionalists advocate a process of "analytical induction" in which small-N comparisons and case studies generate mid-level theories (Skocpol 1985, 3–43). Moreover, they want the case studies to be selected on analytic grounds, and they want the mid-level theories to be correlations and classifications couched in terms of formal concepts and theories. They conceive of history as little more than a series of atomized episodes that can provide data for more timeless variables, mechanisms, and processes.

Given that historical institutionalism restates modernist empiricism, we should not be surprised that it embodies a similar meta-methodology. Institutionalists believe in inductive empiricism. In their view, knowledge is built up on cases that verify or falsify theories. Similarly, institutionalists adopt much the same ontology as earlier modernist empiricists. They ascribe a real existence and causal powers to objects such as institutions and structures: Institutions such as markets, networks, and democracies have intrinsic properties that explain outcomes and events. Finally, while institutionalists sometimes deploy the label "historical" to set themselves up against those who propose general theories, they remain wedded to formal, ahistorical classifications, correlations, and mechanisms.

2.4 Rational Choice

Even as modernist empiricists began restating their approach as an institutionalist alternative to behavioralism, so rational choice theorists had begun to study institutions. Hence a minor scholarly industry now seeks to distinguish between varieties of the new institutionalism (e.g. Hall and Taylor 1996; Pierson and Skocpol 2002; Thelen and Steinmo 1992). At stake in this industry is much the same question as that which split behavioralists and modernist empiricists: What is the role of general theories as a source of hypotheses? On the one hand, rational choice institutionalists echo earlier concerns about hyperfactualism: They complain of a "stockpiling of case studies" (Levi 1988, 197). On the other, historical institutionalists bewail the lack of comparative and historical sensitivity of rational choice in a way that again ignores their own preference for formal explanations rather than historical narratives.

While behavioralism and rational choice assign a similar role to general theory, we should not associate rational choice with the positivist concept of science that inspired behavioralism. To the contrary, the meta-methodology of behavioralism has more in common with institutionalism than with rational choice. Rational choice extends modes of knowing linked to neoclassical economics, which itself was a part of the modernist break with the nineteenth century (cf. Schabas 1990). However, while rational choice is modernist in its rejection of history for atomization and formal models, it can seem to be rationalist rather than empirical. Rational choice is less tied to modernist empiricism than are the other traditions of political science we have considered.

Let us begin by considering epistemology. Rational choice is rightly described as a deductive approach: it derives models as deductions from axioms (Elster 1986; Monroe 1991). Yet, epistemology has as much to do with the nature and justification of valid knowledge as the procedures by which models or explanations are constructed. We should consider, therefore, how rational choice theorists justify their axioms and how they justify applying a model to any particular case. The axioms are usually justified empirically by the claim that they, or more usually the models to which they give rise, correspond to facts about the world. Similarly, the application of models to explain particular cases depends on empirical claims about the beliefs and preferences of the actors standing in relation to one another as the models suggest.

Next consider ontology. The axioms of rational choice are micro-level assumptions about individual action. Rational choice theorists often believe that these assumptions account not only for individual action but also for the institutions that arise out of these actions. Their micro-theory invokes beliefs and preferences in a way that suggests they have no qualms about ascribing existence to unobservable objects. Yet their emphasis on the micro-level often implies that they do not want to ascribe an independent existence or causal properties to objects such as institutions and structures.

Consider, finally, the rational choice view of explanation. Most of the apparently epistemological differences between rational choice and modernist empiricism are better conceived as differences about forms of explanation. Whereas modernist empiricists champion inductive correlations and classifications, rational choice champions deductive models. Equally, however, we should not let this difference obscure the fact that rational choice too rejects historical narratives in favor of formal explanations that straddle time and space.

2.5 Political Science Today

Perhaps we might be reassured to learn that so much of modern political science coalesces around an empiricist epistemology, realist ontology, and formal explanations. Yet before we become too comfortable, we might pause to wonder: Has philosophical thinking too changed so little since the rise of modernist empiricism? Alas, the answer is a ringing "no." Philosophy has long since moved on. As early as the 1970s philosophers were writing surveys of the ways in which various linguistic turns had transformed both the philosophy of science and political theory over the last twenty years (e.g. Bernstein 1976). By the 1990s, after another twenty years had passed, some textbooks in the philosophy of social science were opening with a brief preface on the demise of modernist empiricism and positivism before devoting themselves to introducing undergraduates to the new perspectives and issues that had arisen in their wake (e.g. Fay 1996). When our inherited meta-methodology is so out of date that it barely appears in undergraduate textbooks, surely it is time to reconsider what we are about?

The rest of this chapter examines recent discussions of epistemology, ontology, and explanation. While I provide an overview of broad directions in philosophy, I also make an argument about the rise of meaning holism and its implications for political science. Meaning holism undermines the long entrenched meta-methodological faith in inductive or experimental empiricism, realism, and formal explanations.[2]

3 EPISTEMOLOGY

Political scientists are generally empiricists. Empiricism can be defined as the belief that knowledge comes from experience. While empiricism has an obvious appeal, it often lapses into skepticism. Some skeptics ask how we can know that our experiences are experiences of an independent world. We will not pay much attention to the debates that flow out of such skepticism.[3] Other skeptics want to know how we can assume that patterns found in past experiences will persist in the future. This skepticism poses what is known as the problem of induction. What is the justification for assuming that events in the future will follow similar patterns to those of the past? The problem of induction also applies to attempts to prove theories by appeals to observations. What justification is there for assuming that a generalization based on previous observations will hold for other cases? How can any number of observations of black ravens justify the conclusion that all ravens are black?

The insurmountable problem of induction led philosophers of science to shift their attention from inductive proof to questions about how evidence supports theories.[4] Indeed the idea of inductive logic as a general theory of how to evaluate arguments only really emerged in the early twentieth century as part of a modernist break with nineteenth-century modes of knowing. It then gave rise to theories of confirmation.

---

[2] The arguments I make are in accord with broad shifts in philosophical thought. But philosophy is all about reasoned disagreement, and there are extensive debates about the validity of meaning holism and about its implications. Readers who want to explore the debates in more detail than I am able to here might begin by exploring the introductory philosophical texts to which I refer in the footnotes below. If there are any readers interested in the details of my own views, they might look at Bevir (1999).

[3] General introductions to epistemology usually cover these debates about perception, memory, reason, and skepticism. See, e.g., Audi (2003).

[4] A good introduction to the philosophy of science is Godfrey-Smith (2003).

3.1 Confirmation Theory

Confirmation theory is associated with the logical positivists.[5] Contrary to popular misperception, few logical positivists argued that brute facts proved general claims. Rather, they hoped to provide a logical theory of the way in which evidence can confirm scientific theories. A logical theory is, in this context, an abstract statement of why certain arguments are compelling and even irrefutable. The paradigmatic example is deductive logic, which covers arguments where if the premises are true, the conclusion too must be true. The logical positivists aimed to provide induction with a logical basis akin to that of deduction. This aim had three components. First, inductive logic would be a generalization of deductive logic: Deduction would be the extreme case of a larger inductive spectrum that included partial entailment and partial refutation. Second, probability would provide a conceptual basis for developing a suitable analysis of this larger spectrum of arguments. Third, the resulting spectrum would give an objective logical basis to the relations of premises to conclusion in inductive arguments. So, for the logical positivists, inductive knowledge rested on purely formal, logical relations between propositions. As Rudolf Carnap argued, confirmation was a logical relation between a proposition describing empirical evidence and a proposition describing a hypothesis.

By the mid-1960s not much remained of logical positivism. Arguably the most important reason for its demise was the rise of the kind of holism to be discussed later. For now, we might mention other reasons. The quest for a formal, logical account of induction led the logical positivists to neglect the psychological, social, and historical practice of science; their logical studies did not reflect what scientists actually did. In addition, the logical positivists' attempts to develop an inductive logic ran into a series of insurmountable obstacles. These obstacles—especially Nelson Goodman's "new riddle of induction"—led many philosophers to conclude that there could not be a formal, logical theory of confirmation.[6]

3.2 Falsificationism

The dilemmas confronting logical positivism provide part of the context in which Sir Karl Popper shifted attention from confirmation to refutation (Popper 1959). Popper initially had little interest in the broader issues of language and meaning that had preoccupied the logical positivists. He sought to describe science in a way that would demarcate it from pseudo-science. In addition, Popper believed that inductive logic was a myth. He argued that observations and evidence never confirm a theory. It is worth belaboring what this argument implies, as a surprising number of political

---

[5] Social scientists might be interested to learn that some of the basic ideas of inductive logic come from Keynes (1921). The leading development of confirmation theory was, however, Carnap (1950).

[6] Goodman (1955). As a result of such arguments even when contemporary textbooks use the term "inductive logic," they often do not mean to imply that probability and induction are indeed logical. For an example that also includes interesting discussions of the import of these issues for decision theory and so rational choice see Hacking (2000).

scientists appear to think that Popper lends support for their uses of induction. In Popper's view, it is impossible to confirm a theory to even the slightest degree irrespective of the amount of observations one amasses in accord with it and irrespective of the number of observations it predicts successfully. For Popper, no matter what methods we use, we simply cannot create data or correlations that give us a valid reason even to increase the degree of faith that we place in a theory.

Many of us might worry that scientific knowledge is profoundly threatened by the suggestion that induction and confirmation have no validity. Popper sought to allay such worries by arguing that science depends not on confirmation but on refutation. Science is distinguished from pseudo-science, he argued, by its commitment to falsificationism. In this view, a proposition is scientific if and only if there is an observation (or perhaps a set of observations) that would show it to be false. Science is all about testing hypotheses. Scientists propose theories, deduce observations from them, and then go out and test to see if the prediction works. If our observations are not as predicted, the hypothesis is false. If our observations are as predicted, then we cannot say the hypothesis is true, or even that it is more likely to be true, but we can say that we have not yet falsified it.

3.3 Meaning Holism

So far our philosophical story does not pose many problems for the inherited meta-methodological commitments of political science. Popper's resolute opposition to induction suggests that there is something odd about the way institutionalists appeal to him, for his views actually fit better with the use of statistical and other experiments by political scientists often with a stronger debt to behavioralism.[7] Nonetheless, it is scarcely too neat to suggest that logical positivism provides an account of confirmation that fits well with the inductive empiricism of institutionalists while Popper provides an account of refutation that has a loose fit with the experimental empiricism of the behavioralists.

The problems for the inherited meta-methodology of much political science arise from the rest of our philosophical story. Epistemology and philosophy of science have moved far from the views of the logical positivists and Popper. Arguably the most important move has been that towards holism following the work of philosophers such as Thomas Kuhn (1962), W. V. O. Quine (1961a), and Ludwig Wittgenstein (1972).[8] Meaning holism asserts that the meaning of a proposition depends on the paradigm, web of beliefs, or language game in which it is located. Hence what would have to be the case for a proposition to be true (or false) depends on the other propositions that we hold true.

Meaning holism decisively undermines the earlier concepts of confirmation and refutation. It implies that no set of observations can verify or falsify a proposition.

---

[7] See the frequent references to Popper as inspiring experimentalism in Campbell (1988).

[8] For a comparatively skeptical survey of the utter dominance of various types of holism see Fodor and LePore (1992).

We can reject or retain any proposition in the face of any evidence provided only that we make appropriate changes to the other propositions that we hold true. No proposition can ever confront the world in splendid isolation. We can only evaluate whole bundles of facts, theories, and assumptions. We can present evidence only to overarching research programs or webs of belief, and even then the evidence will be saturated by theories that are part of the relevant webs of belief or research programs.

Meaning holism renders implausible the inductive and experimental empiricisms that are implicit in so much political science. Yet to reject these forms of empiricism is not necessarily to propose out-and-out relativism. Contemporary philosophers have offered a range of alternative accounts of evidence and justified knowledge. To review all these alternatives is beyond the scope of this chapter. We will look only at two of the most prominent among them: Bayesian theories of evidence and comparative approaches to theory choice.

3.4 Bayesianism

The demise of logical positivism led to new theories of the way in which evidence supports scientific theories. Bayesianism has become the main example of the use of probability theory to explore the role of evidence.[9] Bayesianism is the most technical philosophical theory introduced in this chapter. I will try to give a general feel for how it works. For the technically minded, Bayes's theorem states that: $P(h/e) = P(e/h)P(h)/P(e)$. This formula provides a way of calculating the difference that a piece of evidence e makes to the probability of a hypothesis h. It allows us to say that confirmation occurs when the evidence increases the probability of the hypothesis: e confirms h if $P(h/e) > P(h)$. For the less technically minded, the key innovation here is that the probability of a hypothesis being true is no longer defined statically in relation to a given body of evidence; rather, it is defined in terms of the changes made by a series of shifts in accord with Bayes's theorem. This innovation leads to two important features of Bayesianism. First, as one adjusts the probability of one theory, so one simultaneously can adjust the probability of other theories within a wider web. Second, confirmation or justification can appear less as a property of a single proposition relative to given evidence and more as a property of the ideal beliefs at which we would arrive if we continuously adjusted them appropriately. Advocates of Bayesianism argue that these features of the theory overcome the problems associated with taking the prior probabilities of theories to be subjective. They argue that subjective differences get washed out through the constant adjustments: Wherever we start, we all end up at the same teleological end state.

Bayesianism has been subject to various criticisms, most of which are beyond our scope. Perhaps the most important point for us is the limitations of what Bayesianism has to offer. If Bayesianism works, it justifies a process of induction and the beliefs at

---

[9] Short introductions are provided by Godfrey-Smith (2003, ch. 14); and Hacking (2000, ch. 21). Also see Earman (1992).

which we will converge, but the overtly subjectivist account of probabilities leaves it unable to tell us what probability we currently should assign to theories. Likewise— and this is a serious philosophical concern—Bayesianism does not seem to tell us how much relevance we should assign to bits of evidence when assessing competing theories.

3.5 Comparing Theories

The demise of falsificationism led to new accounts of theory choice. Recognition that theories can be tested only as webs of belief inspired attempts to think about domains in which, and criteria by which, to choose among rival webs of belief.[10] These domains and criteria may be seen as either alternatives to Bayesianism or ways of supplementing a Bayesian justification of induction with a viable account of theory choice.

In the philosophy of science, holism arrived forcefully with Kuhn's emphasis on research paradigms. Kuhn insisted that ordinary science occurred within a paradigm that went unquestioned. Most philosophers of science accepted the holism associated with the concept of a paradigm but not Kuhn's idea of a single unified paradigm ruling over any given scientific field. In their view, science is a competition between competing research programs or competing traditions. Hence the question of theory choice comes down to that of how to compare rival traditions.

The trick is, of course, to find valid philosophical ways of generating a domain and criteria of comparison. It might appear that the validity of the domain and criteria requires that they do not privilege a particular framework. But, to some extent, mean- ing holism suggests that such neutrality just is not possible. Hence the validity of the domain or criteria appears to depend instead on their having a suitable relationship to the kind of holism that motivates the turn to comparison as an approach to theory choice. One very common idea is to locate the domain of comparison in the ability of a tradition to narrate itself and its rivals. My own view is that we also might try to generate criteria of comparison as something akin to deductions from holism itself (Bevir 1999, 96–106).

3.6 Issues for Political Science

Why should political scientists worry about the shift from inductive and experimental empiricism to comparative approaches to theory choice? Let me mention just one obvious reason. A comparative approach implies that political scientists are wrong if they think methods—models, regression analyses, etc.—can ever justify causal claims or even the data they generate. Methods merely create data the validity of which is still open to debate. The validity of the data and any related causal claims

---

[10] A useful collection of essays by the main philosophers of science involved is Hacking (1981). The most famous example, and certainly the one most allied to Popper, is Lakatos (1978).

depends on comparisons between rival bundles of facts, theories, and assumptions. Moreover, these comparisons often depend less on methodological rigor than they do on philosophical coherence, theoretical imagination, fruitfulness or breadth, and synergies with other ways of thinking.

4   ONTOLOGY

Now that we have covered the rise of meaning holism, we will be able to move more quickly through questions of ontology and explanation. At issue is the extent to which meaning holism inspires constructivist and historicist positions that are in tension with the meta-methodological assumptions implicit in much political science.

Ontology seeks to answer the question, what exists? More broadly it seeks to describe the basic categories and relationships of existence thereby providing an account of the types of things there are and the manner (or mode) of their being. Ontology thus covers an array of philosophical debates.[11] For a start, there are debates about whether we should ascribe existence to kinds, properties, relationships, mental states, and even propositions. These debates include the well known one between nominalists and realists on the status of universals. Do abstract nouns refer to things that exist of themselves or do they refer only to particular examples or collections of things? Does society exist in itself or does it refer only to objects such as people and events such as their interactions? In addition, there are debates about modes of existence, including temporality, necessity, and possibility. Can an object remain identical with itself even if its parts change over time? Do legislatures remain the same object when all of their members change?

4.1 Naive Realism

Most of us find realism appealing. We believe that science reveals the world to us; it shows us that we live in a world that contains electrons, atoms, waves, and genes. Most of us also believe that the world always contained these objects even when people did not have our knowledge and so did not realize that it did so. By analogy—although, as we will see, far less plausibly—many political scientists believe that social reality has a structure independent of our beliefs. In their view, there are objects such as institutions and social classes, and these objects would exist even if we did not have the words and concepts that refer to them. This naive realism denies social reality is a construct of our concepts.

As naive realists, political scientists claim that there is a world out there. Perhaps there is. But we need to be careful how we unpack this claim. After all, our concepts

---

[11]   General introductions to metaphysics usually cover these debates. See, e.g., Loux (2002).

are part of the world, and when we act to change the world, the world becomes as it is only by virtue of our having acted on certain concepts. Hence we cannot simply claim that the social world exists independently of our concepts or beliefs. What we might say is that the world exists independently of our beliefs except when reality itself is causally dependent on our beliefs. To rewrite realism in this way is, however, to make the ontology of much political science notably more controversial. Naive realism implies that institutions exist, or at least have properties, independent of our concepts and beliefs.

The first half of the twentieth century was a hostile environment for metaphysics, and that environment could make it seem as if scientists might be able to decide ontological issues as they wished or even dismiss them as meaningless.

Logical positivists appealed to verification less as an epistemological position than as a theory of meaning. They argued that ontological propositions are meaningless because they cannot be verified. As we saw earlier, Carnap wanted philosophers to develop formal languages that established a clear relationship between experience and scientific theories. He thus distinguished two ways in which philosophers might pose ontological questions (Carnap 1947). On the one hand, philosophers might ask questions internal to a formal language. But these internal questions are trivial. If we have a formal language in which we introduce numbers, the question of whether it contains numbers is decided. On the other hand, philosophers might then ask questions external to formal languages. They might ask: Are numbers found in reality? But, Carnap continued, the words in external questions are meaningless, for it is only in the context of a formal language that we are able to tie hypotheses, theories, or questions to evidence. To simplify his argument, we might say: Without a formal language, we cannot know what evidence we would need to verify ontological propositions, and if we do not know what evidence would verify a proposition, then that proposition is meaningless.

4.2 Ontological Commitment

A philosophical story that ended with logical positivism would arguably pose few problems for the inherited meta-methodological commitments of political science. The dismissal of ontological questions as meaningless might appear to sanction a neglect of questions about objects and modes of existence. Once again, however, meaning holism transformed the philosophical terrain in a way that proves more troubling.

Holist critiques of the dogmas of empiricism undermined the logical positivists' rejection of ontology as meaningless or trivial internal questions. Consider Quine's use of holism to attack Carnap's distinction between internal and external questions. For Quine, scientific theories constitute a web, where no empirical evidence can ever compel the rejection of a particular part of the web, and yet where no part of the web is immune from empirical evidence. Because no part of the web is immune from evidence, there simply cannot be purely internal questions. Rather, as Quine insisted, the distinction between internal and external questions must fall along with that between analytic and synthetic truths.

While Quine rescued ontology from the attacks of the logical positivists, he did not believe that we could pose ontological questions prior to, or apart from, the rest of our knowledge. Hence he reintroduced ontology as a study of the commitments associated with our best theories. To be more precise, Quine (1961*b*) proposed the slogan: To be is to be the value of a bound variable. This slogan captures the idea that we commit ourselves to the existence of F if and only if we say "there is an F (bound variable) that is . . ." It is, however, one thing to know how we thus commit ourselves to an ontology and another to know what ontology we should commit ourselves to. Quine argued that we might decide ontological matters by examining the logical form of the sentences that make up our best account of the world. An F exists if the logical form of those sentences is such that we quantify over it, that is, if F is a predicate of a property or a relation.

Quine's argument is that we posit the existence of Fs if and only if we say in our best theories that there is an F. It is worth pausing to note that in this view we perfectly reasonably can ascribe existence to unobservable things such as beliefs. It is also worth pausing to note that political scientists still might propose that the logical form of their sentences ascribes existence not only to beliefs, persons, actions, and events, but also to social classes, institutions, and the like.[12] Quine's argument is broadly indifferent as to which ontology we should adopt. It does, however, pose the question: What ontology is entailed by our best theories? I will argue here that meaning holism, as one of our best theories, implies that while social classes, institutions, and the like may be real, they are definitely linguistic constructions.

4.3 Constructivism

Let us look briefly at some very general implications of meaning holism for ontology. Holism implies that the world, as we recognize it, consists of things that we can observe and discuss only because we have the web of beliefs we do. For example, when we observe and discuss malaria conceived as a fever caused by the presence in the body of the protozoan parasite of genus *Plasmodium*, we rely on beliefs about parasites and diseases. Holism thus suggests that any given object or event could not be part of our world unless we had the appropriate beliefs. We could not discuss malaria if we did not have certain beliefs about parasites: We might use the word "malaria" to describe certain symptoms, but we could not discuss malaria conceived as a fever produced by a certain type of parasite. Again, holism thus suggests that things are constructed as real only in particular contexts. We construct malaria as real only with our beliefs

---

[12]   The best-known attempt to approach the ontology of action though logical analysis of the relevant sentences is Davidson (1980*a*). There have also been major developments in logical approaches to modes of existence—see Chellas (1980)—but, alas, I do not understand the more advanced aspects of quantified modal logic well enough to assess their relevance to this chapter.

about parasites. Hence, we can say, more generally, that an object F did not exist at a time T. To echo Quine, we might say that before T, there were no variables to bind F.

The general implication might appear to be that holism entails a constructivist ontology according to which we make the world through our concepts. However, that is not quite the right way of putting it.[13] Holism certainly leads to a constructivist view of the objects in "our world" as we conceive of it. But there are philosophical debates about the relationship of "our world" to "the world" as it is. Some philosophers are reluctant to evoke a real world that lies apart from our world and so is something that by definition we cannot access. Others are equally reluctant to give up their realist intuitions. They want to argue that even if an object F comes to exist only at a time T in our world, it either does or does not exist in the world. Hence they want to postulate "the world" as apart from the world we make through our categories.

Fortunately we need not resolve the philosophical debate about "the world" to grasp the profoundly constructed nature of social things. Instead we can return to the fact that we make the social world by acting on beliefs. Even if we postulate "the world," the social things in it depend on beliefs, and holism implies that these beliefs are themselves socially constructed as part of a wider web of beliefs. Holism thus points toward a type of linguistic constructivism according to which we not only make the social world by our actions but also make the beliefs or concepts on which we act. Our concepts, actions, and practices are products of particular traditions or discourses. Social concepts and things, such as "the working class" or "democracy," do not have intrinsic properties or objective boundaries. They are the artificial inventions of particular languages and societies. Their content depends on the wider webs of meaning that hold them in place.

4.4 Issues for Political Science

Why should political scientists worry about the shift towards constructivism in social ontology? Constructivism suggests that political scientists are generally mistaken if they conceive of institutions or structures as fixed or natural kinds. It challenges the widespread tendency to reify social things, and to ascribe to them an essence that then determines either their other properties or their consequences. Legislatures, democracies, wars, and other social things are meaningful and contingent. We cannot properly identify them—let alone count, correlate, or model them—unless we pay attention to the possibly diverse and changing beliefs of the relevant actors. But let us end our study of ontology, for I am beginning to move on to the ways in which holism overturns formal, ahistorical explanations.

---

[13] For reflections on the complex nature of the constructivist ontology that arises from holism, see Hacking (1999; 2002).

5 FORMS OF EXPLANATION

Political scientists generally evoke institutions and structures as if they were given objects in an attempt to explain why something happened. When concepts such as class, legislature, and democracy are used purely descriptively, they usually can be unpacked as social constructions: We can treat them as simplified terms for patterns of actions based on webs of subjective meanings. In contrast, when these concepts are used to explain actions or outcomes, they often take on a more formal or fixed content: They are reified so they can be treated as causes that either operate independently of the actors' beliefs or stand in for their beliefs. Political scientists sometimes aim just to describe the world, but they more often aspire to provide explanations, and it is this aspiration that encourages them blithely to reify all kinds of social concepts.

The aspiration to explain is, of course, widespread among scientists and lay folk alike. Most of us conceive of our beliefs as giving answers not only to what-questions (what exists? what happened?) but also to why-questions (why is it like that? why did it happen?). Philosophers, in contrast, often find the idea of explanation troubling, or at least a source of puzzles. Consider, for example, the tension between the aspiration to explain and the empiricism avowed by so many political scientists. Empiricists are often skeptical of any claims that go beyond or behind our experiences and purport to discover underlying causes. They are suspicious of explanations that point toward purportedly deep claims about the world as it is rather than the facts of our experience.

5.1 Covering Laws

Arguably we are most likely to be able to reconcile empiricism with explanatory ambitions if we defend a thin concept of explanation. The logical positivists upheld just such a thin concept of explanation that gave it little more content than the Humean idea of experiences of regular successions. According to the logical positivists explanations are a type of argument that appeals to a covering law (Hempel and Oppenheim 1948; Hempel 1942). So, to explain X by reference to A, B, and C is to evoke a covering law (a general proposition) that correlates things of the same type as X with things of the same type as A, B, and C. Hence explanations are just arguments whose premises include not only factual claims but also a law of nature. The relevant arguments might be deductive or inductive provided that they evoked a covering law. The logical positivists' account of explanation thus largely sidesteps the substantive issues about causation that trouble empiricists. It suggests that an *explanandum* is just the conclusion of an argument that has the *explanans* as its premises, where whether or not a particular explanation is good depends on the truth of its premises including the relevant covering law. Questions about the nature of causation are put aside as matters for the analysis of concepts such as "law of nature."

The covering-law theory is no longer a contender in philosophy. It fell before recognition of the asymmetry problem (Bromberger 1966). Explanation is asymmetrical in a way that the covering-law theory is not. The standard example has become that of a flagpole that casts a shadow on the ground. Imagine that we want to explain the length of the shadow. The covering-law theory suggests that we explain it as a deduction from the height of the pole, the position of the sun, a bit of basic trigonometry, and laws of nature (optics). However, we can also reverse the explanation so that it applies to the length of the flagpole. The covering-law theory suggests here that we might explain the length of the flagpole as a deduction from the length of the shadow, the position of the sun, a bit of trigonometry, and the laws of optics. There is no logical difference between the two explanations as they appear given the covering-law theory. The explanation of the height of the flagpole, like the explanation of the length of the shadow, stands as a deduction from premises that include a law of nature. As the example of the flagpole clearly shows, explanations are directional in a way that the covering-law theory just does not capture. Philosophers now take that to be an utterly decisive objection to the covering-law theory.

5.2 Reasons as Causes

The directional nature of explanation suggests that the concept of explanation cannot easily be divorced from causation: When we go in one direction, we have an explanation since X causes Y, whereas when we go in the other, we do not have an explanation since Y does not cause X. The demise of the covering-law theory thus sparked a renewed interest in questions about causation. Some of these questions are very general ones about determinism, conditionality, and causation.[14] Others are more specific to the study of human life. How should we think about the causes of our actions and so the practices and institutions to which these actions give rise?

Discussions of the causes of actions often begin with recognition of intentionality. The concept of intentionality captures the idea that, as we saw earlier, our actions depend on what we believe whether consciously or not. Human life is thus meaningful in a way that purely physical events are not. Recognition of the intentionality of human life poses the question of mental causation: How can mind (or intentionality) make a difference in a world of physical things (atoms, tables, genes, human bodies, etc.)?

Meaning holists generally responded to the question of mental causation in one of two ways, inspired respectively by Wittgenstein and Donald Davidson. The philosophers inspired by Wittgenstein deny actions have causes (e.g. Anscombe 1957; Winch 1958). In their view, causal explanations present events as instances of a lawlike regularity, whereas explanations of actions show how the action fits into larger patterns of belief and rationality. Even though Davidson's argument set him apart from this view, he drew heavily on it (Davidson 1980b; see also Heil and Mele 1995). He too proposed

---

[14] For a useful set of essays see Sosa and Tooley (1993).

that we explain actions in terms of intentionality: We explain actions by reference to a "primary reason" consisting of the belief and pro-attitude (or desire) of the actor. He too accepted that we thereby make actions intelligible by locating them in a larger pattern of belief and rationality. But for Davidson the primary reason for an action is also its cause. Davidson treats a primary reason and an action as distinct events. He then adapts a Wittgensteinian suggestion that actions can be intentional under one description ("I wanted a drink") but not under others ("I knocked the cup over") to argue that the connection between these two events can be described in different ways. Under one description, the connection is a rational one that we cannot assimilate to a lawlike regularity. Under another description the same connection can appear as a lawlike regularity.

Davidson offers us a way of combining folk psychology with physicalism: We can explain actions rationally using folk terms such as belief and desire, while conceiving of the world as composed of physical objects and their interactions. For philosophers, the main questions this view raises are those about the relationship between these mental and physical languages. Davidson himself argued for an "anomalous monism" according to which the mental supervenes on the physical but there are no laws relating them. In this view, any mental event, such as "my wanting to swim," can in principle be paired with a physical event, but no strict law relates "wanting to swim" to a particular type of brain activity (Davidson 1980c). Other philosophers have rejected this argument for various reasons. Some philosophers complain that it leaves the mental with no real causal powers. Others hold to a physicalist vision of a time when folk psychology will be replaced by the language of neuro-science or at least translated into it. For our purposes, however, it seems sufficient to accept that we cannot yet reduce folk psychology to a physical language, so political scientists currently are bound to deploy the kind of rational explanations associated with terms like intentionality, belief, and desire.

5.3 Historicism

Some readers might not yet realize how meaning holism challenges the formal explanations that dominate political science. Rational choice theorists might think that they already explain actions by showing how they are loosely rational given a set of beliefs and desires. Other political scientists might think that they can fairly easily treat their appeals to social categories as stand-ins for appeals to beliefs and desires: Provided they do not reify social categories, they can treat a claim such as "workers generally vote for social democratic parties" as shorthand for a set of claims about the kinds of beliefs and desires workers have and the kind of voting pattern to which these beliefs and desires give rise.

The challenge to formal explanations arises once again from the holism apparent in the idea that rational explanations work by locating an action within a larger web of beliefs or reasons. Holism pushes us to move from formal and ahistorical explanations to contextualizing and historicist ones.

Holism pushes us, firstly, to adopt contextual explanations. It implies that we can properly explain people's beliefs (and so their actions and the practices and institutions to which their actions give rise) only if we locate them in the context of a wider web of beliefs. Holism thus points to the importance of elucidating beliefs by showing how they relate to one another, not by trying to reduce them to categories such as social class or institutional position. We explain beliefs—and so actions and practices—by unpacking the conceptual connections in a web of beliefs, rather than by treating them as variables.

Holism pushes us, secondly, to adopt historicist explanations. It implies that people can grasp their experiences and so adopt new beliefs only against the background of an inherited web of beliefs. Hence we cannot explain why people hold the webs of belief they do solely by reference to their experiences, interests, or social location. To the contrary, even their beliefs about their experiences, interests, and social location will depend on their prior theories. Hence we can explain why they hold the webs of belief they do only by reference to the intellectual traditions that they inherit. Holism suggests, in other words, that social explanation contains an inherently historicist aspect. Even the concepts, actions, and practices that seem most natural to us need to be explained as products of a contingent history.

Perhaps I should admit here that most of the meaning holists I have discussed do not themselves argue for historicism. When they discuss social explanation, they often emphasize the importance of locating an action within a wider web of beliefs that shows it to be loosely rational. Buy they do not suggest the importance of then explaining these webs of belief by locating them against the background of inherited traditions. However, my own philosophical work has attempted not only to bring meaning holism to bear on historical inquiry but also to suggest how meaning holism leads to historicism. It is that latter suggestion that I have now repeated here (Bevir 1999, 187–218).

5.4 Issues for Political Science

Why should political scientists worry about the shift toward contextual and historical forms of explanation? In stark terms, the answer is that it implies that their correlations, classifications, and models are not properly speaking explanations at all. They are, rather, a type of data that we then might go on to explain using contextualizing historical narratives. Correlations and classifications become explanations only if we unpack them as shorthands for narratives about how certain beliefs fit with other beliefs in a way that makes possible particular actions and practices. Similarly, although models appeal to beliefs and desires, they are mere fables that become explanations only when we treat them as accurate depictions of the beliefs and desires that people really held in a particular case (cf. Rubinstein 2006; 1995). Finally, even after we treat correlations, classifications, and models as shorthands for narrative explanations, we then should provide a historical account of the contingent traditions behind these beliefs; we cannot treat the beliefs as epiphenomena explicable in terms of objective facts about the world, social formations, or a purportedly universal rationality.

6 CONCLUSION

As this chapter draws to a close, I hope it has delivered rather more than it first promised. It has certainly tried to clear the underbrush of confusion that arises from reflecting on methods in terms of traditions of political science rather than philosophical subfields and doctrines. Yet, in addition, this chapter has tried to make a start at clearing the underbrush of confusion that arises from political scientists relying on philosophical doctrines that the rise of meaning holism has left looking increasingly implausible. It has argued that political science is too often committed to forms of empiricism, realism, and formal explanation that increasingly lack philosophical plausibility. It has suggested that we need to rethink political science and its methods so as to give greater scope to theory choice, constructivism, and historicism. We might still defend empiricism, but we must recognize that the justification of knowledge depends on comparing whole webs of belief. We might still defend realism, but we must recognize that much of social reality is linguistically constructed. We might still defend naturalism, but we must recognize that the human sciences require historicist forms of explanation.[15]

Let me be clear, the problem is not that holism repudiates any particular method for creating data; it does not. The problem is that holism undermines the dominant meta-methodological commitments in terms of which political scientists think about their data. Holism poses awkward questions about how political scientists should use and explain the data generated by multiple methods. To be harsh, the real problem is that political scientists have not even begun to think about these questions, let alone respond to them and modify their practice accordingly.

It is true that critical and constructivist approaches to political science sometimes try to foreground such questions. Alas, however, other political scientists are prone to dismiss these alternative approaches for lacking methodological rigor—as if the nature and relevance of methodological rigor could be taken as given without bothering to think about the relevant philosophical issues. To be harsher still, therefore, political scientists are in danger of becoming dull technicians, capable of applying the techniques that they learn from statisticians and economists, but lacking any appreciation of the philosophical issues entailed in decisions about when we should use these techniques, the degree of rigor we should want from them, and how we should explain the data they generate.

---

[15] My own view is that historicism entails an antinaturalist view of social explanation but not an antinaturalist ontology. For the antinaturalist view of explanation, see Bevir and Kedar (forthcoming).

Many political scientists have long worried about hyperfactualism—the collection of data without proper theoretical reflection. Today we might also worry about hypermethodologism—the application of methodological techniques without proper philosophical reflection.

REFERENCES

ADCOCK, R., BEVIR, M., and STIMSON, S. (eds.) 2007. *Modern Political Science: Anglo-American Exchanges since 1880*. Princeton, NJ: Princeton University Press.

ANSCOMBE, G. 1957. *Intention*. Oxford: Basil Blackwell.

AUDI, R. 2003. *Epistemology: A Contemporary Introduction*. London: Routledge.

BERNSTEIN, R. 1976. *The Restructuring of Social and Political Theory*. Philadelphia: University of Pennsylvania Press.

BEVIR, M. 1999. *The Logic of the History of Ideas*. Cambridge: Cambridge University Press.

—— and KEDAR, A. forthcoming. Concept formation in political science: an anti-naturalist critique of qualitative methodology. *Perspectives on Politics*.

BROMBERGER, S. 1966. Why-questions. In *Mind and Cosmos*, ed. R. Colodny. Pittsburgh, Pa.: University of Pittsburgh Press.

CAMPBELL, D. 1988. *Methodology and Epistemology for Social Science: Selected Papers*. Chicago: University of Chicago Press.

CARNAP, R. 1947. Empiricism, semantics, and ontology. In *Meaning and Necessity: A Study in Semantics and Modal Logic*. Chicago: University of Chicago Press.

—— 1950. *Logical Foundations of Probability*. Chicago: University of Chicago Press.

CHELLAS, B. 1980. *Modal Logic: An Introduction*. Cambridge: Cambridge University Press.

DAVIDSON, D. 1980*a*. The logical form of action sentences. In *Essays on Actions and Events*. Oxford: Clarendon Press.

—— 1980*b*. Actions, reasons and causes. In *Essays on Actions and Events*. Oxford: Clarendon Press.

—— 1980*c*. Mental events. In *Essays on Actions and Events*. Oxford: Clarendon Press.

EARMAN, J. 1992. *Bayes or Bust? A Critical Examination of Bayesian Confirmation Theory*. Cambridge, Mass.: MIT Press.

EASTON, D. 1953. *The Political System*. Chicago: University of Chicago Press.

ELSTER, J. (ed.) 1986. *Rational Choice*. New York: New York University Press.

FAY, B. 1996. *Contemporary Philosophy of Social Science*. Oxford: Blackwell.

FINER, H. 1921. *Foreign Governments at Work: An Introductory Study*. New York: Oxford University Press.

—— 1932. *Theory and Practice of Modern Government*. London: Methuen.

FODOR, J., and LEPORE, E. 1992. *Holism: A Shopper's Guide*. Oxford: Blackwell.

GODFREY-SMITH, P. 2003. *Theory and Reality: An Introduction to the Philosophy of Science*. Chicago: University of Chicago Press.

GOODMAN, N. 1955. *Fact, Fiction, and Forecast*. Cambridge, Mass.: Harvard University Press.

HACKING, I. 1981. *Scientific Revolutions*. Oxford: Oxford University Press.

—— 1999. *The Social Construction of What?* Cambridge, Mass.: Harvard University Press.

—— 2000. *An Introduction to Probability and Inductive Logic*. Cambridge: Cambridge University Press.

HACKING, I. 2002. Making up people. In *Historical Ontology*. Cambridge, Mass.: Harvard University Press.

HALL, P., and TAYLOR, R. 1996. Political science and the three institutionalisms. *Political Studies*, 44: 936–57.

HEIL J., and MELE, A. (eds.) 1995. *Mental Causation*. Oxford: Oxford University Press.

HEMPEL, C. 1942. The function of general laws in history. *Journal of Philosophy*, 39: 35–48.

——and OPPENHEIM, P. 1948. Studies in the logic of explanation. *Philosophy of Science*, 15: 135–75.

KEYNES, J. 1921. *Treatise on Probability*. London: Macmillan.

KUHN, T. 1962. *The Structure of Scientific Revolutions*. Chicago: University of Chicago Press.

LAKATOS, I. 1978. *Philosophical Writings*, vol. i: *The Methodology of Scientific-Research Programmes*. Cambridge: Cambridge University Press.

LEVI, M. 1988. *Of Rule and Revenue*. Berkeley: University of California Press.

LOUX, M. 2002. *Metaphysics: A Contemporary Introduction*. London: Routledge.

MONROE, K. (ed.) 1991. *The Economic Approach to Politics*. New York: HarperCollins.

PIERSON, P., and SKOCPOL, T. 2002. Historical institutionalism in contemporary political science. In *Political Science: The State of the Discipline*, ed. I. Katznelson and H. Miller. New York: Norton.

POPPER, K. 1959. *The Logic of Scientific Discovery*. New York: Basic Books.

QUINE, W. 1961a. Two dogmas of empiricism. Pp. 20–46 in *From a Logical Point of View*. Cambridge, Mass.: MIT Press.

——1961b. On what there is. In *From a Logical Point of View*. Cambridge, Mass.: MIT Press.

RUBINSTEIN, A. 1995. Microeconomic theory: wonders or miracles. Address to the Israeli Academy of Sciences, 19 December.

——2006. Dilemmas of an economic theorist. *Econometrica*, 74: 865–83.

SCHABAS, M. 1990. *A World Ruled by Number: William Stanley Jevons and the Rise of Mathematical Economics*. Princeton, NJ: Princeton University Press.

SKOCPOL, T. 1985. Bringing the state back in: strategies of analysis in current research. In *Bringing the State Back In*, ed. P. Evans, D. Rueschemeyer, and T. Skocpol. New York: Cambridge University Press.

SOSA, E., and TOOLEY, M. (eds.) 1993. *Causation*. Oxford: Oxford University Press.

THELEN, K., and STEINMO, S. 1992. Historical institutionalism in comparative politics. Pp. 1–32 in S. Steinmo, K. Thelen, and F. Longstreth, *Structuring Politics: Historical Institutionalism in Comparative Analysis*. New York: Cambridge University Press.

WINCH, P. 1958. *The Idea of a Social Science*. London: Routledge and Kegan Paul.

WITTGENSTEIN, L. 1972. *Philosophical Investigations*. Oxford: Basil Blackwell.

CHAPTER 4

AGENT-BASED MODELING

SCOTT DE MARCHI
SCOTT E. PAGE

1 COMPUTATIONAL MODELS AS NUMERICAL METHODS

In mathematics, engineering, and the biological and physical sciences, computational methods have proliferated in recent years due in part to the increase in computing power available to researchers. The ability of computational methods to build upon deductive results has expanded the set of problems researchers can investigate. As a result, in almost every field outside of the social sciences, computational methods now occupy substantial space in the working scientist's bag of tools, and one can see this everywhere from textbooks to the proliferation of clustered computing on campuses. The growth in computational models is also partly caused by demand. Pressing problems ranging from the global (climate change), to the social (disease spread), to the microscopic (protein folding, <http://folding.stanford.edu>) outstrip current mathematical expertise. Owing to their complexity, leading scholars now model each of these problems primarily with computers, eschewing analytics. For more esoteric, academic pursuits such as solving differential equations (Strogatz 2001), producing statistical measures (Gentle 2002), and locating optimal solutions (Judd 1998 and Ballard 1997), using computational methods has also become mainstream.

The question then for social science is not if, but how computational methods can help extend existing results. For statistical work, the answer is easy. Bayesian statistics in our discipline[1] along with preexisting research programs such as Poole and Rosenthal's work on Congress (see Poole 2006 for an overview), illustrate the utility of computational methods. For formal models, however, the answer to the foregoing question remains open to debate within our discipline. There is some belief (particularly among formal theorists themselves; see Tesfatsion 1997; Leombruni and Richiardi 2005) that noncooperative game theory is distinct from other modeling enterprises; investigations of nonequilibrium dynamics or of alternative solution concepts such as the core are not seen as valuable. Baron and Ferejohn (1989), for example, argue that noncooperative bargaining theory takes institutions "seriously" and (unlike prior cooperative models) provides "definite predictions about legislative processes." Diermeier and Krehbiel (2003) extend this argument by asserting that behavioral rules should be fixed (i.e. based on rational choice assumptions), and that "the need for an equilibrium concept [i.e. Nash and its extensions] that is general and flexible enough to model a broad variety of institutions and institutional choices, strongly favors non-cooperative game theory" over other methods.

The case for analytics rests on their *generality* and their capacity to reveal *cause and effect*. Some analytic results hold for classes, e.g. convex or single peaked, of functions. Others hold for parametric families of functions such as Cobb-Douglass utility functions. Computational results hold only for the values tested or, in the best case, statistically for parametric families of functions. Thus, a case can be made that analytic results are more general (e.g. the justly famous Arrow result is both general and explores substantively interesting assumptions). Second, deriving results often reveals cause and effect. It shows how and why assumptions matter. By comparison, computational models can be black boxes.

These critiques have limited merit. Clearly, if a general analytic result can be shown, then by all means it should be. But general results rarely exist and so the standard approach is to simplify the model rather than abandon the methodology. As for the critique that math provides clarity and computational models obscure, reality suggests the opposite. Computational models often provide greater transparency because they can reveal the value of any variable or combination of variables.

At the risk of being provocative, we sense some oppose agent-based and computational methods for other, less scientifically based reasons. Some dislike the methodology because it makes modeling too easy. With a computer, anyone can construct a model and many of these models will be uninformative. Computational models are more flexible, which we see as a good thing, but what this critique misses is that they are also logically consistent owing to the fact that they are programmed. Others question computational approaches because they equate analytic techniques, Nash

---

[1] For an application to the Supreme Court, see Martin and Quinn (2002).

Equilibrium, and purposeful behavior. In fact the latter two are in no way implied by nor do they require mathematics. Yes, equilibria can be derived with mathematics, but they can also emerge computationally.

To date, there has been insufficient commerce between mathematical and computational modelers, so much so that an outside observer might conclude that computational and formal methods are incompatible. Given that this supposed incompatibility of methods does not exist in mathematics or the physical sciences, it is our position that it is not a necessary feature of the social sciences either, but rather a disciplinary choice that will likely be short-lived. Computational models enable scholars to explore richer environments (see, for example, Fowler and Smirnov 2005); they can move beyond Nash Equilibrium to include coalitional deviations (see Page forthcoming), and they can incorporate more realistic behavioral assumptions (Bendor, Diermeier, and Ting 2003). Computational models, therefore, should be seen as a tool that extends the problem domain. In our view, models are models, regardless of the method employed to investigate them.

We provide two examples that will illustrate this point, that highlight the ability of computational methods to extend game-theoretic results. The first example is as simple as possible, so as to provide some general intuition. The second considers a more sophisticated model and better shows the power of computational models to deepen our understanding.

1.1 The Currency Game: Computational Models Used to Expand and Complement Deductive Results

Consider the following example borrowed from Young (2001), who used it as a model to investigate path dependency. N actors in a society must decide among two possible currencies: gold and silver. Initially, the N actors will be randomly assigned gold or silver with equal probability. Let p_t be the proportion of gold users in the population at time t and $(1 - p_t)$ be the silver users. At each subsequent time period, one actor will be chosen by a uniform draw from the population and will make a new decision according to the following rule:

With probability $(1 - \epsilon)$, the actor chooses the more common currency. Formally, if $p_t > 0.5$ (i.e. gold is the dominant currency) the actor chooses gold or remains a gold user if one already; else. The actor behaves similarly if silver is dominant. If $p_t = 0.5$ exactly, the actor continues with whatever currency he or she was using previously. With probability $\epsilon > 0$, a shock occurs and the actor randomly chooses one of the currency. Thus, with a 50 percent probability, he or she switches to the nondominant currency, i.e. makes a mistake. In this model, a natural dependent variable would be the average number of regime shifts one sees over any given time period t. For example, if the game goes on for 100 iterations, how many times would the currency change from one standard to another? This outcome variable is an integer with a range from $[0..t]$. The two main explanatory variable are ϵ (the mutation rate) and N (the population size) with presumably more changes with a higher mutation rate and fewer changes with a larger population.

One can go about solving this problem in two different ways, as outlined in de Marchi (2005). The first approach uses game theory. Using this approach, the currency game generates relatively long periods of convergence characterized by sudden shifts to the alternative currency.[2] Young proves a theorem that states that if you have a suitably large population, a majority of the agents will choose the same currency. Additionally, this majority is largest when ϵ is small. This provides intuition about the currency game, but many readers might not be certain about what the properties of the currency game are for different values of N and ϵ. How large is a "suitably large" population? How small does epsilon have to be? Interpreting this theorem can thus be elusive, even though it is deductively true and even though the game has only two parameters. Young, for example, claims that the currency game is useful in studying path dependent processes, such as competing technologies (see Arthur 1989):

> After an initial shakeout, the process converges quite rapidly to a situation in which most people are carrying the same currency—say, gold. This norm will very likely stay in place for a considerable period of time. Eventually, however, an accumulation of random shocks will "tip" the process into the silver norm. These tipping incidents are infrequent compared to the periods in which one or the other norm is in place (assuming ϵ is small). Moreover, once a tipping incident occurs, the process will tend to adjust quite rapidly to the new norm. This pattern—long periods of stasis punctuated by sudden changes of regime—is known in biology as the *punctuated equilibrium effect*.   (Young 2001, 11–12; emphases in original)

To complement his mathematical results, Young provides graphs of numerical experiments that illustrate multiple regime shifts. For the experiments he details in the text, he relies upon small population sizes ($N = 10$) and a very high mutation rate ($\epsilon = .5$) to generate his intuition about the properties of the game. He runs 30,000 iterations of the model and considers a very small subset of the parameter space in his initial forays into modeling the game. For $N = 10$ and $\epsilon = .5$, $E(\cdot) = 0.015$—in 1,000 iterations of the game, one would expect to see 15 regime shifts. If one considers a larger population and a smaller mutation rate—which more closely mirrors the nature of the real world problem Young uses the currency game to investigate[3]— one quickly discovers that regime shifts never, ever happen. For $N = 100,000$ (still a tiny population) and $\epsilon = .05$ (a reasonably high mutation rate), E (regime shifts) = $6.89E{-}1534$—that is a lot of 0's.

What Young has done is build a simple computational model, which in this case is a straightforward process of translating the dynamics of the game into a programming

---

[2] The formal statement of the theorem is as follows: "Let G be a 2×2 symmetric coordination game with a strictly risk dominant equilibrium, and let Q_N, ϵ be adaptive learning in the playing the field model with population size [N], complete sampling, and error [mutation] rate ϵ, $0 < \epsilon < 1$. For every $\epsilon' > \epsilon$, the probability is arbitrarily high that at least $1 - \epsilon'/2$ of the population is playing the risk dominant equilibrium when [N] is sufficiently large" (Young 2001, 76).

[3] For example, the adoption of competing technologies such as a Wintel computer versus an Apple.

Table 4.1. Results for the currency game

Poisson regression				Number of obs = 1600		
				LR chi2(2) = 19492.69		
				Prob > chi2 = 0.0000		
Log likelihood = −2244.3969				Pseudo R2 = 0.8128		
Num_reg	Coef.	Std.Err.	Z	P> |z|	[95 percent Conf.	Interval]
N_pop	−.0351948	.0007884	−44.64	0.000	−.03674	−.0336496
Mutat_rate	15.4024	.9942932	15.49	0.000	13.45362	17.35118
_cons	−4.148296	.4970227	−8.35	0.000	−5.122443	−3.17415

language like C, python, or Perl—in many respects, this is much easier than constructing a game-theoretic model of comparable complexity. While choices such as the particular computer language are a matter of personal preference, computational models must obey the following strictures:

1. encode the rules of the game as accurately as possible;
2. iterate the computational model through a wide range of parameter values;
3. present a set of statistical results that explain the relationship between the parameters of the model and the dependent variables of interest.

Once this process is accomplished, the results of the computational model produce data in a format that is familiar to social scientists. Each observation is the product of running the model using different parameter choices for N and ϵ, and these data can be used to investigate the role of N and ϵ in predicting mean regime shifts.

As in any statistical work, the problem of choosing a reasonable empirical specification must be faced, though in the case of computational models this is somewhat offset by the ability to generate novel data to test various specifications. One can then use out-of-sample data-sets and make multiple attempts to find a good match. In the case of Young's currency game, a good model is a Poisson regression, which for a large number of observations spans much of the parameter space described by N and ϵ (Table 4.1).

For a Poisson regression, the predicted values are given by e^{xb}. By examining representative values, we can gain a more complete understanding. The output table shows that as N increases, universal adoption of a single currency becomes extremely likely because the likelihood of regime shifts decreases, and regime shifts almost never occur.

Contrasting Young's deductive approach with the computational model, we see that the deductive result gives us a baseline understanding of what the currency game looks like in equilibrium, but it does not tell us much about the dynamics of the system, or even what the system would look like for different parameter values. The computational model extends and deepens our understanding of the deductive result, and generates an empirical model that is both familiar to social scientists (due to the ubiquity of statistics training) and useful in generating intuition about different parameter values. Seen in this way, the deductive and computational approaches are complementary.

1.2 Baron–Ferejohn Bargaining: Computational Models Used to Solve Hard Problems, Search Parameter Spaces, and Investigate Equivalence Classes

Bargaining models occupy a central place in the political science and economics literatures. This prominence is due to two factors. First, these models can be applied in a range of contexts, ranging from cabinet formation in PR systems to coalition behavior within legislatures to alliance structures in the international system. Second, bargaining models produce testable hypotheses which can be explored in both the laboratory setting (Fréchette, Kagel, and Morelli 2005) as well as with macro-level political data (Warwick and Druckman 2006).

Here, we consider the Baron–Ferejohn bargaining model. To call it a single model is not correct. In their original 1989 paper in the *American Political Science Review*, they presented a number of qualitatively distinct games, and those models have, in turn, been extended by other scholars. For example, their infinite-horizon, closed-rule model has received the most attention in the literature. Recently, Snyder, Ting, and Ansolabehere (2005) have advocated for the use of minimum integer weights as a proxy for bargaining power rather than raw votes scores.[4] Subtle changes in assumptions about weights, timing, and parameter create an ensemble of possible models. A crude characterization of these models suggests that they must include:

- discount rate for the value of time
- horizon for the number of periods that bargaining occurs
- minimum integer or raw voting weights
- minimum winning or minimum weight coalitions
- open vs. closed rule for changes in the agreement
- recognition rule (i.e. who proposes a coalition in each time period)
- reversion point if bargaining fails
- stationarity (or not) so that agents do (or do not) incorporate history in their strategies.

The core insight of the formal results derived in the Baron–Ferejohn literature is that the proposer has an advantage (in government coalitions, this is named the *formateur* advantage), but this of itself is not very precise. Ideally, we could make more precise statements of exactly how much of an advantage we would expect to see for a *formateur*.

---

[4] Informally, minimum integer weights are the smallest integer weights that generate a given set of coalitions. E.g. the three-person legislatures {1,1,1}, {2,2,1}, and {99,99,1} generate identical winning coalitions; {1,1,1} is the minimum integer weight representation.

It is important to note that these bargaining games produce brutal combinatorics when one wishes to extent these results to greater than three players. Calculating minimum integer weights, for example, is NP-hard and necessitates the use of computational methods (Strauss 2003). We thus have computational work as a handmaiden to the formal results, but the larger question remains. Has the formal work in this literature yielded a consensus opinion given the large parameter space?

The short answer is "no." Diermeier and Morton (2003), for example, use experiments to test whether subjects adhere to behavior that matches the Baron–Ferejohn model of bargaining. In this model, equilibrium play dictates that the proposer will take a disproportionate share of the pie; in contrast, it might be the case that subjects instead take a piece of the pie proportional to their voting weight in the coalition, regardless of whether they were the proposer or not. Their design relies upon three "different" bargaining games with the following vote totals (all adding to 99) for each of three groups: {34,33,32}, {49,33,17}, and {46,44,9}; and uses a proportional rule for recognition with a finite number of proposal periods. Given these assumptions, each game has a different equilibrium. The problem, of course, is that it is not obvious that these three voting contexts are in fact different games. Their minimum integer weight representations are the same—{1,1,1}—and thus the expected continuation values (the values that each player can expect to receive) would also be the same: 1/3 for each player regardless of their differing vote totals.

Other parameter choices such as an infinite horizon, different recognition rules for selecting the proposer, or a different discount rate would also qualitatively change their expectations. We thus find ourselves in an uncomfortable situation, where minor parameter choices produce a range of dissimilar outcomes that make it difficult to describe Baron–Ferejohn bargaining as a unitary group of models.

In large part, much of the opacity in the Baron–Ferejohn inspired literature can be explained by the fact that in many settings, researchers use simple examples and do not worry overmuch about the parameter choices. Individual modelers pick a set of parameters, prove a result, and fill in a single pin-prick of light in a vast, dark void. Just as with the foregoing example of path dependency and currency adoption, the quality of the intuition generated by this approach to modeling can be quite lacking and computational models are one way to fill in more of this void.

As Laver, de Marchi, and Mutlu (2007) show, computational models extend the reach of existing deductive results by testing different parameterizations. Questions like:

- does a greater vote share always help a party gain cabinet seats?
- what happens if we assume parties prefer coalitions with minimum weight rather than minimum winning partners?
- are nonhomogeneous and homogeneous games the same?
- what happens if the reversion point is not the null vector?

are not easily answered by existing formal models. One needs to span more of the parameter space to address them, and doing this proof by proof is often inefficient.

Additionally, if one plans on testing a formal model, computational models are the glue that makes this enterprise possible.[5] Unless one is completely comfortable with point values chosen in an ad hoc fashion for the above parameters, it is necessary to span as much of the parameter space as possible, if one wants to connect formal models to empirical work. Simply put, measures have error terms, and one needs to know if one's model is immune to such perturbations.

2 COMPUTATIONAL MODELS AS AGENT-BASED MODELS

Unlike the foregoing examples, where computational models are portrayed as a systematic and efficient numerical method for extending the reach of deductive methods, computational models can also investigate problems that are intractable for deductive approaches. Many of the problems that confront the social sciences quickly become very difficult for purely deductive approaches, and it is exactly this kind of complexity that has ushered in a computational era in mathematics and the physical sciences. Faced with a choice between constructing a simple (albeit solvable) game and making a loose analogy to the real-world puzzle we are interested in, and constructing a more realistic computational model (that we can only investigate with statistics), many researchers may wish to follow the latter course. Every form of cooperation is not described by the iterated prisoner's dilemma, and every bargaining situation is not a Rubinstein game. Moreover, every political or economic agent is not able to perform backwards induction in all circumstances.

The main architecture for dealing with these sorts of complex problems is agent-based modeling. This methodology consists of agents who interact according to a set of rules instantiated by a computational algorithm. Often, agents are drawn from a set of heterogeneous types and are situated in a geographic or social structure that takes the form of a network. Agents interact with other agents, and these interactions and the agent information sets are constrained by the networks. Unlike game-theoretic models where the theorist has an end in sight and builds a model that achieves that end point in equilibrium, agent-based modeling starts with the rules and environments that govern behavior, and examines the dynamics that result from these assumptions. This kind of social science is grown from the bottom up, and more emphasis is typically placed on achieving verisimilitude with the assumptions of the

---

[5] The most prominent school of thought on this issue is the *Empirical Implications of Theoretical Models* (EITM) approach to modeling. As put forth in the original 2002 National Science Foundation report, the goal of EITM is to rework the discipline so that the chasm between formal modelers and empirical researchers is bridged, with the hopes that this synthesis will lead to better models that have clearly testable empirical hypotheses.

computational model (Palmer et al. 1994; Epstein and Axtell 1996; Arthur et al. 1997; Epstein 2006; Miller and Page 2007).

It is important to understand that in most cases these are dynamic models in which agents behave purposefully, but do not necessarily follow best response strategies nor do they necessarily choose what would be stage game equilibrium strategies. These agent-based models may produce path dependent outcomes, tipping points, self-organized criticality, or chaos, but in all cases the dynamics of how (or if) you arrive at an equilibrium is of substantive interest. Questions such as how likely the model is to achieve an equilibrium, or how sensitive that equilibrium is to small perturbations in the model, may be investigated with this approach.

Agent-based models thus offer vast possibilities, which can be both a blessing and a curse. On the one hand, agent-based models allow researchers to capture any situation or problem that can be represented in a computational algorithm. Because of this, they offer the flexibility of narrative accounts coupled with the logical consistency of analytic approaches (Holland and Miller 1991). Using more realistic assumptions and building dynamic models allows a wider range of phenomena to be investigated. One recent example is Lodge, Kim, and Taber (2004), who use a state-of-the-art-model of cognition and Annenberg data to predict voter responses to campaign events such as party conventions. In this case, the model's logical consistency enables Lodge, Kim, and Taber to use a far more interesting (and plausible) model of decision-making than is the norm, with enough transparency to see why the voters in the model react to new information in the way that they do.

A risk, as mentioned earlier, is that computational models can contain too many moving parts. The potential even exists for "rigging results" in which the modeler adds assumptions until generating a preferred result. The same critique, of course, also applies to game-theoretic models. One can produce almost any outcome (a Nash equilibrium, a particular set of dynamics, whatever) with the "right" assumptions. A difference between the two is that unlike game-theoretic models, computational models are instantiated in a programming language, and while they look like proofs, they most often contain hundreds or thousands of statements and can be difficult to assess for most researchers. Proving the robustness of a computational result is hard work and reliable methods for accomplishing this is an active research area in the field (Axelrod 1997; Miller 1998; de Marchi 2005; Laver and Sergenti 2007).

As with any methodology, proper usage requires great care and sophistication. Used properly, agent-based models offer substantial potential; nevertheless, methodological concerns exits. Below, we discuss three core concerns: *modeling agents, modeling agent interactions*, and *analyzing system behavior.* We describe how agent-based models differ from and complement mathematical models and conclude with some suggestions for how we might best leverage the strengths of agent based models to advance political science. Throughout, we will use the example of computational models of elections (following Kollman, Miller, and Page 1992; de Marchi 1999; and Laver 2005) to make our points clear.

2.1 Elections as Optimization Problems: Computational Models Used to Describe Candidate and Voter Behavior

Starting with Kollman, Miller, and Page (1992), elections have been a very active area of research in the computational modeling field. Unlike analytic models of elections, where candidates and voters use best response functions and react strategically, computational models of elections treat the problem as a nonstrategic optimization problem for voters and candidates. The electorate has preferences over platforms, but without complete information it is difficult for candidates to know which platforms are preferred. Moreover, the bulk of work on mass electorates indicates that the policy space is at least two-dimensional, and may have additional complexities such as nonseparable or nonsingle peaked preferences over some issues. The fact that candidates resort to polling, focus groups, and political consultants illustrates the immediacy of this problem in the real world, so how would one model candidate behavior?

The famous chaos results of Arrow, McKelvey, Plott, Schofield, and others indicate that, in general, there is no equilibrium, and most efforts to tame this problem have been controversial. Computational models of elections look at candidate behavior from a different perspective. If boundedly rational candidates, with limited computational ability, resources, and incomplete information, had to look for a platform, how would they do it, and what sorts of electoral outcomes would one see?

The first step in building a model of this kind is to structure mass preferences as an electoral landscape. In general terms, this means that the policy space is represented as n dimensions, and an additional dimension captures the aggregate voter utility of each platform. Visually, this electoral landscape forms a geography where high points represent advantageous platforms, and low points disadvantageous platforms. Candidates traverse this landscape with their limited resources using heuristics taken from the optimization literature, and choose the best platform they "see" given limited resources.

One such optimization technique is hillclimbing. Hillclimbing candidates look in a small neighborhood around their current platform, then change platforms to the best neighbor they find. Iterating this algorithm allows candidates to optimize locally and improve their chances in an election, but it is important to realize that local optima can trap such an algorithm. These algorithms are not strategic in a game-theoretic sense, insofar as there is no term in the optimization function for the other candidate's behavior.

This framework was extended by de Marchi (1999; 2003) to include voters with limited attention and varying levels of sophistication using Zaller's RAS model as inspiration. Laver (2005) added parties with more realistic optimization strategies, and mapped the outcomes in the computational model to data from Irish elections. Broadly, however, this class of models has demonstrated a real advantage to incumbency (which stands in contrast to game-theoretic accounts)—like Alchian's evolutionary theory of firm competition, incumbents by definition have been successful at least one time. Whether by luck or because they have a solid underlying algorithm, it is difficult for challengers to unseat them because of the problems posed by searching complicated electoral landscapes. Ensley, Tofias, and de Marchi (2007) provide empirical support for this claim using data from the US case. Thus, we have agents (in this case, candidates), rules (their optimization/search algorithms), and a system (modeled as electoral landscapes) which produces behaviors such as an incumbency advantage. With this example in mind, we will now examine each of these aspects of agent-based models in more detail.

2.2 Agents as Rule-based Objects

An agent-based model consists of a set of computational objects. An agent is defined by a vector of *state variables* along with a set of *rules*. For convenience, we can refer to both states and rules as *attributes*. It will be important to distinguish those state variables that are seen by the other agents from those that are known only to the agents themselves. We refer to the former as *external* and the latter as *internal*. Using this nomenclature, an agent's *action* and *geographic location* belong to its external state, but an agent's *preferences* belong to its internal state. The distinction between internal and external state variables need not be a bright line. An agent's private information could be internal but subsequently learned by other agents.

Agents also contain *rules*. We distinguish between three types of rules: *external rules*, *internal rules*, and *rule-changing rules*. External rules describe how an agent changes its external state variables. These rules depend on the environmental variables, the external states of other agents, and the external and internal state of the agent. For example, if we use the above example of n-party spatial competition, the external state of an agent, in this case a political party, would be the spatial location of its platform. Its external rule would be its rule for changing its platform as a function of its preferences (its internal state), its current position (its external state), the position of the other party (an external state of another agent), and the preferences of the voters over platforms (external states of still other agents).

Agents also have internal rules. These rules change the agent's internal state variables and often use the same arguments as the external state rule. In our model of political competition, a voter's internal state might include a mapping from policies to outcomes. This mapping would determine the voter's preferences. If we assume that winning parties implement their preferred policies, then voters would learn how policies map into outcomes. This learning would be an example of an internal rule. Thus, over time, the model might produce voters who update their policy mappings (Cohen and Axelrod 1984).

Finally, agents can have rule-changing rules. These meta-rules allow the agents to change their internal and external rules, allowing the system to adapt (Vriend 2000). As an example, consider a model of K communities each of which contains N agents who confront a collective action problem. Within each of these communities, agents have external rules that tell them how much to contribute as a function of how much other agents contributed. Selection could occur at the level of agent, where more successful agents reproduce at higher rates. Or selection could occur at the level of community, where more successful communities replace less successful ones. In the latter case, the external rules of the agents in one community are replaced by the external rules of agents in another community. Selection thus changes the distribution of rules that exist in the population.

2.3 Following Rules versus Maximizing Utility

In an agent-based model, the rules governing agent behavior are a focal point of the enterprise (Riolo, Axelrod, and Cohen 2001; Miller and Page 2007). Most agent-based models make no explicit reference to a payoff function. These include Schelling's Tipping Model (1978), the game of life, Axelrod's culture model (1997), Lustick's identity model (Lustick and Miodownik 2000), and some versions of Epstein and Axtell's Sugarscape model (1996). What exactly distinguishes agent-based models from game-theoretic models? On the surface, the difference is not vast. We can, for example, embed agents who use best response functions in an agent-based model. Thus, every equilibrium game-theoretic model can be written as an agent-based model. However, that agent-based model is not very interesting. If we start the model in equilibrium, it stays there. If we do not, best response dynamics often overshoot the equilibrium. Thus, to really compare rational choice models to agent-based models, we should step away from equilibrium models and consider learning models.

So, is there a difference? Let's reconsider political parties competing in a multi-dimensional issue space and compare two possible behavioral rules that an incumbent might apply in their last chance to modify their platform prior to an election. The first rule polls some sample of voters, computes the median of their ideal points, and moves the candidate's position in the direction of that median. The second rule tests a new platform by polling voters in a neighborhood of the existing platform and uses that information to adapt the platform. Both rules seem plausible empirically, yet only the second is consistent with a payoff function. Why? Because even good rules sometimes make stupid mistakes. Assume that the candidate's payoff function is to maximize its probability of winning an election (or its vote total). Consider the last platform modification prior to the election. The incumbent should choose a policy that it believes based on its information produces an expected increase in the probability of winning. With positive probability, the first rule will cause the candidate to choose a platform that it knows—based on previous polls—will do worse than its current platform. It may know this with certainty or it may expect it to be true. This can occur because the candidate is not taking into account what it has previously learned. Thus, in some cases, the first rule results in the incumbent taking an action inconsistent with a utility function. The second rule does not necessarily optimize or seek a best response to the challenger, but it will increase expected utility in all cases.

Our point is a simple one: *actors who follow purposeful rules may sometimes take actions that are not rational given a utility function approach.* Thus, a true adherent to the principles of game theory may therefore see any particular rule-based behavior as ad hoc. We disagree. In many cases, we may know the rules that people follow. And, we might add, that if other players follow rules instead of adhering to utility function-based behavior, it's not clear that following a utility function-based rule makes sense.

Our discussion at this point bears some similarity to the lengthy debate about off-equilibrium play in the centipede game (see Binmore 1996). In this game, imagine your opponent moves first, and does not employ the subgame equilibrium of ending the game—what do you do? Most game theorists would recommend that you follow the equilibrium strategy and end the game, but there is some sense (entirely justified) that playing this strategy would cost you money.

It is worth summarizing how one applies game theory to a problem. First, one needs a representation of the problems that agents confront, and ideally this encoding represents what players know at different points in the game. In game theory, this instantiation is most often an extensive form game, where the innovation of information sets provides a vehicle for understanding how knowledge impacts play. Second, one needs explicit utility functions that represent how players evaluate the outcomes of the game. Last, one needs a solution concept and an algorithm that "solves" a given problem. Game theory typically employs a Nash equilibrium (or a refinement) as the solution concept, and given an extensive form and a utility function, one can apply backwards induction to test for the existence of a Nash equilibrium.

Humans are in many ways limited or less adept than backwards inducing *homo economicus*, and it is also the case that humans typically make choices in difficult environments with limited information. Kahneman and Tversky style experiments point to our obvious flaws in relatively simple tasks; but up the ante a bit by presenting humans with more complicated games and the tables turn quite dramatically. The Ing prize in the boardgame Go, for example, offered just over one million dollars to the first computer player to beat a master level human; when the prize was discontinued in 2000, the best computer player was having difficulty beating eight-year-olds (albeit good eight-year-olds). We "outperform" rational choice players, and there is no reason to suspect that game-theoretic models have much to say about certain (complex) classes of human games and decision contexts. Thus, while computer players modeled after rational choice players have enjoyed significant success in recent years, these successes have been greatest in two-person, zero-sum games.[6]

If the goal is to model people, political parties, organizations, and nations, however, it is fair to ask if the game-theoretic approach is useful in all contexts. Few psychologists believe that utility functions underpin behavioral rules except in a loose sense. Behavior of an organization is probably not best described as optimal relative to an

---

[6] See, for example, the "Man vs. Machine" 2007 poker tournament (<http://poker.cs.ualberta.ca>). Expert humans narrowly defeated the Nash-equilibrium playing computer algorithms designed by the University of Alberta team, but significant limitations were imposed on play. The game was two-person, fixed limit hold-em; no limit, *n*-person, or more complex games such as Omaha would be vastly more challenging.

underlying payoff function but as the expression of tried and true routines and rules that are thought to produce outcomes consistent with broad goals. We do not mean to imply that game-theoretic assumptions of utility function maximization never apply, just that in many contexts, people, organizations, and nations follow rules and these rules need not be maximizing a specific utility function.

We might add that when agents represent collections of individuals, the existence of a utility function or an objective function may be problematic. Diverse preferences need not aggregate into a collective preference ordering. Overall, the premise that we might learn something by saying "here's what we think nations do, let's set those rules loose and see how they aggregate" seems as plausible as saying "here are their payoffs, let's solve for equilibrium."

To summarize, the largest differences between game theory and agent-based modeling are in how agents are characterized and in the solution concepts employed. Game theorists use deductive mathematics. Agent-based modelers use computer science and statistics. Some modelers use both techniques (Bendor, Diermeier, and Ting 2003). But there is no necessary divide between the two methodological approaches. To the extent these differences are seen as vast, it is often due to culture more than anything else.

For example, both game theorists and agent-based modelers capture selection using the replicator equation which assumes that the survival of a particular type of agent increases with its fitness relative to the average fitness in the population. Game theorists use this to solve for *evolutionarily stable strategies,* an equilibrium refinement. Agent-based modelers use the replicator dynamic to create interesting dynamic patterns. According to the replicator equation the probability of a strategy in time $(t + 1)$, p_{t+1}, is proportional to its probability in time t, p_t, times its relative fitness. Formally,

$$p_{t+1} = p_t(f_t/a_t)$$

where f_t equals the fitness of the strategy and a_t equals the average fitness in the population.

We might elevate the general mathematical proofs in this area of research above the computational based models. Were the models the same, we would, but they are not. The agent-based models tend to have more moving parts and include greater realism, and the results of agent-based models include the dynamics of the system (and not just an equilibrium, if one exists).

2.4 Networks, Spaces, Types, and Movement

Agent-based models also allow people and organizations to be placed in social structures or geographies. Cederman (2005) refers to these as *social forms.* A social form is a configuration of actors and rules for interaction along with the structures (possibly multiple) in which they are embedded. These social forms can include social networks and geography and are most commonly modeled using the tools provided by graph theory. Depending on what is being modeled, agents could potentially interact only with agents who either belong to their social network or who are geographically close, or they might only interact with other agents who are both socially connected and geographically close. Alternatively, a modeler might assume that agents have types, and that interactions are type contingent.

The existence of types, or what some call *tags*, leads to a surprising observation: *any model with agents situated in networks or in geographic space is equivalent to a model in which agents have types and interactions are type contingent.* This observation follows from the fact that an agent's type can include its location in a network. This logic also works in reverse. Types can be seen as points in geographic space. Consider for example Axelrod's culture model (1997). In that model, adjacent agents become less likely to interact the further apart their types are. If we map the agent types into Euclidean space, then this assumption becomes equivalent to saying that agents who are far apart do not interact. Type space becomes geographic space.

If geographic space can be recast as a set of types, then agents who move in space can be reconsidered as agents who change their type. Geographic location and types are thus factors in an agent's *contact structure.* The ability of agent-based models to include contingent contact structures is one of their great advantages. Consider two examples. Most mathematical models of markets assume that all economic activity takes place on the head of a pin, which lacks verisimilitude for many markets. Even in virtual markets not everyone is at the computer terminal at all times. And, in markets, distance matters. It can provide rents (Kirman 1997), for example. Similarly, mathematical models of disease often make an assumption of random mixing. These models in effect assume that some random sample of people flies to O'Hare airport. These people interact—some get the disease and some don't—then they fly home. The next week the process repeats itself. In contrast, agent-based models of disease transmission can include geographic and social networks as well as constraints on network interactions (such as flight schedules), and make more accurate predictions than previous models (Epstein et al. 2006).

These contact structures or social forms need not be hardwired into the model; rather, they can emerge from the micro-level agent interactions (Lazer 2001). Cederman's (1997) model of the emergence of nation states provides a good example of emergent contact structures, as does Lustick, Miodownik, and Eidelson's (2004) model of identity formation, Bhavnani's (2003) model of ethnic conflict, and Axelrod et al.'s (1995) model of alliances.

These networks often have empirical relevance. For example, Fowler (2006) examined the Poole and Rosenthal model and asked whether or not co-sponsorship networks mattered in predicting member roll call votes. The null hypothesis would be that they do *not* matter; it is clearly possible that NOMINATE scores explain all the systematic variance. Fowler created a measure of connectedness based on co-sponsorship (see Newman, Barabasi, and Watts 2006 for an overview). Using computational methods, he was then also able to create a visual representation of legislator behavior. Figure 4.1 displays the twenty most and least connected members of the 108th House. The pictures prove to be worth a thousand words. Fowler's empirical

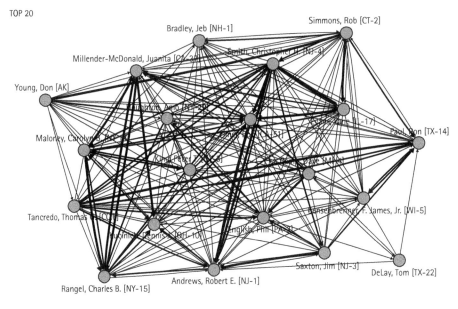

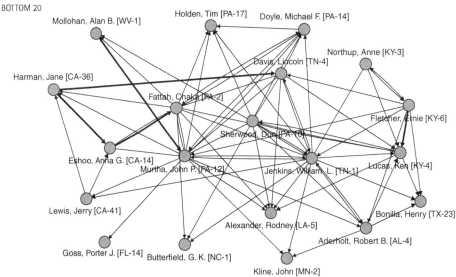

Fig. 4.1. Most and least connected legislators in the 108th House, taken from Fowler (2006). These graphs show connections between the 20 most connected and 20 least connected members of the 108th House. Connections between these two groups and the other legislators are not shown.

analysis reveals that connectedness mattered a great deal, above and beyond the information contained in the NOMINATE scores. In fact, "changing the connectedness of the sponsor by 2 SDs (e.g., from the 95th to the 50th percentile—from very high to average) would change the final passage outcome in 16 percent of the House votes and 20 percent of the Senate votes."

2.5 System Outputs: Complexity and Equilibrium

As we have mentioned, agent-based models are iterative. The modeler defines a set of agents, rules, and the framework or environment they exist in and lets it run. These micro-level interactions produce macro-level behavior in Schelling's sense. The macro-level behavior in turn alters the micro-level interactions that in turn produce new macro-level behavior. These sequences of micro to macro transitions are the output of the model, and as such, they may be investigated by statistical work that ties parameter settings to the results of the computational model through time.

These outputs may or may not be equilibria, however. Given the amount of complexity we see in the real world, we might expect social scientists to leap at the chance to use a tool that might explain or make sense of that complexity. But attachment to purely deductive, equilibrium-based modeling runs deep. The presumption of equilibrium in game-theory models by social scientists rests on strong logical foundations: namely the fixed point theorems of Brouwer and Kakutani which can be used to show that Nash equilibria exist in a wide range of circumstances. These theorems state that a nice map (a continuous function in the case of Brouwer and an upper hemi continuous correspondence in the case of Kakutani) from a nice set (bounded and topologically convex) into itself has a fixed point: a point that maps into itself. Thus, if you swirl your coffee with a wooden stick, when the motion stops at least one coffee molecule will end up in the exact same place that it started.

These theorems can be used to prove the existence of equilibria by thinking of agents' actions as functions of agents' actions. We thus have a map from the space of agents' actions into the space of agents' actions. Formally, we have a mapping from X into X. Provided the set and the map are well behaved, the system has a fixed point: a set of actions such that every agent's action is optimal given the actions of the other agents. These fixed points need not be unique. A system can produce multiple equilibria. For this reason, many analyses rely on equilibrium refinements, which are usually not justified with the same sort of rigor as the rest of the apparatus of game theory.

Proving the existence of equilibria is a helpful first step, but existence alone should not be seen as sufficient for understanding a problem. An equilibrium should also be *stable* and *attainable*. A pencil balancing on its tip is an equilibrium, but not a stable one, and it is difficult to achieve in any case. It is easier to balance a pencil on its eraser, and still easier to balance a square pencil on its side (although not a round one). Stability can be local or global. An equilibrium is *locally stable* if small perturbations in the agent's action return to the equilibrium—this will certainly be true of the square pencil balanced on its side and it is even true for very small perturbations when it is balanced on its eraser, but not on its point. An equilibrium is *globally stable* if any perturbation leads back to that equilibrium. For an equilibrium to be globally stable it must be unique, thus a pencil does not have a global equilibrium

In social science, stability must be defined relative to a behavioral rule. Any local or global equilibrium can be made stable by creating a behavioral rule that says "return to the equilibrium"—friction terms are added to many models to achieve just this purpose, but rules of this sort presume that equilibria are stable. Strict adherence to the idea that actors are self-serving would suggest instead that actors should *naively best respond,* that they take the action that maximizes their payoffs holding everyone else's action fixed. But this rule often overshoots the equilibrium. As mentioned, the prevalence of overshooting is so widespread that most agent-based models rely on a replicator dynamic or a muted best response.

If a system has multiple equilibria, then each will have a basin of attraction given a behavioral rule. For a pencil balanced on its eraser, for example, this basin of attraction is very small since it will remain balanced for only small perturbations, but for a square pencil on its side, bigger perturbations will be possible. The size of the basin of attraction gets us to the issue of attainability. Even if an equilibrium exists, and even if it is stable, it may not be easily attainable. A system with N agents each of whom can take any one of A actions has A^N possible states, that is ignoring the agents having types which influence how they interact. If we add in that each agent can have one of T types, then the system has $A^N T^N$ possible states. We should not assume that a system converges to a particular equilibrium even if it is stable. Thus, if we drop 1,000 round pencils sharpened at both ends on a frictionless surface, we should not expect that they will ever come to an equilibrium—certainly not on their tips and probably not on their sides. They will just keep rolling and rolling around.

As a thought experiment, suppose we take a game-theoretic model and construct an agent-based implementation where the agents will adapt rules with the goal of achieving a best response function. The agents may reach equilibrium. If so, the agent-based model tells us something about equilibrium selection. However, the result instead might be a pattern or a long transient. Does this mean that the agent-based model failed? No. An equilibrium need not be a vortex that attracts the agents. The dynamics created by the behavioral rules could create complex dynamics that take a long time to settle down. If the system is churning, some agents must not be doing well or there may be complex patterns of interactions between agents. The crux of the argument is that if the system is not at an equilibrium, then some agent can improve its payoff by changing its action. But these improvements are defined relative to the status quo. If a lot of agents adapt simultaneously, then not all of the adaptations need to be improving.

Thus, the existence of an equilibrium may not alone be sufficiently informative. We may also want a model that produces the equilibrium based on plausible rules detailing the agent behavior in question. Epstein (2006) refers to this as generative social science: If you didn't grow it, you didn't show it. Concepts from the differential equations/dynamic systems literatures are useful, including techniques such as a Lyapunov function. Many agent-based models with fixed rules have an associated Lyaponuv function. For example, under some assumptions, Schelling's segregation model does, as does the majority rule cellular automata model (Page 1997). Thus, we can prove theorems about the convergence to equilibrium of these agent-based models. Yet, even if we *cannot* prove a theorem, it is far better to have an agent-based model (or two or three; see Bednar and Page 2006) that produces the equilibrium, then to accept the equilibrium's attainability on faith.

3 CONCLUDING REMARKS

Most mathematical analyses of game-theoretic models do not explore the stability and attainability of their equilibria and would be made richer by complementing them with agent-based models that explored those properties. Doing so would identify models in which symmetric equilibria have small basins of attraction or are unstable. We might also identify new equilibria with large basins of attraction that can be solved for analytically. For example, Page and Tassier (2004) used a computational model to show that the Groves Ledyard mechanism had literally billions of inefficient boundary equilibria and that under some assumptions these equilibria had enormous basins of attraction. As their paper shows, the process of creating a computational version of a model forces us to confront hidden assumptions related to boundaries, symmetry, timing, and information.

Agent-based models also permit richer empirical testing. In any situation where we expect to test our model against data, it is desirable to have equivalence classes in the parameter space of our model (de Marchi 2005). If, for example, a small perturbation of any of the parameters or assumptions in our model qualitatively changes the results of the model, it is difficult to imagine we would be able to conduct meaningful empirical tests of these results. All social science data is measured with noise, and to a large degree, we must be able to depend on the results of the model subject to such noise. And as the number of parameters or assumptions in a model increases, the chances we will go wrong (i.e. there is no equivalence class in the model's parameter space) also increases—the combinatorics of ever-larger parameter spaces makes statistical examinations of the results more and more difficult. This gloomy phenomenon is appropriately named the curse of dimensionality, and it applies with equal force to all models, whether they are computational, game-theoretic, or statistical.

Mathematical theorems reveal logical implications of assumptions. If A and B are true, then so is C. Given the often unrealistic assumptions employed by social scientists, the theorems may logically follow but one cannot assume they are of substantive interest. All too often, assumptions are chosen to produce an end result; e.g. we observe warfare or strikes, so we write a bargaining model where asymmetric or imperfect information can lead to these behaviors. Unfortunately, the space of deductive models that produce any given result is infinite; something more is needed to convince us that the particular model settled upon has value. Thus, mathematical models uncover fundamental truths about mathematical objects and not about the real world. The question then becomes not what is a general truth and what is a bunch of examples, but what do we do with them? How are these models—mathematical or computational—useful? To answer these questions we have to return to the question of why we built the models in the first place.

The essence of good modeling is leaving out unnecessary details. However, ignoring important features of real-world phenomena—such as timing or geographic space or the fact that most conflicts are not dyadic—hardly counts as general. The result is only general if these limiting assumptions do not matter. And often they do. Thus, we should focus on the quality of the results and their generality, rather than the method that is employed.

Returning now to the question of usefulness, the bright-eyed person in the front row will respond that one reason we build these models is to empirically test them. A mathematical theorem may say something like *if A is true then B is larger than C*, or it may say that the coefficient on D has a positive or negative value, or it may say that the interaction term E*F has a coefficient that differs significantly from zero. Whatever empirical hypotheses the model produces, we can subject these results to empirical falsification.

Contrast this with a finding from an agent-based model. Suppose that our agent-based model always produces a given phenomenon. We do not have a formal proof that this phenomenon occurs, but this does not mean that we cannot subject the phenomenon to empirical testing (Laver 2005). Nor does it mean that the agent-based model doesn't generalize (Page 2006a). Most of our mathematical models of electoral politics consist of single-dimensional issue spaces. We might prefer having a multitude of examples in higher-dimensional spaces over an equilibrium result in one dimension. Thus, even though it is true that a theorem gives a result for infinite numbers of parameters or even functional forms, and that agent-based models can at best show something to be true for a finite number of cases, the finite cases can span substantial volume in the space of possible assumptions. In sum, if our criterion is empirical validity, the only reason that we'd place more faith in the mathematical model is the possibility of a counter-example to the agent-based model. Perhaps some future run of the model won't produce the phenomenon that we claimed to be true. If this happens, we might ask ourselves whether this makes the model any less valid if most of the time the model produces a phenomenon that also happens to occur in the real world.

Another criterion that we might use to compare agent-based models and mathematical models is whether they provide insights into social processes. Existence theorems rarely provide a lot of transparency. In contrast, an agent-based model may provide intuition. We can probe and test the model to see why it produces what it does. The effort might be especially worthwhile in those cases where a game-theory model relies upon synoptic rationality and the agent-based model makes a more limited rule-based or boundedly rational assumption. Or in cases where the game theorist assumes symmetry for convenience. If the game-theory model cannot account for the phenomenon, then we can ask (and test) whether it makes sense to presume that in this situation people would be more likely to use a simple rule rather than a complex rational calculation or if we can really presume symmetry. A third criterion we might use is how well these models help us to design institutions. Here again, we see the complementary nature of the two approaches. Mathematical models may give us general results, but we must be aware that those are mathematical and not social truths. A mathematical theorem establishes that the revenue generated by an auction does not depend on the auction rules provided that the highest valued bidder wins the object. Thus, an ascending bid auction, a first price auction, and a second price auction all yield the same revenue for the government. Experiments with human subjects and real-world tests show that the auction rules matter (Andreoni and Miller 1995; Hossain and Morgan 2006). Revenue varies depending on the auction design. Empirical regularities need not align with mathematical truth.

The ability of computational models to test the robustness of formal results would be reason alone to add them to our tool kits. But to restrict their use to be as extenders of what we can prove analytically is to ignore their potential to explore the implications of dynamic, spatial models with type-contingent interactions and diversity. Game-theoretic models must be kept analytically tractable and therefore simple. Mathematics proves most powerful when we assume one or two agents or an infinite numbers of agents. In the former case, math works because the problem is simple. In the latter, we can rely on limiting distributions and vanishing marginal effects. But mathematical analysis becomes bogged down in details when we have handfuls to hundreds of heterogeneous agents interacting in a complicated network. This space between two agents and an infinite number of agents happens to be where most social science takes place (Anderson, Arrow, and Pines 1988; Arthur, Durlauf, and Lane 1997; Miller and Page 2007).

For example, models that allow for coalitions of players to deviate are often mathematically intractable. These models lie in this region between two and infinity. If one looks at the formal literatures on bargaining, interstate conflict, or parliamentary behavior, one would come to the conclusion that all interactions are dyadic in nature. In part, this is because the *core*—outcomes for which no subset of agents can collectively improve by deviating—is often empty for interactions with more than two people. The intuition for why it is empty follows from the combinatorics of groupings. Fifty people can form over a million billion coalitions. The core treats each coalition as possible, which is why it has limited purchase. In a computational model, coalitions can emerge, but only limited numbers of them are likely given the constraints introduced by plausible behavioral rules and social or geographical networks. These models need not always focus on elites such as members of Congress. They can also focus on members of ethnic groups who choose whether or not to riot or commit acts of genocide (Backer and Bhavnani 2000; Kuran 1989).

To summarize, if we look at the world and ask ourselves whether it looks to be in equilibrium or to be complex, we cannot help but think it is complex (Jervis 1997). Yet the discipline prizes simple models, which are not likely to produce interesting, complex behavior (Page 2006b). Given that real-world complexity exists and given that we want to understand it, we should have a methodology that allows us to construct models that generate complexity. A methodology consists of both science and art. As a methodology, agent-based modeling should be seen as in its infancy, its enormous potential limited only by the scientific and creative talents of its practitioners.

REFERENCES

ANDERSON, P., ARROW, K., and PINES, D. (eds.) 1988. *The Economy as an Evolving Complex System*. Redwood City, Calif.: Addison-Wesley.

ANDREONI, J., and MILLER, J. 1995. Auctions with adaptive artificial agents. *Games and Economic Behavior*, 10: 39–64.

ARTHUR, B. 1989. Competing technologies, increasing returns, and lock-in by historical events. *Economic Journal*, 99: 116–31.

ARTHUR, W. B., DURLAUF, S., and LANE, D. 1997. *The Economy as an Evolving Complex System II*. Reading, Mass.: Addison-Wesley.

——HOLLAND, J. H., LeBARON, B., PALMER, R. G., and TAYLOR, P. J. 1997. Asset pricing under endogenous expectations in an artificial stock market. In *The Economy as an Evolving Complex System II*, ed. W. B. Arthur, S. Durlauf, and D. Lane. Redwood City, Calif.: Addison-Wesley.

AXELROD, R. 1997. The dissemination of culture: a model with local convergence and global polarization. *Journal of Conflict Resolution*, 41: 203–26.

——MITCHELL, W., THOMAS, R. E., BENNETT, D. S., and BRUDERER, E. 1995. Coalition formation in standard-setting alliances. *Management Science*, 41: 1493–508.

BACKER, D., and BHAVNANI, R. 2000. Localized ethnic conflict and genocide: accounting for differences in Rwanda and Burundi. *Journal of Conflict Resolution*, 44: 283–307.

BALLARD, D. 1997. *An Introduction to Natural Computation*. Cambridge, Mass.: MIT Press.

BARON, D., and FEREJOHN, J. 1989. Bargaining in legislatures. *American Political Science Review*, 83: 1182–202.

BEDNAR, J., and PAGE, S. 2006. Can game(s) theory explain culture? The emergence of cultural behavior within multiple games. *Rationality and Society*, 19: 65–97.

BENDOR, J., DIERMEIER, D., and TING, M. 2003. A behavioral model of turnout. *American Political Science Review*, 97: 261–80.

BHAVNANI, R. 2003. Adaptive agents, political institutions, and civic traditions in modern Italy. *Journal of Artificial Societies and Social Simulation*, 6.

BINMORE, K. 1996. A note on backward induction. *Games and Economic Behavior*, 17: 135–7.

CEDERMAN, L. E. 1997. *Emergent Actors in World Politics*. Princeton, NJ: Princeton University Press.

——2005. Computational models of social forms: advancing generative process theory. *American Journal of Sociology*, 110: 864–93.

COHEN, M., and AXELROD, R. 1984. Coping with complexity: the adaptive value of changing utility. *American Economic Review*, 74: 30–42.

DE MARCHI, S. 1999. Adaptive models and electoral instability. *Journal of Theoretical Politics*, 11: 393–419.

——2003. A computational model of voter sophistication, ideology and candidate position-taking. In *Computational Models in Political Economy*, ed. K. Kollman, J. Miller, and S. Page. Cambridge, Mass.: MIT Press.

——2005. *Computational and Mathematical Modeling in the Social Sciences*. Cambridge: Cambridge University Press.

DIERMEIER, D., and KREHBIEL, K. 2003. Institutionalism as a methodology. *Journal of Theoretical Politics*, 15: 123–44.

——and MORTON, R. 2004. Proportionality versus perfectness: experiments in majoritarian bargaining. In *Social Choice and Strategic Behavior: Essays in the Honor of Jeffrey S. Banks*, ed. D. Austen-Smith and J. Duggan. Berlin: Springer.

DURLAUF, S. 2001. A framework for the study of individual behavior and social interactions. *Sociological Methodology*, 31: 47–87.

ENSLEY, M., TOFIAS, M., and DE MARCHI, S. 2007. Electoral selection and the congressional incumbency advantage: an assessment of district complexity. Presented at the American Political Science Association meetings.

EPSTEIN, J. 2006. *Generative Social Science*. Princeton, NJ: Princeton University Press.

——and AXTELL, R. 1996. *Growing Artificial Societies: Social Science from the Bottom Up.* Cambridge, Mass.: MIT Press

——GOEDECKE, D. M., YU, F., MORRIS, R. J., WAGENER, D. K., and BOBASHEV, G. V. 2006. Pandemic influenza and the value of international travel restrictions. CSED Working Paper No. 46.

FOWLER, J. 2006. Connecting the Congress: a study of cosponsorship networks. *Political Analysis*, 14: 456–87.

——and SMIRNOV, O. 2005. Dynamic parties and social turnout: an agent-based model. *American Journal of Sociology*, 110: 1070–94.

FRÉCHETTE, G., KAGEL, J. H., and MORELLI, M. 2005. Gamson's law versus non-cooperative bargaining theory. *Games and Economic Behavior*, 51: 365–90.

GENTLE, J. 2002. *Elements of Computational Statistics*. New York: Springer-Verlag.

HOLLAND, J., and MILLER, J. 1991. Artificial agents in economic theory. *American Economic Review Papers and Proceedings*, 81: 365–70.

HOSSAIN, T., and MORGAN, J. 2006. . . . Plus shipping and handling: revenue (non)equivalence in field experiments on eBay. *Advances in Economic Analysis and Policy*, 6.

JERVIS, R. 1997 *System Effects: Complexity in Political and Social Life*. Princeton, NJ: Princeton University Press.

JUDD, K. 1997. Computational economics and economic theory: complements or substitutes? *Journal of Economic Dynamics and Control*, 21: 907–42.

——1998. *Numerical Methods in Economics*. Cambridge, Mass.: MIT Press.

KIRMAN, A. 1997. The economy as an interactive system. In *The Economy as a Complex Evolving System II*, ed. W. Arthur, S. Durlauf, and D. Lane. Reading, Mass.: Addison-Wesley.

KOLLMAN, K., MILLER, J., and PAGE, S. 1992. Adaptive parties in spatial elections. *American Political Science Review*, 86: 929–37.

——————1997. Political institutions and sorting in a Tiebout Model. *American Economic Review*, 87: 977–92.

KURAN, T. 1989. Sparks and prairie fires: a theory of unanticipated political revolution. *Public Choice*, 61: 41–74.

LAVER, M. 2005. Policy and the dynamics of political competition. *American Political Science Review*, 99: 263–81.

——and SERGENTI, E. 2007. Agent-based models of party competition: analysis and/or exploration? Presented at the American Political Science Association meetings.

——DE MARCHI, S., and MUTLU, H. 2007. Bargaining in N-party legislatures. Presented at the *American Political Science Association* meetings.

LAZER, D. 2001. The coevolution of individual and network. *Journal of Mathematical Sociology*, 25: 69–108.

LEOMBRUNI, R., and RICHIARDI, M. 2005. Why are economists sceptical about agent-based simulations? *Physica A*, 355: 103–9.

LODGE, M., KIM, S., and TABER, C. 2004. A computational model of political cognition: dynamics of candidate evaluation. Presented at the Midwest Political Science Association meetings.

LUSTICK, I., and MIODOWNIK, D. 2000. Deliberative democracy and public discourse: the agent-based argument repertoire model. *Complexity*, 5: 13–30.

—— —— and EIDELSON, R. J. 2004. Secessionism in multicultural states: does sharing power prevent or encourage it. *American Political Science Review*, 98: 209–29.

MARTIN, A., and QUINN, K. 2002. Dynamic ideal point estimation via Markov Chain Monte Carlo for the US Supreme Court. *Political Analysis*, 10: 134–53.

MILLER, J. 1998. Active nonlinear tests ANTs of complex simulations models. *Management Science*, 44: 820–30.

—— and PAGE, S. 2007. *Complex Adaptive Systems*. Princeton, NJ: Princeton University Press.

NEWMAN, M., BARABASI, A.-L., and WATTS, D. J. 2006. *The Structure and Dynamics of Networks*. Princeton, NJ: Princeton University Press.

PAGE, S. E. 1997. On incentives and updating in agent-based models. *Computational Economics*, 10: 67–87.

—— 2006*a*. Agent-based models. In *The New Palgrave Encyclopedia of Economics*, ed. S. Durlauf and L. Blume. New York: Macmillan.

—— 2006*b*. Type interactions and the rule of six. *Economic Theory*, 30: 223–41.

—— 2007. *The Difference: How the Power of Diversity Creates Better Groups, Firms, Schools, and Societies*. Princeton, NJ: Princeton University Press.

—— forthcoming. Uncertainty, difficulty, and complexity. *Journal of Theoretical Politics*.

—— and TASSIER, T. 2004. Equilibrium selection and stability for the Groves Ledyard Mechanism. *Journal of Public Economic Theory*, 6: 311–35.

PALMER, R., ARTHUR, W., HOLLAND, J., LEBARON, B., and TAYLER, P. 1994. Artificial economic life: a simple model of a stock market. *Physica D*, 75: 264–74.

POOLE, K. 2006. *Spatial Models of Parliamentary Voting*. New York: Cambridge University Press.

RIOLO, R., AXELROD, R., and COHEN, M. 2001. Evolution of cooperation without reciprocity. *Nature*, 414: 441–3.

SCHELLING, T. 1978. *Micromotives and Macrobehavior*. Toronto: George J. McLeod.

SNYDER, J. M., TING, M., and ANSOLABEHERE, S. 2005. Legislative bargaining under weighted voting. *American Economic Review*, 95: 981–1004.

STRAUSS, A. 2003. Applying integer programming techniques to find minimum integer weights of voting games. Department of Electrical Engineering and Computer Science, MIT.

STROGATZ, S. 2001. *Nonlinear Dynamics and Chaos*. Cambridge, Mass.: Perseus.

TESFATSION, L. 1997. How economists can get A-Life. In *The Economy as a Complex Evolving System II*, ed. W. Arthur, S. Durlauf, and D. Lane. Reading, Mass.: Addison-Wesley.

VRIEND, N. 2000. An illustration of the essential difference between individual and social learning, and its consequences for computational analyses. *Journal of Economic Dynamics and Control*, 24: 1–19.

WARWICK, P. V., and DRUCKMAN, J. N. 2006. The portfolio allocation paradox: an investigation into the nature of a very strong but puzzling relationship. *European Journal of Political Research*, 45: 635–65.

YOUNG, P. 2001. *Individual Strategy and Social Structure: An Evolutionary Theory of Institutions*. Princeton, NJ: Princeton University Press.

PART III

CONCEPTS AND MEASUREMENT

CONCEPTS, THEORIES, AND NUMBERS: A CHECKLIST FOR CONSTRUCTING, EVALUATING, AND USING CONCEPTS OR QUANTITATIVE MEASURES

GARY GOERTZ

1 INTRODUCTION

IN this chapter I propose to examine some issues in the evaluation of concepts and quantitative measures. These issues constitute a checklist of considerations when evaluating or constructing concepts and quantitative measures. They are important

I would like to thank Bear Braumoeller, Bruce Bueno de Mesquita, David Collier, Brad Jones, Kevin Sweeney, and Chad Westerland for comments on this chapter. I would like to also thank Scott Bennett and Eric Gartzke for responding to queries regarding the S measure.

questions that the user of concepts and measures should ask when she is planning to construct, evaluate, or use them.[1]

The issues I cover can be grouped into three large categories. The first is that all complex concepts and measures use aggregation procedures. The mathematical operations used in quantitative measures need to represent theoretical considerations on the concept side, what I call the structure of the concept. Rarely do textbooks provide a list of structural or aggregation alternatives. Yet concept and measure validity depends on why and how the dimensions or indicators are aggregated.

The second set of themes deals with important points or zones along the concept or measure scale. Frequently, zero and extreme points play a crucial role in concept and measure construction. Often certain scale points are the focus of the theory to be tested. Similarly, the gray zone in the middle is a site of contention between measures and a place of important choices when dichotomizing.

The third group of considerations deals with the question of equivalence or homogeneity within or between concepts/measures. To code two observations as the "same" reflects decisions about aggregation, zero, and extreme points (among others). Yet rarely do questions about homogeneity of measurement arise. Often one asks if two measures agree on a given observation, but rarely does one ask if one measure is appropriately coding two observations as the same.

For each issue I introduce the basic problem in its general outlines. I then provide a very short example, typically using published research. The end result (see the Checklist at the end for a summary) is a list of considerations that I think should be automatic and standard when using, constructing, and evaluating concepts and quantitative measures.[2]

2 STRUCTURE AND AGGREGATION IN CONCEPTS AND MEASURES

One of the most fundamental operations when constructing concepts and measures (by "measures" I mean henceforth quantitative measures or variables, including dichotomous ones) is that of *structure* or *aggregation*. I prefer the term structure because the concept or measure may not really be an "aggregation," but I will use both terms more or less interchangeably, typically using aggregation when the concept or

---

[1]   The choice of topics arises from work on my book *Social Science Concepts: A User's Guide* (2006). They represent issues that are almost ignored in that book (e.g. the importance of zero points) or those that deserve much more attention than they were given in the book. That book focused on concept construction and only secondarily on quantitative measures. Here I reverse the balance by tilting more toward issues of constructing quantitative measures. The distinction between the two should not be pushed too far, as we shall see many methodological problems really need to be resolved first on the theoretical and conceptual side.

[2]   It should be obvious that the checklist is not exhaustive. Rather, it consists of factors rarely considered but that should be.

measure involves individuals as parts. On the measure side one typically has to aggregate indicators. On the concept side one needs to structure defining characteristics. Hence a central question when evaluating or constructing a concept/measure is why and how this is done.

The qualitative literature on concepts and the quantitative literature on measures differ radically on the default approach to structure and aggregation. These differences reflect the origin of these literatures and where political scientists have borrowed ideas. The quantitative work on measurement—what I would call the Lazarsfeld–Blalock school—borrowed heavily and explicitly from psychology and educational statistics (see Lazarsfeld 1966 for a history). For example, current work on ideal point estimation (e.g. Bafumi et al. 2005) continues this tradition of borrowing from educational testing. The qualitative literature got its ideas from philosophical logic. For example, Sartori's classic 1970 article drew its basic idea of conceptual stretching directly from the classic Cohen and Nagel book (1934) on philosophical logic.

Perhaps the most fundamental difference between these two traditions is the standard way to structure or aggregate a measure or concept. Drawing on philosophical logic (going back to Aristotle) the qualitative literature has structured concepts in terms of necessary and sufficient conditions: Each part is necessary and all the parts together are jointly sufficient. Operationally this means taking the minimum (necessity) or the maximum (sufficiency) of the parts.[3] Quantitative approaches to aggregation most commonly use some additive procedure, either the sum or the mean. When presented with a bunch of indicators of a concept the natural first move is to add them up or take their mean.[4] The key point is that these qualitative and quantitative traditions provide different options on aggregation. Hence when considering a concept or measure one needs to ask about the aggregation technique and whether it is better and more appropriate than other alternatives.

One way to start to bridge the gulf between the qualitative and quantitative schools is to go borrowing from somewhere else. I suggest in this section that a good place to go when thinking about structure and aggregation is the literature on individual or social welfare, well-being, or happiness. This includes a wide range of theoretical and empirical studies from economics, development, psychology, and philosophy. The concepts of individual well-being and social welfare fundamentally deal with aggregation. Social welfare involves by definition aggregating, somehow or another, the welfare of individuals. Individual well-being involves aggregating the various domains of life such as health, family, work, and liberty that constitute individual well-being.

One of the first advantages of using the literature on well-being (individual or social) is that one moves away from the variable–indicator language typical of

---

[3] Davis (2005) criticizes the necessary and sufficient condition view of concepts from the qualitative perspective, but his proposal to use fuzzy logic remains in the domain of logic, albeit a twentieth-century kind.

[4] The big exception to this rule seems to be concepts that are used to collect populations of data. Here the dominant procedure is an implicit, necessary, and sufficient condition structure. Typically, a potential observation must satisfy all the coding rules (the sufficiency condition) and if it fails on one coding rule it is excluded from the population (i.e. necessity). See Sambanis's (2004) survey of civil war concepts and data-sets for examples of this.

discussions of measurement. For example, social welfare is *constituted* by the well-being of individuals in the society. The well-being of individuals is not an indicator, but a constitutive part of social welfare.

Most quantitative scholars are deeply suspicious of language involving words like "constitutive." This is seen as typical of unclear social constructivist thinking. However, the social welfare example illustrates that such language is quite natural and reasonable. For example, Amartya Sen, a prominent player in the economics, philosophy, and development literatures on individual well-being and social welfare, frequently uses this sort of language to discuss the concept of well-being:

> The well-being of a person can be seen in terms of the quality (the "well-ness," as it were) of the person's being. Living may be seen as consisting of a set of interrelated "functionings," consisting of beings and doings. A person's achievement in this respect can be seen as the vector of his or her functionings. The relevant functionings can vary from such elementary things as being adequately nourished, being in good health, avoiding escapable morbidity and premature mortality, etc., to more complex achievements such as being happy, having self-respect, taking part in the life of the community, and so on. The claim is that functionings are *constitutive* of a person's being, and an evaluation of well-being has to take the form of these constitutive elements. (Sen 1992, 39; emphasis in the original).

With such a concept of individual well-being, one must aggregate in some manner or other the various functionings into a global measure.

The literature on international conflict faces the same aggregation problem as the social welfare literature, but on a much reduced scale. Instead of the aggregation of millions of individuals into a society, we have the aggregation of two countries in a dyad. In the one case we have "social" welfare, in the other we have "dyadic" concepts of democracy, trade dependence, and the like. In the former case it is, for example, the problem of aggregating individual utilities into social ones; in the latter, it is aggregating individual levels of, say, democracy, into a dyadic concept.

Table 5.1 gives a brief survey of some common variables in the literature on international militarized conflict. Many or most of these usual suspects will appear in a large-N study of international conflict. The first question of importance when looking at dyadic concepts in this theoretical and empirical context is whether there is aggregation at all. In Table 5.1, I have marked those variables that are inherently dyadic as "relational." Some tangos require two, such as military alliance. These are not an aggregation of country-level variables. If the list in the table is representative, then about half of commonly used variables are not aggregations.[5]

The democracy variable illustrates some of the important issues linking concept theory to quantitative measures. First, it is of note that none of the aggregation measures—including the democracy variable—uses the sum or the average. Given individual democracy levels (on a scale from –10 to 10), why not do the obvious thing

---

[5] Aggregation issues can arise even in these relational variables. For example, if two countries have multiple alliance commitments then one must aggregate them to form a single dyadic alliance measure. Typically the strongest (i.e. maximum) alliance commitment is the aggregation procedure used in this case.

Table 5.1. Dyadic concepts and the study of international conflict

Dyadic concept	Sample citation	Structural relationship	Dominant structure
Democracy	Dixon (1993)	aggregation	weakest link
Trade	Gleditsch (2002)	aggregation	weakest link
Major/minor power	Mousseau (2000)	aggregation	none
Level of development	Hegre (2000)	aggregation	weakest link
Arms race	Sample (2002)	aggregation	none
Alliance	Gibler and Vasquez (1998)	relational	n.a.
Contiguity	Bremer (1992)	relational	n.a.
Power	Organski and Kugler (1980)	relational	n.a.
IGO	Oneal and Russett (1999)	relational	n.a.
Issue, territory	Senese and Vasquez (2003)	relational	n.a.

n.a.—not applicable.
Trade—level of trade dependence.
Level of development—e.g. GNP/capita.
Contiguity—geographical contiguity.
Power—military capabilities.
IGO—memberships in intergovernmental organizations.
Territory—conflict is over territory.

Source: Goertz (2006, 133).

and take the average? Some early work did in fact use some variation on the mean.[6] However, Dixon (1993) made a strong theoretical case that it was the least democratic of the dyad that determined the impact of democracy in the dyad as a whole. The "weakest-link" approach quickly became the standard used in the vast majority of studies on the liberal peace. Others, notably Russett and Oneal (2001), have extended this logic to the trade dependency variable, and Hegre (2000) has used it for the level of development variable.

The democracy variable illustrates that in good research there is a strong theory of the dyadic concept (e.g. dyadic democracy) which is used to the structure of the quantitative measure. One can contrast the strong theory of the democracy variable with another usual suspect, major power status. This variable is my candidate for most popular and least theorized of the common international conflict variables. It seems that about half of the time this is coded as "at least one major power" (i.e. maximum) and about half the time as "both major powers" (i.e. minimum). If one is constantly asking the question "what structure" and "why" then it is less likely that scholars will automatically include such undertheorized variables.

The trade dependency variable is a good example where different structures are used, but these are based on good theoretical positions (which may or may not be

---

[6] Maoz and Russett (1993) use the formula $Dem_{ij} - ((Dem_h + Dem_l)/(Dem_h - Dem_l + 1))$ where Dem_h is the maximum democracy score and Dem_l is the minimum. This is interesting because it is basically a measure of how spread apart the two regime types are. This suggests one potential aggregation category based on the idea of variance; measures of inequality would fall into this category. See Bennett (2005) for another measure of spread between regime types.

born up in empirical analyses). For example, Barbieri (2002) has made a strong case for using the geometric mean as a measure of the salience of trade relationships. Here we have a case where differences between quantitative measures reflect real theoretical differences.

Returning to the literature on individual and social welfare, we can see that the structure question is very much about the weighting of the individual parts. Just as the weakest-link measure of dyadic democracy gives determining weight to the least democratic country, so do various theories of justice give differing weights to individuals in society. For example, theories of (social) justice have very large and direction implications for the measurement of social welfare. A Rawlsian theory puts tremendous weight on the individuals who are least well off in aggregating to the social level. A utilitarian theory in contrast gives every individual equal weight in determining social welfare. As with the dyadic democracy variable, it is a theory (in this case a normative one) that determines the weighting of the individual parts. Often we have weak theory and that results in the equal weighting of the sum or average. However, when we have stronger theory that can often lead to unequal weighting.[7] It is the philosophy of justice and welfare that determines the weighting used in any eventual quantitative measure. A wide variety of aggregation techniques have been used to implement a theory of social welfare, e.g. sum maximization (Harsanyi 1955), lexicographic priorities and maximin (Rawls 1971; Sen 1977), equality (Foley 1967; Nozick 1974; Dworkin 1981), or one of various other combining rules (Varian 1975; Suzumura 1983; Wriglesworth 1985; Baumol 1986; Riley 1987). It is because of the variety of aggregation procedures used that I have suggested the well-being and social welfare literature as a source of inspiration for thinking about how the theory embodied in concepts can be implemented in various quantitative measures.

One concept and aggregation problem Paul Diehl and I have wrestled with over the last ten years is that of the severity of a militarized interstate rivalry (Diehl and Goertz 2000). Here we see the problem of aggregation over time since a rivalry by definition is characterized by a series of militarized interactions. One question is how to aggregate those interactions into a measure of rivalry severity at any given time. One obvious option would be a weighted average of all the previous actions, with each observation exponentially discounted by its elapsed time to the present (basically this is the Crescenzi and Enterline 2001 proposal). I have recently been intrigued by prominent findings in the psychological literature on happiness. Rivalry deals with emotions and feelings of hatred, while happiness deals with the opposite, but both face the same aggregation problem. A prominent finding due to Kahneman and his colleagues (e.g. Kahneman et al. 1993; Kahneman 1999; Oliver 2004) is that current happiness follows a "peak-end" aggregation rule. Basically, current happiness is the average of the happiness at $t - 1$ (i.e. "end") and the maximum happiness (i.e. "peak") over the relevant time period.

---

[7] Sometimes scholars think that by using necessary condition aggregation that no weighting is used. This is clearly incorrect; for an example of this confusion see King and Murray's (2002) measure of "human security." This measure is closely related to work on social welfare.

This is an interesting hybrid structure for a concept/measure: It uses both the average and the maximum. It means that most past periods receive no weight at all, which is the impact of the maximum. It implies that exponential memory models are dramatically off since the peak experience remains very important and shows little decay. I have no idea whether this would make sense for dyadic relationships between states, but it is an interesting aggregation option that I have permanently added to my tool kit.

This brief section on structuring and aggregating concepts and measures suggests that one must first consider the theory embodied in the concept. Then one should survey plausible aggregation and structural relationships that could be applied in a quantitative measure. A key issue throughout is the nature of the weighting scheme implied by the theory and implemented by the measure.

3 ZERO POINTS

The zero point often plays an important role in theoretical and methodological research programs. As prospect theory and our checkbooks show, there is a major difference between positive and negative. Methodologically the existence of zero points has many important implications. A long article could easily be written on zero points; I would like to discuss an example that illustrates some key issues that users of concepts and measures should be asking about when constructing and evaluating measures.

Let me start with a personal anecdote. The zero point plays a large role in some expected utility theories of international conflict. For example, Bueno de Mesquita's (1981) main hypothesis was that a *negative* expected utility was a necessary condition for war initiation. As a result he needed a measure of preferences and utilities that had a zero point. He developed what is known as the τ_b measure of preferences (because it is uses the τ_b statistical measure of association). When Joe Hewitt and I were looking for a measure of "willingness" to initiate a militarized conflict we immediately thought of the τ_b measure. A negative τ_b would be a signal of hostile relationships and hence a willingness to initiate militarized conflict (other factors such as weakness might prevent a country from acting on this willingness). Operationally, willingness was then a negative τ_b score for a dyad.[8]

We first presented this paper at a Peace Science Conference and Bueno de Mesquita was in the audience. In the question period he remarked that we misused his τ_b measure. The reason was that the "nominal" zero in the data (e.g. produced by the EUgene software) was not the "true" zero. The true zero point varies with system size and corresponds to a negative nominal value. As system size goes to infinity the

---

[8] Most often τ_b or S is used as a control variable and hence there are no real theoretical claims regarding it, e.g. Fortna (2003) or Pevehouse (2004).

nominal zero approaches the true zero at zero. The story ends happily with Bueno de Mesquita working with us to develop the appropriate modifications (Goertz 2006, ch. 8).

This anecdote has a number of important lessons.

The first lesson is to ask whether the theory in question does in fact need a zero point. In most uses of τ_b (or its competition S: Signorino and Ritter 1999; see Sweeney and Keshk 2005 for a bibliography of uses of S and τ_b) these measures are treated as interval ones.[9] The zero point plays no role since the hypothesis is usually of the form, the less similar the preferences the more likely war or military conflict. This correlational hypothesis does not require a zero since it only proposes that increasing probability of war with decreasing preference similarity. In this sense Bueno de Mesquita's (e.g. 1981) and our explicit use of the zero point is relatively rare. The moral is that one needs to ask whether zero plays a role in the theory and hence matters in the measure.

The second lesson is that one should ask whether the measure in fact has a zero point. The main alternative to τ_b is the S measure (Signorino and Ritter 1999): Does it have a zero point? If you examine the data as generated by EUgene you would say yes, because the data range from -1 to 1. However, if you look at how the data are generated, the answer is not so obviously yes. Here is a simplified version of the S measure (see Signorino and Ritter 1999 and Sweeney and Keshk 2005 for more details):

$$S_{ij} = 1 - 2 \left(\frac{\sum_{i=1}^{N} |fpp_i - fpp_j|k}{N} \right). \tag{1}$$

The last step in the measure-generating process consists of $1 - 2(\cdot)$ which standardizes the measure into the $[-1,1]$ interval.[10] This is an arbitrary scale transformation so the resulting zero is not a real one. As one can easily see, the range of the substantive part of the measure is $[0,1]$. Instead of zero being a middle point it is in fact an extreme point. For example, Gibler and Rider (2004) use $[0,1]$ S data, which implies that they do not see a zero point in the middle. The second lesson is thus that just because the scale of the measure has zero values does not mean it is a real zero.[11]

This leads to the third lesson: What is the measurement theory that determines the zero point? Recall that Bueno de Mesquita told us that the nominal zero was not the true zero. He must therefore have had a measurement theory about alliance

---

[9] An interesting question is the extent to which this is an issue for Gartzke's (1998) measure of "affinity" which uses Spearman's rank order correlation. Like τ_b this ranges from -1 to 1.

[10] In equation (1) fpp is the "foreign policy preference," k is a standardization parameter which makes the absolute difference in foreign policies range from zero to one. The N in the denominator then makes this the average difference in foreign policies.

[11] For example, many people rescale the polity measure of democracy (Jaggers and Gurr 1995) from its original $[-10,10]$ to $[0,20]$. As an exercise for the reader, I ask whether the zero in either of these ranges could be considered a true zero? A true zero can of course be the lowest or the highest point on a scale. See Bennett (2005) for a variety of examples where the scaling of the polity measure is important. See Beck et al. (2004, 382) who treat the polity scale as ratio.

configurations that he used to determine the true zero point. So one needs always to ask about the theory that determines how to measure the zero point.[12]

Braumoeller (2004) and Brambor, Clark, and Golder (2006) have brought the attention of the political science public to the fact that there are many easy-to-fall-into pitfalls in the use of interaction terms. One important implication of the presence or absence of a zero point is exactly the role ratio variables play in interaction terms.

One issue in interaction term analysis lies in the interpretation of the individual terms of the interaction term, e.g. $\beta_1 X_1$ and $\beta_2 X_2$. Typically, the interpretation is that β_1 is the impact of X_1 when $X_2 = 0$. This then assumes obviously that $X_2 = 0$ really means something. If X_2 is an interval variable then $X_2 = 0$ is completely arbitrary (see Friedrich 1982 and Allison 1977). For example, Gibler and Rider (2004) use S in interaction with level of threat to study alliance reliability. Since level of threat is always greater than zero, it could make a significant difference if S is seen to have a true zero.

In a related manner, standardization of variables with mean zero is common. For example, Beck, King, and Zeng (2004) do this for all the variables in their neural net analysis. These standardized variables are then used in a large variety of interaction terms.

In summary, one needs to ask about the existence or not of zero points. Does the theory need them? Does the use of the variable in interaction terms and the like imply that there is a true zero point?

4 EXTREME POINTS AND IDEAL TYPES

The ideal-type way to construct concepts has a long and distinguished history. In the social sciences it is Max Weber (1949) who made a prominent case for this procedure (e.g. see Burger 1987 for a discussion). While scholars often use ideal types to construct concepts (e.g. Gunther and Diamond 2003), treatment of the methodology of ideal types is almost completely absent from textbooks. We lack analyses of how to construct an ideal type, or what constitutes a good ideal type. In spite of this, one can discern two distinctive characteristics of ideal types as they appear in nature: (1) the ideal type is an extreme point on the continuum, and (2) actual cases of that extreme are rare or nonexistent.

I have argued elsewhere (Goertz 2006, ch. 3) that ideal-type concepts are not really useful once one has a coherent system for constructing concepts. However, the idea of an ideal type does raise an important theoretical and methodological question

---

[12] For example, Sweeney and Keshk (2005) note that if the number of categories used in constructing S increases, the measure moves toward 1. The same is true as the system size increases. Hence, there may be other comparability concerns beyond the existence or not of a zero point.

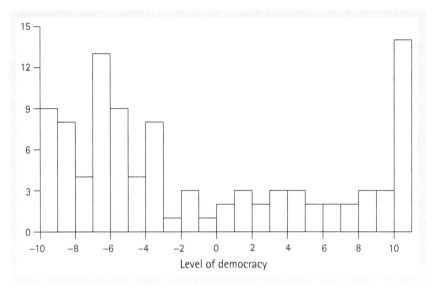

Fig. 5.1. Distribution at extreme points: polity democracy measure

that must be attended to when evaluating and constructing concepts: What is the distribution of cases at the ideal point extreme? Ideal-type concepts are characterized by zero cases at the extreme: Is that a good, bad, or indifferent characteristic? One can ask the contrasting question: Is it good, bad, or indifferent if there are a lot of cases at the extreme?

Figure 5.1 shows the distribution of polity democracy scores (Jaggers and Gurr 1995) for all countries 1816–1999. You will see a high spike at the democracy extreme. When I see a histogram like this my first reaction is to think that the "true" scale really extends further. Because the measure stops too soon we get a piling up cases at the barrier (Gould 1996).[13]

Looking at the polity scores for the United States might confirm the feeling that the scale stops too soon. Beginning in 1870 the United States always receives the maximum score of 10. However, the fact that large parts of the population—e.g. blacks, hispanics, Indians—in some regions, notably the South and Southwest, were either *de jure* or de facto prevented from voting after 1870 suggests that a country could be more democratic than the United States.

The moral here is that one needs to examine the distribution of cases at the extremes. "Ideal typish" concepts and measures with few cases at the extreme might often be a good goal. If our temperature scale maxed out at 100 degrees we would be mismeasuring a lot of temperatures as 100. While not necessarily conclusive evidence against a measure, large concentrations at either extreme need to be consciously justified, not accepted as "that is just what happens when you code the data."

---

[13] See the histograms in Sweeney and Keshk (2005, e.g. figures 3 and 4) for other examples of large spikes at one extreme for the *S* measure.

Table 5.2. Disagreement in the gray zone: level of democracy in Costa Rica, 1901–10

Year	Polity IV	Vanhanen	Gasiorowski	BLM
1901	100	0	0	0
1902	100	0	0	50
1903	100	0	0	50
1904	100	0	0	50
1905	100	0	0	0
1906	100	1	0	0
1907	100	1	0	50
1908	100	1	0	50
1909	100	1	50	50
1910	100	1	50	50

All measures have been rescaled onto the [0,100] interval.

Source: Bowman, Lehoucq, and Mahoney (2005).

5 THE GRAY ZONE

When comparing various concepts and measures one usually finds that correlation coefficients are used to assess similarity. This procedure often dramatically underestimates the dissimilarity of measures. One reason for this is that observations at the ends of the spectrum usually have more weight (in statistical terms, more leverage; Belsley, Kuh, and Welsh 1980) than those in the middle. It is often the case that concepts and measures agree on the extreme cases since they are clear-cut and easy to code, while at the same time disagreeing frequently on cases in the middle. Points in the middle often have a "half fish, half fowl" character that makes them hard to categorize and classify. I call this area the gray zone, because values in it are neither black nor white.

Democracy is a concept where the gray zone often plays a large role in various theoretical contexts ranging from the war-proneness of transitional democracies (e.g. Mansfield and Synder 2002) to successful democratic transitions (e.g. Linz and Stepan 1996). Costa Rica has long been seen as one of the most democratic countries in Latin America. As Table 5.2 illustrates, prominent measures differ significantly on how they code Costa Rica in the crucial first decade of the twentieth century.

When there is a significant number of cases in the gray zone using a correlation coefficient as a measure of similarity can wildly underestimate discrepancies between measures. For example, take the democracy data in Figure 5.1. If one takes the cases at extreme values (i.e. −10 and 10) as given which consists of 23 percent of the data, and then replaces all the observations in between with *independent, random,* and

Table 5.3. Systematic disagreement in the gray zone

X_1	X_2					
	0	1	2	3	4	5
0	50	10	0	0	0	0
1	0	50	40	40	0	0
2	0	0	50	50	40	0
3	0	0	0	50	40	0
4	0	0	0	0	50	10
5	0	0	0	0	0	50

uniform data one still gets a correlation coefficient of almost .5. In short, there can exist extensive disagreement between measures in the gray zone and one can still get quite respectable correlation coefficients.

Suppose that the relationship between the two measures is like that of Table 5.3 (see Goertz 2006, ch. 3 for an example with real data). There is excellent agreement on the extremes but substantial disagreement in the middle. Yet a high correlation of .87 masks differences between the two. Notably measure X_1 is always less than measure X_2 (these kinds of triangular data patterns are not uncommon in comparative research; see also Bennett 2005, figure 1 for a triangular relationship between two dyadic democracy variables). But because a large percentage of observations do lie on the diagonal one will get substantial correlations. This example suggests that there may not only be disagreement on the middle zone, but there is a pattern to that disagreement.

Patterns of disagreement like those of Table 5.3 suggest that the *variance* between two measures changes systematically as one moves away from the extremes and toward the middle. The change in variance is driven once again by agreement at the ends and disagreement in the middle.

Figure 5.2 charts the changes in variance when comparing the polity concept and measure of democracy (Jaggers and Gurr 1995) with Freedom House's concept and measure (Karantycky 2000). To do this I added the scores of the Freedom House variables "political rights" and "civil liberties" which each range from 1 to 7. I then converted them to a −10 to 10 scale which then matches the polity scale. Figure 5.2 gives the variance of the polity scores for all cases where the Freedom House codes a nation-year at a certain level.

We see then at the extremes of autocracy and democracy (i.e. −10 and 10) there is very little variance in polity codings when the Freedom House sees an extreme autocracy or democracy. For example, on the X-axis we see that there is almost no variance in the polity measure cases when the Freedom House codes a maximal democracy (i.e. 10). As we move toward the gray zone in the middle we see that the variation in how polity codes a given nation-year increases significantly: As we move from 10 to 0 the variance increases 1,000-fold from .025 to 22.6. The same

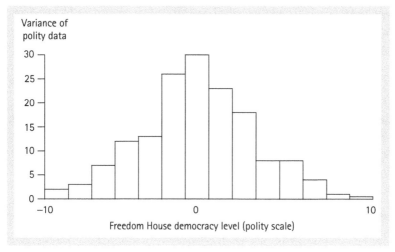

Fig. 5.2. Variance and disagreement in the gray zone

sort of thing happens from the autocracy side, though the increase is "only" by a factor of 10.[14]

A lesson here is that one needs to use multiple criteria to evaluate concepts and measures. In particular, the gray zone needs to be examined independently of the two extremes. Table 5.3 and Figure 5.2 illustrate two patterns that might be quite common. Table 5.3 shows a triangular relationship between measures, while Figure 5.2 shows increasing variance as one moves toward the gray zone.

We need a greater variety of techniques for evaluating concepts and measures. In particular one needs to look closely at particular parts of the concept continuum. This will depend on the theory and hypotheses being tested, but in general the extreme points and the middle always deserve special attention.

6 HOMOGENEITY BETWEEN AND WITHIN CONCEPTS AND MEASURES

A key issue in the analysis of individual concepts as well as the comparison of two or more concepts or measures, is what Przeworski and Teune (1970) called "functional equivalence" or what I prefer to call "concept homogeneity" (Gerring and Thomas 2005 talk about "comparability"). Within a concept or measure one assigns the same value to a potentially large number of observations. The concept

[14] I leave it as an exercise to re-evaluate Przeworski et al.'s (2000, 58–9) argument that their dichotomous coding of democracy produces less error than a continuous measure if error follows the variance as illustrated in Figure 5.2 and the cut point between democracy and autocracy is zero.

homogeneity question is whether all these observations are really instances of the same thing. For example, is the United States receiving a polity score of 10 in 1950 homogeneous or equivalent to its receiving a value of 10 in 2000? The key question in terms of constructing and evaluating concepts and measures then is the degree to which codings within a measure or between measures agree on coding observations as the same.

The homogeneity issue arises as a direct consequence of aggregation. In short, aggregation procedures produce homogeneity claims. For example, in the polity democracy measure there are a variety of ways to get, say, 5. The homogeneity claim is that all these ways are *substitutable* or *equivalent* in terms of causal analyses.

Table 5.3 illustrates the problem with concepts and measures of democracy for Costa Rica. All measures are homogeneous for the years 1909 and 1910. They see the level of democracy being the same for those two years. This is homogeneity *between* concepts, or "relative homogeneity." Posner (2004, 851) remarks that a problem with the Herfindahl index (used to study the impact of ethnic fractionalization) is that it gives quite different fractionalizations the same value. This is homogeneity *within* a measure. These are both important criteria for evaluating concepts and measures.

It is important to note that concept homogeneity is different than examining the extent to which measures or concepts agree on a given observation. For the years 1909–10 all the measures are homogeneous but they disagree radically on the level of democracy. While the degree of agreement on level is certainly correlated with the degree of homogeneity, they are conceptually separate criteria of evaluation.

Figure 5.2 directly assesses the degree of relative homogeneity of the polity and Freedom House measures of democracy. For each level of Freedom House democracy we can determine how homogeneous the polity measure is relative to Freedom House. If the polity measure and data coded democracy homogeneously with regard to Freedom House then the variance of the polity scores would be zero: In other words, polity would code the same value and the variance would be zero. Notice here we are looking at the variation of the scores, not their level. It is possible—if very unlikely—that the level is not the same. In Figure 5.2 we see that when Freedom House codes observations as completely democratic then it is almost certain that polity codes them at the same level. However, once we move into the gray zone the degree of relative homogeneity declines precipitously.

In short, homogeneity is another aspect of comparing within and between various concepts and measures of the same phenomenon. As the comparison of polity with Freedom House illustrates, the degree of relative homogeneity between measures can vary significantly along the continuum from the negative pole to the positive. Looking at the polity scores for the United States over time might suggest that there are homogeneity concerns within the polity measure. Homogeneity comparisons between and within concepts and measures should become standard practice when evaluating different concepts and measures.

7 HOMOGENEITY OF NEGATIVE
OR ZERO CASES

··

We have seen that the zero point can play a key role in constructing and evaluating concepts. The zero *category* can be problematic from a homogeneity perspective, especially for dichotomous variables. Frequently the zero category is a catch-all for all observations that are "not 1." For example, Mahoney and I (2004) have analyzed this problem in the context of choosing the population of "negative" cases, which typically receive zero in a dichotomous coding, e.g. nonsocial revolutions. Sweeney and Keshk (2005) have discussed the same problem in the context of the S measure. In one application of S they use militarized dispute data coded dichotomously. They wonder about the very many zeros (i.e. no dispute) in the data since "the large number of zeros in the MID data may be due to the fact that countries did not have anything to fight about or because they chose to settle any possible conflicts in nonmilitarized ways (expressions of foreign policy preferences), or the large number of zeros may be due to the fact that countries could not engage in MIDs because they were too far apart and did not interact in any way that would give rise to the possibility of a MID (most assuredly not a foreign policy preference revelation)" (Sweeney and Keskh 2005, 174). Similarly, Goertz, Jones, and Diehl (2005) have argued that periods of zero militarized conflict after the end of a rivalry are not homogeneous as they are typically considered in "repeated conflict" studies (e.g. Werner 1999). The first fifteen years or so after the last militarized conflict are different because the rivalry is ending and there is still a possibility of further conflict. However, after those fifteen years the rivalry is over and the dyad drops out of the data-set. In repeated conflict studies the dyad remains in until the end of the period, typically 2001. Hence, Goertz et al. see heterogeneity in the zeros of repeated conflict studies. Thus in a variety of settings, the homogeneity of the "no dispute/war" observations can be called into question.[15]

The Przeworski et al. (2000) analysis of the causes and consequences of democracy illustrates the nature of the problem. Their dichotomous concept of democracy uses the necessary condition aggregation procedure on four dichotomous components. Their concept of democracy states that if a country has a zero value (dichotomously) on any one of the four components, then the country is coded as a nondemocracy. Democracy can be achieved in only one way (i.e. a one on all four components), whereas nondemocracy can occur in fifteen different ways (i.e. $2^4 - 1 = 15$).

The homogeneity hypothesis then becomes the question whether these fifteen different ways of being a nondemocracy have the same consequences for causal inference when introduced into analysis. For example, when assessing the consequences of

---

[15] A potentially useful statistical technique for dealing with the heterogeneity of zeros is Zero-Inflated Poisson (ZIP) regression (e.g., Chin and Quddus 2003). Zeros are modeled to arrive through a "zero-event" state, i.e. where the event basically cannot happen, or through a state where $n > 0$ events can occur.

nondemocracy on fertility rates, as Przeworski et al. (2000) do, can we assume that a country that has zero value on only one of the components is causally equivalent to a country that has a zero value on all four components?

Przeworski et al.'s first analysis of the relationship (2000, 81) between the level of economic development and democracy is a probit analysis with a variety of independent variables which are prominent in the literature. As an exercise, we can examine the homogeneity of the nondemocracy codings and its impact on causal inference using Przeworski et al.'s data and methods.

Given the necessary condition aggregation procedure used, we can easily rank in the zeros in terms of the number—1–4—of components that are equal to zero. One can then empirically evaluate whether the assumption of the conceptual homogeneity of zeros seems confirmed in causal analysis. Since I am also interested in comparing measures, it is useful to take a democracy measure with a structure analogous to Przeworski et al.'s for this exercise.[16]

The "modified polity" measure is one with three dimensions, "Competitiveness of Participation," "Executive Recruitment," and "Constraints on Executive" (see Goertz 2006, ch. 4 for details). The first two dimensions correspond to the two higher-level dimensions of the Przeworski et al. view of democracy which are "Contestation" and "Offices;" the former refers to multiple parties and executive turnover and the latter refers to executive and legislative offices being filled by contested elections.[17] As I have reformulated the polity measure we have three dichotomous dimensions and I require that all three be present for a country to be coded as a democracy. So structurally we have the same basic logic for the Przeworski et al. measure and the modified polity. We also have the same potential problem with the homogeneity of the nondemocracy cases, which can be zero on 1, 2, or 3 dimensions.

As is commonly reported, the correlation between the modified polity and Przeworski et al. measure of democracy is high at .87. Przeworski et al. (2000, 56–7) say that the standard polity measure predicts 91 percent of Przeworski et al. values. If it were not for the above sections, I might claim that since correlations are high the measures are basically the same. Table 5.4 shows that in spite of a .87 correlation when using the modified polity data in Przeworski et al.'s analysis of the causes of democracy, some important differences appear. The first column of Table 5.4 replicates the probit analysis discussed in Przeworski et al. (p. 81).[18] Some variables, notably the key level of development variable, are very similar with both measures of democracy. However, about half of the variables differ significantly in sign or significance level, i.e. Stratification, Catholic, Moslem, and Ethnic Fraction(alization); consistent results show up for Development, New

[16]   The standard polity measure is a weighted average of the five indicators, hence I have preferred to use a modified polity measure with the same logical structure as the Przeworski et al. one.

[17]   The polity measure is unique in its incorporation of constraints on the executive as a core part of the democracy concept. In fact, it is the most heavily weighted of the five indicators used; see Munck and Verkuilen (2002) for a discussion.

[18]   The variable RELDIF—religious fractionalization—is not in the data-set for the book so it does not appear.

Table 5.4. Causal homogeneity of nondemocracy: *democracy and development*

Variable	Przeworski	Polity	Modified Polity Measure		
			One zero	Two zeros	Three zeros
Intercept	−2.7976	−2.0734	.1729	−2.0839	−12.6123
$(Pr > X^2)$	.0001	.0001	.6817	.0001	.0001
Development	.0003	.0003	.0002	.0004	.0018
$(Pr > X^2)$	.0001	.0001	.0001	.0001	.0001
New Colony	−.8490	−1.2740	−3.7547	−1.1456	−11.4318
$(Pr > X^2)$	.0001	.0001	.0001	.0001	.9998
British Colony	1.0167	1.2703	3.4428	1.4706	10.2029
$(Pr > X^2)$	.0001	.0001	.0001	.0001	.9998
Stratification	−.0000	−.1420	−.2386	−.1372	∞^a
$(Pr > X^2)$	.9996	.0018	.0004	.0112	−
Catholic	.0038	−.0004	−.0058	.0000	−.0366
$(Pr > X^2)$	.0005	.7336	.0206	.9951	.0103
Protestant	.0025	.0043	−.0049	.0070	.4853
$(Pr > X^2)$	1028	.0131	.0707	.0010	.0001
Moslem	−.0038	−.0013	.0003	−.0005	.0225
$(Pr > X^2)$	.0030	.3448	.8879	.7571	.0001
Ethnic Fraction	.0163	.0709	−.7415	−.0517	8.4373
$(Pr > X^2)$	.3242	.0472	.0001	.2843	.0001
Global Democracy	4.0812	1.9914	1.1357	1.8348	14.7266
$(Pr > X^2)$	.0001	.0003	.1587	.0031	.0001
N of nondemocracy	2120	1738	346	1258	134

^{a}Results are basically the same when removing the Stratification variable except for the Catholic variable, which changes signs.

Colony, British Colony, and Protestant. Here is then yet another example of how high correlations can mask significant differences, this in the estimation of causal impacts.

The rest of the columns of Table 5.4 examine the impact of homogeneity assumptions of the negative cases. Each of these columns uses a different population of negative cases; for example, "one zero" means that for the negative cases one of the modified polity dimensions is zero but the other two are one. Hence, these negative cases are closer to democracy than the negative cases used in "three zeros" which have zero on all three polity dimensions. The cases of one on the dependent variable remain the same in all of these analyses but the number of zeros varies from column to column (they are given at the bottom of each column).

The probit results in the "one zero" column represent what might be called the "most similar" analysis. These are the negative cases most similar to the positive ones because they are missing only one dimension of democracy. Space constraints prohibit an extensive comparison, but one can look at three things when comparing across columns: (1) sign changes, (2) significance level changes, (3) trends, increasing or decreasing, in parameter estimates. Comparing the "polity" to the "one zero" columns we see that the central economic development variable is consistent. However, the Catholic variable which was insignificant in the polity column is now significantly negative. Overall, four variables vary in important ways between the two columns: Catholic, Protestant, Ethnic Fractionalization, and Global Democracy (ODWP in the Przeworski et al. naming scheme).

When moving further away from democracy by examining the population with two zeros constituting the negative population, we can see a pattern forming that some variables are robust while others are not. Once again the economic Development is very important along with the New Colony, British Colony, and Stratification variables. Again, the religion variables—i.e. Catholic, Protestant, and Moslem, and ethnicity—move a lot.

Moving to the least similar countries—i.e. those with zero on all three dimensions—we see very clear-cut results. All the variables are very important. In fact Stratification is a perfect predictor.[19] All the religion variables are now significant. Hence when we choose the most contrasting set of negative cases we clearly see the impact of variables which are sometimes ambiguous in other comparisons.

Of course, the numbers in Table 5.4 only provide a quick first look at the question of concept homogeneity in a causal setting. A variety of other analyses would be useful in an extended analysis. For example, one might want to run a Poisson or negative binomial regression on the number of zeros for the nondemocracy cases. This would give some idea of the extent to which the independent variables can distinguish between various kinds of nondemocracies. One would want to think about how dramatic and clear the findings tend to be when only using complete nondemocracies; the stratification variable in the "three zeros" column in Table 5.4 perfectly predicts the outcome, though here the small N of nondemocracies may be part of the story.[20]

8 CHECKLIST

When structuring and aggregating concepts and measures there are three related sets of items on a checklist for constructing or evaluating concepts and measures.

- What is the theory embodied in the concept?
- How is that theory translated into a quantitative measure?
- What are the plausible options for aggregation? In particular, what is the weighting scheme to be used?

---

[19] Some software, e.g. Stata, automatically removes these very important variables because of technical problems in statistical estimation. I prefer to include them and indicate their importance with parameter estimates of "∞."

[20] It is striking how the stratification variable was not significant when using the Przeworski et al. democracy variable but was consistently important using the modified polity measure.

In addition to overall evaluations of various concepts and measures, one needs to investigate individual parts or points of the scale or concept continuum.

- Are there big spikes at either extreme? Does that suggest extending the scale?
- Is there a zero point? Does the theory under examination need a zero point?
- Does the zero point or lack thereof play a role in the creation or interpretation of interaction terms?
- What is the theory that determines the zero point?
- What is going on in the gray zone? Is that zone crucial for theory testing?

All concepts and quantitative measures imply homogeneity claims. These need to be investigated.

- When comparing measures are there zones where homogeneity is low (e.g. gray zone)?
- Does homogeneity vary in a systematic manner across the continuum?
- If the measure or concept is dichotomous are there significant concerns about the homogeneity of the negative or zero cases? Should some zeros be removed from the data-set?
- Do concept homogeneity concerns appear in causal analyses? Are some variables more robust in the face of heterogeneity than others?

Of course this checklist is not exhaustive. It is a list of concerns which rarely make it into methodology and research design textbooks and courses. I have tried to illustrate briefly how these issues can arise in common data-sets and concepts. Of course, a lot will depend on the specific theory and hypothesis under investigation. This chapter stresses that it is the lack of integration of theory and methodology which proves problematic. In particular this is true of aggregation and structure problems. Typically they arise because numeric measures are not closely enough tied to the theories they are supposed to embody. The same is true of many of the issues surrounding zero points. In short, one needs continually to ask whether the numeric measures are really doing what the concepts and theories prescribe.

References

ALLISON, P. 1977. Testing for interaction in multiple regression. *American Journal of Sociology*, 83: 144–53.

BAFUMI, J., et al. 2005. Practical issues in implementing and understanding Bayesian ideal point estimation. *Political Analysis*, 13: 171–87.

BARBIERI, K. 2002. *Liberal Illusion: Does Trade Promote Peace?* Ann Arbor: University of Michigan Press.

BAUMOL, W. 1986. *Superfairness.* Cambridge, Mass.: MIT Press.

BECK, N., KING, G., and ZENG, L. 2004. Theory and evidence in international conflict: a response to de Marchi, Gelpi, and Grynaviski. *American Political Science Review*, 98: 379–89.

BELSLEY, D., KUH, E., and WELSH, R. 1980. *Regression Diagnostics: Identifying Influential Data and Sources of Collinearity.* New York: John Wiley and Sons.

BENNETT, D. 2005. Towards a continuous specification of the democracy–autocracy connection. *International Studies Quarterly*, 50: 513–37.

BOWMAN, K., LEHOUCQ, F., and MAHONEY, J. 2005. Measuring political democracy: case expertise, data adequacy, and Central America. *Comparative Political Studies*, 38: 939–70.

BRAMBOR, T., CLARK, W., and GOLDER, M. 2006. Understanding interaction models: improving empirical analyses. *Political Analysis*, 14: 63–82.

BRAUMOELLER, B. 2004. Hypothesis testing and multiplicative interaction terms. *International Organization*, 58: 807–20.

BREMER, S. 1992. Dangerous dyads: interstate war, 1816–1965. *Journal of Conflict Resolution*, 36: 309–41.

BUENO DE MESQUITA, B. 1981. *The War Trap.* New Haven, Conn.: Yale University Press.

BURGER, T. 1987. *Max Weber's Theory of Concept Formation: History, Laws, and Ideal Types.* Durham, NC: Duke University Press.

CHIN, H., and QUDDUS, M. 2003. Modeling count data with excess zeroes: an empirical application to traffic accidents. *Sociological Methods and Research*, 32: 90–116.

COHEN, M., and NAGEL, E. 1934. *An Introduction to Logic and Scientific Method.* New York: Harcourt, Brace.

CRESCENZI, M., and ENTERLINE, A. 2001. Time remembered: a dynamic model of interstate interaction. *International Studies Quarterly*, 45: 409–32.

DAVIS, J. 2005. *Terms of Inquiry: On the Theory and Practice of Political Science.* Baltimore: Johns Hopkins University Press.

DIEHL, P., and GOERTZ, G. 2000. *War and Peace in International Rivalry.* Ann Arbor: University of Michigan Press.

DIXON, W. 1993. Democracy and the management of international conflict. *Journal of Conflict Resolution*, 37: 42–68.

DWORKIN, R. 1981. What is equality? Part 1: equality of welfare, Part 2: equality of resources. *Philosophy and Public Affairs*, 10: 185–246, 283–345.

FOLEY, J. 1967. Resource allocation in the public sector. *Yale Economic Essays*, 7: 73–6.

FORTNA, V. 2003. Inside and out: peacekeeping and the duration of peace after civil and interstate wars. *International Studies Review*, 5: 97–114.

FRIEDRICH, R. 1982. In defense of multiplicative terms in multiple regression equations. *American Journal of Political Science*, 26: 797–833.

GARTZKE, E. 1998. Kant we all just get along? Opportunity, willingness, and the origins of the democratic peace. *American Journal of Political Science*, 42: 1–27.

GERRING, J., and THOMAS, C. 2005. Comparability: a key issue in research design. Presented at the annual meetings of the American Political Science Association.

GIBLER, D., and VASQUEZ, J. 1998. Uncovering the dangerous alliances, 1495–1980. *International Studies Quarterly*, 42: 785–807.

—— and RIDER, T. 2004. Prior commitments: compatible interests versus capabilities in alliance behavior. *International Interactions*, 30: 309–29.

GLEDITSCH, K. 2002. Expanded trade and GDP data. *Journal of Conflict Resolution*, 46: 712–24.

GOERTZ, G. 2006. *Social Science Concepts: A User's Guide.* Princeton, NJ: Princeton University Press.

—— JONES, B., and DIEHL, P. 2005. Maintenance processes in international rivalries. *Journal of Conflict Resolution*, 49: 742–69.

GOULD, S. J. 1996. *Full House: The Spread of Excellence from Plato to Darwin.* New York: Three Rivers Press.

GUNTHER, R., and DIAMOND, L. 2003. Species of political parties: a new typology. *Party Politics*, 9: 167–99.

HARSANYI, J. 1955. Cardinal welfare, individualistic ethics, and interpersonal comparisons of utility. *Journal of Political Economy*, 63: 309–21.

HEGRE, H. 2000. Development and the liberal peace: what does it take to be a trading state? *Journal of Peace Research*, 37: 5–30.

JAGGERS, K., and T. GURR. 1995. Tracking democracy's third wave with the Polity III data. *Journal of Peace Research*, 32: 469–82.

KAHNEMAN, D. 1999. Objective happiness. In *Well-Being: The Foundations of Hedonic Pyschology*, ed. D. Kahneman et al. New York: Russell Sage Foundation.

—— et al. 1993. When more pain is preferred to less: adding a better end. *Psychological Science*, 4: 401–5.

KARATNYCKY, A. (ed.) 2000. *Freedom in the World, 1999–2000*. Washington, DC: Freedom House.

KING, G., and MURRAY, C. 2002. Rethinking human security. *Political Science Quarterly*, 116: 585–610.

LAZARSFELD, P. 1966. Concept formation and measurement in the behavioral sciences: some historical observations. In *Concepts, Theory, and Explanation in the Behavioral Sciences*, ed. G. DiRenzo. New York: Random House.

LINZ, J., and STEPAN, A. 1996. *Problems of Democratic Transition and Consolidation: Southern Europe, South America, and Post-communist Europe*. Baltimore: Johns Hopkins University Press.

MAHONEY, J., and GOERTZ, G. 2004. The Possibility Principle: choosing negative cases in comparative research. *American Political Science Review*, 98: 653–69.

MANSFIELD, E., and SYNDER, J. 2002. Democratic transitions, institutional strength and war. *International Organization*, 56: 297–337.

MAOZ, Z., and RUSSETT, B. 1993. Normative and structural causes of democratic peace, 1946–1986. *American Political Science Review*, 87: 624–38.

MOUSSEAU, M. 2000. Market prosperity, democratic consolidation, and democratic peace. *Journal of Conflict Resolution*, 44: 472–507.

MUNCK, G., and VERKUILEN, J. 2002. Conceptualizing and measuring democracy: evaluating alternative indices. *Comparative Political Studies*, 35: 5–34.

NOZICK, R. 1974. *Anarchy, State and Utopia*. Oxford: Basil Blackwell.

OLIVER, A. 2004. Should we maximise QALYs? A debate with respect to peak-end evaluation. *Applied Health Economics and Health Policy*, 2004: 61–66.

ONEAL, J., and RUSSETT, B. 1999. The Kantian peace: the pacific benefits of democracy, interdependence, and international organizations, 1885–1992. *World Politics*, 52: 1–37.

ORGANSKI, A., and KUGLER, J. 1980. *The War Ledger*. Chicago: University of Chicago Press.

PECENY, M., and BEER, C. 2002. Dictatorial peace? *American Political Science Review*, 96: 15–26.

PEVEHOUSE, J. 2004. Interdependence theory and the measurement of international conflict. *Journal of Politics*, 66: 247–66.

POSNER, D. 2004. Measuring ethnic fractionalization in Africa. *American Journal of Political Science*, 48: 849–63.

PRZEWORSKI, A., et al. 2000. *Democracy and Development: Political Institutions and Well-Being in the World, 1950–1990*. Cambridge: Cambridge University Press.

—— and TEUNE, H. 1970. *The Logic of Comparative Social Inquiry*. New York: John Wiley and Sons.

RAWLS, J. 1971. *A Theory of Justice*. Cambridge, Mass.: Harvard University Press.

RILEY, J. 1987. *Liberal Utilitarianism: Social Choice Theory and J.S. Mill's Philosophy.* Cambridge: Cambridge University Press.

SAMBANIS, N. 2004. What is civil war? Conceptual and empirical complexities of an operational definition. *Journal of Conflict Resolution,* 48: 814–58.

SAMPLE, S. 2002. The outcomes of military buildups: minor states vs. major powers. *Journal of Peace Research,* 39: 669–91.

SARTORI, G. 1970. Concept misformation in comparative politics. *American Political Science Review,* 64: 1033–53.

SEN, A. 1977. On weights and measures: informational constraints in social welfare analysis. *Econometrica,* 45: 1539–72.

——1992. *Inequality Reexamined.* Cambridge, Mass.: Harvard University Press.

SENESE, P., and VASQUEZ, J. 2003. A unified explanation of territorial conflict: testing the impact of sampling bias, 1919–1992. *International Studies Quarterly,* 47: 275–98.

SIGNORINO, C., and RITTER, J. 1999. Tau-b or not tau-b: measuring the similarity of foreign policy positions. *International Studies Quarterly,* 43: 115–44.

SUZUMURA, K. 1983. *Rational Choice, Collective Decisions and Social Welfare.* Cambridge: Cambridge University Press.

SWEENEY, K., and KESHK, O. 2005. The similarity of states: using S to compute dyadic interest similarity. *Conflict Management and Peace Science,* 22: 165–87.

VAREY, C., and KAHNEMAN, D. 1992. Experiences extended across time: evaluation moments and episodes. *Journal of Behavioral Decision Making,* 5: 169–86.

VARIAN, H. 1975. Distributive justice, welfare economics and the theory of fairness. *Philosophy and Public Affairs,* 4: 223–47.

WEBER, M. 1949. "Objectivity" in social science and social policy. In *The Methodology of the Social Sciences.* New York: Free Press.

WERNER, S. 1999. The precarious nature of peace: resolving the issues, enforcing the terms, and renegotiating the settlement. *American Journal of Political Science,* 43: 912–34.

WRIGLESWORTH, J. 1985. *Libertarian Conflicts in Social Choice.* Cambridge: Cambridge University Press.

CHAPTER 6

....

MEASUREMENT

....

SIMON JACKMAN

1 LATENT VARIABLES ARE UBIQUITOUS IN THE SOCIAL SCIENCES

....

MANY problems in the social sciences involve making inferences about quantities that are not directly observable. Here I refer to these quantities as latent states or latent variables. Examples include the ideological dispositions of survey respondents (e.g. Erikson 1990), legislators (Clinton, Jackman, and Rivers 2004), judges (Martin and Quinn 2002), or political parties (Huber and Inglehart 1995); the quantitative, verbal, and analytic abilities of applicants to graduate school (e.g. as measured by scores from the Graduate Record Examination, or GRE); levels of democracy in the world's countries (Gurr and Jaggers 1996); locations in an abstract, latent space used to represent relations in a social network (Hoff, Raftery, and Handcock 2002); elements of public opinion, such as aggregate levels of support for political candidates, at distinct points in time, say, over the course of an election campaign (e.g. Green, Gerber, and De Boef 1999). In each instance, the available data are manifestations (or *indicators*) of the latent quantity and the inferential problem can be stated as follows: Conditional on observable data y, what should we believe about latent quantities x?

For the purposes of this chapter, I refer to inferential problems of this sort as *measurement* problems. Further, I will refer to statistical models that link latent variables and their observed indicators as *measurement models*.

2 THE GOALS OF MEASUREMENT

The success of measurement—the quality of the inferences provided by a measurement model—is usually assessed with reference to two key concepts: *validity* and *reliability*. These concepts have analogs in the theory of parameter estimation. For instance, while measurement uses observed data y to learn about unobserved quantities ξ, parameter estimation uses observed data y to learn about unknown (and hence unobserved) parameters θ. That is, up to a change in nomenclature ("unobserved quantities" versus "unknown parameters"), measurement *is* the same inferential problem as parameter estimation.

Generically, we can represent the relationship between a latent variable ξ_i and an *indicator* of that variable, x_i, with the simple model

$$x_i = \xi_i + \delta_i \qquad (1)$$

where δ_i is *measurement error* and i indexes observational units. As we shall see below, properties of δ_i, such as its mean and variance, are sufficient to charaterize the validity and reliability of an indicator.

The idea that observations are accompanied by measurement error has numerous plausible motivations. Survey research is a domain in which considerations about measurement error seem to arise with great frequency, and is the source of much applied research (e.g. Lessler and Kalsbeek 1992; Tourangeau, Rips, and Rasinski 2000; Biemer et al. 2004). For example, theories of the survey response posit that respondents sample from a set of mentally accessible considerations in furnishing survey responses (e.g. Zaller and Feldman 1992), and so in this view the measurement error δ_i term in equation (1) is actually a form of sampling error: Presumably, if we were to administer the same respondent i the same survey item multiple times (indexed as $j = 1, \ldots, J$), we would acquire different responses x_{ij} even though the underlying trait ξ_i is stable, with measurement error δ_{ij} accounting for the variation. Likewise, it is well known that variation in respondent or interviewer mood, the conditions of the interview (e.g. location, ambient noise, time of day, day of week, season of the year), or characteristics of the interviewer vis-à-vis the respondents (e.g. race, ethnicity, gender) are possible sources of measurement error (e.g. Anderson, Silver, and Abramson 1988; Groves 1989; Kane and Macauley 1993; Kinder and Sanders 1996). It is well known that social desirability—the tendency to give biased responses to survey questions so as to give a favorable self-presentation—gives rise to errors in measurement. Among the many attitudes and behaviors potentially subject to social desirability bias are voter turnout, sexual behavior, employment histories, criminal histories, religious beliefs and practices, drug use, alcohol intake, and exercise regimes (e.g. Sudman and Bradburn 1974; Schaeffer 2000).

More fundamentally, there is also the issue that an indicator x simply is *not* the latent variable of interest ξ: For example, self-reports of church attendance (x), even if accurately reported, are not religiosity (ξ), but are related to religiosity, with equation (1) providing a plausible model for that relationship. Measurement error of the type is hardly exclusive to the domain of survey research or political behavior: As noted in the introduction, many studies of aggregate-level processes in American politics, comparative politics, and international relations make conjectures about unobserved structural variables operationalized with proxies or indicators.

2.1 Validity

Validity is roughly analogous to the notion of unbiasedness in the context of parameter estimation. Bias is a well-defined concept; for instance, if we estimate a parameter θ with the estimator $\hat{\theta}$, then we say $\hat{\theta}$ is an *unbiased* estimator of θ if $E(\hat{\theta}) = \theta$, where usually the expectation is with respect to the random process that generated the data (e.g. a sampling procedure of some kind). In the context of measurement, and using equation (1), we would say x_i is a valid measure of ξ_i if $E(x_i) = \xi_i$, or equivalently, $E(\delta_i) = 0$. That is, errors in measurement are zero, on average, in some sense (e.g. a repeated sampling sense of averaging, in that the measurement errors have zero mean across repeated applications of the measurement process). If this condition holds for all observational units then we could drop the i subscript, writing $E(x) = \xi$ and say that x is a valid measure of ξ.

But in the context of measurement, the term "validity" is often used in other, less formal ways; for some clarification, see Adcock and Collier (2001). But generally, the idea is quite simple: A valid measure actually measures the concept we think it measures, or the concept we want it to measure. Despite the apparent simplicity of this definition, for over seventy years psychometricians have been offering various definitions of validity: e.g.

- *content validity*: Does the measure wholly operationalize the substantive content of the latent construct? For instance, if we are trying to measure democracy among the world's nation states, do the available indicators span all the relevant facets of democracy? In this regard, note that a widely used measure of democracy, the Polity data (e.g. Gurr and Jaggers 1996), use a combination of five indicators of democracy, in an effort to encompass a scholarly consensus as to just what democracy *means*. Of course, to the extent that there is disagreement as to the substantive content of a construct (which is merely another way of saying there is disagreement about the nature of the construct), then valid measurement would seem unattainable.
- *predictive validity*: Does the measure predict things that the latent construct is thought to be a determinant of? For instance, a measure of partisanship ought to be a good predictor of vote choice or other political behaviors and attitudes.
- *convergent validity*: Is the measure closely related to other measures known to be valid measures of the latent construct? For example, the measures of legislators' revealed preferences developed by Clinton, Jackman, and Rivers (2004) correlate strongly with the earlier measures developed by Poole and Rosenthal (1997).

- *discriminant validity*: Is the measure different from measures that it should be different from? For instance, a measure of political efficacy should not be highly correlated with measures of, say, racial prejudice, political ideology, etc. Discriminant validity (sometimes also called divergent validity) is thus the opposite notion to convergent validity. These two senses of validity were introduced by Campbell and Fiske (1959).

Given our focus on measurement as inference for latent variables, it is useful to consider the more general notion of *construct validity*, first promulgated by the American Psychological Association's Committee on Psychological Tests (1950–4). The Committee's work on construct validity was powerfully recapitulated in a separate article by Cronbach and Meehl (1955):

Construct validation is involved whenever a test is to be interpreted as a measure of some attribute or quality which is not "operationally defined."   (282)

And consider also the following sentences from the APA's 1954 Technical Report, quoted in the Cronbach and Meehl (1955) article:

Construct validity is ordinarily studied when the tester has no definite criterion measure of the quality with which he is concerned, and must use indirect measures. Here the trait or quality underlying the test is of central importance, rather than either the test behavior or the scores on the criteria.

Writing forty-five years later, McDonald (1999, 199) notes that construct validity has come to subsume the other forms of validity, and so today:

validation...can be taken to include every form of evidence that the score to some acceptable extent measures a specific attribute....[C]ontent validity, concurrent validity, and validation methods initially associated with "construct" validity are all methods of investigating the extent to which a test score measures the attribute it is used to measure.

That is, there are several species of measurement validity. But at least in the context of latent variables, the term "construct validity" has lost much of the specificity it once had, and today is an umbrella term of sorts.

2.2 Reliability

If bias is the rough analog of measurement validity, then variance is the analog of the *unreliability* of a measure; conversely, precision (the inverse or reciprocal of variance) is the analog of the *reliability* of a measure. That is, suppose a subject has a true latent state ξ, and we have two indicators available, x_A and x_B. Then indicator x_A is (informally) said to be a more reliable measure of ξ than x_B if the measurement error variance of indicator A, $V(x_A)$, is less than the measurement error variance of indicator B, $V(x_B)$. Referring again to equation (1), conditional on the latent variable

ξ_i, the variance of the indicator x_i is just the measurement error variance $V(\delta_i) = \omega_i^2$. Thus, small levels of measurement error variance generate more reliable indicators, and vice versa. In fact, we can define the reliability of an indicator x of ξ as

$$r^2 = V(\xi)/V(x) = \frac{V(\xi)}{V(\xi + \delta)} = \frac{V(\xi)}{V(\xi) + \omega^2} = 1 - \frac{\omega^2}{V(x)} \qquad (2)$$

with an assumption of homoskedasticity ($\omega_i^2 = \omega^2 \forall i$) and no covariance between the latent variable ξ_i and the measurement errors δ_i. The choice of notation here is not accidental, since the reliability is nothing more than the r^2 from the regression implicit in equation (1) (e.g. Lord and Novick 1968, 61). More colloquially, we can see that reliability is simply the proportion of the variance of the observed indicator x that is accounted for by variance in the latent variable ξ. As $\omega^2 \rightarrow 0$, the measurement error is vanishing, and the latent variable ξ dominates the observed measure x, i.e. $V(\xi)/V(x) = r^2 \rightarrow 1$. Conversely, as ω^2 gets larger, the measurement error comes to dominate the observed indicator, the "noise" overwhelming any "signal" from ξ, and $r^2 \rightarrow 0$.

Notice that the definition of reliability given above is not operational as stated. The variance decomposition $V(x) = V(\xi) + \omega^2$ simply isn't identified in most applications; i.e. we observe x and so we can estimate $V(x)$, but absent additional information we simply don't know how much of the observation in x is due to variation in the latent variable ξ or to measurement error. Like all identification problems, additional information is required to solve the problem, either in the form of results from previous research, or by using *multiple indicators* linked to the latent variable via a measurement model. Even with multiple indicators, we observe neither the population variance in x nor the error variance ω^2, but at least we are better placed to estimate these quantities from the information provided by the multiple indicators.

Depending on the availability of the items, there are different ways of assessing reliability. These include:

- *test-retest reliability.* Two items (x_A and x_B) are administered at two different time points. Under the assumption that the latent variable ξ does not change, the correlation between x_A and x_B is an estimate of the reliability of the resulting measure of ξ, x. Guttman (1945) remains an extremely clear and concise treatment of this form of reliability; see also Alwin (2007, 95–148). In particular, see the discussion of the Wiley–Wiley (1970) model, in Section 10, below.
- *inter-rater reliability.* Consider a set of experts or judges $j = 1, \ldots, J$ assigning scores x_{ij} over units $i = 1, \ldots, n$, each with a latent score ξ_i; a well-known example in political science is the Manifestos data (e.g. Budge, Roberstson, and Hearl 1987). In the special case of $J = 2$ experts we have essentially the same idea as with test-retest reliability: The correlation across judges (items) is a measure of the reliability of the resulting measure. In the case of $J > 2$ raters, two popular estimates of inter-rater reliability are (1) the average of the pairwise

correlations among the raters; (2) the intra-class coefficient (ICC), estimated via a variance components model, partitioning the total variance in the scores into components due to between-rater variation and between-subject variation, equivalent to a multi-way analysis of variance. High inter-rater reliability results when the between-rater variation is a small component of the total variation (e.g. Bartko 1966; Shrout and Fleiss 1979).

- *inter-item reliability.* Suppose we have indicators x_j, $j = 1, \ldots, J$, of a latent variable ξ, and we combine the information in the indicators to generate the scale measure z (say, using one of the techniques described below). A measure of the reliability of resulting scale is the average level of correlation among the items, appropriately normalized by the number of items. That is, if the items display high pairwise correlations, then it is likely that the items are tapping the same latent variable. In this sense this measure of inter-item reliability is said to be a measure of "internal reliability" or "internal consistency". Note that these labels are carefully chosen so as to highlight the fact that high levels of inter-item reliability do *not* imply that z is a valid measure of ξ; e.g. just because indicators are highly correlated with one another and so may be construed to measure something (z), more information or assumptions are required before we can say that that "something" is in fact the latent variable of interest ξ. Perhaps the most widely used measure of reliability is an iter-item reliability measure widely known as Cronbach's alpha (1951), although Guttman (1945) provided the same quantity in an earlier article. Cronbach's alpha can be computed in several ways: e.g.

$$\alpha = \frac{J}{J-1} \left(1 - \frac{\sum_{j=1}^{J} V(x_j)}{V(z)} \right),$$ (3)

or a standardized version,

$$\alpha^* = \frac{J\bar{r}}{1 + (J-1)\bar{r}}$$ (4)

where $\bar{r}$ is the average of the $J(J-1)/2$ unique pairwise correlations among the J items. Cronbach developed his reliability measure as a generalization of earlier work by Kuder and Richardson (1937) who considered inter-item reliability with dichotomously scored items.

There are no hard and fast rules for deciding when a scale measure z is reliable on the basis of Cronbach's alpha: again, it is worth stressing that reliability is a matter of degree (i.e. the scale constructed out of J indicators in a given data-set may be more or less reliable than a scale constructed with more or less items, and/or from a different data-set). And indeed, we might well ask how reliable (variable) are reliability assessments (e.g. Fan and Thompson 2001). That said, reliabilities less than .5 are often considered less than acceptable in many settings; indeed, for diagnostic work in psychology and educational testing, scales with Cronbach alpha reliability coefficients of less than .7 or .8 are generally considered too unreliable for use, and reliabilities close to .9 are not all uncommon among some of the more well-studied scales; e.g. see Viswesvaran and Ones (2000) or Yin and Fan (2000).

Just as there is a bias-variance trade-off in parameter estimation (e.g. we might prefer a biased estimator with small variance to an unbiased estimator with higher variance), we can contemplate a similar trade-off between validity and reliability with respect to measurement. Multiple indicators buy us not only the ability to assess reliability (solving the identification problem described above), but also let us generate more reliable measures than we would get from using fewer measures. Of course, adding multiple indicators to a measurement procedure runs the risk of reducing validity: To the extent that the indicators y are measuring things other than ξ, then adding more indicators to the analysis creates some risk of creating a reliable-yet-invalid measure. This is something we have to be alert to with measurement modeling. Imposing restrictions on the parameters in a measurement model is one way to solve these issues, as discussed below: e.g. constraining indicators known to have high validity to have high loadings in a confirmatory factor analysis model, or to have high discrimination parameters in an item-response theory model. In this way we can enjoy the benefits that come from measurement modeling with multiple indicators (measures of latent variables with greater reliability) while ensuring validity remains high.

3 THE USES OF MEASUREMENT

We can identify two distinct uses of measures of latent variables. First, measures of latent variables are used in their own right, as interesting or useful summaries of a broader set of data (the multiple indicators of the latent variable), perhaps with a view to supporting a decision. For example, we rely on scores from standardized tests in making college admissions decisions, and increasingly test scores have become an important determinant of the way governments allocate resources to schools in the United States (e.g. in the wake of 2001 No Child Left Behind Act). In such instances the validity and reliability of measures would seem especially important.

The other use of latent variables is as predictors or response variables (or both) in structural models. Indeed, a large and lively body of methodological work is devoted to models with latent variables under the rubric of "structural equation modeling" (SEM) in the fields such as psychology and sociology (e.g. Bollen 1989); see also the chapter by Bollen, Rabe-Hesketh, and Skrondal in this volume. This modeling approach has never had a particularly strong foothold in political science: important exceptions can be found in work assessing the stability of party identification over time (e.g. Green and Palmquist 1991; Palmquist and Green 1992; Carsey and Layman 2006) and other recent applications include Finkel, Humphries, and Opp (2001), de Figueiredo and Elkins (2003), and Goran (2004). SEMs are essentially unheard of in American economics, and indeed staples of measurement modeling such as factor analysis and item-response modeling are conspicuously absent from econometrics texts. The situation in Europe is somewhat different, where the disciplinary distance between econometrics and psychometrics is much smaller (e.g. Wansbeek and Meijer 2000, with both authors located in the Netherlands). Time series is one of the areas of econometrics where measurement concerns are more central, and we will briefly touch on some of this work and political science applications in Section 10.2. But generally, the standard econometric treatment of measurement (at least in cross-sectional data) is to consider the consequences of analysis with a poorly measured predictor: the so-called "errors-in-variables" problem. We briefly review these results, since they do highlight the inferential risks of ignoring issues to do with measurement.

4 THE COSTS OF IGNORING MEASUREMENT ERROR

Consider the following widespread practice: using an indicator x *as if* it were ξ. The typical example is when the indicator x is used as a "proxy" for ξ in a regression analysis predicting y, giving rise to an "errors-in-variables" problem. To keep ideas simple, we consider the case where x is the only predictor; this particular form of errors-in-variables has been a staple of econometrics texts since at least Tinter (1952), and Fuller (2006) dates the earliest treatment of the topic to Adcock (1877). The researcher is interested in the model $E(\mathbf{y}|\xi) = \xi\beta$, but instead of observing $\xi = (\xi_1, \ldots, \xi_n)'$ the researcher observes $\mathbf{x}$. Note that via equation (1), the model of substantive interest can be re-written as

$$\mathbf{y} = (\mathbf{x} - \delta)\beta + \mathbf{u} = \mathbf{x}\beta + \nu \tag{5}$$

where $\mathbf{u}$ are the disturbances in the "structural" regression of $\mathbf{y}$ on ξ and $\nu = \mathbf{u} - \delta\beta$ is the compound disturbance that arises from using $\mathbf{x}$ in place of ξ. We make the standard assumptions that $E(\xi'\mathbf{u}) = E(\xi'\delta) = E(\delta'\mathbf{u}) = \mathbf{0}$; i.e. the structural regression is correctly specified, and that the measurement error δ does not covary with the structural regressor ξ nor with the structural disturbance $\mathbf{u}$. The problem here is that

$$E(\mathbf{x}'\nu) = E\left[(\xi + \delta)'(\mathbf{u} - \delta\beta)\right]$$
$$= E(\xi'\mathbf{u} - \xi'\delta\beta + \delta'\mathbf{u} - \delta'\delta\beta)$$
$$= -\Omega\beta$$

where $\Omega = V(\delta)$. Now, running a least squares regression of y on x yields $\hat{\beta} = (x'x)^{-1}x'y$ which has expected value

$$E(\hat{\beta}) = \beta + \underbrace{E((x'x)^{-1}x'\nu)}_{\text{bias}} \tag{6}$$

with bias $-\Sigma_x^{-1}\Omega\beta$, where $\Sigma_x = V(x)$. In general, this bias term will not be equal to zero, and has the effect of attenuating the least squares estimate β, on average (i.e. for this simple model, the presense of measurement error tends to result in underestimates of β). One way that this bias-from-measurement-error will be zero is if $\Omega = 0$, which occurs if and only if x is a perfectly reliable indicator of ξ. In fact, as Ω gets large, and measurement error comes to dominate the variability in the proxy x, the term $\Sigma_x^{-1}\Omega \rightarrow 1$, the bias approaches $-\beta$, and $E(\hat{\beta}) \rightarrow 0$ (i.e. a complete attentuation of the estimated effect). Note too that under these assumptions the bias persists asymptotically: i.e. the remedy to the "error-in-variables" problem is not more data, but more reliable data.

It is not uncommon for researchers to interpret these results as follows:

if I use an indicator x in place of the structural variable ξ, then the unreliability of x attenuates the estimate of β, and so conclusions about the effect of ξ are actually conservative; that is, while I have a biased and inconsistent estimate of β, at least I don't have an overestimate.

This is true, but only for the special case considered above, where x is the only variable in a linear regression model, and the measurement error is uncorrelated with everything else. When multiple predictors enter the regression equation and one or more of them are measured with error, and/or when the measurement error is "nonrandom", frankly all bets are off: Signing the biases on particular coefficients of interest becomes harder to do, and sign reversals on regression parameters are not only possible, but quite likely. Work by Achen (1983; 1985) provides one of the more crisp and powerful statements as to the consequences of using poor proxy variables, but it would seem this is a message that needs to be continuously reinforced. To this end, Achen (1983, 74–5) proves the following proposition:

Proposition 1. *Suppose $\beta^* \in \mathbb{R}^k$. Then in a multiple regression setup with k predictors, yielding OLS estimates $\hat{\beta}$, there exists a pattern of measurement error in any one of the predictors such that plim $\hat{\beta} \rightarrow \beta^*$.*

Proof. Achen (1983, 75).   ∎

The implication is rather startling: There exists a pattern of measurement error in one variable (appropriately correlated with other predictors) such that regression results can generate *any* set of results. Now of course, some patterns of measurement error are more likely than others, but the truth is we usually lack firm guidance in generating priors over possible patterns of measurement error.

This result gives rise to another piece of Achen wisdom:

In estimating regression equations, social scientists frequently encounter statistically significant coefficients with the wrong sign. Applied econometrics tests typically assume that the selection of independent variables is to blame, and they recommend search for omitted variables. ... In many practical cases, however, this advice is inappropriate, and the actual cause of the reversed signs is correlated measurement error among the independent variables.

(Achen 1985, 299)

Finally, recall that these results are with respect to a single equation linear regression. Results on the implications of ignoring measurement error in other setups are somewhat rarer: For nonlinear regression models, see Griliches and Ringstad (1970), Amemiya and Fuller (1988), and the book length treatment by Carroll, Ruppert, and Stefasnski (1995), with the latter reference extending its treatment of nonlinear models to include models for discrete responses.

5 Measurement Models

How can we overcome the difficulties posed by modeling with regressors that are actually proxies of structural variables of interest? One solution is to generate better measures of the variables of interest in the first place, since as we saw above, if measurement error decreases, then the scope for it to wreak havoc with regression estimates decreases. Another solution involves correcting regression estimates once we know the reliability of the proxy variable. In both cases, we will rely on measurement models, broadly construed.

Measurement modeling is a huge field, and by necessity this survey will be brief, providing a quick introduction to factor analysis, item-response models, and a very general class of latent variable models.

6 Factor Analysis

Perhaps the best-known measurement model is factor analysis, which dates to the work of Charles Spearman (1904) on intelligence testing. The idea is a familiar one: To the extent that a set of indicators are reliable indicators of a latent variable, they should display high correlations with one another, and analysis of the correlations should reveal this, and provide a basis for assigning scores to subjects on the latent variables or factors (and hence the name of the technique). The book by Harman (1976) contains a useful review of the development of factor analysis within psychology; Lawley and Maxwell (1971) remains an especially valuable reference, combining statistical rigor with clarity and economy of exposition.

Let i index n subjects and j index k indicators. Then the factor analysis model holds that x_{ij} is a combination of $p \leq k$ unobserved factors, each written using the Greek letter ξ: i.e.

$$x_{ij} = \mu_j + \lambda_{j1}\xi_{i1} + \lambda_{j2}\xi_{i2} + \ldots + \lambda_{jp}\xi_{ip} + \delta_{ij} \tag{7}$$

where the λ terms are *factor loadings* to be estimated, μ_j is the mean of x_{ij}, and δ_{ij} is that part of x_{ij} that cannot be accounted for by linear combination of the p underlying factors. It is possible to consider nonlinear or multiplicative factor models (e.g. Jöreskog 1978; Bollen 1989, 403 ff.) but the simple linear, additive structure in equation (7) is by far the more widely used factor analysis model. The factor loadings λ are parameters to be estimated that tap how the unobserved factors account for the observed variables: the larger the values of λ, the more a particular variable is said to "load" on the corresponding factor. In general, factor analytic models are fit with fewer underlying factors than there are variables ($p < k$).

It is typical to drop the intercept terms in factor analysis, since shifts in the mean level of any or all variables is of no consequence when we turn to an analysis of the covariances between items; constrast Jöreskog and Sörbom (1989, ch. 10) and Bollen (1989, 306–11). With the data mean-deviated, we can stack equation (7) over indicators to yield

$$\mathbf{x}_i = \Lambda\boldsymbol{\xi}_i + \boldsymbol{\delta}_i, \tag{8}$$

where $\mathbf{x}_i$ is a k by 1 vector of observed survey responses, Λ is a k by p matrix of factor loadings to be estimated, $\boldsymbol{\xi}_i$ is p by 1 vector of scores on the p underlying factors, and δ is a k by 1 vector of measurement errors. In turn, we can stack equation (8) over respondents to yield

$$\mathbf{X} = \Xi\Lambda' + \Delta, \tag{9}$$

where $\mathbf{X}$ is a n by k matrix of observed survey responses, Ξ is a n by p matrix of scores on the underlying factors, Λ' is the transpose of the k by p matrix of factor loadings, and Δ is a n by k matrix of measurement errors. Make the following assumptions and definitions:

$$E(\Xi'\Delta) = \mathbf{0} \tag{10a}$$

$$E(\Delta'\Delta) = \Theta_\delta \tag{10b}$$

$$E(\Xi'\Xi) = \Phi \tag{10c}$$

$$E(\mathbf{X}'\mathbf{X}) = \Sigma. \tag{10d}$$

The first constraint above is that there is no correlation between the measurement errors and the scores on the underlying factors. The three remaining conditions simply define some variance-covariance matrices of interest: The k by k variance-covariance of the measurement errors is denoted Θ_δ; the p by p variance-covariance matrix of the underlying factors is denoted Φ; and the k by k variance-covariance matrix of the data is denoted Σ. Then equation 9 can be manipulated to yield the following model for the covariance matrix of $\mathbf{X}$, the factor-analysis model:

$$E(\mathbf{X}'\mathbf{X}) = \Sigma = \Lambda\Phi\Lambda' + \Theta_\delta. \qquad (11)$$

That is, the variances and covariances among the observed variables can be decomposed into a component attributable to the underlying factors (and the relationships among those factors), and the measurement error variances and covariances. Quite simply, the statistical problem here is inference for the elements of the matrices on the right-hand side of equation (11)—the parameters constituting the factor analysis model—using the information in the variance-covariance matrix of the observed data.

6.1 Identification Constraints

Constraints are typically needed to make all of these parameters estimable. To see why, note that there are only $k(k+1)/2$ unique elements in Σ (variance-covariance matrices are symmetric), but potentially many more parameters on the right-hand side of equation (11), in Λ, Φ, and Θ_δ, respectively. That is, there are more parameters to estimate than the available pieces of sample information. Common strategies for identifying the factor analytic model are:

1. Make the number of factors, p, small relative to the number of indicators, k. That is, assume there are a relatively small number of factors underlying the data, which is an attractive assumption in any event, on grounds of parsimony.
2. Constrain off-diagonal elements of Θ_δ to zero. For pairs of survey responses reasonably thought to be conditionally independent given the latent variables, then the corresponding off-diagonal element of Θ_δ can be set to zero.
3. Constrain Φ to be an identity matrix, or a diagonal matrix. The former restriction assumes that the underlying factors have equal variances (set to one) and are uncorrelated; this "orthnormal factors" assumption is the default assumption in many popular programs for exploratory factor analysis that produce orthogonal factors. Assuming Φ to be diagonal eases the equal variance restriction, but retains the property that the estimated latent variables (factors) are orthogonal.
4. Constrain elements of Λ to zero; i.e. some variables might reasonably be presumed not to load on a particular factor.
5. Alternatively, one element per column of Λ can be set to 1.0, effectively "labeling" the particular factor with reference to the corresponding indicator. This strategy is especially useful when the researcher has strong beliefs that certain indicators have high validity with respect to the latent variable. In this way the researcher can be sure that the latent variable inherits much of its substantive content (and hence validity) from the corresponding indicator. Conversely, validity

can also be enhanced by ensuring that indicators that are known not to be valid indicators of a particular latent variable do not load on that variable (setting the corresponding element of Λ to zero, as discussed above).

Exploratory factor analysis typically works with a small number of factors relative to the number of variables, but allows all variables to load on all factors. Accordingly, exploratory factor analysis constrains other parts of the model along the lines suggested above: Φ is constrained to be an identity matrix (to yield orthonormal factors), and Θ_δ is constrained to be diagonal. In this case a necessary condition for identification is that

$$\frac{1}{2}k(k+1) \geq kp - \frac{1}{2}p(p-1) + k \iff (k-p)^2 \geq k + p,$$

known as the Lederman (1937) bound. Note that with $p = 1$ (a one-factor model), we require $k \geq 3$ to satisfy this necessary condition for identification.

More interesting models can be estimated by imposing restrictions on the matrix of factor loadings Λ (as discussed above), which allows, say, elements of Φ to be estimated, or even off-diagonal elements of Θ_δ. Factor analytic models of this sort are usually referred to as instances of *confirmatory* factor analysis. See Lawley and Maxwell (1971, ch. 7).

6.2 Estimation via Principal Components

Consider the case where Φ is constrained to be an identity matrix, and so the model in equation (11) reduces to

$$\Sigma = \Lambda\Lambda' + \Theta_\delta. \tag{12}$$

A popular and computationally cheap method for estimating the model parameters exploits the fact that a covariance matrix Σ (i.e. a positive definite, square, symmetric matrix) can be decomposed as

$$\Sigma = Z'\Gamma Z \tag{13}$$

where Γ is a diagonal matrix containing the eigenvalues of Σ in decreasing order ($\gamma_1 \geq \gamma_2 \geq \ldots \geq \gamma_k \geq 0$), and Z is a k by k matrix of orthogonal eigenvectors. Each eigenvector can be usefully considered as a vector of coefficients that could be used forming uncorrelated linear combinations of the X variables. For instance, using the jth eigenvector in this way produces a new variable $y_j = Xz_j$, which is the jth *principal component* of X (i.e. y_j is a n by 1 vector, X is a n by k matrix, and z_j is a k by 1 vector).

Principal components have properties that make them especially useful for factor analysis. The first principal component has the largest variance among all linear combinations of X (note that X variables are often standardized to all have unit variances so as to ensure that a variable with a large variance does not unduly dominate the analysis; this standardization is implicit when performing factor analysis on correlation matrices). The second principal component has the largest variance among linear combinations of $\mathbf{X}$ subject to the constraint that it is uncorrelated with the first principal component, and so on for subsequent principal components.

While there are as many principal components as there are $\mathbf{X}$ variables, the idea behind factor analysis is to come up with a parsimonious representation of the structure underlying the $\mathbf{X}$ variables. In practice, then, only the first few principal components are retained, corresponding to a few factors. For any p factor model (with $p > k$), only the first p eigenvectors in $\mathbf{Z}$ are retained, and so the "full" k dimensional decomposition in equation (13) is not used; i.e. some of the variation in $\mathbf{X}$ is considered random error. The factor analysis model estimated by principal components is

$$\Sigma = \mathbf{Z}_{(p)}\mathbf{Z}'_{(p)} + \Theta_\delta, \tag{14}$$

where $\mathbf{Z}_{(p)}$ is the k by p matrix containing the first p eigenvectors of Σ.

Another important property of factor analysis via principal components is that the model in equation (14) is not unique. Any *rotation* of $\mathbf{Z}$ that preserves its orthogonal structure fits the data just as well as the unrotated solution in equation (14). That is, the principal components factor loadings $\mathbf{Z}_{(p)}$ can be multiplied by a p by p orthogonal matrix $\mathbf{G}$, $\mathbf{GG}' = \mathbf{I}$, to yield $\mathbf{Z}^*_{(p)} = \mathbf{Z}_{(p)}\mathbf{G}$: i.e.

$$\begin{aligned}
\Sigma &= \mathbf{Z}^*_{(p)}\mathbf{Z}^{*'}_{(p)} + \Theta \\
&= (\mathbf{Z}_{(p)}\mathbf{G})(\mathbf{G}'\mathbf{Z}'_{(p)}) + \Theta \\
&= \mathbf{Z}_{(p)}\mathbf{Z}'_{(p)} + \Theta,
\end{aligned}$$

from which we conclude that the factor loadings are identified only up to orthogonal rotations. The problem then becomes one of choosing among rotations that are optimal on other criteria. One popular choice is the *varimax* rotation (Kaiser 1958), which produces factor loadings that have maximal variance, taking on values close to 1 and 0 in absolute value. This helps ensure that the factors are reasonably distinct, with variables tending to load either quite strongly or quite weakly on any given factor. See Lawley and Maxwell (1971, ch. 6) or Harman (1976, chs. 14 and 15) for details.

6.3 Estimation and Inference via Maximum Likelihood

The more modern approach is to estimate the parameters of the factor analysis model via maximum likelihood, first considered by Lawley (1940). Assume that the $\mathbf{x}_i$ are iid multivariate normal $\forall\ i$, i.e. $\mathbf{x}_i \overset{\text{iid}}{\sim} N(\mu, \Sigma)$, and μ is replaced by its sample mean, and is a redundant parameter in the covariance-structure form of the factor analysis model given in equation (11). We then embed the factor analysis model for Σ from equation (11) in the concentrated log likelihood function

$$-\frac{n}{2}\ln|2\pi\Sigma| - \frac{n}{2}\mathrm{tr}(S\Sigma^{-1}) \tag{15}$$

where $S = n^{-1}\sum_{i=1}^{n}(x_i - \bar{x})(x_i - \bar{x})'$; i.e. in evaluating the log likelihood we replace Σ with an estimate based on estimates of Λ, Φ, and Θ_δ via equation (11). Anderson (2003, 14.3) considers properties of the maximum likelihood estimator for the orthonormal factor model ($\Phi = I$); Jöreskog (1967) considers maximum likelihood estimation for the more general model that is commonly referred to as confirmatory factor analysis. A useful summary appears in Mardia, Kent, and Bibby (1979, 264–6).

Inference for individual parameters follows via standard arguments: e.g. when n is large relative to the number of parameters being estimated, the variance-covariance matrix of the MLEs can be well approximated by the inverse of the Hessian matrix of the log-likelihood function evaluated at the MLEs, and central limit theorems apply. The maximum likelihood approach also provides a basis for more general hypothesis testing, such as testing the restrictions in one factor analytic model against a less restrictive alternative model via likelihood ratio tests. This testing framework is often used when assessing the number of factors (or "dimensions") underlying a set of indicators, a question that arises when using factor analysis as an exploratory tool. Useful references include Lawley and Maxwell (1971), Amemiya and Anderson (1990), and Anderson (2003, ch. 14).

Simulation work also suggests some caution be taken in interpreting these tests with factor analysis models (e.g. Bollen 1989, 266 ff.):

- the tests assume that the X variables exhibit no kurtosis (such that the mean-deviated data can be completely characterized with the second moments given in $X'X$, which is true if X is multivariate normal). Browne (1984) considered an asymptotically best, distribution-free, weighted least squares estimator that overcomes some of the difficulties associated with maximum likelihood factor analysis with non-normal indicators; this estimator is used widely when working with ordinal or binary indicators of the sort that often arise in survey data.
- the sample is large; samples less than 50 or even 100 tend to lead to too frequent rejections of null hypotheses; some authors suggest rules-of-thumb such as 5 observations for every free parameter.
- the alternative model is an unrealistic saturated model; perhaps all we want is a model that gives us a reasonable approximation, rather than a comparison against a perfect fit. A high value of the χ^2 test statistic which leads us to reject the null might lead us to estimate more parameters when we already have a reasonable approximation.

6.4 Inference for Latent Variables

Note that the scores on the latent variables, the n-by-p matrix Ξ, are not parameters in the factor analysis model. That is, the likelihood is maximized with respect to the fitted covariance matrix $\Sigma = \Lambda\Phi\Lambda' + \Theta_\delta$. Inference for the latent variables (or "factor scores") is typically done conditional on the MLEs for these parameters, and there is no agreed-upon method for doing this. Textbooks on the subject usually present two methods, so-called "regression" scoring (Thurstone 1935) or Bartlett (1937) scoring. A review appears in Krijnen, Wansbeek, and Ten Berge (1996). For brevity, I consider only regression scoring, which results from assuming the both the mean-deviated indicators $\mathbf{X}$ and the latent variables Ξ have a joint normal density, i.e.

$$\begin{bmatrix} \mathbf{x}_i \\ \boldsymbol{\xi}_i \end{bmatrix} \sim N\left(\begin{bmatrix} \mathbf{0} \\ \mathbf{0} \end{bmatrix}, \begin{bmatrix} \Sigma & \Lambda\Phi \\ \Phi\Lambda' & \Phi \end{bmatrix} \right),$$

from which we can deduce that the conditional density of $\boldsymbol{\xi}_i$ given the indicators $\mathbf{x}_i$ is

$$\boldsymbol{\xi}_i | \mathbf{x}_i \sim N(\Psi^{-1}\Lambda'\Theta_\delta^{-1}\mathbf{x}_i, \Psi^{-1}) \tag{16}$$

where $\Psi^{-1} = \Phi - \Phi\Lambda'\Sigma^{-1}\Lambda\Phi$ (e.g. Wansbeek and Meijer 2000, 163-4). Note that in evaluating equation (16) we replace Ψ, Λ, and Θ_δ with their estimated and/or constrained values.

Moreover, although it may not be obvious from equation (16), the predictions for Ξ are weighting the indicators $\mathbf{X}$ differentially, where both the factor loadings Λ and the measurement error variances (the diagonal elements of Θ_δ) play a role in determining the relative contribution of a particular indicator to the estimate of the latent variable. Indicators with higher loadings and/or smaller error variances make larger relative contributions to the estimate of the latent variables. Only in exceptional circumstances will all the indicators contribute equally to our estimate of the latent variable. In this way we see that one popular approach to building scales in the social sciences—forming equi-weighted sums or averages of a bundle of indicators—corresponds to a special, restrictive case of factor analysis, with the restrictions typically being highly implausible.

6.5 Inference with Latent Variables

Since factor analysis provides estimates (measures) of the latent variable Ξ, $\hat{\Xi} = E(\Xi | \mathbf{X})$, we can use $\hat{\Xi}$ in a structural regression model in place of any one of the $\mathbf{X}$ indicators. This estimate will almost surely be a more reliable indicator of Ξ than any single $\mathbf{X}$ alone, and hence the problems of noisy proxy variables discussed earlier can be mitigated. Moreover, factor analysis also provides an estimate of measurement error variance in any particular indicator (the corresponding element of the diagonal of Θ_δ), or the variance of the proxy measure $\hat{\Xi}$. Armed with this information, it is possible to correct the error-in-variables problem (Section 4): The factor analysis supplies information about the measurement error variance quantity referred to as Ω in equation (6), and it is straightforward to simply substitute this estimate to recover a consistent estimate of the structural parameters of interest in a regression setting. Kapteyn and Wansbeek (1984) refer to this type of two-step procedure as "consistent adjusted least squares" (CALS). Of course, a more general approach is offered by structural equation modeling (SEM), where one or more (exogenous or endogenous) variables in a system of equations may be unobserved, and one is interested primarily in estimating the structural relations between these variables, and perhaps secondarily in inference as to values of the latent variables themselves. In this chapter on measurement per se, we will not pursue the large topic of SEM any further. Useful references include the book by Bollen (1989) and the Bollen, Rabe-Hesketh, and Skrondal chapter in this volume. Indeed, since 1994 there has been a journal devoted to the topic (*Structural Equation Modeling: A Multidisplinary Journal*). Wansbeek and Meijer (2000, ch. 5) provides a remarkably compact and rigorous summary of this large field.

7 ITEM RESPONSE THEORY

Binary indicators are particularly prevalent in the social sciences: Examples include data generated from standardized testing (scored as correct/incorrect), legislative roll call data (recorded as "Yeas" and "Nays"), and the recorded votes of committees and judicial bodies. Analysis of these data often proceeds similarly to factor analysis: What do the observed binary data tell us about the latent scores of the subjects (test-takers, legislators, or judges, as the case may be)? Moreover, what do the binary data tell us about the indicators? The model typically used to analyze data of this type comes from a psychometric subfield known as item-response theory; the resulting measurement model is often referred to as a two-parameter IRT model and is

$$p_{ij} = \Pr(y_{ij} = 1 | \xi_i, \beta_j, a_j) = F(\xi_i \beta_j - a_j) \tag{17}$$

where

- $y_{ij} \in \{0, 1\}$ is the i-th subject's answer to the j-th item (e.g. $y_{ij} = 1$ if correct, $y_{ij} = 0$ if incorrect), where $i = 1, \ldots, n$ indexes respondents and $j = 1, \ldots, m$ indexes items;
- $\xi_i \in \mathbb{R}$ is an unobserved attribute of subject i (typically considered ability in the test-taking context, or ideology in the analysis of legislative data);
- β_j is an unknown parameter, tapping the *item discrimination* of the j-th item, the extent to which the probability of a correct answer responds to change in the latent trait ξ_i;
- a_j is an unknown *item difficulty* parameter, tapping the probability of a correct answer irrespective of levels of political information;
- $F(\cdot)$ is a monotone function mapping from the real line to the unit probability interval, typically the logistic or normal CDF.

A one-parameter version of the model results from setting $\beta_j = 1, \forall j$; i.e. items vary in difficulty, but not in terms of their discrimination, and is often called a Rasch model. A three-parameter version of the model is available, designed to help correct for guessing on standardized tests. Van der Linden and Hambleton (1997) provides a comprehensive survey of IRT models.

Contrast the two-parameter IRT model in equation (17) with factor analysis: The discrimination parameter β_j is similar to a factor loading, although there is no analog to the difficulty parameter α_j in the factor analysis model (which is typically implemented as a model for covariances, in which mean levels and intercept parameters are absent). In addition, in most political science settings we would like to make inferences for the latent variables ξ at the same time as we make inferences for the item parameters β and α; contrast factor analysis in which we typically generate measures of ξ conditional on estimates of the item parameters β and α. For more on the similarities between the IRT models and factor analysis, see Takane and de Leeuw (1987) and Reckase (1997).

The statistical problem here is inference for $\xi = (\xi_1, \ldots, \xi_n)'$, $\beta = (\beta_1, \ldots, \beta_m)$, and $\alpha = (\alpha_1, \ldots, \alpha_m)'$. We form a likelihood for the binary data by assuming that given ξ_i, β_j, and α_j, the binary responses are conditionally independent across subjects and items; this assumption is called "local independence" in the argot of IRT. Thus the likelihood is

$$\mathcal{L} = \prod_{i=1}^{n} \prod_{j=1}^{m} p_{ij}^{y_{ij}} (1 - p_{ij})^{1-y_{ij}} \tag{18}$$

where p_{ij} is defined in equation (17). As it stands, the model parameters are unidentified. For instance, any linear transformation of the ξ_i can be offset by appropriate linear transformations for the β_j and α_j; any obvious case is scale invariance, in which $p_{ij} = F(\xi_i\beta_j - \alpha_j)$ indistinguishable from the model with $p_{ij}^* = F(\xi_i^*\beta_j^* - \alpha_j)$ where $\xi_i^* = c\xi_i$ and $\beta_j^* = \beta_j/c, c \neq 0$. A special type of rotational invariance arises with $c = -1$. Any two linearly independent restrictions on the latent traits is sufficient for at least local identification, in the sense of Rothenberg (1971); a typical example is a mean-zero, unit variance restriction on the ξ_i, while setting at least one pair of (β_j, α_j) item parameters to fixed values is one way of obtaining global identification.

The chief political science use of the IRT model is in the analysis of roll-call data. Operationalizing the Euclidean spatial voting model (Davis, Hinich, and Ordeshook 1970; Enelow and Hinich 1984) gives rise to an IRT model, in which the latent trait corresponds to a legislators' ideal point, and the discrimination and difficulty parameters are functions of the locations of the "Yea" and "Nay" locations; see, e.g., Ladha (1991); Clinton, Jackman, and Rivers (2004). Outside of the roll call context, IRT has been used to assess the measurement properties of survey responses by Delli Carpini and Keeter (1996) and Jackman (2000). Brady (1991) considers IRT-like and factor analytic models for locating candidates and parties in a multidimensional space using data from the 1980 NES; see also Brady (1989), a rare excursion by political methodologists into fully-fledged psychometrics.

Estimation and inference for the two-party IRT model is not trivial, due to the large number of parameters involved in many settings. For instance, in data generated from a contemporary US House of Representatives, there are roughly $n = 450$ ξ_i parameters, and perhaps over a thousand pairs of (β_j, α_j) item parameters, for a total of roughly 2,500 parameters. Higher dimensional versions of the model generate even more parameters, as does pooling across multiple congresses. Data-sets in educational testing can involve many thousands of test-takers and hundreds of items. Baker and Kim (2004) is a book-length treatment of estimation strategies for these models. Popular approaches include marginal maximum likelihood, effectively treating the ξ as nuisance parameters and known only up to a distribution, which is then integrated out of the likelihood over the item parameters (Bock and Aitken 1981); alternating conditional maximum likelihood, used in the NOMINATE algorithms (e.g. Poole and Rosenthal 1997) for analyzing roll-call data; or exploration of the posterior density of the parameters via Markov Chain Monte Carlo methods, pioneered in the context of IRT by Albert (1992) and Patz and Junker (1999), which has since been used to study congressional roll calls (Jackman 2000; 2001; Clinton, Jackman, and Rivers 2004) and decisions of the Supreme Court (Martin and Quinn 2002).

The two-parameter IRT model has been extended in several directions in political science applications. Multidimensional models are routinely fit in the roll-call setting (e.g. Poole and Rosenthal 1997; Londregan 2000; Jackman 2001); Rivers (2003) provides a careful treatment of the identification issue for multidimensional IRT models. IRT models for ordinal responses are routinely deployed in educational testing where they are known as models for "graded responses;" these models are of obvious application in analyzing Likert-type ordinal survey responses or when experts assign ordinal ratings to countries, to party manifestos, to candidates, etc. Examples include an analysis of the ordinal ratings produced by members of graduate admissions committees to generate better measures of applicant quality (Jackman 2004), analysis of a mixture of ordinal and continuous indicators of country-level political and economic risk (Quinn 2004) and analysis of the Polity indicators of country-year levels of democracy (Treier and Jackman 2008). In each of these applications multiple ordinal responses $y_i = (y_{i1}, \ldots, y_{im})'$ are considered indicators of a latent variable ξ_i, and the ordinal IRT model is used as a measurement model for inference about ξ_i. A nonparametric IRT model for ordinal data appears in van Schur (1992).

8 GENERALIZED LATENT VARIABLE MODELING

The factor analytic model and the IRT model are very similar to one another. There are some interesting differences, to be sure. For instance, much of the theory for factor analysis was developed for the case of indicators that are continuous variables, or even more specifically, follow a multivariate normal density; IRT is usually used for binary data, or sometimes ordinal data. These similarities suggest a unifying framework for thinking about measurement modeling, which I now sketch, relying on a Bayesian approach.

Bayesian inference asks the following question: Given data y, what should I believe about parameters θ? Bayes theorem tells us that the posterior density for θ—a formal characterization of one's beliefs over θ after having looked at data y—is proportional to the product of the prior times the likelihood: i.e. $p(\theta|y) \propto p(y|\theta)p(\theta)$ where $p(\theta)$ is a prior density over θ and $p(y|\theta)$ is the likelihood function.

In the specific context of measurement modeling, there are two types of parameters: the latent variables for which we would like measures, ξ, and parameters tapping properties of the indicators (e.g. the Λ, Φ, and Θ_δ parameters in the factor analysis model in equation (11), or the β and α discrimination and difficulty parameters in the two-parameter IRT model). If we denote this second batch of parameters as β, then, generically, measurement modeling can be seen as the problem of inference for $\theta = (\xi, \beta)$. In particular, applying Bayes' Rule, our goal is to compute the joint posterior density $p(\theta|y) = p(\xi, \beta|y) \propto p(y|\xi, \beta)p(\xi, \beta)$. If the latent variables ξ are a priori independent of the item parameters β then the joint prior density simplifies into the product of the two marginal prior densities, i.e. $p(\xi, \beta) = p(\xi)p(\beta)$.

Note that in this approach, the latent variables are placed on the same footing as the item parameters: Both sets of parameters appear in the likelihood for the data, and both sets of parameters are estimated simultaneously from the data, such that uncertainty about one set of parameters propagates into uncertainty over the other. In this way we see that *measurement is merely another form of statistical inference*, in which theory and modeling are vital ingredients; for elaborations of this view (and differing perspectives), see the review provided by Jacoby (1991).

By way of contrast, recall that in factor analysis, predictions for the factor scores are generated conditional on estimates of the parameter in the factor analysis model, meaning we typically underestimate the uncertainty in those parameters; specifically, the terms appearing in the expression for conditional variance of ξ_i in equation (16) are themselves unknown parameters, subject to uncertainty. In the Bayesian approach, keeping track of these different sources of uncertainty is quite straightforward. For instance, if our focus is on measurement per se, the density of interest is the marginal posterior density $p(\xi|y) = \int_{\mathcal{B}} p(\xi, \beta|y)d\beta$, averaging over uncertainty in β ($\beta \in \mathcal{B}$) when we make statements about the measures ξ; modern approaches to Bayesian computation make frequent and creative use of Monte Carlo ideas, meaning that the integration here is not particularly daunting, particularly given advances in desktop computing power.

All manner of measurement models can be considered in this general framework. In addition to factor analysis and IRT, we can also consider several other measurement models; the book by Skrondal and Rabe-Hesketh (2004) shows how a very wide class of statistical models are instances of what they call generalized latent variable modeling. A fully Bayesian approach to SEMs, including measurement modeling, appears in the book by Lee (2007). The measurement models in Jackman (2004) and Quinn (2004) are in this style of generalized latent variable modeling, where the indicators (mixes of discrete and continuous variables) are modeled directly as a function of the latent variables. Likewise, Levendusky, Pope, and Jackman (2008) implement a generalized latent variable model in a study of district-level partisanship, with covariates (district-level census aggregates) supplying additional information about district-level partisanship beyond that in the indicators (vote shares, continuous variables), an example of a fully Bayesian SEM.

In the remainder of this chapter I sketch two examples of models that are usefully considered in this framework: (1) models where the latent variable is discrete (latent class and mixture models); (2) models where the latent variable(s) and its indicators are changing over time.

9 INFERENCE FOR DISCRETE LATENT VARIABLES

Latent class models are due to the seminal work of Lazarsfeld (1950) and later, Goodman (1974) and Haberman (1979). Textbook treatments include McCutcheon (1987), Heinen (1996), and Dayton (1998). The idea is that subjects fall into one of a finite number of discrete categories ("classes"), and that the classes differ with respect to values of the indicator variables. In this respect the latent class model is essentially a special case of a *mixture model*, where the indicators are discrete.

For the latent class model the indicators are cross-classifications of categorical variables (e.g. survey responses), with $\mathbf{y}_i = (y_{i1}, \ldots, y_{iK})'$ being the vector of responses across $k = 1, \ldots, K$ categorical indicator variables for respondent i, with each indicator taking on $l = 1, \ldots, L_k$ unique values. Suppose further that $j = 1, \ldots, m$ indexes the latent classes. Parameters λ_j are proportions, telling us the relative size of classes, with the properties $0 < \lambda_j < 1 \forall j$ and $\sum_{j=1}^{m} \lambda_j = 1$. Thus, conditional on being in class j, let the probability of outcome l on indicator k be θ_{jkl}. Let $z_{ikl} = 1$ if $y_{ik} = l$ and 0 otherwise. Then the probability the respondent gives the particular pattern of responses they actually gave, given that they are in class j, is

$$p(\mathbf{y}_i | i \in j, \boldsymbol{\theta}) = \prod_{k=1}^{K} \prod_{l=1}^{L_k} \theta_{jkl}^{z_{ikl}}.$$

Note the conditional independence assumption at work here: i.e. the probability of a particular response profile is equal to the product of probability of the particular response on a particular variable, given knowledge of the class membership. Indeed, the class membership is presumed to induce this conditional independence structure, just as the latent score is assumed to induce a conditional independence structure for the observed indicators in IRT models and in many factor analytic models. Removing the conditioning on the class membership j (since it is not known a priori) we obtain the density for the data

$$p(\mathbf{y}_i | \Lambda, \boldsymbol{\theta}) = \sum_{j=1}^{m} \lambda_j \prod_{k=1}^{K} \prod_{l=1}^{L_k} \theta_{jkl}^{Z_{ikl}}. \tag{19}$$

Typical examples of latent class analysis appear in biostatistics, where the latent, discrete state is presence or absence of a disease (i.e. a dichotomous latent state). In the social sciences, the latent classes are typically attitudinal states: e.g. tolerant or not (McCutcheon 1985); partisan or ideological categories (e.g. Breen 2000; Blaydes and Linzer 2006), or discrete levels of attitudinal instability, as contemplated by Converse's (1964) "black-and-white" model (e.g. Hill and Kriesi 2001). A useful aggregate-level application of latent class analysis would be in the study of democracy, where some scholars maintain countries either are or are not democratic and the available indicators are typically categorical (e.g. the Polity indicators); e.g. see Alvarez et al. (1996), but contrast Collier and Adcock (1999) and Elkins (2000). Perhaps the most ambitious use of latent class modeling in a political science setting is the work by Quinn et al. (2007) on automated content-coding of congressional speech: This project analyzes some 70 million words over 70,000 documents from seven years of *Congressional Record*, with topic categories as latent classes and word frequencies as the indicators.

Mixture models are more general, at least theoretically, but most applications of mixtures involve mixtures of normals fit to data that are continuous (or can be considered continuous); McLachlan and Peel (2000) and Frühwirth-Schnatter (2006) provide book-length treatments. For example, for a mixture made up of m component normal densities, the density for observation y_i is

$$p(y_i | \Lambda, \boldsymbol{\theta}) = \sum_{j=1}^{m} \lambda_j \, \phi \left(\frac{y_i - \mu_j}{\sigma_j} \right) \tag{20}$$

where $0 < \lambda_j < 1, \forall \, j = 1, \ldots, m, \sum_{j=1}^{m} \lambda_j = 1, \theta_j = (\mu_j, \sigma_j^2)$ are the mean and variance parameters for each of the m components, and ϕ is the standard normal density.

The number of applications using mixture models in political science settings remains relatively small at this stage. Gelman and King (1990) use a mixture of three normal densities to characterize the distribution of vote shares for Democratic candidates across congressional districts, classifying districts into safe Democratic, competitive, and safe Republican seats. Jackman (1995) and Freeman, Hays, and Stix (2000) use a dynamic mixture model due to Hamilton (1990) to allocate time periods to discrete regimes (e.g. high or low volatility periods in public opinion, or different political-economic equilibria in currency markets, respectively); see also the discussion of dynamic measurement models in Section 10.2. These models can be considered measurement models in that they generate inferences for the discrete latent variable ξ_i, an unknown attribute of a subject or observation. Mixtures models extend easily to the case of multivariate observations or mixtures of regression regimes (replacing μ_k in equation (20) with $\mathbf{x}_i \boldsymbol{\beta}_k$) and of course the components need not be normals (examples in the literature include mixtures of Poissons, mixtures of logistic regressions, etc.).

Viewed as measurement models, latent class models and mixture models approach the assignment of individuals to classes/components identically. Let $\xi_{ij} = 1 \iff i \in j$ and 0 otherwise. Then our goal is to compute a posterior density over $\xi_i = (\xi_{i1}, \ldots, \xi_{im})'$, $p(\xi_i|Y)$. Viewed as a special case of the generalized approach to measurement modeling sketched above, we obtain this marginal posterior density as $p(\xi_i|Y) = \int_\Theta p(\xi_i, \theta|Y)d\theta$, acknowledging that uncertainty over θ will generate uncertainty over the class memberships.

With modern software and computing power, latent class and mixture models are not at all difficult to estimate. The EM algorithm (Dempster, Laird, and Rubin 1977) is an obvious candidate for estimation, treating the class membership parameters ξ as missing data: the E step consisting of forming conditional expectations for the "missing" class memberships given current values as other parameters in the model, θ; the M step maximizes the complete data likelihood with respect to θ given the current assignment of cases to categories in ξ. The E step is especially simple for mixture models: e.g. for the m-component of normals in equation (20), given $\theta_k = (\mu_k, \sigma_k^2)$ and $\lambda_k, k = 1, \ldots, m$,

$$E\left(\xi_{ij}|\mathbf{y}_i, \theta\right) = \frac{\lambda_j \phi_{ij}}{\sum_{k=1}^{m} \lambda_k \phi_{ik}} \tag{21}$$

where $\phi_{ik} = \phi((y_i - \mu_k)/\sigma_k)$. Fully Bayesian approaches are also easily implemented via Markov Chain Monte Carlo, replacing each of the steps in the EM algorithm with a round of sampling from the conditional distribution of ξ given the indicators and θ, and then sampling from the conditional distribution of θ given the data and ξ.

Note that mixture models (and, as a special case, latent class models) are easily extended to include covariates that convey information about class memberships, but are not considered indicators of class type per se. The usual formulation is a mulitnomial logit hierarchial model linking covariates $\mathbf{x}_i$ to the probability of class memberships ξ_i. For instance, Linzer and Lewis (2008) provide software for estimating the latent class model as given here, or with covariates also supplying information as to class membership via a hierarchical MNL model. To motivate the model with covariates, Linzer and Lewis (2008) consider data from the 2000 American National Election Study in which respondents were asked to evaluate how well a series of traits—moral, caring, knowledgable, good leader, dishonest, and intelligent—described presidential candidates Al Gore and George W. Bush. Three latent classes are fit to the data ("Gore supporters," "Bush supporters," "neutral") with respondent party identification acting as a covariate in predicting class membership, but not as an indicator per se, consistent with the view that party identification sits causally prior to more concrete political attitudes such as candidate evaluations.

In both latent class and mixture modeling, the number of classes/components is always a pressing question. This is no different to asking how many dimensions/factors one ought to fit in a factor analytic model. There are numerous ways to address this question; McLachlan and Peel (2000, ch. 6) is a comprehensive survey. For example, in addition to the χ^2 likelihood ratio tests described earlier in the context of factor analysis, Linzer and Lewis (2008) use penalized goodness-of-fit measures such as the Akaike (1973) Information Criterion and the Bayesian Information Criterion (Schwartz 1978) in assessing the number of latent classes to fit. In a fully Bayesian setting, the primary model comparison tools include Bayes factors; see Lee (2007) for examples from measurement modeling. In the Bayesian setting, another possibility is also to place a proper prior over the number of components/dimensions in one's model, and then use a simulation algorithm that can increase or decrease the number of components/dimensions "on the fly," such as reversible-jump Markov Chain Monte Carlo; see Robert (1996), Richardson and Green (1997), and Robert, Ryden, and Titterington (2000) for discussion and examples.

10 MEASUREMENT IN A DYNAMIC SETTING

Measurement is not confined to a static setting. Surveys may have a panel design, with the explicit goal of measuring an attitudinal state at multiple time points. At the aggregate level, researchers may be interested in tracking public opinion, perhaps over long periods of time. We first consider the former case, describing one of the more famous measurement models in the social sciences, the Wiley–Wiley (1970) model.

10.1 The Wiley–Wiley model

The Wiley–Wiley model uses three repeated measures of a latent trait to recover estimates of both the reliability and the stability of the underlying trait. The Wiley–Wiley model has become one of the most widely used models for assessing reliability and attitudinal stability, since both these features of the measuring instrument (the survey item) are estimated simultaneously. The Wiley–Wiley model, or variants of it, has been frequently deployed in studies of public opinion and partisanship, where distinguishing random response instability (measurement error) from real attitude change is of special substantive interest; the three-wave panel designs of the National Election Studies are a frequent arena of application for this model.

The Wiley–Wiley model has two parts: a measurement equation for each of the three waves, and a structural or transitional model linking the latent traits across waves of the panel. The measurement equation is simply $x_{it} = \xi_{it} + \delta_{it}$, where i indexes observational units (typically, survey respondents), $t = 1, 2, 3$ index waves of the panel, x_{it} is an observed survey response, ξ_{it} is a latent trait, and δ_{it} is measurement error. The transition equations are

$$\xi_{i2} = \gamma_{21}\xi_{i1} + \epsilon_{i2}, \tag{22a}$$

$$\xi_{i3} = \gamma_{32}\xi_{i2} + \epsilon_{i3}, \tag{22b}$$

defining a first-order Markov process for the latent variables. We impose the restriction that $V(\delta_{it}) = \Theta_\delta, \forall\, i, t$. Further, assume $\text{cov}(\delta_{it}, \delta_{is}) = \text{cov}(\epsilon_{it}, \epsilon_{is}) = 0 \,\forall\, i, t \neq s$ and $\text{cov}(\delta_{it}, \xi_{it}) = 0 \,\forall\, i, t$. With these restrictions, the following six parameters are identified: $\Theta_\delta, \gamma_{21}, \gamma_{22}, V(\xi_1), V(\epsilon_2)$, and $V(\epsilon_3)$. Estimators for these parameters can be obtained as functions of the six unique elements in the variance-covariance matrix of the three indicators, as given in Table 2 of Wiley and Wiley (1970). Moreover, the Wiley–Wiley model is a saturated model: The combination of the six estimated parameters exactly reproduces the variance-covariance matrix of the observed indicators; see Table 1 of Wiley and Wiley (1970). Reliability estimates are simply derived as functions of the fitted parameters: i.e.

$$r_1^2 = V(\xi_1)/[V(\xi_1) + \Theta_\delta] \tag{23a}$$

$$r_2^2 = \frac{\gamma_{21}^2 V(\xi_1) + V(\epsilon_2)}{\gamma_{21}^2 V(\xi_1) + V(\epsilon_2) + \Theta_\delta} \tag{23b}$$

$$r_3^2 = \frac{\gamma_{32}^2[\gamma_{21}^2 V(\xi_1) + V(\epsilon_2)] + V(\epsilon_3)}{\gamma_{32}^2[\gamma_{21}^2 V(\xi_1) + V(\epsilon_2)] + V(\epsilon_3) + \Theta_\delta}, \tag{23c}$$

replacing each parameter with its sample estimate. Stability coefficients (the correlation between ξ_t and ξ_s), are also easily obtained; see equation 8 of Wiley and Wiley (1970).

With more time points, or more indicators, the Wiley–Wiley model can become richer, with fewer parameter restrictions; alternatively, we can estimate an over-identified version of the model. It is important to remember that the Wiley–Wiley model is simply a covariance structure model, a particular kind of confirmatory factor analysis or structural equations model, and the SEM framework provides a convenient framework for estimating the model and variants on it. Jöreskog (1970) refers to the this general class of dynamic latent variable models as "quasi Markov simplex" models. The number of articles using the Wiley–Wiley model, or versions of it, is staggering. For instance, Goren (2005) implements a multiple-indicator version of the model to estimate attitudinal stability over the 1992–94–96 NES panel; Bartels (1993) introduces time-invariant, social-structural variables as covariates in a modified Wiley–Wiley model for media exposure, using three waves of data from the 1980 NES; Markus (1983) uses the 1956–58–60 and 1972–74–76 to estimate the stability of party identification; Green and Palmquist (1990) estimate various Wiley–Wiley type models over four waves of panel data from the 1980 NES; Feldman (1989) estimates a Wiley–Wiley type model with five waves of panel data. A collation of findings using Wiley–Wiley type models across various panel data-sets appears in Green and Palmquist (1994).

10.2 Dynamic Measurement Models for Time Series

Another class of dynamic measurement models has been used widely in political science settings, for the case where the indicators form a time series, rather than a panel. Mathematically, the model does not look that different to the Wiley–Wiley model given above. An observational or measurement equation relates the indicators y_t to the latent state ξ_t:

$$y_t = B_t \xi_t + \gamma_t z_t + \delta_t \tag{24}$$

where B_t and γ_t are unknown parameters, z_t is a vector of exogenous variables, and δ_t is a mean zero disturbance with variance-covariance matrix R_t. The transition equation for the model is

$$\xi_t = F_t \xi_{t-1} + G_t x_t + \epsilon_t, \tag{25}$$

$t = 2, \ldots, T$, where F_t and G_t are unknown parameters, x_t is a vector of exogenous variables, and ϵ_t is a mean zero disturbance with variance-covariance matrix Ω_t. The primary goal of analysis is inference for the latent state variable ξ_t. As written, the model is quite general, allowing either the latent state vector ξ_t or the observational vector y_t to be a vector or a scalar. In this way the model encompasses special cases that sometimes go by distinct names in the literature: e.g. the DYMIMIC (dynamic, multiple indicators, multiple cause) model of Watson and Engle (1983; Engle and Watson 1980) is a special case of this model.

This type of model goes by different names in different parts of the statistics literature: Bayesians refer to this model as dynamic linear model (or DLM), for which West and Harrison (1997) is the standard reference, but see also Carter and Kohn (1994) and Frühwirth-Schnatter (2006); in classical or frequentist statistics, this model is estimated using a Kalman filter (e.g. Harvey 1989).

Applications of this model are reasonably abundant in political science. The typical application involves the analysis of aggregate polling data over time, treating the sampling error accompanying the survey estimates as measurement error δ_t, so to recover underlying trends in the latent variables, and additionally to estimate relationships among multiple latent variables, consistent with a causal, structural relationship. To this end, dynamic measurement models have figured prominently in the work of Stimson and his co-workers on macro-partisanship and dynamic representation: Stimson, Mackuen, and Erikson (1995); Erikson, MacKuen, and Stimson (2002), and, more generally, Stimson's (1991; 2004) work on the dynamics of public opinion. Contrast work by Donald Green and various co-workers making use of the Kalman filter to examine the stability of partisanship in the American electorate: e.g. Green, Palmquist, and Schickler (1998), Green, Gerber, and De Boef (1999), Green and Yoon (2002), and the recapitulation in Green, Palmquist, and Schickler (2002, ch. 4). Beck (1990) also used a KF to estimate the relationship between macroeconomic indicators and presidential approval, using a survey measure of the latter. Baum and Kernell (2001) also use a KF in investigating presidential approval for Franklin Roosevelt. Jackman (2005) uses a DLM to recover not only estimates of a dynamic latent variable (the breakdown of party support over the 2004 Australian federal election campaign), but estimate of house effects (biases specific to each polling organizations; a similar model applied to the case of approval for George W. Bush appears in Beck, Rosenthal, and Jackman 2006).

In these types of political science settings, the general model sketched in equations (24) and (25) dramatically simplifies. First, it is often the case that the latent variable is a scalar (e.g. when tracking support or levels of partisanship for one party, or presidential approval). There are often no exogenous variables z_t in the measurement equation, with the effect of covariates usually posited as working on the latent variable; contrast Jackman (2005) and Beck, Rosenthal, and Jackman (2006) where the measurement equation includes house effects. Simple dynamics are often posited for the latent variable, say a local-level/random-walk model, with $F_t = 1 \forall t$. The effects of covariates x_t are often made time invariant, as is the innovation variance term (i.e. $\Omega_t = \Omega$). For the analysis of survey aggregates, the restriction that $B_t = 1 \forall t$ is sensible, and moreover the stated sample size of the survey supplies information about R_t, the variance of the measurement error. These simplifications mean that many applications of the DLM/KF in political science settings reduce to a simple measurement equation, $y_t = \xi_t + \delta_t$, with $R_t = V(\delta_t) \approx y_t(1 - y_t)/n_t$, say, where $y_t \in [0, 1]$ is an estimate of a population proportion given a random sample of n_t observations, and a similarly simple transition equation $\xi_t = \xi_{t-1} + g x_t + \epsilon_t$, $t = 2, \ldots, T$ with $V(\epsilon_t) = \omega^2 \forall t$.

One of the great strengths of the KF/DLM approach is that it can easily handle the case where the indicators are missing (partially or completely) for any given time point. In such a case inference for ξ_t can proceed with the transitional model given in equation (25); in the case where the indicators y_t are available, both they and lagged and future values of ξ contribute to inferences for ξ_t. This is especially useful in political science settings, where the indicators are typically survey aggregates of some kind, and it is quite typical for surveys to have spotty temporal coverage.

REFERENCES

ACHEN, C. H. 1983. Toward theories of data: the state of political methodology. In *Political Science: The State of the Discipline*, ed. A. W. Finifter. Washington, DC: American Political Science Association.

—— 1985. Proxy variables and incorrect signs on regression coefficients. *Political Methodology*, 11: 299–316.

ADCOCK, R., and COLLIER, D. 2001. Measurement validity: a shared standard for qualitative and quantitative research. *American Political Science Review*, 95: 529–46.

ADCOCK, R. J. 1877. Note on the method of least squares. *Analyst*, 4.

AKAIKE, H. 1973. Information theory and an extension of the maximum likelihood principle. Pp. 267–81 in *Second International Symposium on Information Theory*, ed. B. N. Petrov and F. Csake. Budapest: Akedamiai Kiado.

ALBERT, J. 1992. Bayesian estimation of normal ogive item response curves using Gibbs sampling. *Journal of Educational Statistics*, 17: 251–69.

ALVAREZ, M., CHEIBUB, J. A., LIMONGI, F., and PRZEWORSKI, A. 1996. Classifying political regimes. *Studies in Comparative International Development*, 31: 3–36.

ALWIN, D. F. 2007. *Margins of Error*. Hoboken, NJ: John Wiley and Sons.

AMEMIYA, Y., and ANDERSON, T. W. 1990. Asymptotic chi-square tests for a large class of factor analysis models. *Annals of Statistics*, 18: 1453–63.

—— and FULLER, W. A. 1988. Estimation for the nonlinear functional relationship. *Annals of Statistics*, 16: 147–60.

AMERICAN PSYCHOLOGICAL ASSOCIATION 1954. Technical recommendations for psychological tests and diagnostic techniques. *Psychological Bulletin*, 51: 1–38.

ANDERSON, B. A., SILVER, B. D., and ABRAMSON, P. R. 1988. The effects of race of the interviewer on measures of electoral participation by blacks in SRC national election studies. *Public Opinion Quarterly*, 52: 53–83.

ANDERSON, T. W. 2003. *An Introduction to Multivariate Statistical Analysis*, 3rd edn. Hoboken, NJ: Wiley.

BAKER, F. B., and KIM, S.-H. 2004. *Item Response Theory: Parameter Estimation Techniques*, 2nd edn. New York: Dekker.

BARTELS, L. M. 1993. Messages received: the political impact of media exposure. *American Political Science Review*, 87: 267–85.

BARTKO, J. J. 1966. The intraclass correlation coefficient as a measure of reliability. *Psychological Bulletin*, 19: 3–11.

BARTLETT, M. S. 1937. The statistical conception of mental factors. *British Journal of Psychology*, 28: 97–104.

BAUM, M. A., and KERNELL, S. 2001. Economic class and popular support for Franklin Roosevelt in war and peace. *Public Opinion Quarterly*, 65: 198–229.

BECK, N. 1990. Estimating dynamic models using Kalman filtering. Pp. 121–56 in *Political Analysis*, ed. J. A. Stimson, vol. i. Ann Arbor: University of Michigan Press.

—— ROSENTHAL, H., and JACKMAN, S. 2006. Presidential approval: the case of George W. Bush. Presented to the Annual Meeting of the Society for Political Methodology, University of California, Davis.

BIEMER, P. P., GROVES, R. M., LYBERG, L. E., MATHIOWETZ, N. A., and SUDMAN, S. (eds.) 2004. *Measurement Errors in Surveys*. New York: Wiley.

BLAYDES, L., and LINZER, D. A. 2006. The political economy of women's support for fundamentalist Islam. Paper presented at the Annual Meeting of the American Political Science Association, Philadelphia.

BOCK, R. D., and AITKEN, M. 1981. Marginal maximum likelihood estimation of item parameters: application of an EM algorithm. *Psychometrika*, 46: 443–59.

BOLLEN, K. A. 1989. *Structural Equations with Latent Variables*. New York: Wiley.

BRADY, H. E. 1989. Factor and ideal point analysis for interpersonally incomparable data. *Psychometrika*, 54: 181–202.

—— 1991. Traits versus issues: factor versus ideal-point analysis of candidate thermometer ratings. In *Political Analysis*, ed. J. A. Stimson, vol. ii. Ann Arbor: University of Michigan Press.

BREEN, R. 2000. Why is support for extreme parties underestimated by surveys? A latent class analysis. *British Journal of Political Science*, 30: 375–82.

BROWNE, M. W. 1984. Asymptotically distribution free methods for the analysis of covariance structures. *British Journal of Mathematical and Statistical Psychology*, 37: 62–83.

BUDGE, I., ROBERTSON, D., and HEARL, D. (eds.) 1987. *Ideology, Strategy and Party Change: Spatial Analyses of Post-war Election Programmes in 19 Democracies*. Cambridge: Cambridge University Press.

CAMPBELL, D. T., and FISKE, D. W. 1959. Convergent and discriminant validation by the multitrait-multimethod matrix. *Psychological Bulletin*, 56: 81–105.

CARROLL, R. J., RUPPERT, D., and STEFASNSKI, L. A. 1995. *Measurement Error in Nonlinear Models*. London: Chapman and Hall/CRC.

CARSEY, T. M., and LAYMAN, G. C. 2006. Changing sides or changing minds? Party identification and policy preferences in the American electorate. *American Journal of Political Science*, 50: 464–77.

CARTER, C. K., and KOHN, R. 1994. On Gibbs sampling for state space models. *Biometrika*, 81: 541–53.

CLINTON, J., JACKMAN, S., and RIVERS, D. 2004. The statistical analysis of roll call data. *American Political Science Review*, 98: 355–70.

COLLIER, D., and ADCOCK, R. 1999. Democracy and dichotomies: a pragmatic approach to choices about concepts. *Annual Reviews of Political Science*, 2: 537–65.

CONVERSE, P. E. 1964. The nature of belief systems in mass publics. Pp. 206–61 in *Ideology and Discontent*, ed. D. E. Apter. New York: Free Press.

CRONBACH, L. J. 1951. Coefficient alpha and the internal structure of tests. *Psychometrika*, 16: 297–334.

—— and MEEHL, P. E. 1955. Construct validity in psychological tests. *Psychological Bulletin*, 52: 281–302.

DAVIS, O. A., HINICH, M. J., and ORDESHOOK, P. C. 1970. An expository development of a mathematical model of the electoral process. *American Political Science Review*, 64: 426–48.

DAYTON, C. M. 1998. *Latent Class Scaling Analysis*. Thousand Oaks, Calif.: Sage.

DE FIGUEIREDO, R. J. P., and ELKINS, Z. 2003. Are patriots bigots? An inquiry into the vices of in-group pride. *American Journal of Political Science*, 47: 171–88.

DELLI CARPINI, M. X., and KEETER, S. 1996. *What Americans Know about Politics and Why It Matters*. New Haven, Conn.: Yale University Press.

DEMPSTER, A. P., LAIRD, N. M., and RUBIN, D. B. 1977. Maximum likelihood from incomplete data via the *E M* algorithm. *Journal of the Royal Statistical Society, Series B*, 39: 1–38.

ELKINS, Z. 2000. Gradations of democracy? Empirical tests of alternative conceptualizations. *American Journal of Political Science*, 44: 287–94.

ENELOW, J., and HINICH, M. 1984. *The Spatial Theory of Voting: An Introduction*. New York: Cambridge University Press.

ENGLE, R., and WATSON, M. 1980. A time domain approach to dynamic factor and MIMIC models. *Cahiers du Seminaries d'Économetrie*, 22: 109–25.

ERIKSON, R. S. 1990. Roll calls, reputations, and representation in the U.S. senate. *Legislative Studies Quarterly*, 15: 623–42.

—— MacKUEN, M., and STIMSON, J. A. 2002. *The Macro Polity*. New York: Cambridge University Press.

FAN, X., and THOMPSON, B. 2001. Confidence intervals about score reliability coefficients, please: an *EPM* guidelines editorial. *Educational and Psychological Measurement*, 61: 517–31.

FELDMAN, S. 1989. Measuring issue preference: the problem of response instability. In *Political Analysis*, ed. J. A. Stimson, vol. i, Ann Arbor: University of Michigan Press.

FINKEL, S. E., HUMPHRIES, S., and OPP, K.-D. 2001. Socialist values and the development of democratic support in the former East Germany. *International Political Science Review*, 22: 339–61.

FREEMAN, J. R., HAYS, J. C., and STIX, H. 2000. Democracy and markets: the case of exchange rates. *American Journal of Political Science*, 44: 449–68.

FRÜHWIRTH-SCHNATTER, S. 2006. *Finite Mixture and Markov Switching Models*. New York: Springer.

FULLER, W. A. 2006. Errors in variables. In *Encyclopedia of the Statistical Sciences*, ed. S. Kotz, C. B. Read, N. Balakrishnan, and B. Vidakovic, 2nd edn. Hoboken, NJ: Wiley.

GELMAN, A., and KING, G. 1990. Estimating the consequences of electoral redistricting. *Journal of the American Statistical Association*, 85: 274–82.

GOODMAN, L. A. 1974. Exploratory latent structure analysis using both identifiable and uniden- tifiable models. *Biometrika*, 61: 215–31.

GORAN, P. 2004. Political sophistication and policy reasoning: a reconsideration. *American Journal of Political Science*, 48: 462–78.

—— 2005. Party identification and core political values. *American Journal of Political Science*, 49: 881–96.

GREEN, D. P., GERBER, A. S., and DE BOEF, S. L. 1999. Tracking opinion over time: a method for reducing sampling error. *Public Opinion Quarterly*, 63: 178–92.

—— and PALMQUIST, B. L. 1990. Of artifacts and partisan instability. *American Journal of Political Science*, 34: 872–902.

—— —— 1991. More "tricks of the trade:" reparameterizing LISREL models using negative variances. *Psychometrika*, 56: 137–45.

—— —— 1994. How stable is party identification? *Political Behavior*, 16: 437–66.

—— —— and SCHICKLER, E. 1998. Macropartisanship: a replication and critique. *American Political Science Review*, 92: 883–99.

—— —— —— 2002. *Partisan Hearts and Minds: Political Parties and the Social Identities of Voters*. New Haven, Conn.: Yale University Press.

—— and YOON, D. H. 2002. Reconciling individual and aggregate evidence concerning par- tisan stability: applying time series models to panel survey data. *Political Analysis*, 10: 1–24.

GRILICHES, Z., and RINGSTAD, V. 1970. Error-in-the-variables bias in nonlinear contexts. *Econometrica*, 38: 368–70.

GROVES, R. M. 1989. *Survey Errors and Survey Costs*. New York: Wiley.

GURR, T. R., and JAGGERS. K. 1996. Polity III: regime change and political authority, 1800–1994. Computer file, Inter-university Consortium for Political and Social Research, Ann Arbor.

GUTTMAN, L. 1945. A basis for analyzing test-retest reliability. *Psychometrika*, 10: 255–82.

HABERMAN, S. J. 1979. *Analysis of Quantitative Data*, vol. ii. New York: Academic Press.

HAMILTON, J. D. 1990. Analysis of time series subject to changes in regime. *Journal of Econo- metrics*, 45: 39–70.

HARMAN, H. H. 1976. *Modern Factor Analysis*, rev. 3rd edn. Chicago: University of Chicago Press.

HARVEY, A. C. 1989. *Forecasting, Structural Time Series Models and the Kalman Filter*. New York: Cambridge University Press.

HEINEN, T. 1996. *Latent Class and Discrete Latent Trait Models: Similarities and Differences*. Thousand Oaks, Calif.: Sage.

HILL, J. L., and KRIESI, H. 2001. An extension and test of Converse's "black- and-white" model of response stability. *American Political Science Review*, 95: 397–413.

HOFF, P., RAFTERY, A. E., and HANDCOCK, M. S. 2002. Latent space approaches to social network analysis. *Journal of the American Statistical Association*, 97: 1090–8.

HUBER, J., and INGLEHART, R. 1995. Expert interpretations of party space and party locations in 42 societies. *Party Politics*, 1: 73–111.

JACKMAN, S. 1995. Perception and reality in the American political economy. Ph.D. dissertation. Department of Political Science, Rochester, NY.

—— 2000. Estimation and inference are missing data problems: unifying social science statistics via Bayesian simulation. *Political Analysis*, 8: 307–32.

—— 2001. Multidimensional analysis of roll call data via Bayesian simulation: identification, estimation, inference and model checking. *Political Analysis*, 9: 227–41.

—— 2004. What do we learn from graduate admissions committees? A multiple-rater, latent variable model, with incomplete discrete and continuous indicators. *Political Analysis*, 12: 400–24.

—— 2005. Incumbency advantage and candidate quality. In *Mortgage Nation: The 2004 Australian Election*, ed. M. Simms and J. Warhurst. Perth: API Network/Edith Cowan University Press.

JACOBY, W. G. 1991. *Data Theory and Dimensional Analysis*. Number 07-078 in Quantitative Applications in the Social Sciences. Newbury Park, Calif.: Sage.

JÖRESKOG, K. G. 1967. Some contributions to maximum likelihood factor analysis. *Psychometrika*, 32: 443–82.

—— 1970. Estimation and testing of simplex models. *British Journal of Mathematical and Statistical Psychology*, 23: 121–45.

—— 1978. Structural analysis of covariance and correlation matrices. *Psychometrika*, 43: 443–77.

—— and SÖRBOM, D. 1989. *LISREL 7 User's Reference Guide*. Chicago: Scientific Software International.

KAISER, H. F. 1958. The varimax criterion for analytic rotation in factor analysis. *Psychometrika*, 23: 187–200.

KANE, E. W., and MACAULEY, L. J. 1993. Interviewer gender and gender attitudes. *Public Opinion Quarterly*, 57: 1–28.

KAPTEYN, A., and WANSBEEK, T. J. 1984. Errors in variables: consistent adjusted least squares (CALS) estimation. *Communications in Statistics—Theory and Methods*, 13: 1811–37.

KINDER, D. R., and SANDERS, L. M. 1996. *Divided by Color: Racial Politics and Democratic Ideals*. Chicago: University of Chicago Press.

KRIJNEN, W. P., WANSBEEK, T. J., and TEN BERGE, J. M. F. 1996. Best linear predictors for factor scores. *Communications in Statistics—Theory and Methods*, 25: 3013–25.

KUDER, G. F., and RICHARDSON, M. W. 1937. The theory of the estimation of test reliability. *Psychometrika*, 2: 151–60.

LADHA, K. 1991. A spatial model of voting with perceptual error. *Public Choice*, 78: 43–64.

LAWLEY, D. N. 1940. The estimation of factor loadings by the method of maximum likelihood. *Proceedings of the Royal Society of Edinburgh, Section A*, 60: 64–82.

—— and MAXWELL, A. E. 1971. *Factor Analysis as a Statistical Method*, 2nd edn. London: Butterworths.

LAZARSFELD, P. F. 1950. The logical and mathematical foundations of latent structure analysis. In *Measurement and Prediction*, ed. S. A. Stouffer. New York: John Wiley and Sons.

LEDERMAN, W. 1937. On the rank of the reduced correlational matrix in multiple factor analysis. *Psychometrika*, 2: 85–93.

LEE, S.-Y. 2007. *Structural Equation Modeling: A Bayesian Approach*. Chichester: Wiley.

LESSLER, J. T., and KALSBEEK, W. D. 1992. *Nonsampling Error in Surveys*. New York: Wiley.

LEVENDUSKY, M. S., POPE, J. C., and JACKMAN, S. 2008. Measuring district preferences with implications for the study of U.S. elections. *Journal of Politics*.

LINZER, D. A., and LEWIS, J. 2008. poLCA: an R package for Polytomous Variable Latent Class Analysis. *Journal of Statistical Software*.

LONDREGAN, J. 2000. *Legislative Institutions and Ideology in Chile's Democratic Transition*. New York: Cambridge University Press.

LORD, F. M., and NOVICK, M. R. 1968. *Statistical Theories of Mental Test Scores*. Reading, Mass.: Addison-Wesley.

MARDIA, K. V., KENT, J. T., and BIBBY, J. M. 1979. *Multivariate Analysis*. San Diego: Academic Press.

MARKUS, G. B. 1983. Dynamic modeling of cohort change: the case of political partisanship. *American Journal of Political Science*, 27: 717–39.

MARTIN, A. D., and QUINN, K. M. 2002. Dynamic ideal point estimation via Markov chain Monte Carlo for the U.S. Supreme Court, 1953–1999. *Political Analysis*, 10: 134–53.

McCUTCHEON, A. L. 1985. A latent class analysis of tolerance for nonconformity in the American public. *Public Opinion Quarterly*, 49: 474–88.

—— 1987. *Latent Class Analysis*. Beverly Hills, Calif.: Sage.

McDONALD, R. P. 1999. *Test Theory: A Unified Treatment*. Mahwah, NJ: Lawrence Erlbaum and Associates.

McLACHLAN, G. J., and PEEL, D. 2000. *Finite Mixture Models*. New York: Wiley.

PALMQUIST, B., and GREEN, D. P. 1992. Estimation of models with correlated measurement errors from panel data. In *Sociological Methodology*, ed. P. V. Marsden. Washington, DC: American Sociological Association.

PATZ, R. J., and JUNKER, B. W. 1999. A straightforward approach to Markov Chain Monte Carlo methods for item response models. *Journal of Educational and Behavioral Statistics*, 24: 146–78.

POOLE, K. T., and ROSENTHAL, H. 1997. *Congress: A Political-Economic History of Roll Call Voting*. New York: Oxford University Press.

QUINN, K. 2004. Bayesian factor analysis for mixed ordinal and continuous responses. *Political Analysis*, 12: 338–53.

—— MONROE, B. L., COLARESI, M., CRESPIN, M. H., and RADEV, D. R. 2007. How to analyze political attention with minimal assumptions and costs. Typescript, Department of Government, Harvard University.

RECKASE, M. D. 1997. The past and future of multidimensional item response theory. *Applied Psychological Measurement*, 21: 25–36.

RICHARDSON, S., and GREEN, P. J. 1997. On Bayesian analysis of mixtures with an unknown number of components. *Journal of the Royal Statistical Society Series B-Methodological*, 59: 731–58.

RIVERS, D. 2003. Identification of multidimensional item-response models. Typescript, Department of Political Science, Stanford University.

ROBERT, C. P. 1996. Mixtures of distributions: inference and estimation. Pp. 441–64 in *Markov Chain Monte Carlo in Practice*, ed. W. R. Gilks, S. Richardson, and D. J. Spiegelhalter. London: Chapman and Hall.

—— RYDEN, T., and TITTERINGTON, D. M. 2000. Bayesian inference in hidden Markov models through the reversible jump Markov chain Monte Carlo method. *Journal of the Royal Statistical Society Series B-Statistical Methodology*, 62: 57–75.

ROTHENBERG, T. J. 1971. Identification in parametric models. *Econometrica*, 39: 577–91.

SCHAEFFER, N. C. 2000. Asking questions about threatening topics: a selective overview. In *The Science of Self-Report: Implications for Research and Practice*, ed. A. A. Stone, J. S. Turkkan, C. A. Bachrach, J. B. Jobe, H. S. Kurtzman, and V. S. Cain. Mahwah, NJ: Erlbaum.

SCHWARTZ, G. 1978. Estimating the dimension of a model. *Annals of Statistics*, 6: 461–4.

SHROUT, P. E., and FLEISS, J. L. 1979. Intraclass correlations: uses in assessing rater reliability. *Psychological Bulletin*, 86: 420–8.

SKRONDAL, A., and RABE-HESKETH, S. 2004. *Generalized Latent Variable Modeling: Multilevel, Longitudinal, and Structural Equation Models.* Boca Raton, Fa.: Chapman and Hall/CRC.

SPEARMAN, C. 1904. "General intelligence," objectively determined and measured. *American Journal of Psychology,* 15: 201–93.

STIMSON, J. A. 1991. *Public Opinion in America: Moods, Cycles, and Swings.* Boulder, Colo.: Westview.

—— 2004. *Tides of Consent: How Public Opinion Shapes American Politics.* New York: Cambridge University Press.

—— MACKUEN, M. B., and ERIKSON, R. S. 1995. Dynamic representation. *American Political Science Review,* 89: 543–65.

SUDMAN, S., and BRADBURN, N. M. 1974. *Response Effects in Surveys: A Review and Synthesis.* Number 16 in National Opinion Research Center Monographs in Social Science. Chicago: Aldine.

TAKANE, Y., and DE LEEUW, J. 1987. On the relationship between item response theory and factor analysis of discretized variables. *Psychometrika,* 52: 393–408.

THURSTONE, L. L. 1935. *The Vectors of Mind.* Chicago: University of Chicago Press.

TINTER, G. 1952. *Econometrics.* New York: Wiley.

TOURANGEAU, R., RIPS, L. J., and RASINSKI, K. 2000. *The Psychology of the Survey Response.* New York: Cambridge University Press.

TREIER, S., and JACKMAN, S. 2008. Democracy as a latent variable. *American Journal of Political Science,* 52: 201–17.

VAN DER LINDEN, W. J., and HAMBLETON, R. K. (eds.) 1997. *Handbook of Modern Item Response Theory.* New York: Springer-Verlag.

VAN SCHUR, W. H. 1992. Nonparametric unidimensional unfolding for multicategory data. Pp. 41–74 in *Political Analysis,* ed. J. R. Freeman, vol. iv. Ann Arbor: University of Michigan Press.

VISWESVARAN, C., and ONES, D. S. 2000. Measurement error in "big five favors" personality assessment. *Educational and Psychological Measurement,* 60: 224–35.

WANSBEEK, T., and MEIJER, E. 2000. *Measurement Error and Latent Variables in Econometrics.* Amsterdam: North-Holland.

WATSON, M. W., and ENGLE, R. F. 1983. Alternative algorithms for the estimation of dynamic factor, MIMIC, and time-varying coefficient models. *Journal of Econometrics,* 15: 385–400.

WEST, M., and HARRISON, J. 1997. *Bayesian Forecasting and Dynamic Models.* New York: Springer-Verlag.

WILEY, D. E., and WILEY, J. A. 1970. The estimation of measurement error in panel data. *American Sociological Review,* 35: 112–17.

YIN, P., and FAN, X. 2000. Assessing the reliability of Beck Depression inventory scores. *Educational and Psychological Measurement,* 60: 201–33.

ZALLER, J., and FELDMAN, S. 1992. A simple theory of the survey response: answering questions versus revealing preferences. *American Journal of Political Science,* 36: 579–616.

CHAPTER 7

....

TYPOLOGIES: FORMING CONCEPTS AND CREATING CATEGORICAL VARIABLES

....

DAVID COLLIER

JODY LAPORTE

JASON SEAWRIGHT

1 INTRODUCTION

....

Typologies—understood as organized systems of types—make a fundamental contribution to concept formation and to the construction of categorical variables. Although some scholars might see typologies as part of the qualitative tradition of research, in fact they are also employed by quantitative analysts. This chapter provides

For the larger project of which this chapter is a part, many colleagues have provided valuable comments, including Andrew Bennet, Colin Elman, David Freedman, John Gerring, James Mohaney, Jason Wittenberg, and members of the Berkeley Latin American Politics Research Workshop.

an overview of these multiple contributions of typologies and presents numerous examples from diverse subfields of political science (Table 7.1).

Given our concern with the role of typologies in conceptualization and measurement, the discussion here necessarily focuses on "descriptive" typologies. In such typologies, the cells correspond to specific types or instances of a broader concept. These can be contrasted with "explanatory" typologies,[1] in which the rows and columns are explanatory variables, and the cells contain hypothesized outcomes. Both descriptive and explanatory typologies can, in addition, be used to classify cases.

This distinction between descriptive and explanatory typologies is by no means intended to suggest that descriptive typologies—as with any other form of measurement—are not connected with the formulation and testing of explanatory claims. The contrasting types contained in a particular typology may be the outcome to be explained in a given study, or they may be an explanation that is being formulated and evaluated by the researchers, as we will see in many examples below.

This chapter proceeds as follows. We offer a framework for working with multidimensional typologies, reviewing the building blocks of typologies, and showing how the cell types constitute categorical variables. We then consider the role of typologies in concept formation, the source of the concepts and terms in the cells of the typology, and the role of ideal types. Finally, we examine the contribution of typologies to mapping empirical and theoretical change and to structuring comparison in empirical analysis—with this latter contribution including their role in quantitative as well as qualitative research. We conclude by suggesting norms for the careful use of typologies.

2 THE STRUCTURE OF TYPOLOGIES

This section provides a framework for working with multidimensional typologies[2]—in other words, typologies that involve the cross-tabulation of two or more dimensions to form analytic types.

2.1 The Basic Template

Multidimensional typologies may be understood in terms of several components, which we illustrate with reference to Matland's (1995, 160) conceptualization of policy

---

[1] See Elman (2005) and Bennett and Elman (2006, 465–68). George and Bennett's (2005, ch. 11) discussion of "typological theory" is an important variant of this approach.

[2] These may be contrasted with unidimensional typologies, which are categorical variables organized around a single dimension. See, for example, Krasner's typology of the capacity of national states to shape the formation of international regimes, involving "makers, breakers, and takers" (1977, 52). We focus here on multidimensional typologies given their distinctive contribution to conceptualization and measurement. However, many ideas about multidimensional typologies also apply to unidimensional typologies.

Table 7.1. Inventory of multidimensional typologies

Political regimes
Bicameralism (Lijphart 1984)
Commitment to democracy (Bellin 2000)
Democracy (Lijphart 1968)
Democracy (Weyland 1995)
Democracy, defense against internal threats (Capoccia 2005)
Democracy, pathways to (von Beyme 1996)
Democracy, transitions to (Karl 1990)
Democratization (Collier 1999)
Dictatorships, personalist (Fish 2007)
Leadership authority (Ansell and Fish 1999)
Regime change (Leff 1999)
Regimes (Dahl 1971)
Regimes (Fish 1999)
Regimes (Remmer 1986)
Regimes in Africa (Bratton and van de Walle 1997)
Regimes, authoritarian (Linz 1975)
Regimes, postcommunist (McFaul 2002)
Transitions from authoritarian rule (O'Donnell and Schmitter 1986)

States and state–society relations
Context of contentious politics (Tilly and Tarrow 2007)
Corporatism; policies towards associability (Schmitter 1971)
Corruption (Scott 1972)
Ethnofederal state survival (Hale 2004)
Incorporation of labor movements (Collier and Collier 1991)
Incorporation of the working class (Waisman 1982)
Informal politics (Dittmer and Wu 1995)
Interest representation/aggregation (Schmitter 1974)

Russian elites' perceptions of borrowing (Moltz 1993)
Social policy (Mares 2003)
State economic strategies (Boix 1998)
State intervention in the economy (Levy 2006)
State role in economic development (Evans 1995)
Strike activity (Hibbs 1987)

International relations
Adversaries (Glaser 1992)
Foreign policy decision-making (Schweller 1992)
Governance in trade (Aggarwal 2001)
Great power conflict management (Miller 1992)
Human rights policies (Sikkink 1993)
Organizational forms of information systems (Dai 2002)
Realists (Talliaferro 2000–2001)
Sovereignty (Krasner 1999)
Soviet strategies (Herrmann 1992)
State behavior in the international system (Schweller 1998)
Wars (Vasquez 1993)

American politics, public policy, public law, and organizational/administrative theory
Decentralization (Leonard 1982)
Effect of foreign policy issues on elections (Aldrich, Sullivan, and Borgida 1989)
Issue voters (Carmines and Stimson 1980)
Policemen (Muir 1977)
Policy (Lowi 1972)
Policy decision-making (Kagan 2001)
Policy feedback (Pierson 1993)

Military service (Levi 1997)
Nation states (Haas 2000)
Nation states (Mann 1993)
National unification, regional support for (Ziblatt 2006)
Outcomes of social movements (Gamson 1975)
Revolutions, agrarian (Paige 1975)
Separatist activism (Treisman 1997)
State power (Mann 1993)
States (Ertman 1997)
Transnational coalitions (Tarrow 2005)
Union–government interactions (Murillo 2000)

Parties, elections, and political participation
Electoral mobilization, targeting of rewards for (Nichter 2008)
Market for votes (Lehoucq 2007)
Party regimes (Pempel 1990)
Party systems (O'Dwyer 2004)
Political mobilization (Dalton 2006)
Political parties (Levitsky 2001)

Political economy
Economic transformations (Ekiert and Kubik 1998)
Factor endowments (Rogowski 1989)
Financial regulatory systems (Vitols 2001)
Goods (Mankiw 2001)
National political economy (Hall and Soskice 2001)
National welfare state systems (Sapir 2005)
Political economies (Kullberg and Zimmerman 1999)
Regulatory reforms (Vogel 1996)
Reregulation strategies (Snyder 1999)

Policy implementation (Matland 1995)
Political relationships (Lowi 1970)
Rational administration (Bailey 1994)
Rule application (Kagan 1978)
Rural development (Montgomery 1983)
Voting behavior (Abramson, Aldrich, Paolino, and Rohde 1992)
White house–interest group liaisons (Peterson 1992)

Gender politics
State responses to women's movements (Mazur 2001)
State feminism (Mazur and Stetson 1995)
State feminism (Mazur and McBride 2008)
Women's policy agency activity (Mazur 2001)

Theory and methodology
Explanations of action (Parsons 2006)
Possible outcomes of a hypotheses test (Vogt 2005)
Survey questions (Martin 1984)
Approaches to comparative analysis (Kohli 1995)
Theories of modernization and development (Janos 1986)
Theories of political transformation (von Beyme 1996)
Time horizons in causal analysis (Pierson 2003)
Typologies (Bailey 1992)
Western scholarship on Russia (Fish 1995)

Social relations
Norms (Barton 1955)
Social environment (Douglas 1982)
Sociality, or individual involvement in social life (Thompson, Ellis, and Wildavsky 1990)

Table 7.2. Matland's typology of policy implementation

		Conflict	
		Low	High
Ambiguity	Low	Administrative implementation	Political implementation
	High	Experimental implementation	Symbolic implementation

Source: Adapted from Matland (1995).

implementation (Table 7.2). While these building blocks might seem straightforward, scholars too often limit the analytic potential of their typologies by failing to follow this basic template. In this example, Matland conceptualizes policy implementation by differentiating between level of conflict and level of ambiguity in the implementation process. The elements of his typology are:

(a) *Overarching concept*: The concept that is measured by the typology—in this case, "policy implementation."

(b) *Row and column variables*: These variables are cross-tabulated to form a matrix. In this example the row variable is "ambiguity," because its component categories define the rows, and the column variable is "conflict."

(c) *The matrix*: This cross-tabulation creates the familiar 2 × 2 matrix. Alternatively, more than two categories may be present on each variable, and/or more than two variables can be incorporated, thereby yielding still more cells.

(d) *Types*: The four types located in the cells are the different kinds of policy implementation. These have substantively meaningful labels: administrative, political, experimental, and symbolic. These types give conceptual meaning to each cell, corresponding to their position in relation to the row and column variables.

2.2 Cell Types as Categorical Variables

The cross-tabulation of two or more variables generates four or more cells, thereby creating a new categorical variable that may be nominal, partially ordered,[3] or ordinal. These typology-based categorical variables are conceptualized in terms of two or more dimensions, and thus help to address the concern that the variables employed in a given analysis may hide multidimensionality (Blalock 1982, 109; Jackman 1985, 169; Shively 2005, 32).

Matland's typology, for example, creates a *nominal scale*. The two dimensions of policy implementation—conflict and ambiguity—are ordered in the sense that both

---

[3] See Davey and Priestley (2002, ch. 1).

are given high-low values. Yet the four cells in the typology do not form a scale that measures greater or lesser degrees of policy implementation. The four categories are collectively exhaustive and mutually exclusive, but not ordered. Hence, they are a nominal scale.

By contrast, Dahl's (1971, ch. 1) famous typology of regimes creates a *partially ordered* scale. He builds the typology around the dimensions of public contestation and participation, yielding four basic types. Among the four types—polyarchy, competitive oligarchy, inclusive hegemony, and closed hegemony—polyarchy is the most "democratic," and closed hegemony is the least so. Yet there is no inherent order between the other two types, competitive oligarchy and inclusive hegemony. Hence, this is a partial order.

Finally, the cells in Aldrich, Sullivan, and Borgida's (1989, 136) typology of issue voting constitute an *ordinal scale*. The authors tabulate (1) small- versus large-issue differences between candidates, against (2) low- versus high-salience and accessibility of the issues. Here, one cell corresponds to a low effect, while a second cell corresponds to a high effect of opposing issues on the vote. The other two cells are given the same value: "low to some effect." Thus, a three-category ordinal scale is created.

In all three examples—in which the cell types constitute a nominal, partially ordered, or ordinal scale—the same point remains valid. Regardless of the resulting level of measurement, the two or more dimensions around which the typology is organized are the foundation for the cell types that constitute the scale.

2.3 Mutually Exclusive and Collectively Exhaustive Categories

If typologies are to meet the norms for standard categorical scales, the cells should be mutually exclusive and collectively exhaustive (Bailey 1992, 2188). For the purpose of classification, it is essential that these dual criteria be met; otherwise a given observed case might fit in more than one cell, or might not fit in any cell.

However, some well-known typologies do not meet the standard of mutually exclusive categories. For example, Hirschman's (1970) "exit, voice, and loyalty" has provided a framework for conceptualizing the response to decline in different kinds of organizations. Yet as Hirschman himself points out (1981, 212), these are not mutually exclusive categories. Voice, in the sense of protest or expression of dissatisfaction, can accompany either exit or loyalty.

Hirschman's typology can readily be modified to create mutually exclusive categories. Thus, the initial cell types can be adapted to define the row and column variables in a new 2 × 2 matrix. One dimension would be exit versus loyalty, and the other the exercise versus nonexercise of voice. Two of the cells would be loyalty with or without voice, and the other two would be exit with or without voice. This would produce a new typology which could be used for unambiguously classifying cases. These steps—converting the cell values into categories on one or more dimensions in a revised typology—may be seen as a general solution to the problem that the cells in a typology are not mutually exclusive.

With other typologies, the question arises of whether the categories are collectively exhaustive. This might occur when a typology developed for one set of cases is extended to additional cases. For example, in studies of Latin America, Levitsky (2001, 37) constructs a 2 × 2 typology to identify four types of political parties: personalistic-electoral, electoral-professional, mass-populist, and mass-bureaucratic; and Murillo (2000, 146) identifies four types of union–government interactions: cooperation, opposition, subordination, and resistance. These cell types appear to be collectively exhaustive for the cases under analysis. But if these typologies were applied to a wider range of cases, it seems likely that cases would be encountered that did not fit into these cell types. This should hardly lead to the conclusion that these are failed typologies. Rather, the idea of collectively exhaustive categories must, at least initially, be understood in relation to the domain for which the typology was constructed.

3 Constructing Typologies

To understand the construction of typologies, we must focus on the basic task of concept formation, the issue of where the concepts and terms come from, and the role of ideal types.

3.1 Concept Formation

Various frameworks have been proposed for systematizing concept formation in political science. Among them, that of Sartori (1970; 1984) has been highly influential and provides a useful point of departure here. Sartori challenged scholars to (1) devote careful attention to concepts, in part because they yield the basic "data containers" employed in research; (2) understand the semantic field in which their conceptual reasoning is situated—i.e. the field of concepts and meanings that frame their research; and (3) recognize that concepts can be understood as having a hierarchical structure, involving what has variously been called a ladder of abstraction or a ladder of generality. This recognition helps both with situating concepts in relation to one another, and with adapting them to different domains of comparison. For the present discussion, we use the more self-explanatory label "kind hierarchy" for this structure.[4] An obvious example: A parliamentary democracy is a kind of democracy, which is a kind of political regime.

---

[4] Sartori (1970) called this a ladder of "abstraction," and Collier and Mahon (1993) sought to clarify the focus by calling it a ladder of "generality." We are convinced that it is more self-explanatory to call it a kind hierarchy, a label that fits all of the examples discussed in these earlier studies. For example, Sartori offers the example of staff (in Weber's sense), bureaucracy, and civil service as involving a ladder of generality, but clearly it is also a kind hierarchy; and Collier and Mahon's example of Weberian types of authority likewise constitute a kind hierarchy.

Typologies directly address these three tasks. First of all, scholars who construct typologies necessarily are working systematically with concepts. Moreover, if they employ these typologies to classify cases, then the cells in the typology are, indeed, data containers. Second, typologies focus specifically on the relationships among concepts. We have used the term "overarching concept" to refer to the overall phenomenon measured by the categories in a typology, and we have treated the categories in a typology as a categorical measure of this overarching concept. Explicit discussion of concepts and subtypes, as in a typology, is an important step in mapping out the semantic field.

Finally, the overarching concept and the categorical variable that measures it are related as a kind hierarchy. Let us illustrate this claim with examples already presented in this chapter. Obviously, in Matland's typology, administrative, political, experimental, and symbolic implementation are *kinds* of policy implementation. In Dahl, polyarchies, inclusive hegemonies, competitive oligarchies, and closed hegemonies are *kinds* of political regimes. In Aldrich, Sullivan, and Borgida's typology of the effect of foreign policy issues on elections, the scale contained in their typology provides an ordered characterization of the *kinds* of effects deriving from foreign policy: low, "low to some," and large.

A kind hierarchy may of course have more than two levels. In Collier and Collier's analysis, their typology (1991, 166–7) distinguishes between two *kinds* of incorporation periods: state incorporation and party incorporation. Party incorporation is in turn differentiated into three *kinds:* radical populism, labor populism, and electoral mobilization by a traditional party.

To conclude, scholars who work with typologies can thereby address the basic priorities of concept analysis entailed in a framework such as Sartori's. We thus find a convergence between these two alternative perspectives.

3.2 Where the Concepts and Terms Come from

A key feature of a typology is the specific cell types it establishes—i.e. the concepts located in the cells and the terms to which they correspond. How do researchers select the concepts and terms for each cell?

For some typologies, the analyst simply labels the cells with terms that repeat the corresponding values on the row and column variables. Tilly and Tarrow's (2007, 56) book on contentious politics characterizes contexts of contention by cross-tabulating governmental capacity and regime type. They establish four types of contexts, the names of which simply repeat the categories of the row and column variables: high-capacity undemocratic, high-capacity democratic, low-capacity undemocratic, and low-capacity democratic.

Similarly, Rogowski's (1989, 8) study of commerce and coalitions distinguishes among four main constellations of factor endowments according to whether they involve a high or low land–labor ratio and an advanced or backwards economy. The four cells basically repeat the information presented in the rows and columns so that, for example, a high land–labor ratio and advanced economy correspond to a cell with abundant capital and land but scarce labor. On the other hand, a low land–labor ratio and backward economy correspond to a cell with abundant labor but scarce land and capital.

More commonly, scholars draw terms and concepts from other studies in the particular domain of research. Typologies serve to systematize the meaning of these terms, sometimes by providing a new definition that the researcher finds analytically productive.

For example, Weyland's (1995, 129) typology of democracies borrows common terms from the study of Latin American politics—populism, liberalism, concertation, and *basismo*[5]—and places them within Schmitter and Karl's (1992, 67) dimensions of democracy. These dimensions concern whether the locus of political power is to a greater degree in the state or in society, and whether the dominant principle of aggregation involves numbers (as in the electoral arena) or intensity (as might be the case with powerful elites). Weyland's goal in developing this typology is to provide a framework for understanding opportunities and constraints in pursuing "equity-enhancing reform" in Latin America. He focuses specifically on the opportunities and risks associated with the four types, according to the degree of policy gradualism and the kind of support base that characterize each type. Weyland's example thereby illustrates how a typology can be used to adapt already established dimensions and relatively standard types to a specific analytic purpose.

Researchers may also borrow existing terms, but develop a new meaning for them that helps advance a particular research program. Schmitter's (1974) widely cited typology of interest representation (or intermediation) situated the concept of corporatism in relation to pluralism, monism, and syndicalism. He seeks to persuade scholars that corporatism should be taken seriously as a specific type of interest representation that can be analyzed—based on a large number of dimensions—within a shared framework vis-à-vis these other types. Correspondingly, he advocates treating corporatism as a form of political structure rather than a political ideology, as some other scholars had done. Schmitter's typology played a notable role in refocusing a much wider literature on interest group politics.

Other scholars borrow from preexisting conceptualizations in a less direct way, synthesizing various existing theoretical approaches in order to coin new and useful terms. Kagan (2001, 10) proposes the concept of "adversarial legalism" to describe policy implementation procedures that are both formal and participatory. In developing this concept, he draws on the notion of an "adversarial system," which has been used for several centuries to characterize Anglo-American modes of adjudication, as opposed to the Continental/civil law tradition. Further, he builds on the traditional distinction between legalistic and informal modes of governance. Kagan thus joins these two separate theoretical approaches into a single typology focused on modes of policy implementation.

---

[5] I.e. "bottom-up" political relationships.

These several examples show why the terms and concepts presented in the cells of typologies must be understood in relation to the evolving literature in the given field. Typologies can systematize the meaning of these terms and concepts in novel and analytically productive ways.

3.3 Ideal versus Classificatory Types

Scholars sometimes refer to their analytic categories as ideal types, suggesting that these categories are broad abstractions that may not consistently serve to classify empirical cases. Examples are found in the writings of Schmitter, Luebbert, Weyland, Hall and Soskice, and Levy.[6] However, in these studies the scholars proceed with the classification of cases, such that they are at the same time working with classificatory types.

For instance, in his analysis of political-economic regimes in interwar Europe, Luebbert (1991, 3) states that he is working with ideal types, and then goes on to argue that his categories are valuable for sorting regimes. He states that although "the extent to which the societies corresponded to the idealized model of the regime varied," "it is seldom difficult to locate interwar European societies" in his three categories of liberal democracy, social democracy, and fascism. Schmitter (1974, 94), in conjunction with his elaborate definition of corporatism, makes a similar point about the interplay between abstraction and the concrete utility of his types: "Obviously, such an elaborate definition is an ideal-type." Yet while "no empirically extant system of interest representation may perfectly reproduce all these dimensions, two which I have studied in some detail (Brazil and Portugal) come rather close."[7]

Relatedly, Collier and Collier (1991, 17) frame the discussion in terms of "analytic categories" rather than "ideal types." They emphasize that the kinds of "incorporation periods" they analyze should be thought of as analytic categories, and not as "perfect descriptions of each country" that is placed in a particular category. In their analysis, focused on pairs of countries, they state that

obviously, the two countries within each category are not identical in terms of the defining dimensions, but they are far more similar to one another in terms of these dimensions than they are to the countries identified with the other categories. (1991, 17)[8]

This argument points to one possible reason for evoking ideal types. In some cases these analysts are perhaps not drawing heavily on the Weberian tradition, as

---

[6] Schmitter (1974, 94), Luebbert (1991, 3), Weyland (1995, 128 n. 8), Hall and Soskice (2001, 8), and Levy (2006, 387).

[7] For other examples of type concepts that are initially labeled as ideal types, but then used as classificatory types, see also Weyland (1995, 128 n.8); Hall and Soskice (2001, 8); Levy (2006, 387).

[8] Relatedly, both Rogowski (1989, 6) also Mares (2003) refer to the process of simplification entailed in the generation of dimensions and types, without using the label "ideal type."

might appear to be the case. Rather, they may be indirectly expressing the unease that readily arises when one seeks to fit cases into any scheme of classification. This unease may derive from the recognition that the cases grouped together in any one category usually cannot be understood as perfectly "equal." Rather, the claim is that they do indeed fit in a particular category, and not in another. The resolution here may be a simple recognition that categorization necessarily entails a process of abstraction.

4 PUTTING TYPOLOGIES TO WORK

Careful work with typologies gives structure to empirical comparison and maps change. Typologies also provide a useful bridge between qualitative and quantitative research.

4.1 Structuring Comparison

Well-executed analysis and comparison requires carefully constructing an appropriate analytic framework. Typologies make a valuable and direct contribution to achieving this. For example, Thompson, Ellis, and Wildavsky (1990, 8) employ the grid-group typology, originally developed by Mary Douglas (1982, 191), in their book on cultural theory. Working with the five types generated by the grid-group framework—fatalists, hierarchists, individualists, egalitarians, and hermits—these authors focus throughout their analysis on how individuals in the five categories respond to issues such as apathy, blame, religion, risk, and scarcity.

A further example is found in Mazur (2001, 22), who seeks to understand the interactions between women's social movements and the public sector. Borrowing from Gamson (1975, 29), she distinguishes four types of state response to women's movements: dual response (i.e. achieving both "descriptive" representation and "substantive" representation), co-optation, pre-emption, and no response. In their study, Mazur and her collaborators carry out a sustained application of their typology to eight national cases, and to the European Union, focusing especially on the conditions under which the dual response occurs.

Finally, Collier and Collier (1991, 504)—as noted above—present a typology of the "initial incorporation" of the labor movement in Latin America. Their goal is to differentiate cases according to the interplay between state control and different forms of popular mobilization. Throughout their analysis, alternative constellations of control and mobilization are a central point of reference, and the initial differentiation among cases identified in the incorporation period is explored through the full timespan under investigation.

In these three studies, the typology specifies an overarching concept (political culture, state responses, and initial incorporation), differentiates each overarching concept into analytic categories, and sorts cases accordingly. These typologies thereby provide a systematic basis for organizing key concepts, as well as for comparing cases and framing arguments, and the distinctions contained in the typologies are carried through the entire analysis.

4.2 Mapping Empirical and Theoretical Change

Typologies contribute to conceptualizing and describing new empirical developments. For example, in the literature on party organizations, Duverger (1954) proposes an initial (and very influential) distinction between "mass" and "cadre" parties, a distinction that revolves around three organizational dimensions: (a) broad versus narrow or nonexistent party membership (pp. 62–90); (b) extensive versus weak efforts to educate potential voters about politics and economics (p. 63); and (c) financial cultivation of a broad base of relatively modest contributions versus reliance on a small set of wealthy individual contributors—in Duverger's words, "a few big private donors, industrialists, bankers, or important merchants" (pp. 63–4). Hence, of the eight possible types of parties—derived from dichotomous values on each of the three dimensions—Duverger suggests that only two are empirically significant. The distinction between them grows out of Duverger's immersion in the history of political parties in Europe, where many of the earliest parties had an elite-dominated character notably absent from more recent ones, particularly socialist and communist parties.

Subsequently, Kirchheimer (1966, 184–92) observes that in the 1960s many European parties move away from the organizational pattern of the mass party, without the reliance on social elites that Duverger sees as characteristic of cadre parties. These new parties differ from mass parties in that they shift their ideological appeals from narrow class interests toward policies of potential benefit to majorities within society. At the same time, they seek electoral and other resources from ad hoc coalitions of interest groups, rather than from a mass base or wealthy individuals (1966, 192–5). To capture this configuration, Kirchheimer identifies a new category on the dimension of financial support: support derived from these organized groups. Kirchheimer thus adds the "catch-all" party to previous types.

More recently, Katz and Mair (1995) conclude, through a systematic analysis of party organizations throughout Western Europe, that newer parties have turned away from financial reliance on private individuals (whether wealthy or not) and likewise no longer seek funding from interest groups. Instead, parties obtain financing directly from the state (1995, 15–16). This pattern of funding can encourage cooperation among parties as they jointly seek to establish stable state support that extends beyond the incumbency of one or another party (1995, 17), leading Katz and Mair to designate the emergent organizational pattern as that of the "cartel" party.

In sum, given this understanding of party types in terms of three dimensions, it is specifically the appearance of novel patterns on one of the dimensions—the source of financial support—that yields the emergence of new types. The use of typologies thus helps bring into sharper focus this area of organizational change.

Scholars have also used typologies to capture change over time in the political economy of advanced industrial countries. Since the 1980s, the state's role in the economy has been substantially transformed, and considerable scholarly effort has been devoted to characterizing this transformation. Against the backdrop of prior research by other scholars, Levy (2006, 386) presents a new typology that synthesizes earlier approaches to national political economies, as well as his own perspective on recent patterns of change. Levy characterizes as "market direction" the more comprehensive state role characteristic of the earlier, post-Second World War period, as opposed to "market support," which is more characteristic of economies in the contemporary period. He also introduces a second dimension: the distinction between the authoritative exercise of state power and the use of infrastructural power by the state.

The 2 × 2 typology derived from these dichotomies allows Levy to compare more sharply the characteristics of the earlier versus later state role in the economy. In the earlier period, the cases characterized by an authoritative form of state power were "developmental" states, which engaged in planning, sectoral industrial policy, nationalizations, and selective protectionism. By contrast, the earlier cases characterized by infrastructural state power are labeled "corporatist," involving distinctive forms of cooperation and coordination with societal actors. He classifies postwar France and Japan as developmental states, and postwar Germany and Sweden as corporatist states. However, he suggests that for the more recent period, which corresponds to the categories of "corrective" state and "constructive" state, the assignment of entire countries to the two cells is not meaningful, given the high level of within-country heterogeneity across different policy areas. Instead of focusing on entire countries, Levy classifies specific policies within these two cells. This asymmetry in the unit of analysis within the typology serves to capture what Levy sees as a key shift in the appropriate level of aggregation.

Typologies can also play a role in efforts to reshape scholarly thinking about political realities that evolve *less* than had been anticipated. For example, in conceptualizations of regime types, post-Second World War Spain plays a prominent role in driving an analytic reorientation of this kind. Although many observers interpreted the Spanish fascist regime as being in transition toward democracy, it retained a surprising degree of stability for three decades. This divergence led Anderson (1970, 3) to observe that "the conventional interpretations of Spanish politics should be embarrassing to students of comparative politics." Anderson's own analysis builds on the innovative conceptualization of Linz (1964), who proposes a revision to earlier frameworks that had emphasized the distinction between democracy and totalitarianism, treated either as a dichotomy or a continuum. Linz argues that Spain could not be understood in those terms, and he adds authoritarianism as a distinctive regime type. He defines an authoritarian regime in terms of four dimensions: as a political system with limited pluralism; distinctive mentalities rather than a guiding ideology; limited political mobilization, except potentially at certain points in its development;

and an exercise of power within ill-defined, but in fact quite predictable, limits (Linz 1964, 297). Subsequently, Linz (1975, 278) draws on three of these four dimensions to construct a general typology of authoritarian and totalitarian regimes.

Thus, starting with a specific case that called into question a prior analytic framework, Linz develops a new approach to nondemocratic regimes, based on a much more elaborate, multidimensional framework.

4.3 Typologies and Quantitative Analysis

Far from being incompatible with quantitative research or offering a methodologically inferior form of analysis, typologies play a role in many quantitative studies. In a given piece of research that is predominantly quantitative, a typology—and the categorical variables upon which it is constructed—may help to overcome an impasse in the analysis, to identify a subset of cases on which the researcher wishes to focus, or to draw together the conclusions. In other instances, researchers may use quantitative analysis to assign cases to the cells in a typology.

In Hibbs's (1987, 69) analysis of strikes in eleven advanced industrial countries, a 2 × 2 typology is introduced at a point where quantitative analysis can be pushed no further. Hibbs creates a data-set of strikes in order to analyze long-run trends in their size, duration, and frequency. He uses bivariate correlations to demonstrate that increases in the political power of labor-based and left parties are associated with lower levels of strikes in the decades after the Second World War and hypothesizes that the role of public sector allocation serves as an intervening factor. Hibbs argues that as labor-left parties gain more political power, the locus of distributional conflict shifts from the marketplace to the arena of elections and public policy, thereby making strikes less relevant for trade union actors.

However, the multicollinearity among his variables is so high that—especially given Hibbs's small number of cases—it is not feasible to sort out the causal links. He therefore shifts from bivariate linear correlations to a 2 × 2 typology that cross-tabulates the level of state intervention in the economy against alternative goals of this intervention. For the period up to the 1970s, Hibbs identifies a subset of cases that manifest three patterns: relatively high levels of strikes directed at firms and enterprises (Canada, United States); high levels of strikes which serve as a form of pressure on the government (France, Italy); and a "withering away of the strike" that accompanies the displacement of conflict into the electoral arena (Denmark, Norway, Sweden). Using this typology, he analyzes the outcome in terms of three nonordered categories—in contrast to his overall argument about change in strike level that comes out of the standard correlational treatment.

Vasquez (1993, 73) likewise introduces a typology to resolve what he sees as an impasse in quantitative analyses—in this case, of the causes of war. Using the Correlates of War data, he observes that the literature has produced inconsistent findings in explaining the incidence of war, and he argues that such inconsistencies arise because war is being analyzed at too high a level of aggregation. He identifies eight types of war by cross-tabulating three dimensions: (1) equal versus unequal distribution of national power among belligerent states, (2) limited versus total war, and (3) number of participants. Vasquez uses this typology to focus on a subset of cases, i.e. wars of rivalry. He draws on findings from a wide range of qualitative and quantitative studies to address such questions as why some wars between rivals are limited while others are total, and why some wars of rivalry involve two players while others include more.

Typologies may also synthesize the findings of a quantitative analysis. Aldrich, Sullivan, and Borgida (1989, 136), in their study of the impact of foreign policy platforms on US presidential candidates' vote share, use a typology in this way. Analyzing survey data, they explore the degree to which campaign messages from presidential candidates have resonance with voters: specifically, the degree to which the campaign issues are (1) "available," in the sense that an opinion or position on a given issue is understood, and (2) "accessible," or perceived as relevant by voters. Whereas much of the article employs probit analysis to predict the victory of specific candidates, in the conclusion the authors seek to characterize broader types of elections. They employ a 2 × 2 matrix that classifies presidential elections according to whether there are small versus large differences in candidates' foreign policy stances, and according to the low- versus high-salience/accessibility of foreign policy issues raised in the each election.

Finally, other studies employ quantitative tools, including probit analysis, to place cases in the cells of a typology. Carmines and Stimson (1980, 4) posit a distinction between "easy" issue voting, in which citizens have a deeply embedded preference on a particular issue, and "hard" issue voting, in which citizens' issue preferences depend on a complex decision calculus, typically involving interactions and trade-offs among issues. To test this hypothesis, the authors construct a 2 × 2 typology to describe different types of voters, based on whether, in making a given electoral choice, the voter was swayed by easy versus hard issues. This yields a typology in which the cell types are nonissue voters, easy-issue voters, hard-issue voters, and constrained issue voters. The authors build on probit analysis to place respondents in these four cells, and they use this typology to show how easy- versus hard-issue voting are fundamentally different processes.

5 CONCLUSION

Typologies serve important goals in social science research. Good typologies depend on careful and substantively grounded conceptualization, and they are a basic tool for organizing and analyzing data. The use of typologies is strongly connected to the qualitative tradition of research, yet they play a role in quantitative analysis as well.

Drawing together the discussion above, we propose some guidelines for careful work with typologies. First, the presentation of typologies should be clear and readily understandable, involving either an explicit matrix and/or careful discussion in the text. We have mapped out the building blocks of a good typology, which centrally involve identifying the overall concept being measured, organizing the row and column variables, and establishing the cell types. Typologies that fail to follow this template may end up confusing rather than sharpening the analysis.

Second, the construction of cell types has special importance. Employing vivid names for the types enhances scholarly communication. More fundamentally, careful work with cell types pushes the researcher toward better conceptualization. Furthermore, the cell types, taken together, provide a new variable that measures the concept around which the typology is organized. Scholars should note carefully the level of measurement entailed in this variable. We have discussed three levels that are relevant here—nominal, partially ordered, and ordinal scales. Understanding the substantive content of the typology, and how the categories can be employed, requires a clear grasp of these alternatives.

Third, drawing on conventional discussions of categorical variables, we argue that the criterion of establishing mutually exclusive categories provides a useful norm in constructing typologies. Yet not all analytically interesting typologies meet this standard, and we have shown that a simple reorganization of such typologies can bring them into conformity with this norm.

Fourth, coming back to the distinction between descriptive and explanatory typologies noted at the beginning of this chapter, it is crucial to recognize which is which. One must distinguish carefully between cell types that provide a more differentiated descriptive characterization, as opposed to those that denote explanatory outcomes. Confusion about this distinction distorts the information contained in a typology.

Fifth, we must emphasize once more that this distinction between descriptive and explanatory typologies does not mean that descriptive typologies—again, as with any form of measurement—play no role in formulating and evaluating explanations. In some instances, the categories contained in the typology are the explanatory variable. For example, Thompson, Ellis, and Wildavsky use the categories in the grid-group typology as they seek to explain apathy and perception of risk. Similarly, Dahl introduces his typology of regime types with the central objective of distinguishing alternative trajectories in the movement toward polyarchy. His goal is to explore the hypothesis that different trajectories, as defined in relation to the categories in his typology, have important consequences for long-term regime outcomes.

In other instances, the typology is the outcome to be explained. Among alternative state responses to women's movements, Mazur's typology highlights the pattern of dual response, and she proceeds to consider the conditions under which this particular response occurs—as opposed to the others delineated in the typology. Relatedly, the typology can contribute to a disaggregation of the dependent variable, a disaggregation that the researcher sees as necessary for the explanatory enterprise to proceed. Thus, Vasquez argues that formulating and testing explanations of war cannot advance without a more differentiated conceptualization of war. His typology distinguishes one particular type, on which he then focuses in evaluating alternative explanations.

Thus, among these several guidelines for careful work with typologies, an important priority to keep clearly in view is their contribution to wider goals of formulating and evaluating explanatory claims.

Finally, and more broadly, we have argued that typologies can play a critical role in comparative analysis, and this role should be recognized. Typologies provide the basis for sharpening the theoretical types being investigated in a given study and clarifying the meaning of these types vis-à-vis related concepts. Typologies serve to compare concrete cases, both cross-sectionally and over time, and—as just emphasized—can be critical in the formulation and evaluation of explanatory claims. The adoption of clear norms for using typologies facilitates careful comparative work and helps scholars draw conclusions that are both conceptually sound and analytically productive.

References

ABRAMSON, P. R., ALDRICH J. H., PAOLINO P., and ROHDE D. W. 1992. "Sophisticated" voting in the 1988 presidential primaries. *American Political Science Review*, 86: 55–69.

AGGARWAL, V. K. 2001. Economics: international trade. In *Managing Global Issues: Lessons Learned*, ed. P. J. Simmons and C. de J. Oudraat. Washington, DC: Carnegie Endowment for International Peace.

ALDRICH, J. H., SULLIVAN J. L., and BORGIDA, E. 1989. Foreign affairs and issue voting: do presidential candidates "waltz before a blind audience?" *American Political Science Review*, 83: 123–41.

ANDERSON, C. W. 1970. *The Political Economy of Modern Spain*. Madison: University of Wisconsin Press.

ANSELL, C. K., and FISH, M. S. 1999. The art of being indispensable: noncharismatic personalism in contemporary political parties. *Comparative Political Studies*, 32: 283–312.

BAILEY, K. D. 1992. Typologies. In *Encyclopedia of Sociology*, vol. iv, ed. E. F. Borgatta and M. L. Borgatta. New York: Macmillan.

—— 1994. *Typologies and Taxonomies: An Introduction to Classification Techniques*. Thousand Oaks, Calif. Sage.

BARTON, A. H. 1955. The concept of property-space in social research. In *The Language of Social Research*, ed. P. F. Lazarsfeld and M. Rosenberg. Glencoe, Ill.: Free Press.

BELLIN, E. 2000. Contingent democrats: industrialists, labor, and democratization in late-developing countries. *World Politics*, 52: 175–205.

BENNETT, A., and ELMAN, C. 2006. Qualitative research: recent developments in case study methods. *Annual Review of Political Science*, 9: 455–76.

BLALOCK, H. 1982. *Conceptualization and Measurement in the Social Sciences*. Beverly Hills, Calif.: Sage.

BOIX, C. 1998. *Political Parties, Growth, and Equality: Conservative and Social Democratic Economic Strategies in the World Economy*. Cambridge: Cambridge University Press.

BRATTON, M., and VAN DE WALLE, N. 1997. *Democratic Experiments in Africa: Regime Transitions in Comparative Perspective*. Cambridge: Cambridge University Press.

CAPOCCIA, G. 2005. *Defending Democracy: Reactions to Extremism in Interwar Europe*. Baltimore: Johns Hopkins University Press.

CARMINES, E. G., and STIMSON, J. A. 1980. The two faces of issue voting. *American Political Science Review*, 74: 78–91.

COLLIER, D., and MAHON, J. E., JR. 1993. Conceptual "stretching" revisited: adapting categories in comparative analysis. *American Political Science Review*, 87: 845–55.

COLLIER, R. B. 1999. *Paths toward Democracy: The Working Class and Elites in Western Europe and South America*. Cambridge: Cambridge University Press.

——and COLLIER, D. 1991. *Shaping the Political Arena*. Princeton, NJ: Princeton University Press.

DAHL, R. A. 1971. *Polyarchy: Participation and Opposition*. New Haven, Conn.: Yale University Press.

DAI, X. 2002. Information systems in treaty regimes. *World Politics*, 54: 405–36.

DALTON, R. J. 2006. *Citizen Politics: Public Opinion and Political Parties in Advanced Industrial Democracies*, 4th edn. Washington, DC: CQ Press.

DAVEY, B. A., and PRIESTLEY, H. A. 2002. *Introduction to Lattices and Order*, 2nd edn. Cambridge: Cambridge University Press.

DITTMER, L., and WU, Y.-S. 1995. The modernization of factionalism in Chinese politics. *World Politics*, 47: 467–94.

DOUGLAS, M. 1982. *In the Active Voice*. London: Routledge and Kegan Paul.

DUVERGER, M. 1954. *Political Parties*. London: Methuen and Co.

EKIERT, G., and KUBIK, J. 1998. Contentious politics in new democracies: East Germany, Hungary, Poland and Slovakia, 1989–93. *World Politics*, 50: 547–81.

ELMAN, C. 2005. Explanatory typologies in qualitative studies of international politics. *International Organization*, 59: 293–326.

ERTMAN, T. 1997. *Birth of the Leviathan: Building States and Regimes in Medieval and Early Modern Europe*. Cambridge: Cambridge University Press.

EVANS, P. 1995. *Embedded Autonomy: States and Industrial Transformation*. Princeton, NJ: Princeton University Press.

FISH, M. S. 1995. *Democracy from Scratch: Opposition and Regime in the New Russian Revolution*. Princeton, NJ: Princeton University Press.

——1999. The end of Meciarism. *East European Constitutional Review*, 8: 47–55.

——2007. Really strange regimes: personality cults and personalistic dictatorships in the modern world. Department of Political Science, University of California, Berkeley.

GAMSON, W. A. 1975. *The Strategy of Social Protest*. Homewood, Ill.: Dorsey Press.

GEORGE, A., and BENNETT, A. 2005. *Case Studies and Theory Development in the Social Sciences*. Cambridge, Mass.: MIT Press.

GLASER, C. L. 1992. Political consequences of military strategy: expanding and refining the spiral and deterrence models. *World Politics*, 44: 497–538.

HAAS, E. B. 2000. *Nationalism, Liberalism, and Progress: The Dismal Fate of New Nations*, vol. ii. Ithaca, NY: Cornell University Press.

HALE, H. 2004. Divided we stand: institutional sources of ethnofederal state survival and collapse. *World Politics*, 56: 165–93.

HALL, P. A., and SOSKICE, D. 2001. An introduction to varieties of capitalism. In *Varieties of Capitalism: The Institutional Foundations of Comparative Advantage*, ed. P. A. Hall and D. Soskice. Oxford: Oxford University Press.

HERRMANN, R. K. 1992. Soviet behavior in regional conflicts: old questions, new strategies, and important lessons. *World Politics*, 44: 432–65.

HIBBS, D. A., JR. 1987. *The Political Economy of Industrial Democracies*. Cambridge, Mass.: Harvard University Press.

HIRSCHMAN, A. O. 1970. *Exit, Voice, and Loyalty: Responses to Decline in Firms, Organizations, and States*. Cambridge: Cambridge University Press.

—— 1981. *Essays in Trespassing: From Economics to Politics and Beyond*. Cambridge: Cambridge University Press.

JACKMAN, R. W. 1985. Cross-national statistical research and the study of comparative politics. *American Journal of Political Science*, 29: 161–82.

JANOS, A. 1986. *Politics and Paradigms: Changing Theories of Change in Social Science*. Stanford, Calif.: Stanford University Press.

KAGAN, R. A. 1978. *Regulatory Justice: Implementing a Wage-Price Freeze*. New York: Russell Sage Foundation.

—— 2001. *Adversarial Legalism*. Cambridge, Mass.: Harvard University Press.

KARL, T. L. 1990. Dilemmas of democratization in Latin America. *Comparative Politics*, 22: 1–21.

KATZ, R. S., and MAIR, P. 1995. Changing models of party organization and party democracy: the emergence of the cartel party. *Party Politics*, 1: 5–28.

KIRCHHEIMER, O. 1966. The transformation of West European party systems. In *Political Parties and Political Development*, ed. J. LaPalombara and M. Weiner. Princeton, NJ: Princeton University Press.

KOHLI, A. (ed.) 1995. The role of theory in comparative politics: a symposium. *World Politics*, 48: 1–49.

KRASNER, S. 1977. United States commercial and monetary policy: unraveling the paradox of external strength and internal weakness. In *Between Power and Plenty: Foreign Economic Policies of Advanced Industrial States*, ed. P. J. Katzenstein. Madison: University of Wisconsin Press.

—— 1999. *Sovereignty: Organized Hypocrisy*. Princeton, NJ: Princeton University Press.

KULLBERG, J. S., and ZIMMERMAN, W. 1999. Liberal elites, socialist masses and problems of Russian democracy. *World Politics*, 51: 323–58.

LEFF, C. S. 1999. Democratization and disintegration in multinational states: the breakup of the Communist federations. *World Politics*, 51: 205–35.

LEHOUCQ, F. 2007. When does a market for votes emerge? In *Elections for Sale: The Causes and Consequences of Vote Buying*, ed. F. C. Schaffer. Boulder, Colo.: Lynne Rienner.

LEONARD, D. K. 1982. Analyzing the organizational requirements for serving the rural poor. In *Institutions of Rural Development for the Poor: Decentralization and Organizational Linkages*, ed. D. K. Leonard and D. R. Marshall. Berkeley, Calif.: Institute of International Studies, Research Series No. 49.

LEVI, M. 1997. *Consent, Dissent, and Patriotism*. Cambridge: Cambridge University Press.

LEVITSKY, S. 2001. Organization and labor-based party adaptation: the transformation of Argentine Peronism in comparative perspective. *World Politics*, 54: 27–56.

LEVY, J. D. 2006. *The State after Statism: New State Activities in the Age of Liberalism*. Cambridge, Mass.: Harvard University Press.

LIJPHART, A. 1968. Typologies of democratic systems. *Comparative Political Studies*, 1: 3–44.

—— 1984. *Democracies: Patterns of Majoritarian and Consensus Government in Twenty-one Countries*. New Haven, Conn.: Yale University Press.

Linz, J. 1964. An authoritarian regime: Spain. In *Cleavages, Ideologies and Party Systems: Contributions to Comparative Political Sociology*, ed. E. Allardt and Y. Luttunen. Transactions of the Westermarck Society, vol. 10. Helsinki: Academic Bookstore.

—— 1975. Totalitarian and authoritarian regimes. In *Handbook of Political Science*, vol. iii, ed. F. I. Greenstein and N. W. Polsby. Reading, Mass: Addison-Wesley.

Lowi, T. 1970. Decision making vs. policy making: toward an antidote for technocracy. *Public Administration Review*, 30: 325–34.

—— 1972. Four systems of policy, politics, and choice. *Public Administration Review*, 32: 298–310.

Luebbert, G. M. 1991. *Liberalism, Fascism, or Social Democracy: Social Classes and the Political Origins of Regimes in Interwar Europe*. Oxford: Oxford University Press.

Mankiw, N. G. 2001. *Principles of Economics*, 2nd edn. Fort Worth, Tex.: Harcourt College.

Mann, M. 1993. *The Sources of Social Power, Vol II: The Rise of Classes and Nation-States, 1760–1914*. Cambridge: Cambridge University Press.

Mares, I. 2003. The sources of business interest in social insurance. *World Politics*, 55: 229–58.

Martin, E. 1984. Scheme for classifying survey questions according to their subjective properties. In *Surveying Subjective Phenomena*, vol. i, ed. C. F. Turner and E. Martin. New York: Russell Sage Foundation.

Matland, R. 1995. Synthesizing the implementation literature: the ambiguity-conflict model of policy implementation. *J-Part* (April): 159–70.

Mazur, A. 2001. *State Feminism, Women's Movements, and Job Training: Making Democracies Work in the Global Economy*. New York: Routledge.

—— and McBride, D. E. 2008. State feminism. In *Politics, Gender, and Concepts*, ed. G. Goertz and A. Mazur. Cambridge: Cambridge University Press.

—— and Stetson, D. M. 1995. Conclusion: the case for state feminism. In *Comparative State Feminism*, ed. A. Mazur and D. M. Stetson. London: Sage.

McFaul, M. 2002. The fourth wave of democracy and dictatorship: noncooperative transitions in the postcommunist world. *World Politics*, 54: 212–44.

McKinney, J. C. 1966. *Constructive Typology and Social Theory*. New York: Meredith.

Miller, B. 1992. Great power cooperation in conflict management. *World Politics*, 45: 1–46.

Moltz, J. C. 1993. Divergent learning and the failed politics of Soviet economic reform. *World Politics*, 45: 301–25.

Montgomery, J. D. 1983. Decentralizing integrated rural development activities. In *Decentralization and Development: Policy Implementation in Developing Countries*, ed. G. S. Cheema and D. A. Rondinelli. Beverly Hills, Calif.: Sage.

Muir, W. K., Jr. 1977. *Police: Streetcorner Politicians*. Chicago: University of Chicago Press.

Murillo, M. V. 2000. From populism to neoliberalism: labor unions and market reforms in Latin America. *World Politics*, 52: 135–74.

Nichter, S. 2008. Vote buying or turnout buying? Machine politics and the secret ballot. *American Political Science Review*, 102: 19–31.

O'Donnell, G. A., and Schmitter, P. C. 1986. *Transitions from Authoritarian Rule: Tentative Conclusions about Uncertain Democracies*. Baltimore: Johns Hopkins University Press.

O'Dwyer, C. 2004. Runaway state building: how political parties shape states in postcommunist Eastern Europe. *World Politics*, 56: 520–81.

Paige, J. M. 1975. *Agrarian Revolution: Social Movements and Export Agriculture in the Underdeveloped World*. New York: Free Press.

Parsons, C. 2006. *How to Map Arguments in Political Science*. Oxford: Oxford University Press.

PEMPEL, T. J. 1990. Introduction. In *Uncommon Democracies: The One-Party Dominant Regimes*, ed. T. J. Pempel. Ithaca, NY: Cornell University Press.

PETERSON, M. A. 1992. The presidency and organized interests: White House patterns of interest group liaison. *American Political Science Review*, 86: 612–25.

PIERSON, P. 1993. When effect becomes cause: policy feedback and political change. *World Politics*, 45: 595–628.

—— 2003. Big, slow-moving, and . . . invisible: macrosocial processes in the study of comparative politics. In *Comparative Historical Analysis in the Social Sciences*, ed. J. Mahoney and D. Rueschemeyer. Cambridge: Cambridge University Press.

REMMER, K. L. 1986. Exclusionary democracy. *Studies in Comparative International Development*, 20: 64–85.

ROGOWSKI, R. 1989. *Commerce and Coalitions*. Princeton, NJ: Princeton University Press.

SAPIR, A. 2005. Globalisation and the reform of European social models. Prepared for the ECOFIN Informal Meeting in Manchester, September 9. Accessed at <http://www.bruegel. org/Files/media/PDF/Publications/Papers/EN_SapirPaper080905.pdf>.

SARTORI, G. 1970. Concept misformation in comparative politics. *American Political Science Review*, 64: 1033–53.

—— (ed.) 1984. *Social Science Concepts: A Systematic Analysis*. Beverly Hills, Calif.: Sage.

SCHMITTER, P. C. 1971. *Interest Conflict and Political Change in Brazil*. Stanford, Calif.: Stanford University Press.

—— 1974. Still the century of corporatism? *Review of Politics*, 36: 85–105.

—— and KARL, T. L. 1992. The types of democracy emerging in Southern and Eastern Europe and South and Central America. In *Bound to Change: Consolidating Democracy in East Central Europe*, ed. P. M. E. Volten. New York: Institute for EastWest Studies.

SCHWELLER, R. 1992. Domestic structure and preventive war: are democracies more pacific? *World Politics*, 44: 235–69.

—— 1998. *Deadly Imbalances: Tripolarity and Hitler's Strategy of World Conquest*. New York: Columbia University Press.

SCOTT, J. C. 1972. *Comparative Political Corruption*. Englewood Cliffs, NJ: Prentice Hall.

SHIVELY, W. P. 2005. *The Craft of Political Research*. Upper Saddle River, NJ: Prentice Hall.

SIKKINK, K. 1993. The power of principled ideas: human rights policies in the United States and Western Europe. In *Ideas and Foreign Policy: Beliefs, Institutions, and Political Change*, ed. J. Goldstein and R. O. Keohane. Ithaca, NY: Cornell University Press.

SNYDER, R. 1999. After neoliberalism: the politics of reregulation in Mexico. *World Politics*, 51: 173–204.

TALIAFERRO, J. 2000–1. Security seeking under anarchy: defensive realism revisited. *International Security*, 25: 128–61.

TARROW, S. 2005. *The New Transnational Activism*. Cambridge: Cambridge University Press.

THOMPSON, M., ELLIS, R., and WILDAVSKY, A. 1990. *Cultural Theory*. Boulder, Colo.: Westview.

TILLY, C., and TARROW, S. 2007. *Contentious Politics*. Boulder, Colo.: Paradigm.

TREISMAN, D. S. 1997. Russia's "ethnic revival:" the separatist activism of regional leaders in a postcommunist order. *World Politics*, 49: 212–49.

VASQUEZ, J. A. 1993. *The War Puzzle*. Cambridge: Cambridge University Press.

VITOLS, S. 2001. The origins of bank-based and market-based financial systems: Germany, Japan, and the United States. In *The Origins of Nonliberal Capitalism: Germany and Japan in Comparison*, ed. W. Streeck and K. Yamamura. Ithaca, NY: Cornell University Press.

VOGEL, S. K. 1996. *Freer Markets, More Rules: Regulatory Reform in Advanced Industrial Countries*. Ithaca, NY: Cornell University Press.

VOGT, W. P. 2005. *Dictionary of Statistics of Methodology: A Nontechnical Guide for the Social Sciences*, 3rd edn. Thousand Oaks, Calif.: Sage.

VON BEYME, K. 1996. *Transition to Democracy in Eastern Europe*. New York: St Martin's Press.

WAISMAN, C. H. 1982. *Modernization and the Working Class: The Politics of Legitimacy*. Austin: University of Texas Press.

WEYLAND, K. 1995. Latin America's four political models. *Journal of Democracy*, 6: 125–39.

ZIBLATT, D. 2006. *Structuring the State: The Formation of Italy and Germany and the Puzzle of Federalism*. Princeton, NJ: Princeton University Press.

....

MEASUREMENT VERSUS CALIBRATION: A SET-THEORETIC APPROACH

....

CHARLES C. RAGIN

THIS chapter is organized around the distinction between measurement and calibration, with calibration understood as being more strongly anchored in the theoretical understandings around which a given study is organized. Set theory is a valuable tool for achieving meaningful calibration, and more specifically, fuzzy-set analysis is especially well suited to accomplishing this objective.

Fuzzy sets are relatively new to social science. The first comprehensive introduction of fuzzy sets to the social sciences was offered by Michael Smithson (1987). However, applications were few and far between until the basic principles of fuzzy-set analysis were elaborated through Qualitative Comparative Analysis (QCA; see Ragin 1987; 2000), an analytic system that is fundamentally set-theoretic, as opposed to correlational, in both inspiration and design. The marriage of these two yields fuzzy-set QCA (fsQCA), a family of methods that offers social scientists an alternative to conventional quantitative methods, based almost exclusively on correlational reasoning (see Ragin forthcoming).

The basic idea behind fuzzy sets is easy enough to grasp, but this simplicity is deceptive. A fuzzy-set scales degree of membership (e.g. membership in the set of

Democrats) in the interval from 0.0 to 1.0, with 0.0 indicating full exclusion from a set and 1.0 indicating full inclusion. However, the key to useful fuzzy-set analysis is well-constructed fuzzy sets, which in turn raises the issue of calibration. How does a researcher calibrate degree of membership in a set, for example, the set of Democrats? How should this set be defined? What constitutes full membership? What constitutes full nonmembership? What would a person with 0.75 membership in this set (more in than out, but not fully in) be like? How would this person differ from someone with 0.90 membership?

The main message of this chapter is that fuzzy sets, unlike conventional variables, must be calibrated. Because they must be calibrated, they are superior in many respects to conventional measures, as they are used in both quantitative and qualitative social science. In essence, I argue that fuzzy sets offer a middle path between quantitative and qualitative measurement. However, this middle path is not a compromise between these two; rather, it transcends many of the limitations of both.

1 What is Calibration?

Calibration is a necessary and routine research practice in such fields as chemistry, astronomy, and physics (Pawson 1989, 135–7). In these and other natural sciences, researchers *calibrate* their measuring devices and the readings these instruments produce by adjusting them so that they match or conform to dependably known standards. These standards make measurements directly interpretable (Byrne 2002). A temperature of 20 degrees Celsius is interpretable because it is situated in between 0 degrees (water freezes) and 100 degrees (water boils). By contrast, the calibration of measures according to agreed-upon standards is relatively rare in the social sciences.[1] Most social scientists are content to use uncalibrated measures, which simply show the positions of cases relative to each other. Uncalibrated measures, however, are clearly inferior to calibrated measures. With an uncalibrated measure of temperature, for example, it is possible to know that one object has a higher temperature than another or even that it has a higher temperature than average for a given set of objects, but still not know whether it is hot or cold. Likewise, with an uncalibrated measure of democracy it is possible to know that one country is more democratic than another or more democratic than average, but still not know if it is more a democracy or an autocracy.

[1] Perhaps the greatest calibration efforts have been exerted in the field of poverty research, where the task of establishing external standards (i.e. defining who is poor) has deep policy relevance. Another example of a calibrated measure is the Human Development Index developed by the United Nations and published in its *Human Development Report*. In economics, by contrast, *calibration* has a different meaning altogether. Researchers "calibrate" parameters in models by fixing them to particular values, so that the properties and behavior of other parameters in the model can be observed. This type of calibration is very different from the explicit calibration of measures, the central concern of this chapter.

Calibration is especially important in situations where one condition sets or shapes the context for other conditions. For example, the relationship between the temperature and volume of H_2O changes qualitatively at $0\,°C$ and then again at $100°C$. Volume decreases as temperature crosses $0\,°C$ and then increases as temperature crosses $100\,°C$. The Celsius scale is purposefully calibrated to indicate these "phase shifts," and researchers studying the properties of H_2O know not to examine the relationships between properties of H_2O without taking these two qualitative breakpoints into account. Knowledge of these phase shifts, which is external to the measurement of temperature per se, provides the basis for its calibration.[2]

Context-setting conditions that operate parallel to the phase shifts just described abound in the study of social phenomena. The most basic context-setting condition is the scope condition (Walker and Cohen 1985). When researchers state that a certain property or relationship holds or exists only for cases of a certain type (e.g. only for countries that are "democracies"), they have used a scope condition to define an enabling context. Another example of a context-setting condition in social science is the use of empirical populations as enabling conditions. For instance, when researchers argue that a property or relationship holds only for Latin American countries, they have used an empirically delineated population as a context-setting condition. While the distinction between scope conditions and populations is sometimes blurred, their use as context-setting conditions is parallel. In both usages, they act as conditions that enable or disable specific properties or relationships.

Tests for statistical interaction are usually motivated by this same concern for conditions that alter the relationships between other variables; that is, by this same concern for context-setting conditions. If the effect of X on Y increases from no effect to a substantial effect as the level of a third variable Z increases, then Z operates as a context-setting condition, enabling a relationship between X and Y. Unlike scope conditions and population boundaries, the interaction variable Z in this example varies by level and is not a simple presence/absence dichotomy. While having context-setting conditions vary by level or degree complicates their study, the logic is the same in all three situations. In fact, it could be argued that dichotomous context-setting conditions such as scope conditions are special cases of statistical interaction.

The fact that the interaction variable Z varies by level as a context-setting condition automatically raises the issue of calibration. At what level of Z does a relationship between X and Y become possible? At what level of Z is there a strong connection between X and Y? To answer these questions it is necessary to specify the relevant values of Z, which is a de facto calibration of Z. Over a specific range of values of Z, there is no relation between X and Y, while over another range there is a strong relation between X and Y. Perhaps over intermediate values of Z, there is a weak to moderate relation between X and Y. To specify these values or levels, it is necessary to bring in external, substantive knowledge in some way—to interpret these

---

[2] I thank Henry Brady for pointing out the importance of the idea of "phase shifts" as a way to elaborate my argument.

different levels as context-setting conditions. Unfortunately, researchers who test for statistical interaction have largely ignored this issue and have been content to conduct broad tests of statistical interaction, without attending to issues of calibration and context.

Despite the relevance of calibration to many routine social sciences concerns and practices, it is a topic that has largely been ignored. To set the stage for a discussion of fuzzy sets and their calibration, I first examine common measurement practices in quantitative and qualitative social research. After sketching these practices, I argue that a useful way for social scientists to incorporate measurement calibration into their research is through the use of fuzzy sets. I show further that fuzzy sets resonate with both the measurement concerns of qualitative researchers, where the goal often is to distinguish between relevant and irrelevant variation (that is, to interpret variation), and the measurement concerns of quantitative researchers, where the goal is the precise placement of cases relative to each other.

2 Common Measurement Practices in Quantitative Research

Measurement, as practiced in the social sciences today, remains relatively haphazard and unsystematic, despite the efforts and exhortations of many distinguished scholars (e.g. Duncan 1984; Pawson 1989). The dominant approach is the indicator approach, in which social scientists seek to identify the best possible empirical indicators of their theoretical concepts. For example, national income per capita (in US dollars, adjusted for differences in purchasing power) is often used as an empirical indicator of the theoretical concept of development, applied to countries. In the indicator approach the key requirement is that the indicator must vary across cases, ordering them in a way that is consistent with the underlying concept. The values of national income per capita, for example, must distinguish less developed from more developed countries in a systematic manner.

In this approach fine gradations and equal measurement intervals are preferred to coarse distinctions and mere ordinal rankings. Indicators like income per capita are especially prized not only because they offer fine gradations (e.g. an income per capita value of $5,500 is exactly $100 less than a value of $5,600), but also because the distance between two cases is considered the "same" regardless of whether it is the difference between $1,000 and $2,000 or between $21,000 and $22,000 (i.e. a $1,000 difference).[3] Such interval- and ratio-scale indicators are well-suited for the

---

[3] Actually, there is a world of difference between living in a country with a GNP per capita of $2,000 and living in one with a GNP per capita of $1,000; however, there is virtually no difference between living in one with a GNP per capita of $22,000 and living in one with a GNP per capita of $21,000. Such

most widely used analytic techniques for assessing relationships between variables, such as multiple regression and related linear techniques.[4]

More sophisticated versions of the indicator model use multiple indicators and rely on psychometric theory (Nunnally and Bernstein 1994). The core idea in psychometric theory is that an index that is composed of multiple, correlated indicators of the same underlying concept is likely to be more accurate and more reliable than any single indicator. A simple example: National income per capita could easily overstate the level of development of oil-exporting countries, making them appear to be more developed than they "really are." Such anomalies challenge the face validity of income per capita as an indicator of the underlying concept. However, using an index of development composed of multiple indicators (e.g. including such things as literacy, life expectancy, energy consumption, labor force composition, and so on) would address these anomalies, because many oil-exporting countries have relatively lower scores on some of these alternate indicators of development. Ideally, the various indicators of an underlying concept should correlate very strongly with each other. If they do not, then they may be indicators of different underlying concepts (Nunnally and Bernstein 1994). Only cases with consistently high scores across all indicators obtain the highest scores on an index built from multiple indicators. Correspondingly, only those cases with consistently low scores across all indicators obtain the lowest scores on an index. Cases in the middle, of course, are a mixed bag.

Perhaps the most sophisticated implementation of the indicator approach is through an analytic technique known as structural equation modeling (or "SEM;" see Bollen 1989). SEM extends the use of multiple indicators of a single concept (the basic psychometric model) to multiple concepts and their interrelationships. In essence, the construction of indexes from multiple indicators takes place within the context of an analysis of the interrelationships among concepts. Thus, index construction is adjusted in ways that optimize hypothesized relationships. Using SEM, researchers can evaluate the coherence of their constructed indexes within the context of the model in which they are embedded. Simultaneously, they can evaluate the coherence of the model as a whole.

All techniques in the "indicator" family share a deep reliance upon observed variation, which in turn is almost always sample specific in its definition and construction. As mentioned previously, in the conventional approach the key requirement that an indicator must meet is that it must order cases in a way that reflects the underlying concept. It is important to point out that these orderings are entirely relative in

---

fine points are rarely addressed by researchers who use the conventional indicator approach, but they must be confronted directly in research that uses calibrated measures (e.g. fuzzy sets).

[4] While most textbooks assert that ratio scales are the highest form of measurement because they are anchored by a meaningful zero point, it is important to note that fuzzy sets have three numerical anchors: 1.0 (full membership), 0.0 (full nonmembership), and 0.5 (the crossover point separating "more in" versus "more out" of the set in question). See Ragin (2000). If it is accepted than such "anchoring" signals a higher level of measurement, then it follows that a fuzzy set is a higher level of measurement than a ratio-scale variable.

nature. That is, cases are defined *relative to each other* in the distribution of scores on the indicator (i.e. as having "higher" versus "lower" scores). For example, if the United States' national income per capita is $1,000 higher than Italy's, then the United States correspondingly is considered *relatively* more developed. The greater the gap between countries, the more different their relative positions in the development hierarchy. Furthermore, the definition of "high" versus "low" scores is defined *relative to the observed distribution of scores*, usually conceived as a sample of scores drawn from a well-defined population. Thus, a case with a score that is above the sample's central tendency (usually the mean) has a "high" score; the greater this positive gap, the "higher" the score. Likewise, a case with a score that is below the mean has a "low" score; the greater this negative gap, the "lower" the score. Notice that the use of deviations from sample-specific measures of central tendency offers a crude but passive form of calibration. Its crudeness lies in the fact that the calibration standards (e.g. the mean and standard deviation) vary from one sample to the next and are inductively derived. By contrast, the routine practice in the physical sciences is to base calibration on external, dependably known standards (e.g. the boiling point of water).

At first glance, these conventional practices with respect to the use of indicators in the social sciences appear to be entirely straightforward and uncontroversial. It seems completely reasonable, for example, that countries should be ranked relative to each other and that some measure of central tendency, based on the sample or population in question, should be used to define "high" versus "low" scores. Again, the fundamental requirement of the indicator model is simply variation, which in turn requires only (1) a sample (or population) displaying a variety of scores and (2) a measure of central tendency based on the sample (or population). Note, however, that in this view all variation is considered equally *relevant*.[5] That is, variation in the entire range of the indicator is considered pertinent, with respect to what it reveals about the underlying concept. For example, the two countries at the very top of the income distribution are both "highly developed countries." Yet, the difference that separates them indicates that one is still more "highly developed" than the other. In the indicator approach, this difference is usually taken at face value, meaning that there is usually no attempt to look at the cases and ask whether this difference—or any other difference, regardless of magnitude—is a relevant or meaningful difference with respect to the underlying concept.[6] By contrast, the interpretation of scores relative to agreed upon, external standards is central to measurement calibration. These external standards provide a context for the interpretation of scores.

[5] Of course, researchers sometimes transform their variables (e.g. using logs) in order to reduce skew and shift the weight of the variation. However, such adjustments are relatively uncommon and, in any event, are usually understood mechanistically, as a way to improve the robustness of a model.

[6] Notice also that the idea that variation at either end of a distribution should be de-emphasized or truncated in some way is usually viewed with great suspicion by quantitative researchers because truncating variation tends to attenuate correlations.

3 COMMON MEASUREMENT PRACTICES
IN QUALITATIVE RESEARCH

In conventional quantitative research, measures are indicators of concepts, which in turn are components of models, which in turn are derived from theories. Thus, the quantitative approach to measurement is strongly theory centered. Much qualitative research, by contrast, is more knowledge centered and thus tends to be more grounded in empirical evidence and also more "iterative" in nature. That is, there is an interplay between concept formation and measurement, on the one hand, and research strategy, on the other (see, e.g., Glaser and Strauss 1967). The researcher begins with orienting ideas and broad concepts, and uses empirical cases to help refine and elaborate concepts (Becker 1958). This process of progressive refinement involves an iterative "back-and-forth" movement between ideas and evidence (Katz 1982; Ragin 1994). In this back-and-forth process, researchers specify and refine their empirical indicators and measures.

A simple example: Macro-level researchers often distinguish between countries that experienced "early" versus "late" state formation (see, e.g., Rokkan 1975). Those that developed "early" had certain advantages over those that developed "late" and vice versa. David Laitin (1992, xi), for example, notes that coercive nation-building practices available earlier to monarchs (e.g. the draconian imposition of a national language) are not available to leaders of new states today, in part because of the international censure these policies might generate. But what is "early" state formation? The occurrence of state formation, of course, can be dated. Thus, it is possible to develop a relatively precise ratio-scale measure of the "age" of a state. But most of the variation captured by this simple and direct measure is not relevant to the concept of "early" versus "late" state formation. Suppose, for example, that one state has been around for 500 years and another for 250 years. The first is twice as old as the second, but both are fully "early" when viewed through the lens of accumulated substantive and theoretical knowledge about state formation. Thus, much of the variation captured by the ratio-scale indicator "age" is simply irrelevant to the distinction between "early" versus "late" state formation. "Age in years" must be adjusted on the basis of accumulated substantive knowledge in order to be able to interpret "early" versus "late" in a way that resonates appropriately with existing theory.

Such calibrations are routine in qualitative work, even though they are rarely modeled or even stated explicitly. Indeed, from the perspective of conventional quantitative research, it appears that qualitative researchers skew their measurements to fit their preconceptions. In fact, however, the qualitative researcher's goal is simply to interpret "mere indicators" such as "age in years" in the light of knowledge about cases and the interests of the investigator (e.g. whether a state is "early" or "late" from the standpoint of state formation theory).

A second essential feature of measurement in qualitative research is that it is more case oriented than measurement in quantitative research. This observation goes well beyond the previous observation that qualitative researchers pay more attention to the details of cases. In case-oriented research, the conceptual focus is on specific *kinds* of cases, for example the "developed countries." In variable-oriented research, by contrast, the focus is on dimensions of variation in a defined sample or population of cases, for example variation in level of development across currently constituted nation states. The distinction is subtle but important because cases can vary not only along a given dimension, but also in how well they satisfy the requirements for membership in a category or set. For example, countries vary in how well they satisfy requirements for membership in the set of developed countries—some cases satisfy them fully, some partially, and some not at all. In order to assess how well cases satisfy membership requirements, it is necessary to invoke external standards, for example regarding what it takes for a country to be considered developed. Thus, in the case-oriented view, the key focus is on sets of cases, the members of which can be identified and studied individually (e.g. the "developed countries"). In the variable-oriented view, by contrast, cases are usually understood simply as sites for taking measurements (that is, they are often seen as mere "observations"), which in turn provide the necessary raw material for studying relationships between variables, viewed as cross-case patterns.

It follows that the case-oriented view is more compatible with the idea that measures should be calibrated, for the focus is on the degree to which cases satisfy membership criteria, which in turn are usually externally determined, not inductively derived (e.g. using the sample mean). These membership criteria must reflect agreed-upon standards; otherwise, the constitution of a category or set will be contested. In the variable-oriented view, the members of a population simply vary in the degree to which they express a given trait or phenomenon, and there is usually no special motivation for specifying the criteria for membership in a set or for identifying specific cases as instances. Thus, a key difference between the qualitative approach to measurement and the quantitative approach is that in the qualitative approach meaning is attached to or imposed upon specific measurements, for example what constitutes "early" state formation or what it takes to warrant designation as a developed country. In short, measurement in qualitative research is interpreted.

The qualitative sociologist Aaron Cicourel was an early proponent of the understanding of measurement described here. In his classic text, *Method and Measurement in Sociology*, he argues (1964, 24) that it is necessary to consider the three "media" through which social scientists develop categories and link them to observable properties of objects and events: language, cultural meaning, and the properties of measurement systems. In his view, the problem of establishing equivalence classes (like "democracies" or "developed countries") cannot be seen as independent or separate from problems of language and cultural meaning. He argues (1964, 33):

Viewing variables as quantitative because available data are expressed in numerical form or because it is considered more "scientific" does not provide a solution to the problems of measurement but avoids them in favor of measurement by fiat. Measurement by fiat is not a substitute for examining and re-examining the structure of our theories so that our observations, descriptions, and measures of the properties of social objects and events have a literal correspondence with what we believe to be the structure of social reality.

In simple terms Cicourel argues that measures and their properties must be evaluated in the context of both theoretical and substantive knowledge. The fact that social scientists may possess a ratio-scale indicator of a theoretical concept does not mean that this aspect of "social reality" has the mathematical properties of this type of scale.

Thus, in qualitative research, the idea that social scientists should use external standards to evaluate and interpret their measures has much greater currency than it does in conventional quantitative research. A key difference with quantitative research, however, is that measurement in qualitative research is typically lacking in precision, and the context-sensitive and case-oriented way of measuring that is typical of qualitative research often appears haphazard and unscientific.

4 Fuzzy Sets: A Bridge between the Two Approaches

With fuzzy sets it is possible to have the best of both worlds; namely, the precision that is prized by quantitative researchers and the use of substantive knowledge to calibrate measures that is central to qualitative research. With fuzzy sets, precision comes in the form of quantitative assessments of degree of set membership, which can range from a score of 0.0 (full exclusion from a set) to 1.0 (full inclusion). For example, a country might have a membership score of 0.85 in the set of democracies, indicating that it is clearly more in this set than out, but still not fully in. Substantive knowledge provides the external criteria that make it possible to calibrate measures. This knowledge indicates what constitutes full membership, full nonmembership, and the point at which cases are more "in" a given set than "out" (Ragin 2000; Smithson and Verkuilen 2006).

The external criteria that are used to calibrate measures and translate them into set membership scores may reflect standards based on social knowledge (e.g. the fact that twelve years of education constitutes an important educational threshold), collective social scientific knowledge (e.g. about variation in economic development and what it takes to be considered fully in the set of "developed" countries), or the researcher's own accumulated knowledge, derived from the study of specific cases. These external criteria should be stated explicitly, and they also must be applied systematically and transparently. This requirement separates the use of fuzzy sets from conventional qualitative work, where the standards that are applied usually remain implicit.

Fuzzy sets are able to bridge quantitative and qualitative approaches to measurement because they are simultaneously qualitative and quantitative. Full membership and full nonmembership are qualitative states. In-between these two qualitative states are varying degrees of membership ranging from "more out" (closer to 0.0) to "more in" (closer to 1.0). Fuzzy sets are also simultaneously qualitative and quantitative because they are both case oriented and variable oriented. They are case oriented in their focus on sets and set membership. In case-oriented work, the identity of cases matters, as does the sets to which a case may belong (e.g. the set of democracies). Fuzzy sets are also variable oriented in their allowance for degrees of member-ship and thus for fine-grained variation across cases. This aspect of fuzzy sets also provides a basis for precise measurement, which is greatly prized in quantitative research.

A key difference between a fuzzy set and a conventional variable is how they are conceptualized and labeled. For example, while it is possible to construct a generic variable *years of education*, it is impossible to transform this variable directly into a fuzzy set without first designating and defining a target set of cases. In this instance, the researcher might be interested in the set of individuals with *at least a high school education* or perhaps the set of individuals who are *college educated*. This example makes it clear that the designation of different target sets dictates different calibration schemes. A person who has one year of college education, for example, will have full membership (1.0) in the set of people who are at least high school educated, but this same person clearly has less than full membership in the set of people who are college educated. In a parallel fashion, it is clear that *level of economic development* makes sense as a generic variable, but in order to calibrate it as a fuzzy set, it is necessary to specify a target set, for example the set of *developed countries*. Notice that this requirement—that the researcher designate a target set—not only structures the calibration of the set, it also provides a direct connection between theoretical dis-course and empirical analysis. After all, it is more common for theoretical discourse to be organized around designated sets of cases (e.g. the "developed countries") than it is for it to be organized around generic variables (e.g. "level of economic development").

Finally, these examples clarify a key feature of fuzzy sets central to their calibration—the fact that in order to calibrate a fuzzy set it is necessary for researchers to distinguish between relevant and irrelevant variation. For example, the difference between an individual who has completed one year of college and an individual who has completed two years of college is irrelevant to the set of individuals with at least a high school education, for both of these individuals are fully in this set (membership = 1.0). Their one-year difference is simply not relevant to the target set, as conceptualized and labeled. When calibrating a fuzzy set, variation that is irrelevant to the set must be truncated so that the resulting membership scores faithfully reflect the target set's label. This requirement also establishes a close connection between theoretical discourse and empirical analysis.

The use of external criteria to calibrate fuzzy sets is the primary focus of the remainder of this chapter. I focus specifically on situations where the researcher has a serviceable interval- or ratio-scale indicator of a concept and seeks to transform it into a well-calibrated fuzzy set.

5 TRANSFORMING INTERVAL-SCALE VARIABLES INTO FUZZY SETS

Ideally, the calibration of degree of membership in a set should be based entirely on the researcher's substantive and theoretical knowledge. That is, the collective knowledge base of social scientists should provide the basis for the specification of precise calibrations. For example, armed with an adequate knowledge of development, social scientists should be able to specify the per capita income level that signals "full membership" in the set of developed countries. Unfortunately, the social sciences are still in their infancy, and this knowledge base does not exist. Furthermore, the dominance of variable-oriented research, with its paramount focus on mean-centered variation and on covariation as the key to assessing relationships between case aspects, undermines scholarly interest in substantively based thresholds and benchmarks. While the problem of specifying thresholds and benchmarks has not attracted the attention it deserves, it is not a daunting task. The primary requirement for useful calibration is simply sustained attention to the substantive issues at hand (e.g. what constitutes full membership in the set of developed countries).

Despite the imperfections of the existing knowledge base, it is still possible to demonstrate techniques of calibration. All that is lacking is precise "agreed-upon standards" for calibrating measures. To the extent possible, the calibrations presented here are based on the existing theoretical and substantive literature. Still, the focus is on techniques of calibration, and not on the specific empirical benchmarks used to structure calibration.

The proposed techniques assume that researchers already have at their disposal conventional interval-scale indicators of their concepts, for example per capita national income as an indicator of development. The techniques also assume that the underlying concept can be structured and labeled in set-theoretic terms, for example "degree of membership in the set of developed countries." Notice that this labeling requirement moves the investigation in a decidedly case-oriented direction. "The set of developed countries" identifies specific countries, while "level of development" does not. The latter simply identifies a dimension of cross-national variation.

I present two methods of calibration. The "direct method" focuses on the three qualitative anchors that structure fuzzy sets: the threshold for full membership, the threshold for full nonmembership, and the crossover point. The "indirect method," by contrast, uses regression techniques to estimate degree of set membership based on a six-value coding scheme. Both methods yield precise calibrations of set membership scores based upon either qualitative anchors (direct method) or qualitative groupings (indirect method).

Before discussing the direct method, I should explain that this method uses estimates of the log of the odds of full membership in a set as an intermediate step. While this translation route—using estimates of the log odds of full membership—may seem roundabout, the value of the approach will become clear as the demonstration

Table 8.1. Mathematical translations of verbal labels

1. Verbal label	2. Degree of membership	3. Associated odds	4. Log odds of full membership
Full membership	0.993	148.41	5.0
Threshold of full membership	0.953	20.09	3.0
Mostly in	0.881	7.39	2.0
More in than out	0.622	1.65	0.5
Crossover point	0.500	1.00	0.0
More out than in	0.378	0.61	−0.5
Mostly out	0.119	0.14	−2.0
Threshold of full nonmembership	0.047	0.05	−3.0
Full nonmembership	0.007	0.01	−5.0

proceeds. For now, consider Table 8.1, which shows the different metrics that are used in the demonstration of the direct method. The first column shows various verbal labels that can be attached to differing degrees of set membership, ranging from full nonmembership to full membership. The second column shows the degree of set membership linked to each verbal label. For convenience, degree of membership is rounded to three decimal places. The third column shows the odds of full membership that result from the transformation of the set membership scores (column 2) into the odds of full membership, using the following formula:

odds of membership = (degree of membership)/(1 − (degree of membership))

The last column shows the natural log of the odds reported in column 3. In effect, columns 2 through 4 are different representations of the same numerical values, using different metrics. For example, the membership score attached to "threshold of full membership" is 0.953. Converting it to an odds yields 20.09. Calculating the natural log of 20.09 yields a score of 3.0.[7]

Working in the metric of log odds is useful because this metric is completely symmetric around 0.0 (an odds of 50/50) and suffers neither floor nor ceiling effects. Thus, for example, if a calibration technique returns a value in the log of odds that is either a very large positive number or a very large negative number, its translation to degree of membership stays within the 0.0 to 1.0 bounds, which is a core requirement of fuzzy membership scores. The essential task of calibration using the direct method is to transform interval-scale variables into the log odds metric in a way that respects the verbal labels shown in column 1 of Table 8.1.[8]

---

[7] The values shown for degree of membership in column 2 have been adjusted (e.g. using .993 instead of .999 for full membership) so that they correspond to simple, single-digit entries in column 4.

[8] The procedures for calibrating fuzzy membership scores presented in this chapter are mathematically incapable of producing set membership scores of exactly 1.0 or 0.0. These two membership scores would correspond to positive and negative infinity, respectively, for the log of the odds. Instead, scores that are greater than 0.95 may be interpreted as full membership in the target set, and scores that are less than 0.05 may be interpreted as full nonmembership.

It is important to note that the set membership scores that result from these transformations (ranging from 0.0 to 1.0) are *not* probabilities, but instead should be seen simply as transformations of interval scales into degree of membership in the target set. In essence, a fuzzy membership score attaches a *truth value*, not a probability, to a statement (for example, the statement that a country is in the set of developed countries). The difference between a truth value and a probability is easy to grasp, and it is surprising that so many scholars confuse the two. For example, the *truth value* of the statement "beer is a deadly poison" is perhaps about .05—that is, this statement is almost but not completely out of the set of true statements, and beer is consumed freely, without concern, by millions and millions of people every day. However, these same millions would be quite unlikely to consume a liquid that has a .05 *probability* of being a deadly poison, with death the outcome, on average, in one in twenty beers.

6 THE DIRECT METHOD OF CALIBRATION

The starting point of any set calibration is clear specification of the target set. The focus of this demonstration is the set of developed countries, and the goal is to use per capita national income data to calibrate degree of membership in this set. Altogether, 136 countries are included in the demonstration; Table 8.2 presents data on 24 of these 136 countries, which were chosen to represent a wide range of national income values.

The direct method uses three important qualitative anchors to structure calibration: the threshold for full membership, the threshold for full nonmembership, and the crossover point (see Ragin 2000). The crossover point is the value of the interval-scale variable where there is maximum ambiguity as to whether a case is more in or more out of the target set. For the purpose of this demonstration, I use a per capita national income value of $5,000 as the crossover point. An important step in the direct method of calibration is to calculate the deviations of raw scores (shown in column 1) from the crossover point designated by the investigator ($5,000 in this example). These values are shown in column 2 of Table 8.2. Negative scores indicate that a case is more out than in the target set, while positive scores signal that a case is more in than out.

For the threshold of full membership in the target set, I use a per capita national income value of $20,000, which is a deviation score of $15,000 (compare columns 1 and 2 of Table 8.2). This value corresponds to a set membership score of .95 and a log odds of 3.0. Thus, cases with national income per capita of $20,000 or greater (i.e. deviation scores of $15,000 or greater) are considered fully in the target set, with set membership scores $\geq$ .95 and log odds of membership $\geq$ 3.0. In the reverse direction, the threshold for full nonmembership in the target set is $2,500, which is a deviation score of $-$2,500. This national income value corresponds to a set membership

Table 8.2. Calibrating degree of membership in the set of developed countries: direct method

Country	1. National income	2. Deviations from crossover	3. Scalars	4. Product of 2 × 3	5. Degree of membership
Switzerland	40110	35110.00	.0002	7.02	1.00
United States	34400	29400.00	.0002	5.88	1.00
Netherlands	25200	20200.00	.0002	4.04	.98
Finland	24920	19920.00	.0002	3.98	.98
Australia	20060	15060.00	.0002	3.01	.95
Israel	17090	12090.00	.0002	2.42	.92
Spain	15320	10320.00	.0002	2.06	.89
New Zealand	13680	8680.00	.0002	1.74	.85
Cyprus	11720	6720.00	.0002	1.34	.79
Greece	11290	6290.00	.0002	1.26	.78
Portugal	10940	5940.00	.0002	1.19	.77
Korea, Rep.	9800	4800.00	.0002	.96	.72
Argentina	7470	2470.00	.0002	.49	.62
Hungary	4670	−330.00	.0012	−.40	.40
Venezuela	4100	−900.00	.0012	−1.08	.25
Estonia	4070	−930.00	.0012	−1.12	.25
Panama	3740	−1260.00	.0012	−1.51	.18
Mauritius	3690	−1310.00	.0012	−1.57	.17
Brazil	3590	−1410.00	.0012	−1.69	.16
Turkey	2980	−2020.00	.0012	−2.42	.08
Bolivia	1000	−4000.00	.0012	−4.80	.01
Côte d'Ivoire	650	−4350.00	.0012	−5.22	.01
Senegal	450	−4550.00	.0012	−5.46	.00
Burundi	110	−4890.00	.0012	−5.87	.00

score of .05 and a log odds of −3.0. Thus, cases with national income per capita of $2,500 or lower (i.e. deviation scores of −$2,500 or lower) are considered fully out of the target set, with set membership scores ≤ .05 and log odds of membership ≤ −3.0.

Once these three values (the two thresholds and the crossover point) have been selected, it is possible to calibrate degree of membership in the target set. The main task at this point is to translate the crossover centered national income data (column 2) into the metric of log odds, utilizing the external criteria that have been operationalized in the three qualitative anchors. For deviation scores *above* the crossover point, this translation can be accomplished by multiplying the relevant deviation scores (in column 2 of Table 8.2) by the ratio of the log odds associated with the verbal label for the threshold of full membership (3.0) to the deviation score designated as the threshold of full membership (i.e. 20,000 − 5,000 = 15,000). This ratio is 3/15,000 or .0002. For deviation scores *below* the crossover point, this translation can be accomplished by multiplying the relevant deviation scores (in column 2 of Table 8.2) by the ratio of the log odds associated with the verbal label for the threshold of full nonmembership (−3.0) to the deviation score designated as the threshold of full nonmembership ($2,500 −$5,000 = −$2,500). This ratio is −3/−2500 or .0012. These two scalars are shown in column 3, and the products of columns 2 and 3 are shown in column 4.[9] Thus, column 4 shows the translation of income deviation scores into the log odds metric, using the three qualitative anchors to structure the transformation via the two scalars.

The values in column 4, in effect, are per capita national income values that have been rescaled into values reflecting the log odds of membership in the set of developed countries, in a manner that strictly conforms to the values attached to the three qualitative anchors—the threshold of full membership, the threshold of full nonmembership, and the crossover point. Thus, the values in column 4 are not mere mechanistic rescalings of national income, for they reflect the imposition of external criteria via the three qualitative anchors. The use of such external criteria is the hallmark of measurement calibration.

It is a small step from the log odds reported in column 4 to the degree of membership values reported in column 5. It is necessary simply to apply the standard formula for converting log odds to scores that range from 0.0 to 1.0, namely:

$$\text{degree of membership} = \exp(\log \text{odds})/(1 + \exp(\log \text{odds}))$$

where "exp" represents the exponentiation of log odds to simple odds.[10] Note that the membership values reported in the last column of Table 8.2 strictly conform to the distribution dictated by the three qualitative anchors. That is, the threshold for full membership (0.95) is pegged to an income per capita value of $20,000; the crossover point (0.50) is pegged to an income of $5,000; and so on. For further illustration of the results of the direct method, consider Figure 8.1, which shows a plot of degree of membership in the set of developed countries against per capita national income, using data on all 136 countries included in this demonstration. As the plot shows, the line flattens as it approaches 0.0 (full nonmembership) and 1.0 (full membership), consistent with the conceptualization of degree of set membership. What the plot does not reveal is that most of the world's countries are in the lower-left corner of the plot, with low national incomes and full exclusion from the set of developed countries (i.e. set membership scores ≤ 0.05).

To illustrate the importance of external criteria to calibration, consider using the same national income data (column 1 of Table 8.2) to calibrate degree of membership in the set of countries that are "at least moderately developed." Because the definition of the target set has changed, so too must the three qualitative anchors. Appropriate anchors for the set of "at least moderately developed" countries are: a crossover value

---

[9] These two scalars constitute the slopes of the two lines extending from the origin (0,0) to the two threshold points (15000,3) and (−2500, −3) in the plot of the deviations of national income from the crossover point (X axis) against the log odds of full membership in the set of developed countries (Y axis).

[10] These procedures may seem forbidding. For the mathematically disinclined, I note that the complex set of computational steps depicted in Table 8.2 can be accomplished with a simple *compute* command using the software package fuzzy-set/Qualitative Comparative Analysis (fsQCA; see Ragin, Drass, and Davies 2006).

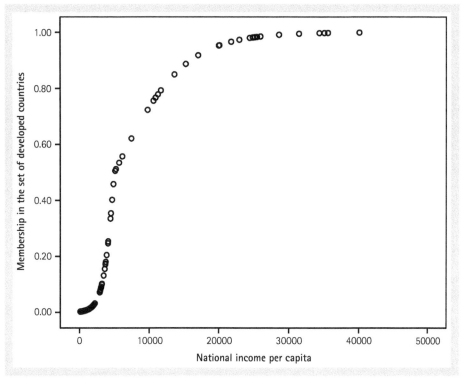

Fig. 8.1. Plot of degree of membership in the set of developed countries against national income per capita: direct method

of $2,500; a threshold of full membership value of $7,500; and a threshold of full nonmembership value of $1,000. The appropriate scalars in this example are 3/5000 for cases above the crossover value, and −3/−1500 for cases below the crossover value. The complete procedure is shown in Table 8.3, using the same cases as in Table 8.2.

The key point of contrast between Tables 8.2 and 8.3 is shown in the last column, the calibrated membership scores. For example, with a national income per capita of $2,980, Turkey has a membership of .08 in the set of developed countries. Its membership in the set of "at least moderately developed" countries, however, is 0.57, which places it above the crossover point. Notice, more generally, that in Table 8.3 there are many more cases that register set membership scores close to 1.0, consistent with the simple fact that more countries have high membership in the set of countries that are "at least moderately developed" than in the set of countries that are fully "developed." The contrast between Tables 8.2 and 8.3 underscores both the knowledge-dependent nature of calibration and the impact of applying different external standards to the same measure (per capita national income). Again, the key to understanding calibration is to grasp the importance of external criteria, which are based, in turn, on the substantive and theoretical knowledge that researchers bring to their research.

Table 8.3. Calibrating degree of membership in the set of "moderately" developed countries: direct method

Country	1. National income	2. Deviations from crossover	3. Scalars	4. Product of 2 × 3	5. Degree of membership
Switzerland	40110	37610	.0006	22.57	1.00
United States	34400	31900	.0006	19.14	1.00
Netherlands	25200	22700	.0006	13.62	1.00
Finland	24920	22420	.0006	13.45	1.00
Australia	20060	17560	.0006	10.54	1.00
Israel	17090	14590	.0006	8.75	1.00
Spain	15320	12820	.0006	7.69	1.00
New Zealand	13680	11180	.0006	6.71	1.00
Cyprus	11720	9220	.0006	5.53	1.00
Greece	11290	8790	.0006	5.27	.99
Portugal	10940	8440	.0006	5.06	.99
Korea, Rep.	9800	7300	.0006	4.38	.99
Argentina	7470	4970	.0006	2.98	.95
Hungary	4670	2170	.0006	1.30	.79
Venezuela	4100	1600	.0006	.96	.72
Estonia	4070	1570	.0006	.94	.72
Panama	3740	1240	.0006	.74	.68
Mauritius	3690	1190	.0006	.71	.67
Brazil	3590	1090	.0006	.65	.66
Turkey	2980	480	.0006	.29	.57
Bolivia	1000	−1500	.0020	−3.00	.05
Côte d'Ivoire	650	−1850	.0020	−3.70	.02
Senegal	450	−2050	.0020	−4.10	.02
Burundi	110	−2390	.0020	−4.78	.01

7 THE INDIRECT METHOD OF CALIBRATION

In contrast to the direct method, which relies on specification of the numerical values linked to three qualitative anchors, the indirect method relies on the researcher's broad groupings of cases according to their degree of membership in the target set. In essence, the researcher performs an initial sorting of cases into different levels of membership, assigns these different levels preliminary membership scores, and then refines these membership scores using the interval-scale data.

Consider again the data on per capita national income, this time presented in Table 8.4. The first and most important step in the indirect method is to categorize cases in a qualitative manner, according to their presumed degree of membership in the target set. These qualitative groupings can be preliminary and open to revision. However, they should be based as much as possible on existing theoretical and

Table 8.4. Calibrating degree of membership in the set of developed countries: indirect method

Country	1. National income	2. Qualitative coding	3. Predicted Value
Switzerland	40110	1.00	1.000
United States	34400	1.00	1.000
Netherlands	25200	1.00	1.000
Finland	24920	1.00	1.000
Australia	20060	1.00	.999
Israel	17090	0.80	.991
Spain	15320	0.80	.977
New Zealand	13680	0.80	.991
Cyprus	11720	0.80	.887
Greece	11290	0.80	.868
Portugal	10940	0.80	.852
Korea, Rep.	9800	0.60	.793
Argentina	7470	0.60	.653
Hungary	4670	0.40	.495
Venezuela	4100	0.40	.465
Estonia	4070	0.40	.463
Panama	3740	0.20	.445
Mauritius	3690	0.20	.442
Brazil	3590	0.20	.436
Turkey	2980	0.20	.397
Bolivia	1000	0.00	.053
Côte d'Ivoire	650	0.00	.002
Senegal	450	0.00	.000
Burundi	110	0.00	.000

Note: 1.00 = fully in the target set; 0.80 = mostly but not fully in the target set; 0.60 = more in than out of the target set; 0.40 = more out than in the target set; 0.20 = mostly but not fully out of the target set; 0.0 = fully out of the target set.

substantive knowledge. The six key qualitative categories used in this demonstration are:[11]

(a) in the target set (membership = 1.0),
(b) mostly but not fully in the target set (membership = 0.8),
(c) more in than out of the target set (membership = 0.6),
(d) more out than in the target set (membership = 0.4),
(e) mostly but not fully out of the target set (membership = 0.2), and
(f) out of the target set (membership = 0.0).

[11] Of course, other coding schemes are possible, using as few as three qualitative categories. The important point is that the scoring of these categories should reflect the researcher's initial estimate of each case's degree of set membership. These qualitative assessments provide the foundation for finer-grained calibration.

These categorizations are shown in column 2 of Table 8.4, using explicit numerical values to reflect preliminary estimates of degree of set membership. These six numerical values are not arbitrary, of course, but are chosen as rough estimates of degree of membership specific to each qualitative grouping. The goal of the indirect method is to rescale the interval-scale indicator to reflect knowledge-based, qualitative groupings of cases, categorized according to degree of set membership. These qualitative interpretations of cases must be grounded in substantive knowledge. The stronger the empirical basis for making qualitative assessments of set membership, the more precise the calibration of the values of the interval-scale indicator as set membership scores.

Note that the qualitative groupings implemented in Table 8.4 have been structured so that they utilize roughly the same criteria used to structure the calibrations shown in Table 8.2. That is, countries with national income per capita greater than $20,000 have been coded as fully in the set of developed countries; countries with income per capita greater than $5,000 have been coded as more in than out; and so on. By maintaining fidelity to the qualitative anchors used in Table 8.2, it is possible to compare the results of the two methods. The direct method utilizes precise specifications of the key benchmarks, while the indirect method requires only a broad classification of cases.

The next step is to use the two series reported in columns 1 and 2 of Table 8.4 to estimate the predicted qualitative coding of each case, using per capita national income as the independent variable and the qualitative codings as the dependent variable. The best technique for this task is a fractional logit model, which is implemented in STATA in the FRACPOLY procedure.[12] The predicted values resulting from this analysis are reported in column 3 of Table 8.4. The reported values are based on an analysis using all 136 cases, not the subset of 24 presented in the table. The predicted values, in essence, constitute estimates of fuzzy membership in the set of developed countries based on per capita national income (column 1) and the qualitative analysis that produced the codings shown in column 2.

Comparison of the set membership scores in column 5 of Table 8.2 (direct method) and column 3 of Table 8.4 (indirect method) reveals great similarities, but also some important differences. First notice that Table 8.2 faithfully implements $20,000 as the threshold for full membership in the set of developed countries (0.95). In Table 8.4, however, this threshold value drops well below New Zealand's score ($13,680). Second, observe that using the indirect method there is a large gap separating Turkey (.397) and the next case, Bolivia (.053). Using the direct method, however, this gap is much narrower, with Turkey at .08 and Bolivia at .01. These differences, which arise despite the use of the same general criteria, follow from the indirectness of

---

[12] In STATA this estimation procedure can be implemented using the commands "fracpoly glm qualcode intervv, family(binomial) link(logit)" and then "predict fzpred" where "qualcode" is the variable that implements the researcher's six-value coding of set membership, as shown in Table 8.4; "intervv" is the name of the interval-scale variable that is used to generate fuzzy membership scores; and "fzpred" is the predicted value showing the resulting fuzzy membership scores. I thank Steve Vaisey for pointing out the robustness of this estimation technique.

the second method and its necessary reliance on regression estimation. Still, if researchers lack the external criteria required by the direct method, the comparison of Tables 8.2 and 8.4 confirms that the indirect method produces useful set membership scores.

8 Using Calibrated Measures

Calibrated measures have many uses. They are especially useful when it comes to evaluating theory that is formulated in terms of set relations. While some social science theory is strictly mathematical, the vast majority of it is verbal. Verbal theory, in turn, is formulated almost entirely in terms of set relations (Ragin 2000; 2006). Unfortunately, social scientists have been slow to recognize this fact. Consider, for example, the statement that "the developed countries are democratic." As in many statements of this type, the assertion is essentially that instances of the set mentioned first (developed countries) constitute a *subset* of instances of the set mentioned second (democracies). (It is common in English to state the subset first, as in the statement "ravens are black.") Close examination of most social science theories reveals that they are composed largely of statements describing set relations, such as the subset relation. These set relations, in turn, may involve a variety of different types of empirical connections—descriptive, constitutive, or causal, among others.

The set relation just described (with developed countries as a subset of democratic countries) is also compatible with a specific type of causal argument, namely that development is sufficient but not necessary for democracy. In arguments of this type, if the cause (development) is present, then the outcome (democracy) should also be present. However, instances of the outcome (democracy) without the cause (development) do not count against or undermine the argument that development is sufficient for democracy (even though such cases dramatically undermine the correlation). Rather, these instances of the outcome without the cause are due to the existence of alternate routes or recipes for that outcome (e.g. the imposition of a democratic form of government by a departing colonial power). Thus, in situations where instances of a causal condition constitute a subset of instances of the outcome, a researcher may claim that the cause is sufficient but not necessary for the outcome.[13]

Before the advent of fuzzy sets (Zadeh 1965; 1972; 2002; Lakoff 1973), many social scientists disdained the analysis of set-theoretic relations because such analyses required the use of categorical-scale variables (i.e. conventional binary or "crisp"

[13] As always, claims of this type cannot be based simply on the demonstration of the subset relation. Researchers should marshal as much corroborating evidence as possible when making any type of causal claim.

sets), which in turn often necessitated the dichotomization of interval and ratio scales. For example, using crisp sets, in order to assess a set-theoretic statement about developed countries, a researcher might be required to categorize countries into two groups, developed and not developed, using per capita national income. Such practices are often criticized because researchers may manipulate breakpoints when dichotomizing interval- and ratio-scale variables in ways that enhance the consistency of the evidence with a set-theoretic claim. However, as demonstrated here, it is possible to calibrate degree of membership in sets and thereby avoid arbitrary dichotomizations.

The fuzzy-subset relation is established by demonstrating that membership scores in one set are consistently less than or equal to membership scores in another. In other words, if for every case degree of membership in set X is less than or equal to degree of membership in set Y, then set X is a subset of set Y. Of course, social science data are rarely perfect and some allowance must be made for these imperfections. It is possible to assess the *degree* of consistency of empirical evidence with the subset relation using the simple formula:

$$\text{Consistency } (X_i \leq Y_i) = \Sigma(\min(X_i, Y_i))/\Sigma(X_i)$$

where X_i is degree of membership in set X; Y_i is degree of membership in set Y; $(X_i \leq Y_i)$ is the subset relation in question; and "min" dictates selection of the lower of the two scores.

For illustration, consider the consistency of the empirical evidence with the claim that the set of developed countries (as calibrated in Table 8.2) constitutes a subset of the set of democracies, using data on all 136 countries. For this demonstration, I use the Polity IV democracy/autocracy measure, which ranges from −10 to +10. (This measure is used because of its popularity, despite its many shortcomings. See, e.g., Goertz 2005, ch. 4.) The calibration of membership in the set of democracies, using the direct method, is shown in Table 8.5. Polity scores for 24 of the 136 countries included in the calibration are presented in column 1 of Table 8.5. These specific cases were selected in order to provide a range of polity scores. Column 2 shows deviations from the crossover point (a polity score of 2), and column 3 shows the scalars used to transform the polity deviation scores into the metric of log odds of membership in the set of democracies. The threshold of full membership in the set of democracies is a polity score of 9, yielding a scalar of 3/7 for cases above the crossover point; the threshold of full nonmembership in the set of democracies is a polity score of −3, yielding a scalar of −3/−5 for cases below the crossover point. Column 4 shows the product of the deviation scores and the scalars, while column 5 reports the calibrated membership scores, using the procedures previously described (see the discussion surrounding Table 8.2).

Applying the formula for set-theoretic consistency described above to all 136 countries, the consistency of the evidence with the argument that the set of developed countries constitutes a subset of the set of democracies is 0.99. (1.0 indicates perfect consistency.) Likewise, the consistency of the evidence with the argument that the set

Table 8.5. Calibrating degree of membership in the set of democratic countries: direct method

Country	1. Polity score	2. Deviations from crossover	3. Scalars	4. Product of 2 × 3	5. Degree of Membership
Norway	10	8.00	0.43	3.43	0.97
United States	10	8.00	0.43	3.43	0.97
France	9	7.00	0.43	3.00	0.95
Korea, Rep.	8	6.00	0.43	2.57	0.93
Colombia	7	5.00	0.43	2.14	0.89
Croatia	7	5.00	0.43	2.14	0.89
Bangladesh	6	4.00	0.43	1.71	0.85
Ecuador	6	4.00	0.43	1.71	0.85
Albania	5	3.00	0.43	1.29	0.78
Armenia	5	3.00	0.43	1.29	0.78
Nigeria	4	2.00	0.43	0.86	0.70
Malaysia	3	1.00	0.43	0.43	0.61
Cambodia	2	0.00	0.60	0.00	0.50
Tanzania	2	0.00	0.60	0.00	0.50
Zambia	1	−1.00	0.60	−0.60	0.35
Liberia	0	−2.00	0.60	−1.20	0.23
Tajikistan	−1	−3.00	0.60	−1.80	0.14
Jordan	−2	−4.00	0.60	−2.40	0.08
Algeria	−3	−5.00	0.60	−3.00	0.05
Rwanda	−4	−6.00	0.60	−3.60	0.03
Gambia	−5	−7.00	0.60	−4.20	0.01
Egypt	−6	−8.00	0.60	−4.80	0.01
Azerbaijan	−7	−9.00	0.60	−5.40	0.00
Bhutan	−8	−10.00	0.60	−6.00	0.00

of "at least moderately developed" countries (as calibrated in Table 8.3) constitutes a subset of the set of democratic countries is 0.95. In short, both subset relations are highly consistent, providing ample support for both statements ("developed countries are democratic" and "countries that are at least moderately developed are democratic"). Likewise, both analyses support the argument that development is sufficient but not necessary for democracy. Note, however, that the set of "at least moderately developed" countries is a much more inclusive set, with higher average membership scores than the set of "developed" countries. It thus offers a more demanding test of the underlying argument. The greater the average membership in a causal condition, the more difficult it is to satisfy the inequality indicating the subset relation ($X_i \leq Y_i$).[14] Thus, using set-theoretic methods it is possible to demonstrate

[14] The two statements differ substantially in their set-theoretic "coverage." Coverage is a gauge of empirical importance or weight (see Ragin 2006). It shows the proportion of the outcome membership scores (in this example, the set of democratic countries) that is "covered" by a causal condition. The coverage of "democratic" countries by "developed" countries is 0.35; however, the coverage of

that membership in the set of countries with a moderate level of development is sufficient for democracy; membership in the set of fully developed countries is not required.

It is extremely difficult to evaluate set-theoretic arguments using correlational methods. There are three main sources of this difficulty:

(1) Set-theoretic statements are about kinds of cases; correlations concern relationships between variables. The statement that developed countries are democratic (i.e. that they constitute a subset of democratic countries) invokes cases, not dimensions of cross-national variation. This focus on cases as instances of concepts follows directly from the set-theoretic nature of social science theory. The computation of a correlation, by contrast, is premised on an interest in assessing how well dimensions of variation parallel each other across a sample or population, not on an interest in a set of cases per se. To push the argument even further: A data-set might not include a single developed country or a single democratic country. Yet, a correlational researcher could still compute a correlation between development and democracy, even though this data-set would be completely inappropriate for such a test.

(2) Correlational arguments are fully symmetric, while set-theoretic arguments are almost always asymmetric. The correlation between development and democracy (treating both as conventional variables) is weakened by the fact that there are many less developed countries that are democratic. However, such cases do not challenge the set-theoretic claim or weaken its consistency. The theoretical argument in question addresses the qualities of developed countries—that they are democratic— and does not make *specific* claims about relative differences between less developed and more developed countries in their degree of democracy. Again, set-theoretic analysis is faithful to verbal formulations, which are typically asymmetric; correlation is not.

(3) Correlations are insensitive to the calibrations implemented by researchers. The contrast between Tables 8.2 and 8.3 is meaningful from a set-theoretic point of view. The set represented in Table 8.3 is more inclusive and thus provides a more demanding set-theoretic test of the connection between development and democracy. From a correlational perspective, however, there is little difference between the two ways of representing development. Indeed, the Pearson correlation between fuzzy membership in the set of developed countries and fuzzy membership in the set of "at least moderately developed" countries is .911. Thus, from a strictly correlational viewpoint, the difference between these two fuzzy sets is slight. The insensitivity of correlation to calibration follows directly from the fact that correlation is computationally reliant on deviations from an inductively derived, sample-specific measure of central tendency—the mean. For this reason, correlation is incapable of analyzing set-theoretic relations and, correspondingly, cannot be used to assess causal sufficiency or necessity.

"democratic" countries by "at least moderately developed" countries is 0.52. These results indicate that the latter gives a much better account of degree of membership in the set of democratic countries.

9 CONCLUSION

This chapter demonstrates both the power of fuzzy sets and the centrality of calibration to their fruitful use. Social scientists have devoted far too much time to measures that indicate only the positions of cases in distributions and not nearly enough time to developing procedures that ground measures in substantive and theoretical knowledge. It is important to be able to assess not only "more versus less" (uncalibrated measurement), but also "a lot versus a little" (calibrated measurement). Not only does the use of calibrated measures ground social science in substantive knowledge, it also enhances the relevance of the results of social research to practical and policy issues. Fuzzy sets are especially powerful as carriers of calibration. They offer measurement tools that transcend the quantitative/qualitative divide in the social sciences.

Current practices in quantitative social science undercut serious attention to calibration. These difficulties stem from reliance on the "indicator approach" to measurement, which requires only variation across sample points and treats all variation as equally meaningful. The limitations of the indicator approach are compounded and reinforced by correlational methods, which are insensitive to calibrations implemented by researchers. Reliance on deviations from the mean tends to neutralize the impact of any direct calibration implemented by the researcher. A further difficulty arises when it is acknowledged that almost all social science theory is set theoretic in nature and that correlational methods are incapable of assessing set-theoretic relations.

The set-theoretic nature of most social science theory is not generally recognized by social scientists today. In tandem with this recognition, social scientists must also recognize that the assessment of set-theoretic arguments and set calibration go hand in hand. Set-theoretic analysis without careful calibration of set membership is an exercise in futility. It follows that researchers need to be faithful to their theories by clearly identifying the target sets that correspond to the concepts central to their theories and by specifying useful external criteria that can be used to guide the calibration of set membership.

REFERENCES

BECKER, H. S. 1958. Problems of inference and proof in participant observation. *American Sociological Review*, 23: 652–60.

BOLLEN, K. 1989. *Structural Equations with Latent Variables*. New York: Wiley Interscience.

BYRNE, D. 2002. *Interpreting Quantitative Data*. London: Sage.

CICOUREL, A. V. 1964. *Method and Measurement in Sociology*. New York: Free Press.

DUNCAN, O. D. 1984. *Notes on Social Measurement*. New York: Russell Sage Foundation.

GLASER, B., and STRAUSS, A. 1967. *The Discovery of Grounded Theory: Strategies for Qualitative Research*. New York: Weidenfeld and Nicolson.

GOERTZ, G. 2005. *Social Science Concepts: A User's Guide*. Princeton, NJ: Princeton University Press.

KATZ, J. 1982. *Poor People's Laywers in Transition*. New Brunswick, NJ: Rutgers University Press.

LAITIN, D. 1992. *Language Repertiores and State Construction in Africa*. New York: Cambridge University Press.

LAKOFF, G. 1973. Hedges: a study in meaning criteria and the logic of fuzzy concepts. *Journal of Philosophical Logic*, 2: 458–508.

NUNNALLY, J., and BERNSTEIN, I. 1994. *Psychometric Theory*. New York: McGraw-Hill.

PAWSON, R. 1989. *A Measure for Measures: A Manifesto for Empirical Sociology*. New York: Routledge.

RAGIN, C. C. 1987. *The Comparative Method: Moving beyond Qualitative and Quantitative Strategies*. Berkeley: University of California Press.

—— 2000. *Fuzzy-Set Social Science*. Chicago: University of Chicago Press.

—— 1994. *Constructing Social Research*. Thousand Oaks, Calif.: Pine Forge.

—— 2006. Set relations in social research: evaluating their consistency and coverage. *Political Analysis*, 14: 291–310.

—— forthcoming. *Redesigning Social Inquiry: Fuzzy Sets and Beyond*. Chicago: University of Chicago Press.

—— DRASS, K. A., and DAVEY, S. 2006. *Fuzzy-Set/Qualitative Comparative Analysis 2.0*. <www.fsqca.com>.

ROKKAN, S. 1975. Dimensions of state formation and nation building: a possible paradigm for research on variations within Europe. In *The Formation of Nation States in Western Europe*, ed. C. Tilly. Princeton, NJ: Princeton University Press.

SMITHSON, M. 1987. *Fuzzy Set Analysis for the Behavioral and Social Sciences*. New York: Springer-Verlag.

SMITHSON, M., and VERKUILEN, J. 2006. *Fuzzy Set Theory*. Thousand Oaks, Calif.: Sage.

WALKER, H., and COHEN, B. 1985. Scope statements: imperatives for evaluating theory. *American Sociological Review*, 50: 288–301.

ZADEH, L. 1965. Fuzzy sets. *Information and Control*, 8: 338–53.

—— 1972. A fuzzy-set-theoretic interpretation of linguistic hedges. *Journal of Cybernetics*, 2: 4–34.

—— 2002. From computing with numbers to computing with words. *Applied Mathematics and Computer Science*, 12: 307–32

CHAPTER 9

THE EVOLVING INFLUENCE OF PSYCHOMETRICS IN POLITICAL SCIENCE

KEITH T. POOLE

PSYCHOMETRICS is a subfield of psychology devoted to the development, evaluation, and application of mental tests of various kinds. These mental tests attempt to measure knowledge, attitudes, personality traits, and abilities. Psychometrics has its origins in the work of Sir Francis Galton (1822–1911), Karl Pearson (1857–1936), and Charles Spearman (1863–1945) in the late nineteenth and early twentieth centuries. Galton's most famous work was *Hereditary Genius* (1869) in which he studied "illustrious" intellects and their families. His biographical data of the descendants of these illustrious intellects showed "regression to the mean" for a number of mental and physical characteristics that he regarded as important. Much of his work in the latter part of the nineteenth century was devoted to eugenics. Galton was interested in measurement and developed a measure of *co-relation* which influenced the development of the correlation coefficient by Karl Pearson. He and Karl Pearson founded the journal *Biometrika* in 1901.

Galton was a major influence on both Karl Pearson and Charles Spearman. Pearson began his professional life as an attorney from 1881 to 1884 but in 1884 he was appointed as a professor of applied mathematics and mechanics at University College,

Table 9.1. Spearman's 1904 (rank-order) correlation matrix

Classics	1.00					
French	.83	1.00				
English	.78	.67	1.00			
Math	.70	.67	.64	1.00		
Pitch	.66	.65	.54	.45	1.00	
Music	.63	.57	.51	.51	.40	1.00

London. He became professor of eugenics in 1911 and was the editor of *Biometrika* from 1902 to 1936. Pearson invented the product moment correlation coefficient which is universally denoted as *r* and he should also be credited with the invention of Principal Components Analysis (what we now would think of as straightforward eigenvalue/eigenvector decomposition). Pearson called it "the method of principal axes" and states the problem quite succinctly: "In many physical, statistical, and biological investigations it is desirable to represent a system of points in plane, three, or higher dimensioned space by the 'best-fitting' straight line or plane" (1901, 559). Remarkably, this also describes the essence of the famous Eckart–Young theorem (Eckart and Young 1936, see below) which is the foundation of general least squares problems (Lawson and Hanson 1974).

Charles Spearman came late to the study of psychology. He began his professional career as an officer in the British army and he served in the 1885 Burmese war and in the Boer War in South Africa. He was forty-three years old when he earned his Ph.D. in psychology at Leipzig in 1906. He held chaired professorships at University College London from 1907 to 1931.

While still a graduate student he published his famous 1904 paper that used *factor analysis* to analyze a correlation matrix between test scores of twenty-two English high school boys for Classics, French, English, Math, Pitch, and Music. This correlation matrix is shown in Table 9.1.

This correlation matrix is historic for two reasons. First, Spearman computed a form of rank-order correlation between each pair of skills across the twenty-two school boys.[1] Second, he applied factor analysis to the matrix of correlations to extract a common or *general* (the "g" factor) factor from the matrix. His method of extracting the g factor was based on his method of "tetrad differences." A tetrad difference is actually the determinant of a 2 by 2 matrix and if there is only one factor then these differences should all be close to zero. For example, using English and Math, the tetrad difference is .78*.67 − .67*.70 or .054. If the tetrad differences are all close to zero then the matrix only has one factor (rank of one). Spearman derived an elaborate formula

---

[1] This rank-order correlation was not what is now known as the Spearman correlation coefficient. He first used the correlation coefficient that would eventually be named for him in a paper published in 1906 (Lovie 1995).

for extracting this g factor from a correlation matrix.[2] The notorious Cyril Burt tried to claim that he invented factor analysis after Spearman's death. However, there is no question that Spearman was the inventor (Lovie and Lovie 1993).

Lewis Leon Thurstone (1887–1955) thought Spearman's one-factor theory of intelligence was wrong. Thurstone was a polymath who earned an engineering degree at Cornell in 1912 and a Ph.D. in psychology at Chicago in 1917 where he became a professor from 1924 to 1952. While an engineering student he invented a flicker-free motion picture projector and briefly worked as an assistant to Thomas Edison in 1912. He made many fundamental contributions to psychological science, the most important of which were multiple factor analysis and the *law of comparative judgment*.

Thurstone generalized Spearman's tetrad differences approach to examine higher order determinants and succeeded in developing a method for extracting multiple factors from a correlation matrix (Thurstone 1931; 1947). Thurstone's theory of intelligence postulated seven rather than one primary mental ability and he constructed tests specific to the seven abilities: verbal comprehension, word fluency, number facility, spatial visualization, associative memory, perceptual speed, and reasoning (Thurstone 1935).

Thurstone also developed the law of comparative judgment. Thurstone's law is more accurately described as a measurement model for a *unidmensional subjective continuum*. Subjects are asked to make a series of $n(n-1)/2$ pairwise comparisons of n stimuli. It is assumed that a subject's response reflects the momentary subjective value associated with the stimulus, and that the probability distribution of these momentary values is normally distributed. It is then possible to recover the underlying continuum or scale by essentially averaging across a group of subjects. If the variances of the stimuli (the *discriminal* dispersions) on the underlying scale are the same (Case 5 of the model), this is equivalent to the requirement of parallel item characteristic curves in the Rasch model. Case 5 of Thurstone's method should yield essentially the same results as the Rasch model for dichotomous data (Andrich 1978).

Although Thurstone developed multiple factor analysis, it was Harold Hotelling (1895–1973) who gave principal components a solid statistical foundation (Hotelling 1933). Hotelling had an eclectic background. He received a BA in journalism in 1919 from the University of Washington and a Ph.D. in mathematics from Princeton in 1924. Reflecting this eclectic background, Hotelling made fundamental contributions in both economics and statistics. In economics Hotelling's famous 1929 paper on the stability of competition is generally recognized as the beginnings of the spatial (geometric) model of voting (see below). It introduced the simple but profound idea that if there are two stores on a street then it is in the interest of each store to locate in the middle (the median walking distance) of the street where each gets one half of the market. Two years later in a 1931 paper Hotelling laid out what has since become labeled "confidence intervals" in an analysis of the use of the Student's t distribution for hypothesis testing.

---

[2] This formula is detailed in Spearman (1927). For a detailed discussion of Spearman's work on the g factor see Jensen (1998).

Hotelling was one of a number of distinguished mathematicians and physicists who made fundamental contributions to the development of psychometrics in the 1930s and 1940s. As fate would have it, a number of these contributors were at the University of Chicago at the same time as Thurstone. Thurstone was the main force behind the founding of the Psychometric Society and its journal *Psychometrika* (Takane 2004). Carl H. Eckart (1902–73), a distinguished quantum physicist (Munk and Preisendorfer 1976), and Gale Young, an applied mathematician, published their landmark paper "The Approximation of One Matrix by Another of Lower Rank" in the very first issue of *Psychometrika* in 1936. Formally, the Eckart–Young theorem is:

Given an n by m matrix $\mathbf{A}$ of rank $r \leq m \leq n$, and its singular value decomposition, $\mathbf{U}\mathit{\Lambda}\mathbf{V}'$, where $\mathbf{U}$ is an n by m matrix, $\mathbf{V}$ is an m by m matrix such that $\mathbf{U}'\mathbf{U}=\mathbf{V}'\mathbf{V}=\mathbf{VV}'=\mathbf{I}$, and $\mathit{\Lambda}$ is an m by m diagonal matrix with the singular values arranged in decreasing sequence on the diagonal

$$\lambda_1 \geq \lambda_2 \geq \lambda_3 \geq \ldots \lambda_m \geq 0$$

then there exists an n by m matrix $\mathbf{B}$ of rank s, $s \leq r$, which minimizes the sum of the squared error between the elements of $\mathbf{A}$ and the corresponding elements of $\mathbf{B}$ when

$$\mathbf{B} = \mathbf{U}\mathit{\Lambda}_s\mathbf{V}'$$

where the diagonal elements of $\mathit{\Lambda}_s$ are

$$\lambda_1 \geq \lambda_2 \geq \lambda_3 \geq \ldots \lambda_s > \lambda_{s+1} = \lambda_{s+2} = \ldots = \lambda_m = 0.$$

The Eckart–Young theorem states that the least squares approximation in s dimensions of a matrix $\mathbf{A}$ can be found by replacing the smallest $m-s$ roots of $\mathit{\Lambda}$ with zeroes and remultiplying $\mathbf{U}\mathit{\Lambda}\mathbf{V}'$. This theorem was never *explicitly* stated by Eckart and Young. Rather, they use two theorems from linear algebra (the key theorem being singular value decomposition[3]) and a very clever argument to show the truth of their result. Later, Keller (1962) independently rediscovered the Eckart–Young theorem.

The Eckart–Young theorem provides a formal justification for the selection of the number of factors in a factor analysis (as well as many other general least squares problems). The Eckart–Young theorem along with the results of Gale Young and Alston Householder (1904–93) published in *Psychometrika* in 1938 provided the foundations for *classical multidimensional scaling*.

Multidimensional scaling (MDS) methods represent measurements of similarity between pairs of stimuli as distances between points in a low-dimensional (usually Euclidean) space. The methods locate the points in such a way that points corresponding to very similar stimuli are located close together, while those corresponding

---

[3] The SVD Theorem was stated by Eckart and Young (1936) in their famous paper, but they did not provide a proof. The first proof that every *rectangular* matrix of real elements can be decomposed into the product of two orthogonal matrices—U and V—and a diagonal matrix $\mathit{\Lambda}$, namely, $\mathbf{U}\mathit{\Lambda}\mathbf{V}'$ as shown in the statement of the Eckart–Young theorem, was given by Johnson (1963). Horst (1963) refers to the singular value decomposition as the *basic structure* of a matrix and discusses the mechanics of matrix decomposition in detail in chapters 17 and 18. A more recent treatment can be found in chapters 1 and 2 of Lawson and Hanson (1974).

to very dissimilar stimuli are located further apart. Warren Torgerson (1924–97) in a 1952 *Psychometrika* paper showed a simple method of MDS based on the work of Eckart and Young (1936) and Young and Householder (1938) (see also Torgerson 1958). The method is elegantly simple. First, transform the observed similarities/dissimilarities into squared distances. (For example, if the matrix is a Pearson correlation matrix subtract all the entries from 1 and square the result.) Next, *double-center* the matrix of squared distances by subtracting from each entry in the matrix the mean of the row, the mean of the column, adding the mean of the matrix, and then dividing by −2. This has the effect of removing the squared terms from the matrix leaving just the cross-product matrix (see Gower 1966). Finally, perform an eigenvalue-eigenvector decomposition to solve for the coordinates.

For example, suppose there are n stimuli and let **D** be the n by n symmetric matrix of squared distances between every pair of the stimuli. Let **Z** be the n by s matrix of coordinates of n points in an s-dimensional Euclidean space that represent the n stimuli and let **Y** be the n by n double centered matrix. The elements of **Y** are:

$$y_{ij} = \frac{(d_{ij}^2 - d_{.j}^2 - d_{i.}^2 + d_{..}^2)}{-2} = (z_i - \bar{z})'(z_j - \bar{z})$$

where $d_{.j}^2$ is the mean of the jth column, $d_{i.}^2$ is the mean of the ith row, $d_{..}^2$ is the mean of the matrix, z_i and z_j are the s length vectors of coordinates for the ith and jth stimuli, and $\bar{z}$ is the s length vector of means for the n stimuli on the s dimensions. Without loss of generality the means can be set equal to zero so that the double-centered matrix is simply

$$\mathbf{Y} = \mathbf{ZZ}'.$$

Let the eigenvalue-eigenvector decomposition be $\mathbf{U}\Lambda\mathbf{U}'$; hence the solution is

$$\mathbf{Z} = \mathbf{U}\Lambda^{1/2}.$$

Torgerson's method is very elegant but similarities/dissimilarities data are rarely measured on a ratio scale. Indeed, it is very likely that data gathered from subjects is at best on an ordinal scale. Roger Shepard (1958) argued that the relationship between the true distance between a pair of stimuli and the observed distance was exponential. That is, if d is the distance between two stimuli then the reported similarity, δ, tends to be e^{-kd}, where $k(k > 0)$ is a scaling constant (Shepard 1958; 1963; 1987; Gluck 1991; Nosofsky 1992; Cheng 2000). This is known as a *response function*. Within psychology, surveys and experiments of how people make similarities and preferential choice judgments show that very simple geometric models appear to structure responses to these tasks (Shepard 1987). When individuals make a judgment of how similar two stimuli are, they appear to base the judgment upon how close the two stimuli are in an abstract psychological space (Nosofsky 1984; 1992; Shepard 1987; Gluck 1991). The dimensions of these psychological spaces correspond to the attributes of the stimuli. A strong regularity is that these psychological spaces are *low dimensional*—very rarely above two dimensions—and that either the stimuli judgments are additive—that is, a city-block metric is being used—or simple Euclidean (Garner 1974; Shepard 1987; 1991; Nosofsky 1992).

Shepard's belief that response functions were exponential led him to develop *non-metric* multidimensional scaling in which distances are estimated that reproduce a weak monotone transformation (or *rank ordering*) of the observed dissimilarities (Shepard 1962a; 1962b). Graphing the "true" (that is, the estimated or reproduced) distances—the *d*'s—versus the observed dissimilarities—the δ's—revealed the relationship between them. This became known as the "Shepard diagram."

Shepard's program worked, but the key breakthrough was Joseph Kruskal's idea of *monotone regression* that lead to the development of a powerful and practical non-metric MDS program (Kruskal 1964a; 1964b; 1965). By the early 1970s this was known under the acronym KYST (Kruskal, Young, and Seery 1973) and is still in use today.

MDS methods can be seen as evolving from factor analysis and Thurstone's unidimensional scaling method with the key difference being that MDS methods are applied to *relational* data; that is, data such as similarities and preferential choice data that can be regarded as *distances*. At the same time that MDS methods were evolving Louis Guttman (1916–87) during the Second World War developed *scalogram analysis* or what is more commonly known as *Guttman Scaling* (Guttman 1944; 1950). A Guttman scale is the basis of all modern skills-based tests. It is a set of items (questions, problems, etc.) that are ranked in order of difficulty so that those who answer correctly (agree) on a more difficult (or extreme) item will also answer correctly (agree) with all less difficult (extreme) items that preceded it.[4] Rasch analysis (more broadly, *item response theory*) is essentially a sophisticated form of Guttman scalogram analysis. They are techniques for examining whether a set of items is *consistent* in the sense that they all measure increasing/decreasing levels of some unidimensional attribute (e.g. mathematical ability; racial prejudice; etc.).

At the same time that Torgerson was developing classical scaling and Guttman was developing scalogram analysis, Clyde Coombs (1912–88) developed *unfolding analysis* (Coombs 1950; 1952; 1958; 1964). Coombs was a student of Thurstone's and received his Ph.D. from the University of Chicago in 1940. After the Second World War Coombs became interested in preferential choice problems where the data consists of subjects' rank orderings of stimuli (Tversky 1992). Coombs came up with the idea of an *ideal point* and a *single-peaked preference function* to account for the observed rank orderings. The idea was to arrange the individuals' ideal points and points representing the stimuli along a scale so that the distances between the ideal points and the stimuli points reproduced the observed rank orderings. Coombs called this an unfolding analysis because the researcher must take the rank orderings and "unfold" them. An individual's rank ordering is computed from her ideal point so that the reported ordering is akin to picking up the dimension (as if it were a piece of string) at the ideal point so that both sides of the dimension fold together to form a line with the individual's ideal point at the end.

---

[4] See van Schuur (1992; 2003) for a discussion of some Guttman-like models. The multidimensional generalization of Guttman scaling is known as Multidimensional Scalogram Analysis (Lingoes 1963). For a survey see Shye (1978, chs. 9–11).

Unfolding analysis deals with relational data and is therefore an MDS method. Both unfolding analysis and scalogram analysis deal with individual's responses to a set of stimuli. But Guttman's model is very different from the unfolding model. In terms of utility theory unfolding analysis assumes a single-peaked (usually symmetric) utility function. That is, utility (the degree of preference) declines with distance from the individual's ideal point. In contrast, Guttman scaling is based on a utility function that is always monotonically increasing or decreasing over the relevant dimension or space. Above some threshold the individual always responds Yes/correct, and below the threshold the individual always responds No/incorrect. The counterpart to an ideal point is the position on the scale where the individual's responses switch from Yes/correct to No/incorrect.

Interestingly, these two very different models are observationally equivalent in the context of parliamentary voting (Weisberg 1968; Poole 2005). In the unfolding model there are two outcomes for every parliamentary motion—one corresponding to Yea and one corresponding to Nay. Legislators vote for the option closest to their ideal points. In one dimension this forms a perfect scalogram (Weisberg 1968). Hence, Guttman scaling methods and their item response theory (IRT) parametric descendants can be used to analyze parliamentary (binary choice) data.

By the mid-1950s factor analysis, Guttman scalogram analysis, and Thurstone's scaling methods had been developed and began to influence political scientists. Duncan MacRae's pathbreaking work on congressional voting (MacRae 1958; 1970) utilized both factor analysis and unidimensional scaling methods at a time when computing resources were very primitive. MacRae used factor analysis to analyze correlation matrices computed between roll calls (usually Yule's Q's) and correlation matrices between legislators to uncover the dimensional structure of roll-call voting. By analyzing the Yule's Q results MacRae was able to construct unidimensional scales for specific issue areas. MacRae proposed the model of roll-call voting that Howard Rosenthal and I implemented as NOMINATE—namely, ideal points for legislators and two policy outcomes per roll call, one for Yea and one for Nay. There is no doubt that MacRae would have estimated this model if computing resources in the 1950s had been up to the task.

Herbert Weisberg in his 1968 Ph.D. dissertation (Weisberg 1968) systematically detailed the interrelationships of existing multivariate methods (most of which came from psychology) that had been used to analyze roll-call voting. In his analysis of factor analysis, Guttman scaling, similarities analysis, and cluster analysis, Weisberg showed the observational equivalence of the ideal point *proximity* model with the Guttman scalogram *dominance* model, and outlined a general framework for analyzing roll-call voting.

In the late 1960s and early 1970s nonmetric MDS began to be used in political science. Beginning in 1968 feeling thermometers were included in the National Election Studies conducted by the University of Michigan. A feeling thermometer measures how warm or cold a person feels toward the stimulus; the measure ranges from 0—very cold and unfavorable opinion—to 100—very warm and favorable opinion—with 50 as a neutral point. In 1968 respondents were asked to give feeling

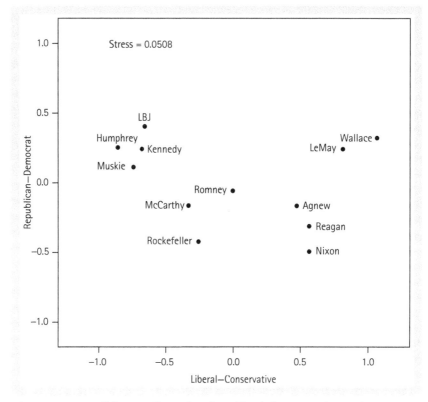

Fig. 9.1. 1968 candidate configuration from Kruskal nonmetric MDS

thermometer ratings to the presidential candidates George Wallace, Hubert Humphrey, and Richard Nixon, along with their vice-presidential running mates and six other political figures. Herbert Weisberg and Jerrold Rusk (1970) computed Pearson correlations between every pair of political figures across the respondents and then used Kruskal's nonmetric MDS procedure (Kruskal 1964a; 1964b) to recover a candidate configuration. This configuration is shown in Figure 9.1.

The availability of the feeling thermometer data led to efforts to apply unfolding methods to them directly. In these models the thermometers were regarded as inverse distances. For example, by subtracting them from 100 these transformed scores could be treated as distances between points representing the candidates and points representing the respondents. Techniques to perform unfolding analyses were developed by psychometricians in the 1960s (Chang and Carroll 1969; Kruskal, Young, and Seery 1973) but the first application of unfolding to thermometers was done by George Rabinowitz (1973; 1976) using his innovative line-of-sight method. Almost at the same time Cahoon (1975) and Cahoon, Hinich, and Ordeshook (1976; 1978), using a statistical model based directly on the spatial model of voting (Davis and Hinich 1966; 1967; Davis, Hinich, and Ordeshook 1970; Enelow and Hinich 1984), also analyzed the 1968 feeling thermometers. Later Poole and Rosenthal (1984) and Brady (1990) developed unfolding procedures that they applied to thermometer scores. Poole (1981; 1984; 1990) and Poole and Daniels (1985) also applied an unfolding procedure to interest group ratings of members of congress.

In the 1980s political scientists began combining techniques from econometrics and statistics with approaches developed by psychometricians. Henry Brady made contributions to the statistical foundations of nonmetric MDS (Brady 1985a) as well as methods for and problems with the analysis of preferences (Brady 1985b; 1989; 1990). Poole and Rosenthal combined the random utility model developed by economists (McFadden 1976), the spatial model of voting, and alternating estimation methods developed in psychometrics (Chang and Carroll 1969; Carroll and Chang 1970; Young, de Leeuw, and Takane 1976; Takane, Young, and de Leeuw 1977)[5] to develop NOMINATE, an unfolding method for parliamentary roll-call data (Poole and Rosenthal 1985; 1991; 1997; Poole 2005).

The NOMINATE model is based on the spatial theory of voting. Legislators have ideal points in an abstract policy space and vote for the policy alternative closest to their ideal point. Each roll-call vote has two policy points—one corresponding to Yea and one to Nay. Consistent with the random utility model, each legislator's utility function consists of (1) a *deterministic* component that is a function of the distance between the legislator and a roll-call outcome; and (2) a *stochastic* component that represents the idiosyncratic component of utility. The deterministic portion of the utility function is assumed to have a normal distribution and voting is probabilistic. An alternating method is used to estimate the parameters. Given starting estimates of the legislator ideal points the roll-call parameters are estimated. Given these roll-call parameters, new legislator ideal points are estimated, and so on. Classical methods of optimization are used to estimate the parameters.[6]

In the 1990s and the early 2000s the availability of cheap, fast computers made simulation methods for the estimation of complex multivariate models practical for the first time[7] and these methods were fused with long-standing psychometric methods. Specifically, Markov Chain Monte Carlo (MCMC) simulation (Metropolis and Ulam 1949; Hastings 1970; Geman and Geman 1984; Gelfand and Smith 1990; Gelman 1992) within a Bayesian framework (Gelman et al. 2000; Gill 2002) can be used to perform an unfolding analysis of parliamentary roll-call data. The general Bayesian MCMC method was introduced into political science by Andrew Martin and Kevin Quinn (Schofield et al. 1998; Quinn, Martin, and Whitford 1999; Martin and Quinn 2002; Quinn and Martin 2002; Martin 2003; Quinn 2004) and Simon Jackman (2000a; 2000b; 2001; Clinton, Jackman, and Rivers 2004).

The primary application of Bayesian MCMC methods in political science has been to unfolding roll-call data from legislatures and courts. Like NOMINATE, the

---

[5] See Jacoby (1991) for an overview and synthesis of the alternating least squares approach in psychometrics.

[6] The work of Heckman and Snyder (1997) is also based on the spatial model and the random utility model. However, even though it uses principal components analysis, it is more accurately classified as an econometrics method than a psychometrics method.

[7] See Hitchcock (2003) for a short history of MCMC simulation.

foundation is the spatial theory of voting and the random utility model. This unfolding approach also uses an alternating structure, only it consists of sampling from conditional distributions for the legislator and roll-call parameters. Technically, this is *alternating conditional sampling* or the *Gibbs sampler* (Geman and Geman 1984; Gelfand and Smith 1990). Thus far the Bayesian MCMC applications have used a quadratic deterministic utility function with most of the applications being one dimensional. With a quadratic deterministic utility function the simple item response model (Rasch 1961) is mathematically equivalent to the basic spatial model if legislators have quadratic utility functions with additive random error (Ladha 1991; Londregan 2000; Clinton, Jackman, and Rivers 2004). This has the effect of making the estimation quite straightforward, as it boils down to a series of linear regressions.

As this is written early in the twenty-first century, the influence of psychometrics shows no sign of abating in political science. The level of sophistication of psychometric applications in political science has steadily increased in the past twenty years. The availability of fast computing has opened up whole new areas of research that were impossible to explore as late as the mid-1980s. In addition, political science methodologists have successfully blended methods from statistics and econometrics with psychometrics to produce unique applications. Heretofore "obscure" methods of estimation are being transmitted between neighboring disciplines much more rapidly than ever before by a younger generation of technically trained scholars. This is an exciting time to be active in applied statistical methods in political science. The coming twenty years should see equally important breakthroughs as massively parallel supercomputing becomes widely available and the information revolution increases the speed of transmission of statistical advances to cadres of ever better trained practitioners.

References

ANDRICH, D. 1978. Relationships between the Thurstone and Rasch approaches to item scaling. *Applied Psychological Measurement*, 2: 449–60.

BRADY, H. E. 1985a. Statistical consistency and hypothesis testing for nonmetric multidimensional scaling. *Psychometrika*, 50: 503–37.

——1985b. The perils of survey research: inter-personally incomparable responses. *Political Methodology*, 11: 269–90.

——1989. Factor and ideal point analysis for interpersonally incomparable data. *Psychometrika*, 54: 181–202.

——1990. Traits versus issues: factor versus ideal-point analysis of candidate thermometer ratings. *Political Analysis*, 2: 97–129.

CAHOON, L. S. 1975. Locating a set of points using range information only. Ph.D. dissertation, Department of Statistics, Carnegie-Mellon University.

—— HINICH, M. J., and ORDESHOOK, P. C. 1976. A multidimensional statistical procedure for spatial analysis. Manuscript, Carnegie-Mellon University.

—— —— —— 1978. A statistical multidimensional scaling method based on the spatial theory of voting. In *Graphical Representation of Multivariate Data*, ed. P. C. Wang. New York: Academic Press.

CARROLL, J. D., and CHANG, J.-J. 1970. Analysis of individual differences in multidimensional scaling via an N-way generalization of "Eckart-Young" decomposition. *Psychometrika*, 35: 283–320.

CHANG, J.-J., and CARROLL, J. D. 1969. How to use MDPREF, a computer program for multidimensional analysis of preference data. *Multidimensional Scaling Program Package of Bell Laboratories*. Bell Laboratories, Murray Hill, NJ.

CHENG, K. 2000. Shepard's universal law supported by honeybees in spatial generalization. *Psychological Science*, 5: 403–8.

CLINTON, J. D., JACKMAN, S. D., and RIVERS, D. 2004. The statistical analysis of roll call data: a unified approach. *American Political Science Review*, 98: 355–70.

COOMBS, C. 1950. Psychological scaling without a unit of measurement. *Psychological Review*, 57: 148–58.

—— 1952. A theory of psychological scaling. *Engineering Research Bulletin*, 34.

—— 1958. On the use of inconsistency of preferences in psychological measurement. *Journal of Experimental Psychology*, 55: 1–7.

—— 1964. *A Theory of Data*. New York: Wiley.

DAVIS, O. A., and HINICH, M. J. 1966. A mathematical model of policy formation in a democratic society. Pp. 175–208 in *Mathematical Applications in Political Science, II*, ed. J. L. Bernd. Dallas: SMU Press.

—— 1967. Some results related to a mathematical model of policy formation in a democratic society. Pp. 14–38 in *Mathematical Applications in Political Science III*, ed. J. Bernd. Charlottesville: University of Virginia Press.

—— HINICH, M. J., and ORDESHOOK, P. C. 1970. An expository development of a mathematical model of the electoral process. *American Political Science Review*, 64: 426–48.

ECKART, C. H., and YOUNG, G. 1936. The approximation of one matrix by another of lower rank. *Psychometrika*, 1: 211–18.

ENELOW, J. M., and HINICH, M. 1984. *The Spatial Theory of Voting*. New York: Cambridge University Press.

GALTON, F. 1869. *Hereditary Genius*. London: Macmillan.

GARNER, W. R. 1974. *The Processing of Information and Structure*. New York: Wiley.

GELFAND, A. E., and SMITH, A. F. M. 1990. Sampling-based approaches to calculating marginal densities. *Journal of the American Statistical Association*, 85: 398–409.

GELMAN, A. 1992. Iterative and non-iterative simulation algorithms. *Computing Science and Statistics*, 24: 433–8.

—— CARLIN, J. B., STERN, H. S., and RUBIN, D. B. 2000. *Bayesian Data Analysis*. New York: Chapman and Hall/CRC.

GEMAN, D., and GEMAN, S. 1984. Stochastic relaxation, Gibbs distributions, and the Bayesian restoration of images. *IEEE Transactions on Pattern Analysis and Machine Intelligence*, 6: 721–41.

GILL, J. 2002. *Bayesian Methods: A Social and Behavioral Sciences Approach*. Boca Raton, Fla: Chapman and Hall/CRC.

GLUCK, M. A. 1991. Stimulus generalization and representation in adaptive network models of category learning. *Psychological Science*, 2: 50–5.

GOWER, J. C. 1966. Some distance properties of latent root and vector methods used in multivariate analysis. *Biometrika*, 53: 325–38.

GUTTMAN, L. L. 1944. A basis for scaling qualitative data. *American Sociological Review*, 9: 139–50.

——1950. The basis for scalogram analysis. In *Measurement and Prediction: The American Soldier*, vol. iv, ed. S. A. Stouffer et al. New York: Wiley.

HASTINGS, W. K. 1970. Monte Carlo sampling methods using Markov chains and their applications. *Biometrika*, 54: 97–109.

HECKMAN, J. J., and SNYDER, J. M. 1997. Linear probability models of the demand for attributes with an empirical application to estimating the preferences of legislators. *Rand Journal of Economics*, 28: 142–89.

HITCHCOCK, D. B. 2003. A history of the Metropolis-Hastings algorithm. *American Statistician*, 57: 254–57.

HORST, P. 1963. *Matrix Algebra for Social Scientists*. New York: Holt, Rinehart and Winston.

HOTELLING, H. 1929. Stability in competition. *Economic Journal*, 39: 41–57.

——1931. The generalization of student's ratio. *Annals of Mathematical Statistics*, 2: 360–78.

——1933. Analysis of a complex statistical variables with principal components. *Journal of Educational Psychology*, 24: 498–520.

JACKMAN, S. D. 2000*a*. Estimation and inference via Bayesian simulation: an introduction to Markov Chain Monte Carlo. *American Journal of Political Science*, 44: 375–404.

——2000*b*. Estimation and inference are "missing data" problems: unifying social science statistics via Bayesian simulation. *Political Analysis*, 8: 307–32.

——2001. Multidimensional analysis of roll call data via Bayesian simulation: identification, estimation, inference and model checking. *Political Analysis*, 9: 227–41.

JACOBY, W. G. 1991. *Data Theory and Dimensional Analysis*. Newbury Park, Calif.: Sage.

JENSEN, A. R. 1998. *The g Factor: The Science of Mental Ability*. Westport, Conn.: Praeger.

JOHNSON, R. M. 1963. On a theorem stated by Eckart and Young. *Psychometrika*, 28: 259–63.

KELLER, J. B. 1962. Factorization of matrices by least-squares. *Biometrika*, 49: 239–42.

KRUSKAL, J. B. 1964*a*. Multidimensional scaling by optimizing a goodness of fit to a nonmetric hypothesis. *Psychometrika*, 29: 1–27.

——1964*b*. Nonmetric multidimensional scaling: a numerical method. *Psychometrika*, 29: 115–29.

——1965. Analysis of factorial experiments by estimating monotone transformations of the data. *Journal of the Royal Statistical Society B*, 27: 251–63.

——and WISH, M. 1978. *Multidimensional Scaling*. Beverly Hills, Calif.: Sage.

——YOUNG, F. W., and SEERY, J. B. 1973. How to use KYST: a very flexible program to do multidimensional scaling and unfolding. *Multidimensional Scaling Program Package of Bell Laboratories*. Bell Laboratories, Murray Hill, NJ.

LADHA, K. K. 1991. A spatial model of legislative voting with perceptual error. *Public Choice*, 68: 151–74.

LAWSON, C. L., and HANSON, R. J. 1974. *Solving Least Squares Problems*. Englewood Cliffs, NJ: Prentice Hall.

LINGOES, J. C. 1963. Multiple scalogram analysis: a set-theoretic model for analyzing dichotomous items. *Education and Psychological Measurement*, 23: 501–24.

LONDREGAN, J. B. 2000. Estimating legislators' preferred points. *Political Analysis*, 8: 35–56.

LOVIE, A. D. 1995. Who discovered Spearman's rank correlation? *British Journal of Mathematical and Statistical Psychology*, 48: 255–69.

—— and Lovie, P. 1993. Charles Spearman, Cyril Burt, and the origins of factor analysis. *Journal of the History of the Behavioral Sciences*, 29: 308–21.

McFadden, D. 1976. Quantal choice analysis: a survey. *Annals of Economic and Social Measurement*, 5: 363–90.

MacRae, D., Jr. 1958. *Dimensions of Congressional Voting*. Berkeley: University of California Press.

—— 1970. *Issues and Parties in Legislative Voting*. New York: Harper and Row.

Martin, A. D. 2003. Bayesian inference for heterogeneous event counts. *Sociological Methods and Research*, 32: 30–63.

—— and Quinn, K. M. 2002. Dynamic ideal point estimation via Markov Chain Monte Carlo for the U.S. Supreme Court, 1953–1999. *Political Analysis*, 10: 134–53.

Metropolis, N. C., and Ulam, S. 1949. The Monte Carlo method. *Journal of the American Statistical Association*, 44: 335–41.

Munk, W. H., and Preisendorfer, R. W. 1976. Carl Henry Eckart. In *Biographical Memoirs V. 48*. Washington, DC: National Academy of Sciences.

Nosofsky, R. M. 1984. Choice, similarity, and the context theory of classification. *Journal of Experimental Psychology: Learning, Memory and Cognition*, 10: 104–14.

—— 1992. Similarity scaling and cognitive process models. *Annual Review of Psychology*, 43: 25–53.

Pearson, K. P. 1901. On lines and planes of closest fit to systems of points in space. *London, Edinburgh and Dublin Philosophical Magazine and Journal*, 6: 559–72.

Poole, K. T. 1981. Dimensions of interest group evaluations of the U.S. Senate, 1969–1978. *American Journal of Political Science*, 25: 49–67.

—— 1984. Least squares metric, unidimensional unfolding. *Psychometrika*, 49: 311–23.

—— 1990. Least squares metric, unidimensional scaling of multivariate linear models. *Psychometrika*, 55: 123–49.

—— 2005. *Spatial Models of Parliamentary Voting*. New York: Cambridge University Press.

—— and Daniels, R. S. 1985. Ideology, party, and voting in the U.S. Congress, 1959–80. *American Political Science Review*, 79: 373–99.

—— and Rosenthal, H. 1984. U.S. presidential elections 1968–1980: a spatial analysis. *American Journal of Political Science*, 28: 282–312.

—— —— 1985. A spatial model for legislative roll call analysis. *American Journal of Political Science*, 29: 357–84.

—— —— 1991. Patterns of congressional voting. *American Journal of Political Science*, 35: 228–78.

—— —— 1997. *Congress: A Political-Economic History of Roll Call Voting*. New York: Oxford University Press.

Quinn, K. M. 2004. Bayesian factor analysis for mixed ordinal and continuous responses. *Political Analysis*, 12: 338–53.

—— and Martin, A. D. 2002. An integrated computational model of multiparty electoral competition. *Statistical Science*, 17: 405–19.

—— —— and Whitford, A. B. 1999. Voter choice in multi-party democracies: a test of competing theories and models. *American Journal of Political Science*, 43: 1231–47.

Rabinowitz, G. 1973. Spatial models of electoral choice: an empirical analysis. Doctoral dissertation, University of Michigan.

—— 1976. A procedure for ordering object pairs consistent with the multidimensional unfolding model. *Psychometrika*, 45: 349–73.

Rasch, G. 1961. On general laws and the meaning of measurement in psychology. *Proceedings of the IV Berkeley Symposium on Mathematical Statistics and Probability*, 4: 321–33.

Ross, J., and Cliff, N. 1964. A generalization of the interpoint distance model. *Psychometrika*, 29: 167–76.

Rusk, J., and Weisberg, H. 1972. Perceptions of presidential candidates. *Midwest Journal of Political Science*, 16: 388–410.

Schofield, N., Martin, A. D., Quinn, K. M., and Whitford, A. B. 1998. Multiparty electoral competition in the Netherlands and Germany: a model based on multinomial probit. *Public Choice*, 97: 257–93.

Shepard, R. N. 1958. Stimulus and response generalization: deduction of the generalization gradient from a trace model. *Psychological Review*, 65: 242–56.

—— 1962a. The analysis of proximities: multidimensional scaling with an unknown distance function, I. *Psychometrika*, 27: 125–39.

—— 1962b. The analysis of proximities: multidimensional scaling with an unknown distance function, II. *Psychometrika*, 27: 219–46.

—— 1963. Analysis of proximities as a technique for the study of information processing in man. *Human Factors*, 5: 33–48.

—— 1987. Toward a universal law of generalization for psychological science. *Science*, 237: 1317–23.

—— 1991. Integrality versus separability of stimulus dimensions: evolution of the distinction and a proposed theoretical basis. In *Perception of Structure*, ed. J. R. Pomerantz and G. Lockhead. Washington, DC: APA.

Shye, S. 1978. *Theory Construction and Data Analysis in the Behavioral Sciences*. San Francisco: Jossey-Bass.

Spearman, C. E. 1904. "General intelligence" objectively determined and measured. *American Journal of Psychology*, 15: 201–93.

—— 1906. "Footrule" for measuring correlation. *British Journal of Psychology*, 2: 89–108.

—— 1927. *The Abilities of Man: Their Nature and Measurement*. New York: Macmillan.

Takane, Y. 2004. Matrices with special reference to applications in psychometrics. *Linear Algebra and Its Applications*, 388C: 341–61.

—— Young, F. W., and de Leeuw, J. 1977. Nonmetric individual differences in multidimensional scaling: an alternating least-squares method with optimal scaling features. *Psychometrika*, 42: 7–67.

Thurstone, L. L. 1927. A law of comparative judgment. *Psychological Review*, 34: 278–86.

—— 1931. Multiple factor analysis. *Psychological Review*, 38: 406–27.

—— 1935. *The Vectors of Mind: Multiple Factor Analysis for the Isolation of Primary Traits*. Chicago: University of Chicago Press.

—— 1947. *Multiple Factor Analysis*. Chicago: University of Chicago Press.

Torgerson, W. S. 1952. Multidimensional scaling: I. theory and method. *Psychometrika*, 17: 401–19.

—— 1958. *Theory and Methods of Scaling*. New York: Wiley.

Tversky, A. 1992. Clyde Hamilton Coombs. In *Biographical Memoirs V.61*. Washington, DC: National Academy of Sciences.

Van Schuur, W. H. 1992. Nonparametric unidimensional unfolding for multicategory data. In *Political Analysis*, vol. iv, ed. J. H. Freeman. Ann Arbor: University of Michigan Press.

—— 2003. Mokken scale analysis: between the Guttman scale and parametric item response theory. *Political Analysis*, 11: 139–63.

Weisberg, H. F. 1968. Dimensional analysis of legislative roll calls. Doctoral dissertation, University of Michigan.

——and RUSK, J. G. 1970. Dimensions of candidate evaluation. *American Political Science Review*, 64: 1167–85.

YOUNG, F. W., DE LEEUW, J., and TAKANE, Y. 1976. Regression with quantitative and qualitative variables: an alternating least squares method with optimal scaling features. *Psychometrika*, 41: 505–29.

YOUNG, G., and HOUSEHOLDER, A. S. 1938. Discussion of a set of points in terms of their mutual distances. *Psychometrika*, 3: 19–22.

PART IV

CAUSALITY AND
EXPLANATION
IN SOCIAL
RESEARCH

CHAPTER 10

....

CAUSATION AND EXPLANATION IN SOCIAL SCIENCE

....

HENRY E. BRADY

1 CAUSALITY

....

HUMANS depend upon causation all the time to explain what has happened to them, to make realistic predictions about what will happen, and to affect what happens in the future. Not surprisingly, we are inveterate searchers after causes. Almost no one goes through a day without uttering sentences of the form *X caused Y* or *Y occurred because of X*. Causal statements explain events, allow predictions about the future, and make it possible to take actions to affect the future. Knowing more about causality can be useful to social science researchers.

Philosophers and statisticians know something about causality, but entering into the philosophical and statistical thickets is a daunting enterprise for social scientists because it requires technical skills (e.g. knowledge of modal logic) and technical information (e.g. knowledge of probability theory) that is not easily mastered. The net payoff from forays into philosophy or statistics sometimes seems small compared to the investment required. The goal of this chapter is to provide a user-friendly synopsis of philosophical and statistical musings about causation. Some technical issues will be discussed, but the goal will always be to ask about the bottom line—how can this information make us better researchers?

Three types of intellectual questions typically arise in philosophical discussions of causality:

- *Psychological and linguistic*—What do we *mean* by causality when we use the concept?
- *Metaphysical or ontological*—What *is* causality?
- *Epistemological*—How do we *discover* when causality is operative?[1]

Four distinct approaches to causality, summarized in Table 10.1, provide answers to these and other questions about causality.[2] Philosophers debate which approach is the right one. For our purposes, we embrace them all. Our primary goal is developing better social science methods, and our perspective is that all these approaches capture some aspect of causality. Therefore, practical researchers can profit from drawing lessons from each one of them even though their proponents sometimes treat them as competing or even contradictory. Our standard has been whether or not we could think of concrete examples of research that utilized (or could have utilized) a perspective to some advantage. If we could think of such examples, then we think it is worth drawing lessons from that approach.

A really good causal inference should satisfy the requirements of all four approaches. Causal inferences will be stronger to the extent that they are based upon finding all the following: (1) Constant conjunction of causes and effects required by the neo-Humean approach. (2) No effect when the cause is absent in the most similar world to where the cause is present as required by the counterfactual approach. (3) An effect after a cause is manipulated. (4) Activities and processes linking causes and effects required by the mechanism approach.

The claim that smoking causes lung cancer, for example, first arose in epidemiological studies that found a correlation between smoking and lung cancer. These results were highly suggestive to many, but this correlational evidence was insufficient to others (including one of the founders of modern statistics, R. A. Fisher). These studies were followed by experiments that showed that, at least in animals, the absence of smoking reduced the incidence of cancer compared to the incidence with smoking when similar groups were compared. But animals, some suggested, are not people. Other studies showed that when people stopped smoking (that is, when the putative cause of cancer was manipulated) the incidence of cancer went down as well. Finally, recent studies have uncovered biological mechanisms that explain the link between smoking and lung cancer. Taken together the evidence for a relationship between smoking and lung cancer now seems overwhelming.

---

[1]   A fourth question is pragmatic: How do we *convince* others to accept our explanation or causal argument? A leading proponent of this approach is Bas van Fraassen (1980). Kitcher and Salmon (1987, 315) argue that "van Fraassen has offered the best theory of the pragmatics of explanation to date, but ... if his proposal is seen as a pragmatic theory of explanation then it faces serious difficulties" because there is a difference between "a theory of the pragmatics of explanation and a pragmatic theory of explanation." From their perspective, knowing how people convince others of a theory does not solve the ontological or epistemological problems.

[2]   Two important books on causality are not covered in this chapter, although the author has profited from their insights. Pearl (2000) provides a comprehensive approach to causality rooted in a Bayesian perspective. Shafer (1996) links decision theory and causal trees in a novel and useful way.

Table 10.1. Four approaches to causality

	Neo-Humean regularity	Counterfactual	Manipulation	Mechanisms and capacities
Major authors associated with the approach	Hume (1739); Mill (1888); Hempel (1965); Beauchamp and Rosenberg (1981)	Weber (1906); Lewis (1973a; 1973b; 1986)	Gasking (1955); Menzies and Price (1993); von Wright (1971)	Harre and Madden (1975); Cartwright (1989); Glennan (1996);
Approach to the symmetric aspect of causality	Observation of constant conjunction and correlation	Truth in otherwise similar worlds of "if the cause occurs then so does the effect" and "if the cause does not occur then the effect does not occur"	Recipe that regularly produces the effect from the cause	Consideration of whether there is a mechanism or capacity that leads from the cause to the effect
Approach to the asymmetric aspect of causality	Temporal precedence	Consideration of the truth of: "if the effect does not occur, then the cause may still occur"	Observation of the effect of the manipulation	An appeal to the operation of the mechanism
Major problems solved	Necessary connection	Singular causation; nature of necessity	Common cause and causal direction	Pre-emption
Emphasis on causes of effects or effects of causes?	Causes of effects (e.g. focus on dependent variable in regressions.)	Effects of causes (e.g. focus on treatment's effects in experiments)	Effects of causes (e.g. focus on treatment's effects in experiments)	Causes of effects (e.g. focus on mechanism that creates effects)
Studies with comparative advantage using this definition	Observational and causal modeling	Experiments; case study comparisons; counterfactual thought experiments	Experiments; natural experiments; quasi-experiments	Analytic models; case studies

2 COUNTERFACTUALS

Causal statements are so useful that most people cannot let an event go by without asking why it happened and offering their own "because." They often enliven these discussions with counterfactual assertions such as "if the cause had not occurred, then the effect would not have happened." A counterfactual is a statement, typically in the subjunctive mood, in which a false or "counter to fact" premise is followed by some assertion about what would have happened if the premise were true. For example, the butterfly ballot was used in Palm Beach County Florida in 2000 and George W. Bush was elected president. A counterfactual assertion might be "if the butterfly ballot had not been used in Palm Beach County in 2000, then George Bush would not have been elected president." The statement uses the subjunctive ("if the butterfly ballot had not been used, ... then George Bush would not have been elected"), and the premise is counter to the facts. The premise is false because the butterfly ballot was used in Palm Beach County in the real world as it unfolded. The counterfactual claim is that without this ballot, the world would have proceeded differently, and George Bush would not have been president. Is this true?

The truth of counterfactuals is closely related to the existence of causal relationships. The counterfactual claim made above implies that there is a causal link between the butterfly ballot (the cause X) and the election of George Bush (the effect Y). The counterfactual, for example, would be true if the butterfly ballot *caused* Al Gore to lose enough votes so that Bush was elected. Then, if the butterfly ballot had not been used, Al Gore would have gotten more votes and won the election.

Another way to think about this is to simply ask what would have happened in the *most similar world* in which the butterfly ballot was not used. Would George Bush still be president? One way to do this would be to rerun the world with the cause eradicated so that the butterfly ballot was not used. The world would otherwise be the same. If George Bush did not become president, then we would say that the counterfactual is true. Thus, the statement that the butterfly ballot *caused* the election of George W. Bush is essentially the same as saying that in the *most similar world* in which the butterfly ballot did not exist, George Bush would have lost. The existence of a causal connection can be checked by determining whether or not the counterfactual would be true in the most similar possible world where its premise is true. The problem, of course, is defining the most similar world and finding evidence for what would happen in it.

Beyond these definitional questions about most similar worlds, there is the problem of finding evidence for what would happen in the most similar world. We cannot rerun the world so that the butterfly ballot is not used. What can we do? Many philosophers have wrestled with this question, and we discuss the problem in detail later in the section on the counterfactual approach to causation.[3] For now, we merely

---

[3] Standard theories of logic cannot handle counterfactuals because propositions with false premises are automatically considered true which would mean that all counterfactual statements, with their false

note that people act as if they can solve this problem because they assert the truth of counterfactual statements all the time.

3 Exploring Three Basic Questions about Causality

Causality is at the center of explanation and understanding, but what, exactly, is it? And how is it related to counterfactual thinking? Somewhat confusingly, philosophers mingle psychological, ontological, and epistemological arguments when they discuss causality. Those not alerted to the different purposes of these arguments may find philosophical discussions perplexing as they move from one kind of discussion to another. Our primary focus is epistemological. We want to know when causality is truly operative, not just when some psychological process leads people to believe that it is operative. And we do not care much about metaphysical questions regarding what causality really is, although such ontological considerations become interesting to the extent that they might help us discover causal relationships.

3.1 Psychological and Linguistic Analysis

Although our primary focus is epistemological, our everyday understanding, and even our philosophical understanding, of causality is rooted in the psychology of causal inference. Perhaps the most famous psychological analysis is David Hume's investigation of what people mean when they refer to causes and effects. Hume (1711–76) was writing at a time when the pre-eminent theory of causality was the existence of a necessary connection—a kind of "hook" or "force"—between causes and their effects so that a particular cause must be followed by a specific effect. Hume looked for the feature of causes that guaranteed their effects. He argued that there was no evidence for the necessity of causes because all we could ever find in events was the contiguity, precedence, and regularity of cause and effect. There was no evidence for any kind of hook or force. He described his investigations as follows in his *Treatise of Human Nature* (1739):

What is our idea of necessity, when we say that two objects are necessarily connected together? .... I consider in what objects necessity is commonly supposed to lie; and finding that it is always ascribed to causes and effects, I turn my eye to two objects supposed to be placed in that

premises, would be true, regardless of whether or not a causal link existed. Modal logics, which try to capture the nature of necessity, possibility, contingency, and impossibility, have been developed for counterfactuals (Lewis 1973a; 1973b). These logics typically judge the truthfulness of the counterfactual on whether or not the statement would be true in the most similar possible world where the premise is true. Problems arise, however, in defining the most similar world.

relation, and examine them in all the situations of which they are susceptible. I immediately perceive that they are *contiguous* in time and place, and that the object we call cause *precedes* the other we call effect. In no one instance can I go any further, nor is it possible for me to discover any third relation betwixt these objects. I therefore enlarge my view to comprehend several instances, where I find like objects always existing in like relations of contiguity and succession. The reflection on several instances only repeats the same objects; and therefore can never give rise to a new idea. But upon further inquiry, I find that the repetition is not in every particular the same, but produces a new impression, and by that means the idea which I at present examine. For, after a frequent repetition, I find that upon the appearance of one of the objects the mind is *determined* by custom to consider its usual attendant, and to consider it in a stronger light upon account of its relation to the first object. It is this impression, then, or *determination*, which affords me the idea of necessity.   (Hume, 1978 [1739], 155)[4]

Thus for Hume the *idea* of necessary connection is a psychological trick played by the mind that observes repetitions of causes followed by effects and then presumes some connection that goes beyond that regularity. For Hume, the major feature of causation, beyond temporal precedence and contiguity, is simply the regularity of the association of causes with their effects, but there is no evidence for any kind of hook or necessary connection between causes and effects.[5]

The Humean analysis of causation became the predominant perspective in the nineteenth and most of the twentieth century, and it led in two directions, both of which focused upon the logical form of causal statements. Some, such as the physicist Ernst Mach, the philosopher Bertrand Russell, and the statistician/geneticist Karl Pearson, concluded that there was nothing more to causation than regularity so that the entire concept should be abandoned in favor of functional laws or measures of association such as correlation which summarized the regularity.[6] Others, such as the philosophers John Stuart Mill (1888), Karl Hempel (1965), and Tom Beauchamp and

---

[4] In the *Enquiry* (1748, 144–5) which is a later reworking of the *Treatise*, Hume says: "So that, upon the whole, there appears not, throughout all nature, any one instance of connexion, which is conceivable by us. All events seem entirely loose and separate. One event follows another; but we never can observe any tye between them. They seem *conjoined*, but never *connected*. And as we can have no idea of any thing, which never appeared to our outward sense or inward sentiment, the necessary conclusion *seems* to be, that we have no idea of connexion or power at all, and that these words are absolutely without meaning, when employed either in philosophical reasonings, or common life.... This connexion, therefore, we feel in the mind, this customary transition of the imagination from one object to its usual attendant, is the sentiment or impression, from which we form the idea of power or necessary connexion."

[5] There are different interpretations of what Hume meant. For a thorough discussion see Beauchamp and Rosenberg (1981).

[6] Bertrand Russell famously wrote that "the word 'cause' is so inextricably bound up with misleading associations as to make its complete extrusion from the philosophical vocabulary desirable.... The law of causality, like so much that passes muster among philosophers, is a relic of a bygone age, surviving like the monarchy, only because it is erroneously supposed to do no harm" (Russell 1918). Karl Pearson rejected causation and replaced it with correlation: "Beyond such discarded fundamentals as 'matter' and 'force' lies still another fetish amidst the inscrutable arcana of even modern science, namely the category of cause and effect. Is this category anything but a conceptual limit to experience, and without any basis in perception beyond a statistical approximation?" (Pearson 1911, vi). "It is this conception of correlation between two occurrences embracing all relationship from absolute independence to complete dependence, which is the wider category by which we have to replace the old idea of causation" (Pearson 1911, 157).

Alexander Rosenberg (1981), looked for ways to strengthen the regularity condition so as to go beyond mere accidental regularities. For them, true cause and effect regularities must be unconditional and follow from some lawlike statement. Their neo-Humean approach improved upon Hume's approach, but as we shall see, there appears to be no way to define lawlike statements in a way that captures all that we mean by causality.

What, then, do we typically mean by causality? In their analysis of the fundamental metaphors used to mark the operation of causality, the linguist George Lakoff and the philosopher Mark Johnson (1980a; 1980b; 1999) describe prototypical causation as "the manipulation of objects by force, the volitional use of bodily force to change something physically by direct contact in one's immediate environment" (1999, 177). Causes bring, throw, hurl, propel, lead, drag, pull, push, drive, tear, thrust, or fling the world into new circumstances. These verbs suggest that causation is forced movement, and for Lakoff and Johnson the "Causation Is Forced Movement metaphor is in a crucial way constitutive of the concept of causation" (187). Causation as forceful manipulation differs significantly from causation as the regularity of cause and effect because forceful manipulation emphasizes intervention, agency, and the possibility that the failure to engage in the manipulation will prevent the effect from happening. For Lakoff and Johnson, causes are forces and capacities that entail their effects in ways that go beyond mere regularity and that are reminiscent of the causal "hooks" rejected by Hume, although instead of hooks they emphasize manipulation, mechanisms, forces, and capacities.[7]

"Causation as regularity" and "causation as manipulation" are quite different notions, but each carries with it some essential features of causality. And each is the basis for a different philosophical or everyday understanding of causality. From a psychological perspective, their differences emerge clearly in research done in the last fifteen years on the relationship between causal and counterfactual thinking (Spellman and Mandel 1999). Research on this topic demonstrates that people focus on different factors when they think causally than when they think counterfactually. In experiments, people have been asked to consider causal attributions and counterfactual possibilities in car accidents in which they imagine that they chose a new route to drive home and were hit by a drunk driver. People's *causal attributions* for these accidents tend to "focus on antecedents that general knowledge suggest would covary with, and therefore predict, the outcome (e.g., the drunk driver)," but *counterfactual thinking* focuses on controllable antecedents such as the choice of route (Spellman and Mandel 1999, 123). Roughly speaking, causal attributions are based upon a regularity approach to causation while counterfactual thinking is based upon a manipulation approach to causation. The regularity approach suggests that drunken drivers typically cause accidents but the counterfactual approach suggests that in this instance the person's

---

[7] As we shall show, two different approaches to causation are conflated here. One approach emphasizes agency and manipulation. The other approach emphasizes mechanisms and capacities. The major difference is the locus of the underlying force that defines causal relationships. Agency and manipulation approaches emphasize human intervention. Mechanism and capacity approaches emphasize processes within nature itself.

choice of a new route was the cause of the accident because it was manipulable by the person. The logic of causal and the logic of counterfactual thinking are so closely related that these psychological differences in attributions lead to the suspicion that both the regularity and the manipulation approaches tell us something important about causation.

3.2 Ontological Questions

Knowing how most people think and talk about causality is useful, but we are ul-timately more interested in knowing what causality actually is and how we would discover it in the world. These are respectively ontological and epistemological ques-tions.[8] Ontological questions ask about the characteristics of the abstract entities that exist in the world. The study of causality raises a number of fundamental ontological questions regarding the *things that are causally related* and the *nature of the causal relation*.[9]

What are the things, the "causes" and the "effects" that are linked by causation? Whatever they are, they must be the same things because causes can also be effects and vice versa. But what are they? Are they facts, properties, events, or something else?[10] The practicing researcher cannot ignore questions about the definition of events. One of the things that researchers must consider is the proper definition of an event,[11] and a great deal of the effort in doing empirical work is defining events suitably. Not surprisingly, tremendous effort has gone into defining wars, revolutions, firms, organizations, democracies, religions, participatory acts, political campaigns, and many other kinds of events and structures that matter for social science re-search. Much could be said about defining events, but we shall only emphasize that defining events in a useful fashion is one of the major tasks of good social science research.

A second basic set of ontological questions concern the nature of the causal rela-tionship. Is causality different when it deals with physical phenomena (e.g. billiard

---

[8] Roughly speaking, philosophy is concerned with three kinds of questions regarding "what is" (ontology), "how it can be known" (epistemology), and "what value it has" (ethics and aesthetics). In answering these questions, twentieth-century philosophy has also paid a great deal of attention to logical, linguistic, and even psychological analysis.

[9] Symbolically, we can think of the causal relation as a statement XcY where X is a cause, Y is an effect, and c is a causal relation. X and Y are the things that are causally related and c is the causal relation. As we shall see later, this relationship is usually considered to be incomplete (not all X and Y are causally related), asymmetric for those events that are causally related (either XcY or YcX but not both), and irreflexive (XcX is not possible).

[10] Events are located in space and time (e.g. "the WWI peace settlement at Versailles") but facts are not ("The fact that the WW I peace settlement was at Versailles"). For discussions of causality and events see Bennett (1988) and for causality and facts see Mellors (1995). Many philosophers prefer to speak of "tropes" which are particularized properties (Ehring 1997). Some philosophers reject the idea that the world can be described in terms of distinct events or tropes and argue for events as enduring things (Harre and Madden 1975, ch. 6).

[11] A potpourri of citations that deal with the definition of events and social processes are Abbott (1983; 1992; 1995), Pierson (2004), Riker (1957), Tilly (1984).

balls hitting one another or planets going around stars) than when it deals with social phenomena (democratization, business cycles, cultural change, elections) that are socially constructed?[12] What role do human agency and mental events play in causation?[13] What can we say about the time structure and nature of causal processes?[14] Our attitude is that social science is about the formation of concepts and the identification of causal mechanisms. We believe that social phenomena such as the Protestant ethic, the system of nation states, and culture exist and have causal implications. We also believe that reasons, perceptions, beliefs, and attitudes affect human behavior. Furthermore, we believe that these things can be observed and measured.

Another basic question about the causal relation is whether it is deterministic or probabilistic. The classic model of causation is the deterministic, clockwork Newtonian universe in which the same initial conditions inevitably produce the same outcome. But modern science has produced many examples where causal relationships appear to be probabilistic. The most famous is quantum mechanics where the position and momentum of particles is represented by probability distributions, but many other sciences rely upon probabilistic relationships. Geneticists, for example, do not expect that couples in which all the men have the same height and all the women have the same height will have children of the same height. In this case, the same set of (observed) causal factors produce a probability distribution over possible heights. We now know that even detailed knowledge of the couple's DNA would not lead to exact predictions. Probabilistic causation, therefore, seems possible in the physical sciences, common in the biological sciences, and pervasive in the social sciences. Nevertheless, following the custom of a great deal of philosophical work, we shall start with a discussion of deterministic causation in order not to complicate the analysis.

3.3 Epistemological Questions

Epistemology is concerned with how we can obtain intellectually certain knowledge (what the Greeks called "episteme"). How do we figure out that X really caused Y? At the dinner table, our admonition not to reach across the table might be met with "I didn't break the glass, the table shook," suggesting that our causal explanation for the broken glass was wrong. How do we proceed in this situation? We would probably try to rule out alternatives by investigating whether someone shook the table, whether there was an earthquake, or something else happened to disturb the glass. The problem here is that there are many possibilities that must be ruled out, and what must be ruled out depends, to some extent, on our definition of causality.

---

[12] For representative discussions see Durkheim (1982), Berger and Luckman (1966), von Wright (1971), Searle (1997), Wendt (1999).

[13] See Dilthey (1961), von Wright (1971, ch. 1), Davidson (2001), Searle (1969), Wendt (1999).

[14] In a vivid set of metaphors, Pierson (2004) compares different kinds of social science processes with tornadoes, earthquakes, large meteorites, and global warming in terms of the time horizon of the cause and the time horizon of the impact. He shows that the causal processes in each situation are quite different.

Learning about causality, then, requires that we know what it is and that we know how to recognize it when we see it. The simple Humean approach appears to solve both problems at once. Two events are causally related when they are contiguous, one precedes another, and they occur regularly in constant conjunction with one another. Once we have checked these conditions, we know that we have a causal connection. But upon examination, these conditions are not enough for causality because we would not say that night causes day, even though day and night are contiguous, night precedes day, and day and night are regularly associated. Furthermore, simple regularities like this do not make it easy to distinguish cause from effect—after all, day precedes night as well as night preceding day so that we could just as well, and just as mistakenly, say that day causes night. Something more is needed.[15] It is this something more that causes most of the problems for understanding causation. John Stuart Mill suggested that there had to be an "unconditional" relationship between cause and effect and modern neo-Humeans have required a "lawlike" relationship, but even if we know what this means[16] (which would solve the ontological problem of causation) it is hard to ensure that it is true in particular instances so as to solve the epistemological problem.

In the following sections, we begin with a review of four approaches of what causality might be. We spend most of our time on a counterfactual definition, mostly amounting to a recipe that is now widely used in statistics. We end with a discussion of the limitations of the recipe and how far it goes toward solving the epistemological and ontological problems.

4 The Humean and Neo-Humean Approach to Causation

4.1 Lawlike Generalities and the Humean Regularity Approach to Causation

Humean and neo-Humean approaches propose logical conditions that must hold for the constant conjunction of events to justify the inference that they have a cause–effect relationship. Specifically, Humeans have explored whether a cause must be sufficient for its effects, necessary for its effects, or something more complicated.

---

[15] Something different might also be needed. Hume himself dropped the requirement for contiguity in his 1748 rewrite of his 1738 work, and many philosophers would also drop his requirement for temporal precedence.

[16] Those new to this literature are presented with many statements about the need for lawfulness and unconditionality which seem to promise a recipe that will insure lawfulness. But the conditions that are presented always seem to fall short of the goal.

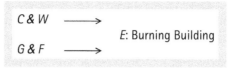

Fig. 10.1. Two sets of INUS conditions

The classic definition shared by Hume, John Stuart Mill, and many others was that "X is a cause of Y if and only if X is sufficient for Y." That is, the cause must always and invariably lead to the effect. Certainly an X that is sufficient for Y can be considered a cause, but what about the many putative causes that are not sufficient for their effect? Striking a match, for example, may be necessary for it to light, but it may not light unless there is enough oxygen in the atmosphere. Is striking a match never a cause of a match lighting? This leads to an alternative definition in which "X is a cause of Y if and only if X is necessary for Y." Under this definition, it is assumed that the cause (such as striking the match) must be present for the effect to occur, but it may not always be enough for the cause to actually occur (because there might not be enough oxygen). But how many causes are even necessary for their effects? If the match does not light after striking it, someone might use a blowtorch to light it so that striking the match is not even necessary for the match to ignite. Do we therefore assume that striking the match is never a cause of its lighting? Necessity and sufficiency seem unequal to the task of defining causation.[17]

These considerations led John Mackie to propose a set of conditions requiring that a cause be an insufficient [I] but necessary [N] part of a condition which is itself unnecessary [U] but exclusively sufficient [S] for the effect. These INUS conditions can be explained by an example. Consider two ways that the effect (E), which is a building burning down, might occur (see Figure 10.1). In one scenario the wiring might short-circuit and overheat, thus causing the wooden framing to burn. In another, a gasoline can might be next to a furnace that ignites and causes the gasoline can to explode. A number of factors here are INUS conditions for the building to burn down. The short circuit (C) and the wooden framing (W) together might cause the building to burn down, or the gasoline can (G) and the furnace (F) might cause the building to burn down. Thus, C and W together are exclusively sufficient [S] to burn the building down, and G and F together are exclusively sufficient [S] to burn the building down. Furthermore, the short circuit and wooden framing (C *and* W) are unnecessary [U], and the gasoline can and the furnace (G *and* F) are unnecessary [U] because the building could have burned down with just one or the other combination of factors. Finally, C, W, G, or F alone is insufficient [I] to burn the building down even though C is necessary [N] in conjunction with W (or vice versa) and G is necessary [N] in conjunction with F (or vice-versa). This formulation allows for the fact that no single cause is sufficient or necessary, but when experts say that a short circuit caused the

[17] And there are problems such as the following favorite of the philosophers: "If two bullets pierce a man's heart simultaneously, it is reasonable to suppose that each is an essential part of a distinct sufficient condition of the death, and that neither bullet is *ceteris paribus* necessary for the death, since in each case the other bullet is sufficient" (Sosa and Tooley 1993, 8–9).

fire they "are saying, in effect that the short-circuit (C) is a condition of this sort, that it occurred, that the other conditions (W) which, conjoined with it, form a sufficient condition were also present, and that no other sufficient condition (such as G *and* F) of the house's catching fire was present on this occasion" (Mackie 1965, 245; letters addded).

From the perspective of a practicing researcher, three lessons follow from the INUS conditions. First a putative cause such as C might not cause the effect E because G *and* F might be responsible. Hence, the burned-down building (E) will not always result from a short circuit (C) even though C could cause the building to burn down. Second, interactions among causes may be necessary for any one cause to be sufficient (C and W require each other and W and G require each other). Third, the relationship between any INUS cause and its effect might appear to be probabilistic because of the other INUS causes. In summary, the INUS conditions suggest the multiplicity of causal pathways and causes, the possibility of conjunctural causation (Ragin 1987), and the likelihood that social science relationships will appear probabilistic even if they are deterministic.[18]

A specific example might help to make these points clearer. Assume that the four INUS factors mentioned above, C, W, G, and F, occur independently of one another and that they are the only factors which cause fires in buildings. Further assume that short circuits (C) occur 10 percent of the time, wooden (W) frame buildings 50 percent of the time, furnaces (F) 90 percent of the time, and gasoline (G) cans near furnaces 10 percent of the time. Because these events are assumed independent of one another, it is easy to calculate that C and W occur 5 percent of the time and that G and F occur 9 percent of the time. (We simply multiply the probability of the two independent events.) All four conditions occur 0.45 percent of the time. (The product of all four percentages.) Thus, fires occur 13.55 percent of the time. This percentage includes the cases where the fire is the result of C and W (5 percent of the time) and where it is the result of G and F (9 percent of the time), and it adjusts downward for double-counting that occurs in the cases where all four INUS conditions occur together (0.45 percent of the time).

Now suppose an experimenter did not know about the role of wooden frame buildings or gasoline cans and furnaces and only looked at the relationship between fires and short circuits. A cross-tabulation of fires with the short circuit factor would yield Table 10.2. As assumed above, short circuits occur 10 percent of the time (see the third column total at the bottom of the table) and as calculated above, fires occur 13.55 percent of the time (see the third row total on the far right). The entries in the interior of the table are calculated in a similar way.[19]

Even though each case occurs because of a deterministic process—either a short circuit and a wooden frame building or a gasoline can and a furnace (or both)— this cross-tabulation suggests a probabilistic relationship between fires and short

---

[18] These points are made especially forcefully in Marini and Singer (1988).

[19] Thus, the entry for short circuits and fires comes from the cases where there are short circuits and wooden frame buildings (5 percent of the time) and where there are short circuits and no wooden frame buildings but there are gasoline cans and furnaces (5 percent times 9 percent).

Table 10.2. Fires by short circuits in hypothetical example (total percentages of each event)

	Not C—no short circuits	C—short circuits	Row totals
Not E—no fires	81.90	4.55	86.45
E—fires	8.10	5.45	13.55
Column totals	90.00	10.00	100.00

circuits. In 4.55 percent of the cases, short circuits occur but no fires result because the building was not wooden. In 8.10 percent of the cases, there are no short circuits, but a fire occurs because the gasoline can has been placed near the furnace. For this table, a standard measure of association, the Pearson correlation, between the effect and the cause is about .40 which is far short of the 1.0 required for a perfect (positive) relationship. If, however, the correct model is considered in which there are the required interaction effects, the relationship will produce a perfect fit.[20] Thus, a misspecification of a deterministic relationship can easily lead a researcher to think that there is a probabilistic relationship between the cause and effect.

INUS conditions reveal a lot about the complexities of causality, but as a definition of it, they turn out to be too weak—they do not rule out situations where there are common causes, and they do not exclude accidental regularities. The problem of common cause arises in a situation where, for example, lightning strikes (L) the wooden framing (W) and causes it to burn (E) while also causing a short in the circuitry (C). That is, $L \rightarrow E$ and $L \rightarrow C$ (where the arrow indicates causation). If lightning always causes a short in the circuitry, but the short never has anything to do with a fire in these situations because the lightning starts the fire directly through its heating of the wood, we will nevertheless always find that C and E are constantly conjoined through the action of the lightning, suggesting that the short circuit caused the fire even though the truth is that *lightning is the common cause of both*.[21] In some cases of common causes such as the rise in barometric pressure followed by the arrival of a storm, common sense tells us that the putative cause (the rise in barometric pressure) cannot be the real cause of the thunderstorm. But in the situation with the lightning, the fact that short circuits have the capacity to cause fires makes it less likely that we will realize that lightning is the common cause of both the short circuits and the fires. We might be better off in the case where the lightning split some of the wood framing of the house instead of causing a short circuit. In that case,

---

[20] If each variable is scored zero or one depending upon whether the effect or cause is present or absent, then a regression equation of the effect on the product (or interaction) of C and W, the product of G and F, and the product of C, W, G, and F will produce a multiple correlation of one indicating a perfect fit.

[21] It is also possible that the lightning's heating of the wood is (always or sometimes) insufficient to cause the fire (not $L \rightarrow E$), but its creation of a short circuit ($L \rightarrow C$) is (always or sometimes) sufficient for the fire ($C \rightarrow E$). In this case, the *lightning is the indirect cause of the fire* through its creation of the short circuit. That is, $L \rightarrow C \rightarrow E$.

we would probably reject the fantastic theory that split wood caused the fire because split wood does not have the capacity to start a fire, but the Humean approach would be equally confused by both situations because it could not appeal, within the ambit of its understanding, to causal capacities. For a Humean, the constant conjunction of split wood and fires suggests causation as much as the constant conjunction of short circuits and fires. Indeed, the constant conjunction of storks and babies would be treated as probative of a causal connection.

Attempts to fix up these conditions usually focus on trying to require "lawlike" statements that are unconditionally true, not just accidentally true. Since it is not unconditionally true that splitting wood causes fires, the presumption is that some such conditions can be found to rule out this explanation. Unfortunately, no set of conditions seem to be successful.[22] Although the regularity approach identifies a necessary condition for describing causation, it basically fails because association is not causation and there is no reason why purely logical restrictions on lawlike statements should be sufficient to characterize causal relationships. Part of the problem is that there are many different types of causal laws and they do not fit any particular patterns. For example, one restriction that has been proposed to ensure lawfulness is that lawlike statements should either not refer to particular situations or they should be derivable from laws that do not refer to particular situations. This would mean that Kepler's first "law" about all planets moving in elliptical orbits around the sun (a highly specific situation!) was not a causal law before Newton's laws were discovered, but it was a causal law after it was shown that it could be derived from Newton's laws. But Kepler's laws were always considered causal laws, and there seems to be no reason to rest their lawfulness on Newton's laws. Furthermore, by this standard, almost all social science and natural science laws (e.g. plate tectonics) are about particular situations. In short, logical restrictions on the form of laws do not seem sufficient to characterize causality.

4.2 The Asymmetry of Causation

The regularity approach also fails because it does not provide an explanation for the asymmetry of causation. Causes should cause their effects, but INUS conditions are almost always symmetrical such that if C is an INUS cause of E, then E is also an INUS cause of C. It is almost always possible to turn around an INUS condition so that an effect is an INUS for its cause.[23] One of the most famous examples of this problem involves a flagpole, the elevation of the sun, and the flagpole's shadow. The

[22] For some representative discussions of the problems see Harre and Madden (1975, ch. 2); Salmon (1990, chs. 1–2); Hausman (1998, ch. 3). Salmon (1990, 15) notes that "Lawfulness, modal import [what is necessary, possible, or impossible], and support of counterfactuals seems to have a common extension; statements either possess all three or lack all three. But it is extraordinarily difficult to find criteria to separate those statements that do from those that do not."

[23] Papineau (1985, 279) provides a demonstration of the symmetry of INUS conditions, and he goes on to suggest a condition for the asymmetry of causation that does not rely on the temporal relationship between causes and effects.

law that light travels in straight lines implies that there is a relationship between the height of the flagpole, the length of its shadow, and the angle of elevation of the sun. When the sun rises, the shadow is long, at midday it is short, and at sunset it is long again. Intuition about causality suggests that the length of the shadow is caused by the height of the flagpole and the elevation of the sun. But, using INUS conditions, we can just as well say that the elevation of the sun is caused by the height of the flagpole and the length of the shadow. There is simply nothing in the conditions that precludes this fantastic possibility.

The only feature of the Humean approach that provides for asymmetry is temporal precedence. If changes in the elevation of the sun precede corresponding changes in the length of the shadow, then we can say that the elevation of the sun causes the length of the shadow. And if changes in the height of the flagpole precede corresponding changes in the length of the shadow, we can say that the height of the flagpole causes the length of the shadow. But many philosophers reject making temporal precedence the determinant of causal asymmetry because it precludes the possibility of *explaining* the direction of time by causal asymmetry and it precludes the possibility of backwards causation. From a practical perspective, it also requires careful measures of timing that may be difficult in a particular situation.

4.3 Summary

This discussion reveals two basic aspects of the causal relation. One is a symmetrical form of association between cause and effect and the other is an asymmetrical relation in which causes produce effects but not the reverse. The Humean regularity approach, in the form of INUS conditions, provides a necessary condition for the existence of the symmetrical relationship,[24] but it does not rule out situations such as common cause and accidental regularities where there is no causal relationship at all. From a methodological standpoint, it can easily lead researchers to presume that all they need to do is to find associations, and it also leads to an underemphasis on the rest of the requirement for a "lawlike" or "unconditional" relationship because it does not operationally define what that would really mean. A great deal of what passes for causal modeling suffers from these defects (Freedman 1987; 1991; 1997; 1999).

The Humean approach does even less well with the asymmetrical feature of the causal relationship because it provides no way to determine asymmetry except temporal precedence. Yet there are many other aspects of the causal relation that seem more fundamental than temporal precedence. Causes not only typically precede their

---

[24] Probabilistic causes do not necessarily satisfy INUS conditions because an INUS factor might only sometimes produce an effect. Thus, the short circuit and the wooden frame of the house might only sometimes lead to a conflagration in which the house is burned down. Introducing probabilistic causes would add still another layer of complexity to our discussion which would only provide more reasons to doubt the Humean regularity approach.

effects, but they also can be used to explain effects or to manipulate effects while effects cannot be used to explain causes or to manipulate them.[25]

Effects also depend upon causes, but causes do not depend upon effects. Thus, if a cause does not occur, then the effect will not occur because effects depend on their causes. The counterfactual, "if the cause did not occur, then the effect would not occur," is true. However, if the effect does not occur, then the cause might still occur because causes can happen without leading to a specific effect if other features of the situation are not propitious for the effect. The counterfactual, "if the effect did not occur, then the cause would not occur," is not necessarily true. For example, where a short circuit causes a wooden frame building to burn down, if the short circuit does not occur, then the building will not burn down. But if the building does not burn down, it is still possible that the short circuit occurred but its capacity for causing fires was neutralized because the building was made of brick. This dependence of effects on causes suggests that an alternative definition of causation might be based upon a proper understanding of counterfactuals.

5 COUNTERFACTUAL DEFINITION OF CAUSATION

In a book *On the Theory and Method of History* published in 1902, Eduard Meyer claimed that it was an "unanswerable and so an idle question" whether the course of history would have been different if Bismarck, then Chancellor of Prussia, had not decided to go to war in 1866. By some accounts, the Austro-Prussian-Italian War of 1866 paved the way for German and Italian unification (see Wawro 1996). In reviewing Meyer's book in 1906, Max Weber agreed that "from the strict 'determinist' point of view" finding out what would have happened if Bismarck had not gone to war "was 'impossible' given the 'determinants' which were in fact present." But he went on to say that "And yet, for all that, it is far from being 'idle' to raise the question what might have happened, if, for example, Bismarck had not decided for war. For it is precisely this question which touches on the decisive element in the historical construction of reality: the causal significance which is properly attributed to this individual decision within the totality of infinitely numerous 'factors' (all of which must be just as they are and not otherwise) if precisely this consequence is to result, and the appropriate position which the decision is to occupy in the historical account" (Weber 1978, 111). Weber's review is an early discussion of the importance of counterfactuals for understanding history and making causal inferences. He argues forcefully that if "history is to raise itself above the level of a mere chronicle of noteworthy events and

---

[25] Hausman (1998, 1) also catalogs other aspects of the asymmetry between causes and effects.

personalities, it can only do so by posing just such questions" as the counterfactual in which Bismarck did not decide for war.[26]

5.1 Lewis's Counterfactual Approach to Causation

The philosopher David Lewis (1973b) has proposed the most elaborately worked out theory of how causality is related to counterfactuals.[27] His approach requires the truth of two statements regarding two distinct events X and Y. Lewis starts from the presumption that X and Y have occurred so that the "counterfactual" statement,[28] "If X were to occur, then Y would occur," is true. The truth of this statement is Lewis's first condition for a causal relationship. Then he considers the truth of a second counterfactual:[29] "If X were not to occur, then Y would not occur either." If this is true as well, then he says that X causes Y. If, for example, Bismarck decided for war in 1866 and, as some historians argue, German unification followed because of his decision, then we must ask: "If Bismarck had not decided for war, would Germany have remained divided?" The heart of Lewis's approach is the set of requirements, described below, that he lays down for the truth of this kind of counterfactual.

Lewis's theory has a number of virtues. It deals directly with singular causal events, and it does not require the examination of a large number of instances of X and Y. At one point in the philosophical debate about causation, it was believed that the individual cases such as "the hammer blow caused the glass to break" or "the assassination of Archduke Ferdinand caused the First World War" could not be analyzed alone because these cases had to be subsumed under a general law ("hammer blows cause glass to break") derived from multiple cases plus some particular facts of the situation in order to meet the requirement for a "lawlike" relationship. The counterfactual approach, however, starts with singular events and proposes that causation can be established without an appeal to a set of similar events and general

---

[26] I am indebted to Richard Swedberg for pointing me towards Weber's extraordinary discussion.

[27] Lewis finds some support for his theory in the work of David Hume. In a famous change of course in a short passage in his *Enquiry Concerning Human Understanding* (1748), Hume first summarized his regularity approach to causation by saying that "we may define a cause to be an object, followed by another, and where all the objects similar to the first, are followed by objects similar to the second," and then he changed to a completely different approach to causation by adding "Or in other words, where if the first object had not been, the second had never existed" (146). As many commentators have noted, these were indeed other words, implying an entirely different notion of causation. The first approach equates causality with the constant conjunction of putative causes and effects across similar circumstances. The second, which is a counterfactual approach, relies upon what would happen in a world where the cause did not occur.

[28] Lewis considers statements like this as part of his theory of counterfactuals by simply assuming that statements in the subjunctive mood with true premises and true conclusions are true. As noted earlier, most theories of counterfactuals have been extended to include statements with true premises by assuming, quite reasonably, that they are true if their conclusion is true and false otherwise.

[29] This is a simplified version of Lewis's theory based upon Lewis (1973a; 1973b; 1986) and Hausman (1998, ch. 6).

laws regarding them.[30] The possibility of analyzing singular causal events is important for all researchers, but especially for those doing case studies who want to be able to say something about the consequences of Stalin succeeding Lenin as head of the Soviet Union or the impact of the butterfly ballot on the 2000 US election.

The counterfactual approach also deals directly with the issue of X's causal "efficacy" with respect to Y by considering what would happen if X did not occur. The problem with the theory is the difficulty of determining the truth or falsity of the counterfactual "If X were not to occur, then Y would not occur either." The statement cannot be evaluated in the real world because X actually occurs so that the premise is false, and there is no evidence about what would happen if X did not occur. It only makes sense to evaluate the counterfactual in a world in which the premise is true. Lewis's approach to this problem is to consider whether the statement is true in the closest possible world to the actual world where X does not occur. Thus, if X is a hammer blow and Y is a glass breaking, then the closest possible world is one in which everything else is the same except that the hammer blow does not occur. If in this world, the glass does not break, then the counterfactual is true, and the hammer blow (X) causes the glass to break (Y). The obvious problem with this approach is identifying the closest possible world. If X is the assassination of Archduke Ferdinand and Y is the First World War, is it true that the First World War would not have occurred in the closest possible world where the bullet shot by the terrorist Gavrilo Princip did not hit the Archduke? Or would some other incident have inevitably precipitated the First World War? And, to add to the difficulty, would this "First World War" be the same as the one that happened in our world?

Lewis's approach substitutes the riddle of determining the similarity of possible worlds for the neo-Humean's problem of determining lawlike relationships. To solve these problems, both approaches must be able to identify similar causes and similar effects. The Humean approach must identify them across various situations in the real world. This aspect of the Humean approach is closely related to John Stuart Mill's "Method of Concomitant Variation" which he described as follows: "Whatever phenomenon varies in any manner, whenever another phenomenon varies in some similar manner, is either a cause or an effect of that phenomenon, or is connected to it through some fact of causation" (Mill 1888, 287).[31] Lewis's theory must also identify similar causes and similar effects in the real world in which the cause does occur and in the many possible worlds in which the cause does not occur. This approach is

---

[30]   In fact, many authors now believe that general causation (involving lawlike generalizations) can only be understood in terms of singular causation: "general causation is a generalisation of singular causation. Smoking causes cancer iff (if and only if) smokers' cancers are generally caused by their smoking" (Mellors 1995, 6–7). See also Sosa and Tooley (1993). More generally, whereas explanation was once thought virtually to supersede the need for causal statements, many philosophers now believe that a correct analysis of causality will provide a basis for suitable explanations (see Salmon 1990).

[31]   The Humean approach also has affinities with Mill's Method of Agreement which he described as follows: "If two or more instances of the phenomenon under investigation have only one circumstance in common, the circumstance in which alone all the instances agree, is the cause (or effect) of the given phenomenon" (Mill 1888, 280).

closely related to Mill's "Method of Difference" in which: "If an instance in which the phenomenon under investigation occurs, and an instance in which it does not occur, have every circumstance in common save one, that one occurring only in the former; the circumstance in which alone the two instances differ, is the effect, or the cause, or an indispensable part of the cause, of the phenomenon" (Mill 1888, 280).[32]

In addition to identifying similar causes and similar effects, the Humean approach must determine if the conjunction of these similar causes and effects is accidental or lawlike. This task requires understanding what is happening in each situation and comparing the similarities and differences across situations. Lewis's approach must identify the possible world where the cause does not occur that is most similar to the real world. This undertaking requires understanding the facts of the real world and the laws that are operating in it. Consequently, assessing the similarity of a possible world to our own world requires understanding the lawlike regularities that govern our world.[33] It seems as if Lewis has simply substituted one difficult task, that of identifying the most similar world for the job of establishing lawfulness.

5.2 The Virtues of the Counterfactual Definition of Causation

Lewis *has* substituted one difficult problem for another, but the reformulation of the problem has a number of benefits. The counterfactual approach provides new insights into what is required to establish causal connection between causes and effects. The counterfactual approach makes it clear that establishing causation does not require observing the universal conjunction of a cause and an effect.[34] One observation of a cause followed by an effect is sufficient for establishing causation if it can be shown that in a most similar world without the cause, the effect does not occur. The counterfactual approach proposes that causation can be demonstrated by simply finding a most similar world in which the absence of the cause leads to the absence of the effect.

Lewis's theory provides us with a way to think about the causal impact of singular events such as the badly designed butterfly ballot in Palm Beach County, Florida that led some voters in the 2000 presidential election to complain that they mistakenly voted for Reform Party candidate Patrick Buchanan when they meant to vote for Democrat Al Gore. The ballot can be said to be causally associated with these mistakes

[32] Mill goes on to note that the Method of Difference is "a method of artificial experiment" (281). Notice that for both the Method of Concomitant Variation and the Method of Difference, Mill emphasizes the association between cause and effect and not the identification of which event is the cause and which is the effect. Mill's methods are designed to detect the symmetric aspect of causality but not its asymmetric aspect.

[33] Nelson Goodman makes this point in a 1947 article on counterfactuals, and James Fearon (1991), in a masterful exposition of the counterfactual approach to research, discusses its implications for counterfactual thought experiments in political science. Also see Tetlock and Belkin (1996).

[34] G. H. von Wright notes that the counterfactual conception of causality shows that the hallmark of a lawlike connection is *"necessity and not universality"* (von Wright 1971, 22).

if in the closest possible world in which the butterfly ballot was not used, the vote for Buchanan was lower than in the real world. Ideally this closest possible world would be a parallel universe in which the same people received a different ballot, but this, of course, is impossible. The next-best thing is a situation where similar people employed a different ballot. In fact, the butterfly ballot was only used for election day voters in Palm Beach County. It was not used by absentee voters. Consequently, the results for the absentee voting can be considered a surrogate for the closest possible world in which the butterfly ballot was not used, and in this absentee voting world, voting for Buchanan was dramatically lower, suggesting that at least 2000 people who preferred Gore—more than enough to give the election to Gore—mistakenly voted for Buchanan on the butterfly ballot.

The difficult question, of course, is whether the absentee voting world can be considered a good enough surrogate for the closest possible world in which the butterfly ballot was not used.[35] The counterfactual approach does not provide us with a clear sense of how to make that judgment.[36] But the framework does suggest that we should consider the similarity of the election day world and the absentee voter world. To do this, we can ask whether election day voters are different in some significant ways from absentee voters, and this question can be answered by considering information on their characteristics and experiences. In summary, the counterfactual perspective allows for analyzing causation in singular instances, and it emphasizes comparison, which seems difficult but possible, rather than the recondite and apparently fruitless investigation of the lawfulness of statements such as "All ballots that place candidate names and punch-holes in confusing arrangements will lead to mistakes in casting votes."

5.3 Controlled Experiments and Closest Possible Worlds

The difficulties with the counterfactual definition are identifying the characteristics of the closest possible world in which the putative cause does not occur and finding an empirical surrogate for this world. For the butterfly ballot, sheer luck led a team of researchers to discover that the absentee ballot did not have the problematic features of the butterfly ballot.[37] But how can we find surrogates in other circumstances?

---

[35] For an argument that the absentee votes are an excellent surrogate, see Wand et al. (1991).

[36] In his book on counterfactuals, Lewis only claims that similarity judgments are possible, but he does not provide any guidance on how to make them. He admits that his notion is vague, but he claims it is not ill-understood. "But comparative similarity is not ill-understood. It is vague—very vague—in a well-understood way. Therefore it is just the sort of primitive that we must use to give a correct analysis of something that is itself undeniably vague" (Lewis 1973a, 91). In later work Lewis (1979; 1986) formulates some rules for similarity judgments, but they do not seem very useful to us and to others (Bennett 1988).

[37] For the story of how the differences between the election day and absentee ballot were discovered, see Brady et al. (2001).

One answer is controlled experiments. Experimenters can create mini-closest-possible worlds by finding two or more situations and assigning putative causes (called "treatments") to some situations but not to others (which get the "control"). If in those cases where the cause C occurs, the effect E occurs, then the first requirement of the counterfactual definition is met: When C occurs, then E occurs. Now, if the situations which receive the control are not different in any significant ways from those that get the treatment, then they can be considered surrogates for the closest possible world in which the cause does not occur. If in these situations where the cause C does not occur, the effect E does not occur either, then the second requirement of the counterfactual definition is confirmed: In the closest possible world where C does not occur, then E does not occur. The crucial part of this argument is that the control situation, in which the cause does not occur, must be a good surrogate for the closest possible world to the treatment.

Two experimental methods have been devised for ensuring closeness between the treatment and control situations. One is classical experimentation in which as many circumstances as possible are physically controlled so that the only significant difference between the treatment and the control is the cause. In a chemical experiment, for example, one beaker holds two chemicals and a substance that might be a catalyst and another beaker of the same type, in the same location, at the same temperature, and so forth contains just the two chemicals in the same proportions without the suspected catalyst. If the reaction occurs only in the first beaker, it is attributed to the catalyst. The second method is random assignment of treatments to situations so that there are no reasons to suspect that the entities that get the treatment are any different, on average, from those that do not. We discuss this approach in detail below.

5.4 Problems with the Counterfactual Definition[38]

Although the counterfactual definition of causation leads to substantial insights about causation, it also leads to two significant problems. Using the counterfactual definition as it has been described so far, the direction of causation cannot be established, and two effects of a common cause can be mistaken for cause and effect. Consider, for example, an experiment as described above. In that case, in the treatment group, when C occurs, E occurs, and when E occurs, C occurs. Similarly, in the control group, when C does not occur, then E does not occur, and when E does not occur, then C does not occur. In fact, there is perfect observational symmetry between cause and effect which means that the counterfactual definition of causation as described so far implies that C causes E *and* that E causes C. The same problem arises with two effects of a common cause because of the perfect symmetry in the situation. Consider, for example, a rise in the mercury in a barometer and thunderstorms. Each is an effect

---

[38] This section relies heavily upon Hausman (1998, especially chs. 4–7) and Lewis (1973b).

of high pressure systems, but the counterfactual definition would consider them to be causes of one another.[39]

These problems bedevil Humean and counterfactual approaches. If we accept these approaches in their simplest forms, we must live with a seriously incomplete theory of causation that cannot distinguish causes from effects and that cannot distinguish two effects of a common cause from real cause and effect. That is, although the counterfactual approach can tell whether two factors A and B are causally connected[40] in some way, it cannot tell whether A causes B, B causes A, or A and B are the effects of a common cause (sometimes called spurious correlation). The reason for this is that the truth of the two counterfactual conditions described so far amounts to a particular pattern of the cross-tabulation of the two factors A and B. In the simplest case where the columns are the absence or presence of the first factor (A) and the rows are the absence or the presence of the second factor (B), then the same diagonal pattern is observed for situations where A causes B or B causes A, or for A and B being the effects of a common cause. In all three cases, we either observe the presence of both factors or their absence. It is impossible from this kind of symmetrical information, which amounts to correlational data, to detect causal asymmetry or spurious correlation. The counterfactual approach as elucidated so far, like the Humean regularity approach, only describes a necessary condition, the existence of a causal connection between A and B, for us to say that A causes B.

Requiring temporal precedence can solve the problem of causal direction by simply choosing the phenomenon that occurs first as the cause, but it cannot solve the problem of common cause because it would lead to the ridiculous conclusion that since the mercury rises in barometers before storms, this upward movement in the mercury must cause thunderstorms. For this and other reasons, David Lewis rejects using temporal precedence to determine the direction of causality. Instead, he claims that when C causes E but not the reverse "then it should be possible to claim the falsity of the counterfactual 'If E did not occur, then C would not occur.'" This counterfactual is different from "if C occurs then E occurs" and from "if C does not occur then E does not occur" which, as we have already mentioned, Lewis believes must both be true when C causes E. The required falsity of "If E did not occur, then C would not occur" adds a third condition for causality. This condition amounts to finding situations in which C occurs but E does not—typically because there is some other condition that must occur for C to produce E. Rather than explore this strategy, we describe a much better way of establishing causal priority in the next section.

---

[39] Thus, if barometric pressure rises, thunderstorms occur and vice versa. Furthermore, if barometric pressure does not rise, then thunderstorms do not occur and vice versa. Thus, by the counterfactual definition, each is the cause of the other. (To simplify matters, we have ignored the fact that there is not a perfectly deterministic relationship between high pressure systems and thunderstorms.)

[40] As implied by this paragraph, there is a causal connection between A and B when either A causes B, B causes A, or A and B are the effects of a common cause. See Hausman (1998, 55–63).

6 EXPERIMENTATION AND THE MANIPULATION APPROACH TO CAUSATION

In an experiment, there is a readily available piece of information that we have overlooked so far because it is not mentioned in the counterfactual approach. The factor that has been manipulated can determine the direction of causality and help to rule out spurious correlation. The manipulated factor must be the cause.[41] It is hard to exaggerate the importance of this insight. Although philosophers are uncomfortable with manipulation and agency approaches to causality because they put people (as the manipulators) at the center of our understanding of causality, there can be little doubt about the power of manipulation for determining causality. Agency and manipulation approaches to causation (Gasking 1955; von Wright 1974; Menzies and Price 1993) elevate this insight into their definition of causation. For Gasking "the notion of causation is essentially connected with our manipulative techniques for producing results" (1955, 483), and for Menzies and Price "events are causally related just in case the situation involving them possesses intrinsic features that *either* support a means-end relation between the events as is, *or* are identical with (or closely similar to) those of another situation involving an analogous pair of means-end related events" (1993, 197). These approaches focus on establishing the direction of causation, but Gasking's metaphor of causation as "recipes" also suggests an approach towards establishing the symmetric, regularity aspect of causation. Causation exists when there is a recipe that regularly produces effects from causes.

Perhaps our ontological definitions of causality should not employ the concept of agency because most of the causes and effects in the universe go their merry way without human intervention, and even our epistemological methods often discover causes, as with Newtonian mechanics or astrophysics, where human manipulation is impossible. Yet our epistemological methods cannot do without agency because human manipulation appears to be the best way to identify causes, and many researchers and methodologists have fastened upon experimental interventions as the way to pin down causation. These authors typically eschew ontological aims and emphasize epistemological goals. After explicitly rejecting ontological objectives, for example, Herbert Simon proceeds to base his initial definition of causality on experimental systems because "in scientific literature the word 'cause' most often occurs in connection with some explicit or implicit notion of an experimenter's intervention in a system" (Simon 1952, 518). When full experimental control is not possible, Thomas Cook and Donald T. Campbell recommend "quasi-experimentation," in which "an abrupt intervention at a known time" in a treatment group makes it possible to compare

---

[41] It might be more correct to say that the cause is buried somewhere among those things that were manipulated or that are associated with the manipulation. It is not always easy, however, to know what was manipulated as in the famous Hawthorne experiments in which the experimenters thought the treatment was reducing the lighting for workers but the workers apparently thought of the treatment as being treated differently from all other workers. Part of the work required for good causal inference is clearly describing what was manipulated and unpacking it to see what feature caused the effect.

the impacts of the treatment over time or across groups (Cook and Campbell 1986, 149). The success of quasi-experimentation depends upon "a world of probabilistic multivariate causal agency in which some manipulable events dependably cause other things to change" (150). John Stuart Mill suggests that the study of phenomena which "we can, by our voluntary agency, modify or control" makes it possible to satisfy the requirements of the Method of Difference ("a method of artificial experiment") even though "by the spontaneous operations of nature those requisitions are seldom fulfilled" (Mill 1888, 281, 282). Sobel champions a manipulation model because it "provides a framework in which the nonexperimental worker can think more clearly about the types of conditions that need to be satisfied in order to make inferences" (Sobel 1995, 32). David Cox claims that quasi-experimentation "with its intervention-ist emphasis seems to capture a deeper notion" (Cox 1992, 297) of causality than the regularity approach.

As we shall see, there are those who dissent from this perspective, but even they acknowledge that there is "wide agreement that the idea of causation as consequential manipulation is stronger or 'deeper' than that of causation as robust dependence" (Goldthorpe 2001, 5). This account of causality is especially compelling if the manip-ulation approach and the counterfactual approach are conflated, as they often are, and viewed as one approach. Philosophers seldom combine them into one perspec-tive, but all the methodological writers cited above (Simon, Cook and Campbell, Mill, Sobel, and Cox) conflate them because they draw upon controlled experi-ments, which combine intervention and control, for their understanding of causality. Through interventions, experiments manipulate one (or more) factor which simpli-fies the job of establishing causal priority by appeal to the manipulation approach to causation. Through laboratory controls or statistical randomization, experiments also create closest possible worlds that simplify the job of eliminating confounding explanations by appeal to the counterfactual approach to causation.

The combination of intervention and control in experiments makes them espe-cially effective ways to identify causal relationships. If experiments only furnished closest possible worlds, then the direction of causation would be indeterminate with-out additional information. If experiments only manipulated factors, then accidental correlation would be a serious threat to valid inferences about causality. Both features of experiments do substantial work.

Any approach to determining causation in nonexperimental contexts that tries to achieve the same success as experiments must recognize both these features. The methodologists cited above conflate them, and the psychological literature on counterfactual thinking cited at the beginning of this chapter shows that our natural inclination as human beings is to conflate them. When considering alternative possi-bilities, people typically consider nearby worlds in which individual agency figures prominently. When asked to consider what could have happened differently in a vignette involving a drunken driver and a new route home from work, subjects focus on having taken the new route home instead of on the factors that led to drunken driving. They choose a cause and a closest possible world in which *their* agency mat-ters. But there is no reason why the counterfactual approach and the manipulation approach should be combined in this way. The counterfactual approach to causation emphasizes possible worlds without considering human agency and the manipulation approach to causation emphasizes human agency without saying anything about possible worlds. Experiments derive their strength from combining both theoretical perspectives, but it is all too easy to overlook one of these two elements in generalizing from experimental to observational studies.[42]

As we shall see in a later section, the best-known statistical theory of causality emphasizes the counterfactual aspects of experiments without giving equal attention to their manipulative aspects. Consequently, when the requirements for causal inference are transferred from the experimental setting to the observational setting, those features of experiments that rest upon manipulation tend to get underplayed.

7 Pre-emption and the Mechanism Approach to Causation

7.1 Pre-emption

Experimentation's amalgamation of the lessons of counterfactual and manipulation approaches to causation produces a powerful technique for identifying the effects of manipulated causes. Yet, in addition to the practical problems of implementing the recipe correctly, the experimental approach does not deal well with two related problems. It does not solve the problem of causal pre-emption which occurs when one cause acts just before and pre-empts another, and it does not so much explain the causes of events as it demonstrates the effects of manipulated causes. In both cases, the experimentalists' focus on the impacts of manipulations in the laboratory instead of on the causes of events in the world, leads to a failure to explain important phenomena, especially those phenomena which cannot be easily manipulated or isolated.

The problem of pre-emption illustrates this point. The following example of pre-emption is often mentioned in the philosophical literature. A man takes a trek across a desert. His enemy puts a hole in his water can. Another enemy, not knowing the action of the first, puts poison in his water. Manipulations have certainly occurred, and the man dies on the trip. The enemy who punctured the water can thinks that she

---

[42] Some physical experiments actually derive most of their strength by employing such powerful manipulations that no controls are needed. At the detonation of the first atom bomb, no one doubted that the explosion was the result of nuclear fission and not some other uncontrolled factor. Similarly, in what might be an apocryphal story, it is said that a Harvard professor who was an expert on criminology once lectured to a class about how all social science evidence suggested that rehabilitating criminals simply did not work. A Chinese student raised his hand and politely disagreed by saying that during the Cultural Revolution, he had observed cases where criminals had been rehabilitated. Once again, a powerful manipulation may need no controls.

caused the man to die, and the enemy who added the poison thinks that he caused the man to die. In fact, the water dripping out of the can pre-empted the poisoning so that the poisoner is wrong. This situation poses problems for the counterfactual approach because one of the basic counterfactual conditions required to establish that the hole in the water can caused the death of the man, namely the truth of the counterfactual "if the hole had not been put in the water can, the man would not have died," is false even though the man did in fact die of thirst. The problem is that the man would have died of poisoning if the hole in the water can had not pre-empted that cause, and the "back-up" possibility of dying by poisoning falsifies the counterfactual.

The pre-emption problem is a serious one, and it can lead to mistakes even in well-designed experiments. Presumably the closest possible world to the one in which the water can has been punctured is one in which the poison has been put in the water can as well. Therefore, even a carefully designed experiment will conclude that the puncturing of the can did not kill the man crossing the desert because the unfortunate subject in the control condition would die (from poisoning) just as the subject in the treatment would die (from the hole in the water can). The experiment alone would not tell us how the man died. A similar problem could arise in medical experiments. Arsenic was once used to cure venereal disease, and it is easy to imagine an experiment in which doses of arsenic "cure" venereal disease but kill the patient while the members of the control group without the arsenic die of venereal disease at the same rate. If the experiment simply looked at the mortality rates of the patients, it would conclude that arsenic had no medicinal value because the same number of people died in the two conditions.

In both these instances, the experimental method focuses on the effects of causes and not on explaining effects by adducing causes. Instead of asking why the man died in his trek across the desert, the experimental approach asks what happens when a hole is put in the man's canteen and everything else remains the same. The method concludes that the hole had no effect. Instead of asking what caused the death of the patients with venereal disease, the experimental method asks whether giving arsenic to those with venereal disease had any net impact on mortality rates. It concludes that it did not. In short, experimental methods do not try to explain events in the world so much as they try to show what would happen if some cause were manipulated. This does not mean that experimental methods are not useful for explaining what happens in the world, but it does mean that they sometimes miss the mark.

7.2 Mechanisms, Capacities, and the Pairing Problem

The pre-emption problem is a vivid example of a more general problem with the Humean account that requires a solution. The general problem is that constant conjunction of events is not enough to "pair-up" particular events even when pre-emption is not present. Even if we know that holes in water cans generally spell trouble for desert travelers, we still have the problem of linking a particular hole in a water can with a particular death of a traveler. Douglas Ehring notes that:

Typically, certain spatial and temporal relations, such as spatial/temporal contiguity, are invoked to do this job. [That is, the hole in the water can used by the traveler is obviously the one that caused his death because it is spatially and temporally contiguous to him.] These singularist relations are intended to solve the residual problem of causally pairing particular events, a problem left over by the generalist core of the Humean account.   (Ehring 1997, 18)

Counterfactual approaches, because they can explain singular causal events, do not suffer so acutely from this "pairing" problem, but the pre-emption problem shows that remnants of the difficulty remain even in counterfactual accounts (Ehring 1997, ch. 1). In both the desert traveler and arsenic examples, the counterfactual account cannot get at the proper pairing of causes and effects because there are two redundant causes to be paired with the same effects. Something more is needed.

The solution in both these cases seems obvious, but it does not follow from the neo-Humean, counterfactual, or manipulation definitions of causality. The solution is to inquire more deeply into what is happening in each situation in order to describe the capacities and mechanisms that are operating. An autopsy of the desert traveler would show that the person died of thirst, and an examination of the water can would show that the water would have run out before the poisoned water could be imbibed. An autopsy of those given arsenic would show that the signs of venereal disease were arrested while other medical problems, associated with arsenic poisoning, were present. Further work might even show that lower doses of arsenic cure the disease without causing death. In both these cases, deeper inquires into the mechanism by which the causes and effects are linked would produce better causal stories.

But what does it mean to explicate mechanisms and capacities?[43] "Mechanisms" we are told by Machamber, Darden, and Craver (2000, 3) "are entities and activities organized such that they are productive of regular changes from start or set-up to finish or termination conditions." The crucial terms in this definition are "entities and activities" which suggest that mechanisms have pieces. Glennan (1996, 52) calls them "parts," and he requires that it should be possible "to take the part out of the mechanism and consider its properties in another context." Entities, or parts, are organized to produce change. For Glennan (52), this change should be produced by "the interaction of a number of parts according to direct causal laws." The biological sciences abound with mechanisms of this sort such as the method of DNA replication, chemical transmission at synapses, and protein synthesis. But there are many mechanisms in the social sciences as well including markets with their methods of transmitting price information and bringing buyers and sellers together, electoral systems with their routines for bringing candidates and voters together in a collective decision-making process, the diffusion of innovation through

---

[43] These approaches are not the same, and those who favor one often reject the other (see, e.g., Cartwright 1989 on capacities and Machamer, Darden, and Craver 2000 on mechanisms). But both emphasize "causal powers" (Harre and Madden 1975, ch. 5) instead of mere regularity or counterfactual association. We focus on mechanisms because we believe that they are a somewhat better way to think about causal powers, but in keeping with our pragmatic approach, we find much that is useful in "capacity" approaches.

social networks, the two-step model of communication flow, weak ties in social networks, dissonance reduction, reference groups, arms races, balance of power, etc. (Hedstrom and Swedberg 1998). As these examples demonstrate, mechanisms are not exclusively mechanical, and their activating principles can range from physical and chemical processes to psychological and social processes. They must be composed of appropriately located, structured, and oriented entities which involve activities that have temporal order and duration, and "an activity is usually designated by a verb or verb form (participles, gerundives, etc.)" (Machamber, Darden, and Craver 2000, 4) which takes us back to the work of Lakoff and Johnson (1999) who identified a "Causation Is Forced Movement metaphor."

Mechanisms provide another way to think about causation. Glennan argues that "two events are causally connected when and only when there is a mechanism connecting them" and "the necessity that distinguishes connections from accidental conjunctions is to be understood as deriving from a underlying mechanism" which can be empirically investigated (64). These mechanisms, in turn, are explained by causal laws, but there is nothing circular in this because these causal laws refer to how the *parts* of the mechanism are connected. The operation of these parts, in turn, can be explained by lower-level mechanisms. Eventually the process gets to a bedrock of fundamental physical laws which Glennan concedes "cannot be explained by the mechanical theory" (65).

Consider explaining social phenomena by examining their mechanisms. Duverger's law, for example, is the observed tendency for just two parties in simple plurality single-member district elections systems (such as the United States). The entities in the mechanisms behind Duverger's law are voters and political parties. These entities face a particular electoral rule (single-district plurality voting) which causes two activities. One is that voters often vote strategically by choosing a candidate other than their most liked because they want to avoid throwing their vote away on a candidate who has no chance of winning and because they want to forestall the election of their least wanted alternative. The other activity is that political parties often decide not to run candidates when there are already two parties in a district because they anticipate that voters will spurn their third party effort.

These mechanisms underlying Duverger's law suggest other things that can be observed beyond the regularity of two-party systems being associated with single-member plurality-vote electoral systems that led to the law in the first place. People's votes should exhibit certain patterns and third parties should exhibit certain behaviors. And a careful examination of the mechanism suggests that in some federal systems that use simple plurality single-member district elections we might have more than two parties, seemingly contrary to Duverger's law. Typically, however, there are just two parties in each province or state, but these parties may differ from one state to another, thus giving the impression, at the national level, of a multiparty system even though Duverger's law holds in each electoral district.[44]

---

[44] This radically simplifies the literature on Duverger's law (see Cox 1997 for more details).

Or consider meterological[45] and physical phenomena. Thunderstorms are not merely the result of cold fronts hitting warm air or being located near mountains; they are the results of parcels of air rising and falling in the atmosphere subject to thermodynamic processes which cause warm humid air to rise, to cool, and to produce condensed water vapor. Among other things, this mechanism helps to explain why thunderstorms are more frequent in areas, such as Denver, Colorado, near mountains because the mountains cause these processes to occur—without the need for a cold air front. Similarly, Boyle's law is not merely a regularity between pressure and volume; it is the result of gas molecules moving within a container and exerting force when they hit the walls of the container. This mechanism for Boyle's law also helps to explain why temperature affects the relationship between the pressure and volume of a gas. When the temperature increases, the molecules move faster and exert more force on the container walls.

Mechanisms like these are midway between general laws on the one hand and specific descriptions on the other hand, and activities can be thought of as causes which are not related to lawlike generalities.[46] Mechanisms typically explicate observed regularities in terms of lower-level processes, and the mechanisms vary from field to field and from time to time. Moreover, these mechanisms "bottom out" relatively quickly—molecular biologists do not seek quantum mechanical explanations and social scientists do not seek chemical explanations of the phenomena they study.

When an unexplained phenomenon is encountered in a science, "Scientists in the field often recognize whether there are known types of entities and activities that can possibly accomplish the hypothesized changes and whether there is empirical evidence that a possible schemata is plausible." They turn to the available types of entities and activities to provide building blocks from which to construct hypothetical mechanisms. "If one knows what kind of activity is needed to do something, then one seeks kinds of entities that can do it, and vice versa" (Machamber, Darden, and Craver 2000, 17).

Mechanisms, therefore, provide a way to solve the pairing problem, and they leave a multitude of traces that can be uncovered if a hypothesized causal relation really exists. For example, those who want to subject Max Weber's hypothesis about the Reformation leading to capitalism do not have to rest content with simply correlating Protestantism with capitalism. They can also look at the detailed mechanism he described for how this came about, and they can look for the traces left by this mechanism (Hedström and Swedberg 1998, 5; Sprinzak 1972).[47]

---

[45] The points in this paragraph, and the thunderstorm example, come from Dessler (1991).

[46] Jon Elster says: "Are there lawlike generalizations in the social sciences? If not, are we thrown back on mere description and narrative? In my opinion, the answer to both questions is No. The main task of this essay is to explain and illustrate the idea of a *mechanism* as intermediate between laws and descriptions" (Elster 1998, 45).

[47] Hedström and Swedberg (1998) and Sorenson (1998) rightfully criticize causal modeling for ignoring mechanisms and treating correlations among variables as theoretical relationships. But it might be worth remarking that causal modelers in political science have been calling for more theoretical thinking (Achen 1983; Bartels and Brady 1993) for at least two decades, and a constant refrain at the annual meetings of the Political Methodology Group has been the need for better "microfoundations."

7.3 Multiple Causes and Mechanisms

Earlier in this chapter, the need to rule out common causes and to determine the direction of causation in the counterfactual approach led us towards a consideration of multiple causes. In this section, the need to solve the problem of pre-emption and the pairing problem led to a consideration of mechanisms. Together, these approaches lead us to consider multiple causes and the mechanisms that tie these causes together. Many different authors have come to a similar conclusion about the need to identify mechanisms (Cox 1992; Simon and Iwasaki 1988; Freedman 1991; Goldthorpe 2001), and this approach seems commonplace in epidemiology (Hill 1965) where debates over smoking and lung cancer or sexual behavior and AIDS have been resolved by the identification of biological mechanisms that link the behaviors with the diseases.

8 Four Approaches to Causality

8.1 What is Causation?

We are now at the end of our review of four causal approaches. We have described two fundamental features of causality. One is the symmetric association between causes and effects. The other is the asymmetric fact that causes produce effects, but not the reverse. Table 10.1 summarizes how each approach identifies these two aspects of causality.

Regularity and counterfactual approaches do better at capturing the symmetric aspect of causation than its asymmetric aspect. The regularity approach relies upon the constant conjunction of events and temporal precedence to identify causes and effects. Its primary tool is essentially the "Method of Concomitant Variation" proposed by John Stuart Mill in which the causes of a phenomenon are sought in other phenomena which vary in a similar manner. The counterfactual approach relies upon elaborations of the "Method of Difference" to find causes by comparing instances where the phenomenon occurs and instances where it does not occur to see in what circumstances the situations differ. The counterfactual approach suggests searching for surrogates for the closest possible worlds where the putative cause does not occur to see how they differ from the situation where the cause did occur. This strategy leads naturally to experimental methods where the likelihood of the independence of assignment and outcome, which ensures one kind of closeness, can be increased by rigid control of conditions or by randomly assigning treatments to cases. None of these methods is foolproof because none solves the pairing problem or gets at the connections between events, but experimental methods typically offer the best chance of achieving closest possible worlds for comparisons.

Causal approaches that emphasize mechanisms and capacities provide guidance on how to solve the pairing problem and how to get at the connections between events. Brady and Collier's emphasis upon causal process observations is in that spirit (2004, ch. 13; see also Freedman, this volume). These observations can be thought of as elucidations and tests of possible mechanisms. And the growing interest in mechanisms in the social sciences (Hedström and Swedberg 1998; Elster 1998) is providing a basis for opening up the black box of the Humean regularity and the counterfactual approaches.

The other major feature of causality, the asymmetry of causes and effects, is captured by temporal priority, manipulated events, and the independence of causes. Each notion takes a somewhat different approach to distinguishing causes from effects once the unconditional association of two events (or sets of events) has been established. Temporal priority simply identifies causes with the events that came first. If growth in the money supply reliably precedes economic growth, then the growth in the money supply is responsible for growth. The manipulation approach identifies the manipulated event as the causally prior one. If a social experiment manipulates work requirements and finds that greater stringency is associated with faster transitions off welfare, then the work requirements are presumed to cause these transitions. Finally, one event is considered the cause of another if a third event can be found that satisfies the INUS conditions for a cause and that varies independently of the putative cause. If short circuits vary independently of wooden frame buildings, and both satisfy INUS conditions for burned-down buildings, then both must be causes of those conflagrations. Or if education levels of voters vary independently of their getting the butterfly ballot, and both satisfy INUS conditions for mistakenly voting for Buchanan instead of Gore, then both must be causes of those mistaken votes.

8.2 Causal Inference with Experimental and Observational Data

Now that we know what causation is, what lessons can we draw for doing empirical research? Table 10.1 shows that each approach provides sustenance for different types of studies and different kinds of questions. Table 10.3 presents a "checklist" based on all of the approaches. Regularity and mechanism approaches tend to ask about the causes of effects while counterfactual and manipulation approaches ask about the effects of imagined or manipulated causes. The counterfactual and manipulation approaches converge on experiments, although counterfactual thought experiments flow naturally from the "possible worlds" perspective of the counterfactual appoach. The regularity approach is at home with observational data, and the mechanism approach thrives on analytical models and case studies.

Which method, however, is the best method? Clearly the gold standard for establishing causality is experimental research, but even that is not without flaws. When they are feasible, well-done experiments can help us construct closest possible worlds and explore counterfactual conditions. But we still have to assume that there is no pre-emption occurring which would make it impossible for us to determine the true

Table 10.3. Causality checklist

General Issues

What is the "cause" (*C*) event? What is the "effect" (*E*) event?

What is the exact causal statement of how *C* causes *E*?

What is the corresponding counterfactual statement about what happens when *C* does not occur?

What is the causal field? What is the context or universe of cases in which the cause operates?

Is this a physical or social phenomenon or some mixture?

What role, if any, does human agency play?

What role, if any, does social structure play?

Is the relationship deterministic or probabilistic?

Neo-Humean Approach

Is there a constant conjunction (i.e. correlation) of cause and effect?

Is the cause necessary, sufficient, or INUS?

What are other possible causes, i.e. rival explanations?

Is there a constant conjunction after controls for these other causes are introduced?

Does the cause precede the effect? In what sense?

Counterfactual Approach

Is this a singular conjunction of cause and effect?

Can you describe a closest possible (most similar) world to where *C* causes *E* but *C* does not occur? How close are these worlds?

Can you actually observe any cases of this world (or something close to it, at least on average)? Again, how close are these worlds?

In this closest possible world, does *E* occur in the absence of *C*?

Are there cases where *E* occurs but *C* does not occur? What factor intervenes and what does this tell us about *C* causing *E*?

Manipulation Approach

What does it mean to manipulate your cause? Be explicit. How would you describe the cause?

Do you have any cases where *C* was actually manipulated? How? What was the effect?

Is this manipulation independent of other factors that influence *E*?

Mechanism and Capacities Approaches

Can you explain, at a lower level, the mechanism(s) by which *C* causes *E*?

Do the mechanisms make sense to you?

What other predictions does this mechanism lead to?

Does the mechanism solve the pairing problem?

Can you identify some capacity that explains the way the cause leads to the effect?

Can you observe this capacity when it is present, and measure it?

What other outcomes might be predicted by this capacity?

What are possible pre-empting causes?

---

impact of the putative cause, and we also have to assume that there are no interactions across units in the treatment and control groups and that treatments can be confined to the treated cases. If, for example, we are studying the impact of a skill training program on the tendency for welfare recipients to get jobs, we should be aware that a very strong economy might pre-empt the program itself and cause those in both the control and treatment conditions to get jobs simply because employers did not care much about skills. As a result, we might conclude that skills do not count for much in getting jobs even though they might matter a lot in a less robust economy. Or if we are studying electoral systems in a set of countries with a strong bimodal distribution of voters, we should know that the voter distribution might pre-empt any impact of the electoral system by fostering two strong parties. Consequently, we might conclude that single-member plurality systems and proportional representation systems both led to two parties, even though this is not generally true. And if we are studying some educational innovation that is widely known, we should know that teachers in the "control" classes might pick up and use this innovation thereby nullifying any effect it might have.

If we add an investigation of mechanisms to our experiments, we might be able to develop safeguards against these problems. For the welfare recipients, we could find out more about their job search efforts, for the party systems we could find out about their relationship to the distribution of voters, and for the teachers we could find out about their adoption of new teaching methods.

Once we go to observational studies, matters get much more complicated. Spurious correlation is a real danger. There is no way to know whether those cases which get the treatment and those which do not differ from one another in other ways. It is very hard to be confident that the requirements for an experiment hold which are outlined in the next section (and in Campbell and Stonley 1966 and Cook and Campbell 1979). Because nothing has been manipulated, there is no surefire way to determine the direction of causation. Temporal precedence provides some information about causal direction, but it is often hard to obtain and interpret it.

9 Going beyond the Neyman–Rubin–Holland Conditions for Causation

9.1 The Neyman–Rubin–Holland (NRH) Theory

Among statisticians, the best-known theory of causality developed out of the experimental tradition. The roots of this perspective are in Fisher (1926) and especially Neyman ([1923] 1990), and it has been most fully articulated by Rubin (1974; 1978) and Holland (1986). In this section, which is more technical than the rest of this chapter, we explain this perspective, and we evaluate it in terms of the four approaches to causality.

There are four aspects of the Neyman–Rubin–Holland (NRH) approach which can be thought of as developing a recipe for solving the causal inference problem by comparing similar possible worlds, if certain assumptions hold. This approach consists of a definition, two assumptions, and a method for satisfying one of the two assumptions:

1. A Counterfactual Definition of Causal Effect—Causal relationships are defined using a counterfactual perspective which focuses on estimating causal effects. This definition alone provides no guidance on how researchers can actually identify causes because it relies upon an unobservable counterfactual. To the extent that the NRH approach considers causal priority, it equates it with temporal priority.

2. An Assumption for Creating Comparable Mini-possible Worlds—Non-interference of Units (SUTVA)—Even if we could observe the outcome for some unit (a person or a country) of both the world with the cause present and without the cause, it is possible that the causal effect would depend upon whether other units received the treatment or did not receive the treatment. For example, the impact of a training program on a child in a family might be different when the child and her sibling received the treatment than when the child alone received the treatment. If this kind of thing happens, then it is very hard to define uniquely what we mean by a "causal effect" because there might be some "interference" across units depending upon which units got the treatment and which did not. The NRH counterfactual possible worlds approach assumes that this kind of interference does not occur by making the Stable Unit Treatment Value Assumption (SUTVA) that treats cases as separate, isolated, closest possible worlds which do not interfere or communicate with one another.

3. An Assumption that Finds a Substitute for Insuring the Identicality of the Counterfactual Situation: The Independence of Assignment and Outcome—The counterfactual possible worlds approach not only assumes that units do not interfere with one another, it also assumes that a world identical to our own, except for the existence of the putative cause, can be imagined. The NHR approach goes on to formulate a set of epistemological assumptions, namely the independence of the assignment of treatment and the outcome or the mean conditional independence of assignment and outcome, that make it possible to be sure that two sets of cases, treatments and controls, only differ on average in whether or not they got the treatment.

4. Methods for Insuring Independence of Assignment and Outcome if SUTVA holds—Finally, the NRH approach describes methods such as unit homogeneity or random assignment for obtaining independence or mean independence of assignment and outcome as long as SUTVA holds.

The definition of a causal effect based upon unobserved counterfactuals was first described in a 1923 paper published in Polish by Jerzy Neyman (1990). Although Neyman's paper was relatively unknown until 1990, similar ideas informed much of the statistical work on experimentation from the 1920s to the present. Rubin (1974; 1978; 1990) and Heckman (1979) were the first to stress the importance of independence of assignment and outcome. A number of experimentalists identified the need for the SUTVA assumption (e.g. Cox 1958). Random assignment as a method for estimating causal effects was first championed by R. A. Fisher in 1925 and 1926. Holland (1986) provides the best synthesis of the entire perspective.

The counterfactual definition of causality rests on the notion of comparing a world with the treatment to a world without it. The fundamental problem of counterfactual definitions of causation is the tension between finding a suitable definition of causation that controls for confounding effects and finding a suitable way of detecting causation given the impossibility of getting perfect counterfactual worlds. As we shall show, the problem is one of relating a *theoretical* definition of causality to an *empirical* one.

9.2 Ontological Definition of Causal Effect Based upon Counterfactuals

Consider a situation in which there is one "unit" A which can be manipulated in some way. Table 10.4 summarizes the situation. Assume that there are two possible manipulations Z_A of the unit, the "control" which we denote by $Z_A = 0$ and the "treatment" which we denote by $Z_A = 1$. Outcomes Y_A are a function $Y_A(Z_A)$ of these manipulations so that the outcome for the control manipulation is $Y_A(0)$ and the outcome for the treatment manipulation is $Y_A(1)$.

According to the NRH understanding of causation, establishing a causal relationship between a treatment Z_A and an outcome $Y_A(Z_A)$ consists of comparing outcomes for the case where the case gets the treatment $Z_A = 1$ and where it does not $Z_A = 0$. Thus we compare:

(a) the value of the outcome variable Y_A for a case that has been exposed to a treatment $Y_A(1)$ with
(b) the value of the outcome variable *for the same case if that case had not been exposed to the treatment* $Y_A(0)$.

In this case, we can define causal impact as follows:

$$E_A = \text{Causal Effect on } A = Y_A(1) - Y_A(0). \tag{1}$$

Note that (a) refers to an actual observation in the treatment condition ("a case that has been exposed to a treatment") so the value $Y_A(1)$ is observed while (b) refers to a counterfactual observation of the control condition ("if that case had not been exposed to the treatment").[48] Because the case was exposed to the treatment, it cannot simultaneously be in the control condition, and the value $Y_A(0)$ is the outcome in the closest possible world where the case was not exposed to the treatment. Although this

---

[48] For simplicity, we assume that the treatment case has been observed, but the important point is not that the treatment is observed but rather that only one of the two conditions can be observed. There is no reason why the situation could not be reversed with the actual observation of the case in the control group and the counterfactual involving the unobserved impact of the treatment condition.

Table 10.4. Possible worlds, outcomes, and causal
effects from manipulation Z for one unit A

	Z_A–Manipulation for Unit A	
POSSIBLE WORLDS:	0 Control	Treatment 1
	$Y_A(0)$	$Y_A(1)$

Outcomes: $Y_A(Z_A)$
Causal Effect: $Y_A(1) - Y_A(0)$
Problem: Only one world observable.

value cannot be observed, we can still describe the conclusions we would draw if we could observe it.

The causal effect E_A for a particular case is the difference in outcomes, $E_A = Y_A(1) - Y_A(0)$, for the case, and if this difference is zero (i.e. if $E_A = 0$), we say the treatment has no net effect.[49] If this difference is nonzero (i.e. E_A is not 0), then the treatment has a net effect. Then, based on the counterfactual approach of David Lewis, there is a causal connection between the treatment and the outcome if two conditions hold. First, the treatment must be associated with a net effect, and second the absence of the treatment must be associated with no net effect.[50]

Although the satisfaction of these two conditions is enough to demonstrate a causal connection, it is not enough to determine the direction of causation or to rule out a common cause. If the two conditions for a causal connection hold, then the third Lewis condition, which establishes the direction of causation and which rules out common cause, cannot be verified or rejected with the available information. The third Lewis condition requires determining whether or not the cause occurs in the closest possible world in which the net effect does not occur. But the only observed world in which the net effect does not occur in the NRH setup is the control

---

[49] Technically, we mean that the treatment has no effect with respect to that outcome variable.

[50] With a suitable definition of effect, one of these conditions will always hold by definition and the other will be determinative of the causal connection. The NRH approach focuses on the Effect of the Treatment ($E = Y(1) - Y(0)$) in which the control outcome $Y(0)$ is the baseline against which the treatment outcome $Y(1)$ is compared. A nonzero E implies the truth of the counterfactual "if the treatment occurs, then the net effect occurs," and a zero E implies that the counterfactual is false. In the NRH setup the Effect for the Control (EC) must always be zero because $EC = (Y(0) - Y(0))$ is always zero. Hence, the counterfactual "if the treatment is absent then there is no net effect" is always true. The focus on the effect of the treatment (E) merely formalizes the fact that in *any* situation one of the two counterfactuals required for a causal connection can always be defined to be true by an appropriate definition of an effect. Philosophers, by custom, tend to focus on the situation where some effect is associated with some putative cause so that it is always true that "if the cause occurs then the effect occurs as well" and the important question is the truth or falsity of "if the cause does not occur then the effect does not occur." Statisticians such as NRH, with their emphasis on the null hypothesis, seem to prefer the equivalent, but reverse, setup where the important question is the truth or falsity of "if the treatment occurs, then the effect occurs." The bottom line is that a suitable definition of effect can always lead to the truth of one of the two counterfactuals so that causal impacts must always be considered comparatively.

condition in which the cause does not occur by *design* so that there is no way to determine whether suppressing the effect would or would not suppress the cause. There is no way to test the third Lewis condition and to show that the treatment causes the net effect.

Alternatively, the direction of causation can be determined (although common cause cannot be ruled out) if the treatment is manipulated to produce the effect. Rubin and his collaborators mention manipulation when they say that "each of the T treatments must consist of a series of actions that could be applied to each experimental unit" (Rubin 1978, 39) and "it is critical that each unit be *potentially exposable* to any one of the causes" (Holland 1986, 946), but their use of phrases such as "could be applied" or "potentially exposable" suggests that they are more concerned about limiting the possible types of causes than with distinguishing causes from effects.[51] To the degree that causal priority is mentioned in the NRH literature, it is established by temporal precedence. Rubin (1974, 689), for example, says that the causal effect of one treatment over another "for a particular unit and an interval t_1 to t_2 is the difference between what would have happened at time t_2 if the unit had been exposed to [one treatment] initiated at time t_1 and what would have happened at t_2 if the unit had been exposed to [another treatment] at t_1." Holland (1986, 980) says that "The issue of temporal succession is shamelessly embraced by the model as one of the defining characteristics of a response variable. The idea that an effect might precede a cause in time is regarded as meaningless in the model, and apparently also by Hume." The problem with this approach, of course, is that it does not necessarily rule out common cause and spurious correlation.[52] In fact one of the limitations and possible confusions produced by the NRH approach is its failure to deal with the need for more information to rule out common causes and to determine the direction of causality.

9.3 Finding a Substitute for the Counterfactual Situation: The Independence of Assignment and Outcome

As with the Lewis counterfactual approach, the difficulty with the NRH definition of causal connections is that there is no way to observe both $Y_A(1)$ and $Y_A(0)$ for any particular case. The typical response to this problem is to find two units A and B which are as similar as possible and to consider various possible allocations of the control and the treatment to the two units. (We shall say more about how to ensure this similarity later; for the moment, simply assume that it can be accomplished.) The

---

[51] Rubin and Holland believe in "NO CAUSATION WITHOUT MANIPULATION" (Holland 1986, 959), which seems to eliminate attributes such as sex or race as possible causes, although Rubin softens this perspective somewhat by describing ways in which sex might be a manipulation (Rubin 1986, 962). Clearly, researchers must consider carefully in what sense some factors can be considered causes.

[52] Consider, for example, an experiment in which randomly assigned special tutoring first causes a rise in self-esteem and then an increase in test scores, but the increase in self-esteem does not cause the increase in test scores. The NRH framework would incorrectly treat self-esteem as the cause of the increased test scores because self esteem is randomly assigned and it precedes and is associated with the rise in test scores. Clearly something more than temporal priority is needed for causal priority.

Table 10.5. Possible worlds, outcomes, and causal effects from manipulations Z for two units A and B

	FOUR POSSIBLE WORLDS			
Manipulations for each unit	$Z_A = 0$, *Control*		$Z_A = 1$, *Treatment*	
	$Z_B = 0$, *Control*	$Z_B = 1$, *Treatment*	$Z_B = 0$, *Control*	$Z_B = 1$, *Treatment*
Outcome value $Y_i(Z_A, Z_B)$, for $i = A$ or B	$Y_A(0,0)$ $Y_B(0,0)$	$Y_A(0,1)$ $Y_B(0,1)$	$Y_A(1,0)$ $Y_B(1,0)$	$Y_A(1,1)$ $Y_B(1,1)$

goal is ultimately to define causal impact as the difference between what happens to A and to B when one of them gets the treatment and the other does not. But, as we shall see, this leads to fundamental problems regarding the definition of causality.

The manipulation for unit A is described by $Z_A = 0$ or $Z_A = 1$ and the manipulation for unit B is described by $Z_B = 0$ or $Z_B = 1$. Table 10.5 illustrates the four possible worlds that could occur based upon the four ways that the manipulations could be allocated. In the first column, both A and B are given the control. In the second column, A gets the control and B gets the treatment. In the third column, A gets the treatment and B gets the control, and in the fourth column, both units get the treatment. The outcomes for these combinations of manipulations are described by $Y_A(Z_A, Z_B)$ and $Y_B(Z_A, Z_B)$.

For each unit, there are then four possible outcome quantities. For example, for A there are $Y_A(0,0)$, $Y_A(0,1)$, $Y_A(1,0)$, and $Y_A(1,1)$. Similarly for B there are $Y_B(0,0)$, $Y_B(0,1)$, $Y_B(1,0)$, and $Y_B(1,1)$. For each unit, there are six possible ways to take these four possible outcome quantities two at a time to define a difference that could be considered the causal impact of Z_A, but not all of them make sense as a definition of the causal impact of Z_A. The six possibilities are listed in Table 10.6.

Table 10.6. Six possible definitions of causal impact on unit A

Four observable quantities: $Y_A(0,0)$, $Y_A(0,1)$, $Y_A(1,0)$, $Y_A(1,1)$
Possible definitions:

$Y_A(0,0) - Y_A(0,1)$	Problem: No manipulation
$Y_A(1,0) - Y_A(1,1)$	of A.
$Y_A(1,1) - Y_A(0,0)$	Problem: Different treatments
$Y_A(1,0) - Y_A(0,1)$	for B.
$Y_A(1,0) - Y_A(0,0) = E_A(Z_B = 0)$	Both good.
$Y_A(1,1) - Y_A(0,1) = E_A(Z_B = 1)$	

For example, each of $[Y_A(0, 0) - Y_A(0, 1)]$ and $[Y_A(1, 0) - Y_A(1, 1)]$ involves a difference where Z_A does not even vary—in the first case Z_A is the control manipulation for both states of the world and in the second case Z_A is the treatment manipulation. Neither of these differences makes much sense as a definition of the causal impact of Z_A.

Two other pairs of differences, $[Y_A(1, 1) - Y_A(0, 0)]$ and $[Y_A(1, 0) - Y_A(0, 1)]$, seem better insofar as they each involve differences in which A received the treatment in one case and the control in the other case, but the manipulation of B differs within each pair. In the first difference, for example, we are comparing the outcome for A in the world in which A gets the treatment and B does not with the world in which A does not get the treatment and B gets it. At first blush, it might seem that it doesn't really matter what happens to B, but a moment's reflection suggests that unless A and B *do not interfere* with one another, it might matter a great deal what happens to B.

Suppose, for example, that A and B are siblings, adjacent plots of land, two students in the same class, two people getting a welfare program in the same neighborhood, two nearby countries, or even two countries united by common language and traditions. Then for treatments as diverse as new teaching methods, propaganda, farming techniques, new scientific or medical procedures, new ideas, or new forms of government it might matter for the A member of the pair what happens to the B member because of causal links between them. For example, if a sibling B is given a special educational program designed to increase achievement, it seems possible that some of this impact will be communicated to the other sibling A, even when A does not get the treatment directly. Or if a new religion or religious doctrine is introduced into one country, it seems possible that it will have an impact on the other country. In both cases, it seems foolish to try to compare the impact of different manipulations of A when different things have also been done to B, unless we can be sure that a manipulation of B has no impact on A or unless we define the manipulation of B as part of the manipulation of A.

This second possibility deserves some comment. If the manipulation of B is part of the manipulation of A, then we really have not introduced a new unit when we decided to consider B as well as A. In this situation we can think of the differences listed above, $[Y_A(1, 1) - Y_A(0, 0)]$ and $[Y_A(1, 0) - Y_A(0, 1)]$, as indicating the impact on A of the manipulation of the combined unit $A + B$. For the first difference, $[Y_A(1, 1) - Y_A(0, 0)]$, the manipulation consists of applying $Z_A = 1$ and $Z_B = 1$ as the treatment to $A + B$ and the $Z_A = 0$ and $Z_B = 0$ as the control to $A + B$. Similar reasoning applies to the second difference, $[Y_A(1, 0) - Y_A(0, 1)]$. There are two lessons to be learned from this discussion. First, it is not as easy as it might seem to define isolated units, and the definition of separate units partly depends upon how they will be affected by the manipulation. Second, it does not make much sense to use $[Y_A(1, 1) - Y_A(0, 0)]$ or $[Y_A(1, 0) - Y_A(0, 1)]$ as the definition of the causal impact of the treatment Z_A on A.

This leaves us with the following pairs which are plausible definitions of the causal effect for each unit, depending upon what happens to the other unit. These pairs are

Table 10.7. Theoretical definitions summarized for units A and B

For unit A:
$$Y_A(1,0) - Y_A(0,0) = E_A(Z_B = 0)$$
$$Y_A(1,1) - Y_A(0,1) = E_A(Z_B = 1)$$
For unit B:
$$Y_B(0,1) - Y_B(0,0) = E_B(Z_A = 0)$$
$$Y_B(1,1) - Y_B(1,0) = E_B(Z_A = 1)$$

summarized in Table 10.7. For example, for A:

$$E_A(Z_B = 0) = Y_A(1, 0) - Y_A(0, 0), \quad \text{and} \tag{2}$$

$$E_A(Z_B = 1) = Y_A(1, 1) - Y_A(0, 1).$$

And for B we have:

$$E_B(Z_A = 0) = Y_B(0, 1) - Y_B(0, 0), \quad \text{and} \tag{3}$$

$$E_B(Z_A = 1) = Y_B(1, 1) - Y_B(1, 0).$$

Consider the definitions for A in (2). Both definitions seem sensible because each one takes the difference between the outcome when A is treated and the outcome when A is not treated, but they differ on what happens to B. In the first case, B is given the control manipulation and in the second case, B is given the treatment manipulation. From the preceding discussion, it should be clear that these might lead to different sizes of effects. The impact of a pesticide on a plot A, for example, might vary dramatically depending upon whether or not the adjacent plot B got the pesticide. The effect of a propaganda campaign might vary dramatically depending upon whether or not a sibling got the propaganda message. As a result, there is no a priori reason why $E_A(Z_B = 0)$ and $E_A(Z_B = 1)$ should be the same thing. The impact on A of a treatment might depend upon what happens to B.

One response to this problem might be simply to agree that $E_A(Z_B = 0)$ and $E_A(Z_B = 1)$ (and $E_B(Z_A = 0)$ and $E_B(Z_A = 1)$) are different and that a careful researcher would want to measure both of them. But how could that be done? Neither can be measured directly because each requires that the unit A both get and not get the treatment, which is clearly impossible. In terms of our notation, the problem is that each difference above involves different values for Z_A and Z_B. For example, $E_A(Z_B = 0)$ which equals $Y_A(1, 0) - Y_A(0, 0)$ involves one state of the world where A gets the treatment and B does not and another state of the world where A does not get the treatment and B does not. Both states of the world cannot occur.

Table 10.8. Observationally feasible definitions of causality

Four states of the world and four possible definitions:
(1) $\{Z_A = 1 \text{ and } Z_B = 1\}$
 Observe $Y_A(1,1)$ and $Y_B(1,1) \rightarrow$ Difference Zero
(2) $\{Z_A = 0 \text{ and } Z_B = 0\}$
 Observe $Y_A(0,0)$ and $Y_B(0,0) \rightarrow$ Difference Zero
(3) $\{Z_A = 1 \text{ and } Z_B = 0\}$
 Observe $Y_A(1,0)$ and $Y_B(1,0) \rightarrow E^*(1,0) = Y_A(1,0) - Y_B(1,0)$
(4) $\{Z_A = 0 \text{ and } Z_B = 1\}$
 Observe $Y_A(0,1)$ and $Y_B(0,1) \rightarrow E^*(0,1) = Y_A(0,1) - Y_B(0,1)$

9.4 Observable Definitions of Causality

As noted earlier, the standard response to this problem is to consider definitions of causal impact that are observable because the relevant quantities can be measured in the same state of the world—thus avoiding the problem of making comparisons across multiple worlds or between the existing world and another, "impossible," world. With two units and a dichotomous treatment, four states of the world are possible: $\{Z_A = 1 \text{ and } Z_B = 1\}$, $\{Z_A = 0 \text{ and } Z_B = 0\}$, $\{Z_A = 1 \text{ and } Z_B = 0\}$, and $\{Z_A = 0 \text{ and } Z_B = 1\}$. These are listed in Table 10.5 along with the two observable quantities, Y_A and Y_B, one for A and one for B, for each state of the world.

The four differences of these two quantities are listed in Table 10.8. Each difference is a candidate to be considered as a measure of causal impact. The differences for the first and second of these four states of the world do not offer much opportunity for detecting the causal impact of Z because there is no variability in the treatment between the two units.[53] Consequently, we consider the differences for the third and fourth cases.

For the state of the world $\{Z_A = 1 \text{ and } Z_B = 0\}$ we can compute the following based upon observable quantities:

$$E^*(1, 0) = Y_A(1, 0) - Y_B(1, 0), \tag{4}$$

where the difference involves terms that occur together in one state of the world. Note that we denote this empirical definition of causality by an asterisk. This difference is computable, but does it represent a causal impact? Intuitively, the problem with using it as an estimate of causal impact is that A and B might be quite different to begin with. Suppose we are trying to estimate the impact of a new teaching method. Person A might be an underachiever while person B might be an overachiever. Hence, even if the method works, person A might score lower on a test after treatment than person B, and the method will be deemed a failure. Or suppose we are trying to determine

---

[53] Consider, for example, the difference $E^*(1, 1) = Y_A(1, 1) - Y_B(1, 1)$ for state of the world $\{Z_A = 1$ and $Z_B = 1\}$. If we make the very reasonable assumption of identicality described below, then $Y_B(1, 1) = Y_A(1, 1)$ so that $E^*(1, 1)$ is always zero which is not a very interesting "causal effect." The same result applies to the state of the world $\{Z_A = 0$ and $Z_B = 0\}$.

the impact of a new voting machine. County A might be very competent at running elections while county B might not be. Consequently, even if the machine works badly, county A with the new system might perform better than county B without it—once again leading to the wrong inference. Clearly $E^*(1, 0)$ alone is not a very good definition of causal impact. One of the problems is that preexisting differences between the units can confound causal inference.

How, then, can $E^*(1, 0)$ be used to make a better causal inference? Surveying the four definitions of causal impact in equations (2) and (3) above, this definition seems most closely related to two of them:

$$E_A(Z_B = 0) = Y_A(1, 0) - Y_A(0, 0), \quad \text{and} \tag{5a}$$

$$E_B(Z_A = 1) = Y_B(1, 1) - Y_B(1, 0). \tag{5b}$$

Consider the first of these, $E_A(Z_B = 0)$. Obviously, $E^*(1, 0)$ will equal $E_A(Z_B = 0)$ if the second term in the expression for $E^*(1, 0)$ which is $Y_B(1, 0)$ equals the second term in the expression for $E_A(Z_B = 0)$ which is $Y_A(0, 0)$. Thus we require that:

$$Y_B(1, 0) = Y_A(0, 0). \tag{6}$$

What conditions will ensure that this is so?

We shall make the transformation of $Y_B(1, 0)$ into $Y_A(0, 0)$ in two steps which are depicted on Table 10.9. If A and B are identical and Z_A and Z_B are identical as well[54] (although we haven't indicated how this might be brought about yet) it might be reasonable to suppose that:

$$Y_B(1, 0) = Y_A(0, 1)[\textit{Identicality of units and treatment or Unit Homogeneity}]. \tag{7}$$

That is, A and B are mirror images of one another so that the impact of $Z_A = 1$ and $Z_B = 0$ on B is the same as the impact of $Z_A = 0$ and $Z_B = 1$ on A.

This assumption is the same as what Holland (1986) calls "unit homogeneity" in which units are prepared carefully "so that they 'look' identical in all relevant aspects" (Holland 1986, 948). This assumption is commonly made in laboratory work where identical specimens are tested or where the impacts of different manipulations are studied for the identical setup. It obviously requires a great deal of knowledge about what makes things identical to one another and an ability to control these factors. It is typically not a very good assumption in the social sciences.

With this assumption, $E^*(1, 0) = Y_A(1, 0) - Y_A(0, 1)$ which is a definition of causality that we discarded earlier because of the possibility that if B gets the treatment when A does not, then A will be affected even when A does not get the treatment. We discarded this definition because, for example, the impact $Y_A(0, 1)$ of the treatment on Amy when Beatrice gets the treatment might be substantial—perhaps

---

[54] By saying that Z_A and Z_B have to be comparable, we mean that $Z_A = 0$ and $Z_B = 0$ are the same thing and $Z_A = 1$ and $Z_B = 1$ are the same thing.

Table 10.9. Linking observational data to theoretical definitions of causality through unit identicality and noninterference of units

Observational	Unit identicality (unit homogeneity)	Noninterference of units (SUTVA)	Theoretical definition
$E^*(1, 0) = Y_A(1, 0) - Y_B(1, 0)$	$Y_B(1, 0) = Y_A(0, 1) \rightarrow Y_A(1, 0) - Y_A(0, 1)$	$Y_A(0, 1) = Y_A(0, 0) \rightarrow Y_A(1, 0) - Y_A(0, 0)$ $Y_A(1, 0) = Y_A(1, 1) \rightarrow Y_A(1, 1) - Y_A(0, 1)$	$E_A(Z_B = 0)$ $E_A(Z_B = 1)$
	$Y_A(1, 0) = Y_B(0, 1) \rightarrow Y_B(0, 1) - Y_B(1, 0)$	$Y_B(1, 0) = Y_B(0, 0) \rightarrow Y_B(0, 0) - Y_B(0, 1)$ $Y_B(0, 1) = Y_B(1, 1) \rightarrow Y_B(1, 1) - Y_B(1, 0)$	$E_B(Z_A = 0)$ $E_B(Z_A = 1)$
$E^*(0, 1) = Y_B(0, 1) - Y_A(0, 1)$	$Y_B(0, 1) = Y_A(1, 0) \rightarrow Y_A(1, 0) - Y_A(0, 1)$	$Y_A(0, 1) = Y_A(0, 0) \rightarrow Y_A(1, 0) - Y_A(0, 0)$ $Y_A(1, 0) = Y_A(1, 1) \rightarrow Y_A(1, 1) - Y_A(0, 1)$	$E_A(Z_B = 0)$ $E_A(Z_B = 1)$
	$Y_A(0, 1) = Y_B(1, 0) \rightarrow Y_B(0, 1) - Y_B(1, 0)$	$Y_B(1, 0) = Y_B(0, 0) \rightarrow Y_B(0, 0) - Y_B(0, 1)$ $Y_B(0, 1) = Y_B(1, 1) \rightarrow Y_B(1, 1) - Y_B(1, 0)$	$E_B(Z_A = 0)$ $E_B(Z_A = 1)$

as much as when Amy gets the treatment alone which is $Y_A(1, 0)$. In that case, $E^*(1, 0)$ seems like a poor definition of the causal impact of Z_A when what we really want is the definition in (5a) above. But to get to that definition, we must suppose that:

$$Y_A(0, 1) = Y_A(0, 0) \ [\textit{Non-interference of units or SUTVA}]. \tag{8}$$

In effect, this requires that we believe that the causal impact of manipulation Z_A on A is not affected by whether or not B gets the treatment. Rubin (1990) calls this the "Stable-Unit-Treatment Value Assumption" (SUTVA). As we have already seen, this is a worrisome assumption, and we shall have a great deal to say about it later.

Similarly, $E^*(1, 0)$ will equal the second definition (5b) above, $E_B(Z_A = 1)$, if the first term in the expression for $E^*(1, 0)$ which is $Y_A(1, 0)$ equals the first term in the expression for $E_B(Z_A = 1)$ which is $Y_B(1, 1)$. Once again, if A and B are identical and Z_A and Z_B are identical then we can suppose that:

$$Y_A(1, 0) = Y_B(0, 1) \ [\textit{Identicality of units and treatment or unit homogeneity}]. \tag{9}$$

In addition we need to assume that the causal impact of manipulation Z_A on B is not affected by whether or not A gets the treatment:

$$Y_B(0, 1) = Y_B(1, 1) \ [\textit{Noninterference of Units or SUTVA}]. \tag{10}$$

To summarize, to get a workable operational definition of causality, we need to assume that one of the following holds true:

$$Y_B(1, 0) = Y_A(0, 1) = Y_A(0, 0), \textit{ or} \tag{11a}$$

$$Y_A(1, 0) = Y_B(0, 1) = Y_B(1, 1). \tag{11b}$$

The first equality in each line holds true if we assume identicality and the second holds true if we assume noninterference (SUTVA). Note that if both (11a) and (11b) are true, then the definitions of $E^*(1, 0)$, $E_A(Z_B = 0)$, and $E_B(Z_A = 1)$ all collapse to one another.

Instead of (4) as the operational definition of causal impact, we might consider the following which is the effect for the state of the world $\{Z_A = 0$ and $Z_B = 1\}$:

$$E^*(0, 1) = Y_B(0, 1) - Y_A(0, 1), \tag{12}$$

where the difference involves terms that occur in only one state of the world. Surveying the four theoretical definitions of causal impact in equations (2) and (3) above, this definition seems most closely related to these two:

$$E_A(Z_B = 1) = Y_A(1, 1) - Y_A(0, 1) \tag{13a}$$

$$E_B(Z_A = 0) = Y_B(0, 1) - Y_B(0, 0), \tag{13b}$$

and these two are the remaining two after the ones in (5) are considered. To make these definitions work, we require, analogously to (11) above, that:

$$Y_B(0, 1) = Y_A(1, 0) = Y_A(1, 1), \ or \tag{14a}$$

$$Y_A(0, 1) = Y_B(1, 0) = Y_B(0, 0), \tag{14b}$$

where as before, the first equality in each line comes from identicality and the second comes from assuming noninterference. Once again, with these assumptions, then the definitions of $E^*(0, 1)$, $E_A(Z_B = 1)$, and $E_B(Z_A = 0)$ collapse into the same thing. And if both (11a,b) and (14a,b) hold, then $E^*(1, 0)$ equals $E^*(0, 1)$, and these definitions are all the same. Table 10.9 summarizes this entire argument.

9.5 Getting around Identicality (Unit Homogeneity) through Average Causal Effect

It is clear that the assumptions of noninterference (SUTVA) and identicality are sufficient to define causality unambiguously, but are they necessary? They are very strong assumptions. Can we do without one or the other? Suppose, for example, that we just assume noninterference so that $Y_A(j, k) = Y_A(j, k')$ and $Y_B(j, k) = Y_B(j, k')$ for $j = 1, 2$ and $k \neq k'$. Then we get the comforting result that the two theoretical definitions of causal impact for A (in (2) above) and the two for B (in (3) above) are identical:

$$E_A(Z_B = 0) = Y_A(1, 0) - Y_A(0, 0) = Y_A(1, 1) - Y_A(0, 1) = E_A(Z_B = 1)$$

$$E_B(Z_A = 0) = Y_B(0, 1) - Y_B(0, 0) = Y_B(1, 1) - Y_B(1, 0) = E_B(Z_A = 1).$$

Table 10.10 depicts this argument (moving from the rightmost column in the table to the second to the right column.) Since these equations hold, we denote the common causal effects as simply E_A and E_B:

$$E_A = E_A(Z_B = 0) = E_A(Z_B = 1)$$

$$E_B = E_B(Z_A = 0) = E_B(Z_A = 1).$$

These assumptions alone, however, will not allow us to link these theoretical definitions with the empirical possibilities $E^*(1, 0)$ and $E^*(0, 1)$. We need some additional assumption such as identicality of A and B which would ensure that $E_A = E_B$.

Can we get around identicality? Consider the following maneuver. Although we cannot observe both $E^*(1, 0)$ and $E^*(0, 1)$ at the same time, consider their average which we shall call the Average Causal Effect or ACE:

$$
\begin{aligned}
ACE &= (1/2)[E^*(1, 0) + E^*(0, 1)] \\
&= (1/2)\{[Y_A(1, 0) - Y_B(1, 0)] + [Y_B(0, 1) - Y_A(0, 1)]\} \\
&= (1/2)\{[Y_A(1, 0) - Y_A(0, 1)] + [Y_B(0, 1) - Y_B(1, 0)]\} \\
&= (1/2)\{[Y_A(1, 0) - Y_A(0, 0)] + [Y_B(0, 1) - Y_B(0, 0)]\}
\end{aligned}
$$

Table 10.10. Linking observational data to theoretical definitions of causality through noninterference of units and average causal effect

Observational →	Noninterference →	Average Causal Effect ← ACE = $[E^*(1, 0) + E^*(0, 1)]/2$	← Noninterference ←	← Theoretical
$E^*(1, 0) = Y_A(1, 0)$ $- Y_B(1, 0)$	$Y_B(1, 0) = Y_B(0, 0)$ $\to Y_A(1, 0) - Y_B(0, 0)$ $Y_A(1,0) = Y_A(1,1)$ $\to Y_A(1, 1) - Y_B(1, 0)$	**Take first and third on left:** ACE = $[Y_A(1, 0) - Y_B(0, 0) + Y_B(0, 1) - Y_A(0, 0)]/2$ = $[Y_A(1, 0) - Y_A(0, 0) + Y_B(0, 1) - Y_B(0, 0)]/2$ = $[E_A + E_B]$ (Using results from panels to right)	$Y_A(1, 0) = Y_A(1, 1)$ $Y_A(0, 0) = Y_A(0, 1)$ Hence: $E_A = E_A(Z_B = 0)$ $= E_A(Z_B = 1)$ $= Y_A(1, *) - Y_A(0, *)$	$E_A(Z_B = 0) = Y_A(1, 0)$ $- Y_A(0, 0)$ $E_A(Z_B = 1) = Y_A(1, 1)$ $- Y_A(0, 1)$
$E^*(0, 1) = Y_B(0, 1)$ $- Y_A(0, 1)$	$Y_A(0, 1) = Y_A(0, 0)$ $\to Y_B(0, 1) - Y_A(0, 0)$ $Y_B(0, 1) = Y_B(1, 1)$ $\to Y_B(1, 1) - Y_A(0, 1)$	**Take second and fourth on left:** ACE = $[Y_A(1, 1) - Y_B(1, 0) + Y_B(1, 1) - Y_A(0, 1)]/2$ = $[Y_A(1, 1) - Y_A(0, 1) + Y_B(1, 1) - Y_B(1, 0)]/2$ = $[E_A + E_B]$ (Using results from panels to right)	$Y_B(0, 1) = Y_B(1, 1)$ $Y_B(0, 0) = Y_B(1, 0)$ Hence: $E_B = E_B(Z_A = 0)$ $= E_B(Z_A = 1)$ $= Y_B(*, 1) - Y_B(*, 0)$	$E_B(Z_A = 0) = Y_B(0, 1)$ $- Y_B(0, 0)$ $E_B(Z_A = 1) = Y_B(1, 1)$ $- Y_B(1, 0)$

where the second line uses the definitions of $E^*(1, 0)$ and $E^*(0, 1)$, the third line is simply algebra, and the last line comes from noninterference. This argument is depicted in Table 10.10 as we move from the first to the second to the third column. As a result, we can write:

$$\text{ACE} = (1/2)[E_A + E_B].$$

Therefore, the ACE represents the average causal impact of Z_A on A and Z_B on B. If identicality (of A to B and Z_A to Z_B) held, then ACE would simply be the causal impact of Z.

Unfortunately, we cannot observe ACE, and we do not want to assume identicality. We can observe either $E^*(1, 0)$ or $E^*(0, 1)$, but not both. We can, however, do the following. We can randomly choose the state of the world, either $\{Z_A = 1 \text{ and } Z_B = 0\}$ or $\{Z_A = 0 \text{ and } Z_B = 1\}$. *Randomization in this way ensures that the treatment is assigned at random.* Once we have done this, we can take the observed value of either $E^*(1, 0)$ or $E^*(0, 1)$ as an estimate of ACE. The virtue of this estimate is that it is a statistically unbiased estimate of the average impact of Z_A on A and Z_B on B. That is, in repeated trials of this experiment (assuming that repeated trials make sense), the expected value of ACE will be equal to the true causal effect. Randomization ensures that we don't fall into the trap of confounding because, in repeated trials, there is no relationship between the assignment of treatment and units.

But the measure has two defects. First, it may be problematic to consider the average impact of Z_A on A and Z_B on B if they are not similar kinds of things. Once we drop identicality, it is quite possible that A and B could be quite different kinds of entities, say a sick person (A) and a well person (B). Then one would be randomly chosen to get some medicine, and the subsequent health (Y) of each person would be recorded. If the sick person A got the medicine then the causal effect E_A would be the difference between the health $Y_A(1, 0)$ of the sick person (after taking the medicine) and the health of the well person $Y_B(1, 0)$. If the well person B got the medicine, then the causal effect E_B would be the difference between the health $Y_B(0, 1)$ of the well person (after taking the medicine) and the health of the sick person $Y_A(0, 1)$. If the medicine works all the time and makes people well, then E_A will be zero (giving the medicine to the sick person will make him like the well person) and E_B will be positive (giving the medicine to the well person will not change her but not giving it to the sick person will leave him still sick)—hence the average effect will be to say that the medicine works, half the time. In fact, the medicine works all the time—when the person is sick. More generally, and somewhat ridiculously, A could be a person and B could be a tree, a dog, or anything. Thus, we need some assumption like the identicality of the units in order for our estimates of causal effect to make any sense. One possibility is that they are randomly chosen from some well-defined population to whom the treatment might be applied in the future.

The second defect of the measure is that it is only correct in repeated trials. In the medical experiment described above, if the well person is randomly assigned the medicine, then the experiment will conclude that the medicine does not work. The usual response to this problem is to multiply the number of units so that the random assignment to treatment group and control group creates groups that are, because of the law of large numbers, very similar, on average. This strategy certainly can make it possible to make statistical statements about the likelihood that an observed difference between the treatment and control groups is due to chance or to some underlying true difference. But it relies heavily upon multiplying the number of units, and it seems that multiplying the number of units brings some risks with it.

9.6 Multiplying the Number of Units and the Noninterference (SUTVA) Assumption

We started this section with a very simple problem in what is called singular causation. We asked: How does manipulation $Z = 1$ affect the outcome Y_A for unit A? Equation (1) provided a very simple definition of what we meant by the causal effect. It is simply $E_A = Y_A(1) - Y_A(0)$. This simple definition foundered because we cannot observe both $Y_A(1)$ and $Y_A(0)$. To solve this problem, we multiplied the number of units. Multiplying the number of units makes it possible to obtain an observable estimate of causal effect by either making the noninterference and identicality assumptions or by making the noninterference assumption and using randomization to achieve random assignment. But these assumptions lead us into the difficulties of defining a population of similar things from which the units are chosen and the problem of believing the noninterference assumption. These problems are related because they suggest that ultimately researchers must rely upon some prior knowledge and information in order to be sure that units or cases can be compared. But how much knowledge is needed? Are these assumptions really problematic? Should we, for example, be worried about units affecting one another?

Yes. Suppose people in a treatment condition are punished for poor behavior while those in a control condition are not. Further suppose that those in the control condition who are "near" (i.e. live in the same neighborhood or communicate regularly with one another) those in the treatment condition are not fully aware that they are exempt from punishment or they fear that they might be made subject to it. Wouldn't their behavior change in ways that it would not have changed if there had never been a treatment condition? Doesn't this mean that it would be difficult, if not impossible, to satisfy the noninterference condition?

In the Cal-Learn experiment in California, for example, teenage girls on welfare in the treatment group had their welfare check reduced if they failed to get passing grades in school. Those in the randomly selected control group were not subject to reductions but many thought they were in the treatment group (probably because they knew people who were in the treatment group) and they appear to have worked to get passing grades to avoid cuts in welfare (Mauldon et al. 2000).[55] Their decision

---

[55] Experimental subjects were told which group they were in, but some apparently did not get the message. They may not have gotten the message because the control group was only a small number of people and almost all teenage welfare mothers in the state were in the treatment group. In these

to get better grades, however, may have led to an underestimate of the impact of Cal-Learn because it reduced the difference between the treatment group and the control group. The problem here is that there is interaction between the units. To rule out these possibilities, Rubin (1990) proposed the "Stable-Unit-Treatment-Value-Assumption (SUTVA)" which, as we have seen, asserts that the outcome for a particular case does not depend upon what happens to the other cases or which of the supposedly identical treatments the unit receives.

Researchers using human subjects have worried about the possibility of interference. Cook and Campbell (1986, 148) mention four fundamental threats to randomized experiments. Compensatory rivalry occurs when control units decide that even though they are not getting the treatment, they can do as well as those getting it. Resentful demoralization occurs when those not getting the treatment become demoralized because they are not getting the treatment. Compensatory equalization occurs when those in charge of control units decide to compensate for the perceived inequities between treatment and control units, and treatment diffusion occurs when those in charge of control units mimic the treatment because of its supposed beneficial effects.

SUTVA implies that each supposedly identical treatment really is identical and that each unit is a separate, isolated possible world that is unaffected by what happens to the other units. SUTVA is the master assumption that makes controlled or randomized experiments a suitable solution to the problem of making causal inferences. SUTVA ensures that treatment and control units really do represent the closest possible worlds to one another except for the difference in treatment. In order to believe that SUTVA holds, we must have a very clear picture of the units, treatments, and outcomes in the situation at hand so that we can convince ourselves that experimental (or observational) comparisons really do involve similar worlds. Rubin (1986, 962) notes, for example, that statements such as "If the females at firm f had been male, their starting salaries would have averaged 20% higher" require much more elaboration of the counterfactual possibilities before they can be tested. What kind of treatment, for example, would be required for females to be males? Are individuals or the firm the basic unit of analysis? Is it possible simply to randomly assign men to the women's jobs to see what would happen to salaries? From what pool would these men be chosen? If men were randomly assigned to some jobs formerly held by women, would there be interactions across units that would violate SUTVA?

Not surprisingly, if the SUTVA assumption fails, then it will be at best hard to generalize the results of an experiment and at worst impossible to even interpret its results. Generalization is hard if, for example, imposing a policy of welfare time-limits on a small group of welfare recipients has a much different impact than imposing it upon every recipient. Perhaps the imposition of limits on the larger group generates a negative attitude toward welfare that encourages job seeking which is not generated

circumstances, an inattentive teenager in the control group could have sensibly supposed that the program applied to everyone. Furthermore, getting better grades seemingly had the desired effect because their welfare check was not cut!

when the limits are only imposed on a few people. Or perhaps the random assignment of a "Jewish" culture to one country (such as Israel) is much different than assigning it to a large number of countries in the same area. In both cases, the pattern of assignment to treatments seems to matter as much as the treatments themselves because of interactions among the units, and the interpretation of these experiments might be impossible because of the complex interactions among units. If SUTVA does not hold, then there are no ways such as randomization to construct closest possible worlds, and the difficulty of determining closest possible worlds must be faced directly.

If SUTVA holds and if there is independence of assignment and outcome through randomization, then the degree of causal connection can be estimated.[56] But there is no direct test that can ensure that SUTVA holds and there are only partial tests of "balance" to ensure that randomization has been done properly. Much of the art in experimentation goes into strategies that will increase the likelihood that they do hold. Cases can be isolated from one another to minimize interference, treatments can be made as uniform as possible, and the characteristics and circumstances of each case can be made as uniform as possible, but nothing can absolutely ensure that SUTVA and the independence of assignment and outcome hold.[57]

9.7 Summary of the NRH Approach

If noninterference across units (SUTVA) holds and if independence of assignment and outcome hold, then mini-closest-possible worlds have been created which can be used to compare the effects in a treatment and control condition. If SUTVA holds, then there are three ways to get the conditional independence conditions to hold:

(a) Controlled experiments in which identicality (unit homogeneity) holds.
(b) Statistical experiments in which random assignment holds.
(c) Observational studies in which corrections are made for covariates that ensure mean conditional independence of assignment and outcome.

The mathematical conditions required for the third method to work follow easily from the Neyman–Holland–Rubin setup, but there is no method for identifying the proper covariates. And outside of experimental studies, there is no way to be sure that conditional independence of assignment and outcome holds. Even if we know about *something* that may confound our results, we may not know about *all* things, and without knowing all of them, we cannot be sure that correcting for some of them

---

[56] If SUTVA fails and independence of assignment and outcome obtains, then causal effects can also be estimated, but they will differ depending on the pattern of treatments. Furthermore, the failure of SUTVA may make it impossible to rely on standard methods such as experimental control or randomization to ensure that the independence of assignment and outcome holds because the interaction of units may undermine these methods.

[57] Although good randomization can make it very likely that there is independence of assignment and outcome.

ensures conditional independence. Thus observational studies face the problem of identifying a set of variables that will ensure conditional independence so that the impact of the treatment can be determined. A great deal of research, however, does this in a rather cavalier way.

Even if SUTVA and some form of conditional independence is satisfied, the NRH framework, like Lewis's counterfactual theory to which it is a close relative, can only identify causal connections. Additional information is needed to rule out spurious correlation and to establish the direction of causation. Appeal can be made to temporal precedence or to what was manipulated to pin down the direction of causation, but neither of these approaches provides full protection against common cause. More experiments or observations which study the impact of other variables which suppress supposed causes or effects may be needed, and these have to be undertaken imaginatively in ways that explore different possible worlds.

REFERENCES

ABBOTT, A. 1983. Sequences of social events. *Historical Methods*, 16: 129–47.

—— 1992. From causes to events. *Sociological Methods and Research*, 20: 428–55.

—— 1995. Sequence analysis: new methods for old ideas. *Annual Review of Sociology*, 21: 93–113.

ACHEN, C. H. 1983. Toward theories of data: the state of political methodology. In *Political Science: The State of the Discipline*, ed. A. Finifter. Washington, DC: American Political Science Association.

BARTELS, L., and BRADY, H. E. 1993. The state of quantitative political methodology. In *Political Science: The State of the Discipline*, 2nd edn., ed. A. Finifter. Washington, DC: American Political Science Association.

BEAUCHAMP, T. L., and ROSENBERG, A. 1981. *Hume and the Problem of Causation*. New York: Oxford University Press.

BENNETT, J. 1988. *Events and Their Names*. Indianapolis: Hackett.

BERGER, P. L., and LUCKMANN, T. 1966. *The Social Construction of Reality: A Treatise in the Sociology of Knowledge*. Garden City, NY: Anchor.

BRADY, H. E., and COLLIER, D. 2004. *Rethinking Social Inquiry: Diverse Tools, Shared Standards*. New York: Rowman and Littlefield.

—— HERRON, M. C., MEBANE, W. R., SEKHON, J. S., SHOTTS, W. S., and WAND, J. 2001. Law and data: the butterfly ballot episode. *PS: Political Science and Politics*, 34: 59–69.

CAMPBELL, D. T., and STANLEY, J. C. 1966. *Experimental and Quasi-Experimental Designs for Research*. Chicago: Rand McNally.

CARTWRIGHT, N. 1989. *Nature's Capacities and Their Measurement*. New York: Oxford University Press.

COOK, T. D., and CAMPBELL, D. T. 1979. *Quasi-Experimentation: Design and Analysis Issues for Field Settings*. Boston: Houghton Mifflin.

—— —— 1986. The causal assumptions of quasi-experimental practice. *Synthese*, 68: 141–180.

COX, D. R. 1958. *The Planning of Experiments*. New York: Wiley.

—— 1992. Causality: some statistical aspects. *Journal of the Royal Statistical Society, Series A (Statistics in Society)*, 155: 291–301.

Cox, G. W. 1997. *Making Votes Count: Strategic Coordination in the World's Electoral Systems*, New York: Cambridge University Press.

Davidson, D. 2001. *Essays on Actions and Events*, 2nd edn. Oxford: Clarendon Press.

Dessler, D. 1991. Beyond correlations: toward a causal theory of war. *International Studies Quarterly*, 35: 337–355.

Dilthey, W. 1961. *Pattern and Meaning in History: Thoughts on History and Society*. New York: Harper.

Durkheim, E. 1982 [1895]. *The Rules of Sociological Method*. New York: Free Press.

Elster, J. 1998. A plea for mechanisms. In *Social Mechanisms*, ed. P. Hedström and R. Swedberg. Cambridge: Cambridge University Press.

Ehring, D. 1997. *Causation and Persistence: A Theory of Causation*. New York: Oxford University Press.

Fearon, J. D. 1991. Counterfactuals and hypothesis testing in political science. *World Politics*, 43: 169–95.

Fisher, R. A., Sir 1925. *Statistical Methods for Research Workers*. Edinburgh: Oliver and Boyd.

—— 1926. The arrangement of field experiments. *Journal of the Ministry of Agriculture*, 33: 503–13.

—— 1935. *The Design of Experiments*. Edinburgh: Oliver and Boyd.

Freedman, D. A. 1987. As others see us: a case study in path analysis. *Journal of Educational Statistics*, 12: 101–223, with discussion.

—— 1991. Statistical models and shoe leather. *Sociological Methodology*, 21: 291–313.

—— 1997. From association to causation via regression. Pp. 113–61 in *Causality in Crisis?* ed. V. R. McKim and S. P. Turner, Notre Dame, Ind.: University of Notre Dame Press.

—— 1999. From association to causation: some remarks on the history of statistics. *Statistical Science*, 14: 243–58.

Gasking, D. 1955. Causation and recipes. *Mind*, 64: 479–87.

Glennan, S. S. 1996. Mechanisms and the nature of causation. *Erkenntnis*, 44: 49–71.

Goldthorpe, J. H. 2001. Causation, statistics, and sociology. *European Sociological Review*, 17: 1–20.

Goodman, N. 1947. The problem of counterfactual conditionals. *Journal of Philosophy*, 44: 113–28.

Harré, R., and Madden, E. H. *c* 1975. *Causal Powers: A Theory of Natural Necessity*. Oxford: B. Blackwell.

Hausman, D. M. 1998. *Causal Asymmetries*. New York: Cambridge University Press.

Heckman, J. J. 1979. Sample selection bias as a specification error. *Econometrica*, 47: 153–62.

Hedström, P., and Swedberg, R. (eds.) 1998. *Social Mechanisms: An Analytical Approach to Social Theory*. New York: Cambridge University Press.

Hempel, C. G. 1965. *Aspects of Scientific Explanation*. New York: Free Press.

Hill, A. B. 1965. The environment and disease: association or causation? *Proceedings of the Royal Society of Medicine*, 58: 295–300.

Holland, P. W. 1986. Statistics and causal inference (in theory and methods). *Journal of the American Statistical Association*, 81: 945–60.

Hume, D. 1739. *A Treatise of Human Nature*, ed. L. A. Selby-Bigge and P. H. Nidditch. Oxford: Clarendon Press.

—— 1748. *An Enquiry Concerning Human Understanding*, ed. T. L. Beauchamp. New York: Oxford University Press.

Kitcher, P., and Salmon, W. 1987. Van Fraassen on explanation. *Journal of Philosophy*, 84: 315–30.

LAKOFF, G. and JOHNSON, M. 1980*a*. Conceptual metaphor in everyday language. *Journal of Philosophy*, 77 (8): 453–86.

—— —— 1980*b*. *Metaphors We Live By*. Chicago: University of Chicago Press.

—— —— 1999. *Philosophy in the Flesh: The Embodied Mind and its Challenge to Western Thought*. New York: Basic Books.

LEWIS, D. 1973*a*. *Counterfactuals*. Cambridge, Mass: Harvard University Press.

—— 1973*b*. Causation. *Journal of Philosophy*, 70: 556–67.

—— 1979. Counterfactual dependence and time's arrow. *Noûs*, Special Issue on Counterfactuals and Laws, 13: 455–76.

—— 1986. *Philosophical Papers*, vol. ii. New York: Oxford University Press.

MACHAMBER, P., DARDEN, L., and CRAVER, C. F. 2000. Thinking about mechanisms. *Philosophy of Science*, 67: 1–25.

MACKIE, J. L. 1965. Causes and conditions. *American Philosophical Quarterly*, 2: 245–64.

MARINI, M. M., and SINGER, B. 1988. Causality in the social sciences. *Sociological Methodology*, 18: 347–409.

MAULDON, J., MALVIN, J., STILES, J., NICOSIA, N., and SETO, E. 2000. Impact of California's Cal-Learn Demonstration Project: final report. UC DATA Archive and Technical Assistance.

MELLORS, D. H. 1995. *The Facts of Causation*. London: Routledge.

MENZIES, P., and PRICE, H. 1993. Causation as a secondary quality. *British Journal for the Philosophy of Science*, 44: 187–203.

MILL, J. S. 1888 *A System of Logic, Ratiocinative and Inductive*, 8th edn. New York: Harper and Brothers.

NEYMAN, J. 1990. On the application of probability theory to agricultural experiments: essay on principles, trans. D. M. Dabrowska and T. P. Speed. *Statistical Science*, 5: 463–80; first pub. in Polish 1923.

PAPINEAU, D. 1985. Causal asymmetry. *British Journal for the Philosophy of Science*, 36: 273–89.

PEARL, J. 2000. *Causality: Models, Reasoning, and Inference*. Cambridge: Cambridge University Press.

PEARSON, K. 1911. *The Grammar of Science*, 3rd edn. rev. and enlarged, Part 1: *Physical*. London: Adam and Charles Black.

PIERSON, P. 2004. *Politics in Time: History, Institutions, and Social Analysis*. Princeton, NJ: Princeton University Press.

RAGIN, C. C. 1987. *The Comparative Method: Moving beyond Qualitiative and Quantitative Strategies*. Berkeley: University of California Press.

RIKER, W. H. 1957. Events and situations. *Journal of Philosophy*, 54: 57–70.

RUBIN, D. B. 1974. Estimating causal effects of treatments in randomized and nonrandomized studies. *Journal of Educational Psychology*, 66: 688–701.

—— 1978. Bayesian inference for causal effects: the role of randomization. *Annals of Statistics*, 6: 34–58.

—— 1986. Statistics and casual inference: comment: which ifs have casual answers. *Journal of the American Statistical Association*, 81: 945–70.

—— 1990. Comment: Neyman (1923) and causal inference in experiments and observational studies. *Statistical Science*, 5: 472–80.

RUSSELL, B. 1918. On the notion of cause. In *Mysticism and Logic and Other Essays*. New York: Longmans, Green.

SALMON, W. C. 1990. *Four Decades of Scientific Explanation*. Minneapolis: University of Minnesota Press.

SEARLE, J. R. 1969. *Speech Acts: An Essay in the Philosophy of Language*. London: Cambridge University Press.

——1997. *The Construction of Social Reality*. New York: Free Press.

SHAFER, G. 1996. *The Art of Casual Conjecture*. Cambridge, Mass.: MIT Press.

SIMON, H. A. 1952. On the definition of the causal relation. *Journal of Philosophy*, 49: 517–28.

——and IWASAKI, Y. 1988. Causal ordering, comparative statics, and near decomposability. *Journal of Econometrics*, 39: 149–73.

SOBEL, M. E. 1995. Causal inference in the social and behavioral sciences. In *Handbook of Statistical Modeling for the Social and Behavioral Sciences*, ed. G. Arminger, C. C. Clogg, and M. E. Sobel. New York: Plenum.

SORENSON, A. B. 1998. Theoretical mechanisms and the empirical study of social processes. In *Social Mechanisms*, ed. P. Hedström and R. Swedberg. Cambridge: Cambridge University Press.

SOSA, E., and TOOLEY, M. 1993. *Causation*. Oxford: Oxford University Press.

SPELLMAN, B. A., and MANDEL, D. R. 1999. When possibility informs reality: counterfactual thinking as a cue to causality. *Current Directions in Psychological Science*, 8: 120–3.

SPRINZAK, E. 1972. Weber's thesis as an historical explanation. *History and Theory*, 11: 294–320.

TETLOCK, P. E., and BELKIN, A. (eds.) 1996. *Counterfactual Thought Experiments in World Politics: Logical, Methodological, and Psychological Perspectives*. Princeton, NJ: Princeton University Press.

TILLY, C. 1984. *Big Structures, Large Processes, Huge Comparison*. New York: Russell Sage Foundation.

VAN FRAASSEN, B. 1980. *The Scientific Image*. Oxford: Clarendon Press.

VON WRIGHT, G. H. 1971. *Explanation and Understanding*. Ithaca, NY: Cornell University Press.

——1974. *Causality and Determinism*. New York: Columbia University Press.

WAND, J. N., SHOTTS, K. W., SEKHON, J. S., MEBANE, W. R., HERRON, M. C., and BRADY, H. E. 1991. The butterfly did it: the aberrant vote for Buchanan in Palm Beach County, Florida. *American Political Science Review*, 95: 793–810.

WAWRO, G. 1996. *The Austro-Prussian War: Austria's War with Prussia and Italy in 1866*. New York: Cambridge University Press.

WEBER, M. 1906 [1978]. *Selections in Translation*, ed. W. G. Runciman, trans. E. Matthews. Cambridge: Cambridge University Press.

WENDT, A. 1999. *Social Theory of International Politics*. Cambridge: Cambridge University Press.

CHAPTER 11

THE NEYMAN– RUBIN MODEL OF CAUSAL INFERENCE AND ESTIMATION VIA MATCHING METHODS

JASJEET S. SEKHON

"CORRELATION does not imply causation" is one of the most repeated mantras in the social sciences, but its full implications are sobering and often ignored. The Neyman–Rubin model of causal inference helps to clarify some of the issues which arise. In this chapter, the model is briefly described, and some consequences of the model are outlined for both quantitative and qualitative research. The model has radical implications for work in the social sciences given current practices. Matching methods, which are usually motivated by the Neyman–Rubin model, are reviewed and their properties discussed. For example, applied researchers are often surprised to

I thank Henry Brady, David Collier, and Rocío Titiunik for valuable comments on earlier drafts, and David Freedman, Walter R. Mebane, Jr., Donald Rubin, and Jonathan N. Wand for many valuable discussions on these topics. All errors are my responsibility.

learn that even if the selection on observables assumption is satisfied, the commonly used matching methods will generally make even linear bias worse unless specific and often implausible assumptions are satisfied.

Some of the intuition of matching methods, such as propensity score matching, should be familiar to social scientists because they share many features with Mill's methods, or canons, of inference. Both attempt to find appropriate units to compare—i.e. they attempt to increase unit homogeneity. But Mill never intended for his canons to be used in the social sciences because he did not believe that unit homogeneity could be achieved in this field (Sekhon 2004a). Because of its reliance on random assignment and other statistical apparatus, modern concepts of experimental design sharply diverge from Mill's deterministic methods. Modern matching methods adopt Mill's key insights of the importance of unit homogeneity to cases where analysts do not control their units precisely. Matching methods, and related methods such as regression discontinuity, drop observations to make inferences more precise as well as less biased because unit homogeneity can be improved by removing some observations from consideration.[1] Dropping observations is almost anathema to most quantitative researchers, but this intuition is wrong with nonexperimental data (Rosenbaum 2005). Case-study research methods in the tradition of Mill contrast sharply with statistical methods, and the hunt for necessary and sufficient causes is generally misplaced in the social sciences given the lack of unit homogeneity.

The key probabilistic idea upon which statistical causal inference relies is conditional probability. But when we are making causal inferences, conditional probabilities are not themselves of direct interest. We use conditional probabilities to learn about counterfactuals of interest—e.g. would Jane have voted if someone from the campaign had not gone to her home to encourage her to do so? One has to be careful to establish the relationship between the counterfactuals of interest and the conditional probabilities one has managed to estimate. Researchers too often forget that this relationship must be established by design and instead rely on statistical models whose assumptions are almost never defended. A regression coefficient is not a causal estimate unless a large set of assumptions are met, and this is no less true of conditional probabilities estimated in other ways such as by matching methods. Without an experiment, natural experiment, a discontinuity, or some other strong design, no amount of econometric or statistical modeling can make the move from correlation to causation persuasive. This conclusion has implications for the kind of causal questions we are able to answer with some rigor. Clear, manipulable treatments and rigorous designs are essential.

1 NEYMAN–RUBIN CAUSAL MODEL

The Neyman–Rubin framework has become increasingly popular in many fields including statistics (Holland 1986; Rubin 2006; 1974; Rosenbaum 2002), medicine

---

[1] Regression discontinuity is discussed in detail by Green and Gerber in this volume.

(Christakis and Iwashyna 2003; Rubin 1997), economics (Abadie and Imbens 2006; Galiani, Gertler, and Schargrodsky 2005; Dehejia and Wahba 2002; 1999), political science (Bowers and Hansen 2005; Imai 2005; Sekhon 2004b), sociology (Morgan and Harding 2006; Diprete and Engelhardt 2004; Winship and Morgan 1999; Smith 1997), and even law (Rubin 2001). The framework originated with Neyman's (1990 [1923]) nonparametric model where each unit has two potential outcomes, one if the unit is treated and the other if untreated. A causal effect is defined as the difference between the two potential outcomes, but only one of the two potential outcomes is observed. Rubin (2006; 1974), among others, including most notably Cochran (1965; 1953), developed the model into a general framework for causal inference with implications for observational research. Holland (1986) wrote an influential review article which highlighted some of the philosophical implications of the framework. Consequently, instead of the "Neyman–Rubin model," the model is often simply called the Rubin causal model (e.g. Holland 1986) or sometimes the Neyman–Rubin–Holland model of causal inference (e.g. Brady, this volume).

Let Y_{i1} denote the potential outcome for unit i if the unit receives treatment, and let Y_{i0} denote the potential outcome for unit i in the control regime. The treatment effect for observation i is defined by $\tau_i = Y_{i1} - Y_{i0}$. Causal inference is a missing data problem because Y_{i1} and Y_{i0} are never both observed. This remains true regardless of the methodology used to make inferential progress—regardless of whether we use quantitative or qualitative methods of inference. The fact remains that we cannot observe both potential outcomes at the same time.

Some set of assumptions have to be made to make progress. The most compelling are offered by a randomized experiment. Let T_i be a treatment indicator: 1 when i is in the treatment regime and 0 otherwise. The observed outcome for observation i is then $Y_i = T_i Y_{i1} + (1 - T_i) Y_{i0}$.[2] Note that in contrast to the usual regression assumptions, the potential outcomes, Y_{i1} and Y_{i1}, are fixed quantities and not random variables.

1.1 Experimental Data

In principle, if assignment to treatment is randomized, causal inference is straightforward because the two groups are drawn from the same population by construction, and treatment assignment is independent of all baseline variables. As the sample size grows, observed and unobserved confounders are balanced across treatment and control groups with arbitrarily high probability. That is, with random assignment, the distributions of both observed and unobserved variables in both groups are equal in expectation. Treatment assignment is independent of Y_0 and Y_1—i.e. $\{Y_{i0}, Y_{i1} \perp\!\!\!\perp T_i\}$, where $\perp\!\!\!\perp$ denotes independence (Dawid 1979). Hence, for $j = 0, 1$,

$$E(Y_{ij} \mid T_i = 1) = E(Y_{ij} \mid T_i = 0) = E(Y_i \mid T_i = j).$$

---

[2] Extensions to the case of multiple discrete treatment are straightforward (e.g. Imbens 2000; Rosenbaum 2002, 300–2).

Therefore, the average treatment effect (ATE) can be estimated by:

$$\tau = E(Y_{i1} \mid T_i = 1) - E(Y_{i0} \mid T_i = 0) \tag{1}$$

$$= E(Y_i \mid T_i = 1) - E(Y_i \mid T_i = 0). \tag{2}$$

The parameter γ can be estimated consistently in an experimental setting because randomization can ensure that observations in treatment and control groups are exchangeable. Randomization ensures that assignment to treatment will not, in expectation, be associated with the potential outcomes.

Even in an experimental setup, much can go wrong which requires statistical adjustment (e.g. Barnard et al. 2003). One of the most common problems which arises is the issue of compliance. People who are assigned to treatment may refuse it, and those assigned to control may find some way to receive treatment. When there are compliance issues, equation (2) then defines the intention-to-treat (ITT) estimand. Although the concept of ITT dates earlier, the phrase probably first appeared in print in Hill (1961, 259). Moving beyond the ITT to estimate the average treatment effect on the treated can be difficult. If the compliance problem is simply that some people assigned to treatment refused it, statistical correction is straightforward and relatively model free. When the compliance problem has a more complicated structure, it is difficult to make progress without making structural assumptions. Statistical corrections for compliance are discussed in detail in Green and Gerber (this volume).

One of the assumptions which randomization by itself does not justify is that "the observation on one unit should be unaffected by the particular assignment of treatments to the other units" (Cox 1958, §2.4). Rubin (1978) calls this "no interference between units" the Stable Unit Treatment Value Assumption (SUTVA). SUTVA implies that the potential outcomes for a given unit do not vary with the treatments assigned to any other unit, and that there are no different versions of treatment. SUTVA is a complicated assumption which is all too often ignored. It is discussed in detail in Brady (this volume).

Brady (this volume) describes a randomized welfare experiment in California where SUTVA is violated. In the experiment, teenage girls in the treatment group had their welfare checks reduced if they failed to obtain passing grades in school. Girls in the control group did not face the risk of reduced payments. However, some girls in the control group thought that they were in the treatment group, probably because they knew girls in treatment (Mauldon et al. 2000). Therefore, the experiment probably underestimated the effect of the treatment.

Some researchers erroneously think that the SUTVA assumption is another word for the usual independence assumption made in regression models. A hint of the problem can be seen by noting that OLS is still unbiased under the usual assumptions even if multiple draws from the disturbance are not independent of each other. When SUTVA is violated, an experiment will not yield unbiased estimates of the causal effect of interest. In the usual regression setup, the correct specification assumption (and not the independence assumption) implicitly deals with SUTVA violations. It is assumed that if there are SUTVA violations, we have the correct model for them.

Note that even with randomization, the assumptions of the OLS regression model are not satisfied. Indeed, without further assumptions, the multiple regression estimator is biased, although the bias goes to zero as the sample size increases. And the regression standard errors can be seriously biased, even asymptotically. For details see Freedman (2008a; 2008b). Intuitively, the problem is that generally, even with randomization, the treatment indicator and the disturbance will be strongly correlated. Randomization does not imply, as OLS assumes, a linear additive treatment effect where the coefficients are constant across units. Researchers should be extremely cautious about using multiple regression to adjust experimental data. Unfortunately, there is a tendency to do just that. One supposes that this is yet another sign, as if one more were needed, of how ingrained the regression model is in our quantitative practice.

The only thing stochastic in the Neyman setup is the assignment to treatment. The potential outcomes are fixed. This is exactly the opposite of many econometric treatments where all of the regressors (including the treatment indicator) are considered to be fixed, and the response variable Y is considered to be a random variable with a given distribution. None of that is implied by randomization and indeed randomization explicitly contradicts it because one of the regressors (the treatment indicator) is explicitly random. Adding to the confusion is the tendency of some texts to refer to the fixed regressors design as an experiment when that cannot possibly be the case.

1.2 Observational Data

In an observational setting, unless something special is done, treatment and nontreatment groups are almost never balanced because the two groups are not ordinarily drawn from the same population. Thus, a common quantity of interest is the average treatment effect for the treated (ATT):

$$\tau \mid (T = 1) = E(Y_{i1} \mid T_i = 1) - E(Y_{i0} \mid T_i = 1). \tag{3}$$

Equation (3) cannot be directly estimated because Y_{i0} is not observed for the treated. Progress can be made by assuming that selection for treatment depends on observable covariates X. Following Rosenbaum and Rubin (1983), one can assume that conditional on X, treatment assignment is unconfounded ($\{Y_0, Y_1 \perp\!\!\!\perp T\} \mid X$) and that there is overlap: $0 < Pr(T = 1 \mid X) < 1$. Together, unconfoundedness and overlap constitute a property known as strong ignorability of assignment which is necessary for identifying the treatment effect. Heckman et al. (1998) shows that for ATT, the unconfoundedness assumption can be weakened to mean independence: $E(Y_{ij} \mid T_i, X_i) = E(Y_{ij} \mid X_i)$.[3]

Then, following Rubin (1974; 1977), we obtain

$$E(Y_{ij} \mid X_i, T_i = 1) = E(Y_{ij} \mid X_i, T_i = 0) = E(Y_i \mid X_i, T_i = j). \tag{4}$$

---

[3] Also see Abadie and Imbens (2006).

By conditioning on observed covariates, X_i, treatment and control groups are balanced. The average treatment effect for the treated is estimated as

$$\tau \mid (T = 1) = E\{E(Y_i \mid X_i, T_i = 1) - E(Y_i \mid X_i, T_i = 0) \mid T_i = 1\}, \qquad (5)$$

where the outer expectation is taken over the distribution of $X_i \mid (T_i = 1)$ which is the distribution of baseline variables in the treated group.

Note that the ATT estimator is changing how individual observations are weighted, and that observations which are outside of common support receive zero weights. That is, if some covariate values are only observed for control observations, those observations will be irrelevant for estimating ATT and are effectively dropped. Therefore, the overlap assumption for ATT only requires that the support of X for the treated observations be a subset of the support of X for control observations. More generally, one would also want to drop treatment observations if they have covariate values which do not overlap with control observations (Crump et al. 2006). In such cases, it is unclear exactly what estimand one is estimating because it is no longer ATT as some treatment observations have been dropped along with some control observations.

It is often jarring for people to observe that observations are being dropped because of a lack of covariate overlap. But dropping observations which are outside of common support not only reduces bias but can also reduce the variance of our estimates. This may be counter-intuitive, but note that our variance estimates are a function of both sample size and unit heterogeneity—e.g. in the regression case, of the sample variance of X and the the mean squared error. Dropping observations outside of common support and conditioning as in equation (5) helps to improve unit homogeneity and may actually reduce our variance estimates (Rosenbaum 2005). Moreover, as Rosenbaum (2005) shows, with observational data, minimizing unit heterogeneity reduces both sampling variability and sensitivity to unobserved bias. With less unit heterogeneity, larger unobserved biases need to exist to explain away a given effect. And although increasing the sample size reduces sampling variability, it does little to reduce concerns about unobserved bias. Thus, maximizing unit homogeneity to the extent possible is an important task for observational methods.

The key assumption being made here is strong ignorability. Even thinking about this assumption presupposes some rigor in the research design. For example, is it clear what is pre- and what is post-treatment? If not, one is unable even to form the relevant questions, the most useful of which may be the one suggested by Dorn (1953, 680) who proposed that the designer of every observational study should ask "[h]ow would the study be conducted if it were possible to do it by controlled experimentation?" This clear question also appears in Cochran's famous Royal Statistical Society discussion paper on the planning of observational studies of human populations (1965). And Dorn's question has become one which researchers in the tradition of the Neyman–Rubin model ask themselves and their students. The question forces the researcher to focus on a clear manipulation and then on the selection problem at hand. Only then can one even begin to think clearly about how plausible the strong ignorability assumption may or may not be. It is fair to say that without answering Dorn's question, one is unsure what the researcher wants to estimate. Since most researchers do not propose an answer to this question, it is difficult to think clearly about the underlying assumptions being made in most applications in the social sciences because one is unclear as to what precisely the researcher is trying to estimate.

For the moment let us assume that the researcher has a clear treatment of interest, and a set of confounders which may reasonably ensure conditional independence of treatment assignment. At that point, one needs to condition on these confounders denoted by X. But we must remember that selection on observables is a large concession; one which should not be made lightly. It is of far greater relevance than the technical discussion which follows on the best way to condition on covariates.

2 MATCHING METHODS

There is no consensus on how exactly matching ought to be done, how to measure the success of the matching procedure, and whether or not matching estimators are sufficiently robust to misspecification to be useful in practice (Heckman et al. 1998). The most straightforward and nonparametric way to condition on X is to exactly match on the covariates. This is an old approach going back to at least Fechner (1966 [1860]), the father of psychophysics. This approach fails in finite samples if the dimensionality of X is large and is simply impossible if X contains continuous covariates. Thus, in general, alternative methods must be used.

Two common approaches are propensity score matching (Rosenbaum and Rubin 1983) and multivariate matching based on Mahalanobis distance (Cochran and Rubin 1973; Rubin 1979; 1980). Matching methods based on the propensity score (estimated by logistic regression), Mahalanobis distance, or a combination of the two have appealing theoretical properties if covariates have ellipsoidal distributions—e.g. distributions such as the normal or t. If the covariates are so distributed, these methods (more generally affinely invariant matching methods[4]) have the property of "equal percent bias reduction" (EPBR) (Rubin 1976a; 1976b; Rubin and Thomas 1992).[5] This property, which is formally defined in Appendix A, ensures that matching methods will reduce bias in all linear combinations of the covariates. If a matching method is not EPBR, then that method will, in general, increase the bias for some linear function of the covariates even if all univariate means are closer in the matched data than the unmatched (Rubin 1976a).

---

[4] Affine invariance means that the matching output is invariant to matching on X or an affine transformation of X.

[5] The EPBR results of Rubin and Thomas (1992) have been extended by Rubin and Stuart (2005) to the case of discriminant mixtures of proportional ellipsoidally symmetric (DMPES) distributions. This extension is important, but it is restricted to a limited set of mixtures. See Appendix A.

2.1 Mahalanobis and Propensity Score Matching

The most common method of multivariate matching is based on Mahalanobis distance (Cochran and Rubin 1973; Rubin 1979; 1980). The Mahalanobis distance between any two column vectors is:

$$md(X_i, X_j) = \left\{ (X_i - X_j)' S^{-1} (X_i - X_j) \right\}^{\frac{1}{2}},$$

where S is the sample covariance matrix of X. To estimate ATT, one matches each treated unit with the M closest control units, as defined by this distance measure, md.[6] If X consists of more than one continuous variable, multivariate matching estimates contain a bias term which does not asymptotically go to zero at $\sqrt{n}$ (Abadie and Imbens 2006).

An alternative way to condition on X is to match on the probability of assignment to treatment, known as the propensity score.[7] As one's sample size grows large, matching on the propensity score produces balance on the vector of covariates X (Rosenbaum and Rubin 1983).

Let $e(X_i) \equiv Pr(T_i = 1 \mid X_i) = E(T_i \mid X_i)$, defining $e(X_i)$ to be the propensity score. Given $0 < Pr(T_i \mid X_i) < 1$ and that $Pr(T_1, T_2, \cdots T_N \mid X_1, X_2, \cdots X_N) = \Pi_{i=1}^{N} e(X_i)^{T_i} (1 - e(X_i))^{(1-T_i)}$, then as Rosenbaum and Rubin (1983) prove,

$$\tau \mid (T = 1) = E \left\{ E(Y_i \mid e(X_i), T_i = 1) - E(Y_i \mid e(X_i), T_i = 0) \mid T_i = 1 \right\},$$

where the outer expectation is taken over the distribution of $e(X_i) \mid (T_i = 1)$. Since the propensity score is generally unknown, it must be estimated.

Propensity score matching involves matching each treated unit to the nearest control unit on the unidimensional metric of the propensity score vector. If the propensity score is estimated by logistic regression, as is typically the case, much is to be gained by matching not on the predicted probabilities (bounded between zero and one) but on the linear predictor, $\hat{\mu} = X\hat{\beta}$. Matching on the linear predictor avoids compression of propensity scores near zero and one. Moreover, the linear predictor is often more nearly normally distributed which is of some importance given the EPBR results if the propensity score is matched along with other covariates.

Mahalanobis distance and propensity score matching can be combined in various ways (Rubin 2001; Rosenbaum and Rubin 1985). It is useful to combine the propensity score with Mahalanobis distance matching because propensity score matching is particularly good at minimizing the discrepancy along the propensity score and Mahalanobis distance is particularly good at minimizing the distance between individual coordinates of X (orthogonal to the propensity score) (Rosenbaum and Rubin 1985).

A significant shortcoming of common matching methods, such as Mahalanobis distance and propensity score matching, is that they may (and in practice, frequently

---

[6] One can do matching with replacement or without. Alternatively one can do optimal full matching (Hansen 2004; Rosenbaum 1991) instead of the greedy matching. But this decision is a separate one from the choice of a distance metric.

[7] The first estimator of treatment effects to be based on a weighted function of the probability of treatment was the Horvitz–Thompson statistic (Horvitz and Thompson 1952).

do) make balance worse across measured potential confounders. These methods may make balance worse, in practice, even if covariates are distributed ellipsoidally symmetric, because EPBR is a property that obtains in expectation. That is, even if the covariates have elliptic distributions, finite samples may not conform to ellipticity, and hence Mahalanobis distance may not be optimal because the matrix used to scale the distances, the covariance matrix of X, can be improved upon.[8] Moreover, if covariates are neither ellipsoidally symmetric nor are mixtures of DMPES distributions, propensity score matching has good theoretical properties only if the true propensity score model is known with certainty and the sample size is large.

The EPBR property itself is limited and in a given substantive problem it may not be desirable. This can arise if it is known based on theory that one covariate has a large nonlinear relationship with the outcome while another does not—e.g. $Y = X_1^4 + X_2$, where X_1 and where both X_1 and X_2 have the same distribution. In such a case, reducing bias in X_1 will be more important than X_2.

Given these limitations, it may be desirable to use a matching method which algorithmically imposes certain properties when the EPBR property does not hold. Genetic Matching does just that.

2.2 Genetic Matching

Sekhon (2008) and Diamond and Sekhon (2005) propose a matching algorithm, Genetic Matching, which maximizes the balance of observed covariates between treated and control groups. Genetic Matching is a generalization of propensity score and Mahalanobis distance matching, and has been used by a variety of researchers (e.g. Bonney and Minozzi 2007; Brady and Hui 2006; Gilligan and Sergenti 2006; Gordon and Huber 2007; Herron and Wand forthcoming; Morgan and Harding 2006; Lenz and Ladd 2006; Park 2006; Raessler and Rubin 2005). The algorithm uses a genetic algorithm (Mebane and Sekhon 1998; Sekhon and Mebane 1998) to optimize balance as much as possible given the data. The method is nonparametric and does not depend on knowing or estimating the propensity score, but the method is improved when a propensity score is incorporated. Diamond and Sekhon (2005) use this algorithm to show that the long-running debate between Dehejia and Wahba (2002; 1997; 1999; Dehejia 2005) and Smith and Todd (2005b; 2005a; 2001) is largely a result of researchers using models which do not produce good balance—even if some of the models get close by chance to the experimental benchmark of interest. They show that Genetic Matching is able quickly to find good balance and reliably recover the experimental benchmark.

The idea underlying the Genetic Matching algorithm is that if Mahalanobis distance is not optimal for achieving balance in a given data-set, one should be able to search over the space of distance metrics and find something better. One way of

---

[8] For justifications of Mahalanobis distance based on distributional considerations see Mitchell and Krzanowski (1985; 1989).

generalizing the Mahalanobis metric is to include an additional weight matrix,

$$d(X_i, X_j) = \left\{ (X_i - X_j)' \left(S^{-1/2}\right)' W S^{-1/2} (X_i - X_j) \right\}^{\frac{1}{2}},$$

where W is a $k \times k$ positive definite weight matrix and $S^{1/2}$ is the Cholesky decomposition of S which is the variance-covariance matrix of X.[9]

Note that if one has a good propensity score model, one should include it as one of the covariates in Genetic Matching. If this is done, both propensity score matching and Mahalanobis matching can be considered special limiting cases of Genetic Matching. If the propensity score contains all of the relevant information in a given sample, the other variables will be given zero weight.[10] And Genetic Matching will converge to Mahalanobis distance if that proves to be the appropriate distance measure.

Genetic Matching is an affinely invariant matching algorithm that uses the distance measure $d()$, in which all elements of W are zero except down the main diagonal. The main diagonal consists of k parameters which must be chosen. Note that if each of these k parameters is set equal to 1 $d()$ is the same as Mahalanobis distance.

The choice of setting the nondiagonal elements of W to zero is made for reasons of computational power alone. The optimization problem grows exponentially with the number of free parameters. It is important that the problem be parameterized so as to limit the number of parameters which must be estimated.

This leaves the problem of how to choose the free elements of W. Many loss criteria recommend themselves, and many can be used with the software which implements Genetic Matching.[11] By default, cumulative probability distribution functions of a variety of standardized statistics are used as balance metrics and are optimized without limit. The default standardized statistics are paired t-tests and bootstrapped nonparametric Kolmogorov–Smirnov tests (Abadie 2002).

The statistics are not used to conduct formal hypothesis tests, because no measure of balance is a monotonic function of bias in the estimand of interest and because we wish to maximize balance without limit. Alternatively, one may choose to minimize some descriptive measure of imbalance such as the maximum gap in the standardized empirical-QQ plots across the covariates. This would correspond to minimizing the D statistic of the Kolmogorov–Smirnov test.

Conceptually, the algorithm attempts to minimize the largest observed covariate discrepancy at every step. This is accomplished by maximizing the smallest p-value at each step.[12] Because Genetic Matching is minimizing the maximum discrepancy observed at each step, it is minimizing the infinity norm. This property holds even

---

[9] The Cholesky decomposition is parameterized such that $S = LL'$, $S^{1/2} = L$. In other words, L is a lower triangular matrix with positive diagonal elements.

[10] Technically, the other variables will be given weights just large enough to ensure that the weight matrix is positive definite.

[11] See <http://sekhon.berkeley.edu/matching>.

[12] More precisely, lexical optimization will be done: all of the balance statistics will be sorted from the most discrepant to the least and weights will be picked which minimize the maximum discrepancy. If multiple sets of weights result in the same maximum discrepancy, then the second-largest discrepancy is examined to choose the best weights. The process continues iteratively until ties are broken.

when, because of the distribution of X, the EPBR property does not hold. Therefore, if an analyst is concerned that matching may increase the bias in some linear combination of X even if the means are reduced, Genetic Matching allows the analyst to put in the loss function all of the linear combinations of X which may be of concern. Indeed, any nonlinear function of X can also be included in the loss function, which would ensure that bias in some nonlinear functions of X is not made inordinately large by matching.

The default Genetic Matching loss function does allow for imbalance in functions of X to worsen as long as the maximum discrepancy is reduced. This default behavior can be altered by the analyst. It is important that the maximum discrepancy be small—i.e. that the smallest p-value be large. The p-values conventionally understood to signal balance (e.g. 0.10) may be too low to produce reliable estimates. After Genetic Matching optimization, the p-values from these balance tests cannot be interpreted as true probabilities because of standard pre-test problems, but they remain useful measures of balance. Also, we are interested in maximizing the balance in the current sample so a hypothesis test for balance is inappropriate.

The optimization problem described above is difficult and irregular, and the genetic algorithm implemented in the R rgenoud package (Mebane and Sekhon 1998) is used to conduct the optimization. Details of the algorithm are provided in Sekhon and Mebane (1998).

Genetic Matching is shown to have better properties than the usual alternative matching methods both when the EPBR property holds and when it does not (Sekhon 2008; Diamond and Sekhon 2005). Even when the EPBR property holds and the mapping from X to Y is linear, Genetic Matching has better efficiency—i.e. lower mean squared error (MSE)—in finite samples. When the EPBR property does not hold, as it generally does not, Genetic Matching retains appealing properties and the differences in performance between Genetic Matching and the other matching methods can become substantial in terms of both bias and MSE reduction. In short, at the expense of computer time, Genetic Matching dominates the other matching methods in terms of MSE when assumptions required for EPBR hold and, even more so, when they do not.

Genetic Matching is able to retain good properties even when EPBR does not hold because a set of constraints is imposed by the loss function optimized by the genetic algorithm. The loss function depends on a large number of functions of covariate imbalance across matched treatment and control groups. Given these measures, Genetic Matching will optimize covariate balance.

3 CASE-STUDY RESEARCH METHODS

Matching designs have long been used by social scientists conducting qualitative research methods. But case-study matching methods often rely on the assumption that the relationships between the variables of interest are deterministic. This is unfortunate because failure to heed the lessons of statistical inference often leads to serious inferential errors, some of which are easy to avoid. The canonical example of deterministic matching designs methods is the set of rules (canons) of inductive inference formalized by John Stuart Mill in his *A System of Logic* (1872).

The "most similar" and the "most different" research designs, which are often used in comparative politics, are variants of Mill's methods (Przeworski and Teune 1970). As such, Mill's methods have been used by generations of social science researchers (Cohen and Nagel 1934), but they contrast sharply with statistical methods. These methods do not lead to valid inductive inferences unless a number of very special assumptions hold. Some researchers seem to be either unaware or unconvinced of these methodological difficulties even though the acknowledged originator of the methods, Mill himself, clearly described many of their limitations.

These canonical qualitative methods of causal inference are only valid when the hypothesized relationship between the cause and effect of interest is *unique* and *deterministic*. These two conditions imply other conditions such as the absence of measurement error which would cease to make the hypothesized causal relationship deterministic at least as we observe it. These assumptions are strict, and they strongly restrict the applicability of the methods. When these methods of inductive inference are not applicable, conditional probabilities should be used to compare the relevant counterfactuals.[13]

For these methods to lead to valid inferences there must be only one possible cause of the effect of interest, the relationship between cause and effect must be deterministic, and there must be no measurement error. If these assumptions are to be relaxed, random factors must be accounted for. Because of these random factors, statistical and probabilistic methods of inference are necessary.

To appreciate how serious these limitations are, consider the case of benchmarking statistical software on modern computer systems—for details see Sekhon (2006). Such computers are Turing machines, hence they are deterministic systems where everything a computer does is in theory observable. To put it another way, your random number generator is not really random. Your pseudorandom numbers are the result of a deterministic algorithm. But notwithstanding the deterministic nature of a computer, methods like those proposed by qualitative researchers for making inferences with deterministic systems are not used in the benchmarking literature. When benchmarking, it is common to match on (and hence eliminate) as many confounders as possible and to report measures of uncertainty and statistical hypothesis tests. Since computers are deterministic, the remaining uncertainty must come from confounders—as opposed to sampling error—which could in theory be observed and hence eliminated. But the system is considered to be so complex that most

---

[13] Needless to say, although Mill was familiar with the work of Laplace and other nineteenth-century statisticians, by today's standards his understanding of estimation and hypothesis testing was simplistic and often erroneous. He did, however, understand that if one wants to make valid empirical inferences, one needs to obtain and compare conditional probabilities when there may be more than one possible cause of an effect or when the causal relationship is complicated by interaction effects.

benchmarking exercises resort to statistical measures of association. Thus, even in this setting where we know we are dealing with a deterministic system, benchmarking exercises rely on statistical measures because of the complexity involved. Certainly society is more complex than a computer, and our social measurements are more prone to error than those of computers.

3.1 Mill's Methods and Conditional Probabilities

Since the application of the five methods Mill discusses has a long history in the social sciences, I am hardly the first to criticize the use of these methods in all but very special circumstances. For example, Robinson, who is well known in political science for his work on the ecological inference problem,[14] also criticized the use of Mill-type methods of analytic induction in the social sciences (Robinson 1951). Robinson's critique did not, however, focus on conditional probabilities nor did he observe that Mill himself railed against the exact use to which his methods have been put. Many other critics will be encountered in the course of our discussion.

Przeworski and Teune, in an influential book, advocate the use of what they call the "most similar" design and the "most different" design (Przeworski and Teune 1970). These designs are variations on Mill's methods. The first is a version of Mill's Method of Agreement, and the second is a *weak* version of Mill's Method of Difference. Although the Przeworski and Teune volume is over thirty years old, their argument continues to be influential. For example, Ragin, Berg-Schlosser, and de Meur in a recent review of qualitative methods make direct supportive references to both Mill's methods and Przeworski and Teune's formulations (Ragin, Berg-Schlosser, and de Meur 1996). However, even when authors such as Ragin et al. recognize that Mill's methods need to be altered for use in the social sciences, they usually follow neither the advice of quantitative methodologists nor Mill's own advice regarding the use of conditional probabilities.[15]

Mill described his views on scientific investigations in *A System of Logic Ratiocinative and Inductive*, first published in 1843.[16] In an often cited chapter (bk. III, ch. 8), Mill formulates five guiding methods of induction: the Method of Agreement, the Method of Difference, the Double Method of Agreement and Difference (also known as the Indirect Method of Difference), the Method of Residues, and the Method of Concomitant Variations. These methods are often counted to be only four because the Double Method of Agreement and Difference may be considered to be just a derivative of the first two methods. This is a mistake because it obscures the tremendous difference between the combined method or what Mill calls the Indirect

---

[14] Ecological inferences are inferences about individual behavior which are based on data of group behavior, called aggregate or ecological data.

[15] For details on the relationship between qualitative comparative analysis and standard regression see Seawright (2004).

[16] For all page referencing I have used a reprint of the eighth edition of *A System of Logic Ratiocinative and Inductive*, first published in 1872. The eighth edition was the last printed in Mill's lifetime. The eighth and third editions were especially revised and supplemented with new material.

Method of Difference and the Direct Method of Difference (Mill 1872, 259). Both the Method of Agreement and the Indirect Method of Difference, which is actually the Method of Agreement applied twice, are limited and require the machinery of probability in order to take chance into account when considering cases where the number of causes may be greater than one or where there may be interactions between the causes (Mill 1872, 344). Other factors not well explored by Mill, such as measurement error, lead to the same conclusion (Lieberson 1991). The Direct Method of Difference is almost entirely limited to the experimental setting. And even in the case of the Direct Method of Difference, chance must be taken into account in the presence of measurement error or if there are interactions between causes which lead to probabilistic relationships between a cause, A, and its effect, a.

Next, we review Mill's first three canons and show the importance of taking chance into account and comparing conditional probabilities when chance variations cannot be ignored.

3.1.1 *First Canon: Method of Agreement*

If two or more instances of the phenomenon under investigation have only one circumstance in common, the circumstance in which alone all the instances agree is the cause (or effect) of the given phenomenon.   (Mill 1872, 255)

Assume that the *possible* causes, i.e. antecedents, under consideration are denoted by A, B, C, D, E, and the effect we are interested in is denoted by a.[17] An antecedent may comprise more than one constituent event or condition. For example, permanganate ion with oxalic acid forms carbon dioxide (and manganous ion). Separately, neither permanganate ion nor oxalic acid will produce carbon dioxide; but if combined, they will. In this example, A may be defined as the presence of both permanganate ion and oxalic acid.

Let us further assume that we observe two instances and in the first we observe the antecedents A, B, C, and in the second we observe the antecedents A, D, E. If we also observe the effect, a, in both cases, we would say, following Mill's Method of Agreement, that A is the cause of a. We conclude this because A was the only antecedent which occurred in both observations—i.e. the observations agree on the presence of antecedent A. This method has eliminated antecedents B, C, D, E as possible causes of a. Using this method, we endeavor to obtain observations which agree in the effect, a, and the supposed cause, A, but differ in the presence of other antecedents.

3.1.2 *Second Canon: Method of Difference*

If an instance in which the phenomenon under investigation occurs, and an instance in which it does not occur, have every circumstance in common save one, that one occurring only in the former; the circumstance in which alone the two instances differ is the effect, or the cause, or an indispensable part of the cause, of the phenomenon.   (Mill 1872, 256)

---

[17]   Following Mill's usage, my usage of the word "antecedent" is synonymous with "possible cause." Neither Mill nor I intends to imply that events *must* be ordered in time to be causally related.

In the Method of Difference we require, contrary to the Method of Agreement, observations resembling one another in every other respect, but differing in the presence or absence of the antecedent we conjecture to be the true cause of a. If our object is to discover the effects of an antecedent A, we must introduce A into some set of circumstances we consider relevant, such as B, C, and having noted the effects produced, compare them with the effects of the remaining circumstances B, C, when A is absent. If the effect of A, B, C is a, b, c, and the effect of B, C is b, c, it is evident, under this argument, that the cause of a is A.

Both of these methods are based on a process of elimination. This process has been understood since Francis Bacon to be a centerpiece of inductive reasoning (Pledge 1939). The Method of Agreement is supported by the argument that whatever can be eliminated is not connected with the phenomenon of interest, a. The Method of Difference is supported by the argument that whatever cannot be eliminated is connected with the phenomenon by a law. Because both methods are based on the process of elimination, they are deterministic in nature. For if even one case is observed where effect a occurs without the presence of antecedent A, we would eliminate antecedent A from causal consideration.

Mill asserts that the Method of Difference is commonly used in experimental science while the Method of Agreement, which is substantially weaker, is employed when experimentation is impossible (Mill 1872, 256). The Method of Difference is Mill's attempt to describe the inductive logic of experimental design. And the method takes into account two of the key features of experimental design, the first being the presence of a manipulation (treatment) and the second a comparison between two states of the world which are in Mill's case exactly alike aside from the presence of the antecedent of interest.[18] The method also incorporates the notion of a relative causal effect. The effect of antecedent A is measured relative to the effect observed in the most similar world without A. The two states of the world we are considering only differ in the presence or absence of A.

The Method of Difference only accurately describes a small subset of experiments. The method is too restrictive even if the relationship between the antecedent A and effect a were to be deterministic. Today we would say that the control group B, C and the group with the intervention A, B, C need not be *exactly* alike (aside from the presence or absence of A). It would be fantastic if the two groups were exactly alike, but such a situation is not only extremely difficult to find but also not necessary. Some laboratory experiments are based on this strong assumption, but a more common assumption, and one which brings in statistical concerns, is that observations in both groups are *balanced* before our intervention. That is, before we apply the treatment, the distributions of both observed and unobserved variables in both groups are equal. For example, if group A is the southern states in the United States and group B is the

---

[18] The requirement of a manipulation by the researcher has troubled many philosophers of science. But the claim is not that causality requires a human manipulation, but only that if we wish to measure the effect of a given antecedent we gain much if we are able to manipulate the antecedent. For example, manipulation of the antecedent of interest allows us to be confident that the antecedent caused the effect and not the other way around—see Brady (this volume).

northern states, the two groups are not balanced. The distribution of a long list of variables is different between the two groups.

Random assignment of treatment ensures, if the sample size is large and if other assumptions are met, that the control and treatment groups are balanced even on un-observed variables.[19] Random assignment ensures that the treatment is uncorrelated with all baseline variables[20] whether we can observe them or not.[21]

Because of its reliance on random assignment, modern concepts of experimental design sharply diverge from Mill's deterministic model. The two groups are not exactly alike in baseline characteristics (as they would have to be in a deterministic setup), but instead, their baseline characteristics have the same distribution. And consequently the baseline variables are uncorrelated with whether a particular unit received treatment or not.

When the balance assumption is satisfied, a modern experimenter estimates the relative causal effect by comparing the conditional probability of some outcome given the treatment minus the conditional probability of the outcome given that the treatment was not received. In the canonical experimental setting, conditional probabilities can be directly interpreted as causal effects.

In the penultimate section of this chapter, I discuss the complications which arise in using conditional probabilities to make causal inferences when randomization of treatment is not possible. With observational data (i.e. data found in nature and not a product of experimental manipulation), many complications arise which prevent conditional probabilities from being directly interpreted as estimates of causal effects. Problems also often arise with experiments which prevent the simple conditional probabilities from being interpreted as relative causal effects. School voucher experiments are a good example.[22] But the problems are more serious with observational data where neither a manipulation nor balance are present.[23]

One of the continuing appeals of deterministic methods for case-study researchers is the power of the methods. For example, Mill's Method of Difference can determine causality with only two observations. This power can only be obtained by assuming that the observation with the antecedent of interest, A, B, C, and the one without, B, C, are exactly alike except for the manipulation of A, and by assuming

---

[19]   Aside from a large sample size, experiments need to also meet a number of other conditions. See Campbell and Stanley (1966) for an overview particularly relevant for the social sciences. An important problem with experiments dealing with human beings is the issue of compliance. Full compliance implies that every person assigned to treatment actually receives the treatment and every person assigned to control does not. Fortunately, if noncompliance is an issue, there are a number of possible corrections which make few and reasonable assumptions—see Barnard et al. (2003).

[20]   Baseline variables are the variables observed before treatment is applied.

[21]   More formally, random assignment results in the treatment being stochastically independent of all baseline variables as long as the sample size is large and other assumptions are satisfied.

[22]   Barnard et al. (2003) discuss in detail a broken school voucher experiment and a correction using stratification.

[23]   In an experiment much can go wrong (e.g. compliance and missing data problems), but the fact that there was a manipulation can be very helpful in correcting the problems—Barnard et al. (2003). Corrections are more problematic in the absence of an experimental manipulation because additional assumptions are required.

deterministic causation and the absence of measurement error and interactions among antecedents. This power makes deterministic methods alluring for case-study researchers, who generally don't have many observations. Once probabilistic factors are introduced, larger numbers of observations are required to make useful inferences. Because of the power of deterministic methods, social scientists with a small number of observations are tempted to rely on Mill's methods. Because these researchers cannot conduct experiments, they largely rely on the Method of Agreement, which we have discussed, and Mill's third canon.

3.1.3 Third Canon: Indirect Method of Difference

If two or more instances in which the phenomenon occurs have only one circumstance in common, while two or more instances in which it does not occur have nothing in common save the absence of that circumstance, the circumstance in which alone the two sets of instances differ is the effect, or the cause, or an indispensable part of the cause, of the phenomenon.

(Mill 1872, 259)

This method arises by a "double employment of the Method of Agreement" (Mill 1872, 258). If we observe a set of observations in all of which we observe a and note that they have no antecedent in common but A, by the Method of Agreement we have evidence that A is the cause of the effect a. Ideally, we would then perform an experiment where we manipulate A to see if the effect a is present when the antecedent A is absent. When we cannot conduct such an experiment, we can instead use the Method of Agreement again. Suppose we can find another set of observations in which neither the antecedent A nor the effect a occur. We may now conclude, by use of the Indirect Method of Difference, that A is the cause of a. Thus, by twice using the Method of Agreement we may hope to establish both the positive and negative instance which the Method of Difference requires. However, this double use of the Method of Agreement is clearly inferior. The Indirect Method of Difference cannot fulfill the requirements of the Direct Method of Difference. For, "the requisitions of the Method of Difference are not satisfied unless we can be quite sure either that the instances affirmative of a agree in no antecedents whatever but A, or that the instances negative of a agree in nothing but the negation of A" (Mill 1872, 259). In other words, the Direct Method of Difference is the superior method because it entails a strong manipulation: We manipulate the antecedents so that we can remove the suspected cause, A, and then put it back at will, without disturbing the balance of what may lead to a. And this manipulation ensures that the only difference in the antecedents between the two observations is the presence of A or its lack.

Researchers are often unclear about these distinctions between the indirect and direct methods of difference. They often simply state they are using the Method of Difference when they are actually only using the Indirect Method of Difference. For example, Skocpol states that she is using both the Method of Agreement and the "more powerful" Method of Difference when she is only using at best the weaker Method of Agreement twice (Skocpol 1979, 36–7). It is understandable that Skocpol is not able to use the Direct Method of Difference since it would be impossible to manipulate the factors of interest. But it is important to be clear about exactly which method one is using.

Mill discusses two other canons: the Method of Residues (Fourth Canon) and the Method of Concomitant Variations (Fifth Canon). We do not review these canons because they are not directly relevant to our discussion.

We have so far outlined the three methods of Mill with which we are concerned. We have also shown that when scholars such as Skocpol assert that they are using the Method of Agreement and the Method of Difference (Skocpol 1979, 37), they are actually using the Indirect Method of Difference, and that this is indeed the weaker sibling of the Direct Method of Difference. This weakness would not be of much concern if the phenomena we studied were simple. However, in the social sciences we encounter serious causal complexities.

Mill's methods of inductive inference are valid only if the mapping between antecedents and effects is *unique* and *deterministic* (Mill 1872, 285–99, 344–50). These conditions allow neither for more than one cause for an effect nor for interactions between causes. In other words, if we are interested in effect *a*, we must assume a priori that only one possible cause exists for *a* and that when *a*'s cause is present, say cause *A*, the effect, *a*, must *always* occur. In fact, these two conditions, of uniqueness and determinism, define the set of antecedents we are considering. This implies, for example, that the elements in the set of causes *A*, *B*, *C*, *D*, *E* must be able to occur independently of each other. The condition is not that antecedents must be independent in the probabilistic sense of the word, but that any one of the antecedents can occur without necessitating the presence or lack thereof of any of the other antecedents. Otherwise, the possible effects of antecedents are impossible to distinguish by these rules.[24] Generalizations of Mill's methods also suffer from these limitations (Little 1998, 221–3).

The foregoing has a number of implications, the most important of which is that for deterministic methods such as Mill's to work there must be no measurement error. For even if there were a deterministic relationship between antecedent *A* and effect *a*, if we were able to measure either *A* or *a* only with some stochastic error, the resulting observed relationship would be probabilistic. It would be probabilistic because it would be possible to observe a case in which we mistakenly think we have observed antecedent *A* (because of measurement error) while not observing *a*. In such a situation the process of elimination would lead us to conclude that *A* is not a cause of *a*.

To my knowledge no modern social scientist argues that the conditions of uniqueness and lack of measurement error hold in the social sciences. However, the question of whether deterministic causation is plausible has a sizeable literature.[25] Most of

---

[24] Mill's methods have additional limitations which are outside the scope of this discussion. For example, there is a set of conditions, call it *Z*, which always exists but is unconnected with the phenomenon of interest. For example, the star Sirius is always present (but not always observable) whenever it rains in Boston. Is the star Sirius and its gravitational force causally related to rain in Boston? Significant issues arise from this question which I do not discuss.

[25] See Waldner (2002) for an overview.

this discussion centers on whether deterministic relationships are possible—i.e. on the ontological status of deterministic causation.[26] Although such discussions can be fruitful, we need not decide the ontological issues in order to make empirical progress. This is fortunate because the ontological issues are at best difficult and may be impossible to resolve. Even if one concedes that deterministic social associations exist, it is unclear how we would ever learn about them if there are multiple causes with complex interactions or if our measures are noisy. The case of multiple causes and complex interactions among deterministic associations would, to us, look probabilistic in the absence of a theory (and measurements) which accurately accounted for the complicated causal mechanisms—e.g. Little (1998, ch. 11). There appears to be some agreement among qualitative and quantitative researchers that there is "complexity-induced probabilism" (Bennett 1998). Thus, I think it is more fruitful to focus instead on the practical issue of how we learn about causes—i.e. on the epistemological issues related to causality.[27]

Focusing on epistemological issues also helps to avoid some thorny philosophical questions regarding the ontological status of probabilistic notions of causality. For example, if one can accurately estimate the probability distribution of A causing a, does that mean that we can explain any particular occurrence of a? Wesley Salmon, after surveying three prominent theories of probabilistic causality in the mid-1980s, noted that "the primary moral I drew was that causal concepts cannot be fully explicated in terms of statistical relationships; in addition, I concluded, we need to appeal to causal processes and causal interactions" (Salmon 1989, 168). I do not think these metaphysical issues ought to concern practicing scientists.

Faced with multiple causes and interactions, what is one to do? There are two dominant responses. The first relies on detailed (usually formal) theories which make precise empirical predictions which distinguish between the theories. Such theories are usually tested by laboratory experiments with such strong manipulations and careful controls that one may reasonably claim to have obtained exact balance and the practical absence of measurement error. Such manipulations and controls allow one to use generalizations of the Method of Difference. A large number of theories in physics offer canonical examples of this approach. Deduction plays a prominent role in this approach.[28]

The second response relies on conditional probabilities and counterfactuals. These responses are not mutually exclusive. Economics, for example, is a field which relies heavily on both formal theories and statistical empirical tests. Indeed, unless the proposed formal theories are nearly complete, there will always be a need to take random factors into account. And even the most ambitious formal modeler will no

---

[26] Ontology is the branch of philosophy concerned with the study of existence itself.

[27] Epistemology is the branch of philosophy concerned with the theory of knowledge, in particular the nature and derivation of knowledge, its scope, and the reliability of claims to knowledge.

[28] Mill places great importance on deduction in the three-step process of "induction, ratiocination, and verification" (Mill 1872, 304). But on the whole, although the term *ratiocinative* is in the title of Mill's treatise and even appears before the term *inductive*, Mill devotes little space to the issue of deductive reasoning.

doubt concede that a complete deductive theory of politics is probably impossible. Given that our theories are weak, our causes complex, and data noisy, we cannot avoid conditional probabilities. Even researchers sympathetic to finding necessary or sufficient causes are often led to probability given these problems (e.g. Ragin 2000).

4 FROM CONDITIONAL PROBABILITIES TO COUNTERFACTUALS

Although conditional probability is at the heart of inductive inference, by itself it isn't enough. Underlying conditional probability is a notion of counterfactual inference. It is possible to have a causal theory that makes no reference to counterfactuals (Brady, this volume; Dawid 2000), but counterfactual theories of causality are by far the norm, especially in statistics. The Method of Difference is motivated by a counterfactual notion: I would like to see what happens both with antecedent A and without A. When I use the Method of Difference, I don't conjecture what would happen if A were absent. I remove A and actually see what happens. Implementation of the method obviously depends on a manipulation. Although manipulation is an important component of experimental research, manipulations as precise as those entailed by the Method of Difference are not possible in the social sciences in particular and with field experiments in general.

We have to depend on other means to obtain information about what would occur both if A is present and if A is not. In many fields, a common alternative to the Method of Difference is a randomized experiment. For example, we could either contact Jane to prompt her to vote as part of a turnout study or we could not contact her. But we cannot observe what would happen if we both contacted Jane and if we did not contact Jane—i.e. we cannot observe Jane's behavior both with and without the treatment. If we contact Jane, in order to determine what effect this treatment had on Jane's behavior (i.e. whether she voted or not), we still have to obtain some estimate of the counterfactual in which we did not contact Jane. We could, for example, seek to compare Jane's behavior with someone exactly like Jane whom we did not contact. The reality, however, is that there is no one exactly like Jane with whom we can compare Jane's turnout decision. Instead, in a randomized experiment we obtain a group of people (the larger the better) and we assign treatment to a randomly chosen subset (to contact) and we assign the remainder to the control group (not to be contacted). We then observe the difference in turnout rates between the two groups and we attribute any differences to our treatment.

In principle the process of random assignment results in the observed and unobserved baseline variables of the two groups being balanced.[29] In the simplest setup,

---

[29] This occurs with arbitrarily high probability as the sample size grows.

individuals in both groups are supposed to be equally likely to receive the treatment, and hence assignment to treatment will not be associated with anything which may also affect one's propensity to vote. In an observational setting, unless something special is done, the treatment and nontreatment groups are almost never balanced.

The core counterfactual motivation is often forgotten when researchers estimate conditional probabilities to make causal inferences. This situation often arises when quantitative scholars attempt to estimate partial effects.[30] On many occasions the researcher estimates a regression and interprets each of the regression coefficients as estimates of causal effects holding all of the other variables in the model constant. For many in the late nineteenth and early twentieth centuries, this was the goal of the use of regression in the social sciences. The regression model was to give the social scientist the control over data which the physicist obtained via precise formal theories and the biologist obtained via experiments. Unfortunately, if one's covariates are correlated with each other (as they almost always are), interpreting regression coefficients to be estimates of partial causal effects is simply asking too much from the model. With correlated covariates, one variable (such as race) does not move independently of other covariates (such as income, education, and neighborhood). With such correlations, it is difficult to posit interesting counterfactuals of which a single regression coefficient is a good estimate.

A good example of these issues is offered by the literatures which developed in the aftermath of the 2000 presidential election. A number of scholars try to estimate the relationship between the race of a voter and uncounted ballots. Ballots are uncounted either because the ballots contain no votes (undervotes) or overvotes (more than the legal number of votes).[31] If one were able to estimate a regression model, for example, which showed that there was no relationship between the race of a voter and her probability of casting uncounted ballots when and only when one controlled for a long list of covariates, it would be unclear what one has found. This uncertainty holds even if ecological and a host of other problems are pushed aside because such a regression model may not allow one to answer the counterfactual question of interest—i.e. "if a black voter became white, would this increase or decrease her chance of casting an uncounted ballot?" What does it mean to change a voter from black to white? Given the data, it is not plausible that changing a voter from black to white would have no implications for the individual's income, education, or neighborhood of residence. It is difficult to conceptualize a serious counterfactual for which this regression result is relevant. Before any regression is estimated, we know that if we measure enough variables well, the race variable itself in 2000 will be insignificant. But in a world where being black is highly correlated with socioeconomic variables, it is not clear what we learn about the causality of ballot problems from a showing that the race coefficient itself can be made insignificant.

There are no general solutions or methods which ensure that the statistical quantities we estimate provide useful information about the counterfactuals of interest.

---

[30] A partial effect is the effect a given antecedent has on the outcome variable net of all the other antecedents—i.e. when all of the other variables "are held constant."

[31] See Herron and Sekhon (2003; 2005) for a review of the literature and relevant empirical analysis.

The solution, which almost always relies on research design and statistical methods, depends on the precise research question under consideration. But all too often the problem is ignored. All too often the regression coefficient itself is considered to be an estimate of the partial causal effect. Estimates of conditional means and probabilities are an important component of establishing causal effects, but are not enough. One has to establish the relationship between the counterfactuals of interest and the conditional probabilities one has managed to estimate.

A large number of other issues are also important when one is examining the quality of the conditional probabilities one has estimated. A prominent example is the extent to which one can combine a given collection of observations. The combining of observations which are actually rather different is one of the standard objections to statistical analysis. But the question of when and how one can legitimately combine observations is and has long been one of the central research questions in statistics. In fact, the original purpose of least squares was to give astronomers a way of combining and weighting their discrepant observations in order to obtain better estimates of the locations and motions of celestial objects (Stigler 1986). Generally used methods, such as robust estimation, still require that the model for combining observations is correct for most of the sample under consideration so they do not get to the heart of the problem (e.g. Bartels 1996; Mebane and Sekhon 2004). This is a subject that political scientists need to pay more attention to.

5   DISCUSSION

....

This chapter has by no means offered a complete discussion of causality and all one has to do in order to demonstrate a causal relationship. There is much more to this than just conditional probabilities and even counterfactuals. For example, it is often important to find the causal mechanism at work, in the sense of understanding the sequence of events which lead from A to a. And I agree with qualitative researchers that case studies are particularly helpful in learning about such mechanisms. Process tracing is often cited as being particularly useful in this regard.[32]

The importance of searching for causal mechanisms is often overestimated by political scientists and this sometimes leads to an underestimate of the importance of comparing conditional probabilities. We do not need to have much or any knowledge about mechanisms in order to know that a causal relationship exists. For example, by the use of rudimentary experiments, aspirin has been known to help with pain since Felix Hoffmann synthesized a stable form of acetylsalicylic acid in 1897. In fact, the bark and leaves of the willow tree (rich in the substance called salicin) have been known to help alleviate pain at least since the time of Hippocrates. But the causal mechanism by which aspirin alleviates pain was a mystery until recently. Only in 1971

---

[32] Process tracing is the enterprise of using narrative and other qualitative methods to determine the mechanisms by which a particular antecedent produces its effects—see George and McKeown (1985).

did John Vane discover aspirin's biological mechanism of action.[33] And even now, although we know how it crosses the blood–brain barrier, we have little idea how the chemical changes in the brain due to aspirin get translated into the conscious feeling of pain relief—after all, the mind–body problem has not been solved. But knowledge of causal mechanisms is important and useful and no causal account can be considered complete without a mechanism being demonstrated or at the very least hypothesized.

The search for causal mechanisms is probably especially useful when working with observational data. But it is still not necessary. In the case of the causal relationship between smoking and cancer, human experiments were not possible yet most (but not all) neutral researchers were convinced of the causal relationship well before the biological mechanisms were known.[34]

In clinical medicine case studies continue to contribute valuable knowledge even though large-N statistical research dominates. Although the coexistence is sometimes uneasy, as noted by the rise of clinical outcomes research, it is nevertheless extremely fruitful and more cooperative than the relationship in political science.[35] One reason for this is that in clinical medicine, researchers reporting cases more readily acknowledge that the statistical framework helps to provide information about when and where cases are informative (Vandenbroucke 2001). Cases can be highly informative when our understanding of the phenomena of interest is very poor, because then we can learn a great deal from a few observations. On the other hand, when our understanding is generally very good, a few cases which combine a set of circumstances that we believed could not exist or, more realistically, were believed to be highly unlikely can alert us to overlooked phenomena. Some observations are more important than others and there sometimes are "critical cases" (Eckstein 1975). This point is not new to qualitative methodologists because there is an implicit (and all too rarely explicit) Bayesianism in their discussion of the relative importance of cases (George and McKeown 1985; McKeown 1999). If one only has a few observations, it is more important than otherwise to pay careful attention to the existing state of knowledge when selecting cases and when deciding how informative they are. In general, as our understanding of an issue improves, individual cases become less important.

The logical fallacy of *cum hoc ergo propter hoc* ("with this, therefore because of this") is committed by social scientists as a matter of course. Looking over a random sample of quantitative articles in the *APSR* over the past thirty years, there appears to be no decline in articles which commit this fallacy. The fallacy is now more often

---

[33] He was awarded the 1982 Nobel Prize for Medicine for this discovery.

[34] R. A. Fisher, one of the fathers of modern statistics and the experimental method, was a notable exception. Without the manipulation offered by an experiment, he remained skeptical. He hypothesized that genetic factors could cause people to both smoke and get cancer, and hence there need not be any causal relationship between smoking and cancer (Fisher 1958a; 1958b).

[35] Returning to the aspirin example, it is interesting to note that Lawrence Craven, a general practitioner, noticed in 1948 that the 400 men he had prescribed aspirin to did not suffer *any* heart attacks. But it was not until 1985 that the US Food and Drug Administration approved the use of aspirin for the purposes of reducing the risk of heart attack. And in 1988 the Physicians' Health Study, a randomized, double-blind, placebo-controlled trial of apparently healthy men, was stopped early because the effectiveness of aspirin had finally been demonstrated (Steering Committee of the Physicians' Health Study Research Group 1989).

committed in a multivariate sense with the use of multiple regression as opposed to correlations or crosstabs. But that does not avoid the problem.

Historically, the matching literature, like much of statistics, has been limited by computational power. What is possible with matching today is nothing like what was possible in 1970 let alone during Mill's time. Not so long ago estimating a logistic regression, the common way today to estimate the propensity score, was prohibitive for all but the smallest of data-sets. Today, as we have seen, we can apply machine learning algorithms to the matching problem. These technical innovations will continue, but history teaches us to be cautious about what the technical advances will bring us. Without a greater focus on experimental research and rigorous observational designs, it is unclear what substantive progress is possible.

APPENDIX A   EQUAL PERCENT BIAS
REDUCTIONS (EPBR)

Affinely invariant matching methods, such as Mahalanobis metric matching and propensity score matching (if the propensity score is estimated by logistic regression), are equal percent bias reducing if all of the covariates used have ellipsoidal distributions (Rubin and Thomas 1992)—e.g. distributions such as the normal or t—or if the covariates are mixtures of proportional ellipsoidally symmetric (DMPES) distributions (Rubin and Stuart 2005).[36]

To formally define EPBR, let Z be the expected value of X in the matched control group. Then, as outlined in Rubin (1976a), a matching procedure is EPBR if

$$E(X \mid T = 1) - Z = \gamma \{E(X \mid T = 1) - E(X \mid T = 0)\}$$

for a scalar $0 \leq \gamma \leq 1$. In other words, we say that a matching method is EPBR for X when the percent reduction in the biases of each of the matching variables is the same. One obtains the same percent reduction in bias for any linear function of X if and only if the matching method is EPBR for X. Moreover, if a matching method is not EPBR for X, the bias for some linear function of X is increased even if all univariate covariate means are closer in the matched data than in the unmatched (Rubin 1976a).

Even if the covariates have elliptic distributions, in finite samples they may not. Then Mahalanobis distance may not be optimal because the matrix used to scale the distances, the covariance matrix of X, can be improved upon.

The EPBR property itself is limited and in a given substantive problem it may not be desirable. This can arise if it is known based on theory that one covariate has a large nonlinear relationship with the outcome while another does not—e.g. $Y = X_1^4 + X_2$, where $X_1 > 1$. In such a case, reducing bias in X_1 will be more important than X_2.

---

[36] Note that DMPES defines a limited set of mixtures. In particular, countably infinite mixtures of ellipsoidal distributions (1) where all inner products are proportional and (2) where the centers of each constituent ellipsoidal distribution are such that all best linear discriminants between any two components are also proportional.

References

ABADIE, A. 2002. Bootstrap tests for distributional treatment effect in instrumental variable models. *Journal of the American Statistical Association*, 97: 284–92.

—— and IMBENS, G. 2006. Large sample properties of matching estimators for average treatment effects. *Econometrica*, 74: 235–67.

BARNARD, J., FRANGAKIS, C. E., HILL, J. L., and RUBIN, D. B. 2003. Principal stratification approach to broken randomized experiments: a case study of school choice vouchers in New York City. *Journal of the American Statistical Association*, 98: 299–323.

BARTELS, L. 1996. Pooling disparate observations. *American Journal of Political Science*, 40: 905–42.

BENNETT, A. 1998. Causal inference in case studies: from Mill's methods to causal mechanisms. Presented at the annual meeting of the American Political Science Association, Atlanta.

BONNEY, J., and MINOZZI, B. C.-W. W. 2007. Issue accountability and the mass public: the electoral consequences of legislative voting on crime policy. Working paper.

BOWERS, J., and HANSEN, B. 2005. Attributing effects to a get-out-the-vote campaign using full matching and randomization inference. Working paper.

BRADY, H., and HUI, I. 2006. Is it worth going the extra mile to improve causal inference? Presented at the 23rd Annual Summer Meeting of the Society of Political Methodology.

CAMPBELL, D. T., and STANLEY, J. C. 1966. *Experimental and Quasi-Experimental Designs for Research*. Boston: Houghton Mifflin.

CHRISTAKIS, N. A., and IWASHYNA, T. I. 2003. The health impact of health care on families: a matched cohort study of hospice use by decedents and mortality outcomes in surviving, widowed spouses. *Social Science and Medicine*, 57: 465–75.

COCHRAN, W. G. 1953. Matching in analytical studies. *American Journal of Public Health*, 43: 684–91.

—— 1965. The planning of observational studies of human populations (with discussion). *Journal of the Royal Statistical Society, Series A*, 128: 234–55.

—— and RUBIN, D. B. 1973. Controlling bias in observational studies: a review. *Sankhyā, Ser. A*, 35: 417–46.

COHEN, M., and NAGEL, E. 1934. *An Introduction to Logic and Scientific Method*. New York: Harcourt, Brace.

COX, D. R. 1958. *Planning of Experiments*. New York: Wiley.

CRUMP, R. K., HOTZ, V. J., IMBENS, G. W., and MITNIK, O. A. 2006. Moving the goalposts: addressing limited overlap in estimation of average treatment effects by changing the estimand. Working paper.

DAWID, A. P. 1979. Conditional independence in statistical theory. *Journal of the Royal Statistical Society, Series B*, 41: 1–31.

—— 2000. Causal inference without counterfactuals (with discussion). *Journal of the American Statistical Association*, 95: 407–24.

DEHEJIA, R. 2005. Practical propensity score matching: a reply to Smith and Todd. *Journal of Econometrics*, 125: 355–64.

—— and WAHBA, S. 1997. Causal effects in non-experimental studies: re-evaluating the evaluation of training programs. Ph.D. dissertation, Harvard University.

—— —— 1999. Causal effects in non-experimental studies: re-evaluating the evaluation of training programs. *Journal of the American Statistical Association*, 94: 1053–62.

DEHEJIA, R., and WAHBA, S. 2002. Propensity score matching methods for nonexperimental causal studies. *Review of Economics and Statistics*, 84: 151–61.

DIAMOND, A., and SEKHON, J. S. 2005. Genetic matching for estimating causal effects: a general multivariate matching method for achieving balance in observational studies. <http://sekhon.berkeley.edu/papers/GenMatch.pdf>

DIPRETE, T. A., and ENGELHARDT, H. 2004. Estimating causal effects with matching methods in the presence and absence of bias cancellation. *Sociological Methods and Research*, 32: 501–28.

DORN, H. F. 1953. Philosophy of inference from retrospective studies. *American Journal of Public Health*, 43: 692–9.

ECKSTEIN, H. 1975. Case study and theory in political science. Pp. 79–137 in *Handbook of Political Science*, vii: *Strategies of Inquiry*, ed. F. I. Greenstein and N. W. Polsby. Reading, Mass.: Addison-Wesley.

FECHNER, G. T. 1966 [1860]. *Elements of Psychophysics*, vol i, trans. H. E. Adler, ed. D. H. Howes and E. G. Boring. New York: Rinehart and Winston.

FISHER, R. A. 1958a. Cancer and smoking. *Nature*, 182: 596.

—— 1958b. Lung cancer and cigarettes? *Nature*, 182: 108.

FREEDMAN, D. A. 2008a. On regression adjustments in experiments with several treatments. *Annals of Applied Statistics*, 2: 176–96.

—— 2008b. On regression adjustments to experimental data. *Advances in Applied Mathematics*, 40: 180–93.

GALIANI, S., GERTLER, P., and SCHARGRODSKY, E. 2005. Water for life: the impact of the privatization of water services on child mortality. *Journal of Political Economy*, 113: 83–120.

GEORGE, A. L., and McKEOWN, T. J. 1985. Case studies and theories of organizational decision-making. Pp. 21–58 in *Advances in Information Processing in Organizations*, ed. R. F. Coulam and R. A. Smith, Greenwich, Conn.: JAI Press.

GILLIGAN, M. J., and SERGENTI, E. J. 2006. Evaluating UN peacekeeping with matching to improve causal inference. Working paper.

GORDON, S., and HUBER, G. 2007. The effect of electoral competitiveness on incumbent behavior. *Quarterly Journal of Political Science*, 2: 107–38.

HANSEN, B. B. 2004. Full matching in an observational study of coaching for the SAT. *Journal of the American Statistical Association*, 99: 609–18.

HECKMAN, J. J., ICHIMURA, H., SMITH, J., and TODD, P. 1998. Characterizing selection bias using experimental data. *Econometrica*, 66: 1017–98.

HERRON, M. C., and SEKHON, J. S. 2003. Overvoting and representation: an examination of overvoted presidential ballots in Broward and Miami-Dade Counties. *Electoral Studies*, 22: 21–47.

—— —— 2005. Black candidates and black voters: assessing the impact of candidate race on uncounted vote rates. *Journal of Politics*, 67: 154–77.

—— and WAND, J. Forthcoming. Assessing partisan bias in voting technology: the case of the 2004 New Hampshire recount. *Electoral Studies*.

HILL, B. 1961. *Principles of Medical Statistics*, 7th edn. London: Lancet.

HOLLAND, P. W. 1986. Statistics and causal inference. *Journal of the American Statistical Association*, 81: 945–60.

HORVITZ, D. G., and THOMPSON, D. J. 1952. A generalization of sampling without replacement from a finite universe. *Journal of the American Statistical Association*, 47: 663–85.

IMAI, K. 2005. Do get-out-the-vote calls reduce turnout? The importance of statistical methods for field experiments. *American Political Science Review*, 99: 283–300.

IMBENS, G. W. 2000. The role of the propensity score in estimating dose-response functions. *Biometrika*, 87: 706–10.

LENZ, G. S., and LADD, J. M. 2006. Exploiting a rare shift in communication flows: media effects in the 1997 British election. Working paper.

LIEBERSON, S. 1991. Small N's and big conclusions: an examination of the reasoning in comparative studies based on a small number of cases. *Social Forces*, 70: 307–20.

LITTLE, D. 1998. *Microfoundations, Method, and Causation*. New Brunswick, NJ: Transaction.

McKEOWN, T. J. 1999. Case studies and the statistical worldview: review of King, Keohane, and Verba's *Designing Social Inquiry: Scientific Inference in Qualitative Research*. *International Organization*, 51: 161–90.

MAULDON, J., MALVIN, J., STILES, J., NICOSIA, N., and SETO, E. 2000. Impact of California's Cal-Learn demonstration project: final report. UC DATA Archive and Technical Assistance.

MEBANE, W. R., JR., and SEKHON, J. S. 1998. Genetic optimization using derivatives (GENOUD). Software Package. <http://sekhon.berkeley.edu/rgenoud>

—— —— 2004. Robust estimation and outlier detection for overdispersed multinomial models of count data. *American Journal of Political Science*, 48: 391–410.

MILL, J. S. 1872. *A System of Logic, Ratiocinative and Inductive: Being a Connected View of the Principles of Evidence and the Methods of Scientific Investigation*, 8th edn. London: Longmans, Green.

MITCHELL, A. F. S., and KRZANOWSKI, W. J. 1985. The Mahalanobis distance and elliptic distributions. *Biometrika*, 72: 464–7.

—— —— 1989. Amendments and corrections: the Mahalanobis distance and elliptic distributions. *Biometrika*, 76: 407.

MORGAN, S. L., and HARDING, D. J. 2006. Matching estimators of causal effects: prospects and pitfalls in theory and practice. *Sociological Methods and Research*, 35: 3–60.

NEYMAN, J. 1990 [1923]. On the application of probability theory to agricultural experiments: essay on principles, section 9, trans. D. M. Dabrowska and T. P. Speed. *Statistical Science*, 5: 465–72.

PARK, J. H. 2006. Causal effect of information on voting behavior from a natural experiment: an analysis of candidate blacklisting campaign in 2000 South Korean National Assembly election. Working paper.

PLEDGE, H. T. 1939. *Science since 1500: A Short History of Mathematics, Physics, Chemistry [and] Biology*. London: His Majesty's Stationery Office.

PRZEWORSKI, A., and TEUNE, H. 1970. *The Logic of Comparative Social Inquiry*. New York: Wiley.

RAESSLER, S., and RUBIN, D. B. 2005. Complications when using nonrandomized job training data to draw causal inferences. *Proceedings of the International Statistical Institute*.

RAGIN, C. C. 2000. *Fuzzy-Set Social Science*. Chicago: University of Chicago Press.

—— BERG-SCHLOSSER, D., and DE MEUR, G. 1996. Political methodology: qualitative methods. Pp. 749–68 in *A New Handbook of Political Science*, ed. R. E. Goodin and H.-D. Klingemann. New York: Oxford University Press.

ROBINSON, W. S. 1951. The logical structure of analytic induction. *American Sociological Review*, 16: 812–18.

ROSENBAUM, P. R. 1991. A characterization of optimal designs for observational studies. *Journal of the Royal Statistical Society, Series B*, 53: 597–610.

—— 2002. *Observational Studies*, 2nd edn. New York: Springer-Verlag.

—— 2005. Heterogeneity and causality: unit heterogeneity and design sensitivity in observational studies. *American Statistician*, 59: 147–52.

ROSENBAUM, P. R., and RUBIN, D. B. 1983. The central role of the propensity score in observational studies for causal effects. *Biometrika*, 70: 41–55.

—— —— 1985. Constructing a control group using multivariate matched sampling methods that incorporate the propensity score. *American Statistician*, 39: 33–8.

RUBIN, D. B. 1974. Estimating causal effects of treatments in randomized and nonrandomized studies. *Journal of Educational Psychology*, 66: 688–701.

—— 1976a. Multivariate matching methods that are equal percent bias reducing, I: some examples. *Biometrics*, 32: 109–20.

—— 1976b. Multivariate matching methods that are equal percent bias reducing, II: maximums on bias reduction for fixed sample sizes. *Biometrics*, 32: 121–32.

—— 1977. Assignment to a treatment group on the basis of a covariate. *Journal of Educational Statistics*, 2: 1–26.

—— 1978. Bayesian inference for causal effects: the role of randomization. *Annals of Statistics*, 6: 34–58.

—— 1979. Using multivariate sampling and regression adjustment to control bias in observational studies. *Journal of the American Statistical Association*, 74: 318–28.

—— 1980. Bias reduction using Mahalanobis-metric matching. *Biometrics*, 36: 293–8.

—— 1997. Estimating causal effects from large data sets using propensity scores. *Annals of Internal Medicine*, 127: 757–63.

—— 2001. Using propensity scores to help design observational studies: application to the tobacco litigation. *Health Services and Outcomes Research Methodology*, 2: 169–88.

—— 2006. *Matched Sampling for Causal Effects*. Cambridge: Cambridge University Press.

—— and STUART, E. A. 2005. Affinely invariant matching methods with discriminant mixtures of proportional ellipsoidally symmetric distributions. Working paper.

—— and THOMAS, N. 1992. Affinely invariant matching methods with ellipsoidal distributions. *Annals of Statistics*, 20: 1079–93.

SALMON, W. C. 1989. *Four Decades of Scientific Explanation*. Minneapolis: University of Minnesota Press.

SEAWRIGHT, J. 2004. Qualitative comparative analysis vis-a-vis regression. Presented at the meeting of the American Political Science Association.

SEKHON, J. S. 2004a. Quality meets quantity: case studies, conditional probability and counterfactuals. *Perspectives on Politics*, 2: 281–93.

—— 2004b. The varying role of voter information across democratic societies. Working paper. <http://sekhon.berkeley.edu/papers/SekhonInformation.pdf>

—— 2006. The art of benchmarking: evaluating the performance of R on Linux and OS X. *Political Methodologist*, 14: 15–19.

—— Forthcoming. Multivariate and propensity score matching software with automated balance optimization: the matching package for R. *Journal of Statistical Software*.

—— and MEBANE, W. R., JR. 1998. Genetic optimization using derivatives: theory and application to nonlinear models. *Political Analysis*, 7: 189–203.

SKOCPOL, T. 1979. *States and Social Revolutions: A Comparative Analysis of France, Russia, and China*. Cambridge: Cambridge University Press.

SMITH, H. L. 1997. Matching with multiple controls to estimate treatment effects in observational studies. *Sociological Methodology*, 27: 305–53.

SMITH, J. A., and TODD, P. E. 2001. Reconciling conflicting evidence on the performance of propensity score matching methods. *AEA Papers and Proceedings*, 91: 112–18.

—— —— 2005a. Does matching overcome LaLonde's critique of nonexperimental estimators? *Journal of Econometrics*, 125: 305–53.

—— —— 2005b. Rejoinder. *Journal of Econometrics*, 125: 365–75.

STEERING COMMITTEE OF THE PHYSICIANS' HEALTH STUDY RESEARCH GROUP 1989. Final report on the aspirin component of the ongoing Physicians' Health Study. *New England Journal of Medicine*, 321: 129–35.

STIGLER, S. M. 1986. *The History of Statistics: The Measurement of Uncertainty before 1900.* Cambridge, Mass.: Harvard University Press.

VANDENBROUCKE, J. P. 2001. In defense of case reports and case series. *Annals of Internal Medicine*, 134: 330–4.

WALDNER, D. 2002. Anti anti-determinism: or what happens when Schrödinger's cat and Lorenz's butterfly meet Laplace's Demon in the study of political and economic development. Presented at the Annual Meeting of the American Political Science Association, Boston.

WINSHIP, C., and MORGAN, S. 1999. The estimation of causal effects from observational data. *Annual Review of Sociology*, 25: 659–707.

ON TYPES OF SCIENTIFIC ENQUIRY: THE ROLE OF QUALITATIVE REASONING

DAVID A. FREEDMAN

ONE type of scientific enquiry involves the analysis of large data-sets, often using statistical models and formal tests of hypotheses. A moment's thought, however, shows that there must be other types of scientific enquiry. For instance, something has to be done to answer questions like the following. How should a study be designed? What sorts of data should be collected? What kind of a model is needed? Which hypotheses should be formulated in terms of the model and then tested against the data?

The answers to these questions frequently turn on observations, qualitative or quantitative, that give crucial insights into the causal processes of interest. Such observations generate a line of scientific enquiry, or markedly shift the direction of

David Collier (Berkeley), Thad Dunning (Yale), Paul Humphreys (University of Virginia), Erich Lehmann (Berkeley), and Janet Macher (Berkeley) made many helpful comments.

the enquiry by overturning prior hypotheses, or provide striking evidence to confirm hypotheses. They may well stand on their own rather than being subsumed under the systematic data collection and modeling activities mentioned above.

Such observations have come to be called "Causal Process Observations" (CPOs). These are contrasted with the "Data Set Observations" (DSOs) that are grist for statistical modeling (Brady and Collier 2004). My object in this chapter is to illustrate the role played by CPOs, and qualitative reasoning more generally, in a series of well-known episodes drawn from the history of medicine.

Why is the history of medicine relevant to us today? For one thing, medical researchers frequently confront observational data that present familiar challenges to causal inference. For another, distance lends perspective, allowing gains and losses to be more sharply delineated. The examples show that an impressive degree of rigor can be obtained by combining qualitative reasoning, quantitative analysis, and experiments when those are feasible. The examples also show that great work can be done by spotting anomalies, and trying to understand them.

1 JENNER AND VACCINATION

The setting is the English countryside in the 1790s. Cowpox, as will be clear from the name, is a disease of cows. The symptoms include sores on the teats. Those who milked the cows often became infected, with sores on their hands; by the standards of the time, the illness is rarely serious. In contrast, smallpox is one of the great killers of the eighteenth century.

In 1796, Edward Jenner took some matter from a cowpox sore on the hand of dairymaid Sarah Nelmes, and inserted it into the arm of an eight-year-old boy, "by means of two superficial incisions, barely penetrating the cutis, each about half an inch long." The boy was "perceptibly indisposed" on the ninth day, but recovered the following day. Six weeks later, Jenner inoculated him with matter taken from a smallpox pustule, "but no disease followed" (Jenner 1798, case XVII).

Jenner published twenty-three case studies to demonstrate the safety and efficacy of "vaccination," as his procedure came to be called: *vacca* is the Latin term for cow, and *vaccinia* is another term for cowpox. Despite initial opposition, vaccination became standard practice within a few years, and Jenner achieved international fame. By 1978, smallpox had been eradicated.

What led Jenner to try his experiment? The eighteenth-century view of disease was quite different from ours. The great Scottish doctor of the time, William Cullen, taught that most diseases were "caused by external influences—climate, foodstuffs, effluvia, humidity, and so on—and...the same external factors could cause different diseases in different individuals, depending on the state of the nervous system" (Porter 1997, 262).

Despite such misconceptions, it was known that smallpox could somehow be communicated from one person to another; moreover a person who contracted smallpox and survived was generally immune to the disease from that point on. As a preventive measure, patients could be deliberately infected (through scratches on the skin) with minute quantities of material taken from smallpox pustules, the idea being to induce a mild case of the disease that would confer immunity later.

This procedure was called "inoculation" or "variolation." It was not free of risk: Serious disease was sometimes caused in the patient, and in people who came into contact with the patient (smallpox is highly contagious). On the other hand, failure to inoculate could easily lead to death from smallpox.

By the early part of the eighteenth century, variolation had reached England. Jenner was a country doctor who performed variolations. He paid attention to two crucial facts—although these facts were not explicable in terms of the medical knowledge of his time. (i) People who had the cowpox never seemed to contract smallpox afterwards, whether they had been inoculated or not. (ii) Some of his patients who had been ill with cowpox in the past still wanted to be inoculated. Such patients reacted very little to inoculation:

what renders the Cox-pox virus so extremely singular, is, that the person who has been thus affected is for ever after secure from the infection of the Small Pox; neither exposure to the variolous effluvia, nor the insertion of the matter into the skin, producing this distemper.

(Jenner 1798, 6)

These two facts led him to a hypothesis: Cowpox created immunity against smallpox. That is the hypothesis he tested, observationally and experimentally, as described above. In our terminology, Jenner vaccinated a boy (case XVII) who showed no response to subsequent inoculation. Immunity to smallpox had been induced by the vaccination.

By "virus," Jenner probably meant "contagious matter," that being a standard usage in his time. Viruses in the modern sense were not to be discovered for another century. By a curious twist, smallpox and cowpox are viral diseases in our sense too.

2 SEMMELWEIS AND PUERPERAL FEVER

The time is 1844 and the place is Vienna. The discovery of microbes as the cause of infectious disease will not be made for some decades. Ignac Semmelweis is an obstetrician in the First Division of the Lying-in Hospital, where medical students are trained. (Midwives are trained in the Second Division.) Pregnant women are admitted to one division or the other, according to the day of the week that they come to the hospital, in strict alternation. Mortality from "puerperal fever" is much higher in the First Division (Semmelweis 1981, 356).

Eventually, Semmelweis discovers the cause. The medical students are doing autopsies, and then examining the "puerperae" (women who are giving birth, or who have just given birth). "Cadaveric particles" are thus transferred to the women, creating a blood-borne infection and causing the disease. In 1847, Semmelweis institutes the practice of disinfection, and mortality plummets (Semmelweis 1981, 393–4).

But how did Semmelweis make his discovery? To begin with, he has to reject conventional explanations, including "epidemic influences," which meant something different then:

epidemic influences... are to be understood [as] certain hitherto inexplicable, atmospheric, cosmic, telluric changes, which sometimes disseminate themselves over whole countrysides, and produce childbed fever in individuals predisposed thereto by the puerperal state. ["Telluric" means earthly.] Now, if the atmospheric-cosmic-telluric conditions of the City of Vienna are so disposed that they cause puerperal fever in individuals susceptible thereto as puerperae, how does it happen that these atmospheric-cosmic-telluric conditions over such a long period of years have carried off individuals disposed thereto as puerperae in the First Clinic, while they have so strikingly spared others also in Vienna, even in the same building in the Second Division and similarly vulnerable as puerperae?   (Semmelweis 1981, 357)

The reasoning is qualitative; and similar qualitative arguments dispose of other theories—diet, ventilation, use of hospital linens, and so forth.

Now he has to discover the real cause. In 1847, his revered colleague Professor Kolletschka is accidentally cut with a knife used in a medico-legal autopsy. Kolletschka becomes ill, with symptoms remarkably similar to puerperal fever; then he dies. Again, qualitative analysis is crucial. Close attention to symptoms and their progression is used to identify Kolletschka's illness with puerperal fever (Semmelweis 1981, 391). Tracing of causal processes comes into play as well:

Day and night this picture of Kolletschka's disease pursued me . . . I was obliged to acknowledge the identity of the disease, from which Kolletschka died, with that disease of which I saw so many puerperae die. . . . I must acknowledge, if Kolletschka's disease and the disease from which I saw so many puerperae die, are identical, then in the puerperae it must be produced by the self-same engendering cause, which produced it in Kolletschka. In Kolletschka, the specific agent was cadaveric particles, which were introduced into his vascular system [the bloodstream]. I must ask myself the question: Did the cadaveric particles make their way into the vascular systems of the individuals, whom I had seen die of an identical disease? This question I answer in the affirmative.   (Semmelweis 1981, 391–2)

Once the cause is discovered, the remedy is not far away: Eliminate the cadaveric particles from the hands that will examine the puerperae. Washing with soap and water is insufficient; chlorine compounds are sufficient (Semmelweis 1981, 392–6). The source of the infectious agent could also be a wound in a living person (Semmelweis 1981, 396).

Semmelweis's work was accepted by few of his contemporaries, due in part to his troubled and disputatious personality, although his picture of the disease was essentially correct. Puerperal fever is a generalized infection, typically caused by bacteria in the group *Streptococcus pyogenes*. These bacteria enter the bloodstream through wounds suffered during childbirth (for instance, at the site where the placenta was attached). Puerperal fever can be—and today it generally is—avoided by proper hygiene.

3 Snow and Cholera

John Snow was a physician in Victorian London. In 1854, he demonstrated that cholera was a water-borne infectious disease, which could be prevented by cleaning up the water supply. The demonstration took advantage of a natural experiment. A large area of London was served by two water companies. The Southwark and Vauxhall company distributed contaminated water, and households served by it had a death rate "between eight and nine times as great as in the houses supplied by the Lambeth company," which supplied relatively pure water (Snow 1965, 86, data in table IX).

What led Snow to design the study and undertake the arduous task of data collection? To begin with, he had to reject the explanations of cholera epidemics that were conventional in his time. The predominant theory attributed cholera to "miasmas;" that is, noxious odors—especially odors generated by decaying organic material. Snow makes qualitative arguments against such theories:

[Cholera] travels along the great tracks of human intercourse, never going faster than people travel, and generally much more slowly. In extending to a fresh island or continent, it always appears first at a sea-port. It never attacks the crews of ships going from a country free from cholera, to one where the disease is prevailing, till they have entered a port, or had intercourse with the shore. Its exact progress from town to town cannot always be traced; but it has never appeared except where there has been ample opportunity for it to be conveyed by human intercourse.   (Snow 1965, 2)

These phenomena are easily understood if cholera is an infectious disease, but hard to explain on the miasma theory. Similarly,

The first case of decided Asiatic cholera in London, in the autumn of 1848, was that of a seaman named John Harnold, who had newly arrived by the *Elbe* steamer from Hamburgh, where the disease was prevailing. . . . Now the next case of cholera, in London, occurred in the very room in which the above patient died.   (Snow 1965, 3)

The first case was infected in Hamburgh; the second case was infected by contact with dejecta from the first case, on the bedding or other furnishings in that fatal room. The miasma theory, on the other hand, does not provide good explanations.

Careful observation of the disease led to the conclusion "that cholera invariably commences with the affection of the alimentary canal" (Snow 1965, 10). A living organism enters the body, as a contaminant of water or food, multiplies in the body, and creates the symptoms of the disease. Many copies of the organism are expelled from the body with the dejecta, contaminate the water supply or the food, then infect other victims. The task is now to prove this hypothesis.

According to Sir Benjamin Ward Richardson, who wrote the introduction to Snow's book, the decisive proof came during the Broad Street epidemic of 1854:

> [Snow] had fixed his attention on the Broad Street pump as the source and centre of the calamity. He advised the removal of the pump-handle as the grand prescription. The vestry [in charge of the pump] was incredulous, but had the good sense to carry out the advice. The pump-handle was removed and the plague was stayed.   (Snow 1965, xxxvi)

The pump-handle as the decisive test is a wonderful fable, which has beguiled many a commentator. But there is a real flaw in Richardson's account.

In fact, contamination at the pump did cause the epidemic, Snow recommended closing the pump, his advice was followed, and the epidemic stopped. However, the epidemic was stopping anyway. Closing the pump had no discernible effect: The episode proves little. Snow explains this with great clarity (Snow 1965, 40–55, see esp. table I on p. 49 and the conclusory paragraph on pp. 51–2). Richardson's account is therefore a classic instance of *post hoc, ergo propter hoc.*

The reality is more interesting than the fable. Snow was intimately familiar with the Broad Street area, because of his medical practice. He says,

> As soon as I became acquainted with the situation and extent of this irruption of cholera, I suspected some contamination of the water of the much-frequented street-pump in Broad Street…but on examining the water, on the evening of 3rd September, I found so little impurity in it of an organic nature, that I hesitated to come to a conclusion.
>
> (Snow 1965, 38–9)

Snow had access to the death certificates at the General Register Office, and drew up a list of the cholera fatalities registered shortly before his inspection of the pump. He then made a house-to-house canvass (the death certificate shows the address of the deceased), and discovered that the cases clustered around the pump, confirming his suspicion.

Later, he made a more complete tally of cholera deaths in the area, which he displayed as a "spot map:" that is, he plotted the locations of cholera fatalities during the epidemic. The clustering is apparent from the map (Snow 1965, 44–5; Cholera Inquiry Committee 1855, 106–9).

There were, however, a number of apparent exceptions, which had to be explained. For example, there was a brewery near the pump; none of the workers contracted the disease: Why not? First, the workers drank beer; second, if water was desired, there was a pump on the premises (Snow 1965, 42).

For another example, a lady in Hampstead contracted cholera: Why? As it turned out, she liked the taste of the water from the Broad Street pump, and had it brought to her house (Snow 1965, 44). Snow gives many other such examples.

Snow's work on the Broad Street epidemic illustrates the power of case studies. Snow's refutation of the usual explanations for cholera, and the development of his own explanation, are other indicators of the power of qualitative reasoning.

The analysis of his natural experiment shows the power of simple quantitative methods and good research design (Snow 1965, 74–86). This was the decisive test of his theory that cholera was a water-borne infectious disease.

In designing the study, however, Snow made some key qualitative steps: (i) seeing that conventional theories were wrong, (ii) formulating the water hypothesis, and (iii) noticing that in 1852, the Lambeth company moved its intake pipe to obtain relatively pure water, while Southwark and Vauxhall continued to draw heavily contaminated water. It took real insight to see—a priori rather than a posteriori—that this difference between the companies allowed the crucial study to be done.

Snow's ideas gained some circulation, especially in England. However, widespread acceptance was achieved only when Robert Koch isolated the causal agent (*Vibrio cholerae*, the comma-shaped bacillus) during the Indian epidemic of 1883. Even then, there were dissenters, with catastrophic results in the Hamburg epidemic of 1892 (Evans 1987).

Inspired by Koch and Louis Pasteur, there was a great burst of activity in microbiology during the 1870s and 1880s. The idea that microscopic life-forms could arise by spontaneous generation was cast aside, and the germ theory of disease was given solid experimental proof.

Besides the cholera vibrio, the bacteria responsible for anthrax (*Bacillus anthracis*) and for tuberculosis (*Mycobacterium tuberculosis*) were isolated, and a vaccine was developed against rabies. However, as we shall see in a moment, these triumphs made it harder to solve the riddle of beriberi. Beriberi is a deficiency disease, but the prestige of the new microbiology made investigators suspicious of any explanation that did not involve microbes.

4 EIJKMAN AND BERIBERI

Beriberi was endemic in Asia, from about 1750 until 1930 or so. Today, the cause is known. People need minute amounts (about one part per million in the diet) of a vitamin called "thiamin." Many Asians eat a diet based on rice, and white rice is preferred to brown.

Thiamin in rice is concentrated in the bran—the skin that gives rice its color. White rice is obtained by polishing away the skin, and with it most of the thiamin; what is left is further degraded by cooking. The diet is then deficient in thiamin, unless supplemented by other foods rich in that substance. Beriberi is the sequel.

In 1888, knowledge about vitamins and deficiency diseases lay decades in the future. That year, Christiaan Eijkman—after studying microbiology with Koch in Berlin—was appointed director of the Dutch Laboratory for Bacteriology and Pathology in the colony of Java, near the city now called Jakarta. His research plan was to use Koch's methods, and show that beriberi was an infectious disease.

Eijkman tried to infect rabbits and then monkeys with blood drawn from beriberi patients. This was unsuccessful. He then turned to chickens. He tried to infect some of the birds, leaving others as controls. After a time, his chickens sickened and many died from a disease he called "polyneuritis" (inflammation of multiple nerves); he judged this disease to be very similar to beriberi in humans. However, the treated chickens and the controls were equally affected.

Perhaps the infection spread from the treated chickens to the controls? To minimize cross-infection, he housed the treated chickens and the controls separately. That had no effect. Perhaps his whole establishment had become infected? To eliminate this possibility, he started work on another, remote experimental station—at which point, the chickens began recovering from the disease.

[Eijkman] wrote "something struck us that had escaped our attention so far." The chickens had been fed a different diet during the five months in which the disease had been developing. In that period (July through November 1889), the man in charge of the chickens had persuaded the cook at the military hospital, without Eijkman being aware of it, to provide him with leftover cooked [white] rice from the previous day, for feeding to the birds. A new cook, who started duty on 21 November, had refused to continue the practice. Thirty years later, Eijkman was to say that "[the new cook] had seen no reason to give military rice to civilian hens."

(Carpenter 2000, 38)

In short, the chickens became ill when fed cooked, polished rice; they recovered when fed uncooked, unpolished rice. This was an accidental experiment, arranged by the two cooks. One of Eijkman's great insights was paying attention to the results, because the cooks' experiment eventually changed the understanding of beriberi.

Eijkman's colleague Adolphe Vorderman undertook an observational study of prisons, to confirm the relevance to humans. Where prisoners were fed polished rice, beriberi was common; with a diet of unpolished rice, beriberi was uncommon. Beriberi is a deficiency disease, not an infectious disease.

The evidence may seem compelling, but that is because we know the answer. At the time, the picture was far from clear. Eijkman himself thought that white rice was poisonous, the bran containing the antidote. Later, he was to reverse himself: Beriberi is an infectious disease, although a poor diet makes people (and chickens) more vulnerable to infection.

In 1896, Gerrit Grijns took over Eijkman's lab (Eijkman suffered from malaria, and had to return to Holland). Among other contributions, after a long series of careful experiments, Grijns concluded that beriberi was a deficiency disease, the missing element in the diet being concentrated in rice bran—and in other foods like mung beans.

In 1901, Grijn's colleague Hulshoff Pol ran a controlled experiment at a mental hospital, showing that mung beans prevented or cured beriberi. In three pavilions out of twelve, the patients were fed mung beans; in three pavilions, other green vegetables. In three pavilions, there was intensive disinfection, and three pavilions were used as controls. The incidence of beriberi was dramatically lower in the pavilions with mung beans.

Still, medical opinion remained divided. Some public health professionals accepted the deficiency hypothesis. Others continued to favor the germ theory, and still others thought the cause was an inanimate poison. It took another ten years or so to reach consensus that beriberi was a deficiency disease, which could be prevented or cured by eating unpolished rice, or enriching the diet in other ways. From a public health perspective, the problem of beriberi might be solved, but the research effort turned to extracting the critical active ingredient in rice bran—no mean challenge, since there is about one teaspoon of thiamin in a ton of bran.

Around 1912, Casimir Funk coined the term "vitamines," later contracted to vitamins, as shorthand for "vital amines." The claim that he succeeded in purifying thiamin may be questionable. But he did guess that beriberi and pellagra were deficiency diseases, which could be prevented by supplying trace amounts of organic nutrients.

By 1926, B. C. P. Jansen and W. F. Donath had succeeded in extracting thiamin (vitamin B1) in pure crystal form. Ten years later, Robert R. Williams and his associates managed to synthesize the compound in the lab. In the 1930s, there were still beriberi cases in the East—and these could be cured by injecting a few milligrams of the new vitamin B1.

5 Goldberger and Pellagra

Pellagra was first observed in Europe in the eighteenth century by a Spanish physician, Gaspar Casal, who found that it was an important cause of ill-health, disability, and premature death among the very poor inhabitants of the Asturias. In the ensuing years, numerous ... authors described the same condition in northern Italian peasants, particularly those from the plain of Lombardy. By the beginning of the nineteenth century, pellagra had spread across Europe, like a belt, causing the progressive physical and mental deterioration of thousands of people in southwestern France, in Austria, in Rumania, and in the domains of the Turkish Empire. Outside Europe, pellagra was recognized in Egypt and South Africa, and by the first decade of the twentieth century it was rampant in the United States, especially in the south.

(Roe 1973, 1)

Pellagra seemed to hit some villages much harder than others. Even within affected villages, many households were spared, but some had pellagra cases year after year. Sanitary conditions in diseased households were primitive: Flies were everywhere. One blood-sucking fly (*Simulium*) had the same geographical range as pellagra, at least in Europe; and the fly was most active in the spring, just when most pellagra cases developed. Many epidemiologists concluded the disease was infectious, and—like malaria or yellow fever—was transmitted from one person to another by insects.

Joseph Goldberger was an epidemiologist working for the US Public Health Service. In 1914, he was assigned to work on pellagra. Despite the climate of opinion described above, he designed a series of observational studies and experiments showing that pellagra was caused by a bad diet, and is not infectious. The disease could be prevented or cured by foods rich in what Goldberger called the P-P (pellagra-preventive) factor.

By 1926, he and his associates had tentatively identified the P-P factor as part of the vitamin B complex. By 1937, C. A. Elvehjem and his associates had identified the P-P factor as niacin, also called vitamin B3 (this compound had been discovered by C. Huber around 1870, but its significance had not been recognized). Since 1940, most of the flour sold in the United States has been enriched with niacin, among other vitamins.

Niacin occurs naturally in meat, milk, eggs, some vegetables, and certain grains. Corn, however, contains relatively little niacin. In the pellagra areas, the poor ate corn—and not much else. Some villages and some households were poorer than others, and had even more restricted diets. That is why they were harder hit by the disease. The flies were a marker of poverty, not a cause of pellagra.

What prompted Goldberger to think that pellagra was a deficiency disease rather than an infectious disease? In hospitals and asylums, the inmates frequently developed pellagra, the attendants almost never—which is unlikely if the disease is infectious, because the inmates could infect the attendants. This observation, although far from definitive, set Goldberger on the path to discovering the cause of pellagra and methods for prevention or cure. The qualitative thinking precedes the quantitative investigation. Pellaga is virtually unknown in the developed world today, although it remains prevalent in some particularly poor countries.

6 McKay and Fluoridation

Dental caries is an infectious, communicable, multifactorial disease in which bacteria dissolve the enamel surface of a tooth ... Soon after establishing his dental practice in Colorado Springs, Colorado, in 1901, Dr. Frederick S. McKay noted an unusual permanent stain or "mottled enamel" (termed "Colorado brown stain" by area residents) on the teeth of many of his patients. After years of personal field investigations, McKay concluded that an agent in the public water supply probably was responsible for mottled enamel. McKay also observed that teeth affected by this condition seemed less susceptible to dental caries.

(Centers for Disease Control 1999, 933; internal citations omitted)

Mottling was caused by something in the drinking water; that was the main hypothesis at the time (McKay and Black 1916, 635). McKay and Black found that mottled teeth were endemic to specific areas. Mottling affected people born in the area, not people who moved to the area after their teeth had been formed. If mottling was prevalent in one area but not in a nearby area, the two areas had different water supplies. These observations supported the water hypothesis, the idea being that the causal agent affects the teeth as they are developing in the body.

McKay and Black could not identify the causal agent in the water, but explained that their chemical analyses

were made according to the standard quantitative form. There are present, however, in waters certain other elements of rarer varieties that exist only in traces, the determination of which requires much elaborate technique and spectroscopic and polariscopic tests, which are beyond the capacities of ordinary chemical laboratories.   (McKay and Black 1916, 904)

As a consequence of mottling, two towns (Oakley in 1925 and Bauxite in 1928) changed the source of their water supply. After the change, newborn children in those towns developed normal teeth. This is, at least in retrospect, striking confirmation of the water hypothesis (McClure 1970, chs. 2–3).

Bauxite was a company town (Aluminum Company of America). H. V. Churchill, an ALCOA chemist, discovered in 1931 that fluorides were naturally present in the original source—a deep well—at relatively high concentrations; he had a spectrograph at the company lab. McKay and Churchill also found high levels of fluorides in the water at several other towns where mottling was endemic, which suggested that fluorides might cause mottling and prevent tooth decay.

H. Trendley Dean, along with others in the US Public Health Service, collected more systematic data on fluorides in the water, mottling, and tooth decay. The data confirmed the associations noted by McKay and Churchill. Moreover, the data indicated that, at lower doses, fluorides in the water could prevent decay without mottling the teeth. (Mottling was unsightly, and carried risks of its own.)

Starting in 1945, community experiments strengthened these conclusions about the role of fluorides, although some controversy remained. Fluoridation of drinking water followed within a few years, and tooth decay in childhood declined precipitously.

7 FLEMING AND PENICILLIN

Alexander Fleming was working at St Mary's Hospital in London, under the direction of Sir Almroth Wright, studying the life cycle of staphylococcus (bacteria that grow in clusters, looking under the microscope like clusters of grapes). Fleming had a number of plates on which he was growing staphylococcus colonies. He left the plates in a corner of his office for some weeks while he was on holiday. When he returned, one of the plates had been contaminated by mold. So far, this is unremarkable. He noticed, however, "that around a large colony of a contaminating mould the staphylococcus colonies became transparent and were obviously undergoing lysis" (Fleming 1929, 226).

Bacteria "lyse" when their cell walls collapse. What caused the lysis? Rather than discarding the plate—the normal thing to do—Fleming thought that the lysis was worth investigating. He did so by growing the mold in broth, watching its behavior, and trying filtered broth on various kinds of bacteria. The mold, a species of *Penicillium*, generated a substance that "to avoid the repetition of the rather cumbersome phrase 'mould broth filtrate' [will be named] 'penicillin'" (Fleming 1929, 227). It was the penicillin that caused the bacteria to lyse. Fleming showed that penicillin destroyed—or at least inhibited the growth of—many kinds of bacteria besides staphylococcus.

Penicillin's therapeutic potential went unrealized until Howard Florey and his associates at Oxford took up the research in 1938 and found processes for purification and larger-scale production. Due to the exigencies of the Second World War, much of the work was done in the United States, where a strain of *Penicillium* that gave high yields was found on a moldy cantaloupe at a market in Peoria. (Industrial-scale development was being done at a nearby Department of Agriculture laboratory under the direction of Kenneth Raper, and people were encouraged to bring in moldy fruit for analysis.)

Penicillin was widely used to treat battlefield injuries, largely preventing gangrene, for example. Along with the sulfa drugs (prontosil was discovered by Gerhard Domagk in 1932) and streptomycin (discovered by Selman Waksman in 1944), penicillin was one of the first of the modern antibiotics.

8 GREGG AND GERMAN MEASLES

Norman Gregg was a pediatric ophthalmologist in Australia. In 1941, he noticed in his practice an unusually large number of infants with cataracts and heart defects. ("Cataracts" make the lens of the eye opaque.) On investigation, he found that many of his colleagues were also treating such cases. The similarity of the cases, and their widespread geographic distribution, led him to guess that the cause must have been exposure to some infectious agent early in the mother's pregnancy, rather than genetics—which was the conventional explanation at the time for birth defects. But what was the infectious agent? This is how Gregg explained his thought process:

> The question arose whether [the cause] could have been some disease or infection occurring in the mother during pregnancy which had then interfered with the developing cells of the lens. By a calculation from the date of the birth of the baby, it was estimated that the early period of pregnancy corresponded with the period of maximum intensity of the very widespread and severe epidemic in 1940 of the so-called German measles.   (Gregg 1941)

Detailed epidemiological research showed that exposure of the mother to German measles in the first or second month of pregnancy markedly increases the risk of birth defects in the baby. The association is generally viewed as causal. Today, there is a vaccine that prevents German measles, and cataracts at birth are exceedingly rare.

9 HERBST AND DES

Herbst and Scully described seven cases of adenocarcinoma of the vagina in adolescent girls. This is an unusual kind of cancer, especially in adolescence. What was the cause? The mother of one patient suggested diethylstibestrol (DES), an artificial hormone often prescribed in those days to prevent miscarriage. Arthur Herbst and his associates were intrigued, but skeptical. They did a case control study, and established a highly significant association, confirmed by a number of other studies, and now accepted as causal.

Two key insights precede any statistical analysis: (i) this is a cluster of cancers worth investigating, and (ii) the cause might have been exposure of the mother during pregnancy—not the daughter after birth—to some toxic substance. A priori, neither point could have been obvious.

10 CONCLUSIONS

In the health sciences, there have been enormous gains since the time of Jenner, many of which are due to statistics. Snow's analysis of his natural experiment shows the power of quantitative methods and good research design. Semmelweis's argument depends on statistics; so too with Goldberger, Dean, Gregg, and Herbst et al.

On the other hand, as the examples demonstrate, substantial progress also derives from informal reasoning and qualitative insights. Recognizing anomalies is important; so is the ability to capitalize on accidents. Progress depends on refuting conventional ideas if they are wrong, on developing new ideas that are better, and on testing the new ideas as well as the old ones. The examples show that qualitative methods can play a key role in all three tasks.

In Fleming's lab, chance circumstances generated an anomalous observation. Fleming resolved the anomaly and discovered penicillin. Semmelweis used qualitative reasoning to reject older theories about the cause of puerperal fever, to develop a new theory from observations on a tragic accident, and to design an intervention that would prevent the disease.

What are the lessons for methodologists in the twenty-first century? Causal inference from observational data presents many difficulties, especially when underlying mechanisms are poorly understood. There is a natural desire to substitute intellectual capital for labor, and an equally natural preference for system and rigor over methods that seem more haphazard. These are possible explanations for the current popularity of statistical models.

Indeed, far-reaching claims have been made for the superiority of a quantitative template that depends on modeling—by those who manage to ignore the far-reaching assumptions behind the models. However, the assumptions often turn out to be unsupported by the data (Duncan 1984; Berk 2004; Brady and Collier 2004; Freedman 2005). If so, the rigor of advanced quantitative methods is a matter of appearance rather than substance.

The historical examples therefore have another important lesson to teach us. Scientific enquiry is a long and tortuous process, with many false starts and blind alleys. Combining qualitative insights and quantitative analysis—and a healthy dose of skepticism—may provide the most secure results.

11 FURTHER READING

....

Brady, Collier, and Seawright (2004) compare qualitative and quantitative methods for causal inference in the social sciences. As they point out,

> it is difficult to make causal inferences from observational data, especially when research focuses on complex political processes. Behind the apparent precision of quantitative findings lie many potential problems concerning equivalence of cases, conceptualization and measurement, assumptions about the data, and choices about model specification...

(Brady, Collier, and Seawright 2004, 9–10)

These authors recommend using a diverse mix of qualitative and quantitative techniques in order to exploit the available information; no particular set of tools is universally best. Causal process observations—including anomalies and results of accidental experiments, even experiments with $N = 1$—can be extremely helpful, as they were in the epidemiological examples discussed here.

The role of anomalies in political science is also discussed by Rogowski (2004). He suggests that scholars in that field may be excessively concerned with hypothesis testing based on statistical models. Scholars may underestimate the degree to which the discovery of anomalies can overturn prior hypotheses and open new avenues of investigation. Anomalies that matter have been discovered in case studies—even when the cases have been selected in ways that do considerable violence to large-N canons for case selection. He also suggests that failure to search for anomalies can lead to a kind of sterility in research programs.

Buck et al. (1989) reprints many of the classic papers in epidemiology; some classic errors are included too. Porter (1997) is a standard reference on history of medicine. Jenner's papers are reprinted in Eliot (1910).

Bazin (2000) discusses the history of smallpox, Jenner's work, and later developments, including the eradication of smallpox; the last recorded cases were in 1977–8. There is a wealth of additional information on the disease and its history in Fenner et al. (1988).

Inoculation was recorded in England by 1721 (Bazin 2000, 13; Fenner et al. 1988, 214–16). However, the practice was described in the journals some years before that (Timonius and Woodward 1714). It was a common opinion in Jenner's time that cowpox created immunity to smallpox (Jenner 1801; Baron 1838, 122).

Over the period 1798–1978, techniques for producing and administering the vaccine were elaborated. As lifespans became longer, it became clear that—contrary to Jenner's teachings—the efficacy of vaccination gradually wore off. Revaccination was introduced. By 1939, the virus in the vaccines was a little different from naturally occurring cowpox virus. The vaccine virus is called "vaccinia" (Bazin 2000, ch. 11; Fenner et al. 1988, chs. 6–7, esp. 278).

Freedman (2005, 6–9) reports on Snow and cholera. For detailed information on Snow's work, see Vinten-Johansen et al. (2003). Evans (1987) gives a historical analysis of the cholera years in Europe. Koch's discovery of the vibrio was anticipated by Filippo Pacini in 1854, but the implications of Pacini's work were not recognized by his contemporaries.

Henry Whitehead was a clergyman in the Soho area. He did not believe that the Broad Street pump—famous for the purity of its water—was responsible for the epidemic. He saw a gap in Snow's argument: The fatalities cluster around the pump, but what about the population in general?

Whitehead made his own house-to-house canvass to determine attack rates among those who drank water from the pump and those who did not. Then he drew up a 2×2 table to summarize the results. The data convinced him that Snow was correct (Cholera Inquiry Committee 1855, 121–33). Snow made this kind of analysis only for his natural experiment.

William Farr, statistical superintendent of the General Register Office, was a leading medical statistician in Victorian England, and a "sanitarian," committed to eliminating air pollution and its sources. He claimed that the force of mortality from cholera in an area was inversely related to its elevation. More specifically, if y is the death rate from cholera in an area and x is its elevation, Farr proposed the equation

$$y = \frac{b}{a + x}.$$

The constants a and b were estimated from the data. The fit to data for 1848–9 was excellent.

An eclectic miasmatist, Farr held the relationship to be causal, explained by atmospheric changes, including attenuation of noxious exhalations from the Thames, changes in vegetation, and changes in the soil. After the London epidemic of 1866, however, he came to accept substantial parts of Snow's theory—without abandoning his own views about miasmas and elevation (Humphreys 1885, 341–84; Eyler 1979, 114–22; Vinten-Johansen et al. 2003, 394). For better or worse, Farr's kind of thinking still has a considerable influence on statistical work in medicine and social science.

There are two informative websites on Snow, Whitehead, and other major figures of the era (these sites were active on September 30, 2007): <http://www.ph.ucla.edu/epi/snow.html>; <http://matrix.msu.edu/~johnsnow>.

Loudon (2000) is highly recommended on puerperal fever; but also see Nuland (1979) for a more sympathetic account of Semmelweis's life. Hare (1970, ch. 7) discusses efforts to control puerperal fever in a London maternity hospital in the 1930s. The strain of *Staphylococcus pyogenes* causing the disease turned out to be a common inhabitant of the human nose and throat. Also see Loudon (2000, 201–4).

A definitive source on beriberi, only paraphrased here, is Carpenter (2000). He gives a vivid picture of a major scientific advance, including discussion of work done before Eijkman arrived in Java.

The discussion of pellagra is based on Freedman, Pisani, and Purves (2007, 15–16). Goldberger's papers are collected in Terris (1964). Goldberger (1914) explains the reasoning that led him to the deficiency-disease hypothesis; Goldberger et al. (1926) identifies the P-P factor as part of the vitamin B complex.

Carpenter (1981) reprints papers by many pellagra researchers, with invaluable commentary. He explains why in Mexico a corn-based diet does not lead to pellagra, discusses the role of tryptophan (an amino acid that can be converted to niacin in the body), and points out the gaps in our knowledge of the disease and the reasons for its disappearance.

The primary papers on fluoridation are McKay and Black (1916), Churchill (1931), and Dean (1938). There is a considerable secondary literature; see, for instance, McClure (1970) and Centers for Disease Control (1999). McKay (1928) is often cited, but seems mainly about another topic: whether enamel in teeth is living tissue.

An excellent source on Fleming is Hare (1970), with Goldsmith (1946) adding useful background. Today, "penicillin" refers to the active ingredient in Fleming's mold broth filtrate.

What is the cell-killing mechanism? In brief, cell walls of most bacteria include a scaffolding constructed from sugars and amino acids. Components of the scaffolding have to be manufactured and assembled when the cells are dividing to form daughter cells. In many species of bacteria, penicillin interferes with the assembly process, eventually causing the cell wall to collapse (Walsh 2003).

Some species of bacteria manufacture an enzyme ("penicillinase") that disables penicillin—before the penicillin can disable the cell. There are other bacterial defense systems too; more generally, there is bacterial resistance to antibiotics. Penicillin inhibits cell wall synthesis by a process that is reasonably well understood, but how does inhibition cause lysis? That is still something of a mystery, although much has been learned (Walsh 2003, 41; Bayles 2000; Giesbrecht et al. 1998).

Penicillin only causes lysis when bacteria are dividing. For this reason among others, a rather unusual combination of circumstances was needed to produce the effect that Fleming noticed on his Petri dish (Hare 1970, ch. 3). Was Fleming merely lucky? Pasteur's epigram is worth remembering: "Dans les champs de l'observation, le hasard ne favorise que les esprits préparés."

Material on Gregg may be hard to find, but see Gregg (1941), Lancaster (1996), and Webster (1998). Gregg (1944) discusses infant deafness following maternal rubella.

On DES, the basic papers are Herbst and Scully (1970) and Herbst, Ulfelder, and Poskanzer (1971), with a useful summary by Colton and Greenberg (1982). Also see

Freedman, Pisani, and Purves (2007, 9–10). DES was an unnecessary tragedy. Doctors who prescribed DES were paying attention to observational studies that showed a positive effect in preventing miscarriage. However, clinical trials showed there was no such effect. DES was banned in 1971 for use in pregnant women.

References

Baron, J. 1838. *The Life of Edward Jenner*, vol. i. London: Henry Colburn; available on Google Scholar, August 27, 2007.

Bayles, K. W. 2000. The bactericidal action of penicillin: new clues to an unsolved mystery. *Trends in Microbiology*, 8: 274–8.

Bazin, H. 2000. *The Eradication of Smallpox*, trans. A. and G. Morgan. London: Academic Press.

Berk, R. A. 2004. *Regression Analysis: A Constructive Critique*. Thousand Oaks, Calif.: Sage.

Brady, H. E., and Collier, D. (eds.) 2004. *Rethinking Social Inquiry: Diverse Tools, Shared Standards*. Lanham, Md.: Rowman and Littlefield.

————— and Seawright, J. 2004. Refocusing the discussion of methodology. Pp. 3–20 in Brady and Collier 2004.

Buck, C., Llopis, A., Nájera, E., and Terris, M. (eds.) 1989. *The Challenge of Epidemiology: Issues and Selected Readings*. Geneva: World Health Organization; available on Google Scholar, August 21, 2007.

Carpenter, K. J. (ed.) 1981. *Pellagra*. Stroudsburg, Pa.: Hutchinson Ross.

————— 2000. *Beriberi, White Rice, and Vitamin B*. Los Angeles: University of California Press.

Centers for Disease Control 1999. Fluoridation of drinking water to prevent dental caries. *Morbidity and Mortality Weekly Report*, 48: 933–40.

Cholera Inquiry Committee 1855. *Report on the Cholera Outbreak in the Parish of St. James, Westminster during the Autumn of 1854*. London: Churchill.

Churchill, H. V. 1931. Occurrence of fluorides in some waters of the United States. *Journal of Industrial and Engineering Chemistry*, 23: 996–8.

Colton, T., and Greenberg, E. R. 1982. Epidemiologic evidence for adverse effects of DES exposure during pregnancy. *American Statistician*, 36: 268–72.

Dean, H. T. 1938. Endemic fluorosis and its relation to dental caries. *Public Health Reports*, 53: 1443–52; reprinted in Buck et al. 1989, 271–87.

Duncan, O. D. 1984. *Notes on Social Measurement*. New York: Russell Sage.

Eliot, C. W. (ed.) 1910. *Scientific Papers: Physiology, Medicine, Surgery, Geology. The Harvard Classics*, vol. 38. New York: P. F. Collier & Son; orig. pub. 1897; available on Google Scholar August 23, 2007.

Evans, R. J. 1987. *Death in Hamburg: Society and Politics in the Cholera Years, 1830–1910*. Oxford: Oxford University Press.

Eyler, J. M. 1979. *Victorian Social Medicine: The Ideas and Methods of William Farr*. Baltimore: Johns Hopkins University Press.

Fenner, F., Henderson, D. A., Arita, I., Jezek, Z., and Ladnyi, I. D. 1988. *Smallpox and its Eradication*. Geneva: World Health Organization. <http://whqlibdoc.who.int/smallpox/9241561106.pdf>

Fleming, A. 1929. On the antibacterial action of cultures of a penicillium, with special reference to their use in the isolation of *B. influenzae*. *British Journal of Experimental Pathology*, 10: 226–36.

FREEDMAN, D. A. 2005. *Statistical Models: Theory and Practice*. New York: Cambridge University Press.

——PISANI, R., and PURVES, R. A. 2007. *Statistics*, 4th edn. New York: W. W. Norton.

GIESBRECHT, P., KERSTEN, T., MAIDHOF, H., and WECKE, J. 1998. Staphylococcal cell wall: morphogenesis and fatal variations in the presence of penicillin. *Microbiology and Molecular Biology Reviews*, 62: 1371–414.

GOLDBERGER, J. 1914. The etiology of pellagra. *Public Health Reports*, 29: 1683–6; reprinted in Buck et al. 1989, 99–102, and in Terris 1964, 19–22.

——WHEELER, G. A., LILLIE, R. D., and ROGERS, L. M. 1926. A further study of butter, fresh beef, and yeast as pellagra preventives, with consideration of the relation of factor P-P of pellagra (and black tongue of dogs) to vitamin B1. *Public Health Reports*, 41: 297–318; reprinted in Terris 1964, 351–70.

GOLDSMITH, M. 1946. *The Road to Penicillin*. London: Lindsay Drummond.

GREGG, N. M. 1941. Congenital cataract following German measles in the mother. *Transactions of the Ophthalmological Society of Australia*, 3: 35–46; reprinted in Buck et al. 1989, 426–34.

——1944. Further observations on congenital defects in infants following maternal rubella. *Transactions of the Ophthalmological Society of Australia*, 4: 119–31.

HARE, R. 1970. *The Birth of Penicillin and the Disarming of Microbes*. London: Allen and Unwin.

HERBST, A. L., and SCULLY, R. E. 1970. Adenocarcinoma of the vagina in adolescence: a report of 7 cases including 6 clear cell carcinomas. *Cancer*, 25: 745–57.

——ULFELDER, H., and POSKANZER, D. C. 1971. Adenocarcinoma of the vagina: association of maternal stilbestrol therapy with tumor appearance in young women. *New England Journal of Medicine*, 284: 878–81; reprinted in Buck et al. 1989, 446–50.

HUMPHREYS, N. A. (ed.) 1885. *Vital Statistics: A Memorial Volume of Selections from the Reports and Writings of William Farr*. London: Edward Stanford; available on Google Scholar, September 23, 2007.

JENNER, E. 1798. *An Inquiry into the Causes and Effects of the Variolae Vaccinae, a Disease Discovered in Some of the Western Counties of England, Particularly Gloucestershire, and Known by the Name of the Cow Pox*. London: printed for the author by Sampson Low; reprinted in Eliot 1910, 151–80.

——1801. *The Origin of the Vaccine Inoculation*. London: D. N. Shury; reprinted in Fenner et al. 1988, 258–61.

LANCASTER, P. A. L. 1996. Gregg, Sir Norman McAlister (1892–1966), ophthalmologist. Pp. 325–7 in *Australian Dictionary of Biography*, vol. xiv, ed. J. Ritchie. Melbourne: Melbourne University Press. <http://www.adb.online.anu.edu.au/biogs/A140370b.htm>

LOUDON, I. 2000. *The Tragedy of Childbed Fever*. Oxford: Oxford University Press.

McCLURE, F. J. 1970. *Water Fluoridation*. Bethesda, Md.: National Institute of Dental Research.

McKAY, F. S. 1928. Relation of mottled enamel to caries. *Journal of the American Dental Association*, 15: 1429–37.

——and BLACK, G. V. 1916. An investigation of mottled teeth: an endemic developmental imperfection of the enamel of the teeth, heretofore unknown in the literature of dentistry. *Dental Cosmos*, 58: 477–84, 627–44, 781–92, 894–904.

NULAND, S. 1979. The enigma of Semmelweis: an interpretation. *Journal of the History of Medicine and Allied Sciences*, 34: 255–72.

PORTER, R. 1997. *The Greatest Benefit to Mankind*. New York: W. W. Norton.

ROE, D. A. 1973. *A Plague of Corn*. Ithaca, NY: Cornell University Press.

ROGOWSKI, R. 2004. How inference in the social (but not the physical) sciences neglects theoretical anomaly. Pp. 75–82 in Brady and Collier 2004.

SEMMELWEIS, I. 1981. *The Etiology, Concept, and Prophylaxis of Childbed Fever*, trans. F. P. Murphy. Birmingham: Classics of Medicine Library; orig. pub. in German 1860.

SNOW, J. 1965. *On the Mode of Communication of Cholera*. New York: Hafner; orig. pub. 1855.

TERRIS, M. (ed.) 1964. *Goldberger on Pellagra*. Baton Rouge: Louisiana State University Press.

TIMONIUS, E., and WOODWARD, J. 1714. An account, or history, of the procuring the small pox by incision, or inoculation; as it has for some time been practised at Constantinople. *Philosophical Transactions*, 29: 72–82.

VINTEN-JOHANSEN, P., BRODY, H., PANETH, N., and RACHMAN, S. 2003. *Cholera, Chloroform, and the Science of Medicine*. New York: Oxford University Press.

WALSH, C. 2003. *Antibiotics: Actions, Origins, Resistance*. Washington, DC: ASM Press.

WEBSTER, W. S. 1998. Teratogen update: congenital rubella. *Teratology*, 58: 13–23.

CHAPTER 13

....

STUDYING MECHANISMS TO STRENGTHEN CAUSAL INFERENCES IN QUANTITATIVE RESEARCH

....

PETER HEDSTRÖM

1 INTRODUCTION

....

SOCIAL scientists and philosophers of science have paid considerable attention to the logic and use of so-called mechanism-based explanations. In this chapter I focus on the role of mechanisms in explanatory social science research, and I highlight various ways by which the study of mechanisms can make quantitative research more useful for causal inference.

This chapter draws upon and further develops some of the core themes in Hedström (2005) and Hedström and Swedberg (1996; 1998). I wish to thank Henry Brady for his useful and insightful comments.

As the terms are being used here, causal inference is not the same as statistical inference. The two types of inference are similar in that they both use "localized" information to draw conclusions about more general phenomena; however the types of phenomena about which one seeks to generalize are not the same and the types of information used also often differ. In statistical inference, one typically uses information obtained from a limited number of observations—usually based on a random sample—to draw conclusions about the likely value of some *parameter* in the population at large such as a regression coefficient or a standard deviation. In causal inference, as the term is being used here, the information being used is not necessarily confined to a specific sample, but a range of different sources of information provide various pieces of the causal puzzle (see also Brady and Collier 2004 and their notion of "causal process observations"). Furthermore, the entity one seeks to generalize about is not the parameter of a statistical model but the *process* by which something has been brought about and the *mechanisms* governing this process. As discussed below, knowing the relevant mechanisms is often important for statistical inference, and statistical estimates and inferences are important for understanding the process by which something has been brought about, but statistical inference and causal inference are different kinds of activities.

The type of "mechanism approach" discussed in this chapter also differs in another important respect from more traditional quantitative approaches. The focus is not on relationships between variables, but on actors, their relationships, and the intended and unintended outcomes of their actions. Properties of actors and/or their social environments often influence the outcomes of individuals' actions. These properties as well as the action outcomes can be measured and represented in the form of variables, but the causality does not operate at the variable level. As discussed in some detail below, since actors, by themselves or in consort with other actors, are the agents of change, causal processes should typically be specified at the actor level.

The chapter is organized as follows. First I describe what I mean by mechanisms and mechanism-based explanations. Then, I focus on three aspects of the role of mechanisms in causal and statistical inference: (i) how an understanding of the mechanisms at work can improve statistical inference by guiding the specification of the statistical models to be estimated; (ii) how mechanisms can strengthen causal inferences by improving our understanding of why individuals do what they do; and (iii) how mechanism-based models can strengthen causal inferences by showing why, acting as they do, individuals bring about the social outcomes they do.[1]

---

[1] In this chapter, "social" outcomes/phenomena and "macro-level" outcomes/phenomena are used as synonymous terms. They refer to collective properties that are not definable by reference to any single member of the collectivity. Important examples of such properties include: (1) typical actions, beliefs, or desires among the members of the collectivity; (2) distributions and aggregate patterns such as spatial distributions and inequalities; (3) topologies of networks that describe relationships among the members of the collectivity; and (4) formal and informal rules that constrain the actions of the members of the collectivity. For a similar definition, see Carlsson (1968).

2 MECHANISMS AND MECHANISM-BASED EXPLANATIONS

The core idea behind the mechanism approach is that we explain by specifying the mechanisms by which that which we wish to explain was brought about. As Elster (1989, 3–4) has expressed it: "To explain an event is to give an account of why it happened. Usually...this takes the form of citing an earlier event as the cause of the event we want to explain.... [But] to cite the cause is not enough: the causal mechanism must also be provided, or at least suggested."[2]

As observed by Mahoney (2001), however, there is no consensus on what is meant by a "mechanism." In fact, at least at a superficial level, there appears to be almost an overabundance of definitions. Philosophers and social scientists have defined the mechanism concept in numerous different ways (e.g. Bhaskar 1978; Bunge 1996; Elster 1999; Gambetta 1998; Glennan 1996; Hedström and Swedberg 1998; Karlsson 1958; Little 1991; Mcadam, Tarrow, and Tilly 2001; Mahoney 2001; Mayntz 2004; Pawson 2000; Salmon 1984; Schelling 1998). Table 13.1 describes some of the most frequently cited definitions.

These definitions differ a great deal from one another. Some refer to causal mechanisms in general, while others refer exclusively to mechanisms of relevance for the social sciences; some are rather precise while others are broad and general; some refer to concrete existing entities while others refer to models or reasoning about such entities. However, despite these differences, they share an important common denominator. Underlying them all is an emphasis on making intelligible the regularities being observed by specifying in detail how they were brought about.

As I have argued in Hedström (2005), the currently most satisfactory conceptual analysis of the mechanism concept is found in Machamer, Darden, and Craver (2000). The spirit of their approach is very similar to the "cogs-and-wheels" approach of Elster (I) and the "social mechanism" approach of Hedström and Swedberg. Following these leads, mechanisms can be said to consist of *entities* (with their properties) and the *activities* that these entities engage in, either by themselves or in concert with other entities. These activities bring about change, and the type of change brought about depends upon the properties of the entities and the way in which the entities are linked to one another. A mechanism, thus defined, refers to a constellation of entities and activities that are organized such that they regularly bring about a particular type of outcome, and we explain an observed outcome by referring to the mechanism by which such outcomes are regularly brought about.

As mentioned above, actors and actions play a privileged role in social science explanations because actors are the entities and actions are the activities that bring

---

[2] Space limitations do not allow for a discussion of other notions of what "explaining" is all about. See Hedström (2005) as well as the chapter by Brady in this volume for a discussion of the alternative notions that appear most relevant for the social sciences.

Table 13.1. Alternative mechanism definitions

Author	Definition	References
Bunge	A mechanism is a process in a concrete system which is capable of bringing about or preventing some change in the system.	Bunge (1997; 2004)
Craver	Mechanisms are entities and activities organized such that they are productive of regular changes from start to finish.	Craver (2001); Machamer, Darden, and Craver (2000)
Elster (I)	A mechanism explains by opening up the black box and showing the cogs and wheels of the internal machinery. A mechanism provides a continuous and contiguous chain of causal or intentional links between the explanans and the explanandum.	Elster (1983a; 1989)
Elster (II)	Mechanisms are frequently occurring and easily recognizable causal patterns that are triggered under generally unknown conditions.	Elster (1998; 1999)
Hedström and Swedberg	A social mechanism is a precise, abstract, and action-based explanation which shows how the occurrence of a triggering event regularly generates the type of outcome to be explained.	Hedström and Swedberg (1996; 1998)
Little	A causal mechanism is a series of events governed by lawlike regularities that lead from the explanans to the explanandum.	Little (1991)
Stinchcombe	A mechanism is a piece of scientific reasoning which gives knowledge about a component of another, ordinarily higher-level theory.	Stinchcombe (1991)

about change. Needless to say, a focus on actors and actions does not mean that extraindividual entities such as "cultures," "institutions," or "social structures" are unimportant; only that actors are needed in order for these types of entities to have any effects. Let us take social structure as an example, and thereby also highlight the fact that social science explanations often refer to mechanisms nested within other mechanisms (see Stinchcombe 1991). Following the social-network tradition in sociology (such as White, Boorman, and Breiger 1976), a social structure here is defined as a network or as a pattern of interactions among a set of individuals which exhibits a certain temporal stability. As shown in numerous studies, such networks are likely to influence the outcomes that the individuals embedded in the structure are likely to bring about (see Strang and Soule 1998 for a review of some of the relevant literature). That is to say, the same entities (individual actors) strung together in different relational patterns can regularly be expected to bring about different types of outcomes. In this sense, different types of relational configurations can be said to constitute different mechanisms (see also Mcadam, Tarrow, and Tilly 2001).

The way in which "structural" mechanisms like these influence aggregate outcomes can be seen most clearly in the study of infectious diseases. As Watts and Strogatz (1998) have shown, even very small changes in the structure of a network can decisively influence the probability that an epidemic will take off. Demonstrating such effects is more difficult in the social sciences because the transmission mechanisms are more complex, but the logic of the processes is similar. Whether the outcome to be explained refers to the size of an epidemic or the extent to which a certain belief is held in the population at large, we explain it (in part) by referring to the mechanism (that is, in this case, to a specific type of network structure) that regularly brings about such outcomes.

Networks, however, cannot produce outcomes in and of themselves. If they are to have any effect, they must influence the ways in which individuals act, and in order to understand how this influence operates, we must specify the mechanisms involved. That is to say, we must explicate the mechanisms that explain the actions of individuals, and the ways in which they are nested within these "structural" mechanisms. These types of action-related mechanisms may also be characterized in terms of their entities (and their properties) and the ways in which the entities are linked to one another. The core entities are different, however, and now include entities such as beliefs, desires, and opportunities of the actors. But the explanatory logic is the same: We explain an observed phenomenon, in this case an individual action, by referring to the mechanism (that is, the constellation of beliefs, desires, opportunities, etc.) by which such actions are regularly brought about.

Why is it so important that we identify the mechanisms that appear to generate the outcomes we observe, whether they be the actions of individuals or collective outcomes that result from the collective or sum total of the actions of numerous individuals? For one thing, identifying the details of the mechanisms tends to produce explanations that are more precise and intelligible. In other words, we can only really understand and explain what we observe by referring to the mechanisms involved.

Another important reason is that focusing on mechanisms tends to reduce theoretical fragmentation. For example, we may imagine numerous theories (of voting, social movements, etc.) that are all based on the same set of mechanisms of action and interaction. By focusing on mechanisms we may avoid unnecessary proliferation of theoretical concepts. We may also be able to place in relief structural similarities between processes that at first glance seem completely dissimilar.

Most social science research is of a nonexperimental kind. In such research, an understanding of the mechanism involved in linking two states or events to one another often is what permits us to conclude that we are dealing with a genuine causal relationship. As Glennan (1996, 65) has emphasized, "two events are causally connected when and only when there is a mechanism connecting them." If we are not able to identify a plausible mechanism, our case for the observed regularity being indicative of a genuine causal relationship is considerably weakened.

In principle, a well-designed experiment can tell us whether a treatment has an impact on an outcome, even if we do not have the faintest idea about the mechanism involved. But as long as we lack knowledge about the mechanism involved, the information obtained from the experiment will have the status of a nonexplanatory causal claim. In practice, because of the difficulties of generalizing results obtained in a laboratory setting to real-life settings, and the practical and ethical difficulties of conducting experiments in real-life settings, true experiments are likely to play a rather minor role in the social sciences also in the future.

3 MECHANISMS AND QUANTITATIVE RESEARCH

As far as nonexperimental research is concerned, survey analysis and the statistical techniques needed for analyzing survey data are invaluable tools. However, as many observers have noted, the use of such data and methods also has contributed to a variable-centered form of analysis that pays scant attention to the processes that are likely to explain observed outcomes. Coleman (1986) aptly described this type of variable-focused research as a form of "individualistic behaviorism." The guiding principle behind such research is the idea that individual behavior of whatever sort can be explained by various individual and environmental "determinants" such as age, gender, class, and ethnicity. The hope is that, by regressing the outcome variable of interest on a set of variables like these, one can identify the causes of the behavior in question. According to Coleman, this type of "causal" explanation of behavior represented a considerable change in the type of explanatory approach used by most social scientists: "One way of describing this change is to say that statistical association between variables has largely replaced meaningful connection between events as the basic tool of description and analysis" (Coleman 1986, 1327–8).

David Freedman has discussed the statistical foundations of this type of causal modeling approach in some detail (e.g. Freedman 1987; 1991; 1999). According to Freedman, the belief of some social scientists in the possibility of estimating causal models is counter-productive. The basic statistical tools of causal modelers, Freedman argues, are based upon a network of highly restrictive stochastic assumptions that are rarely, if ever, met. The basic thrust of Freedman's argument is that social scientists need to think more about underlying social processes, and to look more closely at data unencumbered by the distorting lens of conventional and, according to Freedman, largely irrelevant stochastic models: "In my opinion, the confusion between descriptive and structural models pervades the social-science scholarly literature of the past 20 years, and has distorted the research agenda of a generation" (Freedman 1992, 123). As Freedman has emphasized, at best, such statistical analyses can provide compact descriptive summaries of data, but they cannot in themselves provide causal explanations. Causal inferences should always ride on the strength of the argument, and not on "the magic of least squares" (Freedman 1992).

So where does this leave us? I do not wish to suggest that quantitative empirical research is of minor importance for the social sciences. Quite the contrary. But in order for statistical analyses to provide reliable and useful information, the statistical model must represent reasonably well the process by which the outcome of interest was brought about. In order to arrive at such models, as Sørensen (1998) has argued, we need a different division of labor between social scientists and statisticians than the one that currently predominates. The proper division should be one in which social science theory suggests a mathematical model of a causal process and statistics provides the tools to estimate this model, not, as is common today, that statistics provides models that social scientists use as ad hoc models of social processes (see also Cox 1992; Goldthorpe 2000). One important way in which the study and identification of mechanisms can help to strengthen quantitative research is by providing the basic building blocks of such subject-specific generative models. I will return to this after giving some concrete examples of the types of mechanisms that are likely to be relevant.

Another important way in which a focus on mechanisms can help to strengthen quantitative research is by allowing the identification of models that otherwise could not be identified. Winship and Harding (2008) have shown how this can be done in general, and they illustrate the principles involved with reference to so-called age, period, cohort (APC) models. As is well known, linear APC models cannot be identified because they are exact linear functions of one another, i.e. Age = Period − Cohort. Winship and Harding's core idea is that identification can be achieved by extending the models to include variables that represent the mechanisms by which age, period, and cohort are assumed to influence the outcome to be explained. They have shown how Pearl's (2000) so-called front-door criteria can be used to deal with situations in which there is a perfect linear dependence between some subset of the independent variables. The inclusion of variables representing the relevant mechanisms amounts to expanding the APC model into multiple APC models and this makes it possible to identify the parameters of interest in the original APC model.

4 MECHANISMS AND THE EXPLANATION OF INDIVIDUAL ACTIONS

In addition to being a guide to the types of statistical models that are possible and meaningful to estimate, a focus on mechanisms strengthens causal inferences by helping us to understand why individuals do what they do. Even if we are exclusively interested in large-scale social and political processes, understanding why individuals do what they do is of fundamental importance because it is individuals' actions that make society "tick."

To illustrate what a mechanism-based explanation of action is all about, I will take my point of departure in the so-called DBO theory. According to this theory, desires (D), beliefs (B), and opportunities (O) are the primary entities upon which the analysis of action and interaction is based. That is to say, we can understand why individuals do what they do if we perceive their behavior as being endowed with meaning, that is, that there is an intention that explains why they do what they do (see Elster 1983a; von Wright 1971).

Beliefs and desires are mental events that can be said to cause an action in the sense of providing reasons for the action. A particular combination of desires and beliefs constitutes a "compelling reason" for performing an action. They have a motivational force that allows us to understand, and in this respect to explain the action (see von Wright 1989). Standard rational choice theory is one variant of this theory. It assumes that individuals choose their actions in such a way as to maximize their desires given the constraints imposed by the available opportunities (e.g. utility is maximized with respect to a budget constraint which defines the available opportunities).

Individuals do not act in isolation from one another, however. In order to explain why they do what they do, we must also seek to understand how their beliefs, desires, and opportunities are formed in interaction with other individuals. Simply assuming that beliefs and desires are fixed and unaffected by the actions of others may be plausible in some very specific situations, but it would be an untenable assumption in the general case. Ignoring or misrepresenting the ways in which individuals interact and influence one another often leads to flawed predictions about the social outcomes that a group of individuals are likely to bring about (see, e.g., Holland 1998 for a general discussion). Therefore, we must try to specify mechanisms by which the actions of some may come to influence the beliefs, desires, opportunities, and actions of others.

To the extent that the action of one actor influences the action of another, this influence must be mediated via the action opportunities or mental states of the latter actor. In terms of the DBO theory, the action (or behavior) of the former actor can influence the actions of the latter actor by influencing her desires, beliefs, or opportunities.

Using these basic ideas, we may define more complex "molecular" mechanisms. These molecular mechanisms differ from one another in terms of how these basic entities and activities are linked. Some examples can be seen in Figure 13.1. The letters D, B, O, and A stand for desires, beliefs, opportunities, and actions, and the letters i, j, and k identify different actors.

Taking the mechanisms in the table in order, the first pattern of entities and activities exemplifies *wishful thinking*. As used here, the term wishful thinking denotes a connection between an actor's desires and his or her beliefs that makes the actor believe that what she or he desires is in fact the case (see Davidson 1980). The sour-grapes syndrome, the second type of mechanism, exemplifies the opposite pattern. Here, there is a connection between an actor's beliefs and his or her desires such that the actor only desires what she or he believes she can get (see Elster 1983a).

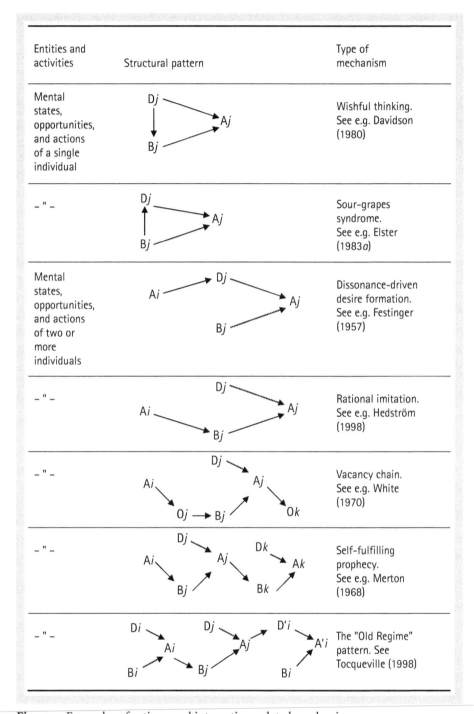

Entities and activities	Structural pattern	Type of mechanism
Mental states, opportunities, and actions of a single individual		Wishful thinking. See e.g. Davidson (1980)
– " –		Sour-grapes syndrome. See e.g. Elster (1983a)
Mental states, opportunities, and actions of two or more individuals		Dissonance-driven desire formation. See e.g. Festinger (1957)
– " –		Rational imitation. See e.g. Hedström (1998)
– " –		Vacancy chain. See e.g. White (1970)
– " –		Self-fulfilling prophecy. See e.g. Merton (1968)
– " –		The "Old Regime" pattern. See Tocqueville (1998)

Fig. 13.1. Examples of action- and interaction-related mechanisms

Dissonance-driven desire formation is a mechanism in which actions of others lead to a change in the focal actor's desires and thus to a change in his or her actions. Festinger's (1957) notion of cognitive dissonance is a classic example. For example, if I desire p but the people I engage with do not, this may cause strong dissonance, particularly if the desire is important to me *and* I value my relationship with these people. One way to eliminate the dissonance would be to persuade them to value p. Another, often easier, way would be to "persuade" oneself that p was not really as desirable as one initially thought.

Rational imitation may be said to occur when one actor's action influences the beliefs and subsequent actions of others. For example, since it is commonly acknowledged that how crowded a restaurant is says something about the dining experience, a large crowd is likely to affect the beliefs and actions of potential diners (see Hedström 1998).

In *vacancy chains*, the actions of some actors create new opportunities and changes in the actions of others. A classic example is Harrison White's (1970) analysis of the vacancy-driven mobility pattern of clergy in the United States. Vacancies occur either when individuals leave their organizations or when new positions are created. When a person fills a vacancy, his or her old position becomes vacant and represents a mobility opportunity to someone else. One of these people will get the job, which will fill that vacancy, but another vacancy is created in this person's old job. This process permits individuals and vacancies to move in different directions, and the mobility process is governed by these chains of opportunity.

The *self-fulfilling prophecy* is a sequential chain of several rational-imitation mechanisms. Merton (1968) focused on the case in which an initially false belief evokes behavior that eventually makes the false belief come true. The example he used was a run on a bank. Once a rumor of insolvency gets started, some depositors are likely to withdraw their savings, acting on the principle that it is better to be safe than sorry. Their withdrawals may hurt the bank's financial viability. But even more importantly, the act of withdrawal in itself *signals* to others that something might be wrong with the bank. This produces even more withdrawals, which further strengthens the belief, and so on. By this mechanism, even an initially sound bank may go bankrupt if enough depositors withdraw their money in the (initially) false belief that the bank is insolvent.

The *"Old Regime" pattern* is a sequential concatenation of rational-imitation and dissonance-driven desire-formation mechanisms ($D_i \rightarrow A_i \rightarrow B_j \rightarrow A_j \rightarrow D'_i \rightarrow A_i$ where $D'_i \neq D_i$). For opportunistic reasons one actor decides to do something she or he does not genuinely desire. Others see the action and the rational-imitation mechanism makes them follow suit. Eventually this feeds back to the first actor such that the actions taken by others produce dissonance and a change in the desires of the first actor. This causes him or her to desire in fact what she or he initially only pretended to want. Such a mechanism was used by Tocqueville to explain the rapid secularization that took place in France at the end of the eighteenth century:

Those who retained their belief in the doctrines of the Church became afraid of being alone in their allegiance and, dreading isolation more than the stigma of heresy, professed to share the sentiment of the majority. So what was in reality the opinion of only a part (though a large one) of the nation came to be regarded as the will of all and for this reason seemed irresistible even to those who had given it this false appearance.   (Tocqueville 1998, 155)

By detailing such mechanisms we arrive at a better understanding of why individuals do what they do. We also have taken an important first step toward understanding how the large-scale social and political outcomes that most of us are particularly interested in explaining are brought about. But to understand what kind of macro-level outcomes micro-processes like these are likely to generate is far from trivial. In the next section, I will briefly discuss some useful approaches for addressing this link between micro and macro.

5 MECHANISMS AND THE EXPLANATION OF MACRO-LEVEL OUTCOMES

As emphasized by Coleman (1986), one of the main hurdles to the development of explanatory theory has been the difficulty of linking individual actions to the social or macro-level outcomes they are likely to bring about. Small and seemingly unimportant changes in the type of mechanisms discussed in the previous section can have considerable consequences for the aggregate social outcomes that a group of individuals is likely to bring about. For this reason, social outcomes cannot simply be "read off" from the properties of the actors that generate them. Even in very small groups in which actors act on the basis of known action logics and where the interaction patterns are fully understood, we often fail to anticipate the social outcomes likely to be brought about (see Schelling 1978 for a range of illuminating examples). Anticipating and explaining the link between the individual and the social is simply too complex for us to handle without the use of some formal analytical tools.

Over the years a range of different models of this kind have been developed, some of which have been enormously influential within the social sciences such Olson's (1965) free-rider model and Downs's (1957) party-competition model. These models were based on highly stylized assumptions, but they were nevertheless of immense value because they offered new insights by identifying mechanisms that were of importance for a range of empirical phenomena. These types of models are purely theoretical in the sense that they identify a specific type of mechanism and show what implications the mechanism can have.

If our purpose instead is to use a formal model for explaining an empirically observed outcome, the details of the model specification become essential. We may, for instance, be able to tell a story that shows how a group of atomistic and rational individuals could have brought about the social outcome we seek to explain, but such an account would not explain why we observed what we observed unless the individuals acted and interacted as assumed in the model (or at least approximately so).[3] Basing the analysis on descriptively false assumptions about the logic of action and interaction may allow us to formulate elegant and parsimonious models, but if such logics are found only in hypothetical worlds much different from our own, explanations based on such assumptions will be fictional in our world. In order to explain we must refer to mechanisms known to be operative in the real-world settings that we are analyzing (Elster 1989).

In many instances, agent-based modeling is an attractive type of formalism for addressing the link between the individual and the social. Agent-based modeling uses computer simulations to assess the social outcomes that groups of virtual actors are likely to bring about, and what distinguishes agent-based analyses from other simulation approaches is that they are actor based, and that they explain social phenomena from the bottom up. That is to say, agent-based models make predictions about social outcomes, given different assumptions about the properties, actions, and interactions among the actors (see Axelrod 1997; Epstein and Axtell 1996, Macy and Willer 2002; and the chapter by de Marchi and Page in the current volume, for a range of examples). Such models may lack the elegance and beauty of mathematical models, but they often have more explanatory power because they do not force the analyst to base the analysis on false assumptions.

Despite the possibilities for bridging the gap between theoretical models and empirical reality that agent-based modeling offers, many agent-based modelers view themselves as pure theorists and pay little or no attention to empirical matters. Macy and Willer, for example, describe agent-based modeling as "a new tool for theoretical research" (2002, 161) and they argue that the core idea behind agent-based modeling is "to perform highly abstract thought experiments that explore plausible mechanisms that may underlie observed patterns" (2002, 147). Similarly, Axelrod argues that agent-based models do not "... aim to provide an accurate representation of a particular empirical application. Instead, the goal of agent-based modeling is to enrich our understanding of fundamental processes that may appear in a variety of applications" (Axelrod 1997, 25).

Although pure thought experiments are of obvious importance, when we are to explain a specific outcome, we must make sure that the mechanisms being modeled have indeed been in operation in this particular case. Furthermore, we must make sure that the more fine-grained detail of the mechanisms seems to correspond to what we know about the real-world case being studied. Unless there is such correspondence

---

[3] It appears essential to make a distinction between descriptively false and descriptively incomplete assumptions. If we have a set A = {a b c d} and we assume that A = {e f}, our assumption would be descriptively false, while if we assume that A = {c d}, our assumption would be descriptively incomplete. In the former case we ascribe to A characteristics which it does not have, while in the latter case we assume A to be what it is only in part; that is, we accentuate certain aspects by ignoring others. While descriptive incompleteness is desirable and unavoidable, descriptively false assumptions are neither.

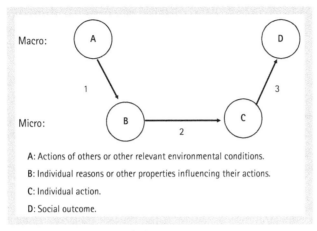

A: Actions of others or other relevant environmental conditions.

B: Individual reasons or other properties influencing their actions.

C: Individual action.

D: Social outcome.

Fig. 13.2. Macro-micro linkages

between model and reality, the analysis will only offer an as-if story of little or no explanatory value.

In Hedström (2005), Yvonne Åberg and I illustrated how one can narrow the gap between model and reality by forging a tighter link between quantitative research and agent-based modeling. Coleman's (1986) so-called micro-macro graph can be used to illustrate the principles involved (see Figure 13.2).

Most of us are engaged in explaining social or macro-level outcomes (**D** in Figure 13.2), and usually we explain such outcomes with references to other social or macro-level phenomena (**A**). But simply relating the two to one another, statistically or otherwise, would lead to a rather superficial explanation since the mechanisms that inform us about how and why they are related cannot be found at this aggregate level. We must instead seek to show how individuals' properties and orientations to action are influenced by the social environments in which they are embedded (link 1).[4] Thereafter, we must seek to show how these properties and orientations to action influence how they act (link 2), and how these actions bring about the social outcomes we seek to explain (link 3).

The essence of the approach advocated by Åberg and me is to use large-scale quantitative data to analyze the details of the first two links in the Coleman graph, and then to incorporate the results of these analyses into an agent-based model that formally represents the core mechanisms believed to be at work (see also Bearman, Moody, and Stovel 2004 for a similar approach linking quantitative research and agent-based modeling). Although this type of approach differs in certain respects from the modal type of agent-based model, the logic of the analysis remains the same. That is to say, it is the actions of and interactions between the agents that generate the social patterns that emerge, and by altering various aspects of the simulation setup one ascertains what effects these changes may have on the outcomes.

---

[4] See Wikström (2007) for a detailed discussion of how such "situational mechanisms" can influence how individuals act.

Space limitations do not allow for a detailed description of this approach, but in all brevity it seeks to closely integrate mechanism-based theories and empirical research, and the way in which this is done can be summarized in the following manner:

1. Start by developing a stylized model that explicates the logic of the mechanism assumed to be operative, and make sure that the model can generate the type of social outcome to be explained. If it can, we have a mechanism-based explanation of the outcome, although the explanation has not yet been empirically verified.
2. For empirical verification, use relevant data to examine the most important bits and pieces of the causal machinery in order to verify that the mechanism actually works as postulated.
3. Make sure that the model generates the type of outcome to be explained even when the model has been modified in the light of (2) and after controls for likely confounders have been introduced.

Only when the explanatory account has passed all of these three stages can we claim to have an empirically verified mechanism-based explanation of a social outcome.

This type of empirically calibrated modeling can accomplish two important tasks. First, it enables a test of the model by examining the extent to which the model brings about the social outcome to be explained, even for realistic parameter values. Second, and more important in this context, it strengthens causal inferences in quantitative research. By embedding the results from a statistical analysis in a theoretical model that represents the core mechanisms believed to be at work, it becomes possible to derive the social outcomes that individuals would bring about were they to act and interact as the results of the empirical analysis suggest that they do.

6 CONCLUDING REMARKS

In this chapter I have focused on the logic of mechanism-based explanations and on how the study of mechanisms can strengthen causal inference. A mechanism, as here defined, refers to a constellation of entities and activities that are organized such that they regularly bring about a particular type of outcome, and we explain an observed outcome by referring to the mechanism by which such outcomes are regularly brought about. I briefly discussed three ways through which a focus on mechanisms can strengthen causal inferences: (1) it can strengthen causal inferences by helping us to decide on what kind of statistical models are at all meaningful to estimate; (2) it can strengthen causal inferences by helping us to understand why individuals do what they do; and (3) it can strengthen causal inferences by helping us to understand why, acting as they do, they bring about the outcomes they do.

Over the last few years there has been a surge of interest in mechanism-based explanations, in political science as well as in sociology. Most of this work has been important and valuable in that it has sought to clarify the distinctiveness of the approach and to apply it empirically. But some of it has been somewhat problematic in that it threatens to strip the approach of all its distinctive features. If a mechanism-based approach simply becomes synonymous with an approach that is attentive to potential causes or to intervening variables, as some recent contributions seem to suggest, adopting a mechanism-based vocabulary simply contributes to an unnecessary proliferation of theoretical concepts. In this chapter I have sought clearly to articulate the guiding principles behind the mechanism approach. This approach is abstract, realistic, and precise, and it explains specific political or social phenomena on the basis of explicitly formulated theories of action and interaction.

REFERENCES

AXELROD, R. M. 1997. *The Complexity of Cooperation: Agent-Based Models of Competition and Collaboration*. Princeton, NJ: Princeton University Press.

BEARMAN, P. S., MOODY, J., and STOVEL, K. 2004. Chains of affection: the structure of adolescent romantic and sexual networks. *American Journal of Sociology*, 110: 44–91.

BHASKAR, R. 1978. *A Realist Theory of Science*. Hassocks: Harvester Press.

BRADY, H. E., and COLLIER, D. (eds.) 2004. *Rethinking Social Inquiry: Diverse Tools, Shared Standards*. Oxford: Rowman and Littlefield.

BUNGE, M. A. 1996. *Finding Philosophy in Social Science*. New Haven, Conn.: Yale University Press.

——1997. Mechanism and explanation. *Philosophy of the Social Sciences*, 27: 410–65.

——2004. How does it work? The search for explanatory mechanisms. *Philosophy of the Social Sciences*, 34: 182–210.

CARLSSON, G. 1968. Change, growth, and irreversibility. *American Journal of Sociology*, 73: 706–14.

COLEMAN, J. S. 1986. Social theory, social research, and a theory of action. *American Journal of Sociology*, 91: 1309–35.

COX, D. R. 1992. Causality: some statistical aspects. *Journal of the Royal Statistical Society, Series A: Statistics in Society*, 155: 291–301.

CRAVER, C. F. 2001. Role functions, mechanisms, and hierarchy. *Philosophy of Science*, 68: 53–74.

DAVIDSON, D. 1980. *Essays on Actions and Events*. Oxford: Clarendon Press.

DOWNS, A. 1957. *An Economic Theory of Democracy*. New York: Harper and Row.

ELSTER, J. 1983a. *Explaining Technical Change: A Case Study in the Philosophy of Science*. Cambridge: Cambridge University Press.

——1983b. *Sour Grapes: Studies in the Subversion of Rationality*. Cambridge: Cambridge University Press.

——1989. *Nuts and Bolts for the Social Sciences*. Cambridge: Cambridge University Press.

——1998. A plea for mechanisms. Pp. 45–73 in *Social Mechanisms: An Analytical Approach to Social Theory*, ed. P. Hedström and R. Swedberg. Cambridge: Cambridge University Press.

——1999. *Alchemies of the Mind: Rationality and the Emotions*. Cambridge: Cambridge University Press.

EPSTEIN, J. M., and AXTELL, R. 1996. *Growing Artificial Societies: Social Science from the Bottom up*. Washington, DC: Brookings Institution Press.

FESTINGER, L. 1957. *A Theory of Cognitive Dissonance*. Stanford, Calif.: Stanford University Press.

FREEDMAN, D. 1987. As others see us: a case study in path analysis. *Journal of Educational Statistics*, 12: 101–28.

—— 1991. Statistical models and shoe leather. *Sociological Methodology*, 21: 291–313.

—— 1992. A rejoinder on models, metaphors, and fables. Pp. 108–25 in *The Role of Models in Nonexperimental Social Science: Two Debates*, ed. J. P. Schaffer. Washington, DC: American Educational Research Association.

—— 1999. From association to causation: some remarks on the history of statistics. *Statistical Science*, 14: 243–58.

GAMBETTA, D. 1998. Concatenations of mechanisms. In *Social Mechanisms: An Analytical Approach to Social Theory*, ed. P. Hedström and R. Swedberg. Cambridge: Cambridge University Press.

GLENNAN, S. S. 1996. Mechanisms and the nature of causation. *Erkenntnis*, 44: 49–71.

GOLDTHORPE, J. H. 2000. *On Sociology: Numbers, Narratives, and the Integration of Research and Theory*. Oxford: Oxford University Press.

HEDSTRÖM, P. 1998. Rational imitation. Pp. 306–27 in *Social Mechanisms: An Analytical Approach to Social Theory*, ed. P. Hedström and R. Swedberg. Cambridge: Cambridge University Press.

—— 2005. *Dissecting the Social: On the Principles of Analytical Sociology*. Cambridge: Cambridge University Press.

—— and SWEDBERG, R. 1996. Social mechanisms. *Acta Sociologica*, 39: 281–308.

—— —— 1998. Social mechanisms: an introductory essay. Pp. 1–31 in *Social Mechanisms: An Analytical Approach to Social Theory*, ed. P. Hedström and R. Swedberg. Cambridge: Cambridge University Press.

HOLLAND, J. H. 1998. *Emergence: From Chaos to Order*. Cambridge, Mass.: Perseus.

KARLSSON, G. 1958. *Social Mechanisms: Studies in Sociological Theory*. Stockholm: Almqvist and Wiksell.

LITTLE, D. 1991. *Varieties of Social Explanation: An Introduction to the Philosophy of Social Science*. Boulder, Colo.: Westview.

MCADAM, D., TARROW, S., and TILLY, C. 2001. *Dynamics of Contention*. Cambridge: Cambridge University Press.

MACHAMER, P., DARDEN, L., and CRAVER, C. F. 2000. Thinking about mechanisms. *Philosophy of Science*, 67: 1–25.

MACY, M. W., and WILLER, R. 2002. From factors to actors: computational sociology and agent-based modeling. *Annual Review of Sociology*, 28: 143–66.

MAHONEY, J. 2001. Beyond correlational analysis: recent innovations in theory and method. *Sociological Forum*, 16: 575–93.

MAYNTZ, R. 2004. Mechanisms in the analysis of social macro-phenomena. *Philosophy of the Social Sciences*, 34: 237–59.

MERTON, R. K. 1968. The self-fulfilling prophecy. Pp. 475–90 in *Social Theory and Social Structure*, ed. R. K. Merton. New York: Free Press.

OLSON, M. 1965. *The Logic of Collective Action: Public Goods and the Theory of Groups*. Cambridge, Mass.: Harvard University Press.

PAWSON, R. 2000. Middle-range realism. *Archives européennes de sociologie*, 41: 283–325.

PEARL, J. 2000. *Causality: Models, Reasoning, and Inference*. Cambridge: Cambridge University Press.

SALMON, W. C. 1984. *Scientific Explanation and the Causal Structure of the World.* Princeton, NJ: Princeton University Press.

SCHELLING, T. C. 1978. *Micromotives and Macrobehavior.* New York: W. W. Norton.

——1998. Social mechanisms and social dynamics. Pp. 32–44 in *Social Mechanisms: An Analytical Approach to Social Theory,* ed. P. Hedström and R. Swedberg. Cambridge: Cambridge University Press.

SØRENSEN, A. B. 1998. Theoretical mechanisms and the empirical study of social processes. Pp. 238–66 in *Social Mechanisms: An Analytical Approach to Social Theory,* ed. P. Hedström and R. Swedberg. Cambridge: Cambridge University Press.

STINCHCOMBE, A. L. 1991. The conditions of fruitfulness of theorizing about mechanisms in social-science. *Philosophy of the Social Sciences,* 21: 367–88.

STRANG, D., and SOULE, S. A. 1998. Diffusion in organizations and social movements: from hybrid corn to poison pills. *Annual Review of Sociology,* 24: 265–90.

TOCQUEVILLE, A. DE 1998. *The Old Regime and the Revolution.* New York: Anchor.

VON WRIGHT, G. H. 1971. *Explanation and Understanding.* Ithaca, NY: Cornell University Press.

——1989. A reply to my critics. In *The Philosophy of George Henrik von Wright,* ed. P. A. Schlipp and L. E. Hahn. La Salle, Ill.: Open Court.

WATTS, D. J., and STROGATZ, S. H. 1998. Collective dynamics of "small world" networks. *Nature,* 393: 440–2.

WHITE, H., BOORMAN, S. A., and BREIGER, R. L. 1976. Social structure from multiple networks: blockmodels of roles and positions. *American Journal of Sociology,* 81: 730–80.

WHITE, H. C. 1970. *Chains of Opportunity: System Models of Mobility in Organizations.* Cambridge, Mass.: Harvard University Press.

WIKSTRÖM, P.-O. 2007. Individuals, settings, and acts of crime: situational mechanisms and the explanation of crime. Ch. 3 in *The Explanation of Crime: Contexts, Mechanisms and Development,* ed. P.-O. Wikström and R. J. Sampson. Cambridge: Cambridge University Press.

WINSHIP, C., and HARDING, D. J. 2008. A mechanism based strategy for the identification of age-period-cohort models. *Sociological Methodology and Research,* 36: 362–401.

PART V

EXPERIMENTS, QUASI-EXPERIMENTS, AND NATURAL EXPERIMENTS

EXPERIMENTATION IN POLITICAL SCIENCE

REBECCA B. MORTON
KENNETH C. WILLIAMS

1 THE ADVENT OF EXPERIMENTAL POLITICAL SCIENCE

EXPERIMENTATION is increasing dramatically in political science. Figure 14.1 shows the number of experimental articles published by decade in three major mainstream journals—the *American Political Science Review* (APSR), *American Journal of Political Science* (AJPS), and *Journal of Politics* (JOP)—from 1950 to 2005.[1] These figures do not include the new use of so-called "survey experiments" and "natural experiments." Moreover, other political science journals have published political experimental articles, such as *Economics and Politics*, *Political Behavior*, *Political Psychology*, *Public Choice*, *Public Opinion Quarterly*, and the *Journal of Conflict Resolution*, as have numerous economics and social psychology journals. Furthermore, a number of political scientists have published experimental work in research monographs; see for example Ansolabehere and Iyengar (1997), Lupia and McCubbins (1998), and Morton and Williams (2001).

As discussed in Kinder and Palfrey (1993), there are a number of reasons for the increase in experimentation in political science in the 1970s and 1980s. We believe that

---

[1] Earlier figures are from McGraw and Hoekstra (1994); more recent ones were compiled by the authors. Note that our figures are significantly greater than those compiled by McDermott (2002).

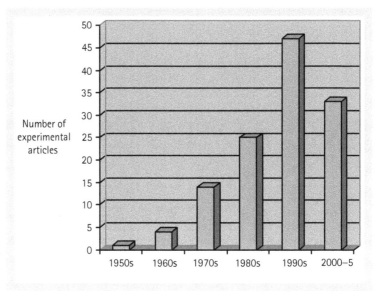

Fig. 14.1. Experimental articles published in APSR, AJPS & JOP 1950–2005

the dominant explanation for the expansion since 1990 is the increase in cheap and easily programmable computer networking technology, for the number of possible experimental designs via laboratory networks and over the internet is hugely greater than what researchers can conduct manually. Computer technology has also led to a greater ability to engage in survey experiments, and to deal with the statistical and other methodological issues that are sometimes involved in field and natural experiments. Technology has transformed political science into an experimental discipline. In this chapter we explore the expanding area of experimental political science and some of the concerns involved in experimentation.[2]

2 WHAT IS AN EXPERIMENT?

2.1 The Myth of the Ideal Experiment

Political science is a discipline that is defined by the substance of what we study—politics. As Beck (2000) remarks, researchers "freely use whatever methodological

---

McDermott's calculations were limited to publications by certain authors according to undefined criteria (established political scientists).

[2] A full and detailed treatment of experimentation in political science cannot be presented in a chapter-length study; we encourage readers to consult Morton and Williams (2008), who expand on the concepts and issues presented here.

solutions are available," drawing from other social sciences like economics, sociology, and psychology—as well as statistics and applied mathematics—to answer substantive questions. Unfortunately, this has led to misinterpretations as experimentalists learn about their method from other disciplines, and few nonexperimentalists have an understanding of advances that have occurred outside political science. The most prominent misconception is that the best experiment is one where a researcher manipulates one variable, called a treatment, while having an experimental group who receives the treatment and a control group who does not, and randomly assigning subjects across groups. This perception arises largely because most nonexperimentalists learn about experiments through the lens of behavioral social science methods formulated in the 1950s. Certainly such a design can be perfect for the case where a researcher is interested in the causal effect of a binary variable that might affect the choices of subjects in some known context, and the researcher is interested in nothing else. But this is rarely true for any significant question in twenty-first-century political science research. Furthermore, the aforementioned advances in technology have changed the nature of experimental research in fundamental ways that researchers writing in the 1950s could not have anticipated. By adhering to an outdated view of what an experiment should be and what is possible with experimentation, political scientists often rule out experimentation as a useful method for many interesting research questions.

There is no perfect or true experiment. The appropriate experimental design depends on the research question, just as is the case with observational data. In fact, the variety of possible experimental designs and treatments is in some ways greater than the range of possibilities with observational data. But how is experimental research different from research with observational data? That is, what is experimental political science?

2.2 How Experimental Data Differs from Observational Data

The defining characteristic of experimental research is intervention by the researcher in the *data-generating process* (DGP), which we define as the source of the data we use in research. In experimental research, the variation in the data is partly a consequence of the researcher's decisions at the design stage before the data are measured. We call the data generated by such intervention *experimental data*. Nonexperimental empirical research involves using only data in which all the variation is a consequence of factors outside of the control of the researcher—that is, the researcher only observes the DGP, but does not intervene in that process.[3] We call this data *observational or nonexperimental data*.

---

[3] This assumes that the researcher measures the data perfectly; clearly choices made in measurement can result in a type of post-DGP intervention.

3 OTHER FEATURES OF EXPERIMENTATION

Beyond intervention, some would contend that control and random assignment are "must have" attributes to an experiment. Below we discuss these two additional features.

3.1 Control

In the out-of-date view of political experimentation, control refers to a baseline treatment that allows a researcher to gather data where he or she has not intervened. But many experiments do not have a clear baseline, and in some cases it is not necessary. For example, suppose a researcher is interested in evaluating how voters choose in a three-party election conducted by plurality rule as compared to how they would choose in an identical three-party election conducted via proportional representation. The researcher might conduct two laboratory elections where subjects' payments depend on the outcome of the election, but some subjects vote in a proportional representation election and others vote in a plurality rule election. The researcher can then compare voter behavior in the two treatments.

In this experiment and many like it, the aspect of control that is most important is not the fact that the researcher has a comparison, but that the researcher can control confounding variables such as voter preferences and candidate identities in order to make the comparison meaningful. To make the same causal inference solely with observational data the researcher would need to do two things: (1) rely on statistical methods to control for observable confounding variables such as control functions in regression equations, proximity scores, or matching methods, and (2) make the untestable assumption that there are no unobservable variables that confound the causal relationship the researcher is attempting to measure.[4] In observational data, things like candidate identities cannot be held constant and it may be impossible to "match" the observable variables. By being able to control these things, an experimentalist can ensure that observable variables are perfectly matched and that many unobservable variables are actually made observable (and made subject to the same matching).

3.2 Random Assignment

Most nonexperimentalists think of random assignment as the principal way that an experimentalist deals with unobservable variables. If subjects are randomly assigned to treatments, then the experimentalist can eliminate—within statistical limits—extraneous factors that can obscure the effects that the experimentalist expects to observe (or not observe), such as voter cognitive abilities, gender differences in voter behavior, and so on. For this reason, experimentalists typically attempt to randomly

---

[4] Morton and Williams (2008) discuss these issues in depth.

assign manipulations as much as possible, and when random assignment is not perfect they employ statistical techniques to account for uncontrolled variables that can be observed.

3.3 Simulations versus Experiments

Occasionally political scientists use the term experiment to refer to a computer simulation that either solves a formal model or explores the implications of an estimated empirical model. We do not include such analyses here. In experimental political science the subjects' choices are independent of the researcher's brain; the subjects affect their own choices in ways that the researcher cannot control. As opposed to simulations, subjects in experiments freely make decisions within the controlled environment constructed by the experimenter.

3.4 Natural Experiments

Sometimes nature acts in a way that is close to how a researcher, given the choice, would have intervened. For example, hurricane Katrina displaced thousands of New Orleans residents and changed the political make-up of the city; it also had an impact on locations that received large numbers of refugees. This event, although devastating to many, provides researchers the opportunity to evaluate theories of how elected representatives respond to changing constituencies, in particular large changes in the racial and ethnic composition of the population. For example, US Census surveys in the spring of 2006 showed that the African-American population in Orleans parish, Louisiana, fell from 36 percent to 21 percent and a study by Tulane University and the University of California, Berkeley, found that the percentage of Latinos in the city doubled from 4 percent to 8 percent as many immigrants filled clean-up jobs. Such situations are called *natural experiments*. In the event of Katrina, it is *as if* nature was composed of two separate personalities: the one that generated most data, and then the interventionist one that occasionally ran experiments like academics, messing up the other personality's data generating process.

4 THE VALIDITY OF EXPERIMENTAL POLITICAL SCIENCE RESEARCH

4.1 Defining Validity

The most important question facing empirical researchers is "what can we believe about what we learn from the data or how valid is the research?" The most definitive recent study of validity is provided in the work of Shadish, Cook, and Campbell (2002) (hereafter SCC). They use the term *validity* as "the approximate truth" of the inference or knowledge claim. As McGraw and Hoekstra (1994) remark, political scientists have adopted a simplistic view of validity based on the early division of Campbell (1957), using internal validity to refer to how robust experimental results are within the experimental data, and external validity to refer to how robust experimental results are outside the experiment.[5] Again, we note that political scientists are adhering to an outdated view, for there are actually many ways to measure the validity of empirical research, both experimental and observational.

SCC divide validity into four types, each of which are explained below: *statistical conclusion validity*, *internal validity*, *construct validity*, and *external validity*. Statistical conclusion validity is defined as whether there is statistically significant covariance between the variables the researcher is interested in, and whether the relationship is sizeable. Internal validity is defined as the determination of whether the relationships the researcher finds within the particular data-set analyzed are causal relationships. It is important to note that this is a much more narrow definition than generally perceived by many political scientists. In fact, Campbell (1986) relabeled internal validity to local molar causal validity.

When some political scientists think of internal validity, particularly with respect to experiments that evaluate formal models or take place in the laboratory, they are referring to construct validity. Construct validity has to do with how valid the inferences of the data are for the theory (or constructs) that the researcher is evaluating. SCC emphasize issues of sampling accuracy—that is, is this an appropriate data-set for evaluating the theory? Is there a close match between what the theory is about and what is happening in the manipulated data-generating process? Thus, when political scientists refer to internal validity they are often referring to a package of three things: statistical conclusion validity, local molar causal validity, and construct validity.

4.2 Are Experiments Externally Valid?

External validity is whether causal inferences established in an empirical analysis hold over variations in persons, settings, treatment variables, and measurement variables. Do the results from one data-set generalize to another? This is a question that is of importance for any empirical researcher, regardless of whether the data-set is experimental or observational. For example, if we study voter turnout in congressional elections, can we generalize from that study to turnout in mayoral elections, or elections in Germany, or elections held in a laboratory? Yet most political scientists rarely worry about the external validity issue with observational data, but *do* worry about it with experimental data.

---

[5] For an example of how the outdated view of validity still dominates discussions of experimentation in political science see McDermott (2002, 35–8).

Political scientists typically assume that external validity means that the data-set used for the analysis must resemble some "natural" or unmanipulated DGP. Since experimentation means manipulation and control of the DGP by the researcher, and an experimental data-set generated through that manipulation and control, then some argue that the results cannot be externally valid by definition. Nevertheless, even in observational data, by choosing variables to measure and study and by focusing on particular aspects of the data, the researcher also engages in manipulation and control through statistical and measurement choices. The researcher who works with observational data simplifies and ignores factors or makes assumptions about those things he or she cannot measure. Thus, the observational data-set is also not natural since it is similarly divorced from the natural DGP; by the same reasoning the results also cannot be externally valid.

It is a mistake to equate external validity with whether a given data-set—used to establish a particular causal relationship—resembles the unmanipulated DGP (which can never be accurately measured or observed). Instead, establishing whether a result is externally valid involves replication of the result across a variety of data-sets. For example, if a researcher discovered that more informed voters were more likely to turnout in congressional elections, and then found this also to be true in mayoral elections, in elections in Germany, and in an experiment with control and manipulation, then we would say the result showed high external validity. The same thing is true with results that originate from experimental analysis. If an experiment demonstrates a particular causal relationship, then whether that relationship is externally valid is determined by examining the relationship across a range of experimental and observational data-sets; it is not ascertained by seeing if the original experimental data-set resembles a hypothesized version of the unmanipulated DGP.

One of the most interesting developments in experimental research has come in laboratory experiments that test the behavioral assumptions in rational choice based models in economics. In order to test these assumptions a researcher must be able to maintain significant control over the choices before an individual and be able to measure subtle differences in preference decisions as these choices are manipulated by the researcher. These things are extremely hard to discern in observational data since it is almost impossible to measure isolated preference changes with enough variation in choices. The robustness of some of the behavioral violations has been established across a wide range of experimental data-sets. An entire new field within economics, behavioral game theory, has evolved as a consequence, with a whole new set of perspectives on understanding economic behavior—this is something that was almost unthinkable twenty years ago. It is odd that many in political science who disagree with assumptions made in rational choice models are also quick to dismiss the experiments which test these assumptions; these critics claim that these experiments do not have external validity, but external validity is really about the robustness of these experiments across different formulations, and not about whether the experiment resembles the hypothesized unmanipulated DGP.

5 DIMENSIONS OF EXPERIMENTATION IN POLITICAL SCIENCE

5.1 Location: Field, Lab, or Web?

A dimension that is especially salient among political scientists, particularly nonexperimentalists, is location. *Laboratory experiments* are experiments where the subjects are recruited to a common location, the experiment is largely conducted at that location, and the researcher controls almost all aspects in the environment in that location, *except* for subjects' behavior. *Field experiments* are experiments where the researcher's intervention takes place in an environment where the researcher has only limited control beyond the intervention conducted, and the relationship between the researcher and the subject is conducted often through variables such as postal delivery times or work schedules of subjects outside of the researcher's control. Furthermore, since many of the individuals in a field experiment that are affected by the researcher are not aware that they are being manipulated, these also raise ethical issues not generally involved in laboratory experiments. For example, in Wantchekon's (2003) experiment in Benin, candidates were induced to vary their campaign messages in order to examine the effects of different messages on voter behavior. But voters were unaware that they were subjects in an experimental manipulation.

5.2 Why Laboratories?

First, laboratory experiments provide a researcher with greater control. For example, suppose that a researcher is conducting a decision-making experiment that evaluates the extent to which different types of campaign advertisements affect voter preferences. In the laboratory, the researcher can show the ads in a specially designed environment that can be held constant across subjects. In the field, however, though subjects can be shown the ads in their homes or via the internet, the researcher loses control over other aspects of the environment in which the ads are watched. If these environmental differences vary systematically with which ads are viewed or if there are other factors that affect the subjects' viewing of the ads, and if these factors are unobservable by the researcher, then the comparison between ads can be more difficult to determine. The advantage of control in the laboratory also extends to group experiments such as the aforementioned one involving a comparison between voters in plurality versus proportional representation systems.

Second, in the laboratory the researcher has the ability to create environments that simply do not exist in observational data. For example, in the laboratory the researcher can conduct group and individual decision-making experiments on specific voting mechanisms that are used very little—if at all—in any country. Many have proposed that approval voting would be a better choice mechanism than plurality or proportional representation,[6] and in the laboratory a researcher can create and conduct elections using new procedures that it would be difficult to convince jurisdictions to adopt on a random basis (as in Bassi 2006).

The third advantage of laboratory experiments is that the researcher can induce a wider range of variation than is possible in the field. For example, suppose a researcher theorizes that voters who choose late in sequential voting elections—like presidential primaries—learn about candidates' policy positions from horse race information about the outcomes of early voting, and that this learning affects their choices in the elections. In the field the researcher can randomly provide horse race information to later voters during a presidential primary contest, and then observe how the provision affects their choices and information measured via survey instruments. But suppose the researcher also expects that the effect is related to the policy positions of the candidates. In the laboratory the researcher can not only provide information randomly, but can also randomly vary the candidates' policy positions to see if the effect is robust to this manipulation; a researcher can do this because the laboratory affords the opportunity to intervene in hundreds of elections, and not just one. Thus, while the number and variety of observations limits the researcher in the field, the experimentalist is able to pick up on subtle differences in prediction of theories.

Independent of these advantages, laboratories are still necessary for some technologies and manipulations. In particular, social scientists are beginning to use fMRI equipment to measure brain activity as subjects make choices (see Dickson and Scheve 2006); currently such equipment is not portable. Other experiments involve subjects in face-to-face interactions—as in some free-form deliberation experiments that test theories about social interaction and discussion. Such experiments would be extremely difficult, if not impossible, to conduct outside of a laboratory.

5.3 Why the Field or the Internet?

Field and internet experiments can potentially focus on either the group or the individual, although most are currently individual decision-making experiments. An early example of a field experiment in political science was Gosnell's (1927) study. By sending postcards containing information on voter registration (the postcards also encouraged individuals to vote) to some voters and not to others, he manipulated the environment of the subjects. However, Gosnell did not randomly assign his treatments. More recently, Gerber and Green (2000) replicated Gosnell's experiments making use of current understandings of statistical inference.

Survey experiments are an increasingly popular type of field (and sometimes internet) experiment in political science. In a particularly noteworthy survey experiment, Sullivan, Pierson, and Marcus (1978) compared the question format used by the National Election Studies prior to 1964 with that used later. Researchers using the data

---

[6] See for example Brams and Fishburn (1983).

had found that the surveys showed significantly different attitudes towards politics over time. But at the same time, the survey questions had changed. Thus, to determine whether attitudes had truly changed, or whether the survey question format changes accounted for the results, Sullivan et al. surveyed the same set of voters but randomly determined which set of questions (pre-1964 or after) each respondent would be asked. The researchers found that the change in the format of the survey implied that the respondents' had different political attitudes, and concluded that the empirical analysis comparing the two time periods was fundamentally flawed.

The most exciting advances in survey experimental design can be found in the work of Paul Sniderman and colleagues with respect to computer-assisted telephone interviewing (CATI) (see Sniderman, Brody, and Tetlock 1991). Using computers, telephone interviewers can randomly assign questions to subjects, thereby manipulating the question environment. The National Science Foundation funded program Time-Sharing Experiments in the Social Sciences (TESS) has facilitated the advancement of survey experiments in political science, providing researchers with a large, randomly selected, diverse subject population for such experiments (not to mention the infrastructure needed for conducting the experiments with this population).[7] For a more comprehensive review of current field experiments, see the chapter by Gerber and Green in this volume.

5.4 Audience or Goal: Theorists, Empiricists, or Policy-makers?

Experiments vary in both the audience that they address and the goal of the analysis. Experimental political scientists have three types of audiences—theorists, empiricists, and policy-makers.[8]

5.4.1 Theory Testing

As in a number of observational studies, some experimentation in political science evaluates nonformal theories. A nonformal theory or model is one in which hypotheses are proposed about the DGP, but the assumptions behind the hypotheses are not precisely stated. One example of such work is that of Lau and Redlawsk's (2001) study, which evaluates a theory from political psychology, hypothesizing that voters use cognitive heuristics in decision-making. Another example of nonformal theory evaluation using experiments is contained in the work of Mutz (2006) who, using both experimental and observational work, challenges arguments of political theorists about the benefits of face-to-face deliberative interactions. The relationship between the theory and experimental data in nonformal theory testing is much the same as the relationship between the theory and observational

---

[7] Arthur Lupia and Diana Mutz have been particularly influential scholars in this field (see, for example, Lupia and McCubbins 1998 and Mutz 2006).

[8] We build on distinctions discussed in Davis and Holt (1993) and Roth (1994).

data in similar evaluations of nonformal theory and is already familiar to political scientists.[9]

Other experimental work in political science, which is recently reviewed in Palfrey (2005), evaluates formal models with experimental data. Fiorina and Plott (1978) is an example of one of the first such experimental tests. A formal theory or model is one in which assumptions made regarding the DGP are explicitly stated and the implications of those assumptions are then solved for (usually) using tools from mathematics. Formal theory testing using experiments is distinctive from most of the empirical research conducted by political scientists for two reasons. First, researchers can use the explicit nature of the model's assumptions to guide the experimental design yielding a close link between the theory and the experimental manipulations. Second, researchers can directly evaluate the underlying assumptions of their theories in experiments, which is not possible when evaluating nonformal theories where the assumptions are not stated or when using observational data to evaluate formal models. Thus we expand on how these experiments proceed in the next sub-section.

5.5 An Example: Theory Testing of Formal Models

In formal models the assumptions are of two types: assumptions about institutional and other exogenous factors such as voting rules, bargaining procedures, preference distributions, and so forth; and assumptions about the behavioral choices of the political actors in the context of these exogenous factors. For example, suppose a formal model considers three-candidate elections. In the model, in plurality rule elections without majority requirements voters are more likely to vote strategically for their second preference but sincerely for their first preference in plurality rule elections with majority requirements. The model makes assumptions about both electoral institutions and voter rationality, and the predictions are behavioral.

An experimentalist can create the electoral institution and then pay subjects based on the outcomes of voting that induce a preference ordering over the candidates. An example of such a payment schedule is shown in Table 14.1. Note that the payoffs are received based on who wins, not based on how a voter chooses. For example, if subjects who are assigned to be Type 1 voted for candidate A, and that candidate wins the election, then that subject would receive $1 for the election period. However, if candidate C wins but candidate B is chosen, the subject would receive only $0.10.

Under the plurality rule, if all voters voted sincerely for the candidate for whom they would receive the highest payoff, then Candidate C would win. But, for example, if voters who are Type 1 vote strategically for B, while the other voters choose sincerely, B would win. Similarly, if voters who are Type 2 vote strategically for A while the other

---

[9] For a more expansive recent review of the political-psychological experimental research, see McDermott (2002). Morton (1999) reviews and discusses the differences between formal and nonformal theory evaluation as well as a number of other examples of such work.

Table 14.1. An example payoff schedule in a voting experiment

Voter types	Winning candidate ($)			
	A	B	C	Number of voters
1	1.00	0.75	0.10	3
2	0.75	1.00	0.10	3
3	0.25	0.25	1.00	4

voters choose sincerely, A would win. As Myerson and Weber (1993) demonstrate, formally the voting situation of all three of these outcomes are equilibria in pure strategies.

Suppose now, however, that there is a majority requirement—that is, in order for a candidate to win, he or she must receive at least 50 percent of the vote. If no candidate receives more than 50 percent of the vote, a run-off election is held between the two top vote receivers. In such a case then, even if all voters vote sincerely in the first round election and candidate C wins that vote, C would have to face either A or B in a run-off (assuming that ties are broken by random draws). In a run-off, either A or B would beat C, so C cannot win. Of course voters of Types 1 and 2 might engage in strategic voting in the first round (as discussed above), thereby avoiding the need for a run-off. Morton and Rietz (2006) formally demonstrate that when there are majority requirements and voters perceive that there is some probability— albeit perhaps small—that their votes can affect the electoral outcome, that the only equilibrium is for voters to vote sincerely in the first stage and let the random draw for second place choose which candidate faces C in a run-off (and then wins the election).

In the end, this theory suggests that strategic voting (in our payoff matrix) is not likely when there are majority requirements, but is possible when these requirements do not exist. These predictions depend on assumptions about payoffs, voting rules, and the distribution of voter types, as well as voter rationality. An experimenter can create a situation that closely matches these theoretical assumptions about payoffs, voting rules, and the distribution of voter types, and then evaluate whether individuals act in accordance with theoretical predictions. The results from such an experiment tell the theorist about the plausibility of their assumptions about human behavior.

5.6 Searching for Facts

Political scientists, like economists, also use experiments to search for facts. For example, as noted in the aforementioned voting game (Table 14.1), when votes are counted according to the plurality rule there are multiple equilibria. Myerson and Weber (1993) conjecture (but do not prove) that campaign contributions and public opinion polls can serve as a coordinating device for voters of Types 1 and 2; that is, they argue that these types of voters would like to coordinate on a common candidate. One way such coordination may be facilitated is by focusing on whichever candidate is ahead in a public opinion poll or in campaign contribution funds prior to the election. However, there is no basis within the Myerson and Weber theory on which to argue that voters will use polls or contributions in this fashion. Researchers have used experiments to see if voters do use polls and campaign contributions to coordinate, and the results support Myerson and Weber's conjecture that polls and contributions can serve as a coordination device (Rietz 2003).

In contrast to the approach of relaxing theoretical assumptions or investigating conjectures in the context of a theoretically driven model as above, some prominent political scientists see searching for facts through experiments as a substitute for theorizing. For example, Gerber and Green (2002) advocate experiments as an opportunity to search for facts with little or no theory, remarking (2002, 820): "The beauty of experimentation is that one need not possess a complete theoretical model of the phenomenon under study. By assigning . . . at random, one guarantees that the only factors that could give rise to a correlation . . . occur by chance alone." Although they go on to recognize the value of having theoretical underpinnings more generally, they clearly see this as simply being more efficient; they do not view a theoretical model as a necessary component in the experimental search for facts.

5.7 The Need for Theory in Experimentation

How necessary is a well-articulated theory for learning from experiments? Is it possible to discover knowledge without theory? Is theorizing merely an aid to experimental political science, but not a requirement? The argument for this position is based on the presumption that causality can be determined without theory—by the trial and error of manipulating various causes and determining their effects through experimentation, facts and nuances can be accumulated that eventually lead to greater knowledge (with or without theory). But what does it mean to measure causality in the experimental setting? Measuring causality *requires* that a researcher think hypothetically or theoretically, having a model of the data-generating process.

To see how theorizing is necessary when searching for facts, consider a simple field experiment on voter information. Suppose that a researcher randomly assigns a set of voters in an upcoming election to a treatment group that receives informative campaign material, and a control group that does not. The researcher then measures how voters in the treated and control groups voted. In order to make a causal inference about the effect of the treatment on voter behavior, researchers who are searching for facts—like Gerber and Green—typically take a Rubin Causal Model approach (hereafter RCM) to establishing causality (see Holland 1988; Rubin 1974). The researcher using an RCM approach to establish a causal inference must hypothesize that for each voter in each group there are two potential behavioral choices: a choice the voter makes when fully informed and a choice a voter makes when uninformed. Of course, because only one state of the world is ever observed for any given voter, the researcher must hypothesize that these counterfactual worlds exist (even though she knows that they do not). Furthermore, the researcher must then make what is called the stable unit treatment assumption (SUTVA), which demands no cross-effects of treatment from one subject onto another's choices, homogeneity of treatment across subjects, and a host of other implicit assumptions about the DGP that are often left unexplored (Morton and Williams 2008). Finally, the researcher must also typically make the untestable assumption that unobservable variables do not confound the effect that she is measuring; that there are no selection effects that interfere with the randomization he is using in the experimental design. In the end, searching for facts—even in field experiments—requires that a researcher theorize. It is not possible to search for facts and discover nuances of the DGP through trial and error without theorizing about that process.

5.8 A Test Bed for Political Methodologists

Searching for facts is not the only way in which experimental research can provide useful information for empirical scholars. Methodologists often test their approaches on simulated data to see if known parameters can be recovered. However, experiments can serve as a *behavioral test bed*. The use of experimental data to test methodologies goes back to at least the work of LaLonde (1986), who compared experimental estimates of the impact of a training program with a range of nonexperimental estimates of the same program. LaLonde found that the nonexperimental estimates varied widely, and that although some came close to the experimental estimates, there was no a priori way for the empirical researcher to determine which estimates were more reliable. This analysis led to many new developments in the econometric literature on the estimation of treatment effects in observational data (for more see Morton and Williams 2008).

More recently, Frechette, Kagel, and Morelli (2005) compare empirical procedures used by Ansolabehere et al. (2005), as well as Warwick and Druckman (2001), to evaluate models of legislative bargaining over ministry divisions when forming governments. Using observational data, researchers can only evaluate the *ex post* distributions and argue that they are the same as predicted by a given theory since it is impossible to observe the secret bargaining process that the legislators typically employ. Ansolabehere et al. (2005) find support for the Baron–Ferejohn legislative bargaining model (see Baron and Ferejohn 1989) with observational data from a cross-section of industrialized democracies. However, using the same data, Warwick and Druckman (2001) find support for a demand-bargaining model (see Morelli 1999).

Which empirical study is correct? Frechette, Kagel, and Morelli use data from laboratory experiments where the underlying bargaining framework was controlled by the researchers. In some treatments the underlying bargaining model is a Baron–Ferejohn game and in others the underlying bargaining model is a demand-bargaining game. In the laboratory, subjects are paid based on their choices, and thus they are induced to have preferences as hypothesized by the two theories. Frechette, Kagel, and Morelli (2005) then take the data from each treatment individually and apply the estimation strategies employed by Ansolabehere et al. and Warwick and Druckman to the experimental data—they do so as if they did not know the underlying bargaining game used in that treatment, as if the data was observational. Frechette, Kagel, and Morelli (2005) find that the empirical estimation strategies fail to distinguish between different bargaining procedures used in the laboratory. Thus, their results show that some standard empirical strategies used by political scientists on observational data are unlikely to identify correctly the underlying bargaining game and explain how two researchers using the same observational data may find support for two different theories of legislative bargaining.

5.9 Experimentalists as Politicians' Assistants

Finally, political scientists also conduct experiments in order to speak to policy-makers. Gosnell's (1927) early field experiment was arguably an attempt to whisper in the ears of princes; it is well known that he was highly involved in everyday politics in his Chicago community. Gerber and Green (2004) have written a book—based on their experimental research—on techniques of mobilizing voters; this is expressly addressed to those involved in election campaigns.

Moreover, Gerber and Green (2002) have argued that the relationship between political experimentalists in field experiments and actors in politics is a potentially interactive one, and that increased experimentation by political scientists will increase the relevance of political science research for political actors. For example, suppose that an interest group is uncertain about which advertising strategy is likely to work in an upcoming election. If the interest group is induced to randomize their advertisements across television markets by an experimentalist, both the experimentalist and the interest group can gain knowledge about the causal effects of such advertisements; presumably, then, the interest group can then use this knowledge to make more efficient future choices.

But should political scientists, as Gerber and Green advocate, increase their focus on experiments that can interest and be directly relevant to the nonacademic community? Certainly, some experiments can serve this purpose. There are certainly questions about politics that are of interest to both academics and nonacademics. But there are risks given that nonacademics may have financial resources to pay for the services of academics; the weight of dollars can impact the choice of which questions are asked, and how they are asked. Furthermore, nonacademics may not be as willing to share information gathered through such research, given that politics is a competitive arena.

6 CONCLUDING REMARKS

Political science is an experimental discipline. Nevertheless, we argue that most political scientists have a view of experimentation that fits with a 1950s understanding of research methodology, and one that especially misunderstands the issue of external validity. These false perceptions lead many political scientists to dismiss experimental work as not being relevant to substantive questions of interest. In this chapter we have provided an analysis of twenty-first-century experimentation in political science, and have demonstrated the wide variety of ways in which experimentation can be used to answer interesting research questions while speaking to theorists, empiricists, and policy-makers.

We expect the use of experimentation techniques to continue to rise in political science, just as it has in other social sciences. In particular, we expect that the technological revolution will continue to expand the opportunities for experimentation in political science in two important ways. First, the expansion of interactive Web-based experimental methods will allow researchers to conduct large-scale experiments testing game-theoretic models that have previously only been contemplated. For example, through the internet, it is possible for researchers to consider how voting rules might affect outcomes in much larger electorates than has been possible in the laboratory. Second, advances in brain-imaging technology will allow political scientists to explore much more deeply the connections between cognitive processes and political decisions. These two types of experiments will join with traditional laboratory and field experiments to transform political science into a discipline where experimental work will one day be as prevalent as traditional observational analyses.

REFERENCES

ANSOLABEHERE, S., and IYENGAR, S. 1997. *Going Negative: How Political Advertisements Shrink and Polarize the Electorate.* New York: Free Press.
——STRAUSS, A., SNYDER, J., and TING, M. 2005. Voting weights and formateur advantages in the formation of coalition governments. *American Journal of Political Science*, 49: 550–63.
BARON, D., and FEREJOHN, J. 1989. Bargaining in legislatures. *American Political Science Review*, 83: 1181–206.
BASSI, A. 2006. Experiments on approval voting. Working paper, New York University.
BECK, N. 2000. Political methodology: a welcoming discipline. *Journal of the American Statistical Association*, 95: 651–4.
BRAMS, S., and FISHBURN, P. 1983. *Approval Voting.* Cambridge, Mass.: Birkhauser.
CAMPBELL, D. T. 1957. Factors relevant to the validity of experiments in social settings. *Psychological Bulletin*, 54: 297–312.

——1986. Science's social system of validity-enhancing collective belief change and the problems of the social sciences. Ch. 19 in *Selected Papers*, ed. E. S. Overman. Chicago: University of Chicago Press.

DAVIS, D., and HOLT, C. 1993. *Experimental Economics*. Princeton, NJ: Princeton University Press.

DICKSON, E., and SCHEVE, K. 2006. Testing the effect of social identity appeals in election campaigns: an fMRI study. Working paper, Yale University.

FIORINA, M., and PLOTT, C. 1978. Committee decisions under majority rule. *American Political Science Review*, 72: 575–98.

FRECHETTE, G., KAGEL, J., and MORELLI, M. 2005. Behavioral identification in coalitional bargaining: an experimental analysis of demand bargaining and alternating offers. *Econometrica*, 73: 1893–937.

GERBER, A., and GREEN, D. 2000. The effects of canvassing, direct mail, and telephone calls on voter turnout: a field experiment. *American Political Science Review*, 94: 653–63.

——2002. Reclaiming the experimental tradition in political science. Pp. 805–32 in *Political Science: State of the Discipline*, ed. I. Katznelson and H. V. Milner. New York: W. W. Norton.

——2004. *Get out the Vote: How to Increase Vote Turnout*. Washington, DC: Brookings.

GOSNELL, H. 1927. *Getting out the Vote: An Experiment in the Stimulation of Voting*. Chicago: University of Chicago Press.

HOLLAND, P. W. 1988. Causal inference, path analysis, and recursive structural equation models (with discussion). Pp. 449–93 in *Sociological Methodology*, ed. C. C. Clogg. Washington, DC: American Sociological Association.

KINDER, D., and PALFREY, T. R. 1993. On behalf of an experimental political science. Pp. 1–42 in *Experimental Foundations of Political Science*, ed. D. Kinder and T. Palfrey. Ann Arbor: University of Michigan Press.

LALONDE, R. 1986. Evaluating the econometric evaluations of training programs. *American Economic Review*, 76: 604–20.

LAU, R. R., and REDLAWSK, D. P. 2001. Advantages and disadvantages of cognitive heuristics in political decision making. *American Journal of Political Science*, 45: 951–71.

LUPIA, A., and McCUBBINS, M. 1998. *The Democratic Dilemma: Can Citizens Learn What They Need to Know?* Cambridge: Cambridge University Press.

McDERMOTT, R. 2002. Experimental methods in political science. *Annual Review of Political Science*, 5: 31–61.

McGRAW, K., and HOEKSTRA, V. 1994. Experimentation in political science: historical trends and future directions. Pp. 3–30 in *Research in Micropolitics*, vol. iv, ed. M. Delli Carpini, L. Huddy, and R. Y. Shapiro. Greenwood, Conn.: JAI Press.

MORELLI, M. 1999. Demand competition and policy compromise in legislative bargaining. *American Political Science Review*, 93: 809–20.

MORTON, R. 1999. *Methods and Models: A Guide to the Empirical Analysis of Formal Models in Political Science*. Cambridge: Cambridge University Press.

——and RIETZ, T. 2006. Majority requirements and strategic coordination. Working paper, New York University.

——and WILLIAMS, K. 2001. *Learning by Voting: Sequential Choices in Presidential Primaries and Other Elections*. Ann Arbor: University of Michigan Press.

——2008. Experimental political science and the study of causality. Unpublished manuscript, New York University.

MUTZ, D. C. 2006. *Hearing the Other Side: Deliberative Versus Participatory Democracy.* Cambridge: Cambridge University Press.

MYERSON, R., and WEBER, R. 1993. A theory of voting equilibria. *American Political Science Review*, 87: 102–14.

PALFREY, T. 2005. Laboratory experiments in political economy. Center for Economic Policy Studies Working Paper No. 111, Princeton University.

RIETZ, T. 2003. Three-way experimental election results: strategic voting, coordinated outcomes and Duverger's Law. In *The Handbook of Experimental Economics Results*, ed. C. R. Plott and V. L. Smith. Amsterdam: Elsevier Science.

ROTH, A. 1994. Introduction to experimental economics. In *Handbook of Experimental Economics*, ed. J. Kagel and A. Roth. Princeton, NJ: Princeton University Press.

RUBIN, D. B. 1974. Estimating causal effects of treatments in randomized and nonrandomized studies. *Journal of Educational Psychology*, 66: 688–701.

SHADISH, W. R., COOK, T. D., and CAMPBELL, D. T. 2002. *Experimental and Quasi-Experimental Designs for Generalized Causal Inference.* Boston, Mass.: Houghton Mifflin.

SNIDERMAN, P. M., BRODY, R. A., and TETLOCK, P. E. 1991. *Reasoning and Choice: Explorations in Political Psychology.* New York: Cambridge University Press.

SULLIVAN, J. L., PIERESON, J. E., and MARCUS, G. E. 1978. Ideological constraint in the mass public: a methodological critique and some new findings. *American Journal of Political Science*, 22: 233–49.

WANTCHEKON, L. 2003. Clientelism and voting behavior: evidence from a field experiment in Benin. *World Politics*, 55: 399–422.

WARWICK, P., and DRUCKMAN, J. 2001. Portfolio salience and the proportionality of payoffs in coalition government. *British Journal of Political Science*, 31: 627–49.

FIELD EXPERIMENTS AND NATURAL EXPERIMENTS

ALAN S. GERBER

DONALD P. GREEN

THIS chapter assesses the strengths and limitations of field experimentation. The chapter begins by defining field experimentation and describing the many forms that field experiments take. The second section charts the growth and development of field experimentation. Third, we describe in formal terms why experiments are valuable for causal inference. Fourth, we contrast the assumptions of experimental and nonexperimental inference, pointing out that the value accorded to observational research is often inflated by misleading reporting conventions. The fifth section discusses the special methodological role that field experiments play insofar as they lay down benchmarks against which other estimation approaches can be assessed. Sixth, we describe two methodological challenges that field experiments frequently confront, noncompliance and attrition, showing the statistical and design implications of each. Seventh, we discuss the study of natural experiments and discontinuities as alternatives to both randomized interventions and conventional nonexperimental research. Finally, we review a list of methodological issues that arise commonly in connection with experimental design and analysis: the role of covariates, planned vs. unplanned comparisons, and extrapolation. The chapter concludes by discussing the ways in which field experimentation is reshaping the field of political methodology.

1 DEFINITION OF FIELD EXPERIMENTATION

Field experimentation represents the conjunction of two methodological strategies, experimentation and fieldwork. Experimentation is a form of investigation in which units of observation (e.g. individuals, groups, institutions, states) are randomly assigned to treatment and control groups. In other words, experimentation involves a random procedure (such as a coin flip) that ensures that every observation has the same probability of being assigned to the treatment group. Random assignment ensures that in advance of receiving the treatment, the experimental groups have the same expected outcomes, a fundamental requirement for unbiased causal inference. Experimentation represents a deliberate departure from observational investigation, in which researchers attempt to draw causal inferences from naturally occurring variation, as opposed to variation generated through random assignment.

Field experimentation represents a departure from laboratory experimentation. Field experimentation attempts to simulate as closely as possible the conditions under which a causal process occurs, the aim being to enhance the external validity, or generalizability, of experimental findings. When evaluating the external validity of political experiments, it is common to ask whether the stimulus used in the study resembles the stimuli of interest in the political world, whether the participants resemble the actors who are ordinarily confronted with these stimuli, whether the outcome measures resemble the actual political outcomes of theoretical or practical interest, and whether the context within which actors operate resembles the political context of interest.

One cannot apply these criteria in the abstract, because they each depend on the research question that an investigator has posed. If one seeks to understand how college students behave in abstract distributive competitions, laboratory experiments in which undergraduates vie for small economic payoffs may be regarded as field experiments. On the other hand, if one seeks to understand how the general public responds to social cues or political communication, the external validity of lab studies of undergraduates has inspired skepticism (Sears 1986; Benz and Meier 2006). These kinds of external validity concerns may subside in the future if studies demonstrate that lab studies involving undergraduates consistently produce results that are corroborated by experimental studies outside the lab; for now, the degree of correspondence remains an open question.

The same may be said of survey experiments. By varying question wording and order, survey experiments may provide important insights into the factors that shape survey response, and they may also shed light on decisions that closely resemble survey response, such as voting in elections. Whether survey experiments provide externally valid insights about the effects of exposure to media messages or other environmental factors, however, remains unclear. What constitutes a field experiment therefore depends on how "the field" is defined. Early agricultural experiments were called field experiments because they were literally conducted in fields. But if the question were how to maximize agricultural productivity of greenhouses, the appropriate field experiment might be conducted indoors.

Because the term "field experiment" is often used loosely to encompass randomized studies that vary widely in terms of realism, Harrison and List (2004, 1014) offer a more refined classification system. "Artefactual" field experiments are akin to laboratory experiments, except that they involve a "non-standard" subject pool. Habyarimana et al. (2007), for example, conduct experiments in which African subjects win prizes depending on how quickly they can open a combination lock; the random manipulation is whether the person who instructs them on the use of such locks is a co-ethnic or member of a different ethnic group. "Framed" field experiments are artefactual experiments that also involve a realistic task. An example of a framed field experiment is Chin, Bond, and Geva's (2000) study of the way in which sixty-nine congressional staffers made simulated scheduling decisions, an experiment designed to detect whether scheduling preference is given to groups associated with a political action committee. "Natural" field experiments unobtrusively assess the effects of realistic treatments on subjects who would ordinarily be exposed to them, typically using behavioral outcome measures. For example, Gerber, Karlan, and Bergan (2009) randomly assign newspaper subscriptions prior to an election and conduct a survey of recipients in order to gauge the extent to which the ideological tone of different papers manifests itself in the recipients' political opinions. For the purposes of this chapter, we restrict our attention to natural field experiments, which have clear advantages over artefactual and framed experiments in terms of external validity. We will henceforth use the term field experiments to refer to studies in naturalistic settings; although this usage excludes many lab and survey experiments, we recognize that some lab and survey studies may qualify as field experiments, depending on the research question.

2 GROWTH AND DEVELOPMENT OF FIELD EXPERIMENTATION

....

Despite the allure of random assignment and unobtrusive measurement, field experimentation has, until recently, rarely been used in political science. Although nonrandomized field interventions date back to Gosnell (1927), the first randomized field experiment to appear in a political science journal was Eldersveld's (1956) study of voter mobilization in the Ann Arbor elections of 1953 and 1954. Assigning voters to receive phone calls, mail, or personal contact prior to election day, Eldersveld examined the marginal effects of different types of appeals, both separately and in combination with one another, using official records to measure voter turnout. The next field experiments, replications of Eldersveld's study (Adams and Smith 1980; Miller, Bositis, and Baer 1981) and a study of the effects of franked mail on constituent opinions of their congressional representative (Cover and Brumberg 1982), appeared a quarter-century later. Although the number of laboratory and survey experiments grew markedly during the 1980s and 1990s, field experimentation remained quiescent. Not a single such experiment was published in a political science journal during the 1990s.

Nor were field experiments part of discussions about research methodology. Despite the fact that political methodology often draws its inspiration from other disciplines, important experiments on the effects of the negative income tax (Pechman and Timpane 1975) and subsidized health insurance (Newhouse 1993) had very little impact on methodological discussion in political science. The most influential research methods textbook, *Designing Social Inquiry* (King, Keohane, and Verba 1994, 125), scarcely mentions experiments in general, noting in passing that experiments are useful insofar as they "provide a useful model for understanding certain aspects of non-experimental design." Books that champion qualitative methods, such as Mahoney and Reuschemeyer (2003), typically ignore the topic of experimental design, despite the fact that random assignment is compatible with—and arguably an important complement to—qualitative outcome and process measurement.

Field experimentation's low profile in political science may be traced to two prevailing methodological beliefs. The first is that field experiments are infeasible. In every stage in the discipline's development, leading political scientists have dismissed the possibility of experimentation. Lowell (1910, 7) declared, "we are limited by the impossibility of experiment. Politics is an observational, not an experimental, science." After the behavioral revolution, the prospects for experimentation were upgraded from impossible to highly unlikely: "The experimental method is the most nearly ideal method for scientific explanation, but unfortunately it can only rarely be used in political science because of practical and ethical impediments" (Lijphart 1971, 684). Textbook discussions of field experiments reinforce this view. Consider Johnson, Joslyn, and Reynolds's description of the practical problems confronting field experimention in the third edition of their *Political Science Research Methods* text:

Suppose, for example, that a researcher wanted to test the hypothesis that poverty causes people to commit robberies. Following the logic of experimental research, the researcher would have to randomly assign people to two groups prior to the experimental treatment, measure the number of robberies committed by members of the two groups prior to the experimental treatment, force the experimental group to be poor, and then to remeasure the number of robberies committed at some later date.   (2001, 133)

In this particular example, the practical difficulties stem from an insistence on baseline measurement (in fact, baseline measurement is not necessary for unbiased inference, thanks to random assignment), while the ethical concerns arise because the intervention is presumed to involve making people poorer rather than making them richer.

The second methodological view that contributed to the neglect of experimentation is the notion that statistical methods can be used to overcome the infirmities of observational data. Whether the methods in question are maximum likelihood estimation, simultaneous equations and selection models, pooled cross-section time series, ecological inference, vector autoregression, or nonparametric techniques such as matching, the underlying theme in most methodological writing is that proper use of statistical methods generates reliable causal inferences. The typical book or essay in this genre describes a statistical technique that is novel to political scientists and then presents an empirical illustration of how the right method overturns the substantive conclusions generated by the wrong method. The implication is that sophisticated analysis of nonexperimental data provides reliable results. From this vantage point, experimental data look more like a luxury than a necessity. Why contend with the expense and ethical encumbrances of generating experimental data?

Long-standing suppositions about the feasibility and necessity of field experimentation have recently begun to change in a variety of social science disciplines, including political science. A series of ambitious studies have demonstrated that randomized interventions are possible. Criminologists have randomized police raids on crack houses in order to assess the hypothesis that public displays of police power deter other forms of crime in surrounding areas (Sherman and Rogan 1995). Chattopadhyay and Duflo (2004) have examined the effects of randomly assigning India's Village Council head positions to women on the kinds of public goods that these rural administrative bodies provide. Economists and sociologists have examined the effects of randomly moving tenants out of public housing projects into neighborhoods with better schools, less crime, and more job opportunities (Kling, Ludwig, and Katz 2005). Hastings et al. (2005) have examined the effects of a "school choice" policy on the academic achievement of students and the voting behavior of parents. Olken (2005) examined the effects of various forms of administrative oversight, including grass-roots participation, on corruption in Indonesia. In political science, use of field experimentation became more widespread after Gerber and Green's (2000) investigation of the mobilizing effects of various forms of nonpartisan campaign communication, with scholars examining voter mobilization campaigns directed at a range of different ethnic groups, in a variety of electoral contexts, and using an array of different campaign appeals (Cardy 2005; Michelson 2003). Experimentation has begun to spread to other subfields, such as comparative politics (Wantchekon 2003; Guan and Green 2006). Hyde (2006), for example, uses random assignment to study the effects of international monitoring efforts on election fraud.

Nevertheless, there remain important domains of political science that lie beyond the reach of randomized experimentation. Although the practical barriers to field experimentation are frequently overstated, it seems clear that topics such as nuclear deterrence or constitutional design cannot be studied in this manner, at least not directly. As a result, social scientists have increasingly turned to natural experiments (as distinct from "natural" field experiments) in which units of observation receive different treatments in a manner that resembles random assignment. Although there are no formal criteria by which to judge whether naturally occurring variation approximates a random experiment, several recent studies seem to satisfy the requirements of a natural experiment. For example, Miguel, Satyanath, and Sergenti (2004) examine the consequences of weather-induced economic shocks on the violent civil conflicts in sub-Saharan Africa, and Ansolabehere, Snyder, and Stewart (2000) use decennial redistricting to assess the "personal vote" that incumbent legislators receive by comparing voters that legislators retain from their old districts to new voters that they acquire through redistricting.

3 Experiments and Inference

The logic underlying randomized experiments—and research designs that attempt to approximate random assignment—is often explicated in terms of a notational system that has its origins in Neyman (1923) and is usually termed the "Rubin Causal Model," after Rubin (1978; 1990). The notational system is best understood by setting aside, for the time being, the topic of experimentation and focusing solely on the definition of causal influence. For each individual i let Y_0 be the outcome if i is not exposed to the treatment, and Y_1 be the outcome if i is exposed to the treatment. The treatment effect is defined as:

$$\tau_i = Y_{i1} - Y_{i0}. \tag{1}$$

In other words, the treatment effect is the difference between two potential states of the world, one in which the individual receives the treatment, and another in which the individual does not. Extending this logic from a single individual to a set of individuals, we may define the average treatment effect (ATE) as follows:

$$ATE = E(\tau_i) = E(Y_{i1}) - E(Y_{i0}). \tag{2}$$

The concept of the average treatment effect implicitly acknowledges the fact that the treatment effect may vary across individuals in systematic ways. One of the most important patterns of variation in τ_i occurs when the treatment effect is especially large (or small) among those who seek out a given treatment. In such cases, the average treatment effect in the population may be quite different from the average treatment effect among those who actually receive the treatment.

Stated formally, the concept of the average treatment effect among the treated (ATT) may be written

$$ATT = E(\tau_i | T_i = 1) = E(Y_{i1} | T_i = 1) - E(Y_{i0} | T_i = 1), \tag{3}$$

where $T_i = 1$ when a person receives a treatment. To clarify the terminology, $(Y_{i1} | T_i = 1)$ is the outcome resulting from the treatment among those who are actually treated, whereas $Y_{i0}|T_i = 1$ is the outcome that would have been observed in the absence of treatment among those who are actually treated. By comparing equations (2) and (3), it is apparent that the average treatment effect is not in general the same as the treatment effect among the treated.

The basic problem in estimating a causal effect, whether the ATE or the ATT, is that at a given point in time each individual is either treated or not: Either Y_1 or Y_0 is observed, but not both. Random assignment solves this "missing data" problem by creating two groups of individuals that are similar prior to application of the treatment. The randomly assigned control group then can serve as a proxy for the outcome that would have been observed for individuals in the treatment group if the treatment had not been applied to them.

Having now laid out the Rubin potential outcomes framework, we now show how it can be used to explicate the implications of random assignment. When treatments are randomly administered, the group that receives the treatment ($T_i = 1$) has the same expected outcome as the group that does not receive the treatment ($T_i = 0$) would if it were treated:

$$E(Y_{i1}|T_i = 1) = E(Y_{i1}|T_i = 0). \tag{4}$$

Similarly, the group that does not receive the treatment has the same expected outcome, if untreated, as the group that receives the treatment, if it were untreated:

$$E(Y_{i0}|T_i = 0) = E(Y_{i0}|T_i = 1). \tag{5}$$

Equations (4) and (5) are termed the independence assumption by Holland (1986) because the randomly assigned value of T_i conveys no information about the potential values of Y_i. Equations (2), (4), and (5) imply that the average treatment effect may be written

$$ATE = E(\tau_i) = E(Y_{i1}|T_i = 1) - E(Y_{i0}|T_i = 0). \tag{6}$$

Because $E(Y_{i1}|T_i = 1)$ and $E(Y_{i0}|T_i = 0)$ may be estimated directly from the data, this equation suggests a solution to the problem of causal inference. The estimator implied by equation (6) is simply the difference between two sample means: the average outcome in the treatment group minus the average outcome in the control group. In sum, random assignment satisfies the independence assumption, and the independence assumption suggests a way to generate empirical estimates of average treatment effects.

Random assignment further implies that independence will hold not only for Y_i, but for any variable X_i that might be measured prior to the administration of the treatment. For example, subjects' demographic attributes or their scores on a pre-test are presumably independent of randomly assigned treatment groups. Thus, one expects the average value of X_i in the treatment group to be the same as the control group; indeed, the entire distribution of X_i is expected to be the same across experimental groups. This property is known as covariate balance. It is possible to gauge the degree of balance empirically by comparing the sample averages for the treatment and control groups. One may also test for balance statistically by evaluating the null hypothesis that the covariates jointly have no systematic tendency to predict treatment assignment. Regression, for example, may be used to generate an F-test to evaluate the hypothesis that the slopes of all predictors of treatment assignment are zero. A significant test statistic suggests that something may have gone awry in the implementation of random assignment, and the researcher may wish to check his or her procedures. It should be noted, however, that a significant test statistic does not prove that the assignment procedure was nonrandom; nor does an insignificant test statistic prove that treatments were assigned using a random procedure. Balance tests provide useful information, but researchers must be aware of their limitations.

We return to the topic of covariate balance below. For now, we note that random assignment obviates the need for multivariate controls. Although multivariate methods may be helpful as a means to improve the statistical precision with which causal effects are estimated, the estimator implied by equation (6) generates unbiased estimates without such controls.

For ease of presentation, the above discussion of causal effects skipped over two further assumptions that play a subtle but important role in experimental analysis. The first is the idea of an *exclusion restriction*. Embedded in equation (1) is the idea that outcomes vary as a function of receiving the treatment per se. It is assumed that assignment to the treatment group only affects outcomes insofar as subjects receive the treatment. Part of the rationale for using placebo groups in experimental design is the concern that subjects' knowledge of their experimental assignment might affect their outcomes. The same may be said for double-blind procedures: When those who implement experiments are unaware of subjects' experimental assignments, they cannot intentionally or inadvertently alter their measurement of the dependent variable.

A second assumption is known as the Stable Unit Treatment Value Assumption, or SUTVA. In the notation used above, expectations such as $E(Y_{i1}|T_i = t_i)$ are all written as if the expected value of the treatment outcome variable Y_{i1} for unit i only depends upon whether or not the unit gets the treatment (whether t_i equals one or zero). A more complete notation would allow for the consequences of treatments T_1 through T_n administered to other units. It is conceivable that experimental outcomes might depend on the values of $t_1, t_2, \ldots, t_{i-1}, t_{i+1}, \ldots, t_n$ as well as the value of t_i:

$$E(Y_{i1}|T_1 = t_1, T_2 = t_2, \ldots, T_{i-1} = t_{i-1}, T_i = t_i, T_{i+1} = t_{i+1}, \ldots, T_n = t_n).$$

By ignoring the assignments to all other units when we write this as $E(Y_{i1}|T_i = t_i)$ we assume away spillovers from one experimental group to the other. Nickerson (2008) and Miguel and Kremer (2004) provide empirical illustrations of instances in which treatments administered to one person have effects on those around them.

Note that violations of SUTVA may produce biased estimates, but the sign and magnitude of the bias depend on the way in which treatment effects spill over across observations (cf. Nickerson 2008). Suppose an experiment were designed to gauge the ATT of door-to-door canvassing on voter turnout. Suppose that, by generating enthusiasm about the upcoming election, treating one person has the effect of increasing their probability of voting by π and the probability that their next-door neighbors vote by π^* (regardless of whether the neighbors are themselves treated). If treatment subjects are as likely as control subjects to live next to a person who receives the treatment, the difference in voting rates in the treatment and control groups provides an unbiased estimate of π even though SUTVA is violated. On the other hand, suppose that canvassers increase voter turnout by conveying information about where to vote. Under this scenario, treating one person has the effect of increasing their probability of voting by π and the probability that their *untreated* next-door neighbors vote by π^*; there is no effect on treated neighbors. This particular violation of SUTVA will boost the turnout rate in the control group and lead to an underestimation of π. As this example illustrates, the direction and magnitude of SUTVA-related bias are often difficult to know *ex ante*, and experimental researchers may wish to assess the influence of spillover effects empirically by randomly varying the density of treatments within different geographic units. Note that SUTVA, like other core assumptions of experimental inference, in fact applies to both experimental and observational research. The next section comments on the points at which the two modes of research diverge and the consequences of this divergence for the interpretation of experimental and observational findings.

4 Contrasting Experimental and Observational Inference

Observational studies compare cases that received the "treatment" (through some unknown selection mechanism) with those that did not receive it. Because random assignment is not used, there are no procedural grounds on which to justify the independence assumption. Without independence, equations (4) and (5) do not hold. We cannot assume that the expected value of the outcomes in the "treatment group," $E(Y_{i1}|T_i = 1)$ equals the expected value of treated outcomes for the control group if treated, $E(Y_{i1}|T_i = 0)$, because the treatment group may differ systematically from the control group in advance of the treatment. Nor can we assume that the expected value of the untreated outcomes in the control group, $E(Y_{i0}|T_i = 0)$ equals the expected value of the untreated outcomes for the treatment group, $E(Y_{i0}|T_i = 1)$. Again, the treatment group in its untreated state may not resemble the control group.

There is no foolproof way to solve this problem. In an effort to eliminate potential confounds, a standard approach is to control for *observable* differences between treatment and control. Sometimes regression is used to control for covariates, but suppose one were to take the idea of controlling for observables to its logical extreme and were to match the treatment and control groups exactly on a set of observable characteristics X. For every value of X, one gathers a treatment and control observation.[1] This matching procedure would generate treatment and control groups that are perfectly balanced in terms of the covariates. However, in order to draw unbiased inferences from these exactly matched treatment and control groups, it is necessary to invoke the ignorability assumption described by Heckman et al. (1998), which stipulates that the treatment and potential outcomes are independent conditional on a set of characteristics X.

$$E(Y_{i1}|X_i, T_i = 1) = E(Y_{i1}|X_i, T_i = 0) \tag{7}$$

$$E(Y_{i0}|X_i, T_i = 0) = E(Y_{i0}|X_i, T_i = 1) \tag{8}$$

Note that these two assumptions parallel the two implications of randomization stated in equations (4) and (5), except that these are conditional on X. From these equations, it is easy to generate expressions for average treatment effects, using the same logic as above.

Analysts of observational data reason along these lines when defending their estimation techniques. It is conventional to assume, for example, that conditional on a set of covariates, individuals who receive treatment have the same expected outcomes as those in the control group. Notice, however, the important difference between the assumptions imposed by experimental and observational researchers. The experimental researcher relies on the properties of a procedure—random assignment—to derive unbiased estimates. The observational researcher, on the other hand, relies on substantive assumptions about the properties of covariates. Whereas the properties of the random assignment procedure are verifiable (one can check the random number generator and review the clerical procedures by which numbers were assigned to units of observation), the validity of the substantive assumptions on which observational inferences rest are seldom verifiable in any direct sense.

Even if one believes that the assumptions underlying an observational inference are probably sound, the mere possibility that these assumptions are incorrect alters the statistical attributes of observational results. Gerber, Green, and Kaplan (2004) show formally that an estimate's sampling distribution reflects two sources of variance: the statistical uncertainty that results when a given model is applied to data and additional uncertainty about whether the estimator is biased. Only the first source of uncertainty is accounted for in the standard errors that are generated by conventional statistical software packages. The second source of uncertainty is ignored. In other words, the standard errors associated with observational results are derived using formulas that are appropriate for experimental data but represent lower bounds when applied to observational data. This practice means that observational results

---

[1] This procedure satisfies the auxiliary assumption that cases with the same X values have a positive probability of being in either treated or control group. This assumption would be violated if treatment assignment were perfectly predicted by X.

are conventionally described in ways that are potentially quite misleading. More specifically, they are misleading in ways that exaggerate the value of observational findings.

This point has been demonstrated empirically. Inspired by the pioneering work of LaLonde (1986), which assessed the correspondence between experimental and observational estimates of the effectiveness of job-training programs, Arceneaux, Gerber, and Green (2006) compare experimental and observational estimates of the effects of phone-based voter mobilization campaigns. Using a sample of more than one million observations, they find the actual root mean squared error associated with the observational estimates to be an order of magnitude larger than their nominal standard errors.

LaLonde-type comparisons expose a seldom-noticed deficiency in political methodology research. Heretofore, methodological debate was premised on the assumption that the value of a casual parameter is unknowable; as a result, the terms of debate hinged on the technical attributes of competing approaches. LaLonde's empirical approach radically alters these debates, for it sometimes turns out that cutting-edge statistical techniques perform quite poorly.

That said, experiments are by no means free from methodological concerns. Field experiments in particular are susceptible to noncompliance and attrition, two problems that convinced some early critics of field experimentation to abandon the enterprise in favor of observational research designs (Chapin 1947). The next sections consider in depth the nature and consequences of these two problems.

5 NONCOMPLIANCE

Sometimes only a subset of those who are assigned to the treatment group are actually treated, or a portion of the control group receives the treatment. When those who get the treatment differ from those who are assigned to receive it, an experiment confronts a problem of noncompliance. In experimental studies of get-out-the-vote canvassing, noncompliance occurs when some subjects who were assigned to the treatment group remain untreated because they are not reached. In clinical trials, subjects may choose to stop a treatment. In studies of randomized election monitoring, observers may fail to follow their assignment; consequently, some places assigned to the treatment group go untreated, while places assigned to the control group receive treatment.

How experimenters approach the problem of noncompliance depends on their objectives. Those who wish to gauge the effectiveness of an outreach program may be content to estimate the so-called "intent-to-treat" effect (ITT); that is, the effect of being randomly assigned to the treatment group after "treatment." At the end of the day, a program's effectiveness is a function of both its effects on those who receive

Table 15.1. Summary of notation distinguishing assigned and received treatments

Actual treatment received	Experimental assignment	
	Treatment group $(Z_i = 1)$	Control group $(Z_i = 0)$
Treated $(T_i = 1)$	$D_1 = 1$	$D_0 = 1$
Not treated $(T_i = 0)$	$D_1 = 0$	$D_0 = 0$

the treatment and the extent to which the treatment is actually administered. Other experimenters may be primarily interested in measuring the effects of the treatment on those who are actually treated. For them, the rate at which any specific program reaches the intended treatment group is of secondary interest. The formal discussion below shows how both the intent-to-treat and treatment-on-treated effects may be estimated from data.

When there is noncompliance, a subject's group assignment, Z_i, is not equivalent to T_i, whether the subject gets treated or not. Angrist, Imbens, and Rubin (1996) extend the notation presented in equations (1) through (6) to the case where treatment group assignment and receipt of treatment can diverge. Let $D_1 = 1$ when a subject assigned to the treatement group is treated, and let $D_1 = 0$ when a subject assigned to the treatment group is not treated. Using this notation, which has been summarized in Table 15.1, we can define a subset of the population, called "Compliers," who get the treatment when assigned to the treatment group but not otherwise. "Compliers" are subjects for whom $D_1 = 1$ and $D_0 = 0$. In the simplest experimental design, in which all those in the treatment group get treated and no one in the control group does, every subject is a Complier. Note that whether a subject is a Complier is a function of both subject characteristics and the particular features of the experiment and is not a fixed attribute of a subject.

When treatments are administered exactly according to plan $(Z_i = T_i, \forall\, i)$, the average causal effect of a randomly assigned treatment can be estimated simply by comparing mean treatment group outcomes and mean control group outcomes. What can be learned about treatment effects when there is noncompliance? Angrist, Imbens, and Rubin (1996) present a set of sufficient conditions for estimating the average treatment effect for the subgroup of subjects who are Compliers. Here we will first present a description of the assumptions and the formula for estimating the average treatment effect for the Compliers. We then elucidate the assumptions using an example.

In addition to the assumption that treatment group assignment Z is random, Angrist et al.'s result invokes the following four assumptions, the first two of which have been mentioned above:

Exclusion restriction. The outcome for a subject is a function of the treatment they receive but is not otherwise influenced by their assignment to the treatment group. In experiments this assumption may fail if subjects change their behavior in response to the treatment group assignment per se (as opposed to the treatment itself) or are induced to do so by third parties who observe the treatment assignment.

Stable Unit Treatment Value Assumption (SUTVA). Whether a subject is treated depends only on the subject's own treatment assignment and not on the treatment assignment of any other subjects. Also, the subject's outcome is a function of his or her treatment assignment and receipt of treatment, and not affected by the assignment of or treatment received by any other subject.

Monotonicity. For all subjects, the probability the subject is treated is at least as great when the subject is in the treatment group as when the subject is in the control group. This assumption is satisfied by design in experiments where the treatment is only available to the treatment group.

Nonzero causal effects of assignment on treatment. The treatment assignment has an effect on the probability that at least some subjects are treated. This is satisfied if the monotonicity assumption is slightly strengthened to require the inequality to be strong for at least some subjects.

Angrist et al. (1996, proposition 1) show that if assumptions 1–4 are satisfied then the effect of the treatment can be expressed as:

$$\frac{E(Y_1 - Y_0)}{E(D_1 - D_0)} = E\left((Y_1 - Y_0)|D_1 - D_0 = 1\right), \tag{9}$$

where Y_j is the outcome when $Z_i = j$, D_j is the value of D when $Z_i = j$, $E(h)$ is the mean value of h in the subject population, and $E(h|g)$ is the mean value of h in the subset of the subject population for which g holds.

The numerator on the left-hand side of equation (9) is the intent-to-treat (ITT) effect of Z on Y, the average causal effect of Z on Y for the entire treatment group, including those who do not get treated. The ITT may be expressed formally as

$$ITT = E(Y_{i1}|Z_i = 1) - E(Y_{i0}|Z_i = 0). \tag{10}$$

The ITT is often used in program evaluation because it takes into account both the treatment effect and the rate at which the treatment is successfully administered. A program may have a weak intent-to-treat effect because the average treatment effect is weak or because the intervention is actually administered to a small portion of those assigned to receive the treatment.

The denominator of equation (9) is the ITT effect of Z on D, the average effect of being placed in the treatment group on the probability a subject is treated. The ratio of these ITT effects equals the average causal effect of the treatment for the Complier population, which is referred to as the Local Average Treatment Effect (LATE). When the control group is never treated, $D_0 = 0$, the LATE is equal to the ATT defined in equation (3).

This proposition has an intuitive basis. Suppose that p percent of those in the treatment group are converted from untreated to treated by their assignment to the treatment group. Suppose that for those whose treatment status is changed by treatment assignment (the subjects in the treatment group who are Compliers), the average change in Y caused by the treatment is Π. How is the average outcome of those subjects assigned to the treatment group changed by the fact that they were given a random assignment to the treatment, rather than the control group?

The observed average value of Y for the treatment group is altered by $p\Pi$, the share of the treatment group affected by the treatment assignment multiplied by the average treatment effect for compliers. If the control group subjects are not affected by the experiment, and the treatment assignment is random, then the difference between the treatment and control group outcome will be on average $p\Pi$. To recover the average effect of the treatment on compliers, divide this difference by p. The average treatment effect on those who are induced to receive treatment by the experiment is therefore equal to the ratio on the left-hand side of (9): the difference in average group outcomes, inflated by dividing this by the change in the probability the treatment is delivered to a subject.

If treatment groups are formed by random assignment, the left-hand side of (9) can be estimated using the sample analogues for the left-hand side quantities. The ITT effect for Y is estimated by the mean difference in outcomes between the treatment and control group and the ITT for D is estimated by the mean difference in treatment rates in the treatment and control group. Equivalently, the LATE can also be estimated using two-stage least squares (2SLS), where subject outcomes are regressed on a variable for receipt of treatment, and treatment assignment is used as an instrument for receipt of treatment. Note that for the simplest case, where no one in the control group is treated and the treatment rate in the treatment group equals c, the LATE is equal to $\frac{ITT_Y}{c}$, where the numerator is the ITT estimate for Y, which is then inflated by the inverse of the treatment rate.

A basic point of Angrist et al.'s analysis is that while some estimate can always be calculated, the estimate is the causal effect of the treatment only when the set of assumptions listed above are satisfied. These conditions are illustrated using an example in which there is failure to treat the treatment group, but treatment is unavailable to the control group. Suppose that after random assignment to treatment and control groups, investigators attempt to contact and then treat the treatment group. The treatment is unavailable to the control group. Examples of this design are get-out-the-vote canvassing experiments, where there is typically failure to treat some of those assigned to the treatment group. Let us now consider how the assumptions presented above apply to this example.

Exclusion restriction. The exclusion restriction is violated when treatment assignment has a direct effect on a subject's outcome. In the example considered here subjects are not aware of their treatment group status (Z), and so they cannot change their behavior based on Z directly. However, it is possible that third parties can observe the treatment assignment. For example, a campaign worker might observe the list of persons assigned to be contacted for get-out-the-vote and then concentrate persuasive messages on these households. This violation of the exclusion restriction causes bias.

SUTVA. Recall that SUTVA requires that the treatment received by a subject does not alter the outcome for other subjects. The SUTVA assumption will fail if, for example, a subject's probability of voting is affected by the treatment of their neighbors. If an experiment that contains multiple members of a household is analyzed at the individual rather than the household level, SUTVA is violated if a subject's probability of voting is a function of whether another member of the household is treated. More generally, spillover effects are a source of violation of SUTVA. If there are decreasing returns to repeat treatments, spillovers will reduce the difference between the average treatment and control group outcomes without changing the recorded treatment rates. As a result, this violation of SUTVA will bias the estimated treatment effect toward zero.

Monotonicity. In the get-out-the-vote example each subject has a zero chance of getting the treatment when assigned to the control group, and therefore monotonicity is satisfied by the experimental design.

Nonzero effect of treatment assignment on the probability of treatment. This assumption is satisfied by the experimental design so long as some members of the assigned treatment group are successfully contacted.

A few final comments on estimating treatment effects when there is noncompliance:

The population proportion of Compliers is a function of population characteristics and the experimental design. The approach presented above produces an estimate of the average treatment effect for Compliers, but which subjects are Compliers may vary with the experimental design. An implication of this is that if the experimental protocols reach different types of subjects and the treatment rates are low, the treatment effect estimate for the same treatment may change across experiments. In order to detect heterogeneous treatment effects, the experimenter may wish to vary the efforts made to reach those assigned to the treatment group.

Generalization of average treatment effects beyond the Compliers requires additional assumptions. When there is noncompliance, the treatment effect estimate applies to Compliers, not the entire subject population. Statements about the effect of treating the entire population require assumptions about the similarity of treatment effects for Compliers and the rest of the subjects.

There is no assumption of homogeneous treatment effects. While both experimental and observational research often implicitly assumes constant treatment effects, the treatment effect estimated by 2SLS is the average treatment effect for Compliers. If homogeneous treatment effects are assumed, then LATE = ATT = ATE.

Given noncompliance, it is sometimes impossible to determine which particular individuals are Compliers. When no members of the control group can get the treatment, which subjects are Compliers can be directly observed, since they are the subjects in the treatment group who get the treatment. However, in situations where it is possible to be treated regardless of group assignment, the exact subjects who are the Compliers cannot be determined. Angrist et al. (1996) offer as an example the natural experiment produced by the Vietnam draft lottery. Those with low lottery numbers were more likely to enter the military than those with high numbers, but some people with high numbers did get "treated." This suggests that some subjects would have joined the military regardless of their draft number. Subjects who get treated regardless of their group assignment are called "Always Takers;" they are people for whom $D_1 = 1$ and $D_0 = 1$. Since some of the subjects assigned to the treatment group are Always Takers, the set of treated subjects in the treatment group is a mix of Always Takers and Compliers. This mix of subjects cannot be divided into Compliers and Always Takers, since an individual subject's behavior in the counterfactual assignment is never observed.

In sum, problems of noncompliance present a set of design challenges for field experimental researchers. Awareness of these problems leads researchers to gather data on levels of compliance in the treatment and control groups, so that local average treatment effects may be estimated. It also encourages researchers to think about which core assumptions—SUTVA, monotonicity, exclusion, and nonzero assignment effects—are likely to be problematic in any given application and to design experiments so as to minimize these concerns.

6 ATTRITION

Less tractable are the problems associated with attrition. Attrition occurs when outcomes are unobserved for certain observations. Consider a simple example of an intervention designed to encourage political parties in closed-list systems to nominate women candidates as regional representatives. The outcomes for this study are $Y = 1$ (a woman is nominated), $Y = 0$ (no women are nominated), and $Y = ?$ (the investigator does not know whether a woman is nominated). Suppose that the experimental results indicate that 50 percent of the jurisdictions in the treatment group had women nominees, 20 percent did not, and 30 percent remain unknown. The corresponding rates for the control group are 40 percent, 20 percent, and 40 percent. In the absence of any other information about these jurisdictions and the reasons why their outcomes are observed or unobserved, this set of results is open to competing interpretations. One could exclude missing data from the analysis, in which case the estimated treatment effect is $.50/(.50 + .20) - .40/(.40 + .20) = .05$. Alternatively, one could assume that those whose outcomes were not observed failed to field women candidates, in which case the estimated treatment effect is .10. Or, following Manski (1990), one could calculate the bounds around the estimated effect by assuming the most extreme possible outcomes. For example, if none of the treatment group's missing observations fielded women candidates, but all of the missing observations in the control group did so, the treatment effect would be $.50 - .80 = -.30$. Conversely, if the missing observations in the treatment group are assumed to be $Y = 1$, but missing observations in the control group are assumed to be $Y = 0$, the estimated treatment effect becomes $.80 - .40 = .40$. As this example illustrates, the bounds $\{-.30, .40\}$ admit an uncomfortably large range of potential values.

The indeterminacy created by attrition can in principle be reduced by imposing some theoretical structure on the data. Imputation models, for example, attempt to use observed covariates to forecast the outcomes for missing values (Imbens and Rubin 1997; Dunn, Maracy, and Tomenson 2005). This approach will generate unbiased estimates under special conditions that may or may not hold for any given application. In situations where data are missing in a fashion that is random conditional on covariates, this approach will be superior to excluding missing data or substituting the unconditional mean. On the other hand, it is possible to construct examples in which imputation exacerbates the problem of bias, as when missing data arise due to systematic factors that are not captured by observed covariates.

Although the consequences of attrition are always to some degree speculative, certain experimental designs are better able than others to allay concerns about attrition. Consider, for example, Howell and Peterson's (2004) analysis of the effects of school vouchers on students' standardized test scores. From a pool of voucher applicants, a subset of voucher recipients was chosen at random. Outcomes were measured by a test administered privately to both voucher recipients and nonrecipients, but recipients were more likely to take the test than nonrecipients. Thus, Howell and Peterson faced a situation in which attrition rates differed between treatment and control groups. The fact that they administered an academic baseline test prior to random assignment enabled them to assess whether attrition was related to academic ability as gauged in the pre-test. This example provides another instance in which covariates, although not strictly necessary for experimental analysis, play a useful role.

7 NATURAL EXPERIMENTS AND DISCONTINUITY DESIGNS

In contrast to randomized experiments, where a randomization procedure ensures unbiased causal inference, natural experiments and regression discontinuity designs use near-random assignment to approximate experimentation. When evaluating near-random research designs, the key methodological issue is whether the treatment is unrelated to unmeasured determinants of the dependent variable. The plausibility of this claim will depend on substantive assumptions. For example, studies of lottery windfalls on consumption (Imbens, Rubin, and Sacerdote 2001) and political attitudes (Doherty, Gerber, and Green 2006) have invoked assumptions about the comparability of lottery players who win varying amounts in distinct lotteries over time. Although plausible, these assumptions are potentially flawed (lottery players may change over time), resulting in biased estimates. Note that the mere possibility of bias means that the reported standard errors potentially understate the mean squared error associated with the estimates for the reasons spelled out in Gerber, Green, and Kaplan (2004).

Regression discontinuity designs attempt to address concerns about bias by looking at sharp breakpoints that make seemingly random distinctions between units that receive a treatment and those that do not. When, for example, one gauges the effects of legislature size on municipal spending by taking advantage of the fact that Scandinavian countries mandate changes in legislature size as a step function of local population size (Pettersson-Lidbom 2004), the key assumption is that the change in legislature size is effectively random in the immediate vicinity of a population threshold that necessitates a change in legislative size. When the legislature changes in size as the municipal population grows from 4,999 to 5,000, is there an abrupt change in municipal spending? A hypothetical example of this kind of discontinuity is illustrated in Figure 15.1. In the vicinity of the discontinuity in legislative size, there is an abrupt shift in government expenditures.[2] The practical problem with this type of design is that the data are typically sparse in the immediate vicinity of a breakpoint, requiring the analyst to include observations that are farther away and therefore potentially contaminated by other factors. The standard remedy for this problem is to control for these factors through use of covariates, such as polynomial functions of the variable (in this example, population size) on which the discontinuity is based. Pettersson-Lidbom (2004) demonstrates the robustness of his estimates across a variety of specifications, but as always there remains a residuum of uncertainty about whether municipal spending patterns reflect unmeasured aspects of population change.

Even if one isolates a causal effect produced by a discontinuity, problems of interpretation remain. Posner (2004) argues that ethnic groups residing on the border of Zambia and Malawi provide an opportunity to study the effects of party competition and ethnic coalitions. The argument is that Chewa and Tumbuka peoples are more in conflict on the Malawi side of the border than the Zambian side, because they together comprise a much larger proportion of the overall Malawi electorate in a winner-takes-all presidential system. Here the issue is one of internal validity. Conceivably, the observed contrast in inter-group relations could be attributed to any difference between the two countries. In an attempt to bolster his interpretation, Posner attempts to rule out differences in economic status, proximity to roads, and colonial history as potential sources of cross-border variation.

---

[2] Pettersson-Lidbom (2004) actually finds little evidence of a link between legislature size and government expenditures in Scandinavia.

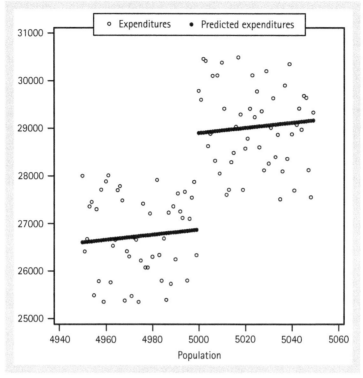

Fig. 15.1. Example of a regression discontinuity

Note: In this hypothetical example, inspired by Pettersson-Lidbom (2004), the number of seats in a local legislature increases abruptly when a town passes the population cutoff of 5,000 residents. The hypothesis tested here is whether local government expenditures (the Y-axis) increase in the vicinity of this breakpoint, presumably due to the exogenous change in legislative size.

8 ASSORTED METHODOLOGICAL ISSUES IN THE DESIGN AND ANALYSIS OF EXPERIMENTS

Various aspects of design, analysis, and inference have important implications for the pursuit of long-term objectives, such as the generation of unbiased research literatures that eventually isolate the causal parameters of interest. This section briefly summarizes several of the leading issues.

8.1 Balance and Stratification

Random assignment is designed to create treatment and control groups that are balanced in terms of both observed and unobserved attributes. As N approaches infinity, the experimental groups become perfectly balanced. In finite samples, random

assignment may create groups that, by chance, are unbalanced. Experimental procedures remain unbiased in small samples, in that there will be no systematic tendency
for imbalance to favor the treatment group. Yet there remains the question of what to
do about the prospect or occurrence of observed imbalances between treatment and
control groups.

If information about covariates is available in advance of an experiment (perhaps
due to the administration of a pre-test), a researcher can potentially reduce sampling
variability of the estimated treatment effect by stratification or blocking. For example,
if gender were thought to be a strong predictor of an experimental outcome, one
might divide the sample into men and women, randomly assigning a certain fraction of each gender group to the treatment condition. This procedure ensures that
gender is uncorrelated with treatment assignment. This procedure may be extended
to include a list of background covariates. Within each type of attribute (e.g. women
over sixty-five years of age, with less than a high school degree), the experimenter
randomly assigns observations to treatment and control groups.

Alternatively, the researcher could stratify after the experiment is conducted by
including the covariates as control variables in a multivariate model. The inclusion
of covariates has the potential to increase the precision with which the treatment
effect is estimated so long as the predictive accuracy of the covariates offsets the loss
of degrees of freedom. The same principle applies also to pre-stratification; adding
the strata-generating covariates as control variables may improve the precision of the
experimental estimates by reducing disturbance variance.

Four practical issues accompany the use of covariates. First, although covariates
potentially make for more precise experimental estimates, the covariates in question
must predict the dependent variable. To the extent that covariates (or nonlinear functions of the covariates or interactions among covariates) have little predictive value,
their inclusion may actually make the treatment estimates less precise. The same goes
for nonparametric methods such as matching, which suspend the usual assumptions
about the linear and additive effects of the covariates, but throw out a certain portion
of the observations for which the correspondence between treatment and control
covariates is deemed to be inadequate. Second, the use of covariates creates the
potential for mischief insofar as researchers have discretion about what covariates to
include in their analysis. The danger is that researchers will pick and choose among
alternative specifications based on how the results turn out. This procedure has the
potential to introduce bias. A third issue concerns potential interactions between the
treatment and one or more covariate. Researchers often find subgroup differences.
Again, the exploration of interactions raises the distinction between planned and
unplanned comparisons. When interactions are specified according to an *ex ante*
plan, the sampling distribution is well defined. When interactions are proposed after
the researcher explores the data, the sampling distribution is no longer well defined.
The results should be regarded as provisional pending confirmation in a new sample.
Fourth, a common use of covariates occurs when the experimenter administers a pre-
test prior to the start of an intervention. Pre-tests, however, may lead subjects to infer
the nature and purpose of the experiment, thereby contaminating the results.

8.2 Publication Bias

An important source of bias that afflicts both observational and experimental re-search is publication bias. If the size and statistical significance of experimental results determine whether they are reported in the scholarly publications, a synthesis of research findings may produce a grossly misleading estimate of the true causal effect. Consider, for example, the distortions that result when an intervention that is thought to contribute to democratic stability is evaluated using a one-tailed hypothesis test. If statistically insignificant results go unreported, the average reported result will exaggerate the intervention's true effect.

Publication bias in experimental research literatures has several tell-tale symptoms. For one-tailed tests of the sort described above, studies based on small sample sizes should tend to report larger treatment effects than studies based on large sample sizes. The reason is that small-N studies require larger effect sizes in order to achieve statistical significance. A similar diagnostic device applies to two-tailed tests; the rela-tionship between sample size and effect size should resemble a funnel. More generally, the observed sampling distribution of experimental results will not conform to the sampling distribution implied by the nominal standard errors associated with the individual studies. Inconclusive studies will be missing from the sampling distribu-tion. The threat of publication bias underscores the tension between academic norms, which often stress the importance of presenting conclusive results, and scientific progress, which depends on unbiased reporting conventions.

8.3 Extrapolation

Any experiment, whether conducted in the lab or field, raises questions about gener-alizability. To what extent do the findings hold for other settings? To what extent do they hold for other dosages or types of interventions? These questions raise important epistemological questions about the conditions under which one can safely generalize beyond the confines of a particular intervention and experimental setting. These questions have been the subject of lively, ongoing debate (Heckman and Smith 1995; Moffitt 2004).

Scholars have approached this issue in two complementary ways. The first is to bring to bear theories about the isomorphism of different treatments and contexts. Often, this type of theoretical argument is based on isolating the essential features of a given treatment or context. For example, one might say of the Gerber et al. (2009) study of the effects of newspaper exposure that the key ingredients are the political topics covered by the newspapers, the manner in which they are presented, the care and frequency with which they are read, and the partisanship and political sophistication of the people who are induced to read as a result of the intervention.

The theoretical exercise of isolating what are believed to be the primary char-acteristics of the treatment, setting, and recipients directs an empirical agenda of experimental extensions. By varying the nature of the treatment, how it is delivered, and to whom, the experimenter gradually assembles a set of empirical propositions about the conditions under which the experimental effect is strong or weak. Note that this empirical agenda potentially unifies various forms of experimental social science by asking whether lab experiments, survey experiments, and natural experiments converge on similar answers and, if not, why the experimental approach generates discrepant results. This process of empirical replication and extension in turn helps refine theory by presenting a set of established facts that it must explain.

8.4 Power and Replication

Often field experiments face practical challenges that limit their size and scope. For example, suppose one were interested in the effects of a political campaign commercial on 100,000 television viewers' voting preferences. Ideally, one would randomly assign small units such as households or blocks to treatment and control groups; as a practical matter, it may only be possible to assign a small number of large geographic units to treatment and control. If individuals living near one another share unobserved attributes that predict their voting preferences, this kind of clustered randomization greatly reduces the power of the study (Raudenbush 1997). Indeed, it is possible to construct examples in which such an experiment has very little chance of rejecting a null hypothesis of no effect.

How should one proceed in this case? Although any given study may have limited diagnostic value, the accumulation of studies generates an informative posterior distribution. Unlike the failure to publish insignificant results, the failure to embark on low-power studies does not lead to bias, but it does slow the process of scientific discovery. In the words of Campbell and Stanley (1963, 3), we must

justify experimentation on more pessimistic grounds—not as a panacea, but rather at the only available route to cumulative progress. We must instill in our students the expectation of tedium and disappointment and the duty of thorough persistence, by now so well achieved in the biological and physical sciences.

9 METHODOLOGICAL VALUE OF EXPERIMENTS

Beyond the substantive knowledge that they generate, field experiments have the potential to make a profound methodological contribution. Rather than evaluate statistical methods in terms of the abstract plausibility of their underlying assumptions, researchers in the wake of LaLonde (1986) have made the performance of statistical methods an empirical question, by comparing estimates based on observational data to experimental benchmarks. Experimentation has been buoyed in part by the lackluster performance of statistical techniques designed to correct the deficiencies of observational data. Arceneaux et al. (2006), for example, find a wide disparity between experimental estimates and estimates obtained using observational methods such as matching or regression. This finding echoes results in labor economics and medicine, where observational methods have enjoyed mixed success in approximating experimental benchmarks (Heckman et al. 1998; Concato, Shah, and Horwitz 2000; Glazerman, Levy, and Myers 2003). By making the performance of observational methods an empirical research question, field experimentation is changing the terms of debate in the field of political methodology.

REFERENCES

ADAMS, W. C., and SMITH, D. J. 1980. Effects of telephone canvassing on turnout and preferences: a field experiment. *Public Opinion Quarterly*, 44: 53–83.

ANGRIST, J. D., IMBENS, G. W., and RUBIN, D. B. 1996. Identification of casual effects using instrumental variables. *Journal of the American Statistical Association*, 91: 444–55.

ANSOLABEHERE, S., SNYDER, J. M., JR., and STEWART, C., III. 2000. Old voters, new voters, and the personal vote: using redistricting to measure the incumbency advantage. *American Journal of Political Science*, 44: 17–34.

ARCENEAUX, K., GERBER, A. S., and GREEN, D. P. 2006. Comparing experimental and matching methods using a large-scale voter mobilization experiment. *Political Analysis*, 14: 1–36.

BENZ, M., and MEIER, S. 2006. Do people behave in experiments as in the field? Evidence from donations. Institute for Empirical Research in Economics Working Paper No. 248.

CAMPBELL, D. T., and STANLEY, J. C. 1963. *Experimental and Quasi-Experimental Designs for Research*. Boston: Houghton Mifflin.

CARDY, E. A. 2005. An experimental field study of the GOTV and persuasion effects of partisan direct mail and phone calls. *Annals of the American Academy of Political and Social Science*, 601: 28–40.

CHAPIN, F. S. 1947. *Experimental Designs in Sociological Research*. New York: Harper and Brothers.

CHATTOPADHYAY, R., and DUFLO, E. 2004. Women as policy makers: evidence from a randomized policy experiment in India. *Econometrica*, 72: 1409–43.

CHIN, M. L., BOND, J. R., and GEVA, N. 2000. A foot in the door: an experimental study of PAC and constituency effects on access. *Journal of Politics*, 62: 534–49.

CONCATO, J., SHAH, N., and HORWITZ, R. I. 2000. Randomized, controlled trials, observational studies, and the hierarchy of research designs. *New England Journal of Medicine*, 342: 1887–92.

COVER, A. D., and BRUMBERG, B. S. 1982. Baby books and ballots: the impact of congressional mail on constituent opinion. *American Political Science Review*, 76: 347–59.

DOHERTY, D., GERBER, A. S., and GREEN, D. P. 2006. Personal income and attitudes toward redistribution: a study of lottery winners. *Political Psychology*, 27: 441–58.

DUNN, G., MARACY, M., and TOMENSON, B. 2005. Estimating treatment effects from randomized clinical trials with noncompliance and loss to follow-up: the role of instrumental variables methods. *Statistical Methods in Medical Research*, 14: 369–95.

ELDERSVELD, S. J. 1956. Experimental propaganda techniques and voting behavior. *American Political Science Review*, 50: 154–65.

GERBER, A. S., and GREEN, D. P., 2000. The effects of canvassing, direct mail, and tele-phone contact on voter turnout: a field experiment. *American Political Science Review*, 94: 653–63.

——— and KAPLAN, E. H. 2004. The illusion of learning from observational research. Pp. 251–73 in *Problems and Methods in the Study of Politics*, ed. I. Shapiro, R. Smith, and T. Massoud. New York: Cambridge University Press.

——— KARLAN, D. S., and BERGAN, D. 2009. Does the media matter? A field experiment measur-ing the effect of newspapers on voting behavior and political opinions. *American Economic Journal: Applied Economics*.

GLAZERMAN, S., LEVY, D. M., and MYERS, D. 2003. Nonexperimental versus experimental estimates of earnings impacts. *Annals of the American Academy of Political and Social Science*, 589: 63–93.

GOSNELL, H. F. 1927. *Getting-out-the-Vote: An Experiment in the Stimulation of Voting*. Chicago: University of Chicago Press.

GUAN, M., and GREEN, D. P. 2006. Non-coercive mobilization in state-controlled elections: an experimental study in Beijing. *Comparative Political Studies*, 39: 1175–93.

HABYARIMANA, J., HUMPHREYS, M., POSNER, D., and WEINSTEIN, J. 2007. *The Co-ethnic Advantage*.

HARRISON, G. W., and LIST, J. A. 2004. Field experiments. *Journal of Economic Literature*, 42: 1009–55.

HASTINGS, J. S., KANE, T. J., STAIGER, D. O., and WEINSTEIN, J. M. 2005. Economic outcomes and the decision to vote: the effect of randomized school admissions on voter participation. Unpublished manuscript, Department of Economics, Yale University.

HECKMAN, J. J., and SMITH, J. A. 1995. Assessing the case for social experiments. *Journal of Economic Perspectives*, 9: 85–110.

——— ICHIMURA, H., SMITH, J., and TODD, P. 1998. Matching as an econometric evaluation estimator. *Review of Economic Studies*, 65: 261–94.

HOLLAND, P. W. 1986. Statistics and causal inference. *Journal of the American Statistical Associ-ation*, 81: 945–60.

HOWELL, W. C., and PETERSON, P. E. 2004. Uses of theory in randomized field trials: lessons from school voucher research on disaggregation, missing data, and the generalization of findings. *American Behavioral Scientist*, 47: 634–57.

HYDE, S. D. 2006. Foreign democracy promotion, norm development and democratization: explaining the causes and consequences of internationally monitored elections. Unpub-lished doctoral thesis, Department of Political Science, University of California, San Diego.

IMBENS, G. W., and RUBIN, D. B. 1997. Bayesian inference for causal effects in randomized experiments with noncompliance. *Annals of Statistics*, 25: 305–27.

——— and SACERDOTE, B. I. 2001. Estimating the effect of unearned income on labor earnings, savings, and consumption: evidence from a survey of lottery winners. *American Economic Review*, 91: 778–94.

JOHNSON, J. B., JOSLYN, R. A., and REYNOLDS, H. T. 2001. *Political Science Research Methods*, 4th edn. Washington, DC: CQ Press.

KING, G., KEOHANE, R. O., and VERBA, S. 1994. *Designing Social Inquiry*. Princeton, NJ: Princeton University Press.

KLING, J. R., LUDWIG, J., and KATZ, L. F. 2005. Neighborhood effects on crime for female and male youth: evidence from a randomized housing voucher experiment. *Quarterly Journal of Economics*, 120: 87–130.

LALONDE, R. J. 1986. Evaluating the econometric evaluations of training programs with exper-imental data. *American Economic Review*, 76: 604–20.

LIJPHART, A. 1971. Comparative politics and the comparative method. *American Political Science Review*, 65: 682–93.

LOWELL, A. L. 1910. The physiology of politics. *American Political Science Review*, 4: 1–15.

MAHONEY, J., and REUSCHEMEYER, D. (eds.) 2003. *Comparative Historical Analysis in the Social Sciences*. New York: Cambridge University Press.

MANSKI, C. F. 1990. Nonparametric bounds on treatment effects. *American Economic Review Papers and Proceedings*, 80: 319–23.

MICHELSON, M. R. 2003. Getting out the Latino vote: how door-to-door canvassing influences voter turnout in rural central California. *Political Behavior*, 25: 247–63.

MIGUEL, E., and KREMER, M. 2004. Worms: identifying impacts on education and health in the presence of treatment externalities. *Econometrica*, 72: 159–217.

——SATYANATH, S., and SERGENTI, E. 2004. Economic shocks and civil conflict: an instrumental variables approach. *Journal of Political Economy*, 112: 725–53.

MILLER, R. E., BOSITIS, D. A., and BAER, D. L. 1981. Stimulating voter turnout in a primary: field experiment with a precinct committeeman. *International Political Science Review*, 2: 445–60.

MOFFITT, R. A. 2004. The role of randomized field trials in social science research: a perspective from evaluations of reforms of social welfare programs. *American Behavioral Scientist*, 47: 506–40.

NEWHOUSE, J. P. 1993. *Free for All? Lessons from the RAND Health Insurance Experiment*. Boston: Harvard University Press.

NEYMAN, J. 1923. On the application of probability theory to agricultural experiments. Essay on principles. Section 9. *Roczniki Nauk Roiniczych*, 10: 1–51; repr. in English in *Statistical Science*, 5 (1990): 463–80.

NICKERSON, D. W. 2008. Is voting contagious? Evidence from two field experiments. *American Political Science Review*, 102: 49–57.

OLKEN, B. A. 2005. Monitoring corruption: evidence from a field experiment in Indonesia. NBER Working Paper 11753.

PECHMAN, J. A., and TIMPANE, P. M. (eds.) 1975. *Work Incentives and Income Guarantees: The New Jersey Negative Income Tax Experiment*. Washington, DC: Brookings Institution.

PETTERSSON-LIDBOM, P. 2004. Does the size of the legislature affect the size of government? Evidence from two natural experiments. Unpublished manuscript, Department of Economics, Stockholm University.

POSNER, D. N. 2004. The political salience of cultural difference: why Chewas and Tumbukas are allies in Zambia and adversaries in Malawi. *American Political Science Review*, 98: 529–45.

RAUDENBUSH, S. W. 1997. Statistical analysis and optimal design for cluster randomized trials. *Psychological Methods*, 2: 173–85.

RUBIN, D. B. 1978. Bayesian inference for causal effects: the role of randomization. *Annals of Statistics*, 6: 34–58.

——1990. Comment: Neyman (1923) and causal inference in experiments and observational studies. *Statistical Science*, 5 (4): 472–80.

SEARS, D. O. 1986. College sophomores in the laboratory: influences of a narrow database on social-psychology's view of human nature. *Journal of Personality and Social Psychology*, 51: 515–30.

SHERMAN, L. W., and ROGAN, D. P. 1995. Deterrent effects of police raids on crack houses: a randomized, controlled experiment. *Justice Quarterly*, 12: 755–81.

WANTCHEKON, L. 2003. Clientelism and voting behavior: evidence from a field experiment in Benin. *World Politics*, 55: 399–422.

PART VI

QUANTITATIVE TOOLS FOR DESCRIPTIVE AND CAUSAL INFERENCE: GENERAL METHODS

CHAPTER 16

....

SURVEY METHODOLOGY

....

RICHARD JOHNSTON

The current situation, seen from the methodological perspective, has elements of being both the best and worst of times.

(Dillman 2002, 473)

SURVEYS may be the most ubiquitous product of political science research, at least for the public at large. They provide essentially our only readings of mass opinion on politics, and can be facts in their own right on the political ground. Indeed, the very act of posing questions and gauging answers is structurally similar to what politicians do as they seek to build and split coalitions.

But are surveys able to carry this burden? Arguably, the statistical foundations of survey research fit the reality of data collection only loosely. One focus of worry is that surveys poorly represent *persons*, starting with the problem of identifying appropriate sampling frames and ending with the problems of unit nonresponse and selection bias. A second concern is with how well surveys represent *opinions*; from measurement error issues—reliability and validity—to item nonresponse to how framing affects response. Finally there is the question of *causal inference*. Although claims of cause and effect are ubiquitous, identification issues are serious. The designs that optimize representation are often not very good at facilitating inference, and vice versa.[1]

---

[1] This chapter focuses on surveys based on probabilistic samples, or samples that purport to serve the same purpose. It thus ignores compelling, but so far rarely used, designs that go beyond random selection. An obvious example would be a snowball sample, which in political science applications is used to gauge network effects (Huckfedlt, Johnson, and Sprague 2004). It also ignores the burgeoning use of the internet for essentially experimental applications, where the role of randomization is more to drive assignment to treatment than selection from the population.

1 Fieldwork Choices

This chapter considers three dimensions of design: the *mode* of fieldwork, the representation of *space*, and the representation of *time*.

1.1 Mode

Four modes present themselves and these strongly constrain what is possible for space and time. Two involve more or less unaided self-administration by the respondent: *paper and pencil* and *internet-based*. Two involve the active intervention of an interviewer: *face-to-face* and *telephone* (but note qualifications for each of these modes later in this paragraph). The humble medium of the self-administered mailback questionnaire underpinned important and still influential early work, notably by McClosky and his colleagues (1958; 1960). It remains the sole mode for Australian Election Studies and is a component of some other national studies. Face-to-face interviewing was the academic norm from the start, however, as with the early Columbia studies (Lazarsfeld, Berelson, and Gaudet 1948; Berelson, Lazarsfeld, and McPhee 1954). It remains the standard for the flagship American National Election Studies (ANES) and is still the dominant mode in national studies elsewhere. But cost considerations drove the commercial sector toward the telephone, such that by the 1980s telephone interviewing was the industry standard. Similar pressures were felt in academic research, and some national election studies have gone over to the telephone in whole or in part. Typically, the mode uses computer-assisted telephone interviewing (CATI), which organizes the clearance of the sample, facilitates direct data entry, and makes randomization both for methodological purposes (for example, to control for order effects among items) and for experimentation in wording and order. Tentative steps are being taken toward eliminating the interviewer with telephone audio computer-assisted self-interviewing, or T-ACASI (Villaroel et al. 2006). Telephone surveys are under increasing challenge, however, and some claim that the wave of the future is the internet. This would be ironic, as in some ways it takes the research community back to the era of paper and pencil (Dennis et al. 2005). For any given study, modes are not mutually exclusive. The telephone-based Canadian Election Studies, for example, also deploy a mailback questionnaire as a cheap way to expand the pool of data points. It is now common for face-to-face interviews to use computer-assisted personal interviewing (CAPI). This serves all the purposes that CATI does for questionnaire management and data entry at the same time as it makes possible self-administration of parts of the instrument, a major advantage for sensitive queries.

Debate now rages over the claims of competing modes, a matter considered below at some length. But the debate is clouded by the difficulty—some would say, impossibility—of distinguishing factors intrinsic to mode from byproducts of sample composition.

1.2 Space

Mode interacts strongly with what is and is not possible in a survey sample's treatment of space. The canonical sample, as idealized in introductory courses, gives each member of the population an equal probability of selection for the sample. Equal probability implies independent probability, the basis for the binomial properties that underpin expectations for means or proportions, for indicators of relationships, and for confidence intervals. The ideal sample is almost impossible of realization, however. Except for certain clearly delimited populations for whom unique locations can be identified (a student population, for instance), real-world sampling is characterized by its degree of derogation from the binomial ideal. At a minimum, sampling is effectively of households with a further protocol required for selection within households.

For face-to-face interviews it is simply unrealistic to make a simple random draw of households. Transportation costs for interviewers dictate that households be clustered, and this affects the statistical properties of the sample. The basic issue is well known: Where the design is clustered, the effective number of observations may be smaller than the actual number. The degree of clustering is indicated by the *intraclass correlation coefficient*, styled originally by Kish (1965) as "roh" (Rate of Heterogeneity) but now, confusingly, named "rho" (ρ), defined as:

$$\rho = \frac{\tau^2}{\tau^2 + \sigma^2}. \tag{1}$$

Where τ^2 is the between-cluster variance, and σ^2 is the within-cluster variance, such that the *effective N* of observations is:

$$\frac{Jn}{1 + (n-1)\rho} \tag{2}$$

where J is the number of clusters and n is the number of observations per cluster.[2] Obviously, to the degree that we rely on clustered data—and the flagship studies tend to do so—we have for years been underestimating standard errors in significance tests. One factor is ρ itself, which is unique to each variable. Most worrisome, however, is the mere fact of clustering, as Stoker and Bowers (2002) show that the power of tests for macro-level effects (for example, from campaign intensity) is affected more by the number of clusters J than by the number of observations per cluster n. Corrections for clustering are now routinely available, but are easiest to apply when clustering is modest. Where J is small and n is large, hierarchical modeling may be required. Stoker and Bowers argue further that "If congressional elections are primarily local affairs...then despite intuition to the contrary, we should be designing national surveys that sample relatively few individuals within relatively many CDs" (2002, 105). But this runs exactly against the cost-saving grain of clustering.

To avoid clustering and yet contain costs, the standard solution has become the telephone. This mode allows an approximation to simple random sampling of

---

[2] Notation in this section is adapted from Stoker and Bowers (2002).

households, and random digit dialing (RDD) techniques get around the problem of unlisted numbers. Pure RDD is rare, for reasons of cost. Even when married to known area codes and exchanges, the universe of potential random four-digit combinations exceeds the total body of active telephone numbers by an order of magnitude. In addition, many active numbers are commercial, and interviewing a respondent initially contacted at a nonresidential number is too great a derogation from equal representation of households. RDD now typically starts with a list of known live noncommercial numbers such that, even if the underlying distribution is biased, draws from it are independent. In principle, the internet and the World Wide Web also cut through the constraints of space, but internet samples have foundered on incomplete penetration of the net, especially to low-income households and the difficulty of finding a way to get a truly random sample.

1.3 Time

Although the preoccupation with time is not as ubiquitous in survey research as preoccupation with space, it is almost as old. Repeated measurement was in fact the strategy employed in the first academic election surveys, by Lazarsfeld and his Columbia colleagues. This is the *panel* design, with each time point designated as a *wave*. The Columbia strategy was to reinterview respondents within the same campaign. The inescapable trade-off was with the overall representativeness of the sample; only a single community could be studied with such temporal density. Representing both space and time was possible only if fieldwork for each wave was itself stretched out. The classic ANES pre-post design is one result. Another has been the inter-election panel, an occasional strategy for the ANES and a more routine one for the British Election Studies.

The defining element in a panel is repeated interviews with the same persons. A common but not a defining feature is the repetition of specific questions. Most of the content in ANES pre-post panels is not repeated between waves. Rather, the second wave evokes retrospection on the event (obviously not possible before the fact) at the same time as it leverages access to respondents to increase the total volume of information extracted from each one. Repetition of questions is a key feature of inter-election panels, for which change is the primary interest. But change was also the central interest of the early Columbia studies, so repetition at the level of the item was a defining feature of their design.

With the advent of internet surveys, panels seem bound to gain prominence. The creation of a high-quality internet sample imposes high up-front costs: At the extreme, it implies a willingness to install the requisite machinery and telephony at the company's expense. This makes sense only if respondents agree to become part of a panel. What is more, with only a minimal workforce of interviewers, it is economical to pay respondents instead. Financial incentives combined with the psychology of precommitment probably will generate higher retention rates than are possible through other modes (Couper 2000). Even where internet surveying is not scrupulous about the representativeness of its respondents, their very online accessibility makes them a panel *malgré eux*.

Time can also be represented in what is otherwise a standard cross-sectional survey. Any cross-section will embody time; the only question is whether it does so self-consciously. Good practice in clearance of a sample requires a willingness to make several attempts to reach a target household, to take daily and weekly rhythms into account in ordering callbacks, and to attempt to convert refusals. Only by such means can the theoretical objective of equal probability of selection be approached. All this takes time and, quite apart from any relationship between respondents' accessibility and their opinions or behavior, this exposes the fieldwork to impact from events. It is increasingly common for fieldwork strategies to recognize this possibility explicitly and turn it to advantage. By dividing the total target sample into replicates, releasing replicates according a prearranged schedule, and subjecting each replicate to the same (ideally, generous) clearance strategy, a respondent's date of interview becomes as much a matter of random selection as his or her original inclusion in the sample. Such a survey, originally designated by Cook and Campbell (1979) as an interrupted time series, has come to be called by political scientists a *rolling cross-section* (hereafter RCS; see Johnston and Brady 2002). The first RCS with weekly release of replicates was conducted in 1984 as a primary-election component of that year's ANES. It became the standard fieldwork strategy for Canadian Election Studies in 1988 (with daily release of replicates), and has since spread to New Zealand, Great Britain, and Germany. It is the distinguishing feature of the (US) National Annenberg Election Study. All these studies make the campaign a central focus. To date, all RCS samples have been drawn by telephone. The face-to-face mode cannot accommodate the daily interweaving of replicates required for proper clearance, although it can work for grosser time scales. The internet can also deliver clearance on a daily basis, and with the 2005 British Election Study and the 2008 National Annenberg Election Study, it became part of the academic world of the RCS. *Any* use of the internet to deliver an RCS implies a melding of that strategy with the panel, however. In this respect, the internet will force the pace of integration between the RCS and the panel designs (Bartels 2006*b*; Brady and Johnston 2006).

2 REPRESENTING PERSONS

2.1 Unit Nonresponse and Selection Bias

How well does a survey represent a population? In general, if the survey is designed to be representative, this question is about *unit nonresponse*, and poor response is an issue to the extent that exclusion from samples produces *selection bias*. Recruiting a respondent to a sample requires three steps, and each step is a potential factor in nonresponse and bias.

The first step is to identify the population by establishing a sampling frame. This is an issue of *coverage*, and some modes offer better coverage than others. Modes featuring in-home administration (mail and face-to-face) are in the strongest position. Almost every person has a dwelling place and reputable houses invest heavily in updating dwelling information. Almost every person in industrialized countries has a telephone. Not all phone numbers are listed, but random-digit dialing and its cousins have largely overcome the listing issue. Unfortunately, an increasing share of telephony consists of mobile, cellular sets that, at the time of writing, pose difficulties for survey houses. This need not matter if each cellular user also has a residential landline. But the percentage of households with landlines varies enormously across countries and is now declining even in Canada and the United States, countries with very deep landline penetration. The internet, in contrast, is increasing its penetration, although it is still well behind the other modes. Additionally, it is usually impossible to identify the internet frame: Apart from delimited institutions (such as universities), there is rarely an equivalent to a census of addresses or telephone numbers, nor is there an equivalent to random digit dialing. For most purposes, identifying a meaningful internet frame requires starting with a household one (Couper 2000).

The second step is to *contact* the respondents. Contact may be most problematic for traditional face-to-face interviewing, as it is affected by population density, the incidence of rental occupancy, crime, ethnic minority status, physical impediments, single-person status, presence of pre-schoolers, and old age (Groves and Couper 1998). For telephone frames, contact has been less problematic. Within modes, rates of contact seem to have held up; indeed for high-quality studies they have gone up (Groves and Couper 1998, ch. 6; but see Steeh et al. 2001). For telephone surveys, the spread of call display and answering machine/voice mail technology has had an equivocal effect. On one hand, it facilitates avoidance of unwanted incoming traffic, which may include survey probes. On the other hand, it reduces the incidence of missed calls and facilitates scheduling. Indeed voice mail/answering machines help survey firms identify residential numbers in what would otherwise be a residual "ring, no answer" category.

The complexity of this account points to the next element in response: Does failure to complete an interview with a household that has voice mail indicate the firm's inability to make contact or the respondent's lack of *cooperation* (Steeh et al. 2001)? Making this distinction is even more difficult for the internet. Cooperation was probably always lower in telephone designs than in face-to-face ones. Shanks, Sanchez, and Marton (1983), reporting what seems to be the only fully controlled comparison of the telephone and face-to-face modes, found a ten-point gap favoring the face-to-face mode in otherwise similarly conducted studies, and substantial telephone under-representation of minorities, low-income households, and poorly educated groups. Mode differences were much smaller for the active electorate, however. Of course, the higher cooperation rate in face-to-face comes at a price: geographical clustering of interviews. To the extent that variables of interest cluster in space, higher cooperation and its attendant avoidance of bias may come at the expense of statistical power.

Across both the telephone and the face-to-face modes, cooperation has clearly declined. Overall rates of decline are difficult to compute, because of the massive variance in the quality and intensity of sample clearance. Luevano (1994) testifies to the challenges of computing response rates even for the flagship ANES. From her calculations and subsequent ones (Bowers and Ensley 2003) it is clear that the ANES response rate has dropped some twenty points in forty years, and that refusals are the culprit.[3]

It is difficult to discuss response rates for internet surveys, given ambiguities in their coverage, contact, and cooperation. Intuitively, this mode would have the lowest response rate if we could but calculate it. In particular, self-selection is the central driving force of most internet samples. Most of the time, however, response rate is an empty category for the internet. Only when contact is initiated by some form of random draw is response rate meaningful.

Do differences and trends in response rates affect analytic results? Much of the discussion turns on commonsense expectations in the face of sample truncation. Actual evidence is harder to come by, precisely because of this truncation. Brehm's (1993) ingenious attempt to recover "phantom" respondents in the NES suggests mainly small univariate differences. Keeter et al. (2000) reach the same conclusion, as do Groves, Presser, and Dipko (2004). Response rates inevitably figure in comparison of modes. Krosnick and Chang (2001) show that self-selected internet samples tend to be more knowledgeable and participative than RDD telephone samples. For relationships among variables, the impact is also usually small, except for models relating to information, interest, turnout, and the impact of class (Brehm 1993).

The most common response to selection bias is to weight cases after the fact. But weighting presupposes known values for the target population. What is the proper target for, say, the electorate? We know, or suspect, that electorates are themselves the product of biased selection. Meanwhile, the respondents from underrepresented groups who actually make it into samples are commonly highly *un*representative of their demographic peers, and upweighting them may only make estimations worse. It is not even clear that weights really eliminate bias (Brehm 1993, 120–1).

More promising is to model selection bias explicitly. Heckman (1976) provides the early insights and proofs. Achen (1986) placed the selection perspective squarely before the political science community and taught us to think of an estimation of substantive interest as an *outcome* equation; preceding it in any properly specified scheme would be a *selection* equation, modeling the process by which cases made it into the sample. The basic insight is that selection bias depends on the response rate and on the correlation between the error terms in the selection and outcome equations, another term designated as ρ. Positive values of ρ, which intuition suggests should be quite common, undermine consistency in outcome coefficients. The first serious implementation of selection estimation was Brehm (1993), with Brehm (2000) as an important extension. But constructing plausible selection estimations is difficult

---

[3] Indeed, contact rates for the ANES have gone up (Groves and Couper 1998).

to impossible, so the techniques have not so far been a panacea. A critical implication of Brehm's work is to demand as much "administrative" information as possible from fieldwork agencies.

All this said, the true net impact of sample truncation is not known. The diagnostics, such as they are, suggest that the situation may not be as dire as all that. Pre-election polls seem to do no worse a job of forecasting than they did in palmier times. Response rates can be raised but at great expense and with only tiny impact on most distributions and parameters (Keeter et al. 2000). There is even a hint that for certain purposes higher response rates make things worse (Visser et al. 1996). More generally, we do not really have a theory of survey response. Brehm (1993) has made a start, by proposing and testing a model of cooperation that turns on potential respondents' relation to strangers, to the interviewer, to the interview, and to themselves (stress, helping orientation, and health). These are useful elements for estimating a selection equation. They are all the more useful to the extent that they are *not* related to substantive factors in an outcome equation. There is a strong hint that variation in such factors is, indeed, largely unrelated to processes of substantive interest to political scientists, except for political participation and interest. But we do not really know, and continuing decline in response rates may be bringing us to a fatal threshold.

Special issues in the representation of persons are presented by panel surveys. On one hand, the panel design can expand the effective power of the sample compared to repeated cross-sections, with consequent benefits for hypothesis testing. In comparison of samples drawn at different times, the standard error that pertains to the temporal comparison is smaller if the same respondents are reinterviewed than if a fresh cross-section is produced. Where each sample is a cross-section, each contains its own cross-sectional variance—true as well as error variance—and this adds error to the between-sample comparison. With a panel, none of this is relevant. The cross-sectional variation is identical between waves, as the individuals are the same. Depending on the error in the measurement of the variable in question, repeated measurement can easily double the effective size of the sample.[4]

The power of panels comes at a price: mortality, sometimes literal. The disappearance of first-wave respondents is a problem akin to unit nonresponse in the overall survey. The volume of panel attrition varies by the interval between waves and is especially acute for the telephone mode. Panel retention may become a special appeal of internet samples, for reasons outlined earlier. Attrition may be particularly amenable to selection estimation, however, on the model of Brehm (1993). A panel does, after all, have a first wave, and this wave commonly yields the administrative information that Brehm especially prizes. So far, however, building selection equations into panel estimations is rare. In part, this reflects the fact that the most frequently used panels have relatively low rates of attrition.

---

[4] Panels that also have supplementary cross-sectional samples can expand the power of cross-sections merely by pooling. But pooling presents problems in its own right, as shown by Bartels (2000).

3 REPRESENTING OPINIONS

3.1 General

Representing a population is one thing, representing opinion is another. Broadly speaking, two issues merit consideration. One is the general *quality* of response, overall and relative to alternative representations. The other is the *distribution* of response, especially on a left–right or liberal–conservative continuum.

The research community has come to see that survey response as not just the error-less mapping of free-standing dispositions onto survey questions and answers. Early on, Converse (1964) questioned the very existence of attitudes on certain issue areas. Achen (1975) challenged Converse but only by transferring the problem to the quality of measurement. As Tourangeau and Rasinski (1988) summarize the issue, generating survey response implicates four tasks: (1) deducing the intent of the question; (2) searching memory for relevant information and retrieving it; (3) integrating the information into a single judgement; and (4) translating the judgement into a response from among the alternatives on offer. In a similar vein, Zaller and Feldman (1992) and Zaller (1992) characterize any given survey response as itself aggregated from lower-level *considerations*. They argue that respondents' aggregation of considerations is governed by three axioms: (1) respondents are commonly ambivalent, as they entertain conflicting considerations; (2) response to a given question is averaged across accessible considerations; and (3) the accessibility of a consideration is a function of how recently it was last evoked.[5]

Respondents thus can, if they choose, do some heavy lifting in deciding how they should respond to a survey stimulus. If they perform each step in the Tourangeau-Rasinski sequence, they may be said to *optimize*. By this is meant not that they are using their time in a maximally efficient way; rather, that they are deploying as many considerations as necessary to emit an equilibrium response, the response they would emit under all (or nearly all) circumstances. How likely are they in fact to do the hard work? As it happens, producing superficially plausible response need not be hard work. Respondents may instead *satisfice*, in Krosnick's terminology (as laid out, for instance, in Krosnick 1999, 547 ff.). By satisficing, Krosnick means doing all four steps carelessly or skipping the retrieval and integration steps altogether. Satisficing manifests itself in the following ways:

- Rank order effects, of either primacy or recency. Primacy effects seem to dominate in visual modes (self-administered questions, including by the internet) and recency effects dominate in aural modes, especially in telephone interviews.

---

[5] Alvarez and Brehm (2002) aim to rehabilitate predispositions, but also show that their anchoring power varies across respondents and issue domains. This leaves the methodological situation roughly as Zaller and Feldman describe it.

- Nondifferentiation, the tendency to repeat the same response. This is a particular affliction of the apparently absolute judgements expressed in rating scales, as opposed to the relative judgements elicited by forced ranking scales.
- Acquiescence, the propensity to agree with an item, regardless of its polarity.
- No-opinion response. Krosnick's (1999) summary shows that facilitating "no opinion" does not, contrary to earlier expectations, improve the quality of response. The implication is that more opinion exists than is commonly thought. "No opinion" response is often just satisficing, the lazy person's escape; respondents should be forced to interrogate themselves more closely.

Item nonresponse is not always distributionally neutral. Berinsky (2004) argues that, apart from measurement considerations, two substantive dimensions govern the probability of a valid, interpretable response. One is cognitive, in that some issues are intrinsically more complicated than others (roughly on the lines adumbrated by Carmines and Stimson 1980). On complicated issues, respondents disproportionately satisfice, most importantly by declining to offer an opinion. This seems to be true of issues, such as support for the welfare state, that implicate educational and class differences. War and peace questions, which potentially engage underlying cleavages, may require elite dissensus for the full measure of popular disagreement to reveal itself (Berinsky 2004, ch. 5; Zaller 1992).

Even domains that pose no particular cognitive challenge may engage a social desirability dimension. The impact of each dimension can be powerfully affected by the balance of elite cues, but only in the sense that respondents are motivated to hide their true opinions behind the "no opinion" alternative. On race and moral questions, Berinsky argues, opinion is more conservative than revealed in surveys. To the extent that the real world of elections and direct democracy permits unequivocally anonymous response in the ballot box, surveys are an imperfect forecasting tool and nasty surprises may lie in store. Selection estimation tools may be the only solution, if any really exists, to compensate for biased nonresponse.

All this raises the question of what true opinion and its distribution might be. Zaller and Feldman paint a picture of survey response (as opposed to public opinion) that is highly dynamic. One might want to posit that only response that is—or has been somehow rendered—insensitive to context, including or especially interview context, counts as true opinion. This implies that the questionnaire context should be made as much as possible like the reflective equilibrium that Fishkin (1995) idealizes in the deliberative poll. Not only is this a contestable proposition but it also begs the question of what a survey is for. To the extent that prediction is the key, perhaps the grubby world of casual opinion is close to the political truth (although, as Berinsky warns, the real truth may be even grubbier).

3.2 Mode Issues

Both the overall quality and the likely distribution of response can be powerfully affected by the mode of data collection. Comparisons, especially distributional ones, are difficult, as differences intrinsic to mode are commonly confounded with other, incidental differences. The most obvious problems have already been mentioned: The internet still does not approximate universal coverage and the mail mode places a premium on cooperation. These tend to produce sophisticated samples but also ones with relatively conservative opinions (Krosnick and Chang 2001; Sanders et al. 2007). Mode comparisons can also be bedeviled by incidental features in the implementation of studies. The focus needs to be on reading versus hearing and typing versus speaking.

On both the quality and the distribution of response, so far as they are affected purely by mode, telephone surveys are the poorest performers and internet and mail questionnaires the best. Face-to-face interviews tend to be the intermediate category, sometimes leaning one way, sometimes the other. On the telephone/face-to-face contrast, Holbrook, Green, and Krosnick (2003) show that satisficing is more ubiquitous in telephone interviews than in face-to-face ones. Krosnick and Chang (2001) effect a telephone/internet comparison and show that internet response generates higher reliabilities and better predictive power than telephone response does. Sanders et al. (2007) complete the triangle, so to speak, by comparing internet and face-to-face modes and claim to find no qualitative difference. Additionally, the internet provides scope for complex visual and audio materials.[6] A drawback closely linked to this advantage is the internet's presumption of literacy (including Web literacy) and the requirement of proficiency with keyboard and mouse (Couper 2000).

A virtue and a defect of both telephone and face-to-face modes is the presence of the interviewer. On one hand, the interviewer can compensate for respondent deficiencies, in particular by supplying clarification, and interviewers can model "professionalism and commitment to task" (Krosnick and Chang 2001, 1). On the other hand, attempts at clarification can go astray as interviewer idiosyncrasies come to the fore. Web administration, in contrast, ensures consistent delivery of questions and answers, if at the price of a lack of opportunity for clarification. Interviewers' task orientation can shade into setting too swift a pace and exerting pressure to move on. Such pressure is an invitation to satisficing. Intuitively, this seems especially problematic for the telephone, but any mode that consumes paid interviewer time will create cost pressure to hurry the respondent along. Finally, the mere presence of the interviewer depresses socially disapproved response. In general, this argues for impersonal modes. But the telephone and face-to-face modes each permit variations that squarely address the issue of social desirability. In principle, the face-to-face mode can deploy CAPI to permit data entry out of the interviewer's sight, simply by turning the laptop around so that the respondent can directly enter responses. Audio computer-assisted self-interviewing (T-ACASI) by telephone promises to do the same for that mode. Villaroel et al. (2006) report, for instance, that self-interviewing produces more admissions of same-sex attraction and experience but less tolerant same-sex attitudes than conventional telephone encounters do.

---

[6] Some of these can now be delivered by CAPI as well.

3.3 Panel Issues

Panel surveys present special but contrasting issues in survey response. On one hand, panel surveys may condition response in ways that make it unrepresentative, especially for the very process that panels uniquely capture: change. Lazarsfeld (1940) identified the possibility of panel conditioning in what appears to be only the second journal article on the method. In the years since, it has become the object of sporadic attention and inconsistent claims. The mere fact of being interviewed before the election accounts for a significant fraction of the discrepancy between ANES turnout reports and official returns (Traugott and Katosh 1979). The implication is that being interviewed energizes voters' civic capacity. This intuition is powerfully confirmed in Sturgis, Allom, and Brunton-Smith (forthcoming), who show that in multiyear surveys engagement continues to increase wave upon wave. On the other hand, Bartels (2000) shows that for variables other than interest and turnout, conditioning does not seem that great. Clinton (2001) finds the same for shorter-term panel sequences in the internet mode.

On the other hand, repetition of items makes it possible to estimate the impact of measurement error on the stability and consistency of response (Achen 1975). This requires at least three survey waves. It also presupposes something that the literature in the preceding paragraph controverts: the stability of reliability estimates from wave to wave (see especially Sturgis, Allom, and Brunton-Smith forthcoming, 7).

4 LONGITUDINAL DESIGNS
AND CAUSAL INFERENCE

For academic political scientists, the representativeness of a survey has not always been the central issue. Indeed, the very first election studies, the Erie County and Elmira studies conducted by Lazarsfeld, Berelson, and their Columbia colleagues, were unapologetic in drawing unrepresentative samples. For these scholars, the challenge was to unravel the tangled web of causality. They sought to represent not so much persons or opinions as processes.

Many causal processes can be unraveled with cross-sectional data, provided that the researcher can make a case from common sense, strong theory, or side information. Most of the claims in the strongly process-oriented Columbia studies rested on such data, after all. But consider as an example *per contra* the image adumbrated in Campbell et al. (1960) of the "funnel of causality." Testing the causal image with the cross-sectional surveys that actually underpinned *The American Voter* was virtually impossible. Notwithstanding advances in *ex post* analytic techniques, it is still not possible with solely cross-sectional data to substantiate causal claims beyond a shadow of a doubt. Miller and Shanks (1996), the sophisticated direct descendant of Campbell et al. (1960), is a case in point. Two kinds of causal claim positively require longitudinal data of some form:

- Impact from an *external* force—a force in history—potentially bearing upon all members of a sample. The problem is obvious: At any single cross-section, no relevant variation across respondents can be observed.
- Impact of shifts in levels or linkages among *intrapersonal* variables. Here the issue of causal priority can be especially tangled.

For external forces, the classic approach in the natural sciences, but also in certain of the social sciences, is to deploy direct application of force and random assignment to experimental treatment. By making treatment a random draw, in effect, causal priority is assured.[7] In the survey context this has involved embedded order or wording experiments, and occasionally interactions between wording and order. The internet mode, to the extent that it relies on the World Wide Web, allows even more elaborate treatments, in particular the deployment of visual effects. Whatever the mode, however, survey experimentation is really about establishing "existence" claims, claims that certain effects are possible. In this sense, survey experimentation does not get us far beyond the laboratory. The question remains whether the experimental effect is also visible out in the field. Indeed, in certain contexts—an election campaign is particularly obvious example—successful experimental induction may indicate precisely that the treatment in question is *not* working in the campaign; if it were, giving or withholding the stimulus should make no difference inside the survey sample (Johnston et al. 1992, 149–52). To get at causal sequences as they actually operate in the real world, we usually need to incorporate real time explicitly. For this we require a panel, a rolling cross-section, or a combination of the two.

4.1 External Forces

To gauge impact originating outside the sample, the rolling cross-section seems especially powerful. Most to the point, the design can stay in the field at low cost and so cover many periods and timescales; it can have, that is, a fine *granularity*. The shorter the period for comparison, the less statistical power the design typically will carry,[8] but depending on how events transpire, the fact that each respondent's day of interview is a random event means that adjoining periods can be merged in the

---

[7] Although there may remain confusion how exactly to label the causal force, that the treatment *is* the causal force will not be in doubt. This is an issue of internal versus external validity.

[8] Zaller (1992) raises the prospect that the RCS can never attain the power necessary to establish communications effects at realistically imaginable sample sizes. His concern seems to be, however, with the noise endemic to tests that condition on respondents' self-reports of media usage. Brady and Johnston (2006) present the issue of power as one that can be addressed by graphical smoothing techniques.

interests of power. Meanwhile, each day's crop of respondents is fresh, so conditioning or attrition is not at issue.[9]

A panel can also capture external impact, of course. Additionally, the panel allows for conditioning the impact on cross-sectional factors, permitting a sophisticated exploration of intervening mechanisms. There is, however, aside from the disadvantages of panel attrition and conditioning, a major problem of granularity. The waves of the panel may not bracket important events that might have an impact, or the representation of time in the panel may be too coarse so that too many events are bracketed making it impossible to capture short-term effects in, say, an election campaign (Brady and Johnston 2006).

4.2 Intrapersonal Variables

Here the panel design carries unquestionable advantages, especially when the task is to sort out rival interpretations for ostensibly similar shifts or in the face of deep endogeneity. Analysis tasks seem to take one or the other of two forms:

- In the simpler variant, "change in X produces change in Y" (Miller 2000).
- In the more complex case, as Miller (2000, 121) puts it, "changes in Y may, in some sense, be 'caused' by X without any change in X."

For the first variant, the panel and the rolling cross-section can both be used, if not with equal power, and the logic for analysis is the same for each design. Finkel (1993) seems to be the first to outline what has come to be the basic setup for capturing this sort of causal relationship. Using notation from Johnston and Brady (2002), the conditional change model takes the following form:

$$Y_{it} = a_1 + \beta_1 B_{it} + \delta_1 Y_{it}^0 + \epsilon_{it} \tag{3}$$

where Y denotes behavior or intent and B some belief relevant to the behavior. Y_{it} denotes the behavior at the later point and Y_{it}^0 the behavior at the start. This model implies:

$$Y_{it}^0 = a_0 + \beta_0 B_{it}^0 + \epsilon_{it}^0 \tag{4}$$

such that, substituting (4) into (3), collecting terms, and simplifying, the conditional relationship can be expressed as:

$$Y_{it} = a_2 + \beta_1 B_{it} + \delta_2 B_{it}^0 + \psi_{it} \tag{5}$$

where $a_2 = a_1 + \delta_1 a_0$; $\delta_2 = \delta_1 \beta_0$; and $\psi_{it} = \delta_1 \epsilon_{it}^0 + \epsilon_{it}$.

The problem is how to capture B_{it}^0. With the panel, the answer is obvious: use the value from the first wave in an estimation that deploys information as relevant from both waves. As Bartels (2000, 3) emphasizes, this is an unimpeachable claim:

[9] Even in studies not designed as an RCS, the date of interview can be leveraged, especially if factors associated with respondent accessibility are also controlled. For certain purposes the timescale can be as coarse as yearly. As examples see Wright (1993) and Bartels (2006a).

The temporal ordering permits the direct analysis of change "where prior opinions appear as explanatory variables."[10] The RCS, by construction, is its own baseline. It is quite inappropriate just to use values of B_{it}, as this confounds time-series and cross-sectional variance. There is no reason to assume that time-series and cross-sectional causal mechanisms are the same (Kramer 1983), and even when they have the same sign, the interpretive significance of a coefficient in this context depends greatly which sort of effect it carries. In a pure RCS, the "baseline," the effective equivalent of B_{it}^0, must be captured inside the daily sample. Johnston and Brady (2002) suggest extracting daily means as the representation of the time-series variable and individual-level residuals from that mean as the cross-sectional variable.[11] This requires heroic assumptions, as Johnston and Brady (2002) admit, but in the pure RCS context the alternative is worse.

The RCS need not be pure, however, and in fact almost never is. The main examples on hand combine the RCS with a panel element. In the Canadian Election Studies, the RCS constitutes the first wave in what is essentially a pre-/post-election panel on the ANES model. The British Election Study is now a multiwave panel, with a campaign RCS as an intermediate element. If at least one wave other than the RCS stands clearly outside the period of primary interest, it can serve as the baseline. It is conceptually cleanest if this wave pre-dates the RCS, but Johnston and Brady (2002) argue that even a post-event wave will serve. This too implies heroic assumptions, but the heroism lies arguably in the simplicity of the change model in (3), rather than in the temporal locus of the baseline.[12] What is more, although putting the baseline after the RCS does not avoid problems of attrition, it does rule out conditioning.

The panel most clearly comes into its own when the prior variable does not change, but instead exerts a gravitational force on the subsequent variable. Formally, this calls for a cross-lag setup, as in Lenz (2005), and this is possible only with multiple waves. It is a pleasing irony that representation of relationships in this domain is clearest with old-fashioned techniques. Miller (2000, 123) argues that to test such a proposition: "... we must stop short of summarizing bivariate distributions as correlation coefficients and retain the detailed presentation of distributions that underlie such coefficients."[13]

There is a final, humble sense in which the panel is useful. Even if we cannot condition our estimation so as to isolate the dynamic elements, we can at least

---

[10] Even where change or an intervening event cannot be captured, panels enable us to eliminate *ex post* rationalization as an interpretation of the coefficient provided, of course, a right-hand side variable is measured in an earlier wave than the left-hand side one.

[11] In terms of equation (5), the daily means stand in for B_{it} and the corresponding coefficient, β_1, captures the time-series effect. The coefficient on the residual, δ_2, must be added to β_1 to capture the full cross-sectional effect.

[12] Subsequent work has shown that the assumptions are even more heroic than those reported in Johnston and Brady (2002) so that those using this estimator should beware of its complexities.

[13] Lenz (2005, n. 7) demonstrates how such relationships can in fact be modeled, but does so in an elegiac tone: "Reluctantly, I follow the norm in priming studies of presenting findings with model-based estimates. Cross-tabs and differences in means reveal essentially the same findings."

minimize rationalization as an explanatory force: a causal claim is more persuasive if the cause precedes the effect, something that only a panel can ensure (Bartels 2006*b*).

5 CONCLUSIONS

The epigraph for this chapter is taken from Don Dillman's 2002 AAPOR presidential address. It seems entirely apt. On one hand, new horizons are opening up for survey research. Not only are analytic possibilities expanding but costs for certain modes are dropping. On the other hand, the theoretical foundations of probabilistic surveying—always more problematic than we were prepared to admit—may be crumbling. Or they may not be.

The advent of the internet and the World Wide Web is dramatically expanding the repertoire for survey research. The Web promises consistent delivery of instrumentation in a context that minimizes social desirability effects even as it affords scope to the experimental imagination. The Web is pushing toward panel designs that are cheap to administer and that promise high reinterview rates. This, together with the mode's power for experimentation, will strengthen our ability to study processes and to make unimpeachable causal claims.

One price, however, may be in representativeness. And representational issues will never go away, at least never *should* go away. With hindsight, it does not seem like an accident that the shift from community-based studies with multiwave panels to nationally representative probability samples coincided with sociology's yielding pride of place in the study of electoral phenomena to political science. Although as a discipline, we do not content ourselves with mere description, we also claim to map causal statements onto a field in which special normative force attaches to majority rule.

But are our techniques letting us down just as we are finally coming to understand them? The decline in response rate is the single most worrisome trend. For the telephone mode, this concern is reinforced by shifts away from landlines. The argument is now afoot that the voluntaristic component of sample selection is overwhelming the probabilistic component. To the extent that this is so, the Sirens' argument goes, we should ask if it is time to accept self-selection as the first stage and then devise probabilistic selection mechanisms for later stages. Or perhaps forget probabilistic models altogether and go for sheer number of respondents, abetted by matching or weighting schemes. To this point, however, the evidence suggests that the forces driving response rate down are largely orthogonal to substantive political choices. Surveys overrepresent political interest and its correlates and so may replicate class and other barriers to political participation. But surveys have always done so, and there is little suggestion that things have gotten worse. It seems premature to abandon the ship of probabilistic sampling, at least for a large part of what we do. But it also seems unwise to be complacent.

REFERENCES

ACHEN, C. H. 1975. Mass political attitudes and the survey response. *American Political Science Review*, 69: 1218–31.

——1986. *The Statistical Analysis of Quasi-Experiments*. Berkeley: University of California Press.

ALVAREZ, R. M., and BREHM, J. 2002. *Hard Choices, Easy Answers: Values, Information, and American Public Opinion*. Princeton, NJ: Princeton University Press.

BARTELS, L. M. 2000. Panel effects in the American national election studies. *Political Analysis*, 8: 1–20.

——2006*a*. Priming and persuasion in presidential campaigns. Pp. 78–112 in *Capturing Campaign Effects*, ed. H. E. Brady and R. Johnston. Ann Arbor: University of Michigan Press.

——2006*b*. Three virtues of panel data for the analysis of campaign effects. In *Capturing Campaign Effects*, ed. H. E. Brady and R. Johnston, Ann Arbor: University of Michigan Press.

BERELSON, B. R., LAZARSFELD, P. F., and MCPHEE, W. N. 1954. *Voting*. Chicago: University of Chicago Press.

BERINSKY, A. J. 2004. *Silent Voices: Public Opinion and Political Participation in America*. Princeton, NJ: Princeton University Press.

BOWERS, J., and ENSLEY, M. J. 2003. *Issues in Analyzing Data from the Dual-Mode 2000 American National Election Study*. ANES Technical Report Series, No. nes010751.

BRADY, H. E., and JOHNSTON, R. 2006. The rolling cross-section and causal attribution. Pp. 164–95 in *Capturing Campaign Effects*, ed. H. E. Brady and R. Johnston. Ann Arbor: University of Michigan Press.

BREHM, J. 1993. *The Phantom Respondents: Opinion Surveys and Political Representation*. Ann Arbor: University of Michigan Press.

——2000. Alternative corrections for sample truncation: applications to the 1988, 1990, and 1992 Senate election studies. *Political Analysis*, 8: 183–99.

CAMPBELL, A., CONVERSE, P. E., MILLER, W. E., and STOKES, D. E. 1960. *The American Voter*. New York: Wiley.

CARMINES, E. G., and STIMSON, J. A. 1980. The two faces of issue voting. *American Political Science Review*, 74: 78–91.

CLINTON, J. D. 2001. Panel bias from attrition and conditioning: a case study of the knowledge networks panel. Presented at the American Association for Public Opinion Research Annual Meeting, Montreal.

CONVERSE, P. E. 1964. The nature of belief systems in mass publics. Pp. 206–61 in *Ideology and Discontent*, ed. D. Apter. New York: Free Press.

COOK, T. D., and CAMPBELL, D. T. 1979. *Quasi-Experimentation: Design and Analysis Issues for Field Settings*. New York: Houghton Mifflin

COUPER, M. P. 2000. Review: web surveys: a review of issues and approaches. *Public Opinion Quarterly*, 64: 464–94.

DENNIS, J. M., CHATT, C., LI, R., MOTTA-STANKO, A., and PULLIAM, P. 2005. Data collection mode effects controlling for sample origins in a panel survey: telephone versus internet. <http://knowledgenetworks.com/ganp/papers/rtimodestudy.html>

DILLMAN, D. A. 2002. Navigating the rapids of change: some observations on survey methodology in the early twenty-first century. *Public Opinion Quarterly*, 66: 473–94.

FINKEL, S. E. 1993. Reexamining the "minimal effects" model in recent presidential campaigns. *Journal of Politics*, 55: 1–21.

FISHKIN, J. S. 1995. *The Voice of the People: Public Opinion and Democracy*. New Haven, Conn.: Yale University Press.

FOWLER, F. J., JR. 2002. *Survey Research Methods*, 3rd edn. Thousand Oaks, Calif.: Sage.

FRICKER, S., GALESIC, M. TOURANGEAU, R., and YAN. T. 2005. An experimental comparison of web and telephone surveys. *Public Opinion Quarterly*, 69: 370–92.

GROVES, R. M., and COUPER, M. P. 1998. *Nonresponse in Household Interview Surveys*. New York: Wiley.

—— PRESSER, S., and DIPKO, S. 2004. The role of topic interest in survey participation decisions. *Public Opinion Quarterly*, 68: 2–31.

HECKMAN, J. J. 1976. The common structure of statistical models of truncation, sample selection, and limited dependent variables and a simple estimator for such models. *Annals of Economic and Social Measurement*, 5: 475–92.

HOLBROOK, A. L., GREEN, M. C., and KROSNICK, J. A. 2003. Telephone versus face-to-face interviewing of national probabilty samples with long questionnaires: comparisons of respondent satisficing and social desirability response bias. *Public Opinion Quarterly*, 67: 79–125.

HUCKFELDT, R., JOHNSON, P. E., and SPRAGUE, J. 2004. *Political Disagreement: The Survival of Diverse Opinions within Communication Networks*. New York: Cambridge University Press.

JOHNSTON, R., and BRADY, H. E. 2002. The rolling cross-section design. *Electoral Studies*, 21: 283–95.

—— BLAIS, A., BRADY, H. E., and CRÊTE, J. 1992. *Letting the People Decide: Dynamics of a Canadian Election*. Montreal: McGill Queen's University Press.

KALTON, G., KASPRZYK, D. K., and MCMILLEN, D. B. 1989. Nonsampling errors in panel surveys. In *Panel Surveys*, ed. D. Kasprzyk. New York: Wiley.

KEETER, S., MILLER, C., KOHUT, A., GROVES, R. M., and PRESSER, S. 2000. Consequences of reducing nonresponse in a national telephone survey. *Public Opinion Quarterly*, 64: 125–48.

KISH, L. 1965. *Survey Sampling*. New York: Wiley.

KRAMER, G. H. 1983. The ecological fallacy revisited: aggregate- versus individual-level findings on economics and elections, and sociotropic voting. *American Political Science Review*, 77: 92–111.

KROSNICK, J. A. 1999. Survey research. *Annual Review of Psychology*, 50: 537–67.

—— and CHANG, L. 2001. A comparison of the random digit dialing telephone survey methodology with internet survey methodology as implemented by knowledge networks and Harris interactive. Ohio State University, unpublished memo.

—— HOLBROOK, A., and PFENT, A. n.d. Response rates in surveys by the news media and government contractor survey research firms. Slides at <http://communication.stanford.edu/faculty/Krosnick/Response% 20rates.pdf.>.

LAZARSFELD, P. F. 1940. "Panel" studies. *Public Opinion Quarterly*, 4: 122–8.

—— BERELSON, B. R., and GAUDET, H. 1948. *The People's Choice*. New York: Columbia University Press.

LENZ, G. S. 2005. Campaign and media attention to an issue causes learning-based effects, not priming. Presented at the annual meeting of the American Political Science Association, Washington, DC.

LUEVANO, P. 1994. *Response Rates in the National Election Studies, 1948–1992*. ANES Technical Report Series, No. nes010162.

MCCLOSKY, H. 1958. Conservatism and personality. *American Political Science Review*, 52: 27–45.

——HOFFMANN, P. J., and O'HARA, R. 1960. Issue conflict and consensus among party leaders and followers. *American Political Science Review*, 54: 406–27.

MILLER, W. E. 2000. Temporal order and causal inference. *Political Analysis*, 8: 119–40.

——and SHANKS, J. M. 1996. *The New American Voter*. Cambridge, Mass: Harvard University Press.

SANDERS, D., CLARKE, H. D., STEWART, M. C., and WHITELEY, P. 2007. Does mode matter for modelling political choice? *Political Analysis*, 15: 257–85.

SHANKS, J. M., SANCHEZ, M., and MORTON, B. 1983. *Alternative Approaches to Survey Data Collection for the National Election Studies*. ANES Technical Report Series, No. nes010120.

STEEH, C., KIRGIS, N., CANNON B., and DeWITT, J. 2001. Are they really as bad as they seem? Nonresponse rates at the end of the twentieth century. *Journal of Official Statistics*, 17: 227–47.

STEENBERGEN, M. R., and JONES, B. S. 2002. Modeling multilevel data structures. *American Journal of Political Science*, 46: 218–37.

STOKER, L., and BOWERS, J. 2002. Designing multi-level studies: sampling voters and electoral contexts. *Electoral Studies*, 21: 235–67.

STURGIS, P., ALLUM, N., and BRUNTON-SMITH, I. forthcoming. Attitudes over time: the psychology of panel conditioning. In *Methodology of Longitudinal Surveys*, ed. P. Lynn. New York: Wiley.

TOURANGEAU, R., and RASINSKI, K. 1988. Cognitive processes underlying context effects in attitude measurement. *Psychological Bulletin*, 103: 299–314.

TRAUGOTT, M. W., and KATOSH, J. P. 1979. Response validity in surveys of voting behavior. *Public Opinion Quarterly*, 43: 359–77.

VILLAROEL, M. A., TURNER, C. F., EGGLESTON, E., AL-TAYYIB, A., ROGERS, S. M., ROMAN, A. M., COOLEY, P. C., and GORDEK, H. 2006. Same-gender sex in the United States: impact of T-Acasi on prevalence estimates. *Public Opinion Quarterly*, 70: 166–96.

VISSER, P. S., KROSNICK, J. A., MARQUETTE, J., and CURTIN, M. 1996. Mail surveys for election forecasting? An evaluation of the *Columbus Dispatch* poll. *Public Opinion Quarterly*, 60: 181–227.

WRIGHT, G. C. 1993. Errors in measuring vote choice in the national election studies, 1952–88. *American Journal of Political Science*, 37: 291–316.

ZALLER, J. 2002. *The Nature and Origins of Mass Opinion*. Cambridge: Cambridge University Press.

——and FELDMAN, S. 1992. A simple theory of survey response: answering questions versus revealing preferences. *American Journal of Political Science*, 36: 579–616.

....

CHAPTER 17

ENDOGENEITY AND STRUCTURAL EQUATION ESTIMATION IN POLITICAL SCIENCE

....

JOHN E. JACKSON

THIS chapter discusses a topic—endogeneity—where the importation of econometric methods substantially advanced the practice of empirical work in political science, enabling important substantive findings. The first section examines why econometrics, and particularly the treatment of endogeneity, proved so valuable for political scientists. The chapter discusses and applies the most prominent methods used to deal with endogeneity. We also include a critique of the critical conditions needed to support the use and interpretation of this method and discuss frequently used diagnostics developed to assess the severity of the problems. The estimation method and diagnostics are illustrated with a running example with data from a previous study of US congressional politics (Jackson and King 1989).

1 ECONOMETRICS AND POLITICAL SCIENCE

The application and refinement of econometric techniques is one of the dominant themes of political methodology for the past forty years. The early expansion of these techniques is well documented by King (1991), Bartels and Brady (1993), and Jackson (1996). The reasons for the rapid and extensive spread of these techniques is fairly easy to understand, in retrospect. Econometric techniques shift attention from the observed data to a model of the behavior being investigated and of the process that likely generated the observed data, referred to as the data-generating process (DGP). This attention is present in the linear model but takes center stage with the subsequent interest in maximum likelihood estimation (MLE). (See King 1989 and econometrics texts such as Greene 2003, ch. 17.) Other chapters discuss MLE and its many extensions in detail and it occupies only a minor part of this chapter. This chapter focuses on one particular but vitally important part of the data-generating model.

1.1 The Linear Model and Observational Data

The experimental paradigm remains the object of emulation based on its ability to vary exogenously the magnitude of treatments among treatment and control groups and to completely randomize the assignment of subjects among the treatment and control groups. See Freedman, Pisani, and Purves (1998, chs. 1 and 2) for an excellent discussion of the requirements and advantages of good experimental design and the perils of observational studies. In many substantively important contexts, however, the experimentalists' manipulations and randomization are impossible. Social scientists are no more likely to be given the license to manipulate an economy to ascertain its impacts on voting or to initiate conflicts to study their duration than medical researchers are to force people to engage in risky behaviors. This leaves many empirical researchers with only observational data where there may not even be any well-defined and distinct treatment and control groups but only variations in the variables of interest.

Enter the linear model, $Y_i = X_i \beta + U_i$. The standard interpretation is that the values of the X_i variables can be treated as fixed and exogenously given, analogously to the treatments in an experimental study. Further, the values of U_i, representing omitted factors, are drawn from distributions with a zero mean for all values of X_i, i.e. $E(U_i) = 0$ for all i, analogously to randomization.[1] When these conditions are satisfied one has the equivalent of a well-designed experiment and the estimated regression coefficients, denoted as b, are unbiased, i.e. $E(b) = \beta$. Additional conditions that further emulate the experimental setting, that the U_i's are iid, establish the linear estimator as the best, meaning minimum variance, unbiased linear estimator.

---

[1] The assumption of a zero mean can be relaxed to be a constant value for all i, which only alters the constant term in the model.

Finally, if the U's are normally distributed these estimates are normally distributed, permitting classical inference tests. With normally distributed U's the coefficients are the maximum likelihood estimates.

This chapter addresses a very specific and central aspect of the DGP assumed in the linear model—the assumption (a fiction for some) that X is equivalent to a fixed set of exogenously determined "treatments" that could be duplicated in an arbitrary number of replications. If the X's are not fixed exogenous treatments the condition that $E(U_i) = 0$ is hard to justify, which means the linear estimator is biased, $E(b - \beta) \neq 0$, and inconsistent, $plim(b - \beta) \neq 0$, negating the justifications for and desirability of the linear model.

1.2 Fixed Treatments and Endogeneity

There are classic situations that render the idea of exogenous and fixed X's questionable if not perfectly ludicrous. One is where variations in the left-hand side variable, the outcome variable, are likely causing changes in one of more of the right-hand side (RHS) variables, a condition referred to as simultaneity. The canonical economic example is the relationship between price and quantity. The demand equation predicts a negative relationship between p and q as larger quantities force lower prices in order to clear the market. The supply equation, on the other hand, predicts a positive association between p and q as higher prices induce more production. Given that one only observes actual quantities sold and the associated prices without direct manipulation of one but not the other it is impossible to estimate either relationship with the linear model described above.

Political science examples are abundant but three examples illustrate the problems well. Jacobson (1978) in a classic article explores how challenger and incumbent campaign expenditures affect the challenger's vote share in the election. He appropriately points out that candidate fundraising, hence expenditures, are not exogenous "treatments" but may be influenced by the expected vote shares. "OLS regression models presuppose . . . that spending produces votes." But "The *expectation* [author's emphasis] that a candidate will do well may bring campaign contributions" (Jacobson 1978, 470). Bartels (1991) offers an excellent critique of the methods chosen by Jacobson and others to confront this endogeneity problem.

A second example is political economists' interest in the effect of institutions on economic outcomes. For example, does a PR form of parliamentary government result in more social welfare spending? In examining this and similar propositions Persson and Tabellini (2003, 114) say, "our inference becomes biased if the variation in constitutional rules used to explain performance is related to the random (unexplained) component of performance. Simultaneity problems can take the form of *reverse causation*, different forms of *selection bias*, and *measurement error* [authors' emphasis]." Their empirical strategy to overcome these biases includes but is not limited to the methods surveyed in this chapter. Acemoglu (2005) has an excellent review and assessment of their methods and models.

The last example is the effort by international relations scholars to estimate models of rivalry and reciprocity, such as arms races and tit-for-tat diplomacy, where the actions of country Y are modeled as a function of the actions of a competitor country, X. But there must be a tit for every tat, meaning the actions of X are not exogenous to the actions of country Y. As Dixon (1986, 434) says, "Although the reciprocity models...depict only the behavior of nation Y, each equation is implicitly paired with a complementary specification for nation X.... The obvious mutual dependency between endogenous variables y_{it} and x_{it} in this two-equation system signals a violation of the basic regression model." Dixon and others then proceed with some of the methods discussed below.

For the purposes of this chapter consider an example drawn from legislative politics. A theory of representation is that representatives' votes should be responsive to the mean preferences within their constituency, $V = \alpha + \beta \bar{P}$ (Achen 1978). Elections are the enforcement mechanism in this argument as representatives who deviate from the mean preference should lose votes and ultimately the election itself. Let *Marg* be representatives' electoral margins and *Dev* measure how much their vote deviates from constituency preferences, $Dev = |V - \bar{P}|$. The punishment model is

$$Marg_i = \gamma_1 Dev_i + X_1 \beta_1 + U_i, \tag{1}$$

with $\gamma_1 < 0$, meaning that increased deviations from constituency preferences lead to smaller electoral margins. X_1 represents other factors that may influence incumbents' vote margins, such as the partisan composition of the district. The difficulty in estimating equation (1) is that *Dev* is unlikely to be exogenously determined. Some congressional scholars (e.g. Kingdon 1973, ch. 2) propose that members with larger electoral margins are freer to deviate from constituency preferences, and may do so. This proposition implies that

$$Dev_i = \gamma_2 Marg_i + X_2 \beta_2 + V_i, \tag{2}$$

with $\gamma_2 > 0$. X_2 describes pressures that lead members to vote differently from their constituents' preferences, such as pressure from party leaders. So, *Marg* and *Dev* in any observational study are simultaneously related, thus violating the linear model's basic assumption. Even if X_1 and X_2 contain all the variables that systematically affect representatives' deviations from constituency preferences and their electoral margins so that $E(i'U_i) = E(X_i'V_i) = 0$, the basic regression model gives biased and inconsistent estimates for γ_1 and γ_2. The simple correlation between *Marg* and *Dev* or a regression with either variable on the RHS and the other on the LHS will not reveal anything about the propensity of elections to function as the reward/punishment mechanism in Achen's model of representation.

The likely endogeneity of an explanatory variable is not limited to cases of simultaneity. There are situations with observational data where it is difficult to believe that one of the X's is fixed and would have the same values in subsequent replications of the "experiment." One must consider carefully the context of the quasi or natural experiment and decide if every X is really determined outside the process being studied.

This is a difficult requirement in many political science studies where some of the right-hand side variables themselves are measures of political behavior or outcomes.

As we will illustrate with our legislative example, representatives' partisanship may be a right-hand side variable in the equation for deviations, as party leaders are likely to be effective at getting members to vote with the party rather than with their constituents. If party is a right-hand side variable in the deviation equation, it is likely endogenous. Each district's representative's party is the result of a series of political factors that may not be fixed, as required by the experimental paradigm being emulated by the linear model. Think about whether representatives' party affiliations are assigned randomly among districts! (See Jackson and King 1989.) Any explanatory variable, such as member partisanship, that cannot be justified as exogenous is implicitly the left-hand side variable in another equation. OLS estimates of an equation with this endogenous variables on the RHS will be consistent only if the stochastic term in this implicit equation is uncorrelated with the stochastic term in the equation being estimated.[2]

The condition of fixed and exogenous X's also fails if any of the right-hand side variables are measured with systematic or random error. The case of random measurement errors is the, relatively, easier one to confront and is the focus of this discussion.[3] Random measurement error does not create endogeneity in the causal way discussed above. It does, however, present identical problems and is approached with the same estimation strategy. Basic texts show that if the correct variables are X_i, but instead one observes $Z_i = X_i + \epsilon_i$ and estimates the model $Y_i = Z_i B + U_i$, the resulting coefficients are biased and inconsistent. Even if only one of K RHS variables is measured with error, all the coefficients, not just the one attached to the erroneous variable, may be biased and inconsistent (Achen 1988).

These situations all lead to conditions that violate the basic assumptions of the linear model.[4] The explanatory, or treatment, variables are now correlated with the stochastic term implicit in the DGP and thus in the measures for Y, which yields biased and inconsistent estimates for the model's coefficients. The textbook treatment of this situation is as Greene (2003) describes, $E[U_i|X_i] \neq 0$ which means that $E[X_i U_i] = \eta$ and $\mathrm{plim}(1/n)(X'U) = \eta$, which has the following implications for the estimated coefficients:

$$E[b|X] = \beta + (X'X)^{-1}X'\eta \neq \beta \quad \text{and}$$

$$\mathrm{plim}\, b = \beta + \mathrm{plim}\left(\frac{X'X}{n}\right)^{-1} \mathrm{plim}\left(\frac{X'\epsilon}{n}\right) = \beta + \Sigma_x^{-1}\eta \neq \beta.$$

This is clearly a failure of the classic paradigm and requires new estimation strategies.

---

[2] These conditions, if met, would imply a hierarchical *and* recursive system, in which case OLS estimates are consistent.

[3] Systematic measurement errors present much greater difficulties and require specialized estimators (see Berinsky 1999; Brady 1988; Jackson 1993) and will not be discussed here.

[4] Other situations may also lead to similar violations. These are often encountered in dynamic models that include lagged values for Y on the right-hand side of the equation and an autocorrelated stochastic term. This chapter does not address these situations, though they can be dealt with in ways similar to the subsequent discussions here.

1.3 OLS Estimates of the Margin and Deviation Relationship

We can illustrate this failure with estimates of the model of legislative margins and deviations. Data for estimating the model come from Jackson and King (1989) and Barone, Ujifusa, and Matthews (1979) and relate to the 1978 session of Congress. Representatives' voting behavior in 1978 is assessed using their ADA and ACA scores, with $V = .5*(ADA - ACA + 100)$. The Jackson and King data contain an estimate of mean constituency preference on income redistribution, $\bar{P}$. Members' deviations are the absolute diffence between their vote score and the proportion of the constituency supporting income redistribution, $Dev = |V - \bar{P}|$. The assumption here is that the mean constituency preference for redistribution assesses the liberalness of the constituency. The absolute difference measures the extent to which the members' votes deviate from this constituency position. The variable *Marg* is incumbents' vote share in the 1978 election (the closer of the primary or general elections). The proposition implicit in Achen's and other representation models is that members who deviate more will have smaller re-election margins.

The model and data are being used to illustrate the methodological problems and estimation procedures associated with endogenous variables. This is not intended as a subtantive study of congressional elections or of representation. Obvious variables are omitted from the analysis that would be required for the latter to be true—such as candidate quality, campaign expenditures, representatives' characteristics, etc. But, in most cases, addition of these variables complicates rather than resolves questions of specification and endogeniety.

The simple correlation between *Marg* and *Dev* is 0.13, a very slight positive association. Do members who deviate more do slightly better in the next election, contradicting theories of representation? Or do larger margins embolden members of Congress, leading to increases in deviations from constituency preferences? Or are *Marg* and *Dev* really uncorrelated? Table 17.1 shows the OLS regressions with margin and deviation as the left-hand side variables. The regressions include additional variables hypothesized to relate to margin and deviation respectively. Partisan advantage is defined as the 1976 Ford vote in the district for incumbent Republicans and $(1 - Ford)$ for Democrats, $Partadv = Repub * Ford + (1 - Repub) * (1 - Ford)$. A South region variable and the gap between the representative's age and the mean age of district voters are included in the vote margin equation along with partisan advantage and deviations. Given a partisan advantage, seats may be safer in the South, and the larger the age gap between representatives and their constituents the more competitive the seat. The deviation equation includes the member's party and population change and income growth. The expectation is that the more a district's demographic composition changed between 1970 and 1978, the greater the possibility that the member's votes became out of synch with district preferences. Party is included as Republicans exhibited higher unity scores than Democrats (CQ 1983), suggesting the Republican leadership may have been more successful at getting members to deviate from constituency preferences. Representatives who did not run for re-election are omitted.

Table 17.1. Ordinary least squares estimates

Variable	Equation			
	Margin		Deviation	
	Coeff.	St. err.	Coeff.	St. err.
Deviation	0.063	0.046		
Margin			0.159	0.042
Part. adv.	0.697	0.077		
Republican			0.152	0.014
South	0.102	0.016		
Age gap	−0.120	0.071		
ΔPop			0.178	0.040
Inc_{78}/Inc_{70}			0.035	0.025
Constant	0.310	0.044	−0.194	0.068
R^2	0.268		0.327	
N	376		376	

Contrary to expectations, deviations from constituency opinion appear to have a positive relationship with electoral margin, suggesting that the more representatives deviate from constituents' preferences, the larger their vote margin. The deviation equation suggests that larger electoral margins are associated with more deviation, as expected. But the hypothesized endogeneity between the two variables makes both results, and the other coefficients, suspect. What to do?

2 INSTRUMENTAL VARIABLES: THEORY

Econometricians working with the linear model recognized the problem posed by endogenous regressors fairly early, which created an extended and creative search for alternative methods and assumptions. The traditional method for dealing with endogenous explanatory variables, and the one of concern in this chapter, is called instrumental variable, or IV, estimation. The method also goes by the name two-stage least squares, as that describes how the estimation was originally done. The statistics are relatively simple in theory, but quite difficult in practice.

2.1 The Instrumental Variables Estimator

The classic model with endogenous RHS variables is

$$y = X\beta + Y\gamma + U = W\delta + U, \tag{3}$$

where y is the outcome variable; X is the matrix of observations on the K truly exogenous variables; Y is the matrix of observations on the M variables suspected to be endogenous for any of the reasons cited above; $W = (X, Y)$; and $\delta' = (\beta', \gamma')$ is the vector of coefficients of interest. The endogeneity problem arises because $\mathrm{plim}\frac{1}{n}(Y'U) \neq 0$.

The theory of IV estimation depends on the existence of a second set of variables, which we denote by Z. Z must contain at least M variables with finite variances and covariances, be correlated with Y, but be uncorrelated with U; i.e.

$$\mathrm{plim}\ \frac{1}{n}Z'Z = \Sigma_{zz}, \quad \text{an } L \times L \text{ finite, positive definite matrix,}$$

$$\mathrm{plim}\ \frac{1}{n}Z'Y = \Sigma_{zy}, \quad \text{an } L \times M \text{ matrix with rank M,}$$

$$\mathrm{plim}\ \frac{1}{n}Z'U = 0.$$

In the simplest case, $L = K$, meaning that there is one "instrument" or Z for each Y. Let $Z^* = (X, Z)$, which is equivalent to letting each of the exogenous variables in X function as its own instrument. In this case, the IV estimator is

$$d_{IV} = (Z^{*'}W)^{-1}(Z^{*'}y). \tag{4}$$

Greene (2003, 76–7) shows that this estimator is consistent with an asymptotic normal distribution.

The situation where one has more instruments than original right-hand side endogenous variables, $L > M$, is handled somewhat differently, though the theory is the same. Since plim $(Z'U)/n = 0$ any set of M variables selected from Z will yield consistent estimates for γ. Further, all M linear combinations of the variables in Z also give consistent estimates. It turns out that the linear combination obtained by regressing each variable in Y on all the variables in Z and using the predicted values for Y from these regressions, denoted as $\hat{Y}$, as the right-hand side variables in the regression with y as the left-hand side variable has the lowest asymptotic variance of any linear combination of the Z's (Brundy and Jorgenson 1971; Goldberger 1973).

This common reference to this method as two-stage least squares, or 2SLS, derives from this process. More formally, denote by a the matrix of coefficients obtained from regressing each variable in Y on the variables in Z and by $\hat{W}$ the matrix $\hat{W} = (X, \hat{Y}) = (X, Za) = [X, Z(Z'Z)^{-1}Z'Y] = Z^*(Z^{*'}Z^*)^{-1}Z^*W$:

Step One : $\hat{Y} = Za = Z(Z'Z)^{-1}(Z'Y)$

Step Two : $d_{2sls} = (\hat{W}'\hat{W})^{-1}(\hat{W}'Y)$

$\qquad\qquad = [(W'Z^*)(Z^{*'}Z^*)^{-1}(Z^{*'}W)]^{-1}[(W'Z^*)(Z^{*'}Z^*)^{-1}(Z^{*'}y)]$

$\qquad\qquad = [W'P_{z^*}W]^{-1}W'P_{z^*}y,$

where $P_{z^*} = Z^*(Z^{*'}Z^*)^{-1}Z^{*'}$. Step two is just estimating the equation

$$y = X\beta + \hat{Y}\gamma + \epsilon. \tag{5}$$

This expression for d_{2sls} reduces to equation (4) if there are exactly as many instruments as variables in Y, i.e. $K = L$.

Some intuition into IV estimation would be helpful before discussing alternative versions. Consider a companion equation to equation (3) that relates the included endogenous variables, Y, to the set of instruments, Z:

$$Y = Z\pi + \epsilon, \tag{6}$$

with $E(Z'\epsilon) = 0$. In the full model discussed in Section 4 these instruments will include the exogenous variables in the structural equations for Y but excluded from the equation for y, equation (3), as well as the exogenous variables in equation (3).[5] For now, we only need the condition that Z is uncorrelated with ϵ plus the previous conditions for instrumental variables that Z is related to Y, meaning that $\pi \neq 0$, and Z is uncorrelated with U.

Substituting equation (6) relating Y to Z into equation (3) for y gives

$$y = X\beta + (Z\pi)\gamma + U + \epsilon\gamma. \tag{7}$$

Were π known we could get unbiased estimates for β and γ in equation (7) by regressing y on X and the product $Z\pi$, assuming the various conditions making U and ϵ uncorrelated with X and Z are satisfied. But, alas, π is not known but only estimated in the first stage regression of Y on Z, $p = (Z'Z)^{-1}Z'Y = \pi + (Z'Z)^{-1}Z'\epsilon$. Substituting $\hat{Y} = Zp$ for $Z\pi$ in equation (7) is the second stage of the 2SLS estimator, shown in equation (5). With this substitution the second stage is estimating the equation

$$y = X\beta + (Zp)\gamma + u + \epsilon\gamma. \tag{8}$$

Equation (8) shows both the attractiveness and limitations of the IV estimator. With an infinite sample the distribution of p collapses at π, or formally plim $p = \pi$, which means that the estimates for β and γ will also collapse about their true values. Hence the consistency result. The IV estimator is biased for finite samples, however, because p is a function of ϵ from the first stage, meaning that Zp and the error term in equation (8) are correlated. These conditions are what makes the IV estimator a biased but consistent estimator for equation (3).

A second important IV estimator is the limited information maximum likelihood estimator, or LIML. Following the notation in Hansen, Hausman, and Newey (2006), the LIML estimator is

$$d_{liml} = (W'P_{z*}W - \tilde{a}W'W)^{-1}(W'P_{z*}y - \tilde{a}W'y), \tag{9}$$

where $\tilde{a}$ is the smallest eigenvalue of the matrix $(\tilde{W}'\tilde{W})^{-1}(\tilde{W}'P_{z*}\tilde{W})$ with $\tilde{W} = (y, W) = (y, X, Y)$.[6] This is the maximum likelihood estimator for d if the stochastic terms are normally distributed. The LIML estimator also has more desirable small

---

[5] In this model equation (6) is referred to as the reduced form equations for Y.

[6] The 2SLS and LIML estimator are special cases of a general estimator referred to as a k-class estimator, which is $d_k = (W'P_{z*}W - \hat{a}W'W)^{-1}(W'P_{z*}y - \hat{a}W'y)$. For the LIML estimator $\hat{a}$ is defined above and for 2SLS $\hat{a} = 0$.

sample properties, as measured by a mean squared error criteria, than 2SLS under many conditions (Donald and Newey 2001). We will consider both the 2SLS and LIML estimators.

There is a further consideration in choosing instruments. The justification for an IV estimator is its consistency, but it is biased in finite samples, as noted previously. Donald and Newey (2001, 1165) give expressions for the mean squared error of the 2SLS and LIML estimators, and Hahn and Hausman (2002) give an expression showing the bias of the 2SLS estimator with one endogenous variable. These errors are proportional to the number of instruments and to the correlation between the error terms in the reduced form, ϵ, and the structural equation, U, and inversely related to the variance of the reduced form error term. There does not seem to be a generalization to equations with more than one endogenous variable, but these proportional relationships should still hold. The implication here is that one should be cautious about selecting both the number and the composition of the instruments. (See Section 3 for a discussion of these concerns.)

2.2 An Example: IV

We can illustrate the use of IV estimation with the model relating to representatives' deviations and electoral margins. Jackson and King propose that representatives' party should be treated as an endogenous variable. Doing so here enables us to illustrate IV estimation with an endogenous right-hand side variable that is not simultaneously related to other endogenous variables. Accordingly we treat members' party as endogenous and use a polynomial with Ford's vote to the third, fourth, and fifth power as instruments:[7]

$$Repub = B_{11} + B_{21}Ford^3 + B_{31}Ford^4 + B_{41}Ford^5 + U_1. \tag{10}$$

This equation can be estimated with OLS as the 1976 Ford vote variables are considered to be exogenous and uncorrelated with the stochastic term in the party equation.

The designation of members' party as an endogenous variable implies that the party electoral advantage variable, which includes members' party, is also endogenous but in a nonlinear manner. This specification permits this example to demonstrate how IV estimation can be used to accommodate nonlinear relationships among the endogenous and exogenous variables. The important works on structural models with nonlinear specifications are Goldfeld and Quandt (1972), Jorgenson and Laffont (1974), Kelejian (1971), and Newey (1990), and see Achen (1986) and Wooldridge (2003) for good discussions of how to apply these results. The key element is to expand the nonlinear parts of the model to find an expression that is linear in the parameters and that includes enough functions of the exogenous variables to

---

[7] In this model *Repub* is being treated as a continuous interval variable, which it is not. The model with polynomial Ford variables gives predicted probabilities that range from −0.02 to 0.97 and whose correlation with the predicted probabilities from a probit model is 0.9988, suggesting this equation very closely approximates the better specified but nonlinear probit model.

function as instruments for the nonlinear term. In the example here the expansion of the party advantage variable is readily done and leads to a clear specification of instruments and estimation strategy for the first stage of the IV procedure. Recall that $Partadv = Repub * Ford + (1 - Repub) * (1 - Ford)$. Substituting the expression for $Repub$ in equation (10) gives

$$Partadv = (1 - B_{11}) + (2B_{11} - 1)Ford - B_{21}Ford^3 + (2B_{21} - B_{31})Ford^4$$

$$+ (2B_{31} - B_{41})Ford^5 + 2B_{41}Ford^6 + (2 * Ford - 1) * U_1. \qquad (11)$$

The coefficients in equation (11) are linear combinations of those in equation (10). The best way to estimate such a system is as a seemingly unrelated regression model (SUR) that incorporates these constraints and allows for the correlation between the error terms in the two equations.[8] The exogenous variables in the *Marg* and *Dev* equations—*South, Age Gap, ΔPop*, and *Δ Inc*—constitute the remaining instruments.

The first-stage equations for *Repub* and *Partadv* are estimated with the SUR model, but with two different specifications. The first specification excludes the exogenous variables from the *Marg* and *Dev* equations, as they are not included in the reduced-form equations for *Repub* and *Partadv*. Achen (1986) suggests that for hierarchical models such as this, exogenous variables from higher-order equations should be excluded for asymptotic efficiency reasons. Most standard procedures, and programs such as Stata, includes all the exogenous variables as instruments in the first-stage equations for all included endogenous variables. Our examples will use both specifications, as the results illustrate questions related to the selection of instruments.

The estimated equations for electoral margin and voting deviations using the IV procedures are shown in Table 17.2. The estimation is done using the 2SLS and LIML estimators. The OLS estimates from Table 17.1 are shown for comparison. The asymptotic coefficient standard errors (Greene 2003, 400) and the corrected standard errors derived in Bekker (1994) and discussed in Hansen, Hausman, and Newey (2006) are presented.[9]

All the IV estimation results for the coefficients relating *Dev* and *Marg*, shown in boldface, differ substantially from the OLS estimates and are in line with the initial propositions. Larger deviations from constituency opinion are associated with decreased electoral margins, with the coefficients ranging from -0.24 to -0.3. Conversely, members with larger margins, and presumably safer seats, deviate more from constituency opinion, with the coefficient likely between 0.4 and 0.5. In all but one set of estimations the 2SLS and LIML estimates are very similar. The exception is

---

[8] The stochastic term in equation (11) is heteroskedastic because of the $(2 * Ford - 1)$ term. Proper GLS estimation requires weighting by the reciprocal of this term, which is not defined for $Ford = 0.5$. This heteroskedasticity is ignored in subsequent estimations as it only affects the efficiency of the first-stage estimations. The IV estimator remains consistent.

[9] The calculations are done in Stata following the expressions given in Hansen et al. (2006, 4). The corrected standard errors do not include the terms related to the third and fourth moments that Hansen et al. write "... are present with some forms of nonnormality."

Table 17.2. Instrumental variable estimates

Variable	OLS coeff	Two-stage least squares			Limited information ML		
		Coeff	s_b(cse)	s_b(asy)	Coeff	s_b(cse)	s_b(asy)
Margin equation–limited instruments							
Deviation	0.063	−0.280	0.133	0.133	−0.314	0.147	0.142
Part. Adv.	0.697	0.673	0.098	0.098	0.668	0.101	0.101
South	0.102	0.123	0.019	0.019	0.125	0.020	0.019
Age Gap	−0.120	−0.071	0.075	0.076	−0.071	0.077	0.077
Constant	0.310	0.396	0.070	0.069	0.408	0.075	0.072
R^2	0.268	0.156			0.132		
Margin equation–all instruments							
Deviation	0.063	−0.261	0.134	0.133	−0.244	0.126	0.128
Part. Adv.	0.697	0.679	0.099	0.098	0.670	0.096	0.097
South	0.102	0.122	0.019	0.019	0.121	0.018	0.019
Age Gap	−0.120	−0.131	0.076	0.076	−0.130	0.075	0.075
Constant	0.310	0.398	0.069	0.068	0.392	0.066	0.067
R^2	0.268	0.169			0.108		
Deviation equation–limited instruments							
Margin	0.159	0.496	0.131	0.128	0.835	0.243	0.237
Republican	0.152	0.227	0.045	0.044	0.338	0.083	0.081
ΔPop	0.178	0.184	0.044	0.045	0.165	0.062	0.062
Inc_{78}/Inc_{70}	0.035	0.046	0.028	0.028	0.048	0.037	0.037
Constant	−0.194	−0.494	0.123	0.120	−0.757	0.208	0.204
R^2	0.327	0.164			−0.428		
Deviation equation–all instruments							
Margin	0.159	0.411	0.112	0.113	0.426	0.119	0.118
Republican	0.152	0.213	0.040	0.040	0.218	0.042	0.041
ΔPop	0.178	0.174	0.044	0.044	0.173	0.044	0.045
Inc_{78}/Inc_{70}	0.035	0.044	0.027	0.027	0.044	0.027	0.027
Constant	−0.194	−0.411	0.108	0.108	−0.423	0.113	0.111
R^2	0.327	0.232			0.219		

the LIML estimate of the *Dev* equation with the limited set of instruments for the *Republican* variable. We discuss this discrepancy in the next section.

The coefficients on partisan advantage and the exogenous variables are quite consistent across all three estimation methods and match expectations, with one exception. The larger the members' partisan advantage the larger their electoral margin, and Southern representatives had safer seats than representatives from outside the South. The OLS estimation and the IV estimations using the full set of instruments suggest that the larger the age gap between representative and constituency, the smaller the electoral margin. The IV estimations with only the Ford vote variables as instruments for *Repub* have much smaller and statistically insignificant coefficients for *Age Gap* though the differences are less than the standard errors of the coefficients.

In the deviation equations, Republicans and members from districts with large population changes and income growth deviated more from constituency opinion than
did Democrats and those from stable districts.

The R^2 are lower in the IV models but this is not a particularly meaningful statistic.
The residuals in the estimated equation are calculated using the observed values
of the RHS endogenous variables, not their predicted values from the first stage.
Subsequent sample statistics—the estimate for σ_u^2, the estimated coefficient standard
errors, and the R^2—all depend on these calculations. By construction the R^2 of the IV
estimates will be smaller than those of the OLS estimates because the latter are chosen
to minimize the sum of squared errors using the observed values of the included
endogenous variables. The R^2 in the OLS estimations, however, do not have much
meaning as we are starting with the premise that because of the endogenity these
OLS coefficients are biased and inconsistent.

These results suggest that one's underlying assumptions about the data-generating
process and the choice of method may have profound, substantive consequences.
In the presence of endogeneity, which may be likely in observational studies, if the
conditions for IV estimation are met, it is possible, in theory, to overcome these
confounding effects. But theory and practice are not always the same thing.

3 INSTRUMENTAL VARIABLES IN PRACTICE

The application of instrumental variables poses several serious, possibly daunting,
issues. The most critical is that the instruments must be independent of the stochastic
term in the equation of interest. The second condition is that the instrument must be
correlated with the variable for which it it being used as the instrument. Bartels (1991),
in a classic discussion of these problems, shows how they affect the asymptotic mean
squared error, AMSE, of the IV estimator. (Also see Bound, Jaeger, and Baker 1995.)
Bartels shows how the AMSE of the IV estimator is related to these two correlations:

$$AMSE\,(b^{IV}) \propto \frac{\rho_{ZU|X}^2 + 1/N}{\rho_{ZY|X}^2},\tag{12}$$

where $\rho_{ZU|X}^2$ is the squared population partial correlation between the instruments
and the stochastic term in the equation being estimated and $\rho_{ZY|X}^2$ is the squared
population partial correlation between the instruments and the endogenous variables
for which they serve as instruments. Bartels makes it clear that it is the partial correlations holding the included exogenous variables, X, constant that are critical. This
requirement is also evident in equation (5). As with any OLS regression the greater
the variance in $\hat{Y}$ and the lower the correlations of $\hat{Y}$ with the variables in X the more
reliable the estimates of γ in the second-stage estimation of equation (5).

Bartels argues that these conditions are problematic in practice, hence the name "quasi-instruments," so users must consider what happens in practice, how to diagnose potential problems, and how best to manage the trade-offs among second-best estimators. The discussion and assessment of weak instruments is also the subject of important work in econometrics over the past decade. These conditions and how one might assess their fit, or lack of, to specific data are discussed and illustrated in this section.

3.1 Correlations of Instruments and Endogenous Variables

We begin the discussion of the practice of IV estimation with the denominator in equation (12) as it is easier to observe and to estimate with available data. The term $\rho^2_{ZY|X}$, referring to the squared population partial correlation, can be estimated by the partial correlation between Z and Y in the sample data. The most direct way to make this assessment is to regress Y on X and Z and then conduct the F-test for the null hypothesis that the coefficients on Z equal zero. There are two weaknesses to this test, however. The first is that the null hypothesis being tested by the F-statistic is not the null hypothesis of interest and one should be most concerned about a type II not a type I error. Rejecting the null hypothesis that the coefficients are zero is not identical to saying they are not zero with some probability of error. Baum, Schaffer, and Stillman (2003) suggest that with one included endogenous variable an F-statistic greater than ten is an appropriate rule of thumb for accepting the alternative hypothesis that the coefficients are not zero.

A second difficulty arises when there is more than one RHS endogenous variable, as in this example. The previous test is designed to ensure that the included endogenous variables are strongly correlated with the excluded exogenous variables, Z, holding constant the included exogenous variables, X. But what if the same variables in Z account for the independent variation in all the included Y's? This effectively means that the coefficients on these included endogenous variables are not really identified, despite appearing to meet the technical criteria.

Shea (1997) presents a test for the strength of the partial relationship between each included endogenous variable and the excluded instruments controlling for the included instruments and the other included endogenous variables. Shea presents a four-step procedure for calculating these statistics, usually referred to as Shea's partial R^2 and denoted as R^2_p. Godfrey (1999) presents a simplified calculation based on the ratios of the coefficients' variances and the R^2 statistics from the OLS and 2SLS estimations respectively. This expression is

$$R^2_p = \left(\frac{\sigma^{ols}_b}{\sigma^{2sls}_b}\right)^2 \left(\frac{\sigma^{2sls}_u}{\sigma^{ols}_u}\right)^2 = \left(\frac{\sigma^{ols}_b}{\sigma^{2sls}_b}\right)^2 \left(\frac{1 - R^2_{2sls}}{1 - R^2_{ols}}\right),$$

where σ_b is the coefficient standard error, σ_u is the standard error of the estimate, and R^2 is the unadjusted centered R-squared from the respective estimated equations. Unfortunately neither Shea nor Godfrey report a test statistic for this partial R-squared

Table 17.3. Tests for instrument relevance

Endogenous Variable		Deviation	Part Advant.	Margin	Republican
1st Stage	R^2	0.165	0.721	0.236	0.255
	$F(K_1, K_2)^a$	8.02	135.59	12.59	17.97
Partial	R^2	0.141	0.713	0.233	0.226
	$F(K_1, K_2)^b$	8.55	182.85	15.87	21.43
Shea's R^2		0.135	0.698	0.156	0.149

^{a} $K_1 = 9$ and $K_2 = 366$ for *Dev* and *Marg* and $K_1 = 7$ and $K_2 = 368$ for *Repub* and *Part Adv.*

^{b} $K_1 = 7$ and $K_2 = 366$ for *Dev* and *Marg* and $K_1 = 5$ and $K_2 = 368$ for *Repub* and *Part Adv.*

so we cannot test the null hypothesis that it is zero, and thus that the instruments for that particular coefficient are irrelevant. In performing these computations one must assure that all estimated standard errors are calculated with the same degrees of freedom.[10]

Table 17.3 reports the R^2 and associated F-statistics for the first-stage regressions, the partial R^2 and associated F-statistics, and the Shea's partial R^2 for the estimations just reported, using the full set of instruments.[11] None of these statistics suggests a problem with how well the necessary instruments correlate with the included endogenous variables. The F-statistic for the partial R^2 for *Dev* is only 8.55, but the P-value for this F with the appropriate degrees of freedom is approximately $1. X 10^{-09}$, which suggests a very low likelihood of a type II error if the null hypothesis of no relationship is rejected. The other F-statistics are even larger. The Shea's partial R^2 statistics range from 0.135 to 0.156, with the value for Partisan Advantage equal to 0.70. On the basis of these statistics we conclude that these instruments adequately meet the standards for relevance, as discussed by Bartels, Bound, and subsequent authors.

3.2 Independence of Instruments and Stochastic Terms

The second critical requirement for consistent IV estimators is independence between the instruments and the stochastic term in the equation being estimated. This is the numerator in Bartels's assessment of the asyptotic mean squared error of the IV estimator, equation (12). This condition is difficult to test in practice as it requires information on the unobservable stochastic term in the equation being estimated.

---

[10] Some 2SLS estimations do not use a degrees of freedom correction in calculating standard errors under the assumption that only the asymptotic properties are of interest. In Stata, for example, the "small" option adjusts for the degrees of freedom in the equation being estimated.

[11] The equations for *Repub* and *Part Adv* have fewer degrees of freedom because following equations (10) and (11) there are only nine coefficients being estimated. The equations for *Dev* and *Marg*, because *Ford* and *Ford*^{6} are included and none of the coefficients are constrained, estimate eleven coefficients.

There are several approaches to approximating this test discussed in this section. All, however, require that the equation being estimated is overidentified, meaning that there are more instruments than included endogenous variables, $L > K$. The first statistic is attributed to Sargan (1958) and is reported as the Sargan statistic. This statistic is the proportion of the sum of squared residuals from the estimated equation that can be "explained" by the full set of instruments:

$$\text{Sargan statistic } = \frac{\hat{u}' Z^*(Z^{*'} Z^*)^{-1} Z^{*'} \hat{u}}{\hat{u}' \hat{u}/n}, \tag{13}$$

where $Z^* = (X, Z)$ and $\hat{u}$ denotes the residuals from the estimated equation using the observed values for the included endogenous variables. Sargan shows that asymptotically this ratio is distributed as a Chi-squared statistic with $(L - K)$ degrees of freedom. If we knew the true values of the stochastic term and if the instruments are truly independent of the stochastic term, this statistic should be zero, meaning that the instruments do not explain any of the residual variance. The Sargan statistic approximates this ratio by using the residuals calculated from the estimated equation. There is also a version of the Sargan statistic that multiplies the ratio by $(n - L)$ rather than n, which is also distributed as a Chi-squared statistic with $(L - K)$ degrees of freedom.

Basmann (1960) proposes a second statistic that compares the same fitted values of the residuals in the Sargan statistic to the unexplained variance in the residuals rather than the total variance of the residuals:

$$\text{Basmann's statistic} = \frac{\hat{u}' Z^*(Z^{*'} Z^*)^{-1} Z^{*'} \hat{u}/(L - K)}{[\hat{u}' \hat{u} - \hat{u}' Z^*(Z^{*'} Z^*)^{-1} Z^{*'} \hat{u}]/(n - L)}. \tag{14}$$

Basmann shows that asymptotically this statistic has an F-distribution with $(L - K)$ and $(n - L)$ degrees of freedom. Basmann and Sargan present other variations on these statistics but the core comparison is the relationship between the residuals in the estimated structural equation and the instrumental variables.

One weakness of these tests is the same as with the tests of instrument relevance. The null hypothesis being tested is that the instruments and stochastic term are uncorrelated, plim $Z'u/n = 0$. If this null is rejected then it is clear that the variables are not adequate instruments. But not rejecting the null is not equivalent to accepting it, which is the critical issue. The smaller the Sargan and/or Basmann statistics the higher the likelihood of getting that value by chance if the null hypothesis is true, and thus the lower the probability of a type II error if the null is accepted. But at the end of the analysis the best that can be said is that these statistics are useful for rejecting the null hypothesis and thus putting the instruments in doubt but are not strong enough for establishing that these instruments are valid.

Table 17.4 shows the Sargan and Basmann statistics for the estimated equations, including the estimations with the limited set of instruments for the *Repub* and *Part Adv* variables. Recall from Table 17.2 that the LIML estimates for the *Dev* equation with the limited set of instruments produced questionable results. The 2SLS and LIML estimations using the full set of instruments in the first-stage estimates for *Repub* and

Table 17.4. Tests for instrument independence

Test (DOF)	Marg		Dev	
	2SLS	LIML	2SLS	LIML
	Full instruments			
Sargan $\chi^2(5)$	1.143	1.213	2.114	2.098
P-Value	0.950	0.944	0.833	0.835
Basmann F(5,366)	0.187	0.198	0.346	0.343
P-Value	0.967	0.963	0.885	0.887
	Limited instruments			
Sargan $\chi^2(5)$	1.844	1.872	2.769	9.963
P-Value	0.870	0.867	0.736	0.076
Basmann F(5,366)	0.301	0.306	0.454	1.665
P-Value	0.912	0.909	0.810	0.142

Part Adv have very low Sargan and Basmann statistics with very high probabilities of occurrence if the null hypothesis of independence is true. The estimates of the *Marg* equation with only the *Ford* variables as instruments for *Part Adv* have similarly low Sargan and Basmann statistics, again suggesting instrument independence.

The questionable results are the limited instrument LIML estimation of the *Dev* equation. We noted earlier that the coefficient on *Marg* was inconsistent with the other estimations and that the estimates fit the observed data very badly. The Sargan and Basmann statistics indicate there is a problem with the assumption that the instruments are uncorrelated with the stochastic term. It is hard to explain these results, as all of the other results with similar specifications and even the 2SLS estimates with the same specifications give more consistent results and have more acceptable summary statistics. There are two things one may want to conclude from these results. Results are sensitive to the choice of instruments, as is also seen in the estimates for the coefficients on *Age gap* in Table 17.2, and estimation method in unexpected ways. This makes the exploration of the robustness of the results to these choices important. It is also the case that some of the diagnostic statistics, such as the assessments of instrument relevance and independence, may reveal problems and should be reported in all studies.

4 FULL INFORMATION ESTIMATION

The previous estimators are limited information estimators because the estimation proceeds one equation at a time. A second estimation strategy, referred to as full information estimation, estimates the entire structural model. This section talks briefly about this strategy and applies it to the running example. The reference to the entire structure means there is an equation of the form of equation (3) for each endogenous variable in the model:

$$y_1 = X_1\beta_1 + Y_1\gamma_1 + U_1 = W_1\delta_1 + U_1$$

$$\vdots \qquad\qquad \vdots$$

$$y_m = X_m\beta_m + Y_m\gamma_m + U_m = W_m\delta_m + U_m \qquad (15)$$

$$\vdots \qquad\qquad \vdots$$

$$y_M = X_M\beta_M + Y_M\gamma_M + U_M = W_M\delta_M + U_M.$$

Assume that $E(X'U) = 0$ and that the U_m's are iid, so that

$$E(U_s U_t') = \Sigma_u, \quad \text{for all } t \ \& \ s = t \qquad (16)$$

$$= 0, \quad \text{otherwise.} \qquad (17)$$

We also assume that the specification of the exogenous and endogenous variables excluded from each equation plus any other a priori constraints are sufficient to meet the identification requirements. (Identification of each equation is required for estimation and is a complex topic that is not addressed in this chapter. The classic work here is Fisher 1966, but see any text, such as Greene 2003, 385–95, or Wooldridge 2003, 211–30.) We discuss two different full information estimation strategies and both parallel those examined above. The first is an extension of the 2SLS estimator to the full model, referred to as Three-stage Least Squares, or 3SLS. The second is a maximum likelihood, or FIML, estimator.

4.1 Three-stage Least Squares

Three-stage Least Squares (Zellner and Theil 1962) stacks each of the M equations in equation (16) into one large $TM \times 1$ system, as shown in equation (18):

$$\begin{pmatrix} y_1 \\ \vdots \\ y_m \\ \vdots \\ y_M \end{pmatrix} = \begin{pmatrix} W_1 & \cdots & 0 & \cdots & 0 \\ \vdots & \ddots & \vdots & \ddots & \vdots \\ 0 & \cdots & W_m & \cdots & 0 \\ \vdots & \ddots & \vdots & \ddots & \vdots \\ 0 & \cdots & 0 & \cdots & W_M \end{pmatrix} \begin{pmatrix} \delta_1 \\ \vdots \\ \delta_m \\ \vdots \\ \delta_M \end{pmatrix} + \begin{pmatrix} U_1 \\ \vdots \\ U_m \\ \vdots \\ U_M \end{pmatrix}. \qquad (18)$$

This expression can be summarized as $Y = W\delta + U$.

Each equation in this system could be estimated by 2SLS using the same IV procedures and instruments discussed above. In this estimation the instruments for each equation are all the exogenous variables in the system, X, so that $\hat{W}_m = (X_m, \hat{Y}_m) = [X_m, X(X'X)^{-1}X'Y_m]$. The 2SLS estimator for each equation is,

$\hat{d}_{2sls} = (\hat{W}'\hat{W})^{-1}\hat{W}'Y$. Unless Σ_u is diagonal, meaning all the stochastic terms are independent of each other, this method loses asymptotic efficiency by not considering these stochastic term covariances. (See Judge et al. 1988, 646–51.) The standard 3SLS estimator uses the residuals from the 2SLS estimation of each equation to form an estimate for the elements in Σ_u, which is the second stage in the 3SLS procedure. The inverse of this estimated variance-covariance matrix is used in a feasible GLS estimation of the full system. Let $\hat{\Sigma}_u^{-1}$ denote this inverted estimated variance-covariance matrix, which following the conditions in equation (17) has the following structure:

$$\hat{\Sigma}_u^{-1} = \begin{pmatrix} \hat{\sigma}^{11}I & \cdots & \hat{\sigma}^{1M}I \\ \vdots & \vdots & \vdots \\ \hat{\sigma}^{1M}I & \cdots & \hat{\sigma}^{MM}I, \end{pmatrix} \qquad (19)$$

where the I are $T \times T$ identity matrices. The 3SLS estimator is

$$\hat{d}_{3sls} = (\hat{W}'\hat{\Sigma}_u^{-1}\hat{W})^{-1}(\hat{W}'\hat{\Sigma}_u^{-1}Y). \qquad (20)$$

This is a specific application of Zellner's (1962) seemingly unrelated regression. Often this process is iterated using the residuals from successive 3SLS estimations to get $\hat{\Sigma}_u$ until convergence is achieved, which is usually fairly rapidly.

The justification for 3SLS depends heavily on its asymptotic properties, even more so than 2SLS. In addition to the conditions required for consistency and the factors that make 2SLS biased in finite samples, with 3SLS the user is relying on the asymptotic condition that the variances and covariances of the stochastic terms in the equations being estimated are given by Σ_u and that the variances and covariances of the residuals from the estimated equations are an adequate approximation of this matrix. But this ignores the fact that the error term in the equation being estimated consists of U_m *and* a term involving the deviations of the estimated reduced form coefficients from their true values. Asymptotically this term goes to zero, but in practice for finite samples it is not zero and thus will contribute to the variance of the error term in the equation being estimated. Whether including the FGLS approximation to Σ_u actually improves efficiency depends on the actual sample and might be open to conjecture.

4.2 Full Information Maximum Likelihood

The full information analog to the LIML estimator uses the assumption that the stochastic terms are normally distributed, i.e. U_i is $N(0, \Sigma_u)$. To develop the FIML estimator, equation (16) is rearranged to give

$$(y_1, \ldots, y_M) = X(\beta_1, \ldots, \beta_M) + Y(\gamma_1, \ldots, \gamma_M) + (U_1, \ldots, U_M), \qquad (21)$$

where Y is a $(T \times M)$ matrix of observations on all the endogenous variables and X is a $(T \times K)$ matrix of observations on all the exogenous variables in the model. β_m is a $(K \times 1)$ vector of coefficients relating y_m to the exogenous variables, which implies that any exogenous variable excluded from this equation has a value of zero in this vector. γ_m is an ($M \times 1$) vector of coefficients relating y_m to the other endogenous variables. Any endogenous variable omitted from the RHS of this equation has a zero coefficient in this vector, including the mth entry, which corresponds to y_m. Equation (22) summarizes this expression:

$$Y\Gamma + XB + U = 0. \tag{22}$$

The matrix Γ has values of -1 on its main diagonal corresponding to the implicit coefficient on y_m in equation (21).

The FIML estimator rearranges equation (22) to isolate the stochastic component:

$$V = -U\Gamma^{-1} = Y + XB\Gamma^{-1}. \tag{23}$$

If the U_i's are normally distributed then V is $N(0, \Gamma^{-1'}\Sigma_u\Gamma^{-1})$. From this, the log likelihood function for the observed data is

$$\log L = -\frac{T}{2}[M\log(2\pi) + \log|\Sigma_v| + tr(\frac{1}{T}\Sigma_v^{-1}V'V)]$$

$$= -\frac{T}{2}\left\{\kappa + \log|\Gamma^{-1'}\Sigma_u\Gamma^{-1}| + tr\left[\frac{1}{T}(\Gamma'\Sigma_u^{-1}\Gamma)(Y + XB\Gamma^{-1})'(Y + XB\Gamma^{-1})\right]\right\}$$

$$= -\frac{T}{2}[\kappa + \log|\Sigma_u| - 2\log|\Gamma| + tr(\Sigma_u^{-1}S)], \tag{24}$$

where $s_{ij} = \frac{1}{T}(Y\Gamma_i + XB_i)'(Y\Gamma_j + XB_j)$. The inclusion of $\log|\Gamma|$ in the likelihood function imposes one more constraint on the model in order to compute the FIML estimator. As the value of this determinant approaches zero, the likelihood function approaches minus infinity, effectively ruling out that particular set of parameter values.

The FIML estimator provides a test of model specification not present in the other estimators if the model is overidentified. The estimated model's fit is based on how well the estimated model predicts the variance-covariance matrix of observed variables. In an exactly identified model the number of parameters being estimated, including the variances and covariances of the stochastic terms, exactly equals the number of entries in the observed variance-covariance matrix. In this case the estimated model will fit the observed matrix perfectly. As additional restrictions are added to the model by specifying that specific variables are excluded from certain equations, i.e. that certain elements of B and Γ are zero, the fit decreases as does the log likelihood function. The test of the overidentifying restrictions then is a function of the difference in the log likelihood functions of the just identified model and the estimated model. Asymptotically minus twice this difference is distributed as a χ^2 variable with degrees of freedom equal to the number of overidentifying restrictions (Jöreskog 1973). A poor fit and accompanying large value for the χ^2 statistic leads to rejection of the null hypothesis that the overidentifying restrictions are satisfied. The functional difference with the Sargan statistic is that this statistic is testing the fit of the whole model, not just the restrictions in an individual equation.

Estimation proceeds by maximizing the expression in equation (24) subject to the constraints and restrictions placed on the model to obtain identification and to conform to any other a priori information about the model. This produces a set of nonlinear simultaneous equations that requires a numerical analysis for solution that is challenging to solve in practice and the discussion of which is beyond the scope of this chapter. The possible presence of sets of parameter values that lead to the condition that $\log |\Gamma| = 0$ further complicates the computational task. These singularities create distinct regions that must be searched separately in order to find the global maximum. The complexity of the computational tasks has led most analysts to use 3SLS more often than FIML. The 3SLS computational advantage actually comes at little cost asymptotically if the stochastic terms are normally distributed. Greene (2003, 409) shows that FIML is also an IV estimator. He then goes on to state that with normally distributed stochastic terms, 3SLS and FIML have identical asymptotic distributions. He also says that small sample properties are "ambiguous" and may differ between the two methods.

4.3 Example: Full Information Estimation

The estimates reported in Table 17.2 were redone using both the 3SLS and FIML procedures.[12] The results are shown in Table 17.5, which includes the estimates for the *Repub* equation. (Coefficients for the *Part Adv* equation are not reported as they are just linear functions of the coefficients in the *Repub* equation. See equation (11)). The table also shows the Sargan statistic calculated for the Margin and Deviation equations. The results from the two methods are remarkably similar, differing by at most 0.012 and in most cases by considerably less, and the estimated asymptotic standard errors are nearly identical as well. A likely explanation for the similarities in results is that the estimated covariances among the stochastic term are quite small, on the order of 0.13 to 0.23. The Sargan statistics are quite low and have a high probability of occurring by chance if the instruments and stochastic terms are independent. The χ^2 test of the whole model with the FIML estimation is 22.61 with 26 degrees of freedom, which has a P-value of 0.665, again suggesting it is probably safe to accept the null hypothesis that the identifying restrictions are consistent with the data and justify the IV variables.

Full information estimators are more susceptible to specification problems, though this sensitivity was not evidenced in this example. Because 2SLS and LIML estimate each equation separately, a misspecification in one equation in the structural system does not influence the estimation of other equations, subject to the requirements that the instruments for the equation being estimated are both relevant and uncorrelated with the stochastic terms in the estimated equation. With the full information methods a misspecification in one equation can affect the estimates of other equations because the 3SLS and FIML procedures try to fit the entire structure. This means

---

[12] The FIML estimation was done using the package LISREL for Windows.

Table 17.5. Full information results

	3SLS		FIML	
	Coeff	s_b(asy)	Coeff	s_b(asy)
Repubican				
$Ford^3/100$	−0.136	0.031	−0.135	0.031
$Ford^4/100$	0.543	0.102	0.542	0.102
$Ford^5/100$	−0.443	0.084	−0.443	0.084
Constant	0.023	0.022	0.023	0.022
R^2	0.250		0.250	
Margin				
Dev	−0.296	0.132	−0.308	0.139
Part Adv	0.685	0.098	0.687	0.097
South	0.119	0.019	0.119	0.018
Age Gap	−0.144	0.075	−0.145	0.075
Constant	0.406	0.067	0.409	0.069
R^2	0.147		0.139	
Sargan $\chi^2(5)$	1.208		1.241	
P-Value	0.944		0.941	
Deviation				
Marg	0.451	0.113	0.464	0.123
Repub	0.218	0.039	0.223	0.042
ΔPop	0.171	0.043	0.170	0.043
ΔInc	0.037	0.026	0.037	0.026
Constant	−0.423	0.104	−0.433	0.113
R^2	0.205		0.191	
Sargan $\chi^2(5)$	1.788		1.844	
P-Value	0.878		0.870	

that the conditions of relevance and independence required of the instrumental variables must be satisfied in every equation (Wooldrige 2003, 199). For these and computational reasons, one of the k-class of limited information estimators seem to be preferred in practice and are more frequently encountered in the literature.

5 COMPARISONS OF ESTIMATORS

This section briefly compares and summarizes the results obtained with the different estimators. The discussion focuses on the relationships between *Dev* and *Marg* estimated in each of their respective equations. Table 17.6 shows the five different estimated relationships between these variables, where first *Marg* and *Dev* are the left-hand side variables. There is little substantive difference among the IV estimations, though the full information estimates are somewhat larger than the limited

Table 17.6. Coefficients with different estimation methods

LHS var.	RHS var.	Estimation method				
		OLS	2SLS	LIML	3SLS	FIML
Marg	Dev	0.063	−0.261	−0.244	−0.296	−0.308
Dev	Marg	0.159	0.411	0.426	0.451	0.464

information estimates. There is even less statistical difference as even the largest difference between the estimates is less than half the magnitude of the standard errors.

The substantial difference is between the OLS and IV estimators, as one would expect if *Marg*, *Dev*, and *Repub* are not exogenous variables, and if the instruments are appropriate. The IV estimates for the effect of voting deviations from constituency preferences on electoral margin range from −0.24 to −0.30, compared to 0.06 with OLS estimation. Conversely, the estimated effect of electoral margin on deviations ranges from 0.41 to 0.46 with the IV estimators, compared to 0.16 for the OLS model. The IV results are more consistent with expectations, particularly in the equations testing the proposition that deviations from constituency preferences are punished in the next election. The final topic is a test of whether RHS variables can be treated as exogenous, and thus which of these estimators is preferred.

If the RHS variables are fully exogenous then the OLS estimator is preferred because it is unbiased, consistent, and efficient and it is possibly the MLE estimator. This gives it a great advantage over less efficient estimators, such as IV. If the RHS variables are not exogenous, then the IV estimators are biased and less efficient but consistent. Specification tests proposed by Durbin (1954), Wu (1973), and Hausman (1978), often referred to as DWH tests, provide information for this choice.[13] Excellent discussions of the versions of these tests are in Baum, Schaffer, and Stillman (2003), Davidson and MacKinnon (1993, 237–42), Greene (2003, 80–3), and Nakamura and Nakamura (1981). The basis for the test is a comparison of the differences in the OLS and IV coefficient values and variances. Denote by b_{iv} the consistent but inefficient IV estimates and by S_{iv} the matrix of estimated asymptotic variances and covariances of these estimates. The null hypothesis is no endogeneity, in which case the OLS estimated coefficients, denoted as b_{ols}, are also consistent but more efficient than the IV estimator. Denote the estimated variances and covariances of these efficient estimates as S_{ols}. The test statistic is

$$H = (b_{iv} - b_{ols})'[S_{iv} - S_{ols}]^{-1}(b_{iv} - b_{ols})$$

$$= n(b_{iv} - b_{ols})'\left[\frac{(\hat{W}'\hat{W})^{-1}}{s_u^2} - \frac{(W'W)^{-1}}{s_u^2}\right]^{-1}(b_{iv} - b_{ols}),$$

---

[13] Hausman's paper and statistic is developed for the general case where one wants to compare a consistent with an efficient but possibly inconsistent estimator, which includes a number of important contexts and is not limited to the case of possible endogeneity and IV estimation.

Table 17.7. Endogeneity tests

	Equation			
	Margin		Deviation	
	Statistic	P-value	Statistic	P-value
$\chi^2(2)$				
2SLS	8.51	0.014	6.88	0.032
3SLS	11.39	0.003	9.47	0.009
F(2,369)				
2SLS	4.85	0.008	3.78	0.024

where following the notation in equation (16), $W = (X_m, Y_m)$ and $\hat{W} = (X_m, \hat{Y}_m)$ and s_u^2 is the estimated variance of the stochastic term. This statistic has a χ-squared distribution with M_m degrees of freedom where M_m denotes the number of LHS endogenous variables.

The variations in the calculations of the H test statistic arise from one's choice of the estimate for s_u^2. One choice is the standard error of the estimate from the OLS estimation, which was Durbin's proposal. A second choice is the estimate from the IV estimation; and a third option is to use each of the estimates in their respective estimates for S.[14] Asymptotically these three ratios should be equal, but in finite samples they will not be. Baum et al., among others, suggest using the OLS estimate as it is the most efficient estimate.

Both Davidson and MacKinnon (1993) and Greene (2003) describe a computationally easier way to test for endogeneity in the IV estimation context. Recall from equation (16) the equation being estimated, $y_m = X_m\beta_m + Y_m\gamma_m + U_m$. Now estimate the equation

$$y_m = X_m\beta_m + Y_m\gamma_m + \hat{Y}_m\alpha + U_m. \tag{25}$$

Wu (1973) and Davidson and MacKinnon (1993) show that the conventional F-test for the null hypothesis $H_0 : \alpha = 0$ is asymptotically equivalent to the DWH test above. This F-statistic has M_m and $(n - K_m - 2 * M_m)$ degrees of freedom where K_m and M_m are the number of included exogenous and endogenous variables. Again, with finite samples this F-statistic will not be identical in its P-value to the versions of the $H \chi^2$ statistics.

Table 17.7 shows the DWH χ^2 and F statistics for the 2SLS equations reported in Table 17.2 and the χ^2 statistic for the 3SLS equations reported in Table 17.5. The χ^2 statistics are computed using the OLS estimates for s_u^2. All results quite clearly reject the null hypothesis that OLS produces asymptotically equivalent but more efficient

---

[14] If the third option is chosen the difference in the matrices of asymptotic variances and covariances may not be positive definite, meaning the generalized inverse must be used in the calculations.

estimates than the different IV estimators at conventional confidence levels. This means that the IV estimators are probably "better" estimates of the joint relationships between *Dev* and *Marg*, being biased and inefficient, but consistent. The DWH statistics for the 3SLS estimation are larger than for the 2SLS, which should be expected as the difference between these estimates for the relationships between *Dev* and *Marg* and the OLS estimates are larger than the differences with the 2SLS estimator. In this particular example the F-tests had smaller P-values than the DWH test. In this example both tests reject the null, but it is possible the DWH test is more conservative on this point than the F-test. Staiger and Stock (1997, 568) argue that the DWH test using the OLS estimate for s_u^2 has more power than the other forms of the test and is recommended if one suspects weak instruments. There seems to be an absence of work comparing the χ^2 and F-test versions of the test, possibly because of Hausman's demonstration that the former can be applied in a number of important estimation contexts.

6 Concluding Remarks

The continuing need to use observational data routinely raises the problem of endogeneity of RHS variables and thus of covariance between these variables and the equation's stochastic term, in violation of a key condition justifying the OLS or GLS estimators. This has been and continues to be a daunting problem for empirical social science researchers. At one point it was hoped that instrumental variables and the associated estimators discussed here constituted a possible and adequate remedy. (See Goldberger and Duncan 1973 for one example.) The difficulty of matching real data to the conditions justifying IV estimation and the estimators' potential small sample biases despite the asymptotic properties has reduced some of this optimism and enthusiasm. These concerns have been augmented by various studies showing the weakness of the IV estimators even with very large data-sets (Bound, Jaeger, and Baker 1995).

Well-founded reservations about the robustness and reliability of the IV estimators are leading some researchers to undertake very creative studies that follow the experimental paradigm. (On experiments see Kinder and Palfrey 1993; and Druckman et al. 2006.) There is also considerable interest in building on the work of statisticians such as Rubin and Rosenbaum to develop techniques to mimic the experimental conditions of treatment and control groups by matching subjects in observational studies. (See Rosenbaum 2001 for an overview and Arceneaux, Gerber, and Green 2006 for a critique of matching methods.) The hope is that these efforts will lead to better tests of causal arguments by avoiding or at least reducing possible endogeneity biases. And one can only applaud and encourage work that expands the methodologist's ability to generate and analyze data in wider contexts.

It is not, however, a situation of replacing one method with another. There will continue to be important substantive questions engaging political science researchers that are not amenable to some of these other methods. Consider the examples given at the beginning of this chapter. Propositions about inter-state rivalry, or the effects of institutions on economic performance, or the consequences of campaign spending are unlikely to be manipulable in an experimental setting. There is also a need to examine how well results obtained in well-controlled laboratory settings apply in nonlaboratory political settings. Thus, in many instances our empirical evidence will continue to be the classic observational study, replete with endogeneity problems. Rather than forgoing analyses of these data and questions because of the reservations about a particular method, it is better to use and to improve those methods in the context of these studies and data. This is surely what stimulates the ongoing work in econometrics to understand better the properties of IV estimators, to develop and use better the diagnostics that help inform judgments about the statistical results, and to encourage the reporting of these newer statistics.

REFERENCES

ACEMOGLU, D. 2005. Constitutions, politics, and economics: a review essay on Persson and Tabellini's *The Economic Effects of Constitutions. Journal of Economic Literature*, 43: 1025–48.

ACHEN, C. H. 1978. Measuring representation. *American Journal of Political Science*, 22: 475–510.

——1986. *The Statistical Analysis of Quasi-Experiments.* Berkeley: University of California Press.

——1988. Proxy variables and incorrect signs on regression coefficients. *Political Methodology*, 11: 299–316.

ARCENEAUX, K., GERBER, A. S., and GREEN, D. P. 2006. Comparing experimental and matching methods using a large-scale vote mobilization experiment. *Political Analysis*, 14: 37–62.

BARONE, M., UJIFUSA, G., and MATTHEWS, D. 1979. *Almanac of American Politics.* New York: E. P. Dutton.

BARTELS, L. M. 1991. Instrumental and quasi-instrumental variables. *American Journal of Political Science*, 35: 777–800.

——and BRADY, H. E. 1993. The state of quantitative political methodology. In *Political Science: The State of the Discipline II*, ed. A. Finifter. Washington, DC: American Political Science Association.

BASMANN, R. 1960. On finite sampling distributions of generalized classical linear identifiability test statistics. *Journal of the American Statistical Association*, 55: 650–9.

BAUM, C. F., SCHAFFER, M. E., and STILLMAN, S. 2003. Instrumental variables and GMM: estimation and testing. *Stata Journal*, 3: 1–31.

BEKKER, P. 1994. Alternative approximations to the distribution of instrumental variable estimators. *Econometrica*, 62: 657–81.

BERINSKY, A. 1999. The two faces of public opinion. *American Journal of Political Science*, 43: 1209–30.

BOUND, J., JAEGER, D. J., and BAKER, R. M. 1995. Problems with instrumental variables estimation when the correlations between the instruments and the endogenous explanatory variable is weak. *Journal of the American Statistical Association*, 90: 443–50.

BRADY, H. 1988. The perils of survey research: interpersonally incomparable responses. *Political Methodology*, 11: 269–91.

BRUNDY, J., and JORGENSON, D. 1971. Consistent and efficient estimation of systems of simultaneous equations by means of instrumental variables. *Review of Economics and Statistics*, 53: 207–24.

CONGRESSIONAL QUARTERLY 1983. *CQ Weekly Report*. 41 (52): 2789.

DAVIDSON, R., and MACKINNON, J. G. 1993. *Estimation and Inference in Econometrics*. New York: Oxford University Press.

DIXON, W. J. 1986. Reciprocity in United States–Soviet relations: multiple symmetry of issue linkage. *American Journal of Political Science*, 30: 421–45.

DONALD, S. G., and NEWEY, W. K. 2001. Choosing the number of instruments. *Econometrica*, 69: 1161–91.

DRUCKMAN, J. N., GREEN, D. P., KUKLINSKI, J. H., and LUPIA, A. 2006. The growth and development of experimental research in political science. *American Political Science Review*, 100: 627–37.

DURBIN, J. 1954. Errors in variables. *Review of the International Statistical Institute*, 22: 23–32.

FISHER, F. M. 1966. *The Identification Problem in Econometrics*. New York: McGraw-Hill.

FREEDMAN, D., PISANI, R., and PURVES, R. 1998. *Statistics*, 3rd edn. New York: W. W. Norton.

GODFREY, L. G. 1999. Instrument relevance in multivariate linear models. *Review of Economics and Statistics*, 81: 550–52.

GOLDBERGER, A. S. 1973. Efficient estimation in overidentified models. Pp. 131–52 in *Structural Equation Models in the Social Sciences*, ed. A. S. Goldberger and O. D. Duncan. New York: Seminar Press.

—— and DUNCAN, O. D. 1973. *Structural Equation Models in the Social Sciences*. New York: Seminar Press.

GOLDFELD, S. M., and QUANDT, R. E. 1972. *Nonlinear Methods in Econometrics*. Amsterdam: North-Holland.

GREENE, W. H. 2003. *Econometric Analysis*, 5th edn. Upper Saddle River, NJ: Prentice Hall.

HAHN, J., and HAUSMAN, J. 2002. New specification test for the validity of instrumental variables. *Econometrica*, 70: 163–89.

HANSEN, C., HAUSMAN, J., and NEWEY, W. K. 2006. Estimation with many instrumental variables. Xerox, Dept. of Economics, MIT.

HAUSMAN, J. A. 1978. Specification tests in econometrics. *Econometrica*, 46: 1251–71.

JACKSON, J. E. 1993. Attitudes, no opinions, and guesses. *Political Analysis*, 5: 39–60.

—— 1996. Political methodology: an overview. In *New Handbook of Political Science*, ed. R. Goodin and H.-D. Klingemann. Oxford: Oxford University Press.

—— and KING, D. C. 1989. Public goods, private interests, and representation. *American Political Science Review*, 83: 1143–64.

JACOBSON, G. C. 1978. The effects of campaign spending in congressional elections. *American Political Science Review*, 72: 469–91.

JÖRESKOG, K. 1973. A general method for estimating a linear structural equation system. In *Structural Equation Models in the Social Sciences*, ed. A. S. Goldberger and O. D. Duncan. New York: Seminar Press.

JORGENSON, D. W., and LAFFONT, J. 1974. Efficient estimation of nonlinear simultaneous equations with additive disturbances. *Annals of Economic and Social Measurement*, 3: 615–40.

JUDGE, G., HILL, G. R. C., GRIFFITHS, W. E., LÜTKEPOHL, H., and LEE, T.-C. 1988. *Introduction to the Theory and Practice of Econometrics*. New York: John Wiley.

KELEJIAN, H. H. 1971. Two stage least squares and econometric systems linear in the parameters but nonlinear in the endogenous variables. *Journal of the American Statistical Association*, 66: 373–4.

KINDER, D. R., and PALFREY, T. R. 1993. *Experimental Foundations of Political Science*. Ann Arbor: University of Michigan Press.

KING, G. 1989. *Unifying Political Methodology*. Cambridge: Cambridge University Press.

——1991. On political methodology. *Political Analysis*, 2: 1–29.

KINGDON, J. W. 1973. *Congressman's Voting Decisions*. New York: Harper and Row.

NAKAMURA, A., and NAKAMURA, M. 1981. On the relationship among several specification tests presented by Durbin, Wu, and Hausman. *Econometrica*, 49: 1583–8.

NEWEY, W. K. 1990. Efficient instrumental variable estimation of nonlinear models. *Econometrica*, 58: 809–37.

PERSSON, T., and TABELLINI, G. 2003. *The Economic Effects of Constitutions*. Cambridge, Mass.: MIT Press.

ROSENBAUM, P. R. 2001. Observational studies: overview. Pp. 10810–15 in *International Encyclopedia of the Social and Behavioral Sciences*, ed. N. Smelser and P. Baltes. New York: Elsevier.

SARGAN, J. 1958. The estimation of economic relationships using instrumental variables. *Econometrica*, 26: 393–415.

SHEA, J. 1997. Instrument relevance in multivariate linear models: a simple measure. *Review of Economics and Statistics*, 79: 348–52.

STAIGER, D., and STOCK, J. H. 1997. Instrumental variables regression with weak instruments. *Econometrica*, 65: 557–86.

WOOLDRIDGE, J. M. 2003. *Econometric Analysis of Cross Section and Panel Data*. Cambridge, Mass.: MIT Press.

WU, D.-M. 1973. Alternative tests of independence between stochastic regressors and disturbances. *Econometrica*, 41: 733–50.

ZELLNER, A. 1962. An efficient method of estimating seemingly unrelated regressions, and tests for aggregation bias. *Journal of the American Statistical Association*, 57: 348–68.

——and THEIL, H. 1962. Three-stage least squares: simultaneous estimation of simultaneous equations. *Econometrica*, 30: 54–78.

CHAPTER 18

....

STRUCTURAL EQUATION MODELS

....

KENNETH A. BOLLEN
SOPHIA RABE-HESKETH
ANDERS SKRONDAL

In 1918 Sewall Wright, a biostatistician, published a paper that examined the bone size of rabbits using a newly created technique called "path analysis." This was the first of many papers by Wright on path analysis and it marks the birth of a statistical modeling procedure that has evolved into what we have come to call Structural Equation Models (SEMs), covariance structure models, path analysis, or latent variable models. We will use the first term, SEMs, to refer to these models, but readers should recognize that the other terms are sometimes employed to refer to the same model.

SEMs are distinguished by several characteristics. One is that SEMs usually have multiple equations and each equation incorporates one or more explanatory variables that are hypothesized to influence the "dependent" or left-hand side endogenous variable. The explanatory variables can be exogenous, predetermined, or endogenous variables. In addition, multiple indicators and latent variables can be part of the model. This enables researchers to study the relation between the latent variables that represent concepts in political science and to model the measurement error that is present in measures of these latent variables. Latent variables are variables specified as part of a hypothesis, but variables for which no direct measures are available in a data-set (Bollen 2002). Liberal democracy of nations, social capital of groups, or political efficacy of individuals are examples of latent variables that are, at best, imperfectly measured. In their most general form SEMs permit variables that have a wide variety of scale types (e.g. continuous, counts, ordinal, nominal, dichotomous). Finally, SEMs are valuable in that nearly all of the statistical models commonly used in the social sciences are special cases of the most general SEMs. Multiple regression, ANOVA, simultaneous equation models, factor analysis, growth curve models, probit regression, etc. are derivable from SEMs and doing so highlights the restrictive assumptions that are part of these other widely used techniques.

In this chapter, we provide an overview of the classic SEMs when the latent and observed variables are continuous and then more recent developments that include categorical, count, and other noncontinuous variables as well as multilevel structural equation models.

1 SEMs with Continuous Responses

In this section we limit our discussion to the situation where both the latent and observed variables are continuous (or nearly so). This is the classic context in which the initial SEMs were developed, so it forms a good starting point. Later in the chapter, we extend the analysis to noncontinuous observed variables. The next section describes the model specification, assumptions, and notation. This is followed by sections on implied moments, identification, estimation, model fit, and respecification.

1.1 Model Specification and Assumptions

Analysts use any one of several notations to present SEMs. The main trade-off in the alternative notations is whether it uses fewer, larger matrices with many zero elements or more matrices with less spareness. We present the latter type by using a modified version of Jöreskog and Sörbom's (1993) LISREL notation for SEMs,[1] the most common notation in the field. It is convenient to distinguish between the *latent variable model* and the *measurement model*. The latent variable model (sometimes called the "structural model") is

$$\eta_i = \alpha_\eta + \mathbf{B}\eta_i + \Gamma\xi_i + \zeta_i \tag{1}$$

where η_i is a vector of latent endogenous variables for unit i, α_η is a vector of intercept terms for the equations, $\mathbf{B}$ is the matrix of coefficients giving the effects of the latent endogenous variables on each other, ξ_i is the vector of latent exogenous variables, Γ is the coefficient matrix giving the effects of the latent exogenous variables on the latent endogenous variables, and ζ_i is the vector of disturbances. The i subscript indexes the ith case in the sample. We assume that $E(\zeta_i) = 0$, $COV(\xi_i', \zeta_i) = 0$, and that $(\mathbf{I} - \mathbf{B})$ is

---

[1] The intercept notation is a slight modification of the LISREL notation to keep them all as αs.

invertible. Exogenous variables are variables that are not explained within the model and that are uncorrelated with all disturbances in the system. Endogenous variables are variables that are directly influenced by other variables in the system other than its disturbance. Two covariance matrices are part of the latent variable model: $\boldsymbol{\Phi}$ the covariance matrix of the exogenous latent variables ($\boldsymbol{\xi}$) and $\boldsymbol{\Psi}$ the covariance matrix of the equation disturbances ($\boldsymbol{\zeta}$). The mean of $\boldsymbol{\xi}$ is $\boldsymbol{\mu}_{\xi}$.

The measurement model links the latent to the observed responses (indicators). It has two equations:

$$\mathbf{y}_i = \boldsymbol{\alpha}_y + \boldsymbol{\Lambda}_y \boldsymbol{\eta}_i + \boldsymbol{\epsilon}_i \tag{2}$$

$$\mathbf{x}_i = \boldsymbol{\alpha}_x + \boldsymbol{\Lambda}_x \boldsymbol{\xi}_i + \boldsymbol{\delta}_i \tag{3}$$

where $\mathbf{y}_i$ and $\mathbf{x}_i$ are vectors of the observed indicators of $\boldsymbol{\eta}_i$ and $\boldsymbol{\xi}_i$, respectively, $\boldsymbol{\alpha}_y$ and $\boldsymbol{\alpha}_x$ are intercept vectors, $\boldsymbol{\Lambda}_y$ and $\boldsymbol{\Lambda}_x$ are matrices of factor loadings or regression coefficients giving the impact of the latent $\boldsymbol{\eta}_i$ and $\boldsymbol{\xi}_i$ on $\mathbf{y}_i$ and $\mathbf{x}_i$, respectively, and $\boldsymbol{\epsilon}_i$ and $\boldsymbol{\delta}_i$ are the unique factors of $\mathbf{y}_i$ and $\mathbf{x}_i$. We assume that the unique factors ($\boldsymbol{\epsilon}_i$ and $\boldsymbol{\delta}_i$) have expected values of zero, covariance matrices of $\boldsymbol{\Theta}_\epsilon$ and $\boldsymbol{\Theta}_\delta$, respectively, and are uncorrelated with each other and with $\boldsymbol{\zeta}_i$ and $\boldsymbol{\xi}_i$.

Figure 18.1 contains the path diagram of a SEM example with three latent variables and eleven observed indicators (see Bollen 1989, 11–20). Path diagrams are a pictorial representation of a system of equations. Following path diagram notation, the observed variables are in boxes and latent variables are in circles. A single-headed arrow indicates an influence from the variable at the base of the arrow to that at the head of the arrow. Doubled-headed curved arrows signify a covariance among the connected variables.

The data have countries as the unit of analysis, but we omit the i subscript here and leave it implicit. The three latent variables are national level of liberal democracy in 1960 (η_1) and 1965 (η_2) and industrialization (ξ_1) in 1960. Using the above latent variable equation (1), this example is

$$\boldsymbol{\eta} = \boldsymbol{\alpha}_\eta + \mathbf{B}\boldsymbol{\eta} + \boldsymbol{\Gamma}\boldsymbol{\xi} + \boldsymbol{\zeta}$$

$$\begin{bmatrix} \eta_1 \\ \eta_2 \end{bmatrix} = \begin{bmatrix} \alpha_{\eta_1} \\ \alpha_{\eta_2} \end{bmatrix} + \begin{bmatrix} 0 & 0 \\ \beta_{21} & 0 \end{bmatrix} \begin{bmatrix} \eta_1 \\ \eta_2 \end{bmatrix} + \begin{bmatrix} \gamma_{11} \\ \gamma_{21} \end{bmatrix} [\xi_1] + \begin{bmatrix} \zeta_1 \\ \zeta_2 \end{bmatrix}. \tag{4}$$

This equation and the assumptions that accompany it are equivalent to the model represented in the path diagram. The covariance matrices are

$$\boldsymbol{\Phi} = [\Phi_{11}] \qquad \boldsymbol{\Psi} = \begin{bmatrix} \Psi_{11} & 0 \\ 0 & \Psi_{22} \end{bmatrix}. \tag{5}$$

The second part of the model is the measurement model. The indicators of liberal democracy are degree of press freedom (y_1 in 1960, y_5 in 1965), freedom of political opposition (y_2, y_6), the fairness of elections (y_3, y_7), and the effectiveness of the elected legislative body (y_4, y_8). The indicators of industrialization in 1960 are logarithm of gross national product per capita (x_1), logarithm of inanimate energy consumption per capita (x_2), and the percentage of the labor force in industry (x_3).

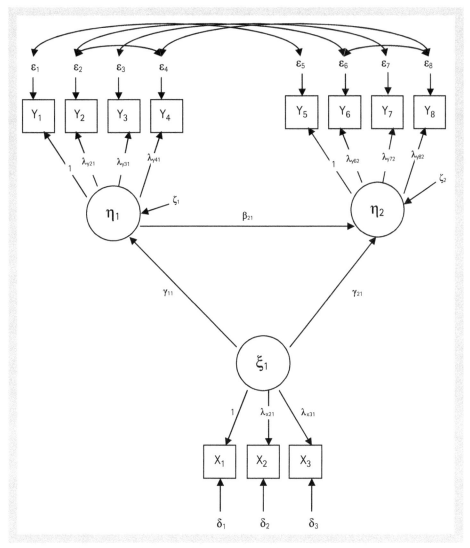

Fig. 18.1. Path diagram of structural equation model

The measurement model for the x variables is

$$\mathbf{x} = \mathbf{a}_x + \Lambda_x \boldsymbol{\xi} + \boldsymbol{\delta}$$

$$\begin{bmatrix} x_1 \\ x_2 \\ x_3 \end{bmatrix} = \begin{bmatrix} 0 \\ a_{x_2} \\ a_{x_3} \end{bmatrix} + \begin{bmatrix} 1 \\ \lambda_{x21} \\ \lambda_{x31} \end{bmatrix} [\xi_1] + \begin{bmatrix} \delta_1 \\ \delta_2 \\ \delta_3 \end{bmatrix} \qquad (6)$$

with a covariance matrix of the unique factors of

$$\Theta_{\boldsymbol{\delta}} = \begin{bmatrix} \Theta_{\delta 11} & 0 & 0 \\ 0 & \Theta_{\delta 22} & 0 \\ 0 & 0 & \Theta_{\delta 33} \end{bmatrix}. \qquad (7)$$

The measurement equation for **y** is similar, except it will be larger since there are eight indicators. Also, $\boldsymbol{\Theta}_\epsilon$, the covariance matrix of the unique factors (ϵ), is 8×8, nondiagonal with nonzero off-diagonal elements (e.g. $(5, 1)$, $(6, 2)$, $(7, 3)$, etc.) to represent the covariances among some of the unique factors as shown in the path diagram.

1.1.1 *Exogenous x Form of Model*

A special form of the general model is useful when there are exogenous *observed* covariates that are measured without error (or with negligible error). In this situation, the measurement model for **x** changes from $\mathbf{x} = \boldsymbol{\alpha}_x + \boldsymbol{\Lambda}_x \boldsymbol{\xi} + \boldsymbol{\delta}$ to $\mathbf{x} = \boldsymbol{\xi}$, and the latent variable (structural) model is now

$$\boldsymbol{\eta} = \boldsymbol{\alpha}_\eta + \mathbf{B}\boldsymbol{\eta} + \boldsymbol{\Gamma}\mathbf{x} + \boldsymbol{\zeta}. \tag{8}$$

We consider two cases of this model. One is when **x** is a vector of fixed, nonrandom variables and the other is when **x** consists of random variables. In either situation, if the conditional distribution, $\mathbf{y} \mid \mathbf{x}$, is multivariate normal, then the distribution or fixed values of **x** are inconsequential for the estimator of the model parameters as long as we are not making inferences about parameters that characterize the distribution of **x**.[2] When discussing the full information estimators for this model below, the distributional assumptions for **y** will be conditional on the values of **x**, a less restrictive assumption than assuming an unconditional multivariate normal distribution for **y** and **x**. We return to this form of the model later when we discuss noncontinuous responses.[3]

1.2 Implied Moment Matrices

Once a model is specified, it is possible to write the population means, variances, and covariances of the observed variables as a function of the parameters in the model. To derive the implied moments, it is useful to work with the reduced-form of the models, where each endogenous variable is a function of only exogenous variables, coefficients, and disturbances. The reduced-form for the latent variable model is

$$\boldsymbol{\eta}_i = (\mathbf{I} - \mathbf{B})^{-1}(\boldsymbol{\alpha}_\eta + \boldsymbol{\Gamma}\boldsymbol{\xi}_i + \boldsymbol{\zeta}_i). \tag{9}$$

The measurement model for the $\mathbf{x}_i$ already is in reduced-form. The reduced-form equation for $\mathbf{y}_i$ is

$$\mathbf{y}_i = \boldsymbol{\alpha}_y + \boldsymbol{\Lambda}_y(\mathbf{I} - \mathbf{B})^{-1}(\boldsymbol{\alpha}_\eta + \boldsymbol{\Gamma}\boldsymbol{\xi}_i + \boldsymbol{\zeta}_i). \tag{10}$$

[2] We also assume that there are no parameter restrictions involving the parameters of the distribution of **x**.

[3] For elements of η to be considered exogenous latent variables, these elements should be regressed on all observed exogenous variables via the Γ matrix. The elements of Γ that correspond to the regression of the latent exogenous variables on the observed exogenous variables should not be regarded as structural coefficients, but more as auxiliary regressions that capture the linear associations between the observed and latent exogenous variables.

Define μ to be the population mean vector of the observed variables, θ to be the vector that contains the parameters in the model, and $\mu(\theta)$ to be the population implied mean vector that is a function of the model parameters. More specifically, in the model in equations (1), (2), and (3) the population implied mean vector is

$$\mu(\theta) = \begin{bmatrix} a_y + \Lambda_y(I - B)^{-1}(a_\eta + \Gamma\mu_\xi) \\ a_x + \Lambda_x\mu_\xi \end{bmatrix}. \tag{11}$$

The top part of the right-hand side vector is the implied mean vector for y and the lower part is the implied mean vector of x.

Similarly, define Σ as the population covariance matrix of the observed variables and $\Sigma(\theta)$ as the implied covariance structure that is a function of the parameters. The implied covariance matrix is fairly complex for the general model, so we partition the matrix to correspond to the implied covariance matrix of y, of x, and of y and x:

$$\Sigma(\theta) = \begin{bmatrix} \Sigma_{yy}(\theta) & \Sigma_{yx}(\theta) \\ \Sigma_{xy}(\theta) & \Sigma_{xx}(\theta) \end{bmatrix}. \tag{12}$$

These parts of the implied covariance matrix are

$$\Sigma_{xx}(\theta) = \Lambda_x\Phi\Lambda_x' + \Theta_\delta \tag{13}$$

$$\Sigma_{xy}(\theta) = \Lambda_x\Phi\Gamma'(I - B)^{-1}\Lambda_y' \tag{14}$$

$$\Sigma_{yy}(\theta) = \Lambda_y(I - B)^{-1}(\Gamma\Phi\Gamma' + \Psi)(I - B)^{-1}\Lambda_y' + \Theta_\epsilon. \tag{15}$$

These equations show the variance and covariance of the observed variables as functions of the model parameters. The equations are sufficiently general that we can find the implied covariance matrix for any SEM. We just substitute the specific matrices for a particular model into these expressions. For instance, the implied covariance matrix for the x variables in the example in Figure 18.1 is

$$\Sigma_{xx}(\theta) = \Lambda_x\Phi\Lambda_x' + \Theta_\delta$$

$$= \begin{bmatrix} 1 \\ \lambda_{x21} \\ \lambda_{x31} \end{bmatrix} [\Phi_{11}] \begin{bmatrix} 1 & \lambda_{x21} & \lambda_{x31} \end{bmatrix} + \begin{bmatrix} \Theta_{\delta11} & 0 & 0 \\ 0 & \Theta_{\delta22} & 0 \\ 0 & 0 & \Theta_{\delta33} \end{bmatrix} \tag{16}$$

and the implied mean vector is

$$\mu_x(\theta) = a_x + \Lambda_x\mu_\xi \tag{17}$$

$$= \begin{bmatrix} 0 \\ a_{x_2} \\ a_{x_3} \end{bmatrix} + \begin{bmatrix} 1 \\ \lambda_{x21} \\ \lambda_{x31} \end{bmatrix} [\mu_{\xi_1}]. \tag{18}$$

If a model specification is valid, then the following mean and covariance structures hold:

$$\mu = \mu(\theta) \tag{19}$$

$$\Sigma = \Sigma(\theta). \tag{20}$$

In other words, there should be an exact match between the population means, variances, and covariances and those implied by the parameters in the model.

These implied moments are useful in estimating and assessing the fit of a model. They also are useful in establishing model identification, a topic to which we now turn.

1.3 Identification

Identification concerns whether it is possible to estimate uniquely values of all the parameters in an SEM. When we can, the model is identified. When we cannot, it is underidentified. Investigating identification is particularly challenging when we have multi-equation models, particularly when this is combined with latent variables and measurement errors. If a parameter in a model is not identified, then there will be two or more values of the parameters that are equally consistent with the data and the researcher will not be able choose among them empirically even if population data were available. Hence, knowing the identification status of a model is important for proper estimation and interpretation of a model. In general, the means (μ), variances, and covariances (Σ) of the observed variables are identified parameters for virtually all observed variables that are part of a model. In the most common situation, the identification question is whether the parameters of the model (e.g. factor loadings, regression coefficients, variances of latent variables) can be written as unique functions of the known-to-be-identified means, variances, or covariances of the observed variables. If "yes," then the parameters and the model are identified. If "no," the model is not identified even if some equations or individual parameters are identified. For instance, it can be shown that if a latent variable has at least three indicators that load exclusively on the latent variable, there are no correlated unique factors, and the factor loading for one indicator is set to one to scale the latent variable, then that part of the model is identified (Bollen 1989, 241–2). Or if a model of observed variables is fully recursive such that it has no errors correlated across equations and there are no feedback effects in the system, then the model is identified (Bollen 1989, 95–8). There are additional rules of identification that apply to classes of simultaneous equations, factor analysis, or general structural equation models with latent variables. For example, there is the rank and order condition for simultaneous equations (Fisher 1966), the FC1 rule for factor analysis models with factor complexity of one and correlated unique factors (Davis 1993), and the "Two-Step Rule" for general SEMs (Bollen 1989, 328–33). But no rule covers all possible SEMs. Empirical checks of *local* identification are available in most SEM software and are based on a test of the singularity of the estimated information matrix of the parameter estimates of a model. Local identification tests will generally, but not always, detect *globally* underidentified models (Bollen 1989, 246–51).

Returning to the industrialization and political democracy example of Figure 18.1, we can use the Two-Step Rule to establish its identification. In the first step, the model is converted to a factor analysis model with three correlated factors so that the structural links among the latent variables are replaced with covariances as in a factor analysis model. Using Davis's (1993) FC1 Rule, we can establish its identification as a factor analysis model and this completes the first step. Turning our attention to the latent variable model and treating it as if it were an observed variable model, this aspect of the model would be identified by the recursive rule. This completes the second step and thereby establishes that the Figure 18.1 model is identified.

Once identification is established, we can consider model estimation.

1.4 Model Estimation

Two broad classes of estimators for SEMs exist: full information estimators and limited information estimators. Full information estimators are dominant in SEM software and we consider these first.

1.4.1 *Full Information Estimators*

Full information estimators are estimators that choose estimates for parameters based on the full system of equations in a model. It is full information in that all relationships in the system including the covariances, variances, and means of exogenous variables and disturbances play a role in developing the estimates. There are a number of full information estimators, but the dominant one is the maximum likelihood (ML) estimator. The ML fitting function in SEMs is

$$F_{ML} = \ln |\Sigma(\theta)| - \ln |S| + \text{tr}[\Sigma^{-1}(\theta)S] - P_z + (\bar{z} - \mu(\theta))'\Sigma^{-1}(\theta)(\bar{z} - \mu(\theta)), \quad (21)$$

where S is the sample covariance matrix, $\bar{z}$ is the vector of the sample means of the observed variables ($\bar{y}$ & $\bar{x}$ stacked in a vector), P_z is the number of observed variables, "ln" is the natural log, $|\cdot|$ is the determinant, and "tr" is the trace of a matrix. The ML estimator, $\hat{\theta}$, is chosen so as to minimize F_{ML}. Like all ML estimators, $\hat{\theta}$ has several desirable properties. It is consistent, asymptotically unbiased, asymptotically efficient, asymptotically normally distributed, and the asymptotic covariance matrix of $\hat{\theta}$ is the inverse of the expected information matrix.

The classic derivation of the ML estimator assumes that all observed variables come from a multinormal distribution. However, a variety of studies have proved that this estimator maintains its properties under less restrictive assumptions. For instance, the ML properties still hold if the observed variables come from a continuous distribution with no excess multivariate kurtosis (e.g. Browne 1984). Alternatively, if the model conforms to equation (8) and has exogenous observed variables, then only the *conditional* distribution of the observed y variables need be multivariate normal (Jöreskog 1973).[4] Furthermore, there are robustness studies that provide conditions

---

[4] The normality assumption for x is innocuous in that identical estimates are produced from the conditional model (with the distribution of x unspecified) and from the unconditional model where the distribution of x is misspecified as multinormal. Only the inferences about the variances, covariances, or means of x might be influenced.

under which the significance tests based on the ML estimator maintain their desirable asymptotic properties even when none of the preceding conditions hold (e.g. Satorra 1990). Finally, there are bootstrapping methods (e.g. Bollen and Stine 1990; 1993) and corrected significance tests (e.g. Arminger and Schoenberg 1989; Satorra and Bentler 1994) that enable significance testing even when the robustness conditions fail. These points on significance testing are a source of great misunderstanding among some who incorrectly assume that SEM estimators are heavily dependent on multivariate normality.

The consequence of structural misspecification is a more serious issue when using ML or other full information estimators. The problem is that a specification error in one equation can introduce bias in the ML estimator of the parameter in another correctly specified equation. This is due to the full information nature of the estimator where the parameter estimator uses information from throughout the system in developing the estimates. This works fine in systems of equations that are correctly specified and in fact this system approach is part of the reason for the ML estimator's asymptotic efficiency. But on the other hand, an error in one part of the system can be propagated through other parts. Given the high likelihood of at least some structural error in models, this is a drawback of full information estimators.

We next turn to limited information estimators.

1.4.2 *Limited Information Estimators*

As the name suggests, limited information estimators do not develop estimates based on the full system of equations. Rather they tend to have an equation-by-equation orientation toward estimation. The limited information estimator is less known in SEMs that include latent variables. Madansky (1964) was an early paper that demonstrated that a limited information instrumental variable (IV) estimator was possible in factor analysis models with uncorrelated unique factors. Hägglund (1982) and Jöreskog (1983) further developed these in factor analysis with uncorrelated unique factors. More recently, Bollen (1996; 2001) has developed an estimator from the Two Stage Least Squares (2SLS) family that applies to the full latent variable SEMs including those with correlated unique factors or errors.

The main requirement of this 2SLS estimator is that each latent variable has a scaling indicator such that

$$y_{1i} = \eta_i + \epsilon_i \tag{22}$$

$$x_{1i} = \xi_i + \delta_i \tag{23}$$

where y_{1i} contains the scaling indicators of η_i and x_{1i} contains the scaling indicators of ξ_i. This implies that $\eta_i = y_{1i} - \epsilon_i$ and $\xi_i = x_{1i} - \delta_i$ and by substituting the right-hand sides of these equations we can eliminate the latent variables from equations (1), (2), and (3) resulting in

$$y_{1i} = \alpha_\eta + By_{1i} + \Gamma x_{1i} + \epsilon_{1i} - B\epsilon_{1i} - \Gamma\delta_{1i} + \zeta_i \tag{24}$$

$$y_{2i} = \alpha_{y_2} + \Lambda_{y_2} y_{1i} - \Lambda_{y_2} \epsilon_{1i} + \epsilon_{2i} \tag{25}$$

$$x_{2i} = a_{x_2} + \Lambda_{x2}x_{1i} - \Lambda_{x2}\delta_{1i} + \delta_{2i}. \tag{26}$$

The end result is a system of equations that consist of observed variables and composite disturbance terms. Generally, most of the equations in this model cannot be consistently estimated with ordinary least squares regression since one or more of the variables in the composite disturbance correlate with the right-hand side variables. An instrumental variable (IV) approach is used to take account of this problem.

To briefly illustrate an IV, consider a simple regression equation, $y_{1i} = a_1 + \gamma_{11}x_{1i} + \zeta_{1i}$ where $COV(x_{1i}, \zeta_{1i}) \neq 0$. Using the Ordinary Least Squares (OLS) estimator of this equation would result in an inconsistent and biased estimator of γ_{11}. However, if there were another variable, say x_{2i}, that has a moderate to strong correlation with x_{1i} but no correlation with ζ_{1i}, then we could regress x_{1i} on x_{2i} and could form the predicted value of $\widehat{x}_{1i}$. The OLS regression of y_{1i} on $\widehat{x}_{1i}$ would provide a consistent estimator of γ_{11}. The resulting estimator would be the IV estimator where x_{2i} is the IV.

Returning to the more general latent variable SEM, a researcher proceeds by selecting the first equation to estimate from the model. The researcher notes which explanatory variables correlate with the composite disturbance. Then, the researcher chooses the *model-implied instrumental variables* of this model. The model-implied instrumental variables (IV) are observed variables that are part of the model and that based on the model structure should not correlate with the disturbance of the equation, but do have a significant association with the problematic explanatory variable(s). This is different from the common approach to IVs where the selection of IVs is somewhat ad hoc. In the 2SLS latent variable approach in Bollen (1996), the model comes first and the observed variables that satisfy the conditions of IVs follow from the model structure. Bollen and Bauer (2004) describe an algorithm that finds the model-implied IVs for a specific model structure, or the researcher can determine this by inspection of the model. Once the IVs are determined for an equation, a 2SLS estimator is applied. The estimator is consistent, asymptotically unbiased, asymptotically normally distributed, and an estimate of the asymptotic covariance matrix of the coefficients is readily available. It also is asymptotically efficient among the equation-by-equation estimators. See Bollen (1996; 2001) for the formula and for more technical details.

1.5 Model Fit

Once a model is estimated, attention turns toward assessing its fit to the data. Model fit has two primary components. The first concerns overall model fit and the second looks at the fit of components of the model. As these terms suggest, overall fit measures are summary measures that characterize the model as a whole; component fit measures assess the fit of pieces of the model.

When using ML and other full information estimators, a chi-square test of overall fit is generally available. For instance, for the ML estimator the test statistic, T_{ML}, is $(N-1)F_{ML}$ where F_{ML} is evaluated at the final estimates $(\hat{\theta})$ of the parameters. When the assumptions of the ML estimator are satisfied, T_{ML} follows an asymptotic chi-square distribution with degrees of freedom of $df = \left(\frac{1}{2}\right) P_z(P_z + 3) - t$ where P_z is the number of observed variables and t is the number of free parameters estimated in the model. The null hypothesis of this chi-square test is $H_o : \mu = \mu(\theta)$ & $\Sigma = \Sigma(\theta)$. A statistically significant test statistic casts doubt on the implied moment structure and the model that gave rise to it. A nonsignificant test statistic is consistent with the model structure.

In practice, $H_o : \mu = \mu(\theta)$ & $\Sigma = \Sigma(\theta)$ is too strict for most models since the test is intolerant of even slight misspecifications and hence in situations with sufficient statistical power (e.g. when N is large) the null hypothesis is nearly always rejected. This has given rise to a wide variety of fit indices that supplement the chi-square test. See, for example, chapters in Bollen and Long (1993) or Hu and Bentler (1998) for rationales, formulas, and discussions of these additional fit indices. Current practice is to report the chi-square test statistic, degrees of freedom, and p-value along with several other fit indices when assessing a model's overall fit.

The component fit of a model sometimes gives a different impression to the overall fit, so it should not be ignored. Aspects of component fit include checks for improper solutions (e.g. negative variance estimates, correlations greater than one), determination of whether the sign and magnitude of coefficients, variances, covariances, and correlations are reasonable, judgments of whether the coefficient of determination of each endogenous variable is sufficiently high, and assessments of whether the rest of the parameter estimates "make sense." For example, a negative variance estimate that is much larger than its estimated standard error suggest structural misspecification of the model even if the overall fit of the model is judged to be satisfactory. Another component fit measure available for each overidentified equation estimated with 2SLS is a test of whether all IVs used in the equation are uncorrelated with the disturbance as is necessary for proper IVs (Bollen 1996). Rejection of the null hypothesis suggests that one or more IVs are correlated with the disturbance. Since these are model-implied IVs, rejection means that the model that led to these IVs is structurally misspecified and needs revision.

If the overall fit or component fit of a model is judged to be inadequate, then this suggests the need to respecify the model.

1.6 Respecification

Respecifications refer to revisions of an initial model. These revisions can range from minor (e.g. introducing a secondary path) to major (e.g. changing the number of latent variables and their relationships). Ideally these changes will be guided by the substantive expertise of the researcher. It is not unusual for a researcher to have alternative structures in mind that might characterize the data. These alternatives can help guide the modifications. There are also empirical methods that researchers use to introduce additional parameters into a model. Chief among these for full information estimators is the Lagrangian Multiplier ("modification indexes") test statistic that is an estimate of the decrease in the chi-square test statistic that would result by freeing a previously fixed parameter in the model. Reliance on the modification index can lead to the introduction of nonsense parameters and difficulty in recovering the true generating model (see MacCallum 1986). The modification index is most useful if used in conjunction with substantive expertise. Other diagnostic tools include covariance residual analysis (e.g. Costner and Schoenberg 1973) and individual case diagnostics (e.g. Bollen and Arminger 1991; Cadigan 1995). The 2SLS test of IVs described in the last section highlights equations that might be misspecified.

These empirically based respecifications push an analysis toward a more exploratory analysis and the significance tests in the respecified models must be interpreted cautiously since they do not take account of the fact that modifications were made to the model in response to previous analysis of the data. However, a respecified model can lay the foundation for a follow-up study with new data that can assess whether it replicates. It generally is better to begin with several alternative plausible models for the same data and to estimate and to compare their fit at the same time than to start with a single model and to modify it afterwards.

2 SEMs with Categorical and Discrete Responses

In practice, indicators measuring latent variables are often dichotomous or ordinal. A common example of ordinal responses are Likert formats where respondents are asked to indicate their agreement with an attitude statement in terms of ordinal categories, for instance, "strongly disagree," "disagree," "agree," and "strongly agree." Dichotomous indicators are legion for instance in ability testing where responses are coded as either 1 (correct) or 0 (incorrect).

There have been two avenues for generalizing linear regression models to handle dichotomous or ordinal responses. The predominant approach in econometrics and psychometrics is to use a standard linear model for an underlying latent continuous response y^*. In the dichotomous case, the observed response y takes the value "1" if y^* exceeds zero and the value "0" otherwise. The predominant approach in statistics and biostatistics is to specify a linear function for a transformation of the probability of a "1" response. We call these two approaches the latent response and generalized linear model formulation, respectively. Both formulations can produce the same models, typically logit and probit models.

The same two avenues were used in generalizing latent variable models for categorical (dichotomous or ordinal) responses. In structural equation modeling the latent response formulation is predominant. In contrast, item response models (typically used in ability testing) are invariably specified via the generalized linear model formulation (e.g. Mellenbergh 1994). Although Takane and de Leeuw (1987) and Bartholomew (1987) pointed out the equivalence of the two formulations for many models, the literatures are still quite separate. For categorical responses it is thus a question of taste which formulation is used. However, for other response types, such as counts, only the generalized linear model formulation can be used.

In structural equation models for continuous responses, a path diagram can be used to represent the model, giving a one-to-one correspondence between model equations and diagram. An appealing feature of the diagrams is that conditional independence properties become apparent at a glance. Using the latent response formulation allows us to show analogous conditional independence relations with noncontinuous observed variables. This is done by replacing each noncontinuous response with the corresponding latent response variable in a path diagram. The threshold model for the relationship between latent and observed responses can be shown in the path diagram as well, but to simplify the figures we will omit this.

2.1 Latent Response Formulation

When the responses are dichotomous or ordinal, it is useful to think of an underlying continuous response that is partitioned or "categorized" into the observed discrete response. There are S_h possible response categories $s = 0, \ldots, S_h - 1$ for item h, the response y_{hi} for subject i is generated as

$$y_{hi} = s \quad \text{if} \quad \kappa_h^s < y_{hi}^* \leq \kappa_h^{s+1},$$

where κ_h^s are threshold parameters, $\kappa_h^0 = -\infty$, $\kappa_h^{S_h} = \infty$. This latent response formulation is illustrated for a hypothetical item h with $S_h = 3$ response categories and $y_{hi}^* \sim N(\nu_{hi}, 1)$ in Figure 18.2. Here ν_{hi} could be some linear function of latent and observed covariates. The response probabilities are given by areas under the normal density curve with mean ν_{hi} and variance 1,

$$\Pr(y_{hi} = s | \nu_{hi}) = \Phi(\kappa_h^{s+1} - \nu_{hi}) - \Phi(\kappa_h^s - \nu_{hi}),$$

where $\Phi(\cdot)$ is the standard normal cumulative distribution function.

The cumulative probability that the response exceeds category s then becomes

$$\Pr(y_{hi} > s | \nu_{hi}) = \Phi(\nu_{hi} - \kappa_h^{s+1}), \tag{27}$$

a cumulative probit model for ordinal responses, known as a graded response model in item response theory (Samejima 1969). For dichotomous items with $S_h = 2$, this becomes the binary probit model, sometimes referred to as a normal ogive model (typically with $\kappa_h^1 = 0$).

An advantage of this formulation is that the same measurement model as given in equation (2) for continuous indicators can be specified for the latent continuous responses $\mathbf{y}_i^*$ underlying the observed responses $\mathbf{y}_i$. Here we specify a more general version that also allows for direct effects of observed covariates $\mathbf{v}_i$ on the latent

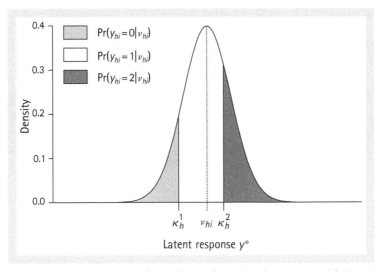

Fig. 18.2. Latent response formulation for ordinal response with $S_h = 3$ categories

responses

$$\mathbf{y}_i^* = \underbrace{\mathbf{a}_{y*} + \Lambda_{y*}\boldsymbol{\eta}_i + \mathbf{K}\mathbf{v}_i}_{v_i} + \boldsymbol{\epsilon}_i,$$

where K is a matrix of regression coefficients. For the structural model, we use the "exogenous x" form introduced in equation (8):

$$\boldsymbol{\eta}_i = \mathbf{a}_\eta + \mathbf{B}\boldsymbol{\eta}_i + \Gamma\mathbf{x} + \boldsymbol{\zeta}. \tag{28}$$

The reason for treating the covariates as exogenous (by conditioning on them) instead of specifying a distribution for them is to avoid making unnecessary distributional assumptions. Unlike the case of multivariate normal $\mathbf{y}_i$, misspecification of the distribution of the covariates will have an impact on inference.

Grouped or interval censored continuous responses such as income brackets ("$0–10,000," "$10,001–30,000," "$30,001–50,000," etc.) can be modeled in the same way by constraining the threshold parameters κ_h^s to equal the limits of the censoring intervals. By allowing unit-specific right-censoring, this approach can be used for discrete time durations, such as length of service in the US Congress (e.g. Box-Steffensmeier and Jones 2004).

By changing the distribution of the elements of $\boldsymbol{\epsilon}_i$ to a logistic distribution, the latent response formulation can also be used to specify logit models popular in item response theory. Models for comparative responses such as unordered categorical responses (such as political parties voted for), rankings, or pairwise comparisons (for instance of candidates or policies) can be formulated in terms of latent responses conceptualized as utilities or utility differences (e.g. Skrondal and Rabe-Hesketh 2003).

2.2 Generalized Linear Model Formulation

The models for categorical and comparative responses described above can also be expressed using a generalized linear model formulation. In addition, this formulation can be used for other response types such as counts for which there is no latent response formulation. Counts are important responses in political science (e.g. King 1988). An example would be the number of US vetoes in the United Nations Security Council each year.

In the generalized linear model formulation, the conditional expectation of the response y_{hi} for indicator h given v_{hi} (a function of x_i and η_i) is "linked" to the linear predictor v_{hi} via a link function $g(\cdot)$,

$$g(\mathrm{E}[y_{hi}|v_{hi}]) = v_{hi}. \tag{29}$$

The linear model discussed in Section 1 for continuous responses uses an identity link whereas the latent response model for dichotomous responses can be expressed as a generalized linear model with a probit link. Other common links are the logit and log links.

The final component in the generalized linear model formulation is the conditional distribution of the response variable given the latent and explanatory variables. This distribution is chosen from the exponential family of distributions; a normal distribution is typically used for continuous responses, a Bernoulli distribution for dichotomous responses, and a Poisson distribution for counts. Alternative distributions for the continuous case are the inverse Gaussian and gamma distributions.

For ordinal responses, the generalized linear model formulation is modified so that the link function is applied to cumulative probabilities instead of expectations:

$$g(\mathrm{P}[y_{hi} > s|v_{hi}]) = v_{hi} - \kappa_i^{s+1}.$$

If $g(\cdot) = \Phi^{-1}(\cdot)$, the probit link, we obtain the model given in (27). A multinomial distribution is then specified for the responses.

In many applications it is necessary to accommodate mixed response types, allowing for different links and/or distributions for different indicators. Such flexibility can generate interesting model types which are not usually thought of as structural equation models. Examples include generalized linear models with covariate measurement error, endogenous treatment models, and joint models for longitudinal data and dropout (e.g. Skrondal and Rabe-Hesketh 2004, ch. 14).

2.3 Implied Moments for y^* and Identification

For models where a latent response formulation can be used, the model-implied mean and covariance structure of y^* is similar to that shown for continuous responses y in Section 1.2. Specifically, the model-implied conditional mean and covariance structure, given v and x, are given by

$$\mu(\theta) = a_{y^*} + Kv + \Lambda_{y^*}(I - B)^{-1}(a_\eta + \Gamma x)$$

and

$$\Sigma_{y^*y^*}(\theta) = \Lambda_{y^*}(\mathbf{I} - \mathbf{B})^{-1}(\Gamma\Phi\Gamma' + \Psi)(\mathbf{I} - \mathbf{B})^{-1}\Lambda'_{y^*} + \Theta_{\epsilon}.$$

Unfortunately, the moment structure of the observed responses $\mathbf{y}$ is generally intractable. This intractability makes investigation of identification along the lines described for the continuous, multivariate normal case impossible. Another difficulty is that higher-order moments must also be considered since the first- and second-order moments are no longer sufficient statistics for the unknown parameters. For these reasons, investigation of identification will in practice often rely on empirical checks such as inspection of the estimated information matrix.

One important exception are models with multivariate normal *latent* responses $\mathbf{y}^*$ since first- and second-order moments of $\mathbf{y}^*$ are tractable in this case and higher-order moments do not provide any information on the model parameters. Since $\mathbf{y}^*$ is not observed, its means and variances are arbitrary (just like the means and variances of latent variables) and can be identified only by imposing restrictions on model parameters. For instance, for an ordinal response, the mean and variance of the corresponding latent response is identified if at least two of its threshold parameters are set to arbitrary constants (typically $\kappa_h^1 = 0$ and $\kappa_h^2 = 1$). A more common approach is not to restrict the thresholds but instead impose appropriate constraints on the intercepts and variances (either the total variance of y_h^* given $\mathbf{x}$ and $\mathbf{v}$ or the variance of ϵ_h).

Theoretically, due to information from higher-order moments, logit models with logistic ϵ may be identified even when the probit version of the model is not. However, we suggest basing consideration of identification on the probit version of the model since information from higher-order moments may be fragile (e.g. Rabe-Hesketh and Skrondal 2001).

2.4 Estimation

For the special case of models with multinormal latent responses (principally probit models), Muthén suggested computationally efficient limited information estimation approaches (e.g. Muthén 1978; Muthén and Satorra 1996) implemented in Mplus (Muthén and Muthén 2004). For instance, consider a structural equation model with dichotomous responses and no observed covariates. Estimation then proceeds by first estimating "tetrachoric correlations" (pairwise correlations between the latent responses). Secondly, the asymptotic covariance matrix of the tetrachoric correlations is estimated. Finally, the parameters of the SEM are estimated using weighted least squares, fitting model-implied to estimated tetrachoric correlations. Here, the inverse of the asymptotic covariance matrix of the tetrachoric correlations serves as weight matrix. This approach provides appropriate asymptotic standard errors and a χ^2 statistic for goodness of fit.

Although this limited information method is very computationally efficient, it can be used only for probit models, not for logit or log-linear models. Furthermore, the approach can currently handle missing data only by listwise deletion which requires that responses are missing completely at random (MCAR). Multiple imputation (e.g. Rubin 1987) can be used to fill in the missing values, but this relies on specifying an appropriate imputation model.

A preferable approach therefore is full information maximum likelihood estimation. Unfortunately, maximum likelihood estimation cannot be based on sufficient statistics such as the empirical covariance matrix (and possibly mean vector) of the observed responses as in the continuous case. Instead, the likelihood must be obtained by somehow "integrating out" the latent variables η. Approaches which work well but are computationally demanding include adaptive Gaussian quadrature (Rabe-Hesketh et al. 2005) implemented for instance in gllamm (Rabe-Hesketh and Skrondal 2008), or Monte Carlo integration (McCulloch 1997).

Bayesian approaches are becoming increasingly popular in structural equation modeling (e.g. Lee and Song 2003) due to the development of feasible estimation via Markov Chain Monte Carlo methods implemented in the BUGS software (Spiegelhalter et al. 1996). In practice, the analysis is rarely truly Bayesian since noninformative prior distributions are specified for the model parameters. In this case, the estimates can be viewed as approximate maximum likelihood estimates.

Skrondal and Rabe-Hesketh (2004) provide an extensive overview of estimation methods for SEMs with categorical, comparative, and discrete responses and related models.

2.5 Application

Political efficacy is a central construct in theories of political attitudes, behavior, and participation. Campbell, Gurin, and Miller (1954) defined political efficacy as:

… the feeling that individual political action does have, or can have, an impact upon the political process … The feeling that political and social change is possible, and that the individual citizen can play a part in bringing about this change.

Here we will consider an analysis of the political efficacy items of the 1974 cross-section of the US subsample of the Political Action Data (Barnes et al. 1979), more fully reported in Skrondal and Rabe-Hesketh (2004, section 10.3). There were six attitude statements, $h = 1, \ldots, 6$:

1. [nos] People like me have no say in what the government does
2. [vot] Voting is the only way that people like me can have any say about how the government runs things
3. [com] Sometimes politics and government seem so complicated that a person like me cannot really understand what is going on
4. [noc] I don't think that public officials care much about what people like me think

5. [tou] Generally speaking, those we elect to Congress in Washington lose touch with the people pretty quickly

6. [int] Parties are only interested in people's votes, but not in their opinions

The responses were rated using a Likert from with four ordered categories (0:Disagree strongly, 1:Disagree, 2:Agree, 3:Agree strongly). The 1707 respondents who responded to at least one efficacy item and had complete covariate information were analyzed under the missing at random (MAR) assumption.

The so-called NES (National Election Studies) model (Miller, Miller, and Schneider 1980) posits two dimensions of political efficacy: one dimension ("internal efficacy") is interpreted as "individuals' self-perceptions that they are capable of understanding politics and competent enough to participate in political acts such as voting," and the other ("external efficacy") as "individuals' beliefs about political institutions rather than perceptions about their own abilities." Miller et al. seem to suggest an "independent clusters" model where [nos], [vot], and [com] measure internal efficacy, whereas [noc], [tou], and [int] measure external efficacy. An alternative model is the "unrestricted" model (Jöreskog 1969) that imposes only a minimal set of identifying restrictions. This model is equivalent to the two-dimensional exploratory factor model in the sense that it is merely a reparameterization. The unrestricted model was preferred to the independent clusters model according to a likelihood ratio test.

The selected model can be written as

$$y_i^* = \Lambda \eta_i + \epsilon_i, \qquad \eta_i \sim N(0, \Psi), \qquad \epsilon_i \sim N(0, I) \tag{30}$$

where

$$\Lambda = \begin{bmatrix} 1 & 0 \\ \lambda_{21} & \lambda_{22} \\ \lambda_{31} & \lambda_{32} \\ \lambda_{41} & \lambda_{42} \\ \lambda_{51} & \lambda_{52} \\ 0 & 1 \end{bmatrix}.$$

In (30) we have set $a_{y*} = 0$ in order to identify all three thresholds κ_h^1, κ_h^2, and κ_h^3 for each item h. Although the selected model relaxes the independent clusters structure, the estimated factor loadings (not shown) suggest that the latent variables η_1 and η_2 can still be loosely interpreted as internal and external political efficacy, respectively.

The model was then extended to allow the means of the latent variables to depend on the following covariates:

- [Black]: a dummy variable for being black (x_{2i}).
- [Educ]: education in years, standardized to zero mean and unit standard deviation (x_{1i}).

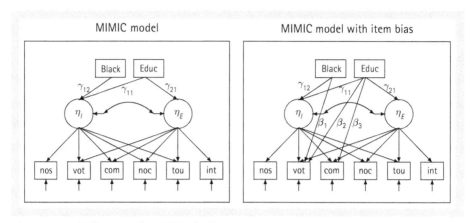

Fig. 18.3. Path diagrams for political efficacy

Specifically, the following MIMIC (Multiple Indicator Multiple Cause) model was specified:

$$\underbrace{\begin{bmatrix} \eta_{1i} \\ \eta_{2i} \end{bmatrix}}_{\boldsymbol{\eta}_i} = \underbrace{\begin{bmatrix} \gamma_{11} & \gamma_{12} \\ \gamma_{21} & \gamma_{22} \end{bmatrix}}_{\boldsymbol{\Gamma}} \underbrace{\begin{bmatrix} x_{1i} \\ x_{2i} \end{bmatrix}}_{\mathbf{x}_i} + \underbrace{\begin{bmatrix} \zeta_{1i} \\ \zeta_{2i} \end{bmatrix}}_{\boldsymbol{\zeta}_i}. \tag{31}$$

It turned out that [Black] had no significant effect on external efficacy, so γ_{22} was set to zero. This model is shown in the left panel of Figure 18.3 (where the latent variables have the subscripts I and E for "internal" and "external").

Note that, in the model above, the covariates affect the responses only indirectly via the latent variables. This assumption can be violated leading to item-bias or differential item functioning (DIF). An item is said to be biased if the response to the item is dependent on extraneous information apart from the latent variables. To investigate item bias, we included direct effects of [Black] and [Educ] on some of the the the items, modifying the measurement model as follows:

$$\mathbf{y}_i^* = \boldsymbol{\Lambda}\boldsymbol{\eta}_i + \mathbf{X}_i\boldsymbol{\beta} + \boldsymbol{\epsilon}_i,$$

where $\boldsymbol{\Lambda}$ is as before and

$$\mathbf{X}_i = \begin{bmatrix} 0 & 0 & 0 \\ x_{1i} & x_{2i} & 0 \\ 0 & 0 & x_{2i} \\ 0 & 0 & 0 \\ 0 & 0 & 0 \\ 0 & 0 & 0 \end{bmatrix}.$$

To determine which covariates have direct effects on which items, competing models were estimated and compared for a random subset of the data (the calibration data) and the chosen model subsequently tested on the remaining subset (the validation data). The resulting model is shown in the right panel of Figure 18.3.

We note from the estimates (not shown here) that [Black] is negatively related to internal political efficacy, whereas [Educ] is positively related to both kinds of political efficacy, as might be expected. There is substantial item bias for two of the internal efficacy items. [Black] has negative direct effects on the response for [vot] and [Educ] has positive direct effects on the responses for [vot] and [com].

3 MULTILEVEL STRUCTURAL EQUATION MODELS

In the models discussed so far, all latent variables and indicators vary between units (typically subjects) and are assumed to be independent across units. The latter assumption is violated in multilevel settings where units are nested in clusters, leading to within-cluster dependence. Examples include voters nested in polling districts, students in schools, or multiple voting occasions nested within voters.

The traditional approach to extending structural equation models to the multilevel setting is to formulate separate within-cluster and between-cluster models (e.g. Longford and Muthén 1992; Poon and Lee 1992; Longford 1993). Let y_{ik} be the vector of continuous responses for unit i in cluster k. Then the within-cluster model is

$$y_{ik} \sim N(\mu_k, \Sigma_W(\theta_W)), \tag{32}$$

where μ_k is the mean vector for cluster k and the within-cluster covariance structure $\Sigma_W(\theta_W)$ is implied by a within-cluster structural equation model. The between-cluster model for the cluster means is

$$\mu_k \sim N(\mu, \Sigma_B(\theta_B)), \tag{33}$$

where μ is the population mean vector and $\Sigma_B(\theta_B)$ is the between-cluster covariance structure implied by a between-cluster structural equation model.

An advantage of this setup is that it allows software for conventional structural equation models to be "tricked" into estimating the model. The basic idea is to fit the within- and between-models to the empirical within-cluster and between-cluster covariance matrices. This must be done in a single analysis since the model-implied within covariance matrix contributes to the expectations of both the empirical within-cluster covariance matrix and the empirical between-cluster covariance matrix. Muthén (1989) suggests an approach which corresponds to maximum likelihood for balanced data where all clusters have the same size n. This approach as well as an ad hoc solution for the unbalanced case are described in detail in Muthén (1994) and Hox (2002). Goldstein (1987; 2003) suggests using multivariate multilevel modeling to estimate Σ_W and Σ_B consistently by either maximum likelihood or restricted maximum likelihood. Using these estimated matrices as input instead of the empirical within- and between-covariance matrices allows within- and between-structural equation models to be fitted independently.

Unfortunately, the standard implementation of the within and between model approach is limited in several ways. First, it does not permit cross-level paths from latent or observed variables at a higher level to latent or observed variables at a lower level. However, cross-level paths from higher- to lower-level latent variables will often be of primary interest. For instance, combining ideas from the two examples discussed previously, consider a multilevel setting where individuals are nested in nations. In this case, the nation-level latent variable liberal democracy could affect the individual-level latent variable political efficacy. A second limitation of the standard approach is that it does not allow for indicators varying at different levels, for instance nation-level indicators for liberal democracy and individual-level indicators for political efficacy. Third, it permits only two levels of nesting; and finally, it is confined to continuous responses.

These limitations are overcome by the *Generalized Linear Latent and Mixed Modeling* (GLLAMM) framework (Rabe-Hesketh, Skrondal, and Pickles 2004; Skrondal and Rabe-Hesketh 2004). Here measurement models can be specified for latent variables varying at different levels with indicators varying at the same or lower levels. Given the latent variables, the measurement models are generalized linear models with possibly different links and distributions for different indicators. The multilevel structural model is given by

$$\eta = \alpha_\eta + \mathbf{B}\eta + \mathbf{\Gamma}\mathbf{x} + \zeta, \tag{34}$$

where η and ζ are now vectors of latent variables for levels 2 (units or subjects), 3 (clusters), 4 (superclusters), etc., up to level L:

$$\eta = (\overbrace{\eta_1^{(2)}, \eta_2^{(2)}, \ldots, \eta_{M_2}^{(2)}}^{\text{Level 2}}, \ldots, \overbrace{\eta_1^{(l)}, \ldots, \eta_{M_l}^{(l)}}^{\text{Level } l}, \ldots, \eta_{M_L}^{(L)})$$

$$\zeta = (\zeta_1^{(2)}, \zeta_2^{(2)}, \ldots, \zeta_{M_2}^{(2)}, \ldots, \zeta_1^{(l)}, \ldots, \zeta_{M_l}^{(l)}, \ldots, \zeta_{M_L}^{(L)}).$$

Here $\mathbf{B}$ and $\mathbf{\Gamma}$ are matrices of regression coefficients. To allow for regression of latent variables on same or higher-level latent variables, but not on lower-level latent variables, $\mathbf{B}$ is specified as block upper triangular, where the blocks correspond to the elements of η varying at a given level.

4 CONCLUSION

The history of SEMs is one of incorporating seemingly diverse models into a single framework. Its entry into the social sciences was originally through sociology in the 1960s and 1970s. A major turning point in the 1970s was the LISREL model and statistical software developed by Karl Jöreskog and Dag Sörbom. The model was a sophisticated synthesis of simultaneous equation models from econometrics with the factor analysis literature developed in psychometrics. The LISREL model was more general and better grounded in statistical theory than were the early latent variable structural equation models that appeared in the sociological literature.

The years since then have been marked by further generalizations of SEMs and advances in statistical software to implement these new approaches. The penetration of SEMs has been high in disciplines such as sociology, psychology, educational testing, and marketing, but lower in economics and political science despite the large potential number of applications. Today, SEMs have begun to enter the statistical literature and to re-enter biostatistics, though often under the name "latent variable models" or "graphical models." As SEMs spread, we expect that they will continue to become more generalized and to see further developments in estimation and the assessment of model fit. Given the abstract nature of many concepts in political science, the presence of measurement error in variables, and the interests in systems of variables, many potential applications of SEMs in political science remain to be explored.

References

ARMINGER, G., and SCHOENBERG, R. 1989. Pseudo maximum likelihood estimation and a test for misspecification in mean and covariance structure models. *Psychometrika*, 54: 409–25.

BARNES, S. H., KAASE, M., ALLERBECK, K. R., FARAH, B. J., HEUNKS, F., INGLEHART, R., JENNINGS, M. K., KLINGEMANN, H. D., MARSH, H., and ROSENMAYR, L. 1979. *Political Action: Mass Participation in Five Western Democracies*. Beverly Hills, Calif.: Sage.

BARTHOLOMEW, D. J. 1987. *Latent Variable Models and Factor Analysis*. Oxford: Oxford University Press.

BOLLEN, K. A. 1989. *Structural Equations with Latent Variables*. New York: John Wiley.

—— 1996. An alternative two stage least squares (2SLS) estimator for latent variable equations. *Psychometrika*, 61: 109–21.

—— 2001. Two-stage least squares and latent variable models: simultaneous estimation and robustness to misspecifications. Pp. 119–38, in *Structural Equation Modeling: Present and Future*, ed. R. Cudeck, S. du Toit, and D. Sörbom. Lincolnwood, Ill.: Scientific Software.

—— 2002. Latent variables in psychology and the social sciences. *Annual Review of Psychology*, 53: 605–34.

—— and ARMINGER, G. 1991. Observational residuals in factor analysis. *Sociological Methodology*, 21: 235–62.

—— and BAUER, D. J. 2004. Automating the selection of model-implied instrumental variables. *Sociological Methods and Research*, 32: 425–52.

—— and LONG, J. S. (eds.) 1993. *Testing Structural Equation Models*. Newbury Park, Calif.: Sage.

—— and STINE, R. A. 1990. Direct and indirect effects: classical and bootstrap estimates of variability. *Sociological Methodology*, 20: 115–40.

—— —— 1993. Bootstrapping goodness-of-fit measures in structural equation models. Pp. 111–35 in *Testing Structural Equation Models*, ed. A. Kenneth and J. S. Long. Newbury Park, Calif.: Sage.

BOX-STEFFENSMEIER, J. M., and JONES, B. S. 2004. *Event History Modeling: A Guide to Social Statistics*. Cambridge: Cambridge University Press.

BROWNE, M. W. 1984. Asymptotically distribution-free methods for the analysis of covariance structures. *British Journal of Mathematical and Statistical Psychology*, 37: 62–83.

CADIGAN, N. G. 1995. Local influence in structural equations models. *Structural Equation Modeling*, 2: 13–30.

CAMPBELL, A., GURIN, G., and MILLER, W. E. 1954. *The Voter Decides*. Evanston, Ill.: Row Peterson.

COSTNER, H. L., and SCHOENBERG, R. 1973. Diagnosing indicator ills in multiple indicator models. Pp. 167–200 in *Structural Equation Models in the Social Sciences*, ed. A. S. Goldberger and O. D. Duncan. New York: Seminar Press.

DAVIS, W. R. 1993. The FC1 rule of identification for confirmatory factor analysis: a general sufficient condition. *Sociological Methods and Research*, 21: 403–37.

FISHER, F. M. 1966. *The Identification Problem in Econometrics*. New York: McGraw-Hill.

GOLDSTEIN, H. 1987. Multilevel covariance component models. *Biometrika*, 74: 430–1.

—— 2003. *Multilevel Statistical Models*, 3rd edn. London: Arnold.

HÄGGLUND, G. 1982. Factor analysis by instrumental variables. *Psychometrika*, 47: 209–22.

HOX, J. 2002. *Multilevel Analysis: Techniques and Applications*. Mahwah, NJ: Erlbaum.

HU, L., and BENTLER, P. M. 1998. Fit indices in covariance structure modeling: sensitivity to underparameterization model misspecification. *Psychological Methods*, 3: 424–53.

JÖRESKOG, K. G. 1969. A general approach to confirmatory maximum likelihood factor analysis. *Psychometrika*, 34: 183–202.

—— 1973. A general method for estimating a linear structural equation. Pp. 85–112 in *Structural Equation Models in the Social Sciences*, ed. A. S. Golderberger and O. D. Duncan, New York: Seminar Press.

—— 1983. Factor analysis as an error-in-variables model. Pp. 185–96 in *Principles of Modern Psychological Measurement*, ed. H. Wainer and S. Messick. Hillsdale, NJ: Lawrence Erlbaum.

—— and SÖRBOM, D. 1993. *LISREL 8*. Mooreseville, Ind.: Scientific Software.

KING, G. 1988. Statistical models for political science event counts. *American Journal of Political Science*, 32: 838–63.

LEE, S.-Y., and SONG, X.-Y. 2003. Bayesian analysis of structural equation models with dichotomous variables. *Statistics in Medicine*, 22: 3073–88.

LONGFORD, N. T. 1993. *Random Coefficient Models*. Oxford: Oxford University Press.

—— and MUTHÉN, B. O. 1992. Factor analysis for clustered observations. *Psychometrika*, 57: 581–97.

MACCALLUM, R. 1986. Specification searcher in covariance structure modeling. *Psychological Bulletin*, 100: 107–20.

MCCULLOCH, C. E. 1997. Maximum likelihood algorithms for generalized linear mixed models. *Journal of the American Statistical Association*, 92: 162–70.

MADANSKY, A. 1964. Instrumental variables in factor analysis. *Psychometrika*, 29: 105–13.

MELLENBERGH, G. J. 1994. Generalized linear item response theory. *Psychological Bulletin*, 115: 300–7.

MILLER, W. E., MILLER, A. H., and SCHNEIDER, E. J. 1980. *American National Election Studies Data Source-Book: 1952–1978*. Cambridge, Mass.: Harvard University Press.

MUTHÉN, B. O. 1978. Contributions to factor analysis of dichotomous variables. *Psychometrika*, 43: 551–60.

—— 1989. Latent variable modeling in heterogeneous populations. *Psychometrika*, 54: 557–85.

—— 1994. Multilevel covariance structure analysis. *Sociological Methods and Research*, 22: 376–98.

—— and SATORRA, A. 1996. Technical aspects of Muthén's LISCOMP approach to estimation of latent variable relations with a comprehensive measurement model. *Psychometrika*, 60: 489–503.

MUTHÉN, L. K., and MUTHÉN, B. O. 2004. *Mplus User's Guide*, 3rd edn. Los Angeles: Muthén and Muthén.

POON, W.-Y., and LEE, S.-Y. 1992. Maximum likelihood and generalized least squares analyses of two-level structural equation models. *Statistics and Probability Letters*, 14: 25–30.

RABE-HESKETH, S., and SKRONDAL, A. 2001. Parameterization of multivariate random effects models for categorical data. *Biometrics*, 57: 1256–64.

—— —— 2008. *Multilevel and Longitudinal Modeling using Stata*. College Station, Tex.: Stata Press.

—— —— and PICKLES, A. 2004. Generalized multilevel structural equation modeling. *Psychometrika*, 69: 167–90.

—— —— —— 2005. Maximum likelihood estimation of limited and discrete dependent variable models with nested random effects. *Journal of Econometrics*, 128: 301–23.

RUBIN, D. B. 1987. *Multiple Imputation for Nonresponse in Surveys*. New York: Wiley.

SAMEJIMA, F. 1969. *Estimation of Latent Trait Ability Using a Response Pattern of Graded Scores*. Bowling Green, Ohio: Psychometric Society.

SATORRA, A. 1990. Robustness issues in structural equation modeling: a review of recent developments. *Quality and Quantity*, 24: 367–86.

—— and BENTLER, P. M. 1994. Corrections to test statistics and standard errors in covariance structure analysis. Pp. 399–419 in *Latent Variables Analysis: Applications for Development Research*, ed. A. von Eye and C. C. Clogg. Newbury Park, Calif.: Sage.

SKRONDAL, A., and RABE-HESKETH, S. 2003. Multilevel logistic regression for polytomous data and rankings. *Psychometrika*, 68: 267–87.

—— —— 2004. *Generalized Latent Variable Modeling: Multilevel, Longitudinal, and Structural Equation Models*. Boca Raton, Fla.: Chapman and Hall/CRC.

SPIEGELHALTER, D. J., THOMAS, A., BEST, N. G., and GILKS, W. R. 1996. *BUGS 0.5 Bayesian Analysis using Gibbs Sampling. Manual (version ii)*. Cambridge: MRC-Biostatistics Unit; available from <http://www.mrc-bsu.cam.ac.uk/bugs/documentation/contents.shtml>.

TAKANE, Y., and DE LEEUW, J. 1987. On the relationship between item response theory and factor analysis of discretized variables. *Psychometrika*, 52: 393–408.

WRIGHT, S. 1918. On the nature of size factors. *Genetics*, 3: 367–74.

CHAPTER 19

....

TIME-SERIES
ANALYSIS

....

JON C. PEVEHOUSE

JASON D. BROZEK

MANY of the political processes we investigate as political scientists are dynamic. Over time, partisanship, macroeconomic conditions, ideologies, public opinion, and foreign policies change. Indeed many of the fundamental questions across all subfields in political science center on change: We are interested in the fact that an actor ends up at point B from point A, but also the process by which they got there. Time-series analysis attempts to model the causes of this change explicitly.

Ironically, however, many analysts treat the dynamic properties of their data as nuisances—violations of the assumptions of ordinary least squares regression which must be expunged from the data. These dynamic properties, however, shed light on the data-generating process. Rather than treat statistical properties such as autocorrelations or trends as problems, the time-series analyst attempts to explicitly model these dynamics as a way to improve inferences using traditional statistical methods, but also to provide a substantive interpretation of them.

To this end, this chapter will outline a brief history of time-series analysis before moving to a review of the basic time-series model.[1] We then discuss stationary models in univariate and multivariate analyses, then explore nonstationary models of each

---

[1] The emphasis in this chapter is on approach and application rather than statistical technique. For a more technical discussion of time-series analysis, see Enders (2004); Lutkepohl (1993); Hamilton (1994). For a discussion focused on social science applications, see Box-Steffensmeier, Freeman, and Pevehouse (forthcoming).

type. We then turn to various issues regarding the analysis of time series including data aggregation and temporal stability. Before concluding, we briefly discuss time-series techniques in the context of panel data.

1 A Brief History of Time Series

Nearly half a millennium ago, merchants recognized consistent trends and variations in their data records of transactions. This recognition gave birth to early time-series analysis. Ironically, it is not a stretch to say that fifteenth-century wheat prices respond to the same seasonal fluctuations, exogenous shocks, and external forces as those in the twenty-first, although the methods to analyze those fluctuations, shocks, and forces have matured considerably.

Unlike correlation and regression, which has roots in mathematics, time-series analysis grew out of commercial need. The Merchant's Rule of Three, or simply using three known variables in a comparison of ratios to find a fourth unknown, found widespread acceptance and application in Europe's mid-seventeenth-century business class. One early practitioner, a clothier named John Graunt, recognized that his "Mathematics of Shop-Arithmetic" could be applied to other social problems, including using data provided by bills of mortality during plague years, "that so the rich might judge of the necessity of their removal, and the Trades-men might conjecture what doings they were to have in their respective dealings" (Graunt 1975 [1662], 17). Graunt undertook an analysis of plague data from London to determine which years had been the deadliest on record. Statistical historian Judy Klein notes that "Graunt's observations on the bills of mortality earned him membership in the Royal Society and posthumous fame as the 'father of statistics'" (Klein 1997, 46).

Graunt and others continued to apply these methods to social issues like birthrates, population gender ratios, surgical effectiveness, and plague deaths. The questions being asked became more difficult to answer with relatively simple tools like the Rule of Three. In the mid-eighteenth century, Daniel Defoe (1968 [1722]) investigated variance in mortality rates and found large differences that seemed to cycle with the seasons.

Graunt and Defoe had constructed and analyzed, if only in a rudimentary way, some of the earliest time-series data. While Graunt also employed serial differencing to identify particularly deadly plague years, the practice of differencing became far more widespread in the mid-nineteenth century, when economic journals like the *Economist* and the *Statist* began tabulating financial indicators in first differences and percentage change from previous period rather than simple absolute values. Robert Giffen, founder of the *Statist*, and William Newmarch, assistant editor of the *Economist* and author of its statistical reviews, were largely responsible for this shift, and helped to propel time-series analysis from commercial applications into mathematical ones.

Around the same time, an economist named Reginald Hooker was making claims that would drive the advancement of time series for the next four decades. Hooker, also interested in seasonal and annual cycles, took first differences for pairs of time series and concluded:

Correlation of the deviations from an instantaneous average (or trend) may be adopted to test the similarity of more or less marked periodic influences. Correlation of the difference between successive values will probably prove most useful in cases where the similarity of the shorter rapid changes (with no apparent periodicity) are the subject of investigation, or where the normal level of one or both series of observations does not remain constant.

(Hooker 1905, 703)

Thus, the idea of separating long-term trends in data from short-term dynamics was born. That is, analysts recognized a difference between data whose mean seemed relatively constant over time (Hooker's "normal level" over time) versus those series whose mean appeared to grow. The concept of mean stationarity thus became important in data analysis. Hooker's observations did not go unnoticed. In separate articles in the same issue of *Biometrika*, William Gossett (writing as Student) and Oscar Anderson disputed Hooker's method of correlating first differences (Student 1914; Anderson 1914). Instead, they proposed the variate difference method, which was a general form of Hooker's method. Their variate difference method entailed differencing variables until the correlation of the nth difference was statistically indistinguishable from the $(n + 1)^{th}$ difference. According to Gossett and Anderson, this method allowed the analyst to remove "variability due to position in time or space and to determine whether there is any correlation between the residual variations" (Student 1914, 180). Their method represented a shift from time-series analysis that saw variables as having an important relationship with time (seasonal variation and annual cycles, for example) to those that saw time (or some form of deterministic trend) as a nuisance to be eliminated so that the true relationship between variables could be discovered.

Around the same time, in the United States, Udny Yule developed a filter for data that removed what was essentially an autoregressive (AR) process.[2] Yule's work noted that the common method of variate differencing destroyed certain interesting oscillations in data, and he noted that "the problem is not to isolate random residuals but oscillations of different durations, and unless the generalized method can be given some meaning in terms of oscillations it is not easy to see what purpose it can serve" (Yule 1921, 504). The importance of these oscillations led Yule to conclude in 1926 that the relationship between a pair of time series could not be described as simply a causal relationship between variables nor a function of time, but was in

---

[2] Yule's filter owed a debt to Russian Eugene Slutzky who had created a moving average (MA) filter to produce a white noise series. See Slutzky (1937); also Gottman (1981).

fact an autoregressive process, "in which successive terms are closely related to one another" (Yule 1926, 6). The "nonsense correlations" indicated in the title of his 1926 article were due to serial correlation in series with short sampling periods. Klein (1997, 286) observes that "Yule's formulation of an autoregressive stochastic process and his suggestion of a disturbance term that took on the statistical properties that before were accorded to variables opened doors for statisticians who had been plagued by problems of economic time series."

In 1938, Herman Wold showed that once autocorrelation, cyclical movements, and nonstationarity were removed from the series—provided the underlying probability structure was constant—any time series can be thought of as white noise process and ordinary least squares regression can be used to estimate relationships. Additionally, Wold pioneered the use of graphs of first- and second-order serial correlation coefficients against time, which he termed correlograms, to model stationarity.

Also called autocorrelation functions (ACF) and partial-autocorrelation functions (PACF), these graphs are critical for the ARIMA (autoregressive integrated moving average) model-fitting procedure (Box and Jenkins 1970). Box and Jenkins contributed greatly to the use of ACF and PACF graphs for uncovering the data-generating process that generate the time-series data analyzed by researchers. The Box–Jenkins approach, covered in greater detail below, is a three-stage process, involving visual inspection of the ACF/PACF plots, estimation of coefficients, and diagnostic checking. These early fundamentals, developed by Yule, Wold, and others, are considered by many to be the foundation of modern time-series analysis.

Throughout the 1950s, 1960s, and 1970s, time-series analysis became more complex as econometricians began to develop more sophisticated techniques for modeling time series with a variety of statistical properties. While we touch on many of these newer developments in the rest of the chapter, three important points can be drawn from this brief review of the early time-series literature. First, real social problems and needs spurred the development of these methods, which meant that analysts were always focused on the data-generating process—one can best understand a problem if the patterns within the data can be appropriately determined and analyzed. Second, early analysts recognized a difference between variation as trend versus variation as substance. Differencing was held out as the key solution, which left only "meaningful" variations in data. Third, the recognition of the importance of differencing was itself controversial. Trends do tell us about the long-term nature of the data-generating process, although the trends may complicate our statistical analyses. Ironically, even after 100 years of improvements on time-series methods, the very same challenges still drive much of the innovation in the field today.

The remainder of this chapter reviews some of the major approaches to time-series modeling, with particular attention to applications in political science. The purpose is not to give the reader an exact sense of *how* to conduct time-series modeling, but by reviewing basic model structures, procedures, and applications, we hope to give a sense of the power (and possible shortcomings) as well as the applicability of these methods to the study of political phenomena.

2 A BASIC TIME-SERIES MODEL

Normally, we assume our regression models have no autocorrelation. That is, the value of a variable at time t is unrelated to its value at $t - 1$. We know in many (if not most) cases, however, this assumption is problematic. Many political processes have inertia, are driven by historical forces, or are guided by institutions that change slowly. What happens if, through either theory or econometric tests, we know our variables are related over time? Taking a univariate model, we can think about taking our variable and decomposing it into distinct parts. So,

$$Y_t = a_0 + \rho_1 Y_{t-1} + e_t \tag{1}$$

where e_t is an independent, identically distributed, mean zero error term. Time-series analysts refer to this e_t as a white noise process and the analysis of these residuals is an important part of any analysis to ensure that there are no temporal dynamics left in the data.

Equation (1) represents an autoregressive process of order 1 (or AR(1)). Thus, the values of e at time t are strongly related to the values of e in the previous period (i.e. errors are correlated over time). Another possibility is that the values of e at time t will be related to some average of its past values:

$$e_t = u_t + \xi_1 u_{t-1} + \xi_2 u_{t-2}. \tag{2}$$

Such a process is labeled a moving average—in equation (2), of order 2—an MA(2). In an MA process, values of a variable "average" over time. In both the case of AR and MA processes, there are important substantive implications of the diagnosis. For example, exogenous shocks in an AR(1) model persist over long periods, dying out slowly.[3] Shocks to a process with an MA(q) error structure persist exactly q periods. Very different interpretations are thus derived from each model: Do perturbations to the model persist over long periods or do they disappear quickly?

A time series may have both autoregressive and moving average components.[4] Conceptually, a time series may be thought of as having several constituent parts: a trend component, a seasonal component, and irregular components. The AR and MA parts of the series are irregular components that can be modeled using a Box–Jenkins methodology that we discuss below. While not every time series will have each component, the goal is to extract the relevant parts out of a given series and analyze these in a substantive fashion.

---

[3] This assumes the value of ρ does not equal 1.

[4] Mathematically, an AR process can be expressed as a higher-order MA process (and vice versa) making the diagnosis of each type a challenge for the analyst. See McCleary and Hay (1980, 56–8). Although in theory one could select a high-order MA model rather than an AR(1), for example, an overriding goal in time-series modeling is to select the most parsimonious model.

2.1 Trends—Deterministic and Stochastic

Many time series have trends (i.e. nonconstant means over time). Indeed as noted in Section 1, most analysts realized their data contained trends and that these were simple linear functions of time. These trends are referred to as deterministic trends since there is no randomness in their movement—there is a seemingly inexorable shift in the mean of the series over time. To handle this problem, one could regress their variable on some linear function (such as time) and analyze the residuals that comprise the irregular part of the time series. Of course, trends may not be linear, but polynomial or of any other functional form. Moreover, the regression to remove the trend may suffer from a number of shortcomings, including outliers (especially if these lie in the first or last observation), that makes this method problematic. Finally, the estimate of the trend in such a model is static—given the changing nature of the data over time, we could ideally obtain a more dynamic estimate of how the series moves over time.

For years, though, most analysts believed that removing linear trends was the key to analyzing their data. Yet, an important body of research began to emphasize that many economic time series did not have a constant mean around a deterministic trend. Rather, there was stochastic variation around a nonconstant mean. Indeed, today most time-series analysts assume that trends are stochastic. Modeling trends as stochastic allows more flexibility in form and estimation thus providing a better fit of a model to the data. The quintessential stochastic trend is the random walk. If, in equation (1) above, rho equals 1, so that the best predictor of the present value is the previous value plus a white noise error, we say that the series is a random walk. A random walk (also referred to as a series with a unit root) is the simplest realization of an integrated, or nonstationary, time series. For these time series, there is no reversion to the mean; each shock to the data creates a permanent (but random) change in the conditional mean. Such a diagnosis is substantively important—shocks to the series do not dissipate over time, but are absorbed (or integrated) into the series.[5]

Not only do nonstationary time series have particular properties that lead to statistical problems like spurious regressions, but because by definition the series violates one of the fundamental assumptions of OLS (errors from one period are not independent from the previous period), the very diagnosis of a random walk requires a distinct set of tools. Initially, many analysts utilized Dickey–Fuller and Augmented Dickey–Fuller tests to diagnose unit roots. While these tests are still common, they are low power tests—the null hypothesis in these tests is the failure to reject that a series is not a random walk.[6] Today, a number of alternative tests exist to diagnose unit roots. For most of these tests the null hypothesis is the rejection of the finding of a unit root, giving them more statistical power. Among the more popular is the Kwiatkowski–Phillips–Schmidt–Shin (KPSS) test.

---

[5] For a more technical introduction to unit roots, see Maddala and Kim (2000). For political science discussions, see Freeman et al. (1998); Durr (1993); and Box-Steffensmeier and Smith (1996).

[6] In other words, a statistically significant test statistic indicates a rejection of the unit root hypothesis. On these tests, see Dickey and Fuller (1979; 1981).

Coping with unit roots or nonstationary series in most cases can be handled by simple differencing. Many of the techniques discussed in the next section rely on this very approach—differencing the variable to remove the stochastic trend, leaving the rest of the irregular component of the series to analyze. Like Yule's early work, however, many contend that differencing removes too much information from the series and that these long-term forces represented by stochastic trends can be incorporated into our models, especially multivariate ones. We return to this in the next section.

More recently, a growing body of research suggests that not only can unit roots lead to problems such as spurious correlations, but levels of integration short of a pure unit root (rho < 1) can also lead to faulty inferences. Research on fractional integration and near-integrated time series has made important contributions in political science. Box-Steffensmeier and Smith (1998) show that the macropartisanship time series is fractionally integrated, suggesting that the series is the result of a data-generating process with a long memory, but also some transitory elements. Thus, macropartisanship measures respond to shocks in terms of "years—not months or decades" (Box-Steffensmeier and Smith 1996, 567). This finding has important implications not only for the modeling of macropartisanship but for how theorists of American politics understand the evolution of political preferences over time. Additional work by Lebo and Clarke (2000) and Lebo, Walker, and Clarke (2000) has shown that most of the typical variables used in political science studies, such as indices of consumer sentiment, presidential approval, and measures of Supreme Court ideology, are fractionally integrated, suggesting that while the memory of these processes is not infinite, they are nonetheless very long. Moreover, to model them appropriately, avoiding pitfalls similar to those of fully integrated data, research must take these fractional properties into consideration.

2.2 Seasonality

Some data-generating processes are seasonal in nature. At some points in time, we may expect values of our variable to increase or decrease in a systematic fashion. For example, unemployment typically falls in the winter, as seasonal, holiday-based employment rises, and rises in the summer as college students flood the job market. To deal with seasonal components in a series, many suggest seasonal differencing. Rather than taking a simple period-by-period difference, the analyst differences by the appropriate time interval (e.g. for monthly data, twelve-months for yearly data, four-month for quarterly data, etc.).[7]

After removing trends (whether deterministic or stochastic) and seasonality, the analyst is left with the irregular component(s) and the white noise (or stochastic) part of the series. The irregular parts can be analyzed using various univariate and

[7] See Enders (2004, 95–9) for additional solutions and an application to holiday-driven money supply policies.

multivariate techniques. Some of these techniques allow for the simultaneous modeling of trends and seasonality, but others require differencing and/or detrending prior to modeling. It is to these techniques that we now turn.

3 MODELING TIME-SERIES DATA

There are a host of methodologies that can be used to analyze time-series data. The choice of the appropriate methodology is dependent on the substantive hypothesis to be tested as well as the properties of the data. Some techniques will be appropriate in analyzing a single time series to determine its dynamic properties and draw substantive conclusions from those findings. Others will be appropriate for an analyst interested in finding the relationship between multiple time series. In every case, one rule of thumb to note always when analyzing any time series is that most statistical techniques within this family are useful only when there are greater than fifty periodic data points to be analyzed since short time series may yield unstable results.

3.1 ARMA and ARIMA Models

Thirty years ago, the phase "time-series analysis" was synonymous with the Box–Jenkins approach (Kennedy 1992, 247–9). Rather than analyze time series in a multivariate setting, Box–Jenkins modeling analyzes a single series for the purpose of understanding the data-generating process as well as forecasting.[8]

The general form of the ARMA model is often labeled an ARMA(p, q) model. If $p = 0$, one is left with an MA(q) model, while if $q = 0$, one has specified an AR(p) model. The purpose of Box–Jenkins modeling is to identify autoregressive and/or moving average components in a time series. This is important not only for substantive reasons (e.g. do shocks to the data-generating process last for long or short periods) but to remove any variation in the variable accounted for by its own past values to facilitate further statistical analysis. This is done through the analysis of correlograms that graph the autocorrelation function (ACF) and partial autocorrelation function (PACF) of a series—the technique pioneered by Wold. Specifically, the ACF graphs the autocorrelation of the series across a number of lags, while the PACF graphs the partial autocorrelations—the autocorrelations at each lag after the correlation of the preceding lag has been controlled for. The normal process of identifying the order of AR or MA processes is to match the correlograms with ideal type graphs of the different processes at different orders (e.g. AR(2), MA(1), etc.). Then, the analyst estimates a statistical model with the appropriate terms and orders, checking the residuals of the model for any remaining temporal dynamics. If

---

[8] For an excellent introduction to ARIMA modeling, see McLeary and Hay (1980), especially ch. 2.

done correctly, the residuals from a properly specific ARMA model should be a white noise process.

This diagnosis process can also be used to help identify other components of the time series such as seasonality and cycles. Also, while not as fine grained as the formal unit root tests previously discussed, correlograms can also assist in the diagnosis of nonstationarity. In cases of nonstationarity, analysts must incorporate a difference (or d) term yielding an autoregressive *integrated* moving average or ARIMA (p, d, q) model. Normally, once the order of integration (noted as d) has been determined, the series is differenced d times (or fractionally differenced if $0 < d < 1$) to arrive at a stationary series, which is then analyzed with normal Box–Jenkins procedures.

One important extension of the ARIMA model is the Box–Taio intervention model, that allows the analyst to test for structural breaks in a time series. Once the underlying data-generating process for a series is identified, one can model whether particular changes, such as new public policies, alter the data-generating process. A classic political science application of the intervention model is Hibbs' (1977) political economy model of macroeconomic policy (as measured by unemployment rates). Hibbs showed, through the use of ARMA techniques, that left-leaning governments in industrial democracies were more likely to respond to social pressures to reduce unemployment, especially in Great Britain and the United States. This work began a long series of debates in comparative political economy concerning the relationship between political partisanship and macroeconomic policy (including unemployment, inflation, and exchange rate policies).[9]

There are numerous examples of ARMA/ARIMA models in political science.[10] Debates over the nature of macropartisanship in American politics have made significant use of ARMA models, including the seminal work of MacKuen, Erikson, and Stimson (1989), which has been built on by Green, Palmquist, and Schickler (1998), as well as Box-Steffensmeier and Smith (1996). In their original work, MacKuen, Erikson, and Stimson (1989) argued that there were meaningful variations in partisan identification over time and these variations were driven by evaluations of the economy and of incumbent presidents. Using ARMA models, they showed that macropartisanship was indeed driven by consumer sentiment, presidential approval (itself modeled as a function of consumer sentiment), and a series of dummy variables for administrations and major political shocks.[11]

The final class of univariate models differs from the rest in terms of what is being modeled. What if the time-series component we are interested in is not only the mean but also the variance? The ARCH (Autoregressive Conditionally Heteroskedastic)

---

[9] Examples include Alt (1985); Oatley (1999); Franzese (2002).

[10] Most recently, analysts have combined ARMA models with the concept of fractionally integrated series to create ARFIMA models.

[11] As discussed below, Box-Steffensmeier and Smith (1996) model macropartisanship as a fractionally integrated time series, generating different substantive interpretations than MacKuen et al. (MES). Green et al. reanalyze the MES data using a variety of measures and suggest macropartisanship does not change as rapidly as MES suggests.

model attempts to model the variance as an important substantive component in the time series. These models, pioneered by Engle (1982), are useful when the residuals from a time-series model contain periods of high and low variance, suggesting that large and small errors cluster together. Thus, if an analyst is interested in modeling the volatility along with the central tendency of a series, ARCH models and its relatives can be quite useful. Many series in political science may even show relatively constant variances on the whole, yet have periods with significant volatility. The ARCH methodology is ideal for the analysis of series like these. In economics, this has meant the analysis of financial data such as exchange rates and inflation.

Fewer applications of ARCH exist in political science relative to the ARIMA model (Leblang and Mukherjee 2004).[12] In American politics, Gronke and Brehm (2002) analyze the volatility of presidential approval. In international relations, Bernhard and Leblang (2000) examine exchange rate volatility as a function of partisanship, elections, and public opinion.[13]

3.2 Vector Autoregression (VAR)

To this point, we have assumed the analyst is interested in questions that concern one variable. Yet political phenomena are rarely simple and most scholars require a multivariate framework to understand the data-generating process at hand. To this end, some who analyze time-series data use a technique known as vector autoregression (VAR). Pioneered by Sims (1980), these models bring very few a priori restrictions to the table. This is in contrast to the vast majority of statistical models that are published in political science, which posit a host of restrictions.[14] Many of these assumed restrictions, however, are untenable, such as assuming that all explanatory variables are exogenous, lag structures are one period, and coefficients are stable across the entire estimation sample.

VAR modelers begin with none of these assumptions. Normally, the analyst starts with a number of time series hypothesized to be interrelated. Rather than arbitrarily select which variables are exogenous and/or the lag length, a VAR analyst will estimate many versions of a VAR then assess which lag structure and model specification provides the best fit to the data. Here, best fit can be determined a number of ways, including various statistical information criteria.[15]

---

[12]   Many applications are in economics and deal with interest rates or exchange rates. See Beine and Laurent (2003); Coporale and McKiernan (1998); Lee and Tse (1991). The extension of ARCH models to a generalized model was by Bollerslev (1987).

[13]   ARCH models should not be confused with the ARCH test, although they are built on identical statistical bases. The ARCH test can be applied to any regression model to test for the heteroskedasticity of errors. While the ARCH model can be used for similar diagnoses, one can also incorporate explanatory variables to model the variance process.

[14]   Freeman, Williams, and Lin (1989) refer to models directly deduced from theory (and its attendant restrictions) as structural models.

[15]   Many time-series analysts use information criteria such as Akaike or Schwartz Bayesian to distinguish model fit. On these criteria in time series, see Enders (2004, 69–70).

Before discussing VAR further, we should note that a closely related approach to VAR in multivariate analysis is Granger causality (Freeman 1990). Granger's idea was that a variable can be considered causal (from a statistical point of view) if past values of it can be used to predict a second variable better than only the past values of the second variable. As usually implemented, this means regressing several lags of a variable (X) on another variable (Y), while controlling for past values of Y. One then conducts a test of joint significance of the coefficient estimate of all the lags of X. If this test (usually an F or a χ^2, depending on sample size) is statistically significant, one can say that "X Granger causes Y" (Freeman 1983).

Indeed, Granger causality tests are often a subset of a VAR estimation. Specifically, a VAR is a series of equations where each variable is regressed on lags of itself and several other variables. Moreover, most (if not all) of the explantory variables are themselves dependent variables. The independent variables are always lagged (avoiding strict simultaneity problems) and because the explanatory variables in each equation are common, OLS can be used to estimate the system of equations (Sims 1980).

What is slightly more complicated in the VAR exercise is hypothesis testing. Due to extensive lag structures and feedback within the system of equations, it is not possible to simply look at one or two coefficient estimates, assess sign and statistical significance, and test hypotheses. Rather, tools known as innovation accounting and variance decomposition assist in this task. Innovation accounting amounts to shocking one variable in the system of equations by a value equal to one standard deviation of the variable, then simulating the moving average response of each equation (see Freeman, Williams, and Lin 1989; Williams 1990). The analyst is then able to see how simulated shocks to one variable influences current and future values of every variable in the system.

A complement to innovation accounting involves examining variance decompositions, which allows the analyst to determine the portion of the error variance of a forecast accounted for by each variable in the model. This also allows one to analyze the substantive influence that each variable has in the system of equations.

The subfield of international relations has a number of applications of the Granger and VAR methodology. Goldstein and Freeman (1990) investigated action-reaction responses between great powers during the cold war. Their modeling of US-Chinese-Soviet relations was able to directly test hypotheses concerning reciprocity—a key concept in international relations theory. They found that the behavior of each superpower during the cold war was reciprocated by the other, whether the behavior was itself cooperative or conflictual, indicating that conflict resolution measures adopted by one side would be rewarded with further cooperation. Goldstein and Pevehouse (1997) used a similar motivation to test reciprocity patterns in the Bosnia conflict. They found that hostility by the United States and NATO caused more cooperative behavior of the Serbians towards the Bosnians, justifying more hard-line policies adopted by Western powers in the conflict.

Although the subfield of international relations has seen the most examples in political science, American politics scholars are increasing their use of the technique.

For example, Americanists have used VAR methods to investigate changes in issue attention as a function of inter-branch dynamics (Fleming, Wood, and Bohte 1999); commercial bank regulation (Krause 1997); and corporate taxation (Williams and Collins 1997) among others.

3.3 Error Correction Models (ECMs)

To this point, we have either assumed that our series were stationary (do not contain unit roots) or if nonstationary, were made stationary before they were analyzed. The diagnosis of unit roots is particularly important in the multivariate context. In a seminal article in economics, Stock and Watson (1988) showed that regression of two nonstationary variables on one another was likely to lead to false inferences about the relationship between the two variables. In addition, some have argued that rather than simply differencing out stochastic trends, these can be modeled, especially in cases where there are common trends between two or more variables. Differencing may throw out important relationships between variables, since any long-run relationship will be lost in differencing (Norpoth 1992, 142).[16]

An alternative approach to modeling multiple time series is the error correction model. A simple error correction model has the following structure:

$$\Delta Y_t = \beta_0 + \beta_1 Y_{t-1} + \beta_2 X_{t-1} + \alpha Z_t + e_t, \tag{3}$$

$$\text{where} \quad Z_t = Y_t - \gamma X_t.$$

Note that the first part of this model is really a VAR in first differences. This allows the analyst to model the short-term perturbations in the relationship between X and Y. The Z term is the error correction component. If two variables are cointegrated, there exists a vector (here gamma, called the cointegrating vector) which yields a stationary series (here, Z_t).[17] The idea is that X and Y are influenced not only by recent values of each other, but by how far apart they drift. This latter relationship is the error correction component of the model. Because the two variables are cointegrated, they move in equilibrium—any movement out of equilibrium will mean a change in the value of one (or both) variables to resume their relationship. The rate at which that movement back to equilibrium takes place is represented by the alpha term in equation X.

Of course, X and Y may not be in equilibrium even though both X and Y are non-stationary. Indeed, most $I(1)$ variables are likely not cointegrated with one another. In

---

[16] Beck (1993) notes that while some suggest econometric tests to determine the need to use ECMs, theory can motivate the use of these models. Even in cases where differencing may remove the cointegration, an analyst may have reason to believe there is a long term relationship between two variables.

[17] It must be the case that X and Y are integrated of the same order, i.e. both $I(1)$, $I(2)$, etc. See Engle and Granger (1987).

these cases, the analyst can revert to VARs after differencing the data. To determine the necessity of using the ECM methodology, Engle and Granger (1987) suggest a four-step procedure: (1) analyze the series for unit roots to ensure integration of the same order; (2) estimate the long-run relationship (the cointegrating vector) between X and Y; (3) use the residuals from the previous stage as the error correction component while estimating a VAR in first differences of X and Y; (4) assess model adequacy and forecasting.

An alternative approach is developed by Johansen.[18] In this methodology, the number of cointegrating relationships between multiple time series is determined by computing the number of characteristic roots of a matrix of parameters from a VAR in first differences. The rank of the matrix is equal to the number of cointegrating vectors. Once the cointegrating vectors are estimated, one can estimate the speed of adjustment parameters, then subject the resulting model to the usual VAR-based innovation accounting procedures.

Within political science, error correction models have proven less common than traditional VARs.[19] Clarke and Stewart (1994) revisit the retrospective and prospective political economy models of presidential approval. Taking on MacKuen, Erikson, and Stimson (1992), they suggest that when controlling for long-term business expectations, opinion concerning the state of the economy has little bearing on presidential approval. Clarke and Stewart show that most of the variables in the MacKuen model contain unit roots. Moreover, Clarke and Stewart find a cointegrating relationship between public approval for the president and five-year prospective evaluations of the economy. Their results suggest that voters' judgments about a president are influenced, in the long run, by their impressions of future economic conditions. Given this equilibrium relationship, we should expect downward shifts in those impressions to be followed closely by declining presidential approval.

Other applications of ECMs have arisen in analyses of US Supreme Court norms over concurrences and dissents (Caldeira and Zorn 1998); conflict and cooperation between the United States and the Soviet Union during the cold war (Ward and Rajmaira 1992); as well as executive–legislative institutional growth patterns in the United States (Krause 2002). Because this methodology allows for more complex dynamics, many analysts find ECMs nicely model a data-generating process with long-term and short-term trends in behavior. As with traditional VAR models, ECMs can be analyzed with impulse response functions and variance decompositions.

---

[18] Stock and Watson (1988) outline a similar methodology. The advantage of the Johansen methodology is that no assumptions are made as to which variables adjust first in the cointegrating process. In the Engle–Granger methodology, one variable must be chosen as a dependent variable to estimate the cointegrating relationship. Such a choice is not required in Johansen, where eigenvalues are calculated based on all variables in the model, yielding an estimated number of cointegrating relationships.

[19] For an excellent introduction to ECMs in politics including applications, see volume 4 of *Political Analysis* (1993); especially articles by Durr; Beck; Ostrom and Smith.

3.4 Data Aggregation and Parameter Instability

When dealing with time-series data, the analyst must often make choices about the level of temporal aggregation in the data. For example, if one is to analyze data on state-to-state political interactions, should one take their snapshot of the process every year, month, or week? In other words, are we interested in variations, such as reactions by states to one another, shifts in public opinion, or changes in economic conditions, as they occur over long or short periods of time? In some cases, data availability will make this decision for us (e.g. cross-national trade data is usually only available on a yearly basis even though trade occurs daily). In other cases, we will have the luxury of having daily or weekly information (e.g. public opinion polls taken by various organizations) that can be averaged or aggregated to longer periods of time should we choose to do so.

As Freeman (1989) notes, however, our choices have important statistical implications. Over-aggregating the data can yield biases in estimation, obscuring the true data-generating process. In some cases, true relationships can be eliminated and in some cases, over-aggregating can create false correlations. As Goldstein (1991) has shown, the substantive implications drawn from arms race and reciprocity models at different levels of temporal aggregation vary widely. Freeman suggests our theories may have "natural time units." Theories concerning budgeting for example will often need yearly data, but action-reaction models from international relations may require more disaggregated data.

Another issue brought to the fore by time-series analyses is parameter stability. Over long periods of time, for example, a statistical model that works well in predicting public opinion between 1945 and 1973 may not work as well from 1973 to the present. While structural modelers often assume stable parameter estimates over an entire sample, the time-series analyst has techniques at their disposal to test this assumption. The Chow (1960) test is often used to test for the structural stability of coefficients. Unlike Box–Taio intervention models or structural break tests in the VAR context, the Chow test is not rooted in time-series econometrics, but is often applied to time-series data and models.[20] More recently, Engle (2002) has developed a class of multivariate models known as dynamic conditional correlation to explicitly model changing correlations over time rather than simply testing for the presence of parameter instability.

3.5 Time-series Regression

Traditionally, those using OLS regression who feared an autoregressive process in their data utilized tests such as the Durbin–Watson d to ensure the independence

---

[20] Caldeira and Zorn (1998) also use structural regime change models in the context of an ECM exercise. The Chow test is essentially an F test comparing the sum of squares of a full sample model to the sum of squares from separate estimates of two sub-samples.

of errors. Failure to meet this OLS assumption results in the need to use some form of generalized least squares (GLS) whereby the rho term is estimated and used as a weight in the variance-covariance matrix. Beck and Katz (1995) have shown that some traditional GLS methods can underestimate standard errors in the context of panel data (particularly when the number of panels is larger than or equivalent to the number of time periods). They suggest OLS with panel-corrected standard errors as a superior alternative within the time-series cross-section context.

Outside of the OLS framework, more techniques are becoming common in the political science realm. In the logit context, Beck, Katz, and Tucker (1998) show the importance of controlling for the temporal properties of binary time-series cross-sectional data, which is essentially event history data (Box-Steffensmeier and Jones 2004). In the context of count models, Brandt and colleagues have developed the Poisson autoregressive (PAR) and the Poisson exponentially weighted moving average (PEWMA) model.[21] Each of these allows for the estimation of traditional count models while controlling for temporal dependence of the count-generating process.

It should also be noted that one important element of any panel data-set is the time-series element.[22] Many of the techniques discussed above, however, are not applicable to panel data-sets. Differencing cannot occur across panels and most panel data-sets in comparative politics and international relations are too short to provide stable estimates for most time-series techniques. Although not common in the political science literature, panel unit root tests exist (see Enders 2004, 225–8) to help identify nonstationarity within some panels in a data-set. Unfortunately, most panel data are cross-section dominant, meaning there are many relatively short time series within the panel. Like all time-series tests, longer series are beneficial to ensure the stability of the test.

4 CONCLUSIONS

While time-series analysis has been with us in some form for nearly 500 years, it is still relatively uncommon compared to other, static statistical techniques within political science. The number of users of time-series techniques in political science is growing. As methods of generating new and longer time series become more common, these techniques will become increasingly ubiquitous. Today, economic data is measured in monthly, daily, even hourly increments creating rich data-sets of interactions among economic actors. Polling data is available on an almost daily basis, while internet news services provide stories for events data hourly. As political scientists move to analyze these rich new data sources, they will necessarily turn to time series.

---

[21] See Brandt et al. (2000) and Brandt and Williams (2001).
[22] For a complete discussion of panel data issues, see Beck, this volume.

As time series becomes increasingly common, political scientists will be able to move away from assumptions of static behavior toward a dynamic understanding of the interactions between political actors, economic forces, and mass publics across the globe. Not only our empirical understandings, but also our theories benefit significantly from these advances. The nature of politics changes over space and over time—while we have long noted the former in our statistical models, we often ignore the latter. Time-series analysis provides a rich set of tools to focus on these very changes, which can only enhance our understanding of the political world.

REFERENCES

ALT, J. 1985. Political parties, world demand, and unemployment. *American Political Science Review*, 79: 1016–40.

ANDERSON, O. 1914. Nochmals über "The elimination of spurious correlation due to position in time or space." *Biometrika*, 10: 269–79.

BECK, N. 1993. The methodology of cointegration. *Political Analysis*, 4: 237–48.

——and KATZ, J. 1995. What to do (and not to do) with time series cross-section data. *American Political Science Review*, 89: 634–47.

————and TUCKER, R. 1998. Taking time seriously: time series–cross-section analysis with a binary dependent variable. *American Journal of Political Science*, 42: 1260–88.

BEINE, M., and LAURENT, S. 2003. Central bank interventions and jumps in double long memory models of daily exchange rates. *Journal of Empirical Finance*, 10: 641–60.

BERNHARD, D., and LEBLANG, W. 2000. Speculative attacks in industrial democracies: the role of politics. *International Organization*, 54: 291–324.

BOLLERSLEV, T. 1987. A conditionally heteroskedastic time series model for speculative prices and rates of return. *Review of Economics and Statistics*, 69: 542–7.

BOX, G., and JENKINS, G. 1970. *Time-Series Analysis: Forecasting and Control*. San Francisco: Holden Day.

BOX-STEFFENSMEIER, J. M., and JONES, B. 2004. *Event History Modeling: A Guide for Social Scientists*. New York: Cambridge University Press.

——and SMITH, R. M. 1996. The dynamics of aggregate partisanship. *American Political Science Review*, 90: 567–80.

————1998. Investigating political dynamics using fractional integration methods. *American Journal of Political Science*, 42: 661–89.

——FREEMAN, J. R., and PEVEHOUSE, J. C. forthcoming. *Time Series Analysis for Social Scientists*. New York: Cambridge University Press.

BRANDT, P. T., and WILLIAMS, J. T. 2001. A linear poisson Autoregressive Model: the Poisson AR(p) Model. *Political Analysis*, 9: 164–84.

——WILLIAMS, J. T., FORDHAM, B. O., and POLLINS, B. 2000. Dynamic modeling for persistent event-count time series. *American Journal of Political Science*, 44: 823–43.

CALDEIRA, G., and ZORN, C. 1998. Of time and consensual norms in the Supreme Court. *American Journal of Political Science*, 42: 874–902.

CAPORALE, T., and McKIERNAN, B. 1998. The Fischer Black Hypothesis: some time series evidence. *Southern Economic Journal*, 64: 765–71.

CHOW, G. 1960. Tests of equality between sets of coefficients in two linear regressions. *Econometrica*, 28: 591–605.

CLARKE, H. D., and STEWART, M. C. 1994. Prospections, retrospections, and rationality: the "bankers" model of presidential approval reconsidered. *American Journal of Political Science*, 38: 1104–23.

DEFOE, D. 1968 [1722]. *A Journal of the Plague Year*, ed. J. Sutherland. New York: Heritage Press.

DICKEY, D., and FULLER, W. 1979. Distribution of the estimators for autoregressive time series with unit root. *Journal of the American Statistical Association*, 74: 427–31.

——1981. Likelihood ratio statistics for autoregressive time series with a unit root. *Econometrica*, 49: 1057–72.

DURR, R. 1993. What moves policy sentiments? *American Political Science Review*, 87: 158–72.

ENDERS, W. 2004. *Applied Econometric Time Series*, 2nd edn. New York: Wiley.

ENGLE, R. 1982. Autoregressive conditional heteroscedasticity with estimates of the variance of United Kingdom inflation. *Econometrica*, 50: 987–1007.

——2002. Dyanmic conditional correlation: a simple class of multivariate generalized autoregressive conditional heteroskedasticity models. *Journal of Business and Economic Statistics*, 20: 339–50.

——and GRANGER, C. W. J. 1987. Cointegration and error correction: representation, estimation, and testing. *Econometrica*, 55: 251–76.

FLEMMING, R., WOOD, B., and BOHTE, J. 1999. Attention to issues in a system of separated powers: the macrodynamics of American policy agendas. *Journal of Politics*, 61: 76–108.

FRANZESE, R. J., JR. 2002. Electoral and partisan cycles in economic policies and outcomes. *Annual Review of Political Science*, 5: 369–421.

FREEMAN, J. 1983. Granger causality and the time series analysis of political relationships. *American Journal of Political Science*, 27: 327–58.

——1989. Systematic sampling, temporal aggregation, and the study of political relationships. In *Political Analysis*, ed. J. Stimson. Ann Arbor: University of Michigan Press.

——1990. Systematic sampling, temporal aggregation and the study of political relationships. *Political Analysis*, 1: 61–88.

——HOUSER, D., KELLSTEDT, P. M., and WILLIAMS, J. T. 1998. Long-memoried processes, unit roots, and causal inference in political science. *American Journal of Political Science*, 42: 1289–327.

——WILLIAMS, J., and LIN, T. 1989. Vector autoregression and the study of politics. *American Journal of Political Science*, 33: 842–77.

GOLDSTEIN, J. S. 1991. Reciprocity in superpower relations: an empirical analysis. *International Studies Quarterly*, 35: 195–209.

——and FREEMAN, J. 1990. *Three Way Street: Strategic Reciprocity in World Politics*. Chicago: University of Chicago Press.

——and PEVEHOUSE, J. 1997. Reciprocity, bullying, and international cooperation: time series analysis of the Bosnian conflict. *American Political Science Review*, 91: 515–29.

GOTTMAN, J. 1981. *Time Series Analysis: A Comprehensive Introduction for Social Scientists*. Cambridge, Mass.: Cambridge University Press.

GRAUNT, J. 1975 [1662]. *Natural and Political Observations Made upon the Bills of Mortality*. Salem, NH: Arno River Press.

GREEN, D., PALMQUIST, B., and SCHICKLER, E. 1998. Macropartisanship: a replication and critique. *American Political Science Review*, 92: 883–99.

GRONKE, P., and BREHM, J. 2002. History, heterogeneity, and presidential approval: a modified ARCH approach. *Electoral Studies*, 21: 425–52.

HAMILTON, J. D. 1994. *Time Series Analysis*. Princeton, NJ: Princeton University Press.

HIBBS, D. 1977. Political parties and macroeconomic performance. *American Political Science Review*, 71: 1467–79.

HOOKER, R. 1905. On the correlation of successive observations. *Journal of the Royal Statistical Society*, 68: 696–703.

KENNEDY, P. 1992. *A Guide to Econometrics*, 3rd edn. Cambridge, Mass.: MIT Press.

KLEIN, J. 1997. *Statistical Visions in Time*. Cambridge: Cambridge University Press.

KRAUSE, G. 1997. Policy preference formation and subsystem behaviour: the case of commercial bank regulation. *British Journal of Political Science*, 27: 525–50.

—— 2002. Separated powers and institutional growth in the presidential and congressional branches: distinguishing between short-run versus long-run dynamics. *Political Research Quarterly*, 55: 27–57.

LEBLANG, D., and MUKHERJEE, B. 2004. Presidential elections and the stock market: comparing Markov-Switching and fractionally integrated GARCH models of volatility. *Political Analysis*, 12: 296–322.

LEBO, M., and CLARKE, H. D. 2000. Modelling memory and volatility: recent advances in the analysis of political time series. *Electoral Studies*, 19: 1–7.

—— WALKER, R. W., and CLARKE, H. D. 2000. You must remember this: dealing with long memory in political analyses. *Electoral Studies*, 19: 31–48.

LEE, T., and TSE, Y. 1991. Term structure of interest rates in the Singapore Asian dollar market. *Journal of Applied Econometrics*, 6: 143–52.

LUTKEPOHL, H. 1993. *Introduction to Multiple Time Series Analysis*. New York: Springer-Verlag.

McCLEARY, R., and HAY, R. A., JR. 1980. *Applied Time Series Analysis for the Social Sciences*. Beverly Hills, Calif.: Sage.

MacKUEN, M., ERIKSON, R., and STIMSON, J. 1989. Macropartisanship. *American Political Science Review*, 83: 1125–42.

——————— 1992. Peasants or bankers? The American electorate and the U.S. economy. *American Political Science Review*, 86: 597–611.

MADDALA, G. S., and KIM, I.-M. 2000. *Unit Roots, Cointegration, and Structural Change*. Cambridge: Cambridge University Press.

NORPOTH, H. 1992. *Confidence Regained: Economics, Mrs. Thatcher, and the British Voter*. Ann Arbor: University of Michigan Press.

OATLEY, T. 1999. Central bank independence and inflation: corporatism, partisanship, and alternative indices of central bank independence. *Public Choice*, 98: 399–413.

SIMS, C. 1980. Macro-economics and reality. *Econometrica*, 48: 1–48.

SLUTZKY, E. 1937. The summation of random causes as the source of cyclic processes. *Econometrica*, 5: 105–20.

STOCK, M., and WATSON, J. 1988. Testing for common trends. *Journal of the American Statistical Association*, 83: 1097–107.

STUDENT (GOSSET, W.) 1914. The elimination of spurious correlation due to position in time or space. *Biometrika*, 10: 179–80.

WARD, M. D., and RAJMAIRA, S. 1992. Reciprocity norms in U.S. foreign policy. *Journal of Conflict Resolution*, 36: 342–68.

WILLIAMS, J. 1990. The political manipulation of the macroeconomic policy. *American Political Science Review*, 84: 767–95.

—— and COLLINS, B. 1997. The political economy of corporate taxation. *American Journal of Political Science*, 41: 208–44.

WOLD, H. 1938. *A Study in the Analysis of Stationary Time Series*. Stockholm: Almqvist and Wiksell.

YULE, G. U. 1921. On the time-correlation problem, and especial reference to the variate-difference correlation method. *Journal of the Royal Statistical Society*, 84: 497–537.

——1926. Why do we sometimes get nonsense-correlations between time series? A study in sampling and the nature of time series. *Journal of the Royal Statistical Society*, 89: 1–63.

CHAPTER 20

....

TIME-SERIES
CROSS-SECTION
METHODS

....

NATHANIEL BECK

TIME-SERIES cross-section (TSCS) data consist of comparable time-series data observed on a variety of units. The paradigmatic applications are to the study of comparative political economy, where the units are countries (often the advanced industrial democracies) and where for each country we observe annual data on a variety of political and economic variables. A standard question for such studies relates to the political determinants of economic outcomes and policies. There have now been hundreds of such studies published.[1]

TSCS data resemble "panel" data, where a large number of units, who are almost invariably survey respondents, are observed over a small number of "waves" (interviews). Any procedure that works well as the number of units gets large should work well for panel data; however, any procedure which depends on a large number of time points will not necessarily work well for panel data. TSCS data typically have the opposite structure to panel data: a relatively small number of units observed for some reasonable length of time. Thus methods that are appropriate for the analysis of panel data are not necessarily appropriate for TSCS data and vice versa.[2]

---

[1] A typical study is Garrett's (1998) analysis of the role of political and labor market variables in determining economic policies and outcomes in fourteen OECD advanced industrial democracies observed annually from 1966 through 1990. Adolph, Butler, and Wilson (2005) provide an inclusive list along with some properties of each data-set analyzed.

[2] Hsiao (2003) is still the best general text for reading about these issues.

All of these types of data are a particular form of "multilevel" (or "hierarchical") data. Multilevel data are organized by grouping lower-level observations in some meaningful way. Thus in the study of education, we may observe students, but students can be thought of as members of a class, and classes can be thought of as members of a school. It is often helpful to think of TSCS data as multilevel data, but with much additional structure.

Political scientists have been familiar with panel data in the guise of election studies for well over half a century. TSCS data has become popular only more recently. Adolph, Butler, and Wilson (2005) examined political science articles in journals indexed in JSTOR. They found relatively few uses of TSCS terminology before 1975, with an explosion of articles using terms related to TSCS analysis starting in the late 1980s. They report that 5 percent of all political science articles from 1996 to 2000 made reference to TSCS or panel terminology and found approximately 200 empirical analyses using TSCS data during that period. Beck and Katz's (1995) methodological discussion of TSCS data is the most heavily cited *American Political Science Review* article published since 1985.

Why the explosive growth in TSCS analyses starting in the mid-1980s? Credit must be given to Stimson's (1985) pioneering essay discussing the importance of both panel and TSCS data in political science. This was the first political science article to discuss general methodological issues related to TSCS data. But it should also be noted that students of comparative politics were ready to hear Stimson's message in 1985.

Most quantitative comparative political science before 1985 consisted of cross-sectional regressions. Researchers interested in the political economy of advanced industrial democracies (Cameron 1978; Lange and Garrett 1985) found themselves running regression on fifteen observations, and hence involved with controversies that relied heavily on whether one particular influential observation (often Norway) completely determined the findings. Since it was not possible to either create more advanced industrial democracies, nor to add nonadvanced industrial democracies to the data-set, the ability to add many additional observations in the temporal domain was clearly attractive (Alvarez, Garrett, and Lange, 1991). TSCS analyses are now the standard in studies of comparative political economy. This, combined with the dyad-year studies of conflict related to the "Democratic Peace" (for example, Maoz and Russett 1993, which is the second-most cited *American Political Science Review* article since 1990), account for much of the popularity of TSCS analyses.

1 EXPLORATORY ANALYSIS

TSCS analysts, like all analysts, should initially examine their data to discern important properties. TSCS data should be examined in the usual ways for whether the data seem to have long tails or skewness, whether there are extreme outliers, and other such issues that must be examined before any regression-type analysis is undertaken. In addition, analysts should examine whether the various cross-sectional units appear similar, whether there is substantial variation in each unit over time, and whether the data show interesting time-series properties. This is most relevant for the dependent variable or variables.

One can look at the time-series properties of the data by usual time-series methods. Thus one can plot the data against time to examine for trends, one can look at correlograms (constructed so as to respect the grouping of the data, which requires a program that is aware of the time-series and cross-sectional properties of the data), and one can look at the autoregression to examine whether the variables have unit roots. While testing for unit roots in such data is a new and active area (Im, Pesaran, and Shin 2003), it surely is easy enough to run an autoregression on TSCS data and see whether the coefficient of the lagged variable is near one.

For exploratory analysis of cross-sectional issues, the best method is the box plot, plotting variables by unit. Since the units are typically both meaningful (countries) and not too numerous (about twenty), much information can be gleaned from these plots. In particular, one can discern if the center and spread of the variables differs by unit, or whether one or a few units are considerably different from the bulk of the units. At that point investigators could consider whether one unit should be dropped from the analysis, or whether this unit to unit heterogeneity (in mean and/or variance) can be modeled.

2 NOTATION

We will work with a single equation setup. While it is possible to extend this to a simultaneous equations framework, such extensions are extremely rare. We use the subscript i to denote unit, and t for time. t always denotes calendar time (typically a year), so that the same t subscript in different units stands for the same time point. The dependent variable is $y_{i,t}$ with the k-vector of independent variables being $x_{i,t}$. A very simple (pooled) model is

$$y_{i,t} = x_{i,t}\beta + \epsilon_{i,t}; i = 1, \ldots, N; t = 1, \ldots, T. \tag{1}$$

This assumes that the data structure is rectangular; that is, each of the N units are observed for the same T time periods. It is easy to handle units that start and end at slightly different time points; data missing in the interior of the time frame can be handled by standard multiple imputation methods (King et al. 2001).

Of course the important issues relate to what independent variables we include to explain y. While one more good predictor of y is worth more than all the various econometric manipulations, we focus on those manipulations, assuming that analysts have done an appropriate job of choosing explanatory variables (and related issues such as functional form).

For the econometric issues, we denote the covariance of the errors by Ω (with variance terms on the diagonal). This is an $NT \times NT$ matrix, with typical element $E(\epsilon_{i,t}\epsilon_{j,s})$. If Ω meets the Gauss–Markov assumptions (that is, all off-diagonal elements are zero and all diagonal elements are identical) then OLS is appropriate and estimation is simple. If the Gauss–Markov assumptions are not met then OLS will still be consistent, but it will not be fully efficient and the reported standard errors will be inaccurate. Much attention has been paid to how the Gauss–Markov assumptions might be violated for TSCS data, and how to improve estimation given those violations. We begin with issues related to the time-series properties of the data, and then consider cross-sectional complications.

3 Dynamic Issues

3.1 Stationary Data

The easiest way to understand the implications of the time-series properties of TSCS data is to remember that for each unit we simply have time-series data, and hence all that we know about time-series data holds (*mutatis mutandis*) for TSCS data. Thus all the standard tests for whether the data are serially independent continue to apply, all the estimation methods for dealing with serially dependent data still work, and all the issues relevant to modeling dynamic processes continue to be relevant.[3] Since TSCS data are often annual, we restrict ourselves here to first-order processes; the generalization to higher-order processes is straightforward.

As always, we can view the dynamics issue as an estimation nuisance or we can treat dynamics as a serious modeling challenge. The latter approach is favored by modern analysts (Hendry, Pagan, and Sargan 1984; Hendry and Mizon 1978). But of course we still need to make sure that the estimation method chosen is appropriate. We begin by noting that dynamic specifications often include a lagged dependent variable. Whether or not the specification contains a lagged dependent variable, OLS is appropriate (at least with respect to time-series issues) so long as the errors are serially independent. It is always appropriate to test for serially correlated errors using a Lagrange multiplier test. This test is easy to implement. One first runs OLS, then regresses the OLS residuals on the lagged values of the residuals (one lag to test for first order serial correlation) and all the other independent variables in the specification, and then compares the statistic NTR^2 to a χ^2 distribution with one

---

[3] For a longer discussion of some of these issues in the context of TSCS data, see Beck and Katz (2004).

degree of freedom. If one fails to reject the null of no serial correlation of the errors, then OLS is appropriate.

If the errors are serially correlated then one can estimate the model by either maximum likelihood or feasible generalized least squares. While iterative methods such as Cochrane–Orcutt may find a local maximum if there is a lagged dependent variable in the specification, this is not usually a problem in practice, and if one is worried, starting the iterations at a few different sets of parameter variables will invariably find the global maximum (Hamilton 1994, 226). But in typical situations the inclusion of a lagged dependent variable in the specification will eliminate almost all serial correlation of the errors (since the lagged dependent variable implicitly includes lagged error terms into the specification).

To see that the use of lagged dependent variables is not fundamentally different from a static model with serially correlated errors, note that both models are a specialized form of the more general "auto-regressive distributed lag" model

$$y_{i,t} = \mathbf{x}_{i,t}\beta + \phi y_{i,t-1} + \mathbf{x}_{i,t-1}\gamma + \epsilon_{i,t}; i = 1, \ldots, N; t = 2, \ldots, T \qquad (2)$$

where the errors are serially independent. The lagged dependent variable model assumes $\gamma = 0$ whereas the model with serially correlated (first-order autoregressive) errors assumes $\gamma = -\beta\phi$. One can always estimate the more general autoregressive distributed lag model and test whether the data support either of the two restrictions on γ. This is easy to do via OLS and surely worth doing in almost all cases.

3.2 Nonstationary Data

There is one additional issue that has important consequences for modeling dynamics: unit roots. In equation (2) ϕ may be very near one. While the exact test statistic for determining whether we can reject that there is a unit root is controversial (Im, Pesaran, and Shin 2003), the presence of unit roots (or nonstationarity) has critical consequences. Estimating a model with either a lagged dependent variable or serially correlated errors in the presence of a unit root can lead to dramatically misleading results (spurious regressions). Thus after estimating a dynamic model one should certainly see if the residuals appear stationary (that is, whether an autoregression of the residuals on their lags shows a coefficient on the lagged residual term near one), as well as examine whether the coefficients on any lagged dependent variable terms are near one. A precise test of the null that the data have no unit roots is much less important than seeing whether certain coefficients are very near one (especially given the large sample sizes, and hence small standard errors, typically seen in TSCS data).

What should analysts do if they find that the data appear to be nonstationary? Clearly they should not ignore the problem. They could simply model the short run; that is, take first differences, giving up on any attempt to model the long run. Alternatively, they could use the various error-correction models associated with the work of Engle and Granger (1987) and Davidson et al. (1978), though almost all the work associated with this approach is for single time-series data rather than TSCS data. Currently this must be marked as an area for further study, though the consequences for ignoring this issue may be grave.

4 Cross-sectional Issues

If, after suitable modeling, we find serially independent errors, there may remain violations of the Gauss–Markov assumptions due to cross-sectional (spatial) complications in the data. In particular, the errors for the different units may have differing variances (panel heteroskedasticity) or may be correlated across units. If there is correlation of errors across the units, it is almost invariably assumed both to not vary over time and to only occur for units observed at the same time point; thus the typical violation allowed for is contemporaneous correlation of the errors. We would expect contemporaneous correlation of the errors to be likely in studies of political economy in open economies; shocks that affect one nation can also be expected to affect its trading partners (either as a common shock or through the unexpected impact on trade).

4.1 Traditional Approaches

Researchers concerned about such spatial violations turned to "feasible generalized least squares" (FGLS). This method uses OLS to estimate the model, then takes the residuals from OLS to estimate the covariance matrix of the errors, Ω, and then, based on that estimate, transforms the data so the resulting transformed observations satisfy the Gauss–Markov assumptions. The FGLS procedure for contemporaneously correlated and panel heteroskedastic errors was derived by Parks (1967).

Beck and Katz (1995) showed that this procedure has extremely poor statistical properties unless $T >> N$, which is rare. Thus this method is seldom used any more. Researchers worried about correcting standard errors due to contemporaneously correlated and panel heteroskedastic errors can use "panel corrected standard errors" (PCSEs) in place of the OLS standard errors.

This consists of using the usual formula for the OLS standard errors when the Gauss–Markov assumption that $\Omega = \sigma^2 I$ is violated. The covariance of the OLS estimate of β in this case is

$$(X'X)^{-1} \left(X' \Omega\, X \right) (X'X)^{-1}. \tag{3}$$

Under the assumptions that the errors at different time points are independent, Ω is a block diagonal matrix, with the blocks down the diagonal being $N \times N$ matrices of the contemporaneous covariances of the errors (and diagonal terms being the unit specific variances). Let $\mathbf{V}$ be this matrix. $\mathbf{V}$ can be estimated using the T replicates of the OLS residuals, $e_{i,t}$ (since the covariance matrix of the errors is assumed to be stable over time). Variances and covariances are estimated in the obvious way (so $\mathbf{V}_{i,j}$ is estimated by $\frac{\sum_{t=1}^{T} e_{i,t} e_{j,t}}{T}$). PCSEs are then the square roots of the diagonal terms of

$$(\mathbf{X}'\mathbf{X})^{-1}\mathbf{X}'\left(\hat{\mathbf{V}}\otimes\mathbf{I}_T\right)\mathbf{X}(\mathbf{X}'\mathbf{X})^{-1} \qquad (4)$$

where $\otimes$ is the Kronecker product. Since the estimate of the $\mathbf{V}$ matrix is based on an average of T replicates, it has good properties for typical TSCS data.

It might appear that this procedure is similar to White's (1982) heteroskedasticity consistent standard errors. But White's procedure is only robust to heteroskedasticity, and does not assume that variances are constant within a unit; it also does not allow for the errors to be contemporaneously correlated. White's procedure also depends heavily on asymptotics, since there is one variance term per observation. With PCSEs there are T observations per estimate, and so as long as T is large the procedure performs well. (The performance of PCSEs is purely a function of T, not N.) Monte Carlo experiments showed that PCSEs are very close to OLS standard errors when the Gauss–Markov assumptions hold, and can be considerably better than OLS standard errors when those assumptions are violated so long as $T > 15$ (Beck and Katz 1995).

4.2 Spatial Insights

PCSEs simply correct the OLS standard errors because the simplifying assumptions of OLS are likely invalid for TSCS data; it clearly would be better to model the process and use that model to improve estimation. Steps along this line can be taken using the ideas of spatial econometrics (Anselin 1988). The FGLS procedure allows for an arbitrary contemporaneous correlation of the errors; by not imposing any structure on these errors an inordinate number of extra parameters must be estimated. Spatial methods allow for a simple parameterization of the correlation of the errors, allowing for better estimation of TSCS data with such errors. This parameterization is known as the "spatially lagged error" model. After examining this, we shall see that an alternative, the "spatial autoregressive" model, may be even more useful.

Spatial methods assume an a priori specified weighting matrix which ties together the errors. Thus it differs from FGLS methods which allow for an arbitrary pattern of correlation of the errors. Of course the spatial methods are only superior if the specified weights are close to being correct. Geographers often assume that geographically nearby units are similar, but any method of weighting can be appropriate. Beck, Gleditsch, and Beardsley (2006) argued that for studies of political economy it is often better to assume that nations are tied together by their level of trade (in proportion to GDP).

Let $\mathbf{W}$ denote the (pre-specified) spatial weighting matrix, which is $NT \times NT$. Letting $w_{i,t,j,s}$ be a typical element of this matrix, the assumption that all error correlations are contemporaneous implies the $w_{i,t,j,s} = 0$ if $t \neq s$. For contemporaneous observations we would have nonzero weights (and by definition $w_{i,t,i,t} = 0$). The weights are then typically normalized to each row sums to one.

The spatially lagged errors model then has

$$y_{i,t} = \mathbf{x}_{i,t}\boldsymbol{\beta} + \epsilon_{i,t} + \lambda \mathbf{W}_{i,t}\boldsymbol{\epsilon}_t \tag{5}$$

where $\mathbf{w}_{i,t}$ corresponds to the row of $\mathbf{W}$ corresponding to unit i and $\boldsymbol{\epsilon}$ is the vector of errors for the other units, both at time t.

Thus there is only one extra parameter, λ, to estimate. Such a model is easy to estimate using standard spatial econometrics packages and usually produces estimates with good properties. If $\lambda = 0$, this reduces to the standard nonspatial linear regression model.

It should be stressed that this setup assumes that the errors are serially independent (perhaps after including some lagged variables in the specification). It also does not allow for panel heteroskedasticity, though this is often not a problem in practice if the dependent variables are suitably measured (say as a proportion of GDP).

The spatial lagged error model assumes that the errors across units are related, but otherwise the observations are independent. Another plausible model is that the dependent variables are linked; if the dependent variable is, say, unemployment, a country will have more unemployment if its trading partners have more unemployment (with weighting matrix as before). If we are willing to assume that these spatial effects occur with a temporal lag, and if there is no remaining serial correlation of the errors, the spatial autoregressive model (also temporally lagged) has

$$y_{i,t} = \mathbf{x}_{i,t}\boldsymbol{\beta} + \gamma \mathbf{W}_{i,t}\mathbf{y}_{t-1} + \epsilon_{i,t} \tag{6}$$

where $\mathbf{y}_{t-1}$ is a vector of the lagged value of y for all the other units. While this spatial autoregressive lag has often been included in specifications based on informal reasoning, it is best to think about this model in the spatial econometrics context. In particular, this model is only easy to estimate if the errors are serially independent (perhaps after inclusion of the temporal lagged $y_{i,t-1}$ in the specification). If the errors are serially independent the model can be estimated by OLS; one simply adjoins to the model the lagged weighted average of the dependent variable for all other units. This simplicity comes from assuming that the spatial lag enters also with a temporal lag. Whether or not this assumption is compelling varies by substantive problem.

5 HETEROGENEOUS UNITS

So far we have assumed a fully pooled model; that is, all units obey the same specification with the same parameter values. There are many ways to allow for unit to unit heterogeneity in equation (1) (or its dynamic counterparts). In keeping with the spirit of TSCS data, we will assume that there is intra-unit homogeneity.

5.1 Fixed Effects

The simplest way to allow for unit heterogeneity is to allow the intercepts to vary by unit, the "fixed effects" model. This has

$$y_{i,t} = \mathbf{x}_{i,t}\boldsymbol{\beta} + f_i + \epsilon_{i,t}. \tag{7}$$

(In this notation there can be no constant term.) This model is easy to estimate by OLS. If the fixed effects are omitted there will be omitted variable bias if the fixed effects both explain y and are correlated with $\mathbf{x}$ (Green, Kim, and Yoon 2001). Researchers should clearly check for the possibility that there are fixed effects by estimating equation (7) and then testing the null hypothesis that all the f_i are equal. This is most easily done via a standard F-test on a model with a constant term and one particular effect dropped, with the null being tested that all the other effects are zero.

The fixed effects model is equivalent to unit centering all observations, so that the only question at issue is whether temporal variation in $\mathbf{x}$ is associated with temporal variation in y; all cross-sectional effects are eliminated by the unit centering. This makes it impossible to estimate the impacts of any variables that do not vary over time; it also becomes almost impossible to estimate the effects of variables that seldom change. This is a serious problem in political economy, where we often care about the impact of institutions, which almost by definition change slowly if at all.

Fortunately it is often the case that well-specified models do not require fixed effects. Ideally one would like to explain the effects by substantive variables, and not simply conclude that Germany grew faster because it was Germany. It will also often be the case that misspecified dynamics may lead to the unnecessary use of fixed effects (Beck and Katz 2001). And it may be better to decide not to include fixed effects if the test of the null of no fixed effects only marginally rejects that null. But where fixed effects are needed in the model, failure to include them can lead to omitted variable bias.

It might appear that random effects would solve the problems caused by fixed effects. Random effects models are similar to equation (7) except the f_i's are seen as draws from a normal distribution. Unfortunately the random effects model assumes that the effects are orthogonal to the independent variables, thus assuming away all the interesting issues which lead to omitted variable bias. While random effect models may be very useful for panel data, they do not deal with the important issues of heterogeneity in TSCS data.

5.2 Assessing Heterogeneity by Cross-validation

A useful tool to examine heterogeneity is cross-validation (leaving out one unit at a time). Cross-validation is a well-known technique for evaluating models by seeing how well they "predict" data that have not already been used to estimate the model

(Stone 1974). Cross-validation can easily be used with TSCS data both to assess models and to see whether some units appear not to pool.

For TSCS data, cross-validation proceeds by estimating the model leaving out one unit, and then using those estimates to "predict" the values of y for the omitted unit. This is done for each unit. Models can then be compared according to the mean squared error of prediction. The idea behind cross-validation is that by examining predictions for data that were not used to estimate the model we can ensure against overfitting. (This becomes more critical as we move to more complicated models with more independent variables or nonlinear functional forms, where it is easier to overfit the data.)

Cross-validation (leaving out a unit at a time) can not only be used to compare models, but can also be used to see if one (or a few) units seem to follow a different pattern than do the bulk of other units. While it is clearly bad practice to simply exclude from data-sets units that fit the model less well, it does make sense to assess whether all units belong in the model. Thus it might make sense to exclude a unit from the analysis if it has *both* large cross-validation prediction errors and might be thought different from other units on some other grounds. Thus, for example, even if Turkey were included in a European Union data-set (at some time in the future), we might suspect that it should not be included in a model of the political economy of advanced democracies. It will often be the case in studies of comparative politics that we know a lot more about the units than just the values of the variables.

Cross-validation is useful for finding whether one or a small number of units should be excluded from the regression. We may also suspect that different units follow different regimes. Thus the older West European countries may not pool with the newer East European members of the European Union. This hunch could be tested by creating an East European dummy variable and then interacting it with all the independent variables with a standard F-test used to assess whether the interaction terms substantially improve goodness of fit. It also might be the case that an East European dummy variable would do as well as the various country fixed effects. The fact that some data-collection organization collects data on a set of units does not mean that those units are sufficiently homogeneous to allow for estimation of the fully pooled model.

5.3 Random Coefficient Models

It is, of course, possible to estimate a model for each unit separately, with

$$y_{i,t} = \mathbf{x}_{i,t}\boldsymbol{\beta}_i + \epsilon_{i,t} \tag{8}$$

(with the appropriate additions for dynamics). If T is large enough it is not ridiculous to estimate N separate time series (and time-series analysis on single countries surely has a long tradition). But T will typically not be large enough for unit time-series analyses to be sensible. (Beck and Katz 2007 found with simulated data that the fully pooled model gives better estimates of the unit β_i even when there is heterogeneity when $T < 30$.) And even for larger T's, separate time-series analyses on each country make it difficult to claim that one is doing comparative politics.

A very nice compromise is the "random coefficients model" (RCM). This allows for unit heterogeneity, but also assumes that the various unit-level coefficients are draws from a common (normal) distribution. Thus the RCM adjoins to equation (8)

$$\beta_i \sim N(\beta, \Gamma) \tag{9}$$

where Γ is a matrix of variance and covariance terms to be estimated. Γ indicates the degree of heterogeneity of the unit parameters ($\Gamma = 0$ indicates perfect homogeneity). An important (and restrictive) assumption is that the stochastic process which generates the β_i is independent of the error process, and is also uncorrelated with the vector of independent variables, although of course this assumption is less restrictive than the assumption of complete homogeneity. The RCM has a venerable heritage, going back at least to Smith (1973); Western (1998) first discussed this model in the context of comparative politics.

While this model is often estimated by Bayesian methods, it is also feasible to estimate it via standard maximum likelihood (Pinheiro and Bates 2000). While until recently it was hard for researchers to estimate the RCM, innovations in commonly used software packages no longer allow for this excuse. Beck and Katz (2007) found that the RCM gave superior estimates of the overall β, whether or not there was significant unit heterogeneity, and also provided good estimates of the unit β_i. These estimates of the β_i are an average of the fully pooled and the separate unit by unit estimates, where the amount of averaging is a function of both how disparate the unit by unit estimates are and the confidence we have in those estimates (their standard errors). Thus the RCM estimates of the β_i "shrink" the unit by unit estimates back toward the pooled estimate, with the degree of shrinkage chosen empirically; alternatively we can talk of improving the low-precision unit by unit estimates by allowing them to "borrow strength" from the other estimates.

Since we would expect there to be some amount of unit heterogeneity, analysts should routinely estimate the RCM. They may then decide there is enough homogeneity to go back to the fully pooled model. Since the RCM provides good estimates of the unit β_i, the method can also be used to see whether the parameters for some unit or units are sufficiently different from the other units that we should not pool the two types of observations.

The RCM is a special case of the multilevel model; yearly data are nested inside countries. Unlike the more general data, the RCM assumes that the lower-level data are connected by being yearly observations (rather than, say, being survey respondents nested by country). Thus one can use all the various dynamic specifications we have discussed as well as the various multilevel methods in analyzing the RCM.

One especially nice feature of the RCM (inherited from the multilevel model) is that we can model the variation of the unit coefficients as a function of unit-level variables. Thus the marginal effect of some $x_{i,t}$ on $y_{i,t}$ can be made dependent on some unit level z_i. In particular, we can make equation (9) more general by

$$\beta_i = \alpha + z_i \kappa + \mu_i \tag{10}$$

where the μ are drawn from k-variate normal distribution. The ability to model the relationship between independent and dependent variables as conditional on unit-level covariates makes the RCM an extremely powerful tool of comparative analysis. It allows us to move from saying that the effect of some variable is different in France and Germany to this impact differs because of some institutional difference between the two nations.

6 BINARY DEPENDENT VARIABLES

So far we have restricted ourselves to models with a continuous dependent variable. This works well in the study of comparative political economy, where the dependent variable is usually an economic policy or outcome. But TSCS data are also common in the study of international relations (Maoz and Russett 1993); here the dependent variable is often dichotomous, with the most common example being whether or not a pair of nations are in conflict in any given year.[4]

The most common data setup in the study of international relations is the "dyad-year" design. This is a form of TSCS data, but the units are pairs of actors (usually pairs of nations) observed over time (usually annually). The dependent variable may be continuous (as in the study of international trade) or binary (as in the study of conflict). The dyads may either be directed or undirected dyads; with directed dyads the dependent variable is what is sent to a receiver (so AB and BA are different dyads) whereas with undirected dyads there is no distinction between sender and receiver (so the dyad AB is the same as the dyad BA).

Dyad-year data present an additional complication over and above standard TSCS data: The dyads AB and AC are not likely to be fully independent. Beck, Gleditsch, and Beardsley (2006) discussed how to use spatial econometric methods to deal with this issue in the context of trade. One simply allows for a spatially lagged error, where

---

[4] One could also have a dependent variable that is ordered or multichotomous. Very little is known about how to estimate such a model, although we shall see below that an event history approach allows researchers to study multichotomous dependent variables. While limited dependent variable panel models are a very active research topic (Wooldridge 2002), there is little corresponding research for TSCS data. Researchers with limited dependent variable TSCS data should surely use Huber's (1967) robust ("sandwich") standard errors, but that is only a band-aid. Beck et al. (2001) discuss some very complicated latent variable approaches, but these are new and unproven. I do not deal further with these complications here. It is also possible to analyze models where the dependent variable is an event count (Cameron and Trivedi 1998), and recent software innovations make estimation of TSCS models with a count dependent variable easier.

dyads containing an overlapping member are considered to be adjacent and others are considered to be nonadjacent. The problem is much more complicated for a binary dependent variable.

Binary TSCS (BTSCS) data present other problems which are likely to be more important. In particular, the lack of a simple residual makes it harder to model either the time-series or the cross-sectional property of the error process. We can think of BTSCS data as generated by realizations of ones and zeros from underlying latent variable, so

$$y_{i,t}^* = \mathbf{x}_{i,t}\boldsymbol{\beta} + \epsilon_{i,t} \tag{11}$$

$$y_{i,t} = \begin{cases} 1 \text{ if } y_{i,t}^* > 0 \\ 0 \text{ otherwise.} \end{cases} \tag{12}$$

While all would be easy if we observed the latent y^*, we do not. Thus we cannot use the "prediction errors" from a logit[5] analysis of the realized y to make inferences about Ω, the covariance matrix of the *latent* errors.

Poirier and Ruud (1988) showed that "ordinary" probit (that is, standard probit analysis assuming serially independent errors in the latent variable) is consistent in the presence of serially correlated errors; ordinary probit is, however, inefficient and produces incorrect standard errors; the same is true for ordinary logit. Poirier and Ruud showed that the standard errors could be corrected by using a robust covariance matrix. Poirier and Ruud's results are for a single time series, but they also hold for the time-series component of BTSCS data. Beck, Katz, and Tucker (1998) showed that using Huber's (1967) robust standard errors assuming that all observations for a unit are correlated provides reasonably correct assessments of the variability of the ordinary logit standard errors, even though the Huber procedure does not take into account that the error structure in a unit should be that of serial correlation. But we can do much better than simply fix the standard errors.

6.1 Event History Approaches

BTSCS data can be seen as sequences of zeros terminated by a one and sequences of ones terminated by a zero. Thus we either can see the data as yearly binary data or as event history data giving the lengths of sequences of ones and zeros, with time-varying covariates.[6] The latter approach is more informative. In event history analysis our interest is in explaining the lengths of spells; that is, the lengths of sequences of zeros terminated by a one. If we remove from the data-set all the sequences of ones after the first one, we have standard discrete time-duration data. This can be analyzed by standard discrete time methods, with the most common being the discrete time version of the Cox (1975) proportional hazards model.

---

[5] Everything said here also holds for probit or other binary variable "link" functions.

[6] See Box-Steffensmeier and Jones (2004) for a general introduction to event history analysis. The rest of this section assumes some familiarity with event history methods and terminology.

Beck, Katz, and Tucker (1998) showed that logit analysis can be seen as estimating the discrete time yearly hazard of transitioning from a zero to a one (peace to conflict) *if* all years with a conflict after the first are removed from the data. The hazard rate is the rate of transitioning from a zero to a one conditional on not having transitioned previously; it is the elimination of the subsequent one observations that enforces this conditioning. Beck, Katz, and Tucker showed that a logit analysis which added a series of dummy variables marking the year since the last event (that is, the number of preceding zeros) is completely analogous to the discrete time Cox model. The years since the last event dummies correspond to the integral over a year of the Cox baseline hazard; since the baseline hazards are unspecified, no information is lost in treating their yearly integrals as a dummy variable.[7] These temporal dummies account, in the logit analysis, for what is known in the event history world as duration dependence; that is, the chance of a spell terminating varies with the length of that spell.

The tie between event history analysis and the yearly logits is seen by noting that the Cox proportion hazards model assumes that the instantaneous hazard rate (the rate at which transitions from zero to one occur in a small time interval given no prior transition) has the form

$$h_i(t) = h_0(t)e^{x_{i,t}\beta} \tag{13}$$

where i refers to units, t refers to continuous time, and $h_0(t)$ is an unspecified baseline hazard function.

We only observe whether or not a transition occurred between time $t - 1$ and t (assuming annual data) and are interested in the probability of a transition in year t, $P(y_{i,t} = 1)$. Assuming no prior transitions, and standard event history formulae, we get

$$P(y_{i,t} = 1) = 1 - \exp(-\int_{t-1}^{t} h_i(\tau)d\tau) \tag{14a}$$

$$= 1 - \exp(-\int_{t-1}^{t} e^{x_{i,t}\beta}h_0(\tau)d\tau) \tag{14b}$$

$$= 1 - \exp(-e^{x_{i,t}\beta}\int_{t-1}^{t} h_0(\tau)d\tau) \tag{14c}$$

Since the baseline hazard is unspecified, we can just treat the integral of the baseline hazard as an unknown constant. Defining

$$a_t = \int_{t-1}^{t} h_0(\tau)d\tau \text{ and} \tag{15}$$

$$\kappa_t = \log(a_t) \tag{16}$$

---

[7] Beck, Katz, and Tucker (1998) consider some refinements of this procedure to enforce smoothness, but all the basics are captured with the dummy variable approach. This section is a condensation of that article which should be consulted for more details.

we then have

$$P(y_{i,t} = 1) = 1 - \exp\left(-e^{x_{i,t}\beta}a_t\right) \tag{17a}$$

$$= 1 - \exp\left(-e^{x_{i,t}\beta+\kappa_t}\right). \tag{17b}$$

This is exactly a binary dependent variable model with a cloglog "link." Thus the Cox proportional hazard in continuous time is *exactly* a binary dependent variable with dummy variables marking the length of the spell and a cloglog link. Since there is seldom reason to prefer one binary link function to another, logit (or probit) should be an adequate substitute for the cloglog model for researchers who are more familiar with logit and probit.

This method allows analysts to assess the impact of the independent variables on either the length of spells of zeros or on the probability of transitioning from a zero to a one given that a unit had not previously transitioned. One might then estimate a completely different model for the lengths of spells of ones or the probability of transitioning from a one to a zero given that a unit had not previously transitioned in this manner. Thus we have one model that determines why dyads remain at peace and another for lengths of conflict; there is no reason those models should be the same. Note that ordinary logit assumes that the same model determines the transition from zero to one and from one to one since in ordinary logit the probability of observing a one is not conditional on whether a unit was previously a one or a zero.

Thinking of BTSCS data as event history data has other advantages. It forces us to think about both left and right censoring. Left censoring is the problem caused by not knowing that the first year of a data-set was the first year of a spell of zeros. There is no easy solution here but at least the event history approach makes the problem clear. Right censoring occurs when a unit ends with a spell of zeros. This causes no problems since a right censored observation is just marked with a string of zeros that do not terminate with a one.

The event history approach also helps deal with dyads that transition several times from zero to one and then back to zero again. In event history analysis this is called repeated spells. The one thing we are sure of is that second spells are usually different from first spells, and so on. Ordinary logit assumes that all spells are identical. The event history approach would lead, at a minimum, to using as an explanatory variable the number of previous transitions from zero to one that a unit has experienced.

Since BTSCS and grouped event history data are identical, it is also possible to use event history methods rather than binary data methods when the former allow for simpler solutions to hard problems. Thus, for example, Jones and Branton (2005) use the Cox proportional hazard model rather than a logit-based method to deal with issues of repeated events and "competing risks" (where a spell can end in one of several ways) in a study of policy innovation in the American states. Note that since competing risk data look exactly like unordered multichotomous data, event history methods can enable researchers to move beyond dichotomous to multichotomous dependent variables.

6.2 Markov Transition Models

The event history approach is very similar to the Markov transition model (Amemiya 1985; Ware, Lipsitz, and Speizer 1988); this approach is best known in political science through the work of Przeworski et al. (2000). Beck et al. (2001) show the similarity of the two approaches. The Markov transition model assumes that the probability of observing a one in the current year is a function of covariates and whether or not a one was observed in the prior year; as in the event history approach there is a different model for transitioning from zero to one and for one remaining one (which is just one minus the probability of a transition from one to zero).

The Markov transition model can be written as:

$$P(y_{i,t} = 1) = \text{logit}(\mathbf{x}_{i,t}\boldsymbol{\beta} + \mathbf{x}_{i,t}y_{i,t-1}\boldsymbol{\gamma}). \tag{18}$$

β is the impact of the independent variables when the prior state of y was zero, while $\beta + \Gamma$ is the similar impact when the prior state of y was one. If $\gamma = 0$ then the probability of being a one currently does not depend on the prior state of y. In that case one can model $P(y_{i,t} = 1)$ without reference to the lagged $y_{i,t-1}$ and so ordinary logit would be appropriate. Note that this is a testable hypothesis, not a necessary assumption.

As with the event history approach, there is no assumption that transitions to one from zero are modeled the same way as transitions from one to zero. Unlike the event history approach, the transition model assumes duration independence and so the transition model is a special case of the event history model. The hypothesis that there is no duration dependence can be tested by an F-test on the null hypothesis that all the spell time dummy variables are zero. But by allowing the transitions from zero to one to differ from the reverse transitions makes the Markov transition model a much more plausible alternative than ordinary logit.

7 CONCLUSION

TSCS (and BTSCS) data present many interesting complications. As always we can treat these complications as an estimation nuisance or as interesting substantive issues to be modeled. The latter approach is usually preferable.

The best way to think about modeling single time series is the best way to think about modeling the time-series component of TSCS data. For the last decade or so a good methodology for time-series data has been well known (based on the autoregressive distributed lag model) and there is no reason not to use that methodology for stationary TSCS data. The data may appear to have unit roots, and at that point analysts should surely consider using the methods associated with analyzing nonstationary data.

On the cross-sectional side the best approach is one based on thinking about cross-sectional issues like a spatial econometrician. Economies are linked, innovations diffuse. These are things to be modeled, not econometric nuisances to be eliminated. There are better and worse ways to eliminate nuisances, but those methods should not be the first choice.

Allowing for parameter heterogeneity is now easy to do and makes much sense. The random coefficient model seems to perform very well and the idea behind it is very attractive. Explaining difference in the effect of the independent variables from unit to unit by unit-level variables is also a very attractive feature of this model. There is no reason not to start with the random coefficient model, and then test for whether there is nontrivial heterogeneity.

Turning to BTSCS data, the key insight is to think about such data as event history data. At that point either the Markov transition model or the logit analysis with the dummy variables counting spell length seem attractive. Thinking about BTSCS data as event history data also leads to a variety of insights that come less easily to those who simply think of this as binary dependent variable data. What is most critical is to realize that understanding the causes of the lengths of sequences of zeros is very different from understanding the length of sequences of ones.

In all cases the critical insight is that TSCS and BTSCS data present a series of interesting issues that must be carefully considered, and not a standard set of nuisances that can be dealt with by a command in some statistical package. There is never a statistical panacea, and there is no such panacea for TSCS or BTSCS data.

REFERENCES

ADOLPH, C., BUTLER, D. M., and WILSON, S. E. 2005. Which time-series cross-section estimator should I use now? Guidance from Monte Carlo experiments. Presented at the Annual Meeting of the American Political Science Association, Washington, DC.

ALVAREZ, R. M., GARRETT, G., and LANGE, P. 1991. Government partisanship, labor organization and macroeconomic performance. *American Political Science Review*, 85: 539–56.

AMEMIYA, T. 1985. *Advanced Econometrics*. Cambridge, Mass.: Harvard University Press.

ANSELIN, L. 1988. *Spatial Econometrics: Methods and Models*. Boston: Kluwer Academic.

BECK, N., EPSTEIN, D., JACKMAN, S., and O'HALLORAN, S. 2001. Alternative models of dynamics in binary time-series–cross-section models: the example of state failure. Presented at the Annual Meeting of the Society for Political Methodology, Emory University.

——GLEDITSCH, K. S., and BEARDSLEY, K. 2006. Space is more than geography: using spatial econometrics in the study of political economy. *International Studies Quarterly*, 50: 27–44.

——and KATZ, J. N. 1995. What to do (and not to do) with time-series cross-section data. *American Political Science Review*, 89: 634–47.

————2001. Throwing out the baby with the bath water: a comment on Green, Kim and Yoon. *International Organization*, 55: 487–95.

————2004. Time series cross section issues: dynamics Presented at the Annual Meeting of the Society for Political Methodology, Stanford University.

BECK, N., and KATZ, J. N. 2007. Random coefficient models for time-series–cross-section data: Monte Carlo experiments. *Political Analysis*, 15: 182–95.

————— and TUCKER, R. 1998. Taking time seriously: time-series–cross-section analysis with a binary dependent variable. *American Journal of Political Science*, 42: 1260–88.

BOX-STEFFENSMEIER, J. M., and JONES, B. S. 2004. *Event History Modeling: A Guide for Political Scientists*. New York: Cambridge University Press.

CAMERON, A. C., and TRIVEDI, P. K. 1998. *Regression Analysis of Count Data*. New York: Cambridge University Press.

CAMERON, D. 1978. The expansion of the public economy: a comparative analysis. *American Political Science Review*, 72: 1243–61.

COX, D. R. 1975. Partial likelihood. *Biometrika*, 62: 269–76.

DAVIDSON, J., HENDRY, D., SRBA, F., and YEO, S. 1978. Econometric modelling of the aggregate time-series relationship between consumers' expenditures and income in the United Kingdom. *Economic Journal*, 88: 661–92.

ENGLE, R., and GRANGER, C. W. J. 1987. Co-integration and error correction: representation, estimation and testing. *Econometrica*, 55: 251–76.

GARRETT, G. 1998. *Partisan Politics in the Global Economy*. New York: Cambridge University Press.

GREEN, D., KIM, S. Y., and YOON, D. 2001. Dirty pool. *International Organization*, 55: 441–68.

HAMILTON, J. 1994. *Time Series Analysis*. Princeton, NJ: Princeton University Press.

HENDRY, D., and MIZON, G. 1978. Serial correlation as a convenient simplification, not a nuisance: a comment on a study of the demand for money by the Bank of England. *Economic Journal*, 88: 549–63.

———— PAGAN, A., and SARGAN, J. D. 1984. Dynamic specification. Ch. 18 in *Handbook of Econometrics*, vol. ii, ed. Z. Griliches and M. Intriligator. Amsterdam: North-Holland.

HSIAO, C. 2003. *Analysis of Panel Data*, 2nd edn. New York: Cambridge University Press.

HUBER, P. J. 1967. The behavior of maximum likelihood estimates under non-standard conditions. Pp. 221–33 in *Proceedings of the Fifth Annual Berkeley Symposium on Mathematical Statistics and Probability*, vol. i, ed. L. M. LeCam and J. Neyman. Berkeley: University of California Press.

IM, K. S., PESARAN, M. H., and SHIN, Y. 2003. Testing for unit roots in heterogeneous panels. *Journal of Econometrics*, 115: 53–74.

JONES, B. S., and BRANTON, R. P. 2005. Beyond logit and probit: Cox duration models of single, repeating and competing events for state policy adoption. *State Politics and Policy Quarterly*, 5: 420–43.

KING, G., HONAKER, J., JOSEPH, A., and SCHEVE, K. 2001. Analyzing incomplete political science data: an alternative algorithm for multiple imputation. *American Political Science Review*, 95: 49–69.

LANGE, P., and GARRETT, G. 1985. The politics of growth: strategic interaction and economic performance in the advanced industrial democracies, 1974–1980. *Journal of Politics*, 47: 792–827.

MAOZ, Z., and RUSSETT, B. M. 1993. Normative and structural causes of democratic peace, 1946–1986. *American Political Science Review*, 87: 639–56.

PARKS, R. 1967. Efficient estimation of a system of regression equations when disturbances are both serially and contemporaneously correlated. *Journal of the American Statistical Association*, 62: 500–9.

PINHEIRO, J. C., and BATES, D. M. 2000. *Mixed Effects Models in S and S-Plus*. New York: Springer.

POIRIER, D. J., and RUUD, P. A. 1988. Probit with dependent observations. *Review of Economic Studies*, 55: 593–614.

PRZEWORSKI, A., ALVAREZ, M., CHEIBUB, J. A., and LIMONGI, F. 2000. *Democracy and Development: Political Regimes and Economic Well-being in the World, 1950-1990*. Cambridge: Cambridge University Press.

SMITH, A. F. M. 1973. A general Bayesian linear model. *Journal of the Royal Statistical Society, Series B*, 35: 67–75.

STIMSON, J. 1985. Regression in space and time: a statistical essay. *American Journal of Political Science*, 29: 914–47.

STONE, M. 1974. Crossvalidatory choice and assessment of statistical prediction. *Journal of the Royal Statistical Society, Series B*, 36: 111–33.

WARE, J. H., LIPSITZ, S., and SPEIZER, F. E. 1988. Issues in the analysis of repeated categorical outcomes. *Statistics in Medicine*, 7: 95–107.

WESTERN, B. 1998. Causal heterogeneity in comparative research: a Bayesian hierarchical modelling approach. *American Journal of Political Science*, 42: 1233–59.

WHITE, H. 1982. Maximum likelihood estimation of misspecified models. *Econometrica*, 50: 1–25.

WOOLDRIDGE, J. M. 2002. *Econometric Analysis of Cross Section and Panel Data*. Cambridge, Mass.: MIT Press.

C H A P T E R   21

....

BAYESIAN ANALYSIS

....

A N D R E W   D .   M A R T I N

1 INTRODUCTION

....

SINCE the early 1990s, Bayesian statistics and Markov Chain Monte Carlo (MCMC) methods have become increasingly used in political science research. While the Bayesian approach enjoyed philosophical cachet up until that point, it was impractical (if not impossible) for applied work. This changed with the onset of MCMC methods, which allowed researchers to use simulation to fit otherwise intractable models. This chapter begins with an introduction to the Bayesian approach for statistical inference, contrasting it with more conventional approaches. I then introduce the Monte Carlo principle and review commonly used MCMC methods. This is followed by a *practical* justification for the use of Bayesian methods in the social sciences, and a number of examples from the literature where Bayesian methods have proven useful. The chapter concludes with a review of modern software for Bayesian inference, and a discussion of the future of Bayesian methods in political science.

This research is supported by the National Science Foundation Methodology, Measurement, and Statistics Section, Grant SES-03-50646. I acknowledge Jong Hee Park, Kyle Saunders, and seminar participants at the University of South Carolina and the University of California, Davis, for their constructive comments about this chapter. R code to replicate the figures will be made available on the author's website <http://adm.wustl.edu>.

2 THE BAYESIAN APPROACH

The Bayesian approach to statistical inference begins at the same place as more conventional approaches: a probability model (also known as a data-generating process). A probability model relates observed data y to a set of unknown parameters θ, with the possible inclusion of fixed, known covariates x. Our data are usually a collection of observations indexed $i = 1, \ldots, n$: $y = \{y_1, y_2, \ldots, y_n\}$. The observed data need not be scalars; in fact, they can be anything supported by the probability model, including vectors and matrices. The probability model has k parameters, which are represented $\theta = (\theta_1, \theta_2, \ldots, \theta_k)$. The covariates, or independent variables, are typically a collection of column vectors: $x = \{x_1, x_2, \ldots, x_n\}$. The probability model can be written $f(y|\theta, x)$, or suppressing the conditioning on the covariates, $f(y|\theta)$. It is important to stress the importance of choosing appropriate probability models. While canonical models exist for certain types of dependent variables, the choice of model is rarely innocuous, and is thus something that should be tested for adequacy.

The linear regression model is, perhaps, the most commonly used probability model in political science. Our dependent variable $y = \{y_1, y_2, \ldots, y_n\}$ is a collection of scalars with domain $y_i \in \mathbb{R}$. Our independent variables can be represented as a collection of column vectors $x = \{x_1, x_2, \ldots, x_n\}$, each of dimension $(K \times 1)$. We typically assume that the conditional distribution of y_i given x_i is normal:

$$y_i | \beta, \sigma^2, x_i \overset{iid}{\sim} \mathcal{N}(x_i'\beta, \sigma^2). \tag{1}$$

This distributional assumption, along with an assumption that the observations are independent, yields a probability model with two parameters: $\theta = \{\beta, \sigma^2\}$. β is a $(K \times 1)$ vector that contains the intercept and slope parameters; σ^2 is the the conditional error variance. The probability model for the linear regression model is thus

$$f(y|\beta, \sigma^2) = \prod_{i=1}^{n} \phi\left(\frac{y_i - x_i'\beta}{\sigma}\right) = \prod_{i=1}^{n} \frac{1}{\sigma\sqrt{2\pi}} \exp\left[-\frac{1}{2\sigma^2}(y_i - x_i'\beta)^2\right]. \tag{2}$$

I will use this probability model as an illustration throughout this chapter.

The purpose of statistical inference is to learn about parameters that characterize the data-generating process given observed data. In the conventional, frequentist approach to statistical inference, one assumes that the parameters are fixed, unknown quantities, and that the observed data y are a single realization of a repeatable process, and can thus be treated as random variables. The goal of the frequentist approach is to produce estimates of these unknown parameters. These estimates are denoted $\hat{\theta}$. The most common way to obtain these estimates is by the method of maximum likelihood (for an introduction to this method for political scientists, see King 1989). This method uses the same probability model, but treats it as a function of the fixed, unknown parameters. For our regression example:

$$\mathscr{L}(\beta, \sigma^2 | \mathbf{y}) \propto f(\mathbf{y} | \beta, \sigma^2) = \prod_{i=1}^{n} \phi \left(\frac{y_i - \mathbf{x}_i' \beta}{\sigma} \right). \tag{3}$$

One maximizes the likelihood function $\mathscr{L}(\cdot)$ with respect the parameters to obtain the maximum likelihood estimates; i.e. the parameter values most likely to have produced the observed data. To perform inference about the parameters, the frequentist recognizes that the estimated parameters $\hat{\theta}$ result from a single sample, and uses the sampling distribution to compute standard errors, perform hypothesis tests, construct confidence intervals, and the like.

When performing Bayesian inference, the foundational assumptions are quite different. The unknown parameters θ are treated as random variables, while the observed data $\mathbf{y}$ are treated as fixed, known quantities. (Both the Bayesian and frequentist approach treat the covariates $\mathbf{x}$ as fixed, known quantities.) These assumptions are much more intuitive; the *unobservable* parameters are treated probabilistically, while the *observed* data are treated deterministically. Indeed, the quantity of interest is the distribution of the parameter θ after having observed the data $\mathbf{y}$. This *posterior distribution* can be written $f(\theta | \mathbf{y})$, and can be computed using Bayes's Theorem:

$$f(\theta | \mathbf{y}) = \frac{f(\mathbf{y} | \theta) f(\theta)}{f(\mathbf{y})}. \tag{4}$$

The posterior distribution is the conditional distribution of the parameters after having observed the data (as opposed to the prior, which is that distribution before having observed the data). The posterior is a formal, probabilistic statement about likely parameter values after observing the data. Bayes's Theorem follows directly from the axioms of probability theory, and is used to relate the conditional distributions of two variables.

One of the three quantities on the right-hand side of equation (4) is familiar: $f(\mathbf{y} | \theta)$ is the likelihood function dictated by the probability model. (The likelihood function plays a crucial role in both frequentist and Bayesian approaches to data analysis; what is done with the likelihood function is what differs between the two approaches.) The second expression in the numerator $f(\theta)$ is called the *prior distribution*. This distribution contains all *ex ante* information about the parameter values available to the researcher before observing the data. Often researchers use noninformative (or minimally informative parameters) such that the amount of prior information included in the analysis is small. The denominator of equation (4) contains the prior predictive distribution:

$$f(\mathbf{y}) = \int_{\theta} f(\mathbf{y} | \theta) f(\theta) d\theta. \tag{5}$$

While this quantity is useful in some settings, such as model comparison, most of the time researchers work up to a constant of proportionality, $f(\theta | \mathbf{y}) \propto f(\mathbf{y} | \theta) f(\theta)$.

The posterior distribution, in essence, translates the likelihood function into a proper probability distribution over the unknown parameters, which can be summarized just as any probability distribution; by computing expected values, standard deviations, quantiles, and the like. What makes this possible is the formal inclusion of prior information in the analysis. For accessible introductions to Bayesian methods see the textbooks by Gill (2002) and Gelman et al. (2004), or the expository articles by Jackman (2000; 2004).

To perform Bayesian inference for the linear regression model, we need to include prior information about our two parameters. These priors can take any form, and are completely at the discretion of the analyst. For the sake of illustration, suppose that β and σ^2 are a priori independent, with the prior information about β encoded in a multivariate normal distribution $\beta \sim \mathcal{N}_K(\mathbf{b}_0, \mathbf{B}_0^{-1})$, and prior information about the inverse of the conditional error variance in a Gamma distribution $\sigma^{-2} \sim \mathcal{G}amma(c_0/2, d_0/2)$. For any application, the analyst would choose values of the hyperparameters $\mathbf{b}_0, \mathbf{B}_0, c_0/2$, and $d_0/2$ that characterize the prior distribution. These priors result in a posterior distribution for the linear regression model:

$$f(\beta, \sigma^2|\mathbf{y}) \propto \prod_{i=1}^{n} \frac{1}{\sigma\sqrt{2\pi}} \exp\left[-\frac{1}{2\sigma^2}(y_i - \mathbf{x}_i'\beta)^2\right] \times f(\beta)f(\sigma^{-2}) \qquad (6)$$

where $f(\beta)$ is the multivariate normal density, and $f(\sigma^{-2})$ is a Gamma density. Getting from a probability model to the posterior distribution is an exercise in taking a probability model, deriving the likelihood function, and positing probabilistic prior beliefs.

So why have Bayesian statistics not been widely used in political science until very recently? Writing down a posterior distribution is a straightforward algebraic exercise, but *summarizing* the distribution is far more complicated. To compute something as simple as the posterior expected value requires integrating the posterior distribution which, except for the most trivial of models, is analytically impossible. We thus require computation methods to summarize posterior distributions, which leads us to simulation methods.

3 MODEL FITTING VIA SIMULATION

Analytically summarizing posterior distributions is typically impossible. Over the last twenty years, Bayesian statisticians have harnessed the Monte Carlo method (Metropolis and Ulam 1949) to perform this summarization numerically. While these methods can be employed to study any distribution, the discussion here will focus solely on Monte Carlo methods commonly used in Bayesian statistics. We are interested in learning about the posterior distribution, $f(\theta|\mathbf{y})$, which I will call the *target* distribution because it is the distribution from which we intend to simulate. (There are other distributions we might be interested in simulating from, including the posterior and prior predictive distributions.) The Monte Carlo method is based on a simple idea: One can learn anything about a target distribution by repeatedly drawing from it and empirically summarizing those draws. For example, we might be interested in computing the posterior expected value, which can be done analytically by computing a high-dimensional integral:

$$E(\theta|\mathbf{y}) = \int_{\Theta} \theta f(\theta|\mathbf{y}) d\theta. \tag{7}$$

If we were able to produce a random sequence of G draws $\theta^{(1)}, \theta^{(2)}, \ldots, \theta^{(G)}$ from $f(\theta|\mathbf{y})$, we could approximate the posterior expected value by taking the average of these draws:

$$E(\theta|\mathbf{y}) = \int_{\Theta} \theta f(\theta|\mathbf{y}) d\theta \approx \frac{1}{G} \sum_{g=1}^{G} \theta^{(g)}.$$

The precision of the estimate depends solely on the quality of the algorithm employed, and the number of draws taken from the target distribution (which is only limited by the speed of one's computer and one's patience). Similar methods can be used to compute the posterior standard deviation or quantiles, probabilities that parameters take particular values, and other quantities of interest. What all of these methods have in common is that they serve to compute high-dimensional integrals using simulation. A great deal of work in numerical analysis is devoted to understanding the properties of algorithms; for such a discussion of commonly used methods in Bayesian statistics, see Tierney (1994).

To use the Monte Carlo method to summarize posterior distributions, it is necessary to have algorithms that are well suited to producing draws from commonly found target distributions. Two algorithms—the Gibbs sampling and Metropolis–Hastings algorithms—have proven to be very useful for applied Bayesian work. Both of these algorithms are *Markov Chain* Monte Carlo methods, which means that the sequence of draws $\theta^{(1)}, \theta^{(2)}, \ldots, \theta^{(G)}$ are dependent; each draw $\theta^{(g+1)}$ depends only on the previous draw $\theta^{(g)}$. The sequence of draws thus forms a Markov chain. Algorithms are constructed such that the Markov Chain converges to the target density (its steady state) regardless of the starting values.

The Gibbs sampling algorithm (Geman and Geman 1984; Gelfand and Smith 1990) uses a sequence of draws from conditional distributions to characterize the joint target distribution. Suppose that our parameter vector θ has three components, making our target distribution $f(\theta_1, \theta_2, \theta_3|\mathbf{y})$. To use the Gibbs sampler, one begins by choosing starting values $\theta_2^{(0)}$ and $\theta_3^{(0)}$ (starting values are usually chosen near the posterior mode or the maximum likelihood estimates). One then repeats, for $g = 1, \ldots, G$ iterations (making sure to store the sequence of draws at each iteration):

Draw $\theta_1^{(g)}$ from $f(\theta_1|\theta_2^{(g-1)}, \theta_3^{(g-1)}, \mathbf{y})$

Draw $\theta_2^{(g)}$ from $f(\theta_2|\theta_1^{(g)}, \theta_3^{(g-1)}, \mathbf{y})$

Draw $\theta_3^{(g)}$ from $f(\theta_3|\theta_1^{(g)}, \theta_2^{(g)}, \mathbf{y})$.

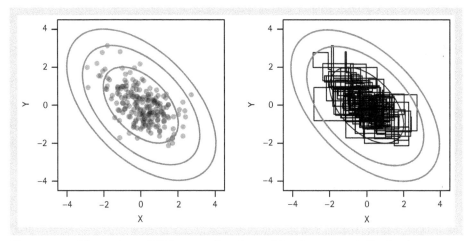

Fig. 21.1. An illustration of Gibbs sampling from a bivariate normal distribution

Note: The target distribution is represented by the grey contour lines. Each cell depicts 200 draws after 100 burn-in iterations, which are discarded. The left-hand cell depicts the individual draws; the right-hand cell shows the trajectory of the sampler.

Since we are always conditioning on past draws, the resultant sequence results in a Markov Chain. When computing Monte Carlo estimates of quantities of interest, like the posterior mean, one discards the first set of "burn-in" iterations to ensure the chain has reached steady state. For the posterior distribution of many common models, these conditional distributions take known forms; e.g. multivariate normal, truncated normal, Gamma, etc. So, while the joint posterior distribution is difficult to simulate from directly, it is easy to simulate from these conditionals.

To illustrate the Gibbs sampling algorithm in practice, Figure 21.1 shows sampling from a bivariate normal distribution $f(X, Y)$, where both X and Y have mean 0 and variance 1, and $\text{cov}(X, Y) = -0.5$. The sampler iteratively draws $Y|X$ and then $X|Y$ from the conditional distributions, each of which take the following form for this example: $f(Y|X) = \mathcal{N}(-0.5X, 0.75)$. What is apparent in Figure 21.1 is that the sampler seems to be sampling from the proper target distribution. The trajectory of the sampler takes a city block pattern because X and Y are updated sequentially. See Casella and George (1992) for an accessible introduction to Gibbs sampling.

The second algorithm that enjoys common use in applied Bayesian statistics is the Metropolis–Hastings algorithm, first introduced by Metropolis et al. (1953) and generalized by Hastings (1979). Chib and Greenberg (1995) provide an accessible introduction to this algorithm. The algorithm has many applications beyond Bayesian statistics; it is commonly used for all sorts of numerical integration and optimization. (It is also the case that the Gibbs sampling algorithm is a special case of the Metropolis–Hastings algorithm.) To simulate from our target distribution $f(\boldsymbol{\theta}|\mathbf{y})$, we again start with sensible starting values: $\theta^{(0)}$. For each iteration of the simulation $g = 1, \ldots, G$, we draw a proposal θ^* from a known proposal distribution $p_g(\theta^*|\theta^{(g-1)})$. One chooses a proposal distribution from which it is easy to sample,

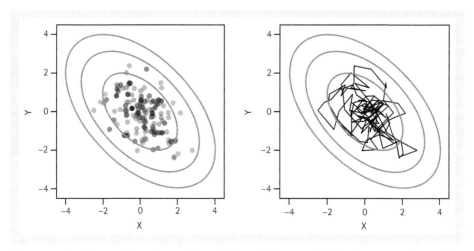

Fig. 21.2. An illustration of an ill-conditioned Metropolis–Hastings sampler with a uniform random walk proposal from a bivariate normal distribution

Note: The target distribution is represented by the grey contour lines. Each cell depicts 200 draws after 100 burn-in iterations, which are discarded. The left-hand cell depicts the individual draws; the right-hand cell shows the trajectory of the sampler.

such as a uniform distribution over a particular region, or a multivariate normal or multivariate-t, centered at the current location of the chain, the posterior mode, or perhaps elsewhere. It is important to choose a proposal distribution such that the chain "mixes well;" i.e. adequately explores the posterior distribution. The convergence diagnostics, discussed below, can be used to determine how well the chain is mixing. For each iteration, we set

$$\theta^{(g)} = \begin{cases} \theta^* & \text{with probability } a^* \\ \theta^{(g-1)} & \text{with probability } (1 - a^*). \end{cases}$$

With a^* defined:

$$a^* = \min\left\{ \frac{f(\theta^*|\mathbf{y})}{f(\theta^{(g-1)}|\mathbf{y})} \frac{p_g(\theta^{(g-1)}|\theta^*)}{p_g(\theta^*|\theta^{(g-1)})}, 1 \right\}.$$

Unlike the Gibbs sampling algorithm, when each move is automatically accepted, one accepts the proposal distribution probabilistically, sometimes moving to a value with a higher density value, sometimes moving to one with a lower density value. Just as with the Gibbs sampling algorithm, the steady state of the Markov chain characterized by this algorithm is the target distribution, in this case the posterior distribution. Figure 21.2 illustrates sampling from the same bivariate normal distribution using Metropolis–Hastings with a uniform random walk proposal with width of two units. In Figure 21.2 we see that this Metropolis–Hastings sampler traverses the space more more slowly; in fact, 30 percent of the time the sampler does not move at all. The size of the proposal distribution is also somewhat small, which keeps the sampler in certain parts of the distribution longer than a better conditioned sampler.

Without being able to plot the target distribution, which in most applications is of high dimension, it would be difficult, if not impossible, to assess whether the chain is sampling from the target distribution. An important part of any Bayesian analysis is assessing the convergence of the simulation results. *Indeed, no Monte Carlo estimates of posterior density summaries can be trusted unless the chain has reached its steady state.* But just as it is impossible to know, in most circumstances, that a numerical optimizer has reached the global maximum likelihood estimate, so too is it impossible to know for sure whether a Markov Chain Monte Carlo algorithm has converged. However, there are a number of methods that can be used to take output from a MCMC sampler and test whether the sequence of draws is consistent with convergence (see the review pieces by Cowles and Carlin 1995; Brooks and Roberts 1998). Each of these convergence diagnostics is based on one of a number of criteria; some look at the marginal posterior distributions to see if the traceplots are stationary (using a number of different tests). Others compare multiple runs from different starting values and using different random number seeds to determine whether the chains converge in such a way as to make their different starting values irrelevant. It is important to note that finding nonconvergence of any parameter means that the entire chain has not converged, and it needs to be run longer (or reimplemented using a different algorithm). Every analyst should use these diagnostic tools before computing any posterior density summaries or reporting results, and results from these diagnostics should be presented in research papers.

I present in Figure 21.3 the traceplots for both X and Y for the simulation results presented above. For this short-run length of 500 iterations neither of these chains passes the standard battery of tests, but by inspection it is clear that the Gibbs sampler is mixing far better than the Metropolis–Hastings chain. A poor mixing chain traverses slowly through the parameter space, and the traceplots will show a close following pattern, as in the right-hand cells of Figure 21.3. (The reader should not take the point that Gibbs sampling works well and Metropolis-Hastings does not; this is solely a feature of the illustration). All of the standard tests for convergence are implemented in the coda (Plummer et al. 2005) package in the R language (R Development Core Team 2005).

4 Practical Advantages of Bayesian Methods

The Bayesian approach to data analysis requires a different set of assumptions and computational tools than the classical approaches typically used in political science. This section provides a number of *practical* advantages of performing Bayesian inference.

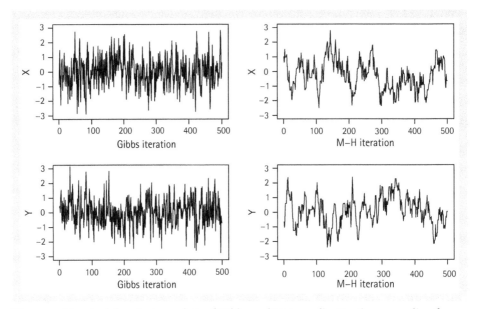

Fig. 21.3. Marginal density traceplots of Gibbs and Metropolis–Hastings sampling from a bivariate normal distribution

Note: These traceplots depict the same simulation results as Figures 21.1 and 21.2, except they depict 500 iterations after 100 burn-in iterations.

4.1 Intuitive Interpretation of Findings

In classical statistics hypothesis tests and confidence intervals are used to perform statisical inference. We choose to reject a null hypothesis when the probability of observing sample data as inconsistent or more inconsistent with a posited null hypothesis is quite low. At base, a rejected null hypothesis (and thus claiming "statistical significance") tells us that an effect exists. Confidence intervals are also used to provide a range of likely values for parameter estimates; i.e. they can be used to make claims about effect sizes. Precisely interpreting confidence intervals is a difficult proposition.

Suppose that for a given sample, we compute a 95 percent confidence interval for parameter θ to be $[3.2, 6.1]$. A question we might want to answer is: What is the probability that θ falls between 3.2 and 6.1? The answer to this question is: "Zero or one—but it is impossible to know." This follows directly from the assumption that, in the classical context, parameters are fixed, unknown, unknowable quantities. Since confidence intervals are computed based on a single sample, and since the observed data y are assumed to be random variables, the end points of the confidence intervals are also random variables. Confidence intervals are constructed such that if we were to repeatedly draw from our population, 95 percent of our confidence intervals (each taking different ranges) would contain the population parameter. (Note that this requires that, at least conceptually, we could resample from the population. This makes sense in survey research, but it is more difficult to believe when modeling data collected about, for example, institutions or markets.) In addition, most frequentist hypothesis tests and confidence intervals require the assumption of an infinitely large sample size. Such asymptotic assumptions are *not* necessary when using the Bayesian approach. Even if one is comfortable with the sample size and the ability to resample from the population, a confidence interval does *not* provide a probabilistic statement about parameter values.

This is quite different in the Bayesian context. It is straightforward to summarize the posterior and compute any number of interesting quantities, *all of which can be treated as probabilities*. Analogous in some ways to a frequentist p-value, the Bayesian analyst can compute the probability that a parameter value is positive or negative. Akin to a confidence interval, one can also write down a range of values that contain the parameter value a certain percentage of the time. Unlike confidence intervals, these Bayesian credible intervals (which are typically computed using the highest posterior density region) can be interpreted probabilistically. A 95 percent Bayesian credible interval for θ of $[3.2, 6.1]$ suggests that, after observing the data, there is a 95 percent chance that the parameter falls between 3.2 and 6.1. Computing these probabilities requires summarizing the posterior density, and is typically done using MCMC methods.

4.2 Quantities of Interest

When analyzing data, parameters of statistical models are typically not the quantities of interest. Indeed, we are typically interested in functions of parameters, such as predicted values (King, Tomz, and Wittenberg 2000). Using Bayesian methods makes it easy to compute many types of quantities of interest, and propagate the uncertainty about parameters into uncertainty about these quantities. One useful example is the posterior predictive distribution, which can be summarized to provide ranges of values for a new datapoint y_{new}:

$$f(y_{new}|y) = \int_{\theta} f(y_{new}|\theta) f(\theta|y) d\theta.$$

Just as with Bayesian credible intervals, these intervals will also be on the scale of probability, and can be interpreted as such.

In the frequentist context, providing confidence intervals for quantities of interest is difficult for nearly all cases except the linear model. To compute these quantities analytically requires the use of the delta method, which can provide arbitrarily precise approximations. There are also simulation-based approaches (King, Tomz, and Wittenberg 2000). In the frequentist context, these intervals suffer the same ills as confidence intervals: They are based on assumptions that the sample size is infinite (such that the sampling distribution is multivariate normal; King, Tomz, and Wittenberg 2000, 352), and require the logic of repeated sampling which is implausible in many political science applications.

The quantities over which one can compute probabilities are limited only by the creativity of the researcher. In the context of estimating latent ideal points for Supreme Court justices, Jackman argues how MCMC methods can be used to perform inference for "comparisons of ideal points, rank ordering the ideal points, the location of the median justice, cutting planes for each bill (or case), residuals, and goodness-of-fit summaries" (Jackman 2004, 499). All of these quantities of interest can be computed using MCMC methods.

4.3 Incorporation of Prior Information

Political scientists typically have a great amount of substantive knowledge gleaned from the political science literature, fieldwork, and journalistic accounts. One advantage of Bayesian methods is the ability to formally include this type of information in a statistical analysis through the use of informative priors. (Related to this is the ability to include results from previous statistical studies by repeatedly using Bayes's Rule, or combining results from a number of studies using meta-analysis.) Western and Jackman (1994) argue that this strategy is particularly germane to the study of comparative politics, where sample sizes are quite low (and, thus, asymptotic properties of estimators have likely not yet kicked in). Translating rich, substantive information into statements about parameters of probability models is a difficult task. Gill and Walker (2005) review the prior elicitation literature, and use some of these tools to translate expert opinion into priors on the marginal effects of various covariates on attitudes toward the judiciary in Nicaragua. One does not need to use informative priors when doing Bayesian inference; indeed, much applied work uses so-called "uninformative" priors, which bring little, if any, information into the analysis. It is important to keep in mind that when using informative priors it is necessary to perform sensitivity analysis to ensure that the prior beliefs are not unduly affecting the results.

4.4 Fitting Otherwise Intractable Models

When performing classical inference, numerical optimization is the computational method used to fit models; one finds parameter values by maximizing some function, in most cases a likelihood function. Bayesian inference, on the other hand, has integration at its core. There are a number of examples where MCMC methods afford the opportunity to fit models that are otherwise difficult, if not impossible, to fit using conventional methods.

Quinn, Martin, and Whitford (1999) use MCMC methods to fit multinomial probit models (MNP) of voter choice in the Netherlands and the UK. These models, which allow for correlated errors in the latent utility specification, are difficult to fit using classical approaches because of the high-dimensional integrals one needs to compute to evaluate the likelihood function (also see the strategic censoring model of Smith 1999). Another example are measurement models, such as the item response model used to uncover ideal points in legislatures (Clinton, Jackman, and Rivers 2004), or the dynamic item response theory model of Martin and Quinn (2002), which allows smooth evolution of ideal points when dealing with multiple cross-sections of data. These models are difficult in the classical context because the number of parameters grows with each additional legislator or bill.

Bayesian methods are also extremely promising in dealing with data that are organized hierarchically. Western (1998) models some cross-sectional time-series data using Bayesian methods. Working with these data in a classical context is difficult because either the number of clusters (e.g. multivariate time-series data), time periods (e.g. panel data), or both (e.g. cross-sectional time-series data as typically used in comparative and international political economy) are small. This does not cause any difficulty in the Bayesian context, which can be modified to deal with other types of complex dependence.

There are also some models that have discrete parameters, which are difficult to deal with in the classical context because the optimization problem is not continuous. One example would be estimating the number of mixture components or the number of dimensions in a latent space model. Green (1995) provides an algorithm suited to these types of problems called reversible jump MCMC. In the time-series context, we might be interested in estimating the number and location of structural breaks in the data. The methods of Chib (1998) are suited to these change point models. In all of these cases, adopting a Bayesian approach and using MCMC for model-fitting opens doors to new types of analyses.

4.5 Model Comparison

Political scientists are typically engaged in comparing explanations of political phenomena. Different explanations often dictate very different models of the observed data y. The Bayesian approach to statistical inference offers an extremely useful tool for model comparison called *Bayes' factors* (Kass and Raftery 1995). Bayes' factors can be used to compare models with different blocks of covariates, models with different functional forms, and can be used with any number of plausible models (because transitivity holds in all pairwise comparisons). As with all quantities in the Bayesian approach, Bayes' factors provide the posterior probability that model M_1 is the true data-generating process compared with model M_2. Since each model contains prior information about the parameters of the model, Bayes' factors are sensitive to the priors chosen. The quantities used to compute Bayes' factors are the prior predictive distribution (see equation (5)), and the prior probabilities assigned to each model (typically one assumes that each model is a priori equally likely). Quinn, Martin, and Whitford (1999) use Bayes' factors to compare two different theoretical models and two different functional forms (multinomial probit and multinomial logit) in their comparative voting study. For an accessible introduction to Bayes' factors for a social science audience see Raftery (1995).

Computing the prior predictive distribution is a difficult task. While there exist MCMC methods that can be used in some situations, others have developed model comparison heuristics that are far easier to compute, such as the Bayesian Information Criterion (Raftery 1995) or the Deviance Information Criterion (Spiegelhalter et al. 2002), which is computed automatically in the WinBUGS software package.

4.6 Missing Data

Missing data is a common problem in political science, and is easily taken into account in the Bayesian context by using data augmentation (Tanner and Wong 1987). Data augmentation works by using the data-generating process as an imputation model. As such, it is easy to estimate models when some of the data y are missing. Not only will the recovered estimates take into account the uncertainty caused by the missing data, but the analyst can access the imputed values, which will average over all parameter uncertainty when producing the values. What about missing data in the covariates x? This is a more difficult problem, because in both the frequentist and Bayesian context the covariates are assumed to be fixed and known. However, given an imputation model for the missing covariates, it is straightforward to adapt an MCMC algorithm to average over the missing covariate information when performing inference about parameters and quantities of interest. The software package WinBUGS automatically performs data augmentation for all missing data y.

4.7 Common Concerns

While there are a number of practical advantages of using Bayesian methods in political science, there are some common concerns, which I detail below with some reactions.

- *Bayesian analysis is far more complicated than classical statistics.* The mathematics that underlie Bayesian methods are no more complicated than those needed to perform classical inference. MCMC algorithms are no more complicated that the numerical optimization and matrix inversion routines. The unfamiliar will always appear more complex than the familiar.
- *Priors are subjective, and they can be used to drive results.* It is true that priors are subjective; but so too are any number of assumptions, including what model to use, what covariates to include or exclude in the analysis, and in what fashion they should relate to the dependent variable. All of these modeling choices are, in a sense, subjective. What is of utmost importance is to *test* all testable assumptions in order to determine which model is best. Bayes' factors are particularly useful in this light. Also, as long as one performs prior sensitivity analysis, it is possible to determine whether the prior or the data are driving results. Simply put, if changing the prior changes the posterior, the data are not informative about the parameter values and the priors are driving the results. Such sensitivity analysis should be an important part of any applied Bayesian work.

- *There is no way to know whether an MCMC algorithm has converged.* This is true. However, there are diagnostics, discussed above, which can be used to determine nonconvergence (Cowles and Carlin 1995; Brooks and Roberts 1998). In the classical context, there is also no way to know whether a numerical optimization algorithm has reached a global maximum in most cases.
- *There is no good software to perform Bayesian inference.* There exists no widely used statistical software for Bayesian inference that compares to commercial products such as SAS, SPSS, or Stata. (This is likely due to the fact that all of these packages were developed before MCMC methods were widely used.) Over the last decade a number of promising software packages have emerged, which I discuss in the following section.

5 Software

Until the late 1990s, those interested in doing applied Bayesian work needed to develop their own MCMC algorithms and write their own software. Much of this work was done in high-level languages like GAUSS, Matlab, R, or S-Plus, or low-level languages like FORTRAN or C. The ability to develop these algorithms and produce software remains an important skill for the applied analyst, as existing software packages are limited in their scope. (It is also the case that developing software is an important part of innovation for those working in the classical paradigm.)

Today there exist two different types of software packages useful for Bayesian inference. The first is the BUGS language. BUGS stands for Bayesian updating using Gibbs sampling. To use BUGS, one writes down a model definition using an R-like syntax. The model definition is then processed, and the program chooses a scheme to sample from the posterior distribution of the model. Here is an example of BUGS syntax for our linear regression model with semi-conjugate priors:

```
1   model {
2     for(i in 1:N) {
3         Y[i] ~ dnorm(mu[i],tau)
4         mu[i] <- inprod(X[i,], beta)
5         }
6
7     for(k in 1:K) {
8         beta[k] ~ dnorm(0,0.001)
9         }
10    tau ~ dgamma(0.001, 0.001)
11    }
```

The first five lines of the code define the probability model. Here each observation y_i is assumed to be distributed conditionally normal with a common precision (inverse variance) τ. Lines 7–10 define the priors, in this case univariate normal for each element of the β, and Gamma for the precision. With this model definition and some data, the BUGS language will use MCMC methods to sample from the posterior. The most commonly used BUGS implementation is the WinBUGS package, which runs only on Microsoft Windows machines (Spiegelhalter et al. 2004). There are two newer implementations of the BUGS language: OpenBUGS (Thomas 2004) which runs on the Linux operating system, and JAGS (Plummer 2005) which is platform independent. The BUGS language works well for most simple models.

The second option is to use contributed software to the R language (R Development Core Team 2005). There are a number packages that are useful for performing applied Bayesian inference. Two general packages that provide model estimation for a number of commonly used models are MCMCpack (Martin and Quinn 2005) and bayesm (Rossi and McCulloch 2005). MCMCpack, for example, uses common R syntax to specify models. Consider the following example code used to fit a linear regression model:

```
posterior <- MCMCprobit(low~age+as.factor(race) + smoke, data=birthwt)
```

The returned object posterior is an mcmc object which can be summarized using the coda package (Plummer et al. 2005). Prior information is included in the model by passing hyperparameter arguments to the model fitting function. The "Bayesian Task View" on the Comprehensive R Archive Network (<http://cran.r-project.org>) contains information about many more packages, including those that fit single models or single classes of models, that are available for the R language.

6 CONCLUSION

Bayesian methods and estimation via Markov Chain Monte Carlo afford a number of advantages to applied political scientists. The methods can be applied in many situations to answer all sorts of substantive questions. Most importantly, all quantities of interest, including parameter estimates, can be stated as probabilities, and as such comport with the manner in which we typically think about estimation.

I conclude this chapter with some thoughts about places for future research, and for promising applications. One area ripe for research is the use of prior information in statistical analyses. Prior elicitation is an underdeveloped field, and there are elicitation problems unique to the study of politics, such as encoding elite opinion or attitudes, or information produced by governmental agencies. Developing new methods for translating that information into formal statements about parameters seems like a promising field of research. So, too, are guidelines for sensitivity analysis. When using informative priors, political scientists need guidance as to testing the dependence of the findings on the included prior information. Another area that needs significant work is statistical software. While the BUGS language and various R packages are promising, there is not yet a lingua franca for applied Bayesian work. This lack of available software makes *doing* Bayesian work more difficult than it otherwise should be. Finally, there are a number of models and methods that are wholly underutilized in political science that I think exhibit great promise. These include mixture models, and those with discrete parameters (such as change point models in the time-series context). Formal model comparison is also rarely performed in political science. Bayes' factors provide an avenue to comparing many different types of models. When dealing with clustered data, such as cross-sectional time-series data, hierarchical models show great promise. These models are easily fit using MCMC, and can be extended to handle many different types of complex dependence. Just as with any statistical tool, Bayesian methods are limited only by the creativity of the practitioner, yet to date the advantages of Bayesian methods have not yet been fully explored in political science.

References

BROOKS, S. P., and ROBERTS, G. O. 1998. Assessing convergence of Markov chain Monte Carlo algorithms. *Statistics and Computing*, 8: 319–35.

CASELLA, G., and GEORGE, E. I. 1992. Explaining the Gibbs sampler. *American Statistician*, 46: 167–74.

CHIB, S. 1998. Estimation and comparison of multiple change-point models. *Journal of Econometrics*, 86: 221–41.

—— and GREENBERG, E. 1995. Understanding the Metropolis–Hastings algorithm. *American Statistician*, 49: 327–36.

CLINTON, J. D., JACKMAN, S., and RIVERS, D. 2004. The statistical analysis of roll call data. *American Political Science Review*, 98: 355–70.

COWLES, M. K., and CARLIN, B. P. 1995. Markov Chain Monte Carlo diagnostics: a comparative review. *Journal of the American Statistical Association*, 91: 883–904.

GELFAND, A. E., and SMITH, A. F. M. 1990. Sampling-based approaches to calculating marginal densities. *Journal of the American Statistical Association*, 85: 398–409.

GELMAN, A., CARLIN, J. B., STERN, H. S., and RUBIN, D. B. 2004. *Bayesian Data Analysis*, 2nd edn. Boca Raton, Fla.: Chapman and Hall/CRC.

GEMAN, S., and GEMAN, D. 1984. Stochastic relaxation, Gibbs distributions, and the Bayesian restoration of images. *IEEE Transactions of Pattern Analysis and Machine Intelligence*, 6: 721–41.

GILL, J. 2002. *Bayesian Methods: A Social and Behavioral Sciences Approach*. Boca Raton, Fla.: Chapman and Hall/CRC.

—— and WALKER, L. D. 2005. Elicited priors for Bayesian model specifications in political science research. *Journal of Politics*, 67: 841–72.

GREEN, P. J. 1995. Reversible jump Markov Chain Monte Carlo computation and Bayesian model determination. *Biometrika*, 82: 711–32.

HASTINGS, W. K. 1979. Monte Carlo sampling methods using Markov Chains and their applications. *Biometrika*, 57: 97–109.

Jackman, S. 2000. Estimation and inference via Bayesian simulation: an introduction to Markov Chain Monte Carlo. *American Journal of Political Science*, 44: 369–98.

—— 2004. Bayesian analysis for political research. *Annual Reviews of Political Science*, 7: 483–505.

Kass, R. E., and Raftery, A. E. 1995. Bayes factors. *Journal of the American Statistical Association*, 90: 773–95.

King, G. 1989. *Unifying Political Methodology: The Likelihood Theory of Statistical Inference*. Cambridge: Cambridge University Press.

—— Tomz, M., and Wittenberg, J. 2000. Making the most of statistical analyses: improving interpretation and presentation. *American Journal of Political Science*, 44: 341–55.

Martin, A. D., and Quinn, K. M. 2002. Dynamic ideal point estimation via Markov Chain Monte Carlo for the U.S. Supreme Court, 1953–1999. *Political Analysis*, 10: 134–53.

—— —— 2005. *MCMCpack: Markov Chain Monte Carlo (MCMC) Package*. R package version 0.6-3. <http://mcmcpack.wustl.edu>

Metropolis, N., and Ulam, S. 1949. The Monte Carlo method. *Journal of the American Statistical Association*, 44: 335–41.

—— Rosenbluth, A. W., Rosenbluth, M. N., Teller, A. H., and Teller, E. 1953. Equation of state calculations by fast computing machines. *Journal of Chemical Physics*, 21: 1087–92.

Plummer, M. 2005. *JAGS: Just Another Gibbs Sampler*. Version 0.8. <http://www-fis.iarc.fr/ martyn/software/jags>

—— Best, N., Cowles, K., and Vines, K. 2005. *coda: Output Analysis and Diagnostics for MCMC*. R package version 0.9-2. <http://www-fis.iarc.fr/coda>

Quinn, K. M., Martin, A. D., and Whitford, A. B. 1999. Voter choice in multi-party democracies: a test of competing theories and models. *American Journal of Political Science*, 43: 1231–47.

R Development Core Team 2005. *R: A Language and Environment for Statistical Computing*. R Foundation for Statistical Computing, Vienna. <http://www.R-project.org>

Raftery, A. 1995. Bayesian model selection in social research. *Sociological Methodology*, 25: 111–96.

Rossi, P., and McCulloch, R. 2005. *bayesm: Bayesian Inference for Marketing/Micro-econometrics*. R package version 2.0-1.

Smith, A. 1999. Testing theories of strategic choice: the example of crisis escalation. *American Journal of Political Science*, 43: 1254–83.

Spiegelhalter, D. J., Best, N. G., Carlin, B. P., and van der Linde, A. 2002. Bayesian measures of model complexity and fit. *Journal of the Royal Statistical Society, B*, 64: 583–639.

—— Thomas, A., Best, N., and Lunn, D. 2004. *WinBUGS*. Version 1.4.1. <http://www.mrc-bsu.cam.ac.uk/bugs/winbugs>

Tanner, M. A., and Wong, W. 1987. The calculation of posterior distributions by data augmentation. *Journal of the American Statistical Association*, 82: 528–50.

Thomas, A. 2004. *OpenBUGS*. <http://mathstat.helsinki.fi/openbugs>

Tierney, L. 1994. Markov Chains for exploring posterior distributions. *Annals of Statistics*, 22: 1701–62.

Western, B. 1998. Causal heterogeneity in comparative research: a Bayesian hierarchical modelling approach. *American Journal of Political Science*, 42: 1233–59.

—— and Jackman, S. 1994. Bayesian inference for comparative research. *American Political Science Review*, 88: 412–23.

PART VII

QUANTITATIVE TOOLS FOR DESCRIPTIVE AND CAUSAL INFERENCE: SPECIAL TOPICS

......

DISCRETE CHOICE METHODS

......

GARRETT GLASGOW
R. MICHAEL ALVAREZ

1 INTRODUCTION

......

A GREAT many political science research questions involve the choices of political agents. These questions arise in most substantive areas of political science. For instance, does a citizen choose to vote in an election or abstain? Does a legislator choose to seek re-election, run for higher office, or retire? Does a country choose to go to war or stay at peace? These kinds of choice situations are known as *discrete choice* problems, so named because political agents are making choices from among a finite set of distinct options. In this chapter we examine the statistical models commonly used by political scientists to study discrete choices.

The first part of this chapter focuses on the "basic" discrete choice models, and is organized around the theoretical choice situations that lead to these models. The first choice situation we consider is the *ordered choice* situation, which assumes that the political agent's choice is determined by some continuous underlying rating of a political item or a propensity to engage in some behavior known as a *latent variable*. We do not observe this latent variable; instead we observe some discrete choice categories related to the latent variable. We begin with the special case of two ordered categories, and show how this leads to the *probit* and *logit* models. For instance, a country might have an underlying propensity to fight with its neighbors, but we only observe two discrete choice categories—war or peace. We then extend this to the case of multiple ordered choice categories, and show how this leads to the *ordered probit* and *ordered logit* models. For instance, an individual might have some underlying level of agreement with a policy position, but we only observe five ordered discrete choice categories offered by a survey question—agree strongly, agree, neither agree nor disagree, disagree, and disagree strongly.

The second choice situation we consider is the *unordered choice* situation. This choice problem generally involves a political agent selecting a political item from among a discrete set of items that have no intrinsic ordering (the choice set). Again, we begin with a special case, in this instance selecting a political item from a choice set of two items, and show that this again leads to the *probit* and *logit* models. An individual choosing which political candidate to vote for in a two-candidate election is an example of this type of choice problem. We then extend this to the case of selecting a political item from a larger choice set, and show how this leads to the *multinomial logit* and *conditional logit* models. An example of a multinomial choice situation is a legislator choosing whether to seek re-election, run for higher office, or retire.

After introducing the basic discrete choice models we consider the estimation and interpretation of these models. We then examine two extensions of the basic discrete choice models commonly seen in political science research—models allowing for heteroskedasticity in the choices made across political agents (such as the *heteroskedastic probit*), and models that estimate substitution patterns across choice alternatives (such as the *multinomial probit* and *mixed logit*). In our conclusion we offer suggestions for further reading.

2 Ordered Choices

2.1 Ordered Choices with Two Categories

We begin by deriving a discrete choice model for the special case of two ordered choices. Examples of this kind of choice problem are an individual choosing to vote for or against a particular political candidate, a country choosing to go to war or stay at peace, and so on. We think of these binary choice categories as ordered because they represent different degrees of feeling (increasing approval leads the individual to vote for the candidate) or propensities to undertake political action (increasing bellicosity leads the country to go to war).

In these cases we generally assume that a political agent's propensity to undertake some action versus do nothing, provide a favorable versus unfavorable evaluation of some political candidate, or some other ordered binary choice is determined by a latent variable y^*, with a threshold dividing this latent variable into two choice categories. We do not observe the agent's position on this latent variable, instead observing y, indicating the choice category the political agent selected. We observe

$y_i = 0$ for agents who are at or below τ, the threshold between choice categories, and $y_i = 1$ for agents above the threshold.

We derive a binary discrete choice model in this case by assuming the latent variable y_i^* is a linear function of a set of some observed variables and coefficients that influence the positions of political agents on the latent variable ($X_i\beta$) and some unobserved stochastic influences (ϵ_i). The latent choice preference is given by

$$y_i^* = X_i\beta + \epsilon_i. \tag{1}$$

Obviously, since y_i^* is unobserved we cannot estimate this equation with OLS. However, we do observe some information about y_i^* that will allow us to determine how the observed characteristics X_i influence choice behavior, because we observe y_i, the choice that agents make, and thus whether they are above the threshold τ. From this we estimate the probability that political agents with particular values of X_i will fall into particular choice categories.

Since y_i^* is latent, we require identifying assumptions in order to estimate the probability that a political agent makes a particular choice. We begin by noting that we cannot obtain a unique estimate for both τ and any constant term (β_0) in the model (since y_i^* is unobserved, we could add an arbitrary constant to both τ and β_0 and still generate the same probability of an observed outcome). A standard identifying assumption is to assume $\tau = 0$. This identifying assumption is arbitrary, and does not influence the estimate of β. With this assumption the probability that agents select the choice category represented by $y_i = 1$ given the observed variables X_i is

$$Pr(y_i = 1|X_i) = Pr(y_i^* > 0|X_i) \tag{2}$$

or, realizing that $y_i^* = X_i\beta + \epsilon_i$, we can rewrite equation (2) as

$$Pr(y_i = 1|X_i) = Pr(X_i\beta + \epsilon_i > 0|X_i). \tag{3}$$

It is clear from equation (3) that the probability that political agents select the choice category denoted by $y_i = 1$ will depend in part on the as-yet undefined error term ϵ_i. Thus, in order to estimate this probability, we must make some additional assumptions about the distribution of ϵ_i. Start by rearranging equation (3) to read

$$Pr(y_i = 1|X_i) = Pr(\epsilon_i > -X_i\beta|X_i). \tag{4}$$

If we assume that the distribution of ϵ_i is symmetric, we can further rearrange this equation to read

$$Pr(y_i = 1|X_i) = Pr(\epsilon_i \leq X_i\beta|X_i). \tag{5}$$

This equation is simply the evaluation of the cumulative density function (CDF) of ϵ_i at $X_i\beta$, which we can express as

$$Pr(y_i = 1|X_i) = F(X_i\beta). \tag{6}$$

We can now calculate the probability that we will observe $y_i = 1$ given the values of X_i by making some assumptions about the distribution of ϵ_i. One possibility is to assume that ϵ_i are drawn from an independently and identically distributed (IID) normal distribution. This results in the binary *probit* model:

$$Pr(y_i = 1|X_i) = \frac{1}{\sqrt{2\pi}} \int_{\epsilon=-\infty}^{X_i\beta/\sigma} \phi(\epsilon)\partial\epsilon = \Phi\left(\frac{X_i\beta}{\sigma}\right) \tag{7}$$

where ϕ is the PDF of the normal distribution, Φ is the CDF of the normal distribution, and σ is the standard deviation of the normal distribution of ϵ_i. As y_i^* is unobserved, we cannot estimate the variance of ϵ_i as we might in the OLS case. Thus, a standard assumption for binary probit models is that $\sigma = 1$.

Another common assumption about the distribution of ϵ_i is that it follows an IID logistic distribution. This results in the binary *logit* model:

$$Pr(y_i = 1|X_i) = \frac{\exp(\mu X_i\beta)}{1 + \exp(\mu X_i\beta)} \tag{8}$$

where μ is a positive scale parameter. As with the binary probit model, we must make an assumption about the variance of this CDF—in this case, we assume $\mu = 1$, which is equivalent to assuming that the variance of ϵ_i is $\frac{\pi^2}{3}$.

Note that estimating a binary probit model involves estimating an integral, while the binary logit is closed form, requiring no integration to solve. Given the computational capabilities of modern computers, this makes little practical difference in the binary choice case. However, differences in ease of estimation between models based on the normal and logistic distributions do emerge in unordered choice settings, as we explain below.

Estimation of a binary logit model will produce estimates of β that are approximately $\sqrt{\pi^2/3}$ times bigger than the corresponding estimates from a binary probit model—however, this difference is due solely to the different assumptions made about the variance of ϵ_i in the two models. In practice there is almost never a substantive difference between the binary logit and binary probit models, and either choice is valid in binary choice cases.

2.2 Ordered Choice with More than Two Categories

Many political science problems involve political agents making choices from more than two ordered choice categories. An example of this kind of choice problem would be asking an individual to rate their ideology on an ordered scale that runs from liberal to conservative. Again, we can think of choices like these as ordered because they represent different degrees of feeling (increasing conservativism leads the individual to select more conservative points on the survey question scale).

Extending the ordered choice models for two categories to ordered choice settings with more than two choice categories is straightforward. Again, we assume that the intensity of feeling or propensity to undertake some action by political agents is determined by a latent variable y_i^*. However, in these cases we assume there is more than one threshold on the latent variable, dividing the latent variable into three or more ordered choice categories. We do not observe a political agent's position on this latent variable, but we do observe y_i, which indicates which choice category a political agent selects. Specifically, we observe

$$y_i = j \text{ if } \tau_{j-1} \leq y_i^* < \tau_j \text{ for } j = 1 \text{ to } J \tag{9}$$

where $\tau_0 = -\infty$ and $\tau_J = \infty$.

We can derive an ordered discrete choice model in this case in a way similar to the derivation of the ordered binary choice model, by assuming the latent variable is a linear function of a set of some observed variables and coefficients that influence the positions of agents on the latent variable and some unobserved stochastic influences:

$$y_i^* = X_i\beta + \epsilon_i. \tag{10}$$

As in the binary case, y_i^* is unobserved, so we must make some identifying assumptions in order to estimate the probability that a political agent makes a particular choice. We cannot obtain unique estimates for all of the thresholds and any constant term (β_0) in the model (since y_i^* is unobserved, we could add an arbitrary constant to all of these terms and still generate the same probability of an observed outcome). Standard identifying assumptions include setting $\tau_1 = 0$ or setting $\beta_0 = 0$—as with the binary case, these assumptions are arbitrary, and do not influence the estimate of β. With one of these identifying assumptions we can estimate the probability that political agents with particular values of X_i will fall into a particular choice category. Under the assumption that $\beta_0 = 0$, the probability that agents select the choice category represented by $y_i = j$ given the observed variables X_i is given by

$$Pr(y_i = j|X_i) = Pr(\tau_{j-1} \leq y_i^* < \tau_j|X_i) \tag{11}$$

or substituting $y_i^* = X_i\beta + \epsilon_i$ and rearranging:

$$Pr(y_i = j|X_i) = Pr(\tau_{j-1} \leq X_i\beta + \epsilon_i < \tau_j|X_i)$$
$$= Pr(\tau_{j-1} - X_i\beta \leq \epsilon_i < \tau_j - X_i\beta|X_i). \tag{12}$$

As the probability that a random variable will fall between two values is the difference between the CDF at those two values, we can rewrite equation (12) as

$$Pr(y_i = j|X_i) = Pr(\epsilon_i < \tau_j - X_i\beta|X_i) - Pr(\epsilon_i < \tau_{j-1} - X_i\beta|X_i)$$
$$= F(\tau_j - X_i\beta|X_i) - F(\tau_{j-1} - X_i\beta|X_i) \tag{13}$$

where F represents the CDF of ϵ_i. These probabilities can be simplified for the lowest and highest choice categories by realizing that $F(\tau_0 - X_i\beta) = F(-\infty - X_i\beta) = 0$, and that $F(\tau_J - X_i\beta) = F(\infty - X_i\beta) = 1$. As with the binary discrete choice models, we can now calculate the probability that $y_i = j$ by making some assumptions about the distribution of ϵ_i. If we make the same assumptions as those made for a binary probit model (ϵ_i is an IID normal distribution with mean zero and unit variance) this leads to an *ordered probit* model. If we make the same assumptions as those made for a binary logit model (ϵ_i is an IID logistic distribution with mean zero and variance $\frac{\pi^2}{3}$), this leads to an *ordered logit* model. As is the case with the binary choice models, there is little to distinguish between the ordered logit and ordered probit models in either ease of estimation or substantive results.

While there is no theoretical maximum to the number of categories in the dependent variable, there is certainly a practical limit beyond which researchers might consider treating the dependent variable as continuous. For instance, the commonly used "thermometer score" survey question is actually an ordered scale with 101 categories, but estimating an ordered logit or probit in this case would be impractical (requiring estimating 100 separate points on the latent variable), and most statistical software places a limit on the number of categories allowed in the dependent variable (for instance, the maximum number of categories allowed in Stata is 50). We are unaware of any agreed upon rule of thumb for a maximum number of ordered categories, although it is rare in practice to see an ordered logit or probit with more than 7–10 categories in the dependent variable.

3 UNORDERED CHOICES

3.1 Unordered Choices for Two Categories

As with our treatment of ordered choices, we begin by deriving a discrete choice model for the special case where there are only two unordered choices. Examples of this kind of choice problem would be an individual choosing which of two political candidates to vote for, a political candidate choosing which of two cities to use as a site for a major campaign speech, and so on. We can think of these binary choice categories as unordered because they represent two distinct items with no intrinsic ordering, in contrast to the binary ordered choice categories considered earlier (which could be considered two different rating categories for the *same* item).

In the unordered choice case we generally assume that political agents assign some kind of relative rating known as a *utility score* to each political item in the choice set, and then agents select the choice category with the highest utility. This theory of choice behavior is known as *random utility maximization (RUM)*, so named because political agents are selecting the choice category that gives them the highest utility, and these utility scores are unobserved, and thus appear random to us as researchers.

Due to the fact that political agents are considering more than one choice, we must keep track of both the characteristics of the political agent and the characteristics of the different choice alternatives (for instance, the issue positions of the various candidates an individual might choose in an election). This makes the derivation of a binary choice model more complicated than in the latent variable case. We derive a binary discrete choice model in this case by assuming that an agent's utility scores are composed of a linear function of a set of observed variables and coefficients specific to the political item j as perceived by agent i $(C_{ij}\lambda)$, a set of observed variables and coefficients specific to the political agent i $(X_i\beta_j)$, and unobserved stochastic influences (e_{ij}). For example, the utility yielded by the choice category denoted by $y = 1$ for agents is given by

$$U_{i1} = X_i\beta_1 + C_{i1}\lambda + e_{i1}. \tag{14}$$

Note that the coefficients for X_i are subscripted by choice category, which allows the political agent's characteristics to influence their utility for different alternatives in different ways. For instance, an individual's partisan identification might increase the utility for a candidate of the same party, but decrease the utility for a candidate of an opposing party.

We do not observe an agent's utility scores, but we do observe y_{ij}, which indicates which choice category the political agent selected. The probability that we will observe agents selecting the choice category represented by $y_i = 1$ over the choice category represented by $y_i = 0$ is given by

$$Pr(y_i = 1|X_i, C_{ij}) = Pr(U_{i1} > U_{i0}) \tag{15}$$

or, realizing that $U_{ij} = X_i\beta_j + C_{ij}\lambda + e_{ij}$, we can rewrite equation (15) as

$$Pr(y_i = 1|X_i, C_{ij}) = Pr(X_i\beta_1 + C_{i1}\lambda + e_{i1} > X_i\beta_0 + C_{i0}\lambda + e_{i0}). \tag{16}$$

It is clear from equation (16) that we will not be able to obtain unique estimates for both β_0 and β_1, since we could add an arbitrary constant to both of these sets of coefficients and still generate the same probability of an observed outcome. A standard identifying assumption is to set $\beta_0 = 0$.

As with our derivation of the binary choice model for ordered alternatives, it is now clear that some assumptions will need to be made about the distribution of the stochastic portion of utility e_{ij} in order to estimate the probability that agents select the choice category denoted by $y_i = 1$. Setting $\beta_0 = 0$, we can rearrange equation (16) to read

$$Pr(y_i = 1|X_i, C_{ij}) = Pr(X_i\beta_1 + (C_{i1} - C_{i0})\lambda > e_{i0} - e_{i1}). \tag{17}$$

This equation is simply the evaluation of the cumulative density function (CDF) of $e_{i0} - e_{i1}$ at $X_i\beta_1 + (C_{i1} - C_{i0})\lambda$, which we can express as

$$Pr(y_i = 1|X_i) = F(X_i\beta_1 + (C_{i1} - C_{i0})\lambda). \tag{18}$$

Just as in the ordered choice case, we can now calculate the probability that we will observe $y_i = 1$ given the values of X_i and C_{ij} by making assumptions about the distribution of e_{ij}. One possibility is to assume that e_{ij} is an IID normal distribution—the difference of two normal distributions is also a normal distribution, so this assumption (and the assumption that $\sigma = 1$) leads to a probit model similar to that presented in equation (7):

$$Pr(y_i = 1|X_i) = \Phi(X_i\beta_1 + (C_{i1} - C_{i0})\lambda).$$ (19)

Another possibility is to assume that e_{ij} follows an IID type I extreme value distribution—the difference of two IID type I extreme value distributions is IID logistic, so this assumption (and the assumption that $\mu = 1$) leads to a logit model similar to that presented in equation (8):

$$Pr(y_i = 1|X_i) = \frac{\exp(X_i\beta_1 + (C_{i1} - C_{i0})\lambda)}{1 + \exp(X_i\beta_1 + (C_{i1} - C_{i0})\lambda)}$$ (20)

Note that if there are no variables that measure the characteristics of the alternatives in the choice set, the probit and logit models presented here are identical to those presented for binary ordered choices above. Including variables that measure the characteristics of alternatives in both the probit and logit models does not require the researcher to do anything beyond calculating $C_{i1} - C_{i0}$ and including this term as an independent variable.

3.2 Unordered Choice with More than Two Categories

Many political science problems also involve political agents making choices from more than two unordered choice categories. Examples of this kind of choice problem would be an individual choosing which of several political parties to vote for, a political candidate choosing which of several cities to use as a site for a major campaign speech, and so on. Again, we can think of these choice categories as unordered because they represent distinct items with no intrinsic ordering.

Extending the unordered choice models for two categories to unordered choice over multiple categories is straightforward. Again, assume that political agents assign utility scores to each political item in the choice set, and select the choice category that yields the highest utility. We do not observe an agent's utility scores, instead observing y_i, which indicates which of the J choice categories the political agent selected. The probability that we observe agents selecting the choice category represented by $y_i = j$ over all other choice categories is

$$Pr(y_i = j|X_i, C_{ij}) = Pr(U_{ij} > U_{ik}) \; \forall \; k \neq j$$ (21)

or, substituting in $U_{ij} = X_i\beta_j + C_{ij}\lambda + e_{ij}$ and rearranging:

$$Pr(y_i = j|X_i, C_{ij}) = Pr(X_i\beta_j + C_{ij}\lambda - X_i\beta_k - C_{ik}\lambda > e_{ik} - e_{ij}) \; \forall \; k \neq j.$$ (22)

As in the binary choice case, we will not be able to obtain unique estimates for each set of β's in the model, since we could add an arbitrary constant to these sets of coefficients and still generate the same probability of an observed outcome. A standard identifying assumption is to pick one choice category as a *baseline category*, and set $\beta = 0$ for that category (the choice of baseline category is arbitrary and does not affect the substantive interpretation of the model).

Once again, we must make some assumptions about the distribution of the stochastic portion of utility e_{ij} in order to estimate the probability that agents select the choice category denoted by $y_i = j$. Assuming that e_{ij} is an IID type I extreme-value distribution (and that $\mu = 1$) leads to a *multinomial logit* model:

$$Pr(y_i = j|X_i) = \frac{\exp(X_i\beta_j + C_{ij}\lambda)}{\sum_{k=1}^{J} \exp(X_i\beta_k + C_{ik}\lambda)}. \tag{23}$$

Many political scientists make a distinction between the multinomial logit and the *conditional logit*. For these researchers the multinomial logit does not include variables that measure the characteristics of the choice alternatives, while conditional logit does contain these variables. We note here that the only difference between these models is in the kinds of variables included in the model, and many research traditions simply refer to both models as multinomial logit.

Assuming that e_{ij} follows an IID normal distribution leads to a special case of the *multinomial probit* (MNP) model. The multinomial probit is a much more difficult model to estimate than a multinomial logit. While the multinomial logit has the closed-form expression presented in equation (23), estimating a multinomial probit involves integrating over a multivariate normal distribution of dimension $J - 1$. Thus, the multinomial probit is generally only used in cases where we want to relax the assumption of an IID error term, as we describe below.

4 Estimation

The discrete choice models discussed above are not typically estimated via OLS because of the nonlinearity of these choice models. Instead, these models are usually estimated through maximum likelihood estimation (MLE). This is done by first creating a likelihood function, and then taking the natural log of this function to create a log likelihood function (we take the natural log of the likelihood function because it is easier to work with).

For instance, the log likelihood of the probit model is

$$\ln L = \sum_i [y_i \ln \Phi(X_i\beta)] + [(1 - y_i) \ln [1 - \Phi(X_i\beta)]]. \tag{24}$$

Maximizing this log likelihood means maximizing the sum of the predicted probabilities assigned to the choices that political agents in fact made. This is done by estimating β to have values such that $X_i\beta$ tends to be large when $y_i = 1$, and small when $y_i = 0$.

The log likelihood functions for all of the models derived above are globally concave and thus relatively easy to maximize, with most current statistical software packages reaching the solution in seconds. However, note that the consistency, normality, and efficiency of MLE depends on asymptotic arguments—the small sample properties of MLE are largely unknown. Thus, researchers should be cautious when using MLE in small samples.

Many common statistical software packages allow researchers to estimate all of the discrete choice models discussed earlier, with the exception of the conditional logit. To our knowledge only LIMDEP, SAS, and Stata offer this option.

5 INTERPRETATION

For all of the discrete choice models discussed above, the relationship between $X_i\beta$ and the choice probabilities depends on a nonlinear function. Thus, the effect of a one-unit change in one independent variable on the choice probabilities will depend on the values of the other independent variables in the model. This means that we cannot interpret the β's in discrete choice models as we would in an OLS setting.

The most common method for interpreting parameter estimates in discrete choice models in political science is through the use of a hypothetical observation. The researcher begins by selecting values for the independent variables in the model that are representative of some case of interest in the study. Setting variables to their mean or modal values is common, although this is not the only possibility—often the researcher will select values for the independent variables that reflect some case of substantive interest. Then, using the estimated values of β and the selected values of X, a baseline probability for $y = 1$ is calculated. For instance, we would interpret the coefficients in a probit model by calculating

$$\hat{Pr}(y = 1|X) = \Phi(\bar{X}\hat{\beta}) \tag{25}$$

where $\bar{X}$ represents the selected values for the independent variables. The influence of a particular independent variable on the probability that $y = 1$ can then be examined by changing the value of this variable while holding all other independent variables constant at $\bar{X}$ and recalculating $\hat{Pr}(y = 1|X)$.

These predicted probabilities can also be calculated fairly easily using some built-in commands in most statistical software packages, such as the "mfx compute" command in Stata, and can even be calculated with a hand calculator in the case of logit probabilities. CLARIFY (King, Tomz, and Wittenberg 2000) is another option, with the added benefit of the ability to calculate standard errors on these predicted probabilities.

6 COMMON EXTENSIONS OF THE BASIC DISCRETE CHOICE MODELS

Many extensions to the basic discrete choice models discussed above have been developed for political science research. Below we examine the two most commonly seen extensions in political science research—models to examine heteroskedasticity in choices across political agents, and models to estimate more realistic substitution patterns across choice alternatives.

6.1 Heteroskedasticity

In some cases there are reasons to suspect there is heteroskedasticity in choices made across political agents. For instance, Alvarez and Brehm (1995) hypothesized that individuals who were ambivalent about allowing abortion would feel a greater sense of internal conflict when making discrete choices related to abortion policy, leading their policy preferences to be more susceptible to external forces that could vary from moment to moment, such as priming effects. In an ideal setting we would simply include these external forces as independent variables in the discrete choice model—however, in this case these forces were unobserved (and perhaps unobservable) in the survey available. Thus, Alvarez and Brehm modeled the effect of these external forces as heteroskedasticity across individuals, with greater variance expected in the error term for ambivalent individuals (those who held conflicting opinions about allowing abortion) as compared to unambivalent individuals (those who held one-sided opinions about abortion).

Accounting for heteroskedasticity is important methodologically as well as substantively. Unlike the OLS case, where violations of the assumption of an IID error term lead to inefficient but unbiased parameter estimates, IID violations in discrete choice models can lead to inconsistent parameter estimates.

Since the error term ϵ_i is unobserved, we cannot directly estimate heteroskedasticity in discrete choice models. Instead, we infer heteroskedasticity through the relationship between $X_i\beta$ and observed choice behavior—as the error variance increases, political agents will be more likely to make choices that differ from those predicted by $X_i\beta$. To see how heteroskedasticity is modeled in a discrete choice setting, consider the binary probit, where the probability that we observe $y_i = 1$ given the values of X_i is

$$Pr(y_i = 1|X_i) = \Phi\left(\frac{X_i\beta}{\sigma}\right) \tag{26}$$

where Φ is the CDF of the normal distribution and σ is the standard deviation of the normally distributed error term. As we do not observe the error term, we must make an identifying assumption about σ—standard probit models generally assume $\sigma = 1$.

The heteroskedastic probit model relaxes this assumption, allowing the variance of the error term to differ across political agents by specifying the variance of the error term as $\sigma_i = \exp(Z_i\gamma)$, where Z_i is a set of observed variables thought to determine the variance of the error term and γ is a set of coefficients to be estimated (the exponential ensures the estimated variance of the error term remains positive). As long as Z_i does not contain a constant term, this model will be identified. The probability that $y_i = 1$ is then given by

$$Pr(y_i = 1|X_i, Z_i) = \Phi\left(\frac{X_i\beta}{\exp(Z_i\gamma)}\right). \tag{27}$$

As the term $\exp(Z_i\gamma)$ increases, it pushes the predicted choice probabilities closer to 0.5 for either alternative, indicating that political agents are more likely to make choices that differ from those predicted by $X_i\beta$—this is what we would expect to see if $\exp(Z_i\gamma)$ measures the variance of the error term. Thus, we interpret a positive coefficient on a variable in Z as indicating that increasing the value of this variable increases the error variance, while interpreting a negative coefficient as indicating that increasing the value of this variable decreases the error variance.

This heteroskedastic probit model is a straightforward generalization of a simple probit, and can be estimated and interpreted in the same way as the basic discrete choice models. Both Stata and LIMDEP include simple commands that allow for the estimation of heteroskedastic probits. This heteroskedastic probit model can easily be generalized to a heteroskedastic ordered probit model (Alvarez and Brehm 1998). Although less commonly seen, heteroskedastic logits and heteroskedastic ordered logits are specified in much the same way as the heteroskedastic probit models, by specifying the logit scale parameter as $\mu = \frac{1}{\exp(Z_i\gamma)}$ rather than $\mu = 1$ (see equation (8)). Models of this type also exist for multiple unordered choices (Dubin and Zeng 1991), although heteroskedasticity in these cases is usually addressed using the approach outlined in the next section.

6.2 Substitution Patterns

In many unordered choice situations researchers are interested in *substitution patterns*, or how political agents might substitute one choice alternative for another as choice options are added to or removed from the choice set. For instance, in a study of voting behavior in the 1992 US presidential election Alvarez and Nagler (1995) examined the possibility that voters viewed Perot as a substitute for Bush. While ideally we could observe all of the characteristics of the candidates that lead voters to view them as similar and include them as independent variables in the discrete choice model, in many cases at least some of these characteristics will be unobserved. Thus, in order to estimate more realistic substitution patterns Alvarez and Nagler modeled these common unobserved attributes as correlations between the unobserved portions of utility for each candidate.

As multinomial logit assumes the unobserved portions of utility are IID, it cannot estimate substitution patterns that take this kind of unobserved similarity between choice alternatives into account. Specifically, MNL (and all other unordered discrete choice models that assume the unobserved portions of utility are IID) imposes the *independence of irrelevant alternatives* (IIA) property on the estimated substitution patterns. IIA requires that the relative odds that a political agent selects one choice alternative over another do not change no matter which other alternatives are added to or deleted from the choice set. A simple Hausman test can be used to determine the validity of the IIA assumption in a multinomial logit model (Hausman and McFadden 1984).

It is easy to imagine political choice settings where this is an unrealistic assumption—any choice situation where political agents might view some choice alternatives as substitutes is likely to violate the IIA assumption. In addition to the substantive motivation, addressing correlations in the error term across choice alternatives is also important methodologically, as violations of the assumption of an IID error term can lead to inconsistent parameter estimates (although some suggest that the inconsistency might be slight in many political choice settings; Dow and Endersby 2004; Quinn, Martin, and Whitford 1999).

Violations of the IIA assumption are most commonly addressed in political science research through discrete choice models that allow the unobserved portion of utility to be correlated across choice alternatives. Specifically, we assume $e_{ij} = Z_{ij}\eta_i + v_{ij}$, where Z_{ij} is an identity matrix of the same dimension as the number of alternatives in the choice set, v_{ij} is an error term that is IID across political agents and alternatives, and η_i is a vector of random terms with mean 0 that varies over political agents and can be correlated across choice alternatives (models that assume IIA implicitly assume $Z_{ij} = 0$). Different assumptions about the distributions of η_i and v_{ij} will lead to different discrete choice models that can estimate realistic substitution patterns.

Assuming that both η_i and v_{ij} are normally distributed leads to the *multinomial probit* model. As the sum of two normal distributions is also normal, the unobserved portion of utility will be normally distributed, leading to the MNP mentioned above. However, as η_i can be correlated across choice alternatives, the unobserved portions of utility for each choice alternative will follow a multivariate normal distribution with a general covariance matrix Σ. Estimating the off-diagonal terms in Σ allows the researcher to examine how the unobserved portions of utility are correlated, and thus which choice alternatives are viewed as substitutes by political agents for unobserved reasons. The probability that political agent i selects choice alternative j is given by integrating over the multivariate normal distribution of the $J - 1$ differences in the unobserved portions of utility (where J is the number of choice alternatives). For instance, if we define $\epsilon_{kj} = e_{ik} - e_{ij}$ and $\bar{U}_j = X_i\beta_j + C_{ij}\lambda$, the probability that political agent i selects alternative 1 from a choice set of three alternatives is given by

$$Pr(y_i = 1 | X_i, C_{ij}) = \int_{\epsilon_{21}=-\infty}^{\frac{\bar{U}_1-\bar{U}_2}{\sqrt{\sigma_1^2+\sigma_2^2-2\sigma_{12}}}} \int_{\epsilon_{31}=-\infty}^{\frac{\bar{U}_1-\bar{U}_3}{\sqrt{\sigma_1^2+\sigma_3^2-2\sigma_{13}}}} \phi(\epsilon_{21}, \epsilon_{31}) \partial\epsilon_{21}\partial\epsilon_{31} \qquad (28)$$

where σ_j^2 denotes the variance of the unobserved portion of utility for alternative j and σ_{jk} denotes the covariance between the unobserved portions of utility for alternatives j and k. Note that one element in Σ must be set to a constant to identify the model, which means that only $[(J(J-1))/2] - 1$ elements in Σ can be estimated.

Assuming that v_{ij} is IID extreme value and that η_i follows a distribution g specified by the researcher leads to the *mixed logit* (MXL) model. Any number of random elements that follow any distribution can be included in η_i, making mixed logit a more general discrete choice model than MNP—in fact, McFadden and Train (2000) demonstrate that mixed logits can be specified to approximate any discrete choice model derived from random utility maximization with the appropriate choices of g and Z. The probability that political agent i selects choice alternative j is given by integrating over the general multivariate distribution of the unobserved portions of utility g:

$$Pr(y_i = j | X_i, C_{ij}) = \int_\eta \left(\frac{\exp(X_i \beta_j + C_{ij}\lambda + Z_{ij}\eta_i)}{\sum_{k=1}^{J} \exp(X_i \beta_k + C_{ik}\lambda + Z_{ik}\eta_i)} \right) g(\eta)\partial\eta. \qquad (29)$$

This equation shows that the choice probability is a mixture of MNL probabilities, with the weight of each particular MNL probability determined by the mixing distribution g (hence the term "mixed logit"). As with the multinomial probit, the unobserved portions of utility in a mixed logit can be specified to follow a multivariate distribution with a general covariance matrix, and estimating the off-diagonal terms in this covariance matrix (subject to the same identification restrictions as the MNP) will allow for more realistic substitution patterns across choice alternatives.

Multinomial probits and mixed logits can also be specified to estimate random coefficients. For instance, Glasgow (2001) hypothesized that the influence of working class membership on vote choice in the 1987 British general election would vary across individuals for unobserved reasons (such as the level of social mobility within an individual's geographic region), and thus specified a mixed logit model for vote choice with random coefficients for the variables indicating working class membership. Random coefficients in these models are specified by including some variables in both X_i and Z_{ij}—in this case the coefficients estimated on the variables in X_i represent the mean of the random coefficient, while the estimated variances on the variables in Z_{ij} represent the variances of the random coefficients. MNPs are restricted to $[(J(J-1))/2] - 1$ normally distributed random coefficients, while MXLs can have any number of random coefficients that follow any distribution.

Unlike the closed form of the MNL, estimation of the MNP and MXL models involves the evaluation of multidimensional integrals. Thus, these models are generally estimated using some kind of simulated maximum likelihood technique, which approximates the multidimensional error distribution through a Monte Carlo technique. LIMDEP, SAS, and Stata allow for estimation of multinomial probits and mixed logits.

It should be noted that multinomial probits and mixed logits are not the only way to relax the IIA assumption and estimate more realistic substitution patterns across choice alternatives. *Generalized extreme value* (GEV) models also allow for correlation across choice alternatives. The most common type of GEV model is the *nested logit*, which divides the choice alternatives into subsets, with IIA holding within each subset, but not across subsets. Although more tractable than either the MNP or MXL, and potentially useful in cases where the researcher has some theory or prior knowledge that allows some choice alternatives to be grouped together, GEV models have not seen many applications in political science.

7 FURTHER READING

Obviously this chapter only provides an overview of the use of discrete choice models in political science, and the interested reader should consult other sources for more details and examples of applications. Long (1997) offers a fairly accessible introduction to the basic discrete choice models discussed here, while more advanced treatments can be found in Ben-Akiva and Lerman (1985) and Train (2003). Jones and Westerland (2006) offer a detailed discussion of the analysis of choices from ordered categories, and present several models not discussed here. For applications of heteroskedastic discrete choice models in political science see the work of Alvarez and Brehm (1995; 1997; 1998). For applications of the multinomial probit to political science problems see Alvarez and Nagler (1995; 1998*a*; 1998*b*), Lacy and Burden (1999), and Schofield et al. (1998). For applications of the mixed logit to political science problems see Glasgow (2001) and Glasgow and Alvarez (2005). Finally, note that there are numerous extensions to the discrete choice methods discussed here that were not covered in this chapter, such as techniques for panel and time-series cross-section (TSCS) data (Hsiao 2003, ch. 7), event history data (Box-Steffensmeier and Jones 2004), censored and truncated dependent variables (Sigelman and Zeng 2000), selection bias (Boehmke 2003), endogeneity in choice models (Alvarez and Glasgow 2000), event counts (King 1989), and models based on distributions other than the normal or logistic (Nagler 1994).

REFERENCES

ALVAREZ, R. M., and BREHM, J. 1995. American ambivalence towards abortion policy: development of a heteroskedastic probit model of competing values. *American Journal of Political Science*, 39: 1055–82.

ALVAREZ, R. M., and BREHM, J. 1997. Are Americans ambivalent towards racial policies? *American Journal of Political Science*, 41: 345–74.

——1998. Speaking in two voices: American equivocation about the Internal Revenue Service. *American Journal of Political Science*, 42: 418–52.

—— and GLASGOW, G. 2000. Two-stage estimation of non-recursive choice models. *Political Analysis*, 8: 147–65.

—— and NAGLER, J. 1995. Economics, issues, and the Perot candidacy: voter choice in the 1992 presidential election. *American Journal of Political Science*, 39: 714–44.

————1998a. Economics, entitlements, and social issues: voter choice in the 1996 presidential election. *American Journal of Political Science*, 42: 1349–63.

————1998b. When politics and models collide: estimating models of multicandidate elections. *American Journal of Political Science*, 42: 55–96.

BEN-AKIVA, M., and LERMAN, S. R. 1985. *Discrete Choice Analysis: Theory and Application*. Cambridge, Mass.: MIT Press.

BOEHMKE, F. J. 2003. Using auxiliary data to estimate selection bias models, with an application to interest groups' use of the direct initiative process. *Political Analysis*, 11: 234–54.

BOX-STEFFENSMEIER, J. M., and JONES, B. S. 2004. *Event History Modeling: A Guide for Social Scientists*. New York: Cambridge University Press.

DOW, J., and ENDERSBY, J. 2004. Multinomial logit and multinomial probit: a comparison of choice models for voting research. *Electoral Studies*, 23: 107–22.

DUBIN, J. A., and ZENG, L. 1991. The heterogeneous logit model. Caltech Social Science Working Paper #759.

GLASGOW, G. 2001. Mixed logit models for multiparty elections. *Political Analysis*, 9: 116–36.

—— and ALVAREZ, R. M. 2005. Voting behavior and the electoral context of government formation. *Electoral Studies*, 24: 245–64.

HAUSMAN, J., and MCFADDEN, D. 1984. Regression-based specification tests for the multinomial logit model. *Econometrica*, 52: 1219–40.

HSIAO, C. 2003. *Analysis of Panel Data*, 2nd edn. New York: Cambridge University Press.

JONES, B. S., and WESTERLAND, C. 2006. Order matters (?): alternatives to conventional practices for ordinal categorical response variables. Presented at the Annual Meetings of the Midwest Political Science Association.

KING, G. 1989. *Unifying Political Methodology: The Likelihood Theory of Statistical Inference*. New York: Cambridge University Press.

—— TOMZ, M., and WITTENBERG, J. 2000. Making the most of statistical analyses: improving interpretation and presentation. *American Journal of Political Science*, 44: 341–55.

LACY, D., and BURDEN, B. C. 1999. The vote stealing and turnout effects of Ross Perot in the 1992 U.S. presidential election. *American Journal of Political Science*, 43: 233–55.

LONG, J. S. 1997. *Regression Models for Categorical and Limited Dependent Variables*. Thousand Oaks, Calif.: Sage.

MCFADDEN, D., and TRAIN, K. 2000. Mixed MNL models for discrete response. *Journal of Applied Econometrics*, 15: 447–70.

NAGLER, J. 1994. Scobit: an alternative estimator to logit and probit. *American Journal of Political Science*, 38: 230–55.

QUINN, K. M., MARTIN, A. D., and WHITFORD, A. B. 1999. Voter choice in a multi-party democracy: a test of competing theories and models. *American Journal of Political Science*, 43: 1231–47.

SCHOFIELD, N., MARTIN, A. D., QUINN, K. M., and WHITFORD, A. B. 1998. Multiparty electoral competition in the Netherlands and Germany: a model based on multinomial probit. *Public Choice*, 97: 257–93.

SIGELMAN, L., and ZENG, L. 2000. Analyzing censored and sample-selected data with Tobit and Heckit models. *Political Analysis*, 8: 167–82.

TRAIN, K. E. 2003. *Discrete Choice Methods with Simulation*. Cambridge: Cambridge University Press.

CHAPTER 23

....

SURVIVAL ANALYSIS

....

JONATHAN GOLUB

WHY does peace last so long between some states while others soon succumb to war? Why are some civil wars brief and others protracted? What makes parliamentary governments durable? How long will a judicial precedent last before being overturned? When one state imposes sanctions on another what determines their duration? Why are some legislative proposals bogged down in endless delays while others experience rapid adoption? These are all examples of important substantive political science questions, and all have one thing in common. In order to answer them researchers have used survival analysis, a quantitative methodology designed to explain why things (war, peace, cabinets, and so on) survive or endure. Over the past decade there has been an explosion in the use of survival analysis as political scientists came to recognize that its application suits many topics of research and has advantages over standard ordinary least squares regression techniques.[1]

This chapter is concerned with ensuring that authors use survival analysis in the most constructive and appropriate way to generate answers to substantive questions. It discusses the main choices researchers face when conducting survival analysis and offers a set of methodological steps that should become standard practice. After introducing the basic terminology that will feature throughout the chapter, I demonstrate that there is little to lose and much to gain by employing Cox models instead of parametric models. I build my argument on theoretical foundations, as well as

I am grateful to the editors for comments on a previous draft of this chapter, and to the many colleagues who kindly made their data available.

[1] For introductions to survival analysis (known also as event history or duration analysis) and detailed expositions of its methodology and advantages over OLS see Allison (1984); Collett (2003); Box-Steffensmeier and Jones (1997; 2004).

a critical evaluation of eighty-four survival analyses published in leading political science journals, forty-five of which I managed to replicate in order to investigate model specification issues.[2]

1 KEY TERMS AND MODEL CHOICES

Given an individual case under observation—a country at peace, a legislative proposal under consideration, a cabinet government in power—the *hazard rate* is, effectively, the probability that at any given point in time the event of interest will occur (e.g. a war starts, a cabinet dissolves, legislation is adopted) given that it has not yet occurred.[3] The *baseline hazard* is the underlying effect the passage of time has on the hazard rate once all independent variables in a model are taken into account. Put another way, the baseline hazard rate is the hazard function for cases whose independent variables are all set to zero.[4] The baseline hazard can take an infinite variety of shapes. For example, with a rising baseline hazard rate (positive *duration dependence*) the probability of an event increases naturally as time passes, regardless of any independent variables. A falling baseline hazard rate (negative duration dependence) signifies that over time the chances of an event occurring decrease.

Researchers face two main choices when specifying a survival model. One relates to the nature of the baseline hazard. In *parametric* models the researcher specifies a particular shape for the baseline hazard, based on their own assumptions about the effect of time. The most commonly chosen parametric models are the Weibull, exponential, Gompertz, gamma, and log-logistic. The estimated "scale" and "shape" parameters then determine the precise form of the baseline hazard, after accounting for all the covariates. Parametric models are referred to as "nested" when one is a specific case of another, for instance the exponential is a special case of the Weibull. Models that require no such assumptions about the baseline and impose no specific distributional form are referred to as semi-parametric, or Cox models. For a Cox model, the baseline hazard rate does not have a parametric form but instead can be estimated from the data.[5]

---

[2] I examined survival analyses published during 1989–2005 in the following journals: *American Political Science Review, American Journal of Political Science, International Organization, World Politics, Journal of Politics, International Studies Quarterly, Journal of Conflict Resolution, Comparative Political Studies, Journal of Peace Research, Political Research Quarterly*, and *British Journal of Political Science*.

[3] Technically, the hazard rate is not really a probability because it can take values greater than one. But when talking about an event occurring in a given period, conditional on it not having occurred yet, it is standard practice for researchers to refer to the hazard rate as a probability (Beck 1998; Bennett 1999, 257; Alt, King, and Signorino 2000, 7; Collett 2003, 11–12).

[4] Similarly, the *baseline survivor function* is the probability of surviving beyond time *t* for an individual when all the covariates are zero.

[5] An important feature of Cox models is that no additional assumptions beyond the model are required to recover and plot the baseline hazard rate. You do not need one model for the coefficients and

The second choice concerns the nature of the covariates. *Time-constant covariates* (TCCs) are variables that retain their initial coding throughout the entire observation period. Examples of TCCs abound: a voter's gender and race, a politician's party affiliation, a nation's geographic position—all of these (normally) remain constant over time. *Time-varying covariates* (TVCs) are independent variables whose values, once assigned at the outset to a given case, can vary throughout the lifetime of the case as it undergoes what are known as *state changes*. Every time a state change occurs for an individual case, its hazard rate "jumps" either up or down to a different level. The hazard rate changes the instant the variable changes value (Box-Steffensmeier and Jones 2004, 108; Cleves, Gould, and Gutierrez 2002, 146). An example of a TVC might be regime status, where this status is an independent variable thought to affect the hazard rate of an individual country engaging in war. Imagine a country that spends twenty years as a dictatorship and then becomes a democracy. In the data-set, the country would retain its initial coding as a dictatorship for the first twenty years, and would need to be recoded as a democracy thereafter. The jump that occurs in this country's hazard rate at twenty years reflects the pacifist (or bellicose) tendencies associated with its new regime status. *Time-dependent coefficients* (TDCs) are associated with variables whose coding remains constant but whose effect undergoes either a decay or accretion function as it changes over the lifetime of an individual. For instance, a country might remain a dictatorship and never undergo a state change to democracy, but the effect that being a dictatorship has on its belligerence could gradually intensify or perhaps fade over the years. Of course a covariate, for example regime status, might be a TVC *and* require a TDC.

The political science literature on survival analysis tends to use the terms "time-varying covariate" and "time-dependent coefficient" interchangeably, when in fact they are analytically distinct (Cleves, Gould, and Guttierez 2002, 147; Therneau and Grambsch 2000, 127, 130). The tendency towards conflation stems in part from the fact that, for both TVCs and TDCs, the passage of time affects the hazard rate—by definition an individual can only undergo a state change, and the effects of being in one state or another can only wear off or intensify, as survival time passes. Nevertheless, conflating the two terms obscures the crucial difference between state changes and decay/accretion functions. One of the most important points emphasized throughout this chapter is that proper handling of TVCs and TDCs virtually eliminates scope for legitimate use of parametric models.

It is useful to visualize the distinction between TVCs and TDCs and examine their individual and combined effects on the hazard rate. Imagine a study with three independent variables, x_1, x_2, x_3. Suppose that x_1 reduces the hazard rate by five units, x_2 increases it by three units, and x_3 increases it by one unit. Suppose further that x_2 requires a TDC: Over time the link between this covariate and the dependent variable slowly wears off. Figure 23.1 shows the hazard functions of four hypothetical

another model (or any further assumptions) for the baseline. This is because *by definition* Cox models provide estimates of the baseline hazard once estimates of the coefficients have been obtained (Collett 2003, ch. 3; Kalbfleisch and Prentice 1980).

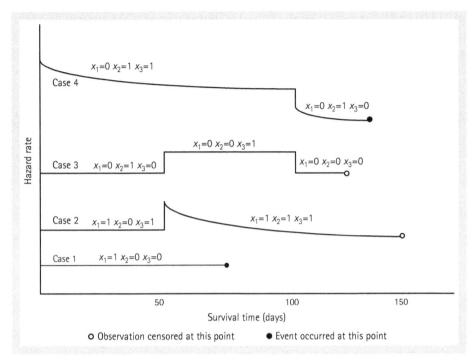

Fig. 23.1. Hazard functions with time-varying covariates and time-dependent coefficients

cases, whether they were still under observation when the study concluded (thus right censored), and the points in time (if any) at which they experienced a change in any of the three independent variables.

As a result of TVCs, state changes occur at $t = 50$ and $t = 100$, with the sudden shift in the value of a covariate causing the hazard rates for cases two, three, and four to jump (either up or down). In contrast, the presence of a TDC causes the hazard rate for cases two and four to fall gradually as a decay function. Notice also that x_2 must be modelled as both a TVC and a TDC: With case two the value of x_2 changes from zero to one at $t = 50$ and the effect of x_3 then erodes over the next hundred days, whereas with case four the coding of x_2 never varies throughout the study and its effect continues to wear off even after the case undergoes a state change with regard to a different independent variable at $t = 100$.

Ignoring TVCs and TDCs produces serious model specification errors because it amounts to using either false or incomplete information about individual cases (Box-Steffensmeier and Jones 2004; Bennett 1999; Box-Steffensmeier and Zorn 2001).[6] Of course TDCs should not be added arbitrarily because their inclusion

---

[6] This does impose certain informational demands on the researcher, but they are manageable, and in any event it is better to include TVCs and do your best to minimize potential measurement error and endogeneity problems with the variety of available methods than to omit them and consciously settle for a model that you know is biased (Box-Steffensmeier and Jones 2004, ch. 8; Collett 2003, ch. 8; Allison 1995, 145–7; Bennett 1999).

could exacerbate multicollinearity and reduce the efficiency of the estimators. In the hypothetical example above, the decay of the hazard rate associated with x_2 for cases two and four could turn out to be extremely gradual, effectively insignificant, so that we would not need to model it (we would, though, still need to treat x_2 as a TVC).

2 THE RELATIVE ADVANTAGES OF COX MODELS

Cox models are superior to parametric models in three main respects. I discuss each in turn.

2.1 More Reliable Treatment of the Baseline Hazard

The baseline hazard can take an infinite variety of shapes. It might be constant, rising, declining, U shaped, bell shaped, bimodal, a step function, and so forth. The choice of shape fundamentally affects the estimated coefficients, and fitting a possibly erroneous baseline to the data can impart enormous bias to the results (Allison 1984; Box-Steffensmeier and Zorn 2001; Bennett 1999; Box-Steffensmeier and Jones 1997; 2004). A particular shape should only be chosen on strong theoretical grounds, and never simply because it proves convenient. Parametric models are often suitable in engineering, for instance, where the basic behaviour of the objects under study— machine parts wearing out or ball bearings overheating—is simple and governed by laws of physics. But in political science it would be difficult to argue that even the strongest theories applied with this sort of logic or regularity. Fortunately, the Cox model alleviates the need to make a potentially incorrect choice because it requires no imposition of a specific form on the baseline hazard function. This is not always recognized, however, and researchers sometimes wrongly choose a parametric model over a Cox because they think that the latter makes extra assumptions.

Researchers often employ graphical and other diagnostic techniques to justify their choice of a particular parametric form, especially plots of the hazard function and the residuals (Collett 2003; Box-Steffensmeier and Jones 2004), but there is no reliable way to determine which form offers the best fit. Relying on raw hazard or survival plots entails the completely untenable assumption that no covariates are related to survival time (Allison 1995, 94), is highly subjective, and provides notoriously misleading inferences (see, for example, Warwick and Easton 1992).[7] Such subjectivity

---

[7] Grofman and Van Roozendaal (1997, 422) relate a wonderful example (about observing the heights of children leaving a school) that illustrates why researchers must undertake multivariate analysis and not merely inspect the shape of raw hazard plots and frequency distributions of events.

also detracts from the use of residual plots. A further serious problem with graphical methods is that that they lack the power to detect departures from the assumed model. This is particularly true of log-cumulative hazard and residual plots, which can produce beautifully straight lines even when the model being fit is quite erroneous (Crowley and Storer 1983; Golub 2007).

For nested models, one can utilize log-likelihood values to conduct a series of formal significance tests that will assess which model provides the better fit, but this method will only distinguish the Weibull or the gamma from the exponential. It says nothing about the relative fit of the Weibull versus the gamma, or the log-logistic versus the exponential, or the Gompertz versus the log-logistic, and so forth, because these models are not nested. One can partly overcome this problem by fitting a parametric model with a general gamma or generalized F distribution, under which the Weibull, log-logistic, exponential, and log-normal are all nested (Kalbfleisch and Prentice 2002, 38–9, 74–8; Box-Steffensmeier and Jones 2004, 86), but a few important distributional forms, such as the Gompertz, would still not be nested.

Researchers can use what is known as Akaike's information criterion (AIC), a statistic that combines information about the log-likelihood value and the number of estimated parameters in each model to compare models that are not nested (the Weibull versus the gamma, for example) (Collett 2003, 81; Box-Steffensmeier and Jones 2004). What must be recognized, though, is that the AIC is inherently limited because it provides only an informal means of discriminating between competing non-nested models. Unlike nested models, where differences in log-likelihood values assume a chi-square distribution, for non-nested models you simply do not know the distribution of differences in AIC values, thus you have no p-values available and no formal significance tests are possible.

The best way to justify a particular parametric form is to compare the estimated coefficients and the respective baseline hazard and survivor functions obtained from fitting a Cox model and the candidate parametric model (Bennett 1999, 262; Box-Steffensmeier and Jones 2004, ch. 4). For the baseline hazard, visual inspection of the resulting plot's shape might suggest the applicability of one parametric form rather than another—a horizontal line would indicate a constant hazard rate and thus an exponential, an inverted "U" would be consistent with a log-linear or a log-logistic model. For the baseline survivor functions, the question is whether the parametric plot matches the Cox plot in terms of how quickly it decreases and at what point it levels off. The chosen parametric form would only be appropriate if it matched the Cox plot quite closely.

Although these techniques are helpful, none deals adequately with the bias inherent in imposing a parametric baseline hazard.[8] To judge whether the parametric

---

[8] Researchers sometimes justify their choice of baseline hazard by fitting a parametric model (usually the Weibull) with gamma heterogeneity. Also known as a "frailty" model, this specification strategy has many attractive features, the most important of which is the ability to allow for omitted variable bias. But because frailty models offer no means of discriminating between non-nested models, and thus do little to attenuate the inherent bias caused by imposing a parametric baseline hazard, they should not be considered substitutes for Cox models (Hougaard 2000). Indeed, Cox models with frailty terms

estimates are "similar" to the Cox estimate can be highly subjective, and if the parametric estimates don't match those of the Cox, the parametric model is wrong (Cleves, Gould, and Guttierez 2002, 184). Likewise, conclusions about the shape of the recovered baselines will remain suspect because even after smoothing a noisy plot, the observer must not only judge the presence of linearity but also draw subtle distinctions between a large number of plausible, complex distributions and just how fast a function decreases or levels off. While it is tempting to settle this by focusing on the question "at what point is the complexity sufficiently unrecognisable to warrant using a Cox model?" the safer approach would be to ask "at what point is the plot sufficiently recognizable *not* to use a Cox model?" The costs of imposing the wrong baseline can be enormous. Only by setting a high threshold for this standard and making widespread use of the flexibility afforded by Cox models can we avoid the potential for seriously biased results.

2.2 Superior Handling of the Proportional Hazards Assumption

The proportional hazards (PH) assumption maintains that the hazard ratio between any two individuals is constant *over their entire survival times*. Stated another way, the assumption requires that "each observation's hazard function follows exactly the same pattern over time" (Box-Steffensmeier and Jones 2004, 132). What has not been fully recognized is that the need to take the PH assumption seriously provides a powerful reason for using Cox models rather than parametric models.

The PH assumption, so commonly associated with the Cox model, applies equally to the entire family of proportional hazards models, which includes the parametric Weibull, exponential, and Gompertz (Collett 2003, ch. 5; Box-Steffensmeier and Zorn 2001; Box-Steffensmeier and Jones 2004).[9] Regrettably, many studies mistakenly choose a parametric model over a Cox because the author believes that only the Cox makes the PH assumption.

It is also essential to recognize that log-logistic models, which are not part of the PH family, make a similar and equally demanding assumption: that the log-odds are proportional (Collett 2003, 225; Klein and Moeschberger 1997, 374). To see this, recall that the survivor function for the log-logistic parametric model is

$$S(t) = 1/[1 + (at)^p] \quad \text{where } a = \exp[-\beta'(x)] \tag{1}$$

---

constitute an interesting area for further research. These models are best considered as providing alternative explanations for nonproportional hazards or for accounting for common effects shared by groups of units.

[9] Two other parametric forms that are not part of the PH family are the gamma and the log-normal. Although these models do not make assumptions about proportionality, they are based on other assumptions. Even under normal circumstances they are each extremely difficult to manipulate and interpret because their hazard functions can only be written in terms of an integral that must be evaluated numerically, and the introduction of nonproportionality only exacerbates the problem.

so that the ratio of the log-odds of survival for any two individuals i and j is

$$\log \frac{\{Si(t)/[1 - Si(t)]\}}{\{Sj(t)/[1 - Sj(t)]\}}. \tag{2}$$

Simplifying this equation we get

$$\log\{Si(t)/[1 - Si(t)]\} - \log\{Sj(t)/[1 - Sj(t)]\} = -\mathrm{plog}(ta_i) + \mathrm{plog}(ta_j)$$

$$= p[\beta'(x_i - x_j)]. \tag{3}$$

Thus the log-logistic model assumes that the ratio of log-odds is proportional, and independent of time, which is precisely the counterpart to the PH assumption made by other parametric forms. Authors worried about PH violations in a Cox model are thus not necessarily safer with a log-logistic, as they sometimes believe.

Violations of the PH (or log-odds) assumption can result in enormous bias and render the estimates meaningless. While there are several ways to identify violations of the PH assumption (Collett 2003, 141, 247), most are highly subjective and unreliable.

For Cox models, though, a simple and powerful detection method was provided by Grambsch and Therneau (1994) and is available as a macro in the Stata software package (Box-Steffensmeier and Zorn 2001). The global test is not very powerful, however, and it has been shown to give a false indication that the PH assumption holds even when tests of the individual covariates reveal significant violations (Box-Steffensmeier, Reiter, and Zorn 2003, 45). I certainly found this to be the case with many of the forty-five replications I performed. When tests of the individual covariates reveal significant violations, one can then relax the PH assumption very easily by including TDCs of the form $\beta^* g(t)$, where $g(t)$ is some function of time (usually $\ln(t)$), without having to modify the structure of the data-set in any way.[10]

With parametric models, by contrast, there exists no adequate way to detect and correct violations of the proportional hazards assumption, since "tests and remedies for nonproportionality in the parametric context are largely nonexistent" (Box-Steffensmeier, Reiter, and Zorn 2003, 40). One test involves fitting what is known as a piecewise model, where one partitions the survival time into several periods and re-estimates the coefficients in each period. The PH assumption only holds if the estimates for each coefficient remain basically unchanged across all periods and if, based on a comparison of log-likelihood values, one cannot distinguish the piecewise model from one without partitions. But "basically unchanged" is highly subjective, and the size of the partitions is arbitrary, so that piecewise models can yield unreliable conclusions about the PH (or log-odds) assumption. And some intervals might have few or no events, which will dramatically inflate the standard errors for

---

[10] It is important to note that specifying the wrong functional form for the covariates can give misleading results about the presence of nonproportional hazards and which covariates require a TDC. As a solution, researchers can use penalized Cox models with splines to accommodate highly complex functional forms and formally test for improved fit. For details and examples see Therneau and Grambsch (2000) and Keele (2005). Although not yet widely available in standard software packages, such penalized models illustrate yet another advantage the Cox has over parametric alternatives.

these intervals. Another possibility is to fit a stratified parametric model, but this only works when the stratifying variables are viewed simply as a nuisance, since you don't obtain estimates for them. And not only can't you test for the effect of the stratifying variables, you can't test for the interaction of these variables with time either. Thus "stratification provides only minimal information about the nature of nonproportional hazards" (Box-Steffensmeier and Jones 2004, 134).

Even if one could reliably detect PH (or log-odds) violations in parametric models, satisfactory corrections are unavailable. Indeed, I know of no examples from political science or any other field where researchers have fit a parametric model with TDCs. Neither did Bill Gould, Head of Development at Stata (personal communication).

So how often might we expect to find violations of the PH (or log-odds) assumption, which in turn would rule out use of a parametric model? Nearly always, since *by definition* the PH assumption no longer holds when a model includes TVCs (Collett 2003, 146, 253; Box-Steffensmeier and Jones 1997, 1433).[11] This is often overlooked because the PH formula is usually presented in a context that assumes no TVCs (Cleves, Gould, and Guttierez 2002, 113; Allison 1995, 113–14). But formally, we can see that whenever TVCs are present, and the coding of the covariates therefore changes with time (equations (4) and (5)), the hazard ratio is no longer constant but rather depends on time (equation (6)):

$$h_i(t) = h_0(t) \exp(B_1 x_{1i} + B_2 x_{2i}(t)) \tag{4}$$

$$h_j(t) = h_0(t) \exp(B_1 x_{1j} + B_2 x_{2j}(t)) \tag{5}$$

$$\frac{h_i(t)}{h_j(t)} = \exp[B_1(x_{1i} - x_{1j}) + B_2(x_{2i}(t) - x_{2j}(t))]. \tag{6}$$

Likewise, a simple extension of equation (2) to include TVCs makes the log-odds in equation (3) depend on time, thus not proportional (Golub 2007).

Figure 23.1, presented earlier, provides a graphical illustration of the fact that every time an individual undergoes a state-change the resulting jump in its hazard rate destroys the proportionality of the hazard ratio. Because of a TVC, the hazard ratios between cases one and two, and between one and three, are no longer proportional after $t = 50$. Of course in theory a covariate might have *precisely* zero affect on the hazard rate, so that a state change would produce no "jump" whatsoever and thus no violation of the PH (or log-odds) assumption. In practice this situation never occurs, and the relevant issue is whether the jump results in a violation that is significant enough to warrant correction with a TDC.

Researchers increasingly recognize that many of the independent variables that interest them are TVCs. Important attributes of the international system and dyadic or multistate relations change over time, such as the presence of bipolarity, the number of existing states, patterns of alliances, the presence of war, patterns of trade,

---

[11] SPSS 11.0 electronic documentation notes under help topics that when "the values of one (or more) of your covariates are different at different time points," then "the proportional hazards assumption does not hold. That is, hazard ratios change across time."

characteristics of neighboring states, and the balance of force in any given conflict. Key attributes of individual states and domestic politics also change over time, such as the level of democratization, regime status, economic conditions, shifting public opinion, and the ideological persuasion of the government. Even the attributes and activities of institutions are subject to change, such as voting rules, membership, and the types of intervention and mediation efforts they employ.

The presumption that no variables undergo state changes is particularly untenable when individual cases under analysis can survive for very long periods of time: four years for cabinets (Warwick 1994); ten years for interstate wars (Bennett and Stam 1996); twenty-seven years for legislative decisions in the European Union (Golub 1999; 2002); fifty years for Supreme Court precedents (Spriggs and Hansford 2001); fifty to sixty years for civil wars, alliances, and political leaders (Regan 2002; Bennett 1997; Bienen and van de Walle 1991); 136 years for interstate rivalries (Bennett 1996); 155 years for spells of peace (Werner 2000); and an astonishing 2,375 years for Maya polities (Cioffi-Revilla and Landman 1999). In all of these situations, the presence of TVCs would violate the PH assumption. And even when there are no TVCs present, we have good reason to suspect that the nature of many political processes will produce violations of the PH assumption (Box-Steffensmeier and Zorn 2001).

In theory, then, the ubiquity of both TDCs and TVCs makes violations of the PH (or log-odds) assumption likely in most situations, which leaves virtually no room for parametric models. My forty-five replications confirmed this. Of the thirty-four studies that included TVCs, Grambsch and Therneau tests for individual covariates revealed that only three had no significant PH violations in any of the models fit.[12] Of the eleven without TVCs, only one had no significant violations in any model. In practice, therefore, parametric models should have been ruled out in over 90 percent of these studies.

2.3 Cox Models are Best for Handling Tied Data

Cases are said to be "tied" when they have either identical event times or identical censored survival times. Ties pose a serious problem for survival analysis, which takes as a central assumption that the hazard function is continuous and thus identical survival times are impossible. Unfortunately, researchers often base their selection of a parametric model over a Cox model on the erroneous belief that parametric models are unaffected by ties. In fact, the ability of Cox models to handle ties constitutes yet another example of their relative superiority. Due to advances in statistics and software in the 1990s, Cox models now allow several readily available methods for approximating the likelihood function in the presence of even heavily tied data (Collett 2003, 67–9; Box-Steffensmeier and Jones 2004, ch. 4). Because they assume

[12] I also discovered that the initial replication of Bennett's (1997) study of alliance duration conducted by Box-Steffensmeier, Reiter, and Zorn (2003), erroneously concluded that there were no PH violations.

continuous survival times, where by definition ties are impossible, and lack such methods of approximation, by their very nature parametric models are rendered inappropriate when data is heavily tied.[13] In political science, where dependent variables are often measured in fairly long units, such as months or quarters or even years, this naturally increases the number of ties in the data and makes it all the more important to use Cox models rather than parametric models.

3 The Illusory Benefits of Parametric Models

There is very little to lose from switching to Cox models. While Cox models do have some limitations, "none of them is serious" (Yamaguchi 1991, 102), and the reputed advantages of parametric models are modest at best.

3.1 Efficiency Concerns do not Justify Parametric Models

Because it is only semiparametric, the Cox uses less information, which can reduce the precision of the estimates. With large samples, though, the efficiency of the Cox very nearly matches parametric models (Yamaguchi 1991, 102; Box-Steffensmeier and Jones 2004, 87). And of course even if the parametric estimates are slightly more precise, they might be totally wrong if the chosen form is incorrect. As noted above, this is likely to be the case in most situations.

3.2 Study of Duration Dependence does not Justify Parametric Models

Many researchers choose a parametric model in order to test competing hypotheses about the nature of duration dependence. Determining which of several theoretically plausible shapes represents the baseline hazard and gaining its precise statistical estimate are so important, some argue, that we should often prefer parametric models to Cox models (Bennett 1999, 262). Provided that the analyst has a strong desire to make inferences about duration dependency, Box-Steffensmeier and Jones tend to agree (2004, 86).

But there are a number of reasons why Cox models actually provide more reliable insight into duration dependence than do parametric models. The main one is that

---

[13] Of course one could fit a parametric model to heavily tied data, in that the software would not prevent it, but the model would still be inappropriate.

precise but inaccurate information about the baseline hazard is clearly not desirable. And the only way to get accurate information is to be certain beforehand that you are fitting the correct parametric form. It is a fundamental mistake to pick a parametric form in a manner that treats the nature of duration dependence as a matter of speculation, which is necessarily the case when one has competing plausible hypotheses. Simply put, "when you do not have a good a priori reason to know the shape of the hazard, you should use [Cox] semiparametric analysis" (Cleves, Gould, and Guttierez 2002, 214). Moreover, the incorporation of TVCs and TDCs often exposes previously incorrect inferences about duration dependence (Bueno de Mesquita and Siverson 1995; Warwick 1994; Box-Steffensmeier, Reiter, and Zorn 2003), and as discussed above these terms make a Cox model preferable to a parametric. The plot of the recovered Cox baseline hazard rate can be noisy, but the application of readily available smoothing methods allows researchers to see the basic pattern more clearly. Thus while Cox models do not provide a single parameter that precisely summarizes the shape of the baseline hazard, they do provide more reliable information about overall duration dependence than do parametric models.

Equally important, Cox models with TDCs return information about the effects of the passage of time that can be more precise and also more valuable than a parametric estimate of general duration dependence. After all, the general duration dependence indicated by the shape and scale parameters is just "unexplained variance in future duration that is statistically related to past duration" (Bennett 1999, 262). If one were capable of including all the relevant covariates in the model, the appearance of duration dependence would vanish (Bennett 1999; Beck 1998). The presence of duration dependence does alert us that important variables have been left out of the model, but apart from this we can draw no clear inferences. Put more pointedly, duration dependence is nothing more than a nuisance (Beck 1998; Box-Steffensmeier and Jones 2004, 22). By contrast, precise estimates of the extent to which individual covariates in the model exhibit duration dependence clearly allow researchers to draw substantive conclusions. This is exactly what TDCs provide, and you can only fit them with Cox models.

3.3 Interest in Forecasting does not Justify Parametric Models

As with other quantitative methods, the estimated coefficients from a survival analysis allow researchers to make predictions about how changes to each of the covariates affect the dependent variable. With either a parametric or a Cox model, one can easily assess the effect on the hazard rate of a unit change in any of the covariates, as well as predict the median survival time for an individual with any particular combination of covariate values, even when the model includes TVCs (Cleves, Gould, and Guttierez 2002, 17, 250; Collett 2003, 270). Likewise, both parametric and Cox models allow researchers to make out-of-sample predictions, in the sense that inferences can be tested against fresh data. When it comes to this gold standard of model validation, neither type of model has an edge.

But there is one particular type of out-of-sample prediction that only parametric models can make, and that is forecasting beyond the last observed survival time. This situation obtains whenever the predicted median survival time of a hypothetical case with a particular set of covariate values exceeds the maximum survival time recorded in the study. Some authors have argued that researchers interested in forecasting what will happen beyond the period of available data should prefer parametric models to Cox models (Box-Steffensmeier and Jones 2004, 86). I disagree for several reasons. Forecasting is perilous business, thus hardly a decisive reason to pick a parametric rather than a Cox model. Standard statistical modeling textbooks rightly caution against forecasting (Montgomery, Peck, and Vining 2001, 5, 11) because predictions beyond the final observation time are very sensitive to model choice and you might have the wrong model. Even with the correct model, predictions are inherently dubious because they depend on tail areas where data is sparse.

Putting aside these serious problems, the actual utility of parametric models in terms of extrapolation is marginal, especially when weighed against the many benefits of Cox models. Out of eighty-four survival studies surveyed, I found only six where political scientists actually said anything about what might happen beyond the final observed survival time. Moreover, in five of these six cases, the forecasts were unreliable because significant PH violations (whether from TVCs or TCCs) should have necessitated use of a Cox model instead. In the sole remaining instance, the forecast was trivial: One government was predicted to last longer were it not for a constitutionally required election, and even then only three months (i.e. 5 percent) beyond the last observed survival time (King et al. 1990, 867).

3.4 Flexible Parametric Models

An alternative to the Cox is to model the baseline hazard parametrically with what are known as spline functions (Royston and Parmar 2002). While this method is certainly superior to standard parametric models, it offers no clear advantages over the Cox, apart from an improved ability to study the (substantively meaningless) baseline hazard, and it comes with some drawbacks. First, the method is no more capable than traditional parametric models of handling heavily tied data. Second, it also makes the PH or proportional log-odds assumption, so one needs to assess and account for the form of duration dependency, which can be cumbersome, especially since there is no equivalent of the Grambsch and Therneau test. Moreover, correcting for nonproportional hazards and interpreting the results is not as straightforward as with the Cox, since these models employ complex interactions between covariates and the spline function rather than $\text{ß}^*g(t)$ terms (Royston and Parmar 2002, 2177, 2183). Finally, the fit of these models can become unstable as the shape of the spline grows more complex (personal communications with Royston, 2003).

4 MAKING THE MOST OF SURVIVAL ANALYSIS

The primary conclusion to draw from the preceding discussion is that in nearly all situations researchers should fit a Cox model rather than a parametric model in order to avoid unreliable estimates. More precisely, the following methodological steps should become standard practice:

1. Fit a Cox model with TVCs as appropriate;
2. Check for violations of the PH assumption by using the Grambsch and Therneau test for individual covariates;
3. If there are no significant PH violations, then recover and inspect the baseline hazard and survivor functions from this model;
4. If there are significant violations, fit a Cox model with TVCs and TDCs;
5. Recover and inspect the baseline hazard from this model to learn about general duration dependence, if desired.

Parametric models should always be treated with caution since they are inherently prone to bias, and should be avoided unless all of the following conditions are satisfied: There are few ties in the data, there are no significant PH violations either intrinsically from the TCCs or automatically from the presence of TVCs, the baseline functions recovered from step three indicate a clearly recognizable shape, and the estimated coefficients from the Cox model in step one match those from the candidate parametric model.

5 CONCLUSION

Survival analysis is poised to become one of the most dominant quantitative methodologies in political science, and rightly so. But to take full advantage of this powerful tool, researchers need to pay close attention to issues of model specification. This chapter has shown that the deficiencies of parametric models are many and varied, and has proposed a set of standard methodological practices to guide future work.

It is essential that researchers distinguish between time-varying covariates, where the coding of the independent variable alters over the lifetime of the case as it undergoes state-changes, and time-dependent coefficients, where the coding of the independent variable remains constant but its effect changes over time. There are good reasons to believe that both are ubiquitous in the processes that interest social scientists.

Except in rare circumstances, researchers should avoid parametric models in favor of Cox models. Parametric models are still commonly used throughout political science, despite their many disadvantages. These models impose a particular form on the baseline hazard rate, and if the chosen form is wrong it can render the results meaningless. This is an inherent risk with parametric models because the baseline hazard might take a form that is extremely complex, and because diagnostic tests to determine the most appropriate form are limited in power and can prove misleading. Compared with Cox models, parametric models are also prone to bias because they can't handle heavily tied data, and can't easily accommodate nonproportional hazards.

There are only three possible reasons why researchers might prefer parametric models over Cox models—to gain more precise estimates, to forecast beyond the final observed survival time, and to obtain a precise estimate of duration dependence—but none is compelling. Efficiency gains from parametric models are modest and the inherent risk of picking an erroneous baseline form means that estimated coefficients, even if precise, are likely to be wrong. Forecasting is notoriously unreliable, is hardly ever done, is precluded in most cases because of the need to incorporate TVCs and TDCs (in only one out of eighty-four studies I examined was a justifiable forecast made), and its utility is far outweighed by the many advantages of Cox models. As to the third reason, parametric estimates of duration dependence are not particularly informative, and moreover they can be precise but wrong. They are almost certain to be wrong when data are heavily tied, there are TVCs, or other sources of nonproportionality. By contrast, a properly specified Cox model returns valuable information about the duration dependence associated with particular covariates as well as more reliable information about overall duration dependence.

In conclusion, then, on both theoretical and practical grounds much greater use should be made of Cox models. This would enable researchers to elicit more useful information from their data, and would facilitate more reliable substantive inferences about important political processes.

References

ALLISON, P. 1984. *Event History Analysis.* Beverly Hills, Calif.: Sage.
——— 1995. *Survival Analysis Using the SAS System.* Cary, NC: SAS Institute.
ALT, J., KING, G., and SIGNORINO, C. 2000. Aggregation among binary, count and duration models: estimating the same quantities for different levels of data. *Political Analysis,* 9: 1–24.
BECK, N. 1998. Modelling space and time: the event history approach. In *Research Strategies in the Social Sciences,* ed. E. Scarborough and E. Tanenbaum. Oxford: Oxford University Press.
BENNETT, S. 1996. Security, bargaining and the end of interstate rivalry. *International Studies Quarterly,* 40: 157–84.
——— 1997. Testing alternative models of alliance duration, 1816–984. *American Journal of Political Science,* 41: 846–78.
——— 1999. Parametric models, duration dependence, and time-varying data revisited. *American Journal of Political Science,* 43: 256–70.

—— and STAM, A. 1996. The duration of interstate wars, 1816–1985. *American Political Science Review*, 90: 239–57.

BIENEN, H., and VAN DE WALLE, N. 1991. *Of Time and Power: Leadership Duration in the Modern World*. Stanford, Calif.: Stanford University Press.

BOX-STEFFENSMEIER, J., and JONES, B. 1997. Time is of the essence: event history models in political science. *American Journal of Political Science*, 41: 1414–61.

—— 2004. *Event History Modeling in Political Science*. Cambridge: Cambridge University Press.

—— REITER, D., and ZORN, C. 2003. Nonproportional hazards and event history analysis in international relations. *Journal of Conflict Resolution*, 47: 33–53.

—— and ZORN, C. 2001. Duration models and proportional hazards in political science. *American Journal of Political Science*, 45: 972–88.

BUENO DE MESQUITA, B., and SIVERSON, R. 1995. War and the survival of political leaders: a comparative study of regime types and political accountability. *American Political Science Review*, 89: 841–55.

CIOFFI-REVILLA, C., and LANDMAN, T. 1999. Evolution of Maya polities in the ancient Mesoamerican system. *International Studies Quarterly*, 43: 559–98.

CLEVES, M., GOULD, W., and GUTTIEREZ, R. 2002. *An Introduction to Survival Analysis Using Stata*. College Station, Tex.: Stata Corporation.

COLLETT, D. 2003. *Modelling Survival Data in Medical Research*, 2nd edn. Boca Raton, Fla.: Chapman and Hall/CRC.

CROWLEY, J., and STORER, B. 1983. Comment on a paper by Aitkin, Laird and Francis. *Journal of the American Statistical Association*, 78: 277–81.

GOLUB, J. 1999. In the shadow of the vote? Decisionmaking in the European Community. *International Organization*, 53: 733–64.

—— 2002. Institutional reform and decisionmaking in the European Union. In *Institutional Challenges in the European Union*, ed. M. Hosli and A. Van Deemen. London: Routledge.

—— 2007. Survival analysis and European Union decisionmaking. *European Union Politics*, 8: 155–79.

GRAMBSCH, P., and THERNEAU, T. 1994. Proportional hazards tests and diagnostics based on weighted residuals. *Biometrika*, 81: 515–26.

GROFMAN, B., and VAN ROOZENDAAL, P. 1997. Review article: modelling cabinet durability and termination. *British Journal of Political Science*, 27: 419–51.

HOUGAARD, P. 2000. *Analysis of Multivariate Survival Data*. New York: Springer.

KALBFLEISCH, J., and PRENTICE, J. 2002. *The Statistical Analysis of Failure Time Data*, 2nd edn. New York: Wiley.

KEELE, L. 2005. Covariate functional form in Cox models. Mimeo.

KING, G., ALT, J., BURNS, N., and LAVER, M. 1990. A unified model of cabinet dissolution in parliamentary democracies. *American Journal of Political Science*, 34: 846–71.

KLEIN, J., and MOESCHBERGER, M. 1997. *Survival Analysis: Techniques for Censored and Truncated Data*. New York: Springer.

MONTGOMERY, D., PECK, E., and VINING, G. 2001. *Introduction to Linear Regression Analysis*, 3rd edn. Wiley: New York.

REGAN, P. 2002. Third-party interventions and the duration of intrastate conflicts. *Journal of Conflict Resolution*, 46: 55–73.

ROYSTON, P., and PARMAR, M. 2002. Flexible parametric models for censored survival data, with applications to prognostic modelling and estimation of treatment effects. *Statistics in Medicine*, July: 1275–97.

Spriggs, J., and Hansford, T. 2001. Explaining the overruling of U.S. Supreme Court precedent. *Journal of Politics*, 63: 1091–111.

Therneau, T., and Grambsch, P. 2000. *Modelling Survival Data: Extending the Cox Model*. New York: Springer.

Warwick, P. 1994. *Government Survival in Parliamentary Democracies*. Cambridge: Cambridge University Press.

——and Easton, S. 1992. The cabinet stability controversy: new perspectives on a classic problem. *American Journal of Political Science*, 36: 122–46.

Werner, S. 2000. The effects of political similarity on the onset of militarised disputes, 1816–1985. *Political Research Quarterly*, 53: 343–74.

Yamaguchi, K. 1991. *Event History Analysis*. Newbury Park, Calif.: Sage.

C H A P T E R 24

....

CROSS-LEVEL/ ECOLOGICAL INFERENCE

....

WENDY K. TAM CHO

CHARLES F. MANSKI

THE cross-level or ecological inference problem has fascinated scholars for nearly a century (Ogburn and Goltra 1919; Allport 1924; Gehlke and Biehl 1934). The problem occurs when one is interested in the behavior of individuals, but has data only at an aggregated level (e.g. precincts, hospital wards, counties). This data limitation creates a situation where the behavior of individuals must be surmised from data on aggregated sets of individuals rather than on individuals themselves. Since the goal is to make inferences from aggregate units that are often derived from an "environmental level" (i.e. geographical/ecological units such as a county or precinct), the term "ecological inference" is used to describe this type of analysis. Relatedly, while it is often the case that one is interested in individual-level behavior, this problem occurs more generally whenever the level of interest is less aggregated than the level of the data. For instance, one might be interested in behavior at the county level when only state-level data are available. Accordingly, the term "cross-level inference" is often used as a synonym for ecological inference.

The ecological inference problem is an especially intriguing puzzle because it is a very long-standing problem with an exceptionally wide-ranging impact. Occurrences are common across many disciplines, and scholars with diverse backgrounds and interests have a stake in approaches to this problem. Political scientists, for instance, confront these issues when they try to detect whether members of different racial groups cast their ballots differently, using only data at the precinct level that identify vote totals and racial demographics but not vote totals broken down by racial categories. In a completely different substantive area, epidemiologists confront identical methodological issues when they seek to explain which environmental factors influence disease susceptibility using only data from counties or hospital wards, rather than individual patients. Economists studying consumer demand and marketing strategies might need to infer individual spending habits from an analysis of sales data from a specific region and the aggregate characteristics of individuals in that region, rather than from data on individuals' characteristics and purchases. These examples are but a few of the myriad applications and fields where the ecological inference problem has emerged.

Not only does the general cross-level inference problem span many fields, the mathematics of ecological inference are also related to important inferential problems in other disciplines, even when the subject matter is not substantially related. For instance, geographers have long been intrigued with the "modifiable areal unit problem" (MAUP), a problem that is isomorphic to the ecological inference problem. MAUP occurs when the estimates at one level of aggregation are different from the estimates obtained at a different level of aggregation (Yule and Kendall 1950; Openshaw and Taylor 1979). Many statisticians and mathematicians have been captivated by Simpson's Paradox (Simpson 1951), which is the reversal in direction of association between two variables when a third ("lurking") variable is controlled. Described in this way, we can see that Simpson's Paradox (and consequently ecological inference) is akin to the omitted variable problem discussed in virtually all econometrics and regression texts. Scholars with a wide variety of methodological backgrounds and training have simultaneously been contributing to a deeper understanding of the nuances behind making cross-level inferences. Their notation and terminology may differ, but the similarity of the underlying problems cannot be denied. These connections are important to note, since scholars so often gain their keenest insight into how to approach a problem of interest by making a foray into an established literature in a field far from their own. The value of tying together methodological developments across disciplinary boundaries can be enormous.

This chapter is intended to be an exposition of some of the main methodological approaches to the ecological inference problem. We present our discussion in two parts. We first pass through a general exposition, with minimal math, and then approach the problem with significantly more mathematical detail. In the first part, we begin by discussing the fundamental indeterminacy of the problem. We then present a framework that coherently binds the variety of approaches that have been proposed to address this problem. Next, we provide an overview of these various approaches and comment on their respective contributions. In the second part, we place the ecological inference problem within the literature of partial identification and discuss recent work generalizing the use of logical bounds on possible solutions as an identification region for the general $r \times c$ problem. Finally, we conclude, cautiously but optimistically, with some admonitions about this fascinating problem that has enthralled decades of scholars from varied disciplines.

1 ECOLOGICAL INFERENCE THEN AND NOW

1.1 Fundamental Indeterminacy

The ecological inference problem is an example of an inverse problem with many "solutions." Accordingly, the problem is defined by ("plagued with" one might lament) a fundamental indeterminacy. Although one may wish to obtain a point estimate or "solution" to the problem, there is not enough information to narrow down the feasible set of estimates to one particular point estimate. This type of problem has been described as "partially identified" because while the available information does not allow one to identify the parameter of interest without the imposition of strong assumptions, it does often allow one to identify a "region" within which the parameter must lie, thus partially identifying the problem. How to proceed with partially identified problems such as the ecological inference problem is not obvious.

For consistency, ease of illustration, and without loss of generality, we will employ the example of racial voting in the United States throughout this chapter. Parallels to other applications should not be difficult to spot. In this voting application, the challenge is to infer how individuals voted from election returns aggregated at the precinct level. Because US elections employ the secret ballot, individual vote choices are unknown. Election returns, however, are reported at the precinct level, and aggregate individual racial categorizations can usually be obtained and merged with the voting data. Hence, for any given precinct, the available data include how many votes each candidate received as well as the precinct's racial composition. The problem can be summed up with a contingency table akin to the one shown in Table 24.1.[1] Here, Y represents vote choice, Z represents racial group, and X represents the precinct. This contingency table represents a single particular precinct. There are I similar tables to represent each of I total precincts in a district.

In this example, there are two racial groups and three candidates, presenting a 2×3 problem. Y takes one of three values, y_1, y_2, or y_3; Z takes one of two values, z_1 or z_2; and X takes one of I values, $x_1, \ldots, x_I$. The known elements of the table are displayed as the so-called marginals, the proportion of the vote each candidate received in a precinct, $P(Y \mid X)$, and the proportion of each racial group in a precinct, $P(Z \mid X)$. The interior cells are conditional probabilities; that is, the probability that we observe a vote choice given a precinct and racial group, $P(Y \mid Z, X)$. Political scientists may be more familiar with notation resembling the lower contingency table in Table 24.1.

---

[1] Note here that we assume that everyone turned out to vote. Of course, this is an unrealistic assumption. In real American elections, substantial proportions of each voter group abstain from voting, which means there is one additional category of vote and the ecological inference problem is more complicated computationally, though not conceptually. For present purposes, ignoring abstention reduces clutter and obscures nothing about the nature of the inference problem. Note also that there is a literature discussing this problem of measurement error (i.e. assuming that our measure of turnout is perfect) in ecological election analysis (Kousser 1973; Loewen 1982; Kleppner 1985; Grofman, Migalski, and Noviello 1985).

Table 24.1. Contingency table for precinct $X = x_1$

	Candidate 1	Candidate 2	Candidate 3	
Group 1	$P(Y = y_1 \mid Z = z_1, X)P(Z = z_1 \mid X)$	$P(Y = y_2 \mid Z = z_1, X)P(Z = z_1 \mid X)$	$P(Y = y_3 \mid Z = z_1, X)P(Z = z_1 \mid X)$	$P(Z = z_1 \mid X)$
Group 2	$P(Y = y_1 \mid Z = z_2, X)P(Z = z_2 \mid X)$	$P(Y = y_2 \mid Z = z_2, X)P(Z = z_2 \mid X)$	$P(Y = y_3 \mid Z = z_2, X)P(Z = z_2 \mid X)$	$P(Z = z_2 \mid X)$
	$P(Y = y_1 \mid X)$	$P(Y = y_2 \mid X)$	$P(Y = y_3 \mid X)$	
	Candidate 1	Candidate 2	Candidate 3	
Group 1	$\beta_{11}z_1$	$\beta_{12}z_1$	$\beta_{13}z_1$	z_1
Group 2	$\beta_{21}z_2$	$\beta_{22}z_2$	$\beta_{23}z_2$	z_2
	y_1	y_2	y_3	

Table 24.2. 2×2 contingency table

	Candidate 1	Candidate 2	
Group 1	$\beta_{11} z_1$	$(1 - \beta_{11}) z_1$	z_1
Group 2	$\beta_{21} z_2$	$(1 - \beta_{21}) z_2$	z_2
	y_1	y_2	

Here, the βs are often referred to as parameters, but they are equivalent to the conditional probabilities shown in the upper contingency table. That is, $\beta_{ij} = P(Y = y_j \mid Z = z_i, X)$. We know, by Bayes's Theorem, that $\beta = P(Y, Z \mid X) = P(Y \mid Z, X) P(Z \mid X)$. Since $P(Z \mid X)$, the proportion of voters in each racial group, is observed via census data, the ecological inference problem boils down to inferring $P(Y \mid Z, X)$, which is not observed. If the ballot had one fewer candidate, it would pose a 2×2 problem, which would be appealing because the mathematics involved for a 2×2 problem are simpler than those for an $r \times c$ problem, where $r > 2$ and/or $c > 2$. However, whether the problem is 2×2 or $r \times c$, the basic inferential problem, which is to infer the conditional probabilities, $P(Y \mid Z, X)$, from the observed values, $P(Y \mid X)$ and $P(Z \mid X)$, does not change. The core issue is that multiple values of the former probabilities are consistent with given values for the latter ones.

We use the simple 2×2 example shown in Table 24.2 to illustrate the indeterminacy. The known elements of this problem are the proportion of voters in each group, z_1 and z_2, and the proportion of votes received by each candidate, y_1 and y_2. The unknown elements are the proportions of each group that voted for each candidate, $\beta_{11}, \beta_{12}, \beta_{21}$, and β_{22}. If we assume that group 1 and group 2 are mutually exclusive and exhaustive, then z_2 is simply $(1 - z_1)$. Similarly, if we assume that all votes were cast for either candidate 1 or candidate 2 and there were no abstentions, then $y_2 = (1 - y_1)$. Usually, there is such a contingency table to describe each areal unit in the data-set. In our voting application, since a set of precincts comprise the voting district in question, one might want to index these values with a further subscript to indicate the precinct. For each precinct, i, then, we have the following relationship:

$$y_{1i} = \beta_{11i} z_{1i} + \beta_{21i}(1 - z_{1i}).$$

This relationship holds exactly for each of the I precincts in the district, yielding a system with I equations (one for each precinct) and $2I$ unknowns (two parameters, β_{11i} and β_{21i}, for each precinct). The available information is that these $2I$ parameters solve the I equations and, moreover, that each parameter takes a value between 0 and 1. The fundamental indeterminacy is that multiple values of the parameters satisfy these restrictions. Note as well that adding observations of further precincts does not change the indeterminacy. Each new precinct adds one more equation to the system and two more parameters to be inferred.

Table 24.3. Duncan and Davis bounds example: employed females by occupation and color for Chicago, 1940

	Not domestic service	Domestic service	
White	[348,578, 376,179] [0.912, 0.984]	[6,073, 33,674] [0.016, 0.088]	382,252 (0.933)
Nonwhite	[0, 27,601] [0.00, 1.00]	[0, 27,601] [0.00, 1.00]	27,601 (0.067)
	376,179 (0.918)	33,674 (0.082)	409,853

1.2 Various Approaches

Despite the fundamental indeterminacy, scholars have nonetheless pursued the ecological inference problem. Certainly, the substantive applications are interesting and important. Although the multifarious approaches to this problem have been distinct, they can be seen as lying along a continuum. The left end of the continuum is characterized by a lack of assumptions, and concomitantly high credibility. Even when no assumptions are imposed, the data can allow one to narrow the range in which the true values of the parameters of interest lie (Duncan and Davis 1953). To move along this continuum, assumptions must be made. At the right end of the continuum are approaches that lead one to a precise point estimate for each parameter. There are, to be sure, many different approaches clustered on the right, in the region of strong and numerous assumptions. In general, one cannot zero in on precise estimates without making restrictive assumptions, and thus trading reduced credibility for increased "precision." Whether or how one settles on a model, with attendant assumptions, in order to narrow the range of estimates is a critical decision that is inextricably tied to the eventual substantive interpretation of the analysis. How to proceed is rarely obvious on the basis of theory alone, and what criteria one should employ is a function of the application at hand, the data, and the costs and benefits associated with different kinds of inferential errors. There are no pat answers, no generic solutions. Instead, each individual project of data analysis merits careful and explicit consideration.

1.2.1 *Ranges*

In some applications, simply narrowing the range in which the possible estimates lie may be sufficient. Duncan and Davis (1953) developed the idea of bounds in an ecological inference problem. Table 24.3 reproduces their example from data for Chicago in 1940.[2] The contingency table shows the breakdown of race and occupation for

---

[2] Note that the interior cells of Table 24.3 are set up a bit differently to Tables 24.1 and 24.2. The interior cells of Table 24.3 give the possible range of the overall number of persons in the cell. We present these different, though obviously related, interior cells to maximize similarity with the Duncan and Davis presentation and to simplify the discussion of how to compute ranges.

females. Usually, we can observe only the marginals of this table. We need to infer the unobservable values in the interior cells from the observed values in the marginals. Given only the marginals, we can surmise nothing more than that the percentage of nonwhites engaged in domestic service spans the entire range from 0 to 100 percent. However, with 33,674 women in domestic service total, and only 27,601 nonwhite women, there cannot be fewer than 6,073 (33,674 − 27,601) white women in domestic service. Hence, the range of whites engaged in domestic service is fairly narrow (1.6 to 8.8 percent). Similarly, the range of whites engaged in nondomestic service is small (91.2 to 98.4 percent). Depending on one's interest with these data, these computed ranges may be sufficient for one's substantive interest in the problem. In the Duncan and Davis framework, the greatest appeal is that no assumptions need be made. Clearly, the best possible outcome is attained when nothing is assumed to define the range of possible estimates, and these computed bounds are sufficient to make the type of inferences that are warranted. Moreover, these bounds are simple to compute:

$$\beta_{11} \in \left[\max\left(0, \frac{Y_1 - (1 - Z_1)}{Z_1} \right), \min\left(\frac{Y_1}{Z_1}, 1 \right) \right]$$

and

$$\beta_{21} \in \left[\max\left(0, \frac{Y_1 - Z_1}{1 - Z_1} \right), \min\left(\frac{Y_1}{1 - Z_1}, 1 \right) \right].$$

It is important to note that even wide bounds may be helpful. This is particularly true if one is interested in gaining a sense of how informative the data are or how much one might need to rely on assumptions to move toward a point estimate. How "wide" or "narrow" bounds are is dependent on the available data and what one wishes to discover. Indeed, a point estimate is not always the end goal. Instead, the true goal is to seek insight into the substantive question of interest. A point estimate (with questionable reliability) is one way of obtaining such insight, but there are other vehicles as well, and having a firm grasp of how informative the data are is an important aspect of the analysis. If one moves directly to a single estimator that yields a point estimate, one is wedded to the strong assumptions that were required to identify the problem. Hence, even though it is rare in real applications to obtain tight bounds on all parameters and it would be unusual that the bounds were sufficient to address all of one's substantive interests, the inherent value of the bounds should not be underestimated. It provides a basis from which to understand how informative the data are without the imposition of questionable assumptions and serves as a domain of consensus among all researchers who may otherwise disagree on the appropriate assumptions for an application.

1.2.2 *Point Estimates*

Although estimating ranges is important and easily integrated in an ecological inference analysis, the information emerging from such an analysis may be insufficiently direct on the substantive question of interest. It may be the case that one needs to narrow the feasible set of estimates further, indeed even to a single point estimate. If so, one has the option of employing an ecological inference model that will yield a point estimate. The tie that binds all models that yield a point estimate is that they rely heavily on strong assumptions. In any particular application, one may have a sense for which assumptions are more tenable, but whether those assumptions hold is never known with certainty. The trade-off is that one obtains a point estimate, which is helpful, but if the assumptions required to narrow the feasible estimates to a single point are wrong, the point estimate will be incorrect and misleading. The potential downside is significant. Accordingly, employing any ecological inference model that yields a point estimate should be approached guardedly with attention to the impact of the assumptions.

Following Robinson's (1950) seminal article demonstrating the lack of agreement between ecological correlation and individual correlation, and the articles which followed Robinson still using ecological correlations as a substitute for individual correlations, Goodman (1953) sought to clarify the problem in the regression context. He cautioned that "*in general* the study of the regression between ecological variables cannot be used as substitutes for the study of the behavior of individuals" (1953, 663). However, "*in very special circumstances* the study of regression between ecological variables may be used to make inferences concerning the behavior of individuals" (1953, 663). His key point is that for regression to yield insight into individual-level behavior, the "constancy assumption" must hold. That is, in our running example, voters in a particular racial group vote similarly regardless of precinct of residence. Goodman (1953, 1959) did not advocate the use of regression for ecological inference, but instead sought to illuminate the strong assumptions required to make such an exercise fruitful.

Consider the two contingency tables in Table 24.4 where the left contingency table represents one precinct, call it "Precinct 1," and the right contingency table represents a second precinct ("Precinct 2"). Consider just the left contingency table for the moment. How might one determine the values of the interior cells given only the information in the marginals? If any one of the four interior cells were known, then one could determine the other three. For instance, if we knew that 100 blacks voted for the

Table 24.4. Assumptions

	Precinct 1				Precinct 2		
	Democrat	Republican			Democrat	Republican	
Black			150 (0.30)	Black			350 (0.449)
White			350 (0.70)	White			430 (0.551)
	300 (0.60)	200 (0.40)	500		400 (0.513)	380 (0.487)	780

Democratic candidate, then $(150 - 100) = 50$ blacks must have voted for the Republican candidate. In a similar calculation, we could determine that $(300 - 100) = 200$ whites voted for the Democratic candidate and so $(350 - 200) = 150$ whites voted for the Republican candidate. If we can set any one of the interior cells to a specific value, the other cells can be determined easily. Without any further information than that contained in the marginals, however, it is impossible to determine a specific value for any of the interior cells with certainty. At this juncture, imposing assumptions is a necessity to move toward a point estimate.

Imposing the Goodman "constancy assumption" (voters in a particular racial group vote similarly regardless of precinct of residence) is one of an innumerable number of ways to proceed. Following this approach, if 50 percent, say, of blacks voted for the Democratic candidate in precinct 1, then outside of random variation, 50 percent of the blacks in precinct 2 voted for the Democratic candidates. Race is a factor associated with vote choice, but precinct, in effect, is not relevant. With our two example precincts, we have a system of two equations:

$$0.6 = 0.3\,\beta_{11} + 0.7\,\beta_{21} \tag{1}$$

$$0.513 = 0.449\,\beta_{12} + 0.551\,\beta_{22},$$

where β_{1j} is the proportion of blacks voting for the Democratic candidate in precinct j and β_{2j} is the proportion of whites voting for the Democratic candidate in precinct j. As we can see, we have two equations and four unknowns. If we impose the constancy assumption across precincts, then $\beta_{11} = \beta_{12}$ and $\beta_{21} = \beta_{22}$, and we can create a system with two equations and two unknowns, $\beta_1 = \beta_{11} = \beta_{12}$ and $\beta_2 = \beta_{21} = \beta_{22}$. It is clear that the system with two equations and two unknowns,

$$0.6 = 0.3\,\beta_1 + 0.7\,\beta_2 \tag{2}$$

$$0.513 = 0.449\,\beta_1 + 0.551\,\beta_2,$$

has a unique solution. Simple algebra leads to the solution, $\beta_1 = 0.1913$ and $\beta_2 = 0.7752$.

While imposing the constancy assumption leads to a "solution," it is questionable in our application, since it implies that contextual factors are irrelevant. The implication is that whites in homogeneously white neighborhoods have exactly the same vote preferences as whites living in predominantly black or otherwise racially diverse neighborhoods. The most appealing aspect of this assumption is that the parameters are identified and a point estimate can be obtained if this assumption is imposed. This appeal is greatly lessened by the least appealing aspect of this identifying assumption, which is that the point estimate may be wrong and grossly misleading.

The role of assumptions is always fundamental, but has been more obvious in some models and less obvious in others. Whether obvious or not, the basic tenets behind the role of assumptions and what they entail for estimation are unyielding. For instance, while the King (1997) ecological inference model is laden with assumptions, the impact and role of these assumptions in determining the point estimate is not transparent. Cho (1998) demonstrates that when the strong assumptions of the King model hold, then that model is appropriate. When the assumptions of the King model are violated, the resulting point estimates and their associated measures of uncertainty are unreliable (see also Rivers 1998; Freedman et al. 1998; 1999; McCue 2001; Cho and Gaines 2004). A key assumption behind the King model is the distributional assumption. King does not impose a "constancy assumption," but his distributional assumption that the parameters or conditional probabilities follow a truncated bivariate normal distribution (TBN) is akin to a "similarity assumption." That is, the percentage of blacks who vote for the Democrat need not be the same across precincts, but the set of estimates for Democratic voting by blacks should follow a truncated bivariate normal distribution so that in most precincts, the percentage congregates around the mean of the TBN. King does not offer any empirical evidence that this distributional assumption is tenable, but he does posit that "[s]ince most areal units were created for administrative convenience and aggregate individuals with roughly similar patterns, ecological observations from the same data sets usually do have a lot in common. Even though Goodman's assumption that [the parameters] are constant over i is usually false, the assumption that they vary but have a single mode usually fits aggregate data" (King 1997, 191–2). Interestingly, Monte Carlo simulations indicate that the King model and OLS yield virtually identical estimates in the vast majority of cases (Cho and Yoon 2001; Anselin and Cho 2002), implying that for substantive purposes, the "similarity assumption" does not differ wildly from the constancy assumption.

Freedman et al. (1991) proposed the neighborhood model to demonstrate the role of assumptions in ecological inference models. His model assumes that voters within a precinct, regardless of race, vote similarly. They did not propose this model as a serious attempt to extract individual-level behavior from aggregate data, but rather to demonstrate that one can arrive at point estimates in a variety of ways and the assumptions that one incorporates in this process heavily influence the eventual outcome. The neighborhood model, in effect, imposes a different type of constancy assumption. Instead of constancy across precincts, it imposes constancy across racial groups. In our simple two-precinct example, then, $\beta_1 = \beta_{11} = \beta_{21}$ and $\beta_2 = \beta_{12} = \beta_{22}$. This approach is another way to convert our system of two equations and four unknowns into a system with two equations and two unknowns. The system (2) then becomes the following

$$0.6 = 0.3\,\beta_1 + 0.7\,\beta_1 \tag{3}$$

$$0.513 = 0.449\,\beta_2 + 0.551\,\beta_2,$$

and the solution is then $\beta_1 = 0.6$ and $\beta_2 = 0.513$. It is simple to see how we can arrive at a unique solution by imposing some type of assumption or constraint. Indeed, there are a very large number of different assumptions that can be imposed and the assumptions completely determine the "solution."

To be sure, many have ventured to explore and propose various assumptions and models for ecological inference. For instance, Hawkes (1969) proposed an aggregated multinomial model where the parameters have fixed multinomial distributions over

Table 24.5. Assumptions

	Democrat	Republican			Democrat	Republican	
Black	30	120	150	Black	70	85	150
White	270	80	350	White	230	120	350
	300	200	500		300	200	500

some number of precincts. Brown and Payne (1986) introduced a random effects model with a specified covariance structure, allowing the parameters to vary over precincts through dependence on precinct-specific covariates and modeling any additional variance through their aggregated compound multinomial distribution. Crewe and Payne (1976) suggested a multiple regression model to account for remaining variation after controlling for race. Calvo and Escolar (2003) presented geographically weighted regressions as a way to account for spatial variation. Indeed, the role of spatial dependence has attracted a flurry of recent scholarship (see, e.g., Anselin and Cho 2002; Wakefield 2003; 2004). Imai, Lu, and Strauss (2008) suggest formulating the problem as a missing data problem. Thomsen (1987) advanced a latent variable logit model where the latent variable is normally distributed and the logits of the marginal values depend linearly on the latent variable. As in some of the previously mentioned models, the Thomsen model assumes that there are some subsets of homogeneous precincts. This is a short list and not nearly an exhaustive one. Since there are innumerable assumptions that one could impose, the possibilities are limitless.

Cho and Judge (2008) highlight the philosophy behind model building in ill-posed situations such as ecological inference. They contend that the most logical way to think through this modeling challenge is to begin with a minimum number of assumptions. The principle is that one should not assume more than one knows, since assumptions, after all, may be incorrect (Judge, Miller, and Cho 2004). In our example precinct 1 in Table 24.4, it is obvious that many different values will be consistent with the observed marginal values. For instance, two possibilities are shown in Table 24.5. How many ways are there to partition the 150 black voters into 30 Democratic votes and 120 Republican votes? This is a simple combinatorial problem, and the answer is $\binom{150}{30}$. Similarly, there are $\binom{350}{270}$ ways to partition the 350 white voters such that there are 270 Democratic votes and 80 Republican votes. So, the number of ways in which we might observe the outcome shown in the left-most table is $\binom{150}{30} \times \binom{350}{270} \approx 8.3 \times 10^{111}$. Similar calculations show that the right-most table is an outcome that could occur with $\binom{150}{70} \times \binom{350}{230} \approx 1.6 \times 10^{140}$ different partitioning of the available voters. Since this latter number is greater than the former number, if we impose no other assumptions, then the outcome in the right-most table must be preferred to the outcome in the left-most table because it can occur in a greater number of ways. Clearly, there is a very large number of outcomes that are consistent with the marginals. However, after assuming as little as possible, the more logical point estimate must be the one most strongly indicated by the data; that is, the point estimate that could occur in the greatest number of ways. This "solution" is not a "magic bullet" in that it will always give the right answer; it is simply a rule for inductive reasoning that leads to the point estimate most strongly indicated by the data at hand.

Lastly, another approach, taken by Cho (2001), is to develop tests for the assumptions underlying the models and to adjust appropriately. So, if the constancy assumption appears untenable, perhaps one should test whether the assumption may hold. This might be done in a manner similar to the way that others have tested for parameter constancy in the switching regressions context. The idea is that voters in racially homogeneous precincts may have different preferences than voters in racially diverse precincts. So, whites in homogeneously white precincts may behave similarly to each other but distinct from whites in racially diverse precincts. In this sense, the constancy assumption may hold among different subsets of data. If one can identify these subsets where constancy can be reasonably assumed, then one can proceed in the usual regression context within homogeneous sets of precincts.

Several works are also helpful in summarizing estimators and discussing the various particularities of their performance. Cleave, Brown, and Payne (1995) and Achen and Shively (1995) are especially noteworthy on this score. These lively debates and discussions have also been visited in other disciplines (see, e.g., Jones 1972; Kousser 1973; Lichtman 1974) as well as across disciplines (Salway and Wakefield 2004). Hanushek, Jackson, and Kain (1974) and Achen and Shively (1995) are also very helpful in illuminating the issues that surround model specifications for the individual and aggregate data and in discussing how the specification for those two levels are related or, unintuitively, unrelated.

2 ECOLOGICAL INFERENCE AS A PROBLEM OF PARTIAL IDENTIFICATION

Each of these many varied approaches to the ecological inference problem brings a unique insight into it. In this section, we highlight an undervisited vantage point from which ecological inference can be viewed. In particular, we discuss the ecological inference problem as a specific instance of a problem of *partial identification of probability distributions*, where the sampling process generating the available data does not fully reveal a distribution of interest. Other familiar partial identification problems include inference with missing data or with errors in measurement, as well as inference on treatment response from observational data. These are problems of identification, rather than of statistical inference, because they persist as sample size increases. They are problems created by the types of data that are available, rather than by the quantity of data. There is a recent and fast-growing literature on partial identification, insights from which are clearly applicable, but underexplored by political scientists. We now turn to discussing how insights from this literature can and should be infused into the study of the ecological inference problem.

A first principle in studying problems of partial identification might be to determine what the sampling process does reveal about the distribution of interest (Manski 1995; 2003). In ecological inference, this means finding a range for the feasible set of estimates. Using the constraints (in our case, the marginal values), we can determine that the distribution of interest must lie in a specific set of feasible distributions, its *identification region*. As we discussed in Section 1.2.1, the identification region may be sufficient for our substantive concerns, but it may not be. Depending on the application at hand, one might proceed to explore what more can be learned when the available data are combined with assumptions that are credible enough to be taken seriously. We say that such assumptions have *identifying power* if they narrow the identification region. Sufficiently strong assumptions may *point-identify*, i.e. fully reveal, the distribution of interest.

Over fifty years ago, the modern literature on ecological inference began to traverse the path suggested by the partial identification literature when Duncan and Davis (1953) demonstrated that the data available in ecological inference imply the bounds on the probabilities $P(Y \mid X, Z)$ that we stated in Section 1.2.1. Contemporaneously, Goodman (1953) showed that the data combined with a specific constancy assumption can point-identify $P(Y \mid X, Z)$, as we showed in Section 1.2.2. However, further work along these lines has not been systematically pursued despite an obvious connection to the partial identification literature. Moreover, these pioneering researchers studied only the relatively simple 2×2 case in which y and z are both binary variables. The general inferential problem has been addressed only recently, in Cross and Manski (2002). We combine their main ideas and findings with our running example to illuminate the manner in which these two literatures are intertwined.

2.1 Inference Using the Data Alone

As we stated earlier, the parameters in an ecological inference application can be understood as conditional probabilities. This framework meshes with the partial identification literature seamlessly, and we continue with the same notation. In particular, let each member j of population J have an outcome y_j in a space Y and covariates (x_j, z_j) in a space $X \times Z$. Let the random variable $(Y, X, Z) : J \to Y \times X \times Z$ have distribution $P(Y, X, Z)$. The general goal is to learn the conditional distributions $P(Y \mid X, Z) \equiv P(Y \mid X = x, Z = z)$, $(x, z) \in X \times Z$. A particular objective may be to determine the mean regression $E(Y \mid X, Z) \equiv E(Y \mid X = x, Z = z)$, $(x, z) \in X \times Z$. We assume only that X and Z are discrete variables, with $P(X = x, Z = z) > 0$ for all $(x, z) \in X \times Z$. The variable Y may be either discrete or continuous.

The joint realizations of (Y, X, Z) are not observable, but data are available from two sampling processes. One process draws persons at random from J and generates observable realizations of (Y, X) but not Z. In our example, voting records reveal (Y, X), the vote received by a certain candidate in a given precinct. The other sampling process draws persons at random and generates observable realizations of (X, Z) but not Y. These data are available from merging racial demographic data from the census with precinct boundaries. The two sampling processes reveal the distributions $P(Y, X)$ and $P(X, Z)$. Ecological inference is the use of this empirical evidence to learn about $P(Y \mid X, Z)$, the propensity to vote for a certain candidate conditional on precinct and race, an unobservable behavior because of the secret ballot. The structure of the ecological inference problem is displayed by the Law of Total Probability:

$$P(Y \mid X) = \sum_{z \in Z} P(Y \mid X, Z = z) \, P(Z = z \mid X). \tag{4}$$

While the bounds, or identification region, for the 2×2 case are relatively simple to compute, the problem becomes much more complex in the $r \times c$ case. We summarize Cross and Manski (2002), who have provided the identification region for the general $r \times c$ case, denoted $H[P(Y \mid X = x, Z)]$. In particular, let Γ_Y denote the space of all probability distributions on Y. Let $x \in X$. Define $P(Y \mid X = x, Z) \equiv [P(Y \mid X = x, Z = z), z \in Z]$. Let $\mid Z \mid$ be the cardinality of Z. Then a $\mid Z \mid$-vector of distributions $[\eta_z, z \in Z] \in (\Gamma_Y)^{|Z|}$ is a feasible value for $P(Y \mid X = x, Z)$ if and only if it solves the finite mixture problem,

$$P(Y \mid X = x) = \sum_{z \in Z} \eta_z P(Z = z \mid X = x). \tag{5}$$

It follows that the identification region for $P(Y \mid X = x, Z)$ using the data alone is the set

$$H[P(Y \mid X = x, Z)] \equiv \big\{ (\eta_z, z \in Z) \in (\Gamma_Y)^{|Z|} : P(Y \mid X = x)$$

$$= \sum_{z \in Z} \eta_z \, P(Z = z \mid X = x) \big\}. \tag{6}$$

Moreover, the identification region for $P(Y \mid X, Z)$ is the Cartesian product $\times_{x \in X} H[P(Y \mid X = x, Z)]$. This holds because the Law of Total Probability (4) restricts $P(Y \mid X, Z)$ across values of Z only, not across values of X. Equation (6) is simple in form but is too abstract to communicate much about the size and shape of the identification region. Hence, practical application requires further study.

A relatively simple result emerges if the objective is inference on $P(Y \mid X = x, Z = z)$ for one specified covariate value $(x, z) \in X \times Z$, or just one precinct and race. In this instance, let $p \equiv P(Z \neq z \mid X = x)$. Cross and Manski show that the identification region for $P(Y \mid X = x, Z = z)$ is the set

$$H[P(Y \mid X = x, Z = z)] = \Gamma_Y \cap [P(Y \mid X = x) - p\,\gamma]/(1 - p), \gamma \in \Gamma_Y. \tag{7}$$

In the special case where Y is binary, this is equivalent to the Duncan and Davis bounds.

Characterization of the identification region is much more involved when the objective is joint inference on the full vector of conditional distributions $P(Y \mid X = x, Z)$, or on the full set of races residing in a precinct. Cross and Manski address an important aspect of this question—the identification region for the mean regression $E(Y \mid X = x, Z)$. Equation (6) implies that the feasible values of $E(Y \mid X = x, Z)$ are

$$\mathbf{H}\left[E(Y \mid X = x, Z)\right] = \left\{\left(\textstyle\int y \, d\eta_z, z \in \mathbf{Z}\right), (\eta_z, z \in \mathbf{Z}) \in \mathbf{H}\left[P(Y \mid X = x, Z)\right]\right\}. \quad (8)$$

Cross and Manski characterize $\mathbf{H}[E(Y \mid X = x, Z)]$ less abstractly than (8) by demonstrating that this is a convex set having finitely many extreme points, which are the expectations of certain $\mid \mathbf{Z} \mid$-tuples of *stacked distributions*. Their result, although still somewhat complex, provides a constructive way to compute the identification region or the bounds for the general $r \times c$ case.

2.2 Assumptions and Instrumental Variables

As we have earlier discussed, bounds or identification regions using the data alone may be helpful, but there are certainly applications where one wishes to reduce the feasible set of estimates further, and perhaps even to a single point estimate. In these cases, one must proceed to impose assumptions. The Goodman constancy assumption is an application of the broad idea of *instrumental variables*, which has been used widely in econometrics from the 1940s onward. Cross and Manski consider two assumptions that use components of X as instrumental variables. Let $X = (V, W)$ and $\mathbf{X} = \mathbf{V} \times \mathbf{W}$. One could assume that Y is mean-independent of V, conditional on (W, Z); that is,

$$E(Y \mid X, Z) = E(Y \mid W, Z). \quad (9)$$

Alternatively, one could assert that Y is statistically independent of V, conditional on (W, Z); that is,

$$P(Y \mid X, Z) = P(Y \mid W, Z). \quad (10)$$

Both assumptions use V as an instrumental variable. Assumption (10) is stronger than (9) unless Y is binary, in which case (9) and (10) are equivalent. In the 2×2 case where Y and Z are both binary, (9) is Goodman's constancy assumption.

Let $w \in \mathbf{W}$. The identification regions for $E(Y \mid W = w, Z)$ under assumptions (9) and (10) can respectively be shown to be

$$\mathbf{H}_w^* \equiv \bigcap_{v \in \mathbf{V}} \mathbf{H}\left[E(Y \mid V = v, W = w, Z)\right] \quad (11)$$

and

$$\mathbf{H}_w^{**} = \left\{\left(\textstyle\int y \, d\eta_z, z \in \mathbf{Z}\right), (\eta_z, z \in \mathbf{Z}) \in \bigcap_{v \in \mathbf{V}} \mathbf{H}\left[P(Y \mid V = v, W = w, Z)\right]\right\}. \quad (12)$$

The corresponding identification regions for $E(Y \mid W, Z)$ are $\times_{w \in W} H^*_w$ and $\times_{w \in W} H^{**}_w$. Observe that set H^*_w and/or H^{**}_w could turn out to be empty. If this occurs, we can conclude that assumption (9) and/or (10) must be incorrect.

Equations (11) and (12) are too abstract to convey a sense of the identifying power of assumptions (9) and (10). Cross and Manski show that a simple *outer identification region* (that is, a set containing the identification region) emerges if one exploits only the Law of Iterated Expectations rather than the full force of the Law of Total Probability. Let assumption (9) hold. Let $w \in W$. Let $\mid V \mid$ denote the cardinality of V. Let $\pi_{(v,w)z} \equiv P(Z = z \mid V = v, W = w)$ and let Π denote the $\mid V \mid \times \mid Z \mid$ matrix whose z-th column is $[\pi_{(v,w)z}, v \in V]$. Let $C^*_w \subset R^{|z|}$ denote the set of solutions $\xi \in R^{|z|}$ to the system of linear equations

$$E(Y \mid V = v, W = w) = \sum_{z \in Z} \pi_{(v,w)z} \, \xi_z, \qquad \forall \; v \in V. \tag{13}$$

Cross and Manski show that $H^*_w \subset C^*_w$. Thus, C^*_w is an outer identification region.

Suppose that the matrix Π has rank $\mid Z \mid$. Then the system of equations (13) has either one solution or none at all. If it has one solution, C^*_w is a singleton, and $H^*_w = C^*_w$. Thus, assumption (9) yields point identification when Π has rank $\mid Z \mid$. In the 2×2 case, C^*_w is the solution to the ecological inference problem developed by Goodman. If (13) has no solutions, then this is a useful diagnostic, and allows one to conclude that assumption (9) is incorrect.

2.3 Structural Prediction

Our discussion thus far may seem highly conceptual and inclined toward intellectual curiosity rather than practical application. However, the abstract study of the ecological inference problem is useful for its insights into structural prediction. For instance, political scientists often want to predict how an observed mean outcome, $E(Y)$, say voting propensity, would change if the covariate distribution were to change from $P(X, Z)$ to some other distribution, say $P^*(X, Z)$; that is, from one set of racial contexts to another. It is common to address this prediction problem under the assumption that the mean regression $E(Y \mid X, Z)$ is *structural*, in the sense that this regression would remain invariant under the hypothesized change in the covariate distribution. Given this assumption, the mean outcome under covariate distribution $P^*(X, Z)$ would be

$$E^*(Y) \equiv \sum_{x \in X} \sum_{z \in Z} E(Y \mid X = x, Z = z) \, P^*(Z = z \mid X = x) \, P^*(X = x).$$

Suppose one wants to compute $E^*(Y)$ and compare it to $E(Y)$. A glaring barrier is that $E(Y \mid X, Z)$ is not point-identified because of the ecological inference problem, and so our understanding of $E^*(Y)$ is limited. A theme that has resonated throughout this chapter is that "limits" are not always as constraining as they may first appear, and that knowing what the limits are can be illuminating in and of itself because they reveal what is based on the known data and clear logic and what lies outside those realms. Our discussion and the findings summarized in Sections 2.1 and 2.2 show what one can learn about $E^*(Y)$. For example, using the data alone, one can conclude that $E^*(Y)$ lies in the set

$$\left\{ \sum_{x \in X} \sum_{z \in Z} \xi_{xz} \, P^*(Z = z \mid X = x) \, P^*(X = x); \right.$$

$$\left. (\xi_{xz}, z \in Z) \in H \left[E(Y \mid X = x, Z) \right], x \in X \right\}. \tag{14}$$

This type of knowledge is helpful particularly for its ability to separate findings based on assumptions and findings that are necessarily true based on data constraints.

To illustrate structural prediction using the data alone, we summarize elements of an empirical application reported in Cross and Manski (1999), a working paper version of their 2002 article. They posed and addressed the counterfactual question: "What would be the outcome of the 1996 U.S. Presidential election if the U.S. population had a different composition, ceteris paribus?" To formalize the question, let x denote a particular state in the US or the District of Columbia. Let Z denote attributes of individual voters possibly associated with voting behavior (e.g. age or race) in state x. Let $Y = \{-1, 0, 1\}$ be the set of vote choices where $Y = 1$ if a person votes Democratic, $Y = -1$ if a Republican vote is cast, and $Y = 0$ otherwise (i.e. minor parties, abstentions, etc.).

In this setting $P(Y \mid X = x)$ is the distribution of voting outcomes in state x, $P(Z \mid X = x)$ is the distribution of voter attributes in the state, and $E(Y \mid Z = z, X = x)$ is the Democratic plurality among voters in state x who have attributes z. Let S_x denote the number of electoral votes allocated to state x. Assuming there are no ties, the Democratic share of the electoral vote is $T \equiv \sum_{x \in X} S_x \cdot 1[E(Y \mid X = x) > 0]$ where $1[\cdot]$ is the indicator function. The number of electors required to win the election is 270.

We know the outcome of the 1996 election, but would that outcome have differed if the composition of the population were different? That is, what would the outcome have been if the distribution of attributes in state x were $P^*(Z \mid X = x)$ and its share of the Electoral College votes were S_x^*? To address this question, we maintain the key assumption that $E(Y \mid \cdot, \cdot)$ is *invariant* in the sense that these conditional expectations remain unchanged under the hypothesized demographic change. This is a nontrivial assumption that hinges on the specification chosen for the covariates Z, but one that seems reasonable to entertain. To interpret this assumption, it may help to consider a behavioral model of the form $Y = f(X, Z, U)$ wherein vote choice is a function, f, of one's state of residence, X, personal attributes, Z, and other factors, U. Then $E(Y \mid \cdot, \cdot)$ is invariant if U is statistically independent of (X, Z) and if the distribution of U remains unchanged under the hypothesized demographic change.

If $E(Y \mid \cdot, \cdot)$ is invariant, the predicted Democratic plurality in state x is

$$E^*(Y \mid X = x) \equiv \sum_{z \in \mathbf{Z}} P^*(Z = z \mid X = x) E(Y \mid X = x, Z = z). \qquad (15)$$

The predicted number of Democratic electoral votes is $T^* \equiv \sum_{x \in \mathbf{X}} S_x^* \times 1[E^*(Y \mid X = x) > 0]$. These formulations make it clear that $[E^*(Y \mid x), x \in \mathbf{X}]$ and thus T^* are functions of $E(Y \mid \cdot, \cdot)$, which is unknown and an instance of the ecological inference problem. The identification region for $E(Y \mid \cdot, \cdot)$ determines the region for T^* and provides the basis for evaluating our counterfactual.

We can obtain data and forecasts for demographic attributes to evaluate our counterfactual from the US Census. In particular, we let our Z covariates be age (two categories: 18–54 years and 55+ years) and ethnicity (white, black, and Hispanic).[3] Table 24.6 reports the bounds on $E^*(Y \mid X)$ in 2004 and 2020. The table shows that the bounds on $E^*(Y \mid X)$ in 2020 are wider than those in 2004 for all states. In 2004 there are twenty-five states where the bound on Democratic plurality is entirely a positive interval, and eleven states where the bound is entirely a negative interval. In 2020 the corresponding number of states is five and zero, respectively. The reason the bounds are wider in 2020 is simple. The forecast change in the distribution of demographic characteristics, $P(Z \mid x)$, for each $x \in \mathbf{X}$ is more pronounced between 1996 and 2020 than between 1996 and 2004. The more $P(Z \mid X = x)$ varies, the less information $P(Y \mid X = x)$ conveys about $E^*(Y \mid X = x)$.

From the bounds on $E^*(Y \mid X = x)$ in a particular state, x, in 2004, we can predict the number of Electoral College seats the Democratic candidate will win in that state. For the twenty-five states where the bound on $E^*(Y \mid X = x)$ is entirely a positive interval, we get the point prediction S_x^* as the number of seats won. And for the eleven states where the bound on $E^*(Y \mid X = x)$ is entirely a negative interval, our point prediction of the number of seats won is zero. In the remaining fifteen states the bound on $E^*(Y \mid X = x)$ straddles zero, and so we obtain no prediction for the number of Electoral College seats won by the Democratic candidate. In the absence of any cross-x or cross-state restrictions, we simply add these bounds, some of which reduce to a point, across all states to obtain the bound on T^*.

3 CONCLUSION

Long ago, Duncan and Davis (1953) pointed out the fundamental indeterminacy in ecological inference. Their simple analysis made clear that aggregate data only

---

[3] In this categorization, Hispanics are all Hispanics regardless of race, blacks are non-Hispanic blacks, and whites are all remaining non-Hispanics. Note also that while these are population figures, we treat them as citizen voting age population figures.

Table 24.6. Bounds on $E^*(y \mid x)$ and T^* in 2004 and 2020

	1996 $E(y \mid x)$	2004 Bound on $E^*(y \mid x)$	2020 Bound on $E^*(y \mid x)$
Northeast			
Connecticut	0.102	[0.055, 0.146]	[−0.053, 0.252]
Maine	0.134	[0.103, 0.168]	[−0.028, 0.309]
Massachusetts	0.184	[0.141, 0.223]	[0.025, 0.346]
New Hampshire	0.057	[0.023, 0.093]	[−0.116, 0.237]
Rhode Island	0.171	[0.131, 0.206]	[0.019, 0.319]
Vermont	0.130	[0.091, 0.172]	[−0.035, 0.308]
New Jersey	0.091	[0.048, 0.130]	[−0.056, 0.231]
New York	0.134	[0.098, 0.167]	[0.014, 0.249]
Pennsylvania	0.045	[0.024, 0.066]	[−0.068, 0.162]
Midwest			
Illinois	0.086	[0.051, 0.120]	[−0.050, 0.222]
Indiana	−0.027	[−0.055, −0.001]	[−0.158, 0.098]
Michigan	0.072	[0.042, 0.104]	[−0.064, 0.218]
Ohio	0.035	[0.007, 0.063]	[−0.097, 0.171]
Wisconsin	0.060	[0.028, 0.091]	[−0.093, 0.221]
Iowa	0.060	[0.034, 0.086]	[−0.078, 0.206]
Kansas	−0.103	[−0.134, −0.072]	[−0.262, 0.046]
Minnesota	0.104	[0.068, 0.140]	[−0.073, 0.290]
Missouri	0.034	[0.013, 0.056]	[−0.099, 0.172]
Nebraska	−0.105	[−0.134, −0.077]	[−0.256, 0.032]
North Dakota	−0.038	[−0.065, −0.013]	[−0.183, 0.100]
South Dakota	−0.021	[−0.034, −0.008]	[−0.171, 0.125]
South			
Delaware	0.076	[0.041, 0.110]	[−0.079, 0.237]
District of Columbia	0.331	[0.299, 0.364]	[0.253, 0.401]
Florida	0.028	[−0.025, 0.078]	[−0.157, 0.209]
Georgia	−0.005	[−0.044, 0.033]	[−0.166, 0.155]
Maryland	0.075	[0.030, 0.117]	[−0.085, 0.233]
North Carolina	−0.022	[−0.060, 0.016]	[−0.183, 0.135]
South Carolina	−0.024	[−0.066, 0.016]	[−0.175, 0.120]
Virginia	−0.009	[−0.058, 0.039]	[−0.172, 0.152]
West Virginia	0.066	[0.035, 0.101]	[−0.057, 0.203]
Alabama	−0.033	[−0.067, −0.001]	[−0.176, 0.102]
Kentucky	0.005	[−0.028, 0.038]	[−0.143, 0.153]
Mississippi	−0.023	[−0.055, 0.008]	[−0.164, 0.113]
Tennessee	0.011	[−0.020, 0.043]	[−0.135, 0.160]
Arkansas	0.080	[0.048, 0.117]	[−0.061, 0.239]
Louisiana	0.069	[0.022, 0.117]	[−0.104, 0.247]
Oklahoma	−0.039	[−0.079, 0.000]	[−0.191, 0.109]
Texas	−0.020	[−0.058, 0.018]	[−0.168, 0.128]

(cont.)

Table 24.6. (*Continued*)

	1996 E(y | x)	2004 Bound on E*(y | x)	2020 Bound on E*(y | x)
West			
Arizona	0.010	[−0.039, 0.059]	[−0.166, 0.186]
Colorado	−0.007	[−0.068, 0.053]	[−0.224, 0.208]
Idaho	−0.108	[−0.159, −0.060]	[−0.320, 0.080]
Montana	−0.018	[−0.070, 0.033]	[−0.231, 0.190]
Nevada	0.004	[−0.053, 0.061]	[−0.186, 0.194]
New Mexico	0.034	[−0.001, 0.068]	[−0.116, 0.184]
Utah	−0.106	[−0.145, −0.074]	[−0.284, 0.046]
Wyoming	−0.078	[−0.133, −0.028]	[−0.284, 0.109]
Alaska	−0.100	[−0.155, −0.039]	[−0.232, 0.050]
California	0.057	[0.003, 0.114]	[−0.085, 0.200]
Hawaii	0.103	[0.079, 0.130]	[0.028, 0.189]
Oregon	0.047	[−0.014, 0.110]	[−0.156, 0.260]
Washington	0.069	[0.017, 0.125]	[−0.116, 0.272]
Democratic electoral votes, T^*	379	[302, 477]	[51, 538]

partially reveal the structure of individual behavior. Nevertheless, their contribution has largely been viewed as limited and an appreciation for the idea of bounds or an identification region has yet to fully emerge. Instead, the bulk of the effort has been directed toward obtaining point estimates or to somehow point identify a problem that is only partially identified. However, empirical researchers should be aware that no solution comes free. Every method yielding point estimates necessarily rests on assumptions that are strong enough to remove the indeterminacy of ecological inference. Researchers contemplating application of any method should carefully consider whether the associated assumptions are credible in their applications.

In our experience, it is rare in practice to find point-identifying assumptions that one can accept with great confidence. The prudent researchers, then, should resist the temptation to embrace any particular estimation method. Instead, the analysis of aggregate data should be a process. First, one should determine what one can learn from the data alone without imposing any assumptions. Then, one should consider various assumptions that have identifying power. A productive approach is to "layer" the assumptions, imposing them sequentially in order of decreasing plausibility. As more assumptions are imposed, one will be able to draw conclusions that are increasingly sharp but decreasingly believable. This process of inference illuminates the respective roles that data and assumptions play in empirical research. Moreover, it enables both researchers and their consumers to adjudicate how best to reconcile the inevitable tension between the strength of conclusions and their credibility.

REFERENCES

ACHEN, C. H., and SHIVELY, W. P. 1995. *Cross-Level Inference.* Chicago: University of Chicago Press.

ALLPORT, F. H. 1924. The group fallacy in relation to social science. *American Journal of Sociology*, 29: 688–703.

ANSELIN, L., and CHO, W. K. T. 2002. Spatial effects and ecological inference. *Political Analysis*, 10: 276–97.

BROWN, P. J., and PAYNE, C. D. 1986. Aggregate data, ecological regression, and voting transitions. *Journal of the American Statistical Association*, 81: 452–60.

CALVO, E., and ESCOLAR, M. 2003. The local voter: a geographically weighted approach to ecological inference. *American Journal of Political Science*, 47: 189–204.

CHO, W. K. T. 1998. Iff the assumption fits...: a comment on the King ecological inference solution. *Political Analysis*, 7: 143–63.

—— 2001. Latent groups and cross-level inferences. *Electoral Studies*, 20: 243–63.

—— and GAINES, B. J. 2004. The limits of ecological inference: the case of split-ticket voting. *American Journal of Political Science*, 48: 152–71.

—— and JUDGE, G. G. 2008. Recovering vote choice from partial incomplete data. *Journal of Data Science*, 6: 155–71.

—— and YOON, A. H. 2001. Strange bedfellows: politics, courts, and statistics: statistical expert testimony in voting rights cases. *Cornell Journal of Law and Public Policy*, 10: 237–64.

CLEAVE, N., BROWN, P. J., and PAYNE, C. D. 1995. Evaluation of methods for ecological inference. *Journal of the Royal Statistical Society, Series A*, 158: 55–72.

CREWE, I., and PAYNE, C. 1976. Another game with nature: an ecological regression model of the British two-party vote ratio in 1970. *British Journal of Political Science*, 6: 43–81.

CROSS, P. J., and MANSKI, C. F. 1999. Regressions, short and long. Presented at the 2000 Econometric Society World Congress. <http://ideas.repec.org/p/ecm/wc2000/0385.html>

—— —— 2002. Regressions, short and long. *Econometrica*, 70: 357–68.

DUNCAN, O. D., and DAVIS, B. 1953. An alternative to ecological correlation. *American Sociological Review*, 18: 665–6.

FIREBAUGH, G. 1978. A rule for inferring individual-level relationships from aggregate data. *American Sociological Review*, 43: 557–72.

FREEDMAN, D., KLEIN, S., SACKS, J., SMYTH, C., and EVERETT, C. 1991. Ecological regression and voting rights. *Evaluation Review*, 15: 673–711.

—— —— OSTLAND, M., and ROBERTS, M. R. 1998. Review of a solution to the ecological inference problem. *Journal of the American Statistical Association*, 93: 1518–22.

—— OSTLAND, M., ROBERTS, M. R., and KLEIN, S. P. 1999. Response to King's comments. *Journal of the American Statistical Association*, 94: 355–7.

GEHLKE, C. E., and BIEHL, K. 1934. Certain effects of grouping upon size of the correlation coefficient in census tract material. *Journal of the American Statistical Association Supplement*, 29: 663–4.

GOOD, I. J. 1963. Maximum entropy for hypothesis formation, especially for multidimensional contingency tables. *Annals of Mathematical Statistics*, 64: 911–34.

GOODMAN, L. A. 1953. Ecological regressions and behavior of individuals. *American Sociological Review*, 18: 663–4.

—— 1959. Some alternatives to ecological correlation. *American Journal of Sociology*, 64: 610–25.

GROFMAN, B., MIGALSKI, M., and NOVIELLO, N. 1985. The "totality of circumstances" test in section 2 of the 1982 extension of the Voting Rights Act: a social science perspective. *Law and Policy*, 7: 209–23.

HAMMOND, J. L. 1973. Two sources of error in ecological correlations. *American Sociological Review*, 38: 764–77.

HANUSHEK, E., JACKSON, J., and KAIN, J. 1974. Model specification, use of aggregate data, and the ecological correlation fallacy. *Political Methodology*, Winter: 89–107.

HAWKES, A. G. 1969. An approach to the analysis of electoral swing. *Journal of the Royal Statistical Association, Series A*, 132: 68–79.

IMAI, K., LU, Y., and STRAUSS, A. 2008. Bayesian and likelihood inference for 2 × 2 ecological tables: an incomplete data approach. *Political Analysis*.

JONES, E. T. 1972. Ecological inference and electoral analysis. *Journal of Interdisciplinary History*, 2: 249–62.

JUDGE, G. G., MILLER, D. J., and CHO, W. K. T. 2004. An information theoretic approach to ecological estimation and inference. Pp. 162–87 in *Ecological Inference: New Methodological Strategies*, ed. G. King, O. Rosen, and M. Tanner. Cambridge: Cambridge University Press.

KING, G. 1997. *A Solution to the Ecological Inference Problem: Reconstructing Individual Behavior from Aggregate Data*. Princeton, NJ: Princeton University Press.

KLEPPNER, P. 1985. *Chicago Divided: The Making of a Black Mayor*. DeKalb: Northern Illinois University Press.

KOUSSER, J. M. 1973. Ecological regression and the analysis of past politics. *Journal of Interdisciplinary History*, 4: 237–62.

LICHTMAN, A. J. 1974. Correlation, regression, and the ecological fallacy: a critique. *Journal of Interdisciplinary History*, 4: 417–33.

LOEWEN, J. 1982. *Social Science in the Courtroom: Statistical Techniques and Research Methods for Winning Class-Action Suits*. Lexington, Mass.: Lexington Books.

MCCUE, K. F. 2001. The statistical foundations of the EI method. *American Statistician*, 55: 102–5.

MANSKI, C. F. 1995. *Identification Problems in the Social Sciences*. Cambridge, Mass.: Harvard University Press.

—— 2003. *Partial Identification of Probability Distributions*. New York: Springer-Verlag.

OGBURN, W. F., and GOLTRA, I. 1919. How women vote: a study of an election in Portland, Oregon. *Political Science Quarterly*, 34: 413–33.

OPENSHAW, S., and TAYLOR, P. 1979. A million or so correlation coefficients: three experiments on the modifiable areal unit problem. Pp. 127–44 in *Statistical Applications in the Spatial Sciences*, ed. N. Wrigley. London: Pion.

PRAIS, S. J., and AITCHISON, J. 1954. The grouping of observations in regression analysis. *Review of the International Institute of Statistics*, 22: 1–22.

RIVERS, D. 1998. Book review: a solution to the ecological inference problem: reconstructing individual behavior from aggregate data. *American Political Science Review*, 92: 442–3.

ROBINSON, W. S. 1950. Ecological correlations and the behavior of individuals. *American Sociological Review*, 15: 351–7.

SALWAY, R., and WAKEFIELD, J. 2004. A comparison of approaches to ecological inference in epidemiology, political science, and sociology. Pp. 303–32 in *Ecological Inference: New Methodological Strategies*, ed. G. King, O. Rosen, and M. Tanner. Cambridge: Cambridge University Press.

SIMPSON, E. H. 1951. The interpretation of interaction in contingency tables. *Journal of the Royal Statistical Society, Series B*, 13: 238–41.

THOMSEN, S. R. 1987. *Danish Elections 1920–1979: A Logit Approach to Ecological Analysis and Inference.* Arhus: Politica.

WAKEFIELD, J. 2003. Sensitivity analyses for ecological regress. *Biometrics*, 59: 9–17.

—— 2004. Ecological inference for 2 × 2 tables. *Journal of the Royal Statistical Society, Series A,* 167: 385–445.

YULE, G. U., and KENDALL, M. G. 1950. *An Introduction to the Theory of Statistics.* London: Griffin.

....

EMPIRICAL MODELS OF SPATIAL INTER-DEPENDENCE

....

ROBERT J. FRANZESE, JR.
JUDE C. HAYS

1 SPATIAL INTERDEPENDENCE IN POLITICAL SCIENCE

....

1.1 The Substantive Range of Spatial Interdependence

UNTIL recently, empirical analyses of spatial interdependence in the social sciences remained largely confined to specialized areas of applied economics (e.g. environmental, urban/regional, real-estate economics) and sociology (i.e. network analysis). However, social-scientific interest in and applications of spatial modeling have burgeoned lately, due partly to advances in theory that imply interdependence and in methodology for addressing it, partly to global substantive changes that have raised at least the perception of and attention to interconnectivity, and likely the actual degree and extent of it, at all levels, from micro/personal to macro/international, and partly to advances in technology for obtaining and working with spatial data. In political science, too, spatial empirical analyses have grown increasingly common;

a very welcome development as many phenomena that political scientists study entail substantively important spatial interdependence.

Perhaps the most extensive classical and contemporary interest in spatial interdependence in political science surrounds the diffusion of policy and/or institutions across national or sub-national governments. The study of policy-innovation diffusion among US states in particular has deep roots and much contemporary interest (e.g. Crain 1966; Walker 1969; 1973; Gray 1973; Bailey and Rom 2004; Boehmke and Witmer 2004; Daley and Garand 2004; Grossback, Nicholson-Crotty, and Peterson 2004; Shipan and Volden 2006; Volden 2006).[1] Similar policy-learning mechanisms underlie some comparative studies of policy diffusion (e.g. Schneider and Ingram 1988; Rose 1993; Meseguer 2004; 2005; Gilardi 2005). Interest in institutional or even regime diffusion is likewise long-standing and recently much reinvigorated in comparative and international politics. Dahl's (1971) classic *Polyarchy*, for instance, (implicitly) references international diffusion among the eight causes of democracy he lists; Starr's (1991) "Democratic Dominoes" and Huntington's (1991) *Third Wave* accord it a central role; and finally, O'Loughlin et al. (1998) and Gleditsch and Ward (2006; 2007) empirically estimate the international diffusion of democracy. Simmons and Elkins (2004), Elkins, Guzman, and Simmons (2006), and Simmons, Dobbin, and Garrett (2006) similarly stress international diffusion as the force behind recent economic liberalizations, as do Eising (2002), Brune, Garrett, and Kogut (2004), Brooks (2005), and many others in recent years.

The substantive range of important spatial-interdependence effects extends well beyond these more obvious contexts of intergovernmental diffusion, however, spanning the subfields and substance of political science. Inside democratic legislatures, e.g., representatives' votes certainly depend on others' votes or expected votes; in electoral studies, election outcomes or candidate qualities or strategies in some contests surely depend on those in others. Outside legislative and electoral arenas, the probabilities and outcomes of coups (Li and Thompson 1975), riots (Govea and West 1981), and/or revolutions (Brinks and Coppedge 2006) in one unit depend in substantively crucial ways on those in others. In microbehavioral work, too, some of the recently surging interest in *contextual effects* surrounds the effects on each respondent's behaviors or opinions of aggregates of others' behaviors and opinions— e.g. those of the respondent's region, community, or social network. Within the mammoth literature on contextual effects in political behavior (Huckfeldt and Sprague 1993 review), recent contributions that stress interdependence include Braybeck and Huckfeldt (2002a; 2002b), Cho (2003), Huckfeldt, Johnson, and Sprague (2005), Cho and Gimpel (2007), Cho and Rudolph (2008), and Lin, Wu, and Lee (2006). In international relations, meanwhile, the interdependence of states' actions essentially defines the subject. States' entry decisions in wars, alliances, or international organizations, for example, heavily depend on how many and who (are expected to)

---

[1]   And between, e.g., Knoke (1982); Caldeira (1985); Lutz (1987); Berry and Berry (1990; 1999); Case, Hines, and Rosen (1993); Berry (1994); Rogers (1995); Mintrom (1997a; 1997b); Mintrom and Vergari (1998); Mossberger (1999); Godwin and Schroedel (2000); Balla (2001); Mooney (2001).

enter.[2] Empirical attention to the inherent spatial interdependence of international relations has been greatest in the work of Ward, Gleditsch, and colleagues (e.g. Shin and Ward 1999; Gleditsch and Ward 2000; Gleditsch 2002; Ward and Gleditsch 2002; Hoff and Ward 2004; Gartzke and Gleditsch 2006; Salehyan and Gleditsch 2006; Gleditsch 2007). In comparative and international political economy also, interdependence is perhaps especially frequently substantively large and central. Simmons and Elkins (2004), Elkins, Guzman, and Simmons (2006), and Simmons, Dobbin, and Garrett (2006) stress cross-national diffusion as the main force behind recent economic liberalizations, for example, as do Eising (2002), Brune, Garrett, and Kogut (2004), Brooks (2005), and many others. In fact, globalization and international economic integration, arguably today's most notable (and indisputably most noted) political-economic phenomena, imply strategic and/or nonstrategic interdependence of domestic politics, policy-makers, and policies. Empirical work emphasizing such globalization-induced interdependencies includes Genschel (2002), Basinger and Hallerberg (2004), Knill (2005), Jahn (2006), Swank (2006), Franzese and Hays (2006b; 2007a; 2007b; 2008), and Kayser (2007).

1.2 Mechanisms of Spatial Interdependence

Spatial interdependence is, in summary, ubiquitous and often quite central throughout the substance of political science. Geographer Waldo Tobler (1930–) puts it simply: *everything is related to everything else, but near things are more related than distant things.* Moreover, as Beck, Gleditsch, and Beardsley (2006) pithily stress titularly: *space is more than geography.* That is, the substantive content of *proximity* in *Tobler's Law*, and so the pathways along which interdependence between units may operate, extend well beyond simple physical distance and bordering (as several examples above illustrate). Elkins and Simmons (2005) and Simmons, Dobbin, and Garrett (2006), for example, define and discuss four mechanisms by which interdependence may arise: coercion, competition, learning, and emulation. *Coercion*, which may be direct or indirect and hard (force) or soft (suasion), encompasses a generally "vertical" pathway by which the powerful induce actions among the weaker. *Competition* refers to interdependence stemming from economic pressures that the actions of each unit place upon others in competition with it or as substitutes for or complements to it. *Learning* entails situations where actors learn from others' actions, in rational-Bayesian or other fashion, something regarding the net appeal of their own alternatives.[3] *Emulation*, lastly, is ritualistic (i.e. neither coerced nor responsive to competition or to learning) following or doing oppositely of others

---

[2] Signorino (1999; 2002) and Signorino and Tarar (2006) also stress the strategic interdependence of international relations in specifying empirical models, as do Signorino and Yilmaz (2003) and Signorino (2003) regarding strategic choice broadly.

[3] For interdependence to arise, what is learned must affect the utilities of actors' choices, but it may be objective or subjective, true/correct or false/incorrect, and may regard the politics, economics, sociology, or any other aspect of those choices.

(e.g. leaders, co-ethnics, co-partisans). Although enumerated specifically for contexts of cross-national diffusion, these four categories nicely span most possible channels of spatial interdependence across its broader substantive domain. We would add a fifth channel, *migration*, wherein components of some units move directly into others, the most obvious example being human im-/emigration, which will tend to generate a direct, mechanical interdependence in addition to strategic ones, only some of which pathways *competition* or *emulation* could cover in Simmons et al.'s (2006) schema.

1.3 A General Theoretical Model of Interdependence

More general-theoretically, one can show that strategic interdependence arises whenever the actions of some unit(s) affect the marginal utility of alternative actions for some other unit(s). (We follow Brueckner 2003 here; see also Braun and Gilardi 2006.) Consider two units (i, j) with (indirect) utilities, (U^i, U^j), from their alternative actions or policies, (p_i, p_j). Due to externalities, i's utility depends on its policy and that of j. For example, imagine two countries with (homogeneous) population preferences regarding, say, the economy and environment. Due to environmental externalities (e.g. pollution spillovers) and economic ones (e.g. regulatory-cost competition), domestic welfare (i.e. net political-economic benefits/utilities to policy-makers) in each country will depend on both countries' actions:

$$U^i \equiv U^i(p_i, p_j); \quad U^j \equiv U^j(p_j, p_i). \tag{1}$$

When unit i chooses its policy, p_i, to maximize its own welfare, this alters the optimal policy in j, and vice versa. For example, i implementing more (less) effective antipollution policy reduces (increases) the need for effective antipollution policy in j due to environmental spillovers. We can express such strategic interdependence between i and j with a pair of best-response functions that give i's optimal policies, p_i^*, as a function of j's chosen policies, and vice versa:

$$p_i^* \equiv \text{Argmax}_{p_i} U^i(p_i, p_j) \equiv R^i(p_j); \quad p_j^* \equiv \text{Argmax}_{p_j} U^j(p_j, p_i) \equiv R^j(p_i). \tag{2}$$

The slopes of these best-response functions indicate whether actions by i induce j to move in the same direction, making i and j *strategic complements*, or in opposite directions as *strategic substitutes*. For instance, antipollution policies are strategic substitutes in their environmental effects as described above. The best-response functions' slopes depend on these ratios of second cross-partial derivatives:

$$\frac{\partial p_i^*}{\partial p_j} = -U^i_{p_i p_j}/U^i_{p_i p_i}; \quad \frac{\partial p_j^*}{\partial p_i} = -U^j_{p_j p_i}/U^j_{p_j p_j}. \tag{3}$$

If the units maximize their utilities, the second-order conditions imply negative denominators in (3). Thus, the slopes depend directly on the signs of the second cross-partial derivatives (i.e. the numerators). If $U^{i,j}_{p_i p_j} > 0$, i.e. if policies are strategic complements, reaction functions slope upward. Regarding any competitive costs of antipollution regulation, e.g. increased (reduced) regulation in i lowers (raises) the costs of regulation in competitors j, and so spurs j to increase (reduce) regulation too. If $U_{p_i p_j}^{i,j} < 0$, policies are strategic substitutes, so reaction functions slope downward, as noted regarding in the environmental benefits of antipollution regulation. If the second cross-partial derivative is zero, strategic interdependence does not materialize and best-response functions are flat.

Generally speaking, then, positive externalities induce strategic-substitute relations, with policies moving in opposite directions as *free-rider* dynamics obtain. Franzese and Hays (2006b) argue and find such free-riding dynamics in EU active-labor-market policies, for instance. Notice, furthermore, that free-rider advantages also confer late-mover advantages and so war-of-attrition (strategic delay and inaction) dynamics are likely. Conversely, negative externalities induce strategic complementarity, with policies moving in the same direction. The common example of tax competition has these features. Tax cuts in one jurisdiction have negative externalities for competitors, thereby spurring them to cut taxes as well. These situations advantage early movers, so *competitive races* can unfold.[4] Other good examples are competitive currency devaluations or trade protection. Early movers in these contexts reap greater economic benefits, so races to move first or earlier are likely. Thus, positive and negative externalities induce strategic-complement and -substitute relations, respectively, which spur competitive races and free-riding, respectively, with their corresponding early- and late-mover advantages that foster strategic rush to go first on the one hand and delays and inaction on the other.

1.4   The Empirical–Methodological Challenges of Spatial Interdependence

A crucial challenge for empirical research, known as *Galton's Problem*,[5] is the great difficulty distinguishing true *interdependence* of units' actions, on the one hand,

---

[4] We eschew the labels *races to the bottom* (or *top*) and *convergence* because these competitive races need not foster convergence on any top, bottom, or mean, and could further divergence (see, e.g., Plümper and Schneider 2006).

[5] Sir Francis Galton originally raised the issue thus: "[F]ull information should be given as to the degree in which the customs of the tribes and races which are compared together are independent. It might be that some of the tribes had derived them from a common source, so that they were duplicate copies of the same original ... It would give a useful idea of the distribution of the several customs and of their relative prevalence in the world, if a map were so marked by shadings and colour as to present a picture of their geographical ranges" (*Journal of the Anthropological Institute of Great Britain and Ireland*, 18: 270, quoted in Darmofal 2006). In <http://en.wikipedia.org/wiki/Galton's_problem>, we find further historical context: "In [1888], Galton was present when Sir Edward Tylor presented a paper at the Royal Anthropological Institute. Tylor had compiled information on institutions of marriage and descent for 350 cultures and examined the correlations between these institutions and measures of societal complexity. Tylor interpreted his results as indications of a general evolutionary sequence, in which institutions change focus from the maternal line to the paternal line as societies become increasingly complex. Galton disagreed, pointing out that similarity between cultures could be due to borrowing, could be due to common descent, or could be due to evolutionary development; he maintained that without controlling for borrowing and common descent one cannot make valid inferences regarding evolutionary development. Galton's critique has become the eponymous *Galton's Problem*, as named by Raoul Naroll (1961; 1965), who proposed [some of] the first statistical solutions."

from the impacts of spatially correlated unit-level factors, of common or spatially correlated exogenous-external factors, and of context-conditional factors involving interactions of unit-level and exogenous-external explanators on the other (call these latter, nonspatial components of the model, this complex of correlated responses to correlated unit-level, contextual, or context-conditional factors, *common shocks*). On the one hand, ignoring or inadequately modeling interdependence processes tends to induce overestimation of the importance of common shocks, thereby privileging unit-level/domestic, contextual/exogenous-external, or context-conditional explanations. On the other hand, if the inherent simultaneity of interdependence is insufficiently redressed, then spatial-lag models (see below) yield misestimates (usually overestimates) of interdependence at the expense of common shocks, especially insofar as such common shocks are inadequately modeled. In other words, summarizing analyses in Franzese and Hays (2004; 2006*a*; 2007*b*), in substantive contexts having any appreciable interdependence, obtaining good estimates (unbiased, consistent, efficient) of coefficients and standard errors and, *a fortiori*, distinguishing domestic/unit-level, exogenous-external/contextual, and context-conditional factor explanations from interdependence ones, *by any empirical-methodological means*, whether qualitative or quantitative, is *not* straightforward.

The first and primary consideration, as we have previously shown analytically for simple cases and via simulations in more realistic ones, are the relative and absolute theoretical and empirical precisions of the spatial and nonspatial parts of the model, i.e. of the *interdependence* part(s) and the *common-shocks* part(s). To elaborate: the relative and absolute accuracy and power with which the empirical specification of the spatial interdependence reflects and can gain leverage in the data upon the actual interdependence mechanisms operating and with which the domestic, exogenous-external, and/or context-conditional parts of the model reflect and gain leverage upon *common-shocks* alternatives crucially affect the empirical attempt to distinguish and evaluate their relative strength because the two mechanisms produce similar effects. This is the crux of Galton's Problem. Inadequacies or omissions in specifying the noninterdependence components of the model tend, intuitively, to induce overestimates of the importance of interdependence and vice versa. Secondarily, even if the common-shocks and interdependence mechanisms are specified properly into the spatial-lag, that (those) regressor(s) will be endogenous (i.e. will covary with residuals), so regression estimates of interdependence strength (or, equally for that matter, attempts to distinguish interdependence from common shocks qualitatively) will suffer simultaneity biases. Conversely to the primary omitted-variable/misspecification biases described first, these secondary simultaneity biases favor overestimating interdependence-strength, which induces biases in the other direction for, i.e. underestimation of, nonspatial factors' effects (*common shocks*).

Methodologically, one can discern two approaches to spatial analysis: spatial statistics and spatial econometrics (Anselin 2006). The distinction regards the relative emphasis in spatial-econometric approaches to theoretical models of interdependence processes (e.g. Brueckner 2003; Braun and Gilardi 2006; Franzese and Hays 2007*a*; 2007*b*; 2008) wherein space may often have broad meaning (Beck, Gleditsch, and Beardsley 2006), well beyond geography and geometry across all

manner of social, economic, or political connection that induces effects from outcomes in some units on outcomes in others. The spatial-lag regression model plays
a starring role in that tradition (Hordijk 1974; Paelinck and Klaassen 1979; Anselin
1980; 1988; 1992; Haining 1990; LeSage 1999). Anselin (2002) notes that such theory-
driven models deal centrally with *substantive* spatial correlation, which suggests a
corresponding approach to model specification and estimation wherein the importance of spatial interdependence is explored primarily by Wald tests upon the
unrestricted spatial-lag model. Spatial-error models, analysis of spatial-correlation
patterns, spatial kriging, spatial smoothing, and the like, characterize the more exclusively data-driven approach and the typically narrower conception of space in
solely geographic/geometric terms in the longer spatial-statistics tradition (initially
inspired by Galton's famous comments (see note 5), and reaching crucial methodological milestones in Whittle 1954; Naroll 1965; 1970; Cliff and Ord 1973; 1981; Besag
1974; Ord 1975; Ripley 1981; Cressie 1993). Anselin (2002) notes that this approach is
often more driven by data problems like measurement error, with spatial correlation
often seen as a *nuisance*, which suggests a different approach to model specification
and estimation wherein the restricted spatial-error model and Lagrange-multiplier
tests are dominant. However, the distinctions are subtle, with considerable and often fruitful cross-fertilization, and both approaches stress the dangers of ignoring
spatial interdependence, namely overconfidence and bias, even for those interested
primarily or even solely in domestic/unit-level or exogenous-external/contextual
matters. Minimally, one should test for spatial interdependence and not proceed
nonspatially unless it truly is negligible; otherwise, estimates of domestic/unit-level,
exogenous-external/contextual, and/or context-conditional phenomena will be exaggerated. Finally, the most important task in any empirical spatial analysis, by either
approach, is the prespecification of the $N \times N$ spatial-weighting matrix, $\mathbf{W}$,[6] whose
elements, w_{ij}, reflect the relative connectivity from unit j to i. As just emphasized,
the relative and absolute accuracy and power with which the spatial-lag weights, w_{ij},
reflect and can gain leverage upon the interdependence mechanisms actually operating empirically and with which the domestic, exogenous-external, and/or context-
conditional parts of the model can reflect and gain leverage upon the *common-shocks*
alternatives critically affect the empirical attempt to distinguish and evaluate their
relative strength because the two mechanisms produce similar effects.

2 SPATIAL AUTOREGRESSIVE MODELS

There are two workhorse regression models in empirical spatial analysis: spatial lag
and spatial error models.

---

[6] Strategies for parameterizing W and estimating such models are of great interest but as yet mostly
remain for future work.

2.1 Spatial Lag Models

Spatial lag models imply spatial externalities in both modeled and unmodeled effects (i.e. the systematic and stochastic components) and are typically motivated by a theoretical model:

$$y = \rho Wy + X\beta + \epsilon \tag{4}$$

$$y = (I - \rho W)^{-1}X\beta + (I - \rho W)^{-1}\epsilon. \tag{5}$$

Note that the multipliers are restricted to be the same. This restriction can be relaxed (discussion below). In the cross-sectional context, the dependent variable, y, is an $N \times 1$ vector of observations; ρ is the spatial autoregressive coefficient, reflecting the overall or average strength of interdependence; and W is an $N \times N$ spatial-weighting matrix, with the elements w_{ij} reflecting the relative connectivity from unit j to i. Wy is a *spatial lag*; i.e. for each observation y_i, Wy gives a weighted sum or average of the y_j, with weights w_{ij}.

2.2 Spatial Error Models

Spatial error models imply that the pattern of spatial dependence is attributable to un-measured covariates (i.e. the stochastic component) only. Spatial error specifications are rarely theory-driven:

$$y = X\beta + \epsilon$$
$$\epsilon = \lambda W\epsilon + u \tag{6}$$

$$y = X\beta + (I - \lambda W)^{-1}u. \tag{7}$$

Note the spatial moving-average (S-MA) alternative to this spatial autoregressive (S-AR) model, $\epsilon = \gamma Wu + u$, implies local autocorrelation or "pockets" of spatial interdependence because the reduced form does not contain and inverse (Anselin 1995; 2003).

2.3 Combined Lag and Error Models

A third model combines the two. Different externalities in modeled and unmodeled effects (a.k.a. systematic and stochastic components) relax the previously noted constraint in the spatial-lag model. The resulting mixed SAR model is

$$y = \rho W_1 y + X\beta + \epsilon$$
$$\epsilon = \lambda W_2 \epsilon + u. \tag{8}$$

Analogously, a mixed SARMA model would be

$$y = \rho W_1 y + X\beta + \epsilon$$
$$\epsilon = \lambda W_2 u + u. \tag{9}$$

3 MODEL SPECIFICATION AND ESTIMATION

In this section we consider ways to specify and estimate spatial autoregressive models with continuous dependent variables and cross-sectional data (we consider models for time-series cross-section and binary-choice contexts below). We begin with OLS estimation and specification testing under the null hypothesis of no spatial dependence. We then turn to the topic of estimating spatial lag models, and finish the section with a discussion of spatial error models. To illustrate the methods, we estimate a model of state-level welfare policy generosity in the US using cross-sectional data from Berry, Fording, and Hanson (2003) on the contiguous forty-eight states.

3.1 OLS with Specification Testing under the Null

One approach to model specification is to estimate a nonspatial model using OLS and then conduct a battery of diagnostic tests on the residuals. This strategy makes sense when one does not have a theoretical model of spatial interdependence, and the spatial dependence in the data (if there is any) is seen primarily as a statistical nuisance. One could also perhaps argue for it on grounds of conservatism in that the approach tests upward from spatial-error models that by nature lack spatial dynamics in the systematic component, wherein one's core theoretical and substantive propositions are usually specified. The diagnostic tests can help identify whether the data-generating process is spatial autoregressive and, in some cases, even detect the nature of the underlying spatial process (i.e. spatial lag vs. spatial error).

One of the most widely known and frequently used diagnostics for spatial correlation is Moran's I:

$$I = \frac{N}{S} \frac{\epsilon'\mathbf{W}\epsilon}{\epsilon'\epsilon}, \text{ where } S = \sum_{i=1}^{N} \sum_{j=1}^{N} w_{ij}. \tag{10}$$

When $\mathbf{W}$ is row-standardized (so row elements sum to one), the expression simplifies to

$$I = \frac{\epsilon'\mathbf{W}\epsilon}{\epsilon'\epsilon}. \tag{11}$$

To test a null of no spatial correlation (in patterns given by $\mathbf{W}$), one can compare a properly standardized Moran's I to the standard normal distribution (Cliff and Ord 1973; Burridge 1980; Kelejian and Prucha 2001).

In addition to Moran's I, several Lagrange multiplier (LM) tests based on OLS residuals exist. The standard LM tests assume that the spatial autoregressive process is either a spatial lag or spatial error model. More precisely, in terms of (8), the standard LM test for the null hypothesis $\rho = 0$ against the spatial lag alternative *assumes* $\lambda = 0$. Likewise, the LM test for $\lambda = 0$ *assumes* $\rho = 0$. The standard, one-directional test against spatial lag alternative is calculated as

$$LM_\rho = \frac{\hat{\sigma}_\epsilon^2 \left(\hat{\epsilon}'\mathbf{W}\mathbf{y}/\hat{\sigma}_\epsilon^2\right)^2}{G + T\hat{\sigma}_\epsilon^2},$$ (12)

where $G = (\mathbf{WX}\hat{\beta})'(\mathbf{I} - \mathbf{X}(\mathbf{X}'\mathbf{X})^{-1}\mathbf{X}')(\mathbf{WX}\hat{\beta})$ and $T = \mathrm{tr}[(\mathbf{W}' + \mathbf{W})\mathbf{W}]$. The standard, one-directional test against spatial error alternative is

$$LM_\lambda = \frac{\left(\hat{\epsilon}'\mathbf{W}\hat{\epsilon}/\hat{\sigma}_\epsilon^2\right)^2}{T}.$$ (13)

The drawback with these tests is that they have power against the incorrect alternative, which means they are usually not helpful for making specification choices. Regardless of whether the true spatial autoregressive process is a lag or error process, both tests are likely to reject the null hypothesis. Anselin et al. (1996) present robust LM tests for spatial dependence that are less problematic in this regard. The robust, one-directional test against spatial error alternative treats ρ in the mixed SAR model, (8), as a nuisance parameter and controls for its effect on the likelihood. The statistic is then calculated as

$$LM_\lambda^* = \frac{\left(\hat{\epsilon}'\mathbf{W}\hat{\epsilon}/\hat{\sigma}_\epsilon^2 - \left[T\hat{\sigma}_\epsilon^2\left(G + T\hat{\sigma}_\epsilon^2\right)^{-1}\right]\hat{\epsilon}'\mathbf{W}\mathbf{y}/\hat{\sigma}_\epsilon^2\right)^2}{T\left[1 - \frac{1}{\hat{\sigma}_\epsilon^2}\left(G + T\hat{\sigma}_\epsilon^2\right)\right]^{-1}}.$$ (14)

The robust, one-directional test against spatial lag alternative is

$$LM_\rho^* = \frac{\hat{\sigma}_\epsilon^2 \left(\hat{\epsilon}'\mathbf{W}\mathbf{y}/\hat{\sigma}_\epsilon^2 - \hat{\epsilon}'\mathbf{W}\hat{\epsilon}/\hat{\sigma}_\epsilon^2\right)^2}{G + T(\hat{\sigma}_\epsilon^2 - 1)}.$$ (15)

The two-directional LM test, finally, can be decomposed into the robust LM test for one alternative (lag or error) and the standard LM test for the other:

$$LM_{\rho\lambda} = LM_\lambda + LM_\rho^* = LM_\rho + LM_\lambda^*.$$ (16)

The one-directional test statistics are distributed χ_1^2 while the two-directional statistic is distributed χ_2^2. Using Monte Carlo simulations, Anselin et al. (1996) show that all five tests have the correct size in small samples. That is, they all reject the null hypothesis at the stated rate when the null is true. The robust LM tests have lower power compared with the standard ones against the correct alternative, but the loss is relatively small and the robust tests are less likely to reject the null against the wrong alternative.

So, for example, when the true data-generating process is a spatial AR error model ($\lambda \neq 0$, $\rho = 0$), rejection rates for LM_λ are about 5 percentage points higher on average across the range of λ than for LM_λ^*. The robustness of LM_ρ^* relative to LM_ρ is clear in this experiment. At $\lambda = .9$, LM_ρ rejects in favor of the incorrect alternative 89.9 percent of the time whereas LM_ρ^* rejects 17.1 percent of the time. The power advantage of the standard LM test is smaller when the true data-generating process is a spatial AR lag model ($\lambda = 0$, $\rho \neq 0$). Rejection rates for LM_ρ are less than 2 percentage points higher on average than for LM_{ρ}^* across the full range of ρ. At $\rho = .9$, LM_{λ} rejects in favor of the incorrect alternative 100 percent of the time whereas LM_{λ}^* rejects 0.6 percent of the time. It seems the reduced power for increased robustness trade-off strongly favors that the robust LM tests be included in the set of diagnostics.[7]

To help illustrate how these tests can be used in empirical research, we present OLS estimates for a nonspatial model of welfare policy generosity in column 1 of Table 25.1. All variables in our illustrative analysis are states' averages over the five years 1986–90. The dependent variable is the maximum monthly AFDC benefit, and the independent variables are the state's poverty rate, average monthly wage in the retail sector, government ideology (ranging from 0 = conservative to 100 = liberal), degree of interparty competition (ranging from .5 = competitive to 1.0 = noncompetitive), tax effort (revenues as a percentage of tax "capacity"), and the portion of AFDC benefits paid by the federal government. We use a standardized binary contiguity-weights matrix, which begins by coding $w_{ij} = 1$ for states i and j that share a border and $w_{ij} = 0$ for states that do not border. Then, we row-standardize (as commonly done in spatial-econometrics) the resulting matrix by dividing each cell in a row by that row's sum. This gives the unweighted average of the dependent variable in "neighboring" (so-defined) states.

The results for our nonspatial model suggest that high tax effort and low party competition are associated with more generous AFDC benefit payments. This seems reasonable. However, if the data exhibit spatial dependence, we need to worry about validity of these inferences. To check this possibility, we implement the diagnostic tests outlined above starting with Moran's I. The value of the standardized Moran-I test statistic is 3.312, which is statistically significant. We can reject the null hypothesis of no spatial dependence. We also include the LM tests. The result of the two-directional test leads to the same conclusion. Both the standard one-directional tests seem, predictably, statistically significant, which unfortunately gives us little guidance for specification. As expected, the robust one-directional tests are more helpful in this regard. The robust test against the spatial lag alternative is statistically significant while the robust test against the spatial error alternative is not. This suggests a spatial lag specification. We conclude with a warning. Ignoring evidence of spatial dependence can be extremely problematic, especially if the data suggest the true source of dependence is a spatial-lag process. In this case, simple OLS is likely to provide inaccurate coefficient estimates, particularly for variables that happen to cluster spatially (e.g. Franzese and Hays 2004; 2006a; 2007b).

3.2 Estimating Lag Models

The spatial lag model has become a very popular specification in social science research. One might arrive at this model via batteries of diagnostic tests or directly

---

[7] See Anselin et al. (1996, tables 3–6). These results are for the $N = 40$ experiments.

Table 25.1. State welfare policy (maximum AFDC benefit)

Independent variables	OLS	Spatial AR lag (S-OLS)	Spatial AR lag (S-2SLS)	Spatial AR lag (S-GMM)	Spatial AR lag (S-MLE)	Spatial AR error (S-MLE)
Constant	54.519 (531.830)	−246.76 (450.75)	−422.09 (437.74)	−500.05 (413.02)	−156.282 (429.130)	676.120 (471.965)
Poverty rate	−6.560 (11.262)	8.04 (10.022)	13.205 (9.977)	7.29 (8.452)	3.657 (8.917)	3.239 (10.062)
Retail wage	−.121 (.226)	.016 (.193)	.089 (.187)	−.008 (.201)	−.025 (.181)	−.344 (.243)
Government ideology	1.513 (1.030)	1.397 (.863)	1.359* (.825)	1.655** (.761)	1.432* (.806)	1.696** (.822)
Inter-party competition	621.799** (290.871)	368.65 (250.55)	286.98 (243.72)	438.9** (197.47)	444.677* (226.911)	263.887 (238.419)
Tax effort	3.357** (1.587)	2.022 (1.364)	1.553 (1.328)	2.397 (1.493)	2.423* (1.262)	2.936* (1.213)
Federal share	−4.405 (5.001)	−5.818 (4.20)	−6.012 (4.014)	−3.654 (3.415)	−5.393 (3.901)	−6.882* (4.099)
Spatial AR		.767*** (.178)	1.069*** (.232)	.840*** (.237)	.537*** (.122)	.565*** (.131)
Moran I-statistic	3.312***					
$LM_{\rho\lambda}$	12.322***					
LM_{ρ}	11.606***					
LM_{ρ}^{*}	6.477**					
LM_{λ}	5.845***					
LM_{λ}^{*}	.716					
Log-likelihood					−270.763	−272.728
Adj.-R²	.461	.622	.595	.606	.510	.588
Obs.	48	48	48	48	48	48

Notes: The spatial lags are generated with a binary contiguity weighting matrix. All the spatial weights matrices are row-standardized. ***Significant at the 1% Level; **Significant at the 5% Level; *Significant at the 10% Level.

from theory. The theory-driven approach starts by estimating the spatial model, and then uses Wald, LR, and related tests to refine the specification. We begin with OLS estimation of spatial lag models, which we label spatial OLS (S-OLS).

3.2.1 *Spatial OLS*

Spatial OLS is inconsistent. To see this, we start by rewriting the spatial lag model as

$$y = Z\delta + \epsilon, \quad \text{where } Z = [Wy \ X] \text{ and } \delta = [\rho \ \beta]'. \tag{17}$$

The matrices Z and δ have dimensions $Nx(k+1)$ and $(k+1)x1$, respectively. The asymptotic simultaneity bias for the S-OLS estimator is given by

$$\text{plim } \hat{\delta} = \delta + \text{plim} \left[\left(\frac{Z'Z}{n}\right)^{-1} \frac{Z'\epsilon}{n} \right]. \tag{18}$$

In the case where Z is a single exogenous regressor, x, $(k = 1, \text{cov }(\epsilon, x) = 0)$, we can rewrite (18) as

$$\text{plim } \hat{\delta} = \begin{bmatrix} \rho \\ \beta \end{bmatrix} + \begin{bmatrix} \frac{\text{var}(x)}{\text{var}(x)\text{var}(Wy)-[\text{cov}(x,Wy)]^2} & \frac{-\text{cov}(x,Wy)}{\text{var}(x)\text{var}(Wy)-[\text{cov}(x,Wy)]^2} \\ \frac{-\text{cov}(x,Wy)}{\text{var}(x)\text{var}(Wy)-[\text{cov}(x,Wy)]^2} & \frac{\text{var}(Wy)}{\text{var}(x)\text{var}(Wy)-[\text{cov}(x,Wy)]^2} \end{bmatrix} \begin{bmatrix} \text{cov}(\epsilon, Wy) \\ \text{cov}(\epsilon, x) \end{bmatrix}. \tag{19}$$

If we define $\Psi = \text{plim}\left(\frac{Z'Z}{n}\right)$ and $\Gamma = \text{plim}\left(\frac{Z'\epsilon}{n}\right)$, and do the matrix multiplication, (19) simplifies to

$$\text{plim } \hat{\delta} = \begin{bmatrix} \rho \\ \beta \end{bmatrix} + \begin{bmatrix} \frac{\Psi_{22}\Gamma_{11}}{|\Psi|} \\ -\frac{\Psi_{12}\Gamma_{11}}{|\Psi|} \end{bmatrix}. \tag{20}$$

Since Ψ is a variance-covariance matrix, its determinant is strictly positive. With positive (negative) spatial dependence in the data, the covariances Ψ_{12} and Γ_{11} are positive (negative), and S-OLS will overestimate (underestimate) ρ and underestimate (overestimate) β. This is one of the analytic results we stressed repeatedly earlier: The simultaneity biases of S-OLS tend to induce exaggerated estimates of interdependence strength and correspondingly deflated estimates of the importance of nonspatial factors.

The S-OLS estimates are provided in column 2 of Table 25.1. Consistent with the results from our diagnostic tests, the estimated coefficient on the spatial lag is large, positive, and statistically significant. The OLS estimates most affected by the switch to a spatial-lag specification are the party-competition and tax-effort coefficients, which become statistically insignificant. Conversely to S-OLS's simultaneity biases, the OLS coefficient estimates on these two variables may, because they cluster spatially, have suffered from omitted variable bias that would have inflated those estimates.

Franzese and Hays (2004; 2006a; 2007b) conclude that spatial OLS, despite its simultaneity, can perform acceptably under low-to-moderate interdependence strength and reasonable sample dimensions. Given our results, S-OLS is clearly preferable to OLS. In this particular case, however, both the size of the spatial-lag coefficient and the fact that no other coefficients are statistically significant should raise concerns about simultaneity bias. We have advised using some consistent estimator under conditions like these. We discuss three consistent estimators below, starting with spatial-2SLS and spatial-GMM.

3.2.2 *Spatial-2SLS and Spatial-GMM*

Spatial-2SLS and spatial-GMM provide consistent estimates for the coefficient on the spatial lag and use spatially weighted values of the exogenous variables in other units as instruments. The latter extends the former to account the heteroskedasticity in the quadratic form of the sample orthogonality conditions. If this particular form of heteroskedasticity is present, the S-GMM estimator yields smaller asymptotic variance than the spatial-2SLS estimator. If it is absent, the two estimators are equivalent.[8] Note that a mixed spatial autoregressive model of the form in (8) would suffer from heteroskedasticity, making S-GMM more efficient for estimating δ. (In this particular case, a generalized S-2SLS estimator using a Cochrane–Orcutt like transformation of the data is also available; see Kelejian and Prucha 1998; 1999).

To see how we estimate the spatial lag model (17) using S-2SLS, define the linear prediction of $\mathbf{W}y$:

$$\widehat{\mathbf{W}y} = \Pi[\Pi'\Pi]^{-1}\Pi'Wy \tag{21}$$

where Π is the full set of *exogenous* variables including, at least, $\mathbf{X}$ and $\mathbf{WX}$. $\mathbf{WX}$ provides *spatial*-instruments.[9] Thus, Π is an $N \times L$ matrix, where $L \geq 2k$. The orthogonality condition for the 2SLS estimator is formally written as $E[\Pi'\epsilon] = 0$. Next, define $\hat{\mathbf{Z}}$ as an $Nx(k + 1)$ matrix of the predicted values of $\mathbf{W}y$ and $\mathbf{X}$,

$$\hat{\mathbf{Z}} = [\widehat{\mathbf{W}y} \ \ \mathbf{X}]. \tag{22}$$

Using this definition, the spatial-2SLS estimator is

$$\hat{\delta}_{S2SLS} = (\hat{\mathbf{Z}}'\hat{\mathbf{Z}})^{-1}\hat{\mathbf{Z}}'y \tag{23}$$

$$\widehat{\mathrm{var}}\left(\hat{\delta}_{S2SLS}\right) = s^2(\hat{\mathbf{Z}}'\hat{\mathbf{Z}})^{-1} \tag{24}$$

where s^2 is calculated from residuals in the original structural model, (17), with $\hat{\delta}_{S2SLS}$ substituted for δ.

---

[8] When the number of excluded exogenous variables exactly equals the number of endogenous variables, the GMM, 2SLS, and ILS estimators are equivalent. Therefore, we could more accurately say that GMM improves on 2SLS when the coefficients in the system/equation are overidentified and heteroskedasticity exists. In this case, we have one endogenous regressor, the spatial lag, in one equation. Provided the number of exogenous variables in X exceeds one, the number of spatial instruments will exceed one, making the coefficient on the spatial lag overidentified.

[9] One can also include higher order spatial instruments in Π—that is, $\{W^2X, W^3X, W^4X, \ldots\}$.

The GMM estimator minimizes a weighted quadratic form of the sample moment conditions derived from the orthogonality assumptions. More specifically, this criterion is

$$q = E\left[\mu(\delta)\Sigma^{-1}\mu(\delta)'\right],\tag{25}$$

with the corresponding moment conditions:

$$\mu(\delta) = \frac{1}{N}\sum_{i=1}^{N}\pi_i\left(y_i - z'_i\delta\right)\tag{26}$$

$$\Sigma = E\left[\mu(\delta)\mu(\delta)'\right] = \frac{1}{N}E\left[\sum_{i=1}^{N}\pi_i\pi'_i(y_i - z'_i\delta)^2\right]$$

$$= \frac{1}{N}\sum_{i=1}^{N}\omega\pi_i\pi_i = \frac{1}{N}\left(\Pi'\Omega\Pi\right).\tag{27}$$

In these equations, π_i is a column vector (lx1) that is the transpose of the ith row of Π (representing the ith observation) and, similarly, z_i is a $(k+1)$x1 vector that is the transpose of the ith row of **Z**. The GMM weighting matrix is calculated by inverting a consistent estimate of the variance-covariance matrix of the moment conditions.[10] White's estimator provides a consistent nonparametric estimate of Σ provided we have a consistent estimator of δ (Anselin 2006). Fortunately, spatial-2SLS can provide these. Thus, the estimate for Σ is

$$\mathbf{S}_0 = \sum_{i=1}^{N}\pi_i\pi'_i\left(y_i - z'_i\hat{\delta}_{\text{S2SLS}}\right)^2\tag{28}$$

and the GMM estimator for δ is

$$\hat{\delta}_{\text{SGMM}} = \left[\mathbf{Z}'\Pi(\mathbf{S}_0)^{-1}\Pi'\mathbf{Z}\right]^{-1}\left[\mathbf{Z}'\Pi(\mathbf{S}_0)^{-1}\Pi'\mathbf{y}\right]\tag{29}$$

$$\widehat{\text{var}}\left(\hat{\delta}_{\text{SGMM}}\right) = \left[\mathbf{Z}'\Pi\left(\hat{\mathbf{S}}_0^{-1}\right)\Pi'\mathbf{Z}\right]^{-1}.\tag{30}$$

We present the S-2SLS and S-GMM estimates for the spatial-lag model of welfare policy generosity in columns 3 and 4 of Table 25.1. The S-2SLS estimates for this particular specification and data-set are troubling as the spatial-lag coefficient estimate exceeds one, giving a nonstationary spatial process. This is a bit surprising when compared with the smaller S-OLS result, given that the S-OLS estimator has likely-inflationary simultaneity biases and S-2SLS likely does not. Of course, this can happen with a single sample and/or if the exogeneity of the instruments is violated.[11] The S-GMM estimates are better. The spatial-lag coefficient estimate

---

[10] The logic here is similar to that behind the WLS estimator. OLS is consistent in the presence of heteroskedasticity, but WLS is more efficient. Likewise, 2SLS is consistent under heteroskedasticty, but GMM is asymptotically more efficient.

[11] Franzese and Hays (2004) show that the exogeneity at issue here is that the y_i must not cause the x_j, a condition we call (no) cross-spatial endogeneity. Such reverse "diagonal" causality seems unlikely

is well below one (though it is still large) and the standard errors are about 5 percent smaller than the S-2SLS standard errors on average, as expected given the likely efficiency of the GMM estimator. The coefficients on government ideology and on party competition are statistically significant. The results suggest that, *ceteris paribus*, welfare benefits are highest in states with noncompetitive party systems and liberal governments.

3.2.3 *Spatial Maximum Likelihood*

Implementing S-ML is not complicated, although the spatial-lag model adds a slight wrinkle to the standard linear additive case, and the maximization can be computationally intense for large samples. To see the minor complication, start by isolating the stochastic component of the spatial-lag model:

$$y = \rho Wy + X\beta + \epsilon \Rightarrow \epsilon = (I - \rho W)y - X\beta \equiv Ay - X\beta. \qquad (31)$$

Assuming *i.i.d.* normality, the likelihood function for ϵ is then just the typical linear one:

$$L(\epsilon) = \left(\frac{1}{\sigma^2 2\pi}\right)^{\frac{N}{2}} \exp\left(-\frac{\epsilon'\epsilon}{2\sigma^2}\right) \qquad (32)$$

which, in this case, will produce a likelihood in terms of y as follows:

$$L(y) = |A| \left(\frac{1}{\sigma^2 2\pi}\right)^{\frac{N}{2}} \exp\left(-\frac{1}{2\sigma^2}(Ay - X\beta)'(Ay - X\beta)\right) \qquad (33)$$

and the log-likelihood takes the form

$$\ln L(y) = \ln|A| - \left(\frac{N}{2}\right)\ln(2\pi) - \left(\frac{N}{2}\right)\ln \sigma^2 - \left(\frac{1}{2\sigma^2}(Ay - X\beta)'(Ay - X\beta)\right). \qquad (34)$$

This still resembles the typical linear-normal likelihood, except that the transformation from ϵ to y is not by the usual factor of 1, but by $|A| = |I - \rho W|$. Since $|A|$ depends on ρ, each recalculation of the likelihood in maximization routine must recalculate this determinant for the updated ρ-values. Ord's (1975) solution to this computational-intensity issue was to approximate $|W|$ by $\prod_i \kappa_i$ because the eigenvector κ in this approximation does not depend on ρ. Then $|I - \rho W| = \prod_i (1 - \kappa_i)$, which requires the estimation routine only to recalculate a product, not a determinant, as it updates.[12] The estimated variance-covariances of parameter estimates follow the

---

to arise in many substantive contexts, although we do note also that spatial correlation among the other regressors plus the typical endogeneity from y to x would create it.

[12]   Unfortunately, the approximation may be numerically unstable (Anselin 1988; 2001; Kelejian and Prucha 1998). On the other hand, S-ML may enjoy a practical advantage over S-2SLS in multiple-W models in that S-ML does not require differentiated instrumentation for each W to gain distinct leverage on its corresponding ρ. The instruments, WX, would differ by virtue of W differing for the alternative interdependence processes, so S-2SLS is estimable for multiple-W models even with identical X in the WX instruments, but we harbor doubts about the practical identification leverage obtainable thereby.

usual ML formula (negative the inverse of Hessian of the likelihood) and so are also functions of $|\mathbf{A}|$. The same approximation serves there.

Typically, estimation proceeds by maximizing a concentrated-likelihood. Given an estimate of the spatial-lag coefficient, ρ, an analytic optimum estimate of the nonspatial coefficients can be found as

$$\hat{\beta} = (\mathbf{X}'\mathbf{X})^{-1}\mathbf{X}'\mathbf{A}\mathbf{y} = (\mathbf{X}'\mathbf{X})^{-1}\mathbf{X}'\mathbf{y} - \rho(\mathbf{X}'\mathbf{X})^{-1}\mathbf{X}'\mathbf{W}\mathbf{y} = \hat{\beta}_0 - \rho.\hat{\beta}_L. \tag{35}$$

Note that the first term in the second two expressions of (35) is just the OLS regression of $\mathbf{y}$ on $\mathbf{X}$, and the second term is just ρ times the OLS regression of $\mathbf{W}\mathbf{y}$ on $\mathbf{X}$. Both of these rely only on observables (except for ρ), and so are readily calculable given some ρ (estimate). Next, define these terms:

$$\hat{\epsilon}_0 = \mathbf{y} - \mathbf{X}\beta_0 \quad \text{and} \quad \hat{\epsilon}_L = \mathbf{W}\mathbf{y} - \mathbf{X}\beta_L. \tag{36}$$

It then follows that

$$\hat{\sigma}^2 = (1/N)(\hat{\epsilon}_0 - \rho\hat{\epsilon}_L)'(\hat{\epsilon}_0 - \rho\hat{\epsilon}_L) \tag{37}$$

is the S-ML estimate of the standard-error of the regression, and

$$\ln L_C(\mathbf{y}) = -\left(\frac{N}{2}\right)\ln \pi + \ln |\mathbf{A}| - \frac{N}{2}\ln\left(\frac{1}{N}(\epsilon_0 - \rho\epsilon_L)'(\epsilon_0 - \rho\epsilon_L)\right) \tag{38}$$

yields the S-ML estimate of ρ which is substituted into (35) to get $\hat{\beta}$. The procedure may be iterated, and estimated variance-covariances of parameter estimates derive from the information matrix as usual, although they could also be bootstrapped.

The S-ML estimates for our spatial lag model of welfare policy generosity are provided in column 5 of Table 25.1. These estimates are mostly similar to the S-GMM estimates. The most noteable difference is in the estimate of ρ. The S-ML coefficient is approximately 36 percent smaller than the S-GMM coefficient, and it is estimated much more precisely, the standard error being about half the size of the S-GMM standard error. Three of the coefficients in this model are statistically significant including the tax effort coefficient. The S-ML estimates imply welfare benefits are systematically larger, all else equal, in states with high taxes, liberal governments, and noncompetitive party systems. Franzese and Hays (2004; 2006a; 2007b) find that S-ML generally outperforms S-2SLS on mean squared error grounds. S-GMM lessens the efficiency advantage for S-ML over the IV class of estimators.

3.3 Estimating Error Models

If specification tests indicate that spatial dependence is of the form in (6), OLS coefficient estimates are consistent, but standard-error estimates will be biased. One could combine OLS coefficient estimates with robust standard errors (e.g. PCSE's:

Beck and Katz 1995; 1996). Another option is to estimate a spatial-error model. In this section we consider the maximum-likelihood estimator for this model. Again, we start by isolating the stochastic component, which in this case is

$$y = X\beta + \epsilon \equiv X\beta + (I - \lambda W)^{-1} u \Rightarrow u = (I - \lambda W)(y - X\beta) \equiv B(y - X\beta). \quad (39)$$

The likelihood for a spatial error process is

$$L(y) = |B| \left(\frac{1}{\sigma^2 2\pi} \right)^{\frac{N}{2}} \exp\left(-\frac{1}{2\sigma^2} (y - X\beta)' B'B(y - X\beta) \right) \quad (40)$$

where $|B| = |I - \lambda W|$, and the log-likelihood takes the form

$$\ln L(y) = \ln |B| - \left(\frac{N}{2} \right) \ln(2\pi) - \left(\frac{N}{2} \right) \ln \sigma^2 - \left(\frac{1}{2\sigma^2} (y - X\beta)' B'B(y - X\beta) \right). \quad (41)$$

We first calculate OLS residuals, and then estimate λ by maximizing the concentrated likelihood:

$$\ln L_C(y) = - \left(\frac{N}{2} \right) \ln(2\pi) + \ln |B| - \frac{N}{2} \ln \left(\frac{1}{N} (\hat{\epsilon}' B'B \hat{\epsilon}) \right). \quad (42)$$

Given λ, the ML estimates for β are calculated using FGLS:

$$\hat{\beta}_{ML} = (X'B'BX)^{-1} X'B'By. \quad (43)$$

The asymptotic variance covariance matrix for $\hat{\beta}_{ML}$ is

$$\text{var}(\hat{\beta}_{ML}) = \hat{\sigma}^2 (X'B'BX)^{-1} \quad (44)$$

where $\hat{\sigma}^2 = (1/N)(\hat{\epsilon}' B'B \hat{\epsilon})$ and $\hat{\epsilon} = y - X\hat{\beta}_{ML}$. The asymptotic variance for λ is

$$\text{var}(\hat{\lambda}) = 2\text{tr}(WB^{-1})^2. \quad (45)$$

The S-ML estimates for the spatial error model of welfare policy generosity are provided in the last column of Table 25.1. We note only that the log-likelihood value for the error model is less than the log-likelihood for the lag model, and this is consistent with the robust LM specification test results.

4 CALCULATING AND PRESENTING SPATIAL EFFECTS

Calculation and presentation of *effects* in empirical models with spatial interdependence, as in any model beyond the purely linear-additive, involve more than simply considering coefficient estimates. In empirical models containing *spatial dynamics*, as in those with only temporal dynamics, coefficients on explanatory variables give only the *pre-dynamic* impetuses to the outcome variable from increases in those variables. This represents the pre-interdependence impetus, which, incidentally, is unobservable if spatial dynamics are instantaneous (i.e. incur within observation period). This section discusses calculation of spatial multipliers, which allow expression of the *effects* of counterfactual shocks across units, and it applies the delta-method to compute standard errors for these *effects*:[13]

$$
\begin{aligned}
\mathbf{y} &= \rho \mathbf{W} \mathbf{y} + \mathbf{X}\boldsymbol{\beta} + \boldsymbol{\epsilon} \\
&= (\mathbf{I_N} - \rho \mathbf{W})^{-1}(\mathbf{X}\boldsymbol{\beta} + \boldsymbol{\epsilon}) \\
&= \begin{bmatrix}
1 & -\rho w_{1,2} \cdots & \cdots & -\rho w_{1,N} \\
-\rho w_{2,1} & 1 & & \vdots \\
\vdots & & \ddots & \vdots \\
\vdots & & 1 & -\rho w_{(N-1),N} \\
-\rho w_{N,1} & \cdots & \cdots -\rho w_{N,(N-1)} & 1
\end{bmatrix}^{-1} (\mathbf{X}\boldsymbol{\beta} + \boldsymbol{\epsilon}). \quad (46) \\
&= \mathbf{M}\,(\mathbf{X}\boldsymbol{\beta} + \boldsymbol{\epsilon})
\end{aligned}
$$

Denote the ith column of $\mathbf{M}$ as $\mathbf{m}_i$ and its estimate as $\hat{\mathbf{m}}_i$. The spatial effects of a one-unit increase in explanatory variable k in country i on country i's and its neighbors' outcomes is $\mathbf{M}\frac{dx_{i,k}\hat{\beta}_{i,k}}{dx_{i,k}}$ or simply, $\mathbf{m}\beta_{ik}$.

The standard errors calculation, using the delta method, is

$$
\text{var}\left(\hat{\mathbf{m}}_i \hat{\beta}_k\right) = \left[\frac{\partial \hat{\mathbf{m}}_i \hat{\beta}_k}{\partial \hat{\theta}}\right] \text{var}\left(\hat{\theta}\right) \left[\frac{\partial \hat{\mathbf{m}}_i \hat{\beta}_k}{\partial \hat{\theta}}\right]', \text{ where } \hat{\theta} = \begin{bmatrix} \hat{\rho} \\ \hat{\beta}_k \end{bmatrix}
$$

$$
\text{and } \left[\frac{\partial \hat{\mathbf{m}}_i \hat{\beta}_k}{\partial \hat{\theta}}\right] = \left[\frac{\partial \hat{\mathbf{m}}_i \hat{\beta}_k}{\partial \hat{\rho}} \quad \mathbf{m}_i\right]. \quad (47)
$$

The vector $\frac{\partial \hat{\mathbf{m}}_i \hat{\beta}_k}{\partial \hat{\rho}}$ is the ith column of $\beta_k \frac{\partial \hat{\mathbf{M}}}{\partial \hat{\rho}}$. Since $\mathbf{M}$ is an inverse matrix, the derivative in equation (47) is calculated as $\frac{\partial \hat{\mathbf{M}}}{\partial \hat{\rho}} = -\hat{\mathbf{M}}\frac{\partial \hat{\mathbf{M}}^{-1}}{\partial \hat{\rho}}\hat{\mathbf{M}} = -\hat{\mathbf{M}}(\mathbf{I} - \rho \mathbf{W})\,\hat{\mathbf{M}} = -\hat{\mathbf{M}}(-\mathbf{W})\hat{\mathbf{M}} = \hat{\mathbf{M}}\mathbf{W}\hat{\mathbf{M}}$. We do not calculate and present the spatial effects implied by the models in Table 25.1. Instead, we concentrate on calculating spatio-temporal effects using one of the panel models in the next section. These spatio-temporal calculations are slightly more complicated than the purely spatial ones.

---

[13] For an excellent discussion of spatial multipliers, see Anselin (2003). For an application (without standard errors), see Kim, Phipps, and Anselin (2003).

5 EXTENSIONS

In this section we consider several newer applications of spatial techniques in empirical political science research: SAR models with multiple lags, SAR models for binary dependent variables, and STAR models for panel data.

5.1 Spatial Autoregressive Models with Multiple Lags

One innovation in the booming literature on policy and institutional diffusion in recent years is the use of spatial autoregressive models with multiple lags to evaluate distinct diffusion mechanisms (Simmons and Elkins 2004; Elkins, Guzman, and Simmons 2006; Lee and Strang 2006). This section briefly highlights some of the difficulties involved in estimating these models, focusing on the linear additive case. Again, there are two main versions of this model. Brandsma and Ketellapper (1979) and Dow (1984) estimate biparametric error models of the form

$$\begin{aligned} y &= X\beta + \epsilon \\ \epsilon &= \lambda_1 W_1 \epsilon + \lambda_2 W_2 \epsilon + u \end{aligned} \tag{48}$$

using the maximum likelihood technique described in Section 3.3 In this case, the concentrated likelihood contains $|B| = |I - \lambda_1 W_1 - \lambda_2 W_2|$ (see (42)). Again, the OLS estimator for β is consistent but inefficient when the spatial dependence takes the form in (48). Lacombe (2004) estimates a biparametric lag model:

$$y = \rho_1 W_1 y + \rho_2 W_2 y + X\beta + \epsilon. \tag{49}$$

As with the single-spatial-lag model, S-OLS estimation of the biparametric model suffers simultaneity bias. However, the problem is potentially worse in the case of multiple spatial lags with its two or more endogenous variables rather than one. To see this, first rewrite the model (without exogenous regressors):

$$y = Z\rho + \epsilon \quad \text{where } Z = [W_1 y \quad W_2 y] \text{ and } \rho = [\rho_1 \quad \rho_2]'. \tag{50}$$

The *asymptotic* simultaneity bias for the S-OLS estimator is given by

$$\text{plim } \hat{\rho} = \rho + \text{plim} \left[\left(\frac{Z'Z}{n} \right)^{-1} \frac{Z'\epsilon}{n} \right] \tag{51}$$

which can be written as

$$\text{plim } \hat{\rho} = \begin{bmatrix} \rho_1 \\ \rho_2 \end{bmatrix} + \begin{bmatrix} \dfrac{\text{var}(W_2 y)}{\text{var}(W_2 y)\text{var}(W_1 y) - [\text{cov}(W_1 y, W_2 y)]^2} & \dfrac{-\text{cov}(W_1 y, W_2 y)}{\text{var}(W_2 y)\text{var}(W_1 y) - [\text{cov}(W_1 y, W_2 y)]^2} \\ \dfrac{-\text{cov}(W_1 y, W_2 y)}{\text{var}(W_2 y)\text{var}(W_1 y) - [\text{cov}(W_1 y, W_2 y)]^2} & \dfrac{\text{var}(W_1 y)}{\text{var}(W_2 y)\text{var}(W_1 y) - [\text{cov}(W_1 y, W_2 y)]^2} \end{bmatrix}$$

$$\times \begin{bmatrix} \text{cov}(\epsilon, W_1 y) \\ \text{cov}(\epsilon, W_2 y) \end{bmatrix}. \tag{52}$$

If we define $\Psi = \text{plim}\left(\frac{Z'Z}{n}\right)$ and $\Gamma = \text{plim}\left(\frac{Z'\epsilon}{n}\right)$, and carry out the matrix multiplication, equation (52) simplifies to

$$\text{plim } \hat{\rho} = \begin{bmatrix} \rho_1 \\ \rho_2 \end{bmatrix} + \begin{bmatrix} \dfrac{\Psi_{22}\Gamma_{11} - \Psi_{12}\Gamma_{21}}{|\Psi|} \\[2ex] \dfrac{\Psi_{11}\Gamma_{21} - \Psi_{12}\Gamma_{11}}{|\Psi|} \end{bmatrix}. \tag{53}$$

Since Ψ is a variance-covariance matrix, its determinant is strictly positive ($[\Psi_{11}\Psi_{22} - \Psi_{12}^2] > 0$). Therefore, if we assume that (1) there is positive spatial dependence (ρ, Ψ_{12}, $\Gamma_{11} > 0$), (2) the spatial lags have the same degree of endogeneity ($\Gamma_{11} = \Gamma_{21}$), and (3) the variance of $W_2 y$ is less than the variance of $W_1 y$ ($\Psi_{22} < \Psi_{11}$), it follows that S-OLS will underestimate ρ_1 and overestimate ρ_2 *asymptotically*.

Fortunately, the maximum likelihood estimator can be implemented in almost the same manner described in Section 3.2.3. In the biparametric case, the error term is

$$\epsilon = (I_N - \rho_1 W_1 - \rho_2 W_2)y - X\beta \equiv Ay - X\beta. \tag{54}$$

With this change, the likelihood function in (38) can be used for estimation. The main practical difficulty in maximizing the concentrated likelihood is calculating the log-determinant of A. Lacombe (2004) addresses this difficulty by calculating $\log|A|$ over a grid of values for ρ_1 and ρ_2 prior to estimation. His routine calls values from this table during the optimization process.

5.2 Spatial Models for Binary Outcomes

The methods for estimating and analyzing spatial latent variable models for categorical data have received significant attention in the literature recently. Much of the methodological research has focused on the spatial probit model (e.g. McMillen 1992; LeSage 2000). This is also one of the most frequently used models in the applied research (Beron, Murdoch, and Vijverberg 2003; Simmons and Elkins 2004). In this section we consider spatial models for binary outcomes, starting with the spatial lag probit model.

5.2.1 *Spatial Lag Probit Models*

The structural model for the spatial probit takes the form

$$y^* = \rho W y^* + X\beta + \epsilon, \tag{55}$$

which can be written in its reduced form as

$$y^* = (I - \rho W)^{-1} X\beta + u \tag{56}$$

where $u = (I - \rho W)^{-1}\epsilon$ and y^* is a latent variable linked to the observed variable y through the measurement equation

$$y_i = \begin{cases} 1 \text{ if } y_i^* > 0 \\ 0 \text{ if } y_i^* \leq 0 \end{cases}. \tag{57}$$

The marginal probabilities are calculated as follows:

$$\Pr(y_i = 1 | \mathbf{x}_i) = \Pr\left((\mathbf{I} - \rho\mathbf{W})_i^{-1}\mathbf{x}'_i\beta + (\mathbf{I} - \rho\mathbf{W})_i^{-1}\epsilon_i > 0\right)$$

or

$$\Pr(y_i = 1 | \mathbf{x}_i) = \Pr\left(u_i < \frac{(\mathbf{I} - \rho\mathbf{W})_i^{-1}\mathbf{x}'_i\beta}{\sigma_i}\right) \tag{58}$$

using the marginal distribution from a multivariate normal with variance-covariance matrix $[(\mathbf{I} - \rho\mathbf{W})'(\mathbf{I} - \rho\mathbf{W})]^{-1}$. The denominator in equation (58), which is the square root of the variance for unit i, is attributable to the heteroskedasticity induced by the spatial dependence. This heteroskedasticity distinguishes the spatial probit from the conventional probit and makes the estimator for the latter inconsistent for the spatial case. The fact that the u_i are interdependent also makes the standard probit estimator inappropriate for the spatial model. One does not sum the log of n one-dimensional probabilities to estimate the model, but rather calculates the log of one n-dimensional normal probability.

Beron et al. (2003) proposed estimation by simulation using recursive importance sampling (RIS), which is discussed extensively in Vijverberg (1997). LeSage (2000) has suggested using Bayesian Markov Chain Monte Carlo (MCMC) methods. The MCMC approach is mostly straightforward. The full conditional distributions are standard except one, and therefore the Gibbs sampler can be used. The parameter ρ has a nonstandard conditional distribution. Metropolis–Hastings sampling is used to draw values from this posterior.

We estimate several spatial lag probits in Table 25.2 using both standard ML and MCMC methods. In keeping with our state welfare spending example, we switch the dependent variable from maximum AFDC benefits to whether a state's CHIP (Children's Health Insurance Program) includes a monthly premium payment (Volden 2006). We keep the same independent variables since this dependent variable also reflects the generosity of the welfare program.

In the first two columns, the models are estimated assuming the spatial lags are exogenous. The model in the first column is estimated using standard ML techniques. The parentheses in this column contain estimated standard errors and the hypothesis tests assume that the asymptotic t-statistics are normally distributed. The models in columns two and three are estimated using MCMC methods with diffuse zero-mean priors. The reported coefficient estimate is the mean of the posterior distribution based on 10,000 observations after a 1,000-observation burn-in period. The number in parentheses is the standard deviation of the posterior distribution. The p-values are also calculated using the posterior. The results in columns two and three are very similar, as they should be given our diffuse priors. Because the estimator used in column two incorrectly treats the spatial lag as exogenous (i.e. like any other right-hand side variable), the likelihood is misspecified and the sampler draws from the wrong posterior distribution for the spatial coefficient ρ. This specification error has serious consequences for drawing inferences about the importance of spatial interdependence.

Table 25.2. State welfare policy (monthly CHIP premium)

Independent variables	Probit MLE	Probit MCMC	Spatial AR lag probit	Spatial AR error probit
Constant	−4.978 (6.260)	−5.163 (6.292)	−5.606 (10.159)	−5.531 (7.337)
Poverty rate	−.244 (.153)	−.265** (.156)	−.374** (.231)	−.243* (.157)
Retail wage	.004 (.003)	.004* (.003)	.006* (.004)	.004* (.003)
Government ideology	.011 (.013)	.011 (.013)	.014 (.020)	.014 (.014)
Inter-party competition	2.174 (3.388)	2.108 (3.478)	1.473 (6.134)	2.636 (3.794)
Tax effort	−.014 (.019)	−.014 (.019)	−.020 (.034)	−.017 (.021)
Federal share	.045 (.063)	.048 (.064)	.065 (.095)	.043 (.066)
Spatial AR	.079 (.798)	.102 (.815)	.200*** (.148)	.297*** (.196)
Pseudo-R^2	.222	.220	.607	.574
Obs.	48	48	48	48

Notes: In the first two columns, the models are estimated assuming the spatial lags are exogenous. The model in the first column is estimated using standard ML techniques. The parentheses in this column contain estimated standard errors and the hypothesis tests assume that the asymptotic t-statistics are normally distributed. The models in columns two through four are estimated using MCMC methods with diffuse zero-mean priors. The reported coefficient estimate is the mean of the posterior density based on 10,000 observations after a 1,000-observation burn-in period. The number in parentheses is the standard deviation of the posterior density. The p-values are also calculated using the posterior density. The last two models are estimated with true spatial estimators described in the text. In third column, 30 of the 10,000 spatial AR coefficients sampled from the posterior distribution were negative. In the fourth column, none of the 10,000 sampled spatial AR coefficients were negative. ***p-value < .01, **p-value < .05, *p-value < .10.

The model in column three is estimated with the true spatial estimator described above. The draws for ρ are taken from the correct (nonstandard) posterior distribution using Metropolis–Hastings. In this case only 30 of the 10,000 spatial AR coefficients sampled from the posterior distribution were negative. Thus, there is strong evidence of positive spatial interdependence in states' decisions to include a monthly premium in their CHIP. In addition, these probit results suggest that a state's poverty rate and average monthly retail wage are also important determinants.

5.2.2 *Spatial Error Probit Models*

The spatial error version of the probit model takes the form

$$\mathbf{y}^* = \mathbf{X}\boldsymbol{\beta} + \mathbf{u}, \tag{59}$$

where $\mathbf{u} = (\mathbf{I} - \lambda\mathbf{W})^{-1}\boldsymbol{\epsilon}$. In this case, the marginal probabilities are calculated as

$$\Pr(y_i = 1|\mathbf{x}_i) = \Pr\left(u_i < \frac{\mathbf{x}'_i\boldsymbol{\beta}}{\sigma_i}\right) \tag{60}$$

using the marginal distribution from a multivariate normal with variance-covariance matrix $[(\mathbf{I} - \lambda\mathbf{W})'(\mathbf{I} - \lambda\mathbf{W})]^{-1}$. The same estimation techniques used for the spatial lag model can be used for the spatial error model. We present estimates for the spatial error model in column four of Table 25.2. In this case, none of the 10,000 sampled spatial AR coefficients were negative. We do not discuss specification tests (*lag* vs. *error*) for the spatial probit, but they are covered in Anselin (2006).

5.3 Spatio-temporal Models for Panel Data

The spatio-temporal autoregressive (STAR) lag model can be written in matrix notation as

$$\mathbf{y} = \rho \mathbf{W}\mathbf{y} + \phi \mathbf{V}\mathbf{y} + \mathbf{X}\beta + \epsilon, \tag{61}$$

where y, the dependent variable, is an $NT \times 1$ vector of cross-sections stacked by periods (i.e. the N first-period observations, then the N second-period ones, and so on to the N in the last period, T).[14] The parameter ρ is the spatial autoregressive coefficient and W is an $NT \times NT$ block-diagonal spatial-weighting matrix. More specifically, we can express this W matrix as the Kronecker product of a $T \times T$ identity matrix and an $N \times N$ weights matrix ($\mathbf{I}_T \otimes \mathbf{W}_N$), with elements w_{ij} of $\mathbf{W}_N$ reflecting the relative degree of connection from unit j to i. Wy is thus the spatial lag; i.e. for each observation y_{it}, Wy gives a weighted sum of the y_{jt}, with weights, w_{ij}, given by the relative connectivity from j to i. Notice how Wy thus directly and straightforwardly reflects the dependence of each unit i's policy dependence on unit j's policy, exactly as in the formal model and theoretical arguments reviewed above. The parameter ϕ is the temporal autoregressive coefficient, and V is an $NT \times NT$ matrix with ones on the minor diagonal, i.e. at coordinates $(N + 1, 1), (N + 2, 2), \ldots, (NT, NT - N)$, and zeros elsewhere, so Vy is the (first-order) temporal lag. The matrix X contains $NT \times k$ observations on k independent variables, and β is a $k \times 1$ vector of coefficients on them. The final term in equation (61), ϵ, is an $NT \times 1$ vector of disturbances, assumed to be independent and identically distributed.[15]

The likelihood for the spatio-temporal model is a straightforward extension of this spatial-lag likelihood. Written in $(N \times 1)$ vector notation, spatio-temporal-model conditional-likelihood is mostly conveniently separable into parts, as seen here:

$$\text{Log } f_{\mathbf{y}_t, \mathbf{y}_{t-1}, \ldots, \mathbf{y}_2 | \mathbf{y}_1} = -\frac{1}{2} N(T - 1)\log\left(2\pi\sigma^2\right) + (T - 1)\log|\mathbf{I} - \rho\mathbf{W}|$$

$$-\frac{1}{2\sigma^2} \sum_{t=2}^{T} \epsilon'_t \epsilon_t \tag{62}$$

where $\epsilon_t = \mathbf{y}_t - \rho\mathbf{W}_N\mathbf{y}_t - \phi\mathbf{I}_N\mathbf{y}_{t-1} - \mathbf{X}_t\beta$.

The issue of stationarity arises in more complicated fashion in spatio-temporal dynamic models than in purely temporally dynamic ones. Nonetheless, the conditions and issues arising in the former are reminiscent of, although not identical to, those

---

[14] With some work, nonrectangular panels and/or missing data are manageable, but we assume rectangularity and completeness for simplicity of exposition.

[15] Alternative distributions of ϵ are possible but add complication without illumination.

arising in the latter. Define $\mathbf{A} = \phi\mathbf{I}$, $\mathbf{B} = \mathbf{I} - \rho\mathbf{W}$, and ω as a characteristic root of $\mathbf{W}$, the statio-temporal process generating the data is covariance stationary if

$$\left|\mathbf{AB}^{-1}\right| < 1$$

or, equivalently, if

$$\begin{cases} |\phi| < 1 - \rho\omega_{max}, \text{ if } \rho \geq 0 \\ |\phi| < 1 - \rho\omega_{min}, \text{ if } \rho < 0 \end{cases}. \tag{63}$$

If W is row-standardized and both the temporal and spatial dependence are positive ($\rho > 0$ and $\phi > 0$), stationarity requires simply that $\phi + \rho < 1$.

Finally, we note that the unconditional (exact) likelihood function, the one that retains the first time-period observations as nonpredetermined, is more complicated (Elhorst 2001; 2003; 2005):

$$\text{Log } f_{y_t,\ldots,y_1} = -\frac{1}{2}NT\log\left(2\pi\sigma^2\right) + \frac{1}{2}\sum_{i=1}^{N}\log\left(\left(1 - \rho\omega_i\right)^2 - \phi^2\right)$$

$$+ (T-1)\sum_{i=1}^{N}\log\left(1 - \rho\omega_i\right) - \frac{1}{2\sigma^2}\sum_{t=2}^{T}\epsilon_t'\epsilon_t - \frac{1}{2\sigma^2}\epsilon_1'\left((\mathbf{B}-\mathbf{A})'\right)^{-1}$$

$$\times \left(\mathbf{B}'\mathbf{B} - \mathbf{B}'\mathbf{A}\mathbf{B}^{-1}\left(\mathbf{B}'\mathbf{A}\mathbf{B}^{-1}\right)'\right)^{-1}(\mathbf{B}-\mathbf{A})^{-1}\epsilon_1 \tag{64}$$

where $\epsilon_1 = \mathbf{y}_1 - \rho\mathbf{W}_N\mathbf{y}_1 - \phi\mathbf{I}_N\mathbf{y}_1 - \mathbf{X}_1\beta$. When T is small, the first observation contributes greatly to the overall likelihood, and the unconditional likelihood should be used to estimate the model. In other cases, the more compact conditional likelihood is acceptable for estimation purposes.

Note that the same condition that complicates ML estimation of the spatio-temporal lag model, namely the first set of observations being stochastic, also invalidates the use of OLS to estimate a model with a temporally lagged spatial lag. The spatio-temporal model with time-lagged dependent variable and time-lagged spatial-lag is

$$\mathbf{y}_t = \eta\mathbf{W}\mathbf{y}_{t-1} + \phi\mathbf{y}_{t-1} + \mathbf{X}_t\beta + \epsilon_t. \tag{65}$$

If the first set of observations is stochastic, the unconditional (exact) log-likelihood is

$$\text{Log } f_{y_t,\ldots,y_1} = -\frac{1}{2}NT\log\left(2\pi\sigma^2\right) + \frac{1}{2}\sum_{i=1}^{N}\log\left(1 - \left(\phi + \eta\omega_i\right)^2\right) - \frac{1}{2\sigma^2}\sum_{t=2}^{T}\epsilon_t'\epsilon_t$$

$$- \frac{1}{2\sigma^2}\epsilon_1'\left((\mathbf{I}-\mathbf{A})'\right)^{-1}\left(\mathbf{I}-\mathbf{A}\mathbf{A}'\right)^{-1}(\mathbf{I}-\mathbf{A})^{-1}\epsilon_1 \tag{66}$$

where $\epsilon_1 = \mathbf{y}_1 - (\phi + \eta\mathbf{W}_N)\mathbf{y}_1 - \mathbf{X}_1\beta$, $\epsilon_t = \mathbf{y}_t - \eta\mathbf{W}_N\mathbf{y}_{t-1} - \phi\mathbf{y}_{t-1} - \mathbf{X}_t\beta$, and $\mathbf{A} = \phi\mathbf{I} + \eta\mathbf{W}$. For the derivation of this likelihood function, see Elhorst (2001, 126–30). Note that the second term in the likelihood function causes the OLS estimator to be biased. Asymptotically ($T \to \infty$), this bias goes to zero.

Table 25.3. State welfare policy (maximum AFDC benefit, 1981–90)

Independent variables	OLS	Spatial AR lag (MLE)	Spatial AR error (MLE)
Poverty rate	−.855 (1.130)	−.911 (1.050)	−.903 (1.198)
Retail wage	.217*** (.036)	.204*** (.034)	.197*** (.037)
Government ideology	.053 (.087)	.059 (.081)	.027 (.083)
Inter-party competition	18.960 (24.046)	25.540 (22.442)	18.633 (22.382)
Tax effort	.388* (.223)	.322 (.208)	.349 (.218)
Federal share	.483 (.521)	.859* (.491)	.750 (.510)
Temporal AR	.663*** (.030)	.628*** (.031)	.666*** (.030)
Spatial AR		.143*** (.044)	.200*** (.058)
Moran I-statistic	3.296***		
$LM_{\rho\lambda}$	11.896***		
LM_{ρ}	9.976***		
LM_{ρ}^{*}	1.446		
LM_{λ}	10.450***		
LM_{λ}^{*}	1.921		
Log-likelihood		−1991.357	−1991.290
Adj.-R^2	.981	.981	.982
Obs.	480	480	480

Notes: All regressions include fixed period and unit effects; those coefficient-estimates suppressed to conserve space. The spatial lags are generated with a binary contiguity weighting matrix. All the spatial weights matrices are row-standardized. ***Significant at the 1% Level; **Significant at the 5% Level; *Significant at the 10% Level.

We present estimates for a panel model of welfare policy generosity in Table 25.3. The data are annual observations from 1981–90 on the contiguous forty-eight states. The dependent variable is the maximum AFDC benefit, and the independent variables remain unchanged. All the regressions include fixed state effects. The first column contains a nonspatial model estimated with OLS. Clearly, from Moran's I statistic and the two-directional LM statistics, there is spatial dependence in the data-set. The diagnostics do not provide clear evidence in favor of a spatial lag or error specification, however. We estimate both with contemporaneous spatial lags. The second column contains a spatio-temporal lag model, and the third column contains a combined temporal lag and spatial error model. Interestingly, the retail wage variable is statistically significant and positive in all three regressions. Once again, the tax effort coefficient becomes statistically insignificant with the change from a nonspatial to spatial specification.

To calculate marginal spatio-temporal effects (noncumulative) or plot the over-time path of the effect of a permanent one-unit change in an explanatory variable (cumulative), and their standard errors, simply solve for **y** in (61):

$$\mathbf{y} = \rho\mathbf{W}\mathbf{y} + \phi\mathbf{V}\mathbf{y} + \mathbf{X}\beta + \epsilon = \left(\rho\mathbf{W} + \phi\mathbf{V}\right)\mathbf{y} + \mathbf{X}\beta + \epsilon$$

$$= \left[\mathbf{I}_{NT} - \rho\mathbf{W} - \phi\mathbf{V}\right]^{-1}\left(\mathbf{X}\beta + \epsilon\right) \equiv \mathbf{M}\left(\mathbf{X}\beta + \epsilon\right). \tag{67}$$

Table 25.4. Spatial effects on AFDC benefits from a $100 counterfactual shock to monthly retail wages in Missouri

Neighbor	Immediate spatial effect	Long-run steady-state effect
Arkansas	.51 [.16, .87]	4.26 [1.01, 7.52]
Illinois	.62 [.19, 1.04]	5.11 [1.25, 8.97]
Iowa	0.52 [.15, .88]	4.37 [.99, 7.75]
Kansas	0.77 [.23, 1.31]	6.38 [1.60, 11.17]
Kentucky	0.44 [.13, .75]	3.68 [.87, 6.50]
Nebraska	0.52 [.15, .89]	4.44 [.99, 7.90]
Oklahoma	0.52 [.15, .89]	4.47 [.96, 7.98]
Tennessee	0.38 [.12, .65]	3.21 [.75, 5.67]

Notes: Effects calculated using estimates from the spatial AR lag model in Table 25.3. Brackets contain a 95% confidence interval.

Denote the ith column of $\mathbf{M}$ as $\mathbf{m}_i$ and its estimate as $\hat{\mathbf{m}}_i$. The spatial effects of a one-unit increase in explanatory variable k in country i are $\mathbf{m}_i \beta_k$ with delta-method standard errors calculated as

$$\text{var}\left(\hat{\mathbf{m}}_i \hat{\beta}_k\right) = \left[\frac{\partial \hat{\mathbf{m}}_i \hat{\beta}_k}{\partial \hat{\theta}} \right] \text{var}\left(\hat{\theta}\right) \left[\frac{\partial \hat{\mathbf{m}}_i \hat{\beta}_k}{\partial \hat{\theta}} \right]', \tag{68}$$

where $\hat{\theta} = \begin{bmatrix} \hat{\rho} \\ \hat{\phi} \\ \hat{\beta}_k \end{bmatrix}$, $\left[\frac{\partial \hat{\mathbf{m}}_i \hat{\beta}_k}{\partial \hat{\theta}} \right] = \left[\frac{\partial \hat{\mathbf{m}}_i \hat{\beta}_k}{\partial \hat{\rho}} \quad \frac{\partial \hat{\mathbf{m}}_i \hat{\beta}_k}{\partial \hat{\phi}} \quad \hat{\mathbf{m}}_i \right]$, and the vectors $\frac{\partial \hat{\mathbf{m}}_i \hat{\beta}_k}{\partial \hat{\rho}}$ and $\frac{\partial \hat{\mathbf{m}}_i \hat{\beta}_k}{\partial \hat{\phi}}$ are the ith columns of $\hat{\beta}_k \hat{\mathbf{M}} \mathbf{W} \hat{\mathbf{M}}$ and $\hat{\beta}_k \hat{\mathbf{M}} \hat{\mathbf{M}}$, respectively. In Table 25.4, we present the immediate and long-run (steady-state) spatial effects on regional AFDC benefits from a permanent $100 increase in monthly retail wages in Missouri using the calculations in equations (67) and (68). The immediate (steady-state) effects range from a low of $0.44 ($3.68) in Kentucky to a high of $0.77 ($6.38) in Kansas.

In Figure 25.1, we present the spatio-temporal effects on AFDC benefits in Missouri from a permanent $100 increase in monthly retail wages in Missouri (with 95 percent C.I.). The marginal effects decay rapidly with most of the total effect experienced within the first two years after the shock. The cumulative ten-year effect is approximately $55.75. In Figure 25.2, we present the spatio-temporal effects on AFDC benefits in Nebraska from a $100 counterfactual increase in monthly retail wages in Missouri (with 95 percent C.I.). The cumulative ten-year effect is about $4.11. Interestingly, the maximum effects in Nebraska are not experienced until one or two years after the initial shock. This serves to highlight an important point, namely that the contemporaneous spatial lag specification does not imply all (or even most) of the spatial effects are instantaneous.

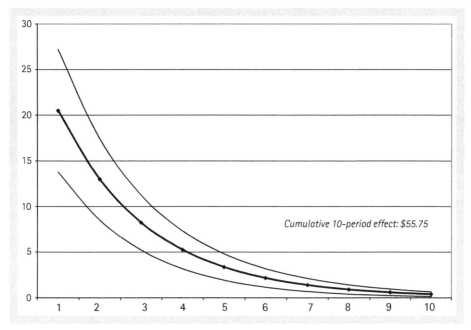

Fig. 25.1. Spatio-temporal effects on AFDC benefits in Missouri from a $100 counterfactual shock to monthly retail wages in Missouri (with 95 percent C.I.)

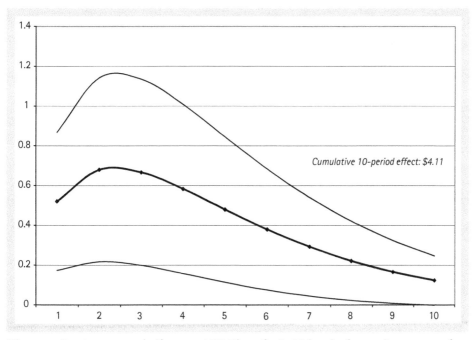

Fig. 25.2. Spatio-temporal effects on AFDC benefits in Nebraska from a $100 counterfactual shock to monthly retail wages in Missouri (with 95 percent C.I.)

6 Conclusions

....

Spatial analysis has become much more common in empirical political science research recently. New theories, data, and technology have all contributed to what is
likely to be a lasting trend in the study of politics. In our view, the incorporation of
spatial models into political science represents a very positive development. After all,
spatial interdependence is an important part of the politics that political scientists
aim to understand. If there is a concern, it is that the applied research on diffusion
and other sources of spatial interdependence is approaching the limits of our methodological knowledge about best practices. This partly reflects the time it takes for new
methods from other disciplines to become standard tools in the political science tool
kit, as seems to be the case, for example, with simulation based estimation, but it
is also due the fact that political scientists ask unique questions and have distinct
methodological needs. In this chapter, we have surveyed some developments with
respect to diagnosing spatial interdependence, specifying and estimating spatial models, and presenting spatial (and spatio-temporal) effects. It is incumbent on applied
researchers to familiarize themselves with these techniques, but it is equally important
for political methodologists to accept the challenge of developing spatial methods for
political science.

References

ANSELIN, L. 1980. Estimation methods for spatial autoregressive structures. Regional Science
    Dissertation and Monograph Series, Cornell University.
——1988. *Spatial Econometrics: Methods and Models.* Boston: Kluwer Academic.
——1992. Space and applied econometrics: introduction. *Regional Science and Urban
    Economics,* 22: 307–16.
——1995. Local indicators of spatial association: LISA. *Geographical Analysis,* 27: 93–115.
——2001. Spatial econometrics. Pp. 310–30 in *A Companion to Theoretical Econometrics,* ed.
    B. Baltagi. Oxford: Basil Blackwell.
——2002. Under the hood: issues in the specification and interpretation of spatial regression
    models. *Agricultural Economics,* 27: 247–67.
——2003. Spatial externalities, spatial multipliers and spatial econometrics. *International
    Regional Science Review,* 26: 153–66.
——2006. Spatial econometrics. Pp. 901–41 in *Palgrave Handbook of Econometrics,* i: *Econo-
    metric Theory,* ed. T. C. Mills and K. Patterson. Basingstoke: Palgrave Macmillan.
——BERA, A., FLORAX, R. J., and YOON, M. 1996. Simple diagnostic tests for spatial depen-
    dence. *Regional Science and Urban Economics,* 26: 77–104.
BAILEY, M., and ROM, M. 2004. A wider race? Interstate competition across health and welfare
    programs. *Journal of Politics,* 66: 326–47.
BALLA, S. 2001. Interstate professional associations and the diffusion of policy innovations.
    American Politics Research, 29: 221–45.

BASINGER, S., and HALLERBERG, M. 2004. Remodeling the competition for capital: how domestic politics erases the race-to-the-bottom. *American Political Science Review*, 98: 261–76.

BECK, N., GLEDITSCH, K. S., and BEARDSLEY, K. 2006. Space is more than geography: using spatial econometrics in the study of political economy. *International Studies Quarterly*, 50: 27–44.

——and KATZ, J. 1995. What to do (and not to do) with time series cross section data in comparative politics. *American Political Science Review*, 89: 634–47.

————1996. Nuisance vs. substance: specifying and estimating time series cross section models. *Political Analysis*, 6: 1–34.

BECK, P., DALTON, R., GREENE, S., and HUCKFELDT, R. 2002. The social calculus of voting: interpersonal, media, and organizational influences on presidential choices. *American Political Science Review*, 96: 57–74.

BERON, K. J., MURDOCH, J. C., and VIJVERBERG, W. P. 2003. Why cooperate? Public goods, economic power, and the Montreal Protocol. *Review of Economics and Statistics*, 85: 286–97.

BERRY, F. S. 1994. Sizing up state policy innovation research. *Policy Studies Journal*, 22: 442–56

——and BERRY, W. 1990. State lottery adoptions as policy innovations: an event history analysis. *American Political Science Review*, 84: 395–415.

————1999. Innovation and diffusion models in policy research. In *Theories of the Policy Process*, ed. P. Sabatier. Boulder, Colo.: Westview.

BERRY, W. D., FORDING, R. C., and HANSON, R. L. 2003. Reassessing the "race to the bottom" in state welfare policy. *Journal of Politics*, 65: 327–49.

BESAG, J. 1974. Spatial interaction and the statistical analysis of lattice systems. *Journal of the Royal Statistical Society, Series B*, 36: 192–225.

BOEHMKE, F., and WITMER, R. 2004. Disentangling diffusion: the effects of social learning and economic competition on state policy innovation and expansion. *Political Research Quarterly*, 57: 39–51.

BRANDSMA, A., and KETELLAPPER, R. H. 1979. A biparametric approach to spatial autocorrelation. *Environment and Planning A*, 11: 51–8.

BRAUN, D., and GILARDI, F. 2006. Taking "Galton's problem" seriously: towards a theory of policy diffusion. *Journal of Theoretical Politics*, 18: 298–322.

BRAYBECK, B., and HUCKFELDT, R. 2002a. Spatially dispersed ties among interdependent citizens: connecting individuals and aggregates. *Political Analysis*, 10: 261–75.

————2002b. Urban contexts, spatially dispersed networks, and the diffusion of political information. *Political Geography*, 21: 195–220.

BRINKS, D., and COPPEDGE, M. 2006. Diffusion is no illusion: neighbor emulation in the third wave of democracy. *Comparative Political Studies*, 39: 463–89.

BROOKS, S. 2005. Interdependent and domestic foundations of policy change: the diffusion of pension privatization around the world. *International Studies Quarterly*, 49: 273–94.

BRUECKNER, J. K. 2003. Strategic interaction among governments: an overview of empirical studies. *International Regional Science Review*, 26: 175–88.

BRUNE, N., GARRETT, G., and KOGUT, B. 2004. The International Monetary Fund and the global spread of privatization. *IMF Staff Papers*, 51: 195–219.

BURRIDGE, P. 1980. On the Cliff–Ord test for spatial autocorrelation. *Journal of the Royal Statistical Society, Series B*, 42: 107–8.

CALDEIRA, G. 1985. The transmission of legal precedent: a study of state supreme courts. *American Political Science Review*, 79: 178–94.

CASE, A., HINES, J., and ROSEN, H. 1993. Budget spillovers and fiscal policy interdependence: evidence from the states. *Journal of Public Economics*, 52: 285–307.

CHO, W. T. 2003. Contagion effects and ethnic contribution networks. *American Journal of Political Science*, 47: 368–87.

——and GIMPEL, J. 2007. Spatial dimensions of Arab American voter mobilization after September 11. *Political Geography*, 26: 330–51.

——and RUDOLPH, T. 2008. Emanating political participation: untangling the spatial structure behind participation. *British Journal of Political Science*, 38: 273–89.

CLIFF, A., and ORD, J. 1973. *Spatial Autocorrelation*. London: Pion.

————1981. *Spatial Processes: Models and Applications*. London: Pion.

CRAIN, R. 1966. Fluoridation: diffusion of an innovation among cities. *Social Forces*, 44: 467–76.

CRESSIE, N. 1993. *Statistics for Spatial Data*. New York: Wiley.

DAHL, R. 1971. *Polyarchy: Participation and Opposition*. New Haven, Conn.: Yale University Press.

DALEY, D., and GARAND, J. 2005. Horizontal diffusion, vertical diffusion, and internal pressure in state environmental policymaking, 1989–1998. *American Politics Research*, 33: 615–44.

DARMOFAL, D. 2006. Spatial econometrics and political science. Society for Political Methodology Working Paper Archive. <http://polmeth.wustl.edu/workingpapers.php>

DOW, M. A. 1984. Biparametric approach to network autocorrelation: Galton's problem. *Sociological Methods and Research*, 13: 201–17.

EISING, R. 2002. Policy learning in embedded negotiations: explaining EU electricity liberalization. *International Organization*, 56: 85–120.

ELHORST, J. P. 2001. Dynamic models in space and time. *Geographical Analysis*, 33: 119–40.

——2003. Specification and estimation of spatial panel data models. *International Regional Science Review*, 26: 244–68.

——2005. Unconditional maximum likelihood estimation of linear and log-linear dynamic models for spatial panels. *Geographical Analysis*, 37: 85–106.

ELKINS, Z., GUZMAN, A., and SIMMONS, B. 2006. Competing for capital: the diffusion of bilateral investment treaties, 1960–2000. *International Organization*, 60: 811–46.

——and SIMMONS, B. 2005. On waves, clusters, and diffusion: a conceptual framework. *Annals of the American Academy of Political and Social Science*, 598: 33–51.

FRANZESE, R., and HAYS, J. 2004. Empirical modeling strategies for spatial interdependence: omitted-variable vs. simultaneity biases. Summer meetings of the Political Methodology Society.

————2006a. Spatio-temporal models for political-science panel and time-series–cross-section data. Summer meetings of the Political Methodology Society.

————2006b. Strategic interaction among EU governments in active-labor-market policymaking: subsidiarity and policy coordination under the European Employment Strategy. *European Union Politics*, 7: 167–89.

————2007a. Empirical models of international capital-tax competition. Pp. 43–72 in *International Taxation Handbook*, ed. G. Gregoriou and C. Read. Amsterdam: Elsevier.

————2007b. Spatial econometric models of cross-sectional interdependence in political science panel and time-series–cross-section data. *Political Analysis*, 15: 140–64.

————2008. Interdependence in comparative politics: theory, empirics, substance. *Comparative Political Studies*, 41: 742–80.

FRIEDEN, J., and ROGOWSKI, R. 1996. The impact of the international economy on national policies: an analytical overview. In *Internationalization and Domestic Politics*, ed. R. O. Keohane. Cambridge: Cambridge University Press.

GARTZKE, E., and GLEDITSCH, K. S. 2006. Identity and conflict: ties that bind and differences that divide. *European Journal of International Relations*, 12: 53–87.

GENSCHEL, P. 2002. Globalization, tax competition, and the welfare state. *Politics and Society*, 30: 245–75.

GILARDI, F. 2005. The institutional foundations of regulatory capitalism: the diffusion of independent regulatory agencies in Western Europe. *Annals of the American Academy of Political and Social Science*, 598: 84–101.

GLEDITSCH, K. S. 2002. *All International Politics is Local: The Diffusion of Conflict, Integration, and Democratization*. Ann Arbor: University of Michigan Press.

—— 2007. Civil war and its spread. In *Handbook on Conflict Resolution*, ed. J. Bercovitch, V. Kremenyuk, and I. W. Zartman. London: Sage.

—— and BEARDSLEY, K. 2004. Nosy neighbors: third party actors in Central American civil conflicts. *Journal of Conflict Resolution*, 48: 379–402.

—— and WARD, M. 2000. War and peace in space and time: the role of democratization. *International Studies Quarterly*, 44: 1–29.

—— —— 2006. Diffusion and the international context of democratization. *International Organization*, 60: 911–33.

—— —— 2007. Diffusion and the spread of democratic institutions. In *The Global Diffusion of Democracy and Markets*, ed. F. Dobbins, G. Garret, and B. Simmons. Cambridge: Cambridge University Press.

GODWIN, M., and SCHROEDEL, J. 2000. Policy diffusion and strategies for promoting policy change: evidence from California local gun control ordinances. *Policy Studies Journal*, 28: 760–76.

GOLDENBERG, E. N., TRAUGOTT, M. W., and BAUMGARTNER, F. K. 1986. Preemptive and reactive spending in U.S. House races. *Political Behavior*, 8: 3–20.

GOVEA, R., and WEST, G. 1981. Riot contagion in Latin America, 1949–1963. *Journal of Conflict Resolution*, 25: 349–68.

GRAY, V. 1973. Innovation in the states: a diffusion study. *American Political Science Review*, 67: 1174–85.

GROSSBACK, L., NICHOLSON-CROTTY, S., and PETERSON, D. 2004. Ideology and learning in policy diffusion. *American Politics Research*, 32: 521–45.

HAINING, R. 1990. *Spatial Data Analysis in the Social and Environmental Sciences*. Cambridge: Cambridge University Press.

HOFF, P., and WARD, M. 2004. Modeling dependencies in international relations networks. *Political Analysis*, 12: 160–75.

HORDIJK, L. 1974. Spatial correlation in the disturbances of a linear interregional model. *Regional Science and Urban Economics*, 4: 117–40.

HUCKFELDT, R., and SPRAGUE, J. 1993. Citizens, contexts, and politics. Pp. 281–303 in *Political Science: The State of the Discipline II*, ed. A. W. Finifter. Washington, DC: APSA.

—— JOHNSON, P. E., and SPRAGUE, J. 2005. Individuals, dyads and networks: autoregressive patterns of political influence. In *The Social Logic of Politics: Personal Networks as Contexts for Political Behavior*, ed. A. S. Zuckerman. Philadelphia: Temple University Press.

HUNTINGTON, S. 1991. *The Third Wave: Democratization in the Late Twentieth Century*. Norman: University of Oklahoma Press.

JAHN, D. 2006. Globalization as "Galton's problem:" the missing link in the analysis of diffusion patterns in welfare state development. *International Organization*, 60: 401–31.

KAYSER, M. A. 2007. Partisan waves: international sources of electoral choice, Unpublished manuscript, University of Rochester. <http://mail.rochester.edu/~mksr/papers/PWaves_ECM_070108.pdf>

KELEJIAN, H. H., and PRUCHA, I. 1998. A generalized spatial two stage least squares procedures for estimating a spatial autoregressive model with autoregressive disturbances. *Journal of Real Estate Finance and Economics*, 17: 99–121.

———— 1999. A generalized moments estimator for the autoregressive parameter in a spatial model. *International Economic Review*, 40: 509–33.

———— 2001. On the asymptotic distribution of the Moran I test statistic with applications. *Journal of Econometrics*, 104: 219–57.

KIM, C.-W., PHIPPS, T. T., and ANSELIN, L. 2003. Measuring the benefits of air quality improvement: a spatial hedonic approach. *Journal of Environmental Economics and Management*, 45: 24–39.

KNILL, C. 2005. Introduction: cross-national policy convergence: concepts, approaches and explanatory factors. *Journal of European Public Policy*, 12: 764–74.

KNOKE, D. 1982. The spread of municipal reform: temporal, spatial, and social dynamics. *American Journal of Sociology*, 87: 1314–39.

KRASNO, J., GREEN, D., and COWDEN, J. 1994. The dynamics of campaign fundraising in House elections. *Journal of Politics*, 56: 459–74.

LACOMBE, D. J. 2004. Does econometric methodology matter? An analysis of public policy using spatial econometric techniques. *Geographical Analysis*, 36: 105–18.

LEE, C. K., and STRANG, D. 2006. The international diffusion of public-sector downsizing: network emulation and theory-driven learning. *International Organization*, 60: 883–909.

LESAGE, J. P. 2000. Bayesian estimation of limited dependent variable spatial autoregressive models. *Geographical Analysis*, 32: 19–35.

—— 1999. Spatial econometrics. <http://rri.wvu.edu/WebBook/LeSage/spatial/spatial.html>

LI, R., and THOMPSON, W. 1975. The "coup contagion" hypothesis. *Journal of Conflict Resolution*, 19: 63–88.

LIN, T. M., WU, C. E., and LEE, F. Y. 2006. "Neighborhood" influence on the formation of national identity in Taiwan: spatial regression with disjoint neighborhoods. *Political Research Quarterly*, 59: 35–46.

LUTZ, J. 1987. Regional leadership patterns in the diffusion of public policies. *American Politics Quarterly*, 15: 387–98.

MCMILLEN, D. P. 1992. Probit with spatial autocorrelation. *Journal of Regional Science*, 32: 335–48.

MESEGUER, C. 2004. What role for learning? The diffusion of privatisation in OECD and Latin American countries. *Journal of Public Policy*, 24: 299–325.

—— 2005. Policy learning, policy diffusion, and the making of a new order. *Annals of the American Academy of Political and Social Science*, 598: 67–82.

MINTROM, M. 1997a. Policy entrepreneurs and the diffusion of innovation. *American Journal of Political Science*, 41: 738–70.

—— 1997b. The state–local nexus in policy innovation diffusion: the case of school choice. *Publius: Journal of Federalism*, 27: 41–59.

—— and VERGARI, S. 1998. Policy networks and innovation diffusion: the case of state education reforms. *Journal of Politics*, 60: 126–48.

MOONEY, C. 2001. Modeling regional effects on state policy diffusion. *Political Research Quarterly*, 54: 103–24.

MOSSBERGER, K. 1999. State–federal diffusion and policy learning: from enterprise zones to empowerment zones. *Publius: Journal of Federalism*, 29: 31–50.

NAROLL, R. 1961. Two solutions to Galton's Problem. *Philosophy of Science*, 28: 15–39.

—— 1965. Galton's problem: the logic of cross-cultural analysis. *Social Research*, 32: 429–51.

—— 1970. What have we learned from cross-cultural surveys? *American Anthropologist*, 72: 1227–88.

O'LOUGHLIN, J., WARD, M., LOFDAHL, C., COHEN, J., BROWN, D., REILLY, D., GLEDITSCH, K., and SHIN, M. 1998. The diffusion of democracy, 1946–1994. *Annals of the Association of American Geographers*, 88: 545–74.

ORD, J. K. 1975. Estimation methods for models of spatial interaction. *Journal of the American Statistical Association*, 70: 120–6.

PAELINCK, J., and KLAASSEN, L. 1979. *Spatial Econometrics*. Farnborough: Saxon House.

PLÜMPER, T., and SCHNEIDER, C. J. 2007. The computation of convergence, or: how to chase a black cat in a dark room. <http://ssrn.com/abstract=955868>

RIPLEY, B. D. 1981. *Spatial Statistics*. New York: Wiley.

ROGERS, E. 1995. *Diffusion of Innovations*. New York: Free Press.

ROSE, R. 1993. *Lesson-Drawing in Public Policy: A Guide to Learning across Time and Space*. London: Chatham House.

SALEHYAN, I., and GLEDITSCH, K. S. 2006. Refugees and the spread of civil war. *International Organization*, 60: 335–66.

SCHNEIDER, A., and INGRAM, H. 1988. Systematically "pinching" ideas: a comparative approach to policy design. *Journal of Public Policy*, 8: 61–80.

SHIN, M., and WARD, M. 1999. Lost in space: political geography and the defense-growth trade-off. *Journal of Conflict Resolution*, 43: 793–816.

SHIPAN, C., and VOLDEN, C. 2006. Bottom-up federalism: the diffusion of antismoking policies from U.S. cities to states. *American Journal of Political Science*, 50: 825–43.

SIGNORINO, C. 1999. Strategic interaction and the statistical analysis of international conflict. *American Political Science Review*, 93: 279–98.

—— 2002. Strategy and selection in international relations. *International Interactions*, 28: 93–115.

—— 2003. Structure and uncertainty in discrete choice models. *Political Analysis*, 11: 316–44.

—— and TARAR, A. 2006. A unified theory and test of extended immediate deterrence. *American Journal of Political Science*, 50: 586–605.

—— and YILMAZ, K. 2003. Strategic misspecification in regression models. *American Journal of Political Science*, 47: 551–66.

SIMMONS, B., DOBBIN, F., and GARRETT, G. 2006. Introduction: the international diffusion of liberalism. *International Organization*, 60: 781–810.

—— and ELKINS, Z. 2004. The globalization of liberalization: policy diffusion in the international political economy. *American Political Science Review*, 98: 171–89.

STARR, H. 1991. Democratic dominoes: diffusion approaches to the spread of democracy in the international system. *Journal of Conflict Resolution*, 35: 356–81.

SWANK, D. 2006. Tax policy in an era of internationalization: explaining the spread of neoliberalism. *International Organization*, 60: 847–82.

VIJVERBERG, W. P. 1997. Monte Carlo evaluation of multivariate normal probabilities. *Journal of Econometrics*, 76: 281–307.

VOLDEN, C. 2006. States as policy laboratories: emulating success in the children's health insurance program. *American Journal of Political Science*, 50: 294–312.

WALKER, J. 1969. The diffusion of innovations among the American states. *American Political Science Review*, 63: 880–99.

—— 1973. Problems in research on diffusion of policy innovations. *American Political Science Review*, 67: 1186–91.

WARD, M., and GLEDITSCH, K. S. 2002. Location, location, location: an MCMC approach to modeling the spatial context of war and peace. *Political Analysis*, 10: 244–60.

WHITTLE, P. 1954. On stationary processes in the plane. *Biometrika*, 41: 434–49.

CHAPTER 26

MULTILEVEL MODELS

BRADFORD S. JONES

1 INTRODUCTION

POLITICAL scientists regularly work with hierarchical or multilevel data and political methodologists have spent a considerable amount of time addressing issues inherent in these kinds of data (cf. Achen and Shively 1995; Boyd and Iverson 1979; Bartels 1996; Jackson 1992; Sprague 1982; Western 1998). In this chapter, I consider broadly a class of "multilevel models." The historical lineage of these models goes back more than fifty years and emerges from disparate perspectives. In econometrics, models for random coefficients using classical methods were considered in the 1960s and brought into prominence with Swamy's (1970) pioneering work. From the Bayesian perspective, initial forays into hierarchical models can be found as early as James and Stein (1961). Treating regression coefficients explicitly as dependent variables has a history in econometrics dating back to Saxonhouse (1976; 1977) and in political science to Boyd and Iverson (1979). The emergence of the "multilevel model" (in education research) extends back to the 1980s (cf. Goldstein 1986) and was brought to prominence with Bryk and Raudenbush (1992). Nevertheless, despite the terminology and techniques, all of these approaches have clear commonalities.

2 MULTILEVEL DATA

Multilevel data structures consist of data measured at multiple levels. For example, one may have survey data collected on individuals, indexed as i. The sample elements, in turn, may reside in distinct geographical units, indexed as j. The j units could be census tracts, counties, states, countries. Data structured in this way are implicitly "hierarchical" insofar as there is a clear nesting of "lower-level" units (i) within "higher-level" units (j). The natural hierarchy of this kind of data structure is why models considered in this chapter are sometimes called hierarchical (non-)linear models. Multilevel data structures need not be hierarchical (Gelman and Hill 2007), however. Some kinds of cross-classification designs or temporal designs may not be obviously hierarchical, yet models considered herein have been usefully applied to these kinds of data structures. Strict maintenance of the concept of hierarchy is unnecessary, though in the discussion that follows, we will proceed as if data are hierarchically structured.

Commonly, researchers are interested in modeling some outcome variable, y_i as a function of lower-and higher-level factors. To fix terminology we refer to units of analysis as comprising either "level-1" units or "level-2" units. Covariates measured at level-1 will be notated by x_i and covariates measured at level-2 will be notated by z_j. The focus in this chapter will primarily be on two-level models. The number of levels in a hierarchy may, of course, extend beyond two levels, though the addition of multiple levels may exacerbate the statistical and interpretative complications of multilevel data structures.

3 POOLING

Imagine an analyst has survey data on an outcome variable of interest as well as data on covariates. Further, suppose these data are collected across countries. In this setting, the country would denote the "j unit" and the respondent would denote the "i unit." If the researcher is interested in modeling the relationship between a response variable y_i and some individual-level covariate, x_i, a garden-variety regression model could be estimated,

$$y_i = \beta_0 + \beta_1 x_i + \epsilon_i. \tag{1}$$

If estimated using all n cases, the researcher is explicitly *pooling* the data. If the data were cross-sectional, as in the case of examining a single administration of a survey, this modeling strategy is equivalent to stacking each survey from country j. The extent to which this modeling strategy is problematic squarely hinges on heterogeneity associated with the j units (Bartels 1996). Optimistically, this approach proceeds as if cross-unit heterogeneity is nonexistent; each of the j units is homogeneous. Frequently, this assumption will be wrong. In the context of (1), unit heterogeneity may induce nonspherical disturbances. Heteroskedasticity may arise because the i observations in the j units are subject to different political conditions or simply because measurement error in x_i varies across j. In either case, the model is agnostic with respect to heterogeneity and so var(ϵ) is no longer a constant, σ^2, but a variable,

σ_i^2. Autocorrelation may arise in this kind of model because the i respondents in unit j may be more alike—hence correlated—with each other than, say, the i respondents in some other unit, k. In the multilevel modeling literature, this sort of correlation structure is sometimes referred to as the intraclass correlation.

Therefore, the usual assumption of zero covariance between disturbances, conditional on the covariates, may not hold. Since the assumption of spherical disturbances is a conditional one, these problems can be mitigated by better specification of (1); for example, inclusion of covariates thought to "explain" or account for unit-wise heterogeneity. Absent this, blissful estimation of (1) in the presence of the kinds of problems commonly yields inefficient and inconsistent standard errors. This, in turn, renders the usual kinds of hypothesis tests invalid. Moreover, because the intraclass correlation will usually be positive (Hox 2002; Kreft and De Leeuw 1998), standard errors will usually be attenuated, thus increasing the chances of a Type-I error (Barcikowski 1981).

Of course recognition of the problems posed by data clustering is nothing new. With respect to the problems posed by heteroskedastic errors, a wide variety of solutions have been proposed to "fix up" the covariance matrix produced by (1). White's heteroskedastic consistent standard errors (White 1980) is a common solution. White's work extended Huber's (1967) results and, as such, the variance estimator given by White (1980) is sometimes referred to as the "Huber–White" or "Huber–White-sandwich" estimator. A variety of simulation evidence has shown White's estimator to be robust to the presence of heteroskedasticity; further, the availability of this correction is now hard-coded into virtually all statistical software packages. White's solution does not account for clustering, however. To see this, note White's heteroskedastic consistent variance estimator is given by

$$\hat{V}_W = (\mathbf{X}'\mathbf{X})^{-1}\left[\sum_{i=1}^{N}(e_i\mathbf{x}_i)'(e_i\mathbf{x}_i)\right](\mathbf{X}'\mathbf{X})^{-1}. \tag{2}$$

Under (2), each observation contributes one variance term and so no adjustment is made to account for the grouping of observations within j units.[1] Fortunately, the foundational results of Huber and White have been extended to account for group-level clustering and thus contemporaneous correlation among observations within clusters.[2] The general form of the variance estimator for clustered data is given by

$$\hat{V}_C = (\mathbf{X}'\mathbf{X})^{-1}\left[\sum_{j=1}^{n_c}\left\{\left(\sum_{i=1}^{n_j}e_i\mathbf{x}_i\right)'\left(\sum_{i=1}^{n_j}e_i\mathbf{x}_i\right)\right\}\right](\mathbf{X}'\mathbf{X})^{-1}, \tag{3}$$

---

[1] In most software packages, equation (2) has a multiplier of $N/N - k$. This multiplier is a finite-sample correction (corrected for lost degrees of freedom due to inclusion of covariates k: Davidson and MacKinnon 1993; see also Franzese 2005 for a extremely clear discussion of these issues).

[2] Interestingly, there is no "foundational" cite for these extensions. Cragg (1983) considered the case of clustered observations. Froot (1989) built on Cragg's work and presented two variance estimators for clustered data. Rogers (1993) derived a variance estimator based on the original Huber (1967) estimator. Finally, Williams (2000) gives a general proof the variance estimator for cluster-correlated data is unbiased.

where n_c corresponds to the number of clusters and n_j corresponds to the number of i-cases within unit j. It is evident from (3) that clustering is explicitly accounted for because the cross-products of the residuals and regressors are computed first within the jth cluster and then summed over the n_j clusters (see Franzese 2005 for further discussion of this).[3] In this sense, it need not be assumed that observations *within* clusters are independent, though it is implicitly assumed that clusters are independent. The point of this discussion is naive pooling of multilevel data frequently results in nonspherical disturbances. Well-understood solutions to this problem are widely available. Therefore, *if* the sole concern with pooling lies with the inducement of nonspherical errors, then the correctives just considered should go far in remedying problems. Yet these correctives do little to exploit information found in multilevel data: here, the hierarchy is a nuisance. Commonly, researchers will be interested in features of the data not easily modeled through the pooling strategy (even with variance corrections) found in (1). This leads to the consideration of multilevel models.

4 Multilevel Models

Implicit in the discussion of the previous section was concern with cross-unit heterogeneity. This sort of heterogeneity might emerge because of unmeasured factors in j. The model in (1) did not explicitly account for any possible heterogeneity associated with j, but the model can be extended to do this. Inclusion of j dummy variables into (1) yields what is sometimes called a "fixed effects" model. The model, given by

$$y_i = \beta_{j[i]} + \beta_1 x_i + \epsilon_i, \tag{4}$$

gives j intercepts, one for each unit.[4] The parameter β_1 is the same for all j and so it is clear that the heterogeneity in (4) is treated as a series of offsets. If x_i is correlated with the fixed effects, then in general $\hat{\beta}_1$ from (4) will differ from $\hat{\beta}_1$ in (1). The fixed effects model has been widely applied but it has some clear drawbacks. First, for small n and large j, the number of degrees of freedom consumed by the fixed effects will be large. Second, covariates that are constants within j cannot be estimated. Third, the relationship between x_i and y may be conditioned by factors measured at level-j; the model in (4) does not directly permit this kind of relationship to exist.

There are a variety of conventional ways to model unit-level relationships. For example, one could estimate separate models for each j unit and then compare

---

[3] The multiplier, which is omitted from (3), for the clustered case is usually taken to be $[N/(N-k)][J/(J-1)]$ (Franzese 2005).

[4] For purposes of estimation, the constant term β_0 would need to be suppressed. Doing so permits estimation of j intercepts. The notation in (4) and in subsequent equations follows the notational conventions used by Gelman and Hill (2007).

coefficients, perhaps using graphical means (cf. Bowers and Drake 2005); however, because the kinds of multilevel data political scientists regularly work with are often unbalanced, some of the j units may have very few individual-level cases compared to others. Thus, parameter estimates for some covariate of interest across the j models may exhibit wide variability, but this variability emanates from sample size differences and not from anything substantively interesting. In lieu of fixed effects or explicit nonpooling, researchers interested in modeling both level-1 and level-2 covariate effects may include factors measured at either level and then proceed by estimating

$$y_i = \beta_0 + \beta_1 x_i + \beta_2 z_j + \epsilon_i. \tag{5}$$

This model has an amalgamation of level-1 (x_i) and level-2 (z_j) factors. Built up in this way, however, the researcher can say little about any conditioning effects level-2 factors have on level-1 factors. Unfortunately, this is often a question of central interest. Nevertheless, this kind of conditioning effect can easily be captured in equation (5) through the inclusion of a multiplicative term:

$$y_i = \beta_0 + \beta_1 x_i + \beta_2 z_j + \beta_3 x_i z_j + \epsilon_i. \tag{6}$$

The "micro" effect is now conditional on the "macro" effect:

$$E(Y \mid x_i, z_j) = \beta_0 + \beta_2 z_1 + (\beta_1 x_i + \beta_3 z_1)x_1 + \epsilon_i \tag{7}$$

(the conditioning effect of the level-1 variable is also retrievable, although with hierarchical data, interest usually centers on the conditioning effect given in the function above). The model in (6) was considered by Boyd and Iverson (1979) as a way to explicitly model contextual relationships. Such relationships are hierarchical in that micro-level factors are conditioned by contextual factors (discussion groups, neighborhood factors, etc.). The conditioning effects given by the interactive model are akin to variable coefficients models; the slope for x_1 is fully conditioned by z_j. As such, there are as many unique conditional slopes as there are j level-2 units (and equally the same number of standard errors: Friedrich 1982; Franzese and Kam 2007).

The problem with model (5), however, is its failure to account for the fact that the overall variance is not only a function of variation among the level-1 units, but also (potentially) variation among the level-2 units. Failure to explicitly account for this renders the "variable coefficient" result shown above problematic: While the micro factor varies with respect to the macro factor, the model assumes this variation is deterministic, not stochastic.

4.1 Random Coefficients Models

Consideration of multiple levels of variation may leads us to models with random coefficients. I begin in the context of a simple one-way ANOVA. Consider the following model:

$$y_i = \beta_{j[i]} + \epsilon_i. \tag{8}$$

In contrast to the standard regression model, the intercept is subscripted by group j, implying β_0 is variable over the j groups. In the standard (unsubscripted) model, a "hard constraint" (Gelman and Hill 2007) is imposed on the j-unit effects in that they all equal a common β. The difference between this model and the "fixed effects" model given in equation (4) is the way $\beta_{j[i]}$ is treated. Under the fixed effects approach, the unit effects are unknown constants that are estimated from the data (Faraway 2006). In lieu of this approach, it is often useful to consider treating $\beta_{j[i]}$ as a random coefficient (Faraway 2006; Gelman 2005). From this perspective, the regression coefficient is assumed to follow some probability distribution, typically the normal distribution (Gelman and Hill 2007):

$$\beta_j \sim \mathrm{N}(\mu_\beta, \sigma_\beta^2), \quad \text{for } j = 1, \ldots, J. \tag{9}$$

Treating β_j as having some probability distribution is what Gelman and Hill (2007) call a "soft constraint" on j-unit variability: The mean effect is estimated but is assumed to have some random variability around it. This variability is attributable to unmeasured factors at level 2. With the distributional assumptions given by (9), the model in (8) is equivalent to a one-way random effects ANOVA (Bryk and Raudenbush 2002; Faraway 2006; Gelman and Hill 2007). To see this explicitly, suppose we treat β_j as a function of a systematic and random component, as in

$$\beta_j = \gamma_{00} + u_{0j}, \tag{10}$$

where γ_{00} gives the mean effect across the sample and u_{0j} gives the residual of group j (i.e. the level-2 unit) from the mean. In (10), u_{0j} accounts for random variation in y due to level-2 factors: If this term is 0 across units, we might conclude unmeasured level-2 factors effectively induce no extra variance in the model. In contrast, departures from 0 imply unmeasured level-2 factors do induce extra variance. In the regression model given by (8), this term constitutes an additional disturbance term. In the parlance of multilevel modeling, equation (8) gives the level-1 model and equation (10) gives the level-2 model. The multilevel model is obtained when we substitute (10) into (8), yielding

$$y_i = \gamma_{00} + u_{0j} + \epsilon_{ij}. \tag{11}$$

While a multilevel model can be expressed as a two-equation system, the model can be summarized as a single reduced-form equation. The interpretation of the model is straightforward: γ_{00} gives the mean; ϵ_{ij} gives the level-1 disturbance; and u_{0j} gives the level-2 disturbance. The additional error term given by u_{0j} separates this model from the standard regression model. Because there are two sources of residual variation, a ratio of these two variances can be constructed and is commonly referred to as the intraclass correlation,

$$\rho = \frac{\sigma_{u_0}^2}{\sigma_{u_0}^2 + \sigma_\epsilon^2}. \tag{12}$$

For two-level models, the ratio in (12) measures the proportion of the total variance that is attributable to level-2 units. Hence, the total variance in the model is

$$\text{var}(y_{ij}) = \sigma_{u_0}^2 + \sigma_\epsilon^2.$$

With respect to distributional assumptions on the errors, we typically will assume

$$\epsilon_{ij} \sim N(0, \sigma_\epsilon^2)$$
$$u_{0j} \sim N(0, \sigma_{u_0}^2).$$

4.2 Random Slopes and Group-level Predictors

Typically, applied workers are interested in the relationship between the response variable and covariates. It is straightforward to extend the basic random ANOVA model. Suppose there is one level-1 factor and one level-2 factor. The unconditional model would be given by

$$y_i = \beta_{j[i]} + \beta_{1j[i]}x_{i1} + \epsilon_{ij}, \tag{13}$$

where $\beta_{1j[i]}$ is the slope coefficient for variable x_{i1}, a level-1 covariate. Further, suppose the constant term, $\beta_{j[i]}$, randomly varies across units as a function of some level-2 factor z_j. Rewriting the unconditional model to account for this, we obtain

$$\beta_{j[i]} = \gamma_{00} + \gamma_{01}z_j + u_{0j}$$
$$\beta_{1j[i]} = \gamma_{10} + u_{1j}. \tag{14}$$

The reduced-form model is given by

$$y_i = (\gamma_{00} + \gamma_{01}z_j + u_{0j}) + (\gamma_{10} + u_{1j})x_i + \epsilon_i,$$

and rearranging terms gives the multilevel model:

$$y_i = \gamma_{00} + \gamma_{10}x_i + \gamma_{01}z_j + u_{1j}x_i + u_{0j} + \epsilon_i. \tag{15}$$

In this model, γ_{00} corresponds to the intercept estimate; γ_{10} corresponds to the slope coefficient for the relationship between x_i and y_i; γ_{01} corresponds to the slope coefficient for the relationship between z_j and y_i; u_{1j} corresponds to the disturbance term for the randomly varying slope coefficient γ_{10}; u_{0j} corresponds to the disturbance term for the random intercept term; and ϵ_i corresponds to the level-1 disturbance term.

It is useful to contrast this model with a garden variety OLS. Under this model, the $u_{..}$ are assumed to be zero and so the model reduces to a simple linear model with a mixture of level-1 and level-2 factors. In standard regression notation, we would posit

$$y_i = \beta_0 + \beta_1 x_i + \beta_2 z_j + \epsilon_i. \tag{16}$$

It is clear the model in equation (14) is more general than the model in equation (16). Under the multilevel model, the regression parameters are assumed to vary across level-2 units. The variance terms (i.e. the $\sigma_{u..}^2$) give information on the degree to which between-unit variance exists. With standard regression, these terms are unestimated and are assumed to be exactly 0.

4.3 Cross-level Interactions

The model in (15) assumes the group-level predictor, z_j, has a direct (unconditional) effect on the response variable; however, it is frequently posited that these kinds of factors "moderate" or conditionalize the relationship between an individual-level factor (i.e. x_i) and y_i. We considered this possibility in the model given by (6). To extend the multilevel model in this way, consider again model (13),

$$y_i = \beta_{j[i]} + \beta_{1j[i]} x_{i1} + \epsilon_{ij}.$$

Now suppose we hypothesize the bivariate relationship between some covariate and the dependent variable is conditioned by another covariate. This would entail specifying the slope from (13) to be a function of a group-level factor, z_j:

$$\beta_{j[i]} = \gamma_{00} + \gamma_{01} z_j + u_{0j}$$

$$\beta_{1j[i]} = \gamma_{10} + \gamma_{11} z_j + u_{1j}. \tag{17}$$

The second equation from (17) gives us the change in $\beta_{1j[i]}$ as a function of covariate z_j. We are explicitly treating the regression slope as conditional on the level-2 factor. The reduced-form model is given by

$$y_i = (\gamma_{00} + \gamma_{01} z_j + u_{0j}) + (\gamma_{10} + \gamma_{11} z_j + u_{1j}) x_i + \epsilon_i,$$

and rearranging terms gives

$$y_i = \gamma_{00} + \gamma_{10} x_i + \gamma_{01} z_j + \gamma_{11} z_j x_i + u_{1j} x_i + u_{0j} + \epsilon_i. \tag{18}$$

In this model, γ_{00} corresponds to the intercept estimate; γ_{10} corresponds to the slope coefficient for the relationship between x_i and y_i when $z_j = 0$; γ_{01} corresponds to the slope coefficient for the relationship between z_j and y_i when $x_i = 0$; γ_{11} corresponds to the interaction between x_i and z_j; u_{1j} corresponds to the disturbance term for the randomly varying slope coefficient γ_{10}; u_{0j} corresponds to the disturbance term for the random intercept term; and ϵ_i corresponds to the level-1 disturbance term. With respect to the interaction between x_i and z_j, because the two covariates are measured at different levels, this kind of term is sometimes called a "cross-level" interaction. It is important to note that when the covariates included in the cross-level interaction are continuous, it is almost always advisable to *mean-center* the covariate. This yields an approximate zero point and makes the parameter more naturally interpretable (Raudenbush and Bryk 2002; Faraway 2006; Gelman and Hill 2007; Hox 2002). To complete the model, we typically assume the following (Goldstein 1995, 17):

$$\epsilon_{ij} \sim N(0, \sigma_\epsilon^2)$$

$$u_{0j} \sim N(0, \sigma_{u_0}^2)$$

$$u_{1j} \sim N(0, \sigma_{u_1}^2),$$

with $\mathrm{cov}(u_{0j}, u_{1j}) = \sigma_{u01}$.

5 ESTIMATION ISSUES

In terms of model matrices, the general two-level model (with cross-level interaction) is given (following Hox's (2002) presentation) by

$$
\begin{bmatrix} y_1 \\ y_2 \\ \vdots \\ y_n \end{bmatrix} = \begin{bmatrix} 1 & x_1 & z_j & z_j x_1 \\ 1 & x_2 & z_j & z_j x_2 \\ \vdots & \vdots & \vdots & \vdots \\ 1 & x_n & z_j & z_j x_n \end{bmatrix} \begin{bmatrix} \gamma_{00} \\ \gamma_{10} \\ \gamma_{00} \\ \gamma_{11} \end{bmatrix} + \begin{bmatrix} 1 & x_1 \\ 1 & x_2 \\ \cdots & \cdots \\ 1 & x_n \end{bmatrix} \begin{bmatrix} u_{oj} \\ u_{1j} \end{bmatrix} + \begin{bmatrix} \epsilon_1 \\ \epsilon_2 \\ \vdots \\ \epsilon_n \end{bmatrix},
$$

and in more succinct form, this yields

$$\mathbf{y} = \mathbf{x}\gamma + \mathbf{W}\mathbf{u} + \epsilon. \tag{19}$$

In the general case, $\mathbf{y}$ is an $n \times 1$ vector for the response variable; $\mathbf{x}$ is an $n \times k$ design matrix for the model parameters γ; γ is an $k \times 1$ vector of model parameters; $\mathbf{W}$ is an $n \times r$ design matrix for the random effects $u_{..}$; $\mathbf{u}$ is an $r \times 1$ vector of random level-2 disturbances; and ϵ is an $n \times 1$ vector of level-1 disturbances. The departure of model (19) from (6) is clear: The presence of the random effects complicates estimation since a mixture of parameters, random and fixed, must be estimated. Estimation of the model, then, entails consideration of $\mathrm{var}(\mathbf{y}) = \mathrm{var}(\mathbf{z}\gamma) + \mathrm{var}(\epsilon) = \sigma^2(\mathbf{z}\mathbf{D}\mathbf{z}') + \sigma^2(\mathbf{I})$, where D is a matrix of variance components (Faraway 2006, 155). The unconditional distribution of y in the normal multilevel model is (equation adapted from Faraway 2006, 155) given by

$$y \sim N(\mathbf{x}\boldsymbol{\beta}, \sigma^2(\mathbf{I} + \mathbf{z}\mathbf{D}\mathbf{z}')),$$

or

$$y \sim N(\mathbf{x}\boldsymbol{\beta}, \sigma^2 V)$$

where $V = \sigma^2(\mathbf{I} + \mathbf{z}\mathbf{D}\mathbf{z}')$. Since V will almost always be unknown, it must be estimated. Once V is estimated, finding estimates of the model parameters, β_k, is straightforward using generalized least squares (or some similar kind of function: Goldstein 1995; Longford 1993; Faraway 2006).

Thus estimation of the variance components is obviously an important issue. In the case of continuous y, most statistical software proceeds in the classical manner using either full maximum likelihood (FMLE) or, more commonly, restricted maximum likelihood (RMLE) methods for the normal model. The major distinction between RMLE and FMLE is that the former accounts for consumed degrees of freedom while the latter does not. FMLE, as is well known (Patterson and Thompson 1971; Longford 1993; Faraway 2006), gives biased estimates of the variances, though this bias decreases with increased sizes of level-2 units (Raudenbush and Bryk 2002; Longford 1993). A variety of algorithms have been proposed for FMLE/RMLE. Among them one the EM algorithm (Dempster, Rubin, and Tsutakawa 1981; see also Raudenbush and Bryk 2002; Longford 1993; Mason, Wong, and Entwistle 1983), iterative generalized least squares for FMLE (Goldstein 1986; 1995), restricted iterative generalized least squares (for RMLE), the Fisher scoring algorithm (proposed by Longford 1987; 1993, for random coefficients models), and Newton–Raphson. As far as choices among these alternatives go, there is no agreed-upon "optimal" way to proceed. In the case of FMLE, Goldstein (1995) and Goldstein and Rasbash (1992) show that Fisher scoring and IGLS are equivalent (for the normal model; see also Kreft and De Leeuw 1998).

In contrast to classical estimation methods, Bayesian methods for multilevel modeling have been widely proposed. Indeed, the literature on Bayesian hierarchical models goes back more than forty years (cf. Hartigan 1969; Hill 1965; Lindley and Smith 1972; Tiao and Zellner 1964). In political science, consideration of Bayesian methods generally (cf. Jackman and Western 1994; Jackman 2000; Quinn, Martin, and Whitford 1999), and for hierarchical data in particular, has been widespread (cf. Gelman and Hill 2007; Gill 2002; Martin 2001). In the Bayesian approach, the unknown parameters, β, γ, $\sigma_{..}$, are assigned a prior distribution. The prior may be informative or uninformative, for example a uniform prior (much more detailed discussion of priors for hierarchical models can be found in Gelman 2006). Following Bayes's Theorem, the likelihood is multiplied by the prior distribution to derive estimates of the posterior distribution of the model parameters. In the multilevel models discussed above, level-1 parameters are conditioned by level-2 parameters. To see the Bayesian approach conceptually, Gill (2002, 352) succinctly summarizes it as

$$\Pr(\beta, \gamma \mid \boldsymbol{D}) \propto L(\beta \mid \boldsymbol{D}) p(\beta \mid \gamma) p(\gamma). \tag{20}$$

Gill (2002) notes that the expression in (20) can be expanded to account for more levels in the hierarchy, for example treating γ as conditioned by level-3 factors. Adding hierarchies adds substantial complication to the model, however (in either the Bayesian or classical case). Goel and DeGroot (1981; cited in Gill 2002, 352) show that the quality of the posterior parameters "decrease at each progressive level of the hierarchical model" (Gill 2002, 352); this assertion is formally proved by Goel (1983; cited in Gill 2002, 352). Computationally, deriving Bayesian estimates of the model parameters entails specifying conditional distributions for the model parameters, specifying starting values for the parameters, and iterating over values for the model parameters. The iterations produces a chain of simulation draws from the posterior. If several chains based on different starting values are jointly run (i.e. multiple simulations), the Bayesian model is said to "converge" when the chains have mixed (Gelman and Hill 2007). Simulating chains and mixing, or evaluating convergence, is computationally demanding. Gibbs samplers, or more generally Markov Chain Monte Carlo (MCMC) techniques, are usually necessary to derive final parameter estimates (Gelman and Hill 2007; Gill 2002; Jackman 2000). Fortunately, the computing environment BUGS (Spiegelhalter et al. 2002) has made MCMC estimation computationally feasible; see also Martin and Quinn's MCMCpack (2007), a package for the R environment.

A third approach to estimation of the multilevel model differs from the above in that an explicit "two-step" strategy is taken to account for data hierarchy. While this two-step approach was considered by Saxonhouse (1976; 1977), political scientists have recently revisited this strategy (cf. Duch and Stevenson 2005; Huber, Kernell, and Leoni 2005; Jusko and Shively 2005; Kedar 2005; Lewis and Linzer 2005). While the details of estimation vary across the authors just cited, the basic thrust of the two-step strategy is the same. In the first step, j regressions are estimated as a function of level-1 covariates:

$$y_{ij} = \beta_{0j} + \beta_{1j}x_i + \epsilon_{ij}. \tag{21}$$

From model (21), the regression parameters, $\hat{\beta}$, are extracted from each model, stacked, and treated as a dependent variable in a model where the covariates are level-2 factors:

$$\hat{\beta}_j = \gamma_0 + \gamma_1 z_j + v_j + u_j. \tag{22}$$

The dual sources of error in (22) come from the fact that the country-specific parameters will be estimated with uncertainty from the first stage as well as in the second stage (this presentation follows Jusko and Shively 2005; Lewis and Linzer 2005 proceed in a different manner). Jusko and Shively (2005) show this strategy is consistent and efficient (for the normal model) and Achen (2005) notes the two-step approach should be asymptotically equivalent to the alternative approaches discussed above (see also Saxonhouse 1977). Beck (2005) argues against the two-step approach noting that "one-step" approaches (like the FMLE/RMLE or Bayesian) will never be worse than the two-step strategy. I discuss these issues in the last section.

6 Extensions

The discussion of the multilevel model to this point has centered on models where the response variable, y_i, is continuous; however, consideration of these kinds of models is not limited to the continuous case. Indeed, most software designed for hierarchical data includes options for estimating binary or multicategorical response models. In the R environment, Bates and Sarkar's (2007) lme4 package utilizes the general linear modeling (GLM) framework. As such, a wide variety of link functions can be considered for multilevel data. Further, the multilevel framework has been extended to survival models as well as count models (cf. Barber et al. 2000; Barber, Murphy, and Verbitsky 2004; Grilli 2005). There is not sufficient space to discuss these developments in detail, though I will discuss the multilevel model in the context of a binary response variable, since such response variables are commonly used in political analysis.

Consider a simple two-level model with binary response variable y and one level-1 covariate, x_i. The structural model is given by

$$y_i = \beta_{j[i]} + \beta_{1j[i]} x_{i1}.$$

If the slope coefficient randomly varies across j and the intercept is treated as a function of a level-2 factor, the level-2 model is

$$\beta_{j[i]} = \gamma_{00} + \gamma_{01} z_j + u_{0j}$$

$$\beta_{1j[i]} = \gamma_{10} + u_{1j}.$$

The full multilevel model is therefore

$$y_i = \gamma_{00} + \gamma_{10} x_i + \gamma_{01} z_j + u_{1j} x_i + u_{0j}. \tag{23}$$

If logistic distribution function is specified for y, then a familiar logit model is obtained (transformed in log-odds):

$$\log\left[\frac{\Pr(y_i)}{1 - \Pr(y_i)}\right] = \gamma_{00} + \gamma_{10} x_i + \gamma_{01} z_j + u_{1j} x_i + u_{0j}, \tag{24}$$

with the complication of the random disturbance terms given by $u_{..}$. The model in (24) is a linear model in the logits and so the parameters are on the logit scale (i.e. are log-odds ratios). The model in (24) can be extended in ways similar to the normal model discussed previously and made to account for greater levels of hierarchy. As in the case of the normal, it is typically assumed that

$$u_{0j} \sim N(0, \sigma_{u_0}^2)$$

$$u_{1j} \sim N(0, \sigma_{u_1}^2).$$

A variety of estimation techniques have been proposed for the multilevel binary response model (Longford 1993 and Rodriguez and Goldman 2001 provide an excellent overview; see also Browne and Draper 2006; Guo and Zhao 2000). The basic issue involves estimating the unconditional distribution of y by integrating out the random effects $u_{..}$. For example, with a simple random-intercepts model (and no group-level predictors), the conditional density is given (following Guo and Zhao 2000) by

$$f(y_i \mid x_i) = \int_{-\infty}^{\infty} f(y_i \mid x_i, u_j) g(u_j) d(u_j). \tag{25}$$

The unconditional density, $f(y \mid x_i)$, however, is what we are interested in. With many random effects, (25) becomes a high-dimensional integral. Three general techniques for estimation of the parameters of interest have been proposed. Numerical methods (like Gaussian quadrature or adaptive quadrature) have been proposed to approximate the integral in (25); quasi-likelihood methods have been proposed to approximate the integrand in (25); and Bayesian methods. Quadrature methods approximate the integral over a number of integration points within the domain of the function. As the number of approximation points increases, the computational burden substantially increases. The GLLAMM package (Rabe-Hesketh and Skrondal 2005; Rabe-Hesketh, Skrondal, and Pickles 2004), which can be implemented in Stata, utilizes the quadrature approach (note also that the Stata module xtlogit uses Gauss–Hermite quadrature: StataCorp 2005). Hedeker and Gibbons (1994) provide a nice overview of quadrature as applied to an ordinal logit model.

Quasi-likelihood methods are more commonly used in standard multilevel software programs. These methods focus on the integrand in (25). With respect to this estimation technique, there are two general varieties employed, penalized quasi-likelihood (PQL) and marginal quasi-likelihood (MQL). The difference in the two methods involves how Taylor series expansions are carried out (Taylor expansions are used to linearize the binary response model). There is not sufficient space to discuss the technical details of these two approximation methods in detail; Longford (1993) and Browne and Draper (2006), among others, provide considerable detail. However, some remarks are in order about implementation. Simulation evidence shows considerable differences can occur in the binary response model between PQL and MQL methods (even greater distinctions can be made if one accounts for the order of the Taylor expansion: see Browne and Draper 2006; Guo and Zhao 2000; Rodriguez and Goldman 2001). Although there is not widespread agreement here, the general advice to offer is that PQL outperforms MQL. This has been found to be particularly true when the within-cluster correlations are very large (Rodriguez and Goldman 2001). In many software packages, for example R's lme4 and SAS's proc mixed, the user can specify which technique to use.

With respect to Bayesian methods, the parameters (both fixed and random) are assigned priors and then multiplied by the likelihood to obtain a posterior distribution. The posterior distribution is then sampled from and updated using a Gibbs sampler. In principal, the approach taken here is similar to that followed for the normal model; however, as Browne and Draper (2006) note, "Gibbs sampling in [random effects logit] models is not straightforward." In their study, they utilize a Gibbs sampler for the variance terms and univariate-update random-walk Metropolis sampling for the fixed effects. The details of either the Gibbs sampler or the Metropolis algorithm are far beyond the scope of this chapter. I recommend Gelman et al. (2003) or Gill (2002) for extensive treatment of these issues. Gelman and Hill (2007) also go into great detail with respect to these approaches and implementation of them in BUGS.

7 LEVEL-1 COEFFICIENTS

To this point, the concern has been with estimating the fixed and random effects from the multilevel model. These parameters will frequently be of primary interest; however, it is often useful to examine the level-1 coefficients directly. In the "two-step" approach discussed above, the "level-1" coefficients are explicitly derived from the first-stage estimation, since these regressions are separate models for each j unit. The separate-models approach has the virtue of giving unbiased estimates of the level-1 coefficients, although the reliability (or precision) of these estimates will decline as the number of level-1 observations within each j unit decreases.

However, in some instances, the number of level-1 cases may in fact be very small. For example, clustering survey respondents within an areal unit (zip code region, county, congressional district, etc.) often produces a hierarchical data structure with many j but few $i \in j$. In lieu of the separate regression approach, it is useful to consider *shrink estimators* (James and Stein 1961; Efron and Morris 1975). The basic concept of a shrink estimator in the context of multilevel data is to treat the level-1 coefficients as a weighted average of, essentially, group means and grand means. In the simple case of the random one-way ANOVA, this implies that if the within-group mean is highly reliable, level-1 estimates of $\beta_{j[i]}$ will be weighted more heavily in terms of the group mean than the grand mean. With random slopes and intercepts, these coefficients will be weighted more heavily in terms of the cluster-level data when the within-unit information gives reliable estimates of the level-1 parameters of interest. When cluster-level data yield low-reliability estimates, level-1 estimates "borrow" information from the full sample. Because of this, Morris (1983) referred to these kinds of estimators as "compromise estimator(s)." The shrink estimator used to derive level-1 coefficients in multilevel models is typically an empirical Bayes (EB) estimator (Carlin and Louis 1996; Efron and Morris 1975; Morris 1983).

The basic concept behind shrink estimators is nicely summarized in Gelman and Hill (2007, 476), who show that

$$\beta_{j[i]} = \omega_j \mu_\beta + (1 - \omega_j)\bar{y}_j, \tag{26}$$

where

$$\omega_j = 1 - \frac{\sigma_\beta^2}{\sigma_\beta^2 + \sigma_y^2/n_j}.$$

Gelman and Hill (2007) refer to this expression as a "pooling factor." It is clear why. When there is "no pooling," the estimate of $\beta_{j[i]}$ will equal the group mean; when there is complete pooling, the group-level coefficient is indistinguishable from the grand mean. Similarly, the variance of the parameter will be affected by the pooling factor in that (following Gelman and Hill 2007, 477, eq. 21.11)

$$\text{var}(\beta_j) = (1 - \omega_j)\sigma_y^2/n_j.$$

This again shows how uncertainty around the level-1 parameter relates to the separation among the j-level units: "borrowing strength" is directly connected to the degree to which the data exhibit pooling.

8 Recommendations and Conclusion

The enterprise of multilevel modeling is far too vast to give adequate coverage here. However, a few concluding remarks and recommendations are in order. Unlike many of the traditional econometric models applied by political scientists where estimation properties are well understood (and may be robust under adverse conditions), the same cannot be said for many of the estimation choices available here. This is *particularly true* with respect to hierarchical nonlinear models. Colossally different estimates may be obtained dependent merely on the choice of estimation technique. Browne and Draper (2006), Guo and Zhao (2000), and Rodriguez and Goldman (2001) demonstrate this with respect to multilevel binary response models. Because of the increasing ease with which software packages allow us to estimate complicated models, failure to take note of "software defaults" can have deleterious consequences. "Deleterious" in this case means one may get fundamentally different parameter estimates contingent on: (a) what the default choice was versus some alternative (this is especially true with PQL and MQL); and (b) which software program/computing environment was actually used. It seems clear that "good practice" with respect to these models will require users to have a "better-than-usual" understanding of what is being estimated and *how* it is being estimated.

Nevertheless, if appropriately applied (or even approximately appropriately applied), these models yield considerable information about model parameters (fixed effects), level-wise variance, and micro-level parameters. Unfortunately, much applied work using multilevel models is often presented as if this extra information was never estimated. Minimally, if random coefficients are posited, the estimated level-2 variances should be presented along with model parameters. Frequently, this is not done. In principle, these terms convey substantive information about variability around the model parameters. "Insignificance" of a level-2 variance term, on its own, may be of some interest. Further discussion and/or interpretation of level-1 coefficients would seem to be of interest. After all, variability across j is one reason multilevel models are considered. Gelman and Hill (2007) provide outstanding coverage of ways to use level-1 information.

Indeed, the explicit consideration of micro-level effects makes the "two-step" strategy discussed above attractive; however, it should be clear that *any* of the estimation techniques permit estimation of the micro-level parameters. With respect to the "two-step" approach versus its alternatives (FMLE/RMLE, MCMC/Bayes, quadrature), then, I agree with Beck's (2005) conclusion that there is not much leverage gained from taking the two-step approach (outside of, perhaps, initial model diagnostics). Achen (2005) makes a compelling case in favor of the two-step approach, noting that political science hierarchical data frequently do not mimic the students-in-classrooms data used by education researchers. That is, at least with comparative politics data, sample sizes are often very large and disparate (see also Bartels 1996) and so concern with "borrowing strength" (or shrink estimators) will not have the same import in this context as in, say, the education research context. Nevertheless, the two-step approach automatically assumes each level-1 coefficient is explicitly nonpooled (in equation (26), $\omega = 0$), which seems to be a strong assumption, one testable inside what Gelman (2005) calls a "full multi-level model." Given the fact that FMLE/RMLE or MCMC/Bayes techniques are getting easier to implement (easy being a relative term) in Stata, R, or BUGS, it is not clear how useful the two-stage strategy will ultimately become.

To conclude, this chapter has attempted to convey the scope of multilevel models but in a very compact way. Many issues were touched upon but not covered in great detail: For example, extension of the GLM framework to hierarchical nonlinear models is an extremely important growth area but was only briefly referenced in the discussion of the binary response model. Also, I did not provide much detailed discussion about modeling decisions involving centering (Hofmann and Gavin 1998) and conditional versus unconditional shrink estimators (Raudenbush and Bryk 2002), although these are clearly important issues. Nevertheless, carefully applied, multilevel models offer great promise for exploiting information in hierarchical data structures. There are a range of alternatives for such data and it bears repeating that sometimes, simpler-to-apply correctives like those discussed in Section 3 will suffice. Often they will not, however, and so extensions of the basic forms given in Sections 4 and 6 will need to be considered.

References

ACHEN, C. H. 2005. Two-step hierarchical estimation: beyond regression analysis. *Political Analysis*, 13: 447–56.

—— and SHIVELY, W. P. 1995. *Cross-Level Inference*. Chicago: University of Chicago Press.

BARCIKOWSKI, R. S. 1981. Statistical power with group mean as the unit of analysis. *Journal of Educational Statistics*, 6: 267–85.

BARTELS, L. 1996. Pooling disparate observations. *American Journal of Political Science*, 40: 905–42.

BARBER, J. S., MURPHY, S. A., and VERBITSKY, N. 2004. Adjusting for time-varying confounding in survival analysis. *Sociological Methodology*, 34: 163–92.

—— —— AXINN, W., and MAPLES, J. 2000. Discrete-time multilevel hazard analysis. *Sociological Methodology*, 30: 201–35.

BATES, D., and SARKAR, D. 2007. lme4: linear mixed-effects models using S4 classes. R package version 0.9975-13.

BECK, N. 2005. Multilevel analysis of comparative data: a comment. *Political Analysis*, 13: 457–8.

BOWERS, J., and DRAKE, K. W. 2005. EDA for HLM: visualization when probabilistic inference fails. *Political Analysis*, 13: 301–26.

BOYD, L. H., JR., and IVERSEN, G. R. 1979. *Contextual Analysis: Concepts and Statistical Techniques*. Belmont, Calif.: Wadsworth.

BROWNE, W. J., and DRAPER, D. 2006. A comparison of Bayesian and likelihood-based methods for fitting multi-level models. *Bayesian Analysis*, 3: 473–514.

BRYK, A. S., and RAUDENBUSH, S. W. 1992. *Hierarchical Linear Models: Applications and Data Analysis Methods*. Newbury Park, Calif.: Sage.

CARLIN, B. P., and LOUIS, T. A. 1996. *Bayes and Empirical Bayes Methods for Data Analysis*. London: Chapman and Hall.

CRAGG, J. 1983. More efficient estimation in the presences of heteroskedasticity of unknown form. *Econometrica*, 51: 751–63.

DAVIDSON, R., and MACKINNON, J. G. 1993. *Estimation and Inference in Econometrics*. New York: Oxford University Press.

DE LEEUW, J., and KREFT, I. 1986. Random coefficient models for multilevel analysis. *Journal of Educational Statistics*, 11: 57–85.

DEMPSTER, A. P., RUBIN, D. B., and TSUTAKAWA, R. K. 1981. Estimation in covariance components models. *Journal of the American Statistical Association*, 76: 341–53.

DUCH, R. M., and STEVENSON, R. 2005. Context and the economic vote: a multilevel analysis. *Political Analysis*, 13: 387–409.

EFRON, B., and MORRIS, C. 1975. Data analysis using Stein's estimator and its generalizations. *Journal of the American Statistical Association*, 70: 311–19.

FARAWAY, J. J. 2006. *Extending the Linear Model with R: Generalized Linear, Mixed Effects and Nonparametric Regression Models*. Boca Raton, Fla.: Chapman and Hall.

FRANZESE, R. J., JR. 2005. Empirical strategies for various manifestations of multilevel data. *Political Analysis*, 13: 430–46.

—— and KAM, C. 2007. *Modeling and Interpreting Interactive Hypotheses in Regression Analysis*. Ann Arbor: University of Michigan Press.

FRIEDRICH, R. J. 1982. In defense of multiplicative terms in multiple regression equations. *American Journal of Political Science*, 26: 797–833.

FROOT, K. A. 1989. Consistent covariance matrix estimation with cross-sectional dependence and heteroskedasticity in financial data. *Journal of Financial and Quantitative Analysis*, 24: 333–55.

GELMAN, A. 2005. Analysis of variance: why it is more important than ever (with discussion). *Annals of Statistics*, 33: 1–53.

—— 2006. Prior distributions for variance parameters in hierarchical models. *Bayesian Analysis*, 1: 514–34.

—— and HILL, J. 2007. *Data Analysis Using Regression and Multi-level/Hierarchical Models*. Cambridge: Cambridge University Press.

—— CARLIN, J. B., STERN, H. S., and RUBIN, D. B. 2003. *Bayesian Data Analysis*, 2nd edn. London: CRC Press.

GIBBONS, R. D., and HEDEKER, D. 1997. Random-effects probit and logistic regression models for three-level data. *Biometrics*, 53: 1527–37.

GILL, J. 2002. *Bayesian Methods for the Social and Behavioral Science*. London: CRC Press.

GOEL, P. K. 1983. Information measures and Bayesian hierarchical models. *Journal of the American Statistical Association*, 78: 408–10.

—— and DEGROOT, M. H. 1981. Information about hyperparameters in hierarchical models. *Journal of the American Statistical Association*, 76: 140–7.

GOLDSTEIN, H. 1986. Multilevel mixed linear model analysis using iterative generalized least squares. *Biometrika*, 74: 43–56.

GOLDSTEIN, H. 1991. Nonlinear multilevel models, with an application to discrete response data. *Biometrika*, 78: 45–51.

—— 1995. *Multilevel Statistical Models*. London: Edward Arnold.

—— and RASBASH, J. 1992. Efficient computational procedures for the estimation of parameters in multilevel models based on iterative generalised least squares. *Computational Statistics and Data Analysis*, 13: 63–71.

GRILLI, L. 2005. The random-effects proportional hazards model with grouped survival data: a comparison between the grouped continuous and continuation ratio versions. *Journal of the Royal Statistical Society, Series A*, 168: 83–94.

GUO, G., and ZHAO, H. 2000. Multilevel modeling for binary data. *Annual Review of Sociology*, 26: 441–62.

HARTIGAN, J. A. 1969. Linear Bayesian methods. *Journal of the Royal Statistical Society, Series B*, 31: 446–54.

HEDEKER, D., and GIBBONS, R. D. 1994. A random-effects ordinal regression model for multilevel analysis. *Biometrics*, 50: 933–44.

HILL, B. M. 1965. Inference about variance components in the one-way model. *Journal of the American Statistical Association*, 60: 806–25.

HOFMANN, D. A., and GAVIN, M. B. 1998. Centering decisions in hierarchical linear models: implications for research in organizations. *Journal of Management*, 24: 623–41.

HOX, J. J. 2002. *Multi-level Analysis: Techniques and Applications*. Mahwah, NJ: Lawrence Erlbaum Associates.

HUBER, P. J. 1967. The behaviour of maximum likelihood estimates under non-standard conditions. *Proceedings of the Fifth Berkeley Symposium on Mathematical Statistics and Probability*, 1: 221–33.

HUBER, J. D., KERNELL, G., and LEONI, E. L. 2005. Institutional context, cognitive resources and party attachments. *Political Analysis*, 13: 365–86.

JACKMAN, S. 2000. Estimation and inference via Bayesian simulation: an introduction to Markov Chain Monte Carlo. *American Journal of Political Science*, 44: 375–404.

—— and WESTERN, B. 1994. Bayesian inference for comparative research. *American Political Science Review*, 88: 412–23.

JACKSON, J. E. 1992. Estimation of models with variable coefficients. *Political Analysis*, 3: 27–49.

JAMES, W., and STEIN, C. 1961. Estimation with quadratic loss. *Proceedings of the Fourth Berkeley Symposium on Mathematical Statistics and Probability*, 1: 311–19.

JUSKO, K. L., and SHIVELY, W. P. 2005. Applying a two-step strategy to the analysis of cross-national public opinion data. *Political Analysis*, 13: 327–44.

KEDAR, O. 2005. How diffusion of power in parliaments affects voter choice. *Political Analysis*, 13: 410–29.

KREFT, I. G. G., and DE LEEUW, J. 1998. *Introducing Multilevel Modeling*. London: Sage.

LEWIS, J. B., and LINZER, D. A. 2005. Estimating regression models in which the dependent variable is based on estimates. *Political Analysis*, 13: 345–64.

LINDLEY, D. V., and SMITH, A. F. M. 1972. Bayes estimates for the linear model (with discussion). *Journal of the Royal Statistical Society, Series B*, 34: 1–41.

LONGFORD, N. T. 1987. A fast scoring algorithm for maximum likelihood estimation in unbalanced mixed models with nested random effects. *Biometrika*, 74: 817–27.

—— 1993. *Random Coefficient Models*. Oxford: Clarendon Press.

MARTIN, A. D. 2001. Congressional decision making and the separation of powers. *American Political Science Review*, 95: 361–78.

—— and QUINN, K. M. 2007. MCMCpack: Markov chain Monte Carlo (MCMC) Package. R package version 0.8–2. <http://mcmcpack.wustl.edu>

MASON, W. M., WONG, G. Y., and ENTWISTLE, B. 1983. Contextual analysis through the multilevel linear model. Pp. 72–103 in *Sociological Methodology 1983–1984*, ed. S. Leinhardt. San Francisco: Jossey-Bass.

MORRIS, C. 1983. Parametric empirical Bayes inference: theory and applications. *Journal of the American Statistical Association*, 78: 47–65.

PATTERSON, H. D., and THOMPSON, R. 1971. Recovery of inter-block information when block sizes are unequal. *Biometrika*, 58: 545–54.

QUINN, K. M., MARTIN, A. D., and WHITFORD, A. B. 1999. Voter choice in multi-party democracies: a test of competing theories and models. *American Journal of Political Science*, 43: 1231–47.

RABE-HESKETH, S., and SKRONDAL, A. 2005. *Multilevel and Longitudinal Modeling Using Stata*. College Station, Tex.: Stata Press.

—— and PICKLES, A. 2004. *GLLAMM Manual*. UC Berkeley Division of Biostatistics Working Paper Series.

RAUDENBUSH, S. W., and BRYK, A. S. 2002. *Hierarchical Linear Models: Applications and Data Analysis Methods*. Thousand Oaks, Calif.: Sage.

RODRIGUEZ, G., and GOLDMAN, N. 2001. Improved estimation procedures for multilevel models with binary response: a case-study. *Journal of the Royal Statistical Society, Series A*, 164: 339–55.

ROGERS, W. 1993. Regression standard errors in clustered samples. *Stata Technical Bulletin*, 13: 19–23.

SAXONHOUSE, G. 1976. Estimated parameters as dependent variables. *American Economic Review*, 66: 178–83.

—— 1977. Regression from samples having different characteristics. *Review of Economics and Statistics*, 59: 234–7.

SPIEGELHALTER, D., THOMAS, A., BEST, N., GILKS, W., and LUNN, S. 2002. BUGS: Bayesian inference using Gibbs sampling. MRC Biostatistics Unit, Cambridge.

SPRAGUE, J. 1982. Is there a micro theory consistent with contextual analysis? In *Strategies of Political Inquiry*, ed. E. Ostrom. Beverly Hills, Calif.: Sage.

STATACORP 2005. *Stata Statistical Software: Release 9.2*. College Station, Tex.: StataCorp LP.

SWAMY, P. A. V. B. 1970. Efficient inference in a random coefficient regression model. *Econometrica*, 38: 311–23.

TIAO, G. C., and ZELLNER, A. 1964. Bayes's Theorem and the use of prior knowledge in regression analysis. *Biometrika*, 51: 219–30.

WESTERN, B. 1998. Causal heterogeneity in comparative research: a Bayesian hierarchical modeling approach. *American Journal of Political Science*, 42: 1233–59.

WHITE, H. 1980. A heteroskedasticity-consistent covariance matrix estimator and a direct test for heteroskedasticity. *Econometrica*, 48: 817–38.

WILLIAMS, R. L. 2000. A note on robust variance estimation for cluster-correlated data. *Biometrics*, 56: 645–6.

PART VIII

QUALITATIVE TOOLS FOR DESCRIPTIVE AND CAUSAL INFERENCE

CHAPTER 27

COUNTERFACTUALS AND CASE STUDIES

JACK S. LEVY

IN Henry James's "The Jolly Corner," Spencer Bryden pursues the ghost of the man he might have been had he not left New York City three decades earlier for a more leisurely life abroad. In Dickens's "A Christmas Carol," Ebenezer Scrooge transforms his life after encountering the Ghost of Christmas Yet to Come and learning how the future would play out if he were to continue his old ways. Robert Frost is less explicit about what he would have encountered on "the road not taken," but he knows that the road less traveled "made all the difference."

Scholars frequently speculate about what might have been in history. Pascal famously wrote that "Cleopatra's nose: had it been shorter, the whole face of the world would have changed." It is often said that the First World War would not have occurred without the assassination of Archduke Ferdinand (Lebow 2007), that the Second World War would not have occurred without Hitler (Mueller 1991), and that the end of the cold war would have been significantly delayed without Gorbachev (English 2007). In a more general theoretical claim, Skocpol (1979) argues that without either peasant revolts or state breakdown, social revolutions will not occur.

Opposition politicians frequently invoke counterfactuals in arguing that if the current administration had acted differently, the country would have been better off. Hillary Clinton later defended her 2002 vote to authorize the president to use force in Iraq by saying that "if we knew then what we know now, there wouldn't have been a vote ... and I certainly wouldn't have voted that way."[1]

[1] NBC, *Today* show, December 18, 2006.

Some historians are skeptical about the analytic utility of counterfactual analysis, and regard it as entertaining "after dinner history" (Ferguson 1999*a*, 15) or a "parlour game" (Carr 1964, 97), but not analytically sound scholarship. Croce (cited in Ferguson 1999*a*, 6) states that it is necessary "to exclude from history the 'conditional' which has no rightful place there...." What is forbidden is ... the "anti-historical and illogical 'if.'" Fischer (1971) includes an index item for "counterfactual questions" in his book *Historians' Fallacies*, but it says "see fictional questions." Fischer describes Fogel's (1964) pathbreaking counterfactual analysis of the impact of railroads on American economic development as a step "down the methodological rathole" and a return to "ancient metaphysical conundrums" (p. 18). Oakeshott (1966, 128–9) argues that if the historian were to consider "what *might* have happened" and treat "great events" or "turning points" as causally "decisive," "the result is not merely bad or doubtful history, but the complete rejection of history... a monstrous incursion of science into the world of history."

Other historians, and most social scientists, recognize that counterfactuals are unavoidable. They understand that "the study of history is a study of causes" (Carr 1964, 87), and they recognize that any causal statement involves assumptions about what did not happen but could have happened. Bueno de Mesquita (1996, 229) argues that in applied game theory "we cannot understand what happened in reality without understanding what did not happen but might have happened under other circumstances." The historian Ferguson (1999*a*, 87) argues that "To understand... [history] as it actually was, we therefore need to understand *how it actually wasn't*—but how, to contemporaries, it might have been."

The question is how to validate counterfactual claims about what would have happened in a hypothetical or alternative world in which the hypothesized cause took on a different value, whether in a particular case or in a more general theoretical relationship. Whereas causal statements are in principle amenable to a direct empirical test, the same is not true for counterfactual statements, since the conditional upon which the counterfactual rests does not exist and cannot be fully realized in order to examine the effects that flow from it (Goodman 1983). In the absence of direct empirical confirmation, by what criteria can we say that some counterfactuals are more legitimate or more valid than others, and for what theoretical purposes? Since we cannot avoid counterfactuals, the question, in response to Oakeshott, is how to introduce science into the world of history in a way that enhances our understanding of history.

I focus on the methodologically normative use of counterfactual arguments to advance causal understanding of the social and political world. This differs from psychologists' more descriptive focus on such cognitive science questions as how people actually use counterfactuals, how they judge the validity of counterfactual arguments, and how their cognitive and motivational biases affect those judgments and influence what kinds of counterfactuals they find most persuasive (Roese and Olson 1995; Tetlock and Belkin 1996; Tetlock and Lebow 2001).

Counterfactuals are relevant in any kind of causal analysis, but I focus primarily on the role of counterfactuals in case study analysis. This subject is particularly important because qualitative-comparative researchers are more likely than quantitative scholars to posit necessary conditions, which automatically generate explicit counterfactuals (Goertz and Starr 2003).

After explaining why counterfactuals are important for history and social science, I identify the criteria by which we can evaluate the utility of counterfactuals for supporting idiographic and nomothetic causal claims. Throughout I assume that counterfactuals are best conceived as a method, to be used in conjunction with other methods, to generate and validate explanations about social and political behavior. The primary goal of studying what did not happen is to better help us to understand what did happen.

1 The Importance of Counterfactuals

I follow Tetlock and Belkin (1996, 4) and define counterfactual as a "subjective conditional in which the antecedent is known or supposed for purposes of argument to be false." It is a "contrary-to-fact" conditional that identifies a "possible" or "alternative" world in which the antecedent did not actually occur.

All causal statements imply some kind of counterfactual. A historical argument that a particular set of conditions, processes, and events caused, influenced, or contributed to a subsequent set of conditions, processes, and events implies that if the antecedent conditions had been different, the outcome would have been different. Similarly, a theoretical statement that x is a cause of y implies that if the value of x were different, the outcome y would be different.[2] The interpretative statement that British and French appeasement of Hitler contributed to the Second World War implies that if Britain and France had stood firm against Hitler the Second World War would not have occurred, or perhaps that it would have been considerably shorter and less destructive. The theoretical proposition that appeasement only encourages further aggression implies the counterfactual that a more hard-line strategy would reduce the likelihood of further aggression.

While all causal statements imply a counterfactual, some counterfactuals are more explicit than others. Historical interpretations and theoretical propositions that posit necessary conditions, which are fairly common in political science and in social science more generally (Goertz and Starr 2003), are particularly explicit about their counterfactual implications. The logical expression of necessary conditions—"if not x then not y"—directly specifies the consequent of a counterfactual world. Necessary condition counterfactuals are central in "window of opportunity" models (Kingdon 1984), "powder keg" models (Goertz and Levy 2007),

---

[2] This is particularly clear if one says that c is a cause of e if the conditional probability that e occurs, given that c occurs, is greater than the unconditional probability that e occurs. For a discussion of statistical approaches to counterfactual analysis see Morgan and Winship (2007).

causal chains involving necessary conditions, and explanations based on path dependency and critical junctures (Mahoney 2000), all of which are common in political science.

Necessary conditions are also important because they are at the core of one of the two leading conceptualizations of causation: x is a cause of y if y would not occur in the absence of x (Lewis 1973).[3] The central role of necessary conditions in causal explanation, particularly in case studies, and the fact that the primary way of testing hypotheses involving necessary conditions is to analyze the validity of the counterfactual associated with it, add significantly to the importance of developing a valid methodology of counterfactual analysis.[4]

Counterfactuals play an essential role in common historiographical debates about whether a particular outcome was inevitable or contingent. The most effective way of supporting an argument that an outcome was contingent is to demonstrate that a slight change could easily have led to a different outcome. An effective way to demonstrate that an outcome was inevitable at a certain point is to demonstrate that there was no change in existing conditions that was both conceivable and capable of leading to a different outcome.

Some theoretical approaches are more explicit than others about their counterfactual implications. A good example is game theory. A game tree specifies exactly what happens if actors make different choices, how other actors react, and the set of possible outcomes. Actors' choices are causally dependent on their expectations of what would happen if they made other choices. "Off the equilibrium path" behavior is a counterfactual prediction.

Since causal statements—whether about particular historical events or about theoretical relationships between variables—imply counterfactuals, the validity of the counterfactual bears on the validity of the original causal proposition. Compelling evidence that Hitler would have initiated a war regardless of whether Britain or France had pursued a strategy of appeasement would falsify the claim that appeasement causally contributed to the Second World War.[5] Evidence that social revolutions sometimes occur in the absence of a peasant revolt and a state crisis would disconfirm Skocpol's (1979) theory of social revolution.

Thus the empirical validation of counterfactual statements is an important step in hypothesis testing. Evidence from several case studies is generally more persuasive than evidence from a single case study in testing a theoretical proposition

---

[3] The alternative conception of causation is the "regularity" model, which includes constant conjunction, temporal precedence, and nonspuriousness. This view is often traced to Hume, but in fact Hume emphasized both conceptions of causation (Goertz and Levy 2007).

[4] While all necessary conditions imply a specific counterfactual, not all counterfactuals imply the presence of necessary conditions. The statement "if not x, then y will still occur" posits a counterfactual, but without a necessary condition. Also, unlike statements of necessary conditions, statements of sufficient conditions do not imply a counterfactual, since "if x then y" says nothing about the consequences of "not x." The widely accepted empirical generalization that a democratic dyad is sufficient for peace implies no counterfactual about what would happen if at least one of two states is not a democracy.

[5] Khong (1996) explores the complexities of validating this counterfactual. Ripsman and Levy (2007) argue that neither British nor French leaders expected that appeasement would avoid war.

(and quantitative researchers argue that statistical evidence is far superior to multiple case studies), but single case studies can also serve this purpose if the hypothesis posits necessary or sufficient conditions, if the hypothesis generates precise predictions, or if the proposition permits a most likely or least likely research design (George and Bennett 2005; Levy 2008).

This point relates to a larger principle about theory construction and research design. The widely accepted injunction to derive as many observable implications as possible from an historical interpretation or theoretical proposition, and to test them against the evidence (King, Keohane, and Verba 1994), applies to a theory's counterfactual implications as well as to its more direct implications.[6] *Ceteris paribus*, the more explicit the counterfactual implications of a theory, the better the theory. A theory that specifies the consequences of both x and not x tells us more about the empirical world than a theory that specifies only the consequences of x.

The preceding discussion emphasizes the utility of counterfactuals in testing both interpretations of individual cases and more general theoretical propositions. The first is more idiographic in orientation, and the second more nomothetic. Interpretations of individual cases can be either inductive or guided by theory.[7] Although theory-guided case studies are presumably more explicit about their counterfactual predictions, at least at the beginning of a research study,[8] inductively driven interpretive case studies can also end up suggesting what would have happened if certain things had been different. Ferguson's (1999b) argument about what would have happened had Britain "stood aside" in the First World War (probably no Bolshevik Revolution, no Second World War, no Holocaust) is based on an inductive case study.

In idiographic case studies, the role of counterfactual analysis is often to explore the question of whether history could have turned out differently, and how alternative worlds might have developed. Such "what if" scenarios include both relative short-term forecasts, such as the consequences of a failed assassination attempt in 1914, and long-term macrohistorical forecasts, such as the plausibility of alternative scenarios through which the rise of the West to a position of world dominance might have been blocked (Tetlock, Lebow, and Parker 2006).

Idiographic counterfactuals can also play a normative role—of passing moral judgment on individual leaders by asking whether or not they could have acted differently under the circumstances (Tetlock and Belkin 1996, 8). Presumably we could not blame a leader for a costly war if a counterfactual analysis were to provide persuasive evidence that the same war would have occurred if another leader had been in power. Neville Chamberlain is widely criticized for his policy of appeasing Hitler, but that

---

[6] Qualitative researchers qualify this argument by de-emphasizing the "as many" phrase and arguing that some observable implications are more important than others for theory testing.

[7] Scholars often mischaracterize the idiographic/nomothetic distinction. Idiographic refers to descriptions or explanations of the particular, whereas nomothetic refers to the construction or testing of general theoretical propositions (Levy 2001).

[8] In the analytic narrative research program (Bates et al. 1998), for example, game-theoretic models are used to guide individual case studies.

judgment rests on the counterfactual argument that another British leader would have acted differently and that the outcome would have been better for Britain, which some scholars have questioned.

Exploring a theory's counterfactual implications can also be useful for theory development. This is a deductive analysis that does not involve empirical case studies.[9] As Tetlock and Belkin (1996) note, "The goal is not historical understanding... [but] to pursue the logical implications of a theoretical framework." For this purpose, the counterfactual conditional itself need not necessarily be plausible, in the sense that we could imagine a path through which it might arise. Such nonplausible counterfactuals are often called "miracle counterfactuals" (Fearon 1996).

Any complete theory specifies the consequences if key causal variables were to take on other values. Economic models specify the consequences for the economy if the Federal Reserve Board were to raise interest rates by a full percent, even if such actions are quite implausible under the circumstances. Computer simulations are used to explore the consequences of possible worlds (including socially complex worlds) that are not really accessible through empirical methods (Cederman 1996). Similar models can be applied historically to trace the consequences of a particular set of initial conditions, however implausible they might be. To assess the contribution of the railroads to American economic growth, Fogel (1964) constructed a model of the American economy and explored how it might have developed in the absence of railroads.

Counterfactual thought experiments can also be used deductively for other purposes, including the pedagogical purposes of encouraging someone to think through the implications of his or her arguments or beliefs, confront uncomfortable arguments, and generally open his or her mind to new ideas. This may help reveal double standards in moral judgment, contradictions in causal beliefs, and the influence of cognitive or motivational biases. This mode of counterfactual analysis combines the descriptive and the normative, in that descriptive/causal knowledge about how people use counterfactuals in making judgments and decisions is used for the normative purpose of inducing them to think in less biased ways about causality and counterfactuals (Tetlock and Belkin 1996, 12–16; Weber 1996; Lebow 2000).

2 CRITERIA FOR EVALUATION

We now turn to the criteria by which we might evaluate the validity of counterfactual arguments in explaining cases or testing theoretical propositions. What kinds of counterfactuals are more legitimate than others for these purposes, recognizing

---

[9] In mathematics, an "indirect proof" or "proof by contradiction" assumes the theorem is false, traces the logical consequences, reveals a contradiction, and concludes that the theorem is true.

that different standards might be appropriate for different theoretical and descriptive purposes?[10]

Counterfactual propositions are similar to other theoretical propositions in that they have premises or initial conditions, hypothesized consequences, and a "covering law" or causal mechanisms explaining how the former leads to the latter. A theoretical proposition must be logically consistent and falsifiable in principle. We generally prefer theories that apply to broader empirical domains, make more (and more varied) predictions about the empirical world, generate substantial support from the empirical evidence, and are consistent with other well-accepted theories (Hempel 1966, ch. 4). Criteria for evaluating counterfactual arguments should be grounded in these widely accepted standards of theory evaluation. These are best organized around the categories of the clarity of the antecedents and consequents, the plausibility of the antecedent, and the conditional probability of the consequent given the antecedent.[11]

2.1 Clarity

Counterfactual arguments must include well-specified antecedents and consequents. The consequent should be more specific than "the outcome would have been different," which is only moderately helpful. Unless we specify *how* it would have been different, the statement is nearly nonfalsifiable and hence not particularly useful. For a counterfactual to be scientifically useful, the consequent must be clearly specified by the analyst, not left to the imagination of the reader.

Necessary condition counterfactuals are quite explicit, since they posit an antecedent of $\sim x$ and a consequent of $\sim y$. To say that war would not have occurred in the absence of an assassination is a powerful statement. It would be more discriminating, and in many ways more useful, to specify whether the absence of war meant peace for several years or peace punctuated by ongoing crises and a high risk of war in the future. With respect to the antecedent, it might have made a difference, in terms of the likely response, if the failed assassination attempt had been discovered or not. Non-necessary condition counterfactuals can also be clear. The statement "if Hitler had been ousted in a coup, the Second World War would still have occurred" has well-specified antecedents and consequents.

While clarity is good, there is a trade-off between the specificity of the consequent and the probability of its occurrence. The more detailed a consequent, the more likely it is to be false. The probability of multiple outcomes is the product of their individual probabilities, and the probability of a single outcome is the product of the individual probabilities of each of the steps leading to it (Lebow 2000, 583). This suggests that

---

[10] The main difference between empirically oriented and deductively oriented counterfactuals is that the latter are not constrained by need for the antecedent to be plausible.

[11] This differs somewhat from the Tetlock and Belkin (1996, 16–31) and Lebow (2000, 577–85) conceptualizations.

counterfactuals that are either too detailed or the result of a long causal chain are likely to be false. Thus at the two extremes counterfactuals are either nonfalsifiable or false. Neither is particularly useful.[12] The best counterfactuals have specific but not too specific antecedents.

Relatedly, arguments suggesting that a particular counterfactual antecedent will lead to a particular consequent with a high degree of certainty are quite suspect. It would be problematic to invoke a counterfactual to demonstrate that history did not have to happen the way it did, only to predict a counterfactual consequent that deterministically flowed from the antecedent, since that would be supporting a statement of contingency with an argument based on determinism.

2.2 Plausibility of the Antecedent

It is widely agreed that for counterfactual arguments to be useful in exploring whether history might have turned out differently, the antecedent must be plausible or realistic as well as well specified. One must be able to imagine how that antecedent might arise. It is not useful to say that 1960s America would have been different if Abraham Lincoln had been president.

For the purposes of assessing causality, counterfactual analysis has the same general task as experimental, statistical, and comparative methods: to organize evidence to show that a change in the value of an outcome variable can be traced to the effects of a change in a causal variable, and not to changes in other variables. Just as experimental research manipulates one variable at a time in a controlled setting, and comparative research tries to select matched cases in which covariation with the outcome variable is limited to a single causal variable, counterfactual analysis ideally posits an alternative world that is identical to the real world in all theoretically relevant respects but one, in order to explore the consequences of that difference.

That is easier said than done, and the same problems that plague comparative research constrain counterfactual analysis as well: In a system of interconnected behavior, a change in one variable reverberates through the system and induces changes in many other variables, so that "we can never do merely one thing" (Hardin, cited in Jervis 1997, 10). In counterfactual thought experiments, as in a matching cases strategy, it is often quite difficult to hold everything else equal. Hence Lebow (2000) questions the utility of "surgical" counterfactuals.

An attempt to assess the impact of US nuclear superiority on the outcome of the Cuban Missile Crisis by imagining the crisis under conditions of Soviet strategic superiority would have to change too much history to be useful. Soviet superiority would be conceivable only if the US economy and technological capacity had been much weaker, if American society did not support a competitive military establishment, and so on. The presence of these other conditions would almost certainly

---

[12] Admittedly, an empirical confirmation of any detailed counterfactual prediction would be particularly compelling precisely because the *ex ante* probability was so low (Popper 1965).

have changed the world in other ways as well (the status of Berlin, for example), further complicating any effort to say that it was Soviet superiority, rather than these other changes, that caused the outcome. Moreover, a Soviet Union with strategic superiority would have had no incentive to put offensive missiles in Cuba in the first place.

As this example suggests, a counterfactual conditional is not complete in itself. It relies on other changes to sustain it. Goodman (1983) called these *connecting principles*, which themselves involve counterfactual propositions about the consequences of those other changes. Any counterfactual analysis needs to specify the secondary counterfactuals, or "enabling counterfactuals" (Lebow 2000), that must be introduced to sustain the primary counterfactual.

A good counterfactual requires that these connecting principles and enabling counterfactuals be specified with reasonable precision (like the primary counterfactual) and that they be consistent with each other and with the antecedent of the primary counterfactual.[13] Goodman (1983, 15) refers to this requirement of logical consistency as *cotenability*.

The counterfactual of Soviet strategic superiority in 1962 fails to satisfy the cotenability criterion. So does the argument that if Nixon had been president during the Cuban Missile Crisis, he would have ordered an air strike rather than a naval blockade. Lebow and Stein (1996) argue persuasively that if Nixon had been president he, unlike Kennedy, would have probably authorized the use of US forces in the Bay of Pigs operation, Castro would have been overthrown, and the Soviets would not have put offensive missiles in Cuba.

In his attempt to assess the likely development of the American economy in the absence of railroads, Fogel (1964) identified other developments that were likely to occur in the absence of railroads, including the introduction of the internal combustion engine and the automobile (along with its demands for iron and other materials) fifty years before its actual appearance. Elster (1978, 204–8) basically argues that this assumption of the early emergence of the automobile is not cotenable with the assumption of the delay of the railroad, since the technology upon which the automobile was based surely would have led to the railroad.[14]

For these reasons, most analysts accept Max Weber's (1949) argument that for the purposes of causal analysis the best counterfactual worlds to examine are those that require as few changes as possible in the real world. This is the "minimal rewrite of history" rule (Tetlock and Belkin 1996), which is defined in terms of the magnitude of the changes as well as their number.[15]

---

[13] Tetlock and Belkin (1996, 21) include consistency with the consequent, which I discuss in the next section on the conditional probability of the consequent given the antecedent.

[14] See also Tetlock and Belkin (1996, 22) and Lebow (2000, 582).

[15] Similarly, King and Zeng (2005) use statistical modeling to demonstrate that whereas the validity of counterfactual propositions positing relatively modest changes in the real world can be evaluated based on the data, "extreme counterfactuals" are quite sensitive to assumptions built into the model that have little to do with the data.

One example of a minimal rewrite counterfactual is the proposition that if George W. Bush had not won the 2000 election, the United States would not have gone to war in Iraq. This counterfactual involves a minimal rewrite of history because one does not have to change much—just a modest number of Florida voters reading their ballots correctly. So the counterfactual's antecedent is quite plausible.[16] The hypothesized consequent (President Al Gore not invading Iraq) is quite plausible but not certain, and the argument would have to include enabling counterfactuals such as how Gore would have reacted to 9/11.

Lebow's (2007) argument that if the assassination attempt against the Archduke had failed the First World War probably would not have occurred is another highly plausible, minimal rewrite counterfactual. The antecedent is quite easy to imagine, as Lebow explains in great detail. Indeed the *ex ante* probability of the alternative world was undoubtedly higher than that of the real world, which is another possible criterion for the evaluation of counterfactuals.[17] Lebow's analysis is particularly useful as an illustration of the value of specifying the *conditions and processes* through which one could get from the real world to the counterfactual world. Another good example of this is Mueller's (1991) detailed assessment of the identity and policy preferences of other possible German leaders who might have held the position of chancellor, to support his argument that in the absence of Hitler the Second World War would not have occurred.

Scholars will disagree, of course, on how minimal a rewrite of history has to be for the antecedent to be considered plausible. There is no single answer to this question, as there may be a trade-off between maximizing the plausibility of a counterfactual by minimizing the number of additional conditions necessary to sustain it, and selecting historically or theoretically meaningful counterfactuals. As the historian Schroeder (2007, 149–50) argues, "a major counterfactual . . . will change too much, and a minor one too little, to help us explain what really did happen and why, and why alternative scenarios failed to emerge."[18] Still, counterfactuals relating to the 1914 assassination and the 2000 American election demonstrate that minimal rewrite counterfactuals can be consequential.

Ferguson (1999a, 86) offers his own answer of how we distinguish plausible and implausible counterfactuals: "We should consider as plausible or probable only those alternatives which we can show on the basis of contemporary evidence that contemporaries actually considered." Ferguson further narrows the range of acceptable counterfactuals by restricting them to "hypothetical scenarios which contemporaries not only considered, but also committed to paper."

The second criterion is unnecessarily restrictive. While paper records of actors' alternative options might provide particularly compelling evidence of choices not made, we should not exclude evidence based on oral interviews with first-hand

---

[16] By contrast, counterfactual claims about the consequences of George W. Bush not winning the 2004 election posit a more problematic antecedent.

[17] The validity of the hypothesized consequent is another, analytically distinct question which I return to later.

[18] See also Weber (1996) and Lebow (2000).

observers. Nor should we be precluded from exploring alternative histories in repressive political systems in which actors are afraid to commit their thoughts to paper or among nonelite groups for which there are no written records.

Even Ferguson's (1999a) first criterion might be too restrictive. It would exclude alternative choices that actors failed to consider, or failed to consider seriously, because of psychological biases, political constraints, or failure of imagination—alternative possibilities that other decision-makers, had they been in office, might have considered (assuming a change in personnel was a plausible antecedent). It is not clear, for example, whether Ferguson's criterion would allow us to consider the consequences of the US responding to the Soviet missiles in Cuba by doing nothing, since they gave that option little or no serious consideration. In addition, some options are formally considered only for political reasons but given no serious thought, as Janis (1982) suggests for many "devil's advocate" arguments.

Schroeder (2007, 151–2) agrees that the counterfactuals actually considered by the actors themselves are important, but recognizes that they are too restrictive. He argues that the historian needs to pose counterfactual questions of his own: "What other decisions and actions could the historical actors have made under the existing circumstances? To what extent did they recognize and consider these? What circumstances made these choices or alternative courses genuinely possible or merely specious and actually unreal? What might the alternative results of these choices have been?" These are precisely the right questions to ask, but even they might be too restrictive. They fail to give enough emphasis to counterfactual possibilities introduced by external events such as assassinations, battles or elections won or lost, fatal illness, personal tragedies, and other highly contingent events (Lebow 2000, 560).[19]

Game theory provides a still more restrictive set of criteria for the selection of acceptable counterfactuals from the enormous number of possible counterfactuals. First of all, game-theoretic models in extensive form specify exactly what will happen if actors were to make different decisions at various choice nodes. All sequences of choices "off the equilibrium path" are possible counterfactuals. But actors did not go down those paths for a reason. In a large class of games, however, there are multiple equilibria, multiple ways all actors could have behaved that were fully consistent with their interests given the constraints of the game. Each of these paths constitutes a fully acceptable counterfactual (Bueno de Mesquita 1996; Weingast 1996).[20]

The consideration of the alternatives that actors did consider or might have considered within a choice-theoretic framework raises an interesting asymmetry in counterfactual analysis. Both events and nonevents generate counterfactuals, but it is often easier to examine event-generated counterfactuals than those generated

---

[19] The outcomes of a small percentage of battles hinge on accidents, luck, insubordination, unexpected weather, and other contingencies, and the long-term political consequences of such reversals of outcome can be profound (Cowley 1999).

[20] The existence of alternative subgame perfect equilibria provides an excellent criterion for good counterfactuals where the specification of the game provides a reasonable fit to the situations faced by actors and choices they consider. We need to remember, however, that the simplifications necessary to create tractable games, including limits on the number of choices available to actors, may be too restrictive in some situations, including those involving enormous social complexity.

by nonevents. We can explore the consequences of a counterfactual failure of the assassination plot in 1914, since there is ample evidence from pre-assassination records of how Austrian and German leaders defined their decision problems and options, and thus how they might have acted. In the absence of an assassination, however, it would be far more difficult to explore the counterfactual possibility of an assassination of the Archduke, since presumably no one at the time gave serious thought to that possibility and what they would do if it happened, and we would have to introduce more secondary counterfactuals that would be somewhat speculative. Similarly, it is easier (though not easy) to explore counterfactuals created by the hypothetical failure of the assassination attempt against Kennedy than those that would have been created by the hypothetical success of the assassination attempt against Reagan. The *ex ante* probability, and hence counterfactual plausibility, of each of these antecedents is quite different.

If the 9/11 plot had failed and gone undetected, and if the US had not invaded Iraq (which is quite plausible but not certain), it would be quite difficult to undertake a counterfactual analysis, set in the absence of 9/11, of the possibility that a major terror attack against the United States originating from Afghanistan might trigger an American war against Iraq in 2003. In a world in which 9/11 (or something like it) had not occurred in 2001 (or soon thereafter), would any of our criteria for evaluating counterfactuals permit the characterization of a 9/11 attack as a plausible antecedent and an American invasion of Iraq as a likely consequent?[21]

2.3 The Conditional Plausibility of the Consequent

Thus far we have emphasized that the characteristics of a useful counterfactual include a well-specified antecedent and consequent and an antecedent or conditional that is plausible, involves a minimal rewrite of history, and is sustainable through conditions that are cotenable with each other and with the antecedent. The next question is whether the antecedent, along with the conditions that are necessary to support it, is likely to lead to the hypothesized consequent. The basic requirement, like those for any theoretical proposition, is that the causal linkages be clearly specified, logically complete, and consistent with the empirical evidence. It is admittedly difficult to separate theoretical and empirical criteria, since social science research is ideally characterized by an ongoing dialogue between theory and evidence (Levy 2007), but listing them separately is useful for our purposes here.

In many ways, the most important requirement for a good counterfactual, besides a plausible antecedent, is a good theory. As Fogel (1964, cited in Tetlock and Belkin 1996, 26) writes, "Counterfactual propositions...are merely inferences from hypothetico-deductive models." The greater the extent to which the hypothesized

---

[21] For an intriguing counterfactual analysis set in a counterfactual world, but one that involves a much more extended timeframe than the one posited here, see Lebow (2006). Imagining a world in which Mozart lived to sixty-five and in which neither of the world wars of the twentieth century occurred, Lebow considers the possibility that an early death of Mozart triggered a chain of historical happenings that led to these events, and considers the critiques and defenses of such a counterfactual.

causal mechanisms leading from a specific antecedent to a particular consequent are consistent with well-established and empirical confirmed theories, the greater the plausibility of the counterfactual. The better the theory—defined in terms of its logical coherence, precision, deductive support from well-established theories, and empirical support—and the more it makes explicit predictions about what will happen under a variety of counterfactual conditions, the better the counterfactual.

For the purposes of evaluating a particular counterfactual proposition, we are more interested in the predictive power of a relevant theory under the specific conditions defined by the antecedent than in its predictive power under a wide range of conditions, although the latter increases our confidence in the former. For this reason, a well-established empirical law, even in the absence of consensus regarding how to explain it theoretically, would also provide useful support for a counterfactual proposition. Admittedly, we have relatively few empirical laws in political science, but some propositions have far more empirical support than others.

Thus *consistency with the empirical evidence* is another criterion for a good counterfactual proposition. Tetlock and Belkin (1996, 27–30) include "consistency with well-established statistical generalizations" as one of their six criteria of a good counterfactual. I would construe evidence more broadly. While statistical (and experimental) evidence is highly desirable—assuming a sufficient number of comparable cases, variables that are operationalizable and measurable over those cases, accessible data, etc.—such evidence is not always available. Comparative studies and, less frequently, single case studies (if based on a compelling most or least likely design) can sometimes provide an adequate evidentiary basis to support a counterfactual proposition, and such evidence, when combined with statistical evidence, can often provide substantially better support than statistical evidence alone (George and Bennett 2005).

Although "direct" support for a specific counterfactual proposition is important, our confidence in its validity is enhanced if the counterfactual generates other theoretical predictions that are also supported. A counterfactual proposition has implications not only for the final outcome, but also for the intervening paths between antecedent and consequent, and those intervening predictions should be specified in advance and tested if at all possible. This is the criterion of *projectibility* (Tetlock and Belkin 1996, 30–1).

Let me return to the point I made above about the likelihood of a counterfactual being a function of the length of the causal chain leading to it. This is just the commonsense notion that short-term predictions are more plausible than long-term predictions, which applies to counterfactual propositions as well as to those with factual antecedents. Even where one finds short-term regularities, the compounding of small uncertainties generates enormous irregularity and unpredictability over the long term. Even deterministic processes can generate highly unpredictable outcomes if they are sensitive to initial conditions, as chaos theory demonstrates.

Fearon (1996) demonstrates this in a compelling way in his discussion of an extremely simple process involving cellular automata that follow rules of behavior that are well understood, precisely specified, but stochastic, with well-defined probabilities of moving from one state to another. He demonstrates how such processes generate local regularities but global unpredictability. Fearon's (1996) analysis leads him to suggest a *proximity* criterion, so that we can assess plausibility "only where the counterfactuals involve causal mechanisms and regularities that are well understood and that are considered at a spatial and temporal range small enough that multiple mechanisms no not interact, yielding chaos" (p. 66).

A related reason for insisting on a proximity criterion is that even if the antecedent is plausible and there are good theoretical and empirical reasons to believe that the presence of the antecedent would lead to predicted consequents with fairly high probability, it is always possible that subsequent developments might return history to its original course, before it was diverted by the hypothesized antecedent. Lebow (2000, 584) labels these "second-order counterfactuals," but I prefer the term *redirecting* counterfactuals, since primary counterfactuals generate numerous secondary counterfactuals and only some of them reroute history back to its original course.

Consider the argument that the Vietcong attack on the US military base at Pleiku in 1965 was a significant cause of US escalation in the Vietnam War. In the absence of that Vietcong attack, however, it is quite plausible to argue that another incident would have occurred, whether randomly or deliberately instigated for strategic advantage, and led to an American escalation. As Bundy argued, "Pleikus are like streetcars." Wait long enough and one will come along.[22] This remark is often used in support of structural arguments and against arguments about the importance of contingency in historical processes.

Another example of a redirecting counterfactual arises with respect to Lebow's (2007) own counterfactual argument that in the absence of the assassination of the Archduke the First World War probably would not have occurred. Lebow argues that in the absence of the assassination, existing trends in the balance of military power that favored Russia would have forced Moltke (or his successor as Chief of the German General Staff) to abandon the Schlieffen Plan and adopt instead a more defensive strategy, which would have eliminated the incentives for preventive or preemptive military action in any crisis that might arise.

This counterfactual is clear and the antecedent constitutes a minimal rewrite. The causal linkages to the consequent are not plausible, however, because they would have probably generated self-refuting strategic behavior. Lebow's assessment of military trends is right on the mark. German military and political leaders would almost certainly have accepted his vision of a 1917 world, and precisely for that reason they never would have allowed that world to come about. The same fears for the future that generated Germany's preventive motivation for war in 1914 (which Lebow implicitly acknowledges) would have led German leaders to initiate or provoke the preventive war they thought they needed before Russia grew too strong (Fischer 1967). This critique, of course, generates its own counterfactual, which would need to be evaluated against Lebow's counterfactual. Fortunately, the expansive literature on the First World War provides enough evidence to resolve this debate, even if not with complete certainty.

---

[22] National Archives and Records Administration, Lyndon Baines Johnson Library, oral interviews of Frederick W. Flott, <http://webstorage1.mcpa.virginia.edu/library/mc/poh/ transcripts/flott_frederick_1984_0927.pdf>.

3 CONCLUSION

All causal statements generate counterfactuals about what would happen if certain variables were to take on different values, and all nonexperimental methodologies must deal with this in one way or the other. I focus here on the role of counterfactuals in case studies. I argue that if counterfactuals are made explicit and used according to scientifically acceptable rules of inference, a study of history as it really wasn't can help us understand history as it really was (to borrow from Ferguson 1999a).

Counterfactuals serve different theoretical and descriptive purposes. Different theoretical goals and normative values call for different trade-offs among various research objectives, and consequently there is no single set of methodological criteria applicable to all counterfactuals. Leaving aside the use of counterfactual thought experiments to stimulate the imagination, which is useful but which follows a different set of rules, I suggest criteria for the evaluation of counterfactuals for the purposes of explaining historical cases or using cases to assess more general theoretical propositions.

The analyst should clearly specify a counterfactual's antecedent, consequent, and the causal linkages between them. Counterfactuals should change as few aspects of the real world as possible in order to isolate their causal effects (the "minimal-rewrite-of-history" rule). The analyst should specify both the "supporting conditions" or "connecting principles" that are needed to sustain the primary counterfactual and the secondary counterfactuals that lead from the antecedent (and its supporting conditions) to the consequent. The consequent should be more specific than "the outcome would have been different," but not so specific that it becomes implausible, given the fact that the probability of a highly specific outcome is far less than the probability of a range of outcomes.

Counterfactual analysis, perhaps even more so than other kinds of analysis, is a theory-driven process. We cannot directly trace the consequences of an unobservable antecedent, so we must rely on theoretical knowledge. The stronger the theory, and the more the analyst can resort to theory or empirical laws to justify his or her hypothesized causal mechanisms linking the antecedent to the consequent, the better the counterfactual. Counterfactuals that generate additional observable implications and that can themselves be "tested" against the evidence provide additional confidence in the validity of the counterfactual. This is the "projectibility" criterion.

Logical consistency is another important criterion. The supporting conditions for a primary factual must be consistent with each other and with the antecedent. Their linkages to the consequent must also be theoretically sensible. It does little good to posit an antecedent that could only lead to the consequent if supported by connecting principles and secondary counterfactuals that were themselves inconsistent with the antecedent. Researchers should be particularly alert to strategic behavior that might return history to its original path ("redirecting counterfactuals")—where actors recognize that the hypothesized consequences of the antecedent are both accurate and undesirable, and act to head off those outcomes.

It would also be inconsistent to try to support an argument that a particular outcome was contingent by demonstrating that a small change in the situation would have invariably led to a different outcome—one cannot support an argument for contingency by invoking a deterministic process. To the extent possible, based on existing theory and empirical evidence, the author should give a sense of the likelihood that the consequent would have followed from the antecedent.

Counterfactual analysis, like any causal analysis, must recognize that uncertainty about initial conditions and the pervasiveness of stochastic behavior limits even the best of our theories to relatively short-term predictions. After that, too many things interact in too many unpredictable ways. The longer the causal chain, the lower the probability of occurrence of the outcome at the end of the chain, particularly given the relative absence of sufficient conditions in social theory. This suggests temporal and spatial "proximity" as an additional criterion for evaluating counterfactuals.

While the application of these criteria might make "after dinner history" somewhat less entertaining, it disciplines the use of counterfactuals and provides an additional methodological tool for evaluating causality in a nonexperimental world in which many confounding variables interact in unpredictable ways.

REFERENCES

BATES, R., GREIF, A., LEVI, M., ROSENTHAL, J.-L., and WEINGAST, B. 1998. *Analytic Narratives*. Princeton, NJ: Princeton University Press.

BUENO DE MESQUITA, B. 1996. Counterfactuals and international afffairs: some insights from game theory. Pp. 211–29 in *Counterfactual Thought Experiments in World Politics*, ed. P. E. Tetlock and A. Belkin. Princeton, NJ: Princeton University Press.

CARR, E. H. 1964. *What is History?* Harmondsworth: Penguin.

CEDERMAN, L.-E. 1996. Rerunning history: counterfactual simulation in world politics. Pp. 247–67 in *Counterfactual Thought Experiments in World Politics*, ed. P. E. Tetlock and A. Belkin. Princeton, NJ: Princeton University Press.

COWLEY, R. 1999. *What If?* New York: G. P. Putnam's Sons.

ELSTER, J. 1978. *Logic and Society*. New York: John Wiley and Sons.

ENGLISH, R. 2007. Perestroika without politics: how realism misunderstands the Cold War's end. Pp. 237–60 in *Explaining War and Peace: Case Studies and Necessary Condition Counterfactuals*, ed. G. Goertz and J. S. Levy. New York: Routledge.

FEARON, J. D. 1996. Causes and counterfactuals in social science: exploring an analogy between cellular automata and historical processes. Pp. 39–67 in *Counterfactual Thought Experiments in World Politics*, ed. P. E. Tetlock and A. Belkin. Princeton, NJ: Princeton University Press.

FERGUSON, N. 1999a. Virtual history: toward a "chaotic" theory of the past. Pp. 1–90 in *Virtual History: Alternatives and Counterfactuals*, ed. N. Ferguson. New York: Basic Books.

——— 1999b. *The Pity of War: Explaining World War I*. New York: Basic Books.

FISCHER, D. 1971. *Historians' Fallacies: Toward a Logic of Historical Thought*. London: Routledge and Kegan Paul.

FISCHER, F. 1967. *Germany's Aims in the First World War*. New York: Norton.

FOGEL, R. 1964. *Railroads and American Economic Growth: Essays in Econometric History.* Baltomore: Johns Hopkins University Press.

GEORGE, A. L., and BENNETT, A. 2005. *Case Studies and Theory Development in the Social Sciences.* Cambridge, Mass.: MIT Press.

GOERTZ, G., and LEVY, J. S. 2007. Causal explanation, necessary conditions, and case studies. Pp. 9–45 in *Explaining War and Peace: Case Studies and Necessary Condition Counterfactuals,* ed. G. Goertz and J. S. Levy. New York: Routledge.

—— and STARR, H. (eds.) 2003. *Necessary Conditions: Theory, Methodology, and Applications.* Lanham, Md.: Rowman and Littlefield.

GOODMAN, N. 1983. *Fact, Fiction, and Forecast,* 4th edn. Cambridge, Mass.: Harvard University Press.

HEMPEL, C. G. 1966. *Philosophy of Natural Science.* Englewood Cliffs, NJ: Prentice Hall.

JANIS, I. L. 1982. *Groupthink,* 2nd rev. edn. Boston: Houghton Mifflin.

JERVIS, R. 1997. *System Effects.* Princeton, NJ: Princeton University Press.

KHONG, Y. F. 1996. Confronting Hitler and its consequences. Pp. 95–118 in *Counterfactual Thought Experiments in World Politics,* ed. P. E. Tetlock and A. Belkin. Princeton, NJ: Princeton University Press.

KING, G., KEOHANE, R., and VERBA, S. 1994. *Designing Social Inquiry.* Princeton, NJ: Princeton University Press.

—— and ZENG, L. 2006. The dangers of extreme counterfactuals. *Political Analysis,* 14: 131–59.

KINGDON, J. 1984. *Agendas, Alternatives, and Public Policies.* Boston: Little, Brown.

LEBOW, R. N. 2000. What's so different about a counterfactual? *World Politics,* 52: 550–85.

—— 2006. If Mozart had died at your age: psychologic versus statistical inference. *Political Psychology,* 27: 157–72.

—— 2007. Contingency, catalysts, and nonlinear change: the origins of World War I. Pp. 85–111 in *Explaining War and Peace: Case Studies and Necessary Condition Counterfactuals,* ed. G. Goertz and J. S. Levy. New York: Routledge.

—— and STEIN, J. G. 1996. Back to the past: counterfactuals and the Cuban missile crisis. Pp. 119–48 in *Counterfactual Thought Experiments in World Politics,* ed. P. E. Tetlock and A. Belkin. Princeton, NJ: Princeton University Press.

LEVY, J. S. 2001. Explaining events and testing theories: history, political science, and the analysis of international relations. Pp. 39–83 in *Bridges and Boundaries: Historians, Political Scientists, and the Study of International Relations,* ed. C. Elman and M. F. Elman. Cambridge, Mass.: MIT Press.

—— 2007. Theory, evidence, and politics in the evolution of research programs. Pp. 177–97 in *Theory and Evidence in Comparative Politics and International Relations,* ed. R. N. Lebow and M. Lichbach. New York: Palgrave Macmillan.

—— 2008. Case studies: types, designs, and logics of inference. *Conflict Management and Peace Science,* 25: 1–18.

LEWIS, D. 1973. *Counterfactuals.* Cambridge, Mass.: Harvard University Press.

MAHONEY, J. 2000. Path dependence in historical sociology. *Theory and Society,* 29: 507–48.

MORGAN, S. L., and WINSHIP, C. 2007. *Counterfactuals and Causal Inference: Methods and Principles for Social Research.* New York: Cambridge University Press.

MUELLER, J. 1991. Changing attitudes towards war: the impact of the First World War. *British Journal of Political Science,* 21: 1–28.

OAKESHOTT, M. 1966. *Experience and its Modes.* London: Cambridge University Press.

POPPER, K. 1965. *The Logic of Scientific Discovery.* New York: Harper Torchbacks.

RIPSMAN, N. M., and LEVY, J. S. 2007. The preventive war that never happened: Britain, France, and the rise of Germany in the 1930s. *Security Studies,* 16: 32–67.

ROESE, N. J., and OLSON, J. M. 1995. *What Might Have Been: The Social Psychology of Counterfactual Thinking*. Mahwah, NJ: Lawrence Erlbaum.

SCHROEDER, P. W. 2007. Necessary conditions and World War I as an unavoidable war. Pp. 147–93 in *Explaining War and Peace: Case Studies and Necessary Condition Counterfactuals*, ed. G. Goertz and J. S. Levy. New York: Routledge.

SKOCPOL, T. 1979. *States and Social Revolutions*. Cambridge: Cambridge University Press.

TETLOCK, P. E., and BELKIN, A. 1996. Counterfactual thought experiments in world politics: logical, methodological, and psychological perspectives. Pp. 1–38 in *Counterfactual Thought Experiments in World Politics*, ed. P. E. Tetlock and A. Belkin. Princeton, NJ: Princeton University Press.

—— and LEBOW, R. N. 2001. Poking counterfactual holes in covering laws: cognitive styles and historical reasoning. *American Political Science Review*, 95: 829–43.

—— —— and PARKER, G. (eds.) 2006. *Unmaking the West: "What If?" Scenarios that Rewrite World History*. Ann Arbor: University of Michigan Press.

WEBER, M. 1949. *The Methodology of the Social Sciences*. Glencoe, Ill.: Free Press.

WEBER, S. 1996. Counterfactuals, past and future. Pp. 268–88 in *Counterfactual Thought Experiments in World Politics*, ed. P. E. Tetlock and A. Belkin. Princeton, NJ: Princeton University Press.

WEINGAST, B. R. 1996. Off-the-path behavior: a game-theoretic approach to counterfactuals and its implications for political and historical analysis. Pp. 230–43 in *Counterfactual Thought Experiments in World Politics*, ed. P. E. Tetlock and A. Belkin. Princeton, NJ: Princeton University Press.

CASE SELECTION FOR CASE-STUDY ANALYSIS: QUALITATIVE AND QUANTITATIVE TECHNIQUES

JOHN GERRING

CASE-study analysis focuses on one or several cases that are expected to provide insight into a larger population. This presents the researcher with a formidable problem of case selection: Which cases should she or he choose?

In large-sample research, the task of case selection is usually handled by some version of randomization. However, in case-study research the sample is small (by definition) and this makes random sampling problematic, for any given sample may be wildly unrepresentative. Moreover, there is no guarantee that a few cases, chosen randomly, will provide leverage into the research question of interest.

In order to isolate a sample of cases that both reproduces the relevant causal features of a larger universe (representativeness) and provides variation along the dimensions of theoretical interest (causal leverage), case selection for very small samples must employ purposive (nonrandom) selection procedures. Nine such methods are discussed in this chapter, each of which may be identified with a distinct case-study "type:" *typical, diverse, extreme, deviant, influential, crucial, pathway, most-similar,* and *most-different.* Table 28.1 summarizes each type, including its general definition, a technique for locating it within a population of potential cases, its uses, and its probable representativeness.

While each of these techniques is normally practiced on one or several cases (the diverse, most-similar, and most-different methods require at least two), all *may* employ additional cases—with the proviso that, at some point, they will no longer offer an opportunity for in-depth analysis and will thus no longer be "case studies" in the usual sense (Gerring 2007, ch. 2). It will also be seen that small-N case-selection procedures rest, at least implicitly, upon an analysis of a larger population of potential cases (as does randomization). The case(s) identified for intensive study is chosen from a population and the reasons for this choice hinge upon the way in which it is situated within that population. This is the origin of the terminology—typical, diverse, extreme, et al. It follows that case-selection procedures in case-study research may build upon prior cross-case analysis and that they depend, at the very least, upon certain assumptions about the broader population.

In certain circumstances, the case-selection procedure may be structured by a quantitative analysis of the larger population. Here, several caveats must be satisfied. First, the inference must pertain to more than a few dozen cases; otherwise, statistical analysis is problematic. Second, relevant data must be available for that population, or a significant sample of that population, on key variables, and the researcher must feel reasonably confident in the accuracy and conceptual validity of these variables. Third, all the standard assumptions of statistical research (e.g. identification, specification, robustness) must be carefully considered, and wherever possible, tested. I shall not dilate further on these familiar issues except to warn the researcher against the unreflective use of statistical techniques.[1] When these requirements are *not* met, the researcher must employ a qualitative approach to case selection.

The point of this chapter is to elucidate general principles that might guide the process of case selection in case-study research, building upon earlier work by Harry Eckstein, Arend Lijphart, and others. Sometimes, these principles can be applied in a quantitative framework and sometimes they are limited to a qualitative framework. In either case, the logic of case selection remains quite similar, whether practiced in small-N or large-N contexts.

Before we begin, a bit of notation is necessary. In this chapter "N" refers to cases, not observations. Here, I am concerned primarily with causal inference, rather than inferences that are descriptive or predictive in nature. Thus, all hypotheses involve at least one independent variable (X) and one dependent variable (Y). For convenience, I shall label the causal factor of special theoretical interest X_1, and the control variable, or vector of controls (if there are any), X_2. If the writer is concerned to explain a puzzling outcome, but has no preconceptions about its causes, then the research will be described as *Y-centered.* If a researcher is concerned to

---

[1] Gujarati (2003); Kennedy (2003). Interestingly, the potential of cross-case statistics in helping to choose cases for in-depth analysis is recognized in some of the earliest discussions of the case-study method (e.g. Queen 1928, 226).

Table 28.1. Techniques of case selection

1. Typical
   - *Definition*: Cases (1 or more) are typical examples of some cross-case relationship.
   - *Cross-case technique*: A low-residual case (on-lier).
   - *Uses*: Hypothesis-testing.
   - *Representativeness*: By definition, the typical case is representative.
2. Diverse
   - *Definition*: Cases (2 or more) illuminate the full range of variation on X_1, Y, or X_1/Y.
   - *Cross-case technique*: Diversity may be calculated by (a) categorical values of X_1 or Y (e.g. Jewish, Catholic, Protestant), (b) standard deviations of X_1 or Y (if continuous), (c) combinations of values (e.g. based on cross-tabulations, factor analysis, or discriminant analysis).
   - *Uses*: Hypothesis generating or hypothesis testing.
   - *Representativeness*: Diverse cases are likely to be representative in the minimal sense of representing the full variation of the population (though they might not mirror the *distribution* of that variation in the population).
3. Extreme
   - *Definition*: Cases (1 or more) exemplify extreme or unusual values of X_1 or Y relative to some univariate distribution.
   - *Cross-case technique*: A case lying many standard deviations away from the mean of X_1 or Y.
   - *Uses*: Hypothesis-generating (open-ended probe of X_1 or Y).
   - *Representativeness*: Achievable only in comparison with a larger sample of cases.
4. Deviant
   - *Definition*: Cases (1 or more) deviate from some cross-case relationship.
   - *Cross-case technique*: A high-residual case (outlier).
   - *Uses*: Hypothesis-generating (to develop new explanations for Y).
   - *Representativeness*: After the case study is conducted it may be corroborated by a cross-case test, which includes a general hypothesis (a new variable) based on the case-study research. If the case is now an on-lier, it may be considered representative of the new relationship.
5. Influential
   - *Definition*: Cases (1 or more) with influential configurations of the independent variables.
   - *Cross-case technique*: Hat matrix or Cook's Distance.
   - *Uses*: Hypothesis-testing (to verify the status of cases that may influence the results of a cross-case analysis).
   - *Representativeness*: Not pertinent, given the goals of the influential-case study.
6. Crucial
   - *Definition*: Cases (1 or more) are most or least likely to exhibit a given outcome.
   - *Cross-case technique*: Qualitative assessment of relative crucialness.
   - *Uses*: Hypothesis-testing (confirmatory or disconfirmatory).
   - *Representativeness*: Often difficult to assess.
7. Pathway
   - *Definition*: Cases (1 or more) that embody a distinct causal path from X_1 to Y.
   - *Cross-case technique*: Cross-tab (for categorical variables) or residual analysis (for continuous variables).
   - *Uses*: Hypothesis-testing (to probe causal mechanisms).
   - *Representativeness*: May be tested by examining residuals for the chosen cases.

(cont.)

Table 28.1. *(Continued)*

8. Most-similar
  ○ *Definition*: Cases (2 or more) are similar on specified variables other than X_1 and/or Y.
  ○ *Cross-case technique*: Matching.
  ○ *Uses*: Hypothesis-generating or hypothesis-testing.
  ○ *Representativeness*: May be tested by examining residuals for the chosen cases.
9. Most-different
  ○ *Definition*: Cases (2 or more) are different on specified variables other than X_1 and Y.
  ○ *Cross-case technique*: The inverse of the most-similar method of large-N case selection (see above).
  ○ *Uses*: Hypothesis-generating or hypothesis-testing (eliminating deterministic causes).
  ○ *Representativeness*: May be tested by examining residuals for the chosen cases.

investigate the effects of a particular cause, with no preconceptions about what these effects might be, the research will be described as *X-centered*. If a researcher is concerned to investigate a particular causal relationship, the research will be described as *X_1/Y-centered*, for it connects a particular cause with a particular outcome.[2] *X-* or *Y*-centered research is exploratory; its purpose is to generate new hypotheses. *X_1/Y-centered* research, by contrast, is confirmatory/disconfirmatory; its purpose is to test an existing hypothesis.

1 Typical Case

In order for a focused case study to provide insight into a broader phenomenon it must be representative of a broader set of cases. It is in this context that one may speak of a *typical-case* approach to case selection. The typical case exemplifies what is considered to be a typical set of values, given some general understanding of a phenomenon. By construction, the typical case is also a representative case.

Some typical cases serve an exploratory role. Here, the author chooses a case based upon a set of descriptive characteristics and then probes for causal relationships. Robert and Helen Lynd (1929/1956) selected a single city "to be as representative as possible of contemporary American life." Specifically, they were looking for a city with

1) a temperate climate; 2) a sufficiently rapid rate of growth to ensure the presence of a plentiful assortment of the growing pains accompanying contemporary social change; 3) an industrial culture with modern, high-speed machine production; 4) the absence of dominance of the city's industry by a single plant (i.e., not a one-industry town); 5) a substantial local artistic

---

[2] This expands on Mill (1843/1872, 253), who wrote of scientific enquiry as twofold: "either inquiries into the cause of a given effect or into the effects or properties of a given cause."

life to balance its industrial activity...; and 6) the absence of any outstanding peculiarities or acute local problems which would mark the city off from the midchannel sort of American community.   (Lynd and Lynd 1929/1956, quoted in Yin 2004, 29–30)

After examining a number of options the Lynds decided that Muncie, Indiana, was more representative than, or at least as representative as, other midsized cities in America, thus qualifying as a typical case.

This is an inductive approach to case selection. Note that typicality may be understood according to the mean, median, or mode on a particular dimension; there may be multiple dimensions (as in the foregoing example); and each may be differently weighted (some dimensions may be more important than others). Where the selection criteria are multidimensional and a large sample of potential cases is in play, some form of factor analysis may be useful in identifying the most-typical case(s).

However, the more common employment of the typical-case method involves a *causal* model of some phenomenon of theoretical interest. Here, the researcher has identified a particular outcome (Y), and perhaps a specific X_1/Y hypothesis, which she wishes to investigate. In order to do so, she looks for a typical example of that causal relationship. Intuitively, one imagines that a case selected according to the mean values of all parameters must be a typical case relative to some causal relationship. However, this is by no means assured.

Suppose that the Lynds were primarily interested in explaining feelings of trust/distrust among members of different social classes (one of the implicit research goals of the *Middletown* study). This outcome is likely to be affected by many factors, only some of which are included in their six selection criteria. So choosing cases with respect to a causal hypothesis involves, first of all, identifying the relevant parameters. It involves, secondly, the selection of a case that has a "typical" value relative to the overall causal model; it is well explained. Cases with untypical scores on a particular dimension (e.g. very high or very low) may still be typical examples of a causal relationship. Indeed, they may be more typical than cases whose values lie close to the mean. Thus, a descriptive understanding of typicality is quite different from a causal understanding of typicality. Since it is the latter version that is more common, I shall adopt this understanding of typicality in the remainder of the discussion.

From a qualitative perspective, causal typicality involves the selection of a case that conforms to expectations about some general causal relationship. It performs as expected. In a quantitative setting, this notion is measured by the size of a case's residual in a large-N cross-case model. Typical cases lie on or near the regression line; their residuals are small. Insofar as the model is correctly specified, the size of a case's residual (i.e. the number of standard deviations that separate the actual value from the fitted value) provides a helpful clue to how representative that case is likely to be. "Outliers" are unlikely to be representative of the target population.

Of course, just because a case has a low residual does not *necessarily* mean that it is a representative case (with respect to the causal relationship of interest). Indeed, the issue of case representativeness is an issue that can never be definitively settled. When one refers to a "typical case" one is saying, in effect, that the *probability* of a case's representativeness is high, relative to other cases. This test of typicality is misleading if the statistical model is mis-specified. And it provides little insurance against errors that are purely stochastic. A case may lie directly on the regression line but still be, in some important respect, atypical. For example, it might have an odd combination of values; the interaction of variables might be different from other cases; or additional causal mechanisms might be at work. For this reason, it is important to supplement a statistical analysis of cases with evidence drawn from the case in question (the case study itself) and with our deductive knowledge of the world. One should never judge a case solely by its residual. Yet, all other things being equal, a case with a low residual is less likely to be unusual than a case with a high residual, and to this extent the method of case selection outlined here may be a helpful guide to case-study researchers faced with a large number of potential cases.

By way of conclusion, it should be noted that because the typical case embodies a typical value on some set of causally relevant dimensions, the variance of interest to the researcher must lie *within* that case. Specifically, the typical case of some phenomenon may be helpful in exploring causal mechanisms and in solving identification problems (e.g. endogeneity between X_1 and Y, an omitted variable that may account for X_1 *and* Y, or some other spurious causal association). Depending upon the results of the case study, the author may confirm an existing hypothesis, disconfirm that hypothesis, or reframe it in a way that is consistent with the findings of the case study. These are the uses of the typical-case study.

2 DIVERSE CASES

A second case-selection strategy has as its primary objective the achievement of maximum variance along relevant dimensions. I refer to this as a *diverse-case* method. For obvious reasons, this method requires the selection of a set of cases—at minimum, two—which are intended to represent the full range of values characterizing X_1, Y, or some particular X_1/Y relationship.[3]

Where the individual variable of interest is categorical (on/off, red/black/blue, Jewish/Protestant/Catholic), the identification of diversity is readily apparent. The investigator simply chooses one case from each category. For a continuous variable,

---

[3] This method has not received much attention on the part of qualitative methodologists; hence, the absence of a generally recognized name. It bears some resemblance to J. S. Mill's Joint Method of Agreement and Difference (Mill 1843/1872), which is to say a mixture of most-similar and most-different analysis, as discussed below. Patton (2002, 234) employs the concept of "maximum variation (heterogeneity) sampling."

the choices are not so obvious. However, the researcher usually chooses both extreme values (high and low), and perhaps the mean or median as well. The researcher may also look for break-points in the distribution that seem to correspond to categorical differences among cases. Or she may follow a theoretical hunch about which threshold values count, i.e. which are likely to produce different values on Y.

Another sort of diverse case takes account of the values of multiple variables (i.e. a vector), rather than a single variable. If these variables are categorical, the identification of causal types rests upon the intersection of each category. Two dichotomous variables produce a matrix with four cells. Three trichotomous variables produce a matrix of eight cells. And so forth. If all variables are deemed relevant to the analysis, the selection of diverse cases mandates the selection of one case drawn from within each cell. Let us say that an outcome is thought to be affected by sex, race (black/white), and marital status. Here, a diverse-case strategy of case selection would identify one case within each of these intersecting cells—a total of eight cases. Things become slightly more complicated when one or more of the factors is continuous, rather than categorical. Here, the diversity of case values do not fall neatly into cells. Rather, these cells must be created by fiat—e.g. high, medium, low.

It will be seen that where multiple variables are under consideration, the logic of diverse-case analysis rests upon the logic of *typological* theorizing—where different combinations of variables are assumed to have effects on an outcome that vary across types (Elman 2005; George and Bennett 2005, 235; Lazarsfeld and Barton 1951). George and Smoke, for example, wish to explore different types of deterrence failure—by "fait accompli," by "limited probe," and by "controlled pressure." Consequently, they wish to find cases that exemplify each type of causal mechanism.[4]

Diversity may thus refer to a range of variation on X or Y, or to a particular combination of causal factors (with or without a consideration of the outcome). In each instance, the goal of case selection is to capture the full range of variation along the dimension(s) of interest.

Since diversity can mean many things, its employment in a large-N setting is necessarily dependent upon how this key term is defined. If it is understood to pertain only to a single variable (X_1 or Y), then the task is fairly simple. A categorical variable mandates the choice of at least one case from each category—two if dichotomous, three if trichotomous, and so forth. A continuous variable suggests the choice of at least one "high" and "low" value, and perhaps one drawn from the mean or median. But other choices might also be justified, according to one's hunch about the underlying causal relationship or according to natural thresholds found in the data, which may be grouped into discrete categories. Single-variable traits are usually easy to discover in a large-N setting through descriptive statistics or through visual inspection of the data.

---

[4] More precisely, George and Smoke (1974, 534, 522–36, ch. 18; see also discussion in Collier and Mahoney 1996, 78) set out to investigate causal pathways and discovered, through the course of their investigation of many cases, these three causal types. Yet, for our purposes what is important is that the final sample includes at least one representative of each "type."

Where diversity refers to particular *combinations* of variables, the relevant cross-case technique is some version of stratified random sampling (in a probabilistic setting) or Qualitative Comparative Analysis (in a deterministic setting) (Ragin 2000). If the researcher suspects that a causal relationship is affected not only by combinations of factors but also by their *sequencing*, then the technique of analysis must incorporate temporal elements (Abbott 2001; Abbott and Forrest 1986; Abbott and Tsay 2000). Thus, the method of identifying causal types rests upon whatever method of identifying causal relationships is employed in the large-N sample.

Note that the identification of distinct case types is intended to identify groups of cases that are internally homogeneous (in all respects that might affect the causal relationship of interest). Thus, the choice of cases within each group should not be problematic, and may be accomplished through random sampling or purposive case selection. However, if there is suspected diversity within each category, then measures should be taken to assure that the chosen cases are typical of each category. A case study should not focus on an atypical member of a subgroup.

Indeed, considerations of diversity and typicality often go together. Thus, in a study of globalization and social welfare systems, Duane Swank (2002) first identifies three distinctive groups of welfare states: "universalistic" (social democratic), "corporatist conservative," and "liberal." Next, he looks within each group to find the most-typical cases. He decides that the Nordic countries are more typical of the universalistic model than the Netherlands since the latter has "some characteristics of the occupationally based program structure and a political context of Christian Democratic-led governments typical of the corporatist conservative nations" (Swank 2002, 11; see also Esping-Andersen 1990). Thus, the Nordic countries are chosen as representative cases within the universalistic case type, and are accompanied in the case-study portion of his analysis by other cases chosen to represent the other welfare state types (corporatist conservative and liberal).

Evidently, when a sample encompasses a full range of variation on relevant parameters one is likely to enhance the representativeness of that sample (relative to some population). This is a distinct advantage. Of course, the inclusion of a full range of variation may distort the actual distribution of cases across this spectrum. If there are more "high" cases than "low" cases in a population and the researcher chooses only one high case and one low case, the resulting sample of two is not perfectly representative. Even so, the diverse-case method probably has stronger claims to representativeness than any other small-N sample (including the standalone typical case). The selection of diverse cases has the additional advantage of introducing variation on the key variables of interest. A set of diverse cases is, by definition, a set of cases that encompasses a range of high and low values on relevant dimensions. There is, therefore, much to recommend this method of case selection. I suspect that these advantages are commonly understood and are applied on an intuitive level by case-study researchers. However, the lack of a recognizable name—and an explicit methodological defense—has made it difficult for case-study researchers to utilize this method of case selection, and to do so in an explicit and self-conscious fashion. Neologism has its uses.

3 Extreme Case

The *extreme-case* method selects a case because of its extreme value on an independent (X_1) or dependent (Y) variable of interest. Thus, studies of domestic violence may choose to focus on extreme instances of abuse (Browne 1987). Studies of altruism may focus on those rare individuals who risked their lives to help others (e.g. Holocaust resisters) (Monroe 1996). Studies of ethnic politics may focus on the most heterogeneous societies (e.g. Papua New Guinea) in order to better understand the role of ethnicity in a democratic setting (Reilly 2000–1). Studies of industrial policy often focus on the most successful countries (i.e. the NICS) (Deyo 1987). And so forth.[5]

Often an extreme case corresponds to a case that is considered to be prototypical or paradigmatic of some phenomena of interest. This is because concepts are often defined by their extremes, i.e. their ideal types. Italian Fascism defines the concept of Fascism, in part, because it offered the most extreme example of that phenomenon. However, the *methodological* value of this case, and others like it, derives from its extremity (along some dimension of interest), not its theoretical status or its status in the literature on a subject.

The notion of "extreme" may now be defined more precisely. An extreme value is an observation that lies far away from the mean of a given distribution. This may be measured (if there are sufficient observations) by a case's "Z score"—the number of standard deviations between a case and the mean value for that sample. Extreme cases have high Z scores, and for this reason may serve as useful subjects for intensive analysis.

For a continuous variable, the distance from the mean may be in either direction (positive or negative). For a dichotomous variable (present/absent), extremeness may be interpreted as *unusual*. If most cases are positive along a given dimension, then a negative case constitutes an extreme case. If most cases are negative, then a positive case constitutes an extreme case. It should be clear that researchers are not simply concerned with cases where something "happened," but also with cases where something did not. It is the rareness of the value that makes a case valuable, in this context, not its positive or negative value.[6] Thus, if one is studying state capacity, a case of state failure is probably more informative than a case of state endurance simply because the former is more unusual. Similarly, if one is interested in incest taboos a culture where the incest taboo is absent or weak is probably more useful than a culture where it is present or strong. Fascism is more important than nonfascism. And so forth. There is a good reason, therefore, why case studies of revolution tend to focus on "revolutionary" cases. Theda Skocpol (1979) had much more to learn from France than from Austro-Hungary since France was more unusual than Austro-Hungary within the population of nation states that Skocpol was

---

[5] For further examples see Collier and Mahoney (1996); Geddes (1990); Tendler (1997).

[6] Traditionally, methodologists have conceptualized cases as having "positive" or "negative" values (e.g. Emigh 1997; Mahoney and Goertz 2004; Ragin 2000, 60; 2004, 126).

concerned to explain. The reason is quite simple: There are fewer revolutionary cases than nonrevolutionary cases; thus, the variation that we explore as a clue to causal relationships is encapsulated in these cases, against a background of nonrevolutionary cases.

Note that the extreme-case method of case selection appears to violate the social science folk wisdom warning us not to "select on the dependent variable."[7] Selecting cases on the dependent variable is indeed problematic if a number of cases are chosen, all of which lie on one end of a variable's spectrum (they are all positive *or* negative), and if the researcher then subjects this sample to cross-case analysis as if it were representative of a population.[8] Results for this sort of analysis would almost assuredly be biased. Moreover, there will be little variation to explain since the values of each case are explicitly constrained.

However, this is not the proper employment of the extreme-case method. (It is more appropriately labeled an extreme-*sample* method.) The extreme-case method actually refers back to a larger sample of cases that lie in the background of the analysis and provide a full range of variation as well as a more representative picture of the population. It is a self-conscious attempt to *maximize* variance on the dimension of interest, not to minimize it. If this population of cases is well understood— either through the author's own cross-case analysis, through the work of others, or through common sense—then a researcher may justify the selection of a single case exemplifying an extreme value for within-case analysis. If not, the researcher may be well advised to follow a diverse-case method, as discussed above.

By way of conclusion, let us return to the problem of representativeness. It will be seen that an extreme case may be typical *or* deviant. There is simply no way to tell because the researcher has not yet specified an X_1/Y causal proposition. Once such a causal proposition has been specified one may then ask whether the case in question is similar to some population of cases in all respects that might affect the X_1/Y relationship of interest (i.e. unit homogeneous). It is at this point that it becomes possible to say, within the context of a cross-case statistical model, whether a case lies near to, or far from, the regression line. However, this sort of analysis means that the researcher is no longer pursuing an extreme-case method. The extreme-case method is purely exploratory—a way of probing possible causes of Y, or possible effects of X, in an open-ended fashion. If the researcher has some notion of what additional factors might affect the outcome of interest, or of what relationship the causal factor of interest might have with Y, then she ought to pursue one of the other methods explored in this chapter. This also implies that an extreme-case method may transform into a different kind of approach as a study evolves; that is, as a more specific hypothesis comes to light. Useful extreme cases at the outset of a study may prove less useful at a later stage of analysis.

---

[7] Geddes (1990); King, Keohane, and Verba (1994). See also discussion in Brady and Collier (2004); Collier and Mahoney (1996); Rogowski (1995).

[8] The exception would be a circumstance in which the researcher intends to disprove a deterministic argument (Dion 1998).

4 DEVIANT CASE

The *deviant-case* method selects that case(s) which, by reference to some general understanding of a topic (either a specific theory or common sense), demonstrates a surprising value. It is thus the contrary of the typical case. Barbara Geddes (2003) notes the importance of deviant cases in medical science, where researchers are habitually focused on that which is "pathological" (according to standard theory and practice). The *New England Journal of Medicine*, one of the premier journals of the field, carries a regular feature entitled Case Records of the Massachusetts General Hospital. These articles bear titles like the following: "An 80-Year-Old Woman with Sudden Unilateral Blindness" or "A 76-Year-Old Man with Fever, Dyspnea, Pulmonary Infiltrates, Pleural Effusions, and Confusion."[9] Another interesting example drawn from the field of medicine concerns the extensive study now devoted to a small number of persons who seem resistant to the AIDS virus (Buchbinder and Vittinghoff 1999; Haynes, Pantaleo, and Fauci 1996). Why are they resistant? What is different about these people? What can we learn about AIDS in other patients by observing people who have built-in resistance to this disease?

Likewise, in psychology and sociology case studies may be comprised of deviant (in the social sense) persons or groups. In economics, case studies may consist of countries or businesses that overperform (e.g. Botswana; Microsoft) or underperform (e.g. Britain through most of the twentieth century; Sears in recent decades) relative to some set of expectations. In political science, case studies may focus on countries where the welfare state is more developed (e.g. Sweden) or less developed (e.g. the United States) than one would expect, given a set of general expectations about welfare state development. The deviant case is closely linked to the investigation of theoretical anomalies. Indeed, to say deviant is to imply "anomalous."[10]

Note that while extreme cases are judged relative to the mean of a single distribution (the distribution of values along a single variable), deviant cases are judged relative to some general model of causal relations. The deviant-case method selects cases which, by reference to some (presumably) general relationship, demonstrate a surprising value. They are "deviant" in that they are poorly explained by the multivariate model. The important point is that deviant-ness can only be assessed relative to the general (quantitative or qualitative) model. This means that the relative deviant-ness of a case is likely to change whenever the general model is altered. For example, the United States is a deviant welfare state when this outcome is gauged relative to societal wealth. But it is less deviant—and perhaps not deviant at all—when certain additional (political and societal) factors are included in the model, as discussed in

---

[9] Geddes (2003, 131). For other examples of casework from the annals of medicine see "Clinical reports" in the *Lancet*, "Case studies" in *Canadian Medical Association Journal*, and various issues of the *Journal of Obstetrics and Gynecology*, often devoted to clinical cases (discussed in Jenicek 2001, 7). For examples from the subfield of comparative politics see Kazancigil (1994).

[10] For a discussion of the important role of anomalies in the development of scientific theorizing see Elman (2003); Lakatos (1978). For examples of deviant-case research designs in the social sciences see Amenta (1991); Coppedge (2004); Eckstein (1975); Emigh (1997); Kendall and Wolf (1949/1955).

the epilogue. Deviance is model dependent. Thus, when discussing the concept of the deviant case it is helpful to ask the following question: *Relative to what general model* (or set of background factors) is Case A deviant?

Conceptually, we have said that the deviant case is the logical contrary of the typical case. This translates into a directly contrasting statistical measurement. While the typical case is one with a low residual (in some general model of causal relations), a deviant case is one with a high residual. This means, following our previous discussion, that the deviant case is likely to be an *un*representative case, and in this respect appears to violate the supposition that case-study samples should seek to reproduce features of a larger population.

However, it must be borne in mind that the primary purpose of a deviant-case analysis is to probe for new—but as yet unspecified—explanations. (If the purpose is to disprove an extant theory I shall refer to the study as crucial-case, as discussed below.) The researcher hopes that causal processes identified within the deviant case will illustrate some causal factor that is applicable to other (more or less deviant) cases. This means that a deviant-case study usually culminates in a general proposition, one that may be applied to other cases in the population. Once this general proposition has been introduced into the overall model, the expectation is that the chosen case will no longer be an outlier. Indeed, the hope is that it will now be *typical*, as judged by its small residual in the adjusted model. (The exception would be a circumstance in which a case's outcome is deemed to be "accidental," and therefore inexplicable by any general model.)

This feature of the deviant-case study should help to resolve questions about its representativeness. Even if it is not possible to measure the new causal factor (and thus to introduce it into a large-N cross-case model), it may still be plausible to assert (based on general knowledge of the phenomenon) that the chosen case is representative of a broader population.

5 INFLUENTIAL CASE

Sometimes, the choice of a case is motivated solely by the need to verify the assumptions behind a general model of causal relations. Here, the analyst attempts to provide a rationale for disregarding a problematic case or a set of problematic cases. That is to say, she attempts to show why apparent deviations from the norm are not *really* deviant, or do not challenge the core of the theory, once the circumstances of the special case or cases are fully understood. A cross-case analysis may, after all, be marred by several classes of problems including measurement error, specification error, errors in establishing proper boundaries for the inference (the scope of the argument), and stochastic error (fluctuations in the phenomenon under study that are treated as random, given available theoretical resources). If poorly fitting cases can be explained away by reference to these kinds of problems, then the theory of interest is that much stronger. This sort of deviant-case analysis answers the question, "What about Case A (or cases of type A)? How does that, seemingly disconfirming, case fit the model?"

Because its underlying purpose is different from the usual deviant-case study, I offer a new term for this method. The *influential case* is a case that casts doubt upon a theory, and for that reason warrants close inspection. This investigation may reveal, after all, that the theory is validated—perhaps in some slightly altered form. In this guise, the influential case is the "case that proves the rule." In other instances, the influential-case analysis may contribute to disconfirming, or reconceptualizing, a theory. The key point is that the value of the case is judged relative to some extant cross-case model.

A simple version of influential-case analysis involves the confirmation of a key case's score on some critical dimension. This is essentially a question of measurement. Sometimes cases are poorly explained simply because they are poorly understood. A close examination of a particular context may reveal that an apparently falsifying case has been miscoded. If so, the initial challenge presented by that case to some general theory has been obviated.

However, the more usual employment of the influential-case method culminates in a substantive reinterpretation of the case—perhaps even of the general model. It is not just a question of measurement. Consider Thomas Ertman's (1997) study of state building in Western Europe, as summarized by Gerardo Munck. This study argues

that the interaction of a) the type of local government during the first period of statebuilding, with b) the timing of increases in geopolitical competition, strongly influences the kind of regime and state that emerge. [Ertman] tests this hypothesis against the historical experience of Europe and finds that most countries fit his predictions. Denmark, however, is a major exception. In Denmark, sustained geopolitical competition began relatively late and local government at the beginning of the statebuilding period was generally participatory, which should have led the country to develop "patrimonial constitutionalism." But in fact, it developed "bureaucratic absolutism." Ertman carefully explores the process through which Denmark came to have a bureaucratic absolutist state and finds that Denmark had the early marks of a patrimonial constitutionalist state. However, the country was pushed off this developmental path by the influence of German knights, who entered Denmark and brought with them German institutions of local government. Ertman then traces the causal process through which these imported institutions pushed Denmark to develop bureaucratic absolutism, concluding that this development was caused by a factor well outside his explanatory framework.

(Munck 2004, 118)

Ertman's overall framework is confirmed insofar as he has been able to show, by an in-depth discussion of Denmark, that the causal processes stipulated by the general theory hold even in this apparently disconfirming case. Denmark is still deviant, but it is so because of "contingent historical circumstances" that are exogenous to the theory (Ertman 1997, 316).

Evidently, the influential-case analysis is similar to the deviant-case analysis. Both focus on outliers. However, as we shall see, they focus on different kinds of outliers.

Moreover, the animating goals of these two research designs are quite different. The influential-case study begins with the aim of confirming a general model, while the deviant-case study has the aim of generating a new hypothesis that modifies an existing general model. The confusion stems from the fact that the same case study may fulfill both objectives—qualifying a general model and, at the same time, confirming its core hypothesis.

Thus, in their study of Roberto Michels's "iron law of oligarchy," Lipset, Trow, and Coleman (1956) choose to focus on an organization—the International Typographical Union—that appears to violate the central presupposition. The ITU, as noted by one of the authors, has "a long-term two-party system with free elections and frequent turnover in office" and is thus anything but oligarchic (Lipset 1959, 70). As such, it calls into question Michels's grand generalization about organizational behavior. The authors explain this curious result by the extraordinarily high level of education among the members of this union. Michels's law is shown to be true for most organizations, but not all. It is true, with qualifications. Note that the respecification of the original model (in effect, Lipset, Trow, and Coleman introduce a new control variable or boundary condition) involves the exploration of a new hypothesis. In this instance, therefore, the use of an influential case to confirm an existing theory is quite similar to the use of a deviant case to explore a new theory.

In a quantitative idiom, influential cases are those that, if counterfactually assigned a different value on the dependent variable, would most substantially change the resulting estimates. They may or may not be outliers (high-residual cases). Two quantitative measures of influence are commonly applied in regression diagnostics (Belsey, Kuh, and Welsch 2004). The first, often referred to as the leverage of a case, derives from what is called the *hat matrix*. Based solely on each case's scores on the independent variables, the hat matrix tells us how much a change in (or a measurement error on) the dependent variable for that case would affect the overall regression line. The second is *Cook's distance*, a measure of the extent to which the estimates of all the parameters would change if a given case were omitted from the analysis. Cases with a large leverage or Cook's distance contribute quite a lot to the inferences drawn from a cross-case analysis. In this sense, such cases are vital for maintaining analytic conclusions. Discovering a significant measurement error on the dependent variable or an important omitted variable for such a case may dramatically revise estimates of the overall relationships. Hence, it may be quite sensible to select influential cases for in-depth study.

Note that the use of an influential-case strategy of case selection is limited to instances in which a researcher has reason to be concerned that her results are being driven by one or a few cases. This is most likely to be true in small to moderate-sized samples. Where N is very large—greater than 1,000, let us say—it is extremely unlikely that a small set of cases (much less an individual case) will play an "influential" role. Of course, there may be influential *sets* of cases, e.g. countries within a particular continent or cultural region, or persons of Irish extraction. Sets of influential observations are often problematic in a time-series cross-section data-set where each unit (e.g. country) contains multiple observations (through time), and hence may have a strong influence on aggregate results. Still, the general rule is: the larger the sample, the less important individual cases are likely to be and, hence, the less likely a researcher is to use an influential-case approach to case selection.

6 CRUCIAL CASE

Of all the extant methods of case selection perhaps the most storied—and certainly the most controversial—is the *crucial-case* method, introduced to the social science world several decades ago by Harry Eckstein. In his seminal essay, Eckstein (1975, 118) describes the crucial case as one "that *must closely fit* a theory if one is to have confidence in the theory's validity, or, conversely, *must not fit* equally well any rule contrary to that proposed." A case is crucial in a somewhat weaker—but much more common—sense when it is most, or least, likely to fulfill a theoretical prediction. A "most-likely" case is one that, on all dimensions *except* the dimension of theoretical interest, is predicted to achieve a certain outcome, and yet does not. It is therefore used to disconfirm a theory. A "least-likely" case is one that, on all dimensions *except* the dimension of theoretical interest, is predicted not to achieve a certain outcome, and yet does so. It is therefore used to confirm a theory. In all formulations, the crucial-case offers a most-difficult test for an argument, and hence provides what is perhaps the strongest sort of evidence possible in a nonexperimental, single-case setting.

Since the publication of Eckstein's influential essay, the crucial-case approach has been claimed in a multitude of studies across several social science disciplines and has come to be recognized as a staple of the case-study method.[11] Yet the idea of any single case playing a crucial (or "critical") role is not widely accepted among most methodologists (e.g. Sekhon 2004). (Even its progenitor seems to have had doubts.)

Let us begin with the confirmatory (a.k.a. least-likely) crucial case. The implicit logic of this research design may be summarized as follows. Given a set of facts, we are asked to contemplate the probability that a given theory is true. While the facts matter, to be sure, the effectiveness of this sort of research also rests upon the formal properties of the theory in question. Specifically, the degree to which a theory is amenable to confirmation is contingent upon how many predictions can be derived from the theory and on how "risky" each individual prediction is. In Popper's (1963, 36) words, "Confirmations should count only if they are the result of *risky predictions*; that is to say, if, unenlightened by the theory in question, we should have expected an

---

[11] For examples of the crucial-case method see Bennett, Lepgold, and Unger (1994); Desch (2002); Goodin and Smitsman (2000); Kemp (1986); Reilly and Phillpot (2003). For general discussion see George and Bennett (2005); Levy (2002); Stinchcombe (1968, 24–8).

event which was incompatible with the theory—and event which would have refuted the theory. Every 'good' scientific theory is a prohibition; it forbids certain things to happen. The more a theory forbids, the better it is" (see also Popper 1934/1968). A risky prediction is therefore one that is highly precise and determinate, and therefore unlikely to be achieved by the product of other causal factors (external to the theory of interest) or through stochastic processes. A theory produces many such predictions if it is fully elaborated, issuing predictions not only on the central outcome of interest but also on specific causal mechanisms, and if it is broad in purview. (The notion of riskiness may also be conceptualized within the Popperian lexicon as *degrees of falsifiability*.)

These points can also be articulated in Bayesian terms. Colin Howson and Peter Urbach explain: "The degree to which h [a hypothesis] is confirmed by e [a set of evidence] depends...on the extent to which $P(e|h)$ exceeds $P(e)$, that is, on how much more probable e is relative to the hypothesis and background assumptions than it is relative just to background assumptions." Again, "confirmation is correlated with how much more probable the evidence is if the hypothesis is true than if it is false" (Howson and Urlbach 1989, 86). Thus, the stranger the prediction offered by a theory—relative to what we would normally expect—the greater the degree of confirmation that will be afforded by the evidence. As an intuitive example, Howson and Urbach (1989, 86) offer the following:

If a soothsayer predicts that you will meet a dark stranger sometime and you do in fact, your faith in his powers of precognition would not be much enhanced: you would probably continue to think his predictions were just the result of guesswork. However, if the prediction also gave the correct number of hairs on the head of that stranger, your previous scepticism would no doubt be severely shaken.

While these Popperian/Bayesian notions[12] are relevant to all empirical research designs, they are especially relevant to case-study research designs, for in these settings a single case (or, at most, a small number of cases) is required to bear a heavy burden of proof. It should be no surprise, therefore, that Popper's idea of "riskiness" was to be appropriated by case-study researchers like Harry Eckstein to validate the enterprise of single-case analysis. (Although Eckstein does not cite Popper the intellectual lineage is clear.) Riskiness, here, is analogous to what is usually referred to as a "most-difficult" research design, which in a case-study research design would be understood as a "least-likely" case. Note also that the distinction between a "must-fit" case and a least-likely case—that, in the event, actually does fit the terms of a theory—is a matter of degree. Cases are more or less crucial for confirming theories. The point is that, in some circumstances, a paucity of empirical evidence may be compensated by the riskiness of the theory.

The crucial-case research design is, perforce, a highly deductive enterprise; much depends on the quality of the theory under investigation. It follows that the theories most amenable to crucial-case analysis are those which are lawlike in their precision,

---

[12] A third position, which purports to be neither Popperian or Bayesian, has been articulated by Mayo (1996, ch. 6). From this perspective, the same idea is articulated as a matter of "severe tests."

degree of elaboration, consistency, and scope. The more a theory attains the status of a causal law, the easier it will be to confirm, or to disconfirm, with a single case. Indeed, risky predictions are common in natural science fields such as physics, which in turn served as the template for the deductive-nomological ("covering-law") model of science that influenced Eckstein and others in the postwar decades (e.g. Hempel 1942).

A frequently cited example is the first important empirical demonstration of the theory of relativity, which took the form of a single-event prediction on the occasion of the May 29, 1919, solar eclipse (Eckstein 1975; Popper 1963). Stephen Van Evera (1997, 66–7) describes the impact of this prediction on the validation of Einstein's theory.

Einstein's theory predicted that gravity would bend the path of light toward a gravity source by a specific amount. Hence it predicted that during a solar eclipse stars near the sun would appear displaced—stars actually behind the sun would appear next to it, and stars lying next to the sun would appear farther from it—and it predicted the amount of apparent displacement. No other theory made these predictions. The passage of this one single-case-study test brought the theory wide acceptance because the tested predictions were unique—there was no plausible competing explanation for the predicted result—hence the passed test was very strong.

The strength of this test is the extraordinary fit between the theory and a set of facts found in a single case, and the corresponding lack of fit between all other theories and this set of facts. Einstein offered an explanation of a particular set of anomalous findings that no other existing theory could make sense of. Of course, one must assume that there was no—or limited—measurement error. And one must assume that the phenomenon of interest is largely invariant; light does not bend differently at different times and places (except in ways that can be understood through the theory of relativity). And one must assume, finally, that the theory itself makes sense on other grounds (other than the case of special interest); it is a plausible general theory. If one is willing to accept these a priori assumptions, then the 1919 "case study" provides a very strong confirmation of the theory. It is difficult to imagine a stronger proof of the theory from within an observational (nonexperimental) setting.

In social science settings, by contrast, one does not commonly find single-case studies offering knockout evidence for a theory. This is, in my view, largely a product of the looseness (the underspecification) of most social science theories. George and Bennett point out that while the thesis of the democratic peace is as close to a "law" as social science has yet seen, it cannot be confirmed (or refuted) by looking at specific causal mechanisms because the causal pathways mandated by the theory are multiple and diverse. Under the circumstances, no single-case test can offer strong confirmation of the theory (George and Bennett 2005, 209).

However, if one adopts a softer version of the crucial-case method—the least-likely (most difficult) case—then possibilities abound. Indeed, I suspect that, *implicitly*, most case-study work that makes a positive argument focusing on a single case (without a corresponding cross-case analysis) relies largely on the logic of the least-likely case. Rarely is this logic made explicit, except perhaps in a passing phrase or two. Yet the deductive logic of the "risky" prediction is central to the case-study enterprise.

Whether a case study is convincing or not often rests on the reader's evaluation of how strong the evidence for an argument might be, and this in turn—wherever cross-case evidence is limited and no manipulated treatment can be devised—rests upon an estimation of the degree of "fit" between a theory and the evidence at hand, as discussed.

Lily Tsai's (2007) investigation of governance at the village level in China employs several in-depth case studies of villages which are chosen (in part) because of their least-likely status relative to the theory of interest. Tsai's hypothesis is that villages with greater social solidarity (based on preexisting religious or familial networks) will develop a higher level of social trust and mutual obligation and, as a result, will experience better governance. Crucial cases, therefore, are villages that evidence a high level of social solidarity but which, along other dimensions, would be judged least likely to develop good governance, e.g. they are poor, isolated, and lack democratic institutions or accountability mechanisms from above. "Li Settlement," in Fujian province, is such a case. The fact that this impoverished village nonetheless boasts an impressive set of infrastructural accomplishments such as paved roads with drainage ditches (a rarity in rural China) suggests that something rather unusual is going on here. Because her case is carefully chosen to eliminate rival explanations, Tsai's conclusions about the special role of social solidarity are difficult to gainsay. How else is one to explain this otherwise anomalous result? This is the strength of the least-likely case, where all other plausible causal factors for an outcome have been minimized.[13]

Jack Levy (2002, 144) refers to this, evocatively, as a "Sinatra inference:" if it can make it here, it can make it anywhere (see also Khong 1992, 49; Sagan 1995, 49; Shafer 1988, 14–6). Thus, if social solidarity has the hypothesized effect in Li Settlement it should have the same effect in more propitious settings (e.g. where there is greater economic surplus). The same implicit logic informs many case-study analyses where the intent of the study is to confirm a hypothesis on the basis of a single case.

Another sort of crucial case is employed for the purpose of *dis*confirming a causal hypothesis. A central Popperian insight is that it is easier to disconfirm an inference than to confirm that same inference. (Indeed, Popper doubted that any inference could be fully confirmed, and for this reason preferred the term "corroborate.") This is particularly true of case-study research designs, where evidence is limited to one or several cases. The key proviso is that the theory under investigation must take a consistent (a.k.a. invariant, deterministic) form, even if its predictions are not terrifically precise, well elaborated, or broad.

As it happens, there are a fair number of invariant propositions floating around the social science disciplines (Goertz and Levy forthcoming; Goertz and Starr 2003). It used to be argued, for example, that political stability would occur only in countries that are relatively homogeneous, or where existing heterogeneities are mitigated by

---

[13] It should be noted that Tsai's conclusions do not rest solely on this crucial case. Indeed, she employs a broad range of methodological tools, encompassing case-study and cross-case methods.

cross-cutting cleavages (Almond 1956; Bentley 1908/1967; Lipset 1960/1963; Truman 1951). Arend Lijphart's (1968) study of the Netherlands, a peaceful country with reinforcing social cleavages, is commonly viewed as refuting this theory on the basis of a single in-depth case analysis.[14]

Granted, it may be questioned whether presumed invariant theories are *really* invariant; perhaps they are better understood as probabilistic. Perhaps, that is, the theory of cross-cutting cleavages is still true, probabilistically, despite the apparent Dutch exception. Or perhaps the theory is still true, deterministically, within a subset of cases that does not include the Netherlands. (This sort of claim seems unlikely in this particular instance, but it is quite plausible in many others.) Or perhaps the theory is in need of reframing; it is true, deterministically, but applies only to cross-cutting *ethnic/racial* cleavages, not to cleavages that are primarily religious. One can quibble over what it means to "disconfirm" a theory. The point is that the crucial case has, in all these circumstances, provided important updating of a theoretical prior.

Heretofore, I have treated causal factors as dichotomous. Countries have either reinforcing or cross-cutting cleavages and they have regimes that are either peaceful or conflictual. Evidently, these sorts of parameters are often matters of degree. In this reading of the theory, cases are *more or less* crucial. Accordingly, the most useful—i.e. most crucial—case for Lijphart's purpose is one that has the most segregated social groups and the most peaceful and democratic track record. In these respects, the Netherlands was a very good choice. Indeed, the degree of disconfirmation offered by this case study is probably greater than the degree of disconfirmation that might have been provided by other cases such as India or Papua New Guinea—countries where social peace has not always been secure. The point is that where variables are continuous rather than dichotomous it is possible to evaluate potential cases in terms of their *degree of crucialness*.

Note that the crucial-case method of case-selection, whether employed in a confirmatory or disconfirmatory mode, cannot be employed in a large-N context. This is because an explicit cross-case model would render the crucial-case study redundant. Once one identifies the relevant parameters and the scores of all cases on those parameters, one has in effect constructed a cross-case model that confirms or disconfirms the theory in question. The case study is thenceforth irrelevant, at least as a means of decisive confirmation or disconfirmation.[15] It remains highly relevant as a means of exploring causal mechanisms, of course. Yet, because this objective is quite different from that which is usually associated with the term, I enlist a new term for this technique.

---

[14] See also the discussion in Eckstein (1975) and Lijphart (1969). For additional examples of case studies disconfirming general propositions of a deterministic nature see Allen (1965); Lipset, Trow, and Coleman (1956); Njolstad (1990); Reilly (2000–1); and discussion in Dion (1998); Rogowski (1995).

[15] Granted, insofar as case-study analysis provides a window into causal mechanisms, and causal mechanisms are integral to a given theory, a single case may be enlisted to confirm or disconfirm a proposition. However, if the case study upholds a posited pattern of X/Y covariation, and finds fault only with the stipulated causal mechanism, it would be more accurate to say that the study forces the *reformulation* of a given theory, rather than its confirmation or disconfirmation. See further discussion in the following section.

7 PATHWAY CASE

One of the most important functions of case-study research is the elucidation of causal mechanisms. But which sort of case is most useful for this purpose? Although all case studies presumably shed light on causal mechanisms, not all cases are equally transparent. In situations where a causal hypothesis is clear and has already been confirmed by cross-case analysis, researchers are well advised to focus on a case where the causal effect of X_1 on Y can be isolated from other potentially confounding factors (X_2). I shall call this a *pathway case* to indicate its uniquely penetrating insight into causal mechanisms. In contrast to the crucial case, this sort of method is practicable only in circumstances where cross-case covariational patterns are well studied and where the mechanism linking X_1 and Y remains dim. Because the pathway case builds on prior cross-case analysis, the problem of case selection must be situated within that sample. There is no standalone pathway case.

The logic of the pathway case is clearest in situations of causal sufficiency—where a causal factor of interest, X_1, is sufficient by itself (though perhaps not necessary) to account for Y's value (o or 1). The other causes of Y, about which we need make no assumptions, are designated as a vector, X_2.

Note that wherever various causal factors are substitutable for one another, each factor is conceptualized (individually) as sufficient (Braumoeller 2003). Thus, situations of causal equifinality presume causal sufficiency on the part of each factor or set of conjoint factors. An example is provided by the literature on democratization, which stipulates three main avenues of regime change: leadership-initiated reform, a controlled opening to opposition, or the collapse of an authoritarian regime (Colomer 1991). The case-study format constrains us to analyze one at a time, so let us limit our scope to the first one—leadership-initiated reform. So considered, a causal-pathway case would be one with the following features: (a) democratization, (b) leadership-initiated reform, (c) no controlled opening to the opposition, (d) no collapse of the previous authoritarian regime, and (e) no other extraneous factors that might affect the process of democratization. In a case of this type, the causal mechanisms by which leadership-initiated reform may lead to democratization will be easiest to study. Note that it is not necessary to assume that leadership-initiated reform *always* leads to democratization; it may or may not be a deterministic cause. But it is necessary to assume that leadership-initiated reform can *sometimes* lead to democratization on its own (given certain background features).

Now let us move from these examples to a general-purpose model. For heuristic purposes, let us presume that all variables in that model are dichotomous (coded as o or 1) and that the model is complete (all causes of Y are included). All causal relationships will be coded so as to be positive: X_1 and Y covary as do X_2 and Y. This allows us to visualize a range of possible combinations at a glance.

Recall that the pathway case is always focused, by definition, on a single causal factor, denoted X_1. (The researcher's focus may shift to other causal factors, but may only focus on one causal factor at a time.) In this scenario, and regardless of how

Table 28.2. Pathway case with dichotomous causal factors

Case types	X_1	X_2	Y
A	1	1	1
B	0	0	0
C	0	1	1
D	0	0	1
E	1	0	0
F	1	1	0
G	1	0	1
H	0	1	0

Notes: X_1 = the variable of theoretical interest. X_2 = a vector of controls (a score of 0 indicates that all control variables have a score of 0, while a score of 1 indicates that all control variables have a score of 1). Y = the outcome of interest. A–H = case types (the N for each case type is indeterminate). G, H = possible pathway cases. Sample size = indeterminate.

Assumptions: (a) all variables can be coded dichotomously (a binary coding of the concept is valid); (b) all independent variables are positively correlated with Y in the general case; (c) X_1 is (at least sometimes) a sufficient cause of Y.

many additional causes of Y there might be (denoted X_2, a vector of controls), there are only eight *relevant* case types, as illustrated in Table 28.2. Identifying these case types is a relatively simple matter, and can be accomplished in a small-N sample by the construction of a truth-table (modeled after Table 28.2) or in a large-N sample by the use of cross-tabs.

Note that the total number of combinations of values depends on the number of control variables, which we have represented with a single vector, X_2. If this vector consists of a single variable then there are only eight case types. If this vector consists of two variables (X_{2a}, X_{2b}) then the total number of possible combinations increases from eight (2^3) to sixteen (2^4). And so forth. However, none of these combinations is relevant for present purposes except those where X_{2a} and X_{2b} have the *same value* (0 or 1). "Mixed" cases are not causal pathway cases, for reasons that should become clear.

The pathway case, following the logic of the crucial case, is one where the causal factor of interest, X_1, correctly predicts Y while all other possible causes of Y (represented by the vector, X_2) make "wrong" predictions. If X_1 is—at least in some circumstances—a sufficient cause of Y, then it is these sorts of cases that should be most useful for tracing causal mechanisms. There are only two such cases in Table 28.2—G and H. In all other cases, the mechanism running from X_1 to Y would be difficult to discern either because X_1 and Y are not correlated in the usual way (constituting an unusual case, in the terms of our hypothesis) or because other confounding factors (X_2) intrude. In case A, for example, the positive value on Y

could be a product of X_1 or X_2. An in-depth examination of this case is not likely to be very revealing.

Keep in mind that because the researcher already knows from her cross-case examination what the general causal relationships are, she knows (prior to the case-study investigation) what constitutes a correct or incorrect prediction. In the crucial-case method, by contrast, these expectations are deductive rather than empirical. This is what differentiates the two methods. And this is why the causal pathway case is useful principally for elucidating causal mechanisms rather than verifying or falsifying general propositions (which are already more or less apparent from the cross-case evidence). Of course, we must leave open the possibility that the investigation of causal mechanisms would invalidate a general claim, if that claim is utterly contingent upon a specific set of causal mechanisms and the case study shows that no such mechanisms are present. However, this is rather unlikely in most social science settings. Usually, the result of such a finding will be a reformulation of the causal processes by which X_1 causes Y—or, alternatively, a realization that the case under investigation is aberrant (atypical of the general population of cases).

Sometimes, the research question is framed as a unidirectional cause: one is interested in why 0 becomes 1 (or vice versa) but not in why 1 becomes 0. In our previous example, we asked why democracies fail, *not* why countries become democratic or authoritarian. So framed, there can be only one type of causal-pathway case. (Whether regime failure is coded as 0 or 1 is a matter of taste.) Where researchers are interested in bidirectional causality—a movement from 0 to 1 as well as from 1 to 0—there are two possible causal-pathway cases, G and H. In practice, however, one of these case types is almost always more useful than the other. Thus, it seems reasonable to employ the term "pathway case" in the singular. In order to determine which of these two case types will be more useful for intensive analysis the researcher should look to see whether each case type exhibits desirable features such as: (a) a rare (unusual) value on X_1 or Y (designated "extreme" in our previous discussion), (b) observable temporal variation in X_1, (c) an X_1/Y relationship that is easier to study (it has more visible features; it is more transparent), or (d) a lower residual (thus indicating a more typical case, within the terms of the general model). Usually, the choice between G and H is intuitively obvious.

Now, let us consider a scenario in which all (or most) variables of concern to the model are continuous, rather than dichotomous. Here, the job of case selection is considerably more complex, for causal "sufficiency" (in the usual sense) cannot be invoked. It is no longer plausible to assume that a given cause can be entirely partitioned, i.e. rival factors eliminated. However, the search for a pathway case may still be viable. What we are looking for in this scenario is a case that satisfies two criteria: (1) it is not an outlier (or at least not an extreme outlier) in the general model and (2) its score on the outcome (Y) is strongly influenced by the theoretical variable of interest (X_1), taking all other factors into account (X_2). In this sort of case it should be easiest to "see" the causal mechanisms that lie between X_1 and Y.

Achieving the second desiderata requires a bit of manipulation. In order to determine which (nonoutlier) cases are most strongly affected by X_1, given all the other parameters in the model, one must compare the size of the residuals for each case in a reduced form model, $Y = \text{Constant} + X_2 + \text{Res}_{\text{reduced}}$, with the size of the residuals for each case in a full model, $Y = \text{Constant} + X_2 + X_1 + \text{Res}_{\text{full}}$. The pathway case is that case, or set of cases, which shows the greatest difference between the residual for the reduced-form model and the full model (ΔResidual). Thus,

$$\text{Pathway} = |\text{Res}_{\text{reduced}} - \text{Res}_{\text{full}}|, \text{ if } |\text{Res}_{\text{reduced}}| > |\text{Res}_{\text{full}}|. \tag{1}$$

Note that the residual for a case must be smaller in the full model than in the reduced-form model; otherwise, the addition of the variable of interest (X_1) pulls the case *away* from the regression line. We want to find a case where the addition of X_1 pushes the case towards the regression line, i.e. it helps to "explain" that case.

As an example, let us suppose that we are interested in exploring the effect of mineral wealth on the prospects for democracy in a society. According to a good deal of work on this subject, countries with a bounty of natural resources—particularly oil—are less likely to democratize (or once having undergone a democratic transition, are more likely to revert to authoritarian rule) (Barro 1999; Humphreys 2005; Ross 2001). The cross-country evidence is robust. Yet as is often the case, the causal mechanisms remain rather obscure. In order to better understand this phenomenon it may be worthwhile to exploit the findings of cross-country regression models in order to identify a country whose regime type (i.e. its democracy "score" on some general index) is strongly affected by its natural-research wealth, all other things held constant. An analysis of this sort identifies two countries— the United Arab Emirates and Kuwait—with high Δ Residual values and modest residuals in the full model (signifying that these cases are not outliers). Researchers seeking to explore the effect of oil wealth on regime type might do well to focus on these two cases since their patterns of democracy cannot be well explained by other factors—e.g. economic development, religion, European influence, or ethnic fractionalization. The presence of oil wealth in these countries would appear to have a strong *independent* effect on the prospects for democratization in these cases, an effect that is well modeled by general theory and by the available cross-case evidence.

To reiterate, the logic of causal "elimination" is much more compelling where variables are dichotomous and where causal sufficiency can be assumed (X_1 is sufficient by itself, at least in some circumstances, to cause Y). Where variables are continuous, the strategy of the pathway case is more dubious, for potentially confounding causal factors (X_2) cannot be neatly partitioned. Even so, we have indicated why the selection of a pathway case may be a logical approach to case-study analysis in many circumstances.

The exceptions may be briefly noted. Sometimes, where all variables in a model are dichotomous, there are no pathway cases, i.e. no cases of type G or H (in Table 28.2). This is known as the "empty cell" problem, or a problem of severe causal multicollinearity. The universe of observational data does not always oblige us with cases that allow us to independently test a given hypothesis. Where variables are continuous, the analogous problem is that of a causal variable of interest (X_1) that has only minimal effects on the outcome of interest. That is, its role in the general model is quite minor. In these situations, the only cases that are strongly affected by X_1—if there are any at all—may be extreme outliers, and these sorts of cases are not properly regarded as providing confirmatory evidence for a proposition, for reasons that are abundantly clear by now.

Finally, it should be clarified that the identification of a causal pathway case does not obviate the utility of exploring other cases. One might, for example, want to compare both sorts of potential pathway cases—G *and* H—with each other. Many other combinations suggest themselves. However, this sort of multi-case investigation moves beyond the logic of the causal-pathway case.

8 MOST-SIMILAR CASES

The most-similar method employs a minimum of two cases.[16] In its purest form, the chosen pair of cases is similar in all respects except the variable(s) of interest. If the study is *exploratory* (i.e. hypothesis generating), the researcher looks for cases that differ on the outcome of theoretical interest but are similar on various factors that might have contributed to that outcome, as illustrated in Table 28.3 (A). This is a common form of case selection at the initial stage of research. Often, fruitful analysis begins with an apparent anomaly: two cases are apparently quite similar, and yet demonstrate surprisingly different outcomes. The hope is that intensive study of these cases will reveal one—or at most several—factors that differ across these cases. These differing factors (X_1) are looked upon as putative causes. At this stage, the research may be described by the second diagram in Table 28.3 (B). Sometimes, a researcher begins with a strong hypothesis, in which case her research design is confirmatory (hypothesis testing) from the get-go. That is, she strives to identify cases that exhibit different outcomes, different scores on the factor of interest, and similar scores on all other possible causal factors, as illustrated in the second (hypothesis-testing) diagram in Table 28.3 (B).

The point is that the purpose of a most-similar research design, and hence its basic setup, often changes as a researcher moves from an exploratory to a confirmatory mode of analysis. However, regardless of where one begins, the results, when published, look like a hypothesis-testing research design. Question marks have been removed: (A) becomes (B) in Table 28.3.

As an example, let us consider Leon Epstein's classic study of party cohesion, which focuses on two "most-similar" countries, the United States and Canada. Canada has highly disciplined parties whose members vote together on the floor of the House of

---

[16] Sometimes, the most-similar method is known as the "method of difference," after its inventor (Mill 1843/1872). For later treatments see Cohen and Nagel (1934); Eggan (1954); Gerring (2001, ch. 9); Lijphart (1971; 1975); Meckstroth (1975); Przeworski and Teune (1970); Skocpol and Somers (1980).

Table 28.3. Most-similar analysis with two case types

Case types	X_1	X_2	Y
(A) Hypothesis-generating (Y-centered):			
A	?	0	1
B	?	0	0
(B) Hypothesis-testing (X_1/Y-centered):			
A	1	0	1
B	0	0	0

X_1 = the variable of theoretical interest. X_2 = a vector of controls. Y = the outcome of interest.

Commons while the United States has weak, undisciplined parties, whose members often defect on floor votes in Congress. In explaining these divergent outcomes, persistent over many years, Epstein first discusses possible causal factors that are held more or less constant across the two cases. Both the United States and Canada inherited English political cultures, both have large territories and heterogeneous populations, both are federal, and both have fairly loose party structures with strong regional bases and a weak center. These are the "control" variables. Where they differ is in one constitutional feature: Canada is parliamentary while the United States is presidential. And it is this institutional difference that Epstein identifies as the crucial (differentiating) cause. (For further examples of the most-similar method see Brenner 1976; Hamilton 1977; Lipset 1968; Miguel 2004; Moulder 1977; Posner 2004.)

Several caveats apply to any most-similar analysis (in addition to the usual set of assumptions applying to all case-study analysis). First, each causal factor is understood as having an independent and additive effect on the outcome; there are no "interaction" effects. Second, one must code cases dichotomously (high/low, present/absent). This is straightforward if the underlying variables are also dichotomous (e.g. federal/unitary). However, it is often the case that variables of concern in the model are continuous (e.g. party cohesion). In this setting, the researcher must "dichotomize" the scoring of cases so as to simplify the two-case analysis. (Some flexibility is admissible on the vector of controls (X_2) that are "held constant" across the cases. Nonidentity is tolerable if the deviation runs counter to the predicted hypothesis. For example, Epstein describes both the United States and Canada as having strong regional bases of power, a factor that is probably more significant in recent Canadian history than in recent American history. However, because regional bases of power should lead to weaker parties, rather than stronger parties, this element of nonidentity does not challenge Epstein's conclusions. Indeed, it sets up a most-difficult research scenario, as discussed above.)

In one respect the requirements for case control are not so stringent. Specifically, it is not usually necessary to *measure* control variables (at least not with a high degree of precision) in order to control for them. If two countries can be assumed to have similar cultural heritages one needn't worry about constructing variables to measure that heritage. One can simply assert that, whatever they are, they are more or less constant across the two cases. This is similar to the technique employed in a randomized experiment, where the researcher typically does not attempt to measure all the factors that might affect the causal relationship of interest. She assumes, rather, that these unknown factors have been neutralized across the treatment and control groups by randomization or by the choice of a sample that is internally homogeneous.

The most useful statistical tool for identifying cases for in-depth analysis in a most-similar setting is probably some variety of matching strategy—e.g. exact matching, approximate matching, or propensity-score matching.[17] The product of this procedure is a set of matched cases that can be compared in whatever way the researcher deems appropriate. These are the "most-similar" cases. Rosenbaum and Silber (2001, 223) summarize:

Unlike model-based adjustments, where [individuals] vanish and are replaced by the coefficients of a model, in matching, ostensibly comparable patterns are compared directly, one by one. Modern matching methods involve statistical modeling and combinatorial algorithms, but the end result is a collection of pairs or sets of people who look comparable, at least on average. In matching, people retain their integrity as people, so they can be examined and their stories can be told individually.

Matching, conclude the authors, "facilitates, rather than inhibits, thick description" (Rosenbaum and Silber 2001, 223).

In principle, the same matching techniques that have been used successfully in observational studies of medical treatments might also be adapted to the study of nation states, political parties, cities, or indeed any traditional paired cases in the social sciences. Indeed, the current popularity of matching among statisticians—relative, that is, to garden-variety regression models—rests upon what qualitative researchers would recognize as a "case-based" approach to causal analysis. If Rosenbaum and Silber are correct, it may be perfectly reasonable to appropriate this large-N method of analysis for case-study purposes.

As with other methods of case selection, the most-similar method is prone to problems of nonrepresentativeness. If employed in a qualitative fashion (without a systematic cross-case selection strategy), potential biases in the chosen case must be addressed in a speculative way. If the researcher employs a matching technique of case selection within a large-N sample, the problem of potential bias can be addressed by assuring the choice of cases that are not extreme outliers, as judged by their residuals in the full model. Most-similar cases should also be "typical" cases, though some scope for deviance around the regression line may be acceptable for purposes of finding a good fit among cases.

---

[17] For good introductions see Ho et al. (2004); Morgan and Harding (2005); Rosenbaum (2004); Rosenbaum and Silber (2001). For a discussion of matching procedures in Stata see Abadie et al. (2001).

Table 28.4. Most-different analysis with two cases

Case types	X_1	X_{2a}	X_{2b}	X_{2c}	X_{2d}	Y
A	1	1	0	1	0	1
B	1	0	1	0	1	1

X_1 = the variable of theoretical interest. X_{2a-d} = a vector of controls.
Y = the outcome of interest.

9 MOST-DIFFERENT CASES

A final case-selection method is the reverse image of the previous method. Here, variation on independent variables is prized, while variation on the outcome is eschewed. Rather than looking for cases that are most-similar, one looks for cases that are *most-different*. Specifically, the researcher tries to identify cases where just one independent variable (X_1), as well as the dependent variable (Y), covary, while all other plausible factors (X_{2a-d}) show different values.[18]

The simplest form of this two-case comparison is illustrated in Table 28.4. Cases A and B are deemed "most different," though they are similar in two essential respects—the causal variable of interest and the outcome.

As an example, I follow Marc Howard's (2003) recent work, which explores the enduring impact of Communism on civil society.[19] Cross-national surveys show a strong correlation between former Communist regimes and low social capital, controlling for a variety of possible confounders. It is a strong result. Howard wonders why this relationship is so strong and why it persists, and perhaps even strengthens, in countries that are no longer socialist or authoritarian. In order to answer this question, he focuses on two most-different cases, Russia and East Germany. These two countries were quite different—in all ways *other than* their Communist experience—prior to the Soviet era, during the Soviet era (since East Germany received substantial subsidies from West Germany), and in the post-Soviet era, as East Germany was absorbed into West Germany. Yet, they both score near the bottom of various cross-national indices intended to measure the prevalence of civic engagement in the current era. Thus, Howard's (2003, 6–9) case selection procedure meets the requirements of the most-different research design: Variance is found on all (or most) dimensions

---

[18] The most-different method is also sometimes referred to as the "method of agreement," following its inventor, J. S. Mill (1843/1872). See also DeFelice (1986); Gerring (2001, 212–14); Lijphart (1971; 1975); Meckstroth (1975); Przeworski and Teune (1970); Skocpol and Somers (1980). For examples of this method see Collier and Collier (1991/2002); Converse and Dupeux (1962); Karl (1997); Moore (1966); Skocpol (1979); Yashar (2005, 23). However, most of these studies are described as *combining* most-similar and most-different methods.

[19] In the following discussion I treat the terms social capital, civil society, and civic engagement interchangeably.

aside from the key factor of interest (Communism) and the outcome (civic engagement).

What leverage is brought to the analysis from this approach? Howard's case studies combine evidence drawn from mass surveys and from in-depth interviews of small, stratified samples of Russians and East Germans. (This is a good illustration, incidentally, of how quantitative and qualitative evidence can be fruitfully combined in the intensive study of several cases.) The product of this analysis is the identification of three causal pathways that, Howard (2003, 122) claims, help to explain the laggard status of civil society in post-Communist polities: "the mistrust of communist organizations, the persistence of friendship networks, and the disappointment with post-communism." Simply put, Howard (2003, 145) concludes, "a great number of citizens in Russia and Eastern Germany feel a strong and lingering sense of distrust of any kind of public organization, a general satisfaction with their own personal networks (accompanied by a sense of deteriorating relations within society overall), and disappointment in the developments of post-communism."

The strength of this most-different case analysis is that the results obtained in East Germany and Russia should also apply in other post-Communist polities (e.g. Lithuania, Poland, Bulgaria, Albania). By choosing a heterogeneous sample, Howard solves the problem of representativeness in his restricted sample. However, this sample is demonstrably *not* representative across the population of the inference, which is intended to cover all countries of the world.

More problematic is the lack of variation on key causal factors of interest— Communism and its putative causal pathways. For this reason, it is difficult to reach conclusions about the causal status of these factors on the basis of the most-different analysis alone. It is possible, that is, that the three causal pathways identified by Howard also operate within polities that never experienced Communist rule.

Nor does it seem possible to conclusively eliminate rival hypotheses on the basis of this most-different analysis. Indeed, this is not Howard's intention. He wishes merely to show that whatever influence on civil society might be attributed to economic, cultural, and other factors does not exhaust this subject.

My considered judgment is that the most-different research design provides minimal leverage into the problem of why Communist systems appear to suppress civic engagement, years after their disappearance. Fortunately, this is not the only research design employed by Howard in his admirable study. Indeed, the author employs two other small-N cross-case methods, as well as a large-N cross-country statistical analysis. These methods do most of the analytic work. East Germany may be regarded as a causal pathway case (see above). It has all the attributes normally assumed to foster civic engagement (e.g. a growing economy, multiparty competition, civil liberties, a free press, close association with Western European culture and politics), but nonetheless shows little or no improvement on this dimension during the post-transition era (Howard 2003, 8). It is plausible to attribute this lack of change to its Communist past, as Howard does, in which case East Germany should be a fruitful case for the investigation of causal mechanisms. The contrast between East and West Germany provides a most-similar analysis since the two polities share virtually everything except a Communist past. This variation is also deftly exploited by Howard.

I do not wish to dismiss the most-different research method entirely. Surely, Howard's findings are stronger with the intensive analysis of Russia than they would be without. Yet his book would not stand securely on the empirical foundation provided by most-different analysis alone. If one strips away the pathway-case (East Germany) and the most-similar analysis (East/West Germany) there is little left upon which to base an analysis of causal relations (aside from the large-N cross-national analysis). Indeed, most scholars who employ the most-different method do so in conjunction with other methods.[20] It is rarely, if ever, a standalone method.[21]

Generalizing from this discussion of Marc Howard's work, I offer the following summary remarks on the most-different method of case analysis. (I leave aside issues faced by *all* case-study analyses, issues that are explored in Gerring 2007.)

Let us begin with a methodological obstacle that is faced by both Millean styles of analysis—the necessity of dichotomizing every variable in the analysis. Recall that, as with most-similar analysis, differences across cases must generally be sizeable enough to be interpretable in an essentially dichotomous fashion (e.g. high/low, present/absent) and similarities must be close enough to be understood as essentially identical (e.g. high/high, present/present). Otherwise the results of a Millean style analysis are not interpretable. The problem of "degrees" is deadly if the variables under consideration are, by nature, continuous (e.g. GDP). This is a particular concern in Howard's analysis, where East Germany scores somewhat higher than Russia in civic engagement; they are both low, but Russia is quite a bit lower. Howard assumes that this divergence is minimal enough to be understood as a difference of degrees rather than of kinds, a judgment that might be questioned. In these respects, most-different analysis is no more secure—but also no less—than most-similar analysis.

In one respect, most-different analysis is superior to most-similar analysis. If the coding assumptions are sound, the most-different research design may be quite useful for *eliminating necessary causes*. Causal factors that do not appear across the chosen cases—e.g. X_{2a-d} in Table 28.4—are evidently unnecessary for the production of Y. However, it does not follow that the most-different method is the *best* method for eliminating necessary causes. Note that the defining feature of this method is the

---

[20] E.g. Collier and Collier (1991/2002); Karl (1997); Moore (1966); Skocpol (1979); Yashar (2005, 23). Karl (1997), which affects to be a most-different system analysis (20), is a particularly clear example of this. Her study, focused ostensibly on petro-states (states with large oil reserves), makes two sorts of inferences. The first concerns the (usually) obstructive role of oil in political and economic development. The second sort of inference concerns variation *within* the population of petro-states, showing that some countries (e.g. Norway, Indonesia) manage to avoid the pathologies brought on elsewhere by oil resources. When attempting to explain the constraining role of oil on petro-states, Karl usually relies on contrasts between petro-states and nonpetro-states (e.g. ch. 10). Only when attempting to explain differences among petro-states does she restrict her sample to petro-states. In my opinion, very little use is made of the most-different research design.

[21] This was recognized, at least implicitly, by Mill (1843/1872, 258–9). Skepticism has been echoed by methodologists in the intervening years (e.g. Cohen and Nagel 1934, 251–6; Gerring 2001; Skocpol and Somers 1980). Indeed, explicit defenses of the most-different method are rare (but see DeFelice 1986).

shared element across cases—X_1 in Table 28.4. This feature does not help one to eliminate necessary causes. Indeed, if one were focused solely on eliminating necessary causes one would presumably seek out cases that register the same outcomes and have maximum diversity on other attributes. In Table 28.4, this would be a set of cases that satisfy conditions X_{2a-d}, but not X_1. Thus, even the presumed strength of the most-different analysis is not so strong.

Usually, case-study analysis is focused on the identification (or clarification) of causal relations, not the elimination of possible causes. In this setting, the most-different technique is useful, but only if assumptions of causal uniqueness hold. By "causal uniqueness," I mean a situation in which a given outcome is the product of only one cause: Y cannot occur except in the presence of X. X is necessary, and in some situations (given certain background conditions) sufficient, to cause Y.[22]

Consider the following hypothetical example. Suppose that a new disease, about which little is known, has appeared in Country A. There are hundreds of infected persons across dozens of affected communities in that country. In Country B, located at the other end of the world, several new cases of the disease surface in a single community. In this setting, we can imagine two sorts of Millean analyses. The first examines two similar communities within Country A, one of which has developed the disease and the other of which has not. This is the most-similar style of case comparison, and focuses accordingly on the identification of a difference between the two cases that might account for variation across the sample. A second approach focuses on communities where the disease has appeared across the two countries and searches for any similarities that might account for these similar outcomes. This is the most-different research design.

Both are plausible approaches to this particular problem, and we can imagine epidemiologists employing them simultaneously. However, the most-different design demands stronger assumptions about the underlying factors at work. It supposes that the disease arises from the *same cause* in any setting. This is often a reasonable operating assumption when one is dealing with natural phenomena, though there are certainly many exceptions. Death, for example, has many causes. For this reason, it would not occur to us to look for most-different cases of high mortality around the world. In order for the most-different research design to effectively identify a causal factor at work in a given outcome, the researcher must assume that X_1—the factor held constant across the diverse cases—is the only possible cause of Y (see Table 28.4). This assumption rarely holds in social-scientific settings. Most outcomes of interest to anthropologists, economists, political scientists, and sociologists have *multiple* causes. There are many ways to win an election, to build a welfare state, to get into a war, to overthrow a government, or—returning to Marc Howard's work—to build a strong civil society. And it is for this reason that most-different analysis is rarely applied in social science work and, where applied, is rarely convincing.

If this seems a tad severe, there is a more charitable way of approaching the most-different method. Arguably, this is not a pure "method" at all but merely a

---

[22] Another way of stating this is to say that X is a "nontrivial necessary condition" of Y.

supplement, a way of incorporating diversity in the sub-sample of cases that provide the unusual outcome of interest. If the unusual outcome is revolutions, one might wish to encompass a wide variety of revolutions in one's analysis. If the unusual outcome is post-Communist civil society, it seems appropriate to include a diverse set of post-Communist polities in one's sample of case studies, as Marc Howard does. From this perspective, the most-different method (so-called) might be better labeled a *diverse-case* method, as explored above.

10 Conclusions

In order to be a case of something broader than itself, the chosen case must be representative (in some respects) of a larger population. Otherwise—if it is purely idiosyncratic ("unique")—it is uninformative about anything lying outside the borders of the case itself. A study based on a nonrepresentative sample has no (or very little) external validity. To be sure, no phenomenon is purely idiosyncratic; the notion of a unique case is a matter that would be difficult to define. One is concerned, as always, with matters of degree. Cases are *more or less* representative of some broader phenomenon and, on that score, may be considered better or worse subjects for intensive analysis. (The one exception, as noted, is the influential case.)

Of all the problems besetting case-study analysis, perhaps the most persistent— and the most persistently bemoaned—is the problem of sample bias (Achen and Snidal 1989; Collier and Mahoney 1996; Geddes 1990; King, Keohane, and Verba 1994; Rohlfing 2004; Sekhon 2004). Lisa Martin (1992, 5) finds that the overemphasis of international relations scholars on a few well-known cases of economic sanctions— most of which failed to elicit any change in the sanctioned country—"has distorted analysts' view of the dynamics and characteristics of economic sanctions." Barbara Geddes (1990) charges that many analyses of industrial policy have focused exclusively on the most successful cases—primarily the East Asian NICs—leading to biased inferences. Anna Breman and Carolyn Shelton (2001) show that case-study work on the question of structural adjustment is systematically biased insofar as researchers tend to focus on disaster cases—those where structural adjustment is associated with very poor health and human development outcomes. These cases, often located in sub-Saharan Africa, are by no means representative of the entire population. Consequently, scholarship on the question of structural adjustment is highly skewed in a particular ideological direction (against neoliberalism) (see also Gerring, Thacker, and Moreno 2005).

These examples might be multiplied many times. Indeed, for many topics the most-studied cases are acknowledged to be less than representative. It is worth reflecting upon the fact that our knowledge of the world is heavily colored by a few "big" (populous, rich, powerful) countries, and that a good portion of the disciplines of economics, political science, and sociology are built upon scholars' familiarity with the economics, political science, and sociology of one country, the United States.[23] Case-study work is particularly prone to problems of investigator bias since so much rides on the researcher's selection of one (or a few) cases. Even if the investigator is unbiased, her sample may still be biased simply by virtue of "random" error (which may be understood as measurement error, error in the data-generation process, or as an underlying causal feature of the universe).

There are only two situations in which a case-study researcher need not be concerned with the representativeness of her chosen case. The first is the influential case research design, where a case is chosen because of its possible influence on a cross-case model, and hence is not expected to be representative of a larger sample. The second is the deviant-case method, where the chosen case is employed to confirm a broader cross-case argument to which the case stands as an apparent exception. Yet even here the chosen case is expected to be representative of a broader set of cases—those, in particular, that are poorly explained by the extant model.

In all other circumstances, cases must be representative of the population of interest in whatever ways might be relevant to the proposition in question. Note that where a researcher is attempting to disconfirm a deterministic proposition the question of representativeness is perhaps more appropriately understood as a question of classification: Is the chosen case appropriately classified as a member of the designated population? If so, then it is fodder for a disconfirming case study.

If the researcher is attempting to confirm a deterministic proposition, or to make probabilistic arguments about a causal relationship, then the problem of representativeness is of the more usual sort: Is case A unit-homogeneous relative to other cases in the population? This is not an easy matter to test. However, in a large-N context the residual for that case (in whatever model the researcher has greatest confidence in) is a reasonable place to start. Of course, this test is only as good as the model at hand. Any incorrect specifications or incorrect modeling procedures will likely bias the results and give an incorrect assessment of each case's "typicality." In addition, there is the possibility of stochastic error, errors that cannot be modeled in a general framework. Given the explanatory weight that individual cases are asked to bear in a case-study analysis, it is wise to consider more than just the residual test of representativeness. Deductive logic and an in-depth knowledge of the case in question are often more reliable tools than the results of a cross-case model.

In any case, there is no dispensing with the question. Case studies (with the two exceptions already noted) rest upon an assumed synecdoche: The case should stand for a population. If this is not true, or if there is reason to doubt this assumption, then the utility of the case study is brought severely into question.

Fortunately, there is some safety in numbers. Insofar as case-study evidence is combined with cross-case evidence the issue of sample bias is mitigated. Indeed, the suspicion of case-study work that one finds in the social sciences today is, in my view, a product of a too-literal interpretation of the case-study method. A case study *tout*

---

[23] Wahlke (1979, 13) writes of the failings of the "behavioralist" mode of political science analysis: "It rarely aims at generalization; research efforts have been confined essentially to case studies of single political systems, most of them dealing . . . with the American system."

court is thought to mean a case study *tout seul*. Insofar as case studies and cross-case studies can be enlisted within the same investigation (either in the same study or by reference to other studies in the same subfield), problems of representativeness are less worrisome. This is the virtue of cross-level work, a.k.a. "triangulation."

11 AMBIGUITIES

Before concluding, I wish to draw attention to two ambiguities in case-selection strategies in case-study research. The first concerns the admixture of several case-selection strategies. The second concerns the changing status of a case as a study proceeds.

Some case studies follow only one strategy of case selection. They are *typical, diverse, extreme, deviant, influential, crucial, pathway, most-similar*, or *most-different* research designs, as discussed. However, many case studies mix and match among these case-selection strategies. Indeed, insofar as all case studies seek representative samples, they are always in search of "typical" cases. Thus, it is common for writers to declare that their case is, for example, both extreme and typical; it has an extreme value on X_1 or Y but is not, in other respects, idiosyncratic. There is not much that one can say about these combinations of strategies except that, where the cases allow for a variety of empirical strategies, there is no reason not to pursue them. And where the same cases can serve several functions at once (without further effort on the researcher's part), there is little cost to a multi-pronged approach to case analysis.

The second issue that deserves emphasis is the changing status of a case during the course of a researcher's investigation—which may last for years, if not decades. The problem is acute wherever a researcher begins in an exploratory mode and proceeds to hypothesis-testing (that is, she develops a specific X_1/Y proposition) or where the operative hypothesis or key control variable changes (a new causal factor is discovered or another outcome becomes the focus of analysis). Things change. And it is the mark of a good researcher to keep her mind open to new evidence and new insights. Too often, methodological discussions give the misleading impression that hypotheses are clear and remain fixed over the course of a study's development. Nothing could be further from the truth. The unofficial transcripts of academia—accessible in informal settings, where researchers let their guards down (particularly if inebriated)—are filled with stories about dead-ends, unexpected findings, and drastically revised theory chapters. It would be interesting, in this vein, to compare published work with dissertation prospectuses and fellowship applications. I doubt if the correlation between these two stages of research is particularly strong.

Research, after all, is about discovery, not simply the verification or falsification of static hypotheses. That said, it is also true that research on a particular topic should move from hypothesis generating to hypothesis-testing. This marks the progress of a field, and of a scholar's own work. As a rule, research that begins with an open-ended (X- or Y-centered) analysis should conclude with a determinate X_1/Y hypothesis.

The problem is that research strategies that are ideal for exploration are not always ideal for confirmation. The extreme-case method is inherently exploratory since there is no clear causal hypothesis; the researcher is concerned merely to explore variation on a single dimension (X or Y). Other methods can be employed in either an open-ended (exploratory) or a hypothesis-testing (confirmatory/disconfirmatory) mode. The difficulty is that once the researcher has arrived at a determinate hypothesis the originally chosen research design may no longer appear to be so well designed.

This is unfortunate, but inevitable. One cannot construct the perfect research design until (a) one has a specific hypothesis and (b) one is reasonably certain about what one is going to find "out there" in the empirical world. This is particularly true of observational research designs, but it also applies to many experimental research designs: Usually, there is a "good" (informative) finding, and a finding that is less insightful. In short, the perfect case-study research design is usually apparent only *ex post facto*.

There are three ways to handle this. One can explain, straightforwardly, that the initial research was undertaken in an exploratory fashion, and therefore not constructed to test the specific hypothesis that is—now—the primary argument. Alternatively, one can try to redesign the study after the new (or revised) hypothesis has been formulated. This may require additional field research or perhaps the integration of additional cases or variables that can be obtained through secondary sources or through consultation of experts. A final approach is to simply jettison, or de-emphasize, the portion of research that no longer addresses the (revised) key hypothesis. A three-case study may become a two-case study, and so forth. Lost time and effort are the costs of this downsizing.

In the event, practical considerations will probably determine which of these three strategies, or combinations of strategies, is to be followed. (They are not mutually exclusive.) The point to remember is that revision of one's cross-case research design is *normal* and perhaps to be expected. Not all twists and turns on the meandering trail of truth can be anticipated.

12 Are There Other Methods of Case Selection?

At the outset of this chapter I summarized the task of case selection as a matter of achieving two objectives: representativeness (typicality) and variation (causal leverage). Evidently, there are other objectives as well. For example, one wishes to identify cases that are *independent* of each other. If chosen cases are affected by each other (sometimes known as Galton's problem or a problem of diffusion), this problem must be corrected before analysis can take place. I have neglected this issue because it is usually apparent to the researcher and, in any case, there are no simple techniques that might be utilized to correct for such biases. (For further discussion of this and other factors impinging upon case selection see Gerring 2001, 178–81.)

I have also disregarded *pragmatic/logistical* issues that might affect case selection. Evidently, case selection is often influenced by a researcher's familiarity with the language of a country, a personal entrée into that locale, special access to important data, or funding that covers one archive rather than another. Pragmatic considerations are often—and quite rightly—decisive in the case-selection process.

A final consideration concerns the *theoretical prominence* of a particular case within the literature on a subject. Researchers are sometimes obliged to study cases that have received extensive attention in previous studies. These are sometimes referred to as "paradigmatic" cases or "exemplars" (Flyvbjerg 2004, 427).

However, neither pragmatic/logistical utility nor theoretical prominence qualifies as a *methodological* factor in case selection. That is, these features of a case have no bearing on the validity of the findings stemming from a study. As such, it is appropriate to grant these issues a peripheral status in this chapter.

One final caveat must be issued. While it is traditional to distinguish among the tasks of case selection and case analysis, a close look at these processes shows them to be indistinct and overlapping. One cannot choose a case without considering the sort of analysis that it might be subjected to, and vice versa. Thus, the reader should consider choosing cases by employing the nine techniques laid out in this chapter *along with* any considerations that might be introduced by virtue of a case's quasi-experimental qualities, a topic taken up elsewhere (Gerring 2007, ch. 6).

References

ABADIE, A., DRUKKER, D., HERR, J. L., and IMBENS, G. W. 2001. Implementing matching estimators for average treatment effects in Stata. *Stata Journal*, 1: 1–18.

ABBOTT, A. 2001. *Time Matters: On Theory and Method*. Chicago: University of Chicago Press.

——and TSAY, A. 2000. Sequence analysis and optimal matching methods in sociology. *Sociological Methods and Research*, 29: 3–33.

——and FORREST, J. 1986. Optimal matching methods for historical sequences. *Journal of Interdisciplinary History*, 16: 471–94.

ACHEN, C. H., and SNIDAL, D. 1989. Rational deterrence theory and comparative case studies. *World Politics*, 41: 143–69.

ALLEN, W. S. 1965. *The Nazi Seizure of Power: The Experience of a Single German Town, 1930–1935*. New York: Watts.

ALMOND, G. A. 1956. Comparative political systems. *Journal of Politics*, 18: 391–409.

AMENTA, E. 1991. Making the most of a case study: theories of the welfare state and the American experience. Pp. 172–94 in *Issues and Alternatives in Comparative Social Research*, ed. C. C. Ragin. Leiden: E. J. Brill.

BARRO, R. J. 1999. Determinants of democracy. *Journal of Political Economy*, 107: 158–83.

BELSEY, D. A., KUH, E., and WELSCH, R. E. 2004. *Regression Diagnostics: Identifying Influential Data and Sources of Collinearity*. New York: Wiley.

BENNETT, A., LEPGOLD, J., and UNGER, D. 1994. Burden-sharing in the Persian Gulf War. *International Organization*, 48: 39–75.

BENTLEY, A. 1908/1967. *The Process of Government*. Cambridge, Mass.: Harvard University Press.

BRADY, H. E., and COLLIER, D. (eds.) 2004. *Rethinking Social Inquiry: Diverse Tools, Shared Standards*. Lanham, Md.: Rowman and Littlefield.

BRAUMOELLER, B. F. 2003. Causal complexity and the study of politics. *Political Analysis*, 11: 209–33.

BREMAN, A., and SHELTON, C. 2001. Structural adjustment and health: a literature review of the debate, its role-players and presented empirical evidence. CMH Working Paper Series, Paper No. WG6: 6. WHO, Commission on Macroeconomics and Health.

BRENNER, R. 1976. Agrarian class structure and economic development in pre-industrial Europe. *Past and Present*, 70: 30–75.

BROWNE, A. 1987. *When Battered Women Kill*. New York: Free Press.

BUCHBINDER, S., and VITTINGHOFF, E. 1999. HIV-infected long-term nonprogressors: epidemiology, mechanisms of delayed progression, and clinical and research implications. *Microbes Infect*, 1: 1113–20.

COHEN, M. R., and NAGEL, E. 1934. *An Introduction to Logic and Scientific Method*. New York: Harcourt, Brace and Company.

COLLIER, D., and MAHONEY, J. 1996. Insights and pitfalls: selection bias in qualitative research. *World Politics*, 49: 56–91.

COLLIER, R. B., and COLLIER, D. 1991/2002. *Shaping the Political Arena: Critical Junctures, the Labor Movement, and Regime Dynamics in Latin America*. Notre Dame, Ind.: University of Notre Dame Press.

COLOMER, J. M. 1991. Transitions by agreement: modeling the Spanish way. *American Political Science Review*, 85: 1283–302.

CONVERSE, P. E., and DUPEUX, G. 1962. Politicization of the electorate in France and the United States. *Public Opinion Quarterly*, 16: 1–23.

COPPEDGE, M. J. 2004. The conditional impact of the economy on democracy in Latin America. Presented at the conference "Democratic Advancements and Setbacks: What Have We Learnt?", Uppsala University, June 11–13.

DEFELICE, E. G. 1986. Causal inference and comparative methods. *Comparative Political Studies*, 19: 415–37.

DESCH, M. C. 2002. Democracy and victory: why regime type hardly matters. *International Security*, 27: 5–47.

DEYO, F. (ed.) 1987. *The Political Economy of the New Asian Industrialism*. Ithaca, NY: Cornell University Press.

DION, D. 1998. Evidence and inference in the comparative case study. *Comparative Politics*, 30: 127–45.

ECKSTEIN, H. 1975. Case studies and theory in political science. In *Handbook of Political Science*, vii: *Political Science: Scope and Theory*, ed. F. I. Greenstein and N. W. Polsby. Reading, Mass.: Addison-Wesley.

EGGAN, F. 1954. Social anthropology and the method of controlled comparison. *American Anthropologist*, 56: 743–63.

ELMAN, C. 2003. Lessons from Lakatos. In *Progress in International Relations Theory: Appraising the Field*, ed. C. Elman and M. F. Elman. Cambridge, Mass.: MIT Press.

—— 2005. Explanatory typologies in qualitative studies of international politics. *International Organization*, 59: 293–326.

EMIGH, R. 1997. The power of negative thinking: the use of negative case methodology in the development of sociological theory. *Theory and Society*, 26: 649–84.

EPSTEIN, L. D. 1964. A comparative study of Canadian parties. *American Political Science Review*, 58: 46–59.

ERTMAN, T. 1997. *Birth of the Leviathan: Building States and Regimes in Medieval and Early Modern Europe*. Cambridge: Cambridge University Press.

ESPING-ANDERSEN, G. 1990. *The Three Worlds of Welfare Capitalism*. Princeton, NJ: Princeton University Press.

FLYVBJERG, B. 2004. Five misunderstandings about case-study research. Pp. 420–34 in *Qualitative Research Practice*, ed. C. Seale, G. Gobo, J. F. Gubrium, and D. Silverman. London: Sage.

GEDDES, B. 1990. How the cases you choose affect the answers you get: selection bias in comparative politics. In *Political Analysis*, vol. ii, ed. J. A. Stimson. Ann Arbor: University of Michigan Press.

—— 2003. *Paradigms and Sand Castles: Theory Building and Research Design in Comparative Politics*. Ann Arbor: University of Michigan Press.

GEORGE, A. L., and BENNETT, A. 2005. *Case Studies and Theory Development*. Cambridge, Mass.: MIT Press.

—— and SMOKE, R. 1974. *Deterrence in American Foreign Policy: Theory and Practice*. New York: Columbia University Press.

GERRING, J. 2001. *Social Science Methodology: A Criterial Framework*. Cambridge: Cambridge University Press.

—— 2007. *Case Study Research: Principles and Practices*. Cambridge: Cambridge University Press.

—— THACKER, S., and MORENO, C. 2005. Do neoliberal policies save lives? Unpublished manuscript.

GOERTZ, G., and STARR, H. (eds.) 2003. *Necessary Conditions: Theory, Methodology and Applications*. New York: Rowman and Littlefield.

—— and LEVY, J. (eds.) forthcoming. Causal explanations, necessary conditions, and case studies: World War I and the end of the Cold War. Manuscript.

GOODIN, R. E., and SMITSMAN, A. 2000. Placing welfare states: the Netherlands as a crucial test case. *Journal of Comparative Policy Analysis*, 2: 39–64.

GUJARATI, D. N. 2003. *Basic Econometrics*, 4th edn. New York: McGraw-Hill.

HAMILTON, G. G. 1977. Chinese consumption of foreign commodities: a comparative perspective. *American Sociological Review*, 42: 877–91.

HAYNES, B. F., PANTALEO, G., and FAUCI, A. S. 1996. Toward an understanding of the correlates of protective immunity to HIV infection. *Science*, 271: 324–8.

HEMPEL, C. G. 1942. The function of general laws in history. *Journal of Philosophy*, 39: 35–48.

HO, D. E., IMAI, K., KING, G., and STUART, E. A. 2004. Matching as nonparametric preprocessing for reducing model dependence in parametric causal inference. Manuscript.

HOWARD, M. M. 2003. *The Weakness of Civil Society in Post-Communist Europe*. Cambridge: Cambridge University Press.

Howson, C., and Urbach, P. 1989. *Scientific Reasoning: The Bayesian Approach*. La Salle, Ill.: Open Court.

Humphreys, M. 2005. Natural resources, conflict, and conflict resolution: uncovering the mechanisms. *Journal of Conflict Resolution*, 49: 508–37.

Jenicek, M. 2001. *Clinical Case Reporting in Evidence-Based Medicine*, 2nd edn. Oxford: Oxford University Press.

Karl, T. L. 1997. *The Paradox of Plenty: Oil Booms and Petro-states*. Berkeley: University of California Press.

Kazancigil, A. 1994. The deviant case in comparative analysis: high stateness in comparative analysis. Pp. 213–38 in *Comparing Nations: Concepts, Strategies, Substance*, ed. M. Dogan and A. Kazancigil. Cambridge: Blackwell.

Kemp, K. A. 1986. Race, ethnicity, class and urban spatial conflict: Chicago as a crucial case. *Urban Studies*, 23: 197–208.

Kendall, P. L., and Wolf, K. M. 1949/1955. The analysis of deviant cases in communications research. In *Communications Research, 1948–1949*, ed. P. F. Lazarsfeld and F. N. Stanton. New York: Harper and Brothers. Reprinted as pp. 167–70 in *The Language of Social Research*, ed. P. F. Lazarsfeld and M. Rosenberg. New York: Free Press.

Kennedy, C. H. 2005. *Single-case Designs for Educational Research*. Boston: Allyn and Bacon.

Kennedy, P. 2003. *A Guide to Econometrics*, 5th edn. Cambridge, Mass.: MIT Press.

Khong, Y. F. 1992. *Analogies at War: Korea, Munich, Dien Bien Phu, and the Vietnam Decisions of 1965*. Princeton, NJ: Princeton University Press.

King, G., Keohane, R. O., and Verba, S. 1994. *Designing Social Inquiry: Scientific Inference in Qualitative Research*. Princeton, NJ: Princeton University Press.

Lakatos, I. 1978. *The Methodology of Scientific Research Programmes*. Cambridge: Cambridge University Press.

Lazarsfeld, P. F., and Barton, A. H. 1951. Qualitative measurement in the social sciences: classification, typologies, and indices. In *The Policy Sciences*, ed. D. Lerner and H. D. Lasswell. Stanford, Calif.: Stanford University Press.

Levy, J. S. 2002. Qualitative methods in international relations. In *Evaluating Methodology in International Studies*, ed. F. P. Harvey and M. Brecher. Ann Arbor: University of Michigan Press.

Lijphart, A. 1968. *The Politics of Accommodation: Pluralism and Democracy in the Netherlands*. Berkeley: University of California Press.

—— 1969. Consociational democracy. *World Politics*, 21: 207–25.

—— 1971. Comparative politics and the comparative method. *American Political Science Review*, 65: 682–93.

—— 1975. The comparable cases strategy in comparative research. *Comparative Political Studies*, 8: 158–77.

Lipset, S. M. 1959. Some social requisites of democracy: economic development and political development. *American Political Science Review*, 53: 69–105.

—— 1960/1963. *Political Man: The Social Bases of Politics*. Garden City, NY: Anchor.

—— 1968. *Agrarian Socialism: The Cooperative Commonwealth Federation in Saskatchewan. A Study in Political Sociology*. Garden City, NY: Doubleday.

—— Trow, M. A., and Coleman, J. S. 1956. *Union Democracy: The Internal Politics of the International Typographical Union*. New York: Free Press.

Lynd, R. S., and Lynd, H. M. 1929/1956. *Middletown: A Study in American Culture*. New York: Harcourt, Brace.

Mahoney, J., and Goertz, G. 2004. The possibility principle: choosing negative cases in comparative research. *American Political Science Review*, 98: 653–69.

MARTIN, L. L. 1992. *Coercive Cooperation: Explaining Multilateral Economic Sanctions.* Princeton, NJ: Princeton University Press.

MAYO, D. G. 1996. *Error and the Growth of Experimental Knowledge.* Chicago: University of Chicago Press.

MECKSTROTH, T. 1975. "Most different systems" and "most similar systems:" a study in the logic of comparative inquiry. *Comparative Political Studies*, 8: 133–77.

MIGUEL, E. 2004. Tribe or nation: nation-building and public goods in Kenya versus Tanzania. *World Politics*, 56: 327–62.

MILL, J. S. 1843/1872. *The System of Logic*, 8th edn. London: Longmans, Green.

MONROE, K. R. 1996. *The Heart of Altruism: Perceptions of a Common Humanity.* Princeton, NJ: Princeton University Press.

MOORE, B., JR. 1966. *Social Origins of Dictatorship and Democracy: Lord and Peasant in the Making of the Modern World.* Boston: Beacon Press.

MORGAN, S. L., and HARDING, D. J. 2005. Matching estimators of causal effects: from stratification and weighting to practical data analysis routines. Manuscript.

MOULDER, F. V. 1977. *Japan, China and the Modern World Economy: Toward a Reinterpretation of East Asian Development ca. 1600 to ca. 1918.* Cambridge: Cambridge University Press.

MUNCK, G. L. 2004. Tools for qualitative research. Pp. 105–21 in *Rethinking Social Inquiry: Diverse Tools, Shared Standards*, ed. H. E. Brady and D. Collier. Lanham, Md.: Rowman and Littlefield.

NJOLSTAD, O. 1990. Learning from history? Case studies and the limits to theory-building. Pp. 220–46 in *Arms Races: Technological and Political Dynamics*, ed. O. Njolstad. Thousand Oaks, Calif.: Sage.

PATTON, M. Q. 2002. *Qualitative Evaluation and Research Methods.* Newbury Park, Calif.: Sage.

POPPER, K. 1934/1968. *The Logic of Scientific Discovery.* New York: Harper and Row.

—— 1963. *Conjectures and Refutations.* London: Routledge and Kegan Paul.

POSNER, D. 2004. The political salience of cultural difference: why Chewas and Tumbukas are allies in Zambia and adversaries in Malawi. *American Political Science Review*, 98: 529–46.

PRZEWORSKI, A., and TEUNE, H. 1970. *The Logic of Comparative Social Inquiry.* New York: John Wiley.

QUEEN, S. 1928. Round table on the case study in sociological research. *Publications of the American Sociological Society, Papers and Proceedings*, 22: 225–7.

RAGIN, C. C. 2000. *Fuzzy-set Social Science.* Chicago: University of Chicago Press.

—— 2004. Turning the tables. Pp. 123–38 in *Rethinking Social Inquiry: Diverse Tools, Shared Standards*, ed. H. E. Brady and D. Collier. Lanham, Md.: Rowman and Littlefield.

REILLY, B. 2000–1. Democracy, ethnic fragmentation, and internal conflict: confused theories, faulty data, and the "crucial case" of Papua New Guinea. *International Security*, 25: 162–85.

—— and PHILLPOT, R. 2003. "Making democracy work" in Papua New Guinea: social capital and provincial development in an ethnically fragmented society. *Asian Survey*, 42: 906–27.

ROGOWSKI, R. 1995. The role of theory and anomaly in social-scientific inference. *American Political Science Review*, 89: 467–70.

ROHLFING, I. 2004. Have you chosen the right case? Uncertainty in case selection for single case studies. Working Paper, International University, Bremen.

ROSENBAUM, P. R. 2004. Matching in observational studies. In *Applied Bayesian Modeling and Causal Inference from an Incomplete-data Perspective*, ed. A. Gelman and X.-L. Meng. New York: John Wiley.

—— and SILBER, J. H. 2001. Matching and thick description in an observational study of mortality after surgery. *Biostatistics*, 2: 217–32.

ROSS, M. 2001. Does oil hinder democracy? *World Politics*, 53: 325–61.

SAGAN, S. D. 1995. *Limits of Safety: Organizations, Accidents, and Nuclear Weapons*. Princeton, NJ: Princeton University Press.

SEKHON, J. S. 2004. Quality meets quantity: case studies, conditional probability and counterfactuals. *Perspectives in Politics*, 2: 281–93.

SHAFER, M. D. 1988. *Deadly Paradigms: The Failure of U.S. Counterinsurgency Policy*. Princeton, NJ: Princeton University Press.

SKOCPOL, T. 1979. *States and Social Revolutions: A Comparative Analysis of France, Russia, and China*. Cambridge: Cambridge University Press.

—— and SOMERS, M. 1980. The uses of comparative history in macrosocial inquiry. *Comparative Studies in Society and History*, 22: 147–97.

STINCHCOMBE, A. L. 1968. *Constructing Social Theories*. New York: Harcourt, Brace.

SWANK, D. H. 2002. *Global Capital, Political Institutions, and Policy Change in Developed Welfare States*. Cambridge: Cambridge University Press.

TENDLER, J. 1997. *Good Government in the Tropics*. Baltimore: Johns Hopkins University Press.

TRUMAN, D. B. 1951. *The Governmental Process*. New York: Alfred A. Knopf.

TSAI, L. 2007. *Accountability without Democracy: How Solidary Groups Provide Public Goods in Rural China*. Cambridge: Cambridge University Press.

VAN EVERA, S. 1997. *Guide to Methods for Students of Political Science*. Ithaca, NY: Cornell University Press.

WAHLKE, J. C. 1979. Pre-behavioralism in political science. *American Political Science Review*, 73: 9–31.

YASHAR, D. J. 2005. *Contesting Citizenship in Latin America: The Rise of Indigenous Movements and the Postliberal Challenge*. Cambridge: Cambridge University Press.

YIN, R. K. 2004. *Case Study Anthology*. Thousand Oaks, Calif.: Sage.

....

INTERVIEWING AND QUALITATIVE FIELD METHODS: PRAGMATISM AND PRACTICALITIES

....

BRIAN C. RATHBUN

INTENSIVE interviewing is a powerful, but unfortunately underused tool in political science methodology. Where it is used, it is generally to add a little color to otherwise stiff accounts. Rarely do researchers talk to more than a handful of respondents. There are numerous practical reasons for this. Gaining access to interview subjects, particularly elites, is often difficult. Interviewing is costly as it often entails traveling great distances, sometimes across national borders. Interviewing often requires tremendous personal investment in language training that might not seem worth it. It is often a risky strategy. Even after the hurdles of access and travel are overcome, informants might reveal little. However, these obstacles cannot fully explain why more political scientists do not utilize interviewing in their research as a major source of data, or even as a supplement to quantitative analysis or archival records.

I maintain that there are two reasons why interviewing is often underused. First, interviewing often runs afoul of methodological tendencies in the discipline. Certain precepts of what I call the naive versions of behavioralism and rationalism make many skeptical about interviewing. Naive behavioralism objects to the status of data derived from interviewing as it is by nature subjective and imprecise, and therefore subject to multiple interpretations. Naive rationalism aims at a framework for understanding politics that privileges structure over agency and often assumes that the political actors of interest view the world objectively and respond the same way to the same stimuli. Both tendencies have the result of privileging some data over others. Most suspect is the kind of information that interviewing is best at ascertaining and that is crucial for many of the most interesting research questions in political science. To the extent that interviewing is endorsed, it is often with some questionable advice and presuppositions: that interview data should always be treated as opinion and not fact, that questions should be indirect and concrete rather than reflective and direct, and that dissembling on the part of respondents is endemic and irremediable. The first section of this article makes the pragmatic case for interviewing. Interviewing, despite its flaws, is often the best tool for establishing how subjective factors influence political decision-making, the motivations of those involved, and the role of agency in events of interest. Behavioralism and rationalism alert us rightly to the importance of rigor in our analyses, but there are steps that can be taken to eliminate some of the concerns about reliability and validity. Skepticism should not be exaggerated.

The second reason why interviewing is often underused is that its practicalities are often not taught. The second portion of this chapter is therefore devoted to assembling in one place the consensus in the literature on the basics of how to undertake interviews, including issues of how to build arguments using interview data, how to structure questionnaires, the proper role to adopt vis-à-vis respondents, and how to gain access to conversation partners. Although advocates propose different techniques for interviewing, the differences are fairly trivial, often just the use of different terms or typologies to describe the same process. There is a striking degree of agreement among proponents once the initial issue of the worth of interviewing data is resolved.

Both tendencies are symbolized perhaps best by the scant attention devoted to interviewing in what is now possibly the most common methodological text in the political discipline, King, Keohane, and Verba's *Designing Social Inquiry* (1994). This book devotes just a single footnote to the issue, a footnote that I argue points in many wrong directions as it is based on the application of the lessons of naive behavioralism to small-N, intensive case-study projects, those where interviewing can have the biggest impact. This chapter will focus on what has come to be known as "semi-structured" interviewing as opposed to "open-ended" interviews more common in ethnography or "close-ended" interviews used in surveys (Mishler 1986). Although ethnography and semi-structured interviewing share a commitment to probing in-depth the experiences of respondents and generally stress context over generalizability, induction over deduction, and complexity over parsimony, true ethnography is rare in modern political science for a variety of reasons. Political science generally involves the explanation of particular events. Participant observation, the most significant feature of ethnography, is generally not even possible as the outcome of interest has usually already taken place (although it can certainly be a fruitful source of new research questions and puzzles). Driven by explanation, political science generally involves the testing of hypotheses, even if they develop inductively over the course of the research process. This requires a more directed research strategy in which researchers seek to uncover some degree of objective truth. The ethnographic style begins with a clean slate and no such presuppositions and is associated with a more relativistic epistemology in which there is no real establishment of fact (Leech 2002, 665). Still there are lessons for ethnographers in the literature on semi-structured interviewing.

1 SKEPTICISM ABOUT INTERVIEWING IN POLITICAL SCIENCE

Methodological trends in modern political science, most notably behavioralism and more recently rational choice, have focused our attention on the importance of rigorous analysis based on principles drawn from the natural sciences. Most critical has been the value of objectivity and theory-driven research. Early behavioralists stressed the importance of freeing explanation from the normative values of the researcher. Data should also be as objective as possible, so that different researchers could agree on the meaning of the same piece of data, the social scientific equivalent of replication. The explanation of political events should be pursued separately from normative theory. And lest personal values should nevertheless influence our results, pure research was given increasing priority over applied research. Quantification was not pursued for its own sake, but rather would improve the precision of data and facilitate objective evaluation. Numbers are a more universal language less prone to differences in interpretation (Easton 1962; Somit and Tanenhaus 1967).

This led naturally to a tendency to focus on observed behavior, rather than unobservables such as mental processes that were more prone to subjective evaluation. Behavioralism of course did not completely eschew studies of political phenomena without observable behavioral implications. It did not go as far as the behaviorists in economics and psychology (Merkl 1969). Nor did it abandon the examination of the effects of the subjective perceptions of political actors on political events. The advances made in public opinion research are an example of both. However, whenever feasible, the possible subjectivity of political actors was to be made more manageable, for instance by the deductive designation of a limited number of response categories in a survey so as to allow objective evaluation, precision, and comparison by the researcher. Behavioralists prefer "structured" interviews, in which the same questions are asked in the same order with a restricted number of answers (Patton 1990, 277–90). This of course also served the goal of capturing the generalizability of political phenomena. Intensive interviewing was simply too costly and time consuming if a survey researcher wanted to gain an overall perspective. A more in-depth approach could be used, however, in early stages to make sure surveys were appropriately designed with questions that adequately measured variables of key concern.

Research was also to be driven by theory. This goal was juxtaposed unfavorably against traditional political science, which was marked by description. Without theory, political science is just journalism (and with a smaller readership). Theories were also to be of a particular sort—generalizable and parsimonious. Scholars should try to explain a lot with a little (Easton 1962; Somit and Tanenhaus 1967). The turn towards generalization was generally associated with a focus on structure over agency. The more that human beings had choice and could change their environment, the less generalizable or parsimonious theories could be (Almond and Genco 1977). Traditionalists responded that politics was far too complex and rich to be captured by general theories. Context mattered tremendously. Behavioralists replied that they missed the forest for the trees. A theoretical rather than an empiricist focus also meant that theories were best deduced from logical principles, rather than inductively built from the ground up with empirical data.

Interviewing does not always stand up well to these standards, as fruitful as they have been for modern political science. While behavioralism is well suited to large-N survey research, its principles have increasingly been applied in naive form to small-N case-study research. Concerns about the scientific status of data drawn from interviews are rarely explicitly stated, but rather are more subtle. They are expressed in advice from faculty advisers to their graduate students or in skepticism about interview data in peer reviews of work submitted to academic journals. Interviewing's faults lie in its inherent emphasis on complexity and context to the detriment of objectivity, parsimony, and generalizability. The very purpose of interviewing is generally to go in-depth in a way that secondhand sources, archives, or surveys do not allow (Berry 2002, 682). Interview subjects are often chosen because of their unique perspective on a particular phenomenon or event. Interviewing is of most use when interviewees have shaped the world around them, often undermining the goal of generalizability. Questions are not standardized across respondents, impeding comparability. The data, generally in the form of quotes or statements by the respondents, are prone to multiple, subjective interpretations by the researcher, making them less reliable. As a result, information culled from interviews has a dubious status, often described merely as the opinion of the respondent rather than fact. Because it cannot be objectively verified, it is less trustworthy. In any case, it is of little use in building the broader arguments that behavioralism is interested in. Interviewing is often regarded as the method used when social scientists do not have fully formed ideas or theories, leading to critiques of inductivism (Mishler 1986, 28).

The usefulness of interviewing has also come increasingly into question with the growing popularity of formal and rational choice frameworks for studying politics. Behavioralists did not deny the importance of unobservables such as motivations, psychology, norms, culture, learning, ethics, all of which might fall under the broader rubric of ideational factors. They merely prefer more observable factors because they lend themselves to more objective analysis akin to the natural sciences. These other factors are not denied, but ignored (Almond and Genco 1977). Rationalists, in contrast, make particular ontological assumptions in their efforts to build general models of politics, most importantly the objectivity of political actors. While they might have varying preferences, all actors placed in the same situation view stimuli similarly, and if they share the same preferences, will respond identically (Mercer 1996; Parsons 2006). The importance of objectivity is different than in behavioralism. For the latter, it is necessary for the researcher. For rationalists, it is necessary for political actors as well. If the situational incentives are the key to explanation, agency is limited, and perception is unproblematic, there is little need for interviewing. Rationalists "eliminate the mind" from analysis (Mercer 2005). They restrict their ontology for the broader methodological goal of generalizable theory (Fearon and Wendt 2002; Almond and Genco 1977). Given that interviewing is often used for deciphering what goes on between the ears, it serves less of a purpose for them. It might be of use for establishing preferences, but rationalists generally prefer the deduction of preferences from broader theories. They adopt the behavioral line about establishing motivations, as they are unobservable (Frieden 1999).

The rising influence of rational choice theory also has a more subtle but perhaps even more important effect. Conceptualizing most political situations as games of strategic interaction has increasingly alerted political scientists to concerns about strategic reconstruction by respondents. Interview data are inherently faulty because respondents have incentives to dissemble. This raises the validity issue in interviewing (Brenner 1985; Berry 2002). Respondents might seek to preserve their reputation and legacy or retain private information in an ongoing bargaining situation. When combined with tendencies discovered by psychologists to want to be perceived in a favorable light or justify one's actions to oneself, there are additional grounds not to trust interview data, not because of its epistemological status as in behavioralism, but because interviewees cannot be trusted. As argued below, this is a particularly vexing problem for students of political science. Politics involves power, which introduces unique dynamics. Political science is interested more than the other social sciences in explaining events, often those with broad social impact. In this sense it has more in common with history. For powerful individuals who often operate in an accountable and public realm, this introduces questions of how accounts are framed. Those formerly involved in politics are concerned about their legacy, those still involved about the public perception of their work. As such, political scientists must be particularly attuned to the issue of strategic reconstruction of events to suit the more vested interests of interviewees.

Paradoxically, the proponents of interviewing add fuel to this skeptical fire. There is a strange meeting of the minds between positivists and relativists. Many books on the method stress that it is not for the researcher to judge the correct view of events. Key proponents of the method discuss the difficulty of a true understanding between interviewer and interviewee because each unwittingly brings assumptions and biases to the conversation (Mishler 1986; Rubin and Rubin 1995). Interviewee data are inherently subjective. This is undoubtedly true, but at the extreme, explanation, however difficult and incomplete, ceases to become the goal of social science. This tendency becomes more pronounced in the literature on ethnography as opposed to semi-structured interviewing. When the research question is the attitudes or perspectives on politics of a particular group, the lack of an evidentiary standard might be appropriate. All are equally entitled to their opinion. But more often political scientists are interested in explaining outcomes, and must make judgements about the accuracy of conflicting accounts. Ironically, relativists end up sounding like positivists when they stress that interview data are more opinion than fact, although they reach that conclusion from different angles. Positivists treat interview data skeptically because objective interpretation is difficult among researchers, relativists because interpretation is an inappropriate imposition of the researcher's subjective views and does not capture the true meaning of the responses. Rationalists assume complete objectivity among the political actors they study. Relativists do the opposite, presuming complete subjectivity to the degree that explanation becomes impossible.

2 THE PRAGMATIC CASE FOR INTERVIEWING

Interviewers must be careful to separate fact from opinion, guard against phoney testimony by their conversation partners, should not let their own theoretical or political beliefs affect their interpretation, and cannot be satisfied with mere impressions. These are all valid concerns. But behavioralism and rationalism, taken to an extreme, can have the pernicious effect of discarding potentially valuable (and often invaluable) information. These rules limit the potential of interviewing significantly. Interviewing has flaws, but on pragmatic grounds, it is often the only means to obtain particular kinds of information. As discussed above, jettisoning interviewing often means restricting the set of independent variables to observable, structural factors. This impoverishes the study of politics to an unacceptable degree. Interviewing is often the best-suited method for establishing the importance of agency or ideational factors such as culture, norms, ethics, perception, learning, and cognition (Aberbach and Rockman 2002, 673; Mishler 1986, 279; Rubin and Rubin 1995, 19). Interviewing is often the most productive approach when influence over the outcome of interest was restricted to a few select decision-makers, creating a bottleneck of political power that increases the importance of agency in the story (and also makes interviewing less costly and time consuming). In short, interviewing, whatever its flaws, is often the best-suited method for gathering data on those characteristics of the social world that differentiate it from the natural world: human beings' effort to intentionally transform their environment on the basis of cognition, reflection, and learning (Almond and Genco 1977).

Interviewing is often necessary for establishing motivations and preferences. Even for those approaches that focus on situational incentives, this is an absolutely critical element of any theory. Without an understanding of desires, even the most rigorous rationalist argument will not be falsifiable if it simply infers preferences from observable behavior and a posited set of situational constraints. It falls into the same trap as folk psychology (Mercer 2005). Desires and beliefs must be measured independent of action. In some instances, interviewing is the only way to do so. For all its problems, interviewing is often more "scientific" than other methods.

Even while interviewing is well suited for discovering preferences and agency, this is not to say that it is not useful at establishing structural causes as well. Interviewing can help establish whether a political actor felt under pressure from forces beyond his or her control, and what those forces were, particularly when there are multiple independent variables in the theoretical mix. To the extent that one is interested, like rationalists, in showing the importance of structural or situational factors in explaining behavior, interviewing can help build the appropriate model. Strategic circumstances might be found by a model to provide the best account for particular action, but are only empirically useful if the model reflects more or less the actual circumstances that decision-makers found themselves in. Interviewing is one, although certainly not the only, way of identifying that situation.

Other methods might provide some insight into these factors, such as archives or memoirs. But interviewing is unique in that it allows the interviewer to ask the questions that he or she wants answered. Memoirs and secondary accounts force the researcher to answer his or her key questions based on what others wanted to write about. Archives sometimes provide insights into the thinking of key individuals, but motivations and agency must be more indirectly established than in interviewing. They require considerable inference and interpretation, raising the reliability issue to a greater degree than in interviewing. Interviewing has the advantage of being perhaps the most directed and targeted method in the qualitative arsenal.

To the extent that interviewing is endorsed by many in the behavioralist and rationalist tradition, it comes with important provisos that are often ill advised and overly constricting. A single passage, taken from a footnote in Keohane, King, and Verba's guide to qualitative research (now standard reading in methodology classes in political science graduate courses), contains many of these:

Be as concrete as possible ... In general and wherever possible, we must not ask an interviewee to do our work for us. It is best not to ask for estimates of causal effects. We must ask for measures of the explanatory and dependent variables, and estimate the causal effects ourselves. We must not ask for motivations, but rather for facts. This rule is not meant to imply that we should never ask people why they did something. Indeed, asking about motivations is often a productive means of generating hypotheses. Self-reported motivations may also be a useful set of observable implications. However, the answers must be interpreted as the interviewee's response to the researcher's question, not necessarily as the correct answer. If questions such as these are to be of use, we should design research so that a particular answer given (with whatever justification, embellishments, lies or selective memories we may encounter) is an observable implication.   (1994, 112 n.)

This quote raises four issues: the extent to which interview data have the status of fact; how tangible questions should be; whether data should be pursued directly; and whether respondents can be trusted to give accurate accounts.

According to these scholars, responses from interviewees cannot be taken as "the correct answer," i.e. data with the status of fact, but rather should be treated as opinions. Motivations are juxtaposed antithetically to facts, indicating a bias in favor of behavior. We should ask for concrete actions, what an interviewee did, rather than his or her overall impression of a situation. But behavior rarely speaks for itself. There are often multiple possible causes and motivations for the same action and outcome. Research is often driven by the desire to explain an already determined and known behavioral outcome, likely due to its intrinsic importance. This means that social scientists will be trying to gauge the effect of competing independent variables with the same expected effect. In these cases behavior does not speak for itself, and the meaning of behavior must be established. There is no substitute for a good research design, but interviewing might often be the only means for establishing causation in these cases, particularly when the phenomenon of study is relatively recent and there are no reliable alternative sources for judging motivation. Although Keohane, King, and Verba (1994) caution us not to ask respondents to estimate causal effects or state their motivations, this seems unwise. Interviews often involve conversations with individuals in a unique position to gauge the importance of multiple and equally plausible causal factors, which any research question of interest generally suffers from. We need not instantly accept those estimates as fact, but when a consensus appears among those in a best position to know, it should be taken very seriously. Presuming that each account is equally valid, as many advocates of interviewing suggest, goes too far, however. Social science requires the researcher to weigh conflicting evidence and offer the best interpretation possible supported by the evidence. Understanding who was in a position to know the true facts of the outcome the researcher is trying to explain is a key factor in balancing different accounts, as it helps separate opinion from fact.

When Keohane et al. recommend concreteness, they mean that questions should be both tangible and indirect. Others do as well (Mishler 1986, 315). In terms of the former, more grounded questions about facts are less subject to multiple interpretations. Answers to concrete questions, such as the temporal sequence of particular actions, are often useful in reconstructing events and mediating between competing arguments. But questions that ask an interviewee to reflect more abstractly about the underlying causes and motivations behind his actions are just as important. In many instances, the researcher already knows about behavior because it has been a matter of public interest and record that led to the selection of the topic in the first place. It is the motivation that is missing. In practical terms, answers to less concrete questions are often easier to obtain, particularly as considerable time may have passed between the interview and the events or outcome in question. Contemporary newspaper accounts or even archives can often provide the facts about what happened on any particular day. To the extent that this is true, interviews should be devoted to allowing respondents to reflect on their experience, which they might only now have had an opportunity to do. Particularly when dealing with elites, respondents are perfectly able to contemplate the broader meaning of their actions just as well as a political scientist, although they do so in less self-consciously theoretical terms. One revealing technique is to ask conversation partners to informally test competing arguments against one another. Rarely are political science theories too complicated to explain to an intelligent layman. The researcher can pose the question as, "Some say X, others say Y, how would you respond to that?" (Mishler 1986, 318). By posing such trade-offs, researchers might encourage interviewees to draw evidence to support their account. This is the best of both worlds, for respondents to explain the broader significance of their actions with actual data about what they did. Another useful method is to ask counterfactuals in the form of "why didn't you do X" or "what if you had done Y in situation Z?" This is a very useful technique for establishing the extent to which structure or agency prevailed. The response might be that one path was more valued than another, or that one path was blocked by some constraint.

Being concrete also means questions should be indirect (McCracken 1988, 21; Brenner 1985, 151). Keohane et al. (1994) recommend for instance not to ask a white conservative whether he is racist, but rather if he would mind if his daughter married a black man (1994, 112 n.). Indirect questions are particularly necessary in instances of what are known as "valence" issues, in which there is only one publicly acceptable position to have on an issue. Any outcome of interest in which politicians might have sought narrower parochial interests at the expense of the broader societal good, which is much of political science, might be so loaded and is a key place to worry about strategic reconstruction. On issues in which there are multiple, publicly acceptable positions, this is less of an issue. Skeptics of interviewing also worry that directed questions put words in the mouth of respondents and are therefore inappropriate. This is a potential worry, and researchers should indicate in their research, perhaps in a footnote, the question to which a quote corresponds if there is a fear of leading respondents.

However, as in journalism, interviewing's payoff is often in the quotation, getting someone on the record, even if it is nonattributable (Mishler 1986, 347). That is, direct statements are more valuable in terms of impact and credibility. And one must remember that interviews with subjects in political science often do have a strategic component, and interviewers must sometimes lead respondents into answering rather than dodging their questions, while simultaneously avoiding giving them the answers. Interviewers should proceed indirectly so as to get a sense of how far respondents will go, but ask follow-up questions, trying to establish more directly what one wants to know. If the interviewee goes so far, one can then safely ask for a confirmation in the form of "I hear you saying that . . . ," without fears of leading the witness, as it were. Questions cannot be purely open ended and undirected. A couple of techniques might be helpful. In cases in which there is a publicly stated position for a particular behavioral outcome but the researcher or others have a suspicion that there was an ulterior motive not flattering to the interviewee, researchers can use presupposition questions in which they indicate their acceptance of the ulterior motive as perfectly natural, assumed, and justifiable (Leech 2002, 666; Mishler 1986, 304). Interviewers might even note that their actions were perfectly understandable in light of the circumstances. They might use euphemisms that take the hard edges off that behavior (Leech 2002, 666). Or they might mention (only honestly!) that other interview subjects have indicated as much to them already. They should then look to see if the subject acquiesces or seeks to correct the assumption. The former is revealing if not concrete proof; the latter provides an opportunity for the interviewer to challenge the account and ask the conversation partner to provide evidence for it.

Although the concern about intentionally (or unintentionally) inaccurate answers is real, it is often overstated (Rubin and Rubin 1995, 225; Berry 2002, 688). When Keohane et al. refer to "justification, embellishments, lies and selective memories," there is almost a presumption of disingenuousness on the part of the respondent. But my experience with interviewing is that dishonesty is not the norm, even among the most high-ranking officials. I was able to solicit evidence on recent issues in national security policy that did not cast subjects in a positive light (Rathbun 2004). Most respondents would rather refuse an appointment than spend the time averting a difficult subject. Interviewees are more likely to commit sins of omission than commission, avoiding deliberate falsehoods and attempting to steer the conversation to other aspects of the subject. For someone who has prepared properly, this becomes obvious. Researchers are not nearly as threatening as journalists. An academic's audience is more limited and is certainly not the average man on the street reading tomorrow's newspaper. This creates difficulty in gaining access to important respondents, but once access is gained, they might be more forthcoming. Interviewees might welcome the chance to explain their actions more fully with fewer fears of being boxed in and quoted out of context (Rubin and Rubin 1995, 105). Those engaged in politics often believe in what they do and are proud of their accomplishments, even when they seem distasteful to some. Certainly the risk of being lied to is surely outweighed by the potential of new and exclusive data. Researchers should not presume interview subjects are telling the truth, but they should not assume they are lying either.

There are a number of other ways of avoiding the perils of strategic reconstruction. Some come from the common sense of journalism. Most simply, when possible, find multiple sources for the same data, either written or interview based (Berry 2002, 680; Rubin and Rubin 1995, 225–7; Brenner 1985, 155). If this is done with other interviews, this reinforces one's belief that what one is hearing is more than just opinion or that it is just a particular interpretation of ambiguous information. And it helps reduce worries that some respondents exaggerate the role they played in the process (Berry 2002, 680). Let them know you are an expert by your questioning, even if it means the gratuitous use of jargon. This tells them you are an informed observer who cannot be easily manipulated (Rubin and Rubin 1995, 197). Confront the respondent with data contrary to his or her point of view, even if you might believe he or she is being straightforward, as this might provide ideas about how to get leverage on multiple causal factors (Rubin and Rubin 1995, 223). The fact that much of the study of politics revolves around conflict in the public sphere also has advantages in gaining more accurate accounts. Interviewees can be challenged with data drawn from the other side of the political spectrum, a standard journalistic technique (Rubin and Rubin 1995, 68–70, 217). This makes the interviewee appear more neutral than if the challenge is issued directly, although interviewers should be careful not to give the impression that they are engaging in the same "gotcha" game as the media. If such an opponent is unavailable, researchers can explicitly refer themselves as a "devil's advocate" in order to be less provocative (Rubin and Rubin 1995, 215). Respondents might be asked to critique their own case, to explain why their adversaries do not accept their account (Berry 2002, 680).

When bias is expected, one can pose some preliminary questions unrelated to the subject that gauge a general ideological approach and allow the researcher to discount certain aspects of testimony, sometimes called "norming" (Rubin and Rubin 1995, 210). Understand the particular bureaucratic, political, or ideological position of your interviewees so you know what biases to expect. Know what the party line might be (Rubin and Rubin 1995, 221). This requires a familiarity with the public record. In improvisational questions, probe differences between the public account and the one you are hearing, but do not despair if they vary. On the contrary, generally this means that you are uncovering something new and exciting. When a researcher finds differences it can yield important new insights about the political context that respondents were negotiating. Follow up on this, as it is important for gauging the significance of structure and agency. Ask why particular arguments were instrumental and why this was necessary. If memories appear weak, ask basic questions about details that allow one to assess the overall credibility of the source (Rubin and Rubin 1995, 84). A researcher might make deliberate mistakes that should be corrected if memories are good (Rubin and Rubin 1995, 219). Finally, if the account has internal contradictions or inconsistencies, let these be known to the respondent and note the adjustments that he or she makes to the story.

3 THE CONSENSUS ON THE PRACTICALITIES OF INTERVIEWING

While there are often disagreements about whether interviews are worthwhile ventures, among those who undertake them there is a general consensus on most points. This section reviews those major points of agreement, proceeding chronologically from preparation to interpretation and writing.

Perhaps the most important lesson for any would-be interviewer is not to begin intensive interviewing without being fully prepared (Brenner 1985, 152). As McCracken writes, "Every qualitative interview is, potentially, the victim of a shapeless inquiry. The scholar who does not control these data will surely sink without a trace" (1988, 22). The interviewer should exhaust all of the secondary sources and publicly available primary sources before beginning (Berry 2002, 680). This allows him or her to work out a puzzle, if one isn't already evident; to figure out what is known and what is not known so questions can be more targeted and efficient; to understand how the debate is framed in different contexts (nation states, cultures, time periods, etc.) in the case that the issue involves political conflict, as it generally does in political science; and to develop expectations about what interview data would be evidence for his or her initial hypothesis or other competitors. In those instances in which research is being undertaken in a new area without a significant paper trail, a political scientist might consider a set of exploratory interviews to get a better sense of the interesting theoretical issues (McCracken 1988, 48), but these should be limited to lower-ranking respondents or those with knowledge of a phenomenon but not directly involved, such as journalists. The researcher should not show up with a year's fellowship in a new place hoping that things will fall into place on the basis of ongoing conversations. They might, but luck will be necessary. An understanding of the literature will not only help the researcher eventually frame his argument in a broader context in the opening passages of an academic work but also provide a benchmark for what is surprising in the interview data he collects (McCracken 1988, 31). A good scholar will read not only the qualitative work in his field but also the quantitative even if he is not a statistical whiz, as it is a source of hypotheses and sometimes an indication of what is yet to be explored due to the inherent limitations of quantitative analyses, such as difficulties in establishing causation.

It is crucial to remember that the literature review, or one's own hypothesis, must be held at arm's length, so that researchers are open, in the true scientific sense, to other possibilities. McCracken calls this "manufacturing distance" (1988, 23) This is particularly important in interviewing as the method is often used when there is a black hole in the evidence about something of theoretical interest, in which case assumptions would be inappropriate. And whereas quantitative analyses might be rerun or a secondary source reread, interviewers often only have one chance with their sources of data. If you are insistent on a particular hypothesis, even if it is not working out, you will waste an experience that cannot be repeated. "A good literature review makes the investigator the master, not the captive, of previous scholarship" (McCracken 1988, 31). Previous theories, or your own, might act as blinders (Rubin and Rubin 1995, 64). This is not only good social science, but any possibility of overturning conventional wisdom benefits the scholar's career!

After the literature review, researchers should establish contact with those who have a particular knowledge of the outcomes of interest. Exploratory interviews are often fine sources of such contacts. It is generally best to begin with low-ranking members of the group you are interested in, whether it be a trade union, government bureaucracy, or social movement. The researcher should talk to anyone who will see him or her. This allows the social scientist to hone and try out different framing of questions, develop and accumulate contacts (sometimes known as "snowballing"), and gather basic information so as to be better prepared for more senior respondents who have less time and tolerance. Initial contact should not be a cold call if it can be avoided. Many recommend a professional letter (Goldstein 2002, 671; Aberbach and Rockman 2002, 674; Peabody et al. 1990, 453).[1] Letterhead conveys a sense of professionalism and status. In closed societies, it is often good to have a local affiliation at a

---

[1] Some note that in developing societies requests for interviews should be made in person if possible, for both cultural and technical reasons. See Rivera, Kozyreva, and Sarovskii (2002).

research center. In more open societies, your own foreign university emblem might be better as it helps you stand out from the flood of mail that many of our conversation partners receive. Explain why the respondent might be of particular help for your project. This provides background but also gives them a sense of relevance that is inevitably flattering (Rubin and Rubin 1995, 103). Tell them they are not obligated to speak on the record or on an attributable basis. When possible, mention the person who referred you and others you have talked to, so as to give yourself a sense of credibility. Preferably the former should be on the same side of any political conflict as your contact, but often the latter can be someone opposed, as this might induce an interest on their part in equal time and setting the record straight that might make them more likely to meet you. Follow up this initial contact with a phone call to the individual or his or her appointments assistant. When possible, allow a large timeframe to set up a meeting, making it harder for the contact to refuse you and enabling the inevitable rescheduling. If possible, have a direct phone number, even a cell phone (Goldstein 2002, 671). Playing phone tag from your hotel room voice mail will prove difficult. Gather the names of the administrative staff as you set up the interview, keep them in your mind as you travel to the interview, and seek them out as you enter or leave the office to thank them directly by name.

Most advocates of interviewing recommend recording interviews (Aberbach and Rockman 2002, 674). Tell your interviewee that you would like to record the interview, and if it might make your work more credible later to identify him or her by name, that you would like for it to be on the record. If this is not possible, inform him or her of your preference for it to be nonattributable, in which you might quote, but not directly identify his or her name. Although recording on the record is often thought to make respondents more circumspect, this presumption is based on an assumption that respondents will not be forthcoming in the first place. As I think this is often overstated, I believe the advantages likely outweigh the disadvantages although every circumstance is different, and they obviously vary by the stakes involved and the local culture. "Senior official" does not have the same cachet in print as "Prime Minister Smith." Having a recorded version of the conversation allows one to think through potential follow-up questions when the conversation takes an interesting turn without worrying about taking down the exact text (Brenner 1985, 154; Berry 2002, 682; Douglas 1985, 83; McCracken 1988, 41). Such a recording allows you to assemble a verbatim transcript that you can make available in an effort to remedy some of the subjective interpretation problems endemic to the method (Brenner 1985, 155; Mishler 1986, 36; Rubin and Rubin 1995, 85). This transparency helps avoid the accusation of massaging and spinning the data. Given that your research question or hypothesis will likely shift as you accumulate information, such a transcript is often invaluable as you have information on record that you might not have thought relevant and noted before in your notes. And given that interviewing is often used to identify the motivation and meaning behind otherwise indeterminate behavior, specific quotations are sometimes the only evidence possible or even moderately convincing. Merely stating your hypothesis and providing a footnote of "Interview with Mr X" is not sufficient. However, allow the interviewee the option of going off the record or not for attribution at any particular point in the interview. They often take it. Make sure you are clear on what you or they mean as "off the record" or "on background" (Goldstein 2002, 671). And take notes so that you do not have to transcribe every single recording, saving that valuable time for particularly evocative conversations.

To the degree possible, the social scientist should inform himself of the role played by that individual in the phenomenon of interest. Let that preparation be known in a brief introduction of yourself and your general research interests. This helps break the ice (Leech 2002, 666; Peabody et al. 1990, 652). Yet the researcher does better not to specifically identify his or her own working hypothesis, whether it be a fully formed argument or just a hunch, as the respondent might be tempted inappropriately to help gather information on behalf of the interviewer or presumptuously dismiss it (and you) (McCracken 1988, 27–8; Aberbach and Rockman 2002, 673). In this sense, Keohane et al. are correct that interviewees should not do our work for us. Use specialized language or acronyms to demonstrate your competence and prompt them to avoid needless background that wastes valuable time (Rubin and Rubin 1995, 77–9). When possible, interview in the language of the interviewee. All of this demonstrates professionalism and gives the sense that the conversation partner is truly valued and important. While politicians might be accustomed to this treatment, other (even powerful) figures might not. The social scientist must strike a balance between formality on the one hand and rapport on the other. Professionalism and a certain distance ensure that the interviewer retains control of the questioning and is taken seriously. Yet too cold a demeanor can inhibit respondents from trusting the interviewer with often sensitive information (McCracken 1988, 26–7). Questioning should be sympathetic, respectful, and nonargumentative, although this does not imply unchallenging, as discussed earlier (Brenner 1985, 157). Yet political science interviewing differs from journalism in that it must be less adversarial. Interviewees might have an obligation to the public interest to sit for an interview with a journalist and they can hardly call it off midstream. That is not the case with academics. Some suggest that an academic demonstrate less of a command of the subject matter than he or she actually has so that respondents do not feel inferior, but this runs the risk of making some feel they are wasting their time (McCracken 1988). Leech's advice to appear knowledgeable, but not as knowledgeable as the interviewee, is probably better (2002, 665).

Researchers should bring a questionnaire to their interviews specifically designed around the unique role played by their particular conversation partner. This helps separate fact from opinion as well as not wasting time with information that could be gathered from other sources (Leech 2002, 666). Interviews should not be entirely improvisational because researchers might forget important questions and not have an opportunity to fill those holes later. But they cannot be too rigidly designed so as to inhibit adaptation. After all, the goal of interviews is rarely simply confirmatory. Social scientists want to be surprised. They are often interviewing in the first place because there are certain things that are just not known. The questionnaire should be a general set of themes, and specifically worded questions that have been found to elicit better responses than others. Do not begin with challenging questions as they might put the respondent on guard and heighten sensitivity to the running tape recorder (McCracken 1988, 38; Mishler 1986, 294; Douglas 1985, 138; Rubin and Rubin 1995, 223). They should be reserved until later after a sense of rapport has been established (but don't wait too long and run out of time) (Leech 2002, 666). But beginning questions should not be tedious either. The interviewer might first try to elicit facts and then as the interviewee loosens up begin with more complex matters of interpretation, motivation, etc., particularly as the former often jogs the memory of events long past (Peabody et al. 1990, 452; Rubin and Rubin 1995, 210). If time is limited, however, focus first on the absolute essentials and then work towards other less important matters (Rubin and Rubin 1995, 200). In these instances, do not ask questions for which information can be obtained from other less busy sources or that you should know the answer to already, thus undermining your credibility (Peabody et al. 1990, 452). Learn the value of nonverbal communication. If an answer is not complete, the researcher can indicate this by remaining silent and nodding his head, both signaling an interest in further explication. If a respondent avoids a question or simply misses it, note this and return to the subject later from a different angle. Have at your disposal some "bridges" that enable you to return to the area of interest in a respectful way (Berry 2002, 681).

When leaving, always ask the conversation partner for other suggestions about whom to talk to. Those directly involved are often in the best position to know who would be uniquely knowledgeable on some aspect of your research topic and can be used as a reference in your request. One should never finish an interview without knowing the next person one wants to talk to. An interviewer should never have crossed off all the names of possible subjects. Also, always ask if he or she would be available for additional questions, either in person, e-mail, or by phone. This is a promise that can be included in a follow-up letter requesting more information that has a better chance of getting past the secretary, especially if you have been previously cordial in your interactions (Rubin and Rubin 1995, 138).

Successive interviews should build on each other. The researcher should constantly be looking over his notes, looking for sources of agreement and disagreement, new themes and causal factors previously untheorized or not mentioned in the literature. Over time, interviews will naturally become less exploratory or inductive and more deductive (Rubin and Rubin 1995, 43; Brenner 1985, 152; McCracken 1988, 45). Scholars will begin to develop more precise hypotheses that they seek to confirm or test the limits of. Questions will become more honed and precise and fewer topics will need to be explored as a narrative emerges. As with all research there will be a point of diminishing returns in which later interviews generate less new information than previous ones, although interviewers should be aware of premature closure (McCracken 1988, 45). This will guide the social scientist in his effort at organizing notes and thoughts once interviewing is complete. With the proper legwork before interviewing and continual reappraisals of the data during the process, researchers can end the data collection phase of research with a well-formed albeit sometimes preliminary idea of the final product.

4 CONCLUSION

Interviewing is a potentially invaluable tool for collecting data that researchers should approach pragmatically, both in terms of how, but also whether, it is conducted. Its financial costs and methodological difficulties are real, but if a political scientist believes there might be some aspect of a phenomenon best captured by directly talking to participants, he or she should not hesitate. Doubts about the status of interview data and the reliability of respondents must be taken into account but can be addressed. These disadvantages rarely outweigh the unique advantages of interviewing: the ability to target questions directly to actual participants and push them for responses in a way that archival or other qualitative research never allows. Although most would agree that interviewing is a kind of art that takes some practice, there is a solid consensus on the practicalities of interviewing. It is no substitute for careful research and investigation of secondary and written primary sources, however. Systematic analysis and meticulous preparation are a must in any kind of analysis.

REFERENCES

ABERBACH, J. D., and ROCKMAN, B. A. 2002. Conducting and coding elite interviews. *Political Science and Politics*, 35: 673–4.

ALMOND, G. A., and GENCO, S. J. 1977. Clocks, clouds and the study of world politics. *World Politics*, 29: 489–522.

BERRY, J. M. 2002. Validity and reliability issues in elite interviewing. *Political Science and Politics*, 35: 679–82.

BRENNER, M. 1985. Intensive interviewing. Pp. 147–62 in *The Research Interview: Uses and Approaches*, ed. M. Brenner, J. Brown, and D. Canter. London: Academic Press.

DOUGLAS, J. D. 1985. *Creative Interviewing*. Beverly Hills, Calif.: Sage.

EASTON, D. 1962. The current meaning of "behavioralism" in political science. Pp. 1–25 in *The Limits of Behavioralism in Political Science*, ed. J. C. Charlesworth. Philadelphia: American Academy of Political and Social Science.

FEARON, J., and WENDT, A. 2002. Rationalism v. constructivism: a skeptical view. In *Handbook of International Relations*, ed. W. Carlsnaes, T. Risse, and B. Simmons. London: Sage.

FRIEDEN, J. A. 1999. Actors and preferences in international relations. Pp. 39–78 in *Strategic Choice and International Relations*, ed. D. A. Lake, and R. Powell. Princeton, NJ: Princeton University Press.

GOLDSTEIN, K. 2002. Getting in the door: sampling and completing elite interviews. *Political Science and Politics*, 35: 669–72.

KING, G., KEOHANE, R., and VERBA, S. 1994. *Designing Social Inquiry: Scientific Inference in Qualitative Research*. Princeton, NJ: Princeton University Press.

LEECH, B. L. 2002. Asking questions: techniques for semistructured interviews. *Political Science and Politics*, 35: 665–8.

McCRACKEN, G. 1988. *The Long Interview*. Qualitative Research Methods, 13. Newbury Park, Calif.: Sage.

MERCER, J. 1996. *Reputation and International Politics*. Ithaca, NY: Cornell University Press.
—— 2005. Rationality and psychology in international politics. *International Organization*, 59: 77–106.
MERKL, P. H. 1969. "Behavioristic" tendencies in American political science. Pp. 141–52 in *Behavioralism in Political Science*, ed. H. Elau. New York: Atherton Press.
MISHLER, E. 1986. *Research Interviewing: Context and Narrative*. Cambridge, Mass.: Harvard University Press.
PARSONS, C. 2006. *The Logics of Interpretation*. Oxford: Oxford University Press.
PATTON, M. Q. 1990. *Qualitative Evaluation and Research Methods*. Newbury Park, Calif.: Sage.
PEABODY, R. L., HAMMOND, S. W., TORCOM, J., BROWN, L. P., THOMPSON, C., and KOLODYNY, R. 1990. Interviewing political elites. *Political Science and Politics*, 23: 451–5.
RATHBUN, B. 2004. *Partisan Interventions: European Party Politics and Peace Enforcement in the Balkans*. Ithaca, NY: Cornell University Press.
RIVERA, S. W., KOZYREVA, P. M., and SAROVSKII, E. G. 2002. Inteviewing political elites: lessons from Russia. *Political Science and Politics*, 35: 683–7.
RUBIN, H. J., and RUBIN, I. S. 1995. *Qualitative Interviewing: The Art of Hearing Data*. Thousand Oaks, Calif.: Sage.
SOMIT, A., and TANENHAUS, J. 1967. *The Development of American Political Science: From Burgess to Behavioralism*. Boston: Allyn and Bacon.

....

PROCESS TRACING: A BAYESIAN PERSPECTIVE

....

ANDREW BENNETT

How are we to judge competing explanatory claims about historical cases? How can we make inferences about which alternative explanations are more convincing, in what ways, and to what degree? How can we make inferences from the explanation of individual historical cases to the general explanatory power and scope conditions of the underlying theories that explanations of cases draw upon? Bayesian logic and case-study methods, particularly methods of within-case analysis such as process tracing, offer two approaches to these questions. Scholars have long recognized that Bayesian analysis is suited to assessing explanations for one or a few cases and for making inferences from the evidence in individual cases to the general viability of theories, and within-case analysis focuses on the historical explanation of individual cases. Recently, experts on qualitative methods have begun to argue that these approaches have much in common (McKeown 2003; Brady and Collier 2004; George and Bennett 2005). The relationship between the two has not been analyzed in any detail, however, nor has there been an analysis of how discussions of Bayesian inference help illuminate the strengths and limits of process tracing. The present chapter seeks to fill these gaps.

This chapter first provides an overview of process tracing, focusing on the dimensions of this method that are relevant to Bayesian logic (for a more complete discussion of process tracing, see George and Bennett 2005). It then briefly summarizes the logic of Bayesian inference, emphasizing the parallels with the logic of process tracing. The chapter illustrates these points with examples from the historical explanation of political events, including the 1898 Fashoda crisis, the end of the First World War, and the end of the cold war. The chapter concludes that Bayesianism helps us understand the strengths of case-study methods, including their potential to develop and test explanations even with limited evidence drawn from one or a few cases, and their limits, including the provisional nature of historical explanations and the challenges of generalizing from small numbers of cases.

1 HISTORICAL EXPLANATION: THREE ILLUSTRATIVE CASES

The social sciences are rife with debates over the historical explanation of particular cases. Consider three historically and theoretically important examples from my own field of international relations, each of which I return to below. In the first, Kenneth Schultz argues that Britain and France were able to avoid war during the Fashoda crisis of 1898 because democratic processes in Britain reinforced the credibility of its coercive diplomatic demands, while those in France undermined the credibility of its willingness to fight. Others attribute the absence of a war over the Fashoda crisis to differences in French and British military power, or to the democratic values held by the two countries (Schultz 2001). In a second example, Hein Goemans argues that in 1916 German leaders became more pessimistic about their prospects for military victory in the First World War but responded by *increasing* their war aims. In his view, this risky gamble was an attempt to seek an even bigger victory that would buy off domestic opponents and allow existing elites to stay in power. Other scholars argue that domestic considerations were unimportant, that Germany did not escalate its war aims, that German leaders did not realize in 1916 that they had little chance of winning, or that changes in German leadership accounted for changes in German policies (Goemans 2000). In a third debate, which I recount in the greatest detail below as it is easier to illustrate process tracing with cases with which one is intimately familiar, I have argued that Soviet leaders changed their foreign policies in the late 1980s for ideational reasons. In brief, I maintain that these leaders were reluctant to use force to stem the Central European revolutions of 1989 because they drew the lesson from their failed interventions in Afghanistan and elsewhere that force is not efficacious in achieving long-term political goals like the support of unpopular governments (Bennett 2005). Others have emphasized instead shifts in the balance of power unfavorable to the Soviet Union (Brooks and Wohlforth 2000–1) or changes in the ruling political coalition inside the Soviet Union (Snyder 1987–8).

The adjudication of such competing historical explanations follows a common pattern. We begin with alternative explanations like those in the previous paragraph. We then consider what kinds of evidence, if found, would strengthen or weaken our confidence in each alternative explanation. Put another way, we consider how strongly each theory anticipates various processes and outcomes, or how surprising it would be from the viewpoint of our prior theoretical expectations to find or to fail to find particular evidence that the hypothesized processes and outcomes took place. Next, we seek out both the expected and the potentially surprising evidence from various sources, taking into account the potential biases that these sources may reflect. After having gathered the available evidence, we update the level of confidence we invest in each of the alternative explanations for the individual case in question. Depending on how this case fits in with our more general theoretical expectations and any earlier empirical findings, the evidence from the case may also lead us to update our confidence in the more general theories lying behind the alternative explanations of the case, and/or our estimate of their scope conditions. This schema for historical explanation is of course oversimplified, and in practice historical explanation can involve many iterations between theoretical conjectures and empirical tests within and across cases. Nonetheless, this logic illustrates much of what is common to both process tracing and Bayesian inference.

2 PROCESS TRACING

Process tracing involves looking at evidence within an individual case, or a temporally and spatially bound instance of a specified phenomenon, to derive and/or test alternative explanations of that case. In other words, process tracing seeks a *historical explanation* of an individual case, and this explanation may or may not provide a theoretical explanation relevant to the wider phenomenon of which the case is an instance. Perhaps the researcher will decide that the best explanation for the case is unique or nearly so, such as a finding that a voter supported a candidate who differed from the voter's party, ideology, and issue preferences simply because the candidate was the voter's sister-in-law. Alternatively, the investigator could uncover and test through process tracing a theoretical hypothesis that helps explain a vast range of cases, including even cases that are dissimilar in many respects to the one initially studied. Charles Darwin's theory of evolutionary selection, for example, derived in part from the study of a few species in the Galapagos Islands, is applicable to all living organisms. It is impossible to judge the generalizability of a theory without an understanding of the hypothesized causal mechanisms it entails, and often this understanding is itself developed through the study of an individual case.

Process tracing thus has both inductive (or theory-generating) and deductive (theory-testing) elements. The balance between the two in any particular study depends on the prior state of development of relevant theories on the phenomenon as well as the researcher's state of knowledge about the phenomenon and the case. If potential alternative explanations of a phenomenon are well established, and if each hypothesis is sufficiently detailed to offer testable predictions on the processes that should have taken place if the hypothesis is to offer a good explanation of the case, then process tracing can proceed largely through deductive theory testing of each alternative explanation (for an example see Schultz 2001, discussed below). If there are no well-specified alternative explanations, however, or if the case is a "deviant" one that does not fit any of the relevant established theories, then process tracing must proceed relatively inductively, through the use of evidence from the case to formulate and possibly later to test new explanations of the case (for an example see Scott 1985). In this regard, while researchers must guard against possible confirmation biases in deriving a theory from a case and then testing it in the same case, it is possible to derive an explanation from a case and then test it against *different and independent evidence* from within that same case. Such evidence provides the possibility of falsifying the new theory as an explanation of the case.

Because process tracing is the technique of looking for the observable implications of hypothesized causal processes within a single case, the researcher engaged in process tracing often looks at a finer level of detail or a lower level of analysis than that of the proposed theoretical explanations.[1] The goal is to document whether the sequence of events or processes within the case fits those predicted by alternative explanations of the case. This is closely analogous to a detective attempting to solve a crime by looking at clues and suspects and attempting to piece together a convincing explanation based on the detailed evidence that bears on means, motives, and opportunity. It is also analogous to a doctor trying to diagnose an illness in an individual patient by taking in the details of the patient's case history and symptoms and applying diagnostic tests that can, for example, distinguish between a viral and a bacterial infection (Gill, Sabin, and Schmid 2005). Indeed, all attempts to diagnose or explain individual or historical cases involve process tracing. This is true not only of social events like the Fashoda crisis, the end of the First World War, and the end of the cold war, but of historical events in the hard sciences, like the origins of a particular rock formation (geology), the extinction of the dinosaurs (evolutionary biology), or the origins of the universe (cosmology).

Some critics have suggested that because process tracing frequently involves looking at a finer degree of detail, it can involve a potential "infinite regress" of studying endless "steps between steps between steps" in a case (King, Keohane, and Verba 1994). Indeed, all process-tracing explanations remain provisional, as they could be disproved by further analysis at a finer degree of detail or at a more aggregate level of analysis, but there are pragmatic limits on how much detail a researcher will go into and how continuous an explanation they will seek. These pragmatic limits include the resources available to the researcher, the importance the researcher places on establishing an explanation of the case with a specified degree of confidence, and the rapidity with which the evidence converges in support of a particular explanation.

[1] Process tracing could take place at a higher level of analysis than the hypothesized causal mechanism as well. One could test an economic theory based on hypothesized mechanisms of individual behavior, for example, by examining aggregate behavior in a market.

Moreover, the theoretical importance of a case can change as our research questions evolve—the Fashoda crisis was all but forgotten by everyone except diplomatic
historians, for example, until the argument that democracies do not fight one another became an important theoretical conjecture and the Fashoda crisis became
a relevant case for testing the alternative mechanisms posited for this hypothesis.
Also, a researcher may choose to end or extend their process tracing based on the
differential theory-building or policy consequences of a Type I error (rejecting a true
explanation) and a Type II error (accepting a false explanation).

In addition, not all pieces of evidence have equal probative value relative to alternative explanations of a case. The more confidently a hypothesis of interest predicts a
particular piece of evidence, and the more unlikely that evidence is from the perspective of alternative explanations, the more we increase our confidence in the hypothesis
of interest if we do indeed find the evidence it predicted. In this regard, Stephen Van
Evera has distinguished among four kinds of tests or evidence representing different
combinations of uniqueness and certitude (Van Evera 1997, 31–2). Unique predictions
are those accounted for only by one of the theories under consideration, while certain
predictions are those that must be unequivocally and inexorably true if an explanation
is true. *Hoop tests* involve evidence that is certain but not unique; failure of such a
test disqualifies an explanation but passage does not greatly increase confidence in
that explanation. Thus, in practice, hoop tests are often used to exclude alternative
hypotheses. Van Evera's apt example of a hoop test is: "Was the accused in the state
on the day of the murder?"

Smoking gun tests are unique but not certain; passage strongly affirms an explanation, but failure does not strongly undermine it. As Van Evera notes, a smoking gun
in the suspect's hands right after a murder strongly implicates the suspect, but the
absence of such a smoking gun does not exonerate a suspect. Smoking gun tests are
therefore usually used to instantiate a hypothesis of interest.

Doubly decisive tests on evidence that is both unique and certain can provide strong
inferences on both the truth and falsity of alternative explanations. Van Evera's example here is that of a bank camera that catches the faces of robbers, thereby implicating
the robbers and exonerating all others.

Finally, *straw in the wind tests* are neither unique nor certain and do not provide
strong evidence for or against the alternative explanations. Thus, in deciding whether
process-tracing evidence is sufficiently convincing to suspend further enquiry into
alternative explanations of a case, what matters is not only the importance attached
to getting the right explanation, but the kinds of evidence the researcher unearths
and the degree of confidence that this evidence allows. A single doubly decisive
piece of evidence may suffice, whereas many straw in the wind tests may still leave
indeterminacy in choosing between two incompatible explanations of a case. It is not
the number of pieces of evidence that matters, but the way in which the evidence
stacks up against the alternative explanations.

Process tracing thus works through both affirmation of explanations, through
evidence consistent with those explanations, and eliminative induction, or the use

of evidence to cast doubt on alternative explanations that do not fit the evidence in a case. This is why it is important to cast the net widely in considering alternative explanations of a case, and to be meticulous and even-handed in gathering and judging the process tracing evidence on all of the potential explanations of a case that scholars have proposed and that extant theories imply. Other standard injunctions for good process-tracing include the desirability of gathering diverse sources and kinds of evidence and of anticipating and accounting for potential biases in the sources of evidence (George and Bennett 2005; Bennett and Elman 2006). These desiderata are especially important in process tracing on social and political phenomena for which participating actors have strong instrumental or ideational reasons for hiding or misrepresenting evidence on their behavior or motives.

The example of Heinz Goemans's research on the end of the First World War illustrates these aspects of process-tracing. Goemans uses process-tracing evidence in the manner Van Evera describes to discount four alternative explanations for Germany's policies on the end of the First World War and to instantiate his own explanation. A first alternative explanation, that Germany should have behaved as a unitary actor and responded only to international considerations, fails a hoop test from Goemans's thorough evidence that Germany's war aims increased even as its prospects for victory diminished. A second argument, that Germany was throughout the war irrevocably committed to hegemony, is also undercut by evidence that German war aims in fact increased. Goemans disproves a third argument, that Germany's authoritarian government made it a "bad learner" impervious to evidence that it was losing the war, with ample indications that German leaders understood very well by late 1916 that their chances for victory were poor. A fourth explanation, that the change in Germany's military leadership led to the change in its war aims, begs the question of why Germany replaced its military leaders in the midst of the war (Goemans 2000, 74–5, 93–105).

Goemans then turns to his own explanation, which is that semi-authoritarian governments like Germany's are likely to gamble on war strategies with a small probability of a resounding victory but a high likelihood of abject defeat when they encounter evidence that they are losing a war. Elites in such regimes engage in this kind of behavior, Goemans argues, because for them negotiating an end to the war on modestly concessionary terms is little different from outright loss in the war. In this view, elites fear that domestic opponents could turn widespread unrest over the government's decision to engage in a costly and unsuccessful war into an opportunity to remove elites from power forcibly. Goemans provides smoking gun evidence for this argument in the case of Germany's escalating war aims. Among many other pieces of evidence, he quotes the German military leader Erich Ludendorff as arguing in a private letter that domestic political reforms would be required to stave off unrest if Germany were to negotiate a concessionary peace. Specifically, the extension of equal voting rights in Prussia "would be worse than a lost war" (Goemans 2000, 114).

3 THE LOGIC OF PROCESS TRACING
AND BAYESIAN INFERENCE

The logic of process tracing outlined above is strikingly similar to that of Bayesian inference. Like process tracing, Bayesian inference can be used to assess competing explanations of individual historical cases. In contrast, frequentist statistical forms of inference need a sufficiently large sample to get off the ground and face difficult challenges in making inferences about individual cases from aggregate data, a task known as the "ecological inference problem."[2] Process tracing and Bayesian inference are also closely analogous in their assertions that some pieces of evidence are far more discriminating among competing explanations than others, and they agree on the criteria that determine the probative value of evidence and on the importance of gathering diverse evidence. A third similarity is that both methods proceed through a combination of affirmative evidence on some hypotheses and eliminative induction of other hypothesized explanations that fail to fit the evidence. These similarities point to the potential strengths of the two approaches: It is possible that greatly differing prior expectations about how best to explain a case will converge as evidence accumulates, and depending on the nature of the evidence vis-à-vis the competing explanations, it *may* be possible to make strong inferences even from a few pieces of evidence in a single case. On the other hand, discussions of the limits of Bayesian inference help illuminate the limitations of process tracing as well. These limitations include the potential for underdetermination of choices among competing explanations and ambiguity on how to generalize from a single case even if it is a most- or least-likely case.

It is also important to note several differences between process tracing and Bayesian analysis. Bayesian analysis does not adequately capture the theory-generating side of process tracing, whereby entirely new hypotheses may occur to the researcher on the basis of a single piece of evidence for which no theory had a clear prior. Another difference is that researchers engaged in process tracing typically use Bayesian logic intuitively, rather than attempting to quantify precisely their priors, the specific probabilities associated with hypotheses and evidence, and the updated probabilities of hypotheses in light of evidence. There are also no case-study methods closely analogous to Bayesian statistical analysis of medium to large numbers of cases. Still, case-study researchers can benefit from a clearer understanding of Bayesian analysis and its application to case studies.

The Bayesian approach to theory testing focuses on updating degrees of belief in the truth of alternative explanations.[3] In other words, Bayesians treat statistical

---

[2] For an optimistic view on addressing and limiting this problem, see King (1997; 1999); for more pessimistic views, see Cho (1998) and Freedman et al. (1998; 1999).

[3] Bayesians often use the metaphor of placing wagers to illustrate how and why beliefs should be updated in light of new information if individuals are to maintain consistent beliefs. In effect, failure to adequately update one's wagers (beliefs) would allow an arbitrager to make a series of sure-winner "Dutch Book" bets. Scientists of course do not (usually) make actual monetary wagers based on their

parameters probabilistically, attaching subjective probabilities to the likelihood that hypotheses are true and then updating these probabilities in the light of new evidence. In contrast, frequentist statistics attaches probabilities to the likelihood of getting similar results from repeated sampling of a population. In frequentist statistics, confirming a hypothesis at the "5 percent level" does not mean that there is a 95 percent chance that the hypothesis is true; rather, it means that only one in twenty random samples from the population would lead just by chance to an estimate of the coefficient of the variable in question that is as different from zero as in the sample first tested (Western 1999, 9).

In Bayes's Theorem, which is derived from Bayes's work even though he did not state the theorem in exactly this form, the probability that a hypothesis H is true in light of evidence E and background knowledge K, or the conditional probability of H given E and K, is as follows:

$$\Pr(H/E \ \& \ K) = \frac{\Pr(H/K) \times \Pr(E/H \ \& \ K)}{\Pr(E/K)}.$$

In other words, the updated probability of a hypothesis being true in light of new evidence ($\Pr(H/E \ \& \ K)$) is equal to the prior probability attached to H (or $\Pr(H/K)$), times the likelihood of the evidence in light of hypothesis H and our background knowledge ($\Pr(E/H \ \& \ K)$), divided by the prior likelihood of E. Thus, the more unlikely a piece of evidence is in light of alternatives to explanation H, the more that evidence increases our confidence that H is true if the evidence proves consistent with H.

This corresponds quite closely with the discussion above of how process-tracing evidence from within a case can be used to update our confidence in alternative explanations of the case, and with the argument that not all evidence is of equal probative value. The more surprising process-tracing evidence proves to be for alternative explanations—that is, the more they fail their hoop tests—the more confidence we gain in the remaining hypotheses. The better that evidence fits the explanation of interest—that is, the more smoking gun tests the explanation passes—the more confidence we gain that the theory of interest explains the case. Evidence that sharply raises confidence in some explanations while markedly reducing confidence in others corresponds with Van Evera's doubly decisive test.

Here again, the analogy to detective work is useful. The sniper team that terrorized the Washington, DC, area in 2002, for example, was finally apprehended after someone called an information hotline and later a local priest claiming to be the sniper. The likelihood of this being true seemed exceedingly low in view of the large number of crank calls on the case, until evidence came to light that substantiated the caller's claim that the recent shootings were linked to an earlier shooting in Montgomery, Alabama. This evidence in turn generated a number of other leads, each of which was highly unlikely to be true unless the caller was in fact involved in the sniper shootings. When all of these otherwise improbable leads proved to be true, they led in turn to information identifying the car in which the sniper(s) could be found, allowing the

theories, but they do in effect wager their professional reputations and their working hours on the likelihood that hypotheses will prove true.

police to apprehend two suspects who were later convicted of the shootings (Bennett 2006, 341–2).

With enough of the right kind of evidence, even researchers who start out with very different prior probabilities on the alternative explanations should converge toward shared expectations (a phenomenon known as the "washing out of priors").[4] Similarly, Bayesian and frequentist analyses should converge on similar answers given sufficient evidence, whereas they may diverge when only a few cases or limited evidence are studied. This still leaves the problem of justifying one's prior probabilities when there is limited evidence, which many view as a key challenge for Bayesian analysis (Earman 1992, 58–9).

Although researchers' differing priors may or may not converge, the logic of Bayesian inference helps illustrate the common intuition that diversity of evidence is useful in testing hypotheses.[5] Repetitive evidence on the same facet or stage of a process soon loses its probative value, as it quickly becomes predictable or expected and can no longer surprise us or push us to change our priors. Independent evidence on a new or different dimension or stage of a hypothesized process, however, retains the potential for surprising us and forcing us to revise our priors. To borrow from the old adage, if something looks like a duck, walks like a duck, sounds like a duck, and so on, it is probably a duck. If we went on looks alone, however, no matter how many angles of vision we employ we can't easily tell a duck from a decoy. An example comes from the work of Yuen Foong Khong, who examined the analogies that American leaders used in making and justifying decisions on the Vietnam War. By assessing the analogies these leaders used in private meetings as well as public settings, and finding a close correspondence between the two (with the exception of analogies to Dien Bien Phu, which leaders did not use in public), Khong was able to reject the hypothesis that analogies were used only in public settings for the purposes of instrumental communication to defend choices made in camera for other reasons (Khong 1992, 58–63). Had Khong confined himself to public statements alone, his analysis would have been far less convincing no matter how many such statements he coded, as public statements alone could have been biased by the instrumental purposes of the actors making these statements. As in process tracing, it is not the

---

[4] There are methods in Bayesian statistical analysis for assessing the sensitivity of results to different priors, and Bayesian Markov Chain Monte Carlo analysis can use diffuse priors so that the results are not strongly affected by the priors (Western 1999, 11; Jackman 2004, 484, 488). There is no equivalent in the informally Bayesian techniques of process tracing, although the convergence on an explanation of a case by researchers who started out with different priors could be construed as an example of the washing out of priors.

[5] For arguments that Bayesianism helps explain the value of diversity of evidence, see Earman (1992, 78–9), Hellman (1997, 202–9); for a critique, see Kruse (1999, 171–4). Even if successful, Bayesian arguments on this point create a potential paradox, known as the problem of "old evidence." The Bayeisan theorem suggests that evidence already known cannot have additional probative value, as it has already been incorporated into the prior estimate of the likely truth of a hypothesis. This means that evidence can have probative value for one person who was previously ignorant of it, but not for another, who knew it already. This can be viewed as either a problem for Bayesianism, or as consistent with the intuition that priors are to some degree subjective and that researchers must guard against confirmation biases that attend old evidence. See Earman (1992, 119–20, 132).

number of cases or of pieces of evidence that matters, but the discriminating power and diversity of evidence vis-à-vis the alternative hypotheses under consideration.

This is quite different from the frequentist logic of inference, and it helps explain why the "degrees of freedom" critique sometimes leveled at case-study methods is woefully misguided. In frequentist statistical inference, the term "degrees of freedom" refers to the number of observations or cases minus the number of estimated parameters, or characteristics of the population being studied. In frequentist studies, this number is crucial, as the higher the degrees of freedom, the more powerful the test is at determining whether the observed variance could have been brought about by chance, and statistical studies simply cannot be done when there are negative degrees of freedom. This has at times led researchers trained in the frequentist tradition to worry that case studies that involve more parameters than cases are inherently indeterminate research designs. Any particular case-study design may in fact prove to be indeterminate in a deeper sense—indeed, as discussed below, Bayesian logic suggests that all research designs are on some level indeterminate—but the determinacy of any particular case-study design is not closely associated with the number of cases or parameters being studied.

The noted methodologist Donald Campbell got this intuition at least partly right when he set out to "correct some of my own prior excesses in describing the case study approach" and reconsidered his earlier critique of case-study methods for allegedly lacking degrees of freedom. Campbell argued that the theory a researcher uses to explain, for example, cultural differences "also generates predictions or expectations on dozens of other aspects of the culture, and he [sic] does not retain the theory unless most of these are also confirmed. In some sense, he [sic] has tested the theory with degrees of freedom coming from the multiple implications of any one theory" (Campbell 1975). Notice, however, that Campbell is still thinking in relatively frequentist terms about the nature of evidence in focusing on the *numbers* of expectations that are or are not met rather than the *probative value and diversity of evidence* relative to the competing hypotheses, as Bayesian logic suggests. The probative value of evidence does not depend on the number of pieces of evidence or the number of cases, but on how the evidence stacks up against competing explanations. A single piece of the right kind of evidence can establish one explanation of a case as highly likely to be true and all other proposed explanations as likely to be wrong, whereas thousands of pieces of evidence that do not discriminate between competing explanations may have no probative value at all. One piece of doubly decisive evidence can outweigh many less decisive bits of seemingly contradictory evidence.

Another parallel is that, in contrast to approaches that emphasize either confirmatory or disconfirming evidence, both process tracing and Bayesian inference proceed through a combination of affirmation of hypotheses consistent with the evidence and eliminative induction of hypothesis that do not fit. As is evident in Bayes's theorem, evidence that is highly unlikely in terms of the alternative hypotheses can raise our posterior estimate of the likely truth of a hypothesis just as evidence consistent with that hypothesis can. This is the root of Sir Arthur Conan Doyle's advice, through his fictional detective Sherlock Holmes, that an investigation "starts upon the supposition that when you have eliminated all which is impossible, then whatever remains, however improbable, must be the truth. It may well be that several explanations remain, in which case one tries test after test until one or other of them has a convincing amount of support" (Doyle 1927, 1011, in "The Blanched Soldier" in *The Case-Book of Sherlock Holmes*; see also Earman 1992, 163–5 on eliminative induction).

Kenneth Schultz provides an excellent example of both affirmative evidence and eliminative induction in his analysis of the 1898 Fashoda crisis between Britain and France. The Fashoda crisis arose over the convergence of British and French expeditionary forces on the town of Fashoda as they raced to lay claim to the Upper Nile Valley. Schultz lays out three alternative explanations that scholars have offered for why the crisis was resolved without a war when France chose to back down from its claims. Neorealists have argued that France backed down short of war simply because Britain's military forces were far stronger, both in the region and globally. Schultz rejects this explanation because it fails to survive a hoop test: It cannot explain why the crisis happened in the first place, why it lasted two months, and why it escalated almost to the point of war, as it should have been obvious from the outset that Britain had military superiority (Schultz 2001, 177). A second argument, that democratic norms and institutions led to mutual restraint, also fails a hoop test in Schultz's view. The British public and British leaders, far from being conciliatory, as traditional democratic peace theories based on the restraining power of democratic norms and institutions would suggest, were belligerent in their rhetoric and actions toward France throughout the crisis (Schultz 2001, 180–3).

Schultz then turns to his own explanation, which is that democratic institutions force democratic leaders to reveal private information about their intentions, making it difficult for democratic leaders to bluff in some circumstances but also making their threats to use force more credible in others. In this view democratic institutions reinforce the credibility of coercive threats when domestic opposition parties and publics support these threats, but they undermine the credibility of threats when domestic groups publicly oppose the use of force. Schultz supports this explanation with smoking gun evidence in its favor. The credibility of Britain's public commitment to take control of the region was resoundingly affirmed by the opposition Liberal Party leader Lord Rosebery (Schultz 2001, 188). Meanwhile, France's Foreign Minister, Theophile Delcasse, initially made public commitments to an intransigent position, but he was quickly undermined by public evidence of apathy and even outright opposition by other domestic political actors (Schultz 2001, 193). After this costly signaling by both sides revealed that Britain had a greater willingness as well as capability to fight for the Upper Nile, within a matter of days France began to back down, leading to a resolution of the crisis in Britain's favor. The close timing of these events, following in the sequence predicted by Schultz's theory, provides strong evidence for his explanation.

Discussions of Bayesian inference also illuminate the limitations of both Bayesianism and process tracing. Foremost among these is the underdetermination thesis (sometimes referred to as the Quine–Duhem problem after the two philosophers of science who called attention to it, Pierre Duhem and Willard Van Orman Quine).

In this view, the choice among competing theories is always underdetermined by evidence, as it is not entirely clear whether evidence falsifies a theory itself or one of the theory's (often implicit) "auxiliary hypotheses" about contextual variables, methods of observation and measurement, and so on. It is also not clear which of the potentially infinite alternative explanations deserves serious consideration, and by definition we cannot consider potentially true alternative hypotheses that we simply have not yet conceived. In Bayes's theorem, these problems arise in the term K, which represents the likelihood of evidence in light of our background knowledge of the alternative hypotheses (or, put another way, the probability of observing E if H is not true). This term is sometimes called the "catchall factor" because it is in effect a grab-bag of all hypotheses other than H, including even those not yet proposed. As it is not actually possible to consider all the potential alternative explanations, Bayesians have gravitated to the pragmatic advice, similar to that offered by proponents of process tracing, that one should cast the net for alternative explanations widely, considering even those explanations that have few proponents if they make different predictions from those of the hypothesis of interest (Earman 1992, 84–5; for a critique see Kruse 1999, 165–71). This remains at best a provisional approach, however, which is one reason that Bayesians never attach 100 percent probability to the likely truth of theories.

Another version of the underdetermination problem is that the evidence might not even allow us to choose decisively between two extant hypotheses that give incompatible explanations. Differences between priors, in other words, may not wash out if there is not adequate evidence, bringing us back to the problem that priors themselves lack any clear justification. As argued above, the severity of this problem in any particular study depends on the nature of the competing hypotheses vis-à-vis the evidence, not on the number of cases or variables—indeed, underdetermination of this sort can be a problem even with many cases and few variables. With the right kind of evidence, some studies may achieve a high degree of confidence in a particular explanation, but there is no general assurance that any given case study will achieve this result.

A third challenge for both Bayesianism and process tracing is that of generalizing from one or a few cases. Bayesian logic can help to some degree with this problem. For example, case-study methodologists have long argued, consistent with Bayesianism, that if a hypothesis appears to accurately explain a tough test case which, a priori, it looked "least likely" to explain, then the hypothesis is strongly affirmed. Conversely, failure to explain a "most likely" case strongly undermines our confidence in a hypothesis. It remains unclear, however, whether these inferences should apply only to the case being studied, to very similar cases to the one studied, or to a broader range of more diverse cases. This kind of inference depends on both our knowledge of the hypothesis, which may itself provide clues on its scope conditions, and our knowledge of the population of cases for which the hypothesis is relevant. These kinds of information must come from either prior knowledge or further study (whether Bayesian or frequentist) of more cases.

To take an example from actual research, my colleagues and I concluded from our study of burden sharing in the 1991 Persian Gulf War that one hypothesis had proved true even in the least-likely cases of Germany and Japan. This was the hypothesis that countries would contribute to an alliance if they were dependent on the alliance leader for their security. In the cases of Germany and Japan, this proved true even though every other hypothesis—the collective action/free riding hypothesis, the domestic politics hypothesis (political opposition at home and a weak state on foreign policy), the "balance of threat" hypothesis—pointed against a substantial contribution by either country. This finding suggested that the alliance dependence hypothesis generally deserved more weight than it had been accorded in the alliance literature, which up to that time was dominated by the collective action hypothesis. In the absence of wider statistical or qualitative studies of more episodes of alliance behavior, however, we could not conclude precisely on the conditions under which or the extent to which an increase in alliance dependence would lead to a specific increase in burden-sharing commitments (Bennett, Lepgold, and Unger 1997).

Finally, there are areas in which Bayesian inference and process tracing are simply different. Bayesianism does not have any equivalent for the generation of new hypotheses from the close process-tracing study of a case. As John Earman has noted, "data-instigated hypotheses call for literally ad hoc responses. When new evidence suggests new theories, a non-Bayesian shift in the belief function may take place" (Earman 1992, 100; see also Hellman 1997, 215). Another issue to which Bayesians have paid less attention than qualitative methodologists is the problem of potential biases in information sources. It is certainly consistent with Bayesianism to discount the likely truth value of evidence that comes from biased or incomplete sources, but most discussions of Bayesian inference do not focus on this problem, perhaps because they usually address examples in the natural sciences in which potential measurement error, rather than intentional obfuscation of evidence by goal-oriented actors, is the most common problem with evidence.

4 AN EXTENDED EXAMPLE: DEBATES ON THE END OF THE COLD WAR

There are many excellent examples of process tracing and Bayesian inference in political science. In the international relations subfield alone these would include but certainly not be limited to books by Drezner (1999), Eden (2006), Evangelista (2002), George and Smoke (1974), Homer-Dixon (2001), Khong (1992), Knopf (1998), Larson (1989), Moravcsik (1998), Sagan (1993), Shafer (1988), Snyder (1984; 1993), Walt (1996), and Weber (1991).[6] I focus here on the historiographical debate on the peaceful

---

[6] For brief descriptions of the research designs by Drezner, George and Smoke, Homer-Dixon, Khong, Knopf, Larson, Owen, Sagan, Shafer, Snyder, and Weber, see George and Bennett (2005, 118–19, 194–7, 302–25); on Evangelista, see Bennett and Elman (2007).

end of the cold war, and particularly the absence of Soviet military interventions in the Eastern European revolutions of 1989. I have contributed to this debate, and it is one on which scholars' prior theoretical expectations have only partially converged. I introduce it here not to convince readers of my own side of this debate, which would require a far more detailed analysis of the competing views and evidence, but to illustrate the kind of Bayesian inference from process-tracing evidence that is involved in such judgments. I also use this example because it is far easier to reconstruct the process-tracing involved in one's own research than to dissect process tracing done by other researchers. I focus here on three of the most prominent explanations for the nonuse of force in 1989: the realist explanation, which emphasizes the changing material balance of power; the domestic politics explanation, which focuses on the changing nature of the Soviet Union's ruling coalition; and the ideational explanation, which highlights the lessons Soviet leaders drew from their recent experiences in using force.

Stephen Brooks and William Wohlforth (Brooks and Wohlforth 2000–1; see also Wohlforth 1994–5; Oye 1996) have constructed the most comprehensive realist/balance of power explanation for Soviet restraint in 1989. Brooks and Wohlforth argue that the decline in Soviet economic growth rates in the 1980s, combined with the Soviet Union's "imperial overstretch" in Afghanistan and its high defense spending burden, was the driving force in Soviet foreign policy retrenchment in the late 1980s. In particular, these authors argue, Soviet leaders were constrained from using force in 1989 because this would have imposed large direct economic and military costs, risked economic sanctions from the West, and forced the Soviet Union to assume the economic burden of the large debts that Eastern European regimes had incurred to the West. In this view, changes in Soviet leaders' ideas about foreign policy were largely determined by changes in their material capabilities.

Jack Snyder has been the foremost proponent of a second hypothesis focused on Soviet domestic politics (Snyder 1987–8). Snyder argues that the long-term shift in the Soviet economy from extensive development (focused on basic industrial goods) to intensive development (involving more sophisticated and information-intensive goods and services) brought about a shift in the ruling Soviet coalition from the military-heavy industry-party complex to light industry and the intelligentsia. This led the Soviet Union to favor improved ties to the West to gain access to technology and trade, which would have been undermined had the Soviet Union used force in 1989. Snyder has not directly applied this argument to Soviet restraint in the use of force in 1989, though he did continue to view sectoral material interests as the driving factor in Soviet policy after 1989 (Snyder 1990).

I have emphasized a third "learning" explanation, namely that Soviet leaders drew lessons from their recent unsuccessful military interventions in Afghanistan and elsewhere that made them doubt the efficacy of using force to resolve long-term political problems (Bennett 1999; 2003; 2005; see also English 2000; 2002; Checkel 1997; Stein 1994).

While scholars agree that the variables highlighted by all three of these hypotheses contributed to the nonuse of force in 1989, there remains considerable disagreement on their relative causal weight, the ways in which they interacted, and the coun-terfactuals that each hypothesis could plausibly sustain. Brooks and Wohlforth, for example, disagree with the "standard view" that "even though decline did prompt change in Soviet foreign policy, the resulting shift could just as easily have been toward aggression or a new version of muddling through and that other factors played a key role in resolving this uncertainty" (Brooks and Wohlforth 2002, 94). In contrast, I find this "standard view" convincing and argue that although the Soviet Union's material decline relative to the West created pressures for foreign policy change, the timing and direction of the foreign policy changes that resulted were greatly influenced by the lessons Soviet leaders drew from their recent failures in the use of force in Afghanistan and elsewhere.

How are we to judge the competing claims of each hypothesis? Nina Tannenwald has offered three relevant process-tracing tests (Tannenwald 2005): First, did ideas correlate with the needs of the Soviet state, actors' personal material interests, or actors' personal experiences and the information to which they were exposed? Sec-ond, did material change precede or follow ideational change? Third, do material or ideational factors better explain which ideas won out? A brief overview of the evidence on each of these points reveals "smoking gun" evidence for both the material and ideational explanations, and a failed "hoop test" for one variant of the material explanation; on the whole, it appears that evidence for sectoral material interests is weakest.

On Tannenwald's first test, the correlation of policy positions with material ver-sus ideational variables, there is some evidence for each explanation, mostly of the "straw in the wind" variety that can only be briefly summarized here. Brooks and Wohlforth argue, citing Soviet Defense Minister Yazov and others, that Soviet con-servatives and military leaders largely did not question Gorbachev's concessionary foreign policies because they understood that the Soviet Union was in dire economic straits and needed to reach out to the West (Brooks and Wohlforth 2000–1). Robert English, pointing to other statements by Soviet conservatives indicating opposition to Gorbachev's foreign policies, concludes instead that "whatever one believes about the old thinkers' acquiescence in Gorbachev's initiatives, it remains inconceivable that they would have launched similar initiatives without him" (English 2002, 78). It is hard to conceive of what "smoking gun" or "hoop test" evidence would look like on this issue, however, as the policy views of any one individual, even an individual as historically important as Gorbachev, cannot definitively show that material incentives rather than ideas were more important in driving and shaping changes in Soviet policies.

More definitive is the hoop-type evidence against Snyder's sectoral interest group explanation: Although Soviet military leaders did at times argue against defense spending cuts, and the conservatives who attempted a coup against Gorbachev in 1990 represented the Stalinist coalition of the military and heavy industry, these actors did *not* argue, even after they had already fallen from power and had little to lose, that force should have been used to prevent the dissolution of the Warsaw Pact in 1989 (Bennett 2005, 104). Indeed, military leaders were among the early skeptics on the use of force in Afghanistan, and many prominent officers with personal experience in Afghanistan resigned their commissions rather than participate in the 1994–7 Russian intervention in Chechnya (Bennett 1999, 339–40).

Tannenwald's second test concerns the timing of material and ideational change. Brooks and Wohlforth have not stated precisely the timeframe within which they believe material decline would have allowed or compelled Soviet foreign policy change, stating only that material incentives shape actions over the "longer run" (2002, 97). The logic of their argument, however, suggests that the Soviet Union could have profitably let go of its Eastern European empire in 1973, by which time nuclear parity guaranteed the Soviet Union's security from external attack and high energy prices meant that the Soviet Union could have earned a higher price for its oil and natural gas on world markets than it got from Eastern Europe. Moreover, the sharpest decline in the Soviet economy came after 1987, by which time Gorbachev had already begun to signal to governments in Eastern Europe that he would not use force to rescue them from popular opposition (Brown 1996, 249). The timing of the ideational explanation coincides much more closely with changes in Soviet foreign policy. Soviet leaders were quite optimistic about the use of force in the developing world in the late 1970s, despite slow Soviet economic growth, but they became far more pessimistic regarding the efficacy of force as their failure in Afghanistan became more apparent (Bennett 1999). Moreover, changes in Soviet leaders' public statements generally preceded changes in Soviet foreign policy, suggesting that ideational change, rather than material interests justified by ad hoc and post hoc changes in stated ideas, were the driving factor (Bennett 1999, 351–2).

The most definitive process-tracing evidence, however, concerns the third question of why some ideas won out over others. Here, there is strong evidence that both material and ideational factors played a role, but one variant of the material explanation appears to have failed a hoop test. Two internal Soviet reports on the situation in Europe in early 1989, one by the International Department (ID) of the Soviet Communist Party and one by the Soviet Institute on the Economy of the World Socialist System (IEMSS in Russian), argued that a crackdown in Eastern Europe would have painful economic consequences for the Soviet Union, including sanctions from the West. The IEMSS report also noted the growing external debts of Soviet allies in Eastern Europe (Bennett 2005, 96–7). At the same time, these reports provide ample evidence for the learning explanation: The IEMSS report warns that a crackdown in Poland could lead to an "Afghanistan in the Middle of Europe" (Bennett 2005, 101), and the ID report argues that "authoritarian methods and direct pressure are clearly obsolete . . . it is very unlikely we would be able to employ the methods of 1956 [the Soviet intervention in Hungary] and 1968 [the Soviet intervention in Czechoslovakia], both as a matter of principle, but also because of unacceptable consequences" (Bennett 2005, 97).

While both material and ideational considerations played a role, there is reason to believe that the latter was predominant in the mind of the key actor, Mikhail Gorbachev. In a meeting on October 31, 1989, just ten days before the Berlin Wall fell, Gorbachev was reportedly "astonished" at hearing from East German leader Egon

Krenz that East Germany owed the West $26.5 billion, almost half of which had been borrowed in 1989 (Zelikow and Rice 1995, 87). Thus, while Gorbachev was certainly concerned about the Soviet economy's performance, the claim that he was in part inhibited from using force in Eastern Europe because of the region's external debts appears to have failed a hoop test.

Finally, counterfactual analysis can shed light on analysts' Bayesian expectations and the need to update them. Jack Snyder carefully and conscientiously outlined in early 1988 the (then) counterfactual future events that would in his view have led to a resurgence of the Stalinist coalition of the military and heavy industry. If Gorbachev's reforms were discredited through poor economic performance, and if the Soviet Union faced "a hostile international environment in which SDI [the Strategic Defense Initiative] was being deployed, Eastern Europe was asserting its autonomy, and Soviet clients were losing their counterinsurgency wars in Afghanistan, Angola, and Ethiopia," Snyder argued, the rise of anti-reform Soviet leaders was much more likely. As it turned out, every one of these conditions except for the deployment of a working SDI system was over-fulfilled within two years, yet apart from the thoroughly unsuccessful coup attempt of 1990, Soviet hardliners never came close to regaining power.

It is also worth considering the counterfactual implications of the material and ideational arguments. The counterfactual of the Brooks–Wohlforth argument is that had Gorbachev's reforms succeeded in dramatically improving Soviet economic production by 1989, the Soviet Union would have been more likely to use force against the revolutions in Eastern Europe. Brooks and Wohlforth have never gone so far as to assert or defend this claim, however. The counterfactual implication of my own argument, and one that I find eminently plausible, is that if Soviet displays and uses of force in Poland in 1980–1, in Afghanistan in 1979 and after, and in other conflicts in the 1970s and 1980s had been considered successes by Soviet leaders in 1989, they would have been far more likely to have threatened and used force to stop the revolutions of 1989. The (apparently) different degrees of belief that we attach to the counterfactual implications of our arguments of course do not constitute evidence on the truth of these arguments, but they do reinforce the point that Bayesian logic's focus on updating degrees of belief through evidence is an apt description of the logic of process tracing as well.

5 CONCLUSION

The logic of Bayesian inference illuminates both the strengths and limitations of process tracing. Among the strengths of both approaches is that it is possible to make strong inferences in just one or a few cases, based on one or a few pieces of the right kind of evidence, if this evidence strongly discriminates between alternative hypotheses in the ways discussed above. Thus, the "Degrees of Freedom" problem is inapplicable to process tracing, even though the more fundamental problem of underdetermination remains. Both approaches are congruent as well, in that they proceed by both affirmation and eliminative induction, that they view some kinds of evidence as far more probative than other kinds of evidence, and that they stress the importance of obtaining diverse evidence on the phenomenon under study.

As for weaknesses, both Bayesianism and process tracing face the problem that prior theoretical expectations may have no absolute justification. With the right kind of evidence differing priors may converge, but in the absence of such evidence they will not. Bayesian logic also serves as a useful reminder that the explanations derived from process tracing are always provisional, which is another way of framing the problem of underdetermination. Because we can never have a full accounting of the background factor of all possible alternative explanations, we should never let our confidence in the likely truth of an explanation equal 100 percent. Moreover, even if the evidence gives us a high degree of confidence in an explanation of a case, Bayesian logic offers only partial help on the challenge of generalizing from a case. Theories that succeed in their least-likely cases may deserve greater weight and scope, and those that fail in most-likely cases may deserve to be rejected or narrowed, but beyond this general conclusion it remains unclear whether or how Bayesian logic can assist in identifying the populations to which an explanation might be applicable, especially in the absence of prior knowledge about such potentially relevant populations.

Bayesianism and process tracing do not overlap completely. There is no Bayesian equivalent for generating a completely new hypothesis from the close process-tracing study of a case. As the example of Darwin's inferences on evolution reminds us, there may also be ways of generalizing from a new hypothesis derived from a case, and from prior knowledge about populations that share some features of the case, that prove to have little to do with Bayesianism. Yet for all their differences, perhaps including those not yet discussed nor discovered (the catchall factor!), the similarities between Bayesian and process-tracing analyses of individual cases, from medical diagnoses to studies of war and peace, reveal the uses and limits of both.

References

BENNETT, A. 1999. *Condemned to Repetition? The Rise, Fall, and Reprise of Soviet-Russian Military Interventionism 1973–1996*. Cambridge, Mass.: MIT Press.

—— 2003. Trust bursting out all over: the Soviet side of German unification. Pp. 175–204 in *Cold War Endgame*, ed. W. Wohlforth. University Park: Pennsylvania State University Press.

—— 2005. The guns that didn't smoke: ideas and the Soviet non-use of force in 1989. *Journal of Cold War Studies*, 7: 81–109.

—— 2006. Stirring the frequentist pot with a dash of Bayes. *Political Analysis*, 14: 339–44.

—— and ELMAN, C. 2006. Qualitative research: recent developments in case study methods. *Annual Review of Political Science*, 9: 455–76.

—— —— 2007. Case study methods in the international relations subfield. *Comparative Political Studies*, 40: 170–95.

BENNETT, A., LEPGOLD, J., and UNGER, D. (eds.) 1997. *Friends in Need: Burden Sharing in the Persian Gulf War*. New York: St Martin's Press.

BRADY, H., and COLLIER, D. 2004. *Rethinking Social Inquiry: Diverse Tools, Shared Standards*. Savage, Md.: Rowman and Littlefield.

BROOKS, S., and WOHLFORTH, W. 2000–1. Power, globalization, and the end of the Cold War: reevaluating a landmark case for ideas. *International Security*, 25: 5–53.

———— 2002. From old thinking to new thinking in qualitative research. *International Security*, 26: 93–111.

BROWN, A. 1996. *The Gorbachev Factor*. Oxford: Oxford University Press.

CAMPBELL, D. 1975. Degrees of freedom and the case study. *Comparative Political Studies*, 8: 178–85.

CHECKEL, J. 1997. *Ideas and International Political Change: Soviet/Russian Behavior and the End of the Cold War*. New Haven, Conn.: Yale University Press.

CHO, W. T. 1998. Iff the assumption fits...: a comment on the King ecological inference solution. *Political Analysis*, 7: 43–163.

DOYLE, A. C. 1927. *The Casebook of Sherlock Holmes*. London: John Murray.

DREZNER, D. 1999. *The Sanctions Paradox: Economic Statecraft and International Relations*. Cambridge: Cambridge University Press.

EARMAN, J. 1992. *Bayes or Bust? A Critical Examination of Bayesian Confirmation Theory*. Cambridge, Mass.: MIT Press.

EDEN, L. 2006. *Whole World on Fire: Organizations, Knowledge, and Nuclear Weapons Devastation*. Ithaca, NY: Cornell University Press.

ENGLISH, R. 2000. *Russia and the Idea of the West: Gorbachev, Intellectuals, and the End of the Cold War*. New York: Columbia University Press.

———— 2002. Power, ideas, and new evidence on the Cold War's end: a reply to Brooks and Wohlforth. *International Security*, 26: 70–92.

EVANGELISTA, M. 2002. *Unarmed Forces: The Transnational Movement to End the Cold War*. Ithaca, NY: Cornell University Press.

FREEDMAN, D. A., KLEIN, S. P., OSTLAND, M., and ROBERTS, M. R. 1998. Review of *A Solution to the Ecological Inference Problem* by G. King. *Journal of the American Statistical Association*, 93: 1518–22.

———— OSTLAND, M., ROBERTS, M. R., and KLEIN, S. P. 1999. Response to King's comment. *Journal of the American Statistical Association*, 94: 355–7.

GEORGE, A. L., and BENNETT, A. 2005. *Case Studies and Theory Development in the Social Sciences*. Cambridge, Mass.: MIT Press.

———— and SMOKE, R. 1974. *Deterrence in American Foreign Policy: Theory and Practice*. New York: Columbia University Press.

GILL, C. J., SABIN, L., and SCHMID, C. H. 2005. Clinicians as natural Bayesians. *British Medical Journal*, 330: 1080–3.

GOEMANS, H. 2000. *War and Punishment: The Causes of War Termination and the First World War*. Princeton, NJ: Princeton University Press.

HELLMAN, G. 1997. Bayes and beyond. *Philosophy of Science*, 64: 191–221.

HOMER-DIXON, T. 2001. *Environment, Scarcity, and Violence*. Princeton, NJ: Princeton University Press.

JACKMAN, S. 2004. Bayesian analysis for political research. *Annual Reviews of Political Science*, 7: 483–505.

KHONG, Y. F. 1992. *Analogies at War: Korea, Munich, Dien Bien Phu and the Vietnam Decisions of 1965*. Princeton, NJ: Princeton University Press.

KING, G. 1997. *A Solution to the Ecological Inference Problem: Reconstructing Individual Behavior from Aggregate Data*. Princeton, NJ: Princeton University Press.

—— 1999. The future of ecological inference research: a comment on Friedman et al. *Journal of the American Statistical Association*, 94: 352–5.

—— KEOHANE, R., and VERBA, S. 1994. *Designing Social Inquiry*. Princeton, NJ: Princeton University Press.

KNOPF, J. 1998. *Domestic Society and International Cooperation: The Impact of Protest on U.S. Arms Control Policy*. Cambridge: Cambridge University Press.

KRUSE, M. 1999. Beyond Bayesianism: comments on Hellman's "Bayes and beyond." *Philosophy of Science*, 66: 165–74.

LARSON, D. W. 1989. *Origins of Containment*. Princeton, NJ: Princeton University Press.

McKEOWN, T. 2003. Case studies and the statistical world view. *International Organization*, 53: 161–90.

MORAVCSIK, A. 1998. *The Choice for Europe: Social Purpose and State Power from Messing to Maastricht*. Ithaca, NY: Cornell University Press.

OYE, K. 1996. Explaining the end of the Cold War: morphological and behavior adaptations to the nuclear peace? Pp. 57–83 in *International Relations Theory and the End of the Cold War*, ed. R. N. Lebow and T. Risse-Kappen. New York: Columbia University Press.

SAGAN, S. 1993. *The Limits of Safety: Organizations, Accidents, and Nuclear Weapons*. Princeton, NJ: Princeton University Press.

SCHULTZ, K. A. 2001. *Democracy and Coercive Diplomacy*. Cambridge: Cambridge University Press.

SCOTT, J. C. 1985. *Weapons of the Weak*. New Haven, Conn.: Yale University Press.

SHAFER, D. M. 1988. *Deadly Paradigms: The Failure of U.S. Counterinsurgency Policy*. Princeton, NJ: Princeton University Press.

SNYDER, J. 1984. *The Ideology of the Offensive: Military Decision Making and the Disasters of 1914*. Ithaca, NY: Cornell University Press.

—— 1987–8. The Gorbachev revolution: a waning of Soviet expansionism? *International Security*, 12: 93–131.

—— 1990. Averting anarchy in the new Europe. *International Security*, 14: 5–41.

—— 1993. *Myths of Empire: Domestic Politics and International Ambition*. Ithaca, NY: Cornell University Press.

STEIN, J. G. 1994. Political learning by doing: Gorbachev as uncommitted thinker and motivated learner. *International Organization*, 48: 155–83.

TANNENWALD, N. 2005. Ideas and explanation: advancing the theoretical agenda. *Journal of Cold War Studies*, 7: 13–42.

VAN EVERA, S. 1997. *Guide to Methods for Students of Political Science*. Ithaca, NY: Cornell University Press.

WALT, S. 1996. *Revolution and War*. Ithaca, NY: Cornell University Press.

WEBER, S. 1991. *Cooperation and Discord in U.S.–Soviet Arms Control*. Princeton, NJ: Princeton University Press.

WESTERN, B. 1999. Bayesian analysis for sociologists: an introduction. *Sociological Methods and Research*, 28: 7–34.

WOHLFORTH, W. 1994–5. Realism and the end of the Cold War. *International Security*, 19: 91–129.

ZELIKOW, P., with RICE, C. 1995. *Germany Unified and Europe Transformed: A Study in Statecraft*. Cambridge, Mass.: Harvard University Press.

....

CASE-ORIENTED CONFIGURA-TIONAL RESEARCH: QUALITATIVE COMPARATIVE ANALYSIS (QCA), FUZZY SETS, AND RELATED TECHNIQUES

....

BENOÎT RIHOUX

With the support of the Fonds National de la Recherche Scientifique—FNRS (Belgium)—FRFC fund. Many ideas in this chapter have been elaborated together with Charles Ragin, and discussed at length with other contributors of an edited textbook on this topic (Rihoux and Ragin 2008).

Most of the points in this chapter, as well as practical descriptions and discussions of the techniques, are further elaborated in two textbooks (Rihoux and Ragin 2008; Schneider and Wagemann 2007; forthcoming). Some software instructions are also available through <http://www.compasss.org>—"software" links.

1 INTRODUCTION

QUALITATIVE comparative analysis (or QCA[1]; Ragin 1987) and linked techniques such as fuzzy sets (Ragin 2000; and this volume) were developed for the analysis of small- and intermediate-N data-sets, typical of those used by researchers in comparative politics and related disciplines. These techniques are designed to unravel causal complexity by applying set-theoretic methods to cross-case evidence. Their central goal is to mimic some of the basic analytic procedures that comparative researchers use routinely when making sense of their cases. The key difference between QCA and traditional case-oriented methods is that with QCA it is possible to extend these basic analytic procedures to the examination of more than a handful of cases. There is no procedural limit on the number of cases that can be studied using QCA.

This chapter offers a conceptually oriented introduction to QCA, also discussing some key technical issues. First, two analytic procedures commonly used by comparative researchers are laid out and contrasted with correlational analysis, the main analytical engine of mainstream quantitative social science. Second, a short description of the state-of-the-art of QCA applications is provided, in terms of discipline, types of cases, models, combinations with other methods, and software development. Next, different uses of QCA are outlined, as well as generic "best practices." Fourth, some key recent evolutions are presented: on the one hand the development, beyond dichotomous "crisp set" QCA (csQCA), of multi-value QCA (mvQCA), fuzzy sets, and fuzzy-set QCA (fsQCA), and on the other hand technical advances and refinements in the use of the techniques. Finally, concluding reflections are offered as to expected developments, upcoming innovations, remaining challenges, expansion of fields of application, and cross-fertilization with other approaches.

2 THE DISTINCTIVENESS OF COMPARATIVE RESEARCH

Researchers in comparative politics and related fields often seek to identify commonalities across cases, focusing on a relatively small number of purposefully selected cases. There are two analytic strategies central to this type of research. The first one is to examine cases sharing a given *outcome* (e.g. consolidated third-wave democracies)

---

[1] Hereafter, QCA is used generically to refer to both csQCA (crisp-set QCA, dichotomous), mvQCA (multi-value QCA), and fsQCA (fuzzy-set QCA, a variant linking fuzzy sets to QCA procedures). All are grouped, together with fuzzy sets, under the "configurational comparative methods" label (Rihoux and Ragin 2008).

and to attempt to identify their shared *conditions*[2] (e.g. the possibility that they share presidential systems). The second one is to examine cases sharing a specific condition or, more commonly, a specific combination of conditions, and to assess whether or not these cases exhibit the same outcome (e.g. do cases that combine party fractionalization, a weak executive, and a low level of economic development all suffer democratic breakdown?). Both strategies are set theoretic in nature. The first is an examination of whether instances of a specific outcome constitute a subset of instances of one or more causal conditions. The second is an examination of whether instances of a specific causal condition or combination of causal conditions constitute a subset of instances of an outcome.

Both strategies are methods for establishing *specific* connections. If it is found, for example, that all (or nearly all[3]) consolidated third-wave democracies have presidential systems, then a specific connection has been established between presidentialism and consolidation—assuming this connection dovetails with existing theoretical and substantive knowledge. Likewise, if it is found that all (or nearly all) third-wave democracies that share a low level of economic development, party fractionalization, and a weak executive failed as democracies, then a specific connection has been established between this combination of conditions and democratic breakdown. Establishing specific connections is not the same as establishing correlations. For example, assume that the survival rate for third-wave democracies with presidential systems is 60 percent, while the survival rate for third-wave democracies with parliamentary systems is 35 percent. Clearly, there is a correlation between these two aspects conceived as variables (presidential versus parliamentary system and survival versus failure). However, the evidence does not come close to approximating a set-theoretic relation: There is evidence of correlation (i.e. a general connection), but not of a specific connection between presidential systems and democratic survival in this example.

As explained in Ragin (2000), the first analytic strategy—identifying conditions shared by cases with the same outcome—is appropriate for the assessment of necessary conditions. The second—examining cases with the same causal conditions to see if they also share the same outcome—is suitable for the assessment of sufficient conditions, especially sufficient combinations of conditions. Establishing conditions that are necessary or sufficient is a long-standing interest of comparative researchers (see, e.g., Goertz and Starr 2002). However, the use of set-theoretic methods to establish explicit connections does not necessarily entail the use of the concepts or the language of necessity and sufficiency, or any other language of causation. A researcher might observe, for example, that instances of democratic breakdown are all ex-colonies without drawing any causal connection from this observation. Demonstrating explicit connections is important to social scientists, whether or not

---

[2] The term *condition* is used generically to designate an aspect of a case that is relevant in some way to the researcher's account or explanation of some *outcome* exhibited by the case. Note that it is not an "independent variable" in the statistical sense.

[3] Neither strategy expects or depends on perfect set-theoretic relations (see Ragin, this volume).

Table 31.1. Cross-tabulation of presence/absence of an outcome against presence/absence of a condition

	Condition absent	Condition present
Outcome present	Cell 1: cases here undermine researcher's argument	Cell 2: cases here support researcher's argument
Outcome absent	Cell 3: cases here support researcher's argument	Cell 4: cases here undermine researcher's argument

they are interested in demonstrating causation. In fact, qualitative analysis in the social sciences is centrally concerned with establishing specific connections.

Correlational methods are not well suited for studying specific connections (Ragin 2000). This mismatch is clearly visible in the simplest form of variable-oriented analysis, the 2×2 cross-tabulation of the presence/absence of an outcome against the presence/absence of an hypothesized cause (Table 31.1).

The correlation (used in the generic sense) focuses simultaneously and equivalently on the degree to which instances of the cause produce instances of the outcome (the number of cases in cell 2 relative to the sum of cells 2 and 4) *and on* the degree to which instances of the absence of the cause are linked to the absence of the outcome (the number of cases in cell 3 relative to the sum of cells 1 and 3). In short, it is an omnibus statistic that rewards researchers for producing an abundance of cases in cell 2 and/or cell 3 and penalizes them for depositing many cases in cell 1 and/or cell 4. Thus, it is a good tool for studying general (correlational) connections.

A researcher interested in specific connections, however, focuses only on some specific components of the information that is conflated in a correlation. For example, comparative researchers interested in causally relevant conditions shared by instances of an outcome would focus on cells 1 and 2. Their goal would be to identify conditions that deposit as few cases as possible in cell 1. Likewise, researchers interested in whether cases that are similar with respect to conditions experience the same outcome would focus on cells 2 and 4. Their goal would be to identify combinations of causal conditions that deposit as few cases as possible in cell 4. It is clear from these examples that the correlation has two major shortcomings when viewed from the perspective of specific connections: (1) it attends only to relative differences (e.g. relative survival rates of presidential versus parliamentary systems); and (2) it conflates different kinds of set-theoretic assessment.

As the bivariate correlation is the foundation of most forms of conventional quantitative social research, including some of the most sophisticated forms of variable-oriented analysis practiced today (Ragin and Sonnett 2004), these sophisticated quantitative techniques eschew the study of explicit connections. QCA, by contrast, is centrally concerned with specific connections. It is grounded in formal logic (Boolean algebra and set-theoretic language), and thus is ideally suited for identifying key set-theoretic relations. An especially useful feature of QCA is its capacity for analyzing complex causation ("multiple conjunctural causation"), defined as a situation where a given outcome may follow from several different combinations of conditions—different causal "paths." Let us consider, for instance, a qualitative outcome such as being fired (or not) from a job. There are different things one could do to get fired: stealing, showing up late, defaming, etc., or all these things combined. The point is that each one of these actions leads one to be fired, and they are all different ways to be fired. In this instance, a single model of the process would be a gross misrepresentation of what happens empirically. It wouldn't mean much to estimate the relative influence of those different actions on the outcome of "being fired," because people get fired for different reasons (or different combinations of reasons), and not because they scored little on stealing plus a little on showing up late at work, etc.

To sum up: With QCA, by examining the fate of cases with different combinations of causally relevant conditions, it is possible to identify the decisive recipes and thereby unravel causal complexity. Note, in this respect, that QCA does not take on board some core assumptions of the mainstream quantitative approach: It does not assume linearity, nor additivity, and it assumes equifinality (i.e. different paths can lead to the same outcome) instead of unit homogeneity (a given factor is assumed to have the same effect on the outcome across all cases) (Rihoux and Ragin 2008; Schneider and Wagemann forthcoming).

The key analytic tool for analyzing causal complexity using QCA is the truth table. It lists the logically possible combinations of conditions and the outcome associated

Table 31.2. Truth table with four conditions (A, B, C, and D) and one outcome (Y)

A	B	C	D	Y[a]
no	no	no	no	no
no	no	no	yes	?
no	no	yes	no	?
no	no	yes	yes	?
no	yes	no	no	no
no	yes	no	yes	no
no	yes	yes	no	?
no	yes	yes	yes	no
yes	no	no	no	?
yes	no	no	yes	?
yes	no	yes	no	?
yes	no	yes	yes	?
yes	yes	no	no	yes
yes	yes	no	yes	yes
yes	yes	yes	no	?
yes	yes	yes	yes	?

[a] Rows with "?" in this column lack cases—the outcome cannot be determined.

with each combination. Table 31.2 illustrates a simple truth table with four dichotomous[4] conditions and sixteen combinations (called *configurations*).

In more complex truth tables the rows (combinations of conditions) may be quite
numerous, for the number of configurations is a geometric function of the number
of conditions (number of causal combinations = 2^k, where k is the number of causal
conditions). The use of truth tables to unravel causal complexity is described in
detail elsewhere (e.g. Ragin 1987; Rihoux and Ragin 2008; Schneider and Wagemann
forthcoming). The essential point is that the truth table elaborates and formalizes one
of the two key analytic strategies of comparative research—examining cases sharing
specific combinations of conditions to see if they share the same outcome. The goal
of truth table analysis is thus to identify specific connections between combinations
of conditions and outcomes.

3 THE STATE OF THE ART[5]

At present, several hundreds of QCA applications have been referenced worldwide, in
several languages.[6] In terms of disciplinary orientation, more than two-thirds of the
applications are found in political science (especially comparative politics and policy
analysis; see Rihoux and Grimm 2006) and sociology. There is also a growing number
of applications in other disciplines such as political economy, management studies,
and criminology. Finally, some applications can be found in history, geography,
psychology, education studies, and various other disciplines.

Although QCA is mainly designed for small- and intermediate-N research, there
is substantial variation across studies in the number of cases. Quite a few applications
have a very small N, between three and six/seven cases. In the intermediate-N range,
most applications are to be found in the broad range from ten to fifty cases. However,
several applications address much more cases, up to large-N designs (e.g. Ishida,
Yonetani, and Kosaka 2006).

The nature of the cases studied is also diverse. In most applications, cases (and outcomes) are macro- or meso-level phenomena, such as policy fields, collective actors,
country or regional characteristics, and so on. There is also substantial variation as
to the number of conditions included in the analysis, though of course there is (or at
least there should be) some connection between the number of cases and the number
of conditions (Rihoux and Ragin 2008). The vast majority of applications consider
between three and six conditions—thus models elaborated for QCA analysis tend to
be parsimonious.

---

[4] The procedures described here are *not* dependent on the use of dichotomies. Truth tables can be
built from dichotomies (csQCA), multichotomies (mvQCA), and also from fuzzy sets (with set
memberships in the interval from 0 to 1).

[5] For more details, see Rihoux (2006); Yamasaki and Rihoux (2008).

[6] A comprehensive list of applications is available through the COMPASSS international
bibliographical database: <http://www.compasss.org>.

Last but not least, one particularly interesting development in QCA applications is the explicit combination with other types of methods, both qualitative and quantitative. Most often, there is already a lot of upstream qualitative work involved in the process of achieving an in-depth understanding of cases (Rihoux and Lobe 2008). With regards to the combination of QCA with other formal—mainly quantitative—methods, several fruitful attempts have been made to confront QCA with some more or less mainstream quantitative techniques such as discriminant analysis, factor analysis, various types of multiple regression, logistic regression, and logit regression.[7]

In terms of software, two major programs have been developed: FSQCA (for csQCA, fsQCA, and fuzzy sets) and TOSMANA (for csQCA and mvQCA). They offer complementary tools, in a quite user-friendly environment. In recent years, some additional tools have been developed. FSQCA now includes routines for truth table analysis of fuzzy-set data (see Ragin 2008, and below), calculations of consistency and coverage measures for both crisp and fuzzy-set analyses (Ragin 2006), and the possibility to derive three different solutions for each analysis: the more complex one, the most parsimonious one, and the intermediate one. TOSMANA now includes graphical aids such as the "visualizer" which produces Venn diagrams, and the "thresholdssetter" which gives a visual grip on the dichotomization or trichotomization thresholds.

4 USES AND BEST PRACTICES

The QCA techniques can be used for at least five different purposes (De Meur and Rihoux 2002; Rihoux and Ragin 2008). (a) They may be used in a straightforward manner simply to summarize data in the form of a truth table, using it as a tool for data exploration. (b) Researchers may take advantage of QCA to check the coherence of their data, mainly through the detection of logical contradictions (i.e. similar combinations of conditions which, however, produce a different outcome in different cases). (c) They can be used to test hypotheses or existing theories. (d) Another use, quite close to the former, is the quick test of any assumption formulated by the researcher—that is, without testing a preexisting theory or model as a whole. This is another way of using QCA techniques for data exploration. (e) Finally, they may be used in the process of developing new theoretical assumptions in the form of hypotheses, following a more inductive approach. Researchers should determine which uses of QCA best suit their research goals. Some of these five uses of QCA are still very much underexploited.

In the last few years, some "best practices" have been more systematically laid out. Here we only discuss some main general guidelines (for more detailed technical

---

[7] For a list, see Rihoux and Ragin (2008). Noteworthy examples include Cronqvist and Berg-Schlosser (2006), Amenta and Poulsen (1996), and Dumont and Bäck (2006).

guidelines see Rihoux and Ragin 2008; Wagemann and Schneider 2007). First, it is advisable to draw on the different functions of the software. Many of these functions are still underused, such as the "hypothesis testing" function (e.g. Peillon 1996), which can be exploited in different ways. Second, technical and reference concepts should be used with care, to avoid confused and imprecise communication. Several misunderstandings—and misplaced critiques of QCA—stem from the misuse of technical terms. One of the most frequent examples is the reference to "independent variables" instead of "conditions" (see footnote 2).

Third, one should never forget the fundamentally configurational logic of QCA (Nomiya 2004). Hence one should never consider the influence of a condition in an isolated manner, especially in the interpretation of the solution of a truth table. Fourth, QCA should never be used in a mechanical manner, but instead as a tool that requires iterative steps (Rihoux 2003). With QCA, there are frequent moves back and forth between the QCA analysis proper (i.e. use of the software) and the cases, viewed in the light of theory. Bottom line: The use of QCA should be both case informed (relying on case-based knowledge: Ragin and Becker 1992) and theory informed. When researchers encounter difficulties, they should explain, as transparently as possible, how they have been resolved. This often implies being transparent about trade-offs, pragmatic choices which may at times seem somewhat arbitrary in real-life research. But at least the reader is informed about the choices that have been made and their rationale. Once again: The QCA programs should never be used in a push-button logic, but rather in a careful, self-conscious way. Needless to say, the same should go with any formal tool—e.g. statistical tools as well—in social science research.

Fifth, one should be careful in the interpretation of the solution of a truth table (called a minimal formula). In particular, it is advisable to be cautious before interpreting a minimal formula in terms of causality. Technically speaking, the formula expresses, more modestly, co-occurrences reflecting *potential* causal connections. It is then up to researchers to decide (relying on their substantive and theoretical knowledge) how far they can go in the interpretation in terms of "causality." Finally, in the research process, it is almost always fruitful to use different methods. At different stages of empirical research, it is often the case that different methods suit different needs. Thus it is advisable to use QCA in some stages, while exploiting other methods (qualitative or quantitative) at other stages. This is not to say that QCA should necessarily be used in a modest way, as it can be used as the main data-analytic tool.

5 Beyond csQCA: mvQCA, Fuzzy Sets, fsQCA, and Other Innovations

Beyond the initial, dichotomous technique (csQCA), which remains the most used so far, two strands of techniques have been developed, allowing us to process more fine-grained-data: mvQCA (multi-value QCA), on the one hand, and fuzzy sets on the other hand, with two variants: fuzzy sets proper, and fsQCA (fuzzy-set QCA), a procedure which links fuzzy sets to truth table analysis.

MvQCA has been developed along with the TOSMANA software (Cronqvist 2005; Cronqvist and Berg-Schlosser 2008). One problem in applying csQCA is the compulsory use of dichotomous conditions, which bears the risk of information loss and may create a large number of contradictory configurations (i.e. configurations with the same condition values, but yet leading to different outcome values). It can also lead to instances where two cases with somewhat different raw values are assigned the same Boolean value and/or two cases with quite similar values are assigned different Boolean values. As the name suggests, mvQCA is an extension of csQCA. It retains the main idea of csQCA, namely to perform a synthesis of a data-set, with the result that cases with the same outcome value are expressed by a parsimonious minimal formula. As in csQCA, the minimal formula contains one or several prime implicants, each of which covers a number of cases with this outcome, while no cases with a different outcome are explained by any of the prime implicants of that minimal formula. The key difference is that mvQCA also enables the inclusion of multi-value conditions. In fact, mvQCA is a generalization of csQCA, because indeed a dichotomous variable is a specific subtype of multi-value variables—it is simply a multi-value variable with only two possible values. In practical terms, the researcher can choose to use more than two values (typically trichotomies, but one can also use four categories or more) for some conditions, hence adding more diversity. MvQCA has already been applied successfully on different sorts of data-sets (e.g. Cronqvist and Berg-Schlosser 2006).

One apparent limitation of the truth table approach, which underlies both csQCA and mvQCA, is that it is designed for conditions that are simple presence/absence dichotomies (the Boolean, csQCA variant) or multichotomies (mvQCA). However, many of the conditions that interest social scientists vary by level or degree. For example, while it is clear that some countries are democracies and some are not, there is a broad range of in-between cases. These countries are not fully in the set of democracies, nor are they fully excluded from this set. Fortunately, there is a well-developed mathematical system for addressing partial membership in sets, fuzzy-set theory, which has been further elaborated for social scientific work by Ragin (2000). Fuzzy sets are especially powerful because they allow researchers to calibrate partial membership in sets using values in the interval between 0 (nonmembership) and 1 (full membership) without abandoning core set-theoretic principles such as, for example, the subset relation. As Ragin (2000) demonstrates, the subset relation is central to the analysis of causal complexity. In many respects fuzzy sets are simultaneously qualitative and quantitative, for they incorporate both kinds of distinctions in the calibration of degree of set membership. Thus, fuzzy sets have many of the virtues of conventional interval-scale variables, but at the same time they permit set-theoretic operations which are outside the scope of conventional variable-oriented analysis.

Fuzzy sets extend crisp sets by permitting membership scores in the interval between 0 and 1. For example, a country (e.g. the United States) might receive a membership score of 1 in the set of rich countries but a score of only 0.9 in the set of democratic countries. The basic idea behind fuzzy sets is to permit the scaling of membership scores and thus allow partial or fuzzy membership. Thus fuzzy membership scores address the varying degree to which different cases belong to a set (including two qualitatively defined states: full membership and full nonmembership), as follows: A fuzzy membership score of 1 indicates full membership in a set; scores close to 1 (e.g. 0.8 or 0.9) indicate strong but not quite full membership in a set; scores less than 0.5 but greater than 0 (e.g. 0.2 and 0.3) indicate that objects are more "out" than "in" a set, but still weak members of the set; and finally a score of 0 indicates full nonmembership in the set.

Thus, fuzzy sets combine qualitative and quantitative assessment: 1 and 0 are qualitative assignments ("fully in" and "fully out," respectively); values between 0 and 1 indicate partial membership. The 0.5 score is also qualitatively anchored, for it indicates the point of maximum ambiguity (fuzziness) in the assessment of whether a case is more "in" or "out" of a set. Note that fuzzy-set membership scores do not simply rank cases relative to each other. Rather, fuzzy sets pinpoint qualitative states while at the same time assessing varying degrees of membership between full inclusion and full exclusion. In this sense, a fuzzy set can be seen as a continuous variable that has been purposefully calibrated to indicate degree of membership in a well-defined set. Such calibration is possible only through the use of theoretical and substantive knowledge, which is essential to the specification of the three qualitative breakpoints: full membership (1), full nonmembership (0), and the crossover point, where there is maximum ambiguity regarding whether a case is more "in" or more "out" of a set (0.5) (Ragin 2008; this volume; Schneider and Wagemann forthcoming). Such calibration should not be mechanical—when specifying the qualitative anchors, the investigator should present a rationale for each breakpoint. In fact the qualitative anchors make it possible to distinguish between relevant and irrelevant variation, especially when one uses quantitative, interval-level data. For instance, variation in GNP per capita among the unambiguously rich countries is *not* relevant to membership in the set of rich countries, at least from the perspective of fuzzy sets. If a country is unambiguously rich, then it is accorded full membership, a score of 1. Similarly, variation in GNP per capita among the unambiguously not-rich countries is also irrelevant to degree of membership in the set of rich countries because these countries are uniformly and completely out of the set of rich countries. Thus, in research using fuzzy sets it is not enough simply to develop scales that show the relative positions of cases on distributions (e.g. a conventional index of wealth such as GNP per capita). Note, finally, that in a fuzzy-set analysis both the outcome and the conditions are represented using fuzzy sets.

However, a limitation of fuzzy sets is that they are not well suited for conventional truth table analysis. With fuzzy sets, there is no simple way to sort cases according to the combinations of conditions they display because each case's array of membership scores may be unique. Ragin (2000) circumvents this limitation by developing an algorithm for analyzing configurations of fuzzy-set memberships that bypasses truth table analysis altogether. While this algorithm remains true to fuzzy-set theory through its use of the containment (or inclusion) rule, it forfeits many of the analytic strengths that follow from analyzing evidence in terms of truth tables. For example, truth tables are very useful for investigating "limited diversity" and the consequences of different "simplifying assumptions" that follow from using different subsets of "logical remainders" to reduce complexity (see Ragin 1987; Ragin and Sonnett 2004; Rihoux and De Meur 2008). Analyses of this type are difficult when not using truth tables as the starting point.

Therefore, Ragin (2008) has built a bridge between fuzzy sets and truth tables, allowing one to construct a conventional Boolean truth table, starting from fuzzy-set data—this procedure is referred to as "fsQCA". It is important to point out that this new technique takes full advantage of the gradations in set membership central to the constitution of fuzzy sets and is not predicated upon a dichotomization of fuzzy membership scores. Rather, the original interval-scale data is converted into fuzzy membership scores (which range from 0 to 1), thereby avoiding dichotomizing or trichotomizing the data (i.e. sorting the cases into crude categories). Actually, fsQCA offers a new way to conduct fuzzy-set analysis. This new analytic strategy is superior in several respects to the initial fuzzy-set strategy developed by Ragin (2000). While both approaches have strengths and weaknesses, the specificity of fsQCA is that it uses the truth table as the key analytic device. A further advantage of this procedure is that it is more transparent. Thus, the researcher has more direct control over the process of data analysis. This type of control is central to the practice of case-oriented research. Technically speaking, once a crisp truth table has been produced (by summarizing the results of multiple fuzzy set assessments), it is then analyzed using Boolean algebra.

Beyond the development of mvQCA, fuzzy sets, and fsQCA, quite a few specific innovations need to be mentioned. A first set of innovations deals with the issue of temporality, which indeed is not "built in" the QCA procedures—actually, from a case-oriented perspective, this is probably the main limitation of QCA so far. Some scholars have attempted to include the time dimension in applying the overall QCA technique, i.e. by specifying sequence considerations in the interpretation of the minimal formulae, by including dynamic considerations in the operationalization of conditions, or by segmenting cases following a chronological logic (e.g. Rihoux 2001; Clément 2005). Some first attempts have also been made to insert temporality into the analytic (software) procedure itself. Duckles, Hager, and Galaskiewicz (2005), using Event Structure Analysis (ESA), first construct some event structures, some of which are operationalized in sequential sub-models for successive QCA minimization procedures. Eventually they elaborate a complete model which enables them to identify some key precipitating factors in the chain of events, at least for some clusters of cases. Another attempt, by Caren and Panofsky (2005), consists in integrating temporality directly into QCA. Using an hypothetically constructed example, they argue that it is possible to develop an extension of QCA (TQCA—temporal QCA) to capture causal sequences. First, they include sequence considerations as a specific case attribute, hence increasing dramatically the number of possible configurations. Second, they place theoretical restrictions to limit the number of possible configurations. Third, they perform a specific form of Boolean minimization, which yields richer minimal formulae which also include sequences and trajectories. In a somewhat other direction, Krook (2006) has made a first attempt to link QCA procedures with an "optimal matching" procedure.

One should also mention the "two-step" procedure initiated by Schneider and Wagemann (2006; forthcoming), which draws a distinction between remote and proximate conditions. Along the same line of enriching and refining the basic QCA procedures, a series of complementary tests have been developed—specifically: testing for the presence of necessary or sufficient conditions, and also assessing the "consistency" and "coverage" of the different elements of the minimal formula (Ragin 2006; Schneider and Wagemann forthcoming). Another adjacent development is the systematization of a procedure (called MSDO/MDSO) which can be used to boil down the number of potential conditions when they are too numerous, while also shedding some light on how cases cluster, before engaging in QCA proper (Berg-Schlosser and De Meur 1997; 2008). Within the QCA procedures themselves, several refinements have also been successfully applied, such as a more informed use of "logical remainders" (nonobserved cases), a specific treatment to solve the so-called "contradictory simplifying assumptions" ("hidden" contradictions which might occur when one uses logical remainders), and so on. The good point here is that these refinements all go in the direction of further enhancing the transparency and solidity of the analysis, and that they have been translated into good practices.

6 CONCLUSION: PROMISES AND OPENINGS

The audience for QCA and its techniques is growing; as are debates about its strengths and limitations. A detailed discussion thereof lies beyond the scope of this chapter (for a full view, see De Meur, Rihoux, and Yamasaki 2008; Ragin and Rihoux 2004[8]). Some key topics of discussion include dichotomization, the use of nonobserved cases (the "logical remainders"), case sensitivity, model specification, causality, and temporality. The bottom line is that many of the critiques are misplaced or overstated, especially those which are formulated from a mainstream quantitative (i.e. statistical) perspective, because they fail to grasp the specificity of the configurational, case-oriented foundation of QCA and its techniques. Of course, there are limitations, as with any technique. It is precisely some of these limitations which foster the development of new tools and ways to enrich QCA.

Quite a few innovations are expected, in the short to medium term, or are already being initiated at present. Some further software innovations will surely be developed within the next few years. Some other efforts are also being undertaken on other platforms, such as the R software (Dusa 2007). Here are some issues on the agenda, which

---

[8] See also issue 2.2. (2004) of the *Qualitative Methods Newsletter* (APSA), as well as issue 40.1. (2005) of *Studies in Comparative International Development*.

will hopefully materialize at some stage in the software developments, through FSQCA, TOSMANA, or other platforms: a more explicit inclusion of the time dimension in the computing procedures; some further improvements in the user-friendliness of the platforms; some interconnections with other software (e.g. importing/exporting data); new ways to visualize the configurations as well as the minimal formulae, etc.

Another particularly promising path consists in small- or intermediate-N research designs in which cases are individuals (micro-level cases). Especially in more participatory research designs, i.e. when researchers are able to engage in regular interaction with the individuals (the "cases") being the object of the study, one may argue that they attain an even better understanding of each individual case than would be the case for meso- or macro-level phenomena. Indeed, they are literally able to interact directly with each and every one of the cases, which would prove much more difficult when cases are meso- or macro-level phenomena (Lobe and Rihoux 2008).

QCA and linked techniques are still quite new tools. They display broad potential in terms of discipline, number of cases, research design, and types of uses. Rather than being a middle path between case-oriented and variable-oriented research, as Ragin (1987) initially argued, all things considered, QCA is more related to case-study methods—especially the crisp, dichotomous version (Rihoux and Lobe 2008). As with any case-oriented methods, a researcher using QCA meets a trade-off between the goals of reaching a certain level of theoretical parsimony, establishing explanatory richness, and keeping the number of cases at a manageable level (George and Bennett 2005). What is specific about QCA, as compared with "focused, structured comparison," is that it enables one to consider a larger number of cases, provided one is willing to accept a certain level of simplification and synthesis necessitated for Boolean or set treatment. Still, in that process, one does not sacrifice explanatory richness, and the possible generalizations which will be produced will always be contingent, in the sense that they only apply to some specific types or clusters of well-delineated cases which operate in specific contexts (George and Bennett 2005).

Naturally, QCA and connected techniques should not be viewed in isolation. They are compatible with other approaches, especially comparative historical analysis (Mahoney and Rueschemeyer 2003; Mahoney and Terrie, this volume) and theory-led case-oriented research (George and Bennett 2005; Bennett, this volume; Gerring 2006; this volume). In addition, much progress can be expected within the next few years, when QCA and connected techniques will hopefully be combined/confronted more systematically with other techniques, be they more qualitative or more quantitative. At the same time, we can also expect some significant further development in terms of software (see above). In addition, dissemination of these techniques is now being extended through some training programs and specialized courses in various institutions. Among other dissemination efforts, a first overarching English-language textbook (Rihoux and Ragin 2008) will make these techniques more accessible to students. Of course neither csQCA, nor mvQCA, fuzzy sets, or fsQCA, solve all problems faced by empirical researchers—no technique should be expected to accomplish this. Yet the application of these techniques is of great analytic value and has potential in many fields across political science and social sciences broadly defined, and in different research designs.

References

AMENTA, E., and POULSEN, J. D. 1996. Social politics in context: the institutional politics theory and social spending at the end of the New Deal. *Social Forces*, 75: 33–60.

BERG-SCHOSSER, D., and DE MEUR, G. 1997. Reduction of complexity for a small-n analysis: a stepwise multi-methodological approach. *Comparative Social Research*, 16: 133–62.

——— 2008. Comparative research design: case and variable selection. In *Configurational Comparative Methods*, ed. B. Rihoux and C. Ragin. Thousand Oaks, Calif.: Sage.

CAREN, N., and PANOFSKY, A. 2005. TQCA: a technique for adding temporality to qualitative comparative analysis. *Sociological Methods and Research*, 34: 147–72.

CLÉMENT, C. 2005. The nuts and bolts of state collapse: common causes and different patterns? COMPASSS Working Paper 2005–32.

CRONQVIST, L. 2005. Introduction to multi-value qualitative comparative analysis (MVQCA). COMPASSS Didactics Paper No. 4.

——— and BERG-SCHLOSSER, D. 2006. Determining the conditions of HIV/AIDS prevalence in sub-Saharan Africa: employing new tools of macro-qualitative analysis. Pp. 145–66 in *Innovative Comparative Methods for Policy Analysis*, ed. B. Rihoux and H. Grimm. New York: Springer.

——— ——— 2008. Multi-value QCA (mvQCA). In *Configurational Comparative Methods*, ed. B. Rihoux and C. Ragin. Thousand Oaks, Calif.: Sage.

DE MEUR, G., and RIHOUX, B. 2002. *L'Analyse quali-quantitative comparée (AQQC-QCA): approche, techniques et applications en sciences humaines*. Louvain-la-Neuve: Academia-Bruylant.

——— RIHOUX, B., and YAMASAKI, S. 2008. Addressing the critiques of QCA. In *Configurational Comparative Methods*, ed. B. Rihoux and C. Ragin. Thousand Oaks, Calif.: Sage.

DUCKLES, B. M., HAGER, M. A., and GALASKIEWICZ, J. 2005. How nonprofits close: using narratives to study organizational processes. Pp. 169–203 in *Advances in Qualitative Organizational Research*, ed. K. D. Elsbach. Greenwich, Conn.: Information Age.

DUMONT, P., and BÄCK, H. 2006. Why so few and why so late? Green parties and the question of governmental participation. *European Journal of Political Research*, 45: s35–68.

DUSA, A. 2007. User manual for the QCA (GUI) package in R. *Journal of Business Research*, 60: 576–86.

GEORGE, A. L., and BENNETT, A. 2005. *Case Studies and Theory Development in the Social Sciences*, Cambridge, Mass.: MIT Press.

GERRING, J. 2006. *Case Study Research: Principles and Practice*. Cambridge: Cambridge University Press.

GOERTZ, G., and STARR, H. 2002. *Necessary Conditions: Theory, Methodology, and Applications*. New York: Rowman and Littlefield.

ISHIDA, A., YONETANI, M., and KOSAKA, K. 2006. Determinants of linguistic human rights movements: an analysis of multiple causation of LHRs movements using a Boolean approach. *Social Forces*, 84: 1937–55.

KROOK, M. L. 2006. Temporality and causal configurations: combining sequence analysis and fuzzy set/qualitative comparative analysis. Presented at the annual APSA meeting, Philadelphia.

LOBE, B., and RIHOUX, B. 2008. The added value of micro-level QCA: getting more out of rich case knowledge. Unpublished manuscript.

MAHONEY, J., and RUESCHEMEYER, D. 2003. *Comparative Historical Research*. Cambridge: Cambridge University Press.

NOMIYA, D. 2004. Atteindre la connaissance configurationnelle: remarques sur l'utilisation précautionneuse de l'AQQC. *Revue Internationale de Politique Comparée*, 11: 131–3.

PEILLON, M. 1996. A qualitative comparative analysis of welfare legitimacy. *Journal of European Social Policy*, 6: 175–90.

RAGIN, C. C. 1987. *The Comparative Method: Moving beyond Qualitative and Quantitative Strategies*. Berkeley: University of California Press.

—— 2000. *Fuzzy-Set Social Science*. Chicago: University of Chicago Press.

—— 2006. Set relations in social research: evaluating their consistency and coverage. *Political Analysis*, 14: 291–310.

—— 2008. Qualitative Comparative Analysis using fuzzy sets (fsQCA). In *Configurational Comparative Methods*, ed. B. Rihoux and C. Ragin. Thousand Oaks, Calif.: Sage.

—— and BECKER, H. 1992. *What is a Case? Exploring the Foundations of Social Inquiry*. Cambridge: Cambridge University Press.

—— and RIHOUX, B. 2004. Replies to commentators: reassurances and rebuttals. *Qualitative Methods: Newsletter of the American Political Science Association Organized Section on Qualitative Methods*, 2: 21–4.

—— and SONNETT, J. 2004. Between complexity and parsimony: limited diversity, counterfactual cases, and comparative analysis. COMPASSS Working Paper 2004–23.

RIHOUX, B. 2001. *Les Partis politiques: organisations en changement. Le test des écologistes*. Paris: L'Harmattan.

—— 2003. Bridging the gap between the qualitative and quantitative worlds? A retrospective and prospective view on qualitative comparative analysis. *Field Methods*, 15: 351–65.

—— 2006. Qualitative comparative analysis (QCA) and related systematic comparative methods: recent advances and remaining challenges for social science research. *International Sociology*, 21: 679–706.

—— and GRIMM, H. (eds.) 2006. *Innovative Comparative Methods for Policy Analysis: Beyond the Quantitative–Qualitative Divide*. New York: Springer/Kluwer.

—— and LOBE, B. 2008. The case for QCA: adding leverage for thick cross-case comparison. In *Handbook of Case Study Methods*, ed. C. C. Ragin and D. Byrne. Thousand Oaks, Calif.: Sage.

—— and RAGIN, C. (eds.) 2008. *Configurational Comparative Methods: Qualitative Comparative Analysis (QCA) and Related Techniques*. Applied Social Research Methods. Thousand Oaks, Calif.: Sage.

SCHNEIDER, C. Q., and WAGEMANN, C. 2006. Reducing complexity in qualitative comparative analysis (QCA): remote and proximate factors and the consolidation of democracy. *European Journal of Political Research*, 45: 751–86.

—— —— forthcoming. *Qualitative Comparative Analysis (QCA) and Fuzzy Sets: A User's Guide*. German-language version (2007), *Qualitative Comparative Analysis (QCA) und Fuzzy Sets*. Opladen: Verlag Barbara Budrich.

WAGEMANN, C., and SCHNEIDER, C. Q. 2007. Standards of good practice in qualitative comparative analysis (QCA) and fuzzy-sets. COMPASSS Working Paper 2007–51.

YAMASAKI, S., and RIHOUX, B. 2008. A commented review of applications. In *Configurational Comparative Methods*, ed. B. Rihoux and C. Ragin. Thousand Oaks, Calif.: Sage.

CHAPTER 32

....

COMPARATIVE-HISTORICAL ANALYSIS IN CONTEMPORARY POLITICAL SCIENCE

....

JAMES MAHONEY
P. LARKIN TERRIE

ALTHOUGH comparative-historical analysis has roots as far back as the founders of modern social science, its place in contemporary political science can be traced to a series of successful books published in the 1960s and 1970s, such as Moore (1966), Bendix (1974), Lipset and Rokkan (1968), Tilly (1975), and Skocpol (1979).

Over the last twenty years, the tradition has sustained momentum in part through the publication of scores of major new books. This scholarship includes work across many of the key substantive areas of comparative politics: social provision and welfare state development (e.g. Esping-Anderson 1990; Hicks 1999; Huber and Stephens 2001; Pierson 1994; Skocpol 1992; Steinmo 1993); state formation and state restructuring (Bensel 1990; Ekiert 1996; Ertman 1997; Tilly 1990; Waldner 1999); economic development and market-oriented adjustment (Bunce 1999; Evans 1995; Haggard 1990; Karl 1997; Kohli 2004; Sikkink 1991); racial, ethnic, and national identities (Lustick

1993; Marx 1998; Yashar 2005); revolutionary change (e.g. Goldstone 1991; Goodwin 2001; Wickham-Crowley 1992); and democratic and authoritarian regimes (Collier 1999; Collier and Collier 1991; Downing 1992; Linz and Stepan 1996; Luebbert 1991; Mahoney 2001; Rueschemeyer, Stephens, and Stephens 1992).

The comparative-historical approach has been strongly identified with the publication of books. Yet beyond these books, key elements of this tradition are also found in a significant portion of published work in scholarly journals on comparative politics—a fact that we empirically demonstrate in this chapter.

While comparative-historical analysis "has claimed its proud place as one of the most fruitful research approaches in modern social science" (Skocpol 2003, 424), it is also true that methodological aspects of the approach are still received skeptically in some quarters. Perhaps most notably, scholars who pursue the statistical testing of hypotheses with large numbers of cases have raised concerns about this tradition. They have argued that, from the standpoint of statistical methodology, this line of enquiry violates well-known aspects of good research design and procedure (e.g. Coppedge 2008; King, Keohane, and Verba 1994; Geddes 1990; 2003; Goldthorpe 1997; Lieberson 1991; 1994; 1998). They use these criticisms as a basis for questioning whether the influential substantive findings produced in this field are, in fact, valid.

In this chapter, we suggest that existing concerns arise from a fundamental misunderstanding of the goals and methods of comparative-historical analysis. This misunderstanding, in turn, is linked to a failure to appreciate basic differences between comparative-historical and statistical analysis. We show that these two research traditions are best understood as adopting distinct research goals, using different methods to achieve these goals, and thus quite justifiably pursuing different kinds of overall research designs. Once basic differences in research orientations are recognized, it becomes clear that advice and criticisms derived solely from a statistical template are not appropriate (see also Brady and Collier 2004; Mahoney and Goertz 2006).

Clarifying the differences between comparative-historical and statistical analysis helps to promote a more fruitful dialogue among scholars. Despite their different research objectives and contrasting methodological tools, researchers representing these different traditions stand to benefit from better understanding one another's methods and research practices. There are at least two reasons why. First, insights from one tradition often can stimulate new and useful ideas for the other tradition. For example, insights about combinatorial causation and equifinality in comparative-historical methods have led to the creation of new statistical methods (Braumoeller 2003; 2004). The same is true of recent writings on necessary and sufficient causes (Clark, Gilligan, and Golder 2006). Likewise, comparing frequentist and Bayesian statistics has stimulated new insights about process tracing in comparative-historical research (Bennett 2006). And statistical techniques have been combined with formal qualitative comparative analysis in creative ways (Ragin 2000).

Second, the proliferation of multimethod research in contemporary political science makes knowledge of a wide range of methods increasingly important. Obviously, scholars who themselves pursue multimethod research should be well schooled in all of the relevant methodological traditions. At the same time, it seems increasingly important that methodologists themselves be able to offer sound advice to scholars who seek to combine statistical and case-study methods, including comparative-historical methods. Obviously, no one methodologist can be expected to be an expert across the board; however, methodologists should know when the limits of their expertise are reached and thus when it is time to defer to specialists in other methodological orientations.

1 THE FIELD OF COMPARATIVE-HISTORICAL ANALYSIS

Many famous books are strongly associated with the comparative-historical tradition. But one might reasonably wonder about the overall commonality of the approach in contemporary political science, including in journals. Does a significant body of literature exist beyond the famous examples? How could we identify such a literature if it did? We address these questions by measuring several traits associated with this tradition and assessing empirically the extent to which these traits are found together in published studies on comparative politics.

As with any research orientation, there are different ways of defining comparative-historical analysis. According to Mahoney and Rueschemeyer (2003), this approach investigates "big questions"—substantively important and large-scale outcomes—that take the form of puzzles about specific cases. In addressing these puzzles, re-searchers are centrally concerned with causal analysis, the examination of processes over time, and use of systematic and contextualized comparison. This understanding of the field is similar to that adopted by Collier (1998) and Skocpol (1979, 36–7; 1984, 1).

In this chapter, we are especially interested in defining the field in terms of char-acteristics that can be empirically measured. With this in mind, we emphasize here three core traits and two secondary traits as features that are important to most work in the field. The three core traits concern explanatory goal, conception of causation, and method of theory testing. On each of these three dimensions, comparative-historical analysis directly contrasts with statistical analysis (see Tables 32.1 and 32.2). Comparative-historical work adopts a causes-of-effects approach to explanation, a necessary and/or sufficient conception of causation, and process tracing to test theo-ries. By contrast, statistical analysis uses an effects-of-causes approach to explanation, an average effects conception of causation, and regression techniques to test theories. In addition to these three main dimensions, two other attributes are often associated with comparative-historical work: the use of a comparative set-theoretic logic and the analysis of temporal sequencing and/or path dependence.[1] In Appendix A, we discuss the definition and measurement of each of these traits.

---

[1] We also coded studies according to whether they adopt a rational choice framework.

Table 32.1. Attributes associated with comparative-historical analysis

Attribute	Definition
Causes-of-effects approach[a]	Research goal is to provide complete explanations of specific outcomes in particular cases.
Necessary/sufficient conception of causation[a]	Study treats individual causal factors or sets of multiple causal factors as necessary/sufficient for the outcome of interest.
Process-tracing method[a]	Study explores the mechanisms, within particular cases, through which potential causal factors are hypothesized to affect an outcome.
Comparative set-theoretic methods	Study tests theory using set-theoretic methods (e.g. Mill's methods of agreement and difference, Boolean algebra).
Temporal processes modeled	Explanation emphasizes the sequencing of independent variables and/or path-dependent processes of change.

[a] Core attribute of comparative-historical analysis.

Table 32.2. Attributes associated with statistical analysis

Attribute	Definition
Effects-of-causes approach	Research goal is to estimate the effects of one or more independent variables on a dependent variable/s across a large number of cases.
Average effects conception of causation	Study treats independent variables as parameters whose average effects can be estimated across the full population of cases.
Regression methods	Regressions are used for theory testing.

With these defining traits at hand, we explored empirically whether a tradition of comparative-historical analysis could be found within the subfield of comparative politics. We gathered data from articles that recently appeared in the major comparative politics journals—*Comparative Political Studies*, *Comparative Politics*, and *World Politics*. We set out to sample approximately 100 articles, evenly distributed, from these journals.[2] To make the sample representative of recent work in comparative politics, we first coded articles from 2005 for each journal. Articles from earlier years were coded if doing so was necessary to obtain a sufficiently large sample for the journal. In order to check the robustness of our results, we also analyzed approximately forty articles on comparative politics from the main discipline-wide journals—the *American Journal of Political Science*, the *American Political Science Review*, and the *Journal of Politics*.[3]

---

[2] The final sample consisted of 107 articles: 30 from *CP*, 38 from *CPS*, and 39 from *WP*. Note that descriptive, theoretical, and methodological articles were excluded from the sample.

[3] This sample consisted of 42 articles: 13 from *AJPS*, 15 from *APSR*, and 14 from *JOP*. These journals were not included in the original sample because the empirical studies they publish are almost exclusively statistical, and as such, they are less representative than the subfield journals of the

Table 32.3. Frequency of attributes associated with comparative-historical analysis

CHA attribute	Percentage of articles
Causes-of-effects approach	55.1
Necessary/sufficient conception of causation	57.9
Process-tracing method	58.9
Comparative set-theoretic methods	43.9
Temporal processes modeled	21.5

Note: Percentage of studies from sample of comparative politics journals ($N = 107$).

The data reveal that all five of the attributes associated with the comparative-historical tradition commonly appear in the comparative politics literature, particularly in the articles published in the subfield journals. Table 32.3 reports the frequency with which each of these attributes appeared in the subfield journals. The three core traits of the field—a causes-of-effects approach to explanation, a necessary/sufficient conception of causation, and a process-tracing methodology—each appear in over half of these articles. The two secondary traits—a comparative set-theoretic logic and a concern with temporal sequencing or path dependence—also appear in a significant proportion of articles. What is more, these attributes are not randomly distributed among the articles in the sample. They have a marked tendency to cluster together, as the factor analysis results in Table 32.4 show. The three core attributes of the comparative-historical field are especially likely to hang together (as are the core attributes of statistical work). The temporal process/path dependence and comparative set-theoretic variables also tend to cluster with these three core attributes, though they exhibit lower factor loadings.

Given the high frequency of each individual attribute and the strength of their tendency to cluster, it is clear that a body of work that can be called comparative-historical analysis is relatively common in the literature on comparative politics. Table 32.5 displays the number of articles from the subfield journal sample that can be classified as comparative-historical analysis according to four possible definitions (articles that have any of the three core attributes associated with statistical work are excluded). Just under half of the articles in this sample have all three of the core attributes. When more restrictive definitions are used, the proportion declines, but a nontrivial percentage of articles still qualify as comparative-historical analysis.

Comparative-historical analysis is, in short, a leading research tradition in the subfield of comparative politics based on prominence of current usage alone. Given this prominent place, it seems quite important that we assess soberly the validity of methodological concerns that have been raised about the tradition.

methodological diversity in comparative politics (Mahoney 2007). Nevertheless, the inclusion of these additional articles did not significantly alter the initial findings. Hence, the factor analysis results presented in Table 32.4 are for the combined sample of articles from both the subfield and discipline-wide journals.

Table 32.4. Factor analysis of methodological attributes

	Factor 1
Causes-of-effects approach	0.9473
Necessary/sufficient conception of causation	0.9428
Process-tracing method	0.8854
Comparative set-theoretic methods	0.7169
Temporal processes modeled	0.4644
Effects-of-causes approach	−0.8654
Average effects conception of causation	−0.9321
Regression methods	−0.9149
Rational choice theory	−0.4490

Note: Results are from principal factors analysis performed on the entire sample of articles ($N = 149$) from comparative politics and discipline journals. Reported is the first factor extracted, which explains 97.48 percent of the total variance in these nine variables (eigenvalue = 5.96).

2 CONCERNS ABOUT METHODOLOGICAL PRACTICES

All observational studies in the social sciences confront important obstacles and potentially are subject to error. However, some analysts have argued that comparative-historical research faces especially grave problems that can be avoided in statistical research (for a recent statement, see Coppedge 2008). The implicit or explicit implication is often that social scientists should pursue statistical research when possible (see also Lijphart 1971). In this section, by contrast, we argue that comparative-historical

Table 32.5. Frequency of comparative-historical articles

Definition of CHA	Percentage of articles
Causes-of-effects * necessary/sufficient * process tracing	49.5
Causes-of-effects * necessary/sufficient * process tracing * comparative set-theoretic methods	36.4
Causes-of-effects * necessary/sufficient * process tracing * temporal processes	18.7
Causes-of-effects * necessary/sufficient * process tracing * comparative set-theoretic methods * temporal processes	14.0

Note: Percentage of studies in sample from comparative politics journals ($N = 107$). The "*" symbol denotes the logical AND.

analysis and statistical analysis pursue different research goals, and that while they both face methodological challenges, they both play an essential role in generating knowledge in political science.

2.1 Selection Bias

Several methodologists have sounded alarm bells about the tendency of qualitative researchers to select cases based on their value on the dependent variable (Achen and Snidal 1989; Geddes 1991; 2003; King, Keohane, and Verba 1994). These stern warnings about deliberately selecting cases because they exhibit certain outcomes are especially applicable to comparative-historical studies, which quite explicitly engage in the practice. On the one hand, of course, selection on the dependent variable in this field is hardly surprising, given that the research goal is precisely the explanation of particular outcomes. If one wishes to explain certain outcomes, it seems natural to choose cases that exhibit those outcomes. On the other hand, however, selecting cases based on their value on the dependent variable will bias findings in statistical research. From this standpoint, the practice seems to violate a basic norm of good research.

To evaluate this concern, when applied to comparative-historical analysis, we need to recognize that the statistical literature on bias deriving from selection on the dependent variable assumes that one wishes to generalize about average causal effects from a sample to a well-defined larger population. In comparative-historical research, however, one seeks to identify realized causal effects in particular cases; generalizing about averages from a sample to a larger population is at most a secondary goal. Insofar as comparative-historical researchers select what can be considered the entire universe of cases, therefore, standard issues of selection bias do not arise, regardless of whether the cases were chosen for their values on the dependent variable (for more extensive discussions, see Collier and Mahoney 1996; Collier, Mahoney, and Seawright 2004).[4]

2.2 Scope and Generalization

These observations raise questions about generalization in comparative-historical analysis. Obviously, comparative-historical researchers cannot simply make up whatever definition of the universe of cases they so choose; the decision to limit a theory's applicability to a particular set of cases should not be arbitrary. One needs to ask, therefore, about the methodological basis for adopting a restrictive understanding of scope. This question is critical because the practice of restricting generalizations to a limited set of cases—not issues of selection bias, as conventionally understood—is

---

[4] Problems of selection bias, as conventionally understood in the statistical literature, arise in comparative-historical studies primarily when analysts seek to generalize their theories beyond the initial cases investigated.

often the real source of concern held by statistical methodologists about case selection in comparative-historical analysis. In particular, given the expansive definition of scope often employed in statistical research, the findings of comparative-historical researchers appear to be derived from a potentially unrepresentative sample of cases that is arbitrarily treated as the full population. Let us then explore these issues of scope and generalization.

Social scientists commonly impose scope restrictions on their findings to avoid problems associated with causal heterogeneity, which generates instability in estimates of causal effects. Indeed, primarily because of causal heterogeneity, social scientists of all traditions rarely develop theories that are intended to apply to all places and times. In addition to issues of causal heterogeneity, the need for stable concepts and measurement leads to the use of scope restrictions in which the analyst excludes cases where conceptual and measurement validity cannot be maintained.

In comparative-historical research, analysts adopt a narrow scope because they believe that causal and conceptual heterogeneity are the norm for their theories when assessed across large populations (Mahoney and Rueschemeyer 2003). But is this belief justified? Here we need to recognize that causal heterogeneity is not an ontological property inherent in a population of cases, but rather a feature of the *relationship* between a specific theory and a population of cases (Seawright and Collier 2004, 276; Goertz and Mahoney 2007). A given population of cases may be heterogeneous vis-à-vis one theory but not another. The same is true of conceptual heterogeneity: Cases may be heterogeneous vis-à-vis some concepts but not others. One key implication is that some types of theories (or concepts) may be more likely than others to produce heterogeneity as the size of the population of cases increases.

There are very good reasons for believing that the type of theories evaluated in comparative-historical analysis is especially likely to generate causal heterogeneity in response to even modest increases in population size. To understand why, we need to compare the problem of missing variables in comparative-historical analysis and statistical analysis. This discussion, in turn, will take us back to the contrasting research goals of the two traditions.

In this tradition, the exclusion of one or more important explanatory variables from a theory is appropriately regarded as a major problem (Ragin 2004, 135–8). This is true because the very goal of this kind of work is to explain particular outcomes in specific cases as completely and adequately as possible. All relevant evidence pertaining to the cases should be gathered and assessed. If theories are missing key variables, or have misspecified key relationships among the variables that are included, these facts count significantly against the arguments posited by the researcher. The failure of previous investigators to consider one or more critical variables in fact provides a common basis for comparative-historical analysts to criticize existing work and build new explanatory theories. Missing variables are thus a constant potential source of causal heterogeneity in this field. Similar arguments can be extended to measurement error, which needs to be addressed and eliminated completely for each specific case, if possible (Ragin 2004). Otherwise, the goal of adequately explaining an outcome in particular cases is compromised. In comparative-historical analysis, indeed, theory falsification often occurs with the change in value of one or a small number of variables. Accordingly, in this mode of research, one needs to strive to avoid measurement error for the cases analyzed, otherwise conceptual heterogeneity problems will likely arise.

There are thus good methodological reasons related to the need to avoid causal and conceptual heterogeneity that explain why comparative-historical researchers restrict the scope of their analysis to a limited number of cases. Given the kind of explanatory theory that these analysts pursue, built around the idea of realized causal effects for particular outcomes, they must quite carefully and deliberately define their population of cases to try to avoid all heterogeneity problems. Once the population is defined, even a modest increase in the number of cases runs the risk of excluding key causal factors relevant to the new cases or introducing measurement problems for the variables that are already included in the theory. Because significant modifications to the theoretical model are often required as new cases are added, the best solution may be to impose restrictive scope conditions that limit generalization.

In statistical analysis, by contrast, the goal of research is typically to estimate the average effects of one or more independent variables. Given this goal, missing variables are not necessarily a problem as long as key assumptions, especially that of conditional independence, still hold. Independent variables that are important for only a small subset of cases may be appropriately considered "unsystematic" and relegated to the error term of a regression model. Indeed, even missing independent variables that are systematically related to the outcome of interest will not necessarily bias estimates of the average effects, as long as conditional independence still applies. Likewise, measurement error in statistical analysis does not raise the kinds of problem that it does in comparative-historical analysis. With large numbers of cases, measurement error is always present and cannot be completely eliminated. However, if one seeks to identify average effects, as statistical analysts do, measurement error is not a devastating problem as long as it is nonsystematic or at least can be adequately modeled in the event that it is systematic. Unbiased estimates of average effects are possible in the presence of measurement error.

The fact that statistical analysis can maintain causal homogeneity even in the presence of missing variables and measurement error allows this kind of research to embrace a more expansive understanding of scope and generalization than the comparative-historical approach. For example, the inclusion of new cases with outcomes that were partially caused by idiosyncratic factors will not necessarily raise any special heterogeneity problems in statistical analysis. As long as assumptions such as conditional independence are valid and measurement error can be modeled, the extension of the scope to include new cases is usually not a problem in statistical research. Not surprisingly, therefore, statistical researchers worry less about issues of heterogeneity as they extend their arguments to new cases.

An important issue arises at this point: If comparative-historical explanations are fragile when new cases are introduced, but statistical explanations are less fragile, does it not also follow that statistical explanations are "superior?" There are two reasons why this conclusion is not correct. The first is that the ability of statistical analysis to adopt a wide scope of generalization is dependent on the validity of key assumptions, especially conditional independence. In contemporary political science, many empirical researchers feel quite comfortable making this assumption with little elaboration. Yet methodologists and statisticians often suggest that the assumption is an unrealistic leap of faith in much of the observational research pursued in the social sciences (Lieberson 1985; Freedman 1991). Insofar as the assumption of conditional independence cannot be sustained, statistical research suffers from unrecognized and unmodeled causal heterogeneity. In other words, it is possible that the expansive understanding of scope adopted in statistical analysis is often not appropriate.

Second, and more important for our purposes, it is essential to remember that comparative-historical researchers and statistical researchers have distinct research goals. If one wishes to explain particular outcomes in specific cases, as comparative-historical researchers do, then one must formulate theories in which it is not possible to easily extend the scope of generalization. The alternative is to reject the research goals of comparative-historical work; that is, to prohibit studies that seek to explain particular outcomes in specific cases and encourage scholars only to ask questions about average effects across large populations. For reasons that we discuss below, this kind of prohibition against asking comparative-historical questions would be extremely costly for social science knowledge. In short, if one is going to remain open to different forms of knowledge accumulation, and allow scholars to ask such questions, then one must be willing to live with the restricted scope that accompanies comparative-historical analysis.

2.3 Assessing Causation with a Small N

Even if the limited scope of comparative-historical enquiry makes good sense, some analysts are still concerned that the small number of cases that fall within this scope does not permit the scientific testing of hypotheses. From a statistical standpoint, a small population poses a degrees of freedom problem and insurmountable obstacles for hypothesis testing. How can researchers ever hope to adjudicate among rival explanations if they select so few cases?

The answer to this question again requires appreciating differences between statistical analysis and comparative-historical analysis. In statistical research, where the goal is to estimate average causal effects, one needs to have enough cases to control for relevant variables and still achieve specified confidence levels. However, with comparative-historical research, the goal is not to generalize about typical effects for a large population. Rather, the goal is to determine whether a given variable *did exert* a causal effect on an outcome in a particular set of cases. Given this goal, researchers need to embrace a distinct understanding of causation and indeed of explanation, which—as we shall now see—obviates the need for a large number of cases to achieve valid causal assessment.

Comparative-historical researchers ask the following question about any potential causal factor: Did it exert an effect (alone or in combination with other variables) on the specific outcomes of interest in the particular set of cases that comprise the population? Sometimes, even a cursory examination will allow one to dispose of certain causal factors that might be generally relevant across a large population of cases. For example, when explaining the emergence of democracy in economically poor India or Costa Rica, the variable of development is clearly not useful (at least not in the usual way), even though it is positively related to democracy in a large sample of cases. In other instances, however, plausible causal factors cannot be so quickly dismissed. Many potential causal factors are "correlated" with the specific outcome of interest. How do researchers adjudicate among these rival explanations that are matched with the outcome of interest?

Researchers in the comparative-historical tradition use the method of process tracing—which involves marshalling "within-case" data—to pass judgement on the validity of rival explanations emphasizing factors that cannot be eliminated through comparative matching techniques. Although here is not the place to discuss at length the mechanics of process tracing (see George and Bennett 2005), a few words are in order. Most basically, process tracing helps one to assess whether a posited causal factor actually exerts a causal effect on a specific outcome. This is done by exploring the mechanisms through which the potential causal factor is hypothesized to contribute to the outcome. If intervening mechanisms cannot be located, then doubt is cast upon the causal efficacy of the factor in question. By contrast, if appropriate intervening mechanisms are found, then one has grounds for believing that the factor in question did exert the effect. Beyond this, process tracing allows one to evaluate hypotheses by considering "sub-hypotheses" that do not necessarily refer to intervening mechanisms but that should be true if the main hypothesis of interest is valid (Mahoney and Villegas 2007).

It bears emphasis that this mode of hypothesis assessment does not require a large number of cases. Rather, like a detective solving a crime, the comparative-historical researcher who uses process tracing draws on particularly important facts from individual cases (see Goldstone 1997; McKeown 1999). Not all pieces of evidence count equally. Some forms of evidence are "smoking guns" that strongly suggest a theory is correct; others are "air-tight alibis" that strongly suggest a theory is not correct (Collier, Brady, and Seawright 2004). For these researchers, a theory is often only one key observation away from being falsified. Yet they may have certain kinds of evidence that suggest that the likelihood of theory falsification ever occurring is small.

Another relevant consideration concerns the conception of causation that is used in comparative-historical explanation. The various small-N comparative methods adopted by these researchers—Mill's methods of agreement and difference, explanatory typologies, and qualitative comparative methods—all assume understandings of causation built around necessary and/or sufficient causes (Ragin 1987; 2000; Mahoney 2000; Goertz and Starr 2003; Elman 2005; George and Bennett 2005).[5] By contrast,

---

[5] Quite often, researchers treat individual causes as parts of a larger combination of causes that are together *jointly sufficient* for the outcome of interest (Mackie 1980). In fact, in this field, distinct

mainstream statistical methods assume forms of symmetrical causation that are not consistent with necessary and/or sufficient causation.

To assess hypotheses about necessary and sufficient causes, including combinations of causes that are jointly sufficient, a large number of cases usually is not needed. One or two cases may be enough for the simple purpose of eliminating (though not confirming) an explanation about necessary and sufficient causation. A medium number of cases is normally needed to achieve statistical confidence about the validity of an explanation that invokes necessary and/or sufficient causation solely by using cross-case matching techniques.[6] In some comparative-historical studies, this medium number of cases is analyzed. However, in small-N studies (e.g. $N = 3$), cross-case analysis is generally combined with process tracing. Because the N needed for necessary and sufficient causation is relatively modest, the "burden" that process tracing must carry in such studies is not overwhelming. Rather, the small-N comparison does some of the work, with process tracing contributing the rest.

3 Implications of the Differences

Our discussion has called attention to fundamental differences between comparative-historical analysis and statistical analysis. On the one hand, an awareness of these differences provides a basis for appreciating their distinctive contributions in political science. On the other hand, these differences raise questions about the extent to which the two research traditions might be meaningfully combined. By way of conclusion, we address these implications.

The kinds of knowledge generated by comparative-historical research and statistical research are clearly different. Comparative-historical studies tell us why particular outcomes happened in specific cases—this is one important sense in which these studies are "historical," though there are others (see Mahoney and Rueschemeyer 2003; Pierson 2004; Skocpol 1984). This historical knowledge, in turn, is relevant for policy and practical reasons. By teaching us about the genesis of outcomes in certain specific cases, the knowledge provides a critical foundation for hypothesizing about the effects of subsequent developments in these cases. Here a comparison with physicians who seek the medical history of their patients is useful. A cardiologist can offer better advice to a patient if the causes of the patient's earlier heart attack are well understood. Analogously, policy-makers can pursue better interventions and

combinations of causes may each be sufficient, such that there are multiple causal paths to the same outcome (see Ragin 1987).

[6] Using Bayesian assumptions, for example, Dion (1998) shows that only five cases may be enough to yield 95% confidence about necessary causes. Using a simple binomial probability test, Ragin (2000, 113–15) shows that if one works with "usually necessary" or "usually sufficient" causes, seven consistent cases are enough to meet this level of significance. Braumoeller and Goertz (2000) offer many examples of case-oriented studies that pass such significance tests.

offer more helpful suggestions if they understand well the causes of prior relevant outcomes in the cases of interest. Indeed, if one understands a particular pattern of causation in a given case, one would seem especially well situated to explore whether the causal pattern might apply to another similar case. These points will be obvious to some, but the tendency for many in the discipline is nevertheless to assume that comparative-historical studies are of mostly historical relevance alone.

The strengths and payoffs of statistical research are different. Whereas comparative-historical analysis is excellent at engaging complex theories with fine-grained over-time evidence, statistical research has the virtue of allowing for the testing of hypotheses about the average effects of particular variables (or specified interactions of variables) within large populations in a way that mimics aspects of a controlled experiment. Findings from large populations may or may not be relevant for thinking about particular cases. For example, a causal variable that promotes a given outcome in the population as a whole might have the opposite effect in a particular case of interest. But statistical findings certainly are relevant for generalizing. Indeed, if one wishes to offer policy advice or recommendations that are intended to—on average—make changes across a large population, the findings generated from statistical methods would seem especially appropriate.

This discussion is not intended to suggest that statistical work is irrelevant for thinking about particular cases. Nor is it meant to suggest that comparative-historical works cannot arrive at quite general findings. Rather, the point is that comparative-historical and statistical studies have different goals, produce different kinds of information, and thus *tend to be* useful for different (though equally valid) purposes.

Given that each tradition has its own distinctive contributions to make, it is not surprising that there would be interest in combining the two, which perhaps could allow for a "best of both worlds" synthesis. While contemporary political scientists often value multimethod research, we nevertheless wish to raise here some cautionary notes about combining comparative-historical analysis and statistical analysis. We believe that the combination is more difficult to achieve than is sometimes suggested, and that multimethod research is not always an improvement over work that is exclusively comparative-historical or exclusively statistical.

When they engage in multimethod research, most analysts still pursue either a causes-of-effects approach or an effects-of-causes approach. In this sense, much multimethod research can be considered *primarily* comparative-historical or *primarily* statistical in orientation. With multimethod work that is primarily comparative-historical, the main goal remains the explanation of specific outcomes in particular cases. The statistical analysis is subservient to this goal. By contrast, with multimethod work that is primarily statistical, the main goal is to estimate average causal effects for a large population. Here one or more case studies are used to service this larger goal. Occasionally, of course, some studies will pursue both goals equally and thus truly cross the divide. However, in our sample, this kind of multimethod research characterized only 8.7 percent of all journal articles.

How is statistical analysis used in multimethod studies that are primarily comparative-historical in orientation? In the most basic way, generalizations from prior statistical research represent background knowledge that comparative-historical analysts must consider as they formulate their own explanatory hypotheses for their case studies. All comparative-historical analysts react to prior general theories relevant to their outcomes, which often entails situating one's argument in relationship to existing statistical knowledge. Beyond this, comparative-historical researchers also may use statistical findings—including findings they generate themselves—in conjunction with process tracing. Much as a detective draws on knowledge of general causal principles to establish a link between suspect and crime, so too a comparative-historical researcher may use existing or newly discovered statistical findings when attempting to establish the mechanisms that connect cause and effect. For example, one might hypothesize that slow increases in grain prices in eighteenth-century France contributed to peasant revolts by deflating rural wages (i.e. the impact of declining grain prices on overall revolts worked through lower wages at the individual level). To develop this idea, a comparative-historical researcher might wish to carry out regression analysis to assess the effects of prices on wages in France—to make sure that the two are, in fact, statistically linked net of other factors (see Goldstone 1991, 188–9). In doing this, the researcher collects a large number of observations from what is, given the perspective of the comparative-historical research design, a single case. Comparative-historical researchers thus may be especially likely to turn to statistical analysis when macro-hypotheses in the small-N research design suggest mechanisms that work at lower levels of analysis. The statistical confirmation of these hypotheses serves the larger goal of validating the small-N argument.

For their part, statistical researchers may draw on the findings from comparative-historical analysis to develop their own hypotheses; comparative-historical work can inspire new ideas about causally relevant factors that can be tested in a statistical model. Statistical researchers may also turn to case studies to determine whether findings make sense when assessed in light of an intensive analysis of specific cases. Through such analyses, statistical researchers can evaluate whether the statistical model is adequate, needs refining and retesting, or is deeply problematic and cannot be salvaged. Although in the course of the case analyses the researcher could potentially seek to develop fully adequate explanations of the particular cases, the overarching goal typically remains estimating the average effects of independent variables of interest for the population as a whole. For instance, in Lieberman's (2005) nested analysis approach, cases are selected not because their outcomes are inherently interesting, but rather because their location with respect to the regression line makes them good candidates for further assessing the validity of the statistical model. The goal of the nested analysis is generating valid knowledge about effects of causes; the comparative-historical evidence is mostly subordinated to the larger statistical design.

Our purpose in noting that one approach typically is subordinated to the other in multimethod research is not intended as a criticism. Rather, we emphasize the point to make it clear that most multimethod research is not equal parts quantitative and qualitative—it is, rather, driven by primarily the goals and orientations of one side or the other. When this point is acknowledged, it becomes clear that multimethod research is an advantage only to the extent that the use of the secondary method actually and effectively supplements the main method of investigation. Statistical studies that offer superficial case studies as supporting evidence do not contribute to the explanation of particular outcomes in those cases. And if the case studies are carried out without attention to good methodological practice, they will not provide a reliable basis for evaluating the statistical model either. By the same token, comparative-historical studies that use regression analysis in the course of process tracing are not necessarily more powerful than comparative-historical studies that do not use any statistical testing. The value added by statistical testing simply depends on what kind of evidence is needed for successful process tracing to be carried out. And the use of regression analysis with process tracing will not be fruitful if the regression analysis is poorly executed.

The message of this discussion is that there is nothing inherently wrong with conducting comparative-historical work that does not include a statistical component (and vice versa). Indeed, for many research projects, an additional secondary analysis using an alternative methodology is unnecessary or inappropriate. Hence, as political science increasingly moves toward and celebrates multimethod research, we believe that some of the best work that is produced in the discipline will eschew this trend and remain squarely centered in the field of comparative-historical analysis.

APPENDIX A: A NOTE ON CODING PROCEDURES

All nine attributes are measured dichotomously as present or absent in a given article. We allow that, in principle, any study could possess any combination of attributes. Brief operational definitions for the nine attributes follow.

(1) *Causes-of-effects approach:* present if a central goal of analysis is to explain one or more specific outcomes in particular cases.
(2) *Effects-of-causes approach:* present if a central goal of analysis is to estimate the extent to which particular independent variables account for variation in the dependent variable for a population as a whole rather than any particular case.
(3) *Necessary and sufficient conception of causation:* present if individual causal factors or sets of multiple causal factors are treated as necessary and/or sufficient for the outcome of interest.
(4) *Average effects conception of causation:* present if individual causes are assumed to exert average symmetrical effects that operate within the population as a whole.
(5) *Process-tracing method:* present if specific pieces of data are used to test the mechanisms through which a potential causal factor is hypothesized to contribute to the outcome of interest.
(6) *Regression method:* present if regression techniques are used to test hypotheses.
(7) *Comparative set-theoretic methods:* present if two or more cases are compared across causal and outcome variables to assess whether potential causal variables can be *logically* eliminated.

(8) *Temporal sequencing or path dependence:* present if the timing or sequencing of independent variables is hypothesized to affect the outcome, or if path-dependent processes are assumed to be present.

(9) *Rational choice framework*: present if theories are either formally or informally deduced from the assumption of rational, goal-oriented actors.

REFERENCES

ACHEN, C. H., and SNIDAL, D. 1989. Rational deterrence theory and comparative case studies. *World Politics*, 41: 143–69.

BENDIX, R. 1974. *Work and Authority in Industry: Ideologies of Management in the Course of Industrialization*. Berkeley: University of California Press.

BENNETT, A. 2006. Stirring the frequentist pot with a dash of Bayes. *Political Analysis*, 14: 339–44.

BENSEL, R. F. 1990. *Yankee Leviathan: The Origins of Central State Authority in America, 1859–1877*. New York: Cambridge University Press.

BRADY, H. E., and COLLIER, D. (eds.) 2004. *Rethinking Social Inquiry: Diverse Tools, Shared Standards*. Lanham, Md.: Rowman and Littlefield.

BRAUMOELLER, B. F. 2003. Causal complexity and the study of politics. *Political Analysis*, 11: 209–33.

——2004. Hypothesis testing and multiplicative interaction terms. *International Organization*, 58: 807–20.

——and GOERTZ, G. 2000. The methodology of necessary conditions. *American Journal of Political Science*, 44: 844–58.

BUNCE, V. 1999. *Subversive Institutions: The Design and the Destruction of Socialism and the State*. Cambridge: Cambridge University Press.

CLARK, W. R., GILLIGAN, M. J., and GOLDER, M. 2006. A simple multivariate test for asymmetric hypotheses. *Political Analysis*, 14: 311–31.

COLLIER, D. 1998. Comparative-historical analysis: where do we stand? *APSA-CP: Newsletter of the Organized Section in Comparative Politics*, 9: 1–2, 4–5.

——BRADY, H. E., and SEAWRIGHT, J. 2004. Sources of leverage in causal inference: toward an alternative view of methodology. Pp. 229–66 in Brady and Collier 2004.

——and MAHONEY, J. 1996. Insights and pitfalls: selection bias in qualitative research. *World Politics*, 49: 56–91.

————and SEAWRIGHT, J. 2004. Claiming too much: warnings about selection bias. Pp. 85–102 in Brady and Collier 2004.

COLLIER, R. B. 1999. *Paths toward Democracy*. New York: Cambridge University Press.

——and COLLIER, D. 1991. *Shaping the Political Arena: Critical Junctures, the Labor Movement, and Regime Dynamics in Latin America*. Princeton, NJ: Princeton University Press.

COPPEDGE, M. 2007. *Approaching Democracy: Research Methods in Comparative Politics*. New York: Cambridge University Press.

DION, D. 1998. Evidence and inference in comparative case study. *Comparative Politics*, 30: 127–46.

DOWNING, B. M. 1992. *The Military Revolution and Political Change: Origins of Democracy and Autocracy in Early Modern Europe*. Princeton, NJ: Princeton University Press.

EKIERT, G. 1996. *The State against Society: Political Crises and their Aftermath in East Central Europe*. Princeton, NJ: Princeton University Press.

ELMAN, C. 2005. Explanatory typologies in qualitative studies of international politics. *International Organization*, 59: 293–326.

ERTMAN, T. 1997. *Birth of the Leviathan: Building States and Regimes in Medieval and Early Modern Europe*. Cambridge: Cambridge University Press.

ESPING-ANDERSON, G. 1990. *The Three Worlds of Welfare Capitalism*. Princeton, NJ: Princeton University Press.

EVANS, P. 1995. *Embedded Autonomy: States and Industrial Transformation*. Princeton, NJ: Princeton University Press.

FREEDMAN, D. A. 1991. Statistical models and shoe leather. In *Sociological Methodology*, ed. P. Marsden. San Francisco: Jossey-Bass.

GEDDES, B. 1990. How the cases you choose affect the answers you get: selection bias in comparative politics. Pp. 131–50 in *Political Analysis*, vol. ii, ed. J. A. Stimson. Ann Arbor: University of Michigan Press.

——1991. Paradigms and sand castles in comparative politics of developing areas. Pp. 45–75 in *Comparative Politics, Policy, and International Relations*, ed. W. Crotty. Evanston, Ill.: Northwestern University Press.

——2003. *Paradigms and Sand Castles: Theory Building in Comparative Politics*. Ann Arbor: University of Michigan Press.

GEORGE, A. L., and BENNETT, A. 2005. *Case Studies and Theory Development in the Social Sciences*. Cambridge, Mass.: MIT Press.

GOERTZ, G., and MAHONEY, J. 2007. Scope in case study research. Manuscript.

——and STARR, H. (eds.) 2003. *Necessary Conditions: Theory, Methodology, and Applications*. Lanham, Md.: Rowman and Littlefield.

GOLDSTONE, J. A. 1991. *Revolution and Rebellion in the Early Modern World*. Berkeley: University of California Press.

——1997. Methodological issues in comparative macrosociology. *Comparative Social Research*, 16: 107–20.

GOLDTHORPE, J. H. 1997. Current issues in comparative macrosociology: a debate on methodological issues. *Comparative Social Research*, 16: 1–26.

GOODWIN, J. 2001. *No Other Way Out: States and Revolutionary Movements, 1945–1991*. Cambridge: Cambridge University Press.

HAGGARD, S. 1990. *Pathways from the Periphery: The Politics of Growth in the Newly Industrializing Countries*. Princeton, NJ: Princeton University Press.

HICKS, A. 1999. *Social Democracy and Welfare Capitalism: A Century of Income Security Politics*. Ithaca, NY: Cornell University Press.

HUBER, E., and STEPHENS, J. D. 2001. *Development and Crisis of the Welfare State: Parties and Policies in Global Markets*. Chicago: University of Chicago Press.

KARL, T. L. 1997. *The Paradox of Plenty: Oil Booms and Petro-States*. Berkeley: University of California Press.

KING, G., KEOHANE, R. O. and VERBA, S. 1994. *Designing Social Inquiry: Scientific Inference in Qualitative Research*. Princeton, NJ: Princeton University Press.

KOHLI, A. 2004. *State-directed Development: Political Power and Industrialization in the Global Periphery*. New York: Cambridge University Press.

LIEBERMAN, E. S. 2005. Nested analysis as a mixed method strategy for comparative research. *American Political Science Review*, 99: 435–52.

LIEBERSON, S. 1985. *Making it Count: The Improvement of Social Research and Theory*. Berkeley: University of California Press.

——1991. Small N's and big conclusions: an examination of the reasoning in comparative studies based on a small number of cases. *Social Forces*, 70: 307–20.

LIEBERSON, S. 1994. More on the uneasy case for using Mill-type methods in small-N comparative studies. *Social Forces*, 72: 1225–37.

—— 1998. Causal analysis and comparative research: what can we learn from studies based on a small number of cases. Pp. 129–45 in *Rational Choice Theory and Large-Scale Data Analysis*, ed. H.-P. Blossfeld and G. Prein. Boulder, Colo.: Westview.

LINZ, J. J., and STEPAN, A. 1996. *Problems of Democratic Transition and Consolidation: Southern Europe, South America, and Post-Communist Europe*. Baltimore: Johns Hopkins University Press.

LIPJHART, A. 1971. Comparative politics and the comparative method. *American Political Science Review*, 65: 682–93.

LIPSET, S. M., and ROKKAN, S. (eds.) 1968. *Party Systems and Voter Alignments: Cross-national Perspectives*. New York: Free Press.

LUEBBERT, G. M. 1991. *Liberalism, Fascism, or Social Democracy: Social Classes and the Political Origins of Regimes in Interwar Europe*. New York: Oxford University Press.

LUSTICK, I. 1993. *Unsettled States, Disputed Lands: Britain and Ireland, France and Algeria, Israel and the West Bank–Gaza*. Ithaca, NY: Cornell University Press.

McKEOWN, T. J. 1999. Case studies and the statistical worldview. *International Organization*, 53: 161–90.

MACKIE, J. L. 1980. *The Cement of the Universe: A Study of Causation*. Oxford: Oxford University Press.

MAHONEY, J. 2000. Strategies of causal inference in small-N analysis. *Sociological Methods and Research*, 28: 387–424.

—— 2001. *The Legacies of Liberalism: Path Dependence and Political Regimes in Central America*. Baltimore: Johns Hopkins University Press.

—— 2007. Debating the state of comparative politics: views from qualitative research. *Comparative Political Studies*, 40: 32–8.

—— and GOERTZ, G. 2006. A tale of two cultures: contrasting qualitative and quantitative research. *Political Analysis*, 14: 227–49.

—— and RUESCHEMEYER, D. 2003. Comparative historical analysis: achievements and agendas. Pp. 3–38 in *Comparative Historical Analysis in the Social Sciences*, ed. J. Mahoney and D. Rueschemeyer. New York: Cambridge University Press.

—— and VILLEGAS, C. 2007. Historical enquiry and comparative politics. Pp. 73–89 in *The Oxford Handbook of Comparative Politics*, ed. C Boix and S. C. Stokes. Oxford: Oxford University Press.

MARX, A. W. 1998. *Making Race and Nation: A Comparison of South Africa, the United States, and Brazil*. Cambridge: Cambridge University Press.

MOORE, B., JR. 1966. *Social Origins of Dictatorship and Democracy: Lord and Peasant in the Making of the Modern World*. Boston: Beacon Press.

PIERSON, P. 1994. *Dismantling the Welfare State? Reagan, Thatcher, and the Politics of Retrenchment*. Cambridge: Cambridge University Press.

—— 2004. *Politics in Time: History, Institutions, and Social Analysis*. Princeton, NJ: Princeton University Press.

RAGIN, C. C. 1987. *The Comparative Method: Moving beyond Qualitative and Quantitative Strategies*. Berkeley: University of California Press.

—— 2000. *Fuzzy-Set Social Science*. Chicago: University of Chicago Press.

—— 2004. Turning the tables: how case-oriented research challenges variable-oriented research. Pp. 123–38 in Brady and Collier 2004.

RUESCHEMEYER, D., STEPHENS, E. H., and STEPHENS, J. D. 1992. *Capitalist Development and Democracy*. Chicago: University of Chicago Press.

SEAWRIGHT, J., and COLLIER, D. 2004. Glossary. Pp. 273–313 in Brady and Collier 2004.

SIKKINK, K. 1991. *Ideas and Institutions: Developmentalism in Brazil and Argentina*. Ithaca, NY: Cornell University Press.

SKOCPOL, T. 1979. *States and Social Revolutions: A Comparative Analysis of France, Russia, and China*. Cambridge: Cambridge University Press.

——1984. Sociology's historical imagination. Pp. 1–21 in *Vision and Method in Historical Sociology*, ed. T. Skocpol. Cambridge: Cambridge University Press.

——1992. *Protecting Soldiers and Mothers: The Political Origins of Social Policy in the United States*. Cambridge, Mass.: Belknap Press of Harvard University Press.

——2003. Doubly engaged social science: the promise of comparative historical analysis. Pp. 407–28 in *Comparative-historical Analysis in the Social Sciences*, ed. J. Mahoney and D. Rueschemeyer. New York: Cambridge University Press.

STEINMO, S. 1993. *Taxation and Democracy: Swedish, British and American Approaches to Financing the Modern State*. New Haven, Conn.: Yale University Press.

TILLY, C. (ed.) 1975. *The Formation of National States in Western Europe*. Princeton, NJ: Princeton University Press.

——1990. *Coercion, Capital, and European States, AD 990–1990*. Cambridge, Mass.: Basil Blackwell.

WALDNER, D. 1999. *State-building and Late Development*. Ithaca, NY: Cornell University Press.

WICKHAM-CROWLEY, T. 1992. *Guerrillas and Revolution in Latin America: A Comparative Study of Insurgents and Regimes since 1956*. Princeton, NJ: Princeton University Press.

YASHAR, D. J. 2005. *Contesting Citizenship in Latin America: The Rise of Indigeneous Movements and the Postiberal Challenge*. New York: Cambridge University Press.

CHAPTER 33

INTEGRATING QUALITATIVE AND QUANTITATIVE METHODS

JAMES D. FEARON

DAVID D. LAITIN

ALMOST by definition, a single case study is a poor method for establishing whether or what empirical regularities exist across cases.[1] To ascertain whether some interesting pattern, or relationship between variables, obtains, the best approach is normally to identify the largest feasible sample of cases relevant to the hypothesis or research question, then to code cases on the variables of interest, and then to assess whether and what sort of patterns or associations appear in the data.

The authors thank the Centro de Estudios Avanzados en Ciencias Sociales at the Juan March Institute in Madrid (and its director, José María Maravall), and the EITM Summer Institute at Berkeley (and its hosts, David Collier, Gary Cox, and Henry Brady) for providing stimulating audiences for earlier versions of this chapter. They thank as well David Freedman for critical commentary. Fearon thanks the Canadian Institute for Advanced Research for its support.

[1] Of course, a single "discrepant" case can disprove a hypothesis asserting a deterministic relationship between two things. But deterministic relationships between variables of interest are at best rare in social science. Eckstein (1975) argues that case studies are, under some conditions, the most efficient method for theory development. But his conditions require theories that make deterministic (i.e. not probabilistic) predictions.

However, with observational data (data not generated by random assignment of presumed causal factors), mere patterns or associations are not enough to allow us to draw inferences about what causes what. The standard approach in large-*N* statistical work in political and other social sciences is to accompany the presentation of associations (often in the form of regression results) with arguments about (a) why the reader should believe that the variation in an independent variable could cause variation in the dependent variable, and (b) why the reader should believe that the association observed in the data is not due to the independent variable happening to vary with some other, actually causal factor. The latter is usually done by adding "control" variables to the regression model, and arguing that one has not omitted important factors that are correlated with the independent variables of interest.[2]

The arguments for (a) and (b) amount to a sort of *story* the researcher tells about the associations observed in the regression results. The arguments, particularly those for (a), are often referred to as a "theory."[3] To some extent these stories can be evaluated as to whether they are deductively valid; that is, whether the conclusions do indeed follow from the premises, and whether the arguments are consistent. For example, it may be that the argument for why one independent variable matters contradicts the argument made on behalf of some other variable. Or it may be that an argument for a particular independent variable is internally inconsistent, confused, or doesn't follow from the premises on closer inspection. However, while a good analysis tells a valid and internally consistent story about the observed correlations, there may be multiple possible consistent stories about particular independent variables, and in general the reader may not know how much weight to put on the researcher's interpretation. Is the researcher's story capturing "what is really going on" in the cases to generate the observed patterns, or is something else driving the results?

At this point case studies can be extremely useful as a method for assessing whether arguments proposed to explain empirical regularities are plausible. One selects particular cases and examines them in greater depth than was required to code values on the outcome and explanatory variables of interest. When the "cases" are sequences of events in different countries or regions, or years in a particular country, or bills proposed in a legislature, and so on, the case study will entail a narrative account of what led to the outcome, including an assessment of what role the proposed causal factors played. In these narratives one typically uses additional data about the beliefs, intentions, considerations, and reasoning of the people who made the choices that produced the outcome, in order to test whether the "higher-level" general story told about many cases is discernible in particular, concrete cases. One can also ask if

---

[2] With regression analysis, there may be additional assumptions that should be justified in order to warrant a causal inference, such as correct functional form and additional assumptions about error variances.

[3] As Wagner (2007) observes, partisans of quantitative social science sometimes seem to mistake a regression equation itself for a theory.

there were important factors omitted from the large-N analysis that might in fact be driving the results. Finally, one can use the finer-grained analysis possible in a narrative account to ask about the validity and accuracy of measures being used in the large-N analysis.

For these several reasons, so-called "multimethod" research has become increasingly popular in political science in recent years, especially in comparative politics (Laitin 1998; Mares 2003; Iversen 1999; Boix 1998) and international relations (Huth 1998; Martin 1994; Schultz 2001; Goemans 2000; Stone 2002; Walters 2001; Fortna 2004; Mansfield and Snyder 2006; Collier and Sambanis 2005; and Doyle and Sambanis 2006).[4] Done well, multimethod research combines the strength of large-N designs for identifying empirical regularities and patterns, and the strength of case studies for revealing the causal mechanisms that give rise to political outcomes of interest.

An important but neglected problem for this research approach is the question of how to choose the cases for deeper investigation. Most work in this vein adopts the implicit criterion of choosing cases that support (or can be argued to support) the researcher's interpretation of the regression results. This criterion need not yield worthless results, since knowing that there are at least *some* cases that show good evidence of the causal mechanisms proposed by the researcher is something. But "cherry picking" by the researcher, or even the perception of cherry picking when it did not occur, will tend to undermine a reader's confidence that the case-study part of the design demonstrates that the researcher's causal story is on target.

In this article we propose that choosing cases for closer study *at random* is a compelling complement in multimethod research to large-N statistical methods in its ability to assess regularities and specify causal mechanisms. We discuss the advantages of random selection (or random selection within strata) for case studies, as well as problems with other possible criteria. These include choosing cases "on the regression line" that appear to fit the researcher's theory well; cases "off the regression line" that do not; "hard" or "critical" cases that are allegedly "tough tests" for the theory to pass; and choosing cases that have particular values on the explanatory factor of interest.

We illustrate what we will call the "random narratives" approach with work in progress we have been doing on the causes of civil war.[5] In Fearon and Laitin (2003), we report the main results of a cross-national statistical analysis of factors that distinguish countries that have had civil war onsets in the period 1945 to 1999. On the basis of these findings, theoretical arguments, and prior, unsystematic reading of diverse cases, we proposed a story about how to interpret why certain factors (such as low per capita income and high country population) are strongly related

---

[4] To our knowledge survey researchers in American politics do not normally do in-depth, unstructured interviews with or ethnographies of particular respondents to assess their theories based on interpreting regression coefficients. In congressional research, ethnographies produced by scholars such as Richard Fenno inspire quantitative work but rarely combine methods with the goal of making better causal inferences.

[5] Two examples of the random narratives are available in Fearon and Laitin (2005).

to civil war risk, whereas other factors (such as ethnic diversity, autocracy, and broad grievances) are not, once one controls for level of economic development. In order to assess this story we randomly selected twenty-five countries, stratified by region and whether or not the country had at least one civil war, and undertook narrative accounts of these countries' civil war experience (or lack thereof) using secondary sources.

In this chapter, we first summarize the findings of our statistical analysis of civil war onsets. We then in Section 2 look more carefully at different criteria for choosing which narratives to tell. In Section 3, we discuss a method for structuring narratives that is complementary to the statistical work. In Section 4 we illustrate in light of our narrative findings the incompleteness of the statistical models we initially ran. In Section 5, we highlight one narrative as an example of its potential yield. In the conclusion, we underline some surprises and advantages of the random narrative approach.

1 STATISTICAL RESULTS

Cross-national statistically based research by us and several other researchers has tended to find little or no support for two well-entrenched theories of civil war onset. First, our data show that by most measures of broad societal grievance— for example, lack of democracy, lack of religious or linguistic rights, or economic inequality—knowing the *level* of grievances in a country does not help differentiate countries susceptible to a civil war from those that are not.[6] Second, our data show that measures of cultural divides (the level of ethnic heterogeneity or the degree of cultural distance) do not help differentiate countries susceptible to a civil war from those that are not, once one controls for level of economic development.

In their stead, we have advanced an argument that points to the conditions that favor insurgency, a technology of military conflict characterized by small, lightly armed bands practicing guerrilla warfare from rural base areas. This perspective ties together a set of variables that correlate with civil war onset. Our interpretation of all of them is that they point to the relative incapacity of a state to quell insurgencies, which may begin at random and be "selected" for growth in countries with favorable conditions, or may be actively encouraged by signs of state weakness. The key variables that are significant and robust in our statistical models are listed below.

---

[6] This is *not* to say that if a state increases the level of grievance for a set of its citizens it can't provoke an insurgency. It may be that some states aggrieve minority groups as much as they can get away with, but some groups will tolerate higher levels of abuse (perhaps due to their weakness). Therefore increasing grievances can lead to insurgency even if levels of grievance across countries vary without implications for civil war onsets.

- Per capita income—we argue that low per capita income matters primarily because it marks states lacking in financial, bureaucratic, military, and police capability.
- Mountainous terrain—we interpret high degrees of mountainous terrain in a country as a tactical advantage to potential insurgents for hiding from government forces.
- Population—large populations require more layers of principals and agents to govern, making it harder for the regime to competently monitor, police, and respond to security threats at the village level.
- Oil—oil increases per capita income and government revenues and so works against insurgency, but controlling for the level of income we expect that oil producers have weaker governmental institutions, inasmuch as oil revenues make it unnecessary to develop intrusive tax bureaus that need to track individual citizens. Oil revenues can also increase the "prize" value of capturing the state or a region.
- Instability—we interpret rapid shifts in the regime type (a two or more change in a single year in the polity score for democracy) as a proxy for weak or weakening central state institutions.
- New state—in the immediate aftermath of independence, due to withdrawal of colonial forces before indigenous institutions have taken root, states are especially fragile. This provides an opportunity for challengers. They may fear that the leaders of the new state cannot commit not to exploit their region or group in the future after the government consolidates. Or they may see that the government cannot commit to provide state benefits in the future worth as much as their short-run expected value for trying to seize power by force now. Unable to hold as credible such commitments, insurgents can take advantage of a window of opportunity to seek secession or capture of the state.
- Anocracy—regimes that mix autocracy with some democratic features (such as a legislature or partly competitive national elections) suggest the presence of political conflict that weakens its ability to counter an internal threat.

A multivariate analysis thereby helped us to address the question of what factors correlate with higher likelihood of civil war onset. Our selection of variables was motivated by reading the literature on civil war, reading about specific cases, and thinking theoretically about the literature and cases using game-theoretic tools (see for example Fearon 1998; Laitin 1995; Fearon and Laitin 1999; Fearon 2004; 2008). We continue to work on formal models of civil war-related interactions in an effort to clarify and deepen the informal arguments we have proposed (e.g. Fearon and Laitin 2007).

Lacking in both approaches, however, is a clear empirical answer as to whether the variables in our statistical and theoretical arguments are actually "doing the work" in raising a country's susceptibility to a civil war onset. This is where case narratives can play an especially valuable role.

2 Choosing Narratives

··

But which narratives to tell? In statistical work, there are some methodological standards for case selection and analysis. In formal and particularly in game-theoretic analysis, there are well-developed rules and standards for what constitutes a well-posed model and proper analysis of it. There is no intellectual consensus, however, on how to choose cases for narrative exposition in a research design that combines statistical and case study evidence.[7] We consider several criteria that have been used in practice or that might be argued to be desirable.

2.1 "Good Cases" for the Researcher's Theory

In practice, perhaps the most common approach is for the researcher to choose "good cases" that nicely illustrate the causal mechanisms that the researcher proposed to explain the broader empirical regularities found in the statistical analysis. This is not an entirely worthless procedure in terms of producing evidence. It tells us that there exist at least some cases showing plausible evidence of the causal mechanisms hypothesized by the researcher. But selection bias is obviously a problem. "Good cases" have been cherry-picked, so it is not clear that they convey much information about the importance of the proposed causal mechanism in explaining the observed patterns. Even worse, what if these are the very cases that led the researcher to propose the causal mechanisms that she hypothesized to explain the statistical patterns in the first place?

In one version of "good case" selection, the researcher tells the reader that one or more of the cases selected for narrative exposition are, in fact, "hard cases" for her theory. It is then argued that received theories predict that the causal mechanism advanced by the author would be especially unlikely to be found in these "hard cases." Invariably, however, the historical narrative shows that the author's proposed causal mechanism is at play or that it trumps other factors stressed by existing theories ("surprisingly").[8] Selection bias is again a major concern. If the reader's prior belief put a great deal of weight on the existing theories, then there may be some evidentiary value (actual surprise) in learning that in at least one case, the author's favored causal mechanism can be argued to have been as or more important. But the reader can also be confident that the researcher would not present a developed "hard case" narrative unless it could be rendered in a way that seemed to support the claims of the researcher's preferred causal mechanism. So readers may be forgiven for thinking

---

[7] Nor is there a consensus on what, given the choice of a particular case, makes for a methodologically strong narrative. Still, most would agree that factual errors and tendentious interpretation make for a bad narrative or case study. Alex George has been a trailblazer in setting criteria for drawing causal inferences from narrative accounts. For his latest (and alas, his last) statement on this, see George and Bennett (2005).

[8] Though they may exist, we are not aware of any published paper or book in which the author asserts that X is a hard case for the preferred theory, and then finds that the case does not support the theory.

that talk of "hard cases" may be as much a rhetorical as a defensible methodological strategy.

Another version of "good case" selection occurs when the researcher selects "easy cases" for the preferred theory. For example, Schultz (2001) chooses for narrative several international crises involving Britain, in part because Britain's Westminster system most closely approximates the way that his theoretical model of crisis bargaining represents domestic politics, and from which Schultz drew his hypotheses about the role of opposition signaling in international disputes. This makes it easier to evaluate whether the causal mechanism at work in the model is at work in the cases. One downside, however, is that we have less information about whether Schultz's mechanism is more general than the sample of cases that led him to his model in the first place.

2.2 Convenience Samples

Another common approach in practice is to choose cases for narrative exposition that are relatively easy for the analyst to research, due to language skills or data availability, in what is sometimes referred to as a convenience sample. This procedure may be justified in some circumstances. The researcher will have to adjudicate trade-offs between the risk of selecting nonrepresentative cases, the accuracy of the narratives (for example, the validity and reliability of the measurement of the variables in question), and the number of cases that can be studied in depth. Representativeness will often be a significant problem for this approach, however, since the cases that are easy for the analyst to research will often be systematically unrepresentative on important variables. For example, in cross-national studies it is normally easier to find the sort of detailed information necessary for a good political narrative for wealthier countries, or for poor countries that happen to have attracted a lot of OECD attention and money for strategic or other reasons.

2.3 Selecting on Variation in the Dependent or Independent Variables

In principle one might select cases for narrative on the basis of values of the dependent variable, on values of an important independent variable, or on some kind of joint variation in both. For example, if the thing to be explained is the occurrence or absence of a phenomenon like democracy, war, rapid economic growth, or post-conflict peace, the researcher might select for close study a few cases where the phenomenon occurred and a few where it did not. Once again, though, we run into a problem of representativeness. If one is selecting a few cases from a larger set, why this one and not another? Why shouldn't the reader be suspicious about selection of "good cases" if no explanation is given for the choice? If an explanation is given and it amounts to convenience sampling, don't we still need to worry about representativeness? We can probably learn something about the proposed theoretical story from these cases and the contrast between them, but are we maximizing the amount? The same concerns apply for a small sample of cases selected on variation in some independent variable.

Another possibility here would be to select cases that show some particular combination on both the dependent variable and on independent variables of interest. For example, in their large-N analysis Mansfield and Snyder (2005) find that democratizing states with "concentrated" political power have been more likely to initiate interstate wars. They explain this with an argument about the incentives for threatened authoritarian elites to use nationalism and conflict for diversionary purposes. For narrative accounts they choose cases of democratizing states that initiated wars, which they call "easiest" for their theory (p. 169), presumably because these exhibit war and democratization together. As they argue, if they were not able to make a plausible case for the operation of their preferred mechanism in these cases, this would strongly undermine their theoretical claims.

Mansfield and Snyder look at all ten countries that were coded as democratizing when they initiated one or more wars, which protects them against the concern that they might have intentionally or unintentionally cherry-picked within this set. And intuitively, it seems plausible that if one's mechanism links the presence of X to phenomenon Y via such-and-such steps, one can learn more empirically about whether the mechanism matters as hypothesized from cases where X and Y occurred than from cases where one or the other did not. If the empirical question is "How often did democratization lead to war by the specific sequence of events that we have proposed?", then these are obviously the only cases one needs to consult. So here is a strong rationale for selecting cases that are not only "on the regression line," but that show a particular combination of values on Y and X.

If a causal mechanism implies specific sequences of events for more than one value of an independent variable, then the same reasoning leads to the suggestion that cases be sampled that are "on the regression line." For example, we proposed that per capita income proxies for several aspects of a state's capability to conduct effective counterinsurgency, relative to insurgent groups' ability to survive. Thus we would expect to find that in rich states nascent insurgent groups are detected and easily crushed by police (or they stay at the level of small, not very effective terrorist groups), while in poor states we should find would-be insurgent groups surviving and growing due to the states' incompetence (e.g. indiscriminate counter-insurgency) and virtual absence from parts of their territory. One could try to evaluate how much of the empirical relationship between income and civil war this mechanism explains by selecting for narratives poor countries that fell into civil war and rich countries that did not.

Of course, selecting on Y and X in this manner still faces the difficulty of *which* cases among those on the regression line. If it is not feasible to write narratives of all such cases, as Mansfield and Snyder did, we still face the problem of cherry-picking, or appearance of selection bias.

Moreover, there are good reasons to think that cases that are *off* the regression line might hold important, if different, information about the mechanisms in question as well. First, recall that the fundamental threat to causal inference in nonexperimental settings is the risk that there are other causes of Y that happen to be correlated with the proposed cause X. Cases off the regression line are more likely to show these other causal mechanisms at work. Seeing what they are and how they work should increase the ability of the researcher to say whether the observed relationship with X is the result of omitted variable bias. In addition, identifying other causes of the phenomenon in particular cases can lead to new hypotheses about general patterns and explanations, to be evaluated in subsequent rounds of research.

Second, narratives of cases off the regression line improve the researchers' chances of understanding why the proposed causal mechanism sometimes fails to operate as theoretically expected. For example, democratization does not always (or in fact, all that often) lead to interstate war—why not? Were authoritarian elites insufficiently threatened in these cases? Were they threatened but judged that there was no good opportunity for diversionary war? What additional variables determine each of these steps? If we accounted for these as well, would the original relationship hold up? In Snyder and Mansfield's study, answering such questions would require narratives of cases of democratization with concentrated political power that failed to produce interstate war.

Third, cases may fall off the regression not only because of the influence of un-measured factors, but due to measurement error in Y or X. Particularly with cross-national data, large-N statistical analyses must often employ crude indicators that can be coded for a large number of cases in a reasonable amount of time. Case narratives can then be used to make rough estimates of the validity and reliability of the large-N indicators, and to estimate how often measurement errors are masking instances where the proposed causal mechanism actually did work as predicted, or where it did not work as predicted but mistakenly got credit in the statistical analysis.

2.4 Selecting Randomly

These several considerations and the general concern about selection bias lead us to propose that *randomly choosing a (relatively) small number of cases for narrative analysis will often be a desirable strategy in "multimethod" research.*

With random selection, the investigator is asked to write narratives for cases that were chosen *for* him or her by a random number generator. The investigator goes from the first case on a list ordered by a random series to some number down the list, in each case using the narrative to ask about what connects or fails to connect the statistically significant independent variables to the coded value on the dependent variable. Most importantly, the researcher is protected against the risks caused by (known or unknown) systematic bias in case selection. In addition, with cases both on and off the regression line, the researcher can ask both about whether the proposed causal mechanisms operated in the cases on the line and about why and whether they failed to operate in cases off the line. If there were missing variables previously unexamined that would have improved the initial statistical analysis, they are probably more likely to be found in cases forced upon the investigator than in cases she or he chose, and the investigator has an unbiased, if small, sample of them. Finally, the researcher has the opportunity to estimate the impact of measurement error in both cases that are well predicted by the statistical model and those that are not.

Of course, there are downsides to random selection as well, most resulting from possible trade-offs against the quality and total number of narratives that can be produced. The researcher may be able to write more and better-quality narratives for cases that she already knows well or for which she has language or other skills. On the other hand, this may itself argue against selecting such cases, since it is more likely that they were consciously or unconsciously already used to generate the theoretical arguments that are being tested. Thus, random cases can have the virtue of serving as out-of-sample tests. In addition, case studies of unfamiliar or obscure events may gain from a fresh reading of the standard literature about a country with an eye to how much mileage can be gotten in understanding outcomes through a special focus on significant independent variables validated from cross-national analysis.

Rather than choosing purely at random, it may be more efficient to stratify on particular variables. For example, if one is interested in evaluating whether one's theoretical account for a particular variable in a cross-sectional study is plausible, then it makes sense to sample cases that have a range of values on this particular variable. Or, as we discuss below, it makes sense to stratify on certain variables, for instance region in a cross-national study, to avoid random selection yielding lots of (say) Eastern European cases but almost no Latin American cases. Still, short of doing case studies for every data point, random selection within strata or values of an independent variable will be warranted for the same reasons just advanced.

To construct the sample for our narrative data-set, we took a random sample of countries stratified by region and by whether the country had experienced a civil war in the period under study (1945–99). The rationale for stratifying by region was to ensure an even distribution across a factor that is correlated with common historical experience, culture, religion, and level of economic development.[9] We distinguished between "war" and "no war" countries for a different reason. We initially expected that there was more to be learned by studying a country that had an outbreak of war at some time than one that never did, because a "war country" has periods of both peace and war (variation), whereas a "no war country" has only peace. There is certainly information in the "no war" cases, and we thought it would be wrong to exclude them entirely. But we wanted to make possible the oversampling of countries that experienced a transition from peace to war, as this provides within country variation

[9] If we had not stratified by region, there was a reasonable probability that at least one region would have been significantly underrepresented, and another overrepresented. Since there are so many common and distinguishing features of the politics and economics of states with "regions" as conventionally described, we wanted to have a better chance of distinguishing the impact of our independent variables from unmeasured, region-specific factors.

on the dependent variable in which, in effect, a great many country-specific factors are controlled for.

While this expectation was to some extent borne out, as we note below we were surprised by how theoretically informative and empirically interesting were the narratives for countries that never had a civil war in the period under study.[10]

3 Structuring the Narratives

From our random selection of cases, we created a graph of predicted probabilities of civil onset by year for all chosen countries. The predicted probabilities were generated using the following (logit) model, using coefficients from the estimations using the data discussed in Fearon and Laitin (2003):

Log odds of onset at time $t = b0 + b1*$Prior war $+ b2*$Per cap Income$\_t - 1$

$+ b3*\log($Population$\_t - 1)$

$+ b4*\log($percent Mountainous$) + b5*$Noncontiguous

$+ b6*$Oil $+ b7*$New state

$+ b8*$Instability in prior 3 years $+ b9*$Anocracy$\_t - 1.$

In other words, we include variables found to be statistically and substantively significant based on that analysis.[11] In generating the predicted probabilities for a given country, we estimate the model *without the data for that country*, so that the experience of the country in question is not being used to shape the predictions for that country.[12] In generating the predicted probabilities, we set "prior war" (which is "1" if there was a civil war in progress in the prior year and zero otherwise) to zero for every year in the country's history, since we did not want to use actual war experience to help predict subsequent war experience. We place a tick on the x axis if in fact there was an ongoing civil war in that country for the given year.

[10] For countries such as Japan and the United States—both in the data-set—we looked for proto-insurgencies (e.g. the Zengakuren protests against Narita airport in Japan; the Aryan Nation militias at Ruby Ridge) to explain in terms of the model how and why they were successfully marginalized.

[11] Noncontiguous territory—not fully justified statistically—was added to the model for the country graphs. Its effects were minor.

[12] We drop all observations for the country, which can be up to 55, depending on how many years the country has been independent since 1945. Changes in predicted probabilities by this procedure were small, giving us confidence that our results did not turn on any single country. Of course, the country's experience has very indirect influence, since it was used in the earlier data analyses that led to this particular model specification. We are merely trying to avoid saying, in effect, "wow the model does great for country X" if part of the reason is that the model is reflecting the experience of country X.

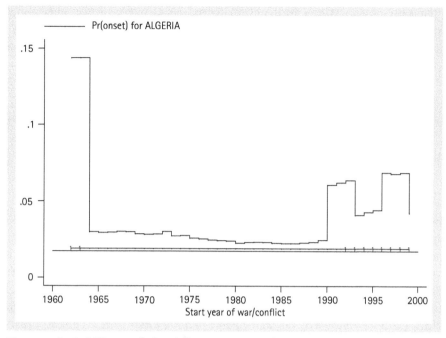

Fig. 33.1. Probability graph for civil war onsets in Algeria

Figure 33.1 illustrates the case of Algeria. Accompanying this graph (Table 33.1) are data on the key variables in comparison to the mean values of the region and the world. Throughout its independent history, Algeria has had a higher predicted probability of onset (.040) than the mean country of the world (.017) and the region as well (.016). We can see that there were two civil war onsets in years that our model predicted heightened susceptibility. Consistent with many other cases, the first civil war coincided with Algeria being a new state and the second civil war coincided with a period of anocracy and instability. Further, there is only one apparent "false positive"

Table 33.1. Key variables for Algeria, and in comparison to regional and world means

Variable	Algeria mean	Regional mean	World mean
Onset probability (predicted)	.040	.016	.017
GDP/capita (in 1985 USD)	2340	5430	3651
Population (in millions)	19.411	11.482	31.787
Mountainous area (as a percentage of total area in country)	15.7	18.6	18.1
Oil (dummy for extensive exports as percentage of total exports)	1	.49	.13
Instability (dummy)	.24	.13	.15
Anocracy (dummy)	.18	.23	.23

in the sense of a sharp rise in the estimated probability of civil war when no war occurred, in 1996–9; and this is fairly excusable given that it occurs during a war in progress, so inclusion of the variable "prior war" in the predictive model would have greatly reduced this "spike."

4 The Incompleteness of Statistical Models

How to interpret this graph and how to bring narrative evidence to bear? A first potential concern is that the predicted probabilities from the model are typically very small. Indeed, some 90 percent of the predicted probabilities (for all countries) fall between .0004 and .05. This is probably as it should be—or as it has to be—for two reasons. First, measured by year of onset, civil war starts are extremely rare. We have only about 127 onsets in nearly 7,000 country years. So, not conditioning on any other factors, the probability of a civil war starting in a randomly selected country year in this period was only about .017. Predicting civil war onset in a given country year from factors that can be coded across a large sample of countries and years is a bit like trying to find a needle in a haystack.

Second, it is virtually impossible to identify factors that are codable for a broad cross-section of countries and that can do an excellent job of predicting in *which year* a civil war will break out, if any. The random narratives reinforced our prior belief that a great deal of essentially random historical contingency is involved in determining whether and exactly when a country will "get" a civil war. Bad luck, idiosyncratic choices by leaders, complicated and *ex ante* unpredictable political and social interactions may all factor into explaining why a particular civil war started at a particular time, or even at all, in a particular country. It is an historian's project, and an admirable project at that, to try to understand such particularities and idiosyncrasies for particular cases. Our social science project, implausible though it may be, is to try to identify some factors and mechanisms that do "travel" across countries and years, raising the risk of civil war onset in a consistent and appreciable manner. This is a difficult task and we do not expect that even in the best case it will be possible to come anywhere close to perfect *ex ante* prediction. (Arguably, we could only do this if the participants themselves could do even better, given that they always have access to much more relevant case-specific information. But many examples suggest that it is quite rare for people and even politicians in a country to be able to forecast with confidence, a full year in advance, that a civil war will begin.)

Several of the key explanatory variables in our statistical model do not change much over time within countries. These variables are mountainousness, per capita income, population, and to some extent oil production. This means that while they may contribute a lot to explaining variation in the propensity for civil war outbreaks *across* countries, they are seriously handicapped for explaining in which year a war will start. The four variables that do (or can) change sharply from year to year— prior war, new state, instability, and anocracy—are all quite crude measures. They are relatively easily coded across a broad cross-section of countries and years, but they do not condition in any sophisticated way on political circumstances or events occurring in the country. While they are statistically and substantively significant as predictors of onset, none of them is diagnostic in the sense that they have empirically been followed by onset with a near certainty. Thus, even when several of these time-varying variables are "on," the predicted probability of civil war breaking out in the very next year may only reach .2 or .3.

So, if one had to bet on civil war starting in a particular year using the model's predicted probabilities, even the country years with some of the highest estimated chances of onset are more likely than not to remain peaceful. The highest probability in the data-set is .51 for Indonesia in 1949 and 1950. After that is Pakistan in 1947 and 1948, with a probability of onset at .35. For all but two cases in the entire data-set, for any given country/year, a betting person should bet against a civil war onset occurring that year.

How then to interpret year-to-year changes in predicted probabilities for a given country, like those seen in Figure 33.1? Relatively large jumps or falls in the graph (as seen, for example, for 1961–2, 1989–90, or 1996–7) correspond to changes on one or more of the sharply time-varying explanatory factors. For each such case we can ask: (1) If the change coincides with or shortly precedes a civil war onset, do we see a causal link from the independent variable to the outcome? (2) If there is no onset, do we see signs of strife or other indications of increased conflict that might have become a civil war (and which appear causally related to the change on the independent variable)? And if so, why didn't the violence escalate to the level of civil war? And (3) if there is no onset and no sign of increased violent conflict, why not? For all these cases we can and should also ask if we have miscoded (measured) the dependent variable or an independent variable, giving too much or too little credit to the model and the theory.

Similarly, for years in which we see an onset but no change in predicted probabilities, what occasioned the onset? Is there some new explanatory factor evident that could be coded across cases? Are there miscodings of variables in the model? If the predicted probability of conflict from the model is high on average (relative to the mean for the region or the world), do we see evidence linking any of the slow-moving variables like income or population and the outcome?

In more statistical terms, one way to interpret the graph of predicted onset probabilities for a given country is to interpret the statistical model as a model of an underlying, unobserved *propensity* for civil war in a given country year. The logit transformation scales the estimated propensity index into the [0, 1] interval as predicted probabilities. With narrative analysis we can try to go beyond assessing the fit of the model by looking at 0/1 outcome predictions, as in the standard quantitative approach to binary outcomes. Instead, to some extent we may be able to assess the model's fit by comparing changes in the predicted propensity of civil war to changes in the actual propensity as judged from the narrative evidence.

Despite difficulties in interpreting blunt variables in case analysis, our narratives of particular countries provide a useful complement and comparison to the statistical model. Before summarizing why they are useful, we will draw from the Algeria narrative to give a specific example of this approach.

5 LEARNING FROM THE NARRATIVES

In the case of Algeria's two civil wars, practitioners in the field of comparative politics committed only to the statistical approach might see the nice fit between model and the real world and then let sleeping dogs lie. Algeria, with its poverty, its oil, its large population, and its mountains, was a likely candidate for civil war. This was especially the case for two periods, 1962–3 and 1991–2, when political factors (being a new state in 1962; political instability and the movement toward anocracy beginning in 1990) pushed the expected probability of civil war well above the world average. And in fact, the onsets of civil war took place precisely when our models showed that Algeria was especially prone to such violence.

Why examine with a fine-toothed comb cases for which no explanation is needed? In our method, however, Algeria was chosen through random selection, and so we could not let this sleeping dog lie. Waking him up proved rewarding.[13]

The civil war onset when Algeria was a new state indeed involved a commitment problem like that we theorized in proposing why the variable New State associates with civil war. Berbers who had prospered under French rule feared a loss of status to Arabs who would be the majority group in the new Algerian state. Furthermore, the local guerrilla units that bore the greatest brunt of the fighting for independence feared marginalization once the regular army entered Algeria from Morocco and Tunisia. If these regional militias did not fight for power in the summer of 1962, they feared marginalization as they did not trust the the new leadership to give them as much as they might be able to take by fighting. Indeed some of these units and at least one from the Berber region took part in the 1962 rebellion.

The narrative also made clear that this "weak state" commitment problem stemmed as well from a factor not previously considered, namely the ineffectiveness of France's transfer of power. France left the scene when the independence movement was divided in several ways, with no clearly dominant force and no general commitment to any constitutional mechanism to decide among them or guarantee future, peaceful chances at power. Independence to a new state without a credible commitment by the former metropole to support the leadership to which it transfers

---

[13]   The full Algeria narrative is available at <http://www.stanford.edu/group/ethnic>.

power yielded a vacuum that drew in insurgents. It was France's inability to commit to Prime Minister Ben Bella rather than just Ben Bella's inability to commit to the future security of minorities that accounted for post-independence violence in 1962.

The civil war coded as beginning in 1992, as our theoretical arguments concerning anocracy and political instability expected, emerged out of the political opening granted by the authoritarian regime in 1990. The opening indicated division within the governing elite and a general sense of weakening in the face of public dissatisfaction and pressure. Clerics in the FIS (Islamic Salvation Front) were emboldened to exploit an economic crisis to challenge the regime in the name of fundamentalist ideals. The commitment problem again appears as critical in the explanation for why there was violence rather than a negotiated or democratic solution—the military regime feared that the first national election lost to the Islamists would be the last election held anytime soon. This is consistent with our theoretical account linking anocracy and political instability (indicated by changed Polity scores) to civil war.

However, a careful look at the civil war that ensued brought into question our interpretation of the impact of per capita income. We have argued that on average, country poverty proxies for a weak central government administration and coercive apparatus, unable to collect information on its own population or to use information strategically to root out insurgents. In the Algerian case, we find a very strong army, one that that had learned much from the experience in fighting the French during the long war of independence. The army was well taken care of and had the resources and will to develop sophisticated counter-insurgency units. So Algeria's moderately low per capita income (versus the regional or world averages) is in this case a poor measure of state coercive capabilities, and civil war occurred despite relatively strong coercive capability.

The narrative suggested, however, another quite different mechanism linking low per capita income and civil war. Area experts have pointed to the earlier closing of the migration outlet to Algerian youth as a causal factor in the onset of the war. Indeed, the rebellion came shortly after France cut off the immigration spigot. Instead of further inciting the anti-immigration program of M. Le Pen and his *Front National* in France, young Algerians that would formerly have been sending back remittances from France were now unemployed and being recruited into the FIS. And so, the low GDP and weak economy in Algeria worked through a second mechanism (available recruits) rather than the first (weak military) to translate high likelihood to actual onset (consistent in this case with Collier and Hoeffler's 2004 interpretation of the role of income).

Since the FIS was a religious mobilization, the narrative almost invited us to ask whether the civil war of 1992 can be explained by some religious factor, even if religion played no role in our statistical analysis. There can be little doubt that Islamic symbols had a powerful emotional impact on the population. In the late 1970s, Muslim activists engaged in isolated and relatively small-scale assertions of fundamentalist principles: harassing women who they felt were inappropriately dressed, smashing establishments that served alcohol, and evicting official imams from their mosques.

The Islamists escalated their actions in 1982, when they called for the abrogation of the National Charter and for the formation of an Islamic government. Amidst an increasing number of violent incidents on campuses, Islamists killed one student. After police arrested 400 Islamists, about 100,000 demonstrators thronged to Friday prayers at a university mosque. Islamists were also able to mobilize large numbers of supporters successfully to demand that the government abrogate rights given to women in the colonial period. And of course, the Islamist political party shocked and awed the military authorities in their impressive first round electoral victory in December 1991 (Metz 1993). Fundamentalism was popular!

However, it is not clear why Islamic fundamentalists confronted the FLN. Algerian nationalism, consequent on the French denial of citizenship to Muslims in the 1870 Cremieux Decree, was always "Islamic" in sentiment. The FLN was never considered, as many in the army command considered themselves, secular and perhaps even anti-Islam. Some FLN leaders were Islamists. The FIS did not represent a deep cultural cleavage in Algeria. In fact, there is a popular pun among Algerians, "le FIS est le fils du FLN" (Quandt 1998, 96–7). The trump in the FIS hand was not its religious devotion or its sole identification with Islam.

Furthermore, a careful examination of the FIS reveals little about Islam as the source for the Algerian rebellion. For one, the clerics followed the urban proletariat into war rather than led them. There is evidence that in fact the clerics sought in the late 1980s to calm the riots in the streets instigated by the unemployed youth (Pelletiere 1992, 6). To be sure, the GIA (the leading insurgent militia) relied on fundamentalist ideology in order to finance the war through the "Islamic rent" paid by Middle East states (Martinez 2000, 198–206, 240). But this was a strategy of raising funds more than a sign of Islamic devotion.

The narrative suggests that it was not Islamic fundamentalism, but rather state strategies in regard to religion that played a vital role in driving the insurgency. After independence, the Algerian government asserted state control over religious activities for purposes of national consolidation and political control. Islam became the religion of the state in the new constitution and the publicly displayed religion of its leaders. No laws could be enacted that would be contrary to Islamic tenets or that would in any way undermine Islamic beliefs and principles. The state monopolized the building of mosques, and the Ministry of Religious Affairs controlled an estimated 5,000 public mosques by the mid-1980s. Imams were trained, appointed, and paid by the state, and the Friday *khutba*, or sermon, was issued to them by the Ministry of Religious Affairs. That ministry also administered religious property, provided for religious education and training in schools, and created special institutes for Islamic learning.

What is the implication of state control over religion? Our statistical analysis of the whole sample found that religious discrimination could not distinguish countries that experienced civil wars from those that did not. But the narrative suggests a different mechanism. The very act of authorizing and subsidizing religious organizations and leaders automatically politicized religious protest. As religious entrepreneurs sought to capture new audiences for their local mosques, they were in fact challenging state authority. Through its subsidization and promotion of Islam, the Algerian authorities opened themselves up to forms of symbolic attack they could not easily repel. By seeking to suppress religious experimentation, the FLN found itself more vulnerable to attack than if it kept entirely out of religious affairs.

In sum, rather than some deep religious message of FIS that articulated with the religious sentiments of the people, it was the situation in which the state sought to co-opt religious opposition that gave that opposition a chance to articulate a clear anti-regime message through renegade mosques. State sponsorship of religion backfired grievously. The Algerian case could thus suggest that state *sponsorship* of religion (rather than *discrimination* against it) raises the probability of civil war.

6 CONCLUSION

Despite some claims to the contrary in the qualitative methods literature, case studies are not designed to discover or confirm empirical regularities. However they can be quite useful—indeed, essential—for ascertaining and assessing the causal mechanisms that give rise to empirical regularities in politics. We have argued that random selection of cases for narrative development is a principled and productive criterion in studies that mix statistical and case-study methods, using the former for identifying regularities, and the latter to assess (or to develop new) explanations of these.

Using the Algerian example, the narratives suggest a return to large-N analysis with several new ideas. First, the variable "new state" might be productively interacted with the capacity of the metropole to commit to the transitional leadership. The expectation is that a strong metropole would better be able to protect the leaders to whom it transferred authority, and thereby deter (at least for a time) potential insurgents. France, in the wake of occupation in the Second World War, the loss of the colonial war in Vietnam, the collapse of the Fourth Republic, and the long war for Algerian independence, was not in a position to manage the transition to the new leadership in Algiers.

This insight emerging from the narrative of a case that was "on the regression line" illuminated a not-so-obvious pattern in vulnerability of new states to civil war onsets. Many countries that received independence in the immediate postwar era when metropoles were devastated (such as in Indonesia, Vietnam, South Asia, and the Palestine Mandate) fell quickly into civil war. Those countries that became new states when the Soviet metropole disintegrated (Azerbaijan, Georgia, and Moldova are examples) were also highly susceptible to civil war onsets. However, those countries that received independence in the 1960s and 1970s in Africa when the metropoles were strong (except for Belgium and Portugal that could not manage the transitions to new leadership in their colonies) were less likely to suffer immediately rebellion. In several of these cases, "commitment problem" wars started several years later, after the colonial power really did stand back. "New state" is more dangerous the weaker the metropole that grants it independence.

Second, the Algeria narrative suggests that we might develop a coding rule for extent of migration by young men to more productive economies for work. The expectation would be that in countries where young men can relatively easily escape unemployment through migration to industrialized countries, insurgent recruitment will be more difficult than otherwise. (Subsequent narratives reported on the relationship of blocked migration opportunities and civil war in Haiti and near civil war in Jamaica; meanwhile open migration opportunities may have helped save Portugal and the Dominican Republic from joining the list of onsets under revolutionary conditions.)

Third, the Algeria narrative suggested a new way to think about the religious sources of insurgency. Instead of modeling hatreds between people of different religions, or of state discrimination against minority religions, it might be more productive to model the relationship between dominant religious authority and the state. The more the state seeks to regulate the dominant religious organization, the more it is setting up a recruitment base against the state within the religious organization. Preliminary data analysis for our large-N data-set gives support to this narrative-inspired conjecture.

There are several more general lessons as well to be learned from the random narrative exercise. Through narrative, it is possible to point to interactions among individual variables that may not matter in a consistent way by themselves, but that jointly may make for civil war susceptibility. It may then be possible to specify more sharply the conditions when a variable will have some theorized effect. It is possible to point to micro-factors for future coding such as tactical decisions by states and by insurgents that are usually ignored in large-N data collection exercises.

As well, the random narrative method allows us to estimate measurement error for variables that are hard to code reliably across large numbers of cases. In the set of narratives we examined through random selection, we found not insubstantial error in the coding of civil war onset, our dependent variable. To give but one example, northern Thailand has been held by area experts to be a zone of peace compared to the mountainous rebellions in neighboring Burma and Laos. A number of civil war lists have thus ignored the northern troubles in Thailand as a possible civil war. As a result of the research that went into the random narrative, however, we found that the northern insurgency clearly passed the death threshold that our scheme determines as a civil war. In general, we estimate that as many as 5 percent of our initial codings on the dependent variable were erroneous. Statistically, if these errors are random, in a logit analysis this will tend to bias effect estimates towards zero. Of course, the errors may not be random—they are surely more likely for relatively low-level civil wars close to whatever death threshold is employed—so a direct advantage of combining narrative analysis with statistical analysis is better measurement and more accurate effect estimates.

These random narratives, in sum, have already proven both troubling and useful as a complement to, or extension of, a large-N analysis of civil war onsets. They suggest a natural way that qualitative work might be integrated into a research program as a complement to rather than as a rival or substitute for quantitative analysis.

REFERENCES

BATES, R., et al. 1998. *Analytic Narratives*. Princeton, NJ: Princeton University Press.

BOIX, C. 1998. *Political Parties, Growth and Equality*. Cambridge: Cambridge University Press.

COLLIER, P., and HOEFFLER, A. 2004. Greed and grievance in civil war. *Oxford Economic Papers*, 56: 563–95.

—— and SAMBANIS, N. 2005. *Understanding Civil War*. 2 vols. Washington, DC: World Bank.

DOYLE, M., and SAMBANIS, N. 2006. *Making War and Building Peace*. Princeton, NJ: Princeton University Press.

ECKSTEIN, H. 1975. Case study and theory in political science. Pp. 94–137 in *Handbook of Political Science*, ed. F. Greenstein and N. Polsby. Reading, Mass.: Addison-Wesley.

ELSTER, J. 1998. A plea for mechanisms. In *Social Mechanisms: An Analytical Approach to Social Theory*, ed. P. Hedstrom and R. Swedberg. Cambridge: Cambridge University Press.

FEARON, J. D. 1998. Commitment problems and the spread of ethnic conflict. In *The International Spread of Ethnic Conflict: Fear, Diffusion, and Escalation*, ed. D. Lake and D. Rothchild. Princeton, NJ: Princeton University Press.

—— 2004. Why do some civil wars last so much longer than others? *Journal of Peace Research*, 41: 275–301.

—— 2008. Economic development, insurgency, and civil war. In *Institutions and Economic Performance*, ed. E. Helpman. Cambridge, Mass.: Harvard University Press.

—— and LAITIN, D. D. 1999. Weak states, rough terrain, and large-scale ethnic violence since 1945. Presented at the Annual Meetings of the American Political Science Association, Atlanta, September 2–5.

—— —— 2003. Ethnicity, insurgency and civil war. *American Political Science Review*, 97: 75–90.

—— —— 2005. Civil war narratives. Estudio/Working Paper 2005/218, Centro de Estudios Avanzados en Ciencias Sociales, Instituto Juan March de Estudios e Investigaciones, June.

—— —— 2007. Civil war terminations. Presented at the 103rd Annual Meeting of the American Political Science Association, Chicago, Aug. 30–Sept. 2.

FORTNA, V. P. 2004. *Peace Time: Cease-fire Agreements and the Durability of Peace*. Princeton, NJ: Princeton University Press.

GEORGE, A., and BENNETT, A. 2005. *Case Studies and Theory Development in the Social Sciences*. Cambridge, Mass.: MIT Press.

GERRING, J. 2006. *Case Study Research: Principles and Practices*. Cambridge: Cambridge University Press.

GOEMANS, H. 2000. *War and Punishment*. Princeton, NJ: Princeton University Press.

GOLDTHORPE, J. 2000. *On Sociology*. Oxford: Oxford University Press.

HUTH, P. 1998. *Standing your Ground: Territorial Disputes and International Conflict*. Ann Arbor: University of Michigan Press.

IVERSEN, T. 1999. *Contested Economic Institutions*. Cambridge: Cambridge University Press.

LAITIN, D. 1995. National revivals and violence. *Archives européennes de sociologie*, 36: 3–43.

—— 1998. *Identity in Formation*. Ithaca, NY: Cornell University Press.

MANSFIELD, E., and SNYDER, J. 2005. *Electing to Fight: Why Emerging Democracies Go to War.* Cambridge, Mass.: MIT Press.

MARES, I. 2003. *The Politics of Social Risk.* Cambridge: Cambridge University Press.

MARTIN, L. 1994. *Coercive Cooperation.* Princeton, NJ: Princeton University Press.

MARTINEZ, L. 2000. *The Algerian Civil War 1990–1998*, trans. J. Derrick. London: Hurst.

METZ, H. (ed.) 1993. *Algeria: A Country Study.* Federal Research Division, Library of Congress, <http://memory.loc.gov/cgi-bin/query2/r?frd/cstdy:@field(DOCID+dz0000>), section on Chadli Bendjedid and Afterward.

PELLETIERE, S. C. 1992. *Mass Action and Islamic Fundamentalism: The Revolt of the Brooms.* Carlisle Barracks, Pa.: US Army War College.

QUANDT, W. B. 1998. *Between Ballots and Bullets.* Washington, DC: Brookings.

SCHULTZ, K. 2001. *Democracy and Coercive Diplomacy.* Cambridge: Cambridge University Press.

STONE, R. 2002. *Lending Credibility.* Princeton, NJ: Princeton University Press.

VAN EVERA, S. 1997. *Guide to Methods for Students of Political Science.* Ithaca, NY: Cornell University Press.

WAGNER, R. H. 2007. *War and the State.* Ann Arbor: University of Michigan Press.

WALTERS, B. 2001. *Committing to Peace.* Princeton, NJ: Princeton University Press.

PART IX

ORGANIZATIONS, INSTITUTIONS, AND MOVEMENTS IN THE FIELD OF METHODOLOGY

CHAPTER 34

....

QUALITATIVE AND MULTIMETHOD RESEARCH: ORGANIZATIONS, PUBLICATION, AND REFLECTIONS ON INTEGRATION

....

DAVID COLLIER

COLIN ELMAN

QUALITATIVE methods in political science have undergone a remarkable transformation.[1] After two decades of relative quiescence, with a fairly stable canon consisting mainly of works published in the 1970s,[2] this branch of methodology has been experiencing a resurgence, and a considerable body of new research and writing has

The authors thank Mark Bevir, Andrew Bennett, Taylor Boas, Henry Brady, John Gerring, Fernando Daniel Hidalgo, Michael Jensen, Jody LaPorte, James Mahoney, Ioana Matesan, and Neal Richardson for helpful comments.

[1] For overviews of this transformation, see Munck (1998); Collier (1998); Bennett and Elman (2006); and *Comparative Political Studies* (2007).

[2] For example, Przeworski and Teune (1970); Sartori (1970); Lijphart (1971; 1975); Vallier (1971); Campbell (1975); Smelser (1976); George (1979).

appeared.[3] The scholars concerned with qualitative research methods are a diverse community. This eclecticism is reflected in the broad range of methods which taken together constitute "qualitative research," including, for example, concept analysis and ethnographic methods, as well as systematic small- to medium-N comparison. Eclecticism is further seen in the increasingly sophisticated use of multiple, complementary methods in composite research designs, based on nesting or the iterated use of alternative qualitative and quantitative strategies. Finally, this eclecticism is evident in the substantial overlap—and the strong interest in exploring the relationship—between what might be thought of as mainstream qualitative methods, and interpretative and constructivist methods. Given this diversity of analytic tools, it is appropriate to designate this area of methodology as involving "qualitative and multi-method research."[4]

Operating as both a cause and an effect of this resurgence, new organizations have emerged to institutionalize these developments within political science. This chapter first provides an overview of the approach to methodology that underpins the idea of qualitative and multimethod work. It then discusses these new organizations, in particular the Organized Section on Qualitative and Multi-Method Research of the American Political Science Association, and the annual Institute for Qualitative and Multi-Method Research. The chapter then reviews patterns of publication, and a conclusion considers briefly the merits of an integrative, versus a separate tracks, approach to coordinating alternative methodologies.

1 THREE MEANINGS OF MULTIMETHOD

....

Qualitative research methods are eclectic, both in their own right and even more so as one considers the links with other research traditions. This leads us to characterize the idea of multimethod in the three different ways just noted: in terms of the increasing diversity of techniques centered in the conventional qualitative tradition; the growing number of interconnections between qualitative and quantitative research tools; and the relationship to interpretative and constructivist approaches.

---

[3] Examples of relevant studies from the 1990s include Fearon (1991); Collier (1993); King, Keohane, and Verba (1994); *Political Methodologist* (1995); *American Political Science Review* (1995); Lustick (1996); Tetlock and Belkin (1996); Van Evera (1997); and Wendt (1999). A small selection of the studies beginning in 2000 would include Ragin (2000); Finnemore and Sikkink (2001); Elman and Elman (2001; 2003); Gerring (2001; 2007); Goertz and Starr (2002); Wedeen (2002); Geddes (2003); Mahoney and Rueschemeyer (2003); Pierson (2004); Brady and Collier (2004); George and Bennett (2005); Goertz (2006); Yanow and Schwartz-Shea (2006); and Guzzini and Leandner (2006).

[4] The field of quantitative methods is, of course, also heterogeneous, and in that sense could also be characterized as multimethod. The key point emphasized throughout this chapter is that juxtaposing the terms "qualitative" and "multimethod" underscores the crucial fact that conventional qualitative methods are not intellectually isolated, but are strongly connected with other methodologies.

With the goal of situating these three perspectives in relation to wider methodological alternatives, we first discuss briefly different understandings of qualitative versus quantitative. This simple dichotomy can sometimes be used unambiguously to differentiate contrasting types of research: for example, large-N studies utilizing structural equation modeling, versus in-depth case studies which might employ within-case process tracing, participant observation, or other forms of ethnographic work.

Yet it is also productive to disaggregate the qualitative–quantitative distinction in terms of four criteria: (1) level of measurement; (2) large versus small N; (3) use of statistical and mathematical tools; and (4) whether the analysis builds on a dense knowledge of one or a few cases, employing what may be called thick analysis,[5] as opposed to the thin analysis characteristic of a great many large-N studies that would routinely be seen as quantitative.[6]

To a substantial extent, these criteria point to major overlaps between what might be understood as qualitative and quantitative approaches. (1) With regard to level of measurement, nominal scales have traditionally been distinctively identified with the qualitative tradition, yet variables at this level of measurement have become quite standard in quantitative research, given the widespread use of logit analysis, probit analysis, and dummy variables in regression studies. (2) Although the size of the N often serves as a good criterion for differentiation, some works of comparative-historical analysis that might be thought of as qualitative in fact analyze many cases,[7] whereas a major tradition of quantitative research on the political economy of advanced industrial countries addresses a smaller number of cases.[8] (3) Although the use of statistical and mathematical tools has long been a hallmark of quantitative research, the extensive use of such tools—for example, in qualitative comparative analysis (QCA), which is strongly anchored in the qualitative tradition—again blurs this distinction.

It is specifically the final criterion, (4) thick analysis, which is especially important in identifying the key differentiating characteristic of qualitative research. Qualitative researchers routinely rely on rich, dense information concerning specific cases. This differentiating characteristic is, in turn, the point of departure for discussing our three contrasting understandings of "multimethod."

1.1 Multimethod: Understood as Diverse Approaches within Conventional Qualitative Methods

With the resurgence of qualitative methods, the suite of available qualitative techniques has expanded—in the framework of a strong reliance on thick knowledge

---

[5] Thick analysis in this sense is understood as related to, but distinct from, Coppedge's (1999) idea of thick concepts, and Geertz's (1973) idea of thick description.

[6] These distinctions are adapted from Collier, Brady, and Seawright (2004, 244–7).

[7] E.g. Rueschemeyer, Stevens, and Stevens (1992); Collier (1999).

[8] For example, a long succession of such studies grew out of the widely cited article by Lange and Garrett (1985).

of cases. These different approaches, along with their practitioners, are increasingly viewed as belonging to a well-defined research community, although advocates of one or another approach may strongly prefer it to the others—and may indeed have serious misgivings about some of the others. Relevant alternatives include the closely related methods of controlled comparison and structured, focused comparison; case-study methodologies; within-case analysis that variously focuses on pattern matching and process tracing; studies with a strong qualitative, historical focus on a temporal dimension, as with research on path dependence; the use of counterfactual analysis; and a spectrum of techniques for data collection, including among many others semi-structured and unstructured interviews, participant observation, archival work, and the systematic analysis of secondary sources. The relevant set of qualitative tools is now sufficiently diverse, and the choices about evaluating and linking these tools sufficiently complex, that the idea of multimethod can certainly be applied to the standard domain of qualitative work.

1.2 Multimethod: Understood as Linking Qualitative, Quantitative, and Statistical Tools

A second understanding refers to the many efforts to connect qualitative methods to quantitative and statistical research procedures. Scholars employ a variety of such tools to reason about necessary causes, and a number of discussions have used probability theory to guide case selection in small-N analysis. The idea of nested designs, the iterated use of qualitative and quantitative methods, and the role of qualitative anomalies in reorienting quantitative research are further examples of this bridging.

1.3 Multimethod: Understood as Conventional Qualitative Methods Vis-à-vis Interpretativism and Constructivism

The third understanding of multimethod concerns the relationship with interpretativism and constructivism. To simplify complex analytic traditions, interpretativism is the analysis of politics focused on the meanings entailed for the actors involved; it adopts an emic (actor-centered) rather than an etic (observer-centered) viewpoint. The related approach of constructivism, which has special importance in the field of international relations, focuses on how the world of politics is socially constituted (or constructed) by these same actors. These two approaches are connected, in that the adequate analysis of the social construction of politics is routinely seen as calling for interpretative tools.[9]

---

[9] Scholars who are unfamiliar with, or skeptical about, interpretative methods might consider the kind of analytic work that goes into generating some major insights in the social sciences: for example, Weber's conception of the protestant ethic (Stryker 2002), Geertz's (1973) interpretation of Balinese social structure through the lens of the cockfight, or Jowitt's (1978) conceptualization of Soviet

Some political scientists would argue that these approaches are consistent with standard research practices.[10] Others maintain it is possible to adopt a distinctive understanding of the subject matter of politics (i.e. ontology), without calling for different methods or stepping outside the domain of conventional social science.[11] Still others argue that a rigorous understanding of interpretativism and constructivism raises such distinctive questions of epistemology and ontology that the contribution of these approaches is lost if they are subsumed within a conventional framework, including the framework of standard qualitative methods.[12] The debate over these alternatives is the third way in which multimethod is a productive designation for the spectrum of methodological concerns under discussion here.

To summarize, the idea of multimethod can be understood as encompassing three different meanings: the heterogeneity of qualitative methods, the interconnections between qualitative and quantitative research procedures, and the relationship with interpretative and constructivist methods. Notwithstanding the diverse character of these several approaches, ultimately they are all anchored in the thick analysis of cases that is distinctively associated with qualitative work.

2 ORGANIZATIONS

The emergence of new organizations in support of qualitative and multimethod research occurred against the backdrop of a larger movement in political science advocating greater methodological pluralism. This shift was reflected in a number of settings, deriving in part from initiatives launched by the presidents and Council of the American Political Science Association. Beginning in the later 1990s, the *American Political Science Review* made a sustained and successful effort to publish articles on a broader range of topics, using a wider variety of methods. During the same period, the APSA inaugurated a new journal, *Perspectives on Politics*, which among other things published integrative review essays on an extensive array of subjects, again underscoring the commitment to a more diverse view of the discipline.

Communism in terms of "charismatic impersonalism." This form of conceptualization, which captures the meaning of political and social action from the standpoint of the actors, involves what may variously be thought of as the creation of ideal types, or the imaginative reconstruction of social action. This reconstruction may well depend on different criteria for evaluating evidence and inference than are found in conventional social science. Yet it would be a great loss if this kind of conceptual work were not a component of the political science enterprise.

[10] A classic, and engagingly overstated, formulation of this position is found in Abel (1977).

[11] Within the international relations literature, see Reus-Smit (2002), as well as various contributions to Katzenstein (1996).

[12] Yanow and Schwartz-Shea (2006). A debate on these issues was published in the *APSA Qualitative Methods Newsletter* 1 (2) (2003): <http://www.asu.edu/clas/polisci/cqrm/Newsletter/Newsletter1.2.pdf>.

This same perspective was articulated by an APSA Task Force on Graduate Education, commissioned in 2002 and co-chaired by Christopher Achen and Rogers Smith. The task force's report, issued in March 2004, includes the observation that:

the complex subject matter of politics must be studied using many methods if we are to obtain the greatly varying sorts of data, form the wide range of descriptive and explanatory concepts, and engage in the many sorts of inferential testing that we need to achieve rigorous analysis.[13]

Relatedly, former APSA president Robert Keohane (2003), in an essay originally written for this task force, articulates the view that rigorous, scientific research is not exclusively the domain of quantitative methods. Keohane argues that:

Our discipline is divided, it seems to me, between those who identify "rigorous" scientific work with quantitative analysis, and those of us who define our field more broadly.... With respect to science, those of us in the latter camp define it not as requiring quantitative analysis but as research that seeks to make necessarily uncertain inferences by using publicly identified methods through public procedures.[14]   (2003, 9)

Correspondingly, Keohane distinguishes between the "technical specialization pole" of the discipline that builds on methods such as game theory and econometrics, and a "contextual knowledge" pole characterized, among other things, by a greater concern with qualitative methods. He then reflects on initiatives that might help ensure that the latter approach has a secure position in the discipline.

In addition to these and other top-down institutional developments that have had important influence, there has been considerable grass-roots support and pressure for greater pluralism in a discipline that was seen as being increasingly narrow and overspecialized.[15]

2.1 APSA Organized Section for Qualitative and Multi-Method Research

The new qualitative/multimethod section[16] emerged in parallel with these wider disciplinary developments, growing out a series of initiatives that started in 1997. Beginning in that year, the long-standing Committee on Conceptual and Terminological Analysis—an official Related Group of APSA—was revitalized. The Committee began to sponsor a growing number of panels, and in 2000 the Committee adapted its name to reflect its wider focus, becoming the Committee on Concepts and Methods. That

---

[13] See <http://www.apsanet.org/imgtest/Final Report Formatted for Distribution.pdf>. Emphasis in the original.

[14] He cites here King, Keohane, and Verba (1994, 7–9).

[15] Certainly the most important and best-known forum for expression of that discontent was the Perestroika discussion listserv (see Monroe 2005).

[16] Prior to the adoption of this name in January 2007, it was called the APSA Qualitative Methods Section. Rather that referring to one name or the other according to the time period, the text below generally refers to the name as of 2007. The same practice is adopted in the discussion below of the Institute for Qualitative and Multi-Method Research.

same year, it began offering a highly successful APSA short course on field methods, a course that as of 2008 was being led by a third cohort of instructors.

In 2003, building on these expanded activities, the further initiative was taken to reorganize the APSA committee as an official Organized Section of the APSA. Support in the discipline for the new section was overwhelming. The petition to form the section was signed by 1,000 APSA members, including twenty-eight former APSA presidents and seven former *APSR* editors. Within a year of its formation the new section had more than 750 members; and as of February 2008 it ranked second in membership among the APSA sections, followed very closely by the Political Methodology Section—whose focus is primarily on quantitative methods.

The new methods section has a strong presence at the annual APSA meeting. The section began in 2003 with an allocation of six panels, and by 2008 the number had risen to twenty-two. The section has continued to sponsor short courses each year—in 2007 these included the ongoing course on Research Design and Field Methods, a day-long course on Interpretative Methods, one on Qualitative Comparative Analysis, and one on Methodological Innovation at the Intersection of Qualitative and Quantitative Methods. In addition to the panels and short courses, the section has sponsored an innovative Methods Café, at which participants can consult with specialists on diverse topics: participant observation, discourse analysis, conversational interviewing, ethnography, feminist methods, research based on sources such as diaries and memoirs, reflexivity and positionality, and the teaching of qualitative-interpretative methods. The members of the section who organized this initiative thereby broke new ground in creating a distinctive approach to offering participants in the annual meeting advice and assistance on methodological issues.

In 2005, the section was one of the first to take part in a new APSA initiative, the annual meeting Working Group. Participants in a working group commit to attending a specified number of panels in a given area of enquiry, in combination with short courses in that same area, as well as one or more special discussion sessions arranged for the members of the working group. The working group thus serves to give greater intellectual coherence to the annual meeting for many attendees. For those who meet the specified requirements of attendance, the APSA awards a certificate. The working groups have proved to be an important forum for training and interaction in the areas of methodology of concern to the section.

Annual awards and the newsletter are other important section activities. Three awards are given for exemplary work that develops and/or applies qualitative and multimethods in books, articles and book chapters, and APSA conference papers. The section publishes a very substantial newsletter. It appears twice a year and has presented what are widely viewed as engaging debates on methodology. John Gerring, as he ended his term as the first editor, observed that his goal had been to offer his readers "the most interesting, innovative, and (it follows) contentious issues in the field of political methodology" (Gerring 2006, 1). The newsletter has published symposia on a wide spectrum of topics, ranging from foundational epistemological issues, to technical questions regarding particular methodologies, to broader disciplinary trends (Table 34.1).

Table 34.1. Selection of symposia published in the newsletter of the APSA section

Combining ethnography and rational choice methodologies. The potential compatibility, strengths, and limitations of the two methodologies, and leverage provided by each in the study of mechanisms.

Concept analysis. Essays on the tradition of concept analysis: exploration and clarification of meanings, and the role of concepts in explanation.

Content and discourse analysis. Comparison of content and discourse analysis as research methods, and discussion of their compatibility with other methods.

Field research strategies. Strengths and challenges of field research; strategies for undertaking and evaluating data collection.

Field research: richness, thickness, and participation. The challenges of, and trade-offs between, different modes of field research. Thick ethnography and participant observation.

George and Bennett's *Case Studies and Theory Development in the Social Sciences*. Essays discussing the contributions and pitfalls of the volume.

Interpretativism. Interpretativism as a qualitative method, its meaning for political science, and its relationship to quantitative survey methods.

Multimethod Work. Essays focused on each subfield of political science, suggesting best practices and the challenges of multimethod research.

Necessary conditions. The challenge of evaluating necessary condition hypotheses, and the requisites for conducting probabilistic tests of necessary condition hypotheses.

The Perestroika movement. The movement for reform within political science and its call for methodological pluralism.

Qualitative comparative analysis (QCA). QCA as a research method, and a comparison of QCA with regression analysis.

Teaching qualitative methods. Approaches to training students in qualitative methods: constraints and trade-offs.

The quantitative/qualitative distinction. Alternative understandings of qualitative methods, the contrast with quantitative methods, and the quantitative/qualitative debate in the United States.

Shapiro's *The Flight from Reality in the Human Sciences*. Discussion of Shapiro's call for problem-driven approaches to political science and for a critical reappraisal in the social sciences.

Overall, the section has been successful beyond anyone's expectations, through its efforts to promote scholarly communication about diverse aspects of methodology, through providing training in research methods, and through preparing scholars to teach qualitative and multimethod research.

2.2 Institute for Qualitative and Multi-Method Research

The institute[17] offers intensive instruction in qualitative/multimethods approaches. It likewise provides participants[18] with the opportunity to present and receive extensive

---

[17] The institute is co-organized by the national Consortium for Qualitative Research Methods.

[18] The term participant rather than student is used here, in part because a significant portion of those who attend the institute are junior-level, and even senior-level, faculty.

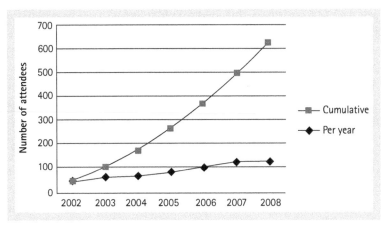

Fig. 34.1. Attendance at the Institute for Qualitative and Multi-Method Research, 2002–8

feedback on research designs—which in most (though not all) cases involve doctoral dissertation research. Each year the sessions span two weeks, with a weekend break. Roughly twenty faculty, drawn from universities across the United States, teach at the institute each year, making it possible to incorporate diverse perspectives on methodology.

2.2.1 *Overview of the Institute*

The original idea for the institute arose from the striking disparity between the wide use of qualitative methods in political science research, and the scarcity in US political science departments of specialized graduate classes teaching these methods. Bennett, Barth, and Rutherford's article[19] on this mismatch called attention to the major role of qualitative methods as a basis for research published in leading political science journals, in contrast to the limited number of qualitative methods courses offered in political science graduate programs. Among the courses offered, many were just one component of a broader scope and methods course, rather than a sustained introduction to qualitative approaches.

The institute has proactively addressed this mismatch. Beginning with forty-five participants in 2002, the number of participants increased to 129 by 2008 (Figure 34.1). The cumulative number of participants has grown accordingly, rising to 630 over the same period.

The curriculum covers a wide spectrum of qualitative/multimethod tools: case studies, field interviewing and ethnography, narrative and interpretative work, and nested research designs that link qualitative and quantitative methods, among many other approaches. The institute explores the uses, techniques, strengths, and limitations of qualitative methods, while emphasizing their complementarity with alternative approaches.

---

[19] This article was widely circulated during the period when the Institute was being formed, and was later published as Bennett, Barth, and Rutherford (2003).

Topics at the 2008 Institute included: research design and fieldwork; debates about standards for causal inference and the logic(s) of explanation; typologies and measurement; concept analysis; process tracing; experiments and natural experiments; historiography and archival research; storing and accessing qualitative data; multi-method research; relationships between qualitative methods and statistical theory; qualitative comparative analysis and fuzzy-set analysis (fs/QCA); conceptualizing culture; temporality, complexity, and critical junctures; and philosophy of science issues relevant to qualitative research, and to understanding these diverse methodological tools.

In addition to lectures attended by all participants, the institute holds breakout sessions that cover topics of particular interest to subgroups of participants, as well as master classes in which authors of well-regarded books discuss how they designed and implemented their research. Examples are drawn from exemplary research in international relations, comparative politics, and American politics.

Participants in the institute are required to prepare a written research design in advance, and sessions focused on the research designs are one of the most valuable parts of the program. On most days, small groups come together for the presentation, discussion, and (constructive) critiquing of the research designs, and to receive feedback from at least one faculty member. These sessions help to reinforce many of the methodological ideas explored in the lectures and breakout sessions, showing how these ideas can be applied in ongoing research.

Beyond the immediate benefits of directly providing participants with training in qualitative/multimethod techniques and helping them with their own research, the institute has had a broader impact. For example, intensive interactions at the institute have established networks of participants who share methodological and substantive interests and who stay closely in touch, often for many years after the institute. In addition, many of the participants go on to teach qualitative and multimethods research tools, and even those who do not directly teach these methods become members of a much enlarged community of scholars trained to use them.

The institute's primary source of funding involves a membership model, parallel to that of the Inter-university Consortium for Political and Social Research at the University of Michigan. However, in the case of ICPSR it is the university that is a member, whereas the institute relies on persuading political science departments to pay for memberships. The expectation was that there was sufficient pent-up demand for training in qualitative methods that political science departments—as well as some research centers on university campuses—would be willing to commit their own funds to pay for membership. They could then nominate one, two, or three of their own students or faculty to attend the institute, according to their level of membership. These membership fees cover all costs of participation, including lodging and meals.

This model has been a great success. In the first year, twenty political science departments and research centers became members, and by January 2008 the number of institutional members had risen to sixty. Participants are also admitted through an open-pool competition for those who either are enrolled in member institutions but are not nominated by them, or who are from nonmember institutions. Using various sources of funding, it is possible to support nine or ten participants per year from this pool. Further evidence of the pent-up demand for this methods training is the fact that each year the institute has received approximately ten applications for each space in the open-pool.

In addition to member subscriptions, financial support has included four grants from the National Science Foundation, as well as funding from Arizona State University. As of the summer of 2008, the Institute moved to the Maxwell School, which is the graduate school of social science at Syracuse University. The Maxwell School, and in particular its Moynihan Institute of Global Affairs, provides long-term support for further broadening the Institute's activities.

2.2.2 *Supporting Advanced Research on Methodology*

From the beginning, the Institute has provided a forum in which methodologists from around the country—including institute faculty, as well as some student/ participants with advanced methodological skills—have come together to discuss their own writing and publications. These interactions have led to co-authored publications, and the institute sees this as a key way in which it fosters methodological innovation.

This interaction has been institutionalized through the formation of a Research Group in Qualitative and Multi-Method Analysis. Each year, this Research Group convenes scholars—especially younger scholars—for intensive discussion of one another's research. These meetings are held on the weekend between the week-long sessions of the regular institute, thereby making it easier—in terms of the logistics of travel—to bring together a strong group of participants. The goal is to create a forum that further improves the quality and analytic value of new work produced in this branch of methodology. NSF support was crucial in launching this initiative.

2.3 Other Organizations Concerned with Qualitative and Multimethod Work

Other organizations have also been significant venues for new work on qualitative methods. The IPSA Committee on Concepts and Methods, which is Research Committee No. 1 of the International Political Science Association, is currently housed at the Centro de Investigación y Docencia Económicas (CIDE) in Mexico, and is dedicated to the promotion of conceptual and methodological discussion in political science. Recognized in 1976 by IPSA at its first research committee (under its former title of Committee on Conceptual and Terminological Analysis), this committee is also affiliated with the International Sociological Association.

Another relevant group is the COMPASSS Research Group (Comparative Methods for the Advancement of Systematic Cross-Case Analysis and Small-n Studies). Its goal is to bring together "scholars and practitioners who share a common interest in theoretical, methodological and practical advancements in a systematic comparative case approach to research which stresses the use of a configurational logic, the existence of multiple causality and the importance of a careful construction of research populations."[20] COMPASSS is headquartered at four Belgian universities—the Université Catholique de Louvain, Université Libre de Bruxelles, Katholieke Universiteit Leuven, and Universiteit Antwerpen—and it also has an active presence at the University of Arizona. An important feature of the research strategies advanced by COMPASSS is Charles Ragin's (1987; 2000) qualitative comparative analysis, and its further development in the form of fuzzy-set analysis (fs/QCA).

In Europe, the University of Essex Summer School in Social Science Data Analysis and Collection is also a significant venue for methods training. Compared for example with ICPSR at the University of Michigan, the Essex summer school has placed greater emphasis on a diverse set of qualitative methods.[21]

3 PUBLICATION

The trajectories of publication in quantitative methods in political science, as opposed to that of the qualitative/multimethod field, have been distinct. As Michael Lewis-Beck and Charles Franklin emphasize in this *Handbook*, at various points quantitative methodologists found it difficult to publish in standard journals the cutting-edge articles that presented their most important, innovative research.

By contrast, this problem has generally not arisen with qualitative/multimethod work. Certainly, there have been occasional disconnects in the review process with journals. In the 1990s, a journal editor might have sent out a qualitative concept analysis article to two reviewers—one a political theorist and the other a quantitative methodologist. Both reviewers, possibly with the best of intentions, might have found the article quite remote from what they saw as standard concerns in work on concepts, or on methodology.

Yet in recent years, mainstream journals have published numerous methodological articles involving qualitative and multimethod approaches, including: the *American Political Science Review, American Journal of Political Science, World Politics, International Organization, Journal of Theoretical Politics, Comparative Political Studies, Comparative Politics, Studies in Comparative International Development, Theory and Society*, and *Political Research Quarterly*—as well as the *Annual Review of Political Science*.

Given the receptivity of these journals, scholars have not felt the need to establish a journal of their own, although they certainly view the newsletter of the APSA

---

[20] See <http://www.compasss.org/Who are we.htm>.
[21] Qualitative methods are also taught at the European Consortium for Political Research's Summer School in Methods and Techniques.

Section—with its wide-ranging debates on methodological issues—as a critical supplement to publications in standard journals.

With respect to book publication, important scholarly presses have also been receptive to qualitative and multimethod work, including Princeton, Cambridge, Chicago, MIT, Cornell, Columbia, Rowman and Littlefield, M. E. Sharpe, Routledge, and Palgrave.

A discussion of publication in the qualitative/multimethod tradition cannot fail to mention the remarkable contribution of Sage Publications in releasing valuable books and monographs, and also publishing journals. One of Sage's newest journals, the *Journal of Mixed Methods Research*, is a good example. In addition to providing an outlet for methodological work by political scientists—for example, Sartori (1984) and Yanow (2000)—the publications by Sage in this area are a major resource for those teaching qualitative and multimethods approaches.

4 CONCLUSION: TOWARD INTEGRATION?

What is the most productive relationship between the qualitative/multimethod field, on the one hand, and quantitative methods, on the other? Is the integration of methodological agendas a plausible future direction, or should these two branches of methodology proceed on what might be thought of as parallel yet separate tracks? Our answer, briefly, is both.

With regard to integration, the single most important, shared accomplishment should immediately be underscored: helping political scientists become more methodologically grounded and rigorous. The objective here is emphatically not to burden the discipline with methodological preoccupations to a degree that is counterproductive. Rather, it is to provide tools for addressing the substantive questions that make political science a worthwhile enterprise.

Major progress in developing such tools has been achieved in recent years. Within this *Handbook*, the coverage of a wide spectrum of quantitative approaches attests to advances in the techniques that this set of methodologists can offer to the discipline. On the qualitative, multimethod side, more than a dozen chapters reflect new research techniques and the integration of older ones into a valuable—and increasingly coherent—set of methodological tools. Together, these two branches of methodology provide substantial new leverage for addressing important substantive topics.

Integration has also been achieved through cooperative efforts at the level of organizations. The relationship between the two corresponding APSA sections has been cordial, and one of mutual support. Evidence of integration includes the joint sponsorship of APSA panels; the summer 2006 special issue of *Political Analysis*, which focused on the relation between qualitative and quantitative methods; and the fact that the faculty at the Institute for Qualitative and Multi-Method Research regularly includes scholars who have advanced statistical skills.

Looking beyond these accomplishments, we argue that the objective of integration, of sustaining dialogue among diverse forms of methodology, should be to develop coherent standards for good research. Scholars should seek shared norms for valuable work—at the same time recognizing that distinct areas of methodology have different standards for evidence and inference, and different criteria for what constitutes rigor. The productive evolution of methodology depends on a shared effort to understand and debate these standards and differences.

While integration is important, for some purposes the idea of separate tracks is appropriate. Charles Franklin (this volume) observes that one goal in forming the APSA Political Methodology Section was to create for quantitative methodologists an organization within which they could "speak to their peers in the technical language of [their] field." This objective is achieved by supporting institutional settings in which the mathematical foundation of their work is well established as a shared language, and in which—within that framework—there is to a reasonable degree a common agenda for future innovation in methods.

The formation of the organizations associated with qualitative/multimethod work reflected in part this same priority: the need for methodologists with convergent skills and objectives to have a meaningful forum for dialogue. Although this group includes some who work with statistical and mathematical tools, for many others the "technical language of their field" is distinct. For a number of scholars, there is a strong and self-conscious commitment to methodological rigor, but of a different kind. This is certainly the case for interpretative approaches, and also for some other practitioners of qualitative methods who have a strong interest in exploring alternative logics-of-inference. Hence, for scholars working with qualitative and multimethod approaches, as for quantitative methodologists, it is valuable to have a separate forum for pursuing their partially distinctive methodological concerns.

Within this framework of parallel organizations, scholars in both traditions receive strong intellectual support for their most fundamental contribution: maintaining a forward-looking dialogue about methodology, and offering to the discipline analytic tools that help answer basic substantive questions about politics.

REFERENCES

ABEL, T. 1977. The operation called *Verstehen*. In *Understanding and Social Inquiry*, ed. F. Dallmayr and T. A. McCarthy, Notre Dame Ind.: University of Notre Dame Press.

American Political Science Review 1995. Symposium on *Designing Social Inquiry*, 89: 454–81.

BENNETT, A., BARTH, A., and RUTHERFORD, K. 2003. Do we preach what we practice? A survey of methods in journals and graduate curricula. *PS: Political Science and Politics*, 36: 373–8.

——and ELMAN, C. 2006. Qualitative research: recent developments in case study methods. *Annual Review of Political Science*, 9: 455–76.

BRADY, H. E., and COLLIER, D. (eds.) 2004. *Rethinking Social Inquiry: Diverse Tools, Shared Standards*. Lanham, Md.: Rowman and Littlefield.

CAMPBELL, D. 1975. Degrees of freedom and the case study. *Comparative Political Studies*, 8: 178–93.

COLLIER, D. 1993. The comparative method. Pp. 105–19 in *Political Science: State of the Discipline II*, ed. A. Finifter. Washington, DC: American Political Science Association.

——1998. Comparative method in the 1990s; and comparative-historical analysis: where do we stand? Letters from the president. *APSA-CP, Newsletter of the APSA Organized Section for Comparative Politics*, 9 (1): 1–5; and (2): 1–5.

——BRADY, H. E., and SEAWRIGHT, J. 2004. Sources of leverage in causal inference: toward an alternative view of methodology. Pp. 229–66 in Brady and Collier 2004.

COLLIER, R. B. 1999. *Paths toward Democracy: Working Class and Elites in Western Europe and South America*. New York: Cambridge University Press.

Comparative Political Studies 2007. Symposium on *Qualitative Methods*, 40: 111–214.

COPPEDGE, M. 1999. Thickening thin concepts and theories: combining large n and small in comparative politics. *Comparative Politics*, 31: 465–76.

ELMAN, C., and ELMAN, M. F. (eds.) 2001. *Bridges and Boundaries: Historians, Political Scientists and the Study of International Relations*. Cambridge, Mass.: MIT Press.

————(eds.) 2003. *Progress in International Relations Theory: Appraising the Field*. Cambridge, Mass.: MIT Press.

FEARON, J. D. 1991. Counterfactuals and hypothesis testing in political science. *World Politics*, 43: 169–95.

FINNEMORE, M., and SIKKINK, K. 2001. Taking stock: the constructivist research program in international relations and comparative politics. *Annual Review of Political Science*, 4: 391–416.

GEDDES, B. 2003. *Paradigms and Sandcastles: Theory Building and Research Design in Comparative Politics*. Ann Arbor: University of Michigan Press.

GEERTZ, C. 1973. *The Interpretation of Cultures: Selected Essays*. New York: Basic Books.

GEORGE, A. L. 1979. Case studies and theory development: the method of structured, focused comparison. Pp. 43–68 in *Diplomacy: New Approaches in History, Theory and Policy*, ed. P. G. Lauren. New York: Free Press.

——and BENNETT, A. 2005. *Case Studies and Theory Development in the Social Sciences*. Cambridge, Mass.: MIT Press.

GERRING, J. 2001. *Social Science Methodology: A Criterial Framework*. Cambridge: Cambridge University Press.

——2006. Letter from the editor. *Qualitative Methods: Newsletter of the American Political Science Association Organized Section on Qualitative Methods*, 4 (1): 1–2.

——2007. *Case Study Research: Principles and Practices*. New York: Cambridge University Press.

GOERTZ, G. 2006. *Social Science Concepts: A User's Guide*. Princeton, NJ: Princeton University Press.

——and STARR, H. (eds.) 2002. *Necessary Conditions: Theory, Methodology, and Applications*. Lanham, Md.: Rowman and Littlefield.

GUZZINI, S., and LEANDNER, A. 2006. *Constructivism and International Relations: Alexander Wendt and his Critics*. New York: Routledge.

JOWITT, K. 1978. *The Leninist Response to National Dependency*. Berkeley: Institute of International Studies, University of California.

KATZENSTEIN, P. J. (ed.) 1996. *The Culture of National Security: Norms and Identity in World Politics*. New York: Columbia University Press.

KEOHANE, R. 2003. Disciplinary schizophrenia: implications for graduate education in political science. *Qualitative Methods: Newsletter of the American Political Science Association Organized Section on Qualitative Methods*, 1 (1): 9–12.

KING, G., KEOHANE, R. O., and VERBA, S. 1994. *Designing Social Inquiry: Scientific Inference in Qualitative Research*. Princeton, NJ: Princeton University Press.

LANGE, P., and GARRETT, G. 1985. The politics of growth: strategic interaction and economic performance in advanced industrial democracies, 1974–1980. *Journal of Politics*, 47: 792–827.

LIJPHART, A. 1971. Comparative politics and the comparative method. *American Political Science Review*, 65: 682–93.

—— 1975. The comparable-cases strategy in comparative research. *Comparative Political Studies*, 8: 158–77.

LUSTICK, I. 1996. History, historiography, and political science: multiple historical records and the problem of selection bias. *American Political Science Review*, 90: 605–18.

MAHONEY, J., and RUESCHEMEYER, D. (eds.) 2003. *Comparative-historical Analysis in the Social Sciences*. Cambridge, Mass.: Cambridge University Press.

MONROE, K. 2005. *Perestroika! The Raucous Rebellion in Political Science*. New Haven, Conn.: Yale University Press.

MUNCK, G. L. 1998. Cannons of research design in qualitative analysis. *Studies in Comparative International Development*, 33: 18–45.

PIERSON, P. 2004. *Politics in Time: History, Institutions, and Social Analysis*. Princeton, NJ: Princeton University Press.

Political Methodologist 1995. Symposium on *Designing Social Inquiry*, 6: 11–19.

PRZEWORSKI, A., and TEUNE, H. 1970. *The Logic of Comparative Social Inquiry*. New York: Wiley.

RAGIN, C. C. 1987. *The Comparative Method: Moving beyond Qualitative and Quantitative Strategies*. Berkeley: University of California Press.

—— 2000. *Fuzzy Set Social Science*. Chicago: University of Chicago Press.

REUS-SMIT, C. 2002. Imagining society: constructivism and the English school. *British Journal of Politics and International Relations*, 4: 487–509.

RUESCHEMEYER, D., STEVENS, E. H., and STEVENS, J. D. 1992. *Capitalist Development and Democracy*. Chicago: University of Chicago Press.

SARTORI, G. 1970. Concept misformation in comparative politics. *American Political Science Review*, 64: 1033–53.

—— 1984. *Social Science Concepts: A Systematic Analysis*. Beverly Hills, Calif.: Sage.

SMELSER, N. J. 1976. *Comparative Methods in the Social Sciences*. Englewood Cliffs, NJ: Prentice Hall.

STRYKER, R. 2002. Interpretive methods: macromethods. In *International Encyclopedia of the Social and Behavioral Sciences*, ed. N. J. Smelser and P. B. Bates. Amsterdam: Elsevier.

TETLOCK P. E., and BELKIN, A. (eds.) 1996. *Counterfactual Thought Experiments in World Politics*. Princeton, NJ: Princeton University Press.

VALLIER, I. (ed.) 1971. *Comparative Methods in Sociology*. Berkeley: University of California Press.

VAN EVERA, S. 1997. *Guide to Methods for Students of Political Science*. Ithaca, NY: Cornell University Press.

WEDEEN, L. 2002. Conceptualizing culture: possibilities for political science. *American Political Science Review*, 96: 713–28.

WENDT, A. 1999. *Social Theory of International Politics*. New York: Cambridge University Press.

YANOW, D. 2000. *Conducting Interpretive Policy Analysis*. Thousand Oaks, Calif.: Sage.

——and SCHWARTZ-SHEA, P. (eds.) 2006. *Interpretation and Method: Empirical Research Methods and the Interpretive Turn*. Armonk, NY: M. E. Sharpe.

CHAPTER 35

··

QUANTITATIVE METHODOLOGY

··

CHARLES H. FRANKLIN

1 INTRODUCTION

··

THE development of political methodology as a field has been closely associated with the development of organizations and institutions that support the field. This chapter focuses on the two organizations most closely associated with quantitative political methodology, the Inter-university Consortium for Political and Social Research (ICPSR) Summer Program and the Society for Political Methodology, which is effectively synonymous with the American Political Science Association (APSA) organized section on Political Methodology.[1] The approach in this chapter emphasizes the role of organizations and institutions in promoting and structuring the development of quantitative methodology in political science. Excellent reviews of the intellectual developments in methodology are available in Achen (1981); King (1990); and Bartels and Brady (1993). The many chapters of this *Handbook* are themselves a profound statement of the intellectual issues in contemporary methodology. The institutions I describe developed out of intellectual pressures and needs, which I briefly highlight, but I am more concerned here with organizations and their role in promoting political methodology.

---

[1] The Society for Political Methodology has the same officers as the organized section. It exists as a separate entity in support of the Summer Methodology Meetings and maintains an extensive working paper archive, newsletter, and website. For our purposes here the Society and the organized section are the same. As a historical matter, the Society existed as the organizer of the Summer Methodology Meetings prior to the formation of the Organized Section.

For historical and intellectual reasons (both good and bad) organizational developments in quantitative methodology proceeded largely apart from developments in qualitative methodology, especially prior to the 1990s which is my focus. The chapter in this volume by Colin Elman reviews those developments and should be seen as the other side of the coin described here. Recent scholarship has seen productive and positive efforts at uniting these different strands of research methodology (King, Keohane, and Verba 1994; Brady and Collier 2004), even if such a union is not visible in this chapter.

Academic institutions develop and are sustained because there are intellectual and professional needs that they serve. The development of "summer programs" in quantitative methods in the 1960s was a response to the needs of a newly quantitative field that lacked a historical foundation of training in statistical techniques. However, as we shall see, these programs persist and thrive because contemporary students remain in need of statistical training outside their home institutions. The development of the Society for Political Methodology and its subsequent twin, the APSA Political Methodology Organized Section, arose from a different intellectual pressure—the need for legitimacy of a subfield and a setting in which methodologists could speak to their peers in the technical language of a field.

The surge in quantitative analysis in political science in the 1960s grew out of the behavioral revolution which required new types of evidence for political research. The skills to carry out this type of research, and the financial resources to conduct national-scale survey research, led to pressures for both access to training and the sharing of data resources. These needs were both met in the development of the Inter-university Consortium for Political Research (ICPR, subsequently renamed the Inter-university Consortium for Political and Social Research (ICPSR)). ICPR made routinely available to political scientists data that had previously required special access, often at the cost of a semester of leave in Ann Arbor. Statistical training that was an integral part of ICPR, the "Summer Program," opened the covers of statistics textbooks for both a new generation of graduate students and for faculty who had received Ph.D.s in an era that treated statistics as a foreign language (literally). Intellectual and professional pressures made acquisition of quantitative skills valuable in the 1960s and later, and this pressure supported the creation and growth of the ICPR Summer Program. Parallel developments in Europe likewise supported and sustained the foundation of the Essex Summer School in Social Science Data Analysis and Collection, founded in 1967, four years after the first Ann Arbor Summer Program.

The pressures that brought about the Society for Political Methodology (SPM) and the APSA organized section were quite different, coming from an already established group of political scientists who felt their work was underappreciated and poorly supported by the professional organizations and conferences of the day. If ICPR and the Ann Arbor and Essex Summer Programs were primarily about skill acquisition, the SPM was about extending the research horizons. SPM set as its goal the development of a political methodology devoted to questions arising from problems unique to political data rather than borrowing solutions from other disciplines whose concerns might only tangentially reflect the concerns of political scientists. SPM was also about extending the boundaries of political methodology by providing settings in which one's research could be valued for its methodological contributions alone, and establishing the full legitimacy of methodology as a field within political science.

My review of these developments will focus on intellectual and organizational forces and will deliberately avoid giving much attention to the efforts of individuals in creating these organizations. A proper history should acknowledge and celebrate the hard work of the many individuals who helped create, nurture, and energize these organizations. Nonetheless my focus here is not on individual contributions but on the broader forces at work.

2 THE DEVELOPMENT OF SUMMER PROGRAMS IN QUANTITATIVE METHODS

The "behavioral revolution" in political science, both in the United States and in Europe, produced a sudden rise in demand for technical analysis skills. A discipline which had only sporadically employed quantitative methods (though with some outstanding exceptions: Rice 1928, for example, and most impressively Gosnell 1927) suddenly found that its most impressive work was being produced by scholars comfortable with Hollerith cards, counter sorters, and even IBM computers. The election studies conducted at the University of Michigan by Angus Campbell and his junior colleagues Philip Converse, Warren Miller, and Donald Stokes culminated in *The American Voter* (Campbell et al. 1960). That book more than any other changed the course of research on American elections.

The American Voter, it must be stressed, was not primarily innovative in its use of "new" analytic methodologies. The cross-tabs and percentages that were the core analytic method were certainly not new, and the survey designs were considerably simpler than the multiwave panel study of Erie County, Ohio in the 1940 election conducted by Lazarsfeld, Berelson, and Gaudet (1944). It was, rather, the psychological theory coupled with the determined empirical testing that set *The American Voter* apart from its predecessors. The psychological theory was exploited over and over throughout the book, from partisanship to impressions of the parties and candidates to the effects of cross-pressures to the crucial role of psychological attachment to groups, rather than mere sociological membership in the groups, that set a new course for electoral studies. And each theoretical assertion was confronted with repeated tests within the data, each probing the evidence in support of the claim. This was not the first exploitation of survey analysis, let alone the first quantitative work, in political science. But the behavioral revolution of the 1950s both supported and was fed by the evident success of the theory and analytic methods of *The American Voter*.

A number of quantitative studies had certainly appeared well before *The American Voter*. The Columbia University studies of the 1940 and 1944 campaigns set the stage for later national surveys but the core methodology and analytic techniques were fully present in those early surveys. Likewise the Michigan Survey Research Center conducted election studies in 1948, resulting in a small book, *The People Elect a President* (Campbell and Kahn 1952), and the 1952 presidential election produced *The Voter Decides* (Campbell, Gurin, and Miller 1954), a more substantial development of what was to come. Yet neither of these studies revolutionized the study of elections in the larger profession. Likewise the earlier empirical studies by V. O. Key that were part of his *Southern Politics* (Key 1949) had contributed to the development of the behavioral revolution, as did Dahl's subsequent study of New Haven politics in *Who Governs?* (Dahl 1961). It is appropriate then to place *The American Voter* within the pantheon of books that forced a new approach to political science, and electoral behavior, without giving it an exaggerated importance.

In the development of quantitative training programs, however, Michigan and the "Michigan election studies" do hold a special place. This place is due to the coincidence of two forces: a monopoly on highly valuable data and an entrepreneurial willingness to give up that monopoly.

By the time *The American Voter* was published, the Michigan Political Behavior Program had amassed the only academic collection of national survey data on US elections then extant. Commercial polls, such as those conducted by the Gallup organization, were not available for scholarly analysis at that time. This was an incredibly valuable commodity within political science. Under the existing norms of the time, the "Michigan election studies" could easily have remained just that— proprietary to Campbell and his co-workers. Yet such was not the case, at least for an academic elite. In the 1959–60 academic year, V. O. Key was given full access to the data collected between 1948 and 1958, as well as office space and research assistance in Ann Arbor to conduct his own analysis of these data (even as *The American Voter* was still in final manuscript preparation).[2] The resulting *Public Opinion and American Democracy* was a major contribution in its own right, but perhaps more importantly it was an exemplar of the power of secondary analysis if access to data were possible.

At the same time it was apparent that standards for graduate training in political science had ill equipped new scholars to exploit the data central to the behavioral revolution. V. O. Key's 1954 *A Primer of Statistics for Political Scientists* explains in its preface and demonstrates by its existence the need for even the most elementary instruction in statistics for political scientists. In addition to a need for introductions to the field of statistics, political scientists also needed to acquire some more specialized skills in data processing, then primarily conducted with punch card counter sorters. The techniques required to produce a two-way table were at the time considerably more complex than introducing students to the "cross-tabs" command is today. By the latter part of the 1950s new skills were just beginning to be demanded, as illustrated once more by *The American Voter*. In 1959 it required special access to an IBM electronic computer, as opposed to counter sorters, to produce the multiple

---

[2] See Key's (1961) preface, pp. viii–ix, for both a description of his access and his acknowledgement of appreciation.

linear regression that underlies the analysis of the "six-component" model of vote choice illustrated by figure 4–2 and described in footnote 6 on page 73 of Campbell et al. (1960). The skills required for this were far in advance of any generally available in political science.

The need for new training opportunities was evident in the 1950s. The Social Science Research Council funded early summer training programs at the SRC in Ann Arbor in 1954 and 1958, introducing students to both survey methodology and techniques of analysis. Similarly Yale University developed a fellowship program allowing advanced graduate students to spend time at the SRC. Such opportunities, however, remained limited and largely unavailable outside of elite academic circles.

Meanwhile, requests for access to the SRC data increased and placed a burden on the Political Behavior Program to meet the demands of reproducing card decks and shipping the boxes of cards, as well as raising the question of who should be allowed access to the data.

By 1962 the accumulated issues of a monopoly on data many political scientists wished to analyze and the need to find financial resources to support the election studies led to the creation of the Inter-university Consortium for Political Research (ICPR). A 1989 report on the then renamed ICPSR neatly summarizes the motivations for creating this institution:

As in all successful collaborations there was to be a two-way flow of benefits within the new consortium. Continually challenged to raise the funds necessary to keep the sequence of electoral surveys in flow, Warren E. Miller and his colleagues of the Political Behavior Program sought in ICPR a device that would generate some funds directly (the initial membership contribution was set at $2500 annually) and more importantly, allow mobilization of the research community in support of major grant applications. Opposite numbers in social science departments, mostly political scientists initially, saw the consortium as a means of acquiring access for themselves and their students to survey data that were too expensive to generate locally and as a means also of developing the analytical and methodological skills necessary for advancement in a social science world that was changing much faster than the formal curriculum. This latter aspect of the consortium plan was to involve the summer training of junior faculty and graduate students and provision of considerable remedial instruction for established faculty as well.   (Blalock 1989)

This captures the entrepreneurial aspects of the early ICPR as well as the collegial willingness to give away what many at the time would have thought of as a private data monopoly. Miller and his colleagues found that by converting a private resource into a public good, they could gain more support for the future enterprise. And political scientists gained access to data they could never collect on their own. Initial membership in ICPR remained limited to the handful of research universities that could both afford the fee and had the research focus that justified such an expense. The charter membership consisted of just eighteen universities.

The second core component of the early ICPR was a summer training program designed to acquaint students with the design and analysis of surveys and political data more generally. Here the ICPR Summer Program was born at the same time as the data dissimilation role of the Consortium. While quantitative training may

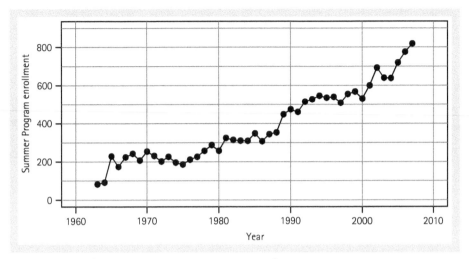

Fig. 35.1. Attendance at ICPSR Summer Program classes, 1963–2006

have advanced somewhat beyond the standards Key had addressed in his 1954 book, there was still a compelling need for training still unavailable within political science departments. If such training was unavailable locally (and implicitly political scientists were unwilling to enroll in classes in statistics departments, few of which were well versed in survey analysis in any case) then Ann Arbor in June and July offered a solution.

The first summer program, held in 1963, drew a substantial eighty-two students and 1964 saw ninety-one attend. But this more than doubled in 1965 to 229 and around 200 or more became the norm through the mid-1970s. The earliest years featured courses in research design and in quantitative analysis, but the scope of the offerings rapidly expanded. By the early 1970s the summer offerings covered a range from introductory statistics through regression to specialized topics such as time series and factor analysis. By the mid-1970s offerings included classes in causal models, exploratory data analysis, and multidimensional scaling. In barely ten years the universe of statistical techniques made available to political scientists had exploded.

This growth in summer courses reflected the tremendous growth in applied statistical methods in the research literature. From simple descriptive statistics, crosstabs, and a rare regression in 1960, by 1975 the profession had discovered and largely borrowed methods such as factor analysis from psychology, time series from statistics, and regression and simultaneous equation models from economics. For more on the explosion on imported techniques during this time see King (1990).

This growth in the breadth of techniques used in the profession seemingly fueled further growth in the Summer Program offerings and attendance. Figure 35.1 illustrates the growth of attendance by a factor of ten between 1963 and 2007. This growth is in part due to good marketing of courses by ICPSR, but also reflects a strong demand which appears unabated even in recent years.

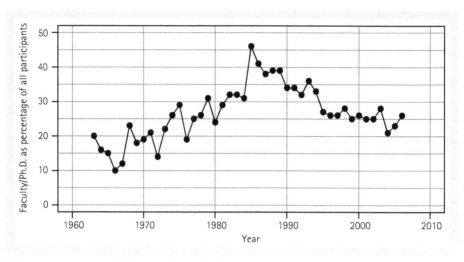

Fig. 35.2. Faculty and Ph.D. participation in ICPSR Summer Program classes, 1963–2006

If the impetus for the Summer Program was the immediate needs of political scientists who lacked newly useful technical skills, we might have expected enrollments to decline over time as graduate programs increasingly included quantitative courses in their local curricula. Certainly few graduate programs included statistics courses in 1960 and a large majority do so now. Few programs now fail to include at least introductions to statistics and multiple regression and most include more advanced courses as well.

Yet there is no evidence in Figure 35.1 that demand for Summer Program classes has abated over time. This implies that whatever growth in quantitative methodology classes has occurred within departments over time has not kept up with the aggregate demand for quantitative training. Of course the changing mix of departments and fields represented in the Summer Program makes any direct inference about political science programs suspect. Likewise, growth of enrollment in graduate programs may well have outstripped Summer Program enrollment growth, so smaller proportions of all graduate students in political science and other social sciences are attending the Summer Program. Nonetheless, it is clear that the social sciences send a steadily increasing number of students to the Summer Program despite the growth of local course options across all the social sciences.

Likewise there has been some change in the mix of participants in the Summer Program, yet not wholesale changes. The early Summer Program explicitly stated the need to offer training to both junior and more senior faculty to help them catch up with the new demands of the field. Yet if graduate training has allowed much greater opportunities for quantitative training over the past forty years, we might expect that fewer and fewer faculty would now require such "remedial" training.

Figure 35.2 shows the percentage of faculty or holders of Ph.D.s within the Summer Program from 1963 through 2006 (the last year for which such data are currently

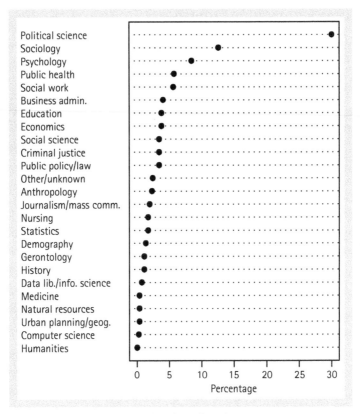

Fig. 35.3. Distribution of participants by discipline in ICPSR Summer Program classes, 2007

available). There was a steady rise in faculty participation through the mid-1980s, suggesting that many faculty did, in that period, find their graduate training insufficient for their professional needs. Since 1985 the rate of faculty participation has declined but has remained close to 25 percent since 1995.[3] If graduate training were providing all the quantitative skills faculty require, then after some forty-four years we might have expected this proportion to have declined.

The mix of disciplines represented in the Summer Program has changed substantially over the years, from almost exclusively political science in the first years to a much more heterogeneous mix today. Figure 35.3 shows that political science remains the largest single discipline represented but stands at just under 30 percent of all participants.[4]

---

[3] Some of the variation in this trend is undoubtedly due to the changing mix of classes sponsored by grants, such as programs in criminal justice, which targeted faculty or Ph.D.s. The basic fact remains that as many as a quarter of participants are holders of the Ph.D.

[4] This of course means that easy inferences about how political science has changed based on Summer Program participation faces an ecological inference fallacy.

2.1 Dynamics of Course Offerings

The earliest days of the Summer Program focused on research design, primarily with surveys, and a single class in quantitative analysis. That rapidly changed as the number of participants increased and the breadth of techniques expanded. By the early 1970s classes included not only introductory statistics but regression and factor analysis. Lectures on mathematics for social scientists (with a focus on matrix algebra and calculus) were also added in the 1970s.

As the structure of the program expanded (exploded) beyond the original needs of novice survey analysts, the structure of the program became clear. The program divided into what came to be called "tracks". Track I classes included introductory classes in mathematics, introductory statistics, and a first class in regression (without matrix algebra). Ancillary lectures also provided an introduction to statistical computing (originally required for those having to use the Michigan Terminal System mainframe operating system and its MIDAS statistical program for the first time and subsequently broadened to cover the range of popular statistical programs such as SAS, SPSS, and Stata in later years).

Track II classes included linear models (with matrix algebra) and a variety of courses focused on such topics as time series, factor analysis, multidimensional scaling, simultaneous equation systems, latent variable models, and more.

Course offerings followed developments in the broad area of social science statistical methods. In the 1970s, Exploratory Data Analysis appeared on the curriculum, following publication of Tukey's book of that name, and stayed on the curriculum 1974–83. Time series, based on Box–Jenkins models, entered the curriculum around 1976.

The early Summer Program emphasis on survey design continued to have a presence in the curriculum. In the 1980s and 1990s courses included The Logic of Data Analysis: Measurement and Design (1982–92), Implications of Sampling Design (1984–8), and Population Estimation (1987–9).

Beginning in the 1980s and 1990s a variety of classes were added (and later dropped) which focused on applications of quantitative techniques to special substantive topics. These classes were in part a response to new directions of topical research and partly driven by the availability of grants to support the courses. Examples include Asian American Research Methods (1980–5), Empirical Research and Gender Issues (1982–3), Latino Research Issues (1987–94), Quantitative Methods of Program Evaluation (1991–2), Quantitative Analysis and the Study of Africa (1996–2001), Quantitative Approaches to the Study of Latin America (1993–7), and Quantitative Research on Race and Ethnicity (since 2006).

Despite the considerable increase in statistical offerings, criticism from the new Society for Political Methodology led to some changes in course offerings. By the late 1980s the curriculum had settled into a pattern of primarily linear models, at various levels, along with dimensional and time-series classes. Around 1986 political scientists began to push for new courses that would cover limited and discrete dependent variables and other topics in which developments were accelerating in the 1980s.

Within a few years the Summer Program added a course in Maximum Likelihood Methods (1990), Hierarchical Models, Categorical Regression, Latent Growth Models, and Non-linear Systems. This refreshing of the curriculum primarily in the 1990s substantially increased the range of offerings while maintaining the place for introductory classes.

Around 2000, an explicit "Track III" was developed. This set of courses was intended to push summer participants to embrace the more challenging topics of recent methodological developments. New classes in this track included Bayesian Methods, Modern Regression, and Advanced Maximum Likelihood along with existing classes on Maximum Likelihood, Categorical Analysis, Lisrel Models, and Game Theory. One of the marks of this new track was an emphasis on computing using the S language and the R statistical program. A two-week lecture course on the S language became an integral part of this effort.

Throughout its history, the Summer Program has maintained a quite stable core of classes, with a dynamic range of additional offerings. The basic introductions to statistics, regression, and computing have remained part of the curriculum since the early 1970s. More advanced or specialized courses have also been offered for most of the program's history, such as time series, dimensional analysis, and structural equation models. And a number of more recent additions have remained on the curriculum for over a decade, such as Maximum Likelihood, Game Theory, Advanced Maximum Likelihood, Hierarchical Linear Models, Categorical Models, and Non-linear Systems. Still other newer classes appear set to remain for the foreseeable future, such as Bayesian Methods and Modern Regression.

Despite that stability, there has also been a highly dynamic set of courses that have come and gone, some for lack of audience and others due to changing interests and funding support. The workshops on quantitative analysis of substantive topics are one example. But statistical offerings have also come and gone: Advanced Analysis of Variance, Event History Analysis, Item Response Theory, Mathematical Statistics (a disappointed effort to add a "high end" probability and inference course to the curriculum in the mid-1990s), Mixed Models, Pooled Time Series Analysis, Resampling Methods, Spatial Analysis and Geographic Information Systems, and Vector Autoregression.

2.2 Why do we Continue to Need Summer Programs?

It is said that the early founders of the ICPSR Summer Program expected it to wither away within a few years.[5] The initial assumption may have been that once a core of political scientists were trained in quantitative methods, they would return to their home universities and teach subsequent generations, making a summer program unnecessary. Whether this was ever really the assumption, the past forty years have

---

[5] Henry Heitowit comments, "Now it can be told: Reminiscences on 80 years at ICPSR," Erik Austin and Henry Heitowit, Panel Presentation at the 2007 ICPSR Meeting of Official Representatives, Ann Arbor, October 18–20, 2007.

demonstrated the growth in demand for summer program instruction, rather than its demise.

Whether true or not, the anecdote raises the question of why summer programs do persist, not only at Ann Arbor but at Essex and in newer short-term programs at Oxford and in programs sponsored by the ECPR.

Perhaps most puzzling is the continued core of introductory courses that remain part of the ICPSR Summer Program. Certainly by now virtually all graduate programs offer at least introductory statistics as part of their curriculum, seeming to obviate the need for such coursework in the summer. In 2007, for example, approximately 85–120 Summer Program students took one of the introductory statistics or introductory regression classes. These students could have come from any discipline, so they may or may not represent a large number of political scientists, but the simple fact that at least an eighth of all 2007 participants chose to take introductory classes shows that there remains an important role for these classes in the program.

There are a number of possible reasons for this persistence of demand. Some students may prefer to focus on substantive courses during the academic year, and concentrate their methodological training during the summer. For these students, the availability of "local" statistical training is not attractive. Another possibility is that these students are disproportionately lacking in mathematical background and so benefit from taking summer courses as either preparation for local courses, or as a means of reviewing coursework they may have taken but not mastered at their home institution.

This last point is strongly supported by overwhelming evidence that many Summer Program participants feel the need for more mathematical training. Over 200 students (a quarter of all participants) attend lectures in either basic mathematics or matrix algebra and calculus. Whether a refresher or a first exposure, this demand makes clear the prevalence of weak mathematical training among social science graduate students. Few undergraduate programs in political science (and most other social sciences outside of economics) require any mathematical training as part of their degree requirements or as a requirement for entry into their graduate programs. Likewise, while many undergraduate programs include a "research methods" class that may include some data analysis, few require a rigorous sequence in statistics. The consequence of this is a divergence between the requirements of an undergraduate degree and the skills required for graduate training.

While only a small minority of undergraduates go on to graduate school in the social sciences, it appears that very few departments provide even a "pre-graduate school" track of suggested courses that would provide their best undergraduates with foundation courses in mathematics or statistics. The result is that the vast majority of social science graduate students require some degree of "remedial" mathematics and statistics training, in the sense that material that could have been covered as an undergraduate must be learned as a graduate student. This lack of training is reflected in the growth of mathematics "bootcamps" in a number of political science programs, and continued demand in the Summer Program.

If something like a quarter of Summer Program students require introductory classes, about three-quarters are prepared for more advanced material. This includes large numbers who take classes in linear regression using matrix algebra. Here students have often had an introduction to regression at their home institution, but frequently one that does not include the more general form allowed by matrix algebra. Since linear models are a fundamental foundation for advanced work, this is a crucial gateway that the Summer Program provides, and for which large demand remains beyond what is provided by home institutions.

Still, over half of Summer Program participants take part in classes devoted to statistical topics beyond that of linear regression. Here the demand seems best explained by the enormous range of statistical methods and models that currently exist and that are emerging. And this is perhaps the explanation for why summer programs remain both popular and necessary beyond the need for introductory classes. The range of statistical models in the social sciences is huge. For students whose primary focus is not methodology (and even for some who are methods specialists) there is a great need for courses in advanced topics that serve their substantive needs.

The 2007 ICPSR Summer Program offered twenty-seven courses *beyond* the level of linear regression in matrix form. Clearly no graduate student has the time to take academic year courses in twenty-seven topics, even in an extended graduate career. Yet each of these courses exists because they provide techniques for addressing a wide range of substantive topics. Likewise, no social science department has the methodological focus to offer more than a handful of these topics in a normal curriculum. By pooling students across the world, summer programs at ICPSR, Essex, and elsewhere provide the mechanism to allow economically feasible instruction in such specialized topics.

For well-prepared students, summer programs offer a relatively quick introduction to advanced topics. In from one to four weeks, students can receive 30–40 hours of instruction, roughly the equivalent of (or even more than) a semester-long course. There are both advantages and disadvantages to this type of course. The daily meetings can enhance instruction because of the continuity from day to day that allows themes to remain apparent that might be lost if stretched over once-a-week classes during the semester. The disadvantage of daily classes is that there is little time for reading and reflection. There is little time to go back and review any points that are missed initially.

One negative aspect of summer courses, but a potential attraction for students, is that the grading may be less demanding than during an academic semester. Given the limits of time, exercises are somewhat less numerous and exams are rare. Likewise there is no time for students to prepare "term" papers during the summer courses. While the quality of the lectures may be high, the opportunities for students to apply the methods are more limited than during an academic semester.

Finally, demand for summer programs may in part benefit from the social nature of summer instruction. Students and faculty alike assemble for the special purpose of taking and teaching quantitative methodology. (The same applies to programs in qualitative methods. See the chapter by Elman, this volume.) Attending the program requires a commitment and some sacrifice by students, and they have this in common with all participants. The camaraderie that forms among Summer Program participants almost certainly enhances the experience and promotes collaborative learning of the material.

2.3 Serving the Needs of Students and the Needs of the Profession

Far from withering away, summer programs in quantitative methodology have only grown with time. They serve vastly increased numbers of students and offer a wide range of courses, from elementary to advanced, and from standard to cutting-edge methodologies.

Some degree of "remedial" instruction in summer programs is likely to remain. This partially reflects the diversity of graduate programs and graduate students, some of whom are likely to continue to require opportunities to learn (or relearn) the basics. This need is not limited to weak programs or weak students. So long as mathematical and statistical training is not required by undergraduate programs in the social sciences, it will inevitably be required as part of graduate training. One might question the desirability of this state of affairs, but despite the "behavioral revolution" of sixty years ago, the nature of undergraduate training in political science (and other social sciences) has not mirrored the changes in graduate education. This means that many graduate students require a venue to acquire basic skills, and summer instruction remains an attractive option.

At the same time, summer programs have made great strides in providing a wide range of courses in advanced and state of the art topics. The ICPSR Summer Program, the Essex Summer School, and others offer topics rarely found on departmental course lists, simply because the requisite skills (both for instructors and for students) are limited and can only be successfully marshalled by pooling across many institutions.

As new techniques are constantly developed in quantitative methods, there will also remain demand for instruction in these new methods. Flexible summer programs are well suited to providing these because they lack permanent faculty and so can add (or drop) classes and instructors with relative ease.

3 THE SOCIETY FOR POLITICAL METHODOLOGY AND APSA ORGANIZED SECTION ON POLITICAL METHODOLOGY

Methodology as a distinct subfield in political science developed slowly in the wake of the behavioral revolution. While growing numbers of political scientists in the 1960s and 1970s used increasingly sophisticated models in their substantive work, relatively few considered themselves primarily "methodologists." Likewise while departments required the services of faculty who could teach quantitative methods, few judged tenure cases primarily on methodological contributions, but rather required the normal substantive contributions to scholarship along with methodological teaching.

The *American Journal of Political Science* early on provided pages for its methodological "Workshop," but there were few other opportunities to publish purely methodological contributions. The "Workshop" section of *AJPS* consisted primarily of expository introductions to techniques, rather than original developments of new statistical approaches. This reflected both the limitations of the methodology field and the interests of the profession in quick introductions to particular techniques.

In a run of eleven volumes from 1974 through 1985, *Political Methodology* provided a journal outlet for methods research. While the journal had a limited circulation and focused more on applications of existing methods than on the development of new techniques, it was the first journal specifically devoted to quantitative methods in political science.

The 1980s saw changes in political methodology as a field. Stimulated in part by a 1977 textbook, Hanushek and Jackson's *Statistical Methods for Social Scientists*, the first serious econometrics textbook aimed at political scientists, more political scientists began to see their role as methodologists as central to their academic identity, rather than simply as a useful skill for teaching and research.

In 1981, Achen's "Towards Theories of Data" appeared (Finifter 1981). This chapter focused on the limitations of political methodology as a field, and focused attention on two unsolved challenges to the discipline, measurement error and the aggregation problem. Achen's argument struck a chord with methodologists in the field, and set the stage for a 1983 Achen paper on ecological inference. The 1983 paper became an example of how political methodology could address fundamental problems of inference in political science that were unlikely to be solved by statisticians outside the field. This in turn illustrated why political science needed a group of scholars committed to fundamental research on methodological issues. In the discussion following the presentation of Achen's paper, sitting on the steps in the Palmer House, a group of methodologists decided to hold a small conference just for methodological issues in the summer of 1984. This was the origin of what has become the "Summer Methods Meeting" and more crucially the development of a self-conscious and activist subfield of political methodology within APSA.

While it is neat to tie the development of the field to the accidents of Achen's presentation in 1983, the developments reflect broader issues and discontents within the small methodology community of the time. If Achen had laid out an intellectual rationale for a subfield specifically devoted to developing new methodologies, a more prosaic need among methodologists was increased outlets for methodological work. Professional conferences provided few if any panels devoted exclusively to methodological papers. The result was that methodology papers competed with substantive ones, or had to appear as disguised topical papers, in order to find space on conference programs. As a result, methodological critique was often limited and purely methodological papers received scant attention.

At the same time, publication outlets remained limited. The *AJPS* "Workshop" typically printed no more than four articles a year, and no other mainstream journal devoted space specifically for methodological work. The niche market in *Political Methodology* suffered from low visibility, including a lack of indexing in the Social Science Citation Index. Even that journal was in its death throes in the early 1980s, ceasing publication in 1985.

A second pressure for a new subfield was that a second generation of methodologists was coming of age. While some of the leaders of the new methodology subfield had attended graduate school in the 1960s, many had Ph.D.s from the 1970s and a few in the 1980s. These were generally not students for whom counter sorters had been a major advance. Rather, they had learned statistical methods from econometrics textbooks by Goldberger or Johnston. Quite a few were also not graduates of undergraduate political science departments but had instead majored in physics or economics or psychology. This background left them somewhat better prepared for statistical studies than the typical undergraduate major in political science. And a few had "grown up" in the new quantitative political science and had absorbed the need for technical training either as undergraduates or as graduate students.

The development of the methodology subfield also reflected the competitive pressures of the post-behavioral revolution era. Standard statistical techniques were routinely applied to political data. Yet the standard techniques often left much to be desired. The ubiquitous dichotomous dependent variables of survey research meant that linear regression was not the best technique available, though it continued to be widely used. New sensitivity to the role of measurement error, and the important consequences it had for substantive conclusions, meant that applied work needed to be more concerned for arcane methodological issues. Simultaneous equations models of political behavior raised issues of identification and specification decisions. All of these areas provided opportunities for methodology both to provide critiques of existing research and to advance improved approaches to inference. Thus there was a market niche for methodology both as a subfield on its own, and as a direct contributor to improving substance through improved methods.

Academic niches can be filled by organized entities, and this was the case with political methodology. Three related developments became the institutional foundations of the new political methodology subfield in 1984 and later.

First, an informal group created a small conference in 1984 that became the first "Summer Methodology Meeting." Attended by less than twenty people, the first meeting provided the forum for methodological research that had been lacking within the existing national and regional professional associations. With a conference devoted exclusively to methodological research, and with sessions conducted entirely by plenary session, with intense discussion, the new conference provided both the opportunity for presentation and the trenchant critique that had been lacking. With a receptive audience, and with blistering criticism to promote hard and careful work, the Summer Methods Meetings provided the opportunity for recognition and the incentive to produce new methodological research. The organizers of this Summer Methodology Meeting became the Society for Political Methodology.

The Summer Methods Meeting also soon developed a training mission. Starting with the fourth Summer Meeting, graduate students were included in the conferences, with grants providing support for their participation. This self-conscious attempt to recruit the next generation of methodologists, and to expose them at an early enough point in their careers that they could properly anticipate the training needed for a career in methodology, distinguished the new methodology group as an entity intent on developing its next generation.

From less than 20 participants at the first Summer Meeting, conference attendance has grown to over 150 in recent years. This mix of faculty and graduate students provides a crucial forum for socialization of graduate students to the subfield and for intellectual stimulation from peers.

The second institutional development was the founding of a new journal devoted to political methodology. It was agreed that the major journals of the profession were unlikely to provide sufficient space for purely methodological work, and that in any case a journal that focused exclusively on methodology would be able to set a higher standard as well as provide a necessary outlet. This new journal, *Political Analysis*, first appeared as an annual volume under the editorship of James Stimson in 1989. The annual nature reflected an initial concern that the volume of high-quality articles might be limited, as well as lack of interest among publishers.

Stimson's introduction to the first volume of *Political Analysis* sets out the mission statement of both the journal and the subfield: "*Political Analysis* aspires to be the publication of record for methodological developments in political science" (Stimson 1989, x). Seven annual volumes followed, publishing about eight articles and a bit over 200 pages in a typical volume. In 1999, *Political Analysis* became a quarterly journal and the volume of articles expanded considerably. Since 2000 the journal has typically published over twenty-five articles and over 400 pages each year. This development has meant that political methodologists have an established outlet for their work, one which is now recognized as an important journal in the field.

The third institutional development was the creation of an organized section for political methodology within the American Political Science Association. Organized sections were introduced within APSA in 1983, and political methodology became the tenth organized section in 1985. As an organized section, political methodology was able to lay claim to panels at the annual meeting of APSA, and was able to eventually bundle subscriptions to *Political Analysis* with membership in the section. For a new field, political methodology experienced very rapid growth, becoming the second-largest organized section based on membership. This organizational role within APSA ensured that space on panels, and control over the content of those panels, would remain within the section's hands. This largely removed the complaint that there were no conference outlets for methodological work (especially with the Summer Meetings in addition to APSA). The organized section was also able to give awards for outstanding work in the field, an important element of professional recognition.

These organizational developments have promoted the development of political methodology for over twenty years now. In that time, the field has grown considerably judged by number of practitioners, number of articles, and by attendance at the Summer Methodology Meetings. On the more critical intellectual front, the field has produced a substantial number of advances since 1984. Among these are new models for ecological inference, scaling of roll-call votes, sample selection models, Bayesian methods, and causal inference to name only a few.

The existence of the Society for Political Methodology has also increased expectations for graduate training, at least among those who see their careers as methodologists. While lack of strong fundamental skills remains a problem at the ICPSR Summer Program, those who seek professional success within methodology are now much better trained as graduate students than was the case twenty years ago. At the first Summer Meeting that welcomed them, graduate students concluded "we have to learn more math." That experience has continued with each successive cohort attending the Summer Meetings, and it has helped raise the ante for political methodology.

Within the profession, political methodology now holds a secure place, if not yet one that is universally welcomed. By its institutional role through the APSA Organized Section, political methodology both literally and figuratively has a seat at the table when conferences are planned, officers elected, and awards handed out. These are critical elements of professional presence and recognition, and they did not exist in 1983. More recently methodology has been added to departmental reputational rankings as a field alongside comparative, IR, theory, and American. This reflects the increased appreciation of the role of methodology within the field, and the extent to which a graduate department is hobbled if it lacks strength in quantitative methods training and research.

Despite these advances, political methodology continues to suffer from the rarity of strong quantitative training at the undergraduate level. Only a handful of students enter graduate school with more than a single semester of calculus or more than one introduction to statistics course. The vast majority of graduate programs spend the first year of methodology training on topics that should be well within the reach of undergraduates, had they only taken the classes. And because few students have strong mathematical training, the amount of time that must be spent on remedial training in math (often in an ad hoc and self-study manner) is substantial and delays or limits the level to which students can rise in statistical training. In this, political science continues to compare unfavorably with economics, in which substantial mathematical and statistical education occurs at the undergraduate level.

These limitations in undergraduate training will continue to hamper the development of political methodology. Excellent students must work harder than they should to catch up once in graduate school. In this area, political methodology may yet not have had the impact on the discipline that it needs to have in order to continue to raise the level of methodological sophistication. It is not necessary that all undergraduate majors in political science take advanced mathematics or statistics. But it is highly desirable that those who might consider graduate careers know that their options will be considerably enhanced by a more sophisticated undergraduate education.

References

ACHEN, C. H. 1981. Toward theories of data. In *Political Science: The State of the Discipline*, ed. A. W. Finifter. Washington, DC: American Political Science Association.

—— 1983. If party ID influences the vote, Goodman's ecological regression is biased (but factor analysis is consistent). Presented at the Annual Meeting of the American Political Science Association, Chicago.

AUSTIN, E. W. 2001. From Hollerith to the Web: a half-century of electronic social science data archives. Presented at the Sawyer Seminar on Archives, Documentation and the Institutions of Social Memory, University of Michigan, February 14.

BARTELS, L. M., and BRADY, H. E. 1993. The state of quantitative political methodology. In *Political Science: The State of the Discipline II*, ed. A. W. Finifter. Washington, DC: American Political Science Association.

BLALOCK, H. M. 1989. Report of the ICPSR Review Committee. ICPSR, June.

BRADY, H. E., and COLLIER, D. (eds.) 2004. *Rethinking Social Inquiry: Diverse Tools, Shared Standards*. Lanham, Md.: Rowman and Littlefield.

CAMPBELL, A., and KAHN, R. L. 1952. *The People Elect a President*. Ann Arbor, Mich.: Institute for Social Research.

—— GURIN, G., and MILLER, W. E. 1954. *The Voter Decides*. Evanston, Ill.: Row, Peterson.

—— CONVERSE, P. E., MILLER, W. E., and STOKES, D. E. 1960. *The American Voter*. New York: John Wiley.

DAHL, R. A. 1961. *Who Governs?* New Haven, Conn.: Yale University Press.

FINIFTER, A. W. (ed.) 1981. *Political Science: The State of the Discipline*. Washington, DC: American Political Science Association.

GOSNELL, H. F. 1927. *Getting out the Vote: An Experiment in the Stimulation of Voting*. Chicago: University of Chicago Press.

HANUSHEK, E. A., and JACKSON, J. E. 1977. *Statistical Methods for Social Scientists*. New York: Academic Press.

KEY, V. O. 1949. *Southern Politics*. New York: Alfred A. Knopf.

—— 1954. *A Primer of Statistics for Political Scientists*. New York: Thomas Y. Crowell.

—— 1961. *Public Opinion and American Democracy*. New York: Alfred A. Knopf.

KING, G. 1990. On political methodology. *Political Analysis*, 2: 1–30.

—— KEOHANE, R. O., and VERBA, S. 1994. *Designing Social Inquiry: Scientific Inference in Qualitative Research*. Princeton, NJ: Princeton University Press.

LAZARSFELD, P., BERELSON, B., and GAUDET, H. 1944. *The People's Choice*. New York: Columbia University Press.

RICE, S. A. 1928. *Quantitative Methods in Politics*. New York: A. A. Knopf.

CHAPTER 36

....

FORTY YEARS OF PUBLISHING IN QUANTITATIVE METHODOLOGY

....

MICHAEL S. LEWIS-BECK

QUANTITATIVE work has had a serious presence in published political science for a long time. David Gow (1985), in reviewing the early history of the discipline (1890–1922), observes that quantification and statistics were well appreciated, particularly by founders John W. Burgess and Richmond Mayo-Smith of the Columbia School. At the University of Chicago, Harold P. Gosnell carried out extensive voting behavior studies in the 1920s and 1930s, publishing results based on correlation, partial correlation, and factor analyses (Gosnell 1990). From a content analysis of *American Political Science Review* (*APSR*) articles, Somit and Tannenhaus (1964, 192) reported that the share of quantitative articles was 11.6 percent, for the period 1946–8. Thus, the practice of quantitative political science has old roots. Still, forty years ago (1965) can be taken as a turning point in the fortunes of the scientific empirical investigation of politics.

The behavioral revolution, given great impetus by *The American Voter* (Campbell et al. 1960), was fully begun. Data analysis had moved completely from hand calculation to computer-driven statistical packages, such as OSIRIS. Training centers, most notably that of the Inter-university Consortium for Political Research (launched in 1962), were springing up. The turbulent politics of the 1960s engaged the hearts and minds of students and faculty. The demand was for "relevant" research, and one form that "relevance" took was the production of sound quantitative answers to important political questions. For the period 1960–6, fully 38 percent of articles in the *APSR* were judged quantitative (Keech and Prothro 1968). For the period 1963–5, that estimate rises to 40.4 percent (Somit and Tannenhaus 1964, 192). King (1991, 4) reports that the annual share of quantitative *APSR* articles went from under 25 percent to over 50 percent in the late 1960s. Interestingly, looking at the graphic he offers, it appears that this take-off began precisely in 1965 (King 1991, figure 1).

As the publication of quantitative political research accelerated, a need appeared for more and better research tools, in particular statistical ones. If nothing else, such tools would allow surer ways to sort things out. Increasingly, there were articles that did not merely *use* data; they went beyond that, and told *how* to analyze data. These "methods" papers, and the forty-year evolution of their pattern of publication from 1965, provide the focus of this chapter. In general, this evolution has been from more general to more specialized outlets. We begin with material in leading general journals, the *APSR* and the *American Journal of Political Science* (*AJPS*). From there, we trace the development of more specialized venues, such as *Political Methodology* (*POM*), *Political Analysis* (*POA*), the *Political Methodologist* (*TPM*), and the Sage *Quantitative Analysis in the Social Sciences* series (*QASS*). Figure 36.1 shows the time lines (start–stop) of these publications.[1] We see that, over time, available scholarly channels for methods publication have tended to become more specialized. This specialization holds out some intriguing future possibilities, which are discussed by way of conclusion.

1 GENERAL JOURNALS: *APSR* AND *AJPS*

In a neglected report, James Hutter (1972, 314–15) examines quantification in the articles (*N* = 576) of seven leading political science journals (*APSR*, *Journal of Politics* (*JOP*), the *Midwest Journal of Political Science* (the *MJPS*), the *Western Political Quarterly*, *World Politics*, the *Journal of Conflict Resolution*, and *Polity*), for the period roughly 1968–70. Overall, 59 percent of these articles contained quantitative data. Two of these journals, the *APSR* and the *MJPS* (now the *AJPS*), were the most quantitative, respectively, with scores of 63 percent and 82 percent. It is fitting,

[1] This study confines itself largely to examination of quantitative methods papers published by political scientists in political science or interdisciplinary outlets. Occasionally, a quantitative methodologist in political science may publish an article in a sociology journal. In the annual *Sociological Methodology* begun in 1969, a few political science names—Hibbs and Rosenthal—appear. In current issues of their journal, *Sociological Methods and Research*, a political science byline may be spotted, e.g. King or Gill. But these are rare events, and always have been. For example, in the initial period under investigation (1965–70), quantitative methods pieces in the leading journal, the *American Sociological Review*, were plentiful; however, none were authored by political scientists. Even rarer is such publication in psychometric, econometric, or statistics journals.

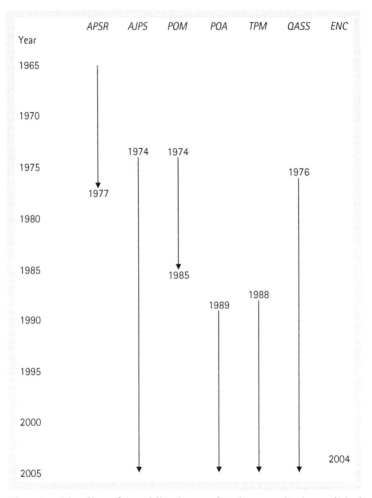

Fig. 36.1. Timelines for publication outlets in quantitative political science, 1965–2005

Note: APSR = American Political Science Review, AJPS = American Journal of Political Science, POM = Political Methodology, POA = Political Analysis, TPM = Political Methodologist, QASS = Sage Quantitative Analysis in the Social Sciences green monograph series, ENCY = Sage Encyclopedia of Social Science Research Methods, and Encyclopedia of Social Measurement.

then, that these two journals should begin our query. (The third of the "Big Three" general journals is *JOP*, which took fourth place in this rating of quantitative papers. Its unique history regarding publication of methods papers is discussed in the footnote.[2])

---

[2] While *JOP* welcomes substantive papers with a quantitative focus, it has published almost no quantitative methods papers per se. From 1965 to 1990, they printed seven such articles. After that, there were none until 2002, when a piece on duration models by Box-Steffensmeier and Zorn (2002) appeared. Then, in 2005, a Bayesian paper by Gill and Walker (2005) was published. These two, more current

Until the mid-1970s, the *APSR* was just about the only place that a political scientist could publish a methods article. By my count, from 1965 to 1977, the *Review* took one to three methods papers a year, with one the modal number. Take as an example our starting year, 1965, when there was a paper on spurious correlation (Beyle 1965) and another on factor analysis and related techniques (MacRae 1965). These articles are fairly typical of the era, in that they are applied, i.e. the method is illustrated in the context of a problem to be solved. Beyle (1965) was trying to figure out the link between contested elections and voter turnout, while MacRae (1965) sought to identify the issue structure in legislative voting. Sometimes the methods issue clearly dominates the substantive issue, such as the various papers on causal modeling (Blalock 1967; 1970; Forbes and Tufte 1968), the paper on ecological inference by Shiveley (1969), or Weisberg's (1974) models of statistical relationships. But, in all cases, the technique was "taught" through explication of substantive research questions.

The *APSR* ceased publishing such methods pieces in 1978 and, but for a few isolated exceptions, continued this policy of exclusion until about 1999, after which it has taken about one a year. The main reason for this demise is the appearance of other relevant outlets, leading among them "The Workshop" of *AJPS*, begun in February 1974. In his inaugural essay on its formation, Donald Stokes (1974*a*, 189) observes that researchers have become more desirous of "formal and precise statement, and more frequent use of statistical and mathematical procedures in data analysis." Therefore, a forum was needed to provide information on "how the methodology in question should be used." He sought three types of articles: expositions of a statistical or mathematical technique; "how-tos" on data acquisition; literature reviews of new concepts. Stokes (1974*b*) himself kicked off The Workshop with a paper of the first type, a lucid exposition of compound paths, which fit nicely with then-current heavy disciplinary attention to causal modeling.

Since that time, The Workshop has been a regular feature in *AJPS*, with the exception of a few blank years (November 1989–August 1990, April–October 2002). Each issue usually contains one, sometimes two, such papers. In the 1970s, a number of classics were published, such as Rabinowitz (1975) on nonmetric multidimensional scaling, or Aldrich and Cnudde (1975) on regression vs. probit analyis. In subsequent years—the 1980s and 1990s—a number of quantitative techniques received careful explication in these pages, e.g. multiplicative models, pooled time series, panel analysis, regression diagnostics, event count models, instrumental variables, questionnaire design, bootstrapping, generalized additive models. For the current period, 2000 to the present, major articles have appeared on Bayesian simulation (Jackman 2000), flexible least squares (Wood 2000), multilevel structures (Steenbergen and Jones 2002), ecological inference (Tam Cho and Gaines 2004), and multinomial models of count data (Mebane and Sekhon 2004). These recent publications demonstrate that The Workshop is continuing to serve as an important outlet for sophisticated papers explicating new methodological techniques.

articles indicate it is possible for quantitative methodologists to submit successfully to *JOP*, and may presage a policy shift.

2 SPECIALIZED JOURNALS: *POLITICAL METHODOLOGY* AND *POLITICAL ANALYSIS*

In the mid-1970s, *APSR* was about to stop publishing methods papers altogether. *AJPS*, with its Workshop, could pick up some of the diverted flow. But it could not meet the growing demand for more journal space for quantitative methods work. Fortunately, at about the same time, winter 1974, the first political science journal devoted exclusively to the study of methods was born—*Political Methodology* (*POM*). The publisher was Gerald Dorfman (Iowa State University and Geron-X) who, at least initially, more or less assembled the bright purple-covered volume in his home garage. Despite this humble beginning, its editors—George Marcus and John Sullivan—were distinguished, as was the editorial board: Hubert Blalock, Donald Campbell, David Easton, Richard Hofferbert, John Jackson, Martin Landau, Donald Matthews, Lester Milbrath, William Riker, W. Phillips Shively, and Edward Tufte.

The first issue covered 142 pages, and contained six articles (Vol. 1, No. 1, 1974). The topics of these papers give a flavor of the new enterprise: intensive analysis (Brown), contextual models (Przeworski), participant observation (Ross and Ross), the ecological correlation fallacy (Hanushek, Jackson, and Kain), problems with aggregate indicators (Cowart), and teaching methodology (Hitlin). These articles conform to the statement of intent soon issued by the journal: "*Political Methodology* is concerned with the entire range of interests and problems centering upon how political inquiry can be conducted" (Vol. 2, No. 4, 1975, 1).

In 1979 slight changes were made to the editorial board, including the addition of the first woman, Dinna Zinnes. The year 1980 saw no publication of the journal, which resumed in 1981. *POM* soon introduced a feature which came to be a characteristic of its successor—the special issue devoted to a single topic. In this case, the special issue dealt with "Modeling" (Vol. 9, No. 1, 1983). The "big change" occurred in 1984, when Christopher Achen assumed the editorship. Gerald Dorfman remained publisher, and the journal kept the same statement of intent. However, Chris appointed a new editorial board, peopled with a new generation of methodologists: Larry Bartels, Nathaniel Beck, Henry Brady, Stanley Feldman, John Freeman, Mel Hinich, Robert Jackman, John Jackson, Steven Rosenstone, Howard Rosenthal, W. Phillips Shively, James Stimson, and Dinna Zinnes. The Achen editorship of *POM* was short-lived, as plans were afoot for a new political methodology journal with a different format.

As noted in Achen's editorial remarks for the last issue (Vol. 11, Nos. 1–2, 1985), the field had experienced "rapid developments" in the last few years. In particular, that year the first summer meeting of the Society for Political Methodology took place in Ann Arbor. The success of the Society led to recognition of political methodology as an official subfield within the American Political Science Association, and to the sponsoring of a new, annual journal—*Political Analysis* (*POA*). With James Stimson as editor and the University of Michigan as publisher, it made its first appearance, Volume 1, 1989. (A mild confusion of dates arises. Volume 2, 1990, as an example, carries the copyright date of 1991.)

POA took over from *POM* as the journal uniquely dedicated to publishing methodological articles in political science. The topics of Volume 2 offer typical fare: political
methodology (King); predicting interstate conflict (Schrodt); measurement error in
two-stage least squares (Green); causality in survey cross-sections (Mebane); factor
vs. ideal-point analysis of candidate thermometer ratings (Brady); selection bias in
comparative politics (Geddes). That volume also featured a special Controversy section, containing a vigorous exchange of views on the R-squared (Achen; King; Lewis-
Beck and Skalaban). Stimson was editor through Volume 3, followed by John Freeman
(Volumes 4–6) and Walter Mebane (Volume 7). The chief difficulty, across this period,
was that *POA* was an annual publication, meaning it was short on space and not able
to respond quickly to change. Thus, the journal moved to a quarterly format, as of
the Winter 2000 volume, with Nathaniel Beck as editor and Westview as publisher.

In the foreword to his first issue (Vol. 8, No. 1), Neal notes that the "quarterly
Political Analysis has the same goals as *Political Methodology* and the annual *Political Analysis*: to advance the field of political methodology, broadly defined" (Beck
1999, iv). His recommendations of articles from the first few issues reflect this broad
definition, and include the following (Beck 1999, iv): Alavarez and Glasgow on two-
state estimation of nonrecursive choice models, Brehm on alternative corrections for
sample truncation, Krause on testing for the strong form of rational expectations,
Miller on dynamic constraint in American public opinion, Poole on nonparametric
unfolding of choice data, Sigelman and Zeng on tobit and heckit models, Sigelman
on publication bias, and Steenbergen on item similarity in scale analysis.

As of Volume 10, the quarterly changed publishers, with Oxford University Press
taking over. This change ushered in a number of special issues on single topics: spatial
models (Vol. 10, No. 3, 2002); experimental methods (Vol. 10, No. 4, 2002); empirical
implication of theoretical models, EITM (Vol. 11, No. 4, 2003). The emphasis on
special issues continued under new editor Robert Erikson, including one on Bayesian
methods (Vol. 12, No. 4, 2004) and another on multilevel modeling for large clusters
(Vol. 13, No. 4, 2005). Erikson (2004, 1) indicated that his assumption of the editorship
"portends no change of mission for *Political Analysis*. . . . This often means technical
discussions of statistical issues—perhaps the development of new techniques appropriate for political science research, or perhaps borrowing from statistical work in
other disciplines." These goals are reflected in his special issues topics just mentioned,
and provide clear signals to would-be submitters.

3 SPECIALIZED NEWSLETTERS: THE
POLITICAL METHODOLOGIST

Looking at political methodology publications, the "new kid on the block" is the
Political Methodologist (*TPM*) newsletter, begun in 1988 under the editorship of
Gary King. It offers a lively and timely forum for methodological ideas and issues.

In an editorial introduction, Gary encourages "contributions of any kind related to political methodology, defined broadly. New items might include brief research reports, requests for data, methodological critiques of published articles, or unusual methodological problems" (King 1989*b*, 1). The table of contents of that issue, as an example, included book reviews, a discussion of graphics, an announcement about the summer methods meeting, an offering of problem sets, treatment of certain computer packages, course syllabi, and a bibliography on AI.

Debates in other parts of the methods literature tend to get picked up in *TPM*. For example, the R-squared debate, which began in the pages of *Political Analysis*, spilled over into a couple of numbers of *TPM* (Vol. 3, No. 2, 1990; Vol. 4, No. 1, 1991). Further, *TPM* occasionally provides statistical expositions, such as the nice one on maximum likelihood estimation by Donald Green (1991). Not infrequently, statistical texts are reviewed. On graduate texts in general, see Vol. 5, No. 1 (1992); on econometrics texts specifically, see Vol. 7, No. 2 (1996); and on undergraduate texts, see Vol. 10, No. 1 (2001).

Editorial leadership has changed a fair amount, and the publication cycle has been somewhat irregular, as happens with newsletters. Michael Alavarez and Nathaniel Beck became editors in 1994 (Vol. 5, No. 2), *TPM* reappearing after a two-year absence. However, the Fall 1994 (Vol. 6, No. 1) issue was a full forty-three pages, and contained a plentiful number of helpful software reviews. In Spring 1996 (Vol. 7, No. 2), Jonathan Nagler took over the editorship. Under his direction, that rare thing in these parts—a qualitative piece—appeared, Katznelson (1997) on historical method.

After a gap of two years, *TPM* re-emerged, with editor Suzanne De Boef (the first female editor in the field of political methodology). Her first issue had a number of computational modeling articles. With respect to editorial policy, she set the newsletter on a regular track, saying it "will arrive in your mailbox twice a year and will contain articles on topics related to teaching, research, section news, and current methodological debates" (DeBoef 2001, 1). As examples of these topics, subsequent issues contained discussions of EITM (Vol. 11, No. 1, 2002) and articles on Bayesian estimation (Vol. 11, No. 2, 2003).

In the spring of 2004, the editorship became a triumvirate—Adam Berinsky, Michael Herron, and Jeffrey Lewis. They maintained the editorial goals of previous editors but with an important twist, worth quoting in full: "we offer the first of what we hope will be several pieces of important original research. With journal space at a premium, more and more of what editors consider 'technical details' ... are relegated to so-called web appendices or can only be found in working papers. It is our intention to provide a broader forum for the interesting methodological advancements that ended up on the cutting room floors of the general interest journals" (Berinsky, Herron, and Lewis 2005, 1). The first offered piece here is by James Snyder, on the scaling of aggregate election returns. This new goal marks a clear departure for *TPM*. Taken as read, it is an encouragement to submit fresh highly technical work to the newsletter, rather than to the journals, where it may have little chance of seeing the light of day. How much change this bold policy will actually effect it is too early to say.

4 PEDAGOGICAL VENUES: THE SAGE QASS SERIES AND ENCYCLOPEDIAS

The Sage Quantitative Applications in the Social Sciences (QASS) series, popularly known as the "little green monographs," has served as a major publication outlet for political science methodologists.[3] The papers are purposefully interdisciplinary, aiming to provide clear, intelligent expositions of quantitative methods, from the most elementary to the most sophisticated. The little green monographs began to appear in 1976, not long after the founding of Sage by Sara Miller McCune and her husband, George Miller. (The "Sage" name actually comes from a combination of the first two letters of the names Sara and George.) Annually, four to five papers, each of about eighty pages in length, are issued. The total number of titles (as of 2005) is 146. Often, a selection of titles is assigned as a set of supplementary readings in a methods class. The series has been quite successful, in the classroom and in the marketplace, with lifetime sales of well over 2,000,000 copies.

Political scientists are major contributors. Until just recently, the editors were exclusively from political science: Eric Uslaner (1976–8), John Sullivan (1979–82), John Sullivan and Richard Niemi (1982–8), and Michael Lewis-Beck (1988–2003). The current editor is Tim Futing Liao, a sociologist. The move to a sociologist is partial recognition of the contributions sociologists have made to QASS. Among the three leading social science disciplines the series serves—political science, psychology, sociology—each provides about one-third of the authors. Political scientists were especially active in the earlier years. The very first title, "Analysis of Variance" (No. 1, 1976), had a political science co-author, Helmut Norpoth. Of the initial fifty monographs (reaching to 1985), almost half had political science authors. Their names, listed chronologically, remain well known in the profession today: Norpoth, Nagel, Asher, Rosenthal, Ostrom, Sullivan, Feldman, Hartwig, Carmines, Markus, McDowall, Lewis-Beck, McIver, Lodge, Huckfeld, Kohfeld, Kuklinski, Achen, Berry, Schrodt, Zagare, Jacob, Aldrich.

Mostly, these pioneering authors wrote excellent papers on bread-and-butter topics. Here is a chronological listing: ANOVA, operations research, causal modeling, ordinal data analysis, basic time series, multiple indicators, exploratory data, reliability and validity, panel analysis, interrupted time series, applied regression, unidimensional scaling, magnitude scaling, dynamic modeling, network analysis, regression interpretation, nonrecursive causal models, microcomputers, game theory, data sources, logit and probit, multiple regression. The intelligent, user-friendly

---

[3] The color of these monographs has always been lime-green. Originally, in the early days of the young company, the lime-green paint was selected for the cover because it was less expensive than other paints. At different points in the life of the series, there was discussion of changing the color. However, that decision was indefinitely deferred, once it was realized that the lime-green cover had become a favorable "brand-identity" for the monographs. Ironically, such lime-green paint is no longer necessarily inexpensive to obtain.

treatments made these many tools available to a wide community of researchers, thereby advancing significantly quantitative investigation.

In 1990, editor Lewis-Beck issued a "call for monographs," in *TPM* (Vol. 3, No. 1, 12–13). He asked for proposals of two types—"fundamental techniques" or "well-known advanced techniques"—and met with some disciplinary success. In the contemporary period, political scientists continue to contribute to the series. Upon examination of the last fifty titles (Nos. 97–146), one counts fifteen political scientists as authors, in chronological order: Lewis-Beck, Finkel, Brown, Hagle, Taber, Timpone, Mooney, Jacoby, Fink, Gates, Humes, Johnson, Gill, Best, Krueger. Their papers cover a mix of topics: elementary data analysis, causal analysis of panel data, chaos and catastrophe theories, basic math, computational modeling, Monte Carlo simulation, statistical graphics, game theory, social choice, generalized linear models, internet data collection.

While political science maintains a strong presence, then, in the QASS series, it is less than earlier years. This mild disciplinary shift away from the little green monographs, which actually first appeared after 1985, seems mostly due to a simple reason: Rival publication outlets came on the scene, namely *Political Analysis* (1989) and the *Political Methodologist* (1988). (The appearance of a brand new series, entitled Analytic Methods for Social Research, might also be mentioned. It is discussed in the footnote.[4])

Besides monographs, another venue for political methodologists has been edited volumes. Older examples are Blalock (1985), Berry and Lewis-Beck (1986), Eulau (1989), and Palfrey (1991). Newer opportunities of this type are handbooks (such as the one in hand) or encyclopedias. With respect to the latter, two have just appeared: the *Encyclopedia of Social Measurement* (Kempf-Leonard 2004), and the *Sage Encyclopedia of Social Science Research Methods* (Lewis-Beck, Bryman, and Liao 2004). The focus here is on the second, which was previewed in *TPM* (Vol. 11, No. 2, 2003, 12), and turned into an especially bountiful opportunity for political scientists. The *Sage Encyclopedia*, a three-volume set, contains almost 1,000 educational essays on research methods and concepts, from Abduction to Z-test. The international, cross-disciplinary editorial board lists two prominent American political scientists, R. Michael Alvarez and Nathaniel Beck. All told, over sixty political scientists wrote at least one, sometimes several, entries.

While this list of citations is too long to complete here, it is worth offering some examples: Beck on time-series analysis, Boehmke on selection bias, Box-Steffensmeier on event history analysis, Clarke on Granger causality, Clinton on the sphericity assumption, De Boef on error correction models, Gill on Bayesian inference, Glasgow on multinomial logit, Green on field experimentation, Herron on Poisson regression,

---

[4] The series Analytical Methods for Social Research is edited by R. Michael Alvarez, Nathaniel L. Beck, and Lawrence L. Wu, and published by Cambridge. Since 2004, it has published four titles, all written by political scientists, on ecological inference (King, Rosen, and Tanner), essential mathematics (Gill), event history (Box-Steffensmeier and Jones), and spatial models (Poole). Each is book length, running over 200 pages.

Jackman on generalized additive models, Kedar on the normal distributon, Katz on asymptotic properties, Nagler on specification, Ondercin on efficiency, Pollins on homoskedasticity, Shannon on the omitted variable, Traugott on public opinion research, Whitten on contingent effects, Wood and Park on the best linear unbiased estimator, and Zorn on generalized estimating equations. This diverse sampling, from scholars at different career stages, illustrates the vibrancy and range of current writing in political methodology.

5 TEXTBOOKS: AN ECONOMETRIC PROBLEM?

Textbooks provide another possible publication outlet for political methodologists. Undergraduate programs in political science now commonly offer an introductory methods class, and certain scholars in the discipline have taken fair advantage of this market. Leading examples are the comprehensive research methods text by Johnson, Joslyn, and Reynolds (2001), and the popular data workbook by Corbett (2001). At the graduate level, however, texts by political methodologists are very scarce. There is the classic stats book by Hanushuk and Jackson (1977), and the more recent work by King (1989a) on maximum likelihood.

However, most political science graduate courses in quantitative methods assign as their main text a volume on econometrics.[5] Johnston (1972), Wonnacott and Wonnacott (1970), and Pindyck and Rubinfeld (1991) used to be popular, but are fading from view. Kmenta (1997) continues to be old reliable. By descending order of difficulty, Greene (2000), Guajarati (1995), and Kennedy (2003) remain in wide use. A relatively new econometrics text, by Wooldridge (2001), appears to be gaining ground. In his thoughtful review of that volume, Krause (2001, 35) notes that the choice of such a textbook depends whether you wish to educate "applied empirical researchers" or "political methodologist[s]." The former are expected to be skillful practitioners, while the latter are expected to advance directly quantitative technique. These advances in technique are beginning to appear in the literature, especially the recent pages of *Political Analysis*. The expectation is that leaders of the current political methodology generation will write texts to replace econometrics texts now in political science classroom use.

---

[5] Political science graduate training in quantitative methods has always borrowed heavily from work in other social sciences. Across the period under study (1965–2005), one can observe this borrowing migrate from sociology and psychology to economics. My own quantitative training (late 1960s–early 1970s) may serve as illustration. In my first stats class in grad school (University of Michigan), we used sociologist Blalock's (1960) classic text. In my second stats class, we used psychologist Hays's (1963) classic text. In my later classes, we focused on econometrics texts, mainly Johnston (1972) and Kmenta (1971).

6 SUMMARY AND CONCLUSIONS

Over the last forty years, publication in quantitative methods for political science has undergone considerable change. In the 1960s, available space was scarce, and essentially confined to the main disciplinary journal, *APSR*. In the 1970s, new venues opened up—the *AJPS* workshop, *Political Methodology*, and the QASS monograph series. Toward the end of the 1980s, *Political Analysis* and the *Political Methodologist* joined the mix. By the early 2000s, different handbooks and encyclopedias also offered their pages to eager political methodologists.

From the vantage point of today, the mid-2000s, a political scientist seeking to publish a paper in quantitative methods has at least five opportunities: the *AJPS* Workshop, *Political Analysis*, the *Political Methodologist*, QASS, or an edited collection (e.g. a new handbook). This array of choices, while not vast, is a far cry from a sole alternative in the mid-1960s. Where political methodologists submit a paper for first review depends, in part, on what they are about. To simplify, are they "missionaries" or "theologians?"

Missionaries translate methodological tools, mainly from statistics or econometrics. They teach research practitioners how to apply these techniques intelligently. Essentially, then, they are popularizers of received wisdom, taking the "good news" to the people. This is an old and honorable tradition. Theologians, in contrast, endeavor to create methodological tools from within political science itself. While they deeply value quantitative work in other fields, they believe the study of politics offers some unique methodological questions and answers. They are specialists, not popularizers. Their first audience, then, is others of like mind, who will understand their original contributions. These contributions, once accepted, could eventually find their way to the practitioner's tool kit. The theological tradition is scarcer, and relatively new, in political science.

Of course neither tradition is in any sense "wrong." Both have their place. And, it must be said that the theological approach, to the extent it is successful, puts the discipline on its own footing. It moves us away from quantitative parasitism, away from any dependency on the methodological innovations within psychology, sociology, and economics. However, the distinction—missionary vs. theologian—does make a difference in terms of where you submit a paper or, put another way, where you are likely to have a paper accepted.[6] For the missionary, a submission to the Workshop or for a QASS volume seems preferred. For the theologian, submission to *Political Analysis* or *TPM* takes preference. Fortunately, the present

---

[6] There is no implication here that the quantitative methodologist must confine himself or herself exclusively to publishing in one journal, or subset of journals. Numerous political methodologists have had papers appear in all, or most, of the multiple venues reviewed here. This has been my own experience, which is perhaps not atypical. (See, as examples, Lewis-Beck 1977; 1978; 1980; 1986; 2001; 2004; Lewis-Beck and Skalaban, 1990.) Thus, even a full-fledged missionary or theologian has opportunities across the board.

dynamics of publication in political methodology provide multiple opportunities for submission, regardless of whether scholars find themselves more in one role than the other.

REFERENCES

ALDRICH, J., and CNUDDE, C. F. 1975. Probing the bounds of conventional wisdom: a comparison of regression, probit, and discriminant analysis. *American Journal of Political Science*, 19: 571–608.

BECK, N. 1999. Editor's foreword. *Political Analysis*, 8: iii–v.

BERINSKY, A., HERRON, M., and LEWIS, J. 2005. Editors' note. *Political Methodologist*, 13: 1.

BERRY, W. D., and LEWIS-BECK, M. S. (eds.) 1986. *New Tools for Social Scientists: Advances and Applications in Research Methods*. Beverly Hills, Calif.: Sage.

BEYLE, T. L. 1965. Contested elections and voter turnout in a local community: a problem in spurious correlation. *American Political Science Review*, 59: 111–16.

BLALOCK, H. M. 1960. *Social Statistics*. New York: McGraw-Hill.

——1967. Causal inferences, closed populations, and measures of association. *American Political Science Review*, 61: 130–6.

——1970. A causal approach to nonrandom measurement error. *American Political Science Review*, 64: 1099–111.

——1985. *Causal Models in the Social Sciences*. New York: Aldine.

BOX-STEFFENSMEIER, J., and ZORN, C. 2002. Duration models for repeated events. *Journal of Politics*, 64: 1069–94.

CAMPBELL, A., CONVERSE, P., MILLER, W., and STOKES, D. 1960. *The American Voter*. New York: Wiley.

CHO, W. K. T., and GAINES, B. J. 2004. The limits of ecological inference: the case of split ticket voting. *American Journal of Political Science*, 48: 152–71.

CORBETT, M. 2001. *Research Methods in Political Science*, 4th edn. Belmont, Calif.: Wadsworth.

DEBOEF, S. 2001. Editor's note. *Political Methodologist*, 10: 1.

ERIKSON, R. 2004. Editor's note. *Political Analysis*, 12: 1–2.

EULAU, H. (ed.) 1989. *Social Science at the Cross-roads*. New York: Agathon.

FORBES, H. D., and TUFTE, E. R. 1968. A note of caution in causal modelling. *American Political Science Review*, 62: 1258–64.

GILL, J., and WALKER, L. D. 2005. Elicited priors for Bayesian model specifications in political science research. *Journal of Politics*, 67: 841–72.

GOSNELL, H. P. 1990. The marriage of math and young political science: some early uses of quantitative methods. *Political Methodologist*, 3: 2–4.

GOW, D. J. 1985. Quantification and statistics in the early years of American political science, 1880–1922. *Political Methodology*, 11: 1–18.

GREEN, D. 1991. Maximum likelihood estimatation for the masses. *Political Methodologist*, 4: 5–11.

GREENE, W. H. 2000. *Econometric Analysis*, 4th edn. New York: Macmillian.

GUAJARATI, D. N. 1995. *Basic Econometrics*, 3rd edn. New York: McGraw-Hill.

HANUSHUK, E., and JACKSON, J. 1977. *Statistical Methods for Social Scientists*. New York: Academic Press.

HAYS, W. L. 1963. *Statistics*. New York: Holt, Rinehart and Winston.

HUTTER, J. L. 1972. Quantification in political science: an examination of seven journals. *Midwest Journal of Political Science*, 16: 313–23.

JACKMAN, S. 2000. Estimation and inference via Bayesian simulation: an introduction to Markov chain Monte Carlo. *American Journal of Political Science*, 44: 375–404.

JOHNSON, J. B., JOSLYN, R. A., and REYNOLDS, H. T. 2001. *Political Science Research Methods*, 4th edn. Washington, DC: CQ Press.

JOHNSTON, J. 1972. *Econometric Methods*. New York: McGraw-Hill.

KATZNELSON, I. 1997. Reflections on history, method, and political science. *Political Methodologist*, 8: 11–13.

KEECH, W., and PROTHRO, J. W. 1968. American government. *Journal of Politics*, 30: 417–42.

KEMPF-LEONARD, K. (ed.) 2004. *Encyclopedia of Social Measurement*. San Diego: Academic Press.

KENNEDY, P. 2003. *A Guide to Econometrics*, 5th edn. Cambridge, Mass.: MIT Press.

KING, G. 1989*a*. *Unifying Political Methodology: The Likelihood Theory of Statistical Inference*. New York: Cambridge University Press.

—— 1989*b*. Editor's note. *Political Methodologist*, 2: 1.

—— 1991. On political methodology. *Political Analysis*, 2: 1–31.

KMENTA, J. 1971. *Elements of Econometrics*. New York: Macmillian.

—— 1997. *Elements of Econometrics*, 2nd edn. Ann Arbor: University of Michigan.

KRAUSE, G. A. 2001. Review of Wooldridge's *Introductory Econometrics*. *Political Methodologist*, 10: 35–6.

LEWIS-BECK, M. S. 1977. The relative importance of socioeconomic and political variables for public policy. *American Political Science Review*, 71: 559–66.

—— 1978. Stepwise regression: a caution. *Political Methodology*, 5: 213–40.

—— 1980. *Applied Regression: An Introduction*. Sage University Papers Series on Quantitative Appliations in the Social Sciences, 07–22. Thousand Oaks, Calif.: Sage.

—— 1986. Interrupted time series. Pp. 209–40 in *New Tools for Social Scientists: Advances and Applications in Research Methods*, ed. M. S. Lewis-Beck and W. D. Berry. Beverly Hills, Calif.: Sage.

—— 2001. Teaching undergraduate methods: overcoming "stat" anxiety. *Political Methodologist*, 10: 7–8.

—— 2004. Regression. Pp. 935–8 in Lewis-Beck, Bryman, and Liao 2004.

—— and SKALABAN, A. 1990. The R-squared: some straight talk. *Political Analysis*, 2: 153–71.

—— BRYMAN, A., and LIAO, T. F. (eds.) 2004. *The Sage Encyclopedia of Social Science Research Methods*. Thousand Oaks, Calif.: Sage.

MACRAE, D. 1965. A method of identifying issues and factions from legislative votes. *American Political Science Review*, 59: 909–26.

MEBANE, W. R., and SEKHON, J. S. 2004. Robust estimation and outlier detection for overdispersed multinomial models of count data. *American Journal of Political Science*, 48: 392–411.

PALFREY, T. R. (ed.) 1991. *Laboratory Research in Political Economy*. Ann Arbor: University of Michigan Press.

PINDYCK, R. S., and RUBINFELD, D. L. 1991. *Econometric Models and Econometric Forecasting*, 3rd edn. New York: McGraw-Hill.

RABINOWITZ, G. B. 1975. An introduction to nonmetric multidimensional scaling. *American Journal of Political Science*, 19: 343–90.

SHIVELY, W. P. 1969. Ecological inference: the use of aggregate data to study individuals. *American Political Science Review*, 63: 1183–96.

SOMIT, A., and TANENHAUS, J. 1964. *The Development of American Political Science*. Boston: Allyn and Bacon.

STEENBERGER, M. R., and JONES, B. 2002. Modeling multilevel data structures. *American Journal of Political Science*, 46: 218–37.

STOKES, D. D. 1974*a*. The Workshop. *American Journal of Political Science*, 18: 189–90.

——1974*b*. Compound paths: an expository note. *American Journal of Political Science*, 18: 191–214.

WEISBERG, H. F. 1974. Models of statistical relationship. *American Political Science Review*, 68: 1638–55.

WONNACOTT, T. H., and WONNACOTT, R. J. 1970. *Econometrics*. New York: Wiley.

WOOD, B. D. 2000. Weak theories and parameter instability: using flexible least squares to take time varying relationships seriously. *American Journal of Political Science*, 44: 603–18.

WOOLDRIDGE, J. 2001. *Introductory Econometrics: A Modern Approach*. Oxford: Oxford Univeristy Press.

....

CHAPTER 37

THE EITM APPROACH: ORIGINS AND INTERPRETATIONS

....

JOHN H. ALDRICH

JAMES E. ALT

ARTHUR LUPIA

MANY scholars seek a coherent approach to evaluating information and converting it into useful and effective knowledge. The term "EITM" ("Empirical Implications of Theoretical Models") refers to such an approach. EITM's initial public use was as the summarizing title of a workshop convened by the National Science Foundation's Political Science program in July 2001.[1] The workshop's goal was to improve graduate and postgraduate training in the discipline in light of the continued growth of an uncomfortable schism between talented theoreticians and innovative empiricists. Since then, the acronym has been applied to a growing range of activities such as summer institutes and scholarship programs. At the time of this writing, the acronym's most common use is as an adjective that describes a distinct scholarly approach in political science. This chapter explains the approach's origins and various ways in which NSF's call to EITM action has been interpreted.

---

[1] We cannot overstate the importance of then-NSF Political Science Director James Granato's leadership in making this happen,

From the late 1960s, a growing number of political scientists turned to increasingly rigorous methods of inference to improve the precision and credibility of their work. Theorists, through the development of a new and intricate class of formal mathematical models, and empiricists, through the development of a new and dynamic class of empirical estimators and experimental designs, made many important contributions to political science over the decades that followed. The precision with which more rigorous theorists could characterize conditional logical relationships amongst a range of factors and the consequent rigor with which empiricists could characterize relations among variables, generated exciting new research agendas and led to the toppling of many previously focal conjectures about cause and effect in politics.

The evolution of game-theoretic, statistical, computational, and experimental forms of inference increased the transparency and replicability of the processes by which political scientists generated causal explanations. In so doing, these efforts revolutionized the discipline and increased its credibility in many important domains. One such domain was the hallways of the National Science Foundation.

At the same time, a problem was recognized. The problem was that the growing sophistication in theory and method were proceeding all too often independently of one another. Many graduate students who obtained advanced training in formal modeling had little or no understanding of the mechanics of empirical inference. Similarly, graduate programs that offered advanced training in statistical methods or experiments often offered little or no training in formal modeling. Few formal theorists and rigorous empiricists shared much in the way of common knowledge about research methods or substantive matters. As a result, they tended not to communicate at all.

There were exceptions, of course. And over the years, intermittent arguments were made about the unrealized potential inferential value that might come from a closer integration of rigorous theorizing and empiricism. But few scholars had the training to capitalize on such opportunities.

The challenge that NSF put to participants in the EITM workshop was to find ways to close the growing chasm between leading-edge formal theory and innovative empirical methodology. Participants were asked to find ways to improve the value and relevance of theoretical work by crafting it in ways that made key aspects of new models more amenable to empirical evaluation. They were also asked to find ways to use methods of empirical inference to generate more effective and informative characterizations of focal model attributes.

The ideas generated at and after this workshop sparked an aggressive response by the National Science Foundation. Since then, NSF Political Science has spent—and continues to spend—a significant fraction of its research budget on EITM activities. The most notable of these activities are its month-long summer institutes which have been held at places like Berkeley, Duke, Harvard, Michigan, UCLA, and Washington University and which have served hundreds of young scholars.

As a result of these and related activities, EITM training now occurs at a growing number of universities around the world. This training not only educates students about highly technical theoretical and empirical work but also encourages them to develop research designs that provide more precise and dynamic answers to critical scientific questions by integrating the two approaches from the very beginning of the work. Most importantly, perhaps, there is a critical mass of scholars (particularly in the discipline's junior ranks) who recognize how this approach can improve the reliability and credibility of their work. New and vibrant scholarly networks are forming around the premise that the EITM approach can be a valuable attribute of research.

EITM, however, has not been without controversy. Some saw it as unnecessary, contending that the theory–empirical gap was natural in origin and impossible to overcome. Others feared that EITM would lead students to have false ideas and expectations about the extent to which formal theories could be evaluated empirically. And, in a particularly infamous example, the *American Journal of Political Science* briefly instituted a policy saying that it would not consider for review articles containing a formal model that did not also include empirical work—with part of the journal's explanation being that they believed such a practice was consistent with the goals of EITM.[2] The *AJPS* policy was widely attacked, opposed by leaders of the EITM movement, and quickly reversed by the journal. However, the episode demonstrated that several years into the endeavor there was still considerable uncertainty about what EITM was and its implications for the future of graduate training and scholarly work in political science. No one disputes that a logically coherent, rigorously tested explanation is desirable, but "what logic" and "which tests" is less obvious.

In what follows, we make a brief attempt to explain why the EITM approach emerged, why it is valuable, and how it is currently understood. With respect to the final point, we contend that EITM has been interpreted in multiple ways. We highlight a subset of extant interpretations and, in the process, offer our own views about the most constructive way forward.[3]

1 DEVELOPMENTS IN POLITICAL SCIENCE: 1960S TO 1990S

Political science is a discipline that shares important attributes with the other sciences. For example, many political scientists are driven by the motive not only to understand relevant phenomena, but also to provide insights that can help humanity more

---

[2] As the journal editors pointed out, they were responding by making a policy that simply instantiated the recurring practices of their reviewers.

[3] While one can debate whether we—the authors of this chapter—speak from a position of authority on what EITM does or should mean (as others may disagree with our emphases and arguments), we do speak from positions of experience. Two of us (Alt and Aldrich—along with Henry Brady and Robert Franzese) founded the first EITM Summer Institute and two of us (Aldrich and Lupia) are the only people to have taught considerable portions of every subsequent version of that institute.

effectively adapt to important challenges. Consequently, many political scientists desire to have their conclusions and arguments attended to and acted upon by others. As a result, many political scientists believe that arguments backed by strong evidence and transparent logic tend to be more credible and persuasive than arguments that lack such attributes, all else constant.

What distinguishes political science from other disciplines is that it focuses on politics. In other words, political scientists are unified by a context, and not by a method. Political science departments typically house faculty with training from a range of traditions. It is not uncommon to see faculty with backgrounds in fields such as economics, journalism, philosophy, psychology, or sociology. As a result, political science is not defined by agreement on which method of inference is best.

For this reason, political scientists tend to be self-conscious about the methods they use (see Thomas 2005 for a review of five recent texts). They must be, because they cannot expect to walk into a broadly attended gathering of colleague-scientists and expect an a priori consensus on whether a particular method is optimal—or even suitable—for the effective examination of a particular problem. Indeed, compared to microeconomics or social psychology, where dominant inferential paradigms exist, consensus on the best way to approach a problem in any comparable subset of political science, including the study of American politics, is rare. Methodological diversity runs deep. So scholars must, as part of their presentational strategies, be able to present a cogent argument as to why the approach they are using is necessary or sufficient to provide needed insights.

This attribute of political science has many important implications. One is that scholars who are trained in a particular research methodology tend to have limited knowledge of other methods. In the case of scholars who use formal models, scholars who use advanced statistical methods, scholars trained in experimental design and inference, and scholars trained in computational models (each of which became far more numerous in political science over the final three decades of the twentieth century), the knowledge gaps with respect to methods other than their own followed the prevailing pattern. However, given the training in logic and inference that scholars must acquire to be competent in formal modeling, experimentation, or the brand of statistics that became known as political methodology, an inconvenient truth existed alongside of the groups' intellectual isolation. The truth was that insufficient interaction between theory and empirics yields irrelevant deductions and false empirical inferences:

Empirical observation, in the absence of a theoretical base, is at best descriptive. It tells one what happened, but not why it has the pattern one perceives. Theoretical analysis, in the absence of empirical testing, has a framework more noteworthy for its logical or mathematical elegance than for its utility in generating insights into the real world. The first exercise has been described as "data dredging," the second as building "elegant models of irrelevant universes." My purpose is to try to understand what I believe to be a problem of major importance. This understanding cannot be achieved merely by observation, nor can it be attained by the manipulation of abstract symbols. Real insight can be gained only by their combination.

(Aldrich 1980)

While many scholars would likely agree with such statements, acting on them was another matter. In the early days of formal modeling in political science, the barrier to closer interactions between formal modeling and political methodology was a lack of "know-how."

Many classic papers of the early formal modeling period recognized the importance of empirical–theoretical integration, but the tools did not exist to allow these scholars to engage in such activities with any rigor. Consider two examples from the first generation of what were widely known as "rational choice" theories.

The decision to turn out to vote and the decision to run for (higher) office were initially formulated in decision-theoretic terms (e.g. Riker and Ordeshook 1968; McKelvey and Ordeshook 1972; and Black 1972; Rohde 1979, respectively). Using decision theory meant that they were formulated as decisions made without consideration of strategic interaction. Only later were they able to be modeled in true game-theoretic settings (e.g. by Palfrey and Rosenthal 1985, and Banks and Kiewiet 1989, respectively). The early modelers did not make that choice because they believed there was no significant strategic interaction (which they may or may not have believed in the first case but certainly did not in the second). Rather, they assumed a decision-theoretic context for at least two reasons. First, that was the technology available for use in addressing those problems. Second, even this technology was sufficient to allow the authors to add to the discipline's stock of theoretically generated knowledge in important ways.[4]

Even when game theory replaced decision theory in these early applications, the models were "primitive" in the sense that they often assumed complete and perfect information. An often unrecognized consequence of these assumptions was that individual behavior was assumed to be deterministic.[5] In retrospect, we can ask why "rational choice" theorists modeled people in these simplistic and evidently empirically false ways. But if we look at the resources that such scholars had available— logical constructs from fields of logic, mathematics, philosophy, and microeconomic theory—there were no better alternatives available for the early formal modeler. For all of the 1960s and most of the 1970s, there was no decision-theoretic or game-theoretic technology that permitted more realistic representations of human perception and cognition. Not until the work of Nobel laureates such as John Harsanyi and Reinhardt Selten was there a widely accepted logical architecture for dealing with incomplete information, asymmetric information, and related problems of perception and cognition.

Even if theory had been able to advance to the Harsanyi/Selten level years or decades earlier, it is not clear how one would have integrated their mechanics or insights into the statistical estimators of the day. Indeed, these early theorists, including William Riker, Richard McKelvey, and Peter Ordeshook, ran experiments as

---

[4] Indeed, both the calculus of voting and of candidacy were systematically and extensively tested in these early papers.

[5] While many methods used by political scientists at this time also made this assumption, the early modelers were explicit about it in ways that are required when developing a model whose logic is transparent and replicable.

a means of evaluating certain aspects of their models empirically (e.g. Riker 1967; McKelvey and Ordeshook 1980; 1982). But such examples were rare and not statistically complex.[6] Rarer still were attempts to evaluate such model attributes using statistical models with an underlying parallel logic sufficient for rigorous evaluation. Intricate estimation of choice models was only beginning to be developed.

McFadden (1977) developed the first model for estimation of discrete choice problems in the early to mid-1970s (something for which he also won a Nobel Prize). His and subsequent work provided rigorous ways to integrate statistical inferences for the testing of hypotheses derived from decision theory. These early statistical models, though, did not extend to testing hypotheses about strategic behavior as derived from game theory. Subsequent advances of this kind in statistical choice models took longer to develop (Aldrich and Alt 2003). Thus, through at least the 1970s, it is arguable that neither game theory nor statistical methodology had the technology to close the gap between the two in any rigorous manner.

In the 1980s and 1990s, theory and method had advanced. Not only were political scientists importing inferential advances from other fields, but they were also creating their own advances—tools and instruments that were of particular value to, and specifically attuned to, the special problems associated with the context of politics. To contribute to such enterprises, an increasing number of faculty and graduate students in political science sought and obtained more intense technical training. While these advances and graduate training trends led to many positive changes in political science, they also fueled the gap between formal theorists and rigorous empiricists. Certainly, widespread perception of such cause and effect was the impetus behind NSF's decision to begin investing in an EITM approach in the 1990s (see, e.g., Brady 2004; Smith 2004; Granato and Scioli 2004).

By the mid-1990s it was possible to point to research agendas that powerfully leveraged the advantages of leading-edge formal modeling and empirical work. There were formal-model-oriented experiments of various kinds (see, e.g., Druckman et al. 2006 for a review) though the number of such efforts remained minuscule in comparison to the number of models produced. There were also notable successes in attempts to leverage the inferential power of high-end game theory and statistical methods such as McKelvey and Palfrey's (1992; 1995) quantal response equilibrium concept and Signorino's (1999) empirical estimation strategy that embedded that equilibrium concept directly into the derivation of therefore-appropriate estimators. However, sparse examples do not a full approach make. As Aldrich and Alt (2003) emphasized, political science articles were less likely than their economics counterparts to connect theory and empirics. But the underlying problem was deeper: Theorists and empirical researchers were not reading, citing, or building upon each other's work.

For the most part, the intellectual streams of formal theorists and rigorous empiricists in the discipline were not converging. Theorists tended to come from and gather at a few focal universities, beginning with the graduate program William Riker

---

[6] By this we mean not just technical sophistication for its own sake, but complex in the sense of permitting insightful inferences about the model's underlying conceptual relations.

founded at the University of Rochester in the 1960s, then extending to departments that housed political scientists and highly technical economic theorists under one roof (such as the interdisciplinary programs at Carnegie Mellon, Cal Tech, and Stanford's Graduate School of Business) and then to departments that employed graduates of such programs. These scholars formed vibrant intellectual communities and could publish in outlets such as *Public Choice*, the *Journal of Political Theory*, and the *Journal of Law, Economics and Organization* (as well as parallel journals in economics) without paying much attention to empirical evaluations of the new models' key attributes.

At roughly the same time that theorists from Rochester and other universities began to make waves, the 1960s saw an explosion of interest in quantitative data by political scientists while the 1970s saw the spread of training in econometrics. The subsequent founding of the Society for Political Methodology, the development of its methods summer conference, and the emergence of the journal *Political Analysis* (from its origin as *Political Methodology*) decisively shifted the standard graduate curriculum in political science toward rigorous inference and the development and use of more appropriate, powerful, and flexible tools, along with more powerful, computer-intensive estimation methods. Later, political scientists with training in experimental design followed suit, designing and conducting a growing range of experiments that were particularly pertinent to key questions in the discipline. Critical masses in departments such as Cal Tech, Minnesota, Yale, and Stony Brook have transformed graduate training in those places through their emphasis on experimental design.

But theorists and empiricists tended to lead parallel rather than integrated existences. By the 1990s, a political science formal theory with its own identity and distinct accomplishments had clearly developed as had a parallel political science statistics. The success of formal modeling and rigorous empirical work in challenging long-held maxims about causality led to increasing demand for training in these areas. But many departments chose to specialize in one method of inference (with training in statistics being more common than training in formal modeling and both being more common than experimental design). While these departments became hotbeds for many valuable scholarly advances, they also fueled increasing specialization. These dynamics also produced increased isolation. Scholars with advanced inferential skills tended to congregate with people like them to the exclusion of others.

Here is one example of this excessive specialization, though we believe there are many. Austen-Smith modeled the income distribution and political choice of taxes under proportional representation in comparison with a first-past-the-post system. Among the implications of his model is that in comparison with a two-party system, legislative bargaining in a three-party PR system results in equilibrium tax rates that are higher, with more equal post-tax income distributions, lower aggregate income, and higher unemployment (Austen-Smith 2000, 1236).

These results are consistent (and inconsistent) with a range of nonformal political science conjectures about the size and consequences of the welfare state, as well as insider–outsider politics (e.g. Rueda 2005). Model features like parties representing specific groups in the labor market or labor market choices responding to tax rates are not unrelated to measures present in the empirical analysis of redistribution. One would think that Austen-Smith's model could inform and advance empirical work. The narrative is clearly argued and the logic expertly presented. At a minimum, the conditional relationships he identifies suggest a variety of modeling changes and evaluating the robustness of causal claims made in the empirical literature. In our view, nothing about the model itself explains why a scholar.google count showed that, from his working paper until the appearance of Iversen and Soskice (2006) last year, a total of five political scientists had cited this paper, none doing empirical evaluation of its conjectures.[7] A generation-long norm of isolation amongst rigorous theorists and empiricists is a more plausible explanation.

The growth of logical rigor—in formal theoretic and statistical contexts—since the 1960s has served political science well. The discipline has seen much progress in theory development and testing. But questions also arose such as, "How much more can be learned if bridges are built, so that young scholars can be systematically trained to use theoretical and empirical methods as complements rather than substitutes?" and "How can we integrate rigorous and coherent hypothesis generation with equally rigorous inference that reflects both the integrity and coherence of the theory and the information within and problems associated with the political process generating the data?" The answers to these questions are the challenge of EITM.

2 INTERPRETATIONS OF THE EITM APPROACH

What value does an EITM approach add, beyond an exhortation to integrate credible theory and rigorous empirical evaluation? A narrow construction emphasizes the major task of science as testing the causal implications of theories against reality. But many suggest views of the research program that are much broader. In this section we present five views of EITM, some that have been presented as self-conscious attempts to formalize boundaries for the approach and two (by Christopher Achen and Richard McKelvey, respectively) that offer important insights despite pre-dating the NSF workshop by years or decades. In the process, we offer some commentary on these various presentations as a means of advancing our own views on the matter.

We begin by illustrating three views drawn from a discussion at the EITM Summer Institute held at Berkeley in 2005. This discussion was led by James Fearon, Henry Brady, and Gary Cox and yielded three views of EITM that are commonly encountered and go beyond the narrow construction.

---

[7] By contrast—or perhaps in the same spirit—seven political science papers, at least two doing empirical work, cited Jackson and Moselle (2002) an equally "difficult" but focal mechanism design for proportional representation.

- View 1. Observing reality and developing theoretical explanations for its causal regularities is just as important as testing those causal implications.
- View 2. Science requires the development and testing of concepts and measurement methods as much as the development of causal theories.
- View 3. A division of labor between deriving and testing of implications must exist, but that division risks overspecialization in which the opportunities of fruitful interactions between theory and empirical work are missed.

As to view 1, rather than a narrow perspective that emphasizes going only from theory to new implications and testing them, going in the opposite direction at the same time (observing reality, developing intuitions and ideas, and positing explanations and theories) is equally important. It is difficult to object to this idea when stated in such generality. But treating the two approaches (theory first, observation first) symmetrically is also problematic. The reason is that scientifically legitimate interpretative claims (i.e. claims whose logic is, at least in principle, transparent and replicable) about the meaning (and any attempt at the labeling) of an observation are impossible in the absence of a categorization scheme that is itself housed in a theory of conceptual relations. In other words, it is hard to claim credibly to observe a causal regularity without an underlying theory.

View 2 is premised on the belief that developing concepts and measurements for theoretical ideas is just as important as developing explanations. Research design develops a test of a theoretical explanation. To do so, the researcher must focus on the empirical relationships between multiple operationalizations of these concepts that grapple with various complexities of the real world. In this account, teaching the conduct of research should be further broadened to consist of testing both the validity of causal relationships *and* the validity of concepts and measurements.

Finally, in view 3, the relative emphasis upon empirical and theoretical work in any one project depends upon both the "production function" for a valuable research paper and the skills of the researcher. Consider three research production functions. "Either one [derivation or testing] alone is enough." That is pure maximization where the accumulation of knowledge is assumed to be simple and additive. Second, "Only as good as the weakest link." This case is rather like a bivariate interaction or, perhaps, like a Leontief production function. But how are we to know whether the problem, when something goes wrong, is due to the elegant model being of an irrelevant universe or due to the data having been dredged too indiscriminately? Thirdly, knowledge is generated by a "Linear production with interactive complementarities." In this view, combining empirical and theoretical work is the best way to advance science because it leads to more than the sum of its parts, though empirical or theoretical work alone also produces great value. Because science is a social process and because people have differing skills, gains from specialization are possible. The danger of specialization, of course, is that nobody will combine theory and method because insufficient numbers of scholars will know how to do so, or how to evaluate others' attempts to do so. The belief of many observers in the late 1990s was that political science suffered from an excess of specialization. It was for this reason that the original EITM conference was called.

2.1 Achen's Approach

To the extent that such views reflect the EITM approach, they are not new or unique in political science. In particular, they echo arguments offered amongst rigorous empiricists decades earlier. For example, Bartels and Brady (1993, 148) argued that in the field of political methodology "there is still far too much data analysis without formal theory—and far too much formal theory without data analysis."

Achen (2002b) set up the problem in the following way, and suggested a way to bring the two together. Starting from a critique of contemporary statistical work—

Too many of the new estimators in political methodology are justified solely because they are one conceivable way to take account of some special feature of the data.... [M]any techniques are available, and...choosing the right one requires consulting the quantitatively sophisticated researchers in a given field (436–7)

he reached the conclusion that

For all our hard work, we have yet to give most of our new statistical procedures legitimate theoretical microfoundations, and we have had difficulty with the real task of quantitative work—the discovery of reliable empirical generalizations. (424)

There were important differences between older and newer styles of quantitative analysis:

The old style...is content with purely statistical derivations from substantively unjustified assumptions. The modern style insists on formal theory. The old style dumps its specification problems into a strangely distributed disturbance term and tries to model the [result]; the new style insists on starting from a formal model plus white noise errors. The old style thinks that if we try two or three familiar estimators...each with some arbitrary list of linear explanatory variables...and one...fits better, then it is...right...The modern style insists that, just because one...fit is better, that does not make them...coherent...Instead a new estimator should be adopted only when formal theory supports it...(440–1)

His conclusion (439) was "That is what microfoundations are for."

But in Achen's view there was still a problem of appropriate domain:

...often the causal patterns are dramatically different across the cases. In those instances, subsetting the sample and doing the statistical analysis separately for each distinct causal pattern is critical. Happily, these causally homogeneous samples will need far fewer control variables. (447)

So not only does quantitative analysis need analogs (measurable devices) that represent formal and empirical concepts, but one might also recommend separating the observations into two or more sorts of theoretically generated sub-samples with modest controls in each: The extra controls are what separate the sub-samples. One can take the model from the formal theory side and add detail on the conditionalities (or on Achen's interactions) or take the statistical model and add some detail on what you don't know. Either way you get enough structure to the model to simplify the theory but still generate expectations and you get enough specification to look for instruments to address identification and endogeneity. Or at least that should be so on enough important cases to make this approach worthwhile.

A related approach to an EITM-based empirical methodology is exemplified by Snyder and Ting (2003), who start from a situation where there are well-established empirical regularities observed over large numbers of previous studies. They develop an account of parties that allows scientific knowledge to cumulate as they find a "minimal" theoretical model that for the first time allows the analyst to deduce all the stylized facts, then additionally derive (at least) one new empirical implication and examine the evidence. Similarly, in a comparative theory-building exercise, Achen (2002a) specified a Bayesian version of the retrospective account of partisanship and showed that one could derive from it many of the same empirical implications that were hallmarks of the social psychological theory of party identification.

2.2 McKelvey's Approach

As we have argued elsewhere (Aldrich, Alt, and Lupia 2007a), no one personified the EITM approach in political science earlier and more effectively than Richard McKelvey. McKelvey is the rare figure who is known to formal modelers as an innovative and seminal figure in the development of their approach in political science and is known to many empirical scholars—principally through the advances presented in McKelvey and Zavoina (1975) and Aldrich and McKelvey (1976)—as an important figure in the advance of rigorous statistical techniques.[8] More importantly, however, he regularly developed theoretical models alongside means for evaluating key aspects of them simultaneously. Since he never published a book-length manuscript, this tendency in his work was difficult to derive from his articles, which did not advertise this point, but a new book-length treatment of his research (Aldrich, Alt, and Lupia 2007b) verifies the pattern.

McKelvey's approach to EITM was different to those described above. A good way to motivate his approach is to begin with a critique of formal theory by Sánchez-Cuenca (2006). His critique highlights attributes of the method that make many nonformal theorists uneasy:

The introduction of rational choice theory in political science [produces]...greater rigor, greater clarity, and the promise of a unified language for the discipline. Yet, rational choice has produced theories that are either far removed from reality or simply implausible, if not false. The problem has to do with the explanatory role of preferences. In economic analysis, the market induces preferences: the entrepreneur maximizes profits and the consumer, given

---

[8] An interesting reflection of the kind of intellectual isolationism described earlier is the fact that this description of McKelvey is surprising to many formal modelers despite the fact that his paper that develops the multinomial probit approach is far and away his most cited work.

her preferences, chooses according to the price system. But out of the market it is more difficult to define the preferences of the actors.

This critique echoes McKelvey's advice to the EITM Workshop (EITM Report 2002). He argued that, because there is no equivalent in political science to general equilibrium theory in economics, there is no central core from which to launch political analysis and perform comparative statics or other stock-in-trade economic methods of analysis. In the ordinary absence of general political equilibrium, he said, theory must incorporate specific details of the situation.

Sánchez-Cuenca also points out that while the consumer is decisive (that is, the consumer obtains what she chooses) the voter is nondecisive, since her vote is one among many and her vote rarely if ever is pivotal in determining the outcome. The result is that many noninstrumental considerations may enter into her decision, and no single easy numeraire like money serves to induce voter preferences. On the politicians' side, preferences may be induced, rather like producers' preferences are. However, there are different bases of induction that may apply, resulting in different types of politicians' preferences (are they seeking to capture political rents, win votes, or create the politician's sense of good public policies?) and perhaps producing different equilibria. This argument is reminiscent of McKelvey's view of institution-based modeling: Standard noncooperative game theory models typically found in the study of institutional politics will have equilibria of the Nash or Nash-with-refinements sort, generally very many of them, each applicable to specific circumstances with limited general applicability elsewhere.

McKelvey thought that this state of affairs would create a role for "applied theory." Empirical modelers might not be able to find a model that they could just plug in and use on any given set of data. He opined that they might have to develop some of the theory themselves, opening up opportunities for those researchers who can "speak both languages" at the empirical and theoretical ends of the spectrum to find common ground in the development of specific models that successfully integrate theoretical and data-generating processes for superior testing.

3 CONCLUSION

The observable implications of formal models, once derived, invite empirical evaluation. The current NSF-sponsored EITM initiative involves a strong commitment to causal inference in service to causal reasoning. At its broadest, it emphasizes addressing well-defined problems with some combination of clearly stated premises, logically coherent theory explaining relations among the premises, and logically coherent empirical work developed to evaluate the premises and/or the relations. Theory is broader than game theory and methods are broader than inference from statistical models and controlled experiments. In addition to game theory, formal models include differential equation dynamic models, simple decision theory, more complicated behavioral decision-making models, and computational models. The empirical tool kit should include not only statistical inference and experiments but also focused analytically-based case studies and computational models.

In the above, we may all be in general agreement. However, we further believe that theory is not independent of empirical investigation. There are so many choices that must be made—questions to ask, parameters to consider, and so on—that a theorist operating in some way independent of understanding and investigating the empirics of the problem at hand will, as a general rule, make incorrect and sterile choices of how to model. But at the same time, estimation requires microfoundations and thus a strong sense of the theory of the problem—the richer that sense the better. In this way, the separation of derivation and testing is false and there is an iterative and integrative process. As a fringe benefit to this view, the prospect that the theorist or the methodologist is somehow favored as the "more important" contributor is reduced. Indeed, it may well be the empirical scholar who bridges the work of theorist and methodologist who is favored.

The idea of EITM is to bring deduction and induction, hypothesis generation and hypothesis testing, close together. That is not quite the same thing as assuming that an individual should be good in all aspects. The challenge is to be able to structure training programs so that theory, methods, and substantive people know enough about each part to be able to work together well. Each has to be able to develop serious competency in (at least) one thing. The required combination of all of these parts is similar to the challenges of creating an effective interdisciplinary research team— each has their own specialized language and technologies, and they must collectively negotiate a common language. Fortunately, it is easier because we share a common context of politics, but only by doing the comparable negotiations can we take that knowledge out to the research frontier.

As a starting point for such negotiations, we close by offering a variant of a list of questions recently posed by de Marchi (2005). He suggests that an appropriate way to begin an effective strategy for evaluating its empirical implications is to ask a series of questions, such as:

1. What are the assumptions/parameters of the model? Do the assumptions spring from a consideration of the problem itself, or are they unrelated to the main logic of the model, chosen arbitrarily, perhaps solely to make derivations possible? Are values chosen for parameters derived from qualitative or quantitative empirical research, or are they chosen arbitrarily, maybe for convenience? How many of the parameters are open, to be "filled in" by data analysis?

2. How sure can we be that the main results of the model are immune to small perturbations of the parameters? That is, is there an equivalence class where the model yields the same results for a neighborhood around the chosen parameters? Alternatively, is the model "brittle," and if so, in what dimensions (that

is, on the basis of perturbations of which parameters)? How central are these particularly brittle parameters to the theoretical questions at hand?

3. Do the results of the model map directly to a dependent variable, or is the author of the model making analogies from the model to an empirical referent? While "toy" models have their place in developing intuition, they are difficult to falsify, and even more difficult to build upon in a cumulative fashion. De Marchi defines "toy" models as a class of simple models without any unique empirical referent. For example, the iterated prisoner's dilemma (IPD) is a simple game that investigates cooperation. He argues that it seems unlikely that all or most of human cooperation is a two-player contest with the exact strategy set of the IPD, and there is enormous difficulty in analogizing from the IPD to actual human behavior with enough precision to do any sort of predictive work.

4. Are the results of the model verified by out-of-sample tests? Are there alternatives to a large-N statistical approach that tests the model directly? Or is the parameter space of the model too large to span with the available data—this is the "curse of dimensionality?" Can one alleviate the impact of this curse by deriving a domain-specific encoding? Or is the specification of limited spheres of relevance just another arbitrary way to make our models appear more complete than they are?

For many people trained in formal modeling or statistics, such questions can be uncomfortable. But our discipline has already embarked on dual processes of enquiry into the development of rigorous theory and empiricism. So the questions, while seemingly inconvenient, will not go away. Nor should they, because underneath the sometimes arcane content of such methodological questions are issues that pertain directly to the substantive relevance of a particular theory or to the substantive generality of an empirical claim. As a discipline, we benefit from being able to offer a growing range of logically coherent and empirically robust explanations of focal political phenomena. Dealing with such questions in an aggressive and straightforward manner is a means to new levels of credibility and influence for political science. Developing a generation of scholars who are up to such challenges is the main goal of the EITM approach and is the reason that the approach merits broad and continuing support.

REFERENCES

ACHEN, C. 2002a. Parental socialization and rational party identification. *Political Behavior*, 24 (2), Special Issue: Parties and Partisanship, Part One: 151–70.

—— 2002b. Towards a new political methodology: microfoundations and ART. *Annual Review of Political Science*, 5: 423–50.

ALDRICH, J. H. 1980. *Before the Convention: Strategies and Choices in Presidential Nomination Campaigns.* Chicago: University of Chicago Press.

ALDRICH, J. H., and ALT, J. 2003. Introduction to the special issue on empirical implications of theoretical models. *Political Analysis*, 11: 309–15.

——— and LUPIA, A. 2007a. Introduction. In Aldrich, Alt, and Lupia 2007b.

——— ——— (eds.) 2007b. *Positive Changes in Political Science: The Legacy of Richard D. McKelvey's Most Influential Writings*. Ann Arbor: University of Michigan Press.

——— and MCKELVEY, R. D. 1977. A method of scaling with applications to the 1968 and 1972 U.S. presidential elections. *American Political Science Review*, 71: 111–30.

AUSTEN-SMITH, D. 2000. Redistributing income under proportional representation. *Journal of Political Economy*, 108: 1235–69.

BANKS, J. S., and KIEWIET, D. R. 1989. Explaining patterns of candidate competition in congressional elections. *American Journal of Political Science*, 33: 997–1015.

BARTELS, L., and BRADY, H. 1993. The state of quantitative political methodology. Pp. 121–59 in *Political Science: The State of the Discipline II*, ed. A. W. Finifter. Washington, DC: American Political Science Association.

BLACK, G. S. 1972. A theory of political ambition: career choices and the role of structural incentives. *American Political Science Review*, 66: 144–59.

BRADY, H. 2004. Introduction to the symposium: two paths to a science of politics. *Perspectives on Politics*, 2: 295–300.

DE MARCHI, S. 2005. *Computational and Mathematical Modeling in the Social Sciences*. New York: Cambridge University Press.

DRUCKMAN, J. N., GREEN, D. P., KUKLINSKI, J. H., and LUPIA, A. 2006. The growth and development of experimental research in the *American Political Science Review*. *American Political Science Review*, 100: 627–36.

EMPIRICAL IMPLICATIONS OF THEORETICAL MODELS REPORT 2002. Political Science Program, National Science Foundation, Dircctorate of Social, Behavioral, and Economic Sciences. Arlington.

GRANATO, J., and SCIOLI, F. 2004. Puzzles, proverbs, and omega matrices: the scientific and social significance of empirical implications of theoretical models (EITM). *Perspectives on Politics*, 2: 313–23.

IVERSEN, T., and SOSKICE, D. 2006. Electoral institutions and the politics of coalitions: why some democracies redistribute more than others. *American Political Science Review*, 100: 165–82.

JACKSON, M., and MOSELLE, B. 2002. Coalition and party formation in a legislative voting game. *Journal of Economic Theory*, 103: 49–87.

MCFADDEN, D. 1974. Conditional logit analysis of qualitative choice behavior. Pp. 105–42 in *Frontiers in Econometrics*, ed. P. Zarembka. New York: Academic Press.

MCKELVEY, R. D., and ORDESHOOK, P. C. 1972. A general theory of the calculus of voting. In *Mathematical Applications in Political Science*, vol. vi, ed. J. Herndon and J. Bernd. Charlottesville: University of Virginia Press.

——— ——— 1980. Vote trading: an experimental study. *Public Choice*, 35: 151–84.

——— ——— 1982. An experimental test of cooperative solution theory for normal form games. In *Political Equilibrium*, ed. P. C. Ordeshook and K. A. Shepsle. Boston: Kluwer-Nijhoff.

——— and PALFREY, T. R. 1992. An experimental study of the centipede game. *Econometrica*, 60: 803–36.

——— ——— 1995. Quantal response equilibria for normal form games. *Games and Economic Behavior*, 10: 6–38.

——— and ZAVOINA, W. 1975. A statistical model for the analysis of ordinal level dependent variables. *Journal of Mathematical Sociology*, 4: 103–20.

PALFREY, T. R., and ROSENTHAL, H. 1985. Voter participation and strategic uncertainty. *American Political Science Review*, 79: 62–78.

RIKER, W. H. 1967. Bargaining in a three-person game. *American Political Science Review*, 61: 642–56.

—— and ORDESHOOK, P. C. 1968. A theory of the calculus of voting. *American Political Science Review*, 62: 25–42.

ROHDE, D. W. 1979. Risk-bearing and progressive ambition: the case of the United States House of Representatives. *American Journal of Political Science*, 23: 1–26.

RUEDA, D. 2005. Insider–outsider politics in industrialized democracies: the challenge to social democratic parties. *American Political Science Review*, 99: 61–74.

SÁNCHEZ-CUENCA, I. 2006. The problem of preferences in the study of politics. Presentation to the IBEI Roundtable "The Study of Politics: From Theory to Empirics and Back," Barcelona, June 22.

SIGNORINO, C. S. 1999. Strategic interaction and the statistical analysis of international conflict. *American Political Science Review*, 93: 279–97.

SMITH, R. 2004. Identities, interests, and the future of political science. *Perspectives on Politics*, 2: 301–12.

SNYDER, J., and TING, M. 2003. Roll calls, party labels, and elections. *Political Analysis*, 11: 419–44.

THOMAS, G. 2005. The qualitative foundations of political science methodology. *Perspectives on Politics*, 3: 855–66.

Name Index

SUBJECT INDEX